D1479629

Frommer's®
Florida 2012

by Lesley Abravanel with Laura Miller

WILEY
John Wiley & Sons, Inc.

Published by:
John Wiley & Sons, Inc.
111 River St.
Hoboken, NJ 07030-5774

ISBN 978-1-118-04599-2 (paper); ISBN 978-1-118-07483-1 (paper); ISBN 978-1-118-11528-2 (ebk); ISBN 978-1-118-11529-9 (ebk); ISBN 978-1-118-11530-5 (ebk)

Editor: Kathleen Warnock, with Stephen Bassman and Lorraine Festa
Production Editor: Heather Wilcox
Cartographer: Guy Ruggiero
Cover Photo Editor: Richard Fox; photo editors: Alden Gewirtz, Cherie Cincilla
Design and Layout by Vertigo Design
Graphics and Prepress by Wiley Indianapolis Composition Services
Front cover photo: ©Daniel Dempster Photography/Alamy Images
Description: Anhinga preening, Anhinga Trail Everglades National Park Florida
Back cover photo: Back (Left): ©Marka/SuperStock, Inc. Miami Beach, yellow convertible; Back (Middle): © Penny Tweedie/Alamy Images, A pair of lovers deck chairs on beach, southern Florida; Back (Right): © M. Timothy O'Keefe/Alamy, Florida Keys: Key lime pie.

For information on our other products and services or to obtain technical support, please contact our Customer Care Department within the U.S. at 877/762-2974, outside the U.S. at 317/572-3993 or fax 317/572-4002.

Wiley also publishes its books in a variety of electronic formats. Some content that appears in print may not be available in electronic formats.

Manufactured in China

5 4 3 2 1

CONTENTS

LIST OF MAPS

ABOUT THE AUTHORS

Lesley Abravanel is a freelance journalist and a graduate of the University of Miami School of Communication. When she isn't combing Florida for the latest hotels, restaurants, and attractions, she is on the lookout for vacationing celebrities, about whom she writes in her weekly nightlife column, "Velvet Underground," and her twice weekly gossip column and daily blog, "Scene In the Tropics," for the *Miami Herald*. She is a contributor to several of the illustrious supermarket tabloids; blogs about the Miami restaurant and bar scene as editor of *Eater Miami*; is the Miami listings editor for BlackBook.com; and is the author of *Frommer's South Florida* and *Frommer's Portable Miami*.

Laura Miller is a freelance writer based in Buffalo, New York, though she's spent countless hours scouring Central Florida's theme parks over the years—both with and without her 5 kids. A family-travel expert who religiously makes several annual pilgrimages to the Land the Mouse Built, she's written extensively about the area for many magazines; operates a family-travel website, **www.travel-insights.com**; and is also the author of *Frommer's Walt Disney World and Orlando*.

HOW TO CONTACT US

In researching this book, we discovered many wonderful places—hotels, restaurants, shops, and more. We're sure you'll find others. Please tell us about them, so we can share the information with your fellow travelers in upcoming editions. If you were disappointed with a recommendation, we'd love to know that, too. Please write to:

Frommer's Florida 2012
John Wiley & Sons, Inc. • 111 River St. • Hoboken, NJ 07030-5774
frommersfeedback@wiley.com

ADVISORY & DISCLAIMER

Travel information can change quickly and unexpectedly, and we strongly advise you to confirm important details locally before traveling, including information on visas, health and safety, traffic and transport, accommodation, shopping, and eating out. We also encourage you to stay alert while traveling and to remain aware of your surroundings. Avoid civil disturbances, and keep a close eye on cameras, purses, wallets and other valuables.

While we have endeavored to ensure that the information contained within this guide is accurate and up-to-date at the time of publication, we make no representations or warranties with respect to the accuracy or completeness of the contents of this work and specifically disclaim all warranties, including without limitation warranties of fitness for a particular purpose. We accept no responsibility or liability for any inaccuracy or errors or omissions, or for any inconvenience, loss, damage, costs or expenses of any nature whatsoever incurred or suffered by anyone as a result of any advice or information contained in this guide.

The inclusion of a company, organization or Website in this guide as a service provider and/or potential source of further information does not mean that we endorse them or the information they provide. Be aware that information provided through some Websites may be unreliable and can change without notice. Neither the publisher or author shall be liable for any damages arising herefrom.

FROMMER'S STAR RATINGS, ICONS & ABBREVIATIONS

Every hotel, restaurant, and attraction listing in this guide has been ranked for quality, value, service, amenities, and special features using a **star-rating system.** In country, state, and regional guides, we also rate towns and regions to help you narrow down your choices and budget your time accordingly. Hotels and restaurants are rated on a scale of zero (recommended) to three stars (exceptional). Attractions, shopping, nightlife, towns, and regions are rated according to the following scale: zero stars (recommended), one star (highly recommended), two stars (very highly recommended), and three stars (must-see).

In addition to the star-rating system, we also use seven feature icons that point you to the great deals, in-the-know advice, and unique experiences that separate travelers from tourists. Throughout the book, look for:

special finds—those places only insiders know about

fun facts—details that make travelers more informed and their trips more fun

kids—best bets for kids and advice for the whole family

special moments—those experiences that memories are made of

overrated—places or experiences not worth your time or money

insider tips—great ways to save time and money

great values—where to get the best deals

The following abbreviations are used for credit cards:

AE	American Express	**DISC**	Discover	**V**	Visa
DC	Diners Club	**MC**	MasterCard		

TRAVEL RESOURCES AT FROMMERS.COM

Frommer's travel resources don't end with this guide. Frommer's website, **www.frommers.com**, has travel information on more than 4,000 destinations. We update features regularly, giving you access to the most current trip-planning information and the best airfare, lodging, and car-rental bargains. You can also listen to podcasts, connect with other Frommers.com members through our active-reader forums, share your travel photos, read blogs from guidebook editors and fellow travelers, and much more.

1

THE BEST OF FLORIDA

There's more than beautifully sunny skies in "The Sunshine State" to recommend a vacation in Florida. You can visit little towns like Apalachicola or a multicultural megalopolis like Miami. You can devour fresh seafood and then work it off bicycling, golfing, or swimming. In St. Augustine, 17th-century history comes alive, while you can make a stop in the Space Age at Cape Canaveral. Florida maintains thousands of acres of wilderness, from Clam Pass County Park in downtown Naples to Everglades National Park, spanning the state's southern tip.

Cities Capital Tallahassee blends modernity with the Old South. Orlando draws families with its theme parks: Walt Disney World, Universal Studios, and SeaWorld. The Gulf Coast seaport of Tampa marks one of the state's growing commercial centers. At Florida's southern tip, Miami draws vacationers with its spicy mix of Latin American and Caribbean culture and steamy nightlife.

Lay of the Land Miles of golden-sand beaches and seaside cottages invite leisurely drives along the Gulf Coast of Florida's Panhandle. In central Florida, you'll find acres of citrus groves. Alligator Alley crosses southern Florida from Naples to Weston, leading cars and bikes past the sawgrass, cypress, and gumbo-limbo trees of the Everglades.

Eating & Drinking Drink freshly squeezed juice or stop at roadside stands for a bag of tangerines. Florida cuisine can mean many things, but we suppose "Floribbean," the fusion of Caribbean and Latin flavors with the local Florida flavors (indigenous fruits and veggies like avocado, star fruit, coconut, Key lime, kumquat, and passion fruit; and fresh seafood like spiny lobster and stone crabs), says it best.

Beaches Family-friendly beaches await visitors in the Panhandle, where long, sun-kissed days include swimming and building sandcastles. Beachcombers collect seashells on Sanibel and Captiva Islands. Drive Florida's surf-sprayed A1A expressway along the Atlantic coast, past lighthouses and bikini beaches from Daytona all the way to Miami. Palm trees and fruity cocktails keep the locals cool and relaxed in the southern islands of the Florida Keys.

Hanging in There After a few rocky years, Florida is bouncing back to normalcy. Florida is never actually "normal," per se, which makes it all that much more fun. Though not entirely recovered from the recession that hit the state almost harder than a category 5 hurricane, Florida has shown signs of rebound—even in the most daunting of times, that is, until 2010's epic BP disaster, in which for most of the spring and summer, crude challenged Hawaiian Tropic as the state's unofficial oil.

The selections in this chapter are just some of the highlights. With an open mind and a sense of adventure, you'll come up with your own "bests."

PREVIOUS PAGE: Colorful flamingos highlight the scene at Homosassa Springs Wildlife State park.

THE best BEACHES

- **Virginia Key** (Key Biscayne): The producers of *Survivor* or *Lost* could shoot their show on this ultrasecluded, picturesque, and deserted key, where people purposely go to not be found. See p. 142.

- **Lummus Park Beach** (South Beach): This beach is world renowned, and better known as **South Beach,** on which seeing, being seen, and, at times, the obscene, go hand-in-hand with the sunscreen and beach towels. The 12th Street section is the beach of choice for gay residents and travelers. This beach has had some of the liveliest parties South Beach has ever seen. See p. 142.

- **Bahia Honda State Park** (Bahia Honda Key): This is one of the nicest and most peaceful beaches in Florida. It's located amid 635 acres of nature trails and a portion of Henry Flagler's railroad. See p. 221.

- **John U. Lloyd Beach State Park** (Dania Beach): Unfettered by high-rise condominiums, T-shirt shops, and hotels, this wonderful beach boasts an untouched shoreline surrounded by a canopy of Australian pine to ensure complete seclusion. See p. 291.

- **Lovers Key State Park** (Fort Myers Beach): You'll have to walk or take a tram through a bird-filled forest of mangroves to this gorgeous, unspoiled beach just a few miles south of busy Fort Myers Beach. Although Sanibel Island gets the accolades, the shelling here is just as good, if not better. See p. 368.

- **Cayo Costa State Park** (off Captiva Island): These days, deserted tropical islands with great beaches are scarce in Florida, but this 2,132-acre barrier strip of sand, pine forest, mangrove swamp, oak hammock, and grassland provides a genuine get-away-from-it-all experience. Access is only by boat from nearby Gasparilla, Pine, and Captiva islands. See p. 394.

Bahia Honda State Park offers all kinds of ecosystems...including a peaceful beach.

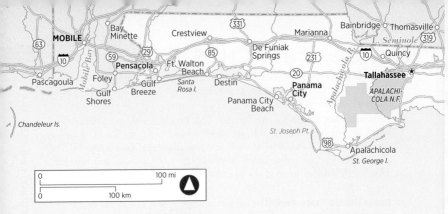

GULF   OF

MEXICO

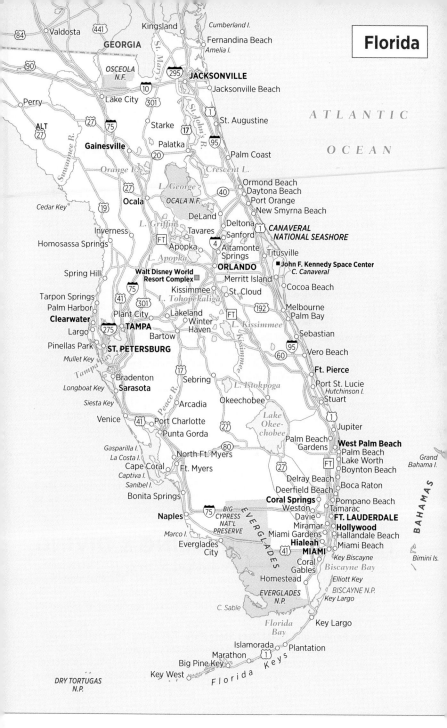

Florida

○ **Caladesi Island State Park** (Clearwater Beach): Even though 3½-mile-long Caladesi Island is in the Tampa Bay area, it has a lovely, relatively secluded beach with soft sand edged in sea grass and palmettos. In the park, there's a nature trail where you might see one of the rattlesnakes, black racers, raccoons, armadillos, or rabbits that live here. The park is accessible only by ferry from Honeymoon Island State Recreation Area, off Dunedin. See p. 457.

○ **Fort DeSoto Park** (St. Petersburg): Where else can you get a good tan *and* a history lesson? At Fort DeSoto Park, you have not only 1,136 acres of five interconnected islands and 3 miles of beaches, but also a fort that's listed on the National Register of Historic Places. There are also nature trails, fishing piers, a 2.25-mile canoe trail, and spectacular views of Tampa Bay and the Gulf. See p. 459.

○ **Siesta Key Beach** (Siesta Key, Sarasota): A public beach with fine white, quartz-crystal sand, Siesta Key is just ¾ mile long but has a huge reputation as one of the state's—and country's—best spots for sand and surf. See p. 471.

○ **Lighthouse Point Park** (Daytona Beach): With 52 acres of pristine land on the north side of Ponce de León Inlet, the park features fishing, nature trails, an observation deck and tower, swimming, and picnicking. A variety of wildlife also calls the park home, including raccoons, possums, skunks, armadillos, shorebirds, and birds of prey. See p. 571.

○ **Gulf Islands National Seashore** (Pensacola): All of Northwest Florida's Gulf shore is one of America's great beaches—an almost uninterrupted stretch of white sand that runs the length of the Panhandle, from Perdido Key to St. George Island. The Gulf Islands National Seashore preserves much of this natural wonder in its undeveloped state. Countless terns, snowy plovers, black skimmers, and other birds nest along the dunes topped with sea oats. East of the national seashore and equally beautiful are **Grayton Beach State Park,** near Destin; and **St. George Island State Park,** off Apalachicola. See p. 651 and 680.

○ **St. Andrews State Park** (Panama City Beach): With more than 1,000 acres of dazzling white sand and dunes, this preserved wilderness demonstrates what Panama City Beach looked like before motels and condominiums lined its shore. Lacy, golden sea oats sway in Gulf breezes and the area is home to foxes and a herd of deer. See p. 672.

THE best SNORKELING & DIVING

○ **Dry Tortugas National Park** (Dry Tortugas): Snorkelers of all levels bubble over when talking about the carpet of white sand that's illuminated by Technicolor tropical fish and living coral at this coral island off of Key West. For divers, nearby off Loggerhead Key is the Schooner wreck, the *Windjammer.* See p. 262.

○ **John Pennekamp Coral Reef State Park** (Key Largo): This is the country's first undersea preserve, with 188 square miles of protected coral reefs. The water throughout much of the park is shallow, so it's a great place for snorkelers to see a vibrant array of coral, including tree-size elkhorn coral and giant brain coral. See p. 205.

Some of the best sights in Florida are underwater, at John Pennekamp Coral Reef State Park.

- **Looe Key National Marine Sanctuary** (Bahia Honda State Park): With 5⅓ square miles of gorgeous coral reef, rock ledges up to 35 feet tall, and a colorful and motley marine community, you may never want to come up for air. See p. 224.

- **Florida Keys:** The Keys Shipwreck Heritage Trail features nine historic sites from Key Largo to Key West. For each of the nine Shipwreck Trail sites there is an underwater site guide available, who provides the shipwreck and mooring buoy positions, history, and a site map, and identifies marine life you can expect to see. See p. 242.

- **Hutchinson Island:** Three artificial reefs off this island provide excellent scenery for divers of any level. The **USS *Rankin,*** sunk in 120 feet of water in 1988, lies 7 miles east-northeast of the St. Lucie Inlet. **Donaldson Reef** consists of a cluster of plumbing fixtures sunk in 58 feet of water. **Ernst Reef,** made from old tires, is a 60-foot dive located 4½ miles east-southeast of the St. Lucie inlet. See chapter 9.

- **Pensacola, Destin, and Panama City:** The military town of Pensacola also happens to have some of the best submerged battleships and even a retired aircraft carrier. In Destin and Panama City, military buffs literally dive into history, studying the ocean floor, which is carpeted with everything from aircraft, tankers, and barges to a hovercraft and a one-time Quonset hut. See chapter 14.

THE best GOLF COURSES

- **Biltmore Hotel** (Miami): The beautiful, rolling, 18-hole golf course designed by Donald Ross at the majestic Biltmore Hotel in Coral Gables is open to the public, and is a favorite of Bill Clinton's. See p. 107.

St. Petersburg's Mangrove Bay is one of the top municipal courses around.

- **Doral Golf Resort and Spa** (Miami): Four championship courses make the Doral one of Miami's best golf destinations. The legendary Blue Monster course hosts the PGA Ford Championship tourney. See p. 104.

- **Fairmont Turnberry Isle Resort & Club** (Aventura, North Miami Beach): These two courses, redesigned in 2008 by Raymond Floyd, are open only to guests, but are among the city's best. See p. 105.

- **PGA National Resort & Spa** (Palm Beach): This rambling resort, the national headquarters of the PGA, is a premier golf destination with five 18-hole courses on more than 2,300 acres. See p. 335.

- **Tiburón Golf Club** (Naples): Greg Norman designed this course's 36 championship holes to play like a British Open—but without the thick thatch rough. The course is now home to the luxurious Ritz-Carlton Golf Resort, Naples. See p. 402.

- **Mangrove Bay Golf Course** (St. Petersburg): One of the nation's top 50 municipal courses, the newly renovated Mangrove Bay course hugs the inlets of Old Tampa Bay and offers 18-hole, par-72 play. See p. 448.

- **The Copperhead Course at Innisbrook, a Salamander Golf & Spa Resort** (Tarpon Springs): *Golfweek* has called this course, with rolling hills and challenging holes, number one in Florida. But novices need not be put off. Each year, 1,000 students flock here for one of the largest resort-owned-and-operated golf schools in North America. Golfers of all abilities come here to play the 600 acres of courses. See p. 466.

- **Walt Disney World** (Orlando): The resorts surrounding the theme parks have 99 regulation holes that let you walk in the footsteps (and share the frustrations) of the game's greatest players. Those with a shorter stroke can play the master miniature courses: Fantasia Gardens and Winter Summerland. Call *C* **407/939-4653** to inquire about golf courses and rates, or try the non-Disney **Golfpac** (*C* **800/486-0948** or 407/260-2288; www.golfpacorlando. com).

o **Ladies Professional Golf Association/LPGA International** (Daytona Beach): This women-friendly course has multiple tee settings, unrestricted tee times, a great pro shop, and state-of-the-art facilities. Designed by Rees Jones, the older course here was chosen as one of the "Top Ten You Can Play" by *Golf* magazine. See p. 572.

o **TPC at Sawgrass** (Ponte Vedra Beach, near Jacksonville): With 99 holes, Pete Dye's The Player's Stadium Course at Sawgrass makes top-10 lists everywhere. The 17th hole, on a tricky island, is one of the most photographed holes in the world. See p. 594.

o **Ocean Hammock Golf Club** (Palm Coast, btw. Daytona Beach and St. Augustine): With 6 of its holes skirting the Atlantic Ocean, the Jack Nicklaus–designed course is the first authentic seaside links built in Florida since the 1920s. Another equally challenging, scenic course was designed by Tom Watson. See p. 595.

o **Omni Amelia Island Plantation** (Amelia Island): This exclusive resort has three of the state's best courses. Long Point Club, designed by Tom Fazio, is the most beautiful and challenging. Pete Dye and Bobby Weed's Amelia Links comprises two courses, Oak Marsh and Ocean Links. Each is open only to resort guests. See p. 625.

o **Bay Point Marriott Golf Resort** (Panama City Beach): Thirty-six holes of championship golf at this Marriott include the Jack Nicklaus–designed Meadows course and Nicklaus Design Course, one of the country's most difficult. See p. 673.

THE best LUXURY RESORTS

o **The Setai** (South Beach; *C* **305/520-6000**): There is no hotel like this anywhere else in Florida. Rough economy or not, this hotel breaks the bank and takes luxury to a new level, with its imported, not imitated, Asian decor and staff, outstanding Pan-Asian cuisine, and celebrity clientele. Who else can afford these prices? See p. 88.

o **The Ritz-Carlton, Key Biscayne** (Key Biscayne; *C* **800/241-3333** or 305/365-4500): In addition to superior services and amenities, this British colonial–style version of the Ritz rises above its casual Key Biscayne surroundings, with a stellar view of the Atlantic Ocean, not to mention an equally impressive 20,000-square-foot spa. See p. 98.

o **Mandarin Oriental, Miami** (Brickell Key, Miami; *C* **305/913-8383**): The swank and stunning Mandarin Oriental features a waterfront location, residential-style rooms, superb service, a spa frequented by J-Lo, and several upscale dining and bar facilities. See p. 101.

o **W South Beach** (South Beach; *C* **305/938-3000**): The W South Beach is considered the brand's signature showpiece and for good reason. All 312 rooms in this visually arresting, Bali meets Miami Beach resort boast ocean

Enjoy old-school luxury at the classic Palm Beach restort, The Breakers.

views and all the trappings of modern hipster society. The hotel's bar and restaurant scene are among the city's hottest, thanks to celebrity clientele who flock to Mr Chow and Wall nightclub. See p. 89.

- **The Atlantic Hotel** (Fort Lauderdale; ☎ **800/325-3589** or 954/567-8020): Set on a golden-sand beach, the Mediterranean-style Atlantic brings a fresh sense of modern luxury to Fort Lauderdale, not to mention a fabulous chef hailing from NYC's Tribeca Grill. See p. 299.

- **The Ritz-Carlton Fort Lauderdale** (Fort Lauderdale; ☎ **800/542-8680** or 954/465-2300): Unparalleled luxury hits Fort Lauderdale beach in the form of this swanky Ritz-Carlton. Formerly and briefly the St. Regis, the Ritz offers everything from beach to butlers. See p. 300.

- **The Breakers Palm Beach** (Palm Beach; ☎ **800/833-3141** or 561/655-6611): This stately, historic hotel epitomizes *la dolce vita*, Palm Beach–style, with an elegant lobby, impeccable service, expansive manicured lawns, and a scenic golf course, the state's oldest. See p. 334.

- **Four Seasons Resort Palm Beach** (Palm Beach; ✆ 800/432-2335 or 561/582-2800): *Exquisite* is often used to describe this posher-than-posh hotel. Luxurious, but hardly stuffy, the Four Seasons was the stay of choice for the quintessential aging rockers of Aerosmith, who took great advantage of post-concert pampering. See p. 334.

- **The Ritz-Carlton, Naples** (Naples; ✆ 888/856-4372 or 239/598-3300): This opulent Mediterranean-style hotel at Vanderbilt Beach is a favorite of affluent types who like standard Ritz amenities such as marble floors, antique art, Oriental rugs, Waterford chandeliers, and British-style high tea. Guests relax in rockers on the verandas or unwind by the heated pool set in a landscaped terrace. See p. 408.

- **Disney's Grand Floridian Resort & Spa** (Lake Buena Vista; ✆ 407/934-7639): This Victorian-style inn has a grand five-story lobby topped by a Tiffany-style glass dome. The glass-enclosed brass cage elevator and Chinese Chippendale aviary are examples of the refined style that runs throughout the entire resort. An orchestra plays big-band music every evening near Victoria & Albert's, the resort's five-star restaurant, and afternoon tea is a daily event. See p. 499.

- **Omni Amelia Island Plantation** (Amelia Island; ✆ 800/834-4900 or 904/261-6161): Set amid magnolias, oak trees, and the Atlantic Ocean, this gracious resort is straight out of the Deep South. It's more rustic than the nearby Ritz, but it has excellent hiking and biking paths, tennis, swimming, horseback riding, and boating. Golfers can enjoy exclusive use of two of Florida's top courses. See p. 625.

THE best ROMANTIC HIDEAWAYS

- **Jules' Undersea Lodge** (Key Largo; ✆ 305/451-2353): Submerge yourself in this single-room Atlantis-like hotel that offers a surprisingly comfortable suit—30 feet under water. Don't worry; there's plenty of breathing room, but you really have to *like* the person you're with to take this plunge. See p. 211.

- **Kona Kai Resort, Gallery & Botanic Garden** (Key Largo; ✆ 800/365-7829 or 305/852-7200): A haven for vacationing adults, Kona Kai features a private beach and stylized, modern rooms and suites amid a 2-acre property, lined with native vegetation and fruit trees. See p. 212.

- **Little Palm Island Resort & Spa** (Little Torch Key; ✆ 800/343-8567 or 305/872-2524): Accessible only by boat, this private 5-acre island is not only remote but also romantic—there are no TVs or telephones in the luxurious thatched cottages. See p. 224.

- **The Moorings Village** (Islamorada; ✆ 305/664-4708): A former coconut plantation, the Moorings features 18 different cottages on 18 stunning acres of beachfront, and lush gardens studded with bougainvillea and coconut palms. See p. 212.

- **La Mer Hotel & Dewey House** (Key West; ✆ 800/354-4455 or 305/296-6577): These picture-postcard turn-of-the-20th-century Victorian and historic homes have spacious, modern British colonial–style rooms overlooking lush gardens and the ocean. See p. 247.

Share your own private island with a loved one at Little Palm Island.

o **Marquesa Hotel** (Key West; ✆**800/869-4631** or 305/292-1919): Don't be fooled by the Marquesa's location on heavily populated Key West: This charming B&B is in a wonderful world of its own, far enough from the tumult, yet close enough if you want it. See p. 248.

o **The Gardens Hotel** (Key West; ✆**800/526-2664** or 305/294-2661): A well-kept secret (until now), the Gardens Hotel is an exotic, lush, serene, and sultry escape from the frat-boy madness that ensues on nearby Duval Street. See p. 245.

o **Sundy House** (Delray Beach; ✆**877/439-9601** or 561/272-5678): With 11 suites surrounded by more than 5,000 species of exotic plants and flowers, gazebos, and flowing streams, Sundy House is a gorgeous getaway that's close enough to access the beach, but still hidden from the mood-ruining madness and conventionality of your typical tourist-class beach hotel. See p. 319.

o **Island's End Resort** (St. Pete Beach; ✆**727/360-5023**): Sitting right on Pass-a-Grille, where the Gulf of Mexico meets Tampa Bay, this little all-cottage retreat is a great hideaway from the crowds of St. Pete Beach. You won't have an on-site restaurant, bar, or other such amenities, but you can step from your cottage right onto the beach. See p. 463.

o **Turtle Beach Resort** (Siesta Key, off Sarasota; ✆**941/349-4554**): Sitting beside the bay, this intimate charmer began life as a traditional Old Florida fishing camp, but today it's one of the state's most romantic retreats. It's a tightly packed place, but high wooden fences surround each unit's private outdoor hot tub, and one-way-mirror walls let you lounge in bed while passersby see only reflections of themselves. See p. 482.

- **The Lodge & Club at Ponte Vedra Beach** (Ponte Vedra Beach, near Jacksonville; ✆ **800/243-4304** or 904/273-9500): Every unit in this intimate hotel has a romantic seat built into its oceanview window, plus a big bathroom with a two-person tub and separate shower. Gas fireplaces in preferred rooms and suites add even more charm. One of the three pools and whirlpools here is reserved exclusively for couples. See p. 614.

- **Casa Marina** (Jacksonville Beach; ✆ **904/270-0025**): The words *luxury* and *Jacksonville* aren't as oxymoronic as it seems when it comes to this 25-room "old-world meets modern oceanfront Jax Beach" hotel. See p. 613.

- **WaterColor Inn** (near Destin; ✆ **866/426-2656** or 850/534-5000): This David Rockwell–designed beachfront boutique hotel feels more like a private beach house. Guest rooms feature a pantry, a walk-in shower with views to the beach, and Adirondack chairs on the balcony. See p. 661.

- **Seaside** (near Destin; ✆ **866/624-1054** or 850/231-1320): The romantic Gulf-front cottages at Seaside were built in the 1980s but evoke the 1880s, in the Victorian-style village of Seaside (a short drive east of Destin), with several cozy cottages designed especially for honeymooners. See p. 660.

THE best FAMILY ATTRACTIONS

- **Jungle Island** (Miami): Adults might think it's overrated and touristy, but kids love it. You'll need to watch your head, however, because hundreds of parrots, macaws, peacocks, cockatoos, and flamingos are flying above. Continuous suitable (but cheesy) shows star bicycle-riding cockatoos, high-flying macaws, and stunt-happy parrots. There are also tortoises, iguanas, and a rare albino alligator on exhibit. Star-struck folk may also want to keep their eyes on the crowds, which tend to draw big-name celebs with toddlers in tow. See p. 172.

- **Miami Children's Museum** (Miami): This museum has hundreds of bilingual, interactive exhibits, along with programs, classes, and learning materials related to arts, culture, community, and communication. It also has a re-creation of the NBC 6 television studio and a working music studio in which aspiring rock stars can lay down tracks and play instruments. See p. 149.

- **Sea Grass Adventures** (Miami): This is not your typical nature tour. With Sea Grass Adventures, you will be able to wade in the water on Key Biscayne with your guide and catch an assortment of sea life in the provided nets. At the end of the program, participants gather on the beach while the guide explains what everyone has just caught, passing the creatures around in miniature viewing tanks. See p. 174.

- **Miami Science Museum** (Miami): The Science Museum features more than 140 hands-on exhibits that explore the mysteries of the universe. Live demonstrations and collections of rare natural-history specimens make a visit here fun and informative. Many of the demos involve audience participation, which can be lots of fun for willing and able kids and adults alike. See p. 149.

- **J. N. "Ding" Darling National Wildlife Refuge** (Sanibel Island): Consisting of more than half of Sanibel Island, this 6,000-plus-acre area of mangrove swamps, winding waterways, and uplands has a 2-mile boardwalk nature trail

Kids can get their hands wet and learn about nature at Sea Grass Adventures.

and a 5-mile, one-way safari-esque **Wildlife Drive** on which you'll view a motley crew of species, including alligators, raccoons, birds, and other wildlife. See p. 378.

o **Busch Gardens Tampa Bay** (Tampa): Although the thrill rides, live entertainment, shops, restaurants, and games get most of the ink at this 335-acre family theme park, Busch Gardens also ranks among the top zoos in the country, with several thousand animals living in naturalistic environments. If you can get them off the roller coasters, kids can find out what all those wild beasts they've seen on the Discovery Channel look like in person. See p. 425.

o **MOSI (Museum of Science and Industry)** (Tampa): The largest educational science center in the Southeast, MOSI has more than 450 interactive exhibits in which the kids can experience hurricane-force winds, defy the laws of gravity, cruise the mysterious world of microbes, explore the human body, and more. The museum is one of very few in the world to feature the articulated remains of a Sauropod dinosaur. They can also watch stunning movies in MOSIMAX, Florida's first IMAX dome theater. See p. 431.

o **The Ringling Circus Museum** (Sarasota): Located within the FSU Ringling Center for the Cultural Arts, this museum isn't clowning around when it comes to telling the history of the circus. Devoted to circus memorabilia, the museum features everything from parade wagons and calliopes to costumes and colorful posters. See p. 476.

o **Universal Studios Florida** (Orlando): Universal Orlando's original theme park (and working movie studio) is filled with rides based on blockbuster movies and hit TV shows. Woody Woodpecker's Kid Zone, with its zippy pint-size coaster, water slide, and water play area (not to mention the numerous attractions aimed at the toddler set), will keep the kids busy for hours. See p. 543.

○ **Universal's Islands of Adventure** (Orlando): Hollywood hits, classic comics, and beloved books spring to life here. Thrill seekers and coaster crazies won't want to miss the Hulk, Spiderman, and the Dragon Challenge (at the Wizarding World of Harry Potter), while the Me Ship Olive, Camp Jurassic, and all things Seussian will thrill the younger set—and that's just a sampling of what awaits you here. See p. 545.

○ **Disney's Magic Kingdom** (Orlando): Opened some 40 years ago, this remains Disney's premier park. Rides and attractions based on classic Disney characters (think princesses like Cinderella, Ariel, and Snow White; adventurers like

Kids can ride on Dr. Seuss characters at Universal Studios.

Peter Pan, Buzz Lightyear—and even Captain Jack) have guests of all ages squealing with delight. Thrill seekers, fear not, as rides like Splash Mountain, Space Mountain, and Pirates of the Caribbean will keep you coming back for more. See p. 526.

○ **Kennedy Space Center** (Cape Canaveral): Despite the changes afoot in the space program, a recent multimillion-dollar renovation and expansion has made this destination a must-see even if the shuttle program is winding down. There is plenty to keep kids and parents busy for at least a full day, including computer games, IMAX films, and dozens of informative displays on the space program. See p. 560.

○ **Daytona International Speedway** (Daytona Beach): Behind-the-scenes tours take speed fans into the garages, the drivers meeting room, the press box, and even the victory lane. Or experience a 200-mph ride on a simulator at **The DAYTONA 500 Experience,** a 60,000-square-foot, state-of-the-art interactive motor-sports attraction where you can learn about the history, color, and excitement of stock car, go-kart, and motorcycle racing in Daytona. See p. 570.

THE best OFFBEAT TRAVEL EXPERIENCES

○ **Jimbo's** (Miami): Located at the end of Virginia Key, in Key Biscayne, on the lagoon where they shot *Flipper*, Jimbo's has become the quintessential, albeit hard-to-find, South Florida watering hole, snack bar, and hangout for an assortment of colorful characters, from shrimpers and yachters to politicos.

Dollar beers and excellent smoked fish are sold from a cooler, vacant shacks serve as backdrops for films, and visitors are able to test their skills in a game of boccie ball. See p. 136.

o **El Palacio de los Jugos:** This Miami institution's Little Havana outpost of fresh-squeezed juices and traditional Cuban fare offers a surrealistic, manic, old-world approach to fast food. See p. 134.

o **People-Watching on South Beach and Worth Avenue** (Miami and Palm Beach): As cliché as the notion of people-watching may seem, it's never the same old scenario on Miami's neon-hued Riviera, where equally colorful locals and luminaries proudly prance as if every day were the Easter parade. See p. 72. In Palm Beach, titled nobility, bejeweled socialites, and an assortment of upper-crust folks put on the Ritz along the city's version of Rodeo Drive. See p. 332.

o **Alabama Jack's** (Key Largo): En route to the Keys, veer off onto Card Sound Road, once the only way to get down there, and follow the Harley-Davidsons to Alabama Jack's. A waterfront biker bar, restaurant, and live-music joint on two barges, on Sundays Alabama Jack's is the place to be for country line dancers, many in full *Hee Haw* regalia; lazy folks whiling away the day over beer, conch fritters, and the best Key lime and peanut butter pie ever; and good ol', interesting folks passin' through. See p. 198.

o **Swimming with the Dolphins at the Dolphin Research Center** (Marathon): Of the four such centers in the continental United States, the Dolphin Research Center is the most impressive. With advance reservations, you can splash around with dolphins in their natural lagoon homes. It's an amazing experience. See p. 203.

Enjoy some tasty conch fritters at Alabama Jack's.

Costumed revelers take over the streets of Key West for Fantasy Fest.

o **Underwater Stay at Jules' Undersea Lodge** (Key Largo): We give this a vote as one of Florida's most romantic rtreats, but this underwater hotel is also, hands down, the most unusual. Where else can you have a pizza delivered via scuba diver? See p. 211.

o **Fantasy Fest** (Key West): Mardi Gras takes a Floridian vacation as the streets of Key West are overtaken by wildly costumed revelers who have no shame and no parental guidance. This weeklong, hedonistic, X-rated Halloween party is *not* for children 17 and under. See p. 38.

o **Columbus Day Regatta** (Biscayne Bay): This unique observation of Columbus Day revolves around a so-called regatta in Biscayne Bay but always ends with participants stripping down to their bare, ahem, necessities and partying at the sandbar in the middle of the bay. There is a boat race at some point of the day, but most people are too preoccupied to notice. See p. 278.

o **Swimming with the Manatees** (Crystal River, north of Clearwater): Some 360 manatees spend the winter in the Crystal River, and you can swim, snorkel, or scuba with them in the natural springs of Kings Bay, about 7 miles north of Homosassa Springs. It's not uncommon to be surrounded in the 72°F (22°C) water by 30 to 40 "sea cows" that nudge and caress you as you swim with them. See p. 450.

o **Wrangling an Alligator** (Orlando): Play trainer for a day and meet some of the toothy stars up-close and *real* personal at Gatorland. You might even get to be part of the show, so hop on and hold on tight! Trainers will snap a photo before the gators snap back! See p. 552.

o **See Who's on the Other Side in Cassadaga** (near Daytona): Billing itself as the Psychic Capital of the World, this 115-year old spiritualist camp composed of psychic mediums, healers, and metaphysical mavens is as off-beat as it comes. See p. 574.

o **Learning to Surf the Big Curls at Ron Jon Surf School** (Cocoa Beach): Even if you don't know how to hang ten, this school will get you riding the waves with the best of them. It provides equipment and lessons for all skill levels—beginner to pro—at the best surf beaches in Florida. See p. 565.

o **Channel Your Inner Picasso at Ruskin Place Artist Colony** (Seaside): Ruskin Place houses an eclectic collection of galleries that are among the most original in the state despite its location in what some find to be (albeit erroneously), a most Stepford-esque community. See p. 656.

THE best SPAS

o **Canyon Ranch** (Miami Beach; ✆ 305/514-7000): If a spa had to go to a spa, this would be the place it would want to go. The largest in Miami with 54 treatment rooms, Canyon Ranch's methods of pampering are among the most high-tech in the biz. See p. 94.

o **Lapis at the Fontainebleau** (Miami Beach; ✆ 305/674-4772): Substance over style, a unique concept in these parts, is what sets Lapis apart, with a focus on stellar treatments over glitz. Among the highlights: mineral water jet pool with red seaweed extract and heated hammam benches and a light massage that, combined with a series of electrical currents, is like a nip/tuck without the nipping.

o **The Spa at Mandarin Oriental** (Miami; ✆ 866/526-6567 or 305/913-8383): If it's good enough for J-Lo, then it must be good enough for the rest of us. But seriously, this star-studded spa isn't the best because of its clientele, but because of its Chinese, Balinese, Indian, and European treatments applied by professionals well versed in the inimitable Mandarin Oriental brand of pampering. See p. 101.

o **The Spa at the Setai** (South Beach; ✆ 305/520-6100): Nirvana is alive and well at the Spa at the Setai, where the philosophy of relaxation is derived from an ancient Sanskrit legend, natural elixirs, eternal youth, and Asian treatments and ingredients such as green tea. See p. 88.

o **The Spa at the Standard** (South Beach; ✆ 305/673-1717): What used to be an old-school, Borscht Belt–style Miami Beach health spa is now one of the hottest, trendiest places to take a Turkish bath in a bona fide *hammam,* let out steam in a cedar sauna, or get spritzed in the hotel's sublime Wall of Sound Shower. See p. 91.

o **The Ritz-Carlton Spa, Key Biscayne** (Key Biscayne; ✆ 305/365-4158): A sublime, 20,000-square-foot West Indies colonial-style Eden, here you can indulge in more than 60 treatments, including the Key Lime Coconut Body Scrub and the Everglades Grass Body Wrap in one of 21 treatment rooms. For a real splurge, the Fountain of Youth Balance treatment is a 6-hour in-dulgence with a facial, massage, manicure, pedicure, shampoo, styling, and lunch served on the oceanfront terrace. See p. 98.

o **ESPA at Acqualina** (Sunny Isles Beach; ✆ 305/918-8000): The first of its kind in the U.S., ESPA features groundbreaking treatments in a stunning, two-story space overlooking the Atlantic. See p. 105.

Ommm...ni Amelia Island Plantation offers yoga classes at its spa.

○ **Harbor Beach Marriott Resort & Spa** (Fort Lauderdale; ℂ 800/222-6543 or 954/525-4000): This $8-million, 22,000-square-foot European spa is the first full-service seaside facility of its kind in Fort Lauderdale. See p. 299.

○ **PGA National Resort & Spa** (Palm Beach Gardens; ℂ 800/633-9150 or 561/627-2000): This lauded golf resort provides the perfect pampering for sore golfers and bored nongolfers, with its Mediterranean Spa offering just about every treatment imaginable, including special ones for pregnant women. See p. 335.

○ **Naples Beach Hotel & Golf Club** (Naples; ℂ 800/237-7600 or 239/261-2222): This modern spa adds complete relaxation to a stay at this venerable hotel, already one of Florida's most relaxing resorts. A deep-body massage followed by a milk-and-honey wrap will leave you on cloud nine, and a special wedding package will have you primed for the big day. See p. 407.

○ **Safety Harbor Resort and Spa** (Tampa Bay area; ℂ 888/237-8772 or 727/726-1161): Tucked away off the beaten track amid moss-draped oaks and cobblestone streets, Safety Harbor is the oldest continually running spa in the United States, and Florida's only spa built around natural healing springs—the feeling is very European. See p. 452.

○ **Omni Amelia Island Plantation** (Amelia Island; ℂ 888/261-6161 or 904/261-6161): The resort's 20-room, all-natural spa features a meditation garden, plus nontoxic, paraben-free products and services, including a few treatments that utilize chocolate as the main ingredient. See p. 625.

THE best LOCAL DINING EXPERIENCES

- **Prime One Twelve** (South Beach; ✆ 305/532-8112): This South of Fifth Street steakhouse sizzles with Kobe-beef hot dogs, aged and oversize steaks, and an unparalleled celebrity clientele that has everyone begging for reservations up to 2 months in advance. While the food may be second to the scene, it is inarguably a quintessential South Beach experience. See p. 114.

- **Michael's Genuine Food & Drink** (Design District; ✆ 305/573-5550): Former *New York Times* dining critic Frank Bruni put Michael's at number 4 on his list of the 10 best new restaurants in the U.S. back in 2008. In 2010, chef/owner Michael Schwartz won a James Beard Award. Today, the restaurant is still one of the hottest reservations in town, thanks to its locally sourced, organic seasonal cuisine, out-of-control desserts, buzzy bar scene, and colorful crowd of foodies, hipsters, celebrities, and assorted culinary dignitaries. See p. 129.

- **Garcia's Seafood Grille & Fish** (downtown Miami; ✆ 305/375-0765): On the Miami River across from the spectacular Miami skyline, Garcia's is an urban oasis of fresh seafood with lots of local flavor. See p. 128.

- **Versailles** (Little Havana; ✆ 305/444-0240): This iconoclastic Cuban diner isn't as swanky as its palatial French namesake, but it is full of mirrors through which you can view the colorful—and audible—Cuban clientele that congregates here for down-home cuisine and hearty conversation. See p. 134.

- **Island Grill** (Islamorada; ✆ 305/664-8400): Located right on the water right before a bridge, Island Grill is *the* place locals go to for fresh fish, views, and live music on any given day or night. See p. 219.

- **Islamorada Fish Company** (Islamorada; ✆ 800/258-2559 or 305/664-9271): We're not sure which is better, the view or the seafood—but whichever it is, it's a winning combination. See p. 218.

- **Blue Heaven** (Key West; ✆ 305/296-8666): What was once a well-kept secret in Key West's Bahama Village is now a popular eatery known for fresh food (it's some of the best in town) and a motley, bohemian crowd. See p. 256.

- **Cap's Place Island Restaurant** (Lighthouse Point; ✆ 954/941-0418): The only way to get to this rustic seafood restaurant, the former bootlegging and gambling hangout of Al Capone, is by boat, but don't be dismayed—it's not the least bit Disneyfied. Churchill, Roosevelt, Marilyn Monroe, and Sylvester Stallone have all indulged in this delicious taste of Old Florida. See p. 309.

- **Farmer's Market Restaurant** (Fort Myers; ✆ 239/334-1687): The retail Farmer's Market next door may be tiny, but the best of the cabbage, okra, green beans, and tomatoes ends up here at this simple eatery, frequented by everyone from business executives to truck drivers. The specialties of the house are such Southern favorites as smoked ham hocks with a bowl of black-eyed peas. See p. 375.

- **Fourth Street Shrimp Store** (St. Petersburg; ✆ 727/822-0325): The outside of this place looks like it's covered with graffiti, but it's actually a gigantic drawing of people eating. Inside, murals on two walls seem to look out on an early-19th-century seaport (one painted sailor permanently peers in to see what you're eating). This is the best and certainly the most interesting bargain in St. Petersburg. See p. 454.

- **Moore's Stone Crab** (Longboat Key, off Sarasota; © 941/383-1748): Set in Longbeach, the old fishing village on the north end of Longboat Key, this popular bayfront restaurant still looks a little like a packing house (it's an offshoot of a family seafood business), but the view of the bay (dotted with mangrove islands) makes a fine complement to stone crabs fresh from the family's own traps. See p. 487.

- **Singleton's Seafood Shack** (Mayport/Jacksonville; © 904/246-4442): This rustic Old Florida fish camp has kept up with the times by offering fresh fish in more ways than just battered and fried, yet it has still managed to retain the charming casualness of a riverside fish camp. Even if you don't want seafood, this spot is worth stopping at, if only for a feel of Old Florida. See p. 617.

- **The Boss Oyster** (Apalachicola; © 850/653-9364): This dockside eatery is a good place to see if what they say about the aphrodisiac properties of Apalachicola oysters is true. The bivalves are served raw, steamed, or under a dozen toppings ranging from capers to crabmeat. You can even steam three dozen oysters and do the shucking yourself. Dine inside or at picnic tables on a screened dockside porch. See p. 684.

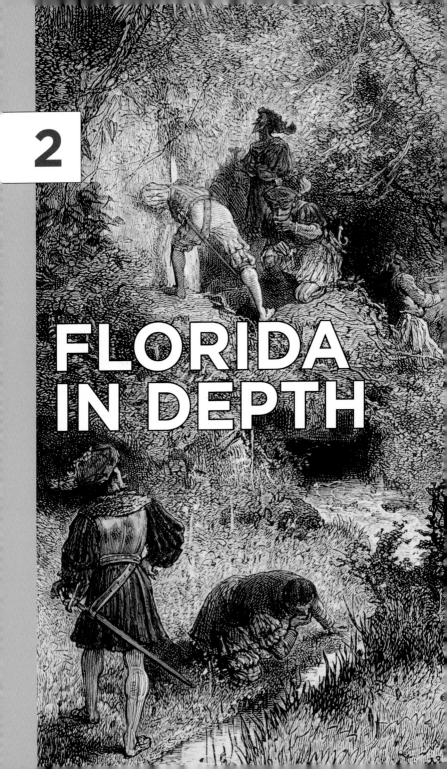

2

FLORIDA IN DEPTH

F lorida isn't just an American swamp turned condo-canyon with pretty palm trees and beaches. And contrary to popular belief, the state's history is a lot richer than its reputation as a haven for retirees, celebrities, and people in dire need of a thaw and a deep, dark tan. From its emergence as a prehistoric swamp, a nexus of Native American culture and civilization, and a 16th-century hot spot for treasure-hunting Spanish explorers to a 21st-century destination of development, politics, and pop culture, Florida has experienced more reincarnations than Shirley MacLaine.

FLORIDA TODAY

Despite the big housing boom that ultimately went bust in 2008, Florida continues to experience some activity in the luxury market. That said, economists predict a dismal economic situation throughout the state well beyond 2010. In October 2009, Florida, along with California and Nevada, posted the highest foreclosure rates in the country. A stunning statistic emerged that in October 2009 a whopping 272 foreclosures were filed by lenders each day—all in the tri-county South Florida area, representing an 8% year-over-year increase from 2008, and a massive 86% increase from 2007.

To make matters worse, unemployment rates in the state skyrocketed, and as of August 2010, the percentage of those out of work in the state rose to a staggering 11.7%. But despite the gloom and doom, thanks to the first-time homebuyer credit, home sales were up in some of the state's most dismal markets—Orlando and Fort Myers.

Optimists, including outgoing governor Charlie Crist, however, saw the glass half-full, telling The *Palm Beach Post* in January 2011, "Something is starting to percolate in Florida's economy," which had many skeptics dubiously agreeing, saying, "Yeah, the Cuban coffee." According to that newspaper, Florida in 2010 was in "the best financial shape it has been in years, despite a sluggish economy that has been a drain on state and local coffers for the past three years." Hotels were seeing an upturn in bookings and new restaurants and diversions opened to sizable crowds. But look at any local newspaper, where headlines one day screamed foreclosures were at record highs and, on another, how real estate sales were booming. Go figure.

Optimism aside, according to economists, however, the job forecast is expected to remain dismal until at least 2012.

In fact, the only boost Florida experienced in 2010 was one in the number of foreclosures, with 1 in 155 households in dire financial straits. In 2009, for the first time in more than 60 years, more people moved out of Florida than moved in; the state experienced a net loss of approximately 58,000 people. A bright spot: 2010 saw a slight rise in population, but the rise was in home *renters*, not owners.

FACING PAGE: **Juan Ponce de León was one of the first European explorers to come to Florida, though he never did find the Fountain of Youth.**

Just when things may have been looking up somewhat came the behemoth known as the BP Oil Disaster. And despite the $25 million the state received for tourist development councils to create ads reflecting the accurate condition of Florida's beaches—that is, that most, if not all, were untouched by the stuff— tourists remained skeptic and, in the summer of 2010, stayed away in droves. After the tar balls settled, however, the tourists trickled back, slowly but surely.

One facet of Florida that didn't seem to be affected by, well, anything was the booming theme park business, which, in 2010, saw a massive sign of improvement and consumer confidence in the form of the multi-zillion-dollar new Harry Potter attraction at Universal Studios in Orlando. As much as the British boy wizard may have saved the theme park biz, the Orlando *Sentinel* reported that the area, as of early 2010, *still* had a long way to go, and that it would be "months or years before the region shakes its hangover from the longest recession since the Great Depression."

South Florida saw a major slowdown in building, condos, hotels, and pretty much everything else. The cranes just stopped and lingered over the cityscape like a movie set on hiatus. Despite the stalling, however, a spate of restaurant openings—high-end, no less—dared to defy the notion that people weren't dining out. For every GOING OUT OF BUSINESS sign So Flo seemed to spit out an opening to balance it out. Drops in hotel rates allowed for a spate of budget-conscious tourists who normally wouldn't have had the opportunities they did after hotels put out their recession-friendly welcome mats.

Over in Southwest Florida, a few homeruns to counter the fact that tourism was indeed down in 2010: The Baltimore Orioles, in their inaugural spring training in Sarasota, drew more than 100,000 fans—most of them out-of-towners. Northeast Florida was also experiencing an upswing. According to the *Florida Times-Union,* in 2010, "Hotels experienced 60 percent-plus occupancy rates for two months in a row in February and March. That hadn't happened since mid-2008, when the downturn was beginning to take hold on the metro area."

Northwest Florida wasn't as fortunate. Before the oil spill threatened the area's beaches, the Panhandle was on a huge high thanks to the opening of the area's brand-new, LEED-certified **Northwest Florida Beaches International Airport** (ECP). Even after the oil spill threatened the area, hotels saw cancellations countered by last-minute reservations. As the oil threatened the area's big Memorial Day Weekend 2010, Southwest Airlines said that flights to the area were full. In early June, Gov. Crist announced a hard-core, 90-day marketing campaign to return tourism to the area's pre–oil spill glory. "Even though there are no physical impacts to Florida's shores from the oil spill," Crist said, "the state's tourism industry, especially in the Panhandle, has already felt a very real economic impact."

As 2011 began, things looked less bleak. "Our belief is that there is nothing that has changed about Florida, its attraction to other states and other countries, and that we're slowly heading back to that same pace," said Amy Baker, coordinator of the Legislature's Office of Economic and Demographic Research. "Over the long run there's still significant growth in our forecast."

FLORIDA HISTORY
Prehistoric Florida

Fourteen thousand years ago, Florida would have made an ideal location for the show *Land of the Lost*—that is, if there were actually dinosaurs down here. Not so much. During the age of dinosaurs, the Florida peninsula was underwater and did not exist as a landmass. Therefore, no dinosaur remains were deposited in the area that became Florida. After the land developed, **Paleo-Indians** arrived from about 13,000 B.C., and they got here by crossing over to North America from Asia. Most of their activity was around the watering holes, and sinkholes and basins in the beds of modern rivers.

Paleo-Indian culture was replaced by, or evolved into, the **Early Archaic** culture around 7900 B.C. There were now more people in Florida, and as they were no longer tied to a few water holes in an arid land, they left their artifacts in many more locations.

The Early Archaic period evolved into the **Middle Archaic** period around 5000 B.C. People started living in villages near wetlands, and favored sites may have been occupied for multiple generations. The **Late Archaic** period started around 3000 B.C., when Florida's climate had reached current conditions and the sea had risen close to its present level. People now lived everywhere fresh- or saltwater wetlands were found. Many people lived in large villages with purpose-built mounds. Fired pottery appeared in Florida by 2000 B.C. By about 500 B.C., the Archaic culture that had been fairly uniform across Florida began to fragment into regional cultures.

The post-Archaic cultures of eastern and southern Florida developed in isolation, and it is likely that the peoples living in those areas at the time of first European contact were descendants of the inhabitants of the areas in Late Archaic times. The cultures of the Florida Panhandle and the north and central Gulf coast of the Florida peninsula were strongly influenced by the Mississippian culture, although there is continuity in cultural history, suggesting that the peoples of those cultures were also descended from the inhabitants of the Archaic period. Cultivation of maize was adopted in the Panhandle and the northern part of the peninsula, but was absent or very restricted in the tribes that lived south of the Timucuan-speaking people (that is, south of a line approximately from present-day Daytona Beach to a point on or north of Tampa Bay).

NATIVE AMERICANS Spanish explorers of the early 16th century were likely the first Europeans to interact with the native population of Florida. The first documented encounter of Europeans with Native Americans of the United States came with the first expedition of **Juan Ponce de León** to Florida in 1513, although he encountered at least one native who spoke Spanish. In 1521, he encountered the **Calusa Indians,** who established 30 villages in the Everglades, during a failed colonization attempt in which they drove off the Europeans.

The Spanish recorded nearly 100 names of groups they encountered, ranging from organized political entities, such as the **Apalachee,** with a population of around 50,000, to villages with no known political affiliation. There were an estimated 150,000 speakers of dialects of the Timucua language, but the **Timucua** were organized only as groups of villages, and did not share a common culture. Other tribes in Florida at the time of first contact included the Ais; Calusa; Jaega; Mayaimi; Tequesta, who lived on the southeast coast of the Everglades; and Tocobaga. All of these tribes diminished in numbers during the period of Spanish control of Florida.

At the beginning of the 18th century, tribes from areas to the north of Florida, supplied, encouraged, and occasionally accompanied by white colonists from the Province of Carolina, raided throughout Florida, burning villages, killing many of the inhabitants, and carrying captives back to Charles Towne to be sold as slaves. Most of the villages in Florida were abandoned, and the survivors sought refuge at St. Augustine or in isolated spots around the state. Some of the Apalachee eventually reached Louisiana, where they survived as a distinct group for at least another century.

The few surviving members of these tribes were evacuated to Cuba when Spain transferred Florida to the British Empire in 1763. The **Seminole,** originally an offshoot of the Creek people who absorbed other groups, developed as a distinct tribe in Florida during the 18th century, and are now represented in the Seminole Nation of Oklahoma, the Seminole Tribe of Florida, and the Miccosukee Tribe of Indians of Florida.

SPANISH RULE Once Ponce de León laid his eyes on Florida in 1513, a slew of competitive conquistadors made futile efforts to find gold there and colonize the region. The first to establish a fort in Florida were the French, actually, but it was ultimately destroyed by the Spanish, who introduced Christianity, horses, and cattle to the region. Unfortunately, they also introduced diseases and conquistador brutality, which ultimately decimated Indian populations. Eager to expand its own American colony collection, Britain led several raids into Florida in the 1700s to overthrow Spanish rule. Among the most notable Spaniards in Florida were the aforementioned de León; **Hernando de Soto,** the most ruthless of the explorers, whose thirst for gold led to the massacre of many Indians; **Panfilo de Narvaez,** whose quest for El Dorado—the land of gold—landed him in Tampa Bay; and **Pedro Menéndez de Avilés,** who founded St. Augustine after defeating the French.

BRITISH RULE The Brits weren't interested in gold: They were all about Florida's bounty of hides and furs. After taking control in 1763, the Brits divided Florida into two. Because Florida was subsidized by the English, Floridians remained loyal to Mother England during the American Revolution—that is, until the Spanish returned and regained West Florida in 1781 and, 2 years later, East Florida. During the Spanish reconquest, American slaves fled to Florida, causing major turmoil between Spain

Ponce de Leon wounded.

Native Americans and European explorers and settlers clashed for decades over the land that became known as Florida.

and the U.S. Combined with Indian raids in the north and an Indian alliance with runaway slaves, Florida was, well, a mess, until **General Andrew Jackson** invaded Spanish Florida, captured Pensacola, and occupied West Florida. Then it was a disaster. Jackson's invasion kicked off the First Seminole War in 1817. Finally, to settle Spain's $5-million debt to the U.S., all Spanish lands east of the Mississippi, including Florida, were ceded to the U.S. in 1819.

AMERICAN RULE Florida became an organized territory of the United States on March 30, 1822. The Americans merged East Florida and West Florida (although the majority of West Florida was annexed to Orleans Territory and Mississippi Territory), and established a new capital in **Tallahassee,** located halfway between the East Florida capital of St. Augustine and the West Florida capital of Pensacola. The boundaries of Florida's first two counties, Escambia and St. Johns, approximately coincided with the boundaries of West and East Florida, respectively.

At this time, the plantation system was adopted by north Florida and because the settlers wanted the best possible land, the federal government tried moving all Indians west of the Mississippi, resulting in the Second and Third Seminole Wars.

THE SEMINOLE WARS Wartime ravaged Florida during the Seminole Wars, a trio of wars between the United States Army and the Seminole Indians and their African-American allies, also known as the Florida Wars. The **First Seminole War** (ca. 1817 or thereabouts—different history books give different dates) was sparked by American slave owners looking for runaway slaves of African and Native American descent who traded weapons with the Brits during the War of 1812. Andrew Jackson led the American response in Florida, commanding an army of 3,000. Jackson divided Florida into two counties, Escambia and St. Johns, and, after establishing county courts and mayors in St. Augustine and Pensacola, left William Pope DuVal as governor.

On March 30, 1822, Florida became an official territory. The **Second Seminole War** (1835–42) erupted as Northern settlers had their eyes on Tallahassee, a Seminole settlement, and in a futile effort to calm the tension, DuVal asked the Seminoles to move south to a 4-million-acre reservation south of present-day Ocala. While their former home became the territory's capital, Jackson became president and again asked the Indians to move, this time west of the Mississippi. They refused and what ensued lasted longer than any war in the U.S. between the American Revolution and the Vietnam War.

The **Third Seminole War** (1855–58) was a sporadic one following Florida's entry into the union and laws sending Indians into reservations in the west. After this final confrontation, many Seminoles retreated to the Everglades, where some of their descendants still live today.

THE CIVIL WAR Following Lincoln's election in 1860, Florida became the third of the original seven states to secede from the Union. But because Florida was so sparsely populated, it contributed more in goods than manpower. The large coastline served as a barrier to the Union Navy, who had a hard time curbing runners from bringing in supplies and materials from foreign suppliers. Union troops occupied major ports like Cedar Key, Jacksonville, Key West,

Visitors can still explore Ft. Pickens in the Pensacola Bay. Union forces retained control of it throughout the Civil War.

and Pensacola. With the exception of Fort Zachary Taylor and Fort Pickens, Confederate forces seized control of every U.S. Army fort in the state.

Confederates put more than 61,000 Florida slaves to work as teamsters transporting supplies, and as laborers in salt mines and fisheries, and many escaped and served the Union, providing them with intelligence on Confederate activity. In 1862, the Union military encouraged slaves in plantation areas to flee their owners.

Increasingly dissatisfied by oppressive drafting policies, Confederate soldiers began to desert to some Florida counties that served as havens for deserters from all Confederate states. These bands of deserters began attacking Confederates and, though many skirmishes did happen in Florida, the only major one to take place during the War's duration was the **Battle of Olustee** near Lake City, in which Union forces eventually retreated, causing the North to question the further Union involvement in what was deemed a "militarily insignificant" Florida.

In January 1865, Union General William Tecumseh Sherman ordered set aside a part of Florida as a home for runaway and freed former slaves, but the order was never enforced and was eventually repealed by President Andrew Johnson. On May 13, 1865, Colonel George Washington Scott surrendered what was left of his active Florida Confederate troops. On May 20, slavery was officially ended in the state as troopers raised the U.S. flag over the state capitol building. Tallahassee was the last Confederate state capital to fall to the Union army.

After meeting the requirements of Reconstruction, including writing a new state Constitution, Florida was readmitted to the United States on July 25, 1868.

UNLOCKING THE KEYS No one knows exactly when the first European set foot on one of the Florida Keys, but as exploration and shipping increased, the islands became prominent on nautical maps. The nearby treacherous coral reefs claimed many actual seafaring "martyrs" from the time of early recorded history. The chain was eventually called "keys," also attributed to the Spanish, from **cayos,** meaning "small islands."

In 1763, the Spanish ceded Florida to the British in a trade for the port of Havana. The treaty was unclear as to the status of the Keys. An agent of the King of Spain claimed that the islands, rich in fish, turtles, and mahogany for shipbuilding, were part of Cuba, fearing that the English might build fortresses and dominate the shipping lanes. The British also realized the treaty was ambiguous, but declared that the Keys should be occupied and defended as part of Florida. The British claim was never officially contested. Ironically, the British gave the islands back to Spain in 1783, to keep them out of the hands of the United States, but in 1821 all of Florida, including the necklace of islands, officially became American territory.

Many of the residents of Key West were immigrants from the Bahamas, known as **"conchs"** (pronounced *conks*), who arrived in increasing numbers after 1830. Many were sons and daughters of British Loyalists who fled to the nearest crown soil during the American Revolution.

In the 20th century, many residents of Key West started referring to themselves as "conchs," and the term is now generally applied to all residents of Key West. Some residents use the term *conch* to refer to a person born in Key West, while the term *freshwater conch* refers to a resident not born in Key West but who has lived in Key West for 7 years or more.

In 1982, Key West and the rest of the Florida Keys briefly declared their "independence" as the **Conch Republic** in a protest over a United States Border Patrol blockade. This blockade was set up on U.S. 1, where the northern end of the Overseas Highway meets the mainland at Florida City. This blockade was in response to the Mariel Boatlift. A 17-mile traffic jam ensued while the Border Patrol stopped every car leaving the Keys, supposedly searching for illegal aliens attempting to enter the mainland United States. This paralyzed the Florida Keys, which rely heavily on the tourism industry. Flags, T-shirts, and other merchandise representing the Conch Republic are still popular souvenirs for visitors to Key West, and the Conch Republic Independence Celebration—including parades and parties—is celebrated every April 23.

BOOMTOWN, FLORIDA After the Civil War, Florida met its best friend—tourism. Although the state's economy was in the dumps, its warm climate and smallish population called out to investors and developers. Railroad barons Henry Flagler and Henry Plant laid their tracks down the east and west coasts of Florida during the late 1880s, offering tourists a not-so-quick escape to paradise, or something close to it. As tourists started pouring down, the economy was stimulated. In February 1888, Florida had a special tourist. President Grover Cleveland, the first lady, and his party visited Florida for a couple of days. He visited the Subtropical Exposition in Jacksonville, where he made a speech supporting tourism to the state; then, he took a train to St. Augustine, meeting Henry Flagler.

Florida's new railroads opened up large areas to development, spurring the Florida land boom of the 1920s. Investors of all kinds, mostly from outside Florida, raced to buy and sell rapidly appreciating land in newly platted communities such as Miami and Palm Beach. A majority of the people who bought land in Florida were able to do so without stepping foot in the state, by hiring people to speculate and buy the land for them. By 1925, the market ran out of buyers to pay the high prices and the boom became a bust. The 1926 Miami hurricane further depressed the real estate market. The Great Depression arrived in 1929; however, by that time, economic decay already consumed much of Florida from the land boom that collapsed 4 years earlier.

VARIATIONS ON A THEME (PARK) Florida's first theme parks emerged in the 1930s and included **Cypress Gardens** (1936), near Winter Haven, and **Marineland** (1938), near St. Augustine. Walt Disney chose Central Florida as the site of his planned Walt Disney World Resort in the 1960s and began purchasing land. In 1971, the first component of the resort, the **Magic Kingdom,** opened and began the dramatic transformation of the Orlando area into a major resort destination. The **Everglades** were finally granted National Park status. Thanks to the work of the Everglades' foremost supporter, Ernest F. Coe, Congress passed a park bill in 1934. Dubbed by opponents as the "alligator and snake swamp bill," the legislation stalled during the Great Depression and World War II. Finally, on December 6, 1947, President Harry S Truman dedicated the Everglades National Park.

In that same year, Marjory Stoneman Douglas first published *The Everglades: River of Grass.* She understood its importance as the major watershed for South Florida and as a unique ecosystem.

ROAD-TRIPPING THROUGH FLORIDA'S FABULOUS '50S Despite the fact that in 1950, producing frozen concentrate of citrus juice became a major industry in the state, things were motoring toward a different trend beginning in

Visitors flocked from all over to see the watery stunts at one of Florida's first theme parks, Cypress Gardens, opened in 1936.

1954 with the completion of the Sunshine Skyway stretching 15 miles across Lower Tampa Bay. In 1955, the state Legislature authorized plans for a state-long turnpike. And in what sealed the deal for the '50s being the decade of Florida transportation, in 1958 a second major federal agency, the National Aeronautics and Space Administration (NASA), began operations at Cape Canaveral.

THE SPACE RACE & CUBAN INFLUX

With the **space race** in full blast, Cape Canaveral brought even more of a boom to Florida in the '60s—especially when Buzz Aldrin and Neil Armstrong blasted off from the so-called Florida Space Coast and onto the moon. Sixties Florida also saw another kind of race,

. . . 3, 2, 1, blast off! An Apollo rocket takes off from Cape Canaveral.

as more than 300,000 **Cubans** fled to Florida when Fidel Castro took over Cuba in 1959. Early arrivals landed in Florida via "freedom flights," but later, refugees risked—and lost—their lives as they made the dangerous 90-mile trip from Cuba to Key West on flimsy rafts. Florida was again in the spotlight in 1962 as the world was on edge during the Cuban Missile Crisis. The large wave of Cubans into South Florida transformed Miami into a major center of commerce, finance, and transportation for all of Latin America. Immigration from Haiti and other Caribbean states continues to the present day.

THE SO-SO '70S After being over the moon about the space race, the '70s had Florida in a bit of a depression beginning in 1971, when Richard M. Nixon ordered a halt to the Cross Florida Barge Canal after $50 million had been spent on the 107-mile structure. On a positive note, Amtrak began operation of service into Orlando as **Walt Disney World** opened its gates on October 1. Things were looking up in '73 when, despite fuel shortages, Florida set an all-time record for influx of visitors, as 26 million people visited the Sunshine State. And after 7½ years and nearly 260,000 refugees, the "freedom flights" from Cuba came to an end on April 7, 1973. The airlifts, bringing refugees into Miami at the rate of 48,000 a year, transformed the ethnic makeup of Dade County by adding at least 100,000 Cubans to the 150,000 already there.

THE GO-GO '80S In 1980, race riots tore Miami apart, and the Mariel Boatlift brought 125,000 Cubans to Florida. Disney opened its $800-million EPCOT center; the next phase of the space program saw the first manned space shuttle launches from Kennedy Space Center (KSC). In 1986, the program was dealt a tragic blow when the space shuttle *Challenger* exploded after takeoff. All seven astronauts aboard were killed. By 1987, the U.S.

Census Bureau estimate indicated that Florida had surpassed Pennsylvania to become the fourth-most-populous state in the nation. The plight of Cubans fleeing their native island was highlighted again in 1980 during the **Mariel Boatlift,** a mass movement of Cubans who departed from Cuba's Mariel Harbor for the U.S. between April 15 and October 31, 1980. The exodus was ended by mutual agreement between the U.S. and Cuba in October 1980. By that time, up to 125,000 Cubans had made the journey to Florida.

END OF THE CENTURY The decade started with the arrival of Panama's dictator, Manuel Noriega, who was being brought to Miami for trial on drug charges. On a more gracious note, Queen Elizabeth II came to Miami and Tampa in 1991, and conferred honorary knighthood on Tampa resident Gen. Norman Schwarzkopf. In 1992, Homestead and adjacent South Florida were devastated on August 24 by the costliest natural disaster in American history, Hurricane Andrew, demanding billions in aid. Bringing the World Series championship to Florida for the first time, the Florida Marlins won it all in 1997.

THIS MILLENNIUM & BEYOND Florida became the battleground of the controversial 2000 U.S. presidential election when a count of the popular votes from Election Day was extremely close and became mired in accusations of fraud and manipulation. Ultimately, the United States Supreme Court let stand the official count, and George W. Bush was declared winner of the election. The mid-2000s were a good time for pro sports in Florida, as the Marlins won another World Series in 2003 and the Tampa Bay Buccaneers won their first (and only) Super Bowl in 2003 as well. The Tampa Bay Lightning won the NHL championship in 2004, and the Miami Heat claimed the NBA title in 2006. Through the first half of the decade, Florida continued to be one of the fastest-growing states in the country, with the economy still depending greatly on tourism, but with expanding industries in business and manufacturing . . . until the economy imploded in 2008, with results that still are being felt and working themselves out.

FLORIDA IN POP CULTURE
Recommended Books & Movies

Florida is an author's dream come true. A state of much diversity (read: bizarre characters, to say the least), Florida practically hangs inspiration from the palm trees. Where to begin? Here's a short list of some of the books that "get" Florida, in her many personas. Happy reading!

FICTION

- *Fiskadoro* (Harper Perennial), by Dennis Johnson: National Book Award winner Johnston's post-apocalyptic perception of nuclear war in the Florida Keys.

- *The Perez Family* (W. W. Norton & Co. Inc.), by Christine Bell: Cuban immigrants from the Mariel Boat Lift exchange their talents for an immigration deal in Miami. See below for the film adaptation.

- *To Have and Have Not* (Scribner), by Ernest Hemingway: One of the many must-reads by Key West's most famous resident.

- *The Yearling* (Collier MacMillan Publishers), by Marjorie Kinnan Rawlings: A classic about life in the Florida backwoods.

- ***Seraph on the Suwanee*** (Harper Perennial), by Zora Neale Hurston: A novel about turn-of-the-20th-century Florida "white crackers."

- ***Nine Florida Stories*** (University Press of Florida), by Marjory Stoneman Douglas: The beloved Florida naturalist's fictional take on Florida, revealing the drama of hurricanes and plane crashes, of kidnappers, escaped convicts, and smugglers.

- ***Rum Punch*** (Harper Torch), by Elmore Leonard: The story of a stewardess, bail bondsman, and gunrunner in Palm Beach County.

- ***Swim to Me*** (Algonquin Books), by Betsy Carter: A novel set in Weeki Wachee about a shy teenager who finds her purpose at the mermaid-happy theme park.

NONFICTION

- ***Miami, the Magic City*** (Centennial Press), by Arva Moore Parks: An authoritative history of the city.

- ***The Everglades: River of Grass*** (Pineapple Press), by Marjory Stoneman Douglas: Eco-maniacs will love this personal account of the treasures of Florida's most famous natural resource.

- ***Celebration USA: Living in Disney's Brave New Town*** (Holt Paperbacks), by Douglas Frantz and Catherine Collins: An eye-opening true story about living in Disney's "model town."

Movies Filmed in Florida

- Clarence Brown's ***The Yearling*** (1946), based on the novel by M. K. Rawlings

- John Huston's ***Key Largo*** (1948), based on the novel by Hemingway (gangsters, hurricanes, and Bogey and Bacall)

Robin Williams and Nathan Lane played a couple who run a Miami nightclub in *The Birdcage.*

- Harry Levin's **Where the Boys Are** (1960; Spring Break in Fort Lauderdale)
- Lawrence Kasdan's **Body Heat** (1981; crime)
- Ron Howard's **Cocoon** (1985), based on a novel by David Saperstein (retirees)
- Tim Burton's **Edward Scissorhands** (1990; modern fairy tale filmed in Dade City and Lakeland)
- Mira Nair's **The Perez Family** (1995; Cuban culture)
- Mike Nichols's **The Birdcage** (1996; South Beach comedy)
- John Singleton's **Rosewood** (1997; African-American culture), based on the historic Rosewood massacre
- Victor Nunez's **Ulee's Gold** (1997; Panhandle family drama)
- Spike Jonze's **Adaptation** (2002), loosely based on Susan Orleans's *The Orchid Thief*

Music of Florida

The Miami recording industry did not begin with Gloria Estefan's Miami Sound Machine, contrary to popular belief. In fact, some major rock albums were recorded in Miami's Criteria Studios. Among them: *Rumours* by Fleetwood Mac and *Hotel California* by the Eagles. Longtime local music entrepreneur Henry Stone and his label, TK Records, created the local indie scene in the 1970s. TK Records produced the R&B group KC and the Sunshine Band, along with soul singers Betty Wright, George McCrae, and Jimmy "Bo" Horne, as well as a number of minor soul and disco hits, many influenced by Caribbean music. In the 1970s and early 1980s, Jacksonville saw a very active music recording scene with Southern rock bands such as Molly Hatchet, the Allman Brothers Band, 38 Special, the Outlaws, and Lynyrd Skynyrd. The Bellamy Brothers also recorded their style of country music in the mid- to late 1970s. They originated from Darby, Florida, just north of Tampa, in Pasco County. Tom Petty is from Gainesville, Florida, while boy band *NSYNC, Britney Spears, Christina Aguilera, and Justin Timberlake were graduates of Orlando's Mickey Mouse Club. In the 2000s, Miami saw an enormous rap boom in the form of Daddy Yankee, Pitbull, Rick Ross, and more.

EATING & DRINKING

Before Florida started evolving into a bona fide gastronomic destination, one respected by eaters and chefs alike, when one used the word *food* in the same sentence as *The Sunshine State,* one of two things may have come to mind: oranges and the Early Bird Special. And while both still play a very important role, pop culturally or otherwise, there's a lot more to Florida food than citrus and $3.99 prime rib, and as the locavore craze continues, in which people prefer to eat or cook with locally sourced ingredients, the following list of foods indigenous to the state can be considered the holy grail for Florida gourmands. If it's true Florida cuisine you are looking for, these are the ingredients you'll want to have, whether in some fancy, fusion restaurant or in a hands-on sea shanty with ice-cold beer, paper napkins, and plastic cutlery.

- Avocado
- Starfruit
- Coconut
- Key lime
- Kumquat
- Hearts of palm
- Mango
- Papaya
- Passion fruit
- Spiny lobster
- Stone crabs

As for the unofficial term "Florida Cuisine," it can mean many things, but we suppose "Floribbean," the fusion of Caribbean and Latin flavors with the aforementioned local Florida flavors, says it best, especially down in South Florida and in Tampa, where the Latin influences are so enormous. Some food snobs shudder at the term and prefer the phrase New World Cuisine, the product of Miami-based chef Norman Van Aken. But it's all semantics. Think cracked conch chowder with orange, saffron, and coconut; or spiny lobster salad with mango . . . mmm.

WHEN TO GO

To a large extent, the timing of your visit will determine how much you'll spend—and how much company you'll have—once you get to Florida. That's because room rates can more than double during so-called high seasons, when countless visitors flock to Florida.

The weather determines the high seasons (see "Weather," below). In subtropical South Florida, **high season** is in the winter, from **mid-December to mid-April,** although if you ask tourism execs, the high season is now creeping further into spring and even, in some parts, summer. On the other hand, you'll be rewarded with incredible bargains if you can stand the heat, humidity, and daily rainstorms of a South Florida summer between June and early September. In North Florida the reverse is true: Tourists flock here during the summer, from Memorial Day to Labor Day.

Hurricane season runs from **June to November,** and, as seen in 2005, the most active hurricane season on record, and 2009, the quietest, you never know what can happen. Pay close attention to weather forecasts during this season and always be prepared.

Presidents' Day weekend in February, Easter week, Memorial Day weekend, the Fourth of July, Labor Day weekend, Thanksgiving, Christmas, and New Year's are busy throughout the state, especially at Walt Disney World and the other Orlando-area attractions, which can be packed any time school is out (see chapter 12, "Walt Disney World & Orlando," for more information on those areas).

Northern and southern Florida share the same **shoulder seasons: April through May,** and **September through November,** when the weather is pleasant throughout Florida and the hotel rates are considerably lower than during the high season. If price is a consideration, these months of moderate temperatures and fewer tourists are the best times to visit.

See the accommodations sections in the chapters that follow for specifics on the local high, shoulder, and off seasons.

WEATHER

Northern Florida has a temperate climate, and even in the warmer southern third of the state, it's subtropical, not tropical. Accordingly, Florida sees more extremes of temperatures than, say, the Caribbean islands.

Spring, which runs from **late March to May,** sees warm temperatures throughout Florida, but it also brings tropical showers.

Summer in Florida extends from **May to September,** when it's hot and very humid throughout the state. If you're in an inland city during these months, you may not want to do anything too taxing when the sun is at its peak. Coastal areas, however, reap the benefits of sea breezes. Severe afternoon thunderstorms are prevalent during the summer heat (there aren't professional sports teams here named Lightning and Thunder for nothing), so schedule your activities for earlier in the day, and take precautions to avoid being hit by lightning during the storms. Those storms, by the way, often start out fierce and end with a rainbow and sunshine, so don't worry, just don't stand under a tree or on a golf course during the main act.

Autumn—about **September through November**—is a great time to visit, as the hottest days are gone and the crowds have thinned out. Unless a hurricane blows through, November is usually Florida's driest month. These days, however, one can never predict 100% sunshine. June through November is hurricane season here, but even if one threatens, the National Weather Service closely tracks the storms and gives ample warning if there's need to evacuate coastal areas.

Winter can get a bit nippy throughout the state and, in recent years, downright freezing, especially in northern Florida. Although snow is rare, the end of 2009 saw flakes falling as far north as Pensacola and as far south as Kendall in South Miami! Speaking of cold in Miami, locals have been known to whip out the coats, hats, and boots when the temperature drops below 80. The "cold snaps" usually last only a few days in the southern half of the state, however, and daytime temperatures should quickly return to the 70s (20s Celsius). Again, that was before all the El Niño/La Niña global warming took effect, so whenever you travel to Florida, bring a jacket. Even in summertime you may need it indoors, when air-conditioning reaches freezing temperatures.

For up-to-the-minute weather info, tune in to cable TV's Weather Channel or check out its website at **www.weather.com**.

HOLIDAYS

Banks, government offices, post offices, and many stores, restaurants, and museums are closed on the following legal national holidays: January 1 (New Year's Day), the third Monday in January (Martin Luther King, Jr., Day), the third Monday in February (Presidents' Day), the last Monday in May (Memorial Day), July 4 (Independence Day), the first Monday in September (Labor Day), the second Monday in October (Columbus Day), November 11 (Veterans' Day/ Armistice Day), the fourth Thursday in November (Thanksgiving Day), and December 25 (Christmas). The Tuesday after the first Monday in November is Election Day, a federal government holiday in presidential-election years (held every 4 years, and next in 2012).

Calendar of Events

For an exhaustive list of events beyond those listed here, check http://events.frommers. com, where you'll find a searchable, up-to-the-minute roster of what's happening in cities all over the world.

JANUARY

Discover Orange Bowl (☎ **305/341-4700;** www.orangebowl.org), Miami. Football fanatics flock to the big Orange Bowl game (now held at Sun Life Stadium, which is much nicer than the recently razed Orange Bowl) on New Year's Day, featuring what seems to be a different corporate sponsor every year and two of the year's best college football teams. Call early if you want tickets; they sell out quickly. First week of January.

Key West Literary Seminar (☎ **888/293-9291;** www.kwls.org), Key West. Literary types have a good reason to put down their books and head to Key West. This 3-day event features a different theme every year, along with a roster of incredible authors, writers, and other literary types. The event is so popular it sells out well in advance, so call early for tickets. Second week of January.

FEBRUARY

Everglades City Seafood Festival (☎ **239/695-2561;** www.everglades seafoodfestival.com), Everglades City. What seems like schools of fish-loving people flock down to Everglades City for a 2-day feeding frenzy in which Florida delicacies from stone crab to gator tails are served from shacks and booths on the outskirts of this quaint Old Florida town. Free admission, but you pay for the food you eat, booth by booth. First full weekend in February.

Speedweeks (☎ **386/254-2700;** www. daytonaintlspeedway.com), Daytona. Nineteen days of events, with a series of races that draw the top names in NASCAR stock car racing, culminate in the Daytona 500. All events take place at the Daytona International Speedway. Especially for the Daytona 500, tickets must be purchased as far as a year in advance; they go on sale January 1 of the prior year. First 3 weeks of February.

Miami International Boat Show (☎ **954/441-3231;** www.miamiboat show.com), Miami Beach. If you don't like crowds, beware, as this show draws a quarter of a million boat enthusiasts to the Miami Beach Convention Center. Some of the world's priciest megayachts, speedboats, sailboats, and schooners are displayed for purchase or for gawking. Mid-February.

South Beach Wine & Food Festival (☎ **877/762-3933;** www.sobewineand foodfest.com), South Beach. A 3-day celebration featuring some of the Food Network's best chefs, who do their thing in the kitchens of various restaurants and at events around town. In addition, there are tastings, lectures, seminars, and parties that are all open to the public—for a price, of course. Last weekend in February.

MARCH

Bike Week (☎ **800/854-1234;** www. officialbikeweek.com), Daytona Beach. This international gathering of motorcycle enthusiasts draws a crowd of more than 200,000. In addition to major races held at Daytona International Speedway (featuring the world's best road racers, motocrossers, and dirt trackers), there are motorcycle shows, beach parties, and the Annual Motorcycle Parade, with thousands of riders. First week in March.

Winter Party (☎ **305/538-5908;** www. winterparty.com), Miami Beach. Gays and lesbians from around the world book trips to Miami far in advance to attend this weekend-long series of parties and events benefiting the Dade Human Rights Foundation. Travel arrangements can be made through Different Roads Travel, the event's official travel company, by calling ☎ **888/ROADS-55** (762-3755), ext. 510. Early March.

Spring Break, Daytona Beach, Miami Beach, Panama City Beach, Key West, and other beaches. College students from all over the United States and Canada flock to Florida for endless partying, wet-T-shirt and bikini contests, free concerts, volleyball tournaments, and more. Three weeks in March.

Calle Ocho Festival (☎ **305/644-8888;** www.carnavalmiami.com), Little Havana. What Carnaval is to Rio, the Calle Ocho Festival is to Miami. This 10-day extravaganza, also called Carnival Miami, features a lengthy block party spanning 23 blocks, with live salsa music, parades, and, of course, tons of savory Cuban delicacies. Those afraid of mob scenes should avoid this party at all costs. Mid-March.

APRIL

Conch Republic Independence Celebration (☎ **305/296-0213;** www. conchrepublic.com), Key West. A 10-day party celebrating the day the Conch Republic seceded from the union. Events include a kooky bed race and drag queen race to mini-golf tournaments, cruiser car shows, and booze, lots of it. Mid-April.

JULY

Lower Keys Underwater Music Fest (☎ **800/872-3722**), Looe Key. When you hear the phrase "the music and the madness," you may think of this amusing aural aquatic event in which boaters head out to the underwater reef at the Looe Key Marine Sanctuary, drop speakers into the water, and pipe in all sorts of music, creating a disco-diving spectacular. Considering the heat at this time of year, underwater is probably the coolest place for a concert. Early July.

Blue Angels Air Show (☎ **800/874-1234** or 850/434-1234; www.visit pensacola.com or www.blueangels.navy. mil), Pensacola. World-famous navy pilots do their aerial acrobatics just 33 feet off Pensacola Beach. Early July.

SEPTEMBER

NKF Labor Day Pro-Am Surfing Festival (☎ **321/459-2200;** www.nkfsurf.com), Cocoa Beach. One of the largest surfing events on the East Coast draws pros and amateurs from around the country. There are also rock-'n'-roll bands and swimsuit contests. Labor Day weekend.

OCTOBER

Biketoberfest (☎ **386/253-RACE** [253-7223]; www.biketoberfest.org), Daytona. Road-racing stars compete at the CCS Motorcycle Championship at Daytona International Speedway. There are parties, parades, concerts, and more. Mid-October.

Clearwater Jazz Holiday (☎ **727/461-5200;** www.clearwaterjazz.com), Clearwater. Top jazz musicians play for 4 days and nights at bayfront Coachman Park in this free musical extravaganza. Mid-October.

Halloween Horror Nights (☎ **800/837-2273** or 407/363-8000; www.universal orlando.com), Orlando. Universal Studios transforms its grounds for 19 nights into haunted attractions with live bands, a psychopath's maze, special shows, and hundreds of ghouls and goblins roaming the streets. The studio closes at dusk, reopening in a new macabre form at 7pm. Full admission is charged for the event, which is geared toward adults. Mid-October to Halloween.

Mickey's Not-So-Scary Halloween Party (☎ **407/934-7639;** www.disneyworld. com), Orlando. At Walt Disney World, guests are invited to trick-or-treat in the Magic Kingdom, starting at 7pm. The party includes parades, storytelling, live music, and a bewitching fireworks display. End of October.

Fantasy Fest (☎ **305/296-1817;** www. fantasyfest.net), Key West. Mardi Gras takes a Floridian holiday as the streets of Key West are overtaken by costumed revelers who have no shame and no parental guidance. This weeklong, hedonistic, X-rated Halloween party is not for children 17 and under. Make reservations in Key West early, as hotels tend to book up quickly during this event. Last week of October.

NOVEMBER

American Sandsculpting Festival (☎ **239/454-7500;** www.sandfestival. com), Fort Myers Beach. Some 50,000 gather to sculpt and to see the world's finest sand castles. First weekend in November.

Miami Book Fair International
(✆ **305/237-3258;** www.miamibookfair. com), Miami. Bibliophiles, literati, and some of the world's most prestigious and prolific authors descend upon Miami for a weeklong homage to the written word, which also happens to be the largest book fair in the United States. The weekend street fair is the best attended of the entire event, in which regular folk mix with wordsmiths such as Tom Wolfe, Nora Ephron, Salman Rushdie, and Jane Smiley while indulging in snacks, antiquarian books, and literary gossip. All lectures are free but fill up quickly, so get there early. Mid-November.

Blue Angels Homecoming Air Show
(✆ **800/874-1234** or 850/434-1234; www.visitpensacola.com or www.blue angels.navy.mil), Pensacola. World-famous Navy pilots do their aerial acrobatics just 33 feet off the beach. Second weekend in November.

DECEMBER

Art Basel Miami Beach (www.art baselmiamibeach.com), Miami Beach/ Design District. Switzerland's most exclusive art fair and the world's most prominent collectors fly south for the winter and set up shop on South Beach and in the Design District with thousands of exhibitions, not to mention cocktail parties, concerts, and containers—as in shipping—that are set up on

the beach and transformed into make-shift galleries. First or second weekend in December.

Edison & Ford Winter Homes Holiday House (✆ **239/334-7419;** www.efwefla. org/home.asp), Fort Myers. Christmas music and thousands of lights hail the holiday season here. At the same time, candles create a spectacular Luminary Trail along the full length of Sanibel Island's Periwinkle Way. First week of December.

Christmas at Walt Disney World (www.disneyworld.com), Orlando. As you would imagine, all of the Disney properties get into the holiday spirit. In the Magic Kingdom, Main Street is lavishly decked out with lights and holly and an 80-foot glistening tree. Call ✆ **407/824-4321** for holiday events, or 934-7639 for travel packages. Throughout December.

Seminole-Hard Rock Winterfest Boat Parade (✆ **954/767-0686;** www. winterfestparade.com), Fort Lauderdale. People who complain that the holiday season just isn't as festive in South Florida as it is in colder parts of the world haven't been to this spectacular boat parade along the Intracoastal Waterway. Forget decking the halls. At this parade, the decks are decked out in magnificent holiday regalia as they gracefully—and boastfully—glide up and down the water. If you're not on a boat, the best views are from waterfront restaurants or anywhere you can squeeze in along the water. Mid-December.

LAY OF THE LAND

Florida. It's a flat state with great beaches and ocean views. But there's more to the state than sunbathing and surfing. The wildlife's pretty spectacular too. And we're not talking about the kind you see barhopping on Duval Street in Key West or spilling out of South Beach clubs as most people are getting up and ready to head to work.

In addition to the usual suspects—the alligator and the crocodile—the Sunshine State is home to a growing list of **endangered species,** including the wild panther, bobcats, and black bears. In fact, a total of 98 species of mammals call Florida home. Among them: armadillos, hogs, shrews, rabbits, possums, coyote, fox, lemurs, monkeys, deer, apes, and bats. Yes, bats. In fact, the Mexican free-tailed bat, the evening bat, and the big brown bat are common sightings everywhere in the state except the Keys and major metropolitan areas. Much cuter than bats are deer, the only native in the state being the **white-tailed deer,** which happens to be the major prey animal of the Florida panther. A smaller subspecies of these are **Key Deer,** which live only in the Keys and are few and far between—only around 800 or so are in existence.

And contrary to popular belief, the "snowbird" is not the official fowl of Florida, a state with hundreds of species of land birds and water birds from vultures, eagles, and ospreys to owls, woodpeckers, pelicans, herons, ducks, loons, and anhingas.

Marine mammals, however, are the true stars of the state, with the **manatee** at the top of the endangered list. According to experts, the highest count of manatee in the state at one time was in 2001 with 3,276. As for Flipper, the most common dolphin in the state is the bottlenose dolphin, while the most frequent orca known to the state is the Atlantic northern white whale. Bottlenose dolphins are not endangered and have a stable future thanks to their adaptability. Climate change, however, is an inevitable factor many species are facing rapidly with little time to adapt. And while some animal activists protest that keeping dolphins in captivity for tourism is cruel, in some cases, the dolphin swims are performed in the ocean with wild dolphins, while other programs are conducted in aquarium environments. Those programs that are neither are what come under fire from the activists.

But back to that alligator. No thanks to global warming, the American alligators are most affected by damage to their habitats. But global warming isn't the only reason the alligator is endangered: Increased levels of dioxins found in the bodies of water are also a key ingredient. Some would also say the alligator is also newly threatened by the recent Burmese python invasion that's straight out of a horror flick. While the python situation is out of control due to irresponsible pet owners who discard them in the Everglades when they become unmanageable, it's not a major factor in the alligator's status as an endangered species.

In December 2009, Congress allotted an additional $15 million to the federal State and Tribal Wildlife Grant program to help bring wildlife action plans into alignment with climate change. For a list of opportunities, sites, and outfitters and guides for wildlife viewing throughout the state, go to **http://myfwc.com/viewing**.

RESPONSIBLE TRAVEL

Florida's biggest attraction isn't a theme park, but rather its natural resources. Thanks to some of the state's initiatives, keeping Florida green is becoming second nature. The **Florida Green Lodging** program, for instance, is a voluntary initiative of the Florida Department of Environmental Protection that designates and recognizes lodging facilities making a commitment to conserving and protecting Florida's natural resources. As of February 19, 2010, there were 621 designated Florida Green Lodging properties. In order to be considered for membership in this very exclusive, green group, motels, hotels, and resorts must educate customers, employees, and the public on conservation; participate in waste reduction, reuse, recycling, water conservation, and energy efficiency; and provide eco-friendly transportation. The designation is valid for 3 years from the date of issue, and all properties are required to submit environmental performance data every year as well as implement at least two new environmental practices from any of the six areas of sustainable operations. For a list of these properties, go to **www.dep.state.fl.us/greenlodging/lodges.htm**

Eco-tourism isn't just a trendy catchphrase when it comes to tourism in Florida. The Florida Fish and Wildlife Conservation Commission estimates that outdoor activities have almost a $10-billion impact on the state's economy. The Everglades is an eco-tourism hot spot where responsible tourism isn't an option but a requirement for anyone visiting or working there. In fact, in 2010, the **Comprehensive Everglades Restoration Plan** began a process that will return some lands previously squandered for development to their formerly pristine, natural conditions.

Similar efforts can be seen throughout the state, such as in North Florida, where the new Northwest Florida Beaches International Airport in Panama Beach is the nation's first Leadership in Energy and Design (LEED)–certified passenger terminal. This "green" airport encompasses 4,000 acres donated by the St. Joe Company that will be part of a landmark conservation effort to include a National Audubon Nature Center. See **www.frommers.com/planning** for more tips on responsible travel.

SPECIAL-INTEREST TRIPS

Bird-watching, boating and sailing, camping, canoeing and kayaking, fishing, golfing, tennis—you name it, the Sunshine State has it. These and other activities are described in the outdoor-activities sections of the following chapters, but here's a brief overview of some of the best places to move your muscles, with tips on how to get more detailed information.

The **Florida Sports Foundation,** 2390 Kerry Forest Pkwy., Ste. 101, Tallahassee, FL 32309 (© **850/488-8347;** fax 850/922-0482; www.flasports. com), publishes free brochures, calendars, schedules, and guides to outdoor pursuits and sports throughout Florida. We've noted some of its specific publications in the sections below.

For excellent color maps of state parks, campgrounds, canoe trails, aquatic preserves, caverns, and more, contact the **Florida Department of Environmental Protection,** Office of Communications, 3900 Commonwealth Blvd., Tallahassee, FL 32399 (© **850/245-2118;** www.dep.state.fl.us). Some of the department's publications are mentioned below.

The Great Outdoors

BIKING & IN-LINE SKATING Florida's relatively flat terrain makes it ideal for bicycling and in-line skating. You can bike right into **Everglades National Park** along the 38-mile-long Main Park Road, and bike or skate from St. Petersburg to Tarpon Springs on the 47-mile-long converted railroad bed known as the **Pinellas Trail.** Many towns and cities have designated routes for cyclists, skaters, joggers, and walkers, such as the pathways running the length of **Sanibel Island;** lovely Bayshore Boulevard in **Tampa; Ocean Drive** on South Beach; and the bike lanes from downtown **Sarasota** out to St. Armands, Lido, and Longboat keys.

BIRD-WATCHING With hundreds of both land- and sea-based species, Florida is one of America's best places for bird-watching—if you're not careful, pelicans will steal your picnic lunch on the historic **Naples Pier.** The **J. N. "Ding" Darling National Wildlife Refuge** is great for watching birds.

With its northeast Florida section now open, the **Great Florida Birding Trail** will eventually cover some 2,000 miles throughout the state. Fort Clinch State Park, on Amelia Island, and Merritt Island National Wildlife Refuge, in Cape Canaveral, are gateways to the northeast trail. Information is available from the Birding Trail Coordinator, Florida Fish & Wildlife Conservation Commission, 620 S. Meridian St., Tallahassee, FL 32399-1600 (✆ **850/922-0664;** fax 850/488-1961; www.floridabirding trail.com). You can download maps from the website.

Many of the state's wildlife preserves have gift shops that carry books about Florida's birds, including the *Florida Wildlife Viewing Guide,* in which authors Susan Cerulean and Ann Morrow profile 96 great parks, refuges, and preserves throughout the state. The guide is also available directly from the publisher, Falcon Press (✆ **888/922-0789;** www.falcbooks.com).

BOATING & SAILING With some 1,350 miles of shoreline, it's not surprising that Florida is a boating and sailing mecca. In fact, you won't be anyplace near the water very long before you see flyers and other advertisements for rental boats and sailboat cruises. Many of them are mentioned in the chapters that follow.

The **Moorings** (✆ **888/952-8420** or 727/530-5651; www.moorings. com), the worldwide sailboat charter company, has its headquarters in Clearwater and its Florida yacht base nearby in St. Petersburg. From St. Pete, experienced sailors can take bareboats as far as the Keys and the Dry Tortugas, out in the Gulf of Mexico.

Key West keeps gaining prominence as a world sailing capital. *Yachting* magazine sponsors the largest winter regatta in America here each January, and smaller events take place regularly.

Even if you've never hauled on a halyard, you can learn the art of sailing at **Steve and Doris Colgate's Offshore Sailing School** (www.off shore-sailing.com), headquartered at the South Seas Plantation Resort & Yacht Harbour on Captiva Island, with an outpost in St. Petersburg. The prestigious **Annapolis Sailing** (www.annapolissailing.com) has bases in St. Petersburg and on Marathon in the Keys.

Florida Boating & Fishing, available free from the Florida Sports Foundation (see the introduction to this section, above), is a treasure-trove of tips on safe boating; state regulations; locations of marinas, hotels, and resorts; marine products and services; and more.

CAMPING Florida is dotted with RV parks (if you own such a vehicle, it's the least expensive way to spend your winters here). But for the best tent camping, look to Florida's national preserves and 110 state parks and recreation areas. Options range from luxury sites with hot-water showers and cable TV hook-ups, to primitive island and beach camping with no facilities whatsoever.

Regular and primitive camping in **St. George Island State Park,** near Apalachicola, is a bird-watcher's dream—plus you'll be on one of the nation's most magnificent beaches. Equally great are the sands at **St. Andrews State Park,** in Panama City Beach (with sites right beside the bay). Other top spots are **Fort DeSoto Park,** in St. Pete Beach (more gorgeous bayside sites); the remarkably preserved **Cayo Costa Island State Park,** between Boca Grande and Captiva Island in Southwest Florida; **Canaveral National Seashore,** near the Kennedy Space Center; **Anastasia State Park,** in St. Augustine; **Fort Clinch State Park,** on Amelia Island; and **Bill Baggs Cape Florida State Park,** on Key Biscayne in Miami. Down in the Keys, the oceanside sites in **Long Key State Park** are about as nice as they get.

In each of these popular campgrounds, reservations are essential, especially during the high season. Florida's state parks take bookings up to 11 months in advance.

The **Florida Department of Environmental Protection,** Division of Recreation and Parks, Mail Station 535, 3900 Commonwealth Blvd., Tallahassee, FL 32399-3000 (✆ **850/245-2118;** www.dep.state.fl.us), publishes an annual guide of tent and RV sites in Florida's state parks and recreation areas.

Pet owners, note: Pets are permitted at some—but not all—state park beaches, campgrounds, and food service areas. Before bringing your animal, check with the department or the individual park to see if your pet will be allowed. And bring your pet's rabies certificate, which is required.

For private campgrounds, the **Florida Association of RV Parks & Campgrounds,** 1340 Vickers Dr., Tallahassee, FL 32303 (✆ **850/562-7151;** fax 850/562-7179; www.floridacamping.com), issues an annual *Camp Florida* directory with locator maps and details about its member establishments in the state.

CANOEING & KAYAKING Canoers and kayakers have almost limitless options for discovery here: picturesque rivers, sandy coastlines, marshes, mangroves, and gigantic Lake Okeechobee. Exceptional trails run through several parks and wildlife preserves, including **Everglades National Park,** Sanibel Island's **J. N. "Ding" Darling National Wildlife Refuge,** and **Briggs Nature Center,** on the edge of the Everglades near Marco Island.

According to the Florida State Legislature, however, the state's official "Canoe Capital" is the Panhandle town of **Milton,** on U.S. 90 near Pensacola. Up here, Blackwater River, Coldwater River, Sweetwater Creek, and Juniper Creek are perfect for tubing, rafting, and paddleboating, as well as canoeing and kayaking.

Another good venue is the waterways winding through the marshes between **Amelia Island** and the mainland.

Many conservation groups throughout the state offer half-day, full-day, and overnight canoe trips. For example, the **Conservancy of Naples** (✆ **239/262-0304;** www.conservancy.org) has a popular series of moonlight canoe trips through the mangroves, among other programs.

Based during the winter at Everglades City, on the park's western border, **North American Canoe Tours, Inc.** (✆ **239/695-3299;** www.evergladesadventures.com), offers weeklong guided canoe expeditions through the Everglades.

The Everglades are a great place to see nature up close from a canoe.

Thirty-six creek and river trails, covering 950 miles altogether, are itemized in the excellent free **Canoe Trails** booklet published by the Florida Department of Environmental Protection, Office of Communications, 3900 Commonwealth Blvd., Tallahassee, FL 32399 (℃ **850/245-2118; www.dep.state.fl.us**).

Specialized guidebooks include *A Canoeing and Kayaking Guide to the Streams of Florida: Volume 1, North Central Florida and Panhandle,* by Elizabeth F. Carter and John L. Pearce; and *Volume 2, Central and Southern Peninsula,* by Lou Glaros and Doug Sphar. Both are published by Menasha Ridge Press (**www.menasharidge.com**).

ECO-ADVENTURES If you don't want to do it yourself, you can observe Florida's flora and fauna on guided field expeditions—and contribute to conservation efforts while you're at it.

The **Sierra Club,** the oldest and largest grass-roots environmental organization in the U.S., offers eco-adventures through its Florida chapters. Recent outings have included canoeing or kayaking through the Everglades, hiking the Florida Trail in America's southernmost national forest, camping on a barrier island, and exploring the sinkhole phenomenon in North-Central Florida. You do have to be a Sierra Club member, but you can join at the time of the trip. Contact the club's national outings office at 85 Second St., 2nd Floor, San Francisco, CA 94105-3441 (℃ **415/977-5500;** www. sierraclub.org).

The Florida chapter of the **Nature Conservancy** has protected 578,000 acres of natural lands in Florida and presently owns and manages 36 preserves. For a small fee, you can join one of its field trips or work parties that take place periodically throughout the year; fees vary from year to year and event to event, so call for more information. Participants get a chance to learn about and even participate in the preservation of the ecosystem. For details on all the preserves and adventures, contact the Nature Conservancy, Florida Chapter, 222 S. Westmonte Dr., Ste. 300, Altamonte Springs, FL 32714 (℃ **407/682-3664;** fax 407/682-3077; www.nature.org).

A nonprofit organization dedicated to environmental research, the **Earthwatch Institute,** 3 Clocktower Place, Ste. 100 (P.O. Box 75), Maynard, MA 01754 (℃ **800/776-0188** or 978/461-0081; www.earthwatch. org), has excursions to survey dolphins and manatees around Sarasota and to monitor the well-being of the whooping cranes raised in captivity and released in the wilds of Central Florida.

Another research group, the **Oceanic Society,** Fort Mason Center, Building E, San Francisco, CA 94123 (℃ **800/326-7491** or 415/441-1106; fax 415/474-3395; www.oceanic-society.org), also has Florida trips among its expeditions, including manatee monitoring in the Crystal River area, north of Tampa.

FISHING In addition to the amberjack, bonito, grouper, mackerel, mahimahi, marlin, pompano, redfish, sailfish, snapper, snook, tarpon, tuna, and wahoo running offshore and in inlets, Florida has countless miles of rivers and streams, plus about 30,000 lakes and springs stocked with more than 100 species of freshwater fish. Indeed, Floridians seem to fish everywhere: off canal banks and old bridges, from fishing piers and fishing fleets. You'll even see them standing alongside the Tamiami Trail (U.S. 41) that cuts across the Everglades—one eye on their line, the other watching for alligators.

Anglers 16 and older need a license for any kind of saltwater or freshwater fishing, including lobstering and spearfishing. Licenses are sold at bait-and-tackle shops around the state.

The **Florida Department of Environmental Protection,** 3900 Commonwealth Blvd., Tallahassee, FL 32399-3000 (✆ **850/245-2118;** www.dep.state.fl.us), publishes the annual *Fishing Lines,* a free magazine with a wealth of information about fishing in Florida, including regulations and licensing requirements. It also distributes free brochures with annual freshwater and saltwater limits. And the Florida Sports Foundation (see the introduction to this section, earlier) publishes *Florida Fishing & Boating,* another treasure-trove of information.

GOLF Florida is the unofficial golf capital of the United States—some say the world—and the **World Golf Hall of Fame** is near St. Augustine. This state-of-the-art museum is worth a visit, even if you're not in love with the game.

One thing is certain: Florida has more golf courses than any other state—more than 1,150 at last count, and growing. We picked some of the best for chapter 1, but suffice it to say that you can tee off almost anywhere, anytime there's daylight. The highest concentrations of excellent courses are in Southwest Flor-ida, around Naples and Fort Myers (more than 1,000 holes!); in the Orlando area (Disney alone has 99 holes open to the public); and in the Panhandle, around Destin and Panama City Beach. It's a rare town in Florida that doesn't have a municipal golf course—even Key West has 18 great holes.

Greens fees are usually much lower at the municipal courses than at privately owned clubs. Whether public or private, greens fees tend to vary greatly, depending on the time of year. You could pay $150 or more at a private course during the high season, but less than half that when the tourists are gone. The fee structures vary so much that it's best to call ahead and ask, and always reserve a tee time as far in advance as possible.

You can learn the game or hone your strokes at one of several excellent golf schools in the state. **David Ledbetter** has teaching facilities in Orlando and Naples, **Fred Griffin** is in charge of the Grand Cypress Academy of Golf at Grand Cypress Resort in Orlando, and you'll find **Jimmy Ballard's** school at the Ocean Reef Club on Key Largo. The Westin Innisbrook Resort at Tarpon Springs has the academy at **Innisbrook, a Salamander Golf & Spa Resort,** while Amelia Island (near Jacksonville) is home to the **Amelia Island Plantation Golf School.**

You can get information about most Florida courses, including current greens fees, and reserve tee times through **Tee Times USA,** P.O. Box 641, Flagler Beach, FL 32136 (✆ **888/GOLF-FLO** [465-3356] or 386/439-0001; www.teetimesusa.com), which publishes a vacation guide with many stay-and-play golf packages.

Florida Golf, published by the Florida Sports Foundation, lists every course in Florida. It's the state's official golf guide and is available from Visit Florida (www.visitflorida.com).

Golfer's Guide magazine publishes monthly editions covering most of Florida. It is available free at local visitor centers and hotel lobbies, or you can contact the magazine at 2 Park Lane, Ste. E, Hilton Head Island, SC 29928 (✆ **800/864-6101** or 843/842-7878; fax 843/842-5743; www.golfersguide.com).

Northwest Florida is covered by **South Coast Golf Guide,** published by Tee and J's Ent., LLC, P.O. Box 11278, Pensacola, FL 32524-1278 (✆ **850/505-7553;** fax 850/505-0057; www.southcoastgolfguide.com).

You can also get more information from the **Professional Golfers' Association (PGA),** 400 Ave. of the Champions, Palm Beach Gardens, FL 33418 (✆ **800/633-9150;** www.pga.com); or from the **Ladies Professional Golf Association (LPGA),** 100 International Golf Dr., Daytona Beach, FL 32124 (✆ **904/254-6200;** www.lpga.com).

More than 700 courses are profiled in **Florida Golf Guide,** by Jimmy Shacky (Open Roads Publishing), available at bookstores for $20.

HIKING Although you won't be climbing any mountains in this relatively flat state, there are thousands of beautiful hiking trails in Florida. The ideal hiking months are October through April, when the weather is cool and dry and mosquitoes are less prominent. Like anywhere else, you'll find trails that are gentle and short, and others that are challenging—some trails in the Everglades require you to wade waist-deep in water!

Most Florida snakes are harmless, but a few have deadly bites, so it's a good idea to avoid them all. If you're venturing into the backcountry, watch out for gators, and don't ever try to feed them (or any wild animal). You risk getting bitten. (They can't tell the difference between the food and your hand.) You're also upsetting the balance of nature, as animals fed by humans lose their ability to find their own food.

The **Florida Trail Association,** 5415 SW 13th St., Gainesville, FL 32608 (✆ **877/HIKE-FLA** [445-3352] or 352/378-8823; www.florida trail.org), maintains a large percentage of the public trails in the state and puts out an excellent book packed with maps, details, and color photos.

For a copy of **Florida Trails,** which outlines the many options, contact **Visit Florida** (www.visitflorida.com). Another resource is **A Guide to Your National Scenic Trails,** from the Office of Greenways and Trails, Department of Environmental Protection, 3900 Commonwealth Blvd., Tallahassee, FL 32399 (✆ **850/245-2118;** www.dep.state.fl.us/gwt). You can also contact the office of **National Forests in Florida,** Woodcrest Office Park, 325 John Knox Rd., Ste. F-100, Tallahassee, FL 32303 (✆ **850/523-8500;** www.southernregion.fs.fed.us/florida).

Finally, **Hiking Florida,** by M. Timothy O'Keefe (Falcon Press; www. falcbooks.com), details 132 hikes in Florida, with maps and photos.

SCUBA DIVING & SNORKELING Divers love the Keys, where you can see magnificent formations of tree-size elkhorn coral and giant brain coral, as well as colorful sea fans and dozens of other varieties, sharing space with 300 or more species of rainbow-hued fish. Reef diving is good all the way from Key Largo to Key West, with plenty of tour operators, outfitters, and dive shops. Particularly worthy are **John Pennekamp Coral Reef State Park** in Key Largo, and **Looe Key National Marine Sanctuary** off Big Pine Key. *Skin Diver* magazine picked Looe Key as the number-one dive spot in North America. Also, the clearest waters in which to view some of the 4,000 sunken ships along Florida's coast are in the Middle Keys and the waters between Key West and the Dry Tortugas. Snorkeling in the Keys is particularly fine between Islamorada and Marathon.

In Northwest Florida, the 100-fathom curve draws closer to the white, sandy Panhandle beaches than to any other spot on the Gulf of Mexico. It's

Special-Interest Trips

FLORIDA IN DEPTH

too far north here for coral, but you can see brilliantly colored sponges and fish and, in Timber Hole, discover an undersea "petrified forest" of sunken planes, ships, and even a railroad car. The battleship USS *Massachusetts* lies in 30 feet of water just 3 miles off Pensacola. Every beach town in Northwest Florida has dive shops to outfit, tour, or certify visitors.

In the Crystal River area, north of the St. Petersburg and Clearwater beaches, you can snorkel with the manatees in the warm spring waters of Kings Bay.

If you want to keep up with what's going on statewide, you can sub-scribe to the monthly magazine *Florida Scuba News* (© 904/783-1610; www.scubanews.com). You might also want to pick up a specialized guidebook. Some good ones include *Coral Reefs of Florida,* by Gilbert L. Voss (Pineapple Press; www.pineapplepress.com), and *The Diver's Guide to Florida and the Florida Keys,* by Jim Stachowicz (Windward Publishing).

TENNIS Year-round sunshine makes Florida great for tennis. There are some 7,700 places to play throughout the state, from municipal courts to exclu-sive resorts. Some municipal facilities—Cambier Park Tennis Center in Na-ples leaps to mind—are comparable to the ones at expensive resorts, except they're free or close to it.

If you can afford it, you can learn from the best in Florida. **Nick Bollettieri** has a sports academy in Bradenton. Safety Harbor Resort and Spa near St. Petersburg has a USTA-approved tennis academy. Amateurs can hobnob with the superstars at **ATP Tour International Headquarters** in Ponte Vedra Beach, near Jacksonville. And **Chris Evert** has her own center in Boca Raton.

The 18 hard courts, 2 grass courts, and 6 clay courts at the **Crandon Tennis Center,** 6702 Crandon Blvd. (© 305/365-2300), get crowded on weekends because they're some of Miami's most beautiful. You'll play on the same courts as Lendl, Graf, Evert, McEnroe, Roddick, Nadal, Federer, and other greats; this is the venue for one of the world's biggest annual ten-nis events, the Sony Ericsson Open. There's a pleasant, if limited, pro shop, plus many good pros. Only four courts are lighted at night, but if you reserve at least 48 hours in advance, you can usually take your pick. Hard-court fees are $4 per person, per hour during the day; $6 per person, per hour at night. Clay-court fees are $7 per person, per hour during daytime only. Grass courts are $11 per person, per hour during daytime only. The courts are open daily from 8am to 9pm.

Famous as the spot where Chris Evert got in her early serves, the **Jimmy Evert Tennis Center,** 701 NE 12th Ave. (off Sunrise Blvd.), Fort Lauderdale (© 954/828-5378), has 18 clay and 3 hard courts (15 light-ed). Her coach and father, James Evert, still teaches young players here, though he is very picky about whom he'll accept. Nonresidents of Fort Lauderdale pay $7.50 an hour per person before 5pm and $9 an hour per person after 5pm.

Other top places at which to learn and play are the **Omni Amelia Island Plantation,** on Amelia Island; **Sanibel Harbour Marriott Resort & Spa,** in Fort Myers, whose 5,500-seat stadium has hosted Davis Cup matches; **South Seas Resort & Yacht Harbour,** on Captiva Island; and the **Naples Grande Resort & Club,** in Naples.

SUGGESTED FLORIDA ITINERARIES

Ask anyone who lives here and they'll tell you: Florida is a long state. If you drive from Jacksonville to the southernmost point in Key West, it'll take 10 hours at least—without traffic. Same goes for the tedious drive from Miami to the Panhandle.

Thankfully, there are flights throughout the state that make exploration much easier. Don't tear your hair out if you can't get from Disney to the Everglades in the same trip. Set your sights on what you want to do and see the most, and simply unwind—this is, after all, a holiday. You can always come back. In fact, return visits are highly encouraged!

The range of possible itineraries is endless; what we've suggested below is a very full program covering Florida over a 2-week period. If possible, you should extend your time—2 weeks is not really enough time if you plan to actually explore the Sunshine State, but if you plan to veg out on a beach, then it's plenty of time—or cut out some of the destinations suggested. You can always tack on one itinerary to the next. We've done our best to keep these itineraries geographically viable and logical. If you need ideas for what to include, you can use the highlights from chapter 1 to work out a route that covers those experiences or sights that really appeal to you. Whatever you finally decide to do, we highly recommend that you at least include a stop at one of Florida's natural wonders, be it the beaches, the Everglades, or the Keys.

Important: Should limited time force you to include only the most obvious stops in your itinerary, you will make contact mainly with those who depend on you to make a living, which regrettably could leave you with a frustrated sense that Florida is one big, long tourist trap. This is why it is so important to *get off the beaten tourist track,* to experience the wacky, the kitschy, the stunning, the baffling, and the fascinating people, places, and things that make this state one of the most popular vacation destinations in the world.

THE REGIONS IN BRIEF

Contrary to popular belief, it's not all sun, sea, sand, and butterfly ballots. Here's a brief rundown of the state's regions to help you plan your itinerary.

MIAMI & MIAMI BEACH Sprawling across the southeastern corner of the state, metropolitan Miami is a city that prides itself on benefiting from its multiple, vibrant personalities as well as its no-passport-necessary international flair. Here you will hear a cacophony of Spanish and many other languages, not to mention accents, spoken all around you, for this area is a melting pot of immigrants from Latin America, the Caribbean, and, undeniably, the northeastern United States in particular. Cross the causeways and you'll come to the sands of Miami Beach, long a resort mecca and home to the hypertrendy South Beach, famous for its Art Deco architecture, nightlife, and celebrity sightings. See chapters 4 and 5 for more information on the Miami area; see p. 72 for descriptions of the different districts within Miami.

FACING PAGE: **You can explore on foot, by bike, or from the water at Bill Baggs State Park in Key Biscayne.**

THE KEYS From the southern tip of the Florida mainland, U.S. 1 travels through a 100-mile-long string of islands stretching from Key Largo to the famous, funky, and laid-back "Conch Republic" of Key West, only 90 miles from Cuba and the southernmost point in the United States (it's always warm down here). While some of the islands are crammed with strip malls and tourist traps, most are dense with unusual species of tropical flora and fauna. The Keys don't have the best beaches in Florida, but the waters here—all in a vast marine preserve—offer the state's best scuba diving and snorkeling, and some of its best deep-sea fishing. See chapter 6 for more information.

EVERGLADES & BISCAYNE NATIONAL PARKS This is not your B-movie swamp. In fact, no Hollywood studio could afford to replicate the stunning beauty found in this national landmark. Encompassing more than 2,000 square miles and 1.5 million acres, Everglades National Park covers the entire southern tip of Florida. The park, along with nearby Big Cypress National Preserve, protects a unique and fragile "River of Grass" ecosystem teeming with wildlife that is best seen by canoe, by boat, or on long or short hikes. To the east of the Everglades is Biscayne National Park, which preserves the northernmost living-coral reefs in the continental United States. See chapter 7 for more information.

THE GOLD COAST North of Miami, the Gold Coast is aptly named, for here are booming Hollywood and Fort Lauderdale, ritzy Boca Raton and Palm Beach—the sun-kissed, glitzy, glamorous, and sandy playgrounds of the rich and famous. Beyond its dozens of gorgeous beaches, the area offers fantastic shopping, entertainment, dining, boating, golfing, and tennis, and many places to relax in beautiful settings. With some of the country's most famous golf courses and even more tennis courts, this area also attracts big-name tournaments. See chapter 8 for more information.

THE TREASURE COAST Despite gaining unprecedented numbers of new residents in recent years, the beach communities running from Hobe Sound north to Sebastian Inlet have successfully and blissfully managed to retain their small-town feel. In addition to a vast array of wildlife (not to be mistaken for nightlife, which is intentionally absent from these parts), the area has a rich and colorful history. Its name stems from a violent 1715 hurricane that sank an entire fleet of treasure-laden Spanish ships. The sea around Sebastian Inlet draws surfers to the largest swells in the state, and the area has some great fishing as well. See chapter 9 for more information.

SOUTHWEST FLORIDA Ever since inventor Thomas Alva Edison built a home here in 1885, some of America's wealthiest families have spent their winters along Florida's southwest coast. They're attracted by the area's subtropical climate, shell-strewn beaches, and intricate waterways winding among 10,000-plus islands. Many charming remnants of Old Florida coexist with modern resorts in the sophisticated riverfront towns of Fort Myers and Naples, and on islands such as Gasparilla, Useppa, Sanibel, Captiva, and Marco. Thanks to some timely preservation, the area has many wildlife refuges, including the "back door" to Everglades National Park. See chapter 10 for more information.

THE TAMPA BAY AREA Halfway down the west coast of Florida lies Tampa Bay, one of the state's most densely populated areas. A busy seaport and commercial center, the city of Tampa is home to Busch Gardens Africa, which is both a major theme park and one of the country's largest zoos. Boasting a unique pier and fine museums, St. Petersburg's waterfront downtown is one of Florida's most pleasant. Most visitors elect to stay near the beaches skirting the narrow barrier islands that run some 25 miles between St. Pete Beach and Clearwater Beach. Across the bay to the south lies Sarasota, one of Florida's prime performing-arts venues, the riverfront town of Bradenton, and another string of barrier islands with great beaches and resorts spanning every price range. See chapter 11 for more information.

WALT DISNEY WORLD & ORLANDO Walt Disney announced plans to build the Magic Kingdom in 1965, a year before his death and 6 years before the theme park opened, changing forever what was then a sleepy Southern town. Walt Disney World claims four distinct parks, two entertainment districts, enough hotels and restaurants to fill a small city, and several smaller attractions, including water parks and miniature-golf courses. Then there are the rapidly expanding Universal Studios Orlando and SeaWorld, as well as many more non-Disney attractions. Orlando is Florida's most popular tourist destination, thanks not only to an animated rodent, but also to those enterprising entertainment venues that have risen to the mouse's challenge. See chapter 12 for more information.

NORTHEAST FLORIDA The northeast section of the state contains the oldest permanent settlement in America—St. Augustine, where Spanish colonists settled more than 4 centuries ago. Today its history comes to life in a quaint historic district. St. Augustine is bordered to the north by Jacksonville, an up-and-coming Sunbelt metropolis with miles of oceanfront beach and beautiful marine views along the St. Johns River. Up on the Georgia border, Amelia Island has two of Florida's finest resorts and its own historic town of Fernandina Beach. To the south of St. Augustine is Daytona Beach, home of the Daytona International Speedway and a maddening Spring Break mecca for the MTV generation. See chapter 13 for more information.

NORTHWEST FLORIDA: THE PANHANDLE Historic roots run deep in Florida's narrow northwest extremity, and Pensacola's historic district, which blends Spanish, French, and British cultures, is a highlight of any visit to today's Panhandle. Despite that, the accents here are decidedly Deep South. So, too, are the powdery, dazzlingly white beaches that stretch for more than 80 miles past the resorts of Pensacola Beach, Fort Walton Beach, Destin, and Panama City Beach. The Gulf Islands National Seashore has preserved much of this beach and its wildlife, and inland are state parks that offer some of the state's best canoeing adventures. All this makes the area a favorite summertime vacation destination for residents of neighboring Georgia and Alabama, with whom Northwest Floridians share many Deep South traditions. Sitting in a pine and oak forest just 30 miles from the Georgia line, the state capital of Tallahassee has a moss-draped, football-loving charm all its own. See chapter 14 for more information.

SOUTH FLORIDA IN 2 WEEKS

Consider this tour to be a South Florida sampler. There's not enough time in 2 weeks to see and do everything, but we've custom-built an itinerary that will provide you with a locals'-eye view of some of the best diversions South Florida is known for. Whether you're a beach bum or a beachcomber, a club hopper or someone who prefers to swing a club, a nature lover or a people-watcher, there's something for everyone on this tour.

DAYS 1 & 2: Arrive in Key West ★★★

After arriving in the so-called Conch Republic (or Margaritaville, if you will), plan to spend a day or two. A full day on the 4 × 2-mile island is plenty for exploring, but if you're into doing the Duval Bar Crawl, you may want to leave yourself a day to recover from that inevitable hangover. Focus most of your sightseeing energy on Old Town, where you'll see stunning, restored Victorian-style homes; lush, tropical greenery; and the old Bahama Village. Be sure not to miss the sunset celebration at Mallory Square, and, if possible, do dinner at Blue Heaven in Bahama Village. Then hit the Duval Street bars if you're so inclined. Spend the next day either relaxing at your hotel pool—we recommend the Gardens Hotel and Simonton Court for a true Key West experience—or exploring the historic seaport and all its shops and Key West kitsch. See chapter 6.

DAY 3: Miami: Coral Gables, Little Havana & South Beach ★★★

Take the 3-hour drive on the Overseas Highway to Miami—one of the most scenic drives you'll ever take, albeit sometimes a boring one. If you've seen it before, consider booking a flight. If you're driving, make a pit stop in Coral Gables about six miles southwest of Miami proper, where you can get a bite to eat at the Latin American Cafeteria or on Miracle Mile, or cool off in the

Watching the sun set in Key West is a beautiful daily ritual.

Venetian Pool. If you like what you see, check into the historic Biltmore Hotel. If not, then at least see the hotel and continue on to Southwest 8th Street, otherwise known as Calle Ocho, the heart of Little Havana. Peruse the cigar stores and the old men playing dominoes in Domino Park. Grab a Cuban coffee at Versailles, and then head north to South Beach to spend the night at one of its trendy (or kitschy) hotels. See chapters 4 and 5.

DAY 4: South Beach ★★★

Wake up early and catch the sunrise on the beach. Have breakfast at the Front Porch Café. Stake your claim on the sand and spend the morning by the water. Hit Lincoln Road for lunch, and then shop there and along Collins Avenue before having a cocktail at the Rose Bar at the Delano, Skybar at the Shore Club, or, for an ocean view with your martini, the Ritz-Carlton South Beach's DiLido Beach Club. If you have the energy, continue north along Collins Avenue to its newest crown jewel, the W South Beach. Marvel at its Miami-meets-Bali decor, have a drink, or just bask in the beauty. Return to your own hotel for a disco nap; wake up around 9pm. If you can't sleep that long, head south, stopping first to marvel at the bay views and unreal, surrealist decor of the Mondrian, and then to Smith & Wollensky to toast the cruise ships leaving the port. Have dinner at Prime 112 if you can snag a reservation, or, for a less pricey, yet still sceney dining experience, the Café at Books and Books, and then hit the clubs and lounges: Wall, LIV, Mansion, Cameo, and Set. Grab a late-night snack at La Sandwicherie, or the 11th Street Diner, and then crash at your hotel. See chapters 5 and 6.

DAY 5: From South Beach to Fort Lauderdale ★★

Have breakfast at the Big Pink or the 11th Street Diner and watch the club kids coming home from the night before. Get in the car and take Fla. A1A north—the scenic route. If you haven't already, stop into the $500-million-plus behemoth known as the Fontainebleau and see if you can feel the spirit of Sinatra and Co. amid all its modern-day glory. Continue north until you hit the recently spruced-up Hollywood Beach Boardwalk, our version of Atlantic City, without the casinos. If you're hungry, have the world's best burger at Le Tub. Continue along A1A until you reach the famous Fort Lauderdale strip. Take a break at the world-famous Elbo Room and watch the action on the beach, or swank it up a bit at the spanking-new W Fort Lauderdale, where views of the ocean are almost as good as the people-watching. Spend the night there or, for a little old-world charm, at the Riverside Hotel on Las Olas Boulevard. See chapters 4, 5, and 8.

DAY 6: Sand, Seminoles & Slots ★★

Hit famous Fort Lauderdale Beach, where Frankie and Annette used to play beach-blanket bingo. Then you might head west to the Seminole Hard Rock Hotel & Casino, where you can catch a concert by a Billboard-charting artist or even Jerry Seinfeld, hit the jackpot on the slots (the hotel claims it pays out $13 million daily!), play a hand or 10 of blackjack and poker, or, for a cheaper alternative, just relax by the pool. It's almost as nice as, if not nicer than, the one at the Hard Rock Hotel in Vegas. Then head out to spot signs of real wildlife in the Everglades. See chapter 8.

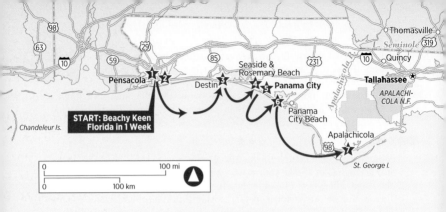

START: Beachy Keen
Florida in 1 Week

Chandeleur Is.

| 0 | 100 mi |
| 0 | 100 km |

G U L F   O F

M E X I C O

UNITED STATES

FLORIDA

■ **START:** South Florida in 2 Weeks
▲ **START:** Florida's Gulf Coast in 1 Week: Relaxing Florida
● **START:** A Week in Florida, Family Style
◆ **START:** 5 Days in Old Historic Florida
★ **START:** Beachy Keen Florida in 1 Week

Note: Bullet numbers indicate days of the itinerary

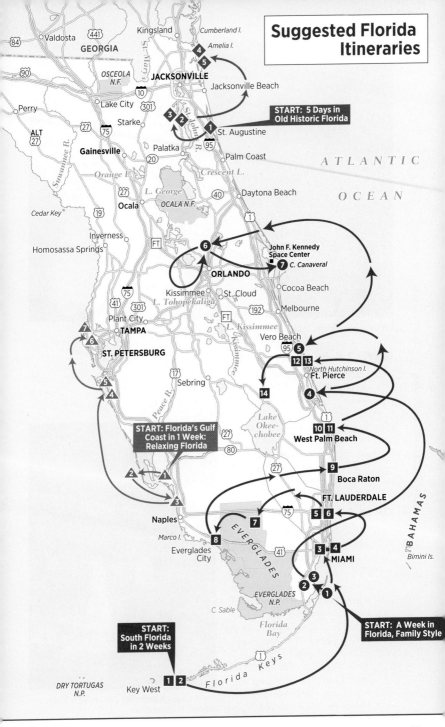

Suggested Florida Itineraries

GEORGIA

Valdosta · 441 · Kingsland · Cumberland I. · Amelia I.

84 · OSCEOLA N.F. · JACKSONVILLE · 4 · 5

90 · Lake City · 10 · Jacksonville Beach

Perry · 301 · 3 · 2 · **START: 5 Days in Old Historic Florida**

75 · Starke · 1 · St. Augustine

ALT 27 · Gainesville · Palatka · 95

Suwannee R. · Orange L. · 20 · Palm Coast · **ATLANTIC**

Cedar Key · Ocala · 19 · L. George · OCALA N.F. · 40 · Crescent L. · **OCEAN**

Inverness · Daytona Beach

Homosassa Springs · FT · 6 · John F. Kennedy Space Center · 7 · C. Canaveral

ORLANDO · 1

Kissimmee · St. Cloud · Cocoa Beach

TAMPA · 75 · 41 · 301 · L. Tohopekaliga · 192 · Melbourne

7 · 6 · Plant City · FT · L. Kissimmee · Vero Beach · 95 · 5

ST. PETERSBURG · 12 · 13 · North Hutchinson I. · Ft. Pierce

5 · 17 · Sebring · 14 · 4

4 · Peace R. · Lake Okeechobee · 1

1 · **START: Florida's Gulf Coast in 1 Week: Relaxing Florida** · 10 · 11 · West Palm Beach

2 · 27 · 80 · 9 · Boca Raton

3 · 27 · 75 · **FT. LAUDERDALE**

Naples · 7 · 5 · 6

Marco I. · 8 · EVERGLADES · 3 · 4 · MIAMI

Everglades City · 41 · **BAHAMAS** · Bimini Is.

START: South Florida in 2 Weeks · C. Sable · 2 · 3 · EVERGLADES N.P. · 1

Florida Bay · **START: A Week in Florida, Family Style**

DRY TORTUGAS N.P. · 1 · 2 · Florida Keys · Key West · 1

55

Explore the Everglades National Park by kayak, swamp buggy, or airboat.

DAYS 7 & 8: Everglades National Park ★★★

Travel 45 minutes west on I-75 to the Seminole Indian Reservation, which encompasses more than 69,000 acres of the Everglades' Big Cypress Swamp. Hop on a swamp buggy at the Billie Swamp Safari to see hogs, bison, gators, and deer. Continue west to Everglades City, check into the Ivey House B&B, and ask owners Sandee and David if they can hook you up with a special, insiders' tour of the 'Glades. See chapters 7 and 8.

DAYS 9 & 10: The Palm Beaches ★★

After leaving charming and historic Everglades City, head east and north to charming, historic, and bustling Delray Beach, where the only alligators you'll likely see are the purses of the ladies who lunch and lounge there. Check into the Sundy House and peruse the hotel's Taru Gardens. The next day, do not miss the Morikami Museum and Japanese Gardens before moving on to West Palm

The Morikami Museum and Gardens offer a Zen moment in Delray Beach.

Beach, where you should check into the Hotel Biba and do a little antiques shopping in downtown West Palm. At night, check out the clubs and restaurants in downtown West Palm, at City Place, or on Clematis Street. Be sure to have a beer and enjoy the view at Bradley's. See chapter 8.

DAY 11: From Mar-A-Lago to the Moon— or Jupiter, at Least ★★

Spend the morning driving around Palm Beach, making sure to stop and catch a glimpse of Donald Trump's palatial Mar-A-Lago. Stop by Worth Avenue to see the ladies with little dogs who lunch and shop. It's the Rodeo Drive of South Florida, truly, and you can't miss the people-watching there. For a glimpse inside a Palm Beach manse, go to the Flagler Museum, where you can explore Whitehall, Standard Oil tycoon Henry Flagler's wedding present to his third wife. Go back to reality and head toward Jupiter (Florida, not the planet!). Check into the PGA National Resort & Spa. See chapter 8.

DAYS 12 & 13: The Treasure Coast

You may not find gold on the Treasure Coast, but you will find Jonathan Dickinson State Park on Hutchinson Island, where you should rent a canoe and explore the many botanical treasures. If you're into snorkeling and diving and feel like delving deeper, check out the USS *Rankin,* an old World War II ship that was sunk in 1988, 7 miles east-northeast of the St. Lucie Inlet. Check into the Hutchinson Island Marriott Beach Resort and Marina, and consider taking the *Loxahatchee Queen* for a 2-hour tour of the area. The next day, head to Vero Beach and Sebastian for a taste of Old Florida. Check into the unique Driftwood Resort or Gloria Estefan's swanky new 94-room boutique hotel, Costa D'Este Beach Resort, and have dinner at Oriente, a Cuban restaurant with Spanish and Creole accents, if your budget allows. If not, just grab a slice of pizza at Nino's Cafe. See chapter 9.

DAY 14: Lake Okeechobee or Bust?

If you can't extend your trip to include a side trip to Lake Okeechobee, consider it for next time. In the meantime, fly home out of either Palm Beach International Airport, 35 miles south of Vero Beach, or the Melbourne International Airport, which is less than 35 miles north of Vero Beach. See chapter 9.

FLORIDA'S GULF COAST IN 1 WEEK

The beaches on the Gulf Coast are infinitely nicer than those in South Florida, with soft sand, stunning sunsets, and a sense of calm that often evades the hustle and bustle of South Florida. A week on the Gulf is akin to spending a month in a city spa. Refreshing and calming, the Gulf Coast is an ideal spot for those looking to recharge their batteries.

DAY 1: Arrive in Fort Myers Beach ★★

Check into the Edison Beach House All Suites Hotel and take in the panoramic Gulf views. Waste no time making a dinner reservation at the Gulf

Get your bubble on at the Bubble Room on Captiva Island.

Shore Grill and The Cottage, where you must try shrimp wrapped in bacon and coated with honey. After dinner, consider hitting the rooftop bar at Beached Whale, a locals' favorite, or Doc Ford's Rum Bar & Grille for some live music. See chapter 10.

DAY 2: Sanibel & Captiva Islands ★★★

Just 14 miles west of Fort Myers are two of Florida's most beautiful islands. Before heading to the wildly kitschy Bubble Room restaurant, be sure to stop at the J. N. "Ding" Darling National Wildlife Refuge, home to alligators, raccoons, otters, and a dazzling array of bird life. Take your car down the Wildlife Drive for a CliffsNotes version of the park. Then call Captiva Cruises and see if there's room for y'all on the next shuttle out to Boca Grande, sort of the Martha's Vineyard of Florida. After touring Boca Grande, return to Sanibel and check into the Casa Ybel Resort, if your budget allows; if not, we highly recommend the Tarpon Tale Inn on Sanibel, or the 'Tween Waters Inn on Captiva. Now you're ready for the Bubble Room, jazz at Ellington's, or our personal fave, live reggae at Jacaranda! See chapter 10.

DAY 3: To Naples ★★

Wake up early and do not miss breakfast and the biscuits at the Sanibel Cafe. If the line's too long, try the delicious corn muffins at Island Cow. Drive south for 40 or so miles, and you'll be in swanky, sleepy Naples. Take the Naples Trolley to get a feel for the place and then, without hesitation, hit the beach before sunset. For a ritzy experience, we recommend the Ritz-Carlton, Naples, one of the best in the entire chain. For a flip-flops-and-T-shirt experience with a hopping bar scene at sunset, you'll love the Naples Beach Hotel & Golf Club. Both have fabulous beaches. After the beach, stroll down 5th Avenue, the city's main drag, where you'll find the only real semblance of nightlife, dining, and shopping. The next morning, head 70 miles north to Sarasota. See chapter 10.

Yes, that's Solomon, standing in front of his Castle.

DAYS 4 & 5: Sarasota ★★★

Sarasota's Siesta Key Beach is one of Florida's best. But if culture is your thing, don't miss the Ringling Museum of Art. If you can't stay at the Ritz-Carlton Sarasota, consider the Captiva Beach Resort on Siesta Key. Do not miss dinner at Euphemia Haye on Longboat Key. Just don't. Also don't miss at least a stop in funky, arty Siesta Key, whose name is quite the antithesis of what it really is. For a fun diversion nearby in Bradenton, stop by the Gamble Plantation and the weird, wacky Solomon's Castle. Before heading to Tampa, have breakfast at the Blue Dolphin Cafe. See chapter 11.

DAYS 6 & 7: Tampa Bay, St. Pete & Clearwater ★★

Because this is the relaxing Gulf Coast itinerary, we won't recommend Busch Gardens Africa unless you're craving roller coasters. The same goes for Ybor City, the hub of Tampa's nightlife. It's rowdy, tacky, and fun, but hardly relaxing. Therefore, we'd like to send you directly to the Saddlebrook Resort–Tampa, where the likes of Jennifer Capriati play tennis, and aspiring Tiger Woods–types play golf. If you prefer to be on the beach, head over to St. Pete Beach and Clearwater, where we recommend the historic Don CeSar Beach Resort & Spa, the Clearwater Beach Marriott Suites on Sand Key, or the boutiquey new Postcard Inn on the Beach in St. Pete Beach. For arty types, the Salvador Dalí Museum in downtown St. Pete is highly recommended. Fly home from Tampa International Airport. See chapter 11.

A WEEK IN FLORIDA, FAMILY-STYLE

Florida is definitely a kid-friendly destination. Contrary to popular belief, not all diversions are animatronic or even remotely animated. Sure, there are the theme parks, the roller coasters, the talking mouse, and Cinderella Castle. We've got Flipper and orca and parrots that play poker. Then there's the Playmobil FunPark. So check out this family-friendly itinerary you may not have experienced yet.

DAY 1: Key Biscayne ★★★

The Ritz-Carlton, Key Biscayne has fabulous children's programs, not to mention pretty cool diversions for adults. If it's in your budget, spend a day checking out the resort (skip the Miami Seaquarium unless the kids want to swim with the dolphins), and, if not, just spend the day at the Marjory Stoneman Douglas Biscayne Nature Center, where the entire family can explore an ancient fossil tidal pool. If there's time left, check out the Bill Baggs Cape Florida State Park and rent a hydrobike. See chapters 4 and 5.

DAYS 2 & 3: Coral Gables ★★★ & South Miami ★★

Get an early start and head south to Homestead's legendary Coral Castle. When the kids have had their fill, head south and grab lunch at the family-friendly, family-run Mexican mainstay, El Toro Taco. On your way to Coral Gables, make a stop at Zoo Miami or Monkey Jungle, depending on your preference in animals, and then clean off that stinky animal scent with a splash in Coral Gables's resplendent, refreshing Venetian Pool. If you're up for it, check out Vizcaya Museum and Gardens, and/or the Miami Science Museum. After working up an appetite, take the kids for burgers at Brickell's bustling Burger & Beer Joint, where no one goes hungry—or thirsty. See chapters 4 and 5.

DAY 4: Miami & Port St. Lucie ★★★

Before leaving Miami, be sure to stop at the Miami Children's Museum, where the kids can spend a few hours channeling their inner grown-up in a bona fide TV and recording studio. If the kids are in the mood for animal antics instead, head across the causeway to Jungle Island. For a more amphibious take on Miami, consider hopping on the Miami Duck Tours "vesicle," a hybrid that's part vessel, part vehicle and looks like a duck. Quacky, to say the least. Then grab a TV dinner at the G-rated Big Pink on South Beach, and let the kids nap en route to Vero Beach. You don't need to stay overnight in Vero, though there is a satellite Disney resort there, Disney's Vero Beach Resort, and the newly renovated family-friendly Club Med Sandpiper Bay on the St. Lucie River. En route to Vero, you may want to take the kids to West Palm Beach's whimsical Playmobil FunPark or on a safari through Lion Country Safari, and then grab lunch at Jupiter's legendary Nick's Tomato Pie. See chapters 4, 5, 8, and 9.

DAY 5: Vero Beach ★★★

As if Club Med or Disney doesn't have enough for the family to do—or not do—if you decide to spend the night in Vero, or even if you don't, you may want to take the kids to McLarty Treasure Museum, where they will marvel at pirate's booty, or to one of the beautiful beaches nearby. See chapter 9.

DAY 6: Arrive in Lake Buena Vista ★★★

Okay, we lied. Sort of. We're sending you in the environs of Disney and friends, but only to check into the coolest kid-friendly hotel possibly in the entire world. The Nickelodeon Suites Resort offers "Kid Suites," with different themes featuring the kids' favorite Nick characters. We know many a family that has traveled here just so the kids could stay in the hotel. If you choose, you can go to Disney World or one of the theme parks. See chapter 12.

SUGGESTED ITINERARIES | A Week in Florida, Family-Style

DAY 7: Spacing Out at Cape Canaveral ★★★

Despite the fact that the shuttle program is in its final countdown, so to speak, the John F. Kennedy Space Center is a must-see for everyone (for now), but especially kids. Not only will you see where rockets and shuttles are launched, but you can also have lunch with an astronaut! Either spend the night here and fly out of the Melbourne International Airport, or make the 3-hour drive back to Miami International Airport. See chapter 13.

Get up close to astronaut artifacts at JFK Space Center.

5 DAYS IN OLD HISTORIC FLORIDA

Many Floridians lament the loss of the days of the plastic pink flamingos, early-bird specials, cracker-style homes (as opposed to Cracker Barrel restaurants), and small, quaint towns. The thing is, they still exist! Old Florida begins in St. Augustine and doesn't end there at all. Here's a sample that promises to take you back to a Florida that would seem ancient even to your grandparents.

DAY 1: St. Augustine ★★★

Walk the boardwalk at pristine Anastasia State park.

The easiest way to hit America's oldest city is to fly into Daytona International Airport. But because this is a tour of Old Florida, we'll have you skip the Daytona Spring Break and NASCAR scene, and head an hour north into the 17th century. Everything in St. Augustine claims to be the oldest whatever—and, in most cases, it's true: the Oldest Store, the Oldest Wooden Schoolhouse, the Oldest House, and more. Pop a multivitamin and skip the overrated Fountain of Youth. Instead, hit Anastasia State Park and see what a beach would look like if it were unfettered by modernization. To really keep with the old theme, we suggest a room at the Casablanca Inn on the Bay, a 1914 house listed on the National Register of Historic Places, or at the circa-1888-meets-21st-century Casa Monica. See chapter 13.

A visit to The Zephaniah Kingsley Plantation gives an idea of plantation life in old Florida.

DAYS 2 & 3: North & South of the St. Johns River ★★

Despite its modern skyline, Jacksonville actually has some serious history. South of the St. Johns River, you will find the Fort Caroline National Memorial, a former 16th-century French Huguenot settlement that was wiped out by the Spanish but preserved in the form of archaeological relics. North of the river is the Zephaniah Kingsley Plantation, or at least the remains of what was once a 19th-century plantation complete with clapboard homes and slave cabins. Check into either the historic House on Cherry Street or, also on the St. Johns, the Inn at Oak Street. See chapter 13.

DAYS 4 & 5: Amelia Island ★★★

With 13 miles of beachfront and restored Victorian homes, Amelia Island is worth the 45-minute drive northeast of downtown Jacksonville. It's another world and, for many, out of this world. Also steeped in history, Amelia Island attracted Oprah Winfrey, who has promised to help restore American Beach, the only beach in the 1930s reserved for African Americans. Nearby is Fernandina Beach, which dates back to the post–Civil War period. Many of the Victorian, Queen Anne, and Italianate homes are listed on the National Register. Nearby, the Palace Saloon claims to be Florida's oldest watering hole, challenging St. Augustine to an ongoing drinking contest! Check into the Amelia Island Plantation for a posh stay, or consider the Florida House Inn, once again, the oldest operating hotel in the entire state. See chapter 13.

BEACHY KEEN FLORIDA IN 1 WEEK

The Panhandle may be known as the Redneck Riviera to some, but to those in the know, the area has some of Florida's best beaches, with undeveloped stretches of powder-white sand that's a hot commodity in the world these days.

DAYS 1 & 2: Gulf Islands National Seashore and Pensacola Beach ★★★

This is, hands down, Florida's best beach. Not only are there 150 miles of protected beach, but there's also a 1,378-acre natural Live Oaks Area full of oaks, pines, and nature trails. Do not leave without hitting the Flora-Bama Lounge, which prides itself on being the "Last Great American Road House." See chapter 14.

DAY 3: Destin Beach ★★

Grayton Beach State Park is a sublime white-sand paradise, with 356 acres of pine forests surrounding a lake. You can camp here to get back to nature, or you can choose to explore Destin's other beaches, such as Henderson Beach State Park and Fort Walton Beach's Okaloosa Island. You can't really go wrong with any of them. The Sandestin Golf and Beach Resort is good for a longer stay, a community unto itself with restaurants, shops, a private 5-mile beach, and, according to the experts, unparalleled golf. Don't get too marooned because you will want to go off property and check out AJ's Seafood & Oyster Bar, the hottest spot on Destin Harbor, famous for its rooftop bar and live music. See chapter 14.

DAYS 4 & 5: Seaside & Rosemary Beach ★★★

Live *The Truman Show* in this stunning, Victorian-style planned community with old-fashioned beach cottages set upon unfettered sand dunes. Just 8 miles east of Seaside is Rosemary Beach, a swanky community of Caribbean-style cottages and old English carriage houses with a stunning private beach and Kodak-worthy Gulf views. Rent a cottage and enjoy the views. Be sure to take a drive up and down scenic 30A and stop for a photo op of the newest planned seaside community, Alys Beach. Or just head to straight to the Red Bar for a cocktail and possible Sheryl Crow sighting. See chapter 14.

DAY 6: Panama City Beach ★★

St. Andrews State Park has 1,000 acres of white sand and dunes, a common theme in the Panhandle. Shell Island is pristine, uninhabited, and known for possessing shells that aren't available for purchase in those touristy souvenir shops. For a little lunch, shopping, or honky-tonking, head to Panama City's brand-new Pier Park, where restaurants, shops, and a bangin' branch of Nashville's Tootsies Orchid Lounge will keep you out of the sun for a few hours and possibly into the night. Spend the night at Bay Point Marriott Golf Resort & Spa. See chapter 14.

DAY 7: Apalachicola ★★

Florida's so-called Last Frontier happens to have one of the country's most amazing beaches, St. George Island State Park. Enjoy the 9 miles of nature

Pensacola Beach is one of the Panhandle's top destinations.

before having to go back to reality. Spend your last night at the Apalachicola River Inn, the town's only waterfront stay, and home of the popular Frog Level Oyster Bar and Boss Oyster, where you'll be treated to some of the best bivalves you've ever had. See chapter 14.

SPECIAL-INTEREST ITINERARY SUGGESTIONS

FOR ART & DESIGN FANATICS Explore the galleries and showrooms in Miami's hip Design District, loosely defined as the area bounded by Northeast 2nd Avenue, Northeast 5th Avenue East and West, and Northwest 36th Street to the south. Just south of the Design District is yet another burgeoning arts district, a sketchy strip of Miami bounded by Northeast 2nd Avenue to the east and Northeast 36th Street to the north, known as Wynwood. Explore at your own risk, preferably during the day.

FOR FOODIES Hungry for knowledge or just hungry? Whatever the case, these comprehensive tours of some of Miami's most delicious neighborhoods and districts will make sure you fill up on all sorts of local and global delicacies. Sure, your souvenir may come in the form of a few extra pounds, but if you like to eat, this is the tour for you. © **786/942-8856.** www.miamiculinary tours.com.

FOR A TASTE OF PRE-CASTRO CUBA Take a ride to Miami's Little Havana, aka Calle Ocho, or Southwest 8th Street. Stroll past Maximo Gomez Park, aka Domino Park, command central for Cuban retirees who sit here all day playing dominoes. Stop and check out the hand rollers at Moore & Bode Cigars, and find trinkets of Yoruba culture at Botanica Begra Francisca before getting perky with a Cuban coffee at Versailles. If you're laying off the caffeine, then head to El Palacio de los Jugos and order a fresh-squeezed *mamey,* papaya, or guava juice.

FOR BIRD-WATCHERS A 70-mile drive from the Jacksonville area is Gainesville's Paynes Prairie Preserve State Park, home to more than 263 bird species, not to mention bison, gators, and snakes. ℂ **866/778-5002.** www.floridastateparks.org/paynesprairie.

FOR KAYAKERS If you can bear the mosquitoes, take a nighttime kayak tour at Merritt Island National Refuge and catch a glimpse of one-celled organisms called dinoflagellates whose lights will guide you on your way—along with an expert guide too, of course.

FOR ENLIGHTENMENT Visit the most powerful lighthouse on the East Coast in Fort Lauderdale's Hillsboro Beach, under which sits a statue of a barefoot mailman. The statue is of Ed Hamilton, who was killed while crossing Hillsboro Inlet. The Hillsboro Lighthouse Preservation Society gives special tours of the grounds and lighthouse four times a year from nearby Pompano Beach. **www.hillsborolighthouse.org.**

FOR DOG LOVERS With appearances on CNN and MTV, it's amazing that Lotta the Surfing Dog even has time to show off for her fans. But if you're in Key West, head to the island's South Beach, where the rat terrier, who learned to surf because she didn't like being in the water, hangs ten on an almost daily basis.

FOR A TOTAL TIME WARP Head 30 minutes north of Fort Myers and you'll eventually end up in the land that development forgot—Pine Island. There are no chain restaurants, no condos, just palm trees, mango orchards, fishing villages, and mom-and-pop restaurants. If the Bahamas hadn't already snagged the name, we'd call this Paradise Island.

FOR A HELL OF A GOOD TIME A trip to Northwest Florida isn't necessarily complete without a stop at **Tate's Hell State Forest,** where legend has it a farmer was lost for 7 days and lived to tell about it. Dubiously named or

Florida is a birder's paradise; here, a blue heron flies low over the waves at St. George Island.

Welcome to Hell? Tate's Hell, that is!

not, the state forest is heaven for those into outdoor recreation and wildlife viewing, with 35 miles of rivers, streams, and creeks ideal for canoeing, boating, and fishing. Endangered species including the bald eagle, Florida black bear, gopher tortoise, and red-cockaded woodpeckers also call this Hell their home.

FOR MILITARY BUFFS Turns out, alligators weren't always the most powerful things in the Everglades. Opened for the first time in 2009 is the Nike Hercules Missile Site in the heart of the national park, which was built during the Kennedy years as a result of the threat of a Soviet-armed Cuba. The 90-minute walking tour takes you through the missile assembly building, the three barns where 12 missiles were stored, and an underground control room. Fascinating!

SOUTH FLORIDA literary tour

Pompano Beach: Author Elmore Leonard took his mother to a small motel on Pompano Beach, which some say was his inspiration for the Coconut Palms Resort Apartments, to where George Moran, the main character in Leonard's 1982 book, *Cat Chaser*, runs. See p. 287.

Dania Beach Pier: Harry Crews used the Dania Pier as a backdrop for a July 4th fireworks display and beauty contest in *Karate Is a Thing of the Spirit*. See Dania Beach's John U. Lloyd Beach State Park on p. 291.

Bahia Mar Beach Resort: Travis McGee, the protagonist in John D. MacDonald's 21 novels (including *The Deep Blue Goodbye*), lived at this resort, 801 Seabreeze Blvd. (© **888/802-2442;** www.bahiamarhotel.com).

Little Haiti: The place where a no-good former oil-burner repairman wanders, in Russell Banks's *Continental Drift*.

Flagler Street: Where Brett Halliday's private eye, Michael Shayne, kept his office.

Hialeah Race Course: The inspiration for Damon Runyon's short story *Pick the Winner*. **www.hialeahparkracing.com**.

Cardozo Hotel: Elmore Leonard's favorite backdrop—as seen in *Get Shorty, La Brava,* and *Rum Punch*— was this hotel, 1300 Ocean Dr., Miami Beach (© **800/782-6500;** www.cardozohotel.com).

Barnacle State Historic Site: James W. Hall's *Hard Aground* transforms the Barnacle into Mangrove House, a place with a sinister history. See p. 153.

Domino Park: Ana Menendez's *In Cuba I Was a German Shepherd* reminisces about Little Havana's most hopping spot, at the southwest corner of 15th Avenue and 8th Street.

Tobacco Road: Miami's oldest bar gets its name from the 1932 novel by Erskine Caldwell. See p. 133.

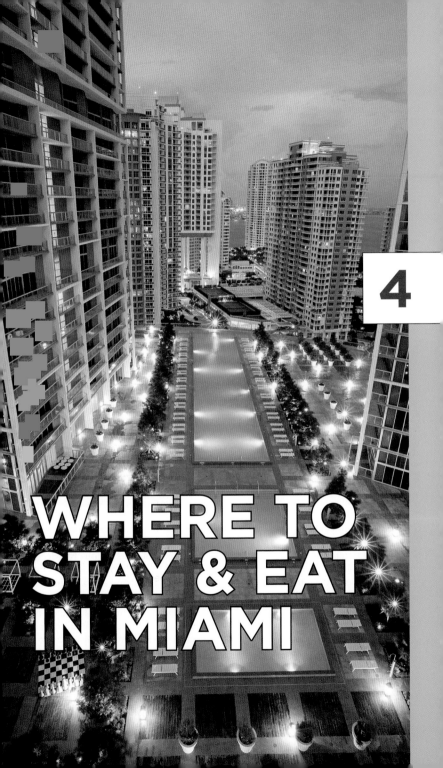

WHERE TO STAY & EAT IN MIAMI

A week in Miami is not unlike watching an unbelievable reality show, only this time it's actually real. Miami: where King James (as in LeBron) chose to play when he fled Cleveland, where rapper Lil Wayne threw his Colin Cowie–designed multi-million-dollar prison release party, and where the paparazzi camp out for days, hoping to catch a glimpse of something or someone fabulous. But that's just a small sample of the surreal, Fellini-esque world that exists way down here at the bottom of the map. Nothing in Miami is ever what it seems.

Things to Do Beyond the whole glitzy, *Us Weekly*–meets–beach–blanket–bacchanalia–as–seen–on–TV scene, Miami has an endless number of sporting, cultural, and recreational activities to keep you entertained. From watersports and sunbathing on **Miami Beach** to alligators in the **Everglades,** Miami lives outdoors. Play golf at **Crandon Park,** watch manatees on **Coconut Grove**'s waterfront, scuba dive off **Jupiter Beach,** or simply soak up the sun. On rainy days, you can school yourself in Dutch and Italian tapestries at the upstanding **Bass Museum of Art** or learn about the city's humble beginnings at the **Historical Museum of Southern Florida.**

Shopping Miami provides an eclectic shopping experience, from designer boutiques at **Bal Harbour** or mainstream chains at **Bayside Marketplace.** Miami likes its megamalls, and one of the best is **Aventura Mall,** which houses a fabulous collection of shops and department stores. Look for new art and furniture in the **Design District,** or take home a little bit of Cuba with a hand-stitched guayabera shirt from **Little Havana.** Pick up incense and Indian imports from **Española Way**'s Mediterranean storefronts, which close to traffic on Sunday afternoons.

Nightlife & Entertainment South Beach is certainly Miami's uncontested nocturnal nucleus, but more and more diverse areas, such as **Midtown/Wynwood, Brickell, South Miami,** and even **Little Havana,** are increasingly providing fun alternatives without the ludicrous cover charges and "fashionably late" hours (the action in South Beach starts after 11pm). Follow Latin grooves to tiny **Española Way** and toast with creative cocktails on **Lincoln Road.** Sip martinis in the swanky bars and lounges in the **Design District,** or watch live jazz, flamenco, and national bands at the **Carnival Performing Arts Centre.**

Where to Eat The economic slowdown did nothing to stop über-high-end restaurants like **Mr Chow** and **STK Miami** from opening to throngs of people who think nothing of dropping hundreds of dollars on dinners that could easily be had at PF Chang's and Applebee's. Downtown and now Midtown Miami saw a boost in activity with the openings of area hot spots like **Zuma** and **Sugarcane Raw Bar Grill.** Also try Cuban along **Calle Ocho,** Haitian in **Overtown,** and casual comfort food at the Grove. Dine at an open-air cafe in **Coral Gables** while enjoying stone crab claws and a mojito, the city's signature drink.

PREVIOUS PAGE: **The Viceroy rises high above Biscayne Bay in downtown Miami.**

ORIENTATION

Arriving

Originally carved out of scrubland in 1928 by Pan American Airlines, **Miami International Airport (MIA)** has become second in the United States for international passenger traffic and 10th in the world for total passengers. Despite the heavy traffic, the airport is quite user-friendly and not as much of a hassle as you'd think. You can change money or use your ATM card at Bank of America, located near the exit. Visitor information is available 24 hours a day at the **Miami International Airport Main Visitor Counter,** Concourse E, second level (✆ 305/876-7000). Information is also available at **www.miami-airport.com**. Because MIA is the busiest airport in South Florida, travelers may want to consider flying into the less crowded **Fort Lauderdale Hollywood International Airport (FLL; ✆ 954/359-1200)**, which is closer to north Miami than MIA, or the **Palm Beach International Airport (PBI; ✆ 561/471-7420)**, which is about 1½ hours from Miami.

GETTING INTO TOWN

Miami International Airport is about 6 miles west of downtown and about 10 miles from the beaches, so it's likely you can get from the plane to your hotel room in less than half an hour. Of course, if you're arriving from an international destination, it will take more time to go through Customs and Immigration.

BY CAR All the major car-rental firms operate off-site branches reached via shuttles from the airline terminals. See the "By Car" section, under "Getting Around," on p. 77, for a list of major rental companies in Miami. If you're arriving late at night, you might want to take a taxi to your hotel and have the car delivered to you the next day.

BY TAXI Taxis line up in front of a dispatcher's desk outside the airport's arrivals terminals. Most cabs are metered, though some have flat rates to popular destinations. The fare should be about $21 to $34 to Coral Gables, $22 to $24 to downtown, and $32 to South Beach, plus tip, which should be about 15% (add more for each bag the driver handles). Depending on traffic, the ride to Coral Gables or downtown takes about 15 to 20 minutes, and to South Beach, 20 to 25 minutes.

BY VAN OR LIMO Group limousines (multipassenger vans) circle the arrivals area looking for fares. Destinations are posted on the front of each van, and a flat rate is charged for door-to-door service to the area marked.

    SuperShuttle (✆ 305/871-2000; www.supershuttle.com) is one of the largest airport operators, charging between $10 and $50 per person for a ride within the county. Its vans operate 24 hours a day and accept American Express, MasterCard, and Visa. This is a cheaper alternative to a cab (if you are traveling alone or with one other person), but be prepared to be in the van for quite some time, as you may have to make several stops to drop off passengers before you reach your own destination. SuperShuttle also has begun service from Palm Beach International Airport to the surrounding communities. The door-to-door, shared-ride service operates from the airport to Stuart, Fort Pierce, Palm Beach, and Broward counties.

    Private limousine arrangements can be made in advance through your local travel agent. A one-way meet-and-greet service should cost $55 to $95 depending on car and destination. Limo services include **Aventura Limousine** (✆ 800/944-9886) and **Limo Miami** (✆ 305/742-5900).

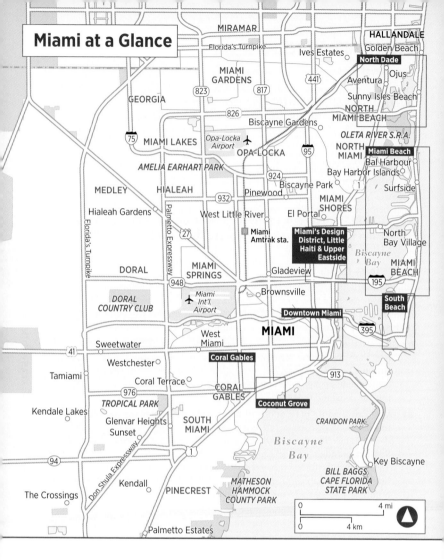

Miami at a Glance

BY PUBLIC TRANSPORTATION Public transportation in South Florida is a major hassle bordering on a nightmare. Painfully slow and unreliable, buses heading downtown leave the airport only once per hour (from the arrivals level), and connections are spotty, at best. It could take about 1½ hours to get to South Beach via public transportation. Journeys to downtown and Coral Gables, however, are more direct. The fare is $2. For those heading to South Beach from the airport, a new bus route, the Airport-Beach Flyer Route, provides direct express service from MIA to Miami Beach and costs $2.35. With only one minor stop en route, the trip to the beach takes about a half-hour. Not bad.

Visitor Information

The most up-to-date information is provided by the **Greater Miami Convention and Visitor's Bureau,** 701 Brickell Ave., Ste. 700, Miami, FL 33131 ((C) **800/933-8448** or 305/539-3000; fax 305/530-3113). Several chambers of commerce in Greater Miami will send out information on their particular neighborhoods.

If you arrive at the Miami International Airport, you can pick up visitor information at the airport's main visitor counter on the second floor of Concourse E. It's open 24 hours a day.

Always check local newspapers for special events during your visit. The city's only daily, the *Miami Herald,* is a good source for current-events listings, particularly the "Weekend" section in Friday's edition. Even better is the free weekly alternative paper the *Miami New Times,* available in bright red boxes throughout the city.

Information on everything from dining to entertainment in Miami is available on the Internet at www.miami.citysearch.com, www.digitalcity.com/southflorida, www.miaminewtimes.com, www.miami.com, and www.miamiherald.com.

City Layout

Miami seems confusing at first, but quickly becomes easy to navigate. The small cluster of buildings that make up the downtown area is at the geographical heart of the city. In relation to downtown, the airport is northwest, the beaches are east, Coconut Grove is south, Coral Gables is west, and the rest of the city is north.

FINDING AN ADDRESS Miami is divided into dozens of areas with official and unofficial boundaries. Street numbering in the city of Miami is fairly straightforward, but you must first be familiar with the numbering system. The mainland is divided into four sections (NE, NW, SE, and SW) by the intersection of Flagler Street and Miami Avenue. Flagler Street divides Miami from north to south, and Miami Avenue divides the city from east to west. It's helpful to remember that avenues generally run north-south, while streets go east-west. Street numbers (1st St., 2nd St., and so forth) start from here and increase as you go farther out from this intersection, as do numbers of avenues, places, courts, terraces, and lanes. Streets in Hialeah are the exceptions to this pattern; they are listed separately in map indexes.

Getting around the barrier islands that make up Miami Beach is easier than moving around the mainland. Street numbering starts with 1st Street, near Miami Beach's southern tip, and goes up to 192nd Street, in the northern part of Sunny Isles. As in the city of Miami, some streets in Miami Beach have numbers as well as names. When those are listed in this book, both name and number are given.

The numbered streets in Miami Beach are not the geographical equivalents of those on the mainland, but they are close. For example, the 79th Street Causeway runs into 71st Street on Miami Beach.

STREET MAPS It's easy to get lost in sprawling Miami, so a reliable map is essential. The **Streetwise Miami Map** (www.streetwisemaps.com) is a full-color map that encompasses all of Miami-Dade County and the maddening Metrorail system. Some maps of Miami list streets according to area, so you'll have to know which part of the city you are looking for before the street can be found.

The Neighborhoods in Brief

SOUTH BEACH—THE ART DECO DISTRICT South Beach's 10 miles of beach are alive with a frenetic, circuslike atmosphere and are center stage for a motley crew of characters, from eccentric locals, seniors, snowbirds, and college students to gender-benders, celebrities, club kids, and curiosity seekers. Individuality is as widely accepted on South Beach as Visa and MasterCard.

Bolstered by a Caribbean-chic cafe society and a sexually charged, tragically hip nightlife, people-watching on South Beach (1st St.–23rd St.) is almost as good as a front-row seat at a Milan fashion show. But although the beautiful people do flock to South Beach, the models aren't the only sights worth drooling over. The thriving Art Deco District within South Beach has the largest concentration of Art Deco architecture in the world (in 1979, much of South Beach was listed in the National Register of Historic Places). The pastel-hued structures are supermodels in their own right—except *these* models improve with age.

MIAMI BEACH In the fabulous '50s, Miami Beach was America's true Riviera. The stomping ground of choice for the Rat Pack and notorious mobsters such as Al Capone, its huge self-contained resort hotels were vacations unto themselves, providing a full day's worth of meals, activities, and entertainment. Then in the 1960s and 1970s, people who fell in love with Miami began to buy apartments rather than rent hotel rooms. Tourism declined, and many area hotels fell into disrepair.

However, since the late 1980s and South Beach's renaissance, Miami Beach has experienced a tide of revitalization. Huge beach hotels, such as the recently renovated and Vegas-esque Fontainebleau and Eden Roc, are finding their niche with new international tourist markets and are attracting large convention crowds. New generations of Americans are quickly rediscovering the qualities that originally made Miami Beach so popular, and they are finding out that the sand and surf now come with a thriving

Vintage cars line the street in front of The Avalon in the Art Deco District.

international city—a technologically savvy city complete with free Wi-Fi with 95% coverage outside, which means on the sand, and 70% indoors up to the second floor of any building.

Before Miami Beach turns into Surfside, there's North Beach, where there are uncrowded beaches, some restaurants, and examples of Miami modernism architecture. For information on North Beach and its slow renaissance, go to **www.gonorthbeach.com**.

Surfside, Bal Harbour, and **Sunny Isles** make up the north part of the beach (island). Hotels, motels, restaurants, and beaches line Collins Avenue and, with some outstanding exceptions, the farther north one goes, the cheaper lodging becomes. Excellent prices, location, and facilities make Surfside and Sunny Isles attractive places to stay, although, despite a slow-going renaissance, they are still a little rough around the edges. Revitalization is in the works for these areas, and, while it's highly unlikely they will ever become as chic as South Beach, there is potential for this, especially as South Beach falls prey to the inevitable spoiler: commercialism. Keep in mind that beachfront properties are at a premium, so many of the area's moderately priced hotels have been converted to condominiums, leaving fewer and fewer affordable places to stay.

In exclusive and ritzy Bal Harbour, few hotels besides the swanky Regent and expected-to-open-in-2012 St. Regis remain amid the many beachfront condominium towers. Instead, fancy homes, tucked away on the bay, hide behind gated communities, and the Rodeo Drive of Miami (known as the Bal Harbour Shops) attracts shoppers who don't flinch at four-, five-, and six-figure price tags.

Note that **North Miami Beach,** a residential area near the Dade-Broward County line (north of 163rd St.; part of North Dade County), is a misnomer. It is actually northwest of Miami Beach, on the mainland, and has no beaches, though it does have some of Miami's better restaurants and shops. Located within North Miami Beach is the posh residential community of **Aventura,** best known for its high-priced condos, the Fairmont Turnberry Isle Resort, and the Aventura Mall.

Note: South Beach, the historic Art Deco District, is treated as a separate neighborhood from Miami Beach.

KEY BISCAYNE Miami's forested and secluded Key Biscayne is technically a barrier island and is not part of the Florida Keys. This island is nothing like its southern neighbors. Located south of Miami Beach, off the shores of Coconut Grove, Key Biscayne is protected from the troubles of the mainland by the long Rickenbacker Causeway and its $1.25 toll.

Largely an exclusive residential community with million-dollar homes and sweeping water views, Key Biscayne also offers visitors great public beaches, a top (read: pricey) resort hotel, world-class tennis facilities, and a few decent restaurants. Hobie Beach, adjacent to the causeway, is the city's premier spot for windsurfing, sailboarding, and jet skiing (see "Watersports," in chapter 5). On the island's southern tip, Bill Baggs State Park has great beaches, bike paths, and dense forests for picnicking and partying.

DOWNTOWN Miami's downtown boasts one of the world's most beautiful cityscapes. Unfortunately, that's about all it offers—for now. During the day, a vibrant community of students, businesspeople, and merchants make their

Bill Baggs State Park on Key Biscayne offers lots of outdoor activities and beautiful vistas.

way through the bustling streets, where vendors sell fresh-cut pineapples and mangoes while young consumers on shopping sprees lug bags and boxes. However, at night, downtown is mostly desolate (except for NE 11th St., where there is a burgeoning nightlife scene) and not a place where you'd want to get lost. The downtown area does have a mall (Bayside Marketplace, where many cruise passengers come to browse), some culture (Metro-Dade Cultural Center), and a few decent restaurants, as well as the sprawling American Airlines Arena (home to the Miami Heat). A slow-going downtown revitalization project in the works promises a cultural arts center, urban-chic dwellings and lofts, and an assortment of hip boutiques, eateries, and bars, all to bring downtown back to a life it never really had. The city has even rebranded the downtown area with a new ad campaign, intentionally misspelling it as DWNTN to inexplicably appeal to hipsters. We don't get it either. The **Downtown Miami Partnership** offers guided historic walking tours daily at 10:30am (© **305/379-7070**). For more information on downtown, go to **www.downtownmiami.com**.

DESIGN DISTRICT With restaurants springing up between galleries and furniture stores galore, the Design District is, as locals say, the new South Beach, adding a touch of New York's SoHo to an area formerly known as downtown Miami's "Don't Go." The district, which is a hotbed for furniture-import companies, interior designers, architects, and more, has also become a player in Miami's ever-changing nightlife. Its bars, lounges, clubs, and restaurants—including one of Miami's best, Michael's Genuine Food & Drink—ranging from überchic and retro to progressive and indie, have helped the area become hipster central for South Beach expatriates and artsy bohemian types. In anticipation of its growing popularity, the district has also banded together to create an up-to-date website, **www.design miami.com**, which includes a calendar of events, such as the internationally lauded Art Basel, which attracts the who's who of the art world. The district is loosely defined as the area bounded by NE 2nd Avenue, NE 5th Avenue East and West, and NW 36th Street to the south.

MIDTOWN/WYNWOOD What used to be called El Barrio is now one of Miami's hippest, still burgeoning areas. Just north of downtown and roughly divided by I-395 to the south, I-195 to the north, I-95 to the west, and Biscayne Boulevard to the east, Wynwood actually includes the Miami Design District, but has developed an identity of its own thanks to an exploding, albeit still very rough and gritty, arts scene made popular by cheap rents and major exposure during Art Basel Miami Beach. While there are still only a very small handful of bars and restaurants, Wynwood is an edgy area for creative types with loft and gallery spaces affordable and aplenty—for now. Also within Wynwood is Midtown Miami, a mall-like town-center complex of apartment buildings surrounded by shops—namely Target—and restaurants. Like its Wynwood neighbor, it's gritty and a work in progress favored by young hipster types who aren't averse to living in transitional neighborhoods.

BISCAYNE CORRIDOR From downtown, near Bayside, to the 70s (affectionately known as the Upper East Side), where trendy curio shops and upscale restaurants are slowly opening, Biscayne Boulevard is aspiring to reclaim itself as a safe thoroughfare where tourists can wine, dine, and shop. Once known for sketchy, dilapidated 1950s- and 1960s-era hotels that had fallen on hard times, this boulevard is getting a boost from residents fleeing the high prices of the beaches in search of affordable housing. They're renovating Biscayne block by block, trying to make this famous boulevard worthy of a Sunday drive.

LITTLE HAVANA If you've never been to Cuba, just visit this small section of Miami and you'll come pretty close. The sounds, tastes, and rhythms are very reminiscent of Cuba's capital city, and some say you don't have to speak a word of English to live an independent life here—even street signs are in Spanish and English.

Cuban coffee shops, tailor and furniture stores, and inexpensive restaurants line Calle Ocho (pronounced *Ka*-yey *O*-choh), SW 8th Street, the region's main thoroughfare. In Little Havana, salsa and merengue beats ring loudly from old record stores while old men in *guayaberas* (loose-fitting cotton short-sleeved shirts) smoke cigars over their daily game of dominoes. The spotlight focused on the neighborhood during the Elián González situation in 2000, but the area was previously noted for the groups of artists and nocturnal types who had moved their galleries and performance spaces here, sparking culturally charged neo-bohemian nightlife.

CORAL GABLES "The City Beautiful," created by George Merrick in the early 1920s, is one of Miami's first planned developments. Houses

Residents and visitors gather at Calle Ocho's Cubana's Café.

here were built in a Mediterranean style along lush, tree-lined streets that open onto beautifully carved plazas, many with centerpiece fountains. The best architectural examples of the era have Spanish-style tiled roofs and are built from Miami *oolite,* native limestone commonly called "coral rock." The Gables's European-flaired shopping and commerce center is home to many thriving corporations. Coral Gables also has landmark hotels, great golfing, upscale shopping to rival Bal Harbour, and some of the city's best restaurants, headed by renowned chefs.

COCONUT GROVE An arty, hippie hangout in the psychedelic '60s, Coconut Grove once had residents who dressed in swirling tie-dyed garb. Nowadays, they prefer the uniform color schemes of Gap. Chain stores, theme restaurants, a megaplex, and bars galore make Coconut Grove a commercial success, but this gentrification has pushed most alternative types out. Ritzier types have now resurfaced here, thanks, in part, to the anti-boho Ritz-Carlton Coconut Grove (p. 108) and the Mayfair, which is in its umpteenth resurgence as a boutique hotel. The intersection of Grand Avenue, Main Highway, and McFarlane Road pierces the area's heart. Right in the center of it all is CocoWalk, filled with boutiques, eateries, and bars. Sidewalks here are often crowded, especially at night, when University of Miami students come out to play.

SOUTHERN MIAMI-DADE COUNTY To locals, South Miami is both a specific area, southwest of Coral Gables, and a general region that encompasses all of southern Dade County, including Kendall, Perrine, Cutler Ridge, and Homestead. For the purposes of clarity, this book has grouped all these southern suburbs under the rubric "Southern Miami-Dade County." The area is heavily residential and packed with strip malls amid a few remaining plots of farmland. Tourists don't usually stay in these parts, unless they are on their way to the Everglades or the Keys. However, Southern Miami-Dade County contains many of the city's top attractions (see chapter 5), meaning that you're likely to spend at least some of your time in Miami here.

GETTING AROUND

Officially, Miami-Dade County has opted for a "unified, multimodal transportation network," which basically means you can get around the city by train, bus, and taxi. However, in practice, the network doesn't work very well. Things have improved somewhat thanks to the $17-billion Peoples' Transportation Plan, which has offered a full range of transportation services at several community-based centers throughout the county, but unless you are going from downtown Miami to a not-too-distant spot, you are better off in a rental car or taxi.

With the exception of downtown Coconut Grove and South Beach, Miami is not a walker's city. Because it is so spread out, most attractions are too far apart to make walking between them feasible. In fact, most Miamians are so used to driving that they do so even when going just a few blocks.

By Public Transportation

BY RAIL Two rail lines, operated by the **Metro-Dade Transit Agency** (© **305/770-3131** for information; www.co.miami-dade.fl.us/mdta), run in concert with each other.

Metrorail, the city's modern high-speed commuter train, is a 21-mile elevated line that travels north-south, between downtown Miami and the southern suburbs. Locals like to refer to this semi-useless rail system as Metro*fail*. If you are staying in Coral Gables or Coconut Grove, you can park your car at a nearby station and ride the rails downtown. However, that's about it. There are plans to extend the system to service Miami International Airport, but until those tracks are built, these trains don't go most places tourists go, with the exception of Vizcaya (p. 154) in Coconut Grove. Metrorail operates daily from about 6am to midnight. The fare is $2.

Metromover, a 4½-mile elevated line, circles the downtown area and connects with Metrorail at the Government Center stop. Riding on rubber tires, the single-car train winds past many of the area's most important attractions and its shopping and business districts. You may not go very far on the Metromover, but you will get a beautiful perspective from the towering height of the suspended rails. System hours are daily from about 6am to midnight, and the ride is free.

BY BUS Miami's suburban layout is not conducive to getting around by bus. Lines operate and maps are available, but instead of getting to know the city, you'll find that relying on bus transportation will acquaint you only with how it feels to wait at bus stops. In short, a bus ride in Miami is grueling. You can get a bus map by mail, either from the Greater Miami Convention and Visitor's Bureau (see "Visitor Information," earlier in this chapter) or by writing the Metro-Dade Transit System, 3300 NW 32nd Ave., Miami, FL 33142. In Miami, call ℂ **305/770-3131** for public-transit information. The fare is $2. When on South Beach, however, consider the **South Beach Local,** a shuttle bus that runs every 12 to 20 minutes from 1st Street all the way to Collins Park at 23rd Street and Collins Avenue for just 25¢ a ride. Look for signs that say SOUTH BEACH LOCAL. Buses run every 13 minutes Monday through Saturday from 10am to 6pm and every 20 minutes from 7:40 to 10am and from 6pm to 1:20am. On Sundays, the bus will come every 13 minutes from noon to 6pm and every 20 minutes from 10am to noon and from 6pm to 1am. It makes several stops, but it's a lot cheaper than a cab.

By Car

Tales circulate about vacationers who have visited Miami without a car, but they are very few indeed. If you are counting on exploring the city, even to a modest degree, a car is essential. Miami's restaurants, hotels, and attractions are far from one another, so any other form of transportation is relatively impractical. You won't need a car, however, if you are spending your entire vacation at a resort, are traveling directly to the Port of Miami for a cruise, or are here for a short stay centered on one area of the city, such as South Beach, where everything is within walking distance and parking is a costly nightmare.

When driving across a causeway or through downtown, allow extra time to reach your destination because of frequent drawbridge openings. Some bridges open about every half-hour for large sailing vessels to make their way through the wide bays and canals that crisscross the city, stalling traffic for several minutes.

RENTALS Miami city is one of the cheapest places in the world to rent a car. Many firms regularly advertise prices in the neighborhood of $150 per week for their economy cars. You should also check with your airline: There are often special discounts when you book a flight and reserve your rental car simultaneously. A minimum age, generally 25, is usually required of renters; some rental agencies have also set maximum ages! A national car-rental broker, **Car Rental Referral Service** (℃ **800/404-4482**), can often find companies willing to rent to drivers between the ages of 21 and 24 and can also get discounts from major companies as well as some regional ones.

National car-rental companies include **Alamo, Avis, Budget, Dollar, Hertz, National,** and **Thrifty.** One excellent company that has offices in every conceivable part of town and offers extremely competitive rates is **Enterprise.** Comparison shop before you make any decisions—car-rental prices can fluctuate more than airfares. Many car-rental companies also offer cellphones or rentals with GPS. It might be wise to opt for these additional safety features (the phone will definitely come in handy if you get lost), although the cost can be exorbitant.

Finally, think about splurging on a convertible. Not only are convertibles one of the best ways to see the beautiful surroundings, but they're also an ideal way to perfect a tan!

PARKING Always keep plenty of quarters on hand to feed hungry meters, most of which have been removed in favor of those pesky parking payment stations where you feed a machine and get a printed receipt to display on your dash. Parking is usually plentiful (except on South Beach and Coconut Grove)—albeit pricey at $1 to $1.50 an hour—but when it's not, be careful: Fines for illegal parking can be stiff, starting at $18 for an expired meter and going way up from there.

In addition to parking garages, whose flat rates are sometimes better bargains than the inevitable ticket you may get from an expired meter, valet services are commonplace and often used. Because parking is such a premium in bustling South Beach as well as in Coconut Grove, prices tend to be jacked up—especially at night and when there are special events (day or night). You can expect to pay an average of $5 to $15 for parking in these areas.

LOCAL DRIVING RULES Florida law allows drivers to make a right turn on a red light after a complete stop, unless otherwise indicated. In addition, all passengers are required to wear seat belts, and children 3 and under must be securely fastened in government-approved car seats.

By Taxi

If you're not planning on traveling much within the city (and especially if you plan on spending your vacation within the confines of South Beach's Art Deco District), an occasional taxi is a good alternative to renting a car and dealing with the parking hassles that come with renting your own car. Taxi meters start at about $2.50 at flag-fall and cost around $2.40 for each additional mile. For specifics on rate increases and surcharges, go to www.taxifarefinder.com.

Major cab companies include **Yellow Cab** (℃ **305/444-4444**) and, on Miami Beach, **Central** (℃ **305/532-5555**).

By Bike

Miami is a biker's paradise, especially on Miami Beach, where the hard-packed sand and boardwalks make it an easy and scenic route. However, unless you are a former New York City bike messenger, you won't want to use a bicycle as your main means of transportation. In 2010, the city of Miami Beach launched **DECOBIKE,** www.decobike.com, a public bike-sharing and rental program including 1,000 custom program bikes at solar-powered, automated rental stations located at all major attractions, shops, hotels, condos, beaches, and civic centers in South Beach, mid-beach, and North Beach.

For more information on bicycles, including where to rent the best ones, see "More Ways to Play, Indoors & Out," in chapter 5.

[Fast FACTS] MIAMI

Area Code The original area code for Miami and all of Dade County is 305. That is still the code for older phone numbers, but all phone numbers assigned since July 1998 have the area code 786 (SUN). For all local calls, even if you're just calling across the street, you must dial the area code (305 or 786) first. Even though the Keys still share the Dade County area code of 305, calls to there from Miami are considered long distance and must be preceded by 1-305. (Within the Keys, simply dial the seven-digit number.) The area codes for Fort Lauderdale are 954 and 754; for Palm Beach, Boca Raton, Vero Beach, and Port St. Lucie, it's 561.

Business Hours Banking hours vary, but most banks are open weekdays from 9am to 3pm. Several stay open until 5pm or so at least 1 day during the week, and most banks feature automated teller machines (ATMs) for 24-hour banking. Most stores are open daily from 10am to 6pm; however, there are many exceptions (noted in "Shopping," in chapter

5, beginning on p. 175). As far as business offices are concerned, Miami is generally a 9-to-5 town.

Dentists If you're in absolute need of a dentist, go to **www.1800dentist. com**. Or call Dr. Edderai, who specializes in emergency dental work and features a 24/7 call dental service at (✆ **305/798-7799;** www.northmiami beachdentist.com).

Doctors In an emergency, call an ambulance by dialing ✆ **911** (a free call) from any phone. The Dade County Medical Association sponsors a **Physician Referral Service** (✆ **305/324-8717**), weekdays from 9am to 5pm.

Emergencies To reach the police, an ambulance, or the fire department, dial ✆ **911** from any phone. No coins are needed. Emergency hot lines include **Crisis Intervention** (✆ **305/358-HELP** [4357] or 305/358-4357) and the **Poison Information Center** (✆ **800/222-1222**).

Internet Access Internet access is available via free Wi-Fi in many parts of the city including downtown and Miami Beach, as

well as Starbucks, and at **Kafka's Cyber Cafe,** 1464 Washington Ave., South Beach (✆ **305/673-9669;** www.kafkas-cafe.com).

Liquor Laws Only adults 21 or older may legally purchase or consume alcohol in the state of Florida. Minors are usually permitted in bars, as long as the bars also serve food. Liquor laws are strictly enforced; if you look young, carry identification. Beer and wine are sold in most supermarkets and convenience stores. Most of the city of Miami's liquor stores are closed on Sunday. Liquor stores in the city of Miami Beach are open daily.

Lost Property If you lost something at the airport, call the **Airport Lost and Found** office (✆ **305/876-7377**). If you lost something on the bus, Metrorail, or Metromover, call **Metro-Dade Transit Agency** (✆ **305/770-3131**). If you lost something anywhere else, phone the **Dade County Police Lost and Found** (✆ **305/375-3366**). You may also want to fill out a police report for insurance purposes.

Newspapers & Magazines The *Miami Herald* is the city's only English-language daily. It is especially known for its extensive Latin American coverage and has a decent Friday "Weekend" entertainment guide. The most respected alternative weekly is the giveaway tabloid, *New Times,* which contains up-to-date listings and reviews of food, films, theater, music, and whatever else is happening in town. Also free, if you can find it, is *Ocean Drive,* an oversize glossy magazine that's limited on text (no literary value) and heavy on ads and society photos. It's what you should read if you want to know who's who and where to go for fun; it's available at a number of chic South Beach boutiques and restaurants. It is also available at newsstands. In the same vein: *Miami Magazine* and *944 Magazine,* also free and available throughout the city.

For a large selection of foreign-language newspapers and magazines, check with any of the large bookstores or try **News Cafe,** 800 Ocean Dr., South Beach (✆ **305/538-6397**). Also check out **Eddie's News,** 1096 Normandy Dr., Miami Beach (✆ **305/866-2661**).

Pharmacies Walgreens Pharmacy has countless locations all over town, including 1845 Alton Rd.

(✆ **305/531-8868**), in South Beach; and 6700 Collins Ave. (✆ **305/861-6742**), in Miami Beach. Then there's **CVS,** which is usually located wherever there's a Walgreens.

Police For emergencies, dial ✆ **911** from any phone. No coins are needed for this call. For other police matters, call ✆ **305/595-6263.**

Post Office The **Main Post Office,** 2200 Milam Dairy Rd., Miami, FL 33152 (✆ **800/275-8777**), is located west of the Miami International Airport. Conveniently located post offices include 1300 Washington Ave. in South Beach and 3191 Grand Ave. in Coconut Grove. There is one central number for all post offices: ✆ **800/275-8777.**

Restrooms Stores rarely let customers use their restrooms, and many restaurants offer their facilities only for their patrons. However, most malls have restrooms, as do many fast-food restaurants. Public beaches and large parks often provide toilets, though in some places you have to pay or tip an attendant. Most large hotels have clean restrooms in their lobbies.

Safety As always, use your common sense and be aware of your surroundings at all times. Don't walk alone at night, and be extra wary when walking or driving though downtown Miami and surrounding areas.

Reacting to several highly publicized crimes against tourists several years ago, local and state governments alike have taken steps to help protect visitors. These measures include special highly visible police units patrolling the airport and surrounding neighborhoods, and better signs on the state's most tourist-traveled routes.

Taxes A 6% state sales tax (plus 1% local tax, for a total of 7% in Miami-Dade County [from Homestead to North Miami Beach]) is added on at the register for all goods and services purchased in Florida. In addition, most municipalities levy special taxes on restaurants and hotels. In Surfside, hotel taxes total 11%; in Bal Harbour, 11%; in Miami Beach (including South Beach), 13%; and in the rest of Dade County, a whopping 13%. Food and beverage tax in Miami Beach, Bal Harbour, and Surfside is 9%; in Miami-Dade restaurants not located inside hotels, it's 8%, and in restaurants located in hotels, 9%.

Time Zone Miami, like New York, is in the **Eastern Standard Time (EST)** zone. Between the second Sunday of March and the first Sunday of November, daylight saving time is adopted, and clocks are set 1 hour ahead. America's eastern seaboard is 5 hours behind Greenwich Mean Time. To find out what time it is, call **☎ 305/324-8811.**

Transit Information For Metrorail or Metromover schedule information, phone **☎ 305/770-3131** or surf over to www.co.miami dade.fl.us/mdta.

Weather Hurricane season in Miami runs June through November. For an up-to-date recording of current weather conditions and forecast reports, call **☎ 305/229-4522.** Also see the "When to Go" section in chapter 2 for more information on the weather.

WHERE TO STAY IN MIAMI

As much a part of the landscape as the palm trees, many of Miami's hotels are on display as if they were contestants in a beauty pageant. The city's long-lasting status on the destination A-list has given rise to an ever-increasing number of upscale hotels, and no place in Miami has seen a greater increase in construction than Miami Beach. Since the area's renaissance, which began in the late 1980s, the beach has turned what used to be a beachfront retirement community into a sand-swept hot spot for the Gucci and Prada set—even in a recession. Contrary to popular belief, however, the beach does not discriminate, and it's the juxtaposition of the chic elite and the hoi polloi that contributes to its allure.

Many of the old hotels from the 1930s, 1940s, and 1950s have been totally renovated, giving way to dozens of "boutique" (small, swanky, and, for the most part, independently owned) hotels. Keep in mind that when a hotel claims that it was just renovated, it can mean that they've completely gutted the building—or just applied a coat of fresh paint or hung a new picture on the wall. Always ask what specific changes were made during a renovation, and be sure to ask if a hotel will be undergoing construction while you're there. You should also find out how near your room will be to the center of the nightlife crowd; trying to sleep directly on Ocean Drive or Collins and Washington avenues, especially during the weekend, is next to impossible, unless your lullaby of choice happens to include throbbing salsa and bass beats.

While South Beach may be the nucleus of all things hyped and hip, it's not the only place with hotels. The advantage to staying on South Beach as opposed to, say, Coral Gables or Coconut Grove is that the beaches are within walking distance, the nightlife and restaurant options are aplenty, and, basically, everything you need is right there. However, staying there is definitely not for everyone. If you're wary, don't worry: South Beach is centrally located and only about a 15- to 30-minute drive from most other parts of Miami.

For a (not that much, but still somewhat) less expensive stay that's only a 10-minute cab ride from South Beach, Miami Beach proper (the area north of 23rd St. and Collins Ave. all the way up to 163rd St. and Collins Ave.) offers a slew of reasonable stays, right on the beach, that won't cost you your kids' college education funds.

What *will* cost you a small fortune are the luxury hotels in the city's financial Brickell Avenue district, the area of choice for expense-account business travelers and camera-shy celebrities trying to avoid the South Beach spotlight.

For a less frenetic, more relaxed, and more tropical experience, the ritzy resort on Key Biscayne exudes an island feel, even though, across the water, a cosmopolitan vibe beckons, thanks to the shimmering, spectacular Miami skyline.

Those who'd rather bag the beach in favor of shopping bags will enjoy North Miami Beach's proximity to the Aventura Mall. For Miami with an Old World European flair, Coral Gables and its charming hotels and exquisite restaurants provide a more prim and proper, well-heeled perspective of Miami than the trendy boutique and condo hotels on South Beach.

SEASONS & RATES South Florida's tourist season is well-defined, beginning in mid-November and lasting until Easter, though if you ask the city's most ardent spin doctors, the season in SoFlo now lasts year-round. It all depends on where and when you're here and what's going on at the time. Hotel prices escalate until about March, after which they begin to decline. During the off season, hotel rates are typically 30% to 50% lower than their winter highs. But timing isn't everything. Rates also depend on your hotel's proximity to the beach and how much ocean you can see from your window. Small motels a block or two from the water can be up to 40% cheaper than similar properties right on the sand.

The rates listed below are broken down into two broad categories: winter (generally, Thanksgiving through Easter) and off season (about mid-May through Aug). The months in between, the shoulder season, should fall somewhere in between the highs and lows, while rates always go up on holidays. Remember, too, that state and city taxes can add as much as 12.5% to your bill in some parts of Miami. Some hotels, especially those in South Beach, also tack on additional service charges, and don't forget that parking is a pricey endeavor.

PRICE CATEGORIES The hotels below are divided first by area and then by price (**Very Expensive, Expensive, Moderate,** or **Inexpensive**). Price categories are based on published rates (or rack rates) for a standard double room during the high season. You should also check with the reservations agent, as many rooms are available above and below the category ranges listed below; and ask about packages, as it's often possible to get a better deal than these "official" rates. Most important, always call the hotel to confirm rates, which may be subject to change without notice because of special events, holidays, or blackout dates.

LONG-TERM STAYS If you plan to visit Miami for a month, a season, or more, think about renting a condominium apartment or a room in a long-term hotel. Long-term accommodations exist in every price category, from budget to deluxe, and in general are extremely reasonable, especially during the off season. Check with the reservation services below, or write a short note to the chamber of commerce in the area where you plan to stay. In addition, many local real estate agents handle short-term rentals (meaning less than a year).

RESERVATION SERVICES Central Reservation Service (© 800/950-0232 or 305/274-6832; www.reservation-services.com) works with many of Miami's hotels and can often secure discounts of up to 40%. It also gives advice on specific locales, especially in Miami Beach and downtown. During holiday time, there may be a 3- to 5-day minimum stay required to use their services. Call for more information.

For bed-and-breakfast information throughout the state, contact **Florida Bed and Breakfast Inns** (© 800/524-1880; www.florida-inns.com). For information on the ubiquitous boutique hotels, check out the **Greater Miami Convention and Visitor's Bureau**'s slick website, **www.miamiboutiquehotels.com**.

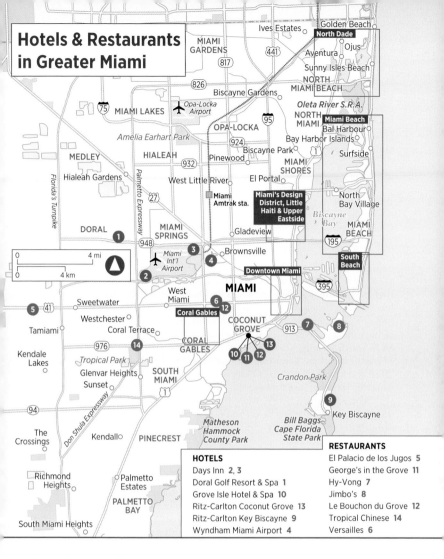

HOTELS
Days Inn **2, 3**
Doral Golf Resort & Spa **1**
Grove Isle Hotel & Spa **10**
Ritz-Carlton Coconut Grove **13**
Ritz-Carlton Key Biscayne **9**
Wyndham Miami Airport **4**

RESTAURANTS
El Palacio de los Jugos **5**
George's in the Grove **11**
Hy-Vong **7**
Jimbo's **8**
Le Bouchon du Grove **12**
Tropical Chinese **14**
Versailles **6**

South Beach

Choosing a hotel on South Beach is similar to deciding whether you'd rather pay $2 for french fries at Denny's or $15 for the same fries—but let's call them *pommes frites,* and add $5 for some fancy salt from a fancy resort town on the Mediterranean—in a pricey haute-cuisine restaurant. It's all about atmosphere. The rooms of some hotels may *look* ultrachic, but they are as comfortable as sleeping on a concrete slab. Once you decide how much atmosphere you want, the choice will be easier. Fortunately, for every chichi hotel in South Beach—and there are many—there are just as many moderately priced, more casual options.

If status is important to you, as it is to many South Beach visitors, then you will be quite pleased with the number of haute hotels in the area. But the times may be a-changin': **Courtyard by Marriott** (📞800/321-2211 or 305/604-8887) maintains a 90-room, moderately priced hotel on a seedy stretch of Washington Avenue, smack in the middle of Clubland, a horror to many a South Beach trend seeker.

For the gay traveler, the 53-room **Lords South Beach,** 1120 Collins Ave. (www.lordssouthbeach.com; 📞877/4484754), has taken over the defunct Hotel Nash with a sleek, stylish, and playful vibe featuring requisite bar, restaurant, and a massive fiberglass polar bear holding a beach ball to greet guests in the lobby. Says owner Brian Gorman, "More than anything else, it's just a safe place where people can meet and have fun and be themselves."

Meanwhile, as a result of the economic downturn, two very popular South Beach hotels faced foreclosure in late 2009 and early 2010. Amid financial disaster, the swanky **Sagamore** (p. 87) was about to team up with the Playboy Club. That deal fell through and in 2011 the hotel seemed to be bouncing back slowly. The **Gansevoort Miami Beach** (p. 85) had accumulated construction debt and looked on the brink of foreclosure—but was rescued in February 2010 by the capable Coral Management (Casa Ybel in Sanibel Island, Sandpearl in Clearwater Beach, among others). So far, so good. It could be even better if Sir Richard Branson has his way and brings Virgin Hotels and some of its $500 million to South Beach. Word is the company is looking for 150- to 400-room "urban properties" to transform into four-star hotels and appealing to the "creative class of high income, well-educated metropolitan travelers." Along similar lines: the **SLS South Beach,** 1701 Collins Ave., a $65-million Philippe Starck–designed, 142-room boutique hotel from billionaire hotelier Sam Nazarian. Expected in 2012, the hotel will feature a branch of L.A. hot spot **Katsuya** and world-class eatery by star-chef José Andrés.

Note: Art Deco hotels, while pleasing to the eye, may be a bit run-down inside. It's par for the course on South Beach, where appearances are, at times, deceiving.

To locate the hotels in this section, see the "Hotels & Restaurants in South Beach" map (p. 86).

VERY EXPENSIVE

Delano ★ Though Beyoncé and Jay Z may choose to sleep at the Setai over Delano these days, it doesn't mean South Beach's original see-and-be-seen hotel is over just yet. The stunning pool area, Rose Bar, Agua Spa, Lenny Kravitz–designed speak-easy The Florida Room, and newly named and decorated **Blue Door Fish** restaurant (p.111) are still studded with the boldface and the beautiful. But today, the Delano, a place where smiles from staffers were once as rare as snow in Miami, is somewhat kinder and gentler. But not entirely—during the worst of the recession, Delano refused to lower its room rates despite the fact that the rooms were empty. They said they'd rather have empty rooms than have budget travelers staying there. Rude or not, it certainly is still pleasantly amusing to look at—with 40-foot sheer white billowing curtains hanging outside, mirrors everywhere, Adirondack chairs, and faux fur–covered beds. Rooms that were once done up sanitarium-style, sterile yet terribly trendy, just received a revamp that boasts a splash of color and reworked bathrooms that went from spartan to spacious.

1685 Collins Ave., South Beach, FL 33139. www.delano-hotel.com. 📞**800/555-5001** or 305/672-2000. Fax 305/532-0099. 194 units, including 1 penthouse. Winter from $495 city view, $1,250 suite, $2,200 bungalow, $4,000 penthouse; off season from $345 city view, $950 suite, $1,000 bungalow, $3,100 penthouse. Extra person $50. AE, DC, DISC, MC, V. Valet parking $37.

Amenities: 3 restaurants; 3 bars; children's program (seasonal); concierge; state-of-the-art gym; large outdoor pool; room service; agua spa. *In room:* A/C, TV/DVD, CD player, hair dryer, minibar, MP3 docking station, Wi-Fi.

Gansevoort Miami Beach ★ No longer affiliated with the hip NYC hotel of the same name, the Gansevoort Miami Beach is still hipster central, but not without a requisite identity crisis. In 2010, it faced foreclosure and auction, fired much of its staff, and ended up in the capable management hands of Coral Hospitality (Casa Ybel in Sanibel Island, Sandpearl in Clearwater, among many others), which has seemingly returned the hotel to a sense of stability. The 340-room hotel features the flagship David Barton Gym and Spa, expansive ocean-view rooftop pool and bar, trendy meatery **STK** (p. 115), chic Chinese restaurant **Philippe,** VIP bar and lounge by the Opium Group, and, inexplicably, a shark tank with 27 types of fish and sharks that spans 50 feet of the lobby, which, compared to the rest of the hotel, is a huge, unsightly letdown. Things are much prettier up top, where a 26,000-square-foot rooftop playground (complete with a 110-ft. elevated swimming pool, bar, and lounge) offers divine views of the ocean, the bay, and downtown. On the main level is a 40,000-square-foot semi-circular oceanfront pool plaza with infinity-edge pool, teak decking, and cabanas. Room furniture screams hot pink, magenta, and yellow, set against charcoal-gray suede walls dotted with pictures of '40s pinup girls. Most rooms have balconies overlooking the ocean.

2377 Collins Ave., South Beach, FL 33139. www.gansevoortmiamibeach.com. © **305/604-1000.** Fax 305/604-6886. 340 units. $250–$595 deluxe double or king; $685–$1,000 suite. AE, DC, DISC, MC, V. Valet parking $15 per night. **Amenities:** 2 restaurants; bar and lounge; beachfront lounge; concierge; fitness center; infinity-edge rooftop pool; room service; spa. *In room:* A/C, TV/ DVD, CD player, hair dryer, minibar, MP3 docking station, Wi-Fi.

Loews Miami Beach Hotel ★ ☺ The Loews is one of the largest hotels on South Beach, consuming an unprecedented 900 feet of oceanfront. This 790-room behemoth is considered an eyesore by many, an architectural triumph by others. In 2010, the resort completed a $50-million renovation, which has whisked the resort from stale to stellar thanks to, among other things, the removal of the ghastly popcorn ceilings in all rooms, renovation of all bathrooms, the removal of the lobby's outdated pineapple-covered staircase in favor of a new re-tail area and wall-size aquarium, and the addition of an old-fashioned ice-cream parlor, boutique, and water features along the hotel's driveway. Rooms are still a bit boxy and bland, nothing to rave about, but they are clean and have new carpets and bedspreads to erase signs of wear and tear from the hotel's heavy traffic. If you can steer your way past all the conventioneers in the lobby, you can escape to the equally massive pool (with an undisputedly gorgeous, landscaped entrance that's more Maui than Miami). In addition to children's fare, such as the Loews Loves Kids program, the hotel hosts fun activities for adults, such as Dive-in Movies at the pool, salsa lessons, and bingo. *Tip:* Rooms facing away from Collins Avenue are much quieter.

1601 Collins Ave., South Beach, FL 33139. www.loewshotels.com. © **800/23-LOEWS** (235-6397) or 305/604-1601. 790 units. Winter from $499 double; off season from $289 double. AE, DC, DISC, MC, V. Valet parking $30. Pets accepted. **Amenities:** 5 restaurants; 2 bars; coffee bar; ice-cream parlor; babysitting; children's programs; concierge; health club; Jacuzzi; sprawling outdoor pool; room service; sauna; spa; watersports equipment/rentals. *In room:* A/C, TV, hair dryer, high-speed Internet access, minibar.

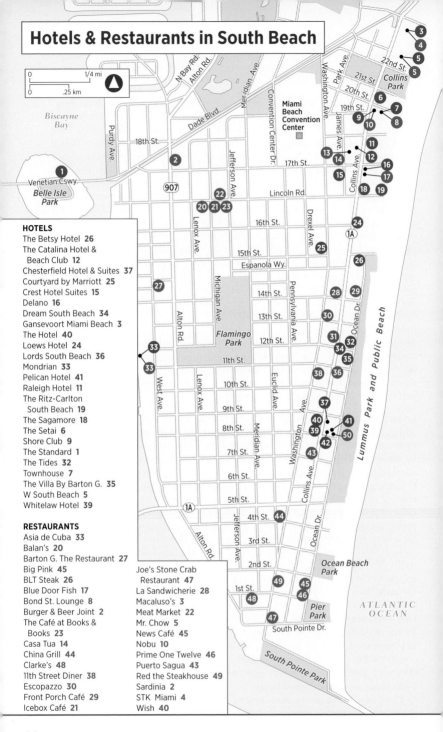

Hotels & Restaurants in South Beach

Biscayne Bay

Venetian Cswy.
Belle Isle Park

Miami Beach Convention Center

Atlantic Ocean

Lummus Park and Public Beach

Ocean Beach Park

Pier Park

South Pointe Park

HOTELS

The Betsy Hotel **26**
The Catalina Hotel & Beach Club **12**
Chesterfield Hotel & Suites **37**
Courtyard by Marriott **25**
Crest Hotel Suites **15**
Delano **16**
Dream South Beach **34**
Gansevoort Miami Beach **3**
The Hotel **40**
Loews Hotel **24**
Lords South Beach **36**
Mondrian **33**
Pelican Hotel **41**
Raleigh Hotel **11**
The Ritz-Carlton South Beach **19**
The Sagamore **18**
The Setai **6**
Shore Club **9**
The Standard **1**
The Tides **32**
Townhouse **7**
The Villa By Barton G. **35**
W South Beach **5**
Whitelaw Hotel **39**

RESTAURANTS

Asia de Cuba **33**
Balan's **20**
Barton G. The Restaurant **27**
Big Pink **45**
BLT Steak **26**
Blue Door Fish **17**
Bond St. Lounge **8**
Burger & Beer Joint **2**
The Café at Books & Books **23**
Casa Tua **14**
China Grill **44**
Clarke's **48**
11th Street Diner **38**
Escopazzo **30**
Front Porch Café **29**
Icebox Café **21**
Joe's Stone Crab Restaurant **47**
La Sandwicherie **28**
Macaluso's **3**
Meat Market **22**
Mr. Chow **5**
News Café **45**
Nobu **10**
Prime One Twelve **46**
Puerto Sagua **43**
Red the Steakhouse **49**
Sardinia **2**
STK Miami **4**
Wish **40**

Mondrian ★★ Much to everyone's surprise, the latest offering from Morgans Hotel Group of Delano fame isn't just another humdrum, been-there-done-that homage to all things painfully trendy. Sure, it's painfully trendy, but it's also refreshingly different. For one, it's located on the western, residential bay side of South Beach, where its neighbors (and its former incarnation) are high-rise condos. Panoramic views of the bay and skyline are stunning. Rooms have been done up with the usual chic trappings and are comfy enough, as they should be, considering someone's grandma used to live there. World-famous design star and *Elle Decor*'s 2006 International Designer of the Year, Marcel Wanders, envisioned the property as Sleeping Beauty's castle, with whimsical adult-playground-style environs. The hotel's so-called "Modern Resort" concept features an **agua spa** (of Delano fame) and Jeffrey Chodorow's **Asia de Cuba** restaurant (p. 110). And while the indoor spaces are swell, it's the outdoor pool area that really must be seen, especially at sundown. Don't miss the lobby's futuristic, ridiculous vending machine from which, if you slide your credit card in, you can actually buy yourself a Bentley. Shop at your own risk.

1100 West Ave., Miami Beach, FL 33139. www.mondrian-miami.com. ℰ **800/606-6090** or 305/514-1500. Fax 305/514-1800. 335 units. Winter $350 studio, $950 deluxe 2-bedroom suite; off season $195 studio, $795 deluxe 2-bedroom suite. AE, DC, DISC, MC, V. Valet parking $37. **Amenities:** Restaurant; 3 bars; babysitting; concierge; fitness center; pool; room service; agua spa; watersports equipment/rentals. *In room:* A/C, TV, high-speed Internet access, kitchenette.

The Ritz-Carlton South Beach ★★ ☺ Far from ostentatious, the Ritz-Carlton South Beach moves away from gilded opulence in favor of the more soothing pastel-washed touches of Deco. Though South Beach is better known for its trendy boutique hotels, the Ritz-Carlton provides comfort to those who might prefer 100% cotton Frette sheets and goose-down pillows to high-style minimalism. The best rooms, by far, are the 72 poolside and oceanview lanai rooms. There's also a trademarked "Tanning Butler" who will spritz you with SPF and water whenever you want. With its impeccable service, an elevated pool with unobstructed views of the Atlantic and live entertainment on weekends, an impressive stretch of sand with a fabulous beach club, and a world-class 16,000-square-foot spa and wellness center, the Ritz-Carlton kicks sand in the faces of some smaller hotels that think they're doing *you* a favor by allowing you to sleep there. Parents love the Ritz Kids program for kids ages 5 through 12; and for gourmands, there's the Ritz's amazing Sunday champagne brunch.

1 Lincoln Rd., South Beach, FL 33139. www.ritzcarlton.com. ℰ **800/241-3333** or 786/276-4000. Fax 786/276-4001. 375 units. Winter $479 standard, $769 junior suite; off season $269 standard, $489 junior suite. AE, DISC, MC, V. Valet parking $36 (overnight), $24 (daily). **Amenities:** 2 restaurants; 2 bars; babysitting; children's program; fitness center; outdoor heated pool; room service; spa; extensive watersports equipment/rentals. *In room:* A/C, TV, hair dryer, high-speed Internet access, minibar.

The Sagamore ★★ Just two doors down from the Delano Hotel is the Sagamore, fabulous in its own right, with an ultramodern lobby-cum-art-gallery-cum-restaurant that's infinitely warmer than your typical pop-art exhibit at the Museum of Modern Art. The hotel doesn't take itself too seriously and boasts a tongue-in-cheek sense of humor that was evidenced when it hosted a Lox and Botox party—no, we're not kidding. Although the lobby and its requisite restaurant, bar, and lounge areas have become command central for the international chic elite and celebrities, the Sagamore's all-suite, apartment-like rooms are havens from the hype, with all the cushy comforts of home and then some. The sprawling outdoor lawn, dotted with cabanas with plasma TVs screening everything from Japanese anime to digital art, pool, and beachfront, makes you realize you're not in Kansas anymore. A branch of Miami's coiffeur to the stars, **Rik Rak,** opened in one of the outdoor bungalows.

1671 Collins Ave., South Beach, FL 33139. www.sagamorehotel.com. © **877/SAGAMORE** (724-2667) or 305/535-8088. Fax 305/535-8185. 93 units. Winter $395–$4,500 suite; off season $195–$1,500 suite. AE, DC, DISC, MC, V. Valet parking $37. **Amenities:** Restaurant; bar; pool bar; concierge; fitness center; pool; room service; spa. *In room:* A/C, TV/VCR/DVD, hair dryer, kitchenette, minibar, MP3 docking station, Wi-Fi.

The Setai ★★★ Asian-inspired Setai is truly for that 1% of society who can afford it—but if you want to splurge, this is where to do it. The celebrity clientele here doesn't have to ask "how much?" but if you're keeping tabs: Suites are $550 to $30,000 for the penthouse, dinners come to around $200 per person (although new "recession friendly" prix-fixe menus start at $50 per person), and drinks (try the one with pork belly–infused Jack Daniels) range from $14 to $20 a pop (although a new Bottle Shock promotion discounts bottles of *vino* by 40%). All of the suites—some are actually condos participating in the condo-hotel program—are gorgeous apartments with floor-to-ceiling windows, full kitchens, and Jacuzzi bathtubs bigger than a small swimming pool. There are 85 regular hotel rooms that are an average of 600 square feet, compared to the suites' 1,300 to 3,500 square feet. All are adorned in sleek Asian decor with over-the-top comforts, including Lavazza espresso makers, Laura Tonatto bathroom amenities, and washer/dryers. The garden area with reflecting pools is lovely, but not as cool as the pool area with a bar serving $18 chicken sandwiches to celebrity clientele. There's also the **Grill,** which features a create-your-own multicourse tapas menu, and the **Restaurant,** its proper name, which is authentically Asian, with stainless-steel tandoori ovens—but with these steep prices and small portions, you may as well buy a ticket to Asia.

2001 Collins Ave., South Beach, FL 33139. www.setai.com. © **305/520-6000.** Fax 305/520-6600. 130 units. Winter $1,150 studio suite, $30,000 penthouse; off season $550 studio suite, price available on request for penthouse. AE, DC, DISC, MC, V. Valet parking $40. **Amenities:** 3 restaurants; 2 bars; concierge; fitness center; 3 pools; room service; spa. *In room:* A/C, TV/DVD, hair dryer, kitchen (1-, 2-, and 3-bedroom suites only), minibar, Wi-Fi.

Shore Club ★ In the fickle world of hot hotels, the Shore Club struggles to hold onto its place at the top, but does okay thanks to Florida's only **Nobu** sushi restaurant (p. 114) and, on certain nights, a celebrity clientele that would fill up an entire issue of *Us Weekly.* Because this hotel is infinitely more cavernous than its hipster neighbors, Delano and the Sagamore (see above), some publicity-shy celebrities such as Janet Jackson and Denzel Washington have been known to call it their home away from home—there are indeed places for them to hide. That said, this is hardly a quiet place for some silent reflection. In fact, during high seasons and Spring Break, it's party central. An outpost of L.A.'s celebrity-laden **SkyBar** reigns supreme, with a Marrakech-meets-Miami motif that stretches throughout the hotel's sprawling pool, patio, and garden areas. Beware of surly doormen if you're not a hotel guest. There's also a branch of L.A.'s—and Robert De Niro's—pricey pasta spot **Ago.** The rooms—most of which have an ocean view—are loaded with state-of-the-art amenities and, frankly, have a bit more personality than those at Delano.

1901 Collins Ave., Miami Beach, FL 33139. www.shoreclub.com. ✆ **877/640-9500** or 305/695-3100. Fax 305/695-3299. 309 units, including 8 bungalows. From $285 superior, $490 suite, $1,500 bungalow. AE, DC, MC, V. Valet parking $42. **Amenities:** 2 restaurants; bar; concierge; 2 outdoor swimming pools; room service; spa. *In room:* A/C, TV, CD player, high-speed Internet access, minibar, MP3 docking station.

The Tides ★★★ This 10-story Art Deco masterpiece reminiscent of a gleaming ocean liner with porthole windows received a massive makeover by trendsetting designer Kelly Wearstler. Rooms have been newly washed in warm earth tones. Also, all rooms are at least twice the size of a typical South Beach hotel room and have a breathtaking panoramic view of the ocean. The penthouses on the 9th and 10th floors are situated at the highest point on Ocean Drive, allowing for a priceless panoramic view of the ocean, the skyline, and the beach. The hotel's Latin-accented restaurant, **La Marea,** is located in the lobby, and is good, but very pricey (in the wake of the recession and thanks to a new chef, prices have dropped about 30%, but we still think it's pricey). Located just off the lobby is the **Coral Bar,** a small and romantic spot for a cocktail or two with the help of its very own rum sommelier. A full selection of spa services is available in rooms and poolside. Best of all, the Tides has what they call "Pool Personal Assistants" who provide magazines, frozen fruits, and chilled water, and will even clean and polish your sunglasses, and "Oceanfront Personal Assistants" who assist in scoring lounges, umbrellas, towels, and picnic baskets if you wish.

1220 Ocean Dr., South Beach, FL 33139. www.tidessouthbeach.com. ✆ **800/439-4095** or 305/604-5070. Fax 305/503-3275. 45 units. Winter $595 studio suites, $1,500–$5,000 penthouse suites; off season $395 studio suites, $1,000–$4,000 penthouse suites. Extra person $100. AE, DC, DISC, MC, V. Valet parking $35. Pets $150 1-time fee including new "Paws" program. **Amenities:** Restaurant; lounge and bar; concierge; fitness room; outdoor heated pool; room service. *In room:* A/C, TV/DVD, CD player, hair dryer, minibar, Wi-Fi.

The Villa By Barton G. The former Versace Mansion got a new name and a new attitude in 2010 when party planner/restaurateur/Miami's PT Barnum Barton G. Weiss signed a decade-long lease to run the all-suite hotel, restaurant, and special-events space. Restyled as The Villa By Barton G., Weiss channels his inner Versace in the decor of the manse's 10 ornate rooms. The restaurant—Weiss's third—dishes up redefined continental cuisine on (what else?) Versace china in the late designer's dining room. Also still intact: the manse's mosaic pool, the bottom of which has Versace's signature Medusa icon created from a thousand mosaic tiles.

1116 Ocean Dr., South Beach, FL 33139. www.thevillabybartong.com. ✆ **305/587-8003.** Fax 305/357-7960. 10 suites. From $795 suite. AE, DISC, MC, V. Valet parking $45 overnight, $25 daily. **Amenities:** Restaurant; 2 private lounges; pool; personal butler service. *In room:* A/C, TV/DVD, hair dryer, iPad, Wi-Fi.

W South Beach ★★★ South Beach's newest "it" girl, the W is so stunning it has been referred to as the Starwood's signature property even though it's hardly the first. A work of art in itself, the property features a Bali–meets–Miami Beach sensibility, with breathtaking landscape design by conceptual design garden artist Paula Hayes, and exclusive artwork by rock-'n'-roll photographer Danny Clinch. W South Beach's stylish guest rooms and suites are soothing in shades of teal and white, enhanced by a fusion of white ceramic wood tiles, soft linens, and glossy acrylic accents. All rooms have a W signature bed with plush pillow-top mattress and feather bed overlay, goose-down duvet and pillows, and 350-thread-count cotton-blend sheets. Expansive glass balconies offer unparalleled and unobstructed views of the beach and ocean. And then there are the amenities, including Florida's first-ever **Mr Chow** restaurant (p. 114), the stellar **Soleà,** three "destination" bars, a secret garden gathering spot for cocktails, a nightclub, and a Bliss spa. Although located directly on the ocean, the pool in its rich wood teak glory is equally picturesque and quite the see-and-be-scene spot. Perhaps the most unique amenities are the full-size tennis and basketball courts with city views. In true W fashion, all we can say is, simply, WOW.

2201 Collins Ave., Miami Beach, FL 33139. www.wsouthbeach.com. ✆ **305/938-3000.** Fax 305/938-3005. 312 units. Winter $599–$999 double, $879–$1,229 suite; off season $399–$799 double, $679–$1,029 suite. AE, DC, DISC, MC, V. Valet parking $35. **Amenities:** 2 restaurants; 3 bars; nightclub; state-of-the-art fitness center; 2 pools; spa; tennis and basketball courts. *In room:* A/C, TV/DVD, CD player, hair dryer, Wi-Fi.

EXPENSIVE

The Betsy Hotel ★ The Betsy is the lone surviving example of Florida Georgian architecture on the famous byway, Ocean Drive. Behind its plantation-style shutters and columned facade, the Betsy Hotel offers a tropical colonial beachside haven. Each room and suite in the oceanfront hotel is a nod to the stately colonial rooms of yesteryear blended with the modern aesthetic of South Beach. The Betsy boasts the South Florida installment of New York's **BLT Steak** restaurant (p. 111) by A-list chef Laurent Tourondel; a roof-deck solarium with Zen garden for sunning, spa services, drinks, and light fare; a well-heeled lobby bar scene; and a private basement lounge that bills itself as the anticelebrity bar, where guests enter by invitation only and reality stars are strictly prohibited, as well they should be. While the beach is a few steps away, the hotel also offers a serene outdoor pool scene.

1440 Ocean Dr., Miami Beach, FL 33139. www.thebetsyhotel.com. ✆ **305/531-3934** or 866/531-8950. Fax 305/531-9009. 63 units. Winter $409–$879 double, $979–$4,000 suite; off season $309–$779 double, $879–$3,500 suite. AE, DC, DISC, MC, V. Valet parking $30. **Amenities:** Restaurant; bar; babysitting; concierge; outdoor pool; room service; roof-deck solarium w/spa services. *In room:* A/C, TV/DVD, CD player, hair dryer, MP3 docking station, Wi-Fi.

Dream South Beach With the economy holding up construction of this NYC import for what seemed to be years, the hotel—which has taken over two landmark Art Deco hotels, the Tudor and the Palmer House—could have changed its name to Nightmare, but instead, it chugged on and became a pleasant reality when it opened in February 2011, featuring 108 rooms, requisite rooftop pool lounge, small full-service Ayurvedic spa, restaurant, and hipster-approved mood lighting. Decor of the hotel is definitely something out of a sound sleep: Modern Moroccan meets late-'70s, Halston-inspired sleek. All rooms feature Skype and Bluetooth-enabled smart phones, MP3 docking station, 380-plus thread count Egyptian cotton linens, and, of course, Wi-Fi.

1111 Collins Ave., Miami Beach, FL 33139. www.dreamsouthbeach.com. ✆ **888/376-7623.** Fax 305/673-4749. 108 units. Winter $299–$479 double, $70 extra for junior suite; off season $219–$299 double, $70 extra for junior suite. AE, DC, DISC, MC, V. Valet parking $35. **Amenities:** Restaurant; bar; babysitting; concierge; rooftop lounge and pool; room service; full service spa. *In room:* A/C, TV/DVD, CD player, hair dryer, MP3 docking station, Wi-Fi.

The Hotel ★ Kitschy fashion designer Todd Oldham whimsically restored this 1939 gem (formerly the Tiffany Hotel) as he would have restored a vintage piece of couture. He laced it with lush, cool colors, hand-cut mirrors, and glass mosaics from his studio, then added artisan detailing, while preserving the terrazzo floors and porthole windows. The small, soundproof rooms are very comfortable and incredibly stylish, though the bathrooms are a bit cramped. Nevertheless, the showers are irresistible, with fantastic rain-shower heads. There's no need to pay more for an oceanfront view here—go up to the rooftop, where the hip and funky **Spire Bar** and pool are located, and you'll have an amazing view of the Atlantic. The hotel's restaurant, **Wish** (p. 116), is one of South Beach's best and most beautiful. New to the hotel: an oceanfront addition of 20 new deluxe rooms and two new 850-square-foot oceanfront terrace suites located at 800 Ocean Dr., above News Café. Oldham-designed rooms feature warm tones of browns, grays, and orange; flatscreen TVs; glass-enclosed showers with oversize shower heads; thick windows to block out the inevitable noise; and separate rates—$225 to $415 off season, $265 to $545 in winter. The addition shares facilities with its sister property.

801 Collins Ave., South Beach, FL 33139. www.thehotelofsouthbeach.com. ✆ **877/843-4683** or 305/531-2222. Fax 305/531-3222. 53 units. Winter $225–$545 suite; off season $195–$415 suite. AE, DC, DISC, MC, V. Valet parking $25 per day. **Amenities:** Restaurant; bar; pool bar; concierge; gym; small pool; room service. *In room:* A/C, TV, hair dryer, MP3 docking station, free Wi-Fi.

Raleigh Hotel ★★ The Raleigh is quintessential old-school Miami Beach with a modern twist. Polished wood, original terrazzo floors, and an intimate martini bar add to the fabulous atmosphere that's favored by fashion photographers, for whom the hotel's fleur-de-lis pool is the favorite subject. In fact, one look at the pool and you'll expect Esther Williams to splash up in a dramatic, aquatic plié. The entire outdoor area is a stunning oasis that elicits oohs and aahs from even the most jaded jet-setters. The cozy bar off the lobby is reminiscent of a place where Dorothy Parker and her Algonquin Round Tablers would have gathered for spirited musings. Rooms have been redone with period furnishings, MP3 docking stations, gourmet minibars, and terrazzo floors (those overlooking the pool and ocean are the most peaceful). The massive penthouse is a favorite among visiting celebrities and authors. But it's the Raleigh's warm, romantic Deco atmosphere that lures people away from chillier, neighboring boutique hotels. Opened in November 2010: **The Royal,** the hot American bistro from chef/restaurateur John DeLucie of NYC's The Lion and Waverly Inn fame.

1775 Collins Ave., Miami Beach, FL 33139. www.raleighhotel.com. ✆ **800/848-1775** or 305/534-6300. Fax 305/538-8140. 104 units. Winter $495–$925 double, $950–$2,750 suite; off season $225–$700 double, $700–$2,000 suite. AE, DC, DISC, MC, V. Valet parking $35. **Amenities:** Restaurant; bar; coffee bar; concierge; pool; room service. *In room:* A/C, TV/DVD, CD player, fridge, hair dryer, minibar, Wi-Fi.

The Standard ★★ The quintessential spa resort, the Standard, owned by hip hotelier Andre Balazs, is housed in Miami Beach's legendary Lido Spa spot, a place that was swinging back in the days when women still wore bathing caps. Today, the hotel is full of all the modern trappings of a swank spa resort, with a bayfront view and a serene location on the Venetian Causeway—walking distance to all the South Beach craziness. Remnants of the atomic age of the fabulous '50s still exist here—the lobby's white-marble walls, terrazzo floors, and stainless steel elevators. Add to that a touch of Scandinavian retro modernism. Whitewashed guest rooms are serviced by roaming carts offering herbal teas and aromatherapy foot baths. There's a cedar sauna; a Turkish hammam; tongue-in-cheek treatments, such as the cellulite-fighting Standard Spanking; a chlorine-free plunge pool, with a 12-foot-tall waterfall and DJ-spun music piped beneath the water; clothing-optional mud baths; and a waterfront restaurant with glorious waterfront views. Anything but standard.

40 Island Ave., Miami Beach, FL 33139. www.standardhotel.com. © **305/673-1717.** Fax 305/673-8181. 105 units. $165–$1,250 suite. AE, DC, DISC, MC, V. Valet parking $25. **Amenities:** Restaurant; bar; concierge; fitness center; pool; limited room service; sauna; spa. *In room:* A/C, TV/DVD, CD player, hair dryer, minibar.

MODERATE

The Catalina Hotel & Beach Club ★★ The Catalina is something straight out of an Austin Powers movie. Groovy, indeed! So much so that the hotel took over the space next door and added 60 more rooms, a rooftop pool, and a funky sushi restaurant, Kung Fu Kitchen & Sushi. Stylish but not at all stuffy, the Catalina is perhaps the only hotel in the area that can pull off using red shag carpeting—though it tends to get a bit mangy. The mod-squad lobby decor gives way to rooms glazed in white with hints of bright colors featuring Tempur-Pedic Swedish mattresses, 300-thread-count Mascioni sheets, goose-down comforters and pillows, iPods, and, of course, flatscreen TVs. The three-building hotel has a happening bar and lounge scene and features a 24-hour restaurant, **Maxine's Bistro & Bar,** with a decidedly European jet-set vibe and a splashy beach club where you can get poolside manicures and pedicures. Request a room in the recently upgraded Maxine building featuring marble bathrooms and espresso wood floors. Free passes to nightclubs and free transportation to and from Miami International are among the many perks here.

If Catalina is sold out, check out its sister hotels: The **Metropole South Beach,** 635 Collins Ave. (www.metropolesouthbeach.com; © **305/672-0009**), an all-suite hotel with one- and two-bedroom suites, is another favorite for hipsters and recording artists—and the cast of *Jersey Shore* for the show's second season. Rates there start at $195 in season and $125 off season. The **Riviera** (© **877/762-3477**), tucked away at 2000 Liberty Ave., on South Beach, features imaginatively designed one-bedroom apartment-like accommodations with full gourmet kitchens; a courtyard pool with a grill and private cabanas, a lobby lounge, a state-of-the-art spa and yoga room, and a sun deck with sweeping views of the city and ocean. Rates include complimentary continental breakfast and beach-chair passes at the beach club and start at $299 in the winter and $159 off-season. Walk to the Catalina to get your happy hour on.

1732 Collins Ave., South Beach, FL 33139. www.catalinahotel.com. © **305/674-1160.** Fax 305/672-8216. 136 units. Winter $225–$290 double; off season $125–$250 double. Rates include unlimited happy-hour cocktails daily 7–8pm, daily beach-chair passes at beach club. AE, DC, MC, V. Valet parking $35. **Amenities:** 2 restaurants; 3 bars; complimentary bike cruisers; 2 pools. *In room:* A/C, TV/VCR, CD player, hair dryer, minibar, free Wi-Fi.

Chesterfield Hotel & Suites ★ This charismatic sliver of a property has won the loyalty of fashion industrialists and romantics alike. Unfortunately, not everyone loves it. Some have complained of the constant construction, apathetic service, and run-down or complete lack of amenities. But if you're in a partying mood, this place is for you. The very central location (1 block from the ocean) and the newly added rooftop sun deck are a plus, especially because the hotel lacks a pool. Most of the rooms are immaculate and reminiscent of a loft apartment;

large bathrooms with big, deep tubs are especially enticing. Rooms have been upgraded with the addition of the Lily & Leon Hotel, the Chesterfield has several different room types, including an 1,800-square-foot penthouse. However, some rooms are dark and have not had such upgrades (we have gotten complaints), and are to be avoided; do not hesitate to ask for a room change. We've also gotten complaints about the music coming from the hotel next door, but you have to realize that if you're staying on Collins or Washington avenues, you're going to hear noise: South Beach isn't known for its quiet, peaceful demeanor. For R&R, try the hotel's day spa, and for good and fast sushi, try the hotel's new sushi bar, **I Love Sushi**, for a quick combo of sushi and sake.

841 Collins Ave., South Beach, FL 33139. www.thechesterfieldhotel.com. ✆ **305/673-3767.** Fax 305/535-9665. 90 units. Winter $175–$245 suite, $395 penthouse; off season $125–$195 suite, $335 penthouse. Extra person $20. AE, DC, MC, V. Valet parking $30. Well-behaved pets accepted. **Amenities:** Restaurant; 2 bars; concierge; reduced rates at local gym; spa. *In room:* A/C, TV, CD player, hair dryer, high-speed Internet access, minibar.

Crest Hotel Suites ★ 🏨 One of South Beach's best-kept secrets, the Crest Hotel has a quietly fashionable, contemporary, relaxed atmosphere with friendly service. Built in 1939, the Crest was restored to preserve its Art Deco architecture, but the interior of the hotel is thoroughly modern, with rooms resembling cosmopolitan apartments. All suites have a living room/dining room area, kitchenette, and executive work space. An indoor/outdoor cafe with terrace and poolside dining isn't besieged with trendy locals, but does attract a younger crowd. Around the corner from the hotel is Lincoln Road, with its sidewalk cafes, gourmet restaurants, theaters, and galleries. In an effort to expand its quiet trendiness, the Crest opened its second hotel, the **South Beach Hotel,** at 236 21st St., in an up-and-coming area near Collins Park that is in the slow throes of a renaissance.

1670 James Ave., Miami Beach, FL 33139. www.crestgrouphotels.com. ✆ **800/531-3880** or 305/531-0321. Fax 305/531-8180. 64 units. Winter $120–$165 double, $211 suite; off season $115 double, $175 suite. Packages available and 10% discount if booked on website. AE, MC, V. **Amenities:** Restaurant; cafe; pool. *In room:* A/C, TV, kitchenette.

Pelican Hotel ★★ Owned by the same creative folks behind the Diesel Jeans company, the fashionable Pelican is South Beach's only self-professed "toy-hotel," in which each of its 30 rooms and suites is decorated as outrageously as some of the area's more colorful drag queens. Each room has been designed daringly and rather wittily by Swedish interior decorator Magnus Ehrland. Countless trips to antiques markets, combined with his wild imagination, have turned room no. 309, for instance, into the "Psychedelic(ate) Girl"; room no. 201 into the "Executive Fifties" suite; and no. 209 into the "Love, Peace, and Leafforest" room. But the most popular room is the tough-to-score no. 215, or the "Best Whorehouse," which is said to have made even former Hollywood madam Heidi Fleiss red with envy. The Ocean Drive location and the hotel's cafe make the Pelican a very popular people-watching spot.

826 Ocean Dr., Miami Beach, FL 33139. www.pelicanhotel.com. ✆ **800/7-PELICAN** (773-5422) or 305/673-3373. Fax 305/673-3255. 30 units. Winter $280–$450 double, $480–$800 oceanfront suite; off season $165–$220 double, $330–$540 oceanfront suite. AE, DC, MC, V. Valet parking $22. **Amenities:** Restaurant; bar; concierge; access to area gyms; room service; Wi-Fi. *In room:* A/C, TV, CD player, fridge w/complimentary water, hair dryer.

Townhouse ★★ New York hipster Jonathan Morr felt that Miami Beach had lost touch with the bons vivants who gave the city its original cachet, so he decided to take matters into his own hands. His solution: this 67-room, five-story so-called shabby-chic hotel. The charm of this hotel is in its clean and simple yet chic design with quirky details: exercise equipment that stands alone in the hallways, free laundry machines in the lobby, and a water bed–lined rooftop. Comfortable, shabby-chic rooms boast L-shaped couches for extra guests (for whom you aren't charged). Though the rooms are all pretty much the same, consider the ones with the partial ocean view. The hotel also offers a rooftop lounge and beach access, with chair and umbrella rentals available. The hotel's basement features the hot sushi spot **Bond St. Lounge** (p. 117).

150 20th St., South Beach, FL 33139. www.townhousehotel.com. ✆ **877/534-3800** or 305/534-3800. Fax 305/534-3811. 69 units. Winter $195–$395 double, $395–$450 penthouse; off season $105–$215 double, $295–$390 penthouse. Rates include Parisian-style (coffee and pastry) breakfast. AE, MC, V. Valet parking $25. **Amenities:** Restaurant; bar; bike rental; workout stations; free Wi-Fi. *In room:* A/C, TV/VCR, CD player, fridge, hair dryer.

Whitelaw Hotel ★ With a slogan that reads, "Clean sheets, hot water, and stiff drinks," the Whitelaw Hotel stands apart from other boutique hotels with its fierce sense of humor. Only half a block from Ocean Drive, this hotel, like its clientele, is full of distinct personalities, pairing such disparate elements as luxurious Belgian sheets with shag carpeting to create an innovative setting. All-white rooms manage to be homey and plush, and not at all antiseptic, with white wood floors, a much-needed improvement from the old linoleum. Bathrooms are pretty small and not that well stocked, and towels are sometimes in short supply, but those who stay here aren't really looking for luxury—they just want to party. Complimentary cocktails in the lobby every night from 7 to 8pm contribute to a very social atmosphere.

808 Collins Ave., Miami Beach, FL 33139. www.whitelawhotel.com. ✆ **305/398-7000.** Fax 305/398-7010. 49 units. Winter $145–$225 double/king; off season $95–$145 double/king. Rates subject to change during special events. Rates include complimentary continental breakfast and free cocktails in the lobby (7–8pm daily). AE, DC, MC, V. Parking $32. **Amenities:** Lounge; free airport pickup (to and from MIA); concierge. *In room:* A/C, TV, CD player, hair dryer, free Wi-Fi.

Miami Beach: Surfside, Bal Harbour, Sunny Isles & North Beach

The area just north of South Beach, known as Miami Beach, encompasses Surfside, Bal Harbour, and Sunny Isles. Unrestricted by zoning codes throughout the 1950s, 1960s, and especially 1970s, area developers went crazy, building ever bigger and more brazen structures, especially north of 41st Street, known as "Condo Canyon." Consequently, there's now a glut of medium-quality condos, with a few scattered holdouts of older hotels and motels casting shadows over the newer, swankier stays emerging on the beachfront.

To locate the hotels in this section, see the map "Hotels & Restaurants in Miami Beach" (p. 96).

VERY EXPENSIVE

Canyon Ranch Miami Beach ★ Opened in late 2008 in the former Carillon Hotel on an unseemly stretch of Collins Avenue, the Miami version of the famous Tucson, Arizona, and Lenox, Massachusetts, spa and wellness hotel is located directly on the beach. If you're looking to drop in excess of, say, $330 for a Japanese bathing ritual, or $350 for an insomnia consultation with a doctor, then this place is for you. The main draw isn't a trendy bar, restaurant, or nightclub, but a 70,000-square-foot health club that includes a two-story rock-climbing wall as well as equipment for testing oxygen saturation and bone density. There's even a $125,000 body scanner that, according to the property's medical director, is the best in the world. The hotel has a full-time medical staff of 11, including a Chinese medicine specialist/acupuncturist, nutritionist, and physical therapist. Because the place operates as a condo as well, every suite—spacious one- and two-bedrooms starting at 720 square feet—has fine furnishings, top electronics, and a designer kitchen. The oceanfront **Canyon Ranch Grill** features all healthy fare. In addition to 750 feet of beach, there are four pools, a reading garden overlooking the ocean, and water-therapy programs. To preserve the tranquil vibe here, cellphone use is prohibited in many of the hotel's public areas.

6900 Collins Ave., Miami Beach, FL 33141. www.canyonranch.com. © **800/742-9000** or 305/514-7000. Fax 305/864-2744. 130 units. Winter suites from $400; off season suites from $295. AE, DISC, MC, V. Valet parking $35. **Amenities:** 3 restaurants; juice and smoothie bar; babysitting; fitness center; 4 outdoor pools; room service; spa. In room: A/C, TV, high-speed Internet, kitchen.

One Bal Harbour ★★★ Formerly a Regent Hotel, which ironically couldn't make it here or on South Beach, this resort may have no big-name affiliation, but it's still big-time luxe. Until the St. Regis finishes completion in the former Sheraton Bal Harbour, this is the only oceanfront resort in the area. The penultimate in luxury, suites are resplendent with mahogany floors, with leather walls, panoramic views of the ocean, and bathrooms with 10-foot floor-to-ceiling windows and, our favorite, a free-standing tub overlooking the ocean. Elevators take you directly into your suite, like a luxury apartment building. A new kids' program pays special attention to trendy tots with all sorts of amenities and classes, including the Nobu cooking class for kids, mini manicures and pedicures, and a VIP card good for sodas and ice cream. A swanky spa, butler service, spectacular pool and 750 feet of beachfront, and restaurant that seems to be in constant transition will cost you a pretty penny; but if you're looking to be doted on hand and foot without lifting a finger—except to pay your bill at the end—this is the place.

10295 Collins Ave., Bal Harbour, FL. 33154. www.oneluxuryhotels.com. © **877/545-5410** or 305/455-5400. Fax 305/866-2419. 124 units. Winter from $700 double; off season from $375 double; penthouse suite $9,000. AE, MC, V. Valet parking $32. **Amenities:** Restaurant; bar; kids programs; concierge; outdoor pool; room service; spa. In room: A/C, TV/DVD/CD player, hair dryer, minibar, Wi-Fi.

EXPENSIVE

Eden Roc Renaissance Miami Beach ★★ Just next door to the mammoth Fontainebleau, this Morris Lapidus–designed flamboyant hotel, which opened in 1956, in 2008 received a $200-million face-lift, nearly doubling its size from 349 to 631 rooms, complete with a new 283-room oceanfront tower; 17 bungalow suites; four pools; two restaurants, including a sceney, swanky steakhouse, **1500°**, featuring the cuisine of executive chef Paula DaSilva, a *Hell's Kitchen* finalist; and a spa. The focal point is now an oasis of pools, water features, and gardens, threaded with walkways and intimate seating areas. If we had a choice between Eden Roc and Fontainebleau, we'd choose the Eden Roc, hands down,

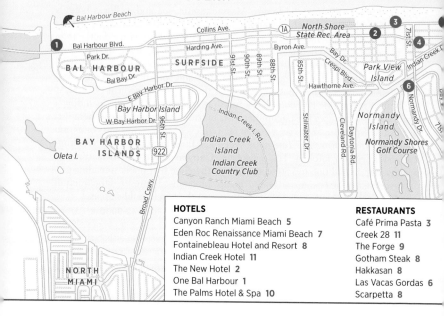

ATLANTIC OCEAN

Bal Harbour Beach

Collins Ave.

North Shore State Rec. Area

Bal Harbour Blvd.

Harding Ave.

Byron Ave.

Park Dr.

BAL HARBOUR

SURFSIDE

Bal Bay Dr.

Park View Island

E Bay Harbor Dr.

Bay Harbor Island

W. Bay Harbor Dr.

Indian Creek I. Rd.

Normandy Island

BAY HARBOR ISLANDS

Oleta I.

Indian Creek Island

Indian Creek Country Club

Normandy Shores Golf Course

Broad Cswy.

NORTH MIAMI

HOTELS	RESTAURANTS
Canyon Ranch Miami Beach 5	Café Prima Pasta 3
Eden Roc Renaissance Miami Beach 7	Creek 28 11
Fontainebleau Hotel and Resort 8	The Forge 9
Indian Creek Hotel 11	Gotham Steak 8
The New Hotel 2	Hakkasan 8
One Bal Harbour 1	Las Vacas Gordas 6
The Palms Hotel & Spa 10	Scarpetta 8

for the seamless service and for a more relaxed, much less Las Vegasy vibe than its neighbor.

4525 Collins Ave., Miami Beach, FL 33140. www.renaissancehotels.com. ☎ **800/327-8337** or 305/531-0000. Fax 305/674-5555. 631 units. Winter $339–$425 double, $394 suite, $750–$1,500 bungalow suites, $2,500–$3,500 penthouse; off season $199–$274 double, $239–$409 suite, $450–$750 bungalows, $1,500 penthouse. Extra person $15. Packages available. AE, DC, DISC, MC, V. Valet parking $24. Pets accepted for a fee. **Amenities:** 2 restaurants; lounge; bar; babysitting; concierge; health club; 4 outdoor pools; room service; spa; watersports equipment/rentals. *In room:* A/C, TV, hair dryer, high-speed Internet, kitchenettes (in suites and penthouse), minibar.

Fontainebleau Hotel and Resort ★ Big changes—$1 *billion* worth—are afoot at Miami Beach's legendary hotel. This grand, Morris Lapidus–designed monolith that once symbolized *Old* Miami decadence reemerged in 2008 as a modern Vegas-style hotel, entertainment, and dining complex featuring all the trappings of a luxury hotel. Choose from the main property or the modern, brand-new all-suite hotel tower, where rooms are plush and posh. A 40,000-square-foot spa and a dramatic oceanfront poolscape are among the many highlights. And while it's a magnet for celebrities who like to disappear into its hugeness, the hotel also brought celebrity chefs as well—with Alfred Portale's **Gotham Steak** (p. 121), Scott Conant's hot New York Italian outpost **Scarpetta** (p. 122), and London's acclaimed Chinese restaurant **Hakkasan** (p. 121) all among the 11 restaurants and lounges. There's also one hotter-than-hot nightclub. Bottom line here: It's huge. And in some ways, it resembles an airport, only airports have the hustle, bustle, and crowd factor. This place is so spread out you may feel like you're in a closed terminal. Although we've received complaints about the service and the emptiness—1,500-plus rooms are hard to fill at these prices and during

this economy—the bars, clubs, and restaurants are almost always packed, so if you're looking for a one-stop hot spot, this is the place to be.

4441 Collins Ave., Miami Beach, FL 33140. www.fontainebleau.com. ✆ **800/548-8886** or 305/538-2000. Fax 305/535-3286. 1,504 units. Winter from $399 double, from $509 suite; off season from $229 double, from $299 suite. AE, DISC, MC, V. Valet parking $32. Pets accepted. **Amenities:** 11 restaurants and lounges; concierge; fitness center; 11 pools w/cabanas; room service; spa. *In room:* A/C, TV/DVD, fax, hair dryer, iMac w/high-speed Internet, kitchenette (in suites), minibar.

MODERATE

Indian Creek Hotel ★ 🎁 Located off the beaten path, the Indian Creek Hotel is a meticulously restored 1936 building with one of the first operating elevators in Miami Beach. Because of its location, which faces the Indian Creek waterway, and its lush landscaping, this place feels like an old-fashioned Key West bed-and-breakfast. The revamped rooms are outfitted in Art Deco furnishings, such as antique writing desks, pretty tropical prints, and small but spotless bathrooms. Just 1 block from a good stretch of sand, the hotel also has a landscaped pool area in the back garden. Although one reader who stayed there complained that the staff was surly, the room was dirty, the lush courtyard was overgrown, and he wasn't informed that he needed a parking pass—obtainable at the hotel—the good news is that there is new ownership and things seem to be running more smoothly. The hotel's restaurant, **Creek 28,** is one of Miami's best-kept secrets, featuring a fusion of Moroccan, Greek, Turkish, and Spanish cuisines with accents of Italy, southern France, Algeria, and Egypt.

2727 Indian Creek Dr. (1 block west of Collins Ave. and the ocean), Miami Beach, FL 33140. www. indiancreekhotel.com. ✆ **800/491-2772** or 305/531-2727. Fax 305/531-5651. 61 units. Winter

$149–$199 double, $269–$289 suite; off season $69–$199 double, $179–$249 suite. Extra person $25. Group packages and summer specials available. AE, DC, DISC, MC, V. **Amenities:** Restaurant; bar; concierge; pool; limited room service. *In room:* A/C, TV/VCR, CD player (in suites), fridge (in suites), hair dryer, Wi-Fi.

The New Hotel ★ 👔 If you drive too fast on Harding Avenue, you will miss this charming, funky boutique hotel located amid North Beach's ramshackle, Art Deco, motel-like apartment buildings. But don't be dismayed by its neighbors, because inside is a secret oasis of all things eco-conscious, stylish, and economically savvy too. The tiny, 10-room New Hotel is located a block from the beach and features comfortably modern rooms with wood floors; Ikea-chic furniture; spacious, colorful bathrooms; and in-room recycling systems. Out back is a nice pool complete with a great gastropub called **Lou's Beer Garden,** which attracts local hipsters as well as visitors. Staff is extremely friendly and accommodating. If you don't mind being off the beaten path and close to the beach and can snag a room here, do so.

7337 Harding Ave., Miami Beach, FL 33140. www.thenewhotelmiami.com. ℂ **305/704-7879.** Fax 305/647-0636. 10 units. Winter $150–$200 double; off season $99–$129 double. AE, DC, MC, V. Public parking nearby $10 a day. **Amenities:** Restaurant; poolside bar; lounge; bike rental; concierge; pool; room service; spa; free Wi-Fi. *In room:* A/C, TV, hair dryer, free high-speed Internet, kitchenette, minibar, MP3 docking station.

The Palms Hotel & Spa ★ Just a stone's throw away from Miami Beach's entertainment district, the Palms Hotel & Spa is ideally located on the beach on the northern, more tranquil side of South Beach. As a sophisticated yet genuine oceanfront resort and recipient of $20 million worth of enhancements, it features lush gardens landscaped with palms and other tropical plants and a large freshwater pool as its centerpiece. Luxurious accommodations—recently redone and featuring fabulous spa-inspired bathrooms—as well as warm and caring service are also signature features of this property. The hotel boasts the Palms Spa, South Florida's only Aveda destination spa, offering a highly personalized experience through Aveda's holistic treatments in five multipurpose treatment rooms and four outdoor treatment cabanas, as well as hair, nail, and makeup services. In its quest to provide a natural and wholesome experience for every guest, the hotel also features an excellent restaurant—**Essensia Restaurant & Lounge,** focusing on utilizing local, organic, and seasonal ingredients. The Palms was also recognized by Florida's Green Lodging Program for demonstrating a commitment to protecting Florida's natural resources.

3025 Collins Ave., Miami Beach, FL 33140. www.thepalmshotel.com. ℂ **800/550-0505** or 305/534-0505. Fax 305/534-0515. 251 units. Winter $239–$639 double, $799 suite; off season $179–$600 double, $659 suite. AE, DC, MC, V. Valet parking $29. **Amenities:** Restaurant; lounge; poolside bar; bike rental; concierge; fitness room; heated pool; 24-hour room service; spa. *In room:* A/C, plasma TV, hair dryer, minibar, MP3 docking station, Wi-Fi.

Key Biscayne

Locals call it the Key, and technically, Key Biscayne, a barrier island, isn't even part of the Florida Keys. A relatively unknown area until Richard Nixon bought a home here in the '70s, Key Biscayne, at 1¼ square miles, is an affluent but hardly lively residential and recreational island known for its pricey homes, excellent beaches, and actor Andy Garcia, who makes his home here. The island is far enough from the mainland to make it feel semiprivate, yet close enough to downtown for guests to take advantage of everything Miami has to offer.

To locate the hotels in this section, see the map "Hotels & Restaurants in Greater Miami" (p. 83).

VERY EXPENSIVE

The Ritz-Carlton Key Biscayne ★★★ ☺ The Ritz-Carlton takes Key
Biscayne to the height of luxury with 44 acres of tropical gardens, a 20,000-square-foot destination spa, and a world-class tennis center under the direction of tennis pro Cliff Drysdale. Decorated in British colonial style, the Ritz-Carlton is straight out of Bermuda, with its impressive flower-laden landscaping. The Ritz Kids programs provide children ages 5 to 12 with fantastic activities, including quality time with the resort's affectionate blue-and-gold macaw mascot, and the 1,200-foot beachfront, named among the Top 10 Beaches in the U.S. by Dr. Stephen "Beach" Leatherman, offers everything from pure relaxation to fishing, boating, or windsurfing. Spacious and luxuriously appointed rooms feature new decor that embodies the resort's island-destination feel and large balconies that overlook the ocean or lush gardens. The oceanview Italian restaurant **Cioppino** is excellent for formal dining, or, if you prefer casual dining, the oceanfront **Cantina Beach** serves great authentic Mexican food and even has a "tequlier"—a sommelier for tequila. The St. Tropez–inspired **Dune Oceanfront Burger Lounge** is ideal for lazy afternoons on the sand with one of their gourmet burgers and a glass of champagne, while the resort's nighttime spot **RUMBAR** hearkens back to Old Havana with an impressive rum selection and light Cuban-inspired fare. The hotel's remote location—just a 10-minute drive from the hustle and bustle—makes it a favorite for those (John Travolta, among others) who want to avoid the hubbub.

455 Grand Bay Dr., Key Biscayne, FL 33149. www.ritzcarlton.com. ✆ **800/241-3333** or 305/365-4500. Fax 305/365-4501. 402 units. Winter $629 double, $1,100 suite; off season $269 double, $525 suite. AE, DC, DISC, MC, V. Valet parking (call for fees). **Amenities:** 4 restaurants; 3 bars; children's programs; concierge; fitness center; 2 outdoor heated pools; room service; spa; tennis center w/lessons available; watersports equipment/rentals. *In room:* A/C, TV, hair dryer, high-speed Internet, minibar.

Downtown

If you've ever read Tom Wolfe's *Bonfire of the Vanities,* you may understand what downtown Miami is all about. If not, it's this simple: Take a wrong turn and you could find yourself in some serious trouble. Desolate and dangerous at night, downtown is trying to change its image, but it's been a long, tedious process. Recently, however, part of the area has experienced a renaissance in terms of nightlife, with several popular dance clubs and bars opening in the environs of NE 11th Street, off Biscayne Boulevard. If you're the kind of person who digs an urban setting, you may enjoy downtown, but if you're looking for shiny, happy Miami, you're in the wrong place (for now). As posh, pricey lofts keep going up faster than the nation's deficit, downtown is about to experience the renaissance it has been waiting for. Keep your eye on this area, and remember that you read it here first: Like orange—or pink, or white, or blue—being the new black, downtown Miami will be the new South Beach. Eventually.

Most downtown hotels cater primarily to business travelers and cruise passengers, although with the slower-than-slow downtown renaissance in progress, a few higher-end luxury hotels opened in the area in late 2010, including a **JW Marriott Marquis,** 55 Biscayne Boulevard Way (www.jwmarriott marquismiami.com; ✆ **305/350-0750**), the hotel chain's hyperluxe hybrid featuring indoor basketball court, hauter-than-thou hotel within a hotel (**Beaux Arts**), and **db Bistro Moderne,** Miami's very first culinary offering from star chef **Daniel Boulud;** and then there's **Tempo Miami, A Rock Resort,** 1100 Biscayne Blvd. (www.rockresorts.com; ✆ **305/396-4082**), attached to one of downtown Miami's vacant condos, and featuring 56 luxurious guest rooms and suites with floor-to-ceiling windows, a gourmet restaurant, an 8,000-square-foot RockResorts Spa, an infinity-edge sunrise swim spa, and a lagoon-style sunset swimming pool.

Although business hotels can be expensive, quality and service are of a high standard. Look for discounts and packages on weekends, when offices are closed and rooms often go empty.

To locate the hotels in this section, see the map "Hotels & Restaurants in Downtown Miami" (p. 101).

VERY EXPENSIVE

EPIC Hotel ★★★ Although it's yet another hotel with adjacent condo (with not nearly as many hotel rooms as condos), the Green Seal and Green Lodging Certified EPIC, a Kimpton Hotel, has its own separate entry and therefore doesn't make you feel like you're intruding on someone's privacy. In fact, it feels as if you are a resident as well in a posh, plush high-rise with stunning views of the Miami skyline and Biscayne Bay. The dramatic hotel lobby—separate from the resident lobby—features 26-foot-high vaulted ceilings, a beautiful white onyx registration desk, glass walls, and shimmering pools, not to mention the first U.S.-based **Zuma** restaurant (p. 126), serving informal (yet überpricey) Japanese dining known as Izakaya. The guest rooms and suites are full of open space and light, offering breathtaking views, exceptional bathroom amenities, and a huge bathroom with open cutout into the bedroom area. Luxury services include an on-site hotel spa by exhale, an expansive outdoor 16th-floor pool deck with private cabanas, two infinity pools, and an excellent seafood restaurant/lounge, **Area 31,** also on the 16th floor. The hotel is extremely pet-friendly, offering beds, bones, and bottled water for your furry friend at no extra cost. EPIC also offers pet sitting, grooming, walking, and massages, which can all be arranged with the concierge. Furthermore, EPIC offers Kimpton's Guppy Love Program, where upon settling in, guests can request a live goldfish to stay overnight in their guest room.

270 Biscayne Blvd. Way, Miami, FL 33131. www.epichotel.com. ✆ **305/424-5226.** Fax 305/424-5232. 411 units. Winter $279–$409 double, $429–$609 suite; off season $229–$409 double, $304–$609 suite. AE, DC, DISC, MC, V. Valet parking $32. **Amenities:** 2 restaurants; concierge; club-level rooms; fitness center; 2 outdoor pools; room service; spa. *In room:* A/C, TV, hair dryer, MP3 docking station, Wi-Fi.

The Four Seasons ★★★ ☺ Deciding between the hyperluxe Mandarin Oriental and the equally luxe, albeit somewhat museum-like, Four Seasons is almost like trying to tell the difference between Eva and Zsa Zsa Gabor. There are some obvious differences and some similarities, but they're kind of subtle. While the architecturally striking Mandarin is located on the semiprivate Brickell Key, the 70-story Four Seasons resembles an office building and is smack in the middle of the business district, making it more of a business hotel than a resort, per se. The rooms and suites are plush, and, as at the Mandarin, service is paramount. Most rooms overlook Biscayne Bay, and while all rooms are cushy, thanks to the hotel's signature "untucked" beds, the bland decor leaves a lot to be

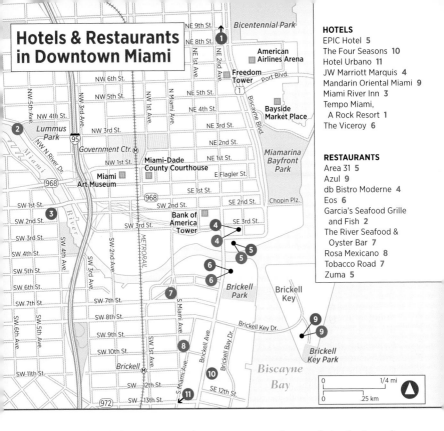

Hotels & Restaurants in Downtown Miami

desired, really. The best rooms are the corner suites with views facing both south and east over the water. There are three gorgeous pools spread out on more than 2 acres. Poolside amenities include fully loaded Kindles for poolside reading and mini spa treatments. Guests at the hotel all have access to—and free classes at—the Sports Club/LA, a gym popular with visiting celebs.

1435 Brickell Ave., Miami, FL 33131. www.fourseasons.com/miami. © **305/358-3535.** Fax 305/358-7758. 260 units. Winter $365–$500 double, $600 suite; off season $250–$355 double, $455 suite. AE, DC, DISC, MC, V. Valet parking $34. **Amenities:** 2 restaurants; 2 bars; concierge; the Sports Club/LA fitness center; outdoor Jacuzzi; 3 outdoor pools; full-service spa. *In room:* A/C, TV, hair dryer, minibar, Wi-Fi.

JW Marriott Marquis ★ Although there are no shortages of Marriotts in the area—especially with the 41-story, 313-room JW Marriott practically up the block—the newest offering from the chain dares to defy the stereotypes by merging two successful brands—the JW Marriott and the Marriott Marquis—into an all-in-one downtown destination that doesn't only cater to business travelers. Located across the street from the much more boutique EPIC, this hotel, one most people didn't think would ever open in a soft economy, is a swankier Marriott, though we think it resembles a grand office building more than anything. Among the highlights: star chef Daniel Boulud's **db Bistro Moderne** (p. 125) and the 19th and 20th "Entertainment Floors," featuring a Jim McLean

Golf School offering personal instruction, golf simulators, putting greens, and pro shop; NBA-approved full-size indoor basketball court; virtual bowling alley; and outdoor heated pool. Rooms are nice and roomy, featuring city or bay views, marble bathrooms, and, our fave, TVs embedded in bathroom mirrors. But wait! There's more. To truly grab that luxury traveler (or NBA star), there's a hotel within a hotel here: **Hotel Beaux Arts,** a glorified concierge level located on the 39th floor, with city and bay views, and private check-in and personal escort to 44 lavishly decorated guest rooms and suites with state-of-the-art video and sound systems throughout, hardwood floors, and Italian-marble bathrooms. Marriott, is that you?

345 Ave. of the Americas., Miami, FL 33131. www.jwmarriottmarquismiami.com. ☎ **305/421-8600** Fax 305/421-8601. 313 units. Winter $365–$500 double, from $679 suite; off season $259–$459 double, $539 suite. AE, DC, DISC, MC, V. Valet parking $32. **Amenities:** 2 restaurants; 2 bars; concierge; the fitness center; outdoor Jacuzzi; heated outdoor pool; full-service spa. *In room:* A/C, TV, hair dryer, minibar, Wi-Fi.

Mandarin Oriental, Miami ★★★ Corporate big shots and celebrities not in the mood for the South Beach spotlight have a high-end luxury hotel to stay in while wheeling and dealing their way through Miami. Catering to business travelers, big-time celebrities (Jennifer Aniston; J-Lo; the late, great Jacko; Will Smith; and so on), and the leisure traveler who doesn't mind spending big bucks, the swank Mandarin Oriental features a waterfront location, recently renovated residential-style rooms with Asian touches (all with balconies), upscale dining, and bathrooms equipped with Aromatherapy Associates products. The waterfront view of the city is the hotel's best asset. The hotel's two restaurants, the high-end **Azul** (p. 124) and the more casual **Café Sambal,** are two of Miami's best, as is the 15,000-square-foot spa, the only official five-star spa in the state, in which traditional Thai massages and ayurvedic treatments are the norm. The hotel is also home to a 20,000-foot white-sand beach club complete with beach butlers and beachside cabana treatments, which is nice, considering that the hotel is 15 minutes from the beach. For those who want to venture out, the Mandarin offers the city's only official "nightlife guide" to lead you to the hot spots. The hotel is also very pet-friendly.

500 Brickell Key Dr., Miami, FL 33131. www.mandarinoriental.com. ☎ **305/913-8383.** Fax 305/913-8300. 326 units. $435–$900 double; $1,300–$6,500 suite. AE, DC, DISC, MC, V. Valet parking $34. Pets welcome. **Amenities:** 2 restaurants; 3 bars; kids' club; concierge; nearby golf; state-of-the-art fitness center; outdoor Jacuzzi; infinity pool; full-service holistic spa; nearby tennis. *In room:* A/C, TV, hair dryer, minibar, Wi-Fi.

Tempo Miami, A Rock Resort Located in the (mostly empty) 67-story Marquis condo building overlooking the MacArthur Causeway, and close to the performing arts center and the arena, is this plush, 56-room hotel with spa, **Amuse Restaurant & Lounge,** a 14th-floor Sky Pool Deck, and unparalleled views of Biscayne Bay and downtown Miami. Much like a condo, there are six different room types and all feature floor-to-ceiling windows (request a room that faces Miami Beach and not I-95, plush linens, and soaking tubs with views (again, make sure you get a room with one). Tempo took a big leap of faith opening in this section of downtown, a haven for vehicular—not pedestrian—traffic, but resting on its luxe Rock Resort laurels and perhaps the excitement and hype surrounding Miami Heat games nearby, it still may be a bit ahead of its, er, time.

1100 Biscayne Blvd., Miami, FL 33129. www.tempomiami.rockresorts.com. © **888/857-7625** or 786/369-0300. Fax 786/369-1052. 56 units. Winter $259–$774 double; off season $223–$574 double. AE, DC, DISC, MC, V. Valet parking $20. **Amenities:** Restaurant; bar; babysitting; pool; spa. *In room:* A/C, TV/DVD, hair dryer, Wi-Fi.

The Viceroy ★ One of the few condo-hotel combos to open before the bust, the trendy Kelly Wearstler–designed Viceroy is located on prime real estate on Biscayne Bay between downtown Miami and trendy Brickell Avenue. The hotel itself occupies its own tower within a three-tower structure and is the only facility to house a 162-room hotel in conjunction with residences. All rooms are full of the modern trappings—Wii and PlayStation gaming systems, DVD players, portable printers, 42-inch flatscreen televisions, and hair- and body-care products by Neil George. Residents and guests alike share exclusive access to the 15th-floor outdoor podium's sweeping recreation area—lounge and deck space, sun deck with cabanas, and a 310-foot infinity pool overlooking the bay. The signature restaurant **Eos** serves an updated Mediterranean menu, with a dining room overlooking the 15th-floor pool, alfresco tables, a fireplace, and waterfront views. **Café Icon** is available for quickie bites in the pool deck. Even better is **Club 50**, the upscale rooftop lounge/restaurant right next to the pool on the 50th floor.

485 Brickell Ave., Miami, FL 33131. www.viceroymiami.com. © **866/720-1991.** 162 units. Winter $200–$400 double; off season $150 double. AE, DC, DISC, MC, V. Valet parking $35. **Amenities:** 2 restaurants; lounge; 500-sq.-ft. state-of-the-art fitness facility; 2 outdoor pools; room service; full-service spa. *In room:* A/C, TV, hair dryer, kitchen or kitchenette, Wi-Fi.

MODERATE

Hotel Urbano A new boutique hotel on the southern, more residential end of Brickell Avenue, Hotel Urbano is a welcome addition to all the haughty high-rises, with just three stories and such style and personality you'd never know you were in a former Hampton Inn. The 65-room Urbano features contemporary decor and a gorgeous, free-form pool with poolside lounge surrounded by private cabanas with a fire pit. Rooms feature city or pool views with big walk-in showers. Artwork displayed throughout the hotel has been selected by William Braemer, curator of Art Fusion Galleries in Miami's Design District. Curious about the art? Tune into the hotel's art channel to get an education on what's displayed. A restaurant offers alfresco dining and Florida cuisine with Cuban accents. Although geared to business travelers, its location just feet away from Key Biscayne's Rickenbacker Causeway and Vizcaya Museum and Gardens, and close to downtown Miami and Brickell nightlife and to all parts south, makes this urbane oasis an excellent—and surprisingly affordable—place to be.

2500 Brickell Ave., Miami, FL 33129. www.hotelurbano.com. © **888/657-3448** or 305/854-2070. Fax 305/856-5055. 65 units. Winter $159–$289 double; off season $109–$169 double. AE, DC, DISC, MC, V. Valet parking $24. **Amenities:** Restaurant; bar; fitness center; pool. *In room:* A/C, TV/DVD, fridge, hair dryer, free Wi-Fi.

Miami River Inn ★★★ 🛏️ The Miami River Inn, listed on the National Register of Historic Places, is a quaint, country-style hideaway (Miami's *only* bed-and-breakfast!), consisting of four cottages smack in the middle of developing downtown Miami. In fact, it's so hidden that most locals don't even know it exists, which only adds to its panache. Every room has hardwood floors and is uniquely furnished with antiques dating from 1908. In one room, you might find a hand-painted bathtub, a Singer sewing machine, and an armoire from the turn of the 20th century, restored to perfection. Thirty-eight rooms have private bathrooms—four have showers only, six have tubs only, and 28 have splendid tub/shower combinations. One- and two-bedroom apartments are available as well. In the foyer, you can peruse a library filled with books about Old Miami. It's close to public transportation, restaurants, and museums, and only 5 minutes from the business district.

118 SW S. River Dr., Miami, FL 33130. www.miamiriverinn.com. © **800/468-3589** or 305/325-0045. Fax 305/325-9227. 38 units. Winter $149–$299 double; off season $89–$149 double. Rates include continental breakfast and parking. Extra person $15. AE, DC, DISC, MC, V. Free parking. Pets accepted for $25 per night. **Amenities:** Babysitting; access to nearby gym facilities; Jacuzzi; small pool. *In room:* A/C, TV, hair dryer (upon request).

West Miami & Airport Area

As Miami continues to grow at a rapid pace, expansion has begun westward, where land is plentiful. Several resorts have taken advantage of the space to build world-class tennis and golf courses. While there's no sea to swim in, a plethora of facilities can definitely make up for the lack of an ocean view.

To locate the hotels in this section, see the map "Hotels & Restaurants in Greater Miami" (p. 83).

EXPENSIVE

Doral Golf Resort and Spa ★ ☺ This sprawling 650-acre resort in a suburban West Miami enclave is all about golf. Doral is where world-class tournaments and the excruciating Blue Monster course have seen even a pre-scandal Tiger frustrated. There's also the Great White Course—the Southeast's first desertscape course, designed by the Shark himself, Greg Norman. Repeat guests usually book the season well in advance. Rooms are spacious, all with private balconies, many overlooking a golf course or garden. Rooms reveal a plantation-style decor with lots of wicker and wood and large marble bathrooms. Enhancements to the golf courses, spa suites, and driving range have also brought the resort up to speed with its competition. In 2009, the **Pritikin Longevity Center & Spa**, a major player in the world of health and wellness, moved in with a state-of-the-art facility featuring private indoor and outdoor saltwater pools, fitness center, indoor and outdoor yoga and meditation centers, indoor and outdoor running tracks, spa, and two Pritikin restaurants. But if you're not in the mood to eat rabbit food, there are six other dining options at the resort, which capped off a $16-million resortwide renewal with the opening of **Mesazul,** a Spanish-style steakhouse, and Bossa Nova Lounge, a Brazilian-style lounge with live music. There's a phenomenal kids' program and the Blue Lagoon water park featuring two 80,000-gallon pools with cascading waterfalls, a rock facade, and a 125-foot water slide. For a spa or golf vacation, the Doral is a great choice. Otherwise, consider investing your money in a hotel that's better located.

4400 NW 87th Ave., Miami, FL 33178. www.doralresort.com. © **800/71-DORAL** (713-6725) or 305/592-2000. Fax 305/594-4682. 693 units. Winter $269 double, $370 suite, $420 1-bedroom suite, $500 2-bedroom suite; off season $119 double, $280 suite, $400 1-bedroom suite, $480 2-bedroom suite. Extra person $35. Golf and spa packages available. AE, DC, DISC, MC, V. Valet parking $17. **Amenities:** 5 restaurants; babysitting; concierge; 5 golf courses and driving range;

Hotels & Restaurants in North Dade

HOTELS
Acqualina **3**
Fairmont Turnbury Isle Resort & Club **1**

RESTAURANTS
Il Mulino New York **3**
Michael Mina's Bourbon Steak **2**
NAOE Miami **5**
Timo **4**

health club; 6 pools; room service; world-class spa; 10 tennis courts. *In room:* A/C, TV, hair dryer, high-speed Internet access.

BARGAIN CHAINS

If you must stay near the airport, consider any of the dozens of moderately priced chain hotels. You'll find one of the cheapest and most recommendable options at either of the **Days Inn** locations at 7250 NW 11th St. and 4767 NW 36th St. (© **800/329-7466** for both, or 305/888-3661 or 305/261-4230, respectively), each about 2 miles from the airport. The larger property on 36th Street offers slightly cheaper rates, with singles starting as low as $69. The 11th Street locale may charge more on weekends, but prices usually start at $70. Prices include free transportation from the airport.

A more luxurious option is the **Wyndham Miami Airport,** at 3900 NW 21st St. (© **305/871-3800**), with rates from about $125 to $225.

North Dade

To locate the hotels in this section, see the map "Hotels & Restaurants in North Dade" (p. 105).

VERY EXPENSIVE

Acqualina ★★★ ☺ Some people are still scratching their heads as to why this luxurious resort opened across the street from a Denny's and T-shirt shops, but once you step inside, you forget that you're even in Miami and feel as if you're on the Italian Riviera. On 4½ beachfront acres, with more than 400 feet of Atlantic coastline, Acqualina is a Mediterranean-style resort towering over all the others, with its baroque fountains, 97 impeccably appointed suites, and a branch of the acclaimed **Il Mulino New York** restaurant. The ESPA is one of Miami's priciest and poshest spas, and while there are three pools just steps away from the beach, the outdoor area is uninspiring. The hotel's **AcquaMarine Program** has a splashy array of marine-biology activities for kids and adults. Best of all, the chance of some teeny-bopper tabloid figure partying here is unlikely. In fact, there's really no scene here at all, which, for some, is bliss.

17875 Collins Ave., Sunny Isles Beach, FL 33160. www.acqualina.com. ✆ **305/918-8000.** Fax 305/918-8100. 97 units. Winter $850–$1,050 double, $1,600–$3,350 suite; off season $475–$675 double, $1,025–$2,000 suite. AE, DC, DISC, MC, V. Valet parking $30. **Amenities:** 2 restaurants; bar; babysitting; concierge; 3 outdoor pools; room service; state-of-the-art spa. *In room:* A/C, TV, CD player, fax, hair dryer, minibar, Wi-Fi.

Fairmont Turnberry Isle Resort & Club ★★★ One of Miami's classiest resorts (along the lines of the Mandarin Oriental), this gorgeous 300-acre retreat has every possible facility for relaxation seekers and active guests, particularly golfers. You'll enjoy spacious guest rooms and suites, golf courses, restaurants, the spa and fitness center, heated pools, a tennis center, and a private ocean club, plus a great kids' program. The main attractions are two Raymond Floyd championship courses, available only to members and guests of the hotel; a Laguna Pool with a water slide, lazy river, and private cabanas; and **Bourbon Steak,** a restaurant by star Chef Michael Mina (p. 123). Be sure to check out the chef's garden along the pathways of the resort. The Willow Stream Spa offers an unabridged menu of treatments. A location in the well-manicured residential and shopping area of Aventura appeals to those who want peace, quiet, and a great mall. A complimentary shuttle bus takes guests to and from the Ocean Club and Aventura Mall.

19999 W. Country Club Dr., Aventura, FL 33180. www.fairmont.com/turnberryisle. ✆ **866/612-7739** or 786/279-6770. Fax 305/933-6560. 392 units. Winter $399–$899 double, $919–$5,500 suite; off season $199–$299 double, $499–$2,700 suite. AE, DC, DISC, MC, V. Valet parking $30. **Amenities:** 4 restaurants; 5 bars and lounges; concierge; 2 golf courses; 3 outdoor pools; room service; state-of-the-art spa and fitness center; 4 clay hydro tennis courts; watersports equipment/rentals. *In room:* A/C, TV/VCR, CD player, fax, fridge (upon request), hair dryer, minibar.

EXPENSIVE

Timo ★★★ ITALIAN/MEDITERRANEAN This hip, haute restaurant is in Sunny Isles, where, not so long ago, Tony Roma's was the hottest eatery. Timo is a stylish Italian/Mediterranean restaurant catering to mostly North Miami Beach locals who have been yearning for something else besides the fabulous Chef Allen's. Among the specialties, try the handcrafted pastas, including Burrata ravioli; seared yellowtail snapper with pumpkin ravioli, sweet corn purée, and crispy sage; and a phenomenal rack of wild boar with roasted cabernet grapes, Marsala, and creamy polenta. Less pricey, less heavy items are also available, such as a delicious ricotta and fontina wood-fired pizza with white truffle oil—perfect for lunch or a happy-hour snack. At Timo, a bistro-meets-lounge atmosphere gives way to a decidedly cool vibe, something that was always conspicuously lacking at Tony Roma's.

17624 Collins Ave., Sunny Isles. 📞 **305/936-1008.** www.timorestaurant.com. Reservations required. Main courses $19–$28. AE, DC, MC, V. Sun–Thurs 11:30am–3pm and 6–10:30pm; Fri–Sat 11:30am–3pm and 6–11pm.

Coral Gables

The Gables, as it's affectionately known, was one of Miami's original planned communities and is still among the city's prettiest, most pedestrian-friendly, albeit preservation-obsessed, neighborhoods. Pristine with a European flair, Coral Gables is best known for its wide array of excellent upscale restaurants of various ethnicities, as well as a hotly contested (the quiet city didn't want to welcome new traffic) shopping megacomplex, with upscale stores such as Nordstrom.

If you're looking for luxury, Coral Gables has a number of wonderful hotels, but if you're on a tight budget, you may be better off elsewhere. One well-priced chain in the area is the **Holiday Inn,** 1350 S. Dixie Hwy. (📞 **800/HOLIDAY** [465-4329] or 305/667-5611), with rates between $100 and $225 depending on the time of year. It's directly across the street from the University of Miami and is popular with families and friends of students.

VERY EXPENSIVE

Biltmore Hotel ★★★ A romantic sense of old-world glamour combined with a rich history permeates the Biltmore as much as the pricey perfume of the guests who stay here. Built in 1926, it's the oldest Coral Gables hotel and is a National Historic Landmark—one of only two operating hotels in Florida to receive that designation. Rising above the Spanish-style estate is a majestic 300-foot copper-clad tower, modeled after the Giralda bell tower in Seville and visible throughout the city. Large Moorish-style rooms are decorated with tasteful decor, European feather beds, Egyptian cotton duvets, writing desks, and some high-tech amenities. The landmark 23,000-square-foot winding pool now has the requisite hipster accessories—the private cabana, alfresco bar, and restaurant. Always a popular destination for golfers, including former president Clinton (who stays in the Al Capone suite), the Biltmore is situated on a lush, rolling, 18-hole Donald Ross course that is as challenging as it is beautiful. Sunday brunch is an equal feat—book early.

1200 Anastasia Ave., Coral Gables, FL 33134. www.biltmorehotel.com. 📞 **800/727-1926** or 305/445-1926. Fax 305/442-9496. 276 units. Winter $395–$895 double; off season $229–$499 double; year-round $659–$6,500 specialty suites. Extra person $20. Special packages available. AE, DC, DISC, MC, V. Valet parking $25; self-parking free. **Amenities:** 4 restaurants; 4 bars; concierge; 18-hole golf course; state-of-the-art health club; outdoor pool; room service; sauna; full-service spa; 10 lit tennis courts. *In room:* A/C, TV, VCR (upon request), fax, hair dryer, high-speed Internet, kitchenette (in tower suites), minibar.

MODERATE

Hotel St. Michel ★ This European-style hotel, in the heart of Coral Gables, is one of the city's most romantic options. The accommodations and hospitality are straight out of old-world Europe, complete with dark-wood-paneled walls, cozy beds, beautiful antiques, and a quiet elegance that seems startlingly out of place in trendy Miami. Everything here is charming—from the brass elevator and parquet floors to the paddle fans. One-of-a-kind furnishings make each room special. Of course, the antiquity is countered with modernity in the form of flatscreen TVs in all rooms. Bathrooms are on the smaller side, but are hardly cramped. All have tub/shower combinations except for two, which have one or the other. If you're picky, request your preference. Guests are treated to fresh fruit upon arrival and enjoy seamless service throughout their stay. A new restaurant, **Gaetano Ristorante,** opened in 2010, replacing the beloved Restaurant St. Michel, serving, strangely, rustic Italian cuisine.

162 Alcazar Ave., Coral Gables, FL 33134. www.hotelstmichel.com. ☎ **800/848-HOTEL** (4683) or 305/444-1666. Fax 305/529-0074. 28 units. Winter $169 double, $199 suite; off season $119 double, $149 suite. Extra person $10. Rates include continental breakfast and fresh fruit daily. AE, DC, MC, V. Self-parking $9. **Amenities:** Bar; lounge; concierge; access to nearby health club; room service; free Wi-Fi in all public areas. *In room:* A/C, TV, hair dryer.

Coconut Grove

This waterfront village hugs the shores of Biscayne Bay, just south of U.S. 1 and about 10 minutes from the beaches. Once a haven for hippies, head shops, and artsy bohemian characters, the Grove succumbed to the inevitable temptations of commercialism and has become a Gap nation, featuring a host of theme and chain restaurants, bars, a megaplex, and lots of stores. Outside the main shopping area, however, you'll find the beautiful remnants of Old Miami in the form of flora, fauna, and, of course, water.

To locate the hotels in this section, see the map "Hotels & Restaurants in Greater Miami" (p. 83).

VERY EXPENSIVE

Grove Isle Hotel and Spa ★ Hidden away in the bougainvillea and lushness of the Grove, the Grove Isle Hotel and Spa is off the beaten path on its own lushly landscaped 20-acre island, just outside the heart of Coconut Grove. The isolated exclusivity of this resort contributes to a country-club vibe, though for the most part, the people here aren't snooty, but just value their privacy and precious relaxation time. Everyone dresses in white and pastels, and if they're not on their way to a set of tennis, they're not in a rush to get anywhere. You'll step into suites that are elegantly furnished, with canopy beds and a patio or balcony overlooking the bay. You'll need to reserve early here—rooms go very fast. The 6,000-square-foot, Indonesian-inspired Spa at Grove Isle is top-notch. Introduced in early 2010, **Gibraltar,** a haute-cuisine restaurant, serves fresh seafood and other regional specialties in a spectacular, elegant dining room, or, better yet, outside on the water.

4 Grove Isle Dr., Coconut Grove, FL 33133. www.groveisle.com. ☎ **800/884-7683** or 305/858-8300. Fax 305/854-6702. 50 units. Winter $299–$399 double, $379–$529 suite; off season $179–$279 double, $279–$399 suite. Packages available. AE, DC, MC, V. Valet parking $17. **Amenities:** Restaurant; babysitting; concierge; large outdoor heated pool; room service; full-service spa; 12 tennis courts. *In room:* A/C, TV/VCR, CD player, hair dryer, high-speed Internet, minibar.

The Ritz-Carlton Coconut Grove, Miami ★ The third and smallest of Miami's Ritz-Carlton hotels is, hands down, the most intimate of its properties, surrounded by 2 acres of tropical gardens and overlooking Biscayne Bay and the Miami skyline. Decorated in the likeness of an Italian villa, the hotel's understated luxury is a welcome addition to an area known for its gaudiness. A room renovation in 2008 saw the addition of Italian damask patterns, Carrara marble bathrooms, and dark Emperador marble-topped dressers that create the feeling of being in a luxurious, private villa. That said, this is more of a business hotel than a vacation or resort property. In addition to the usual Ritz-Carlton standard of service and comfort, the hotel has a tranquil Boutique Spa, and an excellent, cozy Italian trattoria (with footstools for women to put their purses on—how classy!), **Bizcaya**, which is also known for its sublime Sunday Brunch.

3300 SW 27th Ave., Coconut Grove, FL 33133. www.ritzcarlton.com. © **800/241-3333** or 305/644-4680. Fax 305/644-4681. 115 units. Winter $379 double, $479 suite; off season $209 double, $279 suite. AE, DC, DISC, MC, V. Valet parking $24. **Amenities:** Restaurant; pool grill; 2 bars; babysitting; concierge; fitness center; outdoor heated pool; room service; spa. *In room:* A/C, TV, hair dryer, high-speed Internet access, minibar.

WHERE TO EAT IN MIAMI

Don't be fooled by the plethora of superlean model types you're likely to see posing throughout Miami. Contrary to popular belief, dining in this city is as much a sport as plastic surgery and beach yoga. With more than 6,000 restaurants to choose from, dining out in Miami has become a passionate pastime for locals and visitors alike. Our star chefs have fused Californian-Asian with Caribbean and Latin elements to create a world-class flavor all its own: Floribbean. Think mango chutney splashed over fresh swordfish or a spicy sushi sauce served alongside Peruvian seviche.

Formerly synonymous with early-bird specials, Miami's new-wave cuisine now rivals that of San Francisco—or even New York. Nouveau Cuban chef Douglas Rodriguez returned to his roots with a few fabulous South Beach nouveau Latino eateries. In addition, other stellar chefs—such as Michael Schwartz, Michelle Bernstein, and Allen Susser—remain firmly planted in the city's culinary scene, fusing local ingredients into edible masterpieces. Florida foodies rolled out the red carpet for the arrival of Daniel Boulud just as they did for Scott Conant and Alfred Portale at the swanky new Fontainebleau, and Laurent Tourondel at the Betsy on Ocean Drive. A new rumor is cooked up daily about which megachef plans to open in Miami next. This New World cuisine is not only high in calories but also high in price. But if you can manage to splurge at least once, it'll be worth it.

Thanks to a thriving cafe society in both South Beach and Coconut Grove, you can also enjoy a moderately priced meal and linger for hours without having a waiter hover over you. In Little Havana, you can chow down on a meal that serves about six for less than $10. Because seafood is plentiful, it doesn't have to cost you an arm and a leg to enjoy the appendages of a crab or lobster. Don't be put off by the looks of our recommended seafood shacks in places such as Key Biscayne—often, these spots get the best and freshest catches.

Whatever you're craving, Miami's got it—with the exception of decent, affordable Chinese food and a New York–style slice of pizza. If you're craving a scene with your steak, then South Beach is the place to be. Like many cities in Europe and Latin America, it is fashionable to dine late in South Beach, preferably after 9pm, sometimes as late as midnight. Service on South Beach is notoriously slow and arrogant, but it comes with the turf. (Of course, it is possible to find restaurants that defy the notoriety and actually pride themselves on friendly service.) On the mainland—especially in Coral Gables and, more recently, downtown, Midtown, and on Brickell Avenue—you can also experience fine dining without the pretense.

The biggest complaint when it comes to Miami dining isn't the haughtiness, but rather the dearth of truly moderately priced restaurants, especially in South Beach and Coral Gables. It's either really cheap or really expensive; the in-between somehow gets lost in the culinary shuffle. Quick-service diners don't exist here as they do in other cosmopolitan areas. We've tried to cover a range of cuisine in a range of prices. But with new restaurants opening on a weekly basis, you're bound to find an array of savory dining choices for every budget.

Many restaurants keep extended hours in high season (roughly Dec–Apr) and may close for lunch and/or dinner on Monday, when the traffic is slower. Always call ahead, as schedules do change. During the month of August, many Miami restaurants participate in **Miami Spice,** where three-course lunches and dinners are served at affordable prices. Check out **www.miamirestaurant-month.com**. Also, always look carefully at your bill—many Miami restaurants add a 15% to 18% gratuity to your total due to the enormous influx of European tourists who are not accustomed to tipping. Keep in mind that this amount is the *suggested* amount and can be adjusted, either higher or lower, depending on your assessment of the service provided. Because of this tipping-included policy, South Beach waitstaff are best known for their lax or inattentive service. *Feel free to adjust it* if you feel your server deserves more or less.

South Beach

The renaissance of South Beach started in the early '90s and is still continuing as classic cuisine gives in to modern temptation by inevitably fusing with more chic, nouveau developments created by faithful followers and devotees of the Food Network school of cooking. The ultimate result has spawned dozens of first-rate restaurants. In fact, big-name restaurants from across the country have capitalized on South Beach's international appeal and have continued to open branches here with great success. A few old standbys remain from the *Miami Vice* days, but the flock of newcomers dominates the scene, with places going in and out of style as quickly as the tides.

On South Beach, new restaurants are opening and closing as frequently as Emeril says "Bam!" even in an economic downturn. And, ironically, most are upscale. As it's impossible to list them all, we recommend strolling and browsing. Most restaurants post a copy of their menu outside. With very few exceptions, the places on Ocean Drive are crowded with tourists and priced accordingly. You'll do better to venture a little farther onto the pedestrian-friendly streets just west of Ocean Drive.

To locate the restaurants in this section, see the "Hotels & Restaurants in South Beach" map (p. 86).

VERY EXPENSIVE

Asia de Cuba ★ ASIAN/LATIN Located within the remarkably stunning lobby of the Mondrian hotel, this stylish Asian/Latin import from N.Y.C. and L.A. is the latest Miami offering from the China Grill empire. A fusion of Latin and Asian cuisines, the menu features some familiar favorites tweaked from other China Grill eateries and served as new here, including the calamari salad Asia de Cuba, featuring the same crispy calamari as China Grill, only this time with more of a tropical twist with ingredients such as chayote, hearts of palm, and banana. Main courses include the best chicken we've had in a long time—Cuban barbecue chicken with Thai coconut sticky rice, avocado cilantro fruit salsa, and tamarind sauce—and a coconut mustard-seed sustainable Chilean sea bass with crab and corn flan, cilantro *chimichurri,* and jalapeño plum coulis. Definitely not your corner takeout or bodega, nor are the prices, which are steep. But you are paying for prime real estate. Now if only you could just move in.

In the Mondrian, 1100 West Ave., South Beach. ✆ **305/673-1010.** Reservations required. Main courses $35–$76. AE, DC, MC, V. Daily 7am–10:45pm.

Barton G. The Restaurant ★ AMERICAN Set on the quieter west side of South Beach, Barton G.—named after its owner, one of Miami's most famous, over-the-top event-planners—is a place that looks like a trendy restaurant but eats like a show. Here, presentation is paramount. A popcorn-shrimp appetizer is served on a plateful of, yes, popcorn and stuffed into an actual popcorn box. A light, flavorful grilled sea bass is served in a brown paper bag with laundry clips preserving the steam until your server releases the flavor within. Desserts are equally outrageous: A giant plume of cotton candy reminiscent of drag diva Dame Edna's hair is surrounded by white-, dark-, and milk-chocolate-covered popcorn and chocolate-dipped pretzels. There's nothing ordinary about it, which is why athletes and celebrities such as LeBron James, Tom Cruise, and Will Smith are regulars. An elegant, orchid-laden indoor dining room is popular with members of the socialite set, for whom Barton G. has done many an affair, while the bar area and outdoor garden are the places to be for younger trend seekers.

Note: Another show-stopping production, **Prelude by Barton G.,** 1300 Biscayne Blvd. (✆ **305/576-8888**), opened within the Adrienne Arsht Center and features a supper-clubby vibe. Choose your own three-course prix-fixe pre- and post-theater dinners. From swell to swanky, don't miss **The Dining Room at the Villa By Barton G.,** 1116 Ocean Dr. (✆ **305/576-8003**), for impeccable decor and molecular gastronomy in the form of the Villa Salad with frozen Caesar dressing and Colorado rack of lamb accompanied by Greek yogurt jelly cubes dusted with harissa.

1427 West Ave., South Beach. ✆ **305/672-8881.** www.bartong.com. Reservations suggested. Main courses $21–$50. AE, DC, DISC, MC, V. Daily 6pm–midnight.

BLT Steak ★★★ STEAKHOUSE Just when we thought we'd had enough meat, BLT Steak opened its doors in the colonial-chic Betsy Hotel and, without sounding like a James Bond rip-off, we changed our minds—too much meat is never enough if it comes from the hands of Laurent Tourondel and his protégé and chef de cuisine, 20-something Samuel Gorenstein. Unlike other steakhouses, this one is unpretentious and unstuffy, with superb service and a serene setting composed of comfy lobby seating or the preferred outdoor veranda seating, which, at the northern end of Ocean Drive, is actually quite relaxing. The food is outstanding, from the minute they put down the complimentary plate of puffy, fluffy cheesy popovers and chicken liver pâté to your last lingering moment before forcing yourself to leave. Skip the tuna tartare and head straight for a selection of fresh and briny East and West Coast oysters; or, if you don't do mollusks, consider the fantastic *hamachi* with avocado, hearts of palm, and *yuzu* vinaigrette. As for the steaks: They're exceptional, no matter which cut you order. The rib-eye is huge and seasoned perfectly, with marbling so perfect it would have made Liberace cry. Thanks to the meat, side dishes are almost unnecessary, though the creamed spinach jalapeño mashed potatoes are rather irresistible. For mushroom fans, a side order of hard-to-find-in-these-parts hen of the woods mushrooms are a must, too.

1440 Ocean Dr. (in the Betsy Hotel), South Beach. ☎ **305/673-0044.** Reservations recommended. Main courses $26–$85. AE, DC, MC, V. Daily 6–11pm.

Blue Door Fish ★ SEAFOOD After years as the reigning, quintessential South Beach restaurant known more for who's eating there than what they're eating, Blue Door went to sea and returned as the seafood-centric Blue Door Fish. Still at the helm is award-winning chef Claude Troisgros (rhymes with foie gras)—a star in his own right, whose menu eschews the ubiquitous fusion moniker in favor of a more classic French approach to seafood. In addition to raw bar, sushi, steaks, and chops, the menu features highlights such as the Homard Banana, roasted Maine lobster, caramelized banana, brown butter, and cilantro-lime sauce; and Dover Sole, cooked and served on the bone "Claude's way," in almond and caper brown butter and truffled potato foam. In an effort to lure late-night diners, Blue Door introduced a Plat Bleu menu. Besides the $18 croque-monsieur and $18 macaroni and cheese, this menu offers soggy flatbreads for up to $25, duck foie gras for $27, a Cobb salad for $29, and, well, you get the pricey picture. Another option can be found in the Delano: Blue Sea, the lobby sushi bar, is not cheap, with rolls ranging from $14 to $24, but if it's late and you're hungry, it's the better bet. Sunday brunch at Blue Door Fish is enormously popular with locals and tourists alike.

In the Delano Hotel, 1685 Collins Ave., South Beach. ☎ **305/674-6400.** www.chinagrillmgt.com. Reservations recommended for dinner. Main courses $25–$66. AE, DC, MC, V. Daily 7am–4pm and 7pm–midnight (bar until 3am); Plat Bleu menu offered Mon–Wed 11pm–2am and Fri–Sat 11pm–4am; Sun brunch 10:30am–2:30pm.

Casa Tua ★★ 🏠 ITALIAN The stunning Casa Tua is a sleek and chic, country Italian-style establishment set in a refurbished 1925 Mediterranean-style house-cum-hotel. It has several dining areas, including a resplendent outdoor garden, comfy Ralph Lauren–esque living room, and a communal eat-in kitchen whose conviviality does not translate to some of the staff who have been known to turn up a nose at customers. If you're in the market to splurge, the whole Branzino is a huge hit, though we prefer the seared version with black olives, cherry tomatoes, roasted artichokes, and asparagus. Risottos are also highly recommended. Service is, as always with South Beach eateries, inconsistent, ranging from ultra-professional to absurdly lackadaisical. For these prices, they should be wiping our mouths for us. What used to be a fabulous lounge upstairs is now a members-only club, so don't even try to get in.

1700 James Ave., South Beach. ☎ **305/673-1010.** Reservations required. Main courses $20–$100. AE, DC, MC, V. Mon–Sat 7pm–midnight.

China Grill ★ PAN-ASIAN If ever a restaurant could be as cavernous as, say, the Asian continent, this would be it. Formerly a hub of hype and pompous circumstance, China Grill has calmed on the coolness meter despite the infrequent appearance of the likes of J-Lo and Enrique Iglesias, but its cuisine is still sizzling even if it's no longer the newest concept on the block. With an incomparable and dizzying array of amply portioned dishes (such as the outrageous crispy spinach, wasabi mashed potatoes, crispy calamari salad, spicy beef dumplings, lobster pancakes, and a sinfully delicious dessert sampler complete with sparklers), this epicurean journey into the world of near-perfect Pan-Asian cuisine is well worth a stop on any foodie's itinerary. Keep in mind that China Grill is a family-style restaurant and dishes are for sharing. For those who can't stay away from sushi, China Grill also has Dragon, a 40-seat "sushi den" in a private back room with such one-of-a-kind rolls as the Havana Roll—yellowtail snapper, rum, coconut, avocado, and red tobiko—and cocktails such as the Lemongrass Saketini. For those in Fort Lauderdale, there's a China Grill up there now, with water views, at 881 SE 17th St. (☎ **954/759-9950**).

404 Washington Ave., South Beach. ☎ **305/534-2211.** Reservations strongly recommended. Main courses $27–$59. AE, DC, MC, V. Mon–Thurs 11:45am–midnight; Fri 11:45am–1am; Sat 6pm–1am; Sun 6pm–midnight.

Escopazzo ★★★ ITALIAN *Escopazzo* means "I'm going crazy" in Italian, but the only sign of insanity in this externally unassuming Northern Italian eatery is the fact that it seats only 90 and it's one of the best restaurants in town. The wine bottles have it better—the restaurant's cellar holds 1,000 bottles of various vintages. Escopazzo now bills itself as an "Organic Italian Restaurant," a redundant moniker considering the ingredients here have always been the freshest, but newish is a menu of raw vegan and vegetarian appetizers and entrees including vegan raw lasagna of organic marinated tomatoes, zucchini, eggplant, cashew "ricotta," sun-dried tomatoes, and basil pesto. Should you be so lucky as to score a table at this romantic local favorite (choose one in the back dining room that's reminiscent of an Italian courtyard, complete with fountain and faux windows; it's not cheesy at all), you'll have trouble deciding between dishes that will have you swearing off the Olive Garden with your first bite. Standouts are milk and basil dough pasta with baby calamari, chickpeas, tomatoes, and arugula; or grass-fed hanger steak with roasted baby organic veggies in a truffle sauce. The hand-rolled pastas and risotto are near perfection. Eating here is like dining with a big Italian family—it's never boring (the menu changes five or six times a year), the service is excellent, and nobody's happy until you are blissfully full.

1311 Washington Ave., South Beach. ☎ **305/674-9450.** www.escopazzo.com. Reservations required. Main courses $17–$36. AE, MC, V. Mon–Fri 6pm–midnight; Sat 6pm–1am; Sun 6–11pm.

Joe's Stone Crab Restaurant ★ SEAFOOD Unless you grease the palms of one of the stone-faced maitre d's with some stone-cold cash, you'll be waiting for those famous claws for up to 2 hours—if not more. As much a Miami landmark as the beaches themselves, Joe's is a microcosm of the city, attracting everyone from T-shirted locals to a bejeweled Ivana Trump. Whatever you wear, however, will be eclipsed by a kitschy, unglamorous plastic bib that your waiter will tie on you unless you say otherwise. Open only during stone crab season (Oct–May), Joe's reels in the crowds with the freshest (though some disagree and consider Joe's stash subpar to less-assuming area restaurants), meatiest stone crabs and their essential accouterments: creamed spinach and excellent sweet-potato fries. The claws come in medium, large, and jumbo. Some say size doesn't matter; others swear by the jumbo (and more expensive) ones. Whatever you choose, pair them with a savory mustard sauce (a perfect mix of mayo and mustard) or hot butter. Not feeling crabby? The fried chicken and liver and onions on the regular menu are actually considered by many as far superior—they're definitely far cheaper—to the crabs. Oh yes, and save room for dessert. The Key lime pie here is the best in town. If you don't feel like waiting, try **Joe's Takeaway**, which is next door to the restaurant—it's a lot quicker and just as tasty.

11 Washington Ave. (at Biscayne St., just south of 1st St.), South Beach. ℂ **305/673-0365** or 673-4611 for takeout. www.joesstonecrab.com. Reservations not accepted. Market price varies but averages $45–$65. AE, DC, DISC, MC, V. Sun 11:30am–2pm and 4–10pm; Mon–Thurs 11:30am–2pm and 5–10pm; Fri–Sat 11:30am–2pm and 5–11pm. Closed mid-May to mid-Oct.

Meat Market ★★★ STEAKHOUSE As unoriginal yet as telling as its name is, this bustling Lincoln Road steakhouse is one of the city's best—for many things. Thanks to its sexy, loungey vibe, it's a great bar scene and, at times, a bona fide pickup joint or, rather, a meat market. And thanks to a talented chef/co-owner, Sean Brasel, it's also a serious eating place. Raw bar selections such as oysters on the half shell with delicious dipping sauces (habanero cocktail sauce is a favorite) or mahi-mahi with lime, jalapeño, cilantro, and tequila will prepare your taste buds for an epicurean journey that differentiates this meat market from the rest, almost rendering its name a misnomer of sorts. Seafood appetizers such as crispy crab tail bathed in egg batter and pan-fried with passion-fruit butter sauce and sesame-and-*aji-panca* oil make you wonder why they didn't call it Fish Market. That said, the steaks are indeed delicious, too, but we especially love almost each and every one of the 21 side dishes offered—especially the Gouda-filled tater tots. Meat, what?

915 Lincoln Rd., South Beach. ℂ **305/532-0088.** www.meatmarketmiami.com. Reservations required. Main courses $20–$84. AE, MC, V. Daily 6pm–midnight.

Mr Chow ★ CHINESE For whatever reason, celebrities love Michael Chow's exorbitantly priced Chinese cuisine. And we may have liked it as well if it didn't have less flavor than PF Chang's and if our bill for two wasn't pushing $400. Yes, $400 for Chinese food. Of course, you're paying for location, scene, and reputation, which, whether you like it or not, is somewhat stellar. Food critics disagree, but the A-listers of the world don't care. In fact, without celebrities, Mr Chow would be, well, lonely. Pushy, tuxedoed waiters trained in up-selling offer you customized prix-fixe menus upwards of $60 a person as they try to snatch the actual menu out of your hand. Don't fall for it. Order what you want, but order wisely. And maybe eat before. Portions are tiny. Skip the signature green shrimp—they have no taste. Crispy beef is mushy and the white rice should have gold flecks in it at $12 a bowl for two. Don't be fooled by the champagne pushcarts with prices turned such that only a Cirque du Soleil acrobat could see them. And if you do indulge, whatever you do, watch your glass. Refills come fast and furious—at a price. Nothing is free here. After all, they have to pay for that magnificent Swarovski crystal chandelier and plush royal blue carpeting. Yes, the dining room is Kodak-worthy, but is it break-your-bank-account worthy? Hardly. As for our one-star rating? It's for those celebrities who continue to confound us by calling Mr Chow their favorite restaurant.

At the W South Beach, 2201 Collins Ave., South Beach. ℂ **305/695-1695.** www.mrchow.com. Reservations required. Main courses $28–$45 and above. AE, MC, V. Sun–Wed 6–11:30pm; Thurs–Sat 6pm–12:30am.

Nobu ★★ SUSHI When Lady Gaga ate here, no one really noticed. The same thing happened when Jay-Z and Beyoncé canoodled here. Okay, well they noticed, but not for long. It's not because people were purposely trying not to notice, but because the real star at Nobu is the sushi. The raw facts: Nobu has been hailed as one of the best sushi restaurants in the world, with always-packed eateries in New York, London, and Los Angeles. The *Omakase*, or Chef's Choice—a multicourse menu entirely up to the chef for $135 per person—gets consistent raves. Some people, however, say Nobu is overpriced and mediocre. Not being a sushi fan, I can only agree on the fact that it's very expensive. When you do go here, expect to spend at least what Beyoncé probably pays for her plain white Gucci T-shirts. Enjoy the scenery and have fun pretending not to notice, because although you won't wait long for your food to be cooked, you will wait forever to score a table here even if you have a reservation.

At the Shore Club Hotel, 1901 Collins Ave., South Beach. ✆ **305/695-3232.** Reservations suggested. Main courses $26 and above. AE, MC, V. Sun 7–11pm; Mon–Thurs 7pm–midnight; Fri–Sat 7pm–1am.

Prime One Twelve ★★ STEAKHOUSE This frenzied, celebrity-saturated sleek steakhouse is part of the ever-expanding culinary empire of Big Pink and Shoji Sushi, and is the media darling of the exclusive group of restaurants in the hot South of Fifth Street area of South Beach. It's proven recession-proof in 2010, reporting an unheard of *increase* in business and profits to become one of the highest-grossing restaurants in the country. Its clubby ambience and bustling bar (complete with dried strips of bacon in lieu of nuts) play second fiddle to the beef, which is arguably the best in the entire city—although some carnivores say it's all flash and no flesh and prefer BLT Steak, Bourbon Steak, and Capital Grille. The 12-ounce filet mignon is seared to perfection and can be enhanced with optional dipping sauces (for a price): truffle, garlic herb, foie gras, and chipotle. The 22-ounce bone-in rib-eye is a good choice if you can afford it, as is the gigantic 48-ounce porterhouse. Prime One Twelve also features a $20 Kobe-beef hot dog, Kobe-beef sliders—think White Castle on an expense account ($20)—and a $30 Kobe burger that is sheer ecstasy. A powerhouse crowd gathers for lunch and dinner (and reservations are rarer than the yellowfin tuna tartare appetizer), but should you be lucky enough to score such a "prime" reservation, take it without hesitation.

   Note: Also consider Prime's sister restaurant across the street, **Prime Italian,** 101 Ocean Dr. (✆ **305/695-8484**), a pricey red sauce restaurant that's not nearly as much of a scene, but features swift service, outdoor seating, and, yes, an easier reservation to snag. **Prime Fish** is coming soon in the space formerly known as Nemo, 100 Collins Ave. (✆ **305/532-4550**).

112 Ocean Dr. (in the Browns Hotel), South Beach. ✆ **305/532-8112.** www.prime112.com. Reservations recommended. Main courses $20–$88. AE, DISC, MC, V. Mon–Fri 11:30am–3pm; daily 6:30pm–midnight.

Red the Steakhouse ★★ STEAKHOUSE When this high-styled, black-, red-, and stone-walled, clubby-contemporary meatery from Cleveland opened 2 blocks away from Prime One Twelve, people laughed. But it was no joke. Red proved itself and has held its own in the glitzy shadows of its neighbor thanks to spectacularly seasoned steaks that don't taste like those found anywhere else. Purists may sneer at it, but those looking for mad flavor revel in this magical seasoning that is composed of oil, kosher salt, and black peppercorns. Must be a Midwestern thing, some say, but whatever it is, it works. Don't fill up too much on the delicious bread and hearty starters like the savory trio of green peppers stuffed with sweet Italian sausage, but don't pass on them either. And if it's good enough for one of its most repeat customers, Michael Jordan, who is usually holed up in the glass-enclosed private room complete with flatscreen TVs to watch games on, it's good enough for us.

119 Washington Ave., South Beach. ☎ **305/534-3688.** www.redthesteakhouse.com. Reservations required. Main courses $28–$89. AE, DC, MC, V. Sun–Fri 5:30pm–midnight; Sat 5:30pm–2am.

STK ★ STEAKHOUSE After opening delays that lasted several years, STK, the see-and-be-seen "meatery" that's "not your daddy's steakhouse" finally opened off the lackluster lobby of the Gansevoort Miami Beach. Sexy it is, featuring sleek decor, second-floor catwalk perfect for being seen, and glazed screen spanning the restaurant's two stories depicting an abstract shape of a woman's body reflecting off the glass. Because that's just what you want to see when stuffing your face with meat, right? To answer that question is the menu's not-so-tongue-in-cheeky "female friendly portions." Located next to the restaurant is a 2,000-square-foot lounge, Coco DeVille, featuring DJ booth and requisite celebrity clientele. By the looks of things, you understand why it took so long to open. As for the food, some Miami-inspired selections include seared big-eye tuna, with roasted pineapple, habanero chili pepper, and *congri* basmati rice; and pork *mojo cazuela,* with citrus chili *maduros* and yuca. And then there are the steaks, signature cuts of meat in small, medium, and large. As for whether to choose this place over the 400 other sceney steakhouses in Miami, it has one (dis)advantage: that DJ. So if you want your steak with a side of sonic boom, this is the meatery for you.

In the Gansevoort Miami Beach, 2377 Collins Ave., South Beach. ☎ **305/604-6988.** Reservations required. Main courses $24–$65. AE, DC, MC, V. Daily 5:30pm–2am.

Wish ★★★ MEDITERRANEAN Located in the stylish Todd Oldham–designed The Hotel, this is one of the most beautiful, romantic outdoor garden restaurants in South Beach and it was recently spruced up and looks better than ever. Chef Marco Ferraro, who has worked under the toque of Jean-Georges Vongerichten, has taken the restaurant to a new level of taste with a menu he describes as "fresh, seasonal, light, and vibrant." He's putting it mildly. Think New American with Latin and Mediterranean accents. The oven-roasted pork chop with chorizo mashed potato, roasted peppers, grilled eggplant, cilantro, crispy shallots, and Parmesan dressing is exquisite, as is the grilled Maine lobster tail with locally grown pea tendrils, basil, garlic, ginger, dried finger chiles, lemon coriander crema, and pineapple-jicama salsa. And then there are the "electric cocktails," such as the glowing green-apple martini served with psychedelic ice cubes. The only thing you'll wish for after you leave here is to go back!

801 Collins Ave., South Beach. ☎ **305/531-2222.** www.wishrestaurant.com. Reservations recommended. Main courses $29–$39. AE, DC, MC, V. Mon 11:30am–3pm; Tues–Sun 11:30am–3pm and 6–11pm (Fri–Sat to midnight).

EXPENSIVE

Sardinia ★★ ITALIAN A quiet sensation in South Beach terms, Sardinia doesn't need celebrity sightings and publicists to boost its business. And it's not your typical caprese salad and fusilli pasta factory, either. For starters, the cheese and salumi plates will transport you—or at least your palate—to Italy, as will the rest of the innovative menu, consisting of oriechette with wild boar; crunchy fried sweetbreads with Brussels sprouts; and rabbit with Brussels sprouts and beets. Sure, the food's a bit heavy, but it's worth it. As for the scene here, it's all about the food, although the bar is always bustling with people waiting for highly coveted tables. For seafood lovers, don't miss the branzino baked in salt crust.

1801 Purdy Ave., South Beach. ✆ **305/531-2228.** www.sardinia-ristorante.com. Reservations highly suggested. Main courses $11–$40. AE, DC, MC, V. Daily noon–midnight.

MODERATE

Balan's ★ MEDITERRANEAN Balan's provides undeniable evidence that the Brits actually do know a thing or two about cuisine. A direct import from London's Soho, Balan's draws inspiration from various Mediterranean and Asian influences, labeling its cuisine "Mediterrasian." With a brightly colored interior straight out of a mod '60s flick, Balan's is a favorite among the gay and arty crowds, especially on weekends during brunch hours. The moderately priced food is rather good here—especially the double-baked cheese soufflé, citrus tossed mixed greens, Thai red curry, and pan-fried tilapia with Indian garbanzo bean curry and mint yogurt. When in doubt, the restaurant's signature US1 Burger is always a good choice. Adding to the ambience is the restaurant's people-watching vantage point on Lincoln Road. In 2009, Balan's expanded over the causeway and opened a second location at 901 S. Miami Ave., in the bustling Brickell area. In early 2010, they opened a *third* at Biscayne Boulevard and 67th Street in the Upper East Side neighborhood.

1022 Lincoln Rd. (btw. Lenox and Michigan), South Beach. ✆ **305/534-9191.** www.balans.co.uk. Reservations accepted, except for weekend brunch. Main courses, sandwiches, salads $9–$30 (breakfast and dinner specials Mon–Fri). AE, DISC, MC, V. Sun–Thurs 8am–midnight; Fri–Sat 8am–1am; Sat–Sun brunch menu noon–3:30pm.

Big Pink ★ ☺ AMERICAN "Real Food for Real People" is the motto to which this restaurant strictly adheres. Set on what used to be a gritty corner of Collins Avenue, Big Pink—owned by the folks at the higher-end Nemo—is quickly identified by a whimsical Pippi Longstocking–type mascot on a sign outside. Scooters and motorcycles line the streets surrounding the place, which is a favorite among beach bums, club kids, and those craving Big Pink's comforting and hugely portioned pizzas, sandwiches, salads, and hamburgers. The fare is above average, at best, and the menu is massive, but it comes with a good dose of kitsch, such as the "gourmet" spin on the classic TV dinner, which is done perfectly, right down to the compartmentalized dessert. Televisions line the bar area, and the family-style table arrangement (there are several booths too) promotes camaraderie among diners. Outdoor tables are available. Even picky kids will like the food here, and parents can enjoy the family-friendly atmosphere (not the norm for South Beach) without worrying whether their kids are making too much noise.

157 Collins Ave., Miami Beach. ✆ **305/532-4700.** www.mylesrestaurantgroup.com. Salads, sandwiches, burgers, pizzas, main courses $7–$23. AE, DC, MC, V. Sun–Wed 8am–midnight; Thurs 8am–2am; Fri–Sat 8am–5am.

Bond St. Lounge ★ SUSHI A New York City import, the sceney, subterranean Bond St. Lounge is in the basement of the shabby-chic Townhouse Hotel and is packing in hipsters as tightly as the crabmeat in a California roll. Despite its tiny size, Bond St. Lounge's superfresh nigiri and sashimi, and funky sushi rolls such as the sun-dried tomato and avocado or the arugula crispy potato, are worth cramming in here for. As the evening progresses, however, Bond St. becomes more of a bar scene than a restaurant, but sushi is always available at the bar to accompany your sake bloody mary. For those feeling a little claustrophobic downstairs, the **Townhouse** rooftop lounge now serves Bond St. sushi, so you can come up for air and for a roll or two.

Townhouse Hotel, 150 20th St., South Beach. ℂ **305/398-1806.** Reservations recommended. Sushi $6–$20. AE, MC, V. Daily 6pm–2am.

Burger & Beer Joint AMERICAN A refreshing alternative to the throngs of high-end eateries that opened in the area over the past year, B&B is a down-home, family-friendly, well, *burger and beer joint* with no attitude, just great, thick, juicy burgers; fabulously salted skinny fries; beer; cocktails; and, ice-cream sundaes or sodas. Hip without trying too hard, B&B offers all sorts of burgers, from plain and classic iterations (all perfectly cooked at medium rare unless otherwise speci-fied) to those with rock-'n'-roll-inspired monikers: a $39 "Stairway to Heaven," 10 ounces of Wagyu beef, 3 ounces Hudson Valley foie gras, and black truffle demi on a brioche bun; $9 "buck naked" with 10 ounces of prime Angus beef wrapped in lettuce with tomato, grilled red onion, and pickle; or the $12 "Fly Like an Eagle," two turkey patties with homemade stuffing, brown gravy, and cranberry sauce. You can also create your own burgers, with an intimidating list of cheeses, buns, veggies, sauces, and bells and whistles. Before you start with burgers, you may want to try the sassy tempura fried pickles or braised Buffalo wings, which are unlike the ones found in your typical sports bar with meat marinated in a spicy, zippy sauce and falling off the bone. For the insane, try the $75 Mother Burger, a 10-pound patty the size of a manhole, which, if finished within 2 hours, is free. After dinner, check out the back sports bar, which tends to be a bit smoky, or the upstairs lounge with comfy couches and local DJs. A second location of B&B, as it's known by locals, opened at 900 S. Miami Ave. (ℂ **305/523-2244**), in Mary Brickell Village.

1766 Bay Rd., South Beach. ℂ **305/672-3287.** www.burgernbeerjoint.com. No reservations. Burgers $10–$39. AE, DC, MC, V. Daily noon–5pm; Sun–Thurs 5pm–1am; Fri–Sat 5pm–2am.

The Café at Books & Books ★ AMERICAN This sidewalk cafe offers not only some of the best, freshest breakfasts and lunches in town—the egg-and-tuna-salad combo is our favorite, as are the amazing yucca and leek homemade hash browns—but gourmet dinners as well. This is not your chain bookstore's prefab tuna sandwich. Sadly, in 2009, the bookstore became a Diesel store, but the cafe stayed. Chef Bernie Matz gave star chef Douglas Rodriguez his start—enough said. Sandwiches, salads, and burgers are good, but after 5pm the real gourmand comes out in Matz with specials that change often and include things like a juicy flank steak marinated in espresso and brown sugar, seared, sliced, and served with a pineapple-and-onion salsa and a pair of plantain nests smothered in garlicky mojo. The menu also features an impressive selection of vegetarian and vegan options. If you're still inspired to buy a cookbook after your meal, Books & Books set up a small, cozy annex in the back of the courtyard. In 2010, Matz opened **Bernie's L.A. Café,** 1570 Alton Rd. (ℂ **305/535-8003**), a 30-seat spot reflecting more of his Latin roots serving tacos, burgers, seafood cocktails, seviches, tapas, salads, and sandwiches.

933 Lincoln Rd., South Beach. ℂ **305/695-8898.** Main courses $7–$25. AE, MC, V. Daily 9am–11pm.

Clarke's ★ IRISH There's more to this neighborhood pub than pints of Guinness. With a warm, inviting ambience and a gorgeously rich wood bar as the focal point, Clarke's is the only true gastropub in Miami, with excellent fare that goes beyond bangers and mash and delicious burgers, and delves into the gourmet. Highlights include olive oil poached yellowtail snapper with mushroom confit, tomato marmalade, and frisée salad; Sazerac House crab cakes, whose secret recipe hails from owner Laura Cullen's father's New York City landmark, the Sazerac House; and Mom's Montauk-style scallops. If you're not in the mood for full fare, our favorite is the New York–style pretzel, served on a spike with mustard on the side. The vibe here is very friendly, which is why everyone from Miami Heat basketball players to South Beach celebrity types choose Clarke's when they want a low-key night with delicious fare—and even more delicious "dish."

840 1st St., South Beach. ℂ **305/538-9885.** www.clarkesmiamibeach.com. Main courses $6–$27. AE, MC, V. Mon–Fri 5pm–midnight; Sat 11:30am–midnight; Sun 11am–3pm (brunch) and 4pm–midnight.

Macaluso's ★★ ITALIAN This restaurant epitomizes the Italians' love for—and mastery of—savory, plentiful, down-home Staten Island–style food. While the storefront restaurant is intimate and demure in nature, there's nothing delicate about the bold mix of flavors in every meat and pasta dish here. Catch the fantastic clam pie when in season—the portions are huge. Pricier items vary throughout the season but will likely feature fresh fish hand-picked by chef (and owner) Michael, the don of the kitchen, who used to channel the Seinfeld Soup Nazi, refusing special requests, but in light of the economy has since, uh, lightened up. Everyone will recommend favorites such as the rigatoni and broccoli rabe. There are also delicious desserts ranging from homemade anisette cookies to gooey pastries. The wine list is also good. Keep your eyes peeled, as this is a major celeb hot spot, where everyone from Lindsay Lohan to Roger Federer and Billy Joel have been known to eat and kibitz with the chef in the kitchen.

1747 Alton Rd., Miami Beach. ℂ **305/604-1811.** Main courses $15–$40; pizza $10–$20. MC, V. Tues–Sat 6pm–midnight; Sun 6–11pm. After 10:30pm, only pies are served.

INEXPENSIVE

11th Street Diner AMERICAN The only real diner on the beach, the 11th Street Diner is the more interesting alternative to a late-night run to Denny's. Some of Miami's most colorful characters, especially the drunk ones, convene here at odd hours, and your greasy-spoon experience can quickly turn into a three-ring circus. Uprooted from its 1948 Wilkes-Barre, Pennsylvania, foundation, the actual structure was dismantled and rebuilt on a busy—and colorful (a gay bar is right next door, so be on the lookout for flamboyant drag queens)—corner of Washington Avenue. Although it can use a good window cleaning, it remains a popular round-the-clock spot that attracts all walks of life and happens to serve breakfast all day. If you're craving french fries, order them smothered in mozzarella with a side of gravy—a tasty concoction that we call disco fries because of its popularity among starving clubbers.

1065 Washington Ave., South Beach. ℂ **305/534-6373.** www.eleventhstreetdiner.com. Items $4–$19. AE, MC. Daily 24 hr.

Front Porch Café ★ AMERICAN Even after moving from a dreary Art Deco hotel to the more modern Z Ocean Hotel next door, the Front Porch Café is a relaxed local hangout known for cheap breakfasts and, with the new location, drink specials, happy hour, and a bigger dinner menu. Some of the servers tend to be a bit attitudinal and lackadaisical (many are bartenders or club kids by night), so this isn't the place to be if you're in a hurry, especially on the weekends, when the place is packed all day long and lines are the norm. Enjoy home-style French toast with bananas and walnuts, omelets, fresh fruit salads, pizzas, and classic breakfast pancakes that put IHOP to shame. If you're looking to avoid the tourists and prefer to dine with the locals, Front Porch is where it's at for breakfast, lunch, and even dinner.

In the Z Ocean Hotel, 1458 Ocean Dr., South Beach. ✆ **305/531-8300.** Main courses $5–$30. AE, DC, DISC, MC, V. Daily 7am–midnight.

Icebox Café ★ AMERICAN Locals love this place for its homey comfort food—tuna melts, potpies, and eggs for breakfast, lunch, and dinner. Oprah Winfrey singled it out for its desserts, which is really why people raid the Icebox whenever that sweet tooth calls. In the Icebox, you'll discover the best chocolate cake, pound cake, and banana cream pies outside of your grandma's kitchen.

1657 Michigan Ave., South Beach. ✆ **305/538-8448.** Main courses and desserts $3–$10. AE, MC, V. Daily 8am–10:30pm.

La Sandwicherie ★ SANDWICHES You can get mustard, mayo, or oil and vinegar on sandwiches elsewhere in town, but you'd be missing out on all the local flavor. This gourmet sandwich bar, open until the crack of dawn, caters to ravenous club kids, biker types, and the body artists who work in the tattoo parlor next door. For many people, in fact, no night of clubbing is complete without capping it off with a turkey sub from La Sandwicherie.

229 14th St. (behind the Amoco station), South Beach. ✆ **305/532-8934.** Sandwiches and salads $6–$12. AE, MC, V. Daily 9am–5am. Delivery 9:30am–11pm.

News Cafe ★ AMERICAN This South Beach cafe-cum-landmark hasn't fallen off the radar, it's just on a different one, this time as an iconic South Beach figure rather than a currently hip one. The quintessential South Beach experience, News is still au courant, albeit swarming with mostly tourists. Unless it's appallingly hot or rainy out, you should wait for an outside table, where you must be to fully appreciate the experience. Service is abysmal and often arrogant (perhaps because the tip is included), but the menu is reliable, running the gamut from sandwiches and salads to pasta dishes and omelets. Our favorite here is the Middle Eastern platter, a dip lover's paradise, with hummus, tahini, tabbouleh, baba ghanouj, and fresh pita bread. If it's not too busy, feel free to order just a cappuccino—your server may snarl, but that's what News is all about; creative types like to bring their laptops and sit here all day (or all night—this place is open 24 hr. a day). If you're alone and need something to read, there's an extensive collection of national and international newspapers and magazines at the in-house newsstand. The **News Lounge,** at the 55th Street Station off Biscayne Boulevard, 5582 NE 4th Court (✆ **305/758-9932**), has a 100-seat interior video bar, limited bar menu, and 100-seat outdoor space that's open daily from 5pm to 1am, sometimes later.

800 Ocean Dr., South Beach. ✆ **305/538-6397.** www.newscafe.com. Items $5–$30. AE, DC, MC, V. Daily 24 hr.

Puerto Sagua ★ CUBAN/SPANISH This brown-walled diner is one of the only old holdouts on South Beach. Its steady stream of regulars ranges from *abuelitos* (little old grandfathers) and local politicos who meet here every Tuesday morning to hipsters who stop in after clubbing. It has endured because the food is good, if a little greasy. Some of the less heavy dishes are a superchunky fish soup with pieces of whole flaky grouper, chicken, and seafood paella, or marinated kingfish. Also good are most of the shrimp dishes, especially the shrimp in garlic sauce, which is served with white rice and salad. This is one of the most reasonably priced places left on the beach for simple, hearty fare. Our fave? Roast chicken with rice, black beans, and fried plantains. Don't be intimidated by the hunched, older waiters in their white button-down shirts and black pants. If you don't speak Spanish, they're usually willing to do charades. Anyway, the extensive menu, which ranges from BLTs to grilled lobsters to yummy fried plantains, is translated into English. Hurry, before another boutique goes up in its place.

700 Collins Ave., South Beach. ☎ **305/673-1115.** Main courses $10–$24; sandwiches and salads $5–$10. AE, DC, MC, V. Daily 7:30am–2am.

Miami Beach, Surfside, Bal Harbour & Sunny Isles

The area north of the Art Deco District—from about 21st Street to 163rd Street—had its heyday in the 1950s, when huge hotels and gambling halls blocked the view of the ocean. Now many of the old hotels have been converted into condos or budget lodgings, and the bayfront mansions have been renovated by and for wealthy entrepreneurs, families, and speculators. The area has many more residents, albeit seasonal, than visitors. On the culinary front, the result is a handful of superexpensive, traditional establishments as well as a number of value-oriented spots.

To locate the restaurants in this section, see the map "Hotels & Restaurants in Miami Beach" (p. 96).

VERY EXPENSIVE

The Forge Restaurant | Wine Bar ★★★ ORGANIC/STEAK Like many of its most loyal, uh, seasoned customers, The Forge underwent a major nip/tuck and traded its dark roots for a lighter, blonder look and a menu that focuses on organic, locally sourced foods. The bar is stunning in a refreshingly rich, not stark, way, and its electronic dispensing wine system turns oenophiles into kids on a video game bender at the Chuck E. Cheese's, only with booze. Good booze, of course. Thankfully, the old-school wine cellar, one of the country's best, still remains just that. The menu, featuring a whopping 65 items, by chef Dewey LoSasso, offers a modern, largely organic twist on everything, from seafood and salads to pastas and steaks. Yes, the classic Forge Super Steak is still on the menu to the delight of many. This reimagined Forge is nothing like its previous incarnation as a bacchanalian den of decadence, so no more raucous nightclub-esque parties or weekly see-and-be-scene fests. Sure, it's decadent, but it's much more subtly so, just like its customers.

432 Arthur Godfrey Rd. (41st St.), Miami Beach. ☎ **305/538-8533.** Reservations recommended. Main courses $25–$60. AE, DC, MC, V. Sun–Thurs 6pm–midnight; Fri–Sat 6pm–1am.

Gotham Steak ★ STEAKHOUSE NYC's Gotham Bar & Grill chef/owner Alfred Portale's Miami offering is this, a stunning, yet somewhat disappointing steakhouse that fits right into its environs as something with all style yet hardly any substance. The bi-level restaurant is photo-worthy, with a chandelier of hand-blown glass and glass-enclosed wine tower, but as for the food? Uninspired. Steaks, pricey and often overcooked, include a gigantic 20-ounce Brandt Farms rib-eye grilled over hardwood charcoal and finished on a 1,200-degree broiler ($64), an 8-ounce filet mignon that you can get pretty much anywhere these days ($40), and the bargain $27 plate of barbecued pork ribs that a cart on the side of the road in downtown Miami makes better for less than half. Yawn. If you're going to the Fontainebleau, have a drink here, take a few pictures, but save your appetite for one of the other two highly lauded eateries.

In the Fontainebleau, 4441 Collins Ave., Miami Beach. ☏ **305/674-4780.** Reservations required. Main courses $24–$64. AE, DC, MC, V. Daily 6–10:30pm.

Hakkasan ★★★ CHINESE A flashy bastion of the luxe life, this higher-than-high-end haute Chineserie, owned by Michelin-starred chef Alan Yau of London's Hakkasan fame, is a sight to be seen and tasted. Tucked away on the fourth floor of the labyrinthine Fontainebleau, Hakkasan exudes a nightclubby, Vegas vibe with thumping music, scantily clad diners who think they're in Vegas, and screened-off nooks of semiprivate dining areas. There is and has never been a recession in this place, that's for sure. Although we're of the PF Chang's school of Chinese, we can't deny the fact that this is some seriously good, gourmet food. Signature dishes include a fabulous filet of roasted silver cod over tender stalks of *gai lan* (Chinese broccoli) in honey and champagne, roasted duck served in bite-size slices with crisped skin with a savory soy sauce, and red snapper with a spicy scallion soy sauce. For the big splurge, try the Peking duck with 30 grams of Russian osetra caviar at a whopping $198. Service is professional with the exception of one or two aloof types who slipped through the screens. Your best bet is to go with a group of people if you can so you can share dishes. Just watch the drinks—that's where they always get you.

In the Fontainebleau, 4441 Collins Ave., Miami Beach. ☏ **786/276-1388.** Reservations required. Main courses $10–$198. AE, DC, MC, V. Sun and Tues–Wed 6–11pm; Thurs–Sat 6pm–12:30am.

Scarpetta ★★★ ITALIAN Miami Beach's very own version of the wildly popular N.Y.C. Italian restaurant of the same name, Scarpetta has consistently been one of the city's hottest reservations since it opened in late 2008. Chef Scott Conant is a talent and, unlike many star chefs too busy to cook in their own kitchens, he is often found massaging his homemade pasta right here, in his Miami Beach kitchen. And while that kitchen is indeed high-tech, the dining room is a showpiece, with ambient lighting, beautiful chandeliers, banquettes, and an aura that's reminiscent of the first-class dining room in an old-world ocean liner that sailed into the 21st century. Once you are seduced by the room, you may not notice that you're paying $23 for a bowl of the chef's signature spaghetti *pomodoro*—you know, the pasta he was in the kitchen kneading and massaging at 5am? Skip the spaghetti. We've had it twice and it doesn't compare to dishes on the rest of the menu. But first the bread basket, a selection of ciabatta, focaccia, and a stromboli-like round stuffed with salami, mozzarella, and basil, is tempting to polish off, but pace yourself. The polenta served in a silver ramekin alongside a fricassee of mushrooms with a hint of truffle oil will have you wishing you could sail away on this gastronomical vessel and mangia pasta as you sail into the sunset.

In the Fontainebleau, 4441 Collins Ave., Miami Beach. ☏ **305/672-4660.** Reservations required. Main courses $23–$42. AE, DC, MC, V. Sun–Thurs 6–11pm; Fri–Sat 6pm–midnight.

MODERATE

Cafe Prima Pasta ★ ITALIAN Once a small, unknown trattoria on a very trafficky, tacky street, Cafe Prima Pasta has expanded into a place to be for excellent Italian food and quite a bit of fanfare, especially when regular customer Matt Damon comes in. Because a massive waiting line always spilled out onto the street, the cafe expanded to include ample outdoor seating that is set back from the street noise and traffic, thanks to some creative landscaping. The pasta here is homemade, and the kitchen's choice ingredients include ripe, juicy tomatoes; imported olive oil that would cost you a boatload if you bought it in the store; fresh, drippy mozzarella; and fish that tastes as if it has just been caught right out back. The zesty, spicy garlic and oil that is brought out as dip for the bread should be kept with you during your meal, for it doubles as extra seasoning for your food—not that it's necessary. Though tables are packed in, the atmosphere still manages to be romantic. Due to the chef's fancy for garlic, this is a three-Altoid restaurant, so be prepared to pop a few or request that they go light on the garlic.

414 71st St. (half a block east of the Byron movie theater), Miami Beach. ℂ **305/867-0106.** www.primapasta.com. Reservations accepted for parties of 6 or more. Main courses $17–$24; pastas $16–$20. MC, V. Mon–Thurs noon–midnight; Fri noon–1am; Sat 1pm–1am; Sun 5pm–midnight.

Las Vacas Gordas ★★ ARGENTINE STEAKHOUSE Got meat? Or, rather, how do you say it in Spanish, because you may need a translator at this popular Argentine steakhouse, where service doesn't dillydally, nor do they typically speak understandable English. But don't worry, the culture shock wears off once they start to bring out your meat. And meat. And more meat, which explains why the name of the restaurant translates to "The Fat Cows." It's quite a fun experience, actually, as long as you hold off on your food coma—if one of the surly staff catches you snoozing, you're out of there. Specialties are the marinated and grilled steaks, but order carefully. We made the mistake of pointing, like one does in a foreign country when they can't read the menu, and ended up with blood sausage, which is as nasty as it sounds though a delicacy to some. All meats are served with a divine *chimichurri* sauce, but sauces aren't really needed. Neither are sides and salads, but sometimes you'll need something more than red wine to wash your meat down with.

933 Normandy Dr., Miami Beach. ℂ **305/867-1717.** Reservations highly suggested. Main courses $15–$25. MC, V. Daily 6pm–midnight.

North Miami Beach

Although there aren't many hotels in North Dade, the population in the winter months explodes due to the onslaught of seasonal residents from the Northeast. A number of exclusive condominiums and country clubs (including William's Island and Turnberry) breed a demanding clientele, many of whom dine out nightly. That's good news for visitors, who can find superior service and cuisine at value prices.

To locate the restaurants in this section, see the map "Hotels and Restaurants in North Dade" (p. 96).

VERY EXPENSIVE

Michael Mina's Bourbon Steak ★★ STEAKHOUSE Although there's no shortage of steakhouses in Miami, there's nothing like this one. Reminiscent of something out of Las Vegas, everything here is massive—from the stunning all-glass wine cellar that takes up an entire wall, to the sheer size of the place at 7,600 square feet. And then there are the prices. But if you don't mind splurging, a meal at the star chef's first and only South Florida location is worth it. Start off with some oysters on the half shell—East Coast or West Coast, your choice—and then continue with the all-natural farm-raised Angus beef and American Kobe beef. Side dishes are delicious—jalapeño creamed corn, truffled mac and cheese, and a Bourbon Steak trio of Duck Fat Fries comes complimentary to every table, along with a potato focaccia bread with truffle butter and chives. Not in the mood for steak? Some say Mina's bar burgers, including the lamb version with yogurt raita, feta, tomato, and arugula, are the best in town. Well-heeled Aventura residents—including actor James Caan and perma-tanned man George Hamilton—and elegantly dressed hotel guests compose the equally rich crowd.

19999 W. Country Club Dr. (in the Fairmont Turnberry Isle Resort & Club), Aventura. *C* **786/279-6600.** www.michaelmina.net. Reservations recommended. Main courses $26–$79. AE, DC, DISC, MC, V. Mon–Thurs 6–10pm; Fri–Sat 6–11pm; Sun 5–9pm.

NAOE Miami ★★★ SUSHI Simply put, NAOE is Japanese for "OMG omakase." Okay, not really, but chef Kevin Cory sure makes you think so with his exquisitely prepared, hyperfresh sushi and Japanese fare. This may be the closest Miami gets to Tokyo. Take the motto: "It's not fresh, it's alive." Open only Wednesday through Sunday, NAOE serves the chef choice menu ($26) every night. All menus are prepared daily and if you have a special request, you need to make it at least a week in advance. Among the items you may find on your plate or in your bento box: smooth egg custard with soft freshwater eel bits; fresh giant clam sashimi in a tangy *shiso* vinaigrette; in-shell conch dressed in simple soy sauce; sweet, chilled corn-miso soup; salmon belly; saltwater and freshwater eel; *uni* so creamy it's been known to silence even the pickiest of reviewers; and horse mackerel with vinegary soy sauce. It's as authentic as it gets here. Be careful about what you ask for, though, as extras can add up quickly; they charge for fresh grated wasabi. That's fresh stuff, not the tubed stuff, but still.

175 Sunny Isles Blvd. (across from St. Tropez Condominium), Sunny Isles. *C* **305/947-6263.** www.naoemiami.com. Reservations recommended. Tasting menus $26. AE, MC, V. Wed–Sun seatings 6:30 and 9:30pm. Seatings scheduled to change, so call ahead.

Downtown Miami

Downtown Miami is a large, sprawling area divided by the Brickell Bridge into two distinct areas: Brickell Avenue and the bayfront area near Biscayne Boulevard. You shouldn't walk from one to the other—it's quite a distance and unsafe at night. Convenient Metromover stops do adjoin the areas, so it's better to hop on the scenic sky tram (it's closed after midnight).

VERY EXPENSIVE

Azul ★★★ GLOBAL FUSION Azul is one of the most upscale, prettiest—and priciest—waterfront restaurants in town. Like a stunning designer gown, the restaurant's décor is gorgeous, with its waterfront view, high ceilings, walls burnished in copper, and silk-covered chairs. Chef Joel Huff fuses modern European cuisine with American and Asian accents, as seen in dishes such as a loin of Colorado lamb with harrisa, charred eggplant, braised shank *bastila* and feta cheese and "A Study in Tuna Roll," featuring tuna, tempura avocado, Asian

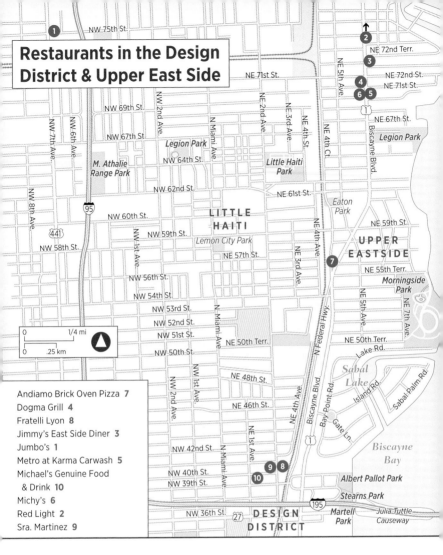

Restaurants in the Design District & Upper East Side

Andiamo Brick Oven Pizza **7**
Dogma Grill **4**
Fratelli Lyon **8**
Jimmy's East Side Diner **3**
Jumbo's **1**
Metro at Karma Carwash **5**
Michael's Genuine Food
 & Drink **10**
Michy's **6**
Red Light **2**
Sra. Martinez **9**

sauces and osetra caviar. Downstairs is the Mandarin's more casual, less expensive **Café Sambal,** an Asian eatery serving breakfast, lunch, and dinner with the same priceless views and a sushi bar.

At the Mandarin Oriental, 500 Brickell Key Dr., Miami. ✆ **305/913-8538.** Reservations strongly recommended. Main courses $24–$55. AE, DC, DISC, MC, V. Mon–Sat 7–11pm.

db Bistro Moderne ★★★ BISTRO Another Manhattan import, db Bistro Moderne, located on the ground floor of the brand-new JW Marriott Marquis, is the more casual offering from star chef Daniel Boulud, a modern French American eatery where "traditional French cuisine meets the flavors of the American market." In other words: hanger steak with oxtail ragout, sun-dried tomatoes, celery root, squash, and garlic pomme purée in a red-wine onion compote; or a phenomenal "Original db Burger," a stop-you-in-your-tracks sirloin burger filled—yes filled—with braised short ribs on a Parmesan bun. Of course, there's lighter fare, from tartes and salads to terrines, charcuterie, raw bar, and pâtés, catering to the ladies-who-lunch crowd. The elegant, dramatic dining room with soaring 16-foot ceilings and cozy banquettes is also conducive to power lunches, celebratory dinners, and dates.

At the JW Marriott Marquis, 345 Ave. of the Americas, Miami. © **305/421-8800.** www.danielnyc. com. Reservations strongly recommended. Main courses $29–$45. AE, DC, DISC, MC, V. Mon–Fri noon–2:30pm; Sun–Mon 5–10pm; Tues–Thurs 5–11pm; Fri–Sat 5pm–midnight; Sun brunch 11am–3pm.

Zuma ★★★ JAPANESE A stunning space bolstered by even more stunning cuisine where traditional Japanese meets modern, Zuma is not your typical sushi and noodle spot. The brainchild of German star chef Rainer Becker, who chose Miami as the city of choice for the restaurant's stateside debut—"We wanted our first Zuma in the USA to be located within an energetic, vibrant, multicultural, and popular city; that to me is Miami"—Zuma is constantly at the top of the "best of" lists, including the exclusive S. Pellegrino list, which rated the restaurant as one of the *world's* best and rightfully so. Based on the traditional Japanese school of cooking known as Izakaya with dishes cooked on a traditional robata grill (an old-school wood grill), menu highlights include prawn and black cod dumplings; sea bass sashimi with yuzu, truffle oil and salmon roe; yellowtail sashimi with green-chili relish, ponzu, and pickled garlic; sliced seared beef with pickled daikon and fresh truffle dressing; pork-belly skewer with yuzu mustard miso; beef skewers with shishito pepper and smoked chili soy; and miso marinated black cod, wrapped in hoba leaf. A $65, $85, $95, or $130 tasting menu (minimum of two people) features the chef's selection of seasonal signature dishes. And, finally, because desserts aren't exactly a Japanese strong point, Zuma's pastry chef hails from, drum roll, France. Welcome to Miami.

In the EPIC Hotel, 270 Biscayne Blvd. Way, Miami. © **305/577-0277.** www.zumarestaurant. com. Reservations necessary. Main courses $26–$55. AE, DC, MC, V. Mon–Sat noon–3pm and 6pm–midnight; Sun 11am–3pm and 6–10pm.

EXPENSIVE

Mercadito Midtown ★ MEXICAN An outpost of a popular New York restaurant, Mercadito has a reputation for serving the best fish tacos (pan-seared tilapia, chile poblano, and tomatillo-garlic mojo), well, ever, and to that we're on the fence. Sometimes they're great, other times they're miles behind the best taco truck in LA. In addition to 10 kinds of tacos, Mercadito has a massive menu of gussied-up Mexican, meant to be shared by the table, and not cheap. For one, you pay for condiments via an open guacamole, salsa, and seviche bar offering a variety of house-made sauces from *mole poblano* to *manzana* (apple, tomatillo, almonds, and habanero). There are also big dishes, like chile relleno, but we say stick with the tacos—maybe the fish, maybe the one with the chicken, sweet potato, and manchego cheese. But go light on the guac—they certainly do in terms of portions. Margaritas are individually muddled and made with 100% blue-agave tequila, and cocktails are quite creative, seamlessly blending all sorts of ingredients from hot sauce to mango, the way that, say, the chef should be doing in the kitchen. A more casual taqueria located adjacent to the main restaurant is a great spot for a beer and a fast taco or 10.

In the Shops at Midtown Miami, 3252 NE 1st Ave. ✆ **305/369-0430.** www.mercaditorestaurants. com. Reservations recommended. Main courses $10–$29. AE, DC, MC, V. Mon–Sat 11:30am–5pm; Sun–Tues 5pm–midnight; Wed–Thurs 5pm–1am; Fri–Sat 5pm–2am.

Michy's ★★ 👔 LATIN Star chef Michelle Bernstein left the fancy confines of the Mandarin Oriental Miami's Azul to open her own, homey 50-seat eatery on Miami's burgeoning Upper East Side. If you drive too fast, you'll miss the small storefront restaurant, a deceiving facade for a whimsical retro orange-and-blue interior where stellar small plates such as ham-and-blue-cheese croquettes are consumed in massive quantities because they're that good. Best of all, everything on the menu comes in half and full portions, so you can either control—or channel—the gluttony. There's also a zingy seviche that changes daily; pan-seared sole with sunchoke purée, baby artichokes, preserved lemon, and olive nage; short ribs "falling off the bone," which it is, with mashed potatoes and butter-braised Brussels sprouts; and, for those whose appetites call for it, on Wednesday nights, all-you-can-eat fried chicken. Fabulous fried chicken. There's nothing ordinary about Michy's, except for the fact that a reservation here is nearly impossible to score if not made weeks in advance.

6927 Biscayne Blvd. ✆ **305/759-2001.** www.michysmiami.com. Reservations recommended. Main courses $15–$30. AE, DC, MC, V. Tues–Thurs noon–3pm and 6–10:30pm; Fri noon–3pm and 6–11pm; Sat 6–11pm; Sun 6–10:30pm.

Sra. Martinez ★★★ TAPAS Housed in a historic post office, this upscale tapas joint, whose name is short for Señora Martinez, features traditional items and several others with Chef Michelle Bernstein's creative flair. Speaking of flair, the menus come folded up inside envelopes in tribute to the venue's original function. Be careful ordering—if you go nuts, your bill could end up costing $40 to $50 a head excluding tax, tip, and booze. That said, some of the standouts include the bacon-wrapped chicken livers; sweetbreads with sticky oranges, soy, and scallions; massive head-on Madagascar prawns grilled and served with cloves of confit garlic and a schmear of a smooth *chimichurri;* and braised oxtail, with Fideo pasta and mascarpone cheese. There are also a few entrees that are excellent, but stick with the tapas extravaganza for the true Sra. Martinez experience. To wash it all down, try one of the amazingly updated takes on old-school cocktail classics, including the sazerac, pisco sour, and bloody mary.

4000 NE 2nd Ave. ✆ **305/573-5474.** www.sramartinez.com. Reservations recommended. Tapas $3.50–$20. Entrees $24–$39. AE, DC, MC, V. Mon–Thurs 6–11pm; Fri–Sat 6pm–2am.

Sugarcane Raw Bar Grill ★★★ SOUTH AMERICAN/ASIAN The darling of Midtown dining, Sugarcane, the spawn of SushiSamba, is a sensational small-plates restaurant that beat Zuma to the punch with Miami's first-ever robata grill. Übertalented chef Timon Balloo presides over three kitchens—one for cooking meats, one for everything else, and a raw bar, seamlessly fusing South American, Asian, and global cuisine into tidy little (and not so little) plates of palate-pleasing excellence. Loud and bustling, the 4,000-plus-square-foot hip, warehouse-style eatery packs in crowds with potent cocktails and signature dishes such as chicken yakitori cooked on the *robata* grill, veal meatballs in sherry-fueled demi-glace, fried goat-cheese croquettes, and my personal faves, white pork buns with apple kimchi and cilantro and grilled, spicy shishito peppers with sea salt and lemon. Most small plates are $10 or less, but be careful. They're so good, and after a few cocktails to boot, you can be looking at a hefty bill. Creative chef Balloo doesn't always stick to the menu, pleasing the staunchest food snobs with his unique spins on ingredients like sweetbreads, tripe, and beef tongue. A huge cocktail crowd gathers at the indoor/outdoor bar and patio area after work and late on weekend nights. Sunday brunch is also extremely popular.

In the Shops at Midtown Miami, 3250 NE 1st Ave. ☎ 786/369-0353. www.sugarcanerawbar grill.com. Reservations recommended. Small plates $5–$10. AE, DC, MC, V. Sun–Wed 11:30am–midnight; Thurs 11:30am–1am; Fri–Sat 11:30am–2am.

MODERATE

Fratelli Lyon ★ ITALIAN We've heard of restaurants housed in markets and even department stores, but this Design District standout appropriately resides in a fabulously industrial modern furniture showroom. And while the not-so-comfy but cool-looking chairs you'll be sitting on may be for sale at an astronomical price, when it comes to the wine and cheese, well, they're bargain-basement in comparison. Owned by a former caterer, Fratelli, as it's known by locals, offers everything from a multitiered platter of antipasti to pizzas, bruschettas, salads, and main courses that include delicious saffron risotto served with boneless *osso buco.* A popular spot for appetizers and wine, Fratelli is also a top spot for lunches among the arty set who live, work, and play in the Design District.

4141 NE 2nd Ave., Miami. ☎ 305/572-2901. Reservations recommended. Main courses $8–$25. AE, DC, DISC, MC, V. Mon–Sat 11:30am–2pm; Mon–Thurs 6–10pm; Fri–Sat 6pm–midnight.

Garcia's Seafood Grille & Fish ★ 🎁 SEAFOOD A good catch on the banks of the Miami River, Garcia's has a great waterfront setting and a fairly simple yet tasty menu of fresh fish cooked in a number of ways—grilled, broiled, fried, or, the best in our opinions, in garlic or green sauce. Meals are quite the deal here, all served with green salad or grouper soup, and yellow rice or french fries. The complimentary fish-spread appetizer is also a nice touch. Because of this, not to mention the great, gritty ambience that takes you away from neon, neo-Miami in favor of the old seafaring days, there's usually a wait for a table. If so, hang out at the bar and order an appetizer of inexpensive stone crabs or famous conch fritters. They also recently opened an upstairs bar and lounge overlooking the river.

398 NW N. River Dr., Miami. ☎ 305/375-0765. http://garciasseafoodgrill.com. Reservations recommended. Main courses $12–$26. AE, DC, DISC, MC, V. Sun–Thurs 11am–10pm; Fri–Sat 11am–11pm.

Gigi ★ ASIAN Although Gigi considers itself a noodle bar, there are only three noodle dishes on the tiny menu. But it doesn't matter. Swarms of foodies and hipsters pack this casual-chic Wynwood spot into the wee hours, when 3 items to decipher from are better than 30. And while the noodles are admittedly deelish—the steak chow fun with mushroom, eggplant, and cabbage broth is a favorite—be sure to check out one of the three rice bowls; crispy soft-shell crab with red coconut curry, basil, mango, and jasmine rice; and any of the many "snacks," including the crispy chicken skin, chicken drumsticks, and pork buns. Portions are small, so prices add up. Beer and wine only.

3470 N. Miami Ave., Miami. ☎ 305/573-1520. www.giginow.com. Reservations not required. Main courses $12–$16. AE, DC, DISC, MC, V. Mon–Thurs 6pm–3am; Fri–Sat 6pm–5am.

Joey's ★★ 🎁 ITALIAN Sometimes you have to go out of your way for good pizza in Florida, even if that means driving into the still-dodgy, yet arty, Wynwood area for it. Owned by the son of South Beach pioneer Tony Goldman, Joey's is carving out yet another ahead-of-its-time visionary type of niche with this cozy,

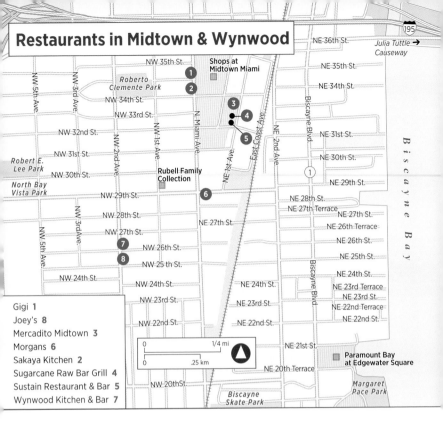

Restaurants in Midtown & Wynwood

Gigi **1**
Joey's **8**
Mercadito Midtown **3**
Morgans **6**
Sakaya Kitchen **2**
Sugarcane Raw Bar Grill **4**
Sustain Restaurant & Bar **5**
Wynwood Kitchen & Bar **7**

minimalistic, industrial-style concrete-floored eatery with an open kitchen, a few tables inside, and an outdoor patio. A full-blown menu of pastas and meat-and-seafood entrees includes dishes like baked cod with eggplant and tomato *gremolata* or lamb chops with juniper-berry reduction, but we personally go there for the pizza. As close to N.Y.-style as you can get, from classic Margherita to a fashionable pie dotted with figs, Gorgonzola, honey, and hot pepper. There are also some nice, reasonably priced Italian wines by the glass. As for the neighborhood, Joey's insists it's on its way. We say take a cab or car straight there, hand the keys to the valet, and enter an oasis of urban evolution.

2506 NW 2nd Ave., Miami. ✆ **305/438-0488.** Reservations recommended. www.joeys wynwood.com. Main courses and pizzas $7–$24. AE, DC, DISC, MC, V. Mon–Wed 11:30am–9:30pm; Thurs 11:30am–10:30pm; Fri–Sat 11:30am–11:30pm.

Michael's Genuine Food & Drink ★★★ NEW AMERICAN The sleek, yet unassuming dining room and serene courtyard seating are constantly abuzz with Design District hipsters, foodies, and celebrities. It's all thanks to chef/owner Michael Schwartz's fresh vision for fabulous food—a stellar, fresh mix of all organic products, some from Schwartz's own stash, including eggs hatched from his own hens. With an emphasis on products sourced from local growers and farmers, the menu, which changes daily, is divided into small, medium, large, and extra-large plates. There are also excellent pizzas, such as the exotic mushroom pizza with cave-aged Gruyère, caramelized onion, fresh thyme, and truffle oil; an astoundingly good Fudge Farms pork chop with Anson Mills cheese grits, pickled onion, and parsley sauce; and our personal favorite, the $4-to-$6 bar menu, featuring crispy hominy with chili and lime, deviled eggs, kimchi, and chicken liver crostini. Book early for Michael's, as it's always crowded. Genuinely. Also enormously popular: Sunday brunch featuring spectacular bloody marys and cocktails, as well as a fantastic assortment of farm-fresh egg dishes; main courses; and Goldsmith's sublime red velvet cupcakes, homemade pop tarts, donuts, and more.

130 NE 40th St., Miami. ℂ **305/573-5550.** www.michaelsgenuine.com. Reservations recommended. Main courses $14–$46. AE, DC, DISC, MC, V. Mon–Fri 11:30am–3pm; Mon–Thurs 5:30–11pm; Fri 5:30pm–midnight; Sat 6pm–midnight; Sun 5:30–10pm.

Red Light ★★ 🎁 CAJUN/CREOLE This one takes the award for the most offbeat location in town, as the on-site restaurant for one of Biscayne Boulevard's grittier motels (which since the restaurant opened is in the process of its own revitalization). If you can ignore the location, not to mention some of the motel's more, uh, colorful clientele, consider Chef Kris Wessell's daring menu instead. Although the place looks like a greasy spoon with vinyl booths and an old-diner vibe, this is gourmet fare on the Boulevard at its finest, with Southern accents. The barbecue shrimp are outstanding, typically themselves sautéed and served in a pan sauce made by sautéing the shrimp heads with butter, lemon, Worcestershire, and Tabasco—served with bread for dipping in the sauce. For an entree, don't miss the quail. A full order features two birds, deboned except for wings and legs, perfectly roasted, and served with Bing cherry peppercorn and Gruyère grits. After dinner, head downstairs and have a cocktail on the shore of the very pungent Little Miami River. It's just par for the offbeat course.

In the Motel Blu, 7700 Biscayne Blvd., Miami. ℂ **305/757-7773.** www.redlightmiami.com. Reservations recommended on weekends. Main courses $8–$20. AE, DC, MC, V. Tues–Sat 6pm–2am.

The River Seafood & Oyster Bar ★★ SEAFOOD A small, yet always packed seafood hot spot next door to Tobacco Road, the River is a buzzy and unpretentious spot for some of the best oysters in town—shipped fresh from all over the world daily—as well as some delicious dishes, including pan-fried snapper filet with roasted garlic chive and pickled asparagus; Maine lobster paella with shrimp, clams, mussels, and scallops; and, for the landlubber, outstanding churrasco skirt steak with *chimichurri* and sour orange mojo yucca frites. A great spot for happy hour, River Oyster's bar is a lively one, where you can suck down some oysters with some seriously stiff drinks or excellent wines. In fact, the bar is the focal point of the restaurant, considering there are so few tables, it's usually standing room only. Good thing is, service at the bar is swift and oftentimes people end up eating there as they wait for that elusive table.

15 SE 10th St. (corner of S. Miami Ave.), Miami. ℂ **305/374-9693.** www.therivermiami.com. Oysters $2.50–$3; main courses $20–$32. AE, MC, V. Mon–Fri 11:30am–5pm; Mon–Thurs 6–10:30pm; Fri 6pm–midnight; Sat 5:30pm–midnight.

Sustain Restaurant + Bar ★★ NEW AMERICAN A restaurant with a conscience almost seems oxymoronic, but when it comes to this modern American Midtown hot spot, it's no joke. With a decor crafted out of recycled and reclaimed materials with fabrics compliant with the U.S. Green Building Council/ LEED (Leadership in Energy & Environmental Design), Sustain isn't just a green facade, but the real deal, with "re-imagined" American fare crafted from locally sourced, regional, artisanal and sustainable outlets, be it a local farmer or one a bit farther away that raises grass-fed beef. Signature dishes include *porchetta,* a traditional Tuscan dish of roasted and herb-enhanced pork, from pasture-raised Berkshire pigs. And for the more vegetable-minded, there's a "50-mile" salad, made with ingredients from within 50 miles of Midtown. And, par for the course, Sustain also has a buzzy, hipster cocktail scene that's indigenous to this burgeoning burg of Miami's dining and nightlife scene.

3252 NE 1st Ave. (in the Shops of Midtown Miami), Miami. © **305/424-9079.** www.sustain miami.com. Main courses $14–$36. AE, MC, V. Daily 11am–3pm; Mon–Wed 5–11pm; Thurs–Sat 5pm–midnight; Sun 5–10pm.

Wynwood Kitchen & Bar ★ AMERICAN Yet another product from urban revitalization visionaries Jessica Goldman Srebnick and her partner and father, Tony Goldman, Wynwood Kitchen & Bar is to Miami what the now-defunct SoHo Kitchen & Bar was to Manhattan back in the '80s. In one word: groundbreaking. The restaurant is part of an art campus that also houses Wynwood Walls, an art park with a collection of more than 18 murals by leading international street artists. Adding to the already successful Goldman-owned Joey's, WKB is another reason besides art galleries to go to the still-gritty, arty Wynwood neighborhood. Described as an "American Brasserie," the 5,000-square-foot, warehousey WKB features a menu of burgers, sandwiches, salads, clay pots, and entrees created by Jean Georges protégé Marco Ferraro; murals by acclaimed graffiti artists Shephard Fairey and Christian Awe; and the requisite hipster bar with creative cocktails named after artists whose works have adorned Wynwood and its surroundings.

2550 NW 2nd Ave., Miami. © **305/722-8959.** http://wynwoodkitchenandbar.com. Burgers, sandwiches, salads $9–$12; main courses $9–$24. AE, MC, V. Mon–Sat 11am–midnight. Bar open until 1am.

INEXPENSIVE

Andiamo Brick Oven Pizza ★ PIZZA Leave it to visionary Mark Soyka (News Cafe, Van Dyke Cafe, Soyka) to turn a retro-style 1960s carwash into one of the city's best pizza places. The brick-oven pizzas are to die for, whether you choose the simple Andiamo pie (tomato sauce, mozzarella, and basil) or the designer combos of pancetta and caramelized onions; hot and sweet sausage with broccoli rabe; or portobello mushrooms with truffle oil and goat cheese. Pizzas come in three sizes: 10-, 13-, and 16-inch. Though the pizza is undeniably delicious here, the most talked-about aspect of Andiamo is the fact that while you're washing down slice after slice, you can get your car washed and detailed at Leo's, the space's original and still-existing occupant out back.

5600 Biscayne Blvd., Miami. © **305/762-5751.** Main courses $3–$15. MC, V. Sun–Thurs 11am–11pm; Fri–Sat 11am–midnight.

Dogma Grill ★★ HOT DOGS A little bit of L.A. comes to a gritty stretch of Biscayne Boulevard in the form of this very tongue-in-cheeky hot dog stand whose motto is "A Frank Philosophy." The brainchild of a former MTV executive, Dogma will change the way you view hot dogs, offering a plethora of choices, from your typical chili dog to Chicago-style, with celery salt, hot peppers, onions, and relish. The tropical version with pineapple is a bit funky but fitting for this stand, which attracts a very colorful, arty crowd from the nearby Design District.

The buns here are softer than feather pillows, and the hot dogs are grilled to perfection. Try the garlic fries and the lemonade too.

7030 Biscayne Blvd., Miami. ☎ **305/759-3433.** www.dogmagrill.com. Main courses $3–$4. No credit cards. Daily 11am–9pm.

Jimmy's East Side Diner ★ DINER The only thing wrong with this quintessential, consummate greasy-spoon diner is that it's not open 24 hours. Other than that, for the cheapest breakfasts in town, not to mention lunches and early dinners, Jimmy's is a dream come true. Try the banana pancakes, corned-beef hash, roasted chicken, or Philly cheesesteak. Located on the newly hip Upper East Side of Biscayne Boulevard, Jimmy's is a very neighborhoody place, where the late Bee Gee Maurice Gibb used to dine every Sunday. Adding to the aging regulars is a new, eclectic contingency of hung-over hipsters for whom Jimmy's is a sweet—and cheap—morning-after salvation.

7201 Biscayne Blvd., Miami. ☎ **305/759-3433.** Main courses $3–$11. No credit cards. Daily 6:30am–4pm.

Jumbo's ★★★ 🎁 SOUL FOOD Open 24 hours daily, this Miami institution is the kind of place where you'll see everyone from Rastafarian musicians and cabdrivers to Lenny Kravitz. It's in a shady neighborhood—Carol City—so if you go there, you're going for only one reason—Jumbo's. Family owned for more than 50 years, Jumbo's is known for its world-famous fried shrimp, fried chicken, catfish fingers, and collard greens. Their motto—"Life is to be enjoyed, not to be endured . . . Making friends is our business"—is spot on. The service is friendly and fun, and there's history here, too. Jumbo's was the first restaurant in Miami to integrate, in 1966, and the first to hire African-American employees, in 1967.

7501 NW 7th Ave., Miami. ☎ **305/751-1127.** Main courses $5–$15. AE, DC, MC, V. Daily 24 hr.

Metro at Karma Car Wash ★ 🎁 BISTRO The funkiest thing to hit Biscayne Boulevard since Dogma, this carwash-cum-bistro is a big hit with the locals who love their SUVs as much as their hot spots. Put your car in for a wash and relax on the outdoor patio, reminiscent of your best friend's backyard, where you can sip from an impressive number of micro beers, wines, and coffees, and snack on delicious fare including sandwiches, salads, and a very good burger made with grass-fed, organic filet mignon. DJs and cocktail parties make it a happening spot from Thursday on, and while we don't encourage you to drink and drive, of course, there's never been a better excuse to shine your car (it's pricey, but they do a spotless job!) while waxing social at the same time.

7010 Biscayne Blvd., Miami. ☎ **305/759-1392.** www.metrobistromiami.com. Sandwiches $12–$14; entrees $15–$23. AE, DC, MC, V. Tapas bar/cafe Wed–Sat 8am–1am. Car wash daily 8am–8pm.

Morgans ★ 🎁 BISTRO Located on a sketchy stretch of up-and-coming Wynwood across from the Shops at Midtown Miami, the cozy, charming Morgans is a welcome respite from the hype and circumstance surrounding this neighborhood. Housed in a two-story lavender house with striped black-and-white awnings and, its crown jewel, a large wraparound terrace, Morgans is where Miamians go for modern comfort food—"Voluptuous Grilled Cheese," sensational skinny fries, brioche French toast, mac and cheese, meatloaf with "smokey mash," and, well, you get the picture. Morgans serves three meals a day, but we prefer the daytime vibe for breakfast, brunch, and lunch. A tiny indoor dining room is minimal, clean, and Ikea-esque, but we highly recommend, when weather permits, grabbing a table on the porch and marveling at the paradox of gritty surroundings and oh-so-cozy confines and cuisine.

28 NE 29th St., Miami. © **305/573-9678.** http://themorgansrestaurant.com. Breakfast, brunch, and lunch $9–$21; dinner main courses $15–$26. AE, DC, MC, V. Tues–Thurs 11am–10pm; Fri 11am–11pm; Sat 8am–5pm and 6–11pm; Sun 8am–5pm.

Sakaya Kitchen ★★★ ASIAN The best no-frills, counter-service spot to hit the city since, well, nothing, Sakaya Kitchen is in a class of its own, serving seriously gourmet Asian fare, from traditional and street-hawker dishes to modern twists on classics. Chef/owner Richard Hales has a serious culinary pedigree, working for the legendary Jean-Georges Vongerichten in N.Y.C., and hasn't slacked in Miami, cooking up divine pork buns starring meat that marinates for 24 hours in a mix of brown sugar, toasted spices, and sesame oil before roasting for yet another 8 hours; Korean-style chicken wings marinated in a spicy Korean chili sauce; baby back ribs with a honey-and-orange glaze; and more. Much more. Sure, you stand in line (the wait is well worth it), order off a chalkboard, and use plastic utensils, but Sakaya Kitchen is the closest thing to Asia in Miami.

In the Shops at Midtown Miami, 3401 N. Miami Ave., Miami. © **305/576-8096.** Main courses $5–$19. AE, DC, MC, V. Sun noon–9pm; Mon–Sat noon–10pm.

Tobacco Road AMERICAN Miami's oldest bar is a bluesy, Route 66–inspired institution favored by barflies, professionals, and anyone else who wishes to indulge in good and greasy bar fare—chicken wings, nachos, and so on—at reasonable prices in a down-home, gritty-but-charming atmosphere. The burgers are also good—particularly the Death Burger, a deliciously unhealthful combo of choice sirloin topped with grilled onions, jalapeños, and pepper-jack cheese (bring on the Tums!). Also a live-music venue, the Road, as it's known by locals, is well traveled, especially during Friday's happy hour and Tuesday's Lobster Night, when 100 1¼-pound lobsters go for only $13 apiece.

626 S. Miami Ave. © **305/374-1198.** www.tobacco-road.com. Main courses $13–$17; burgers and sandwiches $6–$7. AE, DC, MC, V. Mon–Sat 11:30am–5am; Sun noon–5am. Cover $5–$10 Fri–Sat nights.

Little Havana

The main artery of Little Havana is a busy commercial strip called SW 8th Street, or Calle Ocho. Auto-body shops, cigar factories, and furniture stores line this street, and on every corner, there seems to be a pass-through window serving superstrong Cuban coffee and snacks. In addition, many of the Cuban, Dominican, Nicaraguan, Peruvian, and other Latin American immigrants have opened full-scale restaurants ranging from intimate candlelit establishments to bustling stand-up lunch counters.

To locate the restaurants in this section, see the map "Hotels & Restaurants in Greater Miami" (p. 83).

MODERATE

Hy-Vong ★ VIETNAMESE This place is a must in Little Havana, so expect to wait hours for a table and don't even think of mumbling a complaint. This Vietnamese cuisine combines the best of Asian and French cooking with spectacular results. Food at Hy-Vong is elegantly simple and superspicy. Appetizers include small, tightly packed Vietnamese spring rolls, and kimchi, a spicy, fermented cabbage (they ran out of it on our last visit, because we got there too late—so get there early!). Star entrees include pastry-enclosed chicken with watercress cream cheese sauce and fish in tangy mango sauce. Unfortunately, service here is not typically friendly or stellar—in fact, it borders on abysmal, but once you finally get your food, all will be forgotten.

Enjoy the wait with a traditional Vietnamese beer and lots of company. Outside this tiny storefront restaurant, you'll meet interesting students, musicians, and foodies who come for the large, delicious portions.

3458 SW 8th St. (btw. 34th and 35th aves.), Little Havana. ✆ **305/446-3674.** www.hyvong. com. Reservations accepted for parties of 5 or more. Main courses $7–$20. AE, DISC, MC, V. Sun–Thurs 6–11pm; Fri–Sat 6–11:30pm. Closed 2 weeks in Aug.

INEXPENSIVE

El Palacio de los Jugos ★ CUBAN Although the original is on West Flagler Street, this Little Havana outpost of the Cuban culinary landmark is just as good, if not better, serving fresh squeezed juices (guava, papaya, sugar cane, mango), tropical shakes, and some of the most authentic Cuban fare this side of Havana at prices that go back to the days when Havana was a bustling hot spot. Here, you'll find everything from oxtail to roasted chicken, pork ribs, and roast pork, and pretty much anything comes dished from a steam table with a heaping helping of either *arroz con pollo* or red beans and rice. You also get a generous hunk of boiled yuca with its traditional accompaniment of garlic and citrus mojo sauce. They also serve a fantastically cheap breakfast. It's loud, it's frenzied, it's almost 100% in Spanish, and it's one of the most delicious Miami experiences you will have for around five bucks.

14300 SW 8th St., Little Havana. ✆ **305/221-1615.** Juices and main courses $2–$5. No credit cards. Mon–Sat 7am–9pm; Sun 7am–8pm.

Versailles ★ CUBAN Versailles is the meeting place of Miami's Cuban power brokers, who meet daily over *café con leche* to discuss the future of the Cuban exiles' fate. A glorified diner, the place sparkles with glass, chandeliers, murals, and mirrors meant to evoke the French palace. There's nothing fancy here—nothing French, either—just straightforward food from the home country. The menu is a veritable survey of Cuban cooking and includes specialties such as Moors and Christians (flavorful black beans with white rice), *ropa vieja* (shredded beef stew), and fried whole fish. Versailles is the place to come for *mucho* helpings of Cuban kitsch. With its late hours, it's also the perfect place to come after spending your night in Little Havana.

3555 SW 8th St., Little Havana. ✆ **305/444-0240.** Main courses $5–$20; soup and salad $2–$10. DC, DISC, MC, V. Mon–Thurs 8am–2am; Fri 8am–3am; Sat 8am–4:30am; Sun 9am–1am.

Key Biscayne

Key Biscayne is home to the **Ritz-Carlton** (455 Grand Bay Dr., ✆ **305/365-4500;** www.ritzcarlton.com) and some of the world's nicest beaches and parks, yet it is not known for great food. Locals, or "Key rats," as they're known, tend to go off island for meals or takeout, but here is one of the best on-the-island choices.

To locate the restaurant in this section, see the map "Hotels & Restaurants in Greater Miami" (p. 83).

Coconut Grove

Coconut Grove was long known as the artists' haven of Miami, but the rush of developers trying to cash in on the laid-back charm of this old settlement has turned it into something of an overgrown mall. Still, there are several great dining spots both inside and outside the confines of Mayfair and CocoWalk.

To locate the restaurants in this section, see the map "Hotels & Restaurants in Greater Miami" (p. 83).

EXPENSIVE

George's in the Grove ★ FRENCH When the former owner of Le Bouchon du Grove opened his own bistro around the corner, shouts of *"mon Dieu!"* were heard loud and clear. But there's really no comparison. Whereas Le Bouchon is a traditional French bistro, George's is a modern version, with sleek decor and a sleeker champagne-sipping clientele. Entrees range from such classics as French onion soup, ratatouille, and steak frites to a very Miami mango *tarte tatin*. For something unusually good, try the pizza with duck confit, onion jam, aged Gruyère, and fresh shiitake mushrooms. For dessert, people plotz over the Nutella pizza. We're convinced that you can put Nutella on pretty much anything and people will go nuts. Overall, the food is good, but the ambience is better. As the night goes on, the music gets louder, champagne corks start a-popping, and a party scene ensues. If you want romance, go to Le Bouchon; if you want a *Sex and the City* scene, George's is *le place*. In 2010, George's opened in South Miami at 1549 Sunset Dr. (© **305/284-9989**).

3145 Commodore Plaza, Coconut Grove. © **305/444-7878.** www.georgesrestaurants.com. Main courses $13–$40. AE, DC, MC, V. Sun and Tues–Wed 6–11pm; Thurs–Sat 6pm–1am.

Le Bouchon du Grove ★ FRENCH This very authentic bistro is French right down to the waitstaff, who may speak only French to you, forgetting they're in the heart of Coconut Grove, U.S.A. But it matters not. The food, prepared by an animated French (what else?) chef, is good. It used to be superb, but it has fallen off a bit. Still, a delicious starter that's always reliable is the *gratinée Lyonnaise* (traditional French onion soup). Fish is brought in fresh daily; try the pan-seared sea bass *(dos de loup de mer roti)* when it's in season. Though slightly heavy on the oil, it is delivered with succulent artichokes, tomato confit, and seasoned roasted garlic, and it is a gastronomic triumph. The *carre d'agneau roti* (roasted rack of lamb with Provence herbs) is served warm and tender, with a perfect amount of seasoning. There's also an excellent selection of pricey, but drinkable, French and American red and white wines.

3430 Main Hwy., Coconut Grove. © **305/448-6060.** www.lebouchondugrove.com. Reservations recommended. Main courses $20–$30. AE, MC, V. Mon–Thurs 10am–3pm and 5–11pm; Fri 10am–3pm and 5pm–midnight; Sat 8am–3pm and 5pm–midnight; Sun 8am–3pm and 5–11pm.

Coral Gables & Environs

Coral Gables is a foodie's paradise—a city in which you certainly won't go hungry. What Starbucks is to most major cities, excellent gourmet and ethnic restaurants are to Coral Gables, where there's a restaurant on every corner and everywhere in between.

Jimbo's: Miami's Own Seafood Shack

Locals like to keep quiet about **Jimbo's**, Duck Lake Road, Virginia Key (© **305/361-7026**; www.jimbosplace.com), a ramshackle seafood shack that started as a gathering spot for fishermen and has since become the quintessential South Florida watering hole, snack bar, and hangout for those in the know. If ever Miami had a backwoods, this is it, right down to the smoldering garbage can, stray dogs, and chickens. Do *not* get dressed up to come here—you will get dirty. Go to the bathroom before you get here, too, because the porta-potties are absolutely rancid. Grab yourself a dollar can of beer (there's only beer, water, and soda, but you are allowed to bring your own choice of drink if you want) from the cooler and take in the view of the tropical lagoon where they shot *Flipper.* You may even see a manatee or two. Vacant shacks that served as backdrops for films such as *True Lies* surround this hidden enclave, which attracts everyone from shrimpers and politicians to well-oiled beach bums. Oddly enough, there's even a boccie court here, and the owner, Jimbo, may challenge you to a game. Play if you must, but word has it he never loses. Jimbo's smoked fish—marlin or salmon—is the best in town, but be forewarned: There are no utensils or napkins. When I asked for some, the woman said, "Lady, this is a place where you eat with your hands." I couldn't have said it better.

VERY EXPENSIVE

Palme d'Or ★★★ FRENCH Don't be fooled by the ornate setting—yes, it's rich, yes, it's fancy, oozing with old-world elegance, but the cuisine and the service are far from stuffy. Hailed by many as the city's top restaurant, Palme d'Or's New French cuisine is made utterly delicious and accessible via a unique tasting menu showcasing innovative interpretations of classic Continental cuisine, featuring exceptional local ingredients with specialties flown in directly from France and elsewhere. You can order a la carte, but we suggest you go with the prix-fixe menus—three plates at $42, four plates at $54, or five plates at $70. And choosing is tough with Chef Philippe Ruiz's genius in the form of always changing, evolving dishes such as pan-seared Hudson Valley foie gras with caramelized mango and *badiane* spice sauce; seared buffalo tenderloin with truffled potato *galette,* mushrooms, and an aged port-wine reduction; roasted white sturgeon filet with carrot coulis, *masala* spice, and sevruga caviar; braised short ribs with farro risotto, shallots, and carrot confit in a red-wine reduction; and grilled rack of lamb with Caribbean-style sweet potato mousseline, chayote, and aged rum sauce. Service is equally exceptional, almost seamless, making this one of Miami's best, if not the best, upscale dining experiences which, in light of other city restaurants of lesser quality and higher prices, is a deal in comparison.

At the Biltmore Hotel, 1200 Anastasia Ave., Coral Gables. © **305/913-3201.** Reservations recommended. Tasting menus $42–$70; a la carte $14–$20. AE, DC, MC, V. Tues–Sat 6–10:30pm.

EXPENSIVE

Ortanique on the Mile ★★★ NEW WORLD CARIBBEAN Chef Cindy Hutson has truly perfected tantalizing New World Caribbean cuisine. For starters, ask if the pumpkin bisque with a hint of pepper sherry is on the menu. If not, a spicy fried calamari salad is exceptional. Afterward, move on to the tropical mango salad with fresh marinated sable hearts of palm, julienne mango, baby field greens, toasted Caribbean candied pecans, and passion-fruit vinaigrette. For an entree, we recommend the pan-sautéed Bahamian black grouper marinated in teriyaki and sesame oil. It's served with an *ortanique* (an orangelike fruit) orange liqueur sauce and topped with steamed seasoned chayote, zucchini, and carrots on a lemon-orange *boniato*–sweet plantain mash. For dessert, try the chocolate mango tower—layers of brownie, chocolate mango mousse, meringue, and sponge cake, accompanied by mango sorbet and tropical-fruit salsa. Entrees may not be cheap, but they're a lot less than airfare to the islands, which is where most, if not all, of the ingredients hail from.

278 Miracle Mile (next to Actor's Playhouse), Coral Gables. ✆ **305/446-7710.** Reservations requested. Main courses $21–$44. AE, DC, MC, V. Mon–Tues 6–10pm; Wed–Sat 6–11pm; Sun 5:30–9:30pm.

MODERATE

Randazzo's Little Italy ★★★ ITALIAN This old-school, *Godfather*-influenced, *Goodfellas*-inspired, *Sopranos*-style Italian restaurant is a guaranteed knockout and not just because the owner is a former professional boxer, either. Come hungry and leave with your pants unbuttoned as this bustling, fun, and phenomenally garlicky restaurant has a way of making Little Italy seem mammoth thanks to huge portions of traditional favorites—sausage and peppers, meatballs and spaghetti, and rigatoni with vodka sauce, which one critic said was so good it could "bring any homesick Italian-American to tears." The house specialty is spaghetti with Sunday gravy—al dente strands of pasta studded with meatballs the size of wrecking balls (appropriately enough, they will wreck your diet) and large chunks of sweet and hot sausage. Although there are many distractions here, from the cacophonous crowd and gregarious former boxer owner to the TVs showing the aforementioned Italian-themed classics, the focus here is fully on the plate—which, if you finish, will earn you, too, major heavyweight status.

385 Miracle Mile, Coral Gables. ✆ **305/448-7002.** www.randazzoslittleitaly.com. Reservations strongly recommended. Main courses $20–$39. AE, DC, DISC, MC, V. Mon–Fri 11:30am–2:30pm; Mon–Thurs 6–10pm; Fri–Sat 6–11pm.

INEXPENSIVE

Miss Saigon Bistro ★★ VIETNAMESE Unlike Alain Boublil and Claude-Michel Schönberg's bombastic Broadway show, this Miss Saigon is small, quiet, and not at all flashy. Servers at this family-run restaurant will graciously recommend dishes or even have something custom-made for you. The menu is varied and reasonably priced, and the portions are huge—large enough to share. Noodle dishes and soup bowls are hearty and flavorful; caramelized prawns are fantastic, as is the whole snapper with lemon grass and ginger sauce. Despite the fact that there are few tables inside and a hungry crowd usually gathers outside in the street, you won't be rushed through your meal, which is worth savoring. There is also a much larger location at 9503 S. Dixie Hwy., in South Miami's Pinecrest (✆ **305/661-2911**).

148 Giralda Ave. (at Ponce de León and 37th Ave.), Coral Gables. ✆ **305/446-8006.** www.miss saigonbistro.com. Main courses $10–$22. AE, DC, DISC, MC, V. Mon and Wed–Thurs 11:30am–3pm and 5:30–10pm; Tues 11:30am–3pm and 6:30–10pm; Fri 11:30am–3pm and 5:30–11pm; Sat 5:30–11pm; Sun 5:30–10pm.

South Miami & West Miami

Though mostly residential, these areas nonetheless have several eating establishments worth the drive.

EXPENSIVE

Tropical Chinese ★ CHINESE This strip-mall restaurant, way out in West Miami–Dade, is hailed as the best Chinese restaurant in the city. While the food is indeed very good—certainly more interesting than at your typical beef-and-broccoli place—it still seems overpriced. But because good Chinese food in Miami is almost an oxymoronic statement save for some of the fancier restaurants, locals are known to make the trek west for a trip to Tropical. Garlic spinach and prawns in a clay pot are delicious, with the perfect mix of garlic cloves, mushrooms, and fresh spinach. But this isn't your typical Chinese takeout. It's not cheap. Unlike most Chinese restaurants, the dishes here are not large enough to share. Sunday-afternoon dim sum, with all sorts of dumplings, pork buns, and traditional bite-size items carted around to your table, is extremely popular, and lines often snake around the shopping center.

7991 Bird Rd., West Miami. ✆ **305/262-7576.** Reservations highly recommended on weekends. Main courses $10–$49. AE, DC, MC, V. Mon–Fri 11:30am–10:30pm; Sat 11am–11:30pm; Sun 10:30am–10pm. Take U.S. 1 to Bird Rd. and go west on Bird, all the way down to 78th Ave. The restaurant is btw. 78th and 79th on the north side of Bird Rd.

MODERATE

Town Kitchen & Bar ★ AMERICAN A lively neighborhood breakfast, lunch, dinner, and late-night bistro with a great bar scene, Town is where locals gather for good food—everything from Kobe sliders and seafood tacos to meal-worthy salads, seviches, mussel pots, brick-oven pizza, and main plates such as bacon-wrapped prawns, steaks, and hearty pasta dishes. Though we wouldn't necessarily make a special trip to South Miami for a meal at Town, if and when we *are* there, this is the place to eat.

7301 SW 57th Court, South Miami. ✆ **305/740-8118.** www.townkitchenbar.com. Reservations highly recommended on weekends. Burgers, salads, pizzas $9–$14; main courses $15–$33. AE, DC, MC, V. Mon–Fri 11:30am–2am; Sat–Sun 8am–2am.

INEXPENSIVE

El Toro Taco Family Restaurant ★ 🎒 MEXICAN We've put major mileage on our cars since we first stumbled upon this 96-seat, no-frills family-run restaurant a few years ago, when we were lost and very hungry. Deliciously authentic Mexican fare—tacos, enchiladas, and burritos drenched with the freshest and zestiest salsa this side of Baja—is what you'll find here in abundance, although other Mexican fans disagree. It may sound odd to travel from a big city with tons of restaurants to farm country for Mexican food, but trust us: It's so cheap and delicious, it's worth the trip. Corona fans: Don't forget to BYOB.

1 S. Krome Ave., Homestead. ✆ **305/245-8182.** Main courses $2–$15. DISC, MC, V. Tues–Sun 10am–9pm; Fri–Sat 10am–10pm. Take 836 W. (Dolphin Expwy.) toward Miami International Airport. Take Florida Turnpike S. ramp toward Florida City/Key West. Take U.S. 41/SW 8th St. exit (exit 25) and turn left onto SW 8th St. Take SW 8th St. to Krome Ave. (¼ mile) and turn left.

White Lion Cafe ★ 🎁 AMERICAN The quintessence of a quaint off-the-beaten-path eatery in not-so-quaint Miami, the White Lion Cafe is a hidden gem serving Southern-style blue-plate specials, including delicious meatloaf and fried chicken. There's also an extensive entertainment calendar here, with everything from live jazz to karaoke. If you're in the Homestead area en route to or coming from the Keys, it's definitely worth a stop here, where time seems to stand still, at least until the band starts playing.

146 NW 7th St., Homestead. 🕽 **305/248-1076.** www.whitelioncafe.com. Main courses $10–$22. AE, DISC, MC, V. Daily 5pm until "the fat lady sings." Take the 836 E. to the 826 S., at exit 6 make a left and head West on 8th St. (Campbell Dr.), after crossing Krome Ave. take a left at 1st Ave. (the very next light), and turn right on 7th St. The cafe is on the left.

WHAT TO SEE & DO IN MIAMI

5

f there's one thing Miami doesn't have, it's an identity crisis—multiple personalities, maybe, but hardly a crisis. In fact, it's the city's vibrant, multifaceted personality that attracts millions each year from all over the world. South Beach may be on the top of many Miami to-do lists, but the rest of the city—a fascinating assemblage of multicultural neighborhoods, some on the verge of a popularity explosion—should not be overlooked. Once considered "God's Waiting Room," the Magic City now attracts an eclectic mix of old and young, celebs and plebes, American and international, and geek and chic with an equally varied roster of activities.

For starters, Miami boasts some of the world's most natural beauty, with dazzling blue waters, fine sandy beaches, and lush tropical parks. The city's man-made brilliance, in the form of crayon-colored architecture, never seems to fade in Miami's unique Art Deco district. For cultural variation, you can experience the tastes, sounds, and rhythms of Cuba in Little Havana.

As in any metropolis, though, some areas aren't as great as others. Downtown Miami, for instance, is still in the throes of a major, albeit slow, renaissance, in which the sketchier warehouse sections of the city are being transformed into hubs of all things hip. In contrast to this development, however, are the still-poverty-stricken areas of downtown such as Overtown, Liberty City, and Little Haiti (though Overtown is striving to transform itself into the Overtown Historic Village, showcasing its landmarks such as the famous Lyric Theater and the home of DA Dorsey, Miami's first African-American millionaire). While we obviously advise you to exercise caution when exploring the less-traveled parts of the city, we would also be remiss if we were to tell you to bypass them completely.

Lose yourself in the city's nature and its neighborhoods and, best of all, its people—a sassy collection of artists and intellectuals, beach bums and international transplants, dolled-up drag queens and bodies beautiful.

MIAMI'S BEACHES

Perhaps Miami's most popular attraction is its incredible 35-mile stretch of beachfront, which runs from the tip of South Beach north to Sunny Isles, then circles Key Biscayne and numerous other pristine islands dotting the Atlantic. The characteristics of Miami's many beaches are as varied as the city's population: There are beaches for swimming, socializing, or serenity; for family, seniors, or gay singles; some to make you forget you're in the city, others darkened by huge condominiums. Whatever type of beach vacation you're looking for, you'll find it in one of Miami's two distinct beach areas: Miami Beach and Key Biscayne. And in keeping up with technology, Miami Beach is now officially a hot spot—as in a wireless hotspot, offering 95% coverage outdoors (70% indoors) of free Wi-Fi throughout the entire city and, yes, even on the sand.

FACING PAGE: **You can spend the day on the beach, and enjoy more urban pursuits at night in Miami.**

You can bag some rays (and some z's) after a night of partying in Miami Beach.

MIAMI BEACH'S BEACHES Collins Avenue fronts more than a dozen miles of white-sand beach and blue-green waters from 1st to 192nd streets. Although most of this stretch is lined with a solid wall of hotels and condos, beach access is plentiful. There are lots of public beaches here, wide and well maintained, complete with lifeguards, restroom facilities, concession stands, and metered parking (bring lots of quarters). Except for a thin strip close to the water, most of the sand is hard packed—the result of a $10-million Army Corps of Engineers Beach Rebuilding Project meant to protect buildings from the effects of eroding sand.

In general, the beaches on this barrier island (all on the eastern, ocean side of the island) become less crowded the farther north you go. A wooden boardwalk runs along the hotel side of the beach from 21st to 46th streets—about 1½ miles—offering a terrific sun-and-surf experience without getting sand in your shoes. Miami's lifeguard-protected public beaches include 21st Street, at the beginning of the boardwalk; 35th Street, popular with an older crowd; 46th Street, next to the Fontainebleau Hotel; 53rd Street, a narrower, more sedate beach; 64th Street, one of the quietest strips around; and 72nd Street, a local old-timers' spot.

KEY BISCAYNE'S BEACHES If Miami Beach doesn't provide the privacy you're looking for, try Virginia Key and Key Biscayne. Crossing the Rickenbacker Causeway ($1.50 toll), however, can be a lengthy process, especially on weekends, when beach bums and tan-o-rexics flock to the Key. The 5 miles of public beach there, however, are blessed with softer sand and are less developed and more laid-back than the hotel-laden strips to the north. In 2008, Key Biscayne reopened the historic **Virginia Key Beach Park,** 4020 Virginia Beach Dr. (© **305/960-4600**), the former "colored only" beach that opened in 1945 and closed in 1982 because of high maintenance costs. After an $11-million renovation, the 83-acre historic site features picnic tables and grills, shoreline renourishment, a new playground for children with special needs, and a miniature railroad. The beach eventually plans to open a civil rights museum as well. Open from sunrise to sunset daily, with free admission.

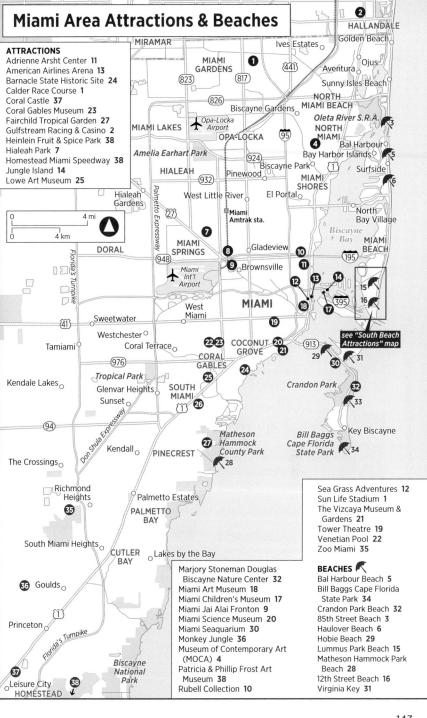

Miami Area Attractions & Beaches

ATTRACTIONS
Adrienne Arsht Center **11**
American Airlines Arena **13**
Barnacle State Historic Site **24**
Calder Race Course **1**
Coral Castle **37**
Coral Gables Museum **23**
Fairchild Tropical Garden **27**
Gulfstream Racing & Casino **2**
Heinlein Fruit & Spice Park **38**
Hialeah Park **7**
Homestead Miami Speedway **38**
Jungle Island **14**
Lowe Art Museum **25**

Sea Grass Adventures **12**
Sun Life Stadium **1**
The Vizcaya Museum & Gardens **21**
Tower Theatre **19**
Venetian Pool **22**
Zoo Miami **35**

BEACHES
Bal Harbour Beach **5**
Bill Baggs Cape Florida State Park **34**
Crandon Park Beach **32**
85th Street Beach **3**
Haulover Beach **6**
Hobie Beach **29**
Lummus Park Beach **15**
Matheson Hammock Park Beach **28**
12th Street Beach **16**
Virginia Key **31**

Marjory Stoneman Douglas Biscayne Nature Center **32**
Miami Art Museum **18**
Miami Children's Museum **17**
Miami Jai Alai Fronton **9**
Miami Science Museum **20**
Miami Seaquarium **30**
Monkey Jungle **36**
Museum of Contemporary Art (MOCA) **4**
Patricia & Phillip Frost Art Museum **38**
Rubell Collection **10**

see "South Beach Attractions" map

THE ART DECO DISTRICT (SOUTH BEACH)

"You know what they used to say? 'Who's Art?'" recalls Art Deco revivalist Dona Zemo. "You'd say, 'This is an Art Deco building,' and they'd say, 'Really, who is Art?'"

How things have changed. This guy Art has become one of the most popular Florida attractions since, well, that mouse named Mickey. The district is roughly bounded by the Atlantic Ocean on the east, Alton Road on the west, 6th Street to the south, and Dade Boulevard (along the Collins Canal) to the north.

Simply put, Art Deco is a style of architecture that, in its heyday of the 1920s and 1930s, used to be considered ultramodern. Today, fans of the style consider it retro fabulous. But while some people may not consider the style fabulous, it's undoubtedly retro. According to the experts, Art Deco made its debut in 1925 at an exposition in Paris in which it set a stylistic tone, with buildings based on early neoclassical styles with the application of exotic motifs such as flora, fauna, and fountains based on geometric patterns. In Miami, Art Deco is marked by the pastel-hued buildings that line South Beach and Miami Beach. But it's a lot more than just color. If you look carefully, you will see the intricacies and impressive craftsmanship that went into each building in Miami back in the '20s, '30s, '40s, and today, thanks to intensive restoration.

Most of the finest examples of the whimsical Art Deco style are concentrated along three parallel streets—Ocean Drive, Collins Avenue, and Washington Avenue—from about 6th to 23rd streets.

After years of neglect and calls for the wholesale demolition of its buildings, South Beach got a new lease on life in 1979. Under the leadership of Barbara Baer Capitman, a dedicated crusader for the Art Deco region, and the Miami Design Preservation League, founded by Baer Capitman and five friends, an area

 walking **BY DESIGN**

The Miami Design Preservation League offers several tours of Miami Beach's historic architecture, all of which leave from the Art Deco Welcome Center at 1001 Ocean Dr., in Miami Beach. A self-guided audio tour (available 7 days a week, 10am–4pm) turns the streets into a virtual outdoor museum, taking you through Miami Beach's Art Deco district at your own leisure, with tours in several languages for just $15 for adults, $10 for seniors. Guided tours conducted by local historians and architects offer an in-depth look at the structures and their history. The 90-minute Ocean Drive and Beyond tour (offered every Wed and Sat at 10:30am) takes you through the district, pointing out the differences between Mediterranean Revival and Art Deco for $20 for adults, $15 for seniors. If you're not blinded by neon, the Thursday-night Art Deco District Up-to-Date Tour (leaving at 6:30pm) will whisk you around for a 90-minute walk, making note of how certain local hot spots were architecturally famous way before the likes of Madonna and Co. entered the scene. The cost is $20 for adults, $15 for seniors. For those who have no time or patience for group tours, there are self-guided ones and even a cellphone tour for that person who can't keep the phone off his or her ears. For more information on tours or reservations, call ✆ **305/672-2014** or log on to www.mdpl.org.

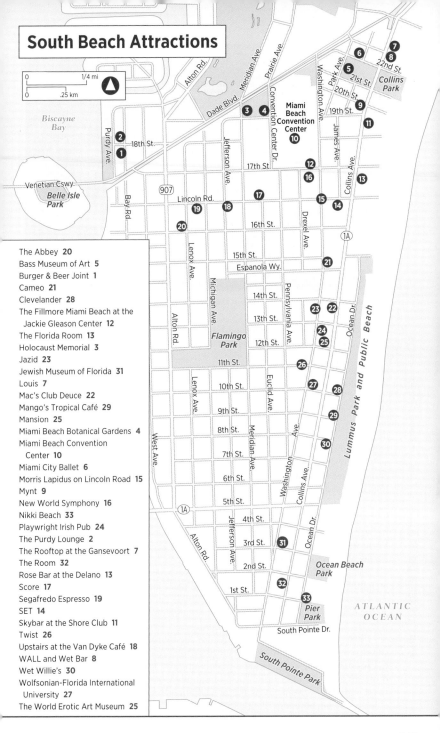

South Beach Attractions

0   1/4 mi
0   .25 km

Biscayne Bay

Venetian Cswy.

Belle Isle Park

Miami Beach Convention Center

Collins Park

Flamingo Park

Lummus Park and Public Beach

Ocean Beach Park

Pier Park

South Pointe Park

ATLANTIC OCEAN

Classic Art Deco architecture is on display at The Carlyle on Collins Avenue.

made up of an estimated 800 buildings was granted a listing on the National Register of Historic Places. Designers then began highlighting long-lost architectural details with soft sherbet shades of peach, periwinkle, turquoise, and purple. Developers soon moved in, and the full-scale refurbishment of the area's hotels was underway.

Not everyone was pleased, though. Former Miami Beach commissioner Abe Resnick said, "I love old buildings. But these Art Deco buildings are 40, 50 years old. They aren't historic. They aren't special. We shouldn't be forced to keep them." But Miami Beach kept those buildings, and Resnick lost his seat on the commission.

Today hundreds of new establishments—hotels, restaurants, and nightclubs—have renovated these older, historic buildings, putting South Beach on the cutting edge of Miami's cultural and nightlife scene.

Exploring the Area

If you're touring this unique neighborhood on your own, start at the **Art Deco Welcome Center,** 1001 Ocean Dr. (© **305/531-3484**), which is run by the Miami Design Preservation League. The only beachside building across from the Clevelander Hotel and bar, the center gives away lots of informational material, including maps and pamphlets, and runs guided tours around the neighborhood. Art Deco books (including *The Art Deco Guide,* an informative compendium of all the buildings here), T-shirts, postcards, mugs, and other paraphernalia are for sale. It's open daily from 10am to 7:30pm.

Take a stroll along **Ocean Drive** for the best view of sidewalk cafes, bars, colorful hotels, and even more colorful people. Another great place for a walk is **Lincoln Road,** which is lined with boutiques, large chain stores, cafes, and funky art and antiques stores. The Community Church, at the corner of Lincoln Road and Drexel Avenue, was the neighborhood's first church and is one of its oldest surviving buildings, dating from 1921.

Or, if you prefer to cruise South Beach in a tiny yellow buggy—part scooter, part golf cart—consider **GoCar,** 1661 James Ave. (© **888/462-2755;** www.go cartours.com), a three-wheeled vehicle for two that comes with a GPS device that not only tracks and tells you where to go, but also prompts a recorded tour that kicks on with every site you cruise by. A 1-hour tour is $49, 3-hour tour is $99, and all-day tour is $150.

MIAMI'S MUSEUM & ART SCENE

Miami has never been known as a cultural mecca as far as museums are concerned, though its reputation is improving thanks to the international attention brought to the scene by such esteemed fairs as Switzerland's Art Basel, which comes to Miami for a few days every December. The focal point of Art Basel is **Collins Park Cultural Center** (www.collinspark.us), which comprises a trio of arts buildings on Collins Park and Park Avenue (off Collins Ave.), bounded by 21st to 23rd streets—the expanded Bass Museum of Art (see below), the new Arquitectonica-designed home of the Miami City Ballet, and the Miami Beach Regional Library, an ultramodern building designed by architect Robert A. M. Stern, with a special focus on the arts. Collins Park, the former site of the Miami Beach Library, returned to its original incarnation as an open space extending to the Atlantic, but it is also now the site of large sculpture installations and cultural activities planned jointly by the organizations that share the space. A few cultural institutions that are part of the emerging Collins Park neighborhood are local arts organization **SoBe Arts** at the Carl Fisher complex; the **Miami Beach Botanical Garden;** the **CANDO Arts Co-Op,** a 5,000-square-foot gallery at 309 23rd St. that's free and open to the public, featuring 12 resident artists, open Thursday and Friday 4 to 7pm and Saturday and Sunday from noon to 6pm; and the Holocaust Memorial. For updates on construction progress and a brochure of all Collins Park venues, check out the neighborhood's comprehensive website.

Bass Museum of Art ★★★ The Bass Museum of Art has expanded and received a dramatically new look, rendering it Miami's most progressive art museum. World-renowned Japanese architect Arata Isozaki designed the magnificent new facility, which has triple the former exhibition space, and added an outdoor sculpture terrace, a museum cafe and courtyard, and a museum shop, among other improvements. In addition to providing space in which to show the permanent collection, exhibitions of a scale and quality not previously seen in Miami will now be featured at the Bass. The museum's permanent collection includes European paintings from the 15th to the early 20th centuries, with special emphasis on northern European art of the Renaissance and baroque periods, including Dutch and Flemish masters. Among the artists in the museum's permanent collection: Jacob Jordaens, Peter Paul Rubens, Gerard Seghers, Ferdinand Bol, and Giovanni Barbagelata. Past exhibitions have included the works of Picasso, Frida Kahlo, and Francois-Marie Banier. The museum also has a lab, the New Information Workshop, making it possible for all aspiring artists to create their own masterpieces on computers free or for a nominal charge.

2121 Park Ave. (1 block west of Collins Ave.), South Beach. © **305/673-7530.** www.bassmuseum. org. Admission $8 adults, $6 students and seniors, free for children 6 and under, free 2nd Thurs of the month 6–9pm. Tues–Wed and Fri–Sat 10am–5pm; Thurs 10am–9pm; Sun 11am–5pm.

Coral Gables Museum This museum is housed in a restored version of the city's original 1930 coral-rock police and fire station and pays homage to the City Beautiful with a 3,000-square-foot gallery, a 5,000-square-foot public plaza, and a permanent, evolving exhibit examining Coral Gables' history. It will likely open its first exhibit in October 2011. Planned programming will have a heavy focus on architecture, urban design, and sustainable development.

285 Aragon Ave., Coral Gables. ✆ **305/910-3996.** www.coralgablesmuseum.org. Admission $7 adults, $4 children 6 and under, free for members. Daily noon–8pm.

Holocaust Memorial ★★★ This heart-wrenching memorial is hard to miss and would be a shame to overlook. The powerful centerpiece, Kenneth Treister's *A Sculpture of Love and Anguish,* depicts victims of the concentration camps crawling up a giant yearning hand stretching up to the sky, marked with an Auschwitz number tattoo. Along the reflecting pool is the story of the Holocaust, told in cut marble slabs. Inside the center of the memorial is a tableau that is one of the most solemn and moving tributes to the millions of Jews who lost their lives in the Holocaust we've seen. You can walk through an open hallway lined with photographs and the names of concentration camps and their victims. From the street, you'll see the outstretched arm, but do stop and tour the sculpture at ground level.

1933 Meridian Ave. (at Dade Blvd.), South Beach. ✆ **305/538-1663.** www.holocaustmmb.org. Free admission. Daily 9am–9pm.

Jewish Museum of Florida ★ Chronicling over 230 years of Jewish heritage and experiences in Florida, the Jewish Museum presents a fascinating look at religion and culture through films, lectures, and exhibits such as Mosaic: Jewish Life in Florida, which features more than 500 photos and artifacts documenting the Jewish experience in Florida since 1763. Housed in a former synagogue, the museum also delves into the Jewish roots of Latin America.

301 Washington Ave., South Beach. ✆ **305/672-5044.** www.jewishmuseum.com. Admission $6 adults, $5 seniors and students, $12 families, free on Sat. Tues–Sun 10am–5pm. Closed Jewish holidays.

Lowe Art Museum ★★ Located on the University of Miami campus, the Lowe Art Museum has a dazzling collection of 8,000 works that include American paintings, Latin American art, Navajo and Pueblo Indian textiles, and Renaissance and baroque art. Traveling exhibits, such as *Wine Spectator* magazine's classic posters of the Belle Epoque, also stop here. For the most part, the Lowe is known for its collection of Greek and Roman antiquities and, as compared to the more modern MOCA, Bass, and Miami Art Museum, features mostly European and international art hailing back to ancient times.

University of Miami, 1301 Stanford Dr. (at Ponce de León Blvd.), Coral Gables. ✆ **305/284-3603.** www.lowemuseum.org. Admission $10 adults, $5 seniors and students with ID. Donation day is 1st Tues of the month. Tues–Wed and Fri–Sat 10am–5pm; Thurs noon–7pm; Sun noon–5pm.

Miami Art Museum ★★★ The Miami Art Museum (MAM) features an eclectic mix of modern and contemporary works by such artists as Eric Fischl, Max Beckmann, Jim Dine, Robert Rauschenberg, Chuck Close, James Rosenquist, Jose Bedia, Marcel Duchamp, and Stuart Davis. Rotating exhibitions span ages and styles, and often focus on Latin American or Caribbean artists. JAM at MAM is the museum's popular happy hour, which takes place on the third Thursday of the month and is tied in to a particular exhibit. Almost as artistic as the works inside the museum is the composite sketch of the people—young and old—who attend these events.

The Miami-Dade Cultural Center, where the museum is housed, is a fortresslike complex designed by Philip Johnson. In addition to the acclaimed Miami Art Museum, the center houses the main branch of the Miami-Dade Public Library, which sometimes features art and cultural exhibits, and the Historical Museum of Southern Florida, which highlights the fascinating history of the area. Unfortunately, the plaza onto which the complex opens is home to many of those in downtown Miami's homeless population, which makes it a bit off-putting but not dangerous. Work has yet to begin on Museum Park, a $200-plus-million project on an underused 29-acre property on the bay in downtown Miami that will become MAM's new home. The 125,000-square-foot Museum Park will include a sculpture garden and spacious galleries as well as the new Miami Science Museum. Estimated completion is sometime in 2013. To check on its status—or lack thereof—go to **www.miamiartmuseum.org/museum_park.asp**.

101 W. Flagler St., Miami. ℂ **305/375-3000.** www.miamiartmuseum.org. Admission $8 adults, $4 seniors, free for children 11 and under. Tues–Fri 10am–5pm; 3rd Thurs of each month 10am–9pm; Sat–Sun noon–5pm. Closed major holidays. From I-95 south, exit at Orange Bowl–NW 8th St. and continue south to NW 2nd St.; turn left at NW 2nd St. and go 1½ blocks to NW 2nd Ave.; turn right.

Miami Children's Museum ★★ ☺ The Children's Museum, located on the MacArthur Causeway, across from Jungle Island, is a modern, albeit odd-looking, 56,500-square-foot facility that includes 14 galleries, classrooms, a parent/teacher resource center, a Kid Smart educational gift shop, a 200-seat auditorium, a Subway restaurant, and an outdoor, interactive play area. The museum offers hundreds of bilingual, interactive exhibits as well as programs, classes, and learning materials related to arts, culture, community, and communication. Even as an adult, I have to say I was tempted to participate in some kids-only activities and exhibitions, such as the miniature Bank of America and Publix Supermarket, and a re-creation of the NBC 6 television studio. There's also a re-creation of a Carnival cruise ship and a gallery of teddy bears from around the world. Perhaps the coolest thing of all is the World Music Studio, in which aspiring rock stars can lay down a few tracks and play instruments.

980 MacArthur Causeway, Miami. ℂ **305/373-5437.** www.miamichildrensmuseum.org. Admission $15 adults and children 13 months and over, $12 Florida residents. Daily 10am–6pm.

Miami Science Museum ★★ ☺ The Miami Science Museum features more than 140 hands-on exhibits that explore the mysteries of the universe. Live demonstrations and collections of rare natural history specimens make a visit here fun and informative. Many of the demos involve audience participation, which can be lots of fun for willing and able kids and adults alike. There is also the Wildlife Center, with more than 175 live reptiles and birds of prey. The adjacent Space Transit Planetarium projects astronomy and laser shows as well as interactive demonstrations of upcoming computer technology and cyberspace features. Call or visit the website for a list of upcoming exhibits and laser shows. Construction began in the fall of 2010 on the museum's new $275-million home at Museum Park (see above), a tri-level natural light and solar-powered homage to high-tech science and technology, including a cone-shaped aquarium tank and an egg-shaped planetarium with views of Biscayne Bay.

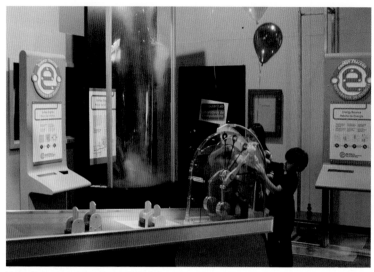

It's hands-on time at the Miami Science Museum.

3280 S. Miami Ave. (just south of the Rickenbacker Causeway), Coconut Grove. ☏ **305/646-4200.** www.miamisci.org. Admission $15 adults; $11 seniors, students, and children 3–12; free for children 2 and under. Daily 10am–6pm; 1st Fri of every month 10am–10pm; call for showtimes (last show 4pm Mon–Fri and 5pm Sat–Sun). Closed Thanksgiving and Christmas.

Museum of Contemporary Art (MOCA) ★★★ MOCA boasts an impressive collection of internationally acclaimed art with a local flavor. It is also known for its forward thinking and ability to discover and highlight new artists. A high-tech screening facility allows for film presentations to complement the exhibitions. Permanent collection includes works by John Baldessari, Dan Flavin, Dennis Oppenheim, Alex Katz, Louise Nevelson, Edward Ruscha, Gabriel Orozco, Julian Schnabel, Zoe Leonard, Nam June Paik, Uta Barth, Teresita Fernandez, Garry Simmons, Jose Bedia, Anna Gaskel, Thomas Hirschhorn, Mariko Mori, John Bock, Pierre Huyghe, Philippe Parreno, Edward Kienholz, Raymond Pettibon, and Matthew Ritchie, plus there are often special exhibitions by such artists as Yoko Ono, Sigmar Polke, and Goya. Guided tours are offered in English, Spanish, French, Creole, Portuguese, German, and Italian. Construction on a 4,000-square-foot expansion of the museum is expected to begin in late 2010 and will include an education wing, a new art storage facility, and enhanced public areas.

770 NE 125th St., North Miami. ☏ **305/893-6211.** Fax 305/891-1472. www.mocanomi.org. Admission $5 adults, $3 seniors and students with ID, free for children 12 and under. Tues by donation. Tues–Sat 11am–5pm; Sun noon–5pm. Closed major holidays.

Patricia and Phillip Frost Art Museum ★★ Housed in a $16-million building designed by architect Yann Weymouth, the Patricia and Phillip Frost Art Museum, located on the campus of Florida International University, was closed to the public until 2009. Today, it is the only art museum in Florida to attempt to exhibit paintings in natural light. The museum has recently begun to present exhibitions in Latin America and is working on future collaborations and partnerships with leading art institutions in those regions. Among the permanent collections is the General Collection, which holds a strong representation of American printmaking from the 1960s and 1970s, photography, pre-Columbian objects dating from A.D. 200 to 500, and a growing number of works by contemporary Caribbean and Latin American artists.

Florida International University, 10975 SW 17th St. © **305/348-2890.** http://thefrost.fiu.edu. Free admission. Tues–Sat 10am–5pm; Sun noon–5pm.

Rubell Family Art Collection ★★★ 🎁 This impressive collection, owned by the Miami hotelier family the Rubells, is housed in a two-story, 40,000-square-foot former Drug Enforcement Agency warehouse in a sketchy area north of downtown Miami. The building looks like a fortress, which is fitting: Inside is a priceless collection of more than 1,000 works of contemporary art by the likes of Keith Haring, Damien Hirst, Julian Schnabel, Jean-Michel Basquiat, Paul McCarthy, Charles Ray, and Cindy Sherman. But *be forewarned:* Some of the art is extremely graphic and may be off-putting to some. The gallery changes exhibitions twice yearly, and there is a seasonal program of lectures, artists' talks, and performances by prominent artists.

95 NW 29th St. (on the corner of NW 1st Ave. near the Design District), Miami. © **305/573-6090.** www.rubellfamilycollection.com. Admission $10 adults, $5 seniors and students. Dec 1–May 31 10am–6pm; by private appointment otherwise.

Wolfsonian–Florida International University ★★★ 🎁 Mitchell Wolfson, Jr., heir to a family fortune built on movie theaters, was known as an eccentric, but we'd call him a pack rat. A premier collector of propaganda and advertising art, Wolfson was spending so much money storing his booty that he decided to buy the warehouse that was housing it. It ultimately held more than 70,000 of his items, from controversial Nazi propaganda to King Farouk of Egypt's match collection. Thrown in the eclectic mix are also zany works from great modernists such as Charles Eames and Marcel Duchamp. Wolfson then gave this incredibly diverse collection to Florida International University. The former 1927 storage facility has been transformed into a museum that is the envy of curators around the world. The museum is unquestionably fascinating and hosts lectures and rather swinging events surrounding particular exhibits. **The Dynamo,** the museum's cafe and shop, is a fun and funky spot serving coffee, wine, beer, and nibbles, whose focal point is a large library shelving system from the late 19th century. The design represents the first modular book-

Visitors check out the cutting-edge art at the Rubell Family Art Collection.

The eclectic collection at the Wolfsonian offers all kinds of art and artifacts.

stacking system ever created. Leave it to the Wolfsonian to make even its restaurant a piece of work!

1001 Washington Ave., South Beach. ℂ **305/531-1001.** www.wolfsonian.org. Admission $7 adults; $5 seniors, students with ID, and children 6–12; free after 6pm on Fri. Sat–Tues noon–6pm; Thurs–Fri noon–9pm.

The World Erotic Art Museum ★ The Hustler store across the street has nothing on this wacky, X-rated museum. Opened in 2005 by then-70-year-old grandmother Naomi Wilzig, the museum features Wilzig's collection of more than 4,000 pieces of erotic art, including Kama Sutra temple carvings from India, peekaboo Victorian figurines that flash their booties, and a prop from the sexual thriller *A Clockwork Orange*. The 12,000-square-foot museum is located above Mansion, a club that's no stranger to erotic art—that is, performance art. This is a great place to spend an hour or two on a rainy day, and more than anything, the stuff is more amusing than sexy or racy.

1205 Washington Ave., South Beach. ℂ **305/532-9336.** www.weam.com. Admission $15 adults, $14 seniors and students. Children 17 and under not admitted. Mon and Wed–Thurs 11am–10pm; Fri–Sun 11am–midnight.

HISTORIC HOMES & SITES

South Beach's well-touted Art Deco District is but one of many colorful neighborhoods that can boast dazzling architecture. The rediscovery of the entire Biscayne Corridor (from downtown to about 80th St. and Biscayne Blvd.) has given light to a host of ancillary neighborhoods on either side, which are filled with Mediterranean-style homes and Frank Lloyd Wright gems. Coral Gables is home to many large and beautiful homes, mansions, and churches that reflect architecture from the 1920s, 1930s, and 1940s. Some of the homes, or portions of their structures, have been created from coral rock and shells. The Biltmore Hotel is also filled with history; see p. 107.

Barnacle State Historic Site ★★ The former home of naval architect and early settler Ralph Middleton Munroe is now a museum in the heart of Coconut Grove. It's the oldest house in Miami and it rests on its original foundation, which sits on 5 acres of natural hardwood forest and landscaped lawns. The house's quiet surroundings, wide porches, and period furnishings illustrate how Miami's first snowbird lived in the days before condomania and luxury hotels. Enthusiastic and knowledgeable state park employees provide a wealth of historical information to those interested in quiet, low-tech attractions such as this one. On Wednesdays from 6 to 7:30pm, they have sunset yoga by the sea. Call for details on the fabulous monthly moonlight concerts during which folk, blues, or classical music is presented and picnicking is encouraged.

3485 Main Hwy. (1 block south of Commodore Plaza), Coconut Grove. ✆ **305/448-9445.** Fax 305/448-7484. Admission $2. Tours $3 adults, $1 children 6–12. Concerts $7 adults, $3 children 6–9, free for children 5 and under. Fri–Mon 9am–4pm. Tours Fri–Mon at 10am, 11:30am, 1pm, and 2:30pm. From downtown Miami, take U.S. 1 south to 27th Ave., make a left, and continue to S. Bayshore Dr.; then make a right, follow to the intersection of Main Hwy., and turn left.

Coral Castle ★ 👫 There's plenty of competition, but Coral Castle is probably the strangest attraction in Florida. In 1923, the story goes, a 26-year-old crazed Latvian, suffering from the unrequited love of a 16-year-old who left him at the altar, immigrated to South Miami and spent the next 25 years of his life carving huge boulders into a prehistoric-looking roofless "castle." It seems impossible that one rather short man could have done all this, but there are scores of affidavits on display from neighbors who swear it happened. Apparently, experts have studied this phenomenon to help figure out how the great pyramids and Stonehenge were built. Rocker Billy Idol was said to have been inspired by this place to write his song "Sweet 16." An interesting 25-minute audio tour guides you through the spot, now on the National Register of Historic Places. Although Coral Castle is overpriced and undermaintained, it's worth a visit when you're in the area, which is about 37 miles from Miami.

28655 S. Dixie Hwy., Homestead. ✆ **305/248-6345.** www.coralcastle.com. Admission $9.75 adults, $6.50 seniors, $5 children 7–12. Group rates available. Sun–Thurs 8am–6pm; Fri–Sat 8am–8pm. Take 836 W (Dolphin Expwy.) toward Miami International Airport. Merge onto 826 S. (Palmetto Expwy.) and take it to the Florida Tpk. toward Homestead. Take the 288th St. exit (#5) and then take a right on S. Dixie Hwy., a left on SW 157th Ave., and then a sharp left back onto S. Dixie Hwy. Coral Castle is on the left side of the street.

Visitors wander the otherworldly grounds of the Coral Castle.

Enjoy a cool dip in a historic Venetian pool.

Venetian Pool ★★★ ☺ Miami's most beautiful and unusual swimming pool, dating from 1924, is hidden behind pastel stucco walls and is honored with a listing in the National Register of Historic Places. Underground artesian wells feed the free-form lagoon, which is shaded by three-story Spanish porticos and has both fountains and waterfalls. It can be cold in the winter months. During summer, the pool's 800,000 gallons of water are drained and refilled nightly, thanks to an underground aquifer, ensuring a cool, *clean* swim. Visitors are free to swim and sunbathe here, just as Esther Williams and Johnny Weissmuller did decades ago. For a modest fee, you or your children can learn to swim during special summer programs.

2701 DeSoto Blvd. (at Toledo St.), Coral Gables. ✆ **305/460-5356.** www.venetianpool.com. Admission $11 for those 13 and older, $6.30 for children 12 and under. Children must be at least 3 (parents must provide proof of child's age with birth certificate) or 38 in. tall to enter. Tues–Fri 11am–5:30pm; Fri–Sat 10am–4:30pm.

The Vizcaya Museum and Gardens ★★★ Sometimes referred to as the "Hearst Castle of the East," this magnificent villa is more Gatsby-esque than anything else you'll find in Miami. It was built in 1916 as a winter retreat for James Deering, cofounder and former vice president of International Harvester. The industrialist was fascinated by 16th-century art and architecture, and his ornate mansion, which took 1,000 artisans 5 years to build, became a celebration of that period. If you love antiques, this place is a dream come true, packed with European relics and works of art from the 16th to the 19th centuries. Most of the original furnishings, including dishes and paintings, are still intact. You will see very early versions of a telephone switchboard, central vacuum-cleaning system, elevators, and fire sprinklers. A free guided tour of the 34 furnished rooms on the first floor takes about 45 minutes. The second floor, which consists mostly of bedrooms, is open to tour on your own. The spectacularly opulent villa wraps itself around a central courtyard. Outside, lush formal gardens, accented with statuary, balustrades, and decorative urns, front an enormous swath of Biscayne Bay. Definitely take the tour of the rooms, but immediately thereafter, you will want to wander and get lost in the resplendent gardens.

3251 S. Miami Ave. (just south of Rickenbacker Causeway), north Coconut Grove. ✆ **305/250-9133.** www.vizcayamuseum.com. Admission $15 adults, $10 seniors, $6 children 6–12, free for children 5 and under. Villa daily 9:30am–5pm (ticket booth closes at 4:30pm). Gardens daily 9:30am–5:30pm.

NATURE PRESERVES, PARKS & GARDENS

The Miami area is a great place for outdoor types, with beaches, parks, nature preserves, and gardens galore. For information on South Florida's two national parks, the Everglades and Biscayne National Park, see chapter 7.

Although South Beach is more known for its sand than its greenery, **South Pointe Park,** 1 Washington Ave. (✆ 305/673-7730), reopened after a $22.4-million renovation that transformed the formerly shabby spot into 18 waterfront acres of green space, walkways, a playground, and an observation deck. It is also home to **Smith and Wollensky** (✆ 305/673-2800), which is one of the best spots from which to view the departing cruise ships in Government Cut.

Reopened in 2009 is the historic **Hialeah Park ★**, 2200 E. 4th Ave. (✆ 305/885-8000; www.hialeahparkracing.com), primarily known for horse racing but also for its legendary flock of neon-pink flamingos, which still roam the property and are definitely worth a photo op. After decades of decay, the park is back and spruced up for the most part, although experts say the restoration of the National Historic Landmark to its former glory will take years and $100 million to complete. Open only for races for now, admission is free. For those who prefer a more historic look, Miami's resident historian Dr. Paul George (see "Specialized Tours," p. 158) offers guided tours of the park for $25 per person. To book a tour, call **305/375-1621** or e-mail citytours@historymiami.org.

You'll know you're at Hialeah when you see the flamingos!

Explore the botanic (and man-made) wonders at the Fairchild Tropical Garden.

At the historic **Bill Baggs Cape Florida State Park ★**, 1200 Crandon Blvd. (© **305/361-5811**), at the southern tip of Key Biscayne about 20 minutes from downtown Miami, you can explore the unfettered wilds and enjoy some of the most secluded beaches in Miami. There's also a historic lighthouse that was built in 1825, which is the oldest lighthouse in South Florida. The lighthouse was damaged during the Second Seminole War (1836) and again in 1861 during the Civil War. Out of commission for a while, it was restored to working lighthouse condition in 1978 by the U.S. Coast Guard. A rental shack leases bikes, hydro-bikes, kayaks, and many more water toys. It's a great place to picnic, but there are also two restaurants on-site: the Lighthouse Café, which serves homemade Latin food, including great fish soups and sandwiches, and the Boater's Grill, offering casual waterfront dining. Just be careful that the raccoons don't get your lunch—the furry black-eyed beasts are everywhere. Wildlife aside, however, Bill Baggs has been consistently rated as one of the top 10 beaches in the U.S. for its 1¼ miles of wide, sandy beaches and its secluded, serene atmosphere. Admission is $8 per car with up to eight people (or $4 for a car with only one person; $2 to enter by foot or bicycle). Open daily from 8am to sunset. Tours of the lighthouse are available every Thursday through Monday at 10am and 1pm. Arrive at least half an hour early to sign up—there is room for only 10 people on each tour. Take I-95 to the Rickenbacker Causeway and take that all the way to the end.

Fairchild Tropical Garden ★★★, at 10901 Old Cutler Rd., in Coral Gables (© **305/667-1651;** www.ftg.org), is the largest of its kind in the continental United States. A veritable rainforest of both rare and exotic plants, as well as 11 lakes and countless meadows, are spread across 83 acres. Palmettos, vine pergola, palm glades, and other unique species create a scenic, lush environment. More than 100 species of birds have been spotted at the garden (ask for a checklist at the front gate), and it's home to a variety of animals. You should not miss the 30-minute narrated tram tour (tours leave on the hour 10am–3pm weekdays and 10am–4pm on weekends) to learn about the various flowers and trees on the grounds. There is also a museum, a cafe, a picnic area, and a gift shop with edible gifts and fantastic books on gardening and cooking. Fairchild often hosts major art exhibits by the likes of Dale Chihuly and Roy Lichtenstein. The 2-acre rainforest exhibit, **Windows to the Tropics,** will save you a trip to the Amazon. Expect to spend a minimum of 2 hours here.

Admission is $20 for adults, $15 for seniors, $10 for children ages 6 to 17, and free for children 5 and under. Open daily, except Christmas, from 9:30am to 4:30pm. Take I-95 south to U.S. 1, turn left onto Le Jeune Road, and follow it straight to the traffic circle; from there, take Old Cutler Road 2 miles to the park.

Named after the late champion of the Everglades, the **Marjory Stoneman Douglas Biscayne Nature Center ★**, 6767 Crandon Blvd., Key Biscayne (✆ **305/361-6767;** www.biscaynenaturecenter.org), is housed in a $4-million facility and offers hands-on marine exploration, hikes through coastal hammocks, bike trips, and beach walks. Local environmentalists and historians lead intriguing trips through the local habitat. Call to reserve a spot on a regularly scheduled weekend tour or program. Be sure to wear comfortable, closed-toe shoes for hikes through wet or rocky terrain. Open daily 10am to 4pm. Admission to the park is $5 per person; admission to the nature center is free. Special programs and tours cost $12 per person. Call for weekend programs. To get there, take I-95 to the Rickenbacker Causeway exit (no. 1) and take the causeway all the way until it becomes Crandon Boulevard. The center is on the east side of the street (the Atlantic Ocean side) and about 25 minutes from downtown Miami.

Because so many people are focused on the beach itself, the **Miami Beach Botanical Garden,** 2000 Convention Center Dr., Miami Beach (✆ **305/673-7256**), remains a secret garden. The lush, tropical 4½-acre garden is a fabulous natural retreat from the hustle and bustle of the silicone-enhanced city. Open Tuesday through Sunday from 9am to 5pm; admission is free.

The **Oleta River State Recreation Area ★★**, 3400 NE 163rd St., North Miami (✆ **305/919-1846**), consists of 993 acres—the largest urban park in the state—on Biscayne Bay. The beauty of the Oleta River, combined with the fact that you're essentially in the middle of a city, makes this park especially worth visiting. With miles of bicycle and canoe trails, a sandy swimming beach, kayak and mountain bike rental shop, Blue Marlin Fish House Restaurant, shaded picnic pavilions, and a fishing pier, Oleta River State Recreation Area allows for an outstanding outdoor recreational experience cloistered from the confines of the big city. There are 14 rustic cabins on the premises that sleep four people. The cost is $55 per night, and guests are required to bring their own linens. Bathrooms and showers are outside, as is a fire circle with a grill for cooking. For reservations, call ✆ **800/326-3521.** It's open daily from 8am to sunset. Admission for pedestrians and cyclists is $2 per person. By car: Driver plus car costs $4; driver plus one to seven passengers and car costs $6. Take I-95 to exit 17 (S.R. 826 E.) and go all the way east until just before the causeway. The park entrance is on your right. Driving time from downtown Miami is about a half-hour.

A testament to Miami's unusual climate, the **Preston B. Bird and Mary Heinlein Fruit and Spice Park ★**, 24801 SW 187th Ave., Homestead (✆ **305/247-5727;** www.fruitandspicepark.org), harbors rare fruit trees that cannot survive elsewhere in the country. If a volunteer is available, you'll learn some fascinating things about this 30-acre living plant museum, where the most exotic varieties of fruits and spices—ackee, mango, Ugli fruits, carambola, and breadfruit—grow on strange-looking trees with unpronounceable names. There are also original coral-rock buildings dating back to 1912. The Strawberry Folk Festival in February and an art festival here in January are among the park's most popular—and populated—events. The best part? You're free to take anything that has *naturally* fallen to the ground (no picking here). If the ground is bare, don't worry. The **Mango Café** in the park's historic Bauer-Mitchell-Neill House

The sight and scent of rare flowers and fruits makes the Heinlein Fruit and Spice Park a beautiful place to visit.

See the city with "Mr. Miami," Dr. Paul George.

features indoor and outdoor garden seating and is open for lunch and late-afternoon dining and serves "Florida Tropical" cuisine—fruit salads, lots of dishes with mango, smoothies, shakes, and, our fave, Florida lobster roll. You'll also find samples of interesting fruits and jellies made from the park's bounty, as well as exotic ingredients and cookbooks in the gift store.

Admission to the spice park is $8 for adults and $2 for children 6 to 11. It's open daily from 9am to 5pm; closed on Christmas. Tours are included in the price of admission and are offered at 11am, 1:30pm, and 3pm. Take U.S. 1 south, turn right on SW 248th Street, and go straight for 5 miles to SW 187th Avenue. The drive from Miami should take 45 minutes to an hour.

ORGANIZED TOURS

Specialized Tours

In addition to the tours listed below, a great option for seeing the city is a tour led by **Dr. Paul George.** Dr. George is a history teacher at Miami-Dade Community College and a historian at the Historical Museum of Southern Florida. He also happens to be "Mr. Miami." There's a variety of tours (including the "Ghostly, Ghastly Vice & Crime Coach Tour," detailed below), all fascinating to South Florida buffs. Tours focus on such neighborhoods as Little Havana, Brickell Avenue, or Key Biscayne, and on themes such as Miami cemeteries, the Miami River, and Stiltsville, the "neighborhood" of houses on stilts in the middle of Biscayne Bay. There are also eco-history coach, walking, boat, and bike tours. The often-long-winded discussions can be a bit much for those who just want a quick look around, but Dr. George certainly knows his stuff. The cost is $25 to $49, and reservations are required (© **305/375-1621;** www.hmsf.org/programs-adult.htm). Tours leave from the Historical Museum at 101 W. Flagler St., downtown. Call for a schedule.

The Design District, Midtown & Wynwood Experience As the Design District and Midtown Miami areas continue to grow, someone saw fit to create a tour to the neighborhoods. More than a tour, however, it's really just a shuttle bus that ferries visitors from their hotels to shops, restaurants, and galleries. Cost is $59 or $69 a person and includes round-trip transportation, a three-course lunch or dinner at participating restaurants, and merchant discounts. Sounds good in theory, but we kind of think it's easier—and cheaper—to take a cab.

C **305/722-4540.** www.designdistrictexperience.com.

Eco-Adventure Tours ★★★ For the eco-conscious traveler, the Miami-Dade Parks and Recreation Department offers guided nature, adventure, and historic tours involving biking, canoeing, snorkeling, hiking, and bird-watching all over the city. Contact them for more information.

C **305/365-3018.** www.miamiecoadventures.com.

Ghostly, Ghastly Vice & Crime Coach Tour ★★★ Visit the past by video and bus to Miami-Dade's most celebrated crimes and criminals from the 1800s to the present, including some sites where the '80s TV series *Miami Vice* was filmed. From the murder spree of the Ashley Gang to the most notorious murders and crimes of the last century, including the murder of designer Gianni Versace, historian Paul George conducts a most fascinating 3-hour tour of scandalous proportions.

Leaves from the Dade Cultural Center, 101 W. Flagler St., Miami. Advance reservations required; call *C* **305/375-1621.** Tickets $44. Held twice a year, usually in Apr and Oct.

Hispanic Heritage Tour This is offered during October only (Hispanic Heritage Month): For those looking to immerse themselves in Miami's rich Latin-American culture, the Herencia Hispana Tour is the ideal way to explore it all. Hop on a bus and zoom past such hotbeds of Latin activity as downtown's Flagler Street, the unavoidable Elián González house, and Little Havana's Domino Park and Tower Theater, among others. Not just a sightseeing tour, this one includes two very knowledgeable, albeit corny, guides who know just when to infuse a necessary dose of humor into the Elián saga, a segment of history that some people may not consider so amusing.

Tours depart from the Steven P. Clark Government Center, 111 NW 1st St. *C* **305/770-3131.** Tours (in Spanish or English, but you must specify which one you require) are free, but advance reservations are required. Tours depart at 9, 9:30, and 10am every Sat in Oct.

Little Havana Cuban Cuisine & Culture Walking Tour ★★★ A historian will guide you through a savory tour of Little Havana, stopping for samples of local cuisine and coffee and even stopping to play dominoes with the locals. Tour also includes a visit to the Bay of Pigs Museum, area social clubs, and a *botanica*, a shop that caters to followers of the Santeria or Voudon religions.

C **305/375-1621.** www.hmsf.org. Tour $25.

Miami Culinary Tours ★★★ There once was a time when Miami was synonymous with early-bird specials and models who didn't eat. Things have changed. Now you can eat your way through the city's most savory neighborhoods, leaving with a few extra pounds to prove it. Miami-as-melting-pot takes on a completely edible meaning thanks to these custom-crafted, specialized tours. Ten years ago, it was inconceivable to eat your way through the Art Deco District, but now you can do just that and marvel at the architecture. And while Little Havana has always been a mouthwatering mecca of Cuban food, thanks to Miami Culinary Tours it's like having your own private Rosetta stone without all the repetition.

Choose from 2½-hour tours of South Beach's or Little Havana's best bites, or Miami Food Tasting Tour, a 3½-hour Cuban-inspired epicurean adventure throughout the city.

✆ **305/942-8856.** www.miamiculinarytours.com. South Beach or Little Havana tours $55; Miami Food Tasting Tour $95.

Miami Duck Tours Hands down, this is the corniest, kookiest tour in the entire city. In fact, the company prefers to call these tours the "Quackiest" way to visit Miami and the beaches. Whatever you call it, it's weird. The *Watson Willy* is the first of several Miami Duck Tours "vesicles," not a body part, but a hybrid name that means part vessel, part vehicle (technical name: Hydra Terra Amphibious Vehicle). Each vesicle seats 49 guests, plus a captain and tour guide, and leaves from Watson Island behind Jungle Island, traveling through downtown Miami and South Beach. If you're image-conscious, you may want to reconsider traveling down Ocean Drive in a duck. That's right, a duck, which is what the vesicle looks like. After driving the streets in the duck, you'll end up cruising Biscayne Bay, past all the swank houses. Embarrassing or downright hilarious, Miami Duck Tours is definitely unique.

1665 Washington Ave., South Beach. ✆ **877/DUCK-TIX** (382-5849). www.ducktoursmiami.com. Tickets $32 adults, $26 seniors and military, $18 children 12 and under.

Redland Tropical Trail Tours ★★★ Check out South Florida farmlands—yes, they do exist in an area near Homestead called the Redlands—on this tour featuring a circuit of stops, tastings, and sightseeing that will take you from gardens and jungles to an orchid farm, an actual working winery, a fruit stand, and more. There's no cost to follow the trail with a map (available on the website) on your own, but call for pricing information for certain attractions found on the trail.

✆ **305/245-9180.** www.redlandtrail.com.

If it quacks like a Duck, you're probably on a tour!

WATERSPORTS

There are many ways to get well acquainted with Miami's wet look. Choose your own adventure from the suggestions listed below.

BOATING Private rental outfits include **Boat Rental Plus,** 2400 Collins Ave., Miami Beach (✆ **305/534-4307**), where powerboats rent for some of the best prices on the beach. Here, you can rent a 21-footer for $69 per hour not including tax or gas, with a 2-hour minimum. A 4-hour rental will get you a free hour. Cruising is permitted only in and around Biscayne Bay (ocean access is prohibited), and renters must be 21 or older to rent a boat. The rental office is at 23rd Street, on the inland waterway in Miami Beach. It's open daily from 10am to sunset. If you want a specific type of boat, call ahead to reserve. Otherwise, show up and take what's available.

For those planning on staying in town a bit longer or more frequently, **Easy Boating Club,** 3301 Rickenbacker Causeway (✆ **305/856-8229;** www.easyboatingclub.com), is a members-only club that lets you hit the high seas for $199 a month plus a $2,500 initiation fee. You get unlimited access to a fabulous fleet of boats without the hassle of maintenance. And, like your best friend or ex-girlfriend, boats are notorious for being high maintenance. With a fleet composed of boats 21 to 23 feet long, The Easy Boating Club has something for everyone, even those whose inner GPS has them a little dazed and confused. An orientation will provide you with explicit instructions on how to maneuver the boat, where to maneuver the boat, good seamanship, and where to find sandbars, canals, restaurants, and other water-based attractions. Also included: basic gear for fishing, tubing, snorkeling, and more.

JET SKIS/WAVERUNNERS Don't miss a chance to tour the islands on the back of your own powerful watercraft. Bravery is, however, a prerequisite, as Miami's waterways are full of speeding jet skiers and boaters who think they're in the Indy 500. Many beachfront concessionaires rent a variety of these popular (and loud) water scooters. The latest models are fast and smooth. **American Watersports,** at the Miami Beach Marina, 300 Alton Rd. (✆ **305/538-7549;** www.jetskiz.com), is the area's most popular spot for jet-ski rental. Rates begin at $60 for a half-hour and $109 for an hour. They also offer fun jet-ski tours past celebrity homes for $119 for the first hour and $60 for the second.

KAYAKING The **Blue Moon Outdoor Center** rents kayaks at 3400 NE 163rd St., in Oleta River Park (✆ **305/957-3040;** www.bluemoonmiami.com). Kayak rentals for self-guided tours include single or tandem kayaks and canoes. All rates are for the first 1½ hours. Rates are $18 for single kayak, $26 for tandem kayak. Canoes are $30. Paddle down several calm water routes and spot blue herons, bottlenose dolphin, and possibly manatees. Kayak instructional classes are offered by ACA (American Canoe Association) certified instructors. There's also stand-up paddleboarding if that's what you're into. Rentals start at $22. The park offers 16 miles of mountain bike trails rated green for easy, blue for intermediate, and black for difficult. Rates for full-suspension mountain bikes begin at $18. Guided eco-tours are available with advance reservation. There are also some really cool monthly full-moon kayak and bike trip, including a bonfire on the beach. Adventure on either a kayak or a bike, or do the combination deal for $75. Afterward, eat at the

5

WHAT TO SEE & DO IN MIAMI

Watersports

Jet skis are a popular (and loud!) way to traverse the Miami waterways.

See Miami from down under (the waterline) with a snorkeling safari.

famous waterfront Blue Marlin Fish House Restaurant for some smoked fish or fresh lobster burgers. Open daily from 9am to sunset. Blue Moon has a second location, **The Loggerhead,** in Broward County at John U. Lloyd Beach State Park in Dania Beach, 6503 N. Ocean Blvd. (© **954/923-6711**), offering kayak, canoe, and standup paddleboard rentals daily from 10am to 5pm. They also offer catering on the beach.

SAILING You can rent sailboats and catamarans through the beachfront concessions desks of several top resorts, such as the Doral Golf Resort and Spa (p. 104).

Aquatic Rental Center, at northern Biscayne Bay in the Pelican Harbor Marina, 1275 NE 79th St. (© **305/751-7514** days, 305/279-7424 evenings; www.arcmiami.com), can also get you out on the water. A 22-foot sailboat rents for $85 for 2 hours, $125 for 3 hours, $150 for a half-day, and $225 for a full day. A Sunfish sailboat for two people rents at $35 per hour. If you've always had a dream to win the America's Cup but can't sail, the able teachers here will get you started. They offer a 10-hour course over 5 days for $400 for one person, or $500 for two.

SCUBA DIVING & SNORKELING In 1981, the U.S. government began a wide-scale project designed to increase the number of habitats available to marine organisms. One of the program's major accomplishments has been the creation of nearby artificial reefs, which have attracted all kinds of tropical plants, fish, and animals. In addition, Biscayne National Park (see the park's section in chapter 7, beginning on p. 278) offers a protected marine environment just south of downtown.

Several dive shops around the city offer organized weekend outings, either to the reefs or to one of more than a dozen old shipwrecks around Miami's shores. Check "Divers" in the Yellow Pages for rental equipment and for a full list of undersea tour operators.

Diver's Paradise, of Key Biscayne, 4000 Crandon Blvd. (© **305/361-3483;** www.keydivers.com), offers one dive expedition per day during the week and two per day on the weekends to the more than 30 wrecks and artificial reefs off the coast of Miami Beach and Key Biscayne. You can take a 3-day certification course for $499, which includes all the dives and gear.

If you already have your C-card, a dive trip costs about $100 if you need equipment, and $60 if you bring your own gear. It's open Tuesday through Friday from 10am to 6pm and Saturday and Sunday from 8am to 6pm. Call ahead for times and locations of dives. For snorkeling, they will set you up with equipment and maps on where to see the best underwater sights. Rental for mask, fins, and snorkel is $60.

South Beach Divers, 850 Washington Ave., Miami Beach (✆ **305/531-6110;** www.south beachdivers.com), will also be

Sailboards stand at attention, ready to hit the water when the wind is right.

happy to tell you where to go under the sea and will provide you with scuba rental equipment as well for $65. You can rent snorkel gear for about $20. They also do dive trips to Key Largo three times a week and do dives off Miami on Sunday at $120 for a two-tank dive or $85 if you have your own equipment. Night dives and trips to the USS *Spiegel Grove,* a dive site in Key Largo, are $10 extra.

The most amusing and apropos South Beach diving spot has to be the **Jose Cuervo Underwater Bar,** located 150 yards southeast of the Second Street lifeguard station—a 22-ton concrete margarita bar that was sunk on May 5, 2000. Nicknamed "Sinko De Mayo," the site is designed with a dive flag roof, six bar stools, and a protective wall of tetrahedrons.

WINDSURFING Many hotels rent windsurfers to their guests, but if yours doesn't have a watersports concession stand, head for Key Biscayne. **Sailboards Miami,** Rickenbacker Causeway, Key Biscayne (✆ **305/361-SAIL** [7245]; www.sailboardsmiami.com), operates out of two big yellow trucks on Windsurfer Beach, the most popular (though our pick for best is Hobie Beach) windsurfing spot in the city. For those who've never ridden a board but want to try it, they offer a 2-hour lesson for $79 that's guaranteed to turn you into a wave warrior, or you get your money back. After that, you can rent a board for $25 to $30 an hour. If you want to make a day of it, a 10-hour prepaid card costs $240 to $290. These cards reduce the price by about $70 for the day. You can use the card year-round, until the time on it runs out. Open Tuesday through Sunday from 10am to 5:30pm. Make your first right after the tollbooth ($^7/_{10}$ of a mile after the tollbooth at the beginning of the causeway—you can't miss it) to find the outfitters. They also rent kayaks.

MORE WAYS TO PLAY, INDOORS & OUT

BIKING The cement promenade on the southern tip of South Beach is a great place to ride. Biking up the beach (either on the beach or along the beach on a cement pathway—which is a lot easier!) is great for surf, sun, sand,

Biking's a great way to see the city and parks and beaches that surround it.

exercise, and people-watching—just be sure to keep your eyes on the road, as the scenery can be most distracting. Most of the big beach hotels rent bicycles, as does the **Miami Beach Bicycle Center,** 601 5th St., South Beach (☏ **305/674-0150;** www.bikemiamibeach.com), which charges $8 per hour, $24 for up to 24 hours, and $80 weekly. It's open Monday through Saturday from 10am to 7pm, Sunday from 10am to 5pm.

For those looking to literally power-bike, **The Electric Bicycle Store,** 1622 Alton Rd., South Beach (☏ **305/508-4040;** www.theelectricbicycle store.com), has just what you need. Choose from either a completely motorized form of cycling or a mix of pedaling and motor power known as "pedal-assist," which is especially easy on the knees. Rates are $65 per day.

Bikers can also enjoy more than 130 miles of paved paths throughout Miami. The beautiful and quiet streets of Coral Gables and Coconut Grove (several bike trails are spread throughout these neighborhoods) are great for bicyclists, where old trees form canopies over wide, flat roads lined with grand homes and quaint street markers.

The terrain in Key Biscayne is perfect for biking, especially along the park and beach roads. If you don't mind the sound of cars whooshing by your bike lane, **Rickenbacker Causeway** is also fantastic, as it is one of the only bikeable inclines in Miami from which you get fantastic elevated views of the city and waterways. However, be warned that this is a grueling ride, especially going up the causeway. **Key Cycling,** 61 Harbor Dr., Key Biscayne (☏ **305/361-0061;** www.keycycling.com), rents mountain bikes for $15 for 2 hours, $24 a day, or $80 a week. It's open Tuesday through Friday from 10am to 7pm, Monday and Saturday from 10am to 6pm, and Sunday from 10am to 3pm.

If you want to avoid the traffic altogether, head out to **Shark Valley** in the Everglades National Park—one of South Florida's most scenic bicycle trails and a favorite haunt of city-weary locals. For more information on Shark Valley and the Everglades, see chapter 7.

Biking note: Children 15 and under are required by Florida law to wear a helmet, which can be purchased at any bike store or retail outlet selling biking supplies.

FISHING Fishing licenses are required in Florida. If you go out with one of the fishing charter boats listed below, you are automatically accredited because the companies are. If you go out on your own, however, you must have a Florida fishing license, which costs $17 for 3 days and $30 for a week. Call ✆ **888/FISH-FLO** (347-4356) or visit www.wildlifelicense.com for more information.

Some of the best surf-casting in the city can be had at **Haulover Beach Park** at Collins Avenue and 105th Street, where there's a bait-and-tackle shop right on the pier. **South Pointe Park,** at the southern tip of Miami Beach, is another popular fishing spot and features a long pier, comfortable benches, and a great view of the ships passing through Government Cut, the deep channel made when the port of Miami was dug.

You can also do some deep-sea fishing in the Miami area. One bargain outfitter, the **Kelley Fishing Fleet,** at the Haulover Marina, 10800 Collins Ave. (at 108th St.), Miami Beach (✆ **305/945-3801;** www.miamibeach fishing.com), has half-day, full-day, and night fishing aboard diesel-powered "party boats." The fleet's emphasis on drifting is geared toward trolling and bottom-fishing for snapper, sailfish, and mackerel. Half-day and night-fishing trips are $40 for adults and $30 for children up to 10 years old, and full-day trips are $60 for adults and $50 for children. Daily departures are scheduled at 9am and 1:45 and 8pm; reservations are recommended.

Also at the Haulover Marina is the charter boat ***Helen C*** (10800 Collins Ave.; ✆ **305/947-4081;** www.fishmiamibeach.com). Although there's no shortage of private charter boats here, Captain Dawn Mergelsberg is a good pick, because she puts individuals together to get a full boat. The *Helen C* is a twin-engine 55-footer, equipped for big-game fish such as marlin, tuna, mahimahi, shark, and sailfish. The cost is $160 per person. Private, full-day trips are available for groups of six people per vessel and cost $1,350; half-days are $750. Group rates and specials are also available. Trips are scheduled for 8am to noon and 1 to 5pm daily; call for reservations. Beginners and children are always welcome.

For a serious fishing charter, Captain Charlie Hotchkiss's ***Sea Dancer*** (✆ **305/775-5534;** www.seadancercharter.com) offers a first-class experience on a 38-foot Luhrs boat complete with tuna tower and air-conditioned cabin. If you're all about big game—marlin, dolphin, tuna, wahoo, swordfish, and sailfish—this is the charter for you. Catch and release or fillet your catch to take home. The *Sea Dancer* also offers two fun water adventures, including a 6-hour Bar Cruz, covering the finest watering holes in Miami and Fort Lauderdale, or a Sandbar Cruz, where the boat drops anchor out by Biscayne Bay's historic Stiltsville, where you'll swim, bounce on a water trampoline, and play sports—all in the middle of the bay. Auto transportation is available to wherever the boat may be docked. Rates are $700 for a half-day and $1,100 for a full day, and $500 for the specialty tours. Tours are also available to Bimini. Call for pricing.

Key Biscayne offers deep-sea fishing to those willing to get their hands dirty and pay a bundle. The competition among the boats is fierce, but the prices are basically the same, no matter which you choose. The going rate is about $400 to $500 for a half-day and $600 to $900 for a full day of fishing. These rates are usually for a party of up to six, and the boats supply you with rods and bait as well as instruction for first-timers. Some will also take you out to the Upper Keys if the fish aren't biting in Miami.

You might also consider the following boats, all of which sail out of the Key Biscayne marina and are in relatively good shape and nicer than most out there: **Sonny Boy** (© 305/361-2217; www.sonnyboysport fishing.com), **Top Hatt** (© 305/361-2528), and **L & H** (© 305/361-9318; www.landhsportfishing.com). Call for reservations.

Bridge fishing in Biscayne Bay is also popular in Miami; you'll see people with poles over almost every waterway. But look carefully for signs telling you whether it's legal to do so wherever you are: Some bridges forbid fishing.

GAMBLING Although gambling is technically illegal in Miami, there are plenty of loopholes that allow all kinds of wagering. Gamblers can try their luck at offshore casinos or on shore at bingo, jai alai, card rooms, horse tracks, dog races, and Native American reservations. The newly reopened **Hialeah Park Racing** (www.hialeahparkracing.com) has thoroughbred and quarter horse racing and, sometime in the near future, because no racetrack in Florida is complete without it, poker and slot machines. For slots and poker, you can check out the **Magic City Casino,** 5 minutes from the airport and downtown Miami at 450 NW 37th Ave. (© **888/56-MAGIC** [566-2442]; www.magiccitycasino.com), but we recommend you stick with the brand-new casino at **Calder Casino & Race Course,** located by Sun Life Stadium at 21001 NW 27th Ave. in Miami Gardens (© **305/625-1311;** www.calderracecourse.com), featuring 1,200 slot machines, poker, and horse racing. You can also drive up to Broward County, where the **Seminole Hard Rock Hotel and Casino** (www.seminolehardrock.com), **Seminole Casino Coconut Creek** (www.seminolecoconutcreekcasino.com), **Mardi Gras Racetrack and Gaming** (www.playmardigras.com), **Isle Casino & Racing** (www.pompano-park.isleofcapricasinos.com), and the new and still expanding **Gulfstream Park Casino and Racing** (www.gulfstreampark.com) in Hallandale offer slots, poker, and, in the cases of Hard Rock and Gulfstream, blackjack too.

Despite the Hard Rock in Hollywood's behemoth presence on the gambling circuit (and its many imitators), some people prefer the less flashy **Miccosukee Indian Gaming,** 500 SW 177th Ave. (off S.R. 41, in West Miami, on the outskirts of the Everglades; © **800/741-4600** or 305/222-4600), where a touch of Vegas meets West Miami. This tacky casino isn't Caesar's Palace, but you can play tab slots, high-speed bingo (watch out for the serious blue-haired players who will scoff if you make too much noise or if you win before they do), and even poker (with more tables added now that they're competing with Seminole Hard Rock; see above). With more than 85,000 square feet of playing space, the complex even provides overnight accommodations for those who can't get enough of the thrill and don't want to make the approximately 1-hour trip back to downtown Miami. Take the Florida Turnpike south toward Florida City/Key West. Take the SW 8th Street exit (#25) and turn left onto SW 8th Street. Drive for about 3½ miles and then turn left onto Krome Avenue, and left again at 177th Street; you can't miss it.

It's post time at Gulfstream Park Casino and Racing.

GOLF There are more than 50 private and public golf courses in the Miami area. Contact the **Greater Miami Convention and Visitor's Bureau** (*C* **800/ 933-8448;** www.miamiandbeaches.com) for a list of courses and costs.

The best hotel courses in Miami are found at the **Doral Golf Resort and Spa** (p. 104), home of the legendary Blue Monster course, as well as the Gold Course, designed by Raymond Floyd; the Great White Shark Course; and the newest course, the former Silver Course, refinished by Jim McLean and known as the Jim McLean Signature course, which, according to experts, has one of the toughest starting holes in the entire state.

Other hotels with excellent golf courses include the **Fairmont Turnberry Isle Resort & Club** (p. 105), with two Robert Trent Jones, Sr.– designed courses for guests and members, and the **Biltmore Hotel ★★★** (p. 107), which is our pick for best public golf course because of its modest greens fees and an 18-hole, par-71 course located on the hotel's spectacular grounds. It must be good: Despite his penchant for privacy, former president Bill Clinton prefers teeing off at this course more than any other in Miami!

Otherwise, the following represent some of the area's best public courses. **Crandon Park Golf Course,** formerly known as the Links, 6700 Crandon Blvd., Key Biscayne (*C* **305/361-9129;** www.crandongolfclub. com), is the number-one-ranked municipal course in the state and one of the top five in the country. The park is situated on 200 bayfront acres and offers a pro shop, rentals, lessons, carts, and a lighted driving range. The course is open daily from dawn to dusk; greens fees (including cart) range from $70 to $165, depending on the season, for nonresidents and include a cart. Special twilight rates are also available.

One of the most popular courses among real enthusiasts is the **Doral Park Golf and Country Club,** 5001 NW 104th Ave., West Miami (*C* **305/591-8800**); it's not related to the Doral Hotel or spa. Call to book in advance, as this challenging, semiprivate 18-holer is extremely popular with locals. The course is open from 6:30am to 6pm during the winter and until 7pm during the summer. Cart and greens fees vary, so call *C* **305/592- 2000,** ext. 2104, for information.

Known as one of the best in the city, the **Country Club of Miami,** 6801 Miami Gardens Dr., at NW 68th Avenue, North Miami (© **305/829-8456;** www.golfmiamicc.com), has three 18-hole courses of varying degrees of difficulty. You'll encounter lush fairways, rolling greens, and some history, to boot. The west course, designed in 1961 by Robert Trent Jones, Sr., and updated in the 1990s by the PGA, was where Jack Nicklaus played his first professional tournament and Lee Trevino won his first professional championship. The course is open daily from 7am

Doral Park is one of the Miami area's most popular golf courses.

to sunset. Cart and greens fees are $25 to $75, depending on the season and tee times. Special twilight rates are available.

The recently renovated **Miami Beach Golf Club,** 2301 Alton Rd., South Beach (© **305/532-3350;** www.miamibeachgolfclub.com), is a gorgeous, 79-year-old course that, par for the, er, course in Miami Beach, received a $10-million face-lift. Miami Heat players and Matt Damon have been known to tee off here. Greens fees range from $100 to $200, depending on the season.

SWIMMING There is no shortage of water in the Miami area. See the Venetian Pool listing (p. 154) and the "Miami's Beaches" section on p. 141 for descriptions of good swimming options.

TENNIS Hundreds of tennis courts in South Florida are open to the public for a minimal fee. Most courts operate on a first-come, first-served basis and are open from sunrise to sunset. For information and directions, call the **City of Miami Beach Recreation, Culture, and Parks Department** (© **305/673-7730**) or the **City of Miami Parks and Recreation Department** (© **305/575-5256**). Of the 590 public tennis courts throughout Miami, the three hard courts and seven clay courts at the **Crandon Tennis Center,** 6702 Crandon Blvd. (© **305/361-5263**), are the best and most beautiful. Because of this, they often get crowded on weekends. You'll play on the same courts as Lendl, Graf, Evert, McEnroe, Federer, the Williams sisters, and other greats; this is also the venue for one of the world's biggest annual tennis events, the Sony Ericsson Open. There's a pleasant, if limited, pro shop, plus many good pros. Only four courts are lit at night, but if you reserve at least 24 to 48 hours in advance, you can usually take your pick. Hard courts cost $4 per person per hour during the day, $6 per person per hour at night. Clay courts cost $7 per person per hour during the day. Grass courts are $11 per person per hour. There are no night hours on the clay or grass courts. The courts are open Monday through Friday from 8am to 9pm, Saturday and Sunday until 6pm.

Other courts are pretty run-of-the-mill and can be found in most neighborhoods. We do, however, recommend the **Miami Beach public courts at Flamingo Park,** 1001 12th St., in South Beach (© 305/673-7761), where there are 19 clay courts that cost $5 per person an hour for Miami Beach residents and $10 per person an hour for nonresidents. Playing at night adds an extra $1.50 "light fee." It's first-come, first-served. Open 8am to 9pm Monday through Friday, 8am to 8pm Saturday and Sunday.

Hotels with the best tennis facilities are the Biltmore, Fairmont Turnberry Isle Resort & Club, Doral Golf Resort and Spa, and Inn and Spa at Fisher Island.

SPECTATOR SPORTS

Check the *Miami Herald*'s sports section for a daily listing of local events and the paper's Friday "Weekend" section for comprehensive coverage and in-depth reports. For last-minute tickets, call the venue directly, as many season ticket holders sell singles and return unused tickets. Expensive tickets are available from brokers or individuals listed in the classified sections of the local papers. Some tickets are also available through **Ticketmaster** (© 305/358-5885; www.ticketmaster.com).

BASEBALL The **Florida Marlins** shocked the sports world in 1997 when they became the youngest expansion team to win a World Series, but then floundered as their star players were sold off by former owner Wayne Huizenga. The team shocked the sports world again in 2003 by winning the World Series, and turned many of Miami's apathetic sports fans into major-league ball fans. The Marlins are not as good as they were anymore after trading away some of their best players, and every day there's a new rumor that the team either is looking to move to another state or will move to their new home in the zillion-dollar (actually $525 million and counting) new baseball stadium opening sometime in 2012 in the space formerly known as the Orange Bowl. The Maine Marlins? Sounds fishy. Anyway, if you're interested in catching a game, *be warned:* The summer heat in Miami can be unbearable, even in the evenings. The new stadium, whenever it opens, will feature a retractable roof to make things more bearable.

In the meantime, home games are held at **Sun Life Stadium,** 2269 NW 199th St., North Miami Beach (© 305/623-6200). Tickets cost from $4 to $50. Box office hours are Monday to Friday from 8:30am to 5:30pm and before games; tickets are also available through Ticketmaster. The team currently holds spring training in Melbourne, Florida.

BASKETBALL The **Miami Heat** (© 786/777-1000) is one of Miami's hottest tickets, especially since the team won the NBA championship in 2006 and thanks to the powerhouse trifecta composed of Dwyane Wade, LeBron James, and Chris Bosh making it to the league finals in 2011. Courtside seats are full of visiting celebrities. The season lasts from October to April, with most games beginning at 7:30pm. The team plays in the brand-new waterfront **American Airlines Arena,** downtown on Biscayne Boulevard. Tickets are $10 to $100 or much more. Box office hours are Monday through Friday from 10am to 5pm (until 8pm on game nights); tickets are also available through Ticketmaster (© 305/358-5885).

LEFT: The Heat is on in Miami since LeBron James joined the team; ABOVE: The Dolphins are Miami's favorite seagoing mammal (and NFL team).

CAR RACING **Homestead-Miami Speedway,** One Speedway Blvd., Homestead (✆ 866/409-7223 or 866/409-RACE [7223]; www.homestead miamispeedway.com), made history in 2009 when it become the first venue ever to host all of North America's premier motorsports championships: the IndyCar, Grand-Am, and Firestone Indy Lights Series; and NASCAR's Sprint Cup, Nationwide, and Camping World Truck Series. Even when the major races aren't going on here, you can channel your inner speed demon via open-to-the-public events that allow regular folk to put the pedal to the metal, including **Hooked on Driving** (www.hookedondriving.com) and **Florida Track Days** (www.floridatrackdays.com). The track also features private club–level seating. Tickets to all events vary.

FOOTBALL Miami's golden boys are the **Miami Dolphins,** the city's most recognizable team, followed by thousands of "dolfans." The team plays at least eight home games during the season, between September and December, at **Sun Life Stadium,** 2269 NW 199th St., North Miami Beach (✆ 305/620-2578). In 2009, in an effort to boost ticket sales, the stadium formerly known as Dolphin Stadium was renamed Land Shark Stadium after the beer licensed to Anheuser-Busch by hit maker Jimmy Buffett, whose presence is still heavy at Dolphins games even though the deal expired at the final whistle blow of the Orange Bowl in December 2009. Besides Buffett, an impressive roster of celebrity "co-owners" of the team were also announced, including local faves Gloria and Emilio Estefan, Jennifer Lopez and Marc Anthony, and Fergie from the Black Eyed Peas. Because of this, the home games now feature an "orange carpet," on which owners and their famous friends prance before star-struck fans. Free concerts before games also bring big names thanks to the Buffett connection. And a satellite branch of Fontainebleau hot spot LIV—yes, a nightclub within the stadium—has yet to prove whether the only high rollers who can afford the steep cocktail and bottle prices are busy playing on the field. As for whether this star power actually has helped the team, well, that's to be decided.

Tickets cost $20 and much, much more. The box office is open Monday through Friday from 8:30am to 5:30pm; tickets are also available through Ticketmaster (© **305/358-5885;** www.ticketmaster.com).

HORSE RACING Located on the Dade–Broward County border in Hallandale (just north of North Miami Beach/Aventura) is **Gulfstream Racing & Casino,** at U.S. 1 and Hallandale Beach Boulevard (© **305/454-7000;** www.gulfstreampark.com), South Florida's very own version of Churchill Downs, but without the hats. This horse track is a haven for serious gamblers and voyeurs alike. Large purses and important races are commonplace at this sprawling suburban course, and the track is typically crowded, especially after receiving a multimillion-dollar face-lift that has added to the park a brand-new flashy casino, nightclubs, restaurants (including **Ola Cuba,** a midrange restaurant by star chef Douglas Rodriguez, and a popular beer restaurant, **Yardhouse**), and stores in the massive work in progress known as the **Village at Gulfstream Park.** Admission and parking are free. January 3 through April 23, post times are 1:15pm Wednesday through Sunday. The track is closed Mondays and Tuesdays, though the casino remains open. If you're hungry, South Florida's venerable Christine Lee's Chinese restaurant is housed here.

Hialeah Park, 2200 E. 4th Ave. (© **305/885-5000;** www.hialeah parkracing.com), is a National Historic Landmark that reopened in 2009 with a 20-day race season in November and another one in December. Though initially limited to shorter—and less glamorous—quarter horse races, Hialeah Park aspires to add thoroughbred events in the future. Fans of racing have been patient and will wait it out. After all, it is the racetrack where champions like Seabiscuit, who made his racing debut at Hialeah Park on January 19, 1935, made history. Then there's **Calder Casino & Race Course,** located by Sun Life Stadium at 21001 NW 27th Ave. in Miami Gardens (© **305/625-1311;** www.calderracecourse.com). Owned by the venerable Churchill Downs, Calder first opened as a horse-racing track back in 1971 and has been one of the most successful parimutuel franchises in the state's history. While horse racing and simulcast wagering are its mainstays, in order to keep up with the competition, Calder added a casino in January 2010. And while not exactly racing, a newish event that takes place on the sands of South Beach is the **Miami Beach Polo Cup,** featuring hard-core sand-kicking polo matches, a parade of the ponies down the beach, and chic parties. General admission to matches throughout the weekend is free to the public, while VIP tickets are available for those seeking more than a view from the sidelines and for coveted events outside of the arena. Visit **www.miamipolo.com**.

JAI ALAI Jai alai, sort of a Spanish-style indoor lacrosse, was introduced to Miami in 1924 and is regularly played in two Miami-area frontons (the buildings in which jai alai is played). Although the sport has roots stemming from ancient Egypt, the game, as it's now played, was invented by Basque peasants in the Pyrenees mountains during the 17th century. Players use *cesetas,* curved wicker baskets strapped to their wrists, to hurl balls, called *pelotas,* at speeds that sometimes exceed 170 mph. Spectators, who are protected behind a wall of glass, place bets on the evening's players. The Florida Gaming Corporation owns the jai alai operations throughout the state, making betting on this sport as legal as buying a lottery ticket.

Jai alai originated in the Basque country of northern Spain, where players used church walls as their courts. The game looks something like lacrosse, with rules similar to handball or tennis. It's played on a court with numbered lines. What makes the game unique, however, is the requirement that the ball must be returned in one continuous motion. The server must bounce the ball behind the serving line and, with the basket, must hurl the ball to the front wall, with the aim being that, upon rebound, the ball will bounce between lines four and seven. If it doesn't, it is an under- or overserve and the other team receives a point.

The **Miami Jai Alai Fronton,** 3500 NW 37th Ave., at NW 35th Street (© **305/633-6400**), is America's oldest fronton, dating from 1926. It schedules 13 games per night, which typically last 10 to 20 minutes, but can occasionally go much longer. Admission is free. There are year-round games. On Wednesday, Thursday, and Sunday, there are matinees only, which run from noon to 5:30pm. Friday, Saturday, and Monday, there are matinees in addition to evening games, from 7pm to midnight. The fronton is closed on Tuesday. This is the main location where jai alai is played in Miami. The other South Florida jai alai venue is in Dania, near the Fort Lauderdale–Hollywood International Airport. See "Jai Alai Explained" above.

ANIMAL PARKS

For a tropical location, Miami's got a lot of nontropical animals to see, and we're not talking about the motorists on I-95. Everything from dolphins and alligators to lions, tigers, and bears call Miami home (most in parks, some in nature). Call the parks to inquire about discount packages or coupons, which may be offered at area retail stores or in local papers.

Jungle Island ★ ☺ Not exactly an island and not quite a jungle, Jungle Island is an excellent diversion for the kids and for animal lovers. While the island doubles as a protected bird sanctuary, the very pricey 19-acre park features an Everglades exhibit, a petting zoo, and several theaters, jungle trails, and aviaries. Watch your heads because flying above are hundreds of parrots, macaws, peacocks, cockatoos, and flamingos. Continuous shows star bicycle-riding cockatoos, high-flying macaws, and numerous stunt-happy parrots. One of the most popular shows is Tale of the Tiger, featuring awesome animals. Jungle Island also features the only African penguins in South Florida as well as a liger—part lion, part tiger—and endangered baby lemurs. There are also tortoises, iguanas, and a rare albino alligator on exhibit. The park's website sometimes offers downloadable discount coupons, so take a look before you visit because you definitely won't want to pay full price for this park, which has the nerve to charge for parking. If you do get your money's worth and see all the shows and exhibits, expect to spend upwards of 4 hours here. *Note:* The former South Miami site of (Parrot) Jungle Island is now known as **Pinecrest Gardens,** 11000 Red Rd. (© **305/669-6942**), which features a petting zoo, a mini water park, lake, natural hammocks, and banyan caves. Open daily from 8am until sunset; admission is free.

1111 Parrot Jungle Trail, Watson Island (on the north side of MacArthur Causeway/I-395). © **305/372-3822.** www.jungleisland.com. Admission $33 adults, $31 seniors, $25 children 3–10, free for military personnel with valid ID. Parking $8 per vehicle. Mon–Fri 10am–5pm; Sat–Sun 10am–6pm. From I-95, take I-395 E. (MacArthur Causeway); make a right on Parrot Jungle Trail, which is the 1st exit after the bridge. Follow the road around and under the causeway to the parking garage on the left side.

Miami Seaquarium ★ ☺ ✋ If you've been to Orlando's SeaWorld, you may be disappointed with Miami's version, which is considerably smaller and not as well maintained. It's hardly a sprawling Seaquarium, but you will want to arrive early to enjoy the effects of its mild splash. You'll need at least 3 hours to tour the 35-acre oceanarium and see all four daily shows, starring a number of showy ocean mammals. You can cut your visit to 2 hours if you limit your shows to the better, albeit corny, *Flipper Show* and *Killer Whale Show.* The highly regarded Dolphin Encounter allows visitors to touch and swim with dolphins in the Flipper Lagoon. The program costs $139 per person, $45 per adult observer, $36 per child observer ages 3 to 9, and is offered daily at 12:15 and 3:15pm. Children must be at least 52 inches tall to participate. Reservations are necessary for this program. Call © **305/365-2501** in advance for reservations. The Seaquarium also debuted a new sea lion show and a Stingray Touch Pool.

4400 Rickenbacker Causeway (south side), en route to Key Biscayne. © **305/361-5705.** www. miamiseaquarium.com. Admission $36 adults, $27 children 3–9, free for children 2 and under. Parking $8. Daily 9am–6pm (ticket booth closes at 4pm).

Monkey Jungle ★ Personally, we think this place is nasty. It reeks, the monkeys are either sleeping or in heat, and it's really far from the city, even farther than the zoo. But if primates are your thing and you'd rather pass on the zoo, you'll be in paradise. You'll see rare Brazilian golden lion tamarins and Asian macaques. There are no cages to restrain the antics of the monkeys as they swing, chatter, and play their way into your heart. Screened-in trails wind through acres of "jungle," and daily shows feature the talents of the park's most progressive pupils. People who come here are not monkeying around—many of the park's frequent visitors are scientists and anthropologists. In fact, an interesting archaeological exhibition excavated from a Monkey Jungle sinkhole displays 10,000-year-old artifacts, including human teeth and animal bones. A somewhat amusing attraction here, if you can call it that, is the Wild Monkey Swimming Pool, a show in which you get to watch monkeys diving for food. If you can stand the humidity, the smell, and the bugs (flies, mosquitoes, and so on), expect to spend about 2 hours here. The park's website sometimes offers downloadable discount coupons, so if you have Internet access, take a look before you visit.

14805 SW 216th St., South Miami. © **305/235-1611.** www.monkeyjungle.com. Admission $30 adults, $28 seniors and active-duty military, $24 children 4–12. Daily 9:30am–5pm (tickets sold until 4pm). Take U.S. 1 south to SW 216th St., or from Florida Tpk., take exit 11 and follow the signs.

Kids can see the variety of marine life at Sea Grass Adventures.

Sea Grass Adventures ★ ☺ 🐟 Even better than the Seaquarium is Sea Grass Adventures, in which a naturalist from the Marjory Stoneman Douglas Biscayne Nature Center introduces ($12 per person) kids and adults to an amazing variety of creatures that live in the sea-grass beds of the Bear Cut Nature Preserve near Crandon Beach on Key Biscayne. You will be able to wade in the water with your guide and catch an assortment of sea life in nets provided by the guides. At the end of the program, participants gather on the beach while the guide explains what everyone has just caught, passing the creatures around in miniature viewing tanks. Call for available dates, times, and reservations.

Marjory Stoneman Douglas Biscayne Nature Center, 6767 Crandon Blvd., Key Biscayne. ✆ **305/361-6767.** Free admission to the center. Daily 10am–4pm.

Zoo Miami ★★ ☺ This 330-acre complex is quite a distance from Miami proper and the beaches—about 45 minutes—but worth the trip. Isolated and never really crowded, it's also completely cageless—animals are kept at bay by cleverly designed moats. This is a fantastic spot to take younger kids; there are wonderful play areas, and safari cycles for rent, and the zoo offers several daily programs designed to educate and entertain, like the Wildlife Show and Zoo Scene Investigations Show. Mufasa and Simba (of Disney fame) were modeled on a couple of Zoo Miami's lions. Other residents include chimpanzees, Komodo dragons, koalas, kangaroos, and meerkats. The air-conditioned monorail and tram tours offer visitors a nice overview of the park. The zoo is always upgrading its facilities, including the impressive aviary, Wings of Asia. Cool activities include the Samburu Giraffe Feeding Station, where, for $2, you get to feed the giraffes veggies; the Kaziranga Camp Rhino Encounter, where you can touch, brush, and feed an Indian rhino for $5; and Humpy's Camel Rides, where you can hop on a camel for $5. Opened in December 2008, Amazon & Beyond features jaguars, anacondas, giant river otters, harpy eagles, a stingray touch tank, two interactive water-play areas, the Flooded Forest building with a unique display of a forest before and during flood times, and an indoor Cloud Forest that houses reptiles. At 27 acres and a cost of $50 million, this exhibit is massive and makes Zoo Miami the third zoo in the country to have giant river otters, one of its keystone species. Private tours and overnights are also available

You'll have an elephant time at Zoo Miami.

for those who really want to commune with nature. *Note:* The distance between animal habitats can be great, so you'll do *a lot* of walking here. There are benches, shaded gazebos, cool misters, a water-shooting mushroom, and two water-play areas strategically positioned throughout the zoo so you can escape the heat when you need to. Also, because the zoo can be miserably hot during summer months, plan these visits in the early morning or late afternoon. Expect to spend all day here if you want to see it all.

12400 SW 152nd St., Miami. *℅* **305/251-0400.** www.zoomiami.org. Admission $16 adults, $12 children 3–12. Daily 9:30am–5:30pm (ticket booth closes at 4pm). Free parking. From U.S. 1 south, turn right on SW 152nd St., and follow signs about 3 miles to the entrance. From FL Tpk. S., take exit 16 west to the entrance.

SHOPPING

If you're not into sunbathing and outdoor activities, or you just can't take the heat, you'll be in good company in one of Miami's many malls—and you are not likely to emerge empty-handed. In addition to the strip malls, Miami offers a choice of megamalls, from the upscale Village of Merrick Park and mammoth Aventura Mall to the ritzy Bal Harbour Shops and touristy yet scenic Bayside Marketplace (just to name a few).

Miami also offers more unique shopping spots, such as the up-and-coming Biscayne Corridor, where funky boutiques dare to defy Gap, and Little Havana, where you can buy hand-rolled cigars and *guayaberas*.

You may want to order the Greater Miami Convention and Visitors Bureau's *Shop Miami: A Guide to a Tropical Shopping Adventure*. Although it is limited to details on the bureau's paying members, it provides some good advice and otherwise unpublished discount offers. The glossy little pamphlet is printed in English, Spanish, and Portuguese, and provides information on transportation from hotels, translation services, and shipping. Call *℅* **800/283-2707** or 305/539-3000 for more information.

Shopping Hours & Taxes

As a general rule, shop hours are Monday through Saturday from 10am to 6pm, and Sunday from noon to 5pm. Many stores stay open late (until 9pm or so) 1 night of the week, usually Thursday. Shops in Coconut Grove are open until 9pm Sunday through Thursday, and even later on Friday and Saturday. South Beach's stores also stay open later—as late as midnight. Department stores and shopping malls keep longer hours as well, with most staying open from 10am to 9 or 10pm Monday through Saturday, noon to 6pm on Sunday. With all these variations, you may want to call specific stores to find out their hours.

The 7% state and local sales tax is added to the price of all nonfood purchases. Food and beverage in hotels and restaurants are subject to the resort tax, which is 6% in Miami/South Beach, 9% in Bal Harbour, and 3% in the rest of Miami-Dade County.

Shopping Areas

Most of Miami's shopping happens at the many megamalls scattered from one end of the county to the other. However, excellent boutique shopping and browsing can be found in the following areas (see "The Neighborhoods in Brief," on p. 72, for more information):

AVENTURA On Biscayne Boulevard between Miami Gardens Drive and the county line at Hallandale Beach Boulevard is a 2-mile stretch of major retail stores including Target, Best Buy, DSW, Bed Bath & Beyond, Loehmann's, Marshall's, Ross Dress For Less, Filene's Basement, Old Navy, Sports Authority, and more. Also here is the mammoth Aventura Mall, housing a fabulous collection of shops and restaurants. Nearby in Hallandale Beach, the Village at Gulfstream Park is a new outdoor dining, shopping, and entertainment complex at the ever-expanding racetrack.

BISCAYNE CORRIDOR ★ Amid the ramshackle old motels of yesteryear exist several funky, kitschy, and arty boutiques along the stretch of Biscayne Boulevard from 50th Street to about 79th Street known as the Biscayne Corridor. Everything from hand-painted tank tops to expensive Juicy Couture sweat suits can be found here, but it's not just about fashion: Several furniture stores selling antiques and modern pieces exist along here as well, so look carefully, as you may find something here that would cause the appraisers on *Antiques Road Show* to lose their wigs. For more mainstream creature comforts—Target, PetSmart, Loehmann's, Marshall's, and West Elm—a new complex called the Shops at Midtown Miami has opened on a gritty yet developing street at North Miami Avenue and NE 36th Street.

CALLE OCHO For a taste of Little Havana, take a walk down 8th Street between SW 27th Avenue and SW 12th Avenue, where you'll find some lively street life and many shops selling cigars, baked goods, shoes, furniture, and record stores specializing in Latin music. For help, take your Spanish dictionary.

COCONUT GROVE Downtown Coconut Grove, centered on Main Highway and Grand Avenue, and branching onto the adjoining streets, is one of Miami's most pedestrian-friendly zones. The Grove's wide sidewalks, lined with cafes and boutiques, can provide hours of browsing pleasure. Coconut Grove is best known for its chain stores (Gap, Victoria's Secret, Bath & Body Works, and so on) and some funky holdovers from the days when the Grove was a bit more bohemian, plus some good sidewalk cafes and lively bars.

Buy hand-rolled cigars at shops like Cuba Tobacco Cigar Company in Calle Ocho.

DESIGN DISTRICT Although it's still primarily an interior design, art, and furniture hub, Design District is slowly adding retail to its roster with a few funky and fabulous boutiques catering to those who don't necessarily have to ask, "How much?"

DOWNTOWN MIAMI If you're looking for discounts on all types of goods—especially watches, fabric, buttons, lace, shoes, luggage, and leather—Flagler Street, just west of Biscayne Boulevard, is the best place to start. We wouldn't necessarily recommend buying expensive items here, as many stores seem to be on the shady side and do not understand the word *warranty*. However, you can still have fun here as long as you are a savvy shopper and don't mind haggling. Most signs are printed in English, Spanish, and Portuguese; however, many shopkeepers may not be entirely fluent in English. Mary Brickell Village, a 192,000-square-foot urban entertainment center west of Brickell Avenue and straddling South Miami Avenue between 9th and 10th streets downtown, hasn't been so quick to emerge as a major shopping destination as much as it is a dining and nightlife one with a slew of trendy restaurants, bars, a few boutiques, and the requisite Starbucks—a sure sign that a neighborhood has been revitalized.

MIRACLE MILE (CORAL GABLES) Actually only a half-mile long, this central shopping street was an integral part of George Merrick's original city plan. Today the strip still enjoys popularity, especially for its bridal stores, ladies' shops, haberdashers, and gift shops. Recently, newer chain stores, such as Barnes & Noble, Old Navy, and Starbucks, have been appearing on the Mile. The hyperupscale **Village of Merrick Park,** a mammoth, 850,000-square-foot outdoor shopping complex between Ponce de León Boulevard and Le Jeune Road, just off the Mile, houses Nordstrom, Neiman Marcus, Armani, Gucci, Jimmy Choo, and Yves St. Laurent, to name a few.

SOUTH BEACH ★ South Beach has come into its own as far as trendy shopping is concerned. While the requisite stores such as Gap and Banana Republic have anchored here, several higher-end stores have also opened on the southern blocks of Collins Avenue, which has become the Madison Avenue of Miami. For the hippest clothing boutiques (including Armani Exchange, Ralph Lauren, Intermix, Benetton, Levi's, Barneys Co-Op, Diesel, Guess, Club Monaco, Kenneth Cole, and Nicole Miller, among others), stroll along this pretty strip of the Art Deco District.

Take a break from shopping the Miracle Mile in a gracious outdoor café.

For those who are interested in a little more fun with their shopping, consider South Beach's legendary Lincoln Road. This pedestrian mall, originally designed in 1957 by Morris Lapidus, recently underwent a multimillion-dollar renovation, restoring it to its former glory. Here shoppers find an array of clothing, books, tchotchkes, and art, as well as a menagerie of sidewalk cafes flanked on one end by a multiplex movie theater and, at the other, by the Atlantic Ocean.

MIAMI AFTER DARK

With all the hype, you'd expect Miami to have long outlived its 15 minutes of fame by now. But you'd be wrong. Miami's nightlife, in South Beach *and,* slowly but surely, downtown and its urban environs, is hotter than ever before—and getting cooler with the opening of each funky, fabulous watering hole, lounge, and club. Not always cool, however, is the presence of ubiquitous, closely guarded velvet ropes used to often erroneously create an air of exclusivity. Don't be fooled or intimidated by them—*anyone* can go clubbing in the Magic City, and throughout this section, we've provided tips to ensure that you gain entry to your desired venue.

South Beach is certainly Miami's uncontested nocturnal nucleus, but more and more diverse areas, such as the Design District, Midtown/Wynwood, Brickell, South Miami, and even Little Havana, are increasingly providing fun alternatives without the ludicrous cover charges, "fashionably late" hours of operation (things don't typically get started on South Beach until after 11pm), lack of sufficient self-parking, and outrageous drink prices that are standard in South Beach.

While South Beach dances to a more electronic beat, other parts of Miami dance to a Latin beat—from salsa and merengue to tango and cha-cha. However, if you're looking for a less frenetic good time, Miami's bar scene has something for everyone, from haute hotel bars to sleek, loungey watering holes.

Parts of downtown, such as the Biscayne Corridor, the Miami River, Midtown, Wynwood, and the Design District, are undergoing a trendy makeover a la New York City's Meatpacking District. Cool lounges, bars, and clubs are popping up and providing the "in" crowds with a newer, more urban-chic nocturnal pasture.

But if the possibility of a celebrity sighting in one of the city's lounges, bars, or clubs doesn't fulfill your cultural needs, Miami also provides a variety of first-rate diversions in theater, music, and dance, including a world-class ballet (under the aegis of Edward Villella), a recognized symphony, and a talented opera company. The circa-2006 Cesar Pelli–designed, $446-million Adrienne Arsht Center for the Performing Arts is the focal point for the arts, created to prove to the world that Miami isn't as shallow and devoid of culture as people once thought.

For up-to-date listing information, and to make sure the club of the moment hasn't expired, check the *Miami Herald*'s "Weekend" section, which runs on Friday, or the more comprehensive listings in *New Times,* Miami's free alternative weekly, available each Wednesday; or visit **www.miami.com** online.

Bars & Lounges

There are countless bars and lounges in and around Miami (most require proof that you are 21 or older to enter), with the highest concentration on trendy South Beach. The selection here is a mere sample. Keep in mind that many of the popular bars—and the easiest to get into—are in hotels (with a few notable exceptions—see below). For a clubbier scene, if you don't mind making your way through hordes of inebriated club kids, a stroll on Washington Avenue will provide you with ample insight into what's hot and what's not. Just hold on to your bags. It's not dangerous, but occasionally a few shady types manage to slip into the crowd. Another very important tip when in a club: *Never put your drink down out of your sight*—there have been unfortunate incidents in which drinks have

The Adrienne Arsht Center lights up Miami's performing arts scene.

been spiked with illegal chemical substances. For a less hard-core, more collegiate nightlife, head to Coconut Grove. Oh, yes, and when going out in South Beach, make sure to take a so-called disco nap, as things don't get going until at least 11pm. If you go earlier, be prepared to face an empty bar or club. Off of South Beach and in hotel bars in general, the hours are fashionably earlier, with the action starting as early as, say, 7pm.

The Abbey Dark, dank, and hard to find, this local microbrewery is a favorite for locals looking to escape the $20 candy-flavored martini scene. Best of all, there's never a cover and it's always open until 5am, perfect for those pesky and insatiable hops cravings that pop up at 3 or 4am. 1115 16th St., South Beach. ✆ 305/538-8110.

Bardot 🏆 Modeled after the basement of a rock star circa 1972, Bardot is Miami proper's hottest new scene despite the fact that it prides itself on being the antithesis of being sceney. A mixed crowd of young and old, gay and straight, and everything in between is what you'll find at this off-the-beaten-path lounge–cum–speak-easy located in the back of a Midtown furniture store. Shag carpeting, comfy couches, and decor straight out of *That '70s Show* make for a very comfy backdrop for cocktailing, listening to live music, and watching what may be, at the time of this writing, Miami's most colorful hipster crowd. 3456 N. Miami Ave., Miami. ✆ **305/576-5570.** www.bardotmiami.com.

Burger & Beer Joint Although downstairs at this bustling, well, burger and beer joint, is more about food, in back is a sports bar complete with flatscreen TVs to catch the latest game. Not in the mood for athletics? Consider the lounge upstairs where a chilled-out scene attracts everyone from barflies and models to overly full diners from downstairs looking to veg out on the couches. 1766 Bay Rd., South Beach. ✆ **305/672-3287.** www.burgernbeerjoint.com.

Clevelander If wet-T-shirt contests and a fraternity-party atmosphere are your thing, then this Ocean Drive mainstay is your kind of place. Popular with tourists and locals who like to pretend they're tourists, the Clevelander, which was the recent recipient of much-needed renovations, attracts a lively, sporty crowd of only adults (the burly bouncers *will* confiscate fake IDs) who have no interest in being part of a scene, but, rather, like to take in the very revealing scenery. A great time to check out the Clevelander is on a weekend afternoon, when beach Barbies and Kens line the bar for a post-tanning beer or frozen cocktail. 1020 Ocean Dr., South Beach. ✆ **305/531-3485.** www.clevelander.com.

DRB Miami A tiny spot across the street from the performing arts center, DRB—Democratic Republic of Beer—is where Miami meets Williamsburg, Brooklyn, with an unabridged list of microbrews from all over the world, a better-than-average bar menu, and a crowd of hops-loving hipsters sporting ironic facial hair and quoting Kafka. 255 NE 14th St., Miami. ✆ **305/372-4565.** www.drbmiami.com.

Electric Pickle A tiny bar with upstairs lounge and a parking lot out back that doubles as its outdoor area, Electric Pickle is the unofficial clubhouse of Miami's indie music scene, where the long-running Brit-pop, hipster-happy one-nighter Pop Life takes up residence every Saturday. We completely recommend the place if that's your scene, but go at your own risk as its host neighborhood is still very dodgy. 2826 N. Miami Ave., Wynwood. ✆ **305/456-5613.**

The Florida Room The Florida Room is a dimly chandelier-lit den of "old-school Florida decor meets swanky cruise ship lounge"—a place of 200 maximum capacity—where everyone from young hipsters and swanky sophisticates to the Golden Girls would go for a fancy night out, where Rue McClanahan's feisty, randy Blanche would climb atop the Lucite piano, channeling Michelle Pfeiffer in *The Fabulous Baker Boys*. Designed by rocker Lenny Kravitz, the interior of this subterranean speak-easy is the antithesis of the sleek, stark hotel in which it resides, and for that, we love it. 1685 Collins Ave. (in the Delano), South Beach. ℭ **305/672-2000.** www.delano-hotel.com.

Stargazing in Miami

The most popular places for celebrity sightings include Louis, Mansion, LIV, WALL, Mondrian, the Florida Room, Skybar, the Rose Bar at Delano, and, when it comes to stars gazing at other stars, Miami Heat basketball games. That or, when it comes to edgier, under-the-radar celebs, Mac's Club Deuce around 5 in the morning.

Louis Another product of the Opium Group, Louis is, if you will, the French foreign exchange student where Louis XVI meets South Beach's reigning royalty on the nightlife circuit. Boasting (and we do mean boasting) a French sensibility—and attitude—Louis, located on the street level at the Gansevoort South, has been known to host everyone from Lindsay Lohan to Marilyn Manson to a few unsuspecting, low-key folks thrown in to throw you off. 2325 Collins Ave. ℭ **305/531-4600.** www.louismiami.com. Cover $30 and up.

Mac's Club Deuce Standing amid an oasis of trendiness, Mac's Club Deuce is the quintessential dive bar, with cheap drinks and a cast of characters ranging from your typical barfly to your atypical drag queen. It's got a well-stocked jukebox, friendly bartenders, and a pool table. Best of all, it's an insomniac's dream, open daily from 8am to 5am. 222 14th St., South Beach. ℭ **305/673-9537.**

Mynt A massive 6,000-square-foot place, Mynt is nothing more than a huge living room in which models, celebrities, locals, and assorted hangers-on bask in the green glow to the beat of very loud lounge and dance music. If you want to dance—or move, for that matter—this is not the place in which to do so. It's all about striking a pose in here. Unless you know the person at the door, be prepared to be ridiculed, emasculated, and socially shattered, as you may be forced to wait outside upward of an hour. If that's the case, forget it; it's not worth it. Wait next door at the Greek place for a celebrity sighting, as you'll have a better chance of seeing people from there instead of just waiting in the melee at the door. 1921 Collins Ave., South Beach. ℭ **786/276-6132.** www.myntlounge.com. Cover $10–$20.

Playwright Irish Pub Bono came here once when U2 was in town, not because it's such an authentic Irish pub, but because the bar was showing some European soccer match—and serves pints of Guinness. A great pre- or post-club spot, Playwright is one of the few places in town that also features live music from time to time. 1265 Washington Ave., South Beach. ℭ **305/534-0667.** www.playwrightirishpub.com.

The Purdy Lounge With the exception of a wall of lava lamps, Purdy is not unlike your best friend's basement, featuring a pool table and a slew of board games such as Operation to keep the attention-deficit-disordered from getting bored. It even has a bingo and spelling bee night! Because it's a no-nonsense bar with relatively cheap cocktails (by South Beach standards), Purdy gets away with not having a star DJ or fancy bass-heavy Bose sound system. A CD player somehow does the trick. With no cover and no attitude, a line is inevitable (it gets crowded inside), so be prepared to wait. Saturday night has become the preferred night for locals, while Friday night's happy hour draws a young professional crowd on the prowl. 1811 Purdy Ave. at Sunset Harbor, South Beach. ℂ 305/531-4622. www.purdylounge.com.

The Rooftop at the Gansevoort Possibly the best thing about the Gansevoort is the hotel's rockin' rooftop pool lounge, where on any given day or night, scantily clad scene- (and bikini-) chasers can be found either in or out of the water, sipping colorful cocktails to the tune of DJ-spun music. 2399 Collins Ave., South Beach. ℂ 305/604-1000.

The Room It's beer and wine only at this South of Fifth hideaway, where locals and N.Y. expats (there are a few Rooms in N.Y.C.) come to get away from the insanity just a few blocks away. The beer selection is comprehensive, with brews from almost everywhere in the world. The wine is not so great, but there's no whining here at this tiny, industrial-style, candlelit spot that doesn't have a DJ—just a CD player spinning indie tunes—or those pesky Paris Hilton sightings. 100 Collins Ave., South Beach. ℂ 305/531-6061. www.theotheroom.com.

Segafredo Espresso Although Segafredo is technically a cafe, it has become an integral part of Miami's nightlife as command central for Euros who miss that very special brand of European cafe society. Not in the mood for a club or bar, but want to hear great music, sip a few cocktails, snack on delicious sandwiches and pizza, and sit outside and people-watch? This is the place. European lounge music, tons of outdoor tables on a prime corner of Lincoln Road, and always a mob scene make 'Fredo one of our—and many other Miamians'—favorite nocturnal diversions. Although South Beach boasts the original, another Segafredo, with different owners, a larger food menu, and separate nightclub, is open in the Brickell Area, at 1421 S. Miami Ave., and another cafe opened on Espanola Way on South Beach and in South Miami at 5800 SW 73rd St. 1040 Lincoln Rd., South Beach. ℂ 305/673-0047.

Skybar at The Shore Club Skybar lives up to its name in terms of loftiness, something this place has perfected better than anyone else, whether at its original L.A. location or the sprawling South Beach location at the Shore Club. If you're not a hotel guest, not Beyoncé, or not on the "list," or if you're a guy with several other guys and no girls, forget about it. For those of you who can't get in, the Skybar is basically the entire backyard area of the Shore Club, consisting of several areas, including the Moroccan-themed garden area, the hip-hop-themed indoor Red Room, the Sand Bar by the beach, and the Rum Bar by the pool. Sunday-afternoon pool parties are a magnet for celebs and locals alike. Popular on any given night, Skybar is yet another brilliant example of how hotelier Ian Schrager has managed to control the hipsters in a most Pavlovian way. At the Shore Club, 1901 Collins Ave., South Beach. ℂ 305/695-3100. www.shoreclub.com.

Transit Lounge It's hard to locate, but once you do find Transit Lounge, you'll be happy you did. Reminiscent of what locals describe as "a real big-city lounge," Transit is cavernous, featuring a huge bar, tons of cozy couches and tables, board games, a funky crowd, and, hallelujah, live music. 1729 SW 1st Ave., Miami. ℂ 305/377-4628. www.transitlounge.us.

Wet Bar at the W South Beach As wholly unoriginal as the name is, the poolside Wet Bar along with the secret-garden Grove and lobby-level Living Room at the fabulous new W South Beach are among the city's most stylish, creative, and

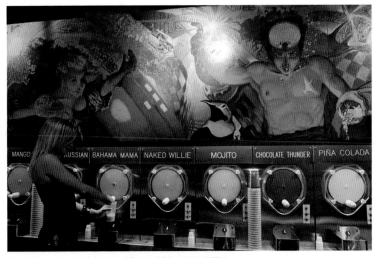
Choose from the colorfully named frozen drinks at Wet Willie's.

buzz-worthy nightspots thanks to a stellar combo of master mixologists who shake and stir up some of the most creative—and pricey—cocktails you'll ever drink, celebrities and locals who drink them, and resplendent settings with Facebook-worthy photo-op backdrops. 2201 Collins Ave., South Beach. ℂ **305/938-3000.**

Wet Willie's With such telling drinks as Call a Cab, this beachfront oasis is not the place to go if you have a long drive ahead of you. A well-liked pre- and post-beach hangout, Wet Willie's inspires serious drinking. Popular with the Harley-Davidson set, tourists, and beachcombers, this bar is best known for its rooftop patio (get there early if you plan to get a seat) and its half-nude bikini beauties. 760 Ocean Dr., South Beach. ℂ **305/532-5650.**

Bowling Alleys

Think of it as the Big Lebowski meets Studio 54, because in Miami, this is not your Sunday-afternoon ESPN bowling tournament. As much a fun rainy-day activity as it is with the kids, bowling in Miami gives new meaning to partying in the gutter.

Lucky Strike Lanes South Beach's only bowling alley is a pricey blast for adults and children, with 14 lanes, two pool tables, free Wi-Fi (to cheat on bowling?), a pulsating nightclub-esque soundtrack, a full bar, TVs, and a restaurant. Kids are allowed only up until 9pm, after which time Lucky Strike turns into a 21-and-over scene. 1691 Michigan Ave. ℂ **305/532-0307.** www.bowlluckystrike.com. $45–$55 per hour depending on day and time, including shoe rental. Mon–Thurs 11:30am–1am; Fri 11:30am–2am; Sat 11am–2am; Sun 11am–1am.

Splitsville Luxury Lanes & Dinner Lounge Located at Sunset Place, Splitsville is South Miami's Lucky Strike, with 12 lanes, six pool tables, a full-service restaurant, TVs, and multiple bars. Like Lucky Strike, no youth age 20 and under are allowed after 8pm, when the place turns into a thumping club scene until 5am. Unlike Lucky Strike, Splitsville is affordable, and because of that, there's usually a wait list for a lane. Luckily, there are plenty of other distractions

Strike up a conversation (or spare a moment for a drink) at Splitsville.

to keep you busy while you wait. 5701 Sunset Dr. ☎ **305/665-5263.** www.splitsvillelanes. com. $6 per person per game, $4 for shoe rental. Mon–Thurs 4pm–2am; Fri–Sat 11am–5am; Sun 11am–2am.

Strike Miami Located at the Dolphin Mall, this one is Miami's biggest bowling alley, with 34 lanes and, like the others, a nightclub setting. This one, owned by N.Y.C.'s famed Bowlmor, even has glow-in-the-dark bowling. Food, bars, TVs, you get the picture. It's 18 and over after 9pm. In the Dolphin Mall, 11401 NW 12 St. ☎ **305/594-0200.** www.bowlmor.com. $30–$40 per hour depending on day and time, including shoe rental. Mon–Thurs 4pm–1am; Fri noon–3am; Sat 11am–3am; Sun 11am–1am.

Dance Clubs

Clubs are as much a cottage industry in Miami as is, say, cheese in Wisconsin. Clubland, as it is known, is a way of life for some. On any given night in Miami, there's something going on—no excuses are needed to throw a party here. Short of throwing a glamorous event for the grand opening of a new gas station, Miami is very party hearty, celebrating everything from the fact that it's Tuesday night to the debut of a hot new DJ.

To keep things fresh in Clubland, local promoters throw 1-nighters, which are essentially parties with various themes or motifs, from funk to fashion. Because these change so often, we can't possibly list them here. Word of mouth, local advertising, and listings in the free weekly *New Times,* www.miami.city-search.com, or the "Weekend" section of the *Miami Herald* are the best ways to find out about these ever-changing events.

SAVING MONEY, TIME & SANITY AT SOUTH BEACH CLUBS Before you get all decked out to hit the town as soon as the sun sets, consider the fact that Miami is a very late town. Things generally don't get started here before 11pm. The Catch-22 is that if you don't arrive on South Beach early enough, you may find yourself driving around aimlessly for parking (meters are jacked up to as much as $1.50 per **hour** on weekend nights), as it is very limited outside of absurd $20-plus valet charges. Municipal lots fill up quickly, so your best bet is to arrive on South Beach somewhat early and kill time by strolling around, having something to eat, or sipping a cocktail in a hotel bar. Another advantage of arriving a bit earlier than the crowds is that some clubs don't charge a cover before 11pm or midnight, which could save you a wad of cash over time.

Most clubs are open every night of the week, though some are open only Thursday to Sunday and others are open only Monday through Saturday. Call ahead to get the most up-to-date information possible: Things change very quickly around here, and a call in advance can help you make sure that the dance club you're planning to go to hasn't become a video arcade.

Cover charges are very haphazard, too. If you're not on the ubiquitous guest list (ask your concierge to put you on the list—he or she usually has the ability to do so, which won't help you with the wait to get in, but will eliminate the cover charge), you may have to fork over a ridiculous $20 to walk past the ropes. Don't fret, though. There are many clubs and bars that have no cover charge—they just make up for it by charging $20 for a martini!

LIV The latest in Miami's celebrity-saturated nightlife, LIV (as in, "celebrities live for LIV") and Blade are the recently revamped Fontainebleau's dance club and subterranean lounge–slash–pool bar, respectively. Because they're new, they're at the top of the A-list and among the hardest to get into. Go early even if it means lining up in the lobby. In the cavernous LIV, expect to see celebs ensconced in visible VIP areas. A new sister club, Arkadia, opened on the floor below LIV in October 2010, but it's hardly beneath its older sibling in terms of star power and club cachet. Two separate entrances, two totally different vibes, two times the fun. 4441 Collins Ave., South Beach. ✆ **305/538-2000.** www.livnightclub.com. Cover $10–$50.

Mansion A product of the same team behind the utterly addictive Opium Group (see above), this place is a massive multilevel lounge that, according to the owners and promoters, is entirely "VIP," meaning you'd best know someone to get in or else you'll be among the masses outside and not even close to the manse. DJs, models, and celebrities galore—ubiquitous Paris Hilton, Britney Spears, Lindsay Lohan, Justin Timberlake, Beyoncé, Jay-Z, and more—not to mention high ceilings, wood floors, brick walls, and a decidedly nonsmoky interior—make this Mansion, despite its cheesy name, a *must* on the list of see-and-be-scensters. Open Tuesday through Sunday from 11pm to 5am. 1235 Washington Ave., South Beach. ✆ **305/531-5535.** www.theopiumgroup.com. Cover $10–$40.

Dancers pack the floor at LIV.

Nikki Beach What the Playboy Mansion is to L.A., the Nikki Beach is to South Beach—but if you want a locals scene, you won't find it here. The allure is mostly for visiting tourists who love to gawk at their fellow half-naked ladies and men actually venturing into the daylight on Sunday (around 4pm, which is ungodly in this town) to see, be seen, and, at times, be obscene. At night, it's very "Brady Bunch goes to Hawaii," with a sexy Tiki hut/Polynesian theme, albeit rated R. Also located within this bastion of hedonism is the second-floor nightclub for those who want to dance on an actual dance floor and not sand. The club recently debuted a new spruced-up dining room serving very massive portions of "global cuisine," but we'd stick with cocktails. 101 Ocean Dr., South Beach. ☏ **305/538-1111**. www.nikkibeach.com. Cover $10–$20.

SET The Opium Group's undisputed "it" child, SET is *the* place to be, at least at the time of this writing. A luxurious lounge with chandeliers and design mag–worthy decor is always full of trendsetters, celebs, and wannabes. Where you really want to be, however, is upstairs, in the private VIP room, where Britney Spears was seen downing purple hooter shots. A classy place that doesn't designate the behavior of its patrons, SET is also known for a ruthless door policy. Ask your hotel concierge to get you in or else you may find yourself standing on the wrong side of the velvet ropes wasting precious vacation time. 320 Lincoln Rd., South Beach. ☏ **305/531-2800**. www.setmiami.com. Cover $20.

WALL The W South Beach's requisite velvety roped-off hipster nightclub run by—who else—the Opium Group in collaboration with some other heavy hitters in the Miami club scene, WALL is a place you definitely want to bang up against if you're into that very VIP scene complete with couches reserved for only those dropping thousands on booze even in a recession. With its mirrored walls and flashy ambience, a night in WALL is not unlike what we think it would feel like to spin around inside a disco ball. 2201 Collins Ave., South Beach. ☏ **305/938-3000**.

Live Music

Unfortunately, Miami's live music scene is not thriving. Instead of local bands garnering devoted fans, local DJs are more admired, skyrocketing much more easily to fame—thanks to the city's lauded dance-club scene. However, there are still several places that strive to bring Miami up to speed as far as live music is concerned. You just have to look—and listen—for it a bit more carefully. The following is a list of places where you can, from time to time, catch some live acts.

Churchill's Hideaway British expatriate Dave Daniels couldn't live in Miami without a true English-style pub, so he opened Churchill's Hideaway, the city's premier space for live rock music. Filthy and located in a rather unsavory neighborhood, Churchill's is committed to promoting and extending the lifeline of the lagging local music scene. A fun no-frills crowd hangs out here. Bring earplugs with you, as it is deafening once the music starts. Monday is open-mic night, while Wednesday is reserved for ladies' wrestling. 5501 NE 2nd Ave., Little Haiti. ☏ **305/757-1807**. www.churchillspub.com. Cover up to $6.

Grand Central The newest addition to Miami's ever-burgeoning yet still somewhat underground indie music scene, Grand Central is, indeed, the Grand Central of live indie acts who flock here from around the world to perform for adoring hipster fans. 697 N. Miami Ave., Downtown Miami. ☏ **305/377-2277**. www.grandcentralmiami.com. Cover varies depending on who's performing.

Grab a table and listen to some blues at Tobacco Road.

Jazid Smoky, sultry, and illuminated by flickering candelabras, Jazid is the kind of place where you'd expect to hear Sade's "Smooth Operator" on constant rotation. Instead, however, you'll hear live jazz (sometimes acid jazz), soul, and funk. An eclectic mix of mellow folk convenes here for a much-needed respite from the surrounding Washington Avenue mayhem. 1342 Washington Ave., South Beach. ☎ **305/673-9372.** www.jazid.net. Cover free–$10.

Tobacco Road Al Capone used to hang out here when it was a speakeasy. Now locals flock here to see local bands perform, as well as national acts such as George Clinton and the P-Funk All-Stars, Koko Taylor, and the Radiators. Tobacco Road (the proud owner of Miami's very first liquor license) is small and gritty, and meant to be that way. Escape the smoke and sweat in the backyard patio, where air is a welcome commodity. The downright-cheap nightly specials, such as the $11 lobster on Tuesday, are quite good and served until 2am; the bar is open until 5am. 626 S. Miami Ave. (over the Miami Ave. Bridge, near Brickell Ave.), Downtown. ☎ **305/374-1198.** www.tobacco-road.com. Cover Thurs–Sat $5–$10.

Upstairs at the Van Dyke Cafe The cafe's jazz bar, located on the second floor, resembles a classy speak-easy in which local jazz performers play to an intimate, enthusiastic crowd of mostly adults and sophisticated young things, who often huddle at the small tables until the wee hours. 846 Lincoln Rd., South Beach. ☎ **305/534-3600.** www.thevandykecafe.com. Cover Sun–Thurs $5, Fri–Sat $10 for a seat; no cover at the bar.

The Gay & Lesbian Scene

Miami and the beaches have long been host to what is called a "first-tier" gay community. Similar to the Big Apple, the Bay Area, or LaLa land, Miami has had a large alternative community since the days when Anita Bryant used her citrus power to boycott the rise in political activism in the early '70s. Well, things have changed and Miami-Dade now has a gay-rights ordinance.

Newcomers intending to party in any bar, whether downtown or certainly on the beach, will want to check ahead for the schedule, as all clubs must have a gay or lesbian night to pay their rent. Miami Beach, in fact, is a capital of the gay circuit party scene, rivaling San Francisco, Palm Springs, and even the mighty Sydney, Australia, for tourist dollars. However, ever since South Beach got bit by the hip-hop bug, many of Miami's gays have been crossing county lines into Fort Lauderdale, where there are, surprisingly, many more gay establishments.

Mova Just off Lincoln Road, Mova (formerly Halo) is the beach's newer, boutiquey gay lounge. Smoke free and überstylish, Mova is open nightly until 3am

Where the boys are: Score, in South Beach.

and features DJs and a daily buy-one-get-one-free happy hour from 3 to 6pm. 1625 Michigan Ave., South Beach. No phone.

The Palace   Just steps away from the men preening on the 12th Street Beach (p. 3) is this gay bar and drag show venue, which loudly and proudly plants its rainbow flag on the Ocean Drive sidewalk, much to the curiosity of the guests quietly lounging at The Tides hotel next door. Snag a sidewalk table before a show

THE rhythm IS GONNA GET YOU

Are you feeling shy about hitting a Latin club because you fear your two left feet will stand out? Then take a few lessons from one of the following dance companies or dance teachers. They offer individual and group lessons to dancers of any origin who are willing to learn. These folks have made it their mission to teach merengue and flamenco to non-Latinos and Latino left-foots, and are among the most reliable, consistent, and popular ones in Miami. So what are you waiting for?

Thursday and Friday nights at **Bongo's Cuban Café** (pictured, American Airlines Arena, 601 Biscayne Blvd., Downtown; ✆ **786/777-2100**) are amazing showcases for some of the city's best salsa dancers, but amateurs need not be intimidated, thanks to the instructors from Latin Groove Dance Studios, who are on hand to help you with your two left feet. Lessons are free.

At **Ballet Flamenco La Rosa** (in the Performing Arts Network [PAN] building, 13126 W. Dixie Hwy., North Miami;

✆ **305/899-7730**; www.panmiami. org), you can learn to flamenco, salsa, or merengue. This is the only professional flamenco company in the area. They charge $15 per class.

Nobody teaches salsa like **Luz Pinto** (✆ **786/281-9747**; www.latin-heat. com). She teaches 7 days a week and, trust us, with her, you'll learn cool turns easily. She charges $50 for a private lesson and is the only instructor who doesn't charge extra if you want to share the lesson with a partner or (usually Fri–Sat 6pm and Sun 11am and 4pm) if you want Tiffany Fantasia to get all up in your Cobb salad. 1200 Ocean Dr. ☎ **305/531-7234.** www.palacesouthbeach. com.

Score There's a reason this Lincoln Road hotbed of gay activity is called Score. In addition to the huge pickup scene, Score offers a multitude of bars, dance floors, lounge areas, and outdoor tables, in case you need to come up for air. Sunday afternoon tea dances are legendary. 727 Lincoln Rd., South Beach. ☎ **305/535-1111.** www.scorebar.net.

Twist One of the most popular bars (and hideaways) on South Beach, this recently expanded bar (which is literally right across the street from the police station) has a casual yet lively atmosphere. 1057 Washington Ave., South Beach. ☎ **305/538-9478.** www.twistsobe.com.

Latin Clubs

Considering that Hispanics make up a large part of Miami's population and that there's a huge influx of Spanish-speaking visitors, it's no surprise that there are some great Latin nightclubs in the city. Plus, with the meteoric rise of the international music scene based in Miami, many international stars come through the offices of MTV Latino, SONY International, and a multitude of Latin TV studios based in Miami—and they're all looking for a good club scene on weekends. Most of the Anglo clubs also reserve at least 1 night a week for Latin rhythms.

Hoy Como Ayer Formerly known as Cafe Nostalgia, the Little Havana hangout dedicated to reminiscing about Old Cuba, Hoy Como Ayer is like the Brady Bunch of Latin hangouts—while it was extremely popular with old-timers in

partners. She also teaches group classes at PAN on Miami Beach. She teaches everything from classic to hip wedding dances to ballroom, disco, and merengue, as well L.A.-style and Casino-style salsa, popularized in the 1950s in Cuba. You will be impressed with how well and quickly Luz can teach you to have fun and feel great dancing. Call her for more information.

Angel Arroyo has been teaching salsa to the clueless out of his home (at 16467 NE 27th Ave., North Miami Beach; ☎ **305/949-7799**) for the past 10 years. Classes are $55 per person or couple. He traditionally teaches Monday and Wednesday nights, but call ahead to check for any schedule and rate changes.

its Cafe Nostalgia incarnation, it is now experiencing a resurgence among the younger generation seeking its own brand of nostalgia. Its Thursday-night party, *Fuacata* (slang for "Pow!"), is a magnet for Latin hipsters, featuring classic Cuban music mixed in with modern DJ-spun sound effects. Open Thursday to Sunday from 9pm to 4am. 2212 SW 8th St. (Calle Ocho), Little Havana. ℂ **305/541-2631.** Cover Thurs–Sun $10.

Mango's Tropical Café Claustrophobic types do not want to go near Mango's—ever. One of the most popular spots on Ocean Drive, this outdoor enclave of Latin liveliness shakes with the intensity of a Richter-busting earthquake. Mango's is *Cabaret,* Latin-style. Nightly live Brazilian and other Latin music, not to mention scantily clad male and female dancers, draws huge gawking crowds in from the sidewalk. But pay attention to the music, if you can: Incognito international musicians often lose their anonymity and jam with the house band on stage. Open daily from 11am to 5am. 900 Ocean Dr., South Beach. ℂ **305/673-4422.** www.mangostropicalcafe.com. Cover $5–$15.

The Performing Arts

Highbrows and culture vultures complain that there is a dearth of decent cultural offerings in Miami. What do locals tell them? Go back to New York! However, in recent years, Miami's performing arts scene has improved greatly. The city's Broadway Series features Tony Award–winning shows (the touring versions, of course), which aren't always Broadway caliber, but usually pretty good and not nearly as pricey. Local arts groups such as the Miami Light Project, a not-for-profit cultural organization that presents performances by innovative dance, music, and theater artists, have had huge success in attracting big-name artists such as Nina Simone and Philip Glass to Miami. Also, a burgeoning bohemian movement in Little Havana has given way to performance spaces that are nightclubs in their own right.

THEATER

The **Actors' Playhouse,** a musical theater at the newly restored Miracle Theater at 280 Miracle Mile, Coral Gables (ℂ **305/444-9293;** www.actorsplayhouse. org), is a grand 1948 Art Deco movie palace with a 600-seat main theater and a smaller theater/rehearsal hall that hosts a number of excellent musicals for children throughout the year. In addition to these two theaters, the Playhouse recently added a 300-seat children's balcony theater. Tickets run from $10 to $52.

The **GableStage,** at the Biltmore Hotel (p. 107), Anastasia Avenue, Coral Gables (ℂ **305/445-1119;** www.gablestage.org), stages at least one Shakespearean play, one classic, and one contemporary piece a year. This well-regarded theater usually tries to secure the rights to a national or local premiere as well. Tickets cost $38 to $43. GableStage announced in 2009 that it would take over the abandoned, landmark Coconut Grove Playhouse using $20 million in designated county improvement funds to create a larger, 600-seat theater. Construction is expected to start in 2012 and end in 2014.

The **Jerry Herman Ring Theatre** is on the main campus of the University of Miami in Coral Gables (ℂ **305/284-3355**). The University's Department of Theater Arts uses this stage for advanced-student productions of comedies, dramas, and musicals. Faculty and guest actors are regularly featured, as are contemporary works by local playwrights. Performances are usually scheduled

Tuesday through Saturday during the academic year. In the summer, don't miss "Summer Shorts," a selection of superb one-acts. Tickets sell for $10 to $18.

The **New Theatre**, 4120 Laguna St., Coral Gables (✆ **305/443-5909**; www.new-theatre.org), prides itself on showing renowned works from America and Europe. As the name implies, you'll find mostly contemporary plays, with a few classics thrown in. Performances are staged Thursday through Sunday year-round. Tickets are $35 on Thursday, $40 on Friday and Saturday, and $35 to $40 on Sunday. If tickets are available on the day of the performance—and they usually are—students pay half-price.

CLASSICAL MUSIC

In addition to a number of local orchestras and operas (see below), which regularly offer quality music and world-renowned guest artists, each year brings a slew of classical-music special events and touring artists to Miami. The **Concert Association of Florida** (**CAF**; ✆ **877/433-3200**) produces one of the most important and longest-running series. Known for more than a quarter of a century for its high-caliber, star-packed schedules, CAF regularly arranges the best "serious" music concerts for the city. Season after season, the schedules are punctuated by world-renowned dance companies and seasoned virtuosi such as Itzhak Perlman, Andre Watts, and Kathleen Battle. Because CAF does not have its own space, performances are usually scheduled in the Miami-Dade County Auditorium or the Jackie Gleason Theater of the Performing Arts (see the "Major Venues" section below). The season lasts October through April, and ticket prices range from $20 to $70.

New World Symphony ★ This organization, led by artistic director Michael Tilson Thomas, is a steppingstone for gifted young musicians seeking professional careers. The orchestra specializes in innovative, energetic performances,

The Frank Gehry–designed home of the New World Symphony opened with great fanfare in 2011.

and often features renowned guest soloists and conductors. The season lasts from October to May, during which time there are many free concerts. In the fall of 2010, the NWS moved to its spectacular new $200-million-plus Frank Gehry–designed campus featuring practice rooms, rehearsal rooms, technology suites, and a grand performance space. Even if you're not into the music, this is something to see. 500 17th St., South Beach. ✆ **305/673-3330.** www.nws.org. Tickets free to $60. Rush tickets (remaining tickets sold 1 hr. before performance) $20. Students $10 (1 hr. before concerts; limited seating).

OPERA

Florida Grand Opera Around for more than 60 years, this company regularly features singers from top houses in both America and Europe. All productions are sung in their original language and staged with projected English supertitles. Tickets become scarce when Placido Domingo comes to town. The season runs roughly from November to April, with five performances each week. In 2007, the opera moved into more upscale headquarters in the **Sanford and Dolores Ziff Ballet Opera House at the Arsht Center for the Performing Arts.** Box office: 1300 Biscayne Blvd., Miami. ✆ **305/949-6722.** www.fgo.org. Tickets $19–$175. Student discounts available.

DANCE

Several local dance companies train and perform in the Greater Miami area. In addition, top traveling troupes regularly stop at the venues listed below. Keep your eyes open for special events and guest artists.

Ballet Flamenco La Rosa For a taste of local Latin flavor, see this lively troupe perform impressive flamenco and other styles of Latin dance on Miami stages. (They also teach Latin dancing—see the earlier "The Rhythm Is Gonna Get You" box.) 13126 W. Dixie Hwy., North Miami. ✆ **305/899-7729.** www.balletflamencolarosa.com. Tickets $20 at door; $15 in advance; $8 for students and seniors.

Miami City Ballet This artistically acclaimed and innovative company, directed by Edward Villella, features a repertoire of more than 60 ballets, many by George Balanchine, and has had more than 20 world premieres. The company's three-story center features eight rehearsal rooms, a ballet school, a boutique, and ticket offices. The City Ballet season runs from September to April. Ophelia and Juan Jr. Roca Center, Collins Ave. and 22nd St., South Beach. ✆ **305/929-7000,** or 929-7010 for box office. www.miamicityballet.org. Tickets $10–$175.

Major Venues

The **Colony Theater,** 1040 Lincoln Rd. in South Beach (✆ **305/674-1040**), which has become an architectural showpiece of the Art Deco District, opened in 2006 after a $4.3-million renovation that added wing and fly space, improved access for those with disabilities, and restored the lobby to its original Art Deco look.

At the 1,700-seat **Gusman Center for the Performing Arts,** 174 E. Flagler St., downtown Miami (✆ **305/372-0925**), seating is tight, and so is funding, but the sound is superb. In addition to hosting the Miami Film Festival, the elegant Gusman Center features pop concerts, plays, film screenings, and special events. The auditorium was built as the Olympia Theater in 1926, and its ornate palace interior is typical of that era, complete with fancy columns, a huge pipe organ, and twinkling "stars" on the ceiling.

Not to be confused with the Gusman Center (above), the **Gusman Concert Hall,** 1314 Miller Dr., at 14th Street, Coral Gables (📞 305/284-6477), is a roomy 600-seat hall that gives a stage to the Miami Chamber Symphony and a varied program of university recitals.

The newly revamped **Fillmore Miami Beach at the Jackie Gleason Theater,** located in South Beach at Washington Avenue and 17th Street (📞 305/673-7300), may be a mouthful, but when it comes to live music, it truly rocks. In addition to its very modern Hard Rock–meets–Miami Beach decor, complete with requisite bars, chandeliers, and an homage to the original legendary Fillmore in San Francisco, Fillmore, which was taken over by Live Nation, brings major talent to the beach, from Kid Rock and Fall Out Boy to comediennes Sarah Silverman and Lisa Lampanelli. Fillmore also hosts various awards shows, from the Food Network Awards to the Fox Sports Awards.

Last, but definitely not least, the **Adrienne Arsht Center for the Performing Arts,** 1300 Biscayne Blvd. (📞 786/468-2000), opened in late 2006 after a whopping $446-million tab. In 2008, philanthropist Adrienne Arsht donated $30 million to the financially troubled center, renaming it the Adrienne Arsht Center for the Performing Arts of Miami-Dade County (or the Arsht Center, for short). Included: The 2,400-seat **Sanford and Dolores Ziff Ballet Opera House** and the 2,200-seat **Knight Concert Hall** are Miami venues for the **Concert Association of Florida, Florida Grand Opera, Miami City Ballet,** and **New World Symphony,** as well as premier venues for a wide array of local, national, and international performances, ranging from Broadway musicals and visiting classical artists to world and urban music, Latin concerts, and popular entertainment from many cultures. The **Studio Theater,** a flexible black-box space designed for up to 200 seats, hosts intimate performances of contemporary theater, dance, music, cabaret, and other entertainment. The **Peacock Education Center** acts as a catalyst for arts education and enrichment programs for children and adults. Finally, the **Plaza for the Arts** is a magnificent setting for outdoor entertainment, social celebrations, and informal community gatherings.

Designed by world-renowned architect Cesar Pelli, the Carnival Center is the focal point of a planned Arts, Media, and Entertainment District in mid-Miami. The complex is wrapped in limestone, slate, decorative stone, stainless steel, glass curtain walls, and tropical landscaping, and was completed in mid-2006. Newly opened within the complex is a bona fide restaurant, **Prelude by Barton G.** (📞 305/357-7900; www.preludebybartong.com), an old-school yet modern supper club featuring prix-fixe pre- and post-theater menus. The biggest joke in town, however, is that after spending all that money, the planners forgot to include parking facilities. As a result, valet parking is available for $10 to $20 or you can park at the Marriott nearby, but it's truly a pain; so to make things easy, just take a cab. It'll cost you the same and you won't have to deal with traipsing across Biscayne Boulevard in your fine theater threads. For more information, check out the website at **www.arshtcenter.org.**

6

THE KEYS & THE DRY TORTUGAS

T he drive from Miami to the Keys is a slow descent into an unusual but breathtaking American ecosystem: On either side, for miles ahead, are nothing but emerald waters. (On weekends, however, you will also see plenty of traffic in front of and in back of you.) Strung out across the Atlantic Ocean like loose strands of cultured pearls, more than 400 islands make up this 150-mile-long necklace.

Despite the usually calm landscape, these rocky islands can be treacherous, as tropical storms, hurricanes, and tornadoes are always possibilities. The exposed coast poses dangers to those on land as well as at sea.

When Spanish explorers Juan Ponce de León and Antonio de Herrera sailed amid these craggy, dangerous rocks in 1513, they and their men dubbed the string of islands "Los Martires" (The Martyrs) because they thought the rocks looked like men suffering in the surf. It wasn't until the early 1800s that rugged and ambitious pioneers, who amassed great wealth by salvaging cargo from ships sunk nearby, settled the larger islands (legend has it that these shipwrecks were sometimes caused by "wreckers," who removed navigational markers from the shallows to lure unwitting captains aground). At the height of the salvaging mania (in the 1830s), Key West boasted the highest per-capita income in the country.

However, wars, fires, hurricanes, mosquitoes, and the Depression took their toll on these resilient islands in the early part of the 20th century, causing wild swings between fortune and poverty. In 1938, the spectacular Overseas Highway (U.S. 1) was finally completed atop the ruins of Henry Flagler's railroad (which was destroyed by a hurricane in 1935, leaving only bits and pieces still found today), opening the region to tourists, who had never before been able to drive to this sea-bound destination. These days, the highway connects more than 30 of the populated islands in the Keys. The hundreds of small, undeveloped islands that surround these "mainline" Keys are known locally as the "backcountry" and are home to dozens of exotic animals and plants. Therein lie some of the most renowned outdoor sporting opportunities, from bonefishing to spearfishing and—at appropriate times of the year—diving for lobsters and stone crabs. To get to the backcountry, you must take to the water—a vital part of any trip to the Keys. Whether you fish, snorkel, dive, or cruise, include some time on a boat in your itinerary; otherwise, you haven't truly seen the Keys.

Of course, people go to the Keys for the peaceful waters and year-round warmth, but the sea and the teeming life beneath and around it are the main attractions here: Countless species of brilliantly colored fish can be found swimming above the ocean's floor, and you'll discover a stunning abundance of tropical and exotic plants, birds, and reptiles.

The warm, shallow waters (deeper and rougher on the eastern/Atlantic side of the Keys) nurture living coral that supports a complex, delicate ecosystem of plants and animals—sponges, anemones, jellyfish, crabs, rays, sharks, turtles, snails, lobsters, and thousands of types of fish. This vibrant underwater habitat

FACING PAGE: **The emerald waters of the Keys offer activities, light, and beauty.**

The Florida Keys

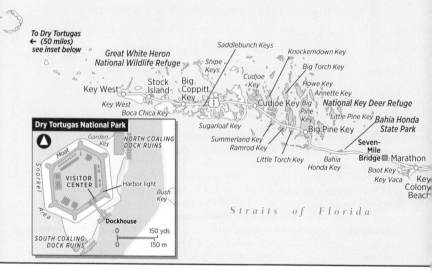

thrives on one of the few living tropical reefs on the entire North American continent. As a result, anglers, divers, snorkelers, and watersports enthusiasts of all kinds come to explore.

Heavy traffic has taken its toll on this fragile ecoscape, but conservation efforts are underway (traffic laws are strictly enforced on Deer Key, for example, due to deer crossings that have been contained, thanks to newly installed fences). In fact, environmental efforts in the Keys exceed those in many other high-traffic visitor destinations.

Although the atmosphere throughout the Keys is that of a laid-back beach town, don't expect many impressive beaches. Nice beaches are mostly found in a few private resorts, though there are some small, sandy strips in John Pennekamp Coral Reef State Park, Bahia Honda State Park, and Key West. One great exception is Sombrero Beach, in Marathon (p. 200), which is well maintained by Monroe County and is larger and considerably nicer than other beaches in the Keys.

The Keys are divided into three sections, both geographically and in this chapter. The Upper and Middle Keys are closest to the Florida mainland, so they are popular with weekend warriors who come by boat or car to fish or relax in such towns as Key Largo, Islamorada, and Marathon. Farther on, just beyond the impressive Seven-Mile Bridge (which actually measures 6½ miles), are the Lower Keys, a small, unspoiled swath of islands teeming with wildlife. Here, in the protected regions of the Lower Keys, is where you're most likely to catch sight of the area's many endangered animals—with patience, you may spot the rare eagle, egret, or Key deer. You should also keep an eye out for alligators, turtles, rabbits, and a huge variety of birds.

Key West, the most renowned—and last—island in the Lower Keys, is the southernmost point in the continental United States (made famous by Ernest Hemingway). This tiny island is the most popular destination in the Florida Keys,

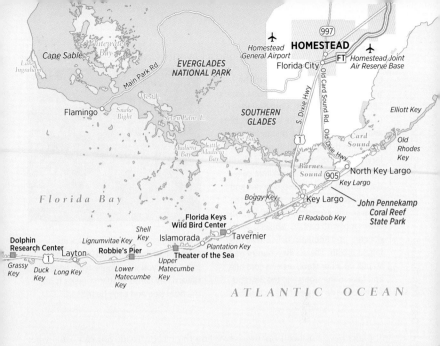

overrun with cruise ship passengers and day-trippers, as well as franchises and T-shirt shops. More than 1.6 million visitors pass through it each year. Still, this "Conch Republic" has a tightly knit community of permanent residents who cling fiercely to their live-and-let-live attitude—an atmosphere that has made Key West famously popular with painters, writers, and free spirits, despite the recent influx of money-hungry developers who want to turn Key West into Palm Beach south.

The last section in this chapter is devoted to the Dry Tortugas, a national park located 68 nautical miles from Key West.

Exploring the Keys by Car

After you've left the Florida Turnpike and landed on U.S. 1, which is also known as the Overseas Highway (see "Getting There" under "Essentials," below), you'll have no trouble negotiating these narrow islands, as only one main road connects the Keys. The scenic, lazy drive from Miami can be very enjoyable if you have the patience to linger and explore the diverse towns and islands along the way. If you have the time, we recommend allowing at least 2 days to work your way down to Key West, and 3 or more days once there.

Encouraging you to slow down is the new $21-million, 106-mile **Florida Keys Overseas Heritage Trail,** a work in progress that is creating a scenic, multiuse paved trail for bikers, hikers, runners, fishermen, and sightseers running parallel to the Overseas Highway and extending from Key Largo all the way down to Key West. With 66 of the 106 miles already completed and 12 miles of trail and five bridges under construction, the rest of the trail is still under design and scheduled for completion by 2013.

Most of U.S. 1 is a narrow two-lane highway, with some wider passing zones along the way. The speed limit is usually 55 mph (35–45 mph on Big Pine Key and in some commercial areas). There has been talk of expanding the highway,

but plans have not been finalized. Even on the narrow road, you can usually get from downtown Miami to Key Largo in just over an hour. If you're determined to drive straight through to Key West, allow at least 3½ hours. Weekend travel is another matter entirely: When the roads are jammed with travelers from the mainland, the trip can take upwards of 5 to 6 hours (when there's an accident, traffic is at an absolute standstill). We *strongly* urge you to avoid driving anywhere in the Keys on Friday afternoon or Sunday evening.

Most addresses in the Keys (except in Key West and parts of Marathon) are delineated by **mile markers** (MM), small green signs on the roadside that announce the distance from Key West. The markers start at no. 127, just south of the Florida mainland. The zero marker is in Key West, at the corner of Whitehead and Fleming streets. Addresses in this chapter are accompanied by a mile marker (MM) designation when appropriate.

THE UPPER & MIDDLE KEYS

58 miles SW of Miami

The Upper Keys are a popular year-round refuge for South Floridians, who take advantage of the islands' proximity to the mainland. This is the fishing and diving capital of America, and the swarms of outfitters and billboards never let you forget it.

Key Largo, once called Rock Harbor but renamed to capitalize on the success of the 1948 Humphrey Bogart film (which wasn't filmed here), is the largest Key and is more developed than its neighbors to the south. Dozens of chain hotels, restaurants, and tourist information centers service the water enthusiasts who come to explore the nation's first underwater state park, **John Pennekamp Coral Reef State Park,** and its adjacent marine sanctuary. **Islamorada,** the unofficial capital of the Upper Keys, has the area's best atmosphere, food, fishing, entertainment, and lodging. It's an unofficial "party capital" for mainlanders seeking a quick tropical excursion. Here (Islamorada is actually composed of four islands), nature lovers can enjoy walking trails, historic exploration, and big-purse fishing tournaments. For a more tranquil, less party-hearty experience, other Keys besides Key West and Islamorada are better choices. **Marathon,** smack in the middle, is known as the heart of the Keys and is one of the most populated. But don't judge it by its main drag. To appreciate Marathon you need to go beyond U.S. 1. It is part fishing village, part tourist center, part nature preserve. This area's highly developed infrastructure includes resort hotels, a commercial airport, and a highway that expands to four lanes.

Essentials

GETTING THERE From Miami International Airport (there is also an airport in Marathon), take Le Jeune Road (NW 42nd Ave.) to Route 836 West. Follow signs to the Florida Turnpike South, about 7 miles. The turnpike extension connects with U.S. 1 in Florida City. Continue south on U.S. 1. For a scenic option, take Card Sound Road, south of Florida City, a backcountry drive that reconnects with U.S. 1 in upper Key Largo. The view from Card Sound Bridge is spectacular and well worth the $1 toll.

If you're coming from Florida's west coast, take Alligator Alley to the Miami exit and then turn south onto the turnpike extension. The turnpike ends in Florida City, at which time you will be dumped directly onto the two-lane U.S. 1, which leads to the Keys. Have around $15 for the tolls. If you take U.S. 1 straight down and bypass the turnpike, it's free, but a lot longer.

Greyhound (© 800/231-2222; www.greyhound.com) has three buses leaving Miami for Key West every day, with stops in Key Largo, Tavernier, Islamorada, Marathon, Big Pine Key, Cudjoe Key, Sugarloaf, and Big Coppit on the way south. Prices range from $39 to $50 one-way and $77 to $98 round-trip; the trip takes from 1 hour and 40 minutes to 4 hours and 40 minutes, depending on how far south you're going. Seats fill quickly in season, so come early. It's first-come, first-served.

Once you've arrived in the Keys, let **Flying Dog Helicopters** (© 866/425-4743; www.flyingdoghelicopters.com) take you on 10- to 20-minute helicopter tours of the Upper and Middle Keys from their base at Holiday Isle in Islamorada, featuring aerial views of sandbars, reefs, sharks, and more. Price ranges from $70 to $155 per person.

VISITOR INFORMATION Make sure you get your information from an official not-for-profit center. The **Key Largo Chamber of Commerce,** U.S. 1 at MM 106, Key Largo, FL 33037 (© 800/822-1088 or 305/451-1414; fax 305/451-4726; www.keylargo.org), runs an excellent facility, with free direct-dial phones and plenty of brochures. Headquartered in a handsome clapboard house, the chamber operates as an information clearinghouse for all of the Keys and is open daily from 9am to 6pm.

The **Islamorada Chamber of Commerce,** housed in a little red caboose, U.S. 1 at MM 82.5, P.O. Box 915, Islamorada, FL 33036 (© 800/322-5397 or 305/664-4503; fax 305/664-4289; www.islamorada chamber.com), offers maps and literature on the Upper Keys.

You can't miss the big, blue visitor center at MM 53.5, **Greater Marathon Chamber of Commerce,** 12222 Overseas Hwy., Marathon, FL 33050 (© 800/262-7284 or 305/743-5417; fax 305/289-0183; www. floridakeysmarathon.com). Here you can receive free information on local events, festivals, attractions, dining, and lodging.

On your smartphone, check out the **Florida Keys App** available for the iPhone, iPod touch, and iPad. With it, users can access information to weather, events, venues, and maps, as well as GPS and audio driving tours. Best of all, the app is free.

Outdoor Sights & Activities

Anne's Beach (MM 73.5, on Lower Matecumbe Key, at the southwest end of Islamorada) is more picnic spot than full-fledged beach, but die-hard tanners congregate on this lovely, tiny strip of coarse sand that was damaged beyond recognition by storms in 1998. The place has been spruced up a bit, even the restrooms, which are (for now) clean and usable.

A better choice for real beaching is **Sombrero Beach ★★**, in Marathon, at the end of Sombrero Beach Road (near MM 50). This wide swath of un-cluttered beachfront actually benefited from Hurricane George in 1998, with generous deposits of extra sand and a face-lift courtesy of the Monroe County Tourist Development Council. More than 90 feet of sand is dotted with palms, Australian pines, and royal poincianas, as well as with grills, clean restrooms, and Tiki huts for relaxing in the shade. It's also a popular nesting spot for turtles that lay their eggs at night.

If you're interested in seeing the Keys in their natural, pre–modern de-velopment state, you must venture off the highway and take to the water. Two backcountry islands that offer a glimpse of the "real" Keys are **Indian Key** and **Lignumvitae Key ★★★**. Visitors come here to relax and enjoy the islands' col-orful birds and lush hammocks (elevated pieces of land above a marsh).

Named for the lignum vitae ("wood of life") trees found there, Lignumvitae Key supports a virgin tropical forest, the kind that once thrived on most of the Upper Keys. Human settlers imported "exotic" plants and animals, irrevocably changing the botanical makeup of many backcountry islands and threatening much of the indigenous wildlife. Over the past 25 years, however, the Florida Department of Natural Resources has successfully re-moved most of the exotic vegetation from this key, leaving the 280-acre site much as it existed in the 18th century. The island also holds the Matheson House, a historic structure built in 1919 that has survived numerous hurricanes. You can go inside, but it's interesting only if you appreciate the coral rock of which the house is made. It's a museum dedi-cated to the history, nature, and topogra-phy of the area. More interesting are the **Botanical Gardens,** which surround the house and are a state preserve. Lignumvitae Key has a visitor center at MM 88.5 (✆ **305/664-2540**).

You can get back to nature at Lignumvitae Key.

Indian Key, a much smaller island on the Atlantic side of Islamorada, was occupied by Native Americans for thousands of years before European settlers arrived. The 10-acre historic site was also the original seat of Dade County before the Civil War. You can see the ruins of the previous settlement and tour the lush grounds on well-marked trails (off Indian Key Fill, Overseas Hwy., MM 79). For more information on Indian Key, call the Florida Park Service (✆ **305/664-4815**) or check out www. abfla.com/parks/indiankey/indiankey.html.

If you want to see both islands, plan to spend at least half a day. You can rent your own powerboat from **Robbie's Rent-A-Boat,** U.S. 1 at MM 77.5 (on the bay side), on Islamorada. It's then a $1 admission fee to each island, which includes an hour-long guided tour by park rangers. This is a good option if you're a confident boater. We also recommend Robbie's **ferry service.** A visit to Lignumvitae Key costs $20 for adults and $15 for kids 12 and under, which includes the $1 park admission. For a ride to Indian Key, take the 2½-hour Florida Bay Eco-Nature Tour, which costs $35 for adults and $20 for children 12 and under. The ferry is a more economical, easier way to enjoy the beauty of the islands. The runabouts, which carry up to six people, usually depart from Robbie's Pier (p. 204) Thursday through Monday at 10am and 2pm for Lignumvitae Key, but when demand is low and mosquitoes are high, the ferry runs only from Friday to Sunday from 10am to 2pm. In high season, you may need to book 2 days before departure. Robbie's also does eco-tours, 2-hour trips through passages among the sea-grass beds that rim the many protected shallow bays. You'll get to cruise among the hundreds of small, uninhabited mangrove and hardwood hammock islands, which host an amazing variety of wildlife and create the island network of the Florida Bay. Call ✆ **305/664-4815** for information from the park service; or call ✆ **305/664-9814** or visit Robbie's.

Crane Point Hammock ★★ ☺ 🎁 Crane Point Hammock is a little-known but worthwhile stop, especially for those interested in the rich botanical and archaeological history of the Keys. This privately owned, 64-acre nature area is considered one of the most important historic sites in the Keys. It contains what is probably the last virgin thatch-palm hammock in North America, as well as a rainforest exhibit and an archaeological site with prehistoric Indian and Bahamian artifacts.

Crane Point Hammock provides a habitat to wildlife large and small.

Also headquarters for the Florida Keys Land and Sea Trust, the hammock's impressive nature museum has simple, informative displays of the Keys' wildlife, including a walk-through replica of a coral-reef cave and life-size dioramas with tropical birds and Key deer. Kids can make art projects, see 6-foot-long iguanas, climb through a scaled-down pirate ship, and touch a variety of indigenous aquatic and landlubber creatures.

5550 Overseas Hwy. (MM 50), Marathon. ✆ **305/743-9100.** www.cranepoint.net. Admission $13 adults, $11 seniors 66 and over, $8.50 students, free for children 5 and under. Mon–Sat 9am–5pm; Sun noon–5pm.

Pigeon Key ★★ At the curve of the old bridge on Pigeon Key is an intriguing historic site that has been under renovation since late 1993. This 5-acre island once served as the camp for the crew that built the old railway in the early 20th century, and later served as housing for the bridge builders. From here, the vista includes the vestiges of Henry Flagler's old Seven-Mile Bridge and the one on which traffic presently soars, as well as many old wooden cottages and a tranquil stretch of lush foliage and sea. If you miss the shuttle tour from the Pigeon Key visitor center or would rather walk or bike to the site, it's about 2½ miles. Either way, you may want to bring a picnic to enjoy after a brief self-guided walking tour and a museum visit to what has become an homage to Flagler's railroad, featuring artifacts and photographs of the old bridge. An informative 28-minute video of the island's history is shown every hour starting at 10am. Parking is available at the Knight's Key end of the bridge, at MM 48, or at the visitor center at MM 47, on the ocean side.

East end of the Seven-Mile Bridge near MM 47, Marathon. ✆ **305/743-5999.** www.pigeonkey. net. Admission $11 adults, $8.50 children 12 and under. Prices include shuttle transportation from the visitor center. Daily 10am–3pm; shuttle tours run hourly 10am–4pm.

Seven-Mile Bridge ★★★ A stop at the Seven-Mile Bridge is a rewarding and relaxing break on the drive south. Built alongside the ruins of oil magnate Henry Flagler's incredible Overseas Railroad, the "new" bridge (btw. MMs 40 and 47) is considered an architectural feat. The apex of the wide-arched span, completed

Seven-Mile Bridge crosses the waters between the Middle and Lower Keys.

in 1985 at a cost of more than $45 million, is the highest point in the Keys. The new bridge and its now-defunct neighbor provide excellent vantage points from which to view the stunning waters of the Keys. In the daytime, you may want to walk, jog, or bike along the 4-mile stretch of old bridge. Or you may join local anglers, who catch barracuda, yellowtail, and dolphin (the fish, not the mammal) on what is known as "the longest fishing pier in the world." Parking is available on both sides of the bridge.

Btw. MMs 40 and 47 on U.S. 1. ℂ **305/289-0025.**

Visiting with the Animals

Dolphin Research Center ★★★ ☺ Of the several such centers in the continental United States (all located in the Keys), the Dolphin Research Center is a nonprofit facility and one of the most organized and informative. Although some people argue that training dolphins is cruel and selfish, this is one of the most respected of the institutions that study and protect the mammals. Trainers at the center will also tell you that the dolphins need stimulation and enjoy human contact. They certainly seem to. They nuzzle and seem to smile and kiss the people who get to interact with them in daily interactive programs. The "family" of 19 dolphins swims in a 90,000-square-foot natural saltwater pool carved out of the shoreline. If you can't get into an interactive program, you can watch the sessions that cover a variety of topics from fun facts about dolphins, to therapeutic qualities of dolphins, to research projects in progress. Because the Dolphin Encounter swimming program is the most popular, advanced reservations are required and can be made up to 6 months in advance. The cost is $189 per person. If you're not brave enough to swim with the dolphins or if you have a child under 5 (not permitted to swim with dolphins), try the Dolphin Dip program, in which participants stand on a submerged platform from which they can "meet and greet" the critters. A participating adult must hold children younger than 5. Cost for this program is $104 per person (free for children 4 and under).

   Note: Swimming with dolphins has both its critics and its supporters. You may want to visit the Whale and Dolphin Conservation Society's website at **www.wdcs.org**.

U.S. 1 at MM 59 (on the bay side), Marathon. ℂ **305/289-1121.** www.dolphins.org. Admission $20 adults, $17 seniors, $14 children 4–12. Daily 9am–4:30pm. Narrated behavior sessions with bottlenose dolphins and sea lions and educational presentations approximately every half-hour.

Florida Keys Wild Bird Center ★ Wander through lush canopies of mangroves on wooden walkways to see some of the Keys' most famous residents—the large variety of native birds, including broad-wing hawks, great blue and white herons, roseate spoonbills, cattle egrets, and pelicans. This not-for-profit center operates as a hospital for the many birds that have been injured by accident or disease. In 2002, the World Parrot Mission was established here, focusing on caring for parrots and educating the public about the birds. Visit at feeding time, usually about 3:30pm, when you can watch the dedicated staff feed the hundreds of hungry birds.

U.S. 1 at MM 93.6 (bay side), Tavernier. ℂ **305/852-4486.** www.fkwbc.org. Donations suggested. Daily sunrise–sunset.

Robbie's Pier ★★★ ✦ One of the best and definitely one of the cheapest attractions in the Upper Keys is the famed Robbie's Pier. Here the fierce steely tarpons, a prized catch for backcountry anglers, have been gathering for the past 20 years. You may recognize these prehistoric-looking giants that grow up to 200

Here you go, little fishy! You can feed the tarpons at Robbie's Pier.

pounds; many are displayed as trophies and mounted on local restaurant walls. To see them live, head to Robbie's Pier, where tens and sometimes hundreds of these behemoths circle the shallow waters waiting for you to feed them. Robbie's Pier also offers ranger-led boat tours and guided kayak tours to Indian Key, where you can go snorkeling or just bask in the glory of your surroundings.

U.S. 1 at MM 77.5, Islamorada. ℂ **305/664-9814.** www.robbies.com. Admission to see the tarpon $1. Bucket of fish to feed them $3. Daily 8am–5pm. Make a hard-right U-turn off the highway, then it's a short drive before you'll see a HUNGRY TARPON restaurant sign. Robbie's driveway is just before the restaurant.

Theater of the Sea ★ ☺ Established in 1946, the Theater of the Sea is one of the world's oldest marine zoos. Recently refurbished, the park's dolphin and sea lion shows are entertaining and informative, especially for children. If you want to swim with dolphins and haven't booked well in advance, you may be able to get into this place with just a few hours' notice, as opposed to the more rigid Dolphin Research Center in Marathon (see above). While the Dolphin Research Center is a legitimate, scientific establishment, Theater of the Sea is more like a theme-park attraction. That's not to say the dolphins are mistreated, but it's not as educational and professional as the Dolphin Research Center. Theater of the Sea also permits you to swim with sea lions. (Children 4 and under cannot participate.) There are twice-daily 4-hour adventure and snorkel cruises that cost $69 for adults and $45 for children ages 3 to 12, during which you can learn about the history and ecology of the marine environment.

U.S. 1 at MM 84.5, Islamorada. ℂ **305/664-2431.** www.theaterofthesea.com. Admission $27 adults, $19 children 3–12. Dolphin swim $175; sea lion swim $135. Reservations are a must. Daily 10am–5pm (ticket office closes at 4pm).

Two Exceptional State Parks

One of the best places to discover the diverse ecosystem of the Upper Keys is its most famous park, **John Pennekamp Coral Reef State Park** ★★★, located on U.S. 1 at MM 102.5, in Key Largo (ℂ **305/451-6300;** www.pennekamp

park.com). Named for a former *Miami Herald* editor and conservationist, the 188-square-mile park, which celebrated its 50th anniversary in 2010, is the nation's first undersea preserve: It's a sanctuary for part of the only living coral reef in the continental United States.

Because the water is extremely shallow, the 40 species of coral and more than 650 species of fish here are accessible to divers, snorkelers, and glass-bottom-boat passengers. To experience this park, visitors must get in the water—you can't see the reef from the shore. Your first stop should be the visitor center, which has a mammoth 30,000-gallon saltwater aquarium that re-creates a reef ecosystem. At the adjacent dive shop, you can rent snorkeling and diving equipment and join one of the boat trips that depart for the reef throughout the day. Visitors can also rent motorboats, sailboats, sailboards, and canoes. The 2½-hour glass-bottom-boat tour is the best way to see the coral reefs if you don't want to get wet. Watch for the lobsters and other sea life residing in the fairly shallow ridge walls beneath the coastal waters. **Remember:** These are protected waters, so you can't remove anything from them.

Canoeing around the park's narrow mangrove channels and tidal creeks is also popular. You can go on your own in a rented canoe or, in winter, sign up for a tour led by a local naturalist. Hikers have two short trails from which to choose: a boardwalk through the mangroves, and a dirt trail through a tropical hardwood hammock. Ranger-led walks are usually scheduled daily from the end of November to April. Call ✆ **305/451-1202** for schedule information and reservations.

Park admission is $8 per vehicle of two to eight passengers, $4 for a single driver, $2 for pedestrians and bicyclists, plus a 50¢ Monroe County surcharge per person. On busy weekends, there's often a line of cars waiting to get into the park. On your way in, ask the ranger for a map. Glass-bottom-boat tours cost $24 for adults and $17 for children 11 and under. Tours depart three times daily, at 9:15am, 12:15pm, and 3pm. Snorkeling tours are $30 for adults and $25 for

Explore the living coral at John Pennekamp State Park.

children 17 and under; masks, fins, and snorkels cost $7 and the snorkel is yours to keep. Canoes rent for $12 per hour; kayaks are $12 per hour for a single, $17 per hour for a double. For experienced boaters only, four different sizes of reef boats (powerboats) rent for $160 to $210 for 4 hours, and $259 to $359 for a full day; call ✆ **305/451-6325** for information. A minimum $400 deposit (or more, depending on boat size) is required. The park's boat-rental office is open daily from 8am to 5pm (last boat rented at 3pm); phone for tour and dive times. Reservations are recommended for all of the above. Also see below for more options on diving, fishing, and snorkeling off these reefs.

Long Key State Recreation Area ★★★, U.S. 1 at MM 68, Long Key (✆ **305/664-4815;** www.floridastateparks.org/longkey), is one of the best places in the Middle Keys for hiking, camping, snorkeling, and canoeing. This 965-acre site is situated atop the remains of an ancient coral reef. At the entrance gate, ask for a free flyer describing the local trails and wildlife.

Three nature trails can be explored via foot or canoe. The Golden Orb Trail is a 40-minute walk through mostly plants; the Layton Trail is a 15-minute walk along the bay; and the Long Key Canoe Trail glides along a shallow-water lagoon. The excellent 1.5-mile canoe trail is short and sweet, allowing visitors to loop around the mangroves in about an hour. Long Key is also a great spot to stop for a picnic if you get hungry on your way to Key West. Campsites are available along the Atlantic Ocean. The swimming and saltwater fishing (license required) are top-notch here, as is the snorkeling, which is shallow and on the shoreline of the Atlantic. For novices, educational programs on the aforementioned are available, too.

THE 10 "keymandments"

The Keys have always attracted independent spirits, from Ernest Hemingway and Tennessee Williams to Jimmy Buffett, Zane Grey, and local hero Mel Fisher. Writers, artists, and freethinkers have long drifted down here to escape.

Although you'll generally find a very laid-back and tolerant code of behavior in the Keys, some rules do exist. Be sure to respect the 10 "Keymandments" while you're here, or suffer the consequences.

- Don't anchor on a reef. (Reefs are alive.)

- Don't feed the animals. (They'll want to follow you home.)

- Don't trash our place (or we'll send Bubba to trash yours).

- Don't touch the coral. (After all, you don't even know them. Some pose a mild risk of injury to you as well.)

- Don't speed (especially on Big Pine Key, where deer reside and tar-and-feathering is still practiced).

- Don't catch more fish than you can eat. (Better yet, let them go. Some of them support schools.)

- Don't collect conch. (This species is protected by Bubba.)

- Don't disturb the birds' nests. (They find it very annoying.)

- Don't damage the sea grass (and don't even think about making a skirt out of it).

- Don't drink and drive on land or sea. (There's nothing funny about it.)

Railroad builder Henry Flagler created the Long Key Fishing Club here in 1906, and the waters surrounding the park are still popular with game fishers. In summer, sea turtles lumber onto the protected coast to lay their eggs. Educational programs are available to view this phenomenon.

Admission is $5 per car of two to eight people, $4 for a single-occupant vehicle, $2 per pedestrian or bicyclist, plus 50¢ per person Monroe County Surcharge (except for the Layton Trail, which is free). The recreation area is open daily from 8am to sunset. You can rent canoes at the trail head for about $5 per hour, $10 each additional hour. The nearest place to rent snorkel equipment is **Holiday Isle,** 84001 U.S. 1, Islamorada (© **800/327-7070**).

Watersports from A to Z

There are hundreds of outfitters in the Keys who will arrange all kinds of water activities, from cave dives to parasailing. If those recommended below are booked up or unreachable, ask the local chamber of commerce for a list of qualified members.

BOATING In addition to the rental shops in the state parks, you'll find dozens of outfitters along U.S. 1 offering a range of runabouts and skiffs for boaters of any experience level. **Captain Pip's,** U.S. 1 at MM 47.5, Marathon (© **800/707-1692** or 305/743-4403; www.captainpips.com), charges $195 to $300 per day. Overnight accommodations are available and include a free boat rental: 2-night minimum $250 to $450 in season and $225 to $415 off season; weekly $1,185 to $2,595. Rooms are Key West comfortable and charming, with ceiling fans, tile floors, and pine paneling. But the best part is that every room comes with an 18- to 21-foot boat for your use during your stay. **Robbie's Rent-a-Boat,** U.S. 1 at MM 77.5, Islamorada (© **305/664-9814;** www.robbies.com), rents 18- to 26-foot motorboats with engines ranging from 60 to 130 horsepower. Boat rentals are $135 to $185 for a half-day and $185 to $235 for a full day.

Not in the mood for a full boat, but want to see the Keys by water? Consider **SeaMonster Watersports,** 3390 Gulfview Ave., Marathon (© **305/743-6541**), whose 2-hour jet-ski tours will take you to the Seven-Mile Bridge, Key Vaca, and Pigeon Key. Tours are $130 per jet ski and carry up to three to four passengers including children.

CANOEING & KAYAKING We can think of no better way to explore the uninhabited backcountry on the Gulf side of the Keys than by kayak or canoe, as you can reach places that big boats just can't get to because of their large draft. Manatees will sometimes cuddle up to the boats, thinking them to be another friendly species.

Many area hotels rent kayaks and canoes to guests, as do the outfitters listed here. **Florida Bay Outfitters,** U.S. 1 at MM 104, Key Largo (© **305/451-3018;** www.kayakfloridakeys.com), rents canoes and sea kayaks for use in and around John Pennekamp Coral Reef State Park for $35 to $75 for a half-day, $45 to $90 for a full day. **Florida Keys Kayak and Sail,** U.S. 1 at MM 75.5, Islamorada (© **305/664-4878;** www.robbies.com), at Robbie's Pier, offers backcountry tours, botanical-preserve tours of Lignumvitae Key, historic-site tours of Indian Key, and sunset tours through the mangrove tunnels and saltwater flats. Tour rates are from $39 to $49; rental rates range from $15 per hour to $45 per day for a single kayak, and $20 per hour to $60 per day for a double kayak.

Get hands on with the local sealife in a kayak off Key Largo.

Reflections Nature Tours (☎ 305/872-4668; www.floridakeys kayaktours.com) is a small mobile company that specializes in kayak tours through the Lower Keys. Guided kayak excursions cost $50 per person for a 3-hour tour, $40 per person for a 2-hour full-moon tour. The 3-hour custom tours start at $125 for one person and $195 for two people. All tours are by appointment only. Kayak rentals are $45 for a single kayak all day and $60 for a full-day tandem. For the same price as a single kayak, you can rent a paddleboard. They also offer paddleboard tours, lessons, and custom kayak sailing and fishing excursions.

Nature lovers can slip through the silent backcountry waters off Key West and the Lower Keys in a kayak, discovering the flora and fauna that make up the unique Keys ecosystem, on **Blue Planet Kayak Tours'** (☎ 305/294-8087; www.blue-planet-kayak.com) starlight tour. All excursions are led by an environmental scientist. The starlight tours last between 2½ and 3 hours. No previous kayaking experience is necessary. Cost for the guided kayak adventure is $50 per person.

FISHING **Robbie's Partyboats & Charters,** U.S. 1 at MM 77.5, Islamorada (☎ 305/664-8070 or 664-8498; www.robbies.com), located at Robbie's Marina on Lower Matecumbe Key, offers day and night deep-sea and reef-fishing trips aboard a 65-foot party boat. Big-game fishing charters are also available, and "splits" are arranged for solo fishers. Party-boat fishing costs about $35 for a half-day morning tour ($3 for rod-and-reel rental); it's $40 if you want to go back out on an afternoon tour. Charters run about $950 for three-quarters of a day, $1,050 for a full day. Phone for information and reservations.

Bud n' Mary's Fishing Marina, U.S. 1 at MM 79.8, Islamorada (☎ 800/742-7945 or 305/664-2461; www.budnmarys.com), one of the largest marinas between Miami and Key West, is packed with sailors offering backcountry fishing charters. This is the place to go if you want to stalk tarpon, bonefish, and snapper. If the seas are not too rough, deep-sea and coral fishing trips can also be arranged. Charters cost $375 for a half-day, $550 for a full day; splits begin at $75 per person.

SCUBA DIVING & SNORKELING Just 6 miles off Key Largo is a U.S. Navy Landing Ship Dock, the latest artificial wreck site to hit the Keys—or, rather, to be submerged 130 feet *below* the Keys.

The **Florida Keys Dive Center,** U.S. 1 at MM 90.5, Tavernier (© **305/852-4599;** www.floridakeysdivectr.com), takes snorkelers and divers to the reefs of John Pennekamp Coral Reef State Park and environs every day. PADI (Professional Association of Diving Instructors) training courses are available for the uninitiated. While some people have complained that employees are rude here, others disagree; decide for yourself. Tours leave at 8am and 12:30pm; the cost is $38 per person to snorkel (plus $10 rental fee for mask, snorkel, and fins), and $60 per person to dive (plus an extra $19 if you need to rent all the gear. Add $10 to that $19 if you're going on a major "heavy metal" dive to sites such as *Spiegel Grove.*

At **Hall's Dive Center & Career Institute,** U.S. 1 at MM 48.5, Marathon (© **305/743-5929;** www.hallsdiving.com), snorkelers and divers can dive at Looe Key, Sombrero Reef, Delta Shoal, Content Key, or Coffins Patch. Tours are scheduled daily at 9am and 1pm. You'll spend 1 hour at each of two sites per tour. It's $40 per person to snorkel (gear included), $35 for children, and $55 to $65 per person (weights included) to dive (tanks $7.50 to $15 each).

The **Key Largo Scuba Shack,** 97684 Overseas Hwy., in the Seafarer Resort at MM 97.8 (© **305/735-4313;** www.keylargoscubashack.com), will take 6 to 10 divers on a 37-foot Burpee dive vessel on once-daily three-tank, dive-master-guided trips to explore the area's reefs and wrecks. Rates range from $40 to $160 per person.

Where to Stay

U.S. 1 is lined with chain hotels in all price ranges. In the Upper Keys, the best moderately priced option is the **Harborside Inn Key Largo,** off U.S. 1 at MM 100, Key Largo (www.ramadakeylargo.com; © **305/451-3939**), which has a waterfront heated pool, marina with tour boats and boat rentals and a Tiki bar, and is just 3 miles from John Pennekamp Coral Reef State Park. Another good Upper Keys option is **Days Inn Oceanfront Resort,** U.S. 1 at MM 82.5 (www.days innflakeys.com; © **800/DAYS-INN** [329-7466] or 305/664-3681). In the Middle Keys, the **Siesta Motel,** 7425 Overseas Hwy., MM 54 in Marathon (www.siestamotel.net; © **305/743-5671**), offers reasonably priced, very clean oceanside rooms. New in 2010, the **Holiday Inn Express & Suites,** 13201 Overseas Hwy. (www.hiexpress.com; © **888/465-4329** or 305/289-0222), a smoke-free and pet-friendly hotel featuring free hot breakfast, marina, Tiki bar, large outdoor pool, and free Wi-Fi.

Because the real beauty of the Keys lies mostly beyond the highways, there is no better way to see this area than by boat. So why not stay in a floating hotel? Especially if you're traveling with a group, houseboats can be economical. To rent a houseboat, contact **Houseboat Vacations,** 85944 Overseas Hwy., Islamorada (© **305/664-4009;** www.floridakeys.com/houseboats). Rates are from $1,112 to $1,350 for 3 nights. Boats accommodate up to six people.

Those wondering what may have happened to many of the condos that were built before the real estate bust take the **Indigo Bay Hotel,** 81450 Overseas Hwy., Islamorada (www.indigobayhotel.com; © **305/664-0082**), a former condo which quickly changed gears and reopened as a hotel in the summer of

2010 featuring 25 contemporary cottages, a 14-slip marina and nightly rates beginning at $250 with a 3-night minimum.

For other options, consider the recommendations below.

VERY EXPENSIVE

Cheeca Lodge & Spa ★★★ ☺ Located on 27 lush acres of beachfront, this rambling resort sports one of the only golf courses in the Upper Keys and much more. Rooms have the amenities of a world-class resort in a very laid-back setting. After a renovation following a fire which temporarily shut the property down, upgrades/improvements include new Premier Suites, 840-square-foot rooms with huge balconies, floor-to-ceiling glass walls opening to ocean or island views, open-air round spa tubs for two, and glass rain showers. Also revamped is the lobby, which includes a new bar, 2,400 square feet of retail shops, and the restaurants **Nikai Sushi Bar,** serving the raw goods along with Asian-inspired fare, and a revamped signature restaurant, **Atlantic's Edge,** which is now under the creative direction of James Beard–approved chef Dean Max of 3030 Ocean fame in Fort Lauderdale. Standard guest rooms still feature West Indies–style decor, marble bathrooms, plasma TVs, and wireless DSL. **The Spa at Cheeca** offers products from fair-trade sources as well as a variety of massage therapies, skin care, body treatments, a fitness room, and butler-serviced poolside cabanas. Cheeca also offers tennis, a 9-hole Jack Nicklaus–designed golf course, eco-tours, sunset cruises, snorkel excursions, boats with seasoned guides for back-country fishing, the Camp Cheeca children's environmental program, and much more. The $39 daily resort fee may seem steep, but it's worth it, including unlimited tennis, golf, fishing rods, bicycles, beach shade cabanas, sea kayaks, valet parking, Wi-Fi, exercise classes, in-room Starbucks coffee service and bottled water, housekeeping gratuity, local calls, daily newspaper, and fax services.

U.S. 1 at MM 82 (P.O. Box 527), Islamorada, FL 33036. www.cheeca.com. © **305/664-4651.** Fax 305/664-2893. 212 units. In season Superior $599–$1,099, Luxury $599–$1,399, Premier $899–$999; off season Superior $199–$599, Luxury $249–$549, Premier $399–$499. AE, DC, DISC, MC, V. **Amenities:** Restaurant; sushi bar; 2 lounges (1 poolside); babysitting; bike rental; children's nature programs; concierge; 9-hole golf course; 5 Jacuzzis; 2 outdoor heated pools; saltwater lagoon; limited room service; full-service spa; 6 lighted hard tennis courts; watersports equipment/rentals. *In room:* A/C, TV/DVD, CD player, hair dryer, Internet access, kitchenette (in suites), minibar.

Hawks Cay Resort ★★★ ☺ Set on its own 60-acre island in the Middle Keys, when it comes to activities, this resort is far superior to Cheeca Lodge. In addition to sailing, fishing, snorkeling, diving, SNUBA, and water-skiing, guests have the opportunity to interact directly with dolphins in the resort's Dolphin Connection program. (You'll need to reserve a spot well in advance.) Guest rooms are large, with spacious bathrooms, island-style furniture, and private balconies with ocean or tropical views. There are also 225 hyperposh villas modeled after the kitschy 1950s concept of the "boatel," the recipients of a sophisticated redesign. The 7,000-square-foot **Calm Waters Spa** provides stellar treatments. Organized children's activities include marine- and ecology-inspired programs. A $35-million renovation in 2008 included a veranda and a new lobby incorporating direct water views, a bar and lounge, and a vastly expanded main resort pool featuring new landscaping, multitiered sun terrace, and private butlered cabanas. Fine-dining options include a Nuevo-Latino restaurant and bar featuring hard-to-find rums. In 2010, the resort opened a kiteboarding and stand-up-paddleboarding shop, featuring lessons and tours. There's also a $99 personalized Segway tour of the resort's grounds for those who don't like to miss out on anything.

61 Hawks Cay Blvd., at MM 61, Duck Key, FL 33050. www.hawkscay.com. © **877/667-0763** or 305/743-7000. Fax 305/743-5215. 402 units, including 225 2-, 3-, and 4-bedroom villas. Winter $329–$539 double, $549–$1,300 suite, $519–$1,400 villa; off season $279–$459 double, $479–$900 suite, $449–$1,000 villa. Packages available. AE, DC, DISC, MC, V. **Amenities:** 4 restaurants; lounge; bike rental; children's programs ($48–$75 per child); concierge; exercise room; Jacuzzi; 5 outdoor heated pools; room service; full-service spa; 8 tennis courts (6 hard, 2 clay, 2 lighted); watersports equipment/rentals. *In room:* A/C, TV, fridge, hair dryer, Internet access.

EXPENSIVE

Casa Morada ★★ 🏨 The closest thing to a boutique hotel in the Florida Keys, Casa Morada is the brainchild of a trio of New York women who used to work for hip hotelier Ian Schrager. This 16-suite property is a hipster haven tucked away off a sleepy street and radiates serenity and style in an area where serenity is aplenty, but style is elusive. Sitting on 1¾ acres of prime bayfront, the hotel features a limestone grotto, a freshwater pool, and poolside beverage service. Each of the cool rooms has either a private garden or a terrace—request the one with the open-air Jacuzzi that faces the bay. While the decor is decidedly island, think St. Barts rather than, say, Gilligan's. There's no on-site restaurant, a complimentary breakfast is served daily, and there's free yoga Wednesday to Sunday at 8:30am. Enjoy free use of bikes, boccie balls, and board games. Despite the games, this place is not recommended for kids.

136 Madeira Rd., Islamorada, FL 33036. www.casamorada.com. © **888/881-3030** or 305/664-0044. Fax 305/664-0674. 16 units. Winter $329–$659 double; off season $249–$509 double. Rates include continental breakfast. AE, DISC, MC, V. From U.S. 1 S., at MM 82.2, turn right onto Madeira Rd. and continue to the end of the street. The hotel is on the right. Friendly pets are welcome. **Amenities:** Complimentary bike use; freshwater pool. *In room:* A/C, TV/DVD, CD player, hair dryer, minibar.

Jules' Undersea Lodge ★★★ 🏨 Staying here is an experience of a lifetime—if you're brave enough to take the plunge. Originally built as a research lab, this small underwater compartment, which rests on pillars on the ocean floor, now operates as a two-room hotel. As expensive as it is unusual, Jules' is most popular with diving honeymooners. To get inside, guests swim 21 feet under the structure and pop up into the unit through a 4 × 6-foot "moon pool" that gurgles soothingly all night long. The 30-foot-deep underwater suite consists of two separate bedrooms that share a common living area. Room service will deliver your meals, daily newspapers, and even a late-night pizza in waterproof containers, at no extra charge. If you don't have time or a desire to spend the night, you can hang out and explore the lodge for 3 hours for $125 to $165 per person.

51 Shoreland Dr., Key Largo, FL 33037. www.jul.com. © **305/451-2353.** Fax 305/451-4789. 2 units. $375–$475 per person. Rates include breakfast and dinner, as well as all equipment and unlimited scuba diving in the lagoon for certified divers. Packages available. AE, DISC, MC, V. From U.S. 1 S., at MM 103.2, turn left onto Transylvania Ave., across from the Central Plaza shopping mall. *In room:* A/C, kitchenette.

Kona Kai Resort, Gallery & Botanic Garden ★★★ 🏨 This little haven is an exquisite, adults-only waterfront property right on Florida Bay—a location that offers a stunning sunset view overlooking Everglades National Park. Highly stylized, modern rooms and suites dot the lush 2-acre property, brimming with native vegetation and fruit-bearing trees from which you're free to sample. An orchid house has more than 350 flowers. Lounge chairs, hammocks, a beachfront freshwater pool (heated in winter and cooled in summer), complimentary bottled water and fresh fruit poolside, a Jacuzzi, and one of the largest private beaches on the island make Kona Kai perfect for relaxation. For the more adventurous, Kona Kai's complimentary concierge services will organize excursions to the Everglades and the backcountry as well as fishing, snorkeling, diving, paddleboarding, and more. Kayaks, paddleboats, tennis, Wi-Fi, CD/DVD libraries, and parking are all included at no extra charge. In-room or beachfront massage and private yoga are available. For meals, two restaurants are within walking distance and the exceptional staff will give you insider tips—and discounts—to their favorite local eateries and watering holes. A fine art gallery doubles as the lobby.

97802 Overseas Hwy. (U.S. 1 at MM 97.8), Key Largo, FL 33037. www.konakairesort.com. ✆ **800/365-7829** or 305/852-7200. 11 units. Winter $308–$561 double and 1-bedroom suite, $736–$940 2-bedroom suite; off season $211–$454 double and 1-bedroom suite, $552–$656 2-bedroom suite. AE, DISC, MC, V. Free parking. Children 15 and under not permitted. **Amenities:** Concierge; Jacuzzi; heated/cooled pool; in-room and on-beach spa treatments; lighted tennis court; watersports equipment/rentals; Wi-Fi. *In room:* A/C, TV/DVD, CD player, fridge, hair dryer, full kitchen (suites only), no phone.

The Moorings Village ★★★ 🏕 You'll never see another soul on this 18-acre resort, a former coconut plantation, if you choose not to. There isn't even maid service unless you request it. The whitewashed units, from cozy cottages to three-bedroom houses, are spacious with fully equipped kitchens and rustic, yet modern, decor. Most have washers and dryers, and all have CD players and DVD players; ask when you book. The real reason to come to this resort is to relax on the 1,000-plus-foot beach (one of the only real beaches around). You'll also find a great pool, a hard tennis court, and a few kayaks and sailboards, but no motorized water vehicles in the waters surrounding the hotel. There's no room service or restaurant, but Morada Bay and Pierres across the street are excellent. This is a place for people who like each other a lot. Leave the kids at home unless they're extremely well behaved and not easily bored.

123 Beach Rd., near MM 81.5, on the ocean side, Islamorada, FL 33036. www.moorings village.com. ✆ **305/664-4708.** Fax 305/664-4242. 18 units. Winter $325 small cottage, $650 1-bedroom house, $800 2-bedroom house, $1,500 3-bedroom oceanfront house; off season $250 small cottage, $450 1-bedroom house, $550 2-bedroom house, $1,100 3-bedroom oceanfront house. AE, MC, V. **Amenities:** Outdoor heated pool; spa; tennis court; watersports equipment. *In room:* A/C, TV/DVD, CD player, hair dryer, kitchen.

Tranquility Bay Beach House Resort ★★★ ☺ Tranquility Bay sits on a tropically landscaped 12 acres on the Gulf of Mexico and worlds away from the busy, not-so-pretty main stretch of Marathon's U.S. 1. You'll feel like you're in your own beach house—literally, with gorgeous two- and three-bedroom conch-style cottages all with water views. All of them come equipped with everything a techno-savvy beach bum needs—even washers and dryers. Every beach house has spacious porches with French doors, wooden deck chairs, and 180-degree views of the water. The restaurant, **Butterfly Café,** is just as fine, with seasonal seafood menus. The resort has an on-site watersports center featuring jet skiing, kayaking, and boat rentals, as well as two swimming pools, gazebos, a great lawn with putting green, and a beachfront Tiki bar. Activities from adventure fishing to snorkeling and spa services can be arranged with the front-desk staff. *Note:*

This is a smoke-free resort. Smoking is not permitted on porches or most of the grounds, only in designated areas.

2600 Overseas Hwy., Marathon, FL 33036. www.tranquilitybay.com. © **305/289-0888.** Fax 305/289-0667. 87 units. Winter $349–$699 double; off season $249–$599 double. AE, DC, MC, V. **Amenities:** Fitness center; 2 outdoor heated pools; spa services; watersports equipment/rentals. *In room:* A/C, TV/DVD, CD player, hair dryer, kitchen, Wi-Fi.

MODERATE

Banana Bay Resort & Marina ★★ 🎒 It doesn't look like much from the sign-cluttered Overseas Highway, but once you enter the lush, 10-acre grounds of Banana Bay, you'll realize you're in one of the most bucolic and best-run properties in the Upper Keys. The resort is a beachfront maze of two-story buildings hidden among banyans and palms, with moderately sized rooms, many with private balconies. An activity area has horseshoe pits, a boccie court, barbecue grills, and a giant lawn chessboard. The pool is one of the largest freshwater pools in the Keys. The kitschy restaurant serves three meals a day, indoors and poolside. The hotel also rents bikes, boats, WaveRunners, kayaks, day-sailing dinghies, and bait and tackle. Another amenity is **Pretty Joe Rock,** the hotel's private island, available for long weekends and weekly rentals. On it is a two-bedroom, two-bathroom cottage that's ideal for romantic escapes. Banana Bay is family-friendly, but for an adults-only resort, there's **Banana Bay Resort,** at 2319 N. Roosevelt Blvd., in Key West (© **305/296-6925**), which doesn't allow children.

U.S. 1 at MM 49.5, Marathon, FL 33050. www.bananabay.com. © **800/BANANA-1** (226-2621) or 305/743-3500. Fax 305/743-2670. 60 units. Winter $185–$245 double; off season $105–$225 double. Rates include continental breakfast. 3- and 7-night honeymoon and wedding packages available. AE, DC, DISC, MC, V. **Amenities:** Restaurant; bar; bike rentals; Jacuzzi; pool; tennis courts; watersports equipment/rentals. *In room:* A/C, TV, fridge, hair dryer.

Conch Key Cottages ★★ 🎒 Here's your chance to play castaway in the Keys. Occupying its own private microisland just off U.S. 1, Conch Key Cottages is a place to get away from it all. The cottages exude a sense of bohemian luxury (not an oxymoron) and old Florida architecture with tin roofs and Dade County Pine. Located miles from neon-hued tourist traps and towering hotels, the cottages offer solitude. The romantic, beachfront cottages are situated on a small natural sandy beach just steps from the ocean. The two-bedroom oceanview stilt cottages, the gardenview cottage, and the marina/sunset cottage are the most spacious, well designed, and tailor-made for families. On one side of the pool is an adorable studio cottage for two with a private Jacuzzi in a tropical garden. At the entrance to the compound are a total of four very comfy island rooms and apartments with garden views. On the other side of the pool are a handful of efficiency apartments that are similarly outfitted but don't enjoy beach frontage. All units feature full-size kitchens plus a microwave, coffeemaker, toaster, juicer and blender, utensils, dishes, pots and pans, and outside individual barbecue grills with charcoal and lighter fluid. The cottages are impeccably clean and well appointed with luxury linens and daily housekeeping service. Other fantastic amenities include free use of kayaks; a check-in gift of chocolates; a delicious complimentary continental breakfast of fresh muffins, bagels and croissants, coffee, and tea delivered to your door; and an unlimited supply of fresh Florida oranges that you can juice right in your own cottage. A heated pool is surrounded by lush foliage and, for those who break out in hives when they have no connection to the real world, free Wi-Fi.

Private Island off U.S. 1 at MM 62.3, Marathon, FL 33050. www.conchkeycottages.com. ☎ **800/330-1577** or 305/289-1377. Fax 305/743-8661. 13 cottages. $110–$499 depending on occupancy and time of year. Rates include complimentary continental breakfast daily. AE, DISC, MC, V. **Amenities:** Concierge; heated pool; free Wi-Fi. *In room:* A/C, TV, hair dryer, full kitchen, no phone.

Key Largo Grande ★ A short drive from Miami, this Hilton-run property is an ideal escape for a weekend or longer, situated on 13 acres of forest and the Gulf and featuring recently revamped rooms, most with water views. Forget the pools—there are two, a kids' and an adults' pool, in the middle of the parking lot—and although it is hidden by trees and a waterfall, you will want to spend your time on the private, white-sand beach where you can partake in watersports activities, walk on nature trails, lounge on chairs, or hang out at the Tiki bar. It's very peaceful and beautiful, which you'd never know from its motel-esque facade. There's a restaurant on-site and it's okay—stick to area restaurants if you can or, better yet, bring some snacks and stick them in the in-room fridge. Once you see the beach here, you may not want to leave for a food run.

97000 S. Overseas Hwy., Key Largo, FL 33037. www.keylargoresort.com. ☎ **888/871-3437** or 305/852-5553. Fax 305/852-8669. 200 units. Winter $129–$299 double; $259–$429 suite; off season $119–$199 double; $249–$419 suite. AE, DISC, MC, V. **Amenities:** Restaurant; 3 bars; children's activities; Jacuzzi; 2 outdoor pools; 2 tennis courts; watersports equipment/rentals. *In room:* A/C, TV, fridge, hair dryer, Internet access.

Lime Tree Bay Resort Motel The only place to stay in the tiny town of Layton (pop. 183), Lime Tree is midway between Islamorada and Marathon and is on a pretty piece of waterfront graced with hundreds of mature palm trees and tropical foliage. It prides itself on its promise of no hustle, no valets, and, most amusingly, no bartenders in Hawaiian shirts! Motel rooms and efficiencies have tiny bathrooms with showers, but are clean and well maintained. The best deal is the two-bedroom bayview suite: A spacious living area with new furnishings leads to a large private deck overlooking the Gulf. There's also a full kitchen and two full bathrooms. Fifteen efficiencies and suites have kitchenettes. Pretty cool in its own right is the Zane Grey Suite (named after the famous author and screenwriter, who lived right around the corner), a two-bedroom, one-bathroom unit with the best views and a second-story location with private stairs.

U.S. 1 at MM 68.5, Layton, Long Key, FL 33001. www.limetreebayresort.com. ☎ **800/723-4519** or 305/664-4740. Fax 305/664-0750. 36 units. Winter $117–$375 double; summer $100–$320 double; off season $89–$290 double. AE, DC, DISC, MC, V. **Amenities:** Restaurant; Jacuzzi; small outdoor pool; tennis court; Wi-Fi in business center. *In room:* A/C, TV, fridge, kitchenette (in some).

Pines and Palms ★★★ Looking for a beachfront cottage or, better yet, an oceanfront villa, but don't want to spend your (future) child's college fund? This is the place. Cheery, one- to three-bedroom cozy cottages, Atlantic views, and a private beachfront with hammocks and a pool give way to a relaxed, tropical paradise. Service is friendly and accommodating. All rooms and cottages have full kitchens and balconies, and are ideal for extended stays. Although there's no restaurant, the staff will be happy to bring a barbecue to your patio so you can grill out by the beach. There's usually a 2-night minimum.

MM 80.4 (ocean side), Islamorada, FL 33036. www.pinesandpalms.com. ☎ **800/624-0964** or 305/664-4343. 25 units. $89–$219 double; $129–$299 suite; $159–$459 cottage; $399–$579 villa. AE, MC, V. **Amenities:** Bike rental; heated freshwater pool; watersports equipment/rentals. *In room:* A/C, fridge, kitchen (in most).

INEXPENSIVE

Ragged Edge Resort ★★ This oceanfront property's Tahitian-style units are spread along more than half a dozen gorgeous, grassy waterfront acres. All are immaculately clean and comfortable, and most are outfitted with full kitchens and tasteful furnishings. There's no bar, restaurant, or staff to speak of, but the retreat's affable owner is happy to lend bicycles and give advice on the area's offerings. A large dock attracts boaters and a variety of local and migratory birds. An outdoor heated freshwater pool is a bonus for those months when the temperature gets a bit chilly.

243 Treasure Harbor Rd. (near MM 86.5), Islamorada, FL 33036. www.ragged-edge.com. ℂ **800/436-2023** or 305/852-5389. 11 units. $69–$99 double; $109–$259 suite. AE, MC, V. **Amenities:** Free use of bikes; outdoor pool. *In room:* A/C, fridge, kitchen (in most).

CAMPING

John Pennekamp Coral Reef State Park ★★ One of Florida's best parks (p. 205), Pennekamp has 47 well-separated campsites, half of which are available by advance reservation. The tent sites are small but equipped with restrooms, hot water, and showers. Note that the local environment provides fertile breeding grounds for insects, particularly in late summer, so bring repellent. Two man-made beaches and a small lagoon attract many large wading birds. Reservations are held until 5pm; the park must be notified of late arrival by phone on the check-in date. Pennekamp opens at 8am and closes around sundown. In 2010 the campground closed until April 2011 for a construction project to enhance the grounds.

U.S. 1 at MM 102.5 (P.O. Box 487), Key Largo, FL 33037. www.pennekamppark.com. ℂ **305/451-1202.** Reservations: Reserve America (ℂ **800/326-3521**). 47 campsites. $36 (with electricity) per site, 8 people maximum. Park entry $8 per vehicle with driver (plus 50¢ per person Monroe County Surcharge). Yearly permits and passes available. AE, DISC, MC, V. No pets.

Long Key State Park ★ The Upper Keys' other main state park is more secluded than its northern neighbor—and more popular. All sites are located oceanside and surrounded by narrow rows of trees and nearby restroom facilities. Reserve well in advance, especially in winter.

U.S. 1 at MM 67.5 (P.O. Box 776), Long Key, FL 33001. www.floridastateparks.org/longkey. ℂ **305/664-4815.** 60 sites. $36 per site for 1–8 people; $5 per vehicle (plus 50¢ per person Monroe County Surcharge). AE, DISC, MC, V. No pets.

Where to Dine

Not known as a culinary hot spot (though it's improving), the Upper and Middle Keys do have some excellent restaurants, most of which specialize in seafood. The landmark **Green Turtle Inn** (below) is alive and well, featuring classic and contemporary Florida cuisine by star chef Andy Niedenthal, a full bar and tasting station, custom catering, gourmet to go, and a Green Turtle product line, all in a beautiful, rustic environment. The restaurant is flanked by an art gallery and sportfishing outfitter, making it a one-stop shop for locals and fun-loving tourists.

Often, visitors (especially those who fish) take advantage of accommodations that have kitchen facilities and cook their own meals. Some restaurants will even clean and cook your catch, for a fee.

VERY EXPENSIVE

Atlantic's Edge ★★★ SEAFOOD Continuing its award-winning culinary tradition, albeit with a modern twist, the 21st-century version of Atlantic's Edge under the culinary direction of chef Dean Max (of 3030 Ocean in Fort Lauderdale) is a welcome addition to the Upper Keys dining scene. Max has packed his modern American seafood and taken it with him down to the Keys. Signature dishes include whole fried Florida Keys fresh fish with chili aioli, citron vinaigrette, and house-made tartar sauce; and Florida Keys barrel fish with Parmesan risotto, wild mushrooms, and greens in a lemon thyme sauce. With an emphasis on farm-to-table ingredients and, of course, the freshest seafood possible, Atlantic's Edge takes things to the, uh, max, and puts on an impressive show. Speaking of shows, the revamped restaurant itself is stunning, with views of its namesake and a gorgeous glassed-in wine cellar featuring more than 150 wines selected by the chef.

Cheeca Lodge, U.S. 1 at MM 82, Islamorada. ✆ **305/664-4651.** Reservations recommended. Main courses $23–$52. AE, DC, MC, V. Daily 7am–5pm and 6–10pm.

Pierre's ★★★ FRENCH The two-story British West Indies–style plantation home that houses this exquisite French restaurant is only part of the dramatic effect of a dinner at Pierre's. Inside, you'll find more design drama—in a good way—in the form of an eclectic mix of Moroccan, Indian, and African artifacts. Lighting is dim, with candlelight and Tiki torches outside, and it's completely romantic—especially outdoors on the second-floor veranda overlooking the water. The food challenges the setting, with amazing flavors and gorgeous presentation. The tempura lobster tail with hearts of palm hash, soy glaze, and wasabi crème fraîche, and the Florida Keys Hogfish Meunière with roasted creamer potatoes, pattypan squash, and baby zucchini are to die for. Desserts are divine, and if you can't decide what to have, order the Valrhona Chocolate Fondue with biscotti, *pâté a choux,* lemon sugar cookies, strawberries, and mandarin oranges. After dinner, head downstairs to the Green Flash Lounge, where you'll find a laid-back cocktail scene, with locals and visitors marveling at the exquisite, priceless setting. Pierre's also hosts a fabulous, monthly Full Moon Party with its casual-dining sister, Morada Bay Beach Café.

U.S. 1 at MM 81.6 (bay side), Islamorada. ✆ **305/664-3225.** www.pierres-restaurant.com. Main courses $28–$40. AE, MC, V. Sun–Thurs 6–10pm; Fri–Sat 6–11pm. Lounge open at 5pm daily. Restaurant closed Tues during summer.

EXPENSIVE

Barracuda Grill ★ SEAFOOD This small, casual spot serves good seafood, steaks, and chops, although lately we've heard some complaints that the food is not worthy of the hefty prices. Some favorites are the Caicos gold conch, braised pork shank, and mangrove snapper and mango. Try the appetizer of tipsy olives, marinated in gin or vodka, to kick-start your meal. For fans of spicy food, go for the red-hot calamari. Decorated with barracuda-themed art, the restaurant also features a well-priced American wine list with lots of California vintages.

U.S. 1 at MM 49.5 (bay side), Marathon. ✆ **305/743-3314.** Main courses $15–$30. AE, MC, V. Wed–Sat 6–10pm.

Butterfly Café ★★★ SEAFOOD In the stunning Tranquility Bay resort, Butterfly Café is the newest gourmet hot spot in the Middle Keys, with water views and a stellar menu of fresh local seafood. Among the dishes not to miss: horseradish-encrusted grouper; and Cuban-spiced, grilled pork chops with garlic, lime, and cumin and served with black beans and rice. Service is very friendly and knowledgeable, and desserts are to die for. Save room for the sticky toffee pudding and nutty-crust Key lime pie with white chocolate mousse. Open for breakfast, lunch, and dinner, but Sunday brunch is especially spectacular. Don't miss the tropical French toast.

2600 Overseas Hwy., in the Tranquility Bay Resort, Marathon. ☎ **305/289-0888.** www.tranquility bay.com. Main courses $18–$37. AE, MC, V. Daily 7–10am and 11:30am–10pm; Sun brunch 10:30am–2:30pm.

Green Turtle Inn ★★★ SEAFOOD The legend is back, but this time with a gourmet market and cuisine cooked with locally farmed vegetables and micro-greens. While it may not be a throwback to the old Florida Keys, Green Turtle, helmed by star chef Andy Niedenthal, remains a must for anyone looking for a fabulous dining experience. Some old menu items remain—the famous turtle chowder with pepper sherry, and luscious conch chowder. But the new menu items are nothing to sneer at either. Small plates, including pan-seared scallops with goat cheese–whipped potatoes, sherry-vinegar brown butter, white truffle oil, and sizzled leeks, make for satisfying main courses, but don't miss entrees such as fresh diver scallops with sautéed spinach, mushrooms, chive beurre blanc, white truffle oil, and shaved pecorino over papardelle. And do not pass up the chocolate decadence mousse cake! After dinner, check out the art gallery and gourmet shop. Green Turtle also serves excellent breakfast (try the coconut French toast) and lunch (we love the fried-green-tomato BLT).

81219 Overseas Hwy., at MM 81.2, Islamorada. ☎ **305/664-2006.** www.greenturtlekeys.com. Main courses $20–$38. AE, MC, V. Daily 7–10am and 11:30am–10pm.

Marker 88 ★★★ SEAFOOD An institution in the Upper Keys, Marker 88 has been pleasing locals and visitors since it opened in the 1970s. New chefs and own-ers have infused a new life into the place and the menu, which still utilizes fresh fruits, local ingredients, and fish caught in the Keys' waters. Among the menu highlights are the crispy yellowtail meunière, sautéed and finished with a Key lime butter; and mahi Martinique, sautéed and topped with sweet basil, grilled ba-nanas, and garlic butter. The waitresses, who are pleasant enough, require a bit of patience, but the food—not to mention the spectacular Gulf views—is worth it.

U.S. 1 at MM 88 (bay side), Islamorada. ☎ **305/852-9315.** www.marker88.info. Reservations sug-gested. Main courses $24–$36; burgers and sandwiches $10–$15. AE, DC, DISC, MC, V. Tues–Sun 5–11pm. Closed Sept.

Ziggie and Mad Dog's ★★★ STEAKHOUSE When former Miami Dolphins player Jim Mandich, aka Mad Dog, bought Ziggie's Crab Shack from Sigmund "Ziggie" Stockie, he decided to keep the ex-owner's name up there with his own. These days, people are mad for this fine Florida Keys steak and chop house. Casually elegant, Ziggie and Mad Dog's is quite the Upper Keys scene, attracting everyone from locals and tourists to day-trippers looking for something more than a ramshackle fish shack. If you're starving, we dare you to order the 28-ounce Czonka Porterhouse named after Mandich's fellow 'fins teammate Larry Csonka. People also rave about the bone-in rib-eye and the mac and cheese. Service is friendly and the vibe is fun. Sports fans love it here not because of the games on in the bar, but because many of Mandich's famous athlete friends come here.

83000 Overseas Hwy., Islamorada. ☎ **305/664-3391.** www.ziggieandmaddogs.com. Reserva-tions suggested. Main courses $20–$42. AE, DC, DISC, MC, V. Daily 5:30–10pm.

MODERATE

Lazy Days ★ SEAFOOD/BAR FARE Making good on its name, this laid-back oceanfront eatery is the quintessence of Keys lifestyle. But chef/owner Lupe is far from lazy, preparing excellent fresh seafood, seafood pastas, vegetar-ian pastas, sandwiches, steaks, and chicken. He'll even cook your own catch. A popular happy hour at the bar from 4 to 6pm features three-for-$1 appetizers. Lazy Days is so popular that Lupe and co-owner Michelle Ledesma have opened **Lazy Days South,** featuring an identical menu and waterfront seating at the Marathon Marina (📞 **305/289-0839**).

79867 Overseas Hwy., Islamorada. 📞 **305/664-5256.** www.lazydaysrestaurant.com. Reservations not usually required. Main courses $15–$26; lighter fare and appetizers $7–$12. AE, DC, DISC, MC, V. Sun–Thurs 11am–9:30pm; Fri–Sat 11am–10pm.

Lorelei Restaurant and Cabana Bar ★ SEAFOOD/BAR FARE Follow the siren call of the enormous roadside mermaid—you won't be dashed onto the rocks. This big old fish house and bar, with excellent views of the bay, is a great place for a snack, a meal, or a beer. A good-value menu focuses mainly on seafood; in season, lobster is the way to go. Other fare includes the standard clam chowder, fried shrimp, and doughy conch fritters. For those tired of fish, the menu offers a few beef options, but we say the simpler the better. Food is definitely trumped by ambience. The outside bar has live music every evening, and you can order snacks and light meals from a limited menu.

U.S. 1 at MM 82, Islamorada. 📞 **305/664-4656.** www.loreleifloridakeys.com. Reservations not usually required. Main courses $15–$22; sandwiches $9–$11. AE, DC, DISC, MC, V. Daily 7am–10:30pm. Outside bar serves breakfast 7–11am; lunch/appetizer menu 11am–9pm. Bar closes at midnight.

INEXPENSIVE

Calypso's Seafood Grill ★★ 📖 SEAFOOD With a motto proudly declaring, "Yes, we know the music is loud and the food is spicy. That's the way we like it!" you know you're in a typical Keys eatery. Thankfully, the food is anything but, with inventive seafood dishes in a casual and rustic waterside setting. Among the house specialties is cracked conch and steamed clams; but if you're not too hot, try the she-crab soup. It's exceptional. If it's offered, try the deep-fried corn and the hog snapper however they prepare it. It's outstanding! The prices are surprisingly reasonable, but the service may be a bit more laid-back than you're used to.

1 Seagate Blvd. (near MM 99.5), Key Largo. 📞 **305/451-0600.** Main courses $10–$20. No credit cards. Wed–Thurs and Sun–Mon 11:30am–10pm; Fri–Sat 11:30am–11pm. From the south, turn right at the blinking yellow lights near MM 99.5 to Ocean Bay Dr., and then turn right. Look for the blue vinyl-sided building on the left.

Islamorada Fish Company ★★ SEAFOOD Pick up a cooler of stone crab claws in season (mid-Oct to Apr), or try the great fried-fish sandwiches. A few hundred yards up the road (at MM 81.6) is Islamorada Fish Company Restaurant & Bakery, the newer establishment, which looks like an average diner but has fantastic seafood, pastas, and breakfasts. Locals gather here for politics and gossip as well as grits, oatmeal, omelets, and pastries. Keep your eyes open while dining outside—the last time we were here, baby manatees were floating around, waiting for their close-ups.

U.S. 1 at MM 81.5 (up the street from Cheeca Lodge), Islamorada. 📞 **800/258-2559** or 305/664-9271. www.islamoradafishco.com. Reservations not accepted. Main courses $11–$22; sandwiches $9–$14. DISC, MC, V. Sun–Thurs 11am–9pm; Fri–Sat 11am–10pm.

Island Grill ★ SEAFOOD If you drive too fast over Snake Creek Bridge, you may miss one of the best Keys dining experiences around. Just under the bridge and on the bay, Island Grill is a locals' favorite, with an expansive outdoor deck and bar and cozy waterfront dining room serving some fresh fare, including their famous tuna nachos, guava barbecued shrimp, and graham cracker–crusted cala-mari. There are also salads, sandwiches—try the lobster roll—and entrees, in-cluding a whole yellowtail snapper with Thai sweet chili sauce that's out of this world. Bring your own catch, and they'll cook and prepare it for you—served family-style with veggies and rice for only $12. Live entertainment almost every night brings in a great, colorful Keys crowd. Although they serve breakfast too, we say skip the food and just stick to the bloody marys.

MM 88.5 (ocean side at Snake Creek Bridge), Islamorada. © **305/664-8400.** www.keysisland grill.com. Reservations not necessary. Main courses $14–$26; sandwiches $7–$14. Sun–Thurs 11am–10pm; Fri–Sat 11am–11pm.

Key Largo Conch House Restaurant & Coffee Bar ★★ AMERICAN A funky, cozy, off-the-beaten-path hot spot for breakfast, lunch, and dinner, Key Largo Conch House is exactly that—a house set amid lush foliage, complete with resident dog, parrot, wraparound veranda for outdoor dining, and a warm and inviting indoor dining room reminiscent of your grandma's. Food is fresh and fabulously priced—from the heaping $14 plate of Mom's Lasagna, to $9-to-$14 twists on the usual eggs Benedict, including our favorite, the crab cakes Benedict. Featured on the Food Network, Conch House should be a feature on everyone's trip down to the Keys, if not just for a cup of excellent coffee and a slice of home-made Key lime pie. It's also one of the few pet-friendly restaurants in the area.

U.S. 1 at MM 100, Key Largo. © **305/453-4844.** www.keylargocoffeehouse.com. Reservations recommended. Main courses $12–$29; wraps and sandwiches $8–$13. AE, DC, DISC, MC, V. Daily 7am–10pm.

Snapper's ★ SEAFOOD A locals' waterfront favorite, Snapper's serves fresh seafood caught by local fishermen—or by you, if you dare! The blackened mahi-mahi is exceptional and a bargain, complete with salad, vegetable, and choice of starch. There's also live music nightly and a lively, colorful—and deliciously ca-sual—crowd. A popular Sunday brunch features live jazz from the barge out back and a make-your-own-bloody-mary bar. Kids love feeding the tarpon off the docks, and for those who just can't stay away from work, there's free Wi-Fi, indoors and out. If you caught a big one, clean it and they will cook it for you at $12 for 8 ounces a person. For an even more casual dining experience, check out the Turtle Club, the entirely outdoor, waterfront bar and grill located out back and featuring live music and a more casual menu of sandwiches, snacks, and pub grub.

139 Seaside Ave., at MM 94.5, Key Largo. © **305/852-5956.** www.snapperskeylargo.com. Main courses $12–$28; sandwiches $8–$14. DISC, MC, V. Sun–Thurs 11am–9pm; Fri–Sat 11am–10pm.

The Upper & Middle Keys After Dark

Nightlife in the Upper Keys tends to start before the sun goes down, often at noon, as most people—visitors and locals alike—are on vacation. Also, many anglers and sports-minded folk go to bed early.

Hog Heaven, MM 85.3, just off the main road on the ocean side, Islamorada (© **305/664-9669**), opened in the early 1990s, the joint venture of young locals tired of tourist traps. This whitewashed biker bar is a welcome respite from the neon-colored cocktail circuit. It has a waterside view and diver-sions such as big-screen TVs and video games. The food isn't bad, either. The atmosphere is cliquish because most patrons are regulars, so start up a game of pool to break the ice. Open daily from 11am to 4am.

No trip to the Keys is complete without a stop at the **Tiki Bar at the Holiday Isle Resort,** U.S. 1 at MM 84, Islamorada (✆ **305/664-2321**). Hundreds of revelers visit this oceanside spot for drinks and dancing at any time of day, but the live rock starts at 8:30pm. The thatched-roof Tiki Bar draws a mix of thirsty people, all in pursuit of a good time. In the afternoon and early evening (when everyone is either sunburned, drunk, or just happy to be dancing to live reggae), head for **Kokomo's,** next door. It often closes at 7:30pm on weekends (5:30pm on weekdays), so arrive early. For information, call the Holiday Isle Resort. Rumor has it that developers are going to raze the Tiki Bar to make way for condos, but loyal booze hounds are raising hell over it, and some are trying to have the Tiki Bar declared a Florida landmark! Stay tuned.

Locals and tourists mingle at the outdoor cabana bar at **Lorelei** (see "Where to Dine," earlier in this chapter). Most evenings after 5pm, you'll find local bands playing on a thatched-roof stage—mainly rock or reggae, and sometimes blues.

Woody's Saloon and Restaurant, U.S. 1 at MM 82, Islamorada (✆ **305/664-4335**), is a lively, loud, raunchy, local legend serving up mediocre pizzas, buck-naked strippers, and live bands almost every night. The house band, Big Dick and the Extenders, showcases a 300-pound Native American who does a lewd, rude, and crude routine of politically incorrect jokes and songs starting at 9pm Tuesday through Sunday. He is a legend. By the way, don't think you're lucky if you're offered the front table: It's the target seat for Big Dick's haranguing. Avoid the lame karaoke on Sunday and Monday evenings. There's a small cover most nights. Drink specials, contests, and Big Dick keep this place packed until 4am almost every night. *Note:* This place is not for the faint of heart, but more for those from the Howard Stern School of Nightlife.

For a more subdued atmosphere, try the stained-glass and mahogany-wood bar and club at **Zane Grey's,** on the second floor of World Wide Sportsman, MM 81.5 (✆ **305/664-4244**). Outside, enjoy a view of the calm waters of the bay; inside, soak up the history of real longtime anglers. It's open from 11am to at least 11pm (later on weekends). Call to find out who's playing on Friday and Saturday nights, when there's live entertainment and no cover.

THE LOWER KEYS

128 miles SW of Miami

Unlike their neighbors to the north and south, the Lower Keys (including **Big Pine, Sugarloaf,** and **Summerland**) are devoid of rowdy Spring Break crowds, boast few T-shirt and trinket shops, and have almost no late-night bars. What they do offer are the best opportunities to enjoy the vast natural resources on land and water that make the area so rich. Stay overnight in the Lower Keys, rent a boat, and explore the reefs—it might be the most memorable part of your trip.

Essentials

GETTING THERE See "Essentials" for the Upper and Middle Keys (p. 199) and continue south on U.S. 1. The Lower Keys start at the end of the Seven-Mile Bridge. There are also airports in Marathon and Key West.

VISITOR INFORMATION Big Pine and Lower Keys Chamber of Commerce, ocean side of U.S. 1 at MM 31 (P.O. Box 430511), Big Pine Key, FL 33043 (✆ **800/872-3722** or 305/872-2411; fax 305/872-0752; www. lowerkeyschamber.com), is open Monday through Friday from 9am to 5pm, and Saturday from 9am to 3pm. The pleasant staff will help with anything a traveler may need. Call, write, or stop in for a comprehensive, detailed information packet.

What to See & Do

Once the centerpiece (these days, it's Big Pine Key) of the Lower Keys and still a great asset is **Bahia Honda State Park ★**, U.S. 1 at MM 37.5, Big Pine Key (*C* 305/872-2353; www.bahiahondapark.com or www.floridastateparks. org/bahiahonda/default.cfm), which has one of the most beautiful coastlines in South Florida. Bahia (pronounced *Bah*-ya) Honda is a great place for hiking, bird-watching, swimming, snorkeling, and fishing. The 524-acre park encompasses a wide variety of ecosystems, including coastal mangroves, beach dunes, and tropical hammocks. There are miles of trails packed with unusual plants and animals, plus a small white-sand beach. Shaded seaside picnic areas are fitted with tables and grills. Although the beach is never wider than 5 feet, even at low tide, this is the Lower Keys' best beach area.

True to its name (Spanish for "deep bay"), the park has relatively deep waters close to shore—perfect for snorkeling and diving. Easy offshore snorkeling here gives even novices a chance to lie suspended in warm water and simply observe diverse marine life passing by. Or else head to the stunning reefs at Looe Key, where the coral and fish are more vibrant than anywhere else in the United States. Snorkeling trips go from the Bahia Honda concessions to Looe Key National Marine Sanctuary (4 miles offshore). They depart twice daily (9:30am and 1:30pm) March through September and cost $30 for adults, $25 for children 6 to 17, and $8 for equipment rental. Call *C* 305/872-3210 for a schedule.

Entry to the park is $8 per vehicle of two to eight passengers, $4 for a solo passenger, $2 per pedestrian or bicyclist, free for children 5 and under, with a 50¢-per-person Monroe County Surcharge. Open daily from 8am to sunset.

The most famous residents of the Lower Keys are the tiny Key deer. Of the estimated 300 existing in the world, two-thirds live on Big Pine Key's **National Key Deer Refuge ★**. To get your bearings, stop by the rangers' office at the Winn-Dixie Shopping Plaza, near MM 30.5 off U.S. 1. They'll give you an informative brochure and map of the area. The refuge is open Monday through Friday from 8am to 5pm.

If the office is closed, head out to the **Blue Hole,** a former quarry now filled with the fresh water that's vital to the deer's survival. To get there, turn right at Big Pine Key's only traffic light at Key Deer Boulevard (take the left fork immediately after the turn) and continue 1½ miles to the observation-site parking lot, on your left. The .5-mile **Watson Hammock Trail,** about ⅓ mile past the Blue Hole, is the refuge's only marked footpath. The deer are more active in cool hours, so try coming out to the path in the early morning or late evening to catch a glimpse of these gentle dog-size creatures. There is an observation deck from which you can watch and photograph the protected species. Refuge lands are open daily from a half-hour before sunrise to a half-hour after sunset. Don't be surprised to see a lazy alligator warming itself in the sun, particularly in outlying areas around the Blue Hole. If you do see a gator, do not go near it, do not touch it, and do not provoke it. Keep your distance; if you must get a photo, use a zoom lens. Also, whatever you do, do not feed the deer—it will threaten their survival. Call the **park office** (*C* 305/872-2239) to find out about the infrequent free tours of the refuge, scheduled throughout the year.

Outdoor Activities

BIKING The Lower Keys are a great place to get off busy U.S. 1 to explore the beautiful back roads. On Big Pine Key, cruise along Key Deer Boulevard (at MM 30). Those with fat tires can ride into the National Key Deer Refuge. Many lodgings offer bike rentals.

BIRD-WATCHING A stopping point for migratory birds on the Eastern Flyway, the Lower Keys are populated with many West Indian bird species, especially in spring and fall. The small, vegetated islands of the Keys are the only nesting sites in the U.S. for the white-crowned pigeon. They're also some of the few breeding places for the reddish egret, roseate spoonbill, mangrove cuckoo, and black-whiskered vireo. Look for them on Bahia

FROM TOP: Snorkeling is also a favorite activity off Big Pine Key; you'll see the dear little Key deer in Keys.

Honda Key and the many uninhabited islands nearby.

BOATING Dozens of shops rent powerboats for fishing and reef exploring. Most also rent tackle, sell bait, and have charter captains available. **Florida Keys Boat Rental** (© **305/664-2003;** www.keysboat.com) offers an impressive selection of boats from $125 to $450 for a half-day and $105 to $650 for a full day. They also offer kayaks and paddleboats for eco-tours.

CANOEING & KAYAKING The Overseas Highway (U.S. 1) touches on only a few dozen of the many hundreds of islands that make up the Keys. To really see the Lower Keys, rent a kayak or canoe—perfect for these shallow waters. **Reflections Kayak Nature Tours,** operating out of the Old Wooden

Bridge Fishing Camp, 1791 Bogie Dr., MM 30, Big Pine Key (© **305/872-4668;** www.floridakeyskayaktours.com), offers fully outfitted backcountry wildlife tours, either on your own or with an expert. The expert, U.S.C.G.-licensed Captain Bill Keogh, wrote the book on the subject. *The Florida Keys Paddling Guide* (Countryman Press), which he wrote in 2004, covers all the unique ecosystems and inhabitants, as well as launches and favorite routes from Key Biscayne to the Dry Tortugas National Park. The 3-hour kayak tours cost $50 per person. An extended 4-hour backcountry tour for two to six people costs $125 per person and uses a mother ship to ferry kayaks and paddlers to the remote reaches of the refuge. Reservations are required.

FISHING A day spent fishing, either in the shallow backcountry or in the deep sea, is a great way to ensure a fresh-fish dinner, or you can release your catch and just appreciate the challenge. Whichever you choose, **Strike Zone Charters,** U.S. 1 at MM 29.5, Big Pine Key (© **305/872-9863;** www.strikezonecharter.com), is the charter service to call. Prices for fishing boats start at $650 for a half-day and $850 for a full day with the possibility of a $50 fuel surcharge added to the cost. If you have enough anglers to share the price (they take up to six people), it isn't too steep. The outfitter may also be able to match you with other interested visitors. Strike Zone also offers daily trips to Looe Key National Marine Sanctuary on a glass-bottom boat. The 2-hour trip costs $25 for viewing, $35 for snorkeling, and $45 for scuba diving, all with a $3-per-person fuel charge. Strike Zone's 5-hour **Eco Island** excursion offers a vivid history of the Keys from the glass-bottom boat. The tour stops for snorkeling and light tackle fishing and docks at an island for their famous island fish cookout. Cost is $55 per person plus an additional $3 surcharge for fuel, including mask, snorkel, fins, vests, rods, reel, bait, fishing licenses, food, and all soft drinks.

HIKING You can hike throughout the flat, marshy Keys on both marked trails and meandering coastlines. The best places to trek through nature are **Bahia Honda State Park,** at MM 29.5, and **National Key Deer Refuge,** at MM 30 (for more information on both, see "What to See & Do," above). Bahia Honda Park has a free brochure describing an excellent self-guided tour along the Silver Palm Nature Trail. You'll traverse hammocks, mangroves, and sand dunes, and cross a lagoon. The walk (less than a mile) explores a great cross section of the natural habitat in the Lower Keys and can be done in less than half an hour.

SNORKELING & SCUBA DIVING Snorkelers and divers should not miss the Keys' most dramatic reefs at the **Looe Key National Marine Sanctuary.** Here you'll see more than 150 varieties of hard and soft coral—some centuries old—as well as every type of tropical fish, including gold and blue parrotfish, moray eels, barracudas, French angels, and tarpon. **Looe Key Dive Center,** U.S. 1 at MM 27.5, Ramrod Key (© **305/872-2215;** www.diveflakeys.com), offers a mind-blowing 5-hour tour aboard a 45-foot catamaran with two shallow 1-hour dives for snorkelers and scuba divers. Snorkelers pay $44, children 6 and under pay $34; divers pay $84 for three dives, $69 for two. Snorkeling equipment is available for rent for $10; diving-equipment rental prices range from $14 to $29. On Wednesday and Saturday, you can do a fascinating dive to the *Adolphus Busch, Sr.,* a shipwreck off Looe Key in 100 feet of water, for $50 with $30 per additional diver. (See "What to See & Do," above, for other diving options.)

Where to Stay

There are a number of cheap, fairly unappealing fish shacks along the highway for those who want bare-bones accommodations. So far, there are no national hotel chains in the Lower Keys. For information on lodging in cabins or trailers at local campgrounds, see "Camping," below.

VERY EXPENSIVE

Little Palm Island Resort & Spa ★★★ This exclusive island escape—host to presidents, royalty, and even Howard Stern—is not just a place to stay while in the Lower Keys; it is a destination all its own. Built on a private 5½-acre island, it's accessible only by boat or seaplane. Guests stay in thatched-roof duplexes amid lush foliage and flowering tropical plants—and Key deer, which are to this island what cats are to Key West. Many bungalows have ocean views and private decks with hammocks. Inside, the romantic suites have all the comforts of a swank beach cottage, but without phones, TVs, or alarm clocks. Mosquitoes can be a problem, even in winter. (Bring spray and lightweight, long-sleeved clothing.) Known for a stellar spa and innovative and pricey food, Little Palm also hosts visitors just for dinner, brunch, or lunch. If you're staying on the island, opt for the full American plan, which includes three meals a day.

Launch is on the ocean side of U.S. 1 at MM 28.5, Little Torch Key, FL 33042. www.littlepalm island.com. ✆ **800/343-8567** or 305/872-2524. Fax 305/872-4843. 30 units. Winter $840–$1,695 double; off season $640–$1,595 double. Rates include transportation to and from the island and unlimited (nonmotorized) watersports. Meal plans include 2 meals daily for $125 per person per day, 3 meals at $140 per person. AE, DC, DISC, MC, V. No children 15 and under. **Amenities:** Restaurant; bar; courtesy van from Key West or Marathon airport; concierge; health club; 2 pools; limited room service; spa; watersports equipment/rentals. *In room:* A/C, hair dryer, Internet access, minibar, no phone.

INEXPENSIVE

Parmer's Resort ★ Parmer's, a fixture for more than 20 years, is known for its charming hospitality and helpful staff. This downscale resort offers modest but comfortable cottages, each of them unique. Some are waterfront, many have kitchenettes, and others are just a bedroom. The Wahoo room (no. 26), a one-bedroom efficiency, is especially nice, with a small sitting area that faces the water. All units have been recently updated and are very clean. Many can be combined to accommodate families. The hotel's waterfront location, not to mention the fact that it's only a half-hour from Key West, almost makes up for the fact that you must pay extra for maid service.

565 Barry Ave, MM 28.5, Little Torch Key, FL 33042. www.parmersresort.com. ✆ **305/872-2157.** Fax 305/872-2014. 45 units. Winter $134–$194 double, from $174 efficiency; off season $99–$129 double, from $129 efficiency. Rates include continental breakfast. AE, DISC, MC, V. From U.S. 1, turn right onto Barry Ave. Resort is ½ mile down on the right. **Amenities:** Heated pool. *In room:* A/C, TV.

CAMPING

Bahia Honda State Park ★★★ (www.floridastateparks.org/bahiahonda/default.cfm; ✆ **800/326-3521**) offers some of the best camping in the Keys. It is as loaded with facilities and activities as it is with campers. But don't be discouraged by its popularity—this park encompasses more than 500 acres of land, 80 campsites spread throughout three areas, and three spacious, comfortable duplex cabins. Cabins hold up to eight guests each and come complete with linens, kitchenettes, wraparound terraces, barbecue pits, and rocking chairs. For one to four people, camping costs about $36 per site. Depending on the season, cabin prices range from $120 to $160.

Another excellent value can be found at the **KOA Sugarloaf Key Resort ★★**, near MM 20. This oceanside facility has 200 fully equipped sites, with water, electricity, and sewer, which rent for about $89 a night (no-hookup sites cost about $55). Or you can pitch a tent on the 5 acres of waterfront property. Or stay in a shiny Airstream trailer which sleeps up to four people for $170 a night. This place is especially nice because of its private beaches and access to diving, snorkeling, and boating; its grounds are also well maintained. In addition, the resort rents travel trailers: The 25-foot Dutchman sleeps six and costs about $150 a day. For details, contact the resort at P.O. Box 420469, Summerland Key, FL 33042 (www.koa.com; © **800/562-7731** or 305/745-3549; fax 305/745-9889).

Where to Dine

There aren't many fine-dining options in the Lower Keys, with the exception of the **Dining Room at Little Palm Island,** MM 285, Little Torch Key (© **305/872-2551**), where you'll be wowed with gourmet French Caribbean fare that looks like a meal but tastes like a vacation (see above for the hotel listing). You need to take a ferry to this chichi private island, where you can indulge at the oceanside restaurant even if you're not staying.

MODERATE

Mangrove Mama's Restaurant SEAFOOD/CARIBBEAN As the locals who come daily for happy hour will tell you, this is a Lower Keys institution and a dive in the best sense of the word (the restaurant is a shack that used to have a gas pump as well as a grill). Guests share the property with stray cats and some miniature horses out back. It's run-down, but in a charming Keys sort of way—they serve beer in a jelly glass. A handful of tables, inside and out, are shaded by banana trees and palm fronds. Fish is the menu's mainstay, although soups, salads, sandwiches, and omelets are also good. Grilled-chicken and club sandwiches are tasty alternatives to fish, as are meatless chef's salads and spicy barbecued baby back ribs. The restaurant is under new ownership, which some say has let the place slip a bit, though they still rock their Sunday brunch with amazing crab Benedict.

U.S. 1 at MM 20, Sugarloaf Key. © **305/745-3030.** www.mangrovemamasrestaurant.com. Main courses $19–$29; lunch $9–$11; brunch $5–$15. MC, V. Daily 11am–3pm and 5:30–10pm.

INEXPENSIVE

Coco's Kitchen ★ CUBAN/AMERICAN This storefront has been dishing out black beans, rice, and shredded beef for more than 10 years. The owners, who are actually from Nicaragua, cook not only superior Cuban food, but also local specialties, Italian dishes, and Caribbean choices. Specialties include fried shrimp, whole fried yellowtail, and Cuban-style roast pork (available only on Sat). The best bet is the daily special, which may be roasted pork or fresh grouper, served with rice and beans or salad and crispy fries. Top off the huge meal with a rich caramel-soaked flan.

283 Key Deer Blvd. (in the Winn-Dixie Shopping Center), Big Pine Key. © **305/872-4495.** http://cocoskitchen.com. Main courses $8.50–$17; breakfast $2.75–$8; lunch $3.75–$6. MC, V. Tues–Sun 7am–3pm. Turn right at the traffic light near MM 30.5; stay in the left lane.

No Name Pub PUB FARE/PIZZA This hard-to-find funky old bar out in the boondocks (tagline: You Found It) serves snacks and sandwiches until 11pm on most nights, and drinks until midnight. Pizzas are tasty—try one topped with local shrimp. Or consider a bowl of chili with all the fixings. Everything is served on paper plates. Locals hang out at the rustic bar, one of the Keys' oldest bars blanketed with thousands of autographed dollar bills, drinking beer and listening to a jukebox heavy with 1980s tunes.

¼ mile south of No Name Bridge on N. Watson Blvd., Big Pine Key. ℭ **305/872-9115.** www. nonamepub.com. Pizzas $6–$18; subs $5–$9. MC, V. Daily 11am–11pm. Turn right at Big Pine's only traffic light (near MM 30.5) onto Key Deer Blvd. Turn right on Watson Blvd. At the stop sign, turn left. Look for a small wooden sign on the left marking the spot.

The Lower Keys After Dark

Although the mellow islands of the Lower Keys aren't exactly known for wild nightlife, there are some friendly bars and restaurants where locals and tourists gather. **No Name Pub** (listed above in "Where to Dine") is one of the best. One of the most scenic is **Parrotdise Waterfont,** Barry Avenue near MM 28.5 (ℭ **305/872-9989;** www.parrotdisewaterfront.com), the only waterfront restaurant between Key West and Marathon. The place is enclosed with windows looking out onto the water where there's a shark pond for those who are curious. Great food (even sushi) is served from 10:30am to 10pm, and the bar closes around midnight. The place even has its own brand of wine, which is currently being marketed in France, of all places. Parrotdise attracts an odd mix of bikers and blue-hairs daily, and is a great place to overhear local gossip and colorful metaphors. Pool tables are the main attraction, but there's also live music some nights. The drinks are reasonably priced, and the food isn't too bad, either.

KEY WEST ★★★

159 miles SW of Miami

Key West is the land of the eternal vacation. It seems the sun is always shining here, making the island a perfect destination for sunbathers, fishermen, divers, and motorcyclists. Munch on fresh seafood, watch the jugglers in Mallory Square, and have another margarita.

Things to Do The preferred leisure activity in Key West is relaxing. Visitors inclined toward more active pursuits head to the docks, where divers explore submarine reefs, and anglers head off from **Garrison Bight Marina** in hopes of landing sailfish and tarpon in the azure waters of the Gulf of Mexico.

Shopping You'll soon become convinced the predominant island souvenir is a tacky T-shirt. But if you can make it past the crude shirts, you'll discover a nice supply of bathing suits, strappy sandals, and sunglasses along Duval Street. Head to **Cigar Alley** between Front and Greene streets for a stogie rolled by Cuban immigrants.

Nightlife & Entertainment When the sun begins to drop, Sunset Celebration goes into full swing in **Mallory Square.** Magicians, jugglers, and one-man bands entertain the crowds each evening as the sun tints the sky and waves with orange and purple. After dark, do the **Duval Street** crawl. Favorite bars include Sloppy Joe's, reputed to be an old Hemingway haunt, and Hog's Breath Saloon.

Restaurants & Dining For a dinner of "conch fusion cuisine," stop in at Hot Tin Roof, in the Ocean Key Resort. Or head off the beaten track to enjoy a fish dinner at Hogfish Bar and Grill, where tattooed bikers and yacht owners alike gather to eat freshly caught fish at picnic tables.

Essentials

GETTING THERE For directions by car, see "Essentials" (p. 199) for the Upper and Middle Keys and continue south on U.S. 1. When entering Key West, stay in the far-right lane onto North Roosevelt Boulevard, which becomes Truman Avenue in Old Town. Continue for a few blocks and you'll find yourself on **Duval Street ★**, in the heart of the city. If you stay to the left, you'll also reach the city center after passing the airport and the remnants of historic houseboat row, where a motley collection of boats once made up one of Key West's most interesting neighborhoods.

Sunset's time to celebrate at Mallory Square.

Several regional airlines fly nonstop (about 55 min.) from Miami to Key West. **American Eagle** (© 800/433-7300), **Continental** (© 800/525-0280), **Delta** (© 800/221-1212), and **US Airways Express** (© 800/428-4322) land at the recently expanded **Key West International Airport,** South Roosevelt Boulevard (© 305/296-5439), on the southeastern corner of the island.

Greyhound (© 800/231-2222; www.greyhound.com) has buses leaving Miami for Key West every day for about $39 to $50 one-way and $77 to $98 round-trip. Seats fill up in season, so come early. The ride takes about 4½ hours.

You can also get to Key West from Ft. Myers or Marco Island via the **Key West Express** (© 866/KW-FERRY [593-3779]; www.seakeywest.com), a 155-foot-long catamaran that travels to Key West at 40 mph. The Big Cat features two enclosed cabins, sun seated deck, observation deck, satellite TV, and full galley and bar. Prices range from $85 one-way and $145 round-trip per person.

GETTING AROUND Old Town Key West has limited parking, narrow streets, and congested traffic, so driving is more of a pain than a convenience. Unless you're staying in one of the more remote accommodations, consider trading in your car for a bicycle. The island is small and flat as a board, which makes it easy to negotiate, especially away from the crowded downtown area. Many tourists choose to cruise by moped, an option that can make navigating the streets risky, especially because there are no helmet laws in Key West. Hundreds of visitors are seriously injured each year, so be careful and spend the extra few bucks to rent a helmet.

Key West

RESTAURANTS

Alonzo's Oyster Bar/
A&B Lobster House **5**
Antonia's **30**
Banana Café **53**
Blue Heaven **33**
Café Marquesa **25**
Fausto's Food Palace **27**
Hot Tin Roof **3**
Island Dogs Bar **4**
La Trattoria/ Virgilio's **28**
Louie's Backyard/
Upper Deck Lounge **45**
Michael's **22**
Nine One Five **55**
Pepe's **17**
Sarabeth's **26**
Seven Fish **37**
Turtle Kraals Wildlife Grill **18**
White Street Bistro **40**

Mallory Square

GULF OF MEXICO

TRUMAN ANNEX

Fort Zachary Taylor State Park ↓

HOTELS

Ambrosia **47**
Ambrosia Key West **24**
Angelina Guest House **32**
Big Ruby's **29**
Casa Marina, A Waldorf Astoria
  Resort **42**
Curry Mansion Inn **15**
Eden House **20**
The Gardens Hotel **31**

The Grand Guesthouse **41**
Hyatt Key West Resort & Spa **1**
Island City House Hotel **21**
Key West Hostel & Seashell Motel **44**
La Mer Hotel & Dewey House **49**
La Pensione **38**
Marquesa Hotel **25**
Ocean Key Resort and Spa **3**
Orchid Key Inn **54**
Pearl's Rainbow **52**

Pier House Resort and Caribbean Spa **2**
The Reach, A Waldorf Astoria
  Resort **46**
Seascape, An Inn **36**
Silver Palms Inn **39**
Simonton Court **16**
Southernmost on the Beach **48**
Southernmost Point Guest House **50**
The Westin Key West Resort & Marina **9**
Westwinds Inn **19**

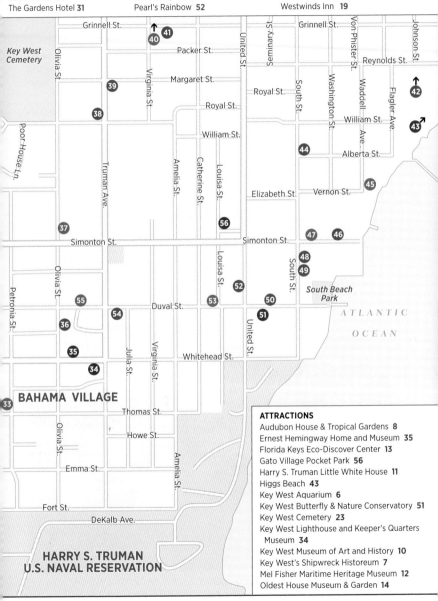

ATTRACTIONS

Audubon House & Tropical Gardens **8**
Ernest Hemingway Home and Museum **35**
Florida Keys Eco-Discover Center **13**
Gato Village Pocket Park **56**
Harry S. Truman Little White House **11**
Higgs Beach **43**
Key West Aquarium **6**
Key West Butterfly & Nature Conservatory **51**
Key West Cemetery **23**
Key West Lighthouse and Keeper's Quarters
  Museum **34**
Key West Museum of Art and History **10**
Key West's Shipwreck Historeum **7**
Mel Fisher Maritime Heritage Museum **12**
Oldest House Museum & Garden **14**

Rates for simple one-speed cruisers start at about $10 per day. Mopeds start at about $20 for 2 hours, $35 per day, and $100 per week. The best shops include the **A&M Scooter and Bicycle Center,** 523 Truman Ave. (✆ **305/294-4556;** www.amscooterskeywest.com); the **Moped Hospital,** 601 Truman Ave. (✆ **866/296-1625;** www.mopedhospital.com); and **Tropical Bicycles & Scooter Rentals,** 1300 Duval St. (✆ **305/294-8136**). The **Bike Shop,** 1110 Truman Ave. (✆ **305/294-1073;** www.the bikeshopkeywest.com), rents cruisers for $12 per day, $60 per week; a $150 deposit is required.

PARKING Parking in Key West's Old Town is limited, but there is a well-placed **municipal parking lot** at Simonton and Angela streets, just behind the firehouse and police station. If you've brought a car, you may want to stash it here while you enjoy the very walkable downtown part of Key West.

VISITOR INFORMATION The **Key West Chamber of Commerce,** 402 Wall St., Key West, FL 33040 (✆ **800/527-8539** or 305/294-2587; www.key westchamber.com), provides both general and specialized information. The lobby is open daily from 8:30am to 6pm; phones are answered from 8am to 8pm. The **Key West Visitor Center** (✆ **800/LAST-KEY** [527-8539]) is the area's best for information on accommodations, goings-on, and restaurants; it's open Monday through Friday from 8am to 5:30pm, Saturday and Sunday from 8:30am to 5pm. Gay travelers may want to call the **Key West Business Guild** (✆ **305/294-4603**), which represents more than 50 guesthouses and B&Bs, as well as many other gay-owned businesses (ask for its color brochure).

While you're in one of the above offices, be sure to pick up a free copy of *Sharon Wells' Walking & Biking Guide to Historic Key West*. Though we still couldn't find all the spots we wanted to in the Key West Cemetery (p. 234) while using the guide, it was helpful for historic descriptions

Scooters are a popular way to get around Key West.

throughout town. Sharon Wells also leads guided walking tours around the island. For information, call her at ☎ **305/294-8380** or go to www.seekey west.com.

ORIENTATION A mere 2 × 4-mile island, Key West is simple to navigate, even though there's no real order to the arrangement of streets and avenues. As you enter town on U.S. 1 (Roosevelt Blvd.), you will see most of the moderate chain hotels and fast-food restaurants. The better restaurants, shops, and outfitters are crammed onto Duval Street, the main thoroughfare of Key West's Old Town. On surrounding streets, many inns and lodges are set in picturesque Victorian/Bahamian homes. On the southern side of the island are the coral-beach area and some of the larger resort hotels.

The area called Bahama Village is the furthest thing from a tourist trap, but can be a bit spotty at night if you aren't familiar with the area. With several newly opened, trendy restaurants and guesthouses, this hippie-ish neighborhood, complete with street-roaming chickens and cats, is the roughest and most urban you'll find in the Keys. You might see a few drug deals on street corners, but they're nothing to be overly concerned about: It looks worse than it is, and resident business owners tend to keep a vigilant eye out. The area is actually quite funky and should be a welcome diversion from the Duvalian mainstream.

Seeing the Sights

Key West's greenest attraction, the **Florida Keys Eco-Discovery Center,** overlooking the waterfront at the Truman Annex (35 E. Quay Rd.; ☎ **305/809-4750;** http://floridakeys.noaa.gov/eco_discovery.html), features 6,000 square feet of interactive exhibits depicting Florida Keys underwater and upland habitats—with emphasis on the ecosystem of North America's only living contiguous barrier coral reef, which parallels the Keys. Kids dig the interactive yellow submarine while adults seem to get into the cinematic depiction of an underwater abyss. Free admission. Open 9am to 4pm daily except Sunday and Monday.

Before shelling out for any of the dozens of worthwhile attractions in Key West, we recommend getting an overview on either of the two comprehensive island tours, the **Conch Tour Train** (p. 236) or the **Old Town Trolley** (p. 237). There are simply too many attractions and historic houses to list. We've highlighted our favorites below, but we encourage you to seek out others.

Audubon House & Tropical Gardens ★★ This well-preserved 19th-century home stands as a prime example of early Key West architecture. Named after renowned painter and bird expert John James Audubon, who is said to have visited the house in 1832, the graceful two-story structure is a retreat from the bustle of Old Town. Included in the price of admission is a self-guided, half-hour audio tour that spotlights rare Audubon prints, antiques, historical photos, and tropical gardens. With voices of several characters from the house's past, the tour never gets boring—though it is a bit hokey at times. Even if you don't want to explore the grounds and home, check out the gift shop, which sells a variety of fine mementos at reasonable prices. Expect to spend 30 minutes to an hour.

205 Whitehead St. (btw. Greene and Caroline sts.). ☎ **305/294-2116.** www.audubonhouse.com. Admission $12 adults, $5 children 6–12, $7.50 students of any age. Daily 9:30am–5pm (last entry at 4:30pm).

East Martello Museum and Gallery

Adjacent to the airport, the East Martello Museum is in a Civil War–era brick fort that itself is worth a visit. The museum contains a bizarre variety of exhibits that do a thorough job of interpreting the city's intriguing past. Historic artifacts include model ships, a deep-sea diver's wooden air pump, a crude raft from a Cuban "boat lift," a supposedly haunted doll, and a horse-drawn hearse. Exhibits illustrate the Keys' history of salvaging, sponging, and cigar making. After seeing the galleries (which should take 45–60 min.), climb a steep spiral staircase to the top of the lookout tower for good views over the island and ocean. A member of the Key West Art and Historical Society, East Martello has two cousins: the **Key West Museum of Art and History,** 281 Front St. (✆ **305/295-6616**), and

The décor is reminiscent of the artist at the Audubon House.

the **Key West Lighthouse Museum** (p.234). Expect to spend 1 to 2 hours.

3501 S. Roosevelt Blvd. ✆ **305/296-3913.** www.kwahs.com/martello.htm. Admission $6 adults, $5 seniors, $3 children 8–12. Daily 9:30am–4:30pm (last entry at 4pm). Closed Christmas.

Ernest Hemingway Home and Museum ★

Hemingway's handsome stone Spanish colonial house, built in 1851 and designated a literary landmark by the American Library Association in 2010, was one of the first on the island to be fitted with indoor plumbing and a built-in fireplace. It also has the first swimming pool built on Key West (look for the penny that Hemingway pressed into the cement). The author owned the home from 1931 until his death in 1961, and lived here with about 50 cats, whose descendants, including the famed six-toed felines, still roam the premises. It was during those years that the Nobel Prize–winning author wrote some of his most famous works, including *For Whom the Bell Tolls, A Farewell to Arms,* and *The Snows of Kilimanjaro.* Fans may want to take the optional half-hour house tour to see his study as well as rooms with glass cabinets that store certain artifacts, books, and pieces of mail addressed to him. It's interesting (to an extent) and included in the price of admission. If you don't take the tour or you have no interest in Hemingway, the price of admission is a waste of money, except for the lovely architecture and garden. If you're feline phobic (or allergic), beware: There are cats everywhere. Guided tours are given every 15 minutes, and expect to spend an hour on the property.

907 Whitehead St. (btw. Truman Ave. and Olivia St.). ✆ **305/294-1136.** Fax 305/294-2755. www.hemingwayhome.com. Admission $12 adults, $6 children 6 and over. Daily 9am–5pm. Limited parking.

Harry S. Truman Little White House ★★

President Truman used to refer to the White House as the "Great White Jail." On temporary leave from the Big House, Truman discovered the serenity of Key West and made his escape to what became known as the Little White House, which is open to the public for

Descendents of Hemingway's cats still live in his former Key West home.

touring. The house is fully restored; the exhibits document Truman's time in the Keys. Tours run every 15 minutes and last between 45 and 50 minutes, so plan to spend more than an hour here. For fans of all things Oval Office–related, there's a presidential gift shop on the premises.

111 Front St. ✆ **305/294-9911.** www.trumanlittlewhitehouse.com. Admission $15 adults, $13 seniors, $5 children 5-12. Daily 9am-4:30pm.

Key West Aquarium ★★ ☺ The oldest attraction on the island, the Key West Aquarium is a modest but fascinating place. A long hallway of eye-level displays showcases dozens of varieties of fish and crustaceans. Kids can touch sea cucumbers and sea anemones in a shallow tank. The Touch Tank allows for a hands-on experience with harmless sea creatures, and the Atlantic Shores Exhibit features a cross section of a near-shore mangrove environment and a 50,000-gallon tank that's home to a variety of tropical fish and game fish. If possible, catch one of the free guided tours—you can witness the dramatic feeding frenzy of the sharks, tarpon, barracudas, stingrays, and turtles. Expect to spend 1 to 1½ hours here.

1 Whitehead St. (at Mallory Sq.). ✆ **305/296-2051.** www.keywestaquarium.com. Admission $12 adults, $5 children 4-12. Website offers tickets for $1 less. Look for discount coupons at local hotels, at Duval St. kiosks, and from trolley and train tours. Daily 10am-6pm; tours at 11am and 1, 3, and 4pm.

Key West Butterfly & Nature Conservatory ★★ ☺ In a 13,000-square-foot pavilion, this attraction has nature lovers flitting with excitement, thanks to the 5,000-square-foot, glass-enclosed butterfly aviary as well as a gallery, learning center, and gift shop exploring all aspects of the butterfly world. Inside, more than 1,500 butterflies and 3,500 plants, including rare orchids, and even fish and turtles coexist in a controlled climate. You'll walk freely among the butterflies. Expect to spend about an hour inside.

1316 Duval St. ✆ **305/296-2988.** www.keywestbutterfly.com. Admission $12 adults, $9 seniors, $8.50 children 4-12. Daily 9am-5pm; last ticket sold at 4:30pm.

Key West Cemetery ★★★ 🎁 This funky cemetery is the epitome of quirky Key West: irreverent and humorous. Many tombs are stacked several high, condominium-style, because the rocky soil made digging 6 feet under nearly impossible for early settlers. Epitaphs reflect residents' lighthearted attitudes toward life and death. I TOLD YOU I WAS SICK is one of the more famous, as is the tongue-in-cheek widow's inscription AT LEAST I KNOW WHERE HE'S SLEEPING TONIGHT. Pick up a copy of *Sharon Wells' Walking & Biking Guide to Historic Key West* (p. 231). Some of the inscriptions are hard to find even with the free walking-tour guide, but this place is fun to explore. Plan to spend 30 minutes to an hour or more, depending on how morbid your curiosity is.

Entrance at the corner of Margaret and Angela sts. Free admission. Daily dawn–dusk.

Key West Lighthouse & Keeper's Quarters Museum ★ When the Key West Lighthouse opened in 1848, it signaled the end of a profitable era for the pirate salvagers who looted reef-stricken ships. The story of this and other area lighthouses is illustrated in a small museum that was formerly the keeper's quarters. It's worth mustering the energy to climb the 88 claustrophobic steps to the top, where you'll be rewarded with magnificent panoramic views of Key West and the ocean. Expect to spend 30 minutes to an hour.

938 Whitehead St. ℂ **305/295-6616.** www.kwahs.com. Admission $10 adults, $9 seniors and locals, $5 children 7–12. Daily 9:30am–4:30pm.

Key West's Shipwreck Historeum You'll see more impressive artifacts at Mel Fisher's museum, but for the morbidly curious, shipwrecks should rank right up there with car wrecks. For those of you who can't help but look, this museum is the place to be for everything you ever wanted to know about shipwrecks and more. See movies, artifacts, and a real-life wrecker, who will be happy to indulge your curiosity about the wrecking industry that preoccupied the early pioneers of Key West. Depending on your level of interest, you can expect to spend up to 2 hours here.

1 Whitehead St. (at Mallory Sq.). ℂ **305/292-8990.** Fax 305/292-5536. www.shipwreck historeum.com. Admission $12 adults, $5 children 4–12. Website sells tickets for $1 less. Shows daily every half-hour 9:45am–4:45pm.

You can visit with the tiny inhabitants of the Butterfly Conservatory.

Mel Fisher Maritime Heritage Museum ★★ This museum honors local hero Mel Fisher, whose death in 1998 was mourned throughout South Florida and who, along with a crew of other salvagers, found a multimillion-dollar treasure-trove in 1985 aboard the wreck of the Spanish galleon *Nuestra Señora de Atocha*. If you're into diving, pirates, and sunken treasures, check out this small museum, full of doubloons, pieces of eight, emeralds, and solid-gold bars (one of them you can

Nautical artifacts are on display at the Keeper's Quarters.

lift!). A 1700 English merchant slave ship, the only tangible evidence of the transatlantic slave trade, is on view on the museum's second floor. An exhibition telling the story of more than 1,400 African slaves captured in Cuban waters and brought to Key West for sanctuary is the museum's latest, most fascinating exhibit to date. Expect to spend 1 to 3 hours.

200 Greene St. ℂ **305/294-2633.** www.melfisher.org. Admission $12 adults, $11 students and seniors, $6 children 6–12. Daily 9:30am–5pm. Take U.S. 1 to Whitehead St. and turn left on Greene.

Oldest House Museum & Garden ★ Dating from 1829, this old New England Bahama House has survived pirates, hurricanes, fires, warfare, and economic ups and downs. The one-and-a-half-story home was designed by a ship's carpenter and incorporates many features from maritime architecture, including portholes and a ship's hatch designed for ventilation before the advent of air-conditioning. Especially interesting is the detached kitchen building outfitted with a brick "beehive" oven and vintage cooking utensils. Though not a must-see on the Key West tour, history and architecture buffs will appreciate the finely preserved details and the glimpse of a slower, easier time in the island's life. Plan to spend 30 minutes to an hour.

322 Duval St. ℂ **305/294-9501.** www.oirf.org. Free admission. Daily 10am–4pm.

Organized Tours

BY TRAM & TROLLEY-BUS Yes, it's more than a bit hokey to sit on this 60-foot tram of yellow cars, but it's worth it—at least once. The city's whole story is packed into a neat, 90-minute package on the **Conch Tour Train,** which covers the island and all its rich, raunchy history. In operation since 1958, the cars are open-air, which can make the ride uncomfortable in bad weather. The engine of the "train" is a propane-powered jeep disguised as a locomotive. Tours depart from both Mallory Square and the Welcome Center, near where U.S. 1 becomes North Roosevelt Boulevard, on the less-developed side of the island. For information, call ℂ **305/294-5161** or go to www.

conchtourtrain.com. The cost is $29 for adults, $26 for seniors, free for children 12 and under. Tickets are cheaper on the website. Daily departures are every half-hour from 9am to 4:30pm.

The **Old Town Trolley** is the choice in bad weather or if you're staying at one of the hotels on its route. Humorous drivers maintain a running commentary as the enclosed trolley loops around the island's streets past all the major sights. Trolley buses depart from Mallory Square and other points around the island, including many area hotels. For details, call ℭ **305/296-6688** or visit www.trolley-tours.com. Tours are $29 for adults, $26 for seniors, and free for children 12 and under. Tickets are cheaper on the website. Departures are daily every half-hour (though not always on the half-hour) from 9am to 4:30pm. New from Old Town Trolley: **Ghosts & Gravestones Frightseeing Tour,** a 90-minute look at Key West's scariest sites and stories. Tours depart from 501 Front St. at 6:30 and 8pm. Tickets are $30 per person and children 12 and under are not recommended to attend.

Whichever you choose, both of these historic, trivia-packed tours are well worth the price of tickets.

BY AIR Conch Republic Air Force, at Key West Airport, 3469 S. Roosevelt Blvd. (ℭ **305/294-8687;** www.keywestbiplanes.com), offers open-cockpit biplane rides over Key West and the coral reef in a 1942 Waco. The rides

---

A Smokin' Park

Though Key West has a rich hippie history, a new park pays homage to cigars, not that other funny cigarette. **Gato Village Pocket Park,** 616 Louisa St., pays homage to the island's once-flourishing cigar-making industry. Located on the site of a former cigar maker's cottage in what was once called Gatoville—a housing community built by cigar baron Eduardo Gato for his factory workers—the park features a re-creation of the cottage's front porch and facade, a 13-foot-tall metal cigar and signage telling the community's ashy history.

Tour Key West by the Conch Train.

accommodate two passengers in the forward cockpit, but true thrill-seekers will also enjoy a spin in a Pitts Special S-2C, which does loops, rolls, and sideways figure eights. For the photographer, they offer a 1941 J-3 Cub for superslow flight over Key West and the coral reef; dual instruction, tail-wheel checkouts, and banner towing in the Cub are also available. For war-bird enthusiasts, there's the 1944 North American T-6 Texan, originally used for advanced fighter training in World War II. Company owner Fred Cabanas was decorated in 1991, after he spotted a Cuban airman defecting to the United States in a Russian-built MIG fighter. Sightseeing flights cost $135 to $850 depending on duration.

BY BIKE Besides walking, one of the best ways to explore Key West is by bike. Thanks to **Eaton Bikes,** 830 Eaton St. (✆ 305/294-8188; www.eaton bikes.com), you can pedal around the Old Town district on a 2-hour bicycle tour led by a knowledgeable guide who will offer insight into everything from Key West's seafaring history to architecture, foliage, and even local gossip. Included in the $30-per-person tour are locally sourced refreshments, bike, and helmet. Tours go three times weekly. Call for time information.

BY BOAT The catamarans and the glass-bottom boat of **Fury Water Adventures,** 237 Front St. (✆ 305/296-6293; www.furycat.com), depart on daytime coral-reef tours and evening sunset cruises (call for times). Reef trips cost $40 per adult, $20 per child 6 to 12; sunset cruises are $49 per adult and $30 per child 6 to 12. Prices are cheaper on the website.

The schooner *Western Union* (✆ 305/292-9830; www.schooner westernunion.org) was built in 1939 and served as a cable-repair vessel until it was designated the flagship of the city of Key West and began day, sunset, and charter sailings. In 2010, the schooner received a million-dollar renovation. Sunset sailings are especially memorable and include entertainment, cocktails, and cannon fire. Prices vary; inquire for details.

A new boat tour combines Florida Keys sunsets with delectable Keys cuisine. **Sunset Culinaire Tours** (✆ 305/296-0982; www.sunset culinaire.com) is a cruise aboard the vessel *RB's Lady* and includes a tour of Key West harbor as the sun sinks below the horizon, and a three-course gourmet dinner (including beer or wine) prepared by chef Brian Kirkpatrick. The vessel departs from Sunset Marina, off U.S. 1 at 5555 College Rd., at 5:30pm nightly. Boarding time is 5pm and the cost is $85 per person.

OTHER TOURS Sharon Wells (✆ 305/294-0566; www.kwlightgallery.com), historian, artist, and owner of the KW Light Gallery, leads a slew of great tours throughout the island, focusing on things as diverse as literature, architecture, and places connected with the island's gay and lesbian culture.

Not necessarily a tour, per se, but a special-interest trip, **Key West Wellness Retreats** offers 5-night stays at **Rose Lane Villas,** 522 Rose Lane (✆ 800/294-2170; www.roselanevillas.com), a collection of private condos complete with full kitchen, free Wi-Fi, and shared pool. Each stay includes nutrition and fitness evaluations, poolside Pilates, reflexology, yoga, skin-care sessions, and mangrove kayaking excursions. Prices start at $1,499 per person.

For a lively look at Key West, try the **Key West Pub Crawl** (✆ 305/744-9804; www.keywestwalkingtours.com), a tour of the island's most famous bars. It's given on Tuesday and Friday nights at 8pm, lasts 2½ hours, costs $30, and includes five (!) drinks. Another fun option is the 1-mile, 90-minute **ghost tour** (✆ 305/294-WALK [294-9255];

Take a cruise on the *Western Union*, under full sail.

www.hauntedtours.com), leaving daily at 8 and 9pm from the Holiday Inn La Concha, 430 Duval St. Cost is $15 for adults and $10 for children 11 and under. This spooky and interesting tour gives participants insight into many old island legends.

Key West's **Ghosts and Legends Tour** (© 866/622-4467 or 305/294-1713; www.keywestghosts.com) is a fun, 90-minute narrated tour of the island and spirits that don't come in a plastic cup or mug. You'll walk through the shadowy streets and lanes of Old Town, stopping at allegedly haunted Victorian mansions, and learning about island pirate lore, voodoo superstitions and rituals, a count who lived with the corpse of his beloved, and other bizarre yet true aspects of this eerie place. Tours depart nightly from the Porter House Mansion on the corner of Duval and Caroline Street. Space is limited and reservations are required. Tickets are $18 for adults and $10 for children.

Since the early 1940s, Key West has been a haven for gay luminaries such as Tennessee Williams and Broadway legend Jerry Herman. The **Gay and Lesbian Historic Trolley Tour,** created by the Key West Business Guild, showcases the history, contributions, and landmarks associated with the island's flourishing gay and lesbian culture. Highlights include Williams's house, the art gallery owned by Key West's first gay mayor, and a variety of guesthouses whose gay owners fueled the island's architectural-restoration movement. The 70-minute tour takes place Saturday at 10:50am, starting and ending at City of Key West parking lot, corner of Simonton Street and Angela Street. Look for the trolley with the rainbow flags. The cost is $20 to $25. Call © 305/294-4603 or go to www.gaykeywestfl.com/featureevent.cfm?id=16.

Outdoor Activities

BEACHES Key West actually has a few small beaches, although they don't compare with the state's wide natural wonders up the coast; the Keys' beaches are typically narrow and rocky. Here are your options: Smathers Beach, off South Roosevelt Boulevard, west of the airport; Higgs Beach, along

Atlantic Boulevard, between White Street and Reynolds Road; and Fort Zachary Beach, located off the western end of Southard Boulevard.

A magnet for partying teenagers, **Smathers Beach** is Key West's largest and most over-populated. Despite the number of rowdy teens, the beach is actually quite clean. If you go early enough in the morning, you may notice people sleeping on the beach from the night before.

Higgs Beach is a favorite among Key West's gay crowds, but what many people don't know is that beneath the sand is an unmarked cemetery of African slaves who died while waiting for freedom. Higgs has a playground and tennis courts, and is near the minute Rest Beach, which is ac-

A Key West ghost tour might be a haunting experience.

tually hidden by the White Street pier. The sand here is coarse and rocky and the water tends to be a bit mucky, but if you can bear it, Higgs is known as a great snorkeling beach. If it's sunbathing you want, skip Higgs and go to Smathers.

Although there is an entrance fee ($6 per car of two to eight, $4 single-occupant vehicle, $2 pedestrians and bicyclists, plus 50¢ per person for Monroe County Surcharge), we recommend the beach at **Fort Zachary Taylor State Park,** as it has a great historic fort; a Civil War museum; and a large picnic area with tables, barbecue grills, restrooms, and showers. Large trees scattered across 87 acres provide shade for those who are reluctant to bake in the sun.

BIKING & MOPEDING A popular mode of transportation for locals and visitors, bikes and mopeds are available at many rental outlets in the city. Escape the hectic downtown scene and explore the island's scenic side streets by heading away from Duval Street toward South Roosevelt Boulevard and the beachside enclaves along the way.

FISHING As any angler will tell you, there's no fishing like Keys fishing. Key West has it all: bonefish, tarpon, dolphin, tuna, grouper, cobia, and more—sharks too.

Step aboard a small exposed skiff for an incredibly diverse day of fishing. In the morning, you can head offshore for sailfish or dolphin (the fish, not the mammal), and then by afternoon get closer to land for a shot at tarpon, permit, grouper, or snapper. Here in Key West, you can probably pick up more cobia—one of the best fighting and eating fish around—than anywhere else in the world. For a real fight, ask your skipper to go for the tarpon—the greatest fighting fish there is, famous for its dramatic "tail walk" on the water after it's hooked. Shark fishing is also popular.

You'll find plenty of competition among the charter-fishing boats in and around Mallory Square. You can negotiate a good deal at **Charter Boat Row**, 1801 N. Roosevelt Ave. (across from the Shell station), home to more than 30 charter-fishing and party boats. Just show up to arrange your outing, or call **Garrison Bight Marina** (✆ 305/292-8167) for details.

The advantage of the smaller, more expensive charter boats is that you can call the shots. They'll take you where you want to go, to fish for what you want to catch. These "light tackles" are also easier to maneuver, which means you can go to backcountry spots for tarpon and bonefish, as well as out to the open ocean for tuna and dolphin fish. You'll really be able to feel the fish, and you'll get some good fights too. Larger boats, for up to six or seven people, are cheaper and are best for kingfish, billfish, and sailfish. For every kind of fishing charter, from flats and offshore to backcountry and wreck fishing, call **Almost There Sportfishing Charters** (✆ 800/795-9448; www.almostthere.net).

The huge commercial party boats are more for sightseeing than serious angling, though you can be lucky enough to get a few bites at one of the fishing holes. One especially good deal is the ***Gulfstream III*** (✆ 305/296-8494; www.gulfstreamiiifishing.com), an all-day charter that goes out daily from 11am to 4:30pm. You'll pay $55 for adults, $52 for seniors, $35 for kids 11 and under, and the price includes rod, bait, tackle, and license. This 65-foot party boat usually has at least 30 other anglers. Bring your own cooler or buy snacks onboard. Beer and wine are allowed.

Serious anglers should consider the light-tackle boats that leave from **Oceanside Marina**, on Stock Island at 5950 Peninsula Ave., 1½ miles off U.S. 1 (✆ 305/294-4676). It's a 20-minute drive from Old Town on the Atlantic side. There are more than 30 light-tackle guides, which range from

Lots of folks get around town on their bikes.

Come home from a charter fishing trip with something for dinner...

flatbed, backcountry skiffs to 28-foot open boats. There are also a few larger charters and a party boat that goes to the Dry Tortugas. Call for details.

For a light-tackle outing with a very colorful Key West flair, call **Capt. Bruce Cronin** (© 305/294-4929; www.fishbruce.com) or **Capt. Ken Harris** (© 305/294-8843; www. kwextremeadventures.com), two of the more famous (and pricey) captains working these docks for more than 20 years. You'll pay from $750 for a full day, usually about 8am to 4pm, and from $500 for a half-day. For a comprehensive list of Florida Keys fishing guides, go to www.ccaflorida.org/guides/keys_guides.html.

Reel Deals on Fishing

When looking for the best deals on fishing excursions, know that the bookers from the kiosks in town generally take 20% of a captain's fee in addition to an extra monthly fee. You can usually save yourself money by booking directly with a captain or by going straight to one of the docks.

GOLF The area's only public golf club is **Key West Golf Club** (© 305/294-5232; www.keywestgolf.com), an 18-hole course at the entrance to the island of Key West at MM 4.5 (turn onto College Rd. to the course entrance). Designed by Rees Jones, the course, which was renovated in 2008, has plenty of mangroves and water hazards on its 6,526 yards. It's open to the public and has a new pro shop. Call ahead for tee-time reservations. Rates are $95 per player during off season and $165 in season, or $70 off season and $95 in season after 2:30pm, including cart.

KAYAKING **Lazy Dog Adventure,** 5114 Overseas Hwy. (© 305/295-9898; http://lazydog.com), operates a first-rate, 2-hour daily kayaking tour through the backcountry of Key West for $35 per person. For the really adventurous, they also offer a 4-hour kayak and snorkel tour combo through the mangroves and backcountry for $60 per person.

SCUBA DIVING One of the area's largest scuba schools, **Dive Key West, Inc.,** 3128 N. Roosevelt Blvd. (© 800/426-0707 or 305/296-3823; www.divekeywest.com), offers instruction at all levels; its dive boats take participants to scuba and snorkel sites on nearby reefs.

Key West Marine Park (© 305/294-3100), the newest dive park along the island's Atlantic shore, incorporates no-motor "swim-only" lanes marked by buoys, providing swimmers and snorkelers with a safe way to explore the waters. The park's boundaries stretch from the foot of Duval Street to Higgs Beach.

Wreck dives and night dives are two of the special offerings of **Lost Reef Adventures,** 261 Margaret St. (© 800/952-2749 or 305/296-9737; www.lostreefadventures.com). Regularly scheduled runs and private charters can be arranged. Phone for departure information.

In 2009, the ***General Hoyt S. Vandenberg,*** a 524-foot former U.S. Air Force missile tracking ship, was sunk 6 miles south of Key West to create an artificial reef. For a map of the **Florida Keys Shipwreck Heritage Trail,** an entire network of wrecks from Key Largo to Key West, go to http://floridakeys.noaa.gov/sanctuary_resources/shipwreck_trail/welcome.html.

For hard-core and high-tech wreck divers, check out the **Wreck Trek Passport Program,** www.fla-keys.com/diving/wrecktrek, spotlighting the Florida Keys Shipwreck Trail from Key Largo to Key West and allowing certified divers to explore the trail and be rewarded for logging back-to-back wreck dives through January 1, 2012. Dive passport highlights nine shipwrecks. After completing all nine dives, passport holders are entered into a drawing for grand prizes including dive equipment and dive-and-stay hotel packages. Even if you don't compete, it's worth a look just for the trail information alone.

Shopping

You'll find all kinds of unique gifts and souvenirs in Key West, from coconut postcards to Key lime pies. On Duval Street, T-shirt shops outnumber almost any other business. If you must get a wearable memento, be careful of unscrupulous salespeople. Despite efforts to curtail the practice, many shops have been known to rip off un-

Cigar Alley is where you can watch how the stogies are made by hand.

witting shoppers. It pays to check the prices and the exchange rate before signing any sales slips. You are entitled to a written estimate of any T-shirt work before you pay for it.

At Mallory Square, you'll find the **Clinton Street Market,** an overly air-conditioned mall of kiosks and stalls designed for the many cruise ship passengers who never venture beyond this supercommercial zone. There are some coffee and candy shops, and some high-priced hats and shoes. There's also a free and clean restroom.

Once the main industry of Key West, cigar making is enjoying renewed success at the handful of factories that survived the slow years. Stroll through **Cigar Alley** (while on Greene St., go 2 blocks west and you'll hit Cigar Alley, also known as Pirate's Alley), where you will find *viejitos* (little old men) rolling fat stogies just as they used to do in their homeland across the Florida Straits. Stop at the **Conch Republic Cigar Factory,** 512 Greene St. (© **305/295-9036;** www.conch-cigars.com), for an excellent selection of imported and locally rolled smokes, including the famous El Hemingway. Remember, buying or selling Cuban-made cigars is illegal. Shops advertising "Cuban cigars" are usually referring to domestic cigars made from tobacco grown from seeds that were brought from Cuba decades ago. To be fair, though, many premium cigars today are grown from Cuban seed tobacco—only it is grown in Latin America and the Caribbean, not Cuba.

If you're looking for local or Caribbean art, you'll find nearly a dozen galleries and shops on Duval Street between Catherine and Fleming streets. There are also some excellent shops on the side streets. One worth seeking out is the **Haitian Art Co.,** 1100 Truman Ave. (© **305/296-8932;** www.haitian-art-co.com), where you can browse through room upon room of original paintings from well-known and obscure Haitian artists, in a range of prices from a few dollars to a few thousand. Also check out **Cuba, Cuba!** at 814 Duval St. (✆ **305/295-9442;** www.cubacubastore.com), where you'll see paintings, sculpture, and photos by Cuban artists, as well as books and art from the island.

From sweet to spicy, **Peppers of Key West,** 602 Greene St. (✆ **305/295-9333;** www.peppersofkeywest.com), is a hot-sauce lover's heaven, with hundreds of variations, from mild to brutally spicy. Grab a seat at the tasting bar and be prepared to let your taste buds sizzle. *Tip:* Bring beer, and they'll let you taste some of their secret sauces!

Literature and music buffs will appreciate the many bookshops and record stores on the island. **Key West Island Bookstore,** 513 Fleming St. (✆ **305/294-2904**), carries new, used, and rare books, and specializes in fiction by residents of the Keys, including Ernest Hemingway, Tennessee Williams, Shel Silverstein, Ann Beattie, Richard Wilbur, and John Hersey. The bookstore is open daily from 10am to 9pm.

For anything else, from bed linens to candlesticks to clothing, go to downtown's oldest and most renowned department store, **Fast Buck Freddie's,** 500 Duval St. (✆ **305/294-2007**). For the same merchandise at reduced prices, try **Half Buck Freddie's ★**, 726 Caroline St. (✆ **305/294-2007**), where you can shop for out-of-season bargains and "rejects" from the main store.

Also check out **KW Light Gallery,** 534 Fleming St. (✆ **305/294-0566;** www.kwlightgallery.com), for high-quality contemporary photography as well as historic images and other artwork relating to the Keys or to the concept of light and its varied interpretations. The gallery is open Thursday through Tuesday from 10am to 6pm (10am–4pm in summer). Owner/photographer/painter Sharon Wells also gives historic tours of Key West so inquire while you're inside for the inside scoop.

Hot stuff! Get it in all kinds of varieties at Peppers of Key West.

Where to Stay

You'll find a wide variety of places to stay in Key West, from resorts with all the amenities to seaside motels, quaint bed-and-breakfasts, and clothing-optional guesthouses. You can almost always find a place to stay at the last minute, unless you're in town during the most popular holidays: Fantasy Fest (around Halloween), when Mardi Gras meets South Florida for the NC-17 set and most hotels have outrageous rates and 5-night minimums; Hemingway Days (in July), when Papa is seemingly and eerily alive and well; and Christmas and New Year's—or for a big fishing tournament (many are held Oct–Dec) or a boat-racing tourney. However, you may want to book early, especially in winter, when prime properties fill up and many require 2- or 3-night minimum stays. Prices at these times are extremely high. Finding a decent room for less than $100 a night is a real trick.

Another suggestion, and our recommendation, is to call **Vacation Key West** (©**800/595-5397** or 305/295-9500; www.vacationkw.com), a wholesaler that offers discounts of 20% to 30% and is skilled at finding last-minute deals. It represents mostly larger hotels and motels, but can also place visitors in guesthouses. The phones are answered Monday through Friday from 9am to 6pm, and Saturday from 11am to 2pm. **Key West Innkeepers Association** (©**800/492-1911** or 305/292-3600; www.keywestinns.com) can also help you find lodging in any price range from among its members and affiliates.

GLBT travelers may want to call the **Key West Business Guild** (©**305/294-4603;** www.gaykeywestfl.com), which represents more than 50 guesthouses and B&Bs in town, as well as many other gay-owned businesses. Be advised that most gay guesthouses have a clothing-optional policy. One of the most elegant and popular is **Big Ruby's,** 409 Applerouth Lane (www.bigrubys.com; ©**800/477-7829** or 305/296-2323), located on a little alley just off Duval Street. Rates start at $215 double in peak season and $129 off season. A low cluster of buildings surrounds a lush courtyard where a hearty breakfast is served each morning and wine is poured at dusk. The all-male guests hang out by the pool, tanning in the buff.

For women mostly and their male friends and/or family members, **Pearl's Rainbow,** 525 United St. (www.pearlsrainbow.com; ©**800/74-WOMYN** [749-6696] or 305/292-1450), is a large, fairly well-maintained guesthouse with lots of privacy and amenities, including two pools and two hot tubs. Rates range from $79 to $369.

VERY EXPENSIVE

The Gardens Hotel ★★★ 🏨 At last, the true Garden of Eden has been located—and it's on Angela Street in Key West. Once a private residence, the Gardens Hotel (whose main house is listed on the National Register of Historic Places) is hidden amid exotic gardens. Behind the greenery is a Bahamian-style hideaway with luxuriously appointed rooms in the main house, garden and courtyard rooms in the carriage house, and one ultrasecluded cottage. Though the place is within walking distance of frenetic Duval Street, you may not want to leave. A free-form pool is centered in the courtyard, where a Tiki bar serves libations. The Jacuzzi is hidden behind foliage. Guest rooms have hardwood floors, plantation beds with Tempur-Pedic mattresses, and marble bathrooms. Winding brick pathways leading to secluded seating areas in the private gardens make for an idyllic getaway. On Sunday afternoons the hotel features live jazz in the gardens. New to the hotel: the **d'Vine Wine Gallery,** an on-site wine bar offering 36 different vintages open daily and also to non–hotel guests from 5 to 10pm. *Note:* If you plan to party, do not stay here—guests tend to be on the quieter, more sophisticated side.

526 Angela St., Key West, FL 33040. www.gardenshotel.com. ℰ **800/526-2664** or 305/294-2661. Fax 305/292-1007. 17 units. Winter $300–$415 double, $495–$675 suite; off season $175–$325 double, $225–$395 suite. Rates include continental breakfast. AE, DC, MC, V. **Amenities:** Bar; pool. *In room:* A/C, TV, hair dryer.

Ocean Key Resort and Spa ★★ You can't beat the location of this 100-room resort, at the foot of Mallory Square, the epicenter of the sunset ritual. Ocean Key also features a Gulf-side heated pool and the lively Sunset Pier, where guests can wind down with cocktails and live music. Guest rooms are huge and luxuriously appointed, with living and dining areas, oversize Jacuzzis, and views of the Gulf, the harbor, or Mallory Square and Duval Street. The two-bedroom suite is 1,200 square feet and has a full kitchen, three beds, and a large private balcony. The property is adorned in classic Key West decor, from the tile floors and hand-painted furniture to the pastel art. The Indonesian-inspired **SpaTerre** is perhaps the best in town. The resort's restaurant, **Hot Tin Roof** (p. 254), is one of Key West's best. New to the resort, **The Liquid Lounge** is a VIP pool lounge featuring private cabanas, dipping pool, whirlpool, and nightclub-style bottle service and music.

Zero Duval St. (near Mallory Docks), Key West, FL 33040. www.oceankey.com. ℰ **800/328-9815** or 305/296-7701. Fax 305/292-2198. 100 units. Winter $379–$679 double, $479–$1,149 suite; off season $239–$439 double, $319–$639 suite. AE, DC, MC, V. **Amenities:** 2 restaurants; 3 bars; babysitting; bike rental; concierge; heated pool; room service; watersports equipment/rentals. *In room:* A/C, TV, hair dryer, minibar, Wi-Fi.

The Westin Key West Resort & Marina ★★ In the heart of Old Town, The Westin Key West Resort & Marina is next to Mallory Square and within walking distance of Duval Street. Featuring large rooms with all the modern conveniences, most of the 178 rooms and suites have ocean views and balconies. Bistro 245 serves ample breakfasts and a huge Sunday brunch. Visit the Westin Sunset Pier for the nightly Sunset Celebration, with live performers and outdoor dining. The Westin's sister property, **Sunset Key Guest Cottages, A Westin Resort ★★★** (www.westinsunsetkeycottages.com; ℰ **888/477-7SUN** [7786] or 305/292-5300; fax 305/292-5395), features 39 luxurious cottages just 10 minutes by boat from Key West. Check in at The Westin Key West Resort & Marina and take a 10-minute launch ride to the secluded island of Sunset Key, where there is a white sandy beach, free-form pool with whirlpool jets, two tennis courts, spa, and stunning beachfront Latitudes restaurant. Cottages are equipped with full kitchens, high-tech entertainment centers, and one, two, three, or four bedrooms. Grocery shopping services are available upon request. Guests at Sunset Key have access to all the amenities at The Westin Key West Resort & Marina. For a nominal fee, guests of The Westin Key West Resort & Marina can enjoy the beach on Sunset Key; however, access is limited and on a first-come, first-served basis.

245 Front St., Key West, FL 33040. www.westinkeywestresort.com. ℰ **800/221-2424** or 305/294-4000. Fax 305/294-4086. 217 units, including cottages. Winter $399–$659 double, $499–$1,149. suite; off season $229–$459 double, $329–$829 suite. Sunset Key Cottage: winter $659–$3,695; off season $595–$3,695. AE, DC, DISC, MC, V. Valet parking $22 per day; self-parking $20 per day. Pets up to 40 lb. allowed at The Westin Key West Resort & Marina only.

Amenities: 5 restaurants; 3 bars; bike rental; concierge; fitness room; Jacuzzi; outdoor heated pool; limited room service; watersports equipment/rentals. *In room:* A/C, TV, hair dryer, Wi-Fi.

EXPENSIVE

Casa Marina, A Waldorf Astoria Resort ★ ☺ After a dramatic $44-million renovation, Casa Marina is the only resort in Key West to offer a pleasing mix of both historic architecture *and* modern Key West vibe. Supremely located on the south side of the island, spanning more than 1,000 feet of private beach, the Casa Marina features sweeping lawns, a grand veranda, and a new "water walk" leading from the historic lobby to the water's edge. Recently revitalized rooms with sun-soaked balconies overlook the Atlantic and historic Old Town Key West. Elegant artwork and furnishings are complemented by luxurious bedding and soothing earth tones. One- and two-bedroom oceanview suites have stellar views and separate living areas. In addition to the beach itself, there are also two outdoor pools, a full-service spa, and an outdoor restaurant. Nightly movies shown at the pool with free popcorn and snacks cater to families with kids.

1500 Reynolds St., Key West, FL 33040. www.casamarinaresort.com. ☏ **866/397-6342** or 305/296-3535. Fax 305/296-3008. 311 units. Winter $249–$499 double, $349–$799 suite; off season $149–$399 double, $249–$699 suite. AE, DC, MC, V. **Amenities:** Restaurant; bar; bike rental; concierge; fitness center; 2 pools; room service; spa; watersports equipment/rentals. *In room:* A/C, TV, hair dryer, high-speed Internet, minibar.

Curry Mansion Inn ★★ 🎁 This charismatic inn is the former home of the island's first millionaire, a once-penniless Bahamian immigrant who made a fortune as a pirate. Owned today by Al and Edith Amsterdam, the Curry Mansion is now on the National Register of Historic Places, but you won't feel like you're staying in a museum—it's rather like a wonderfully warm home. Rooms are sparsely decorated, with wicker furniture, four-poster beds, and pink walls—call it Key West minimalism meets Victorian. The dining room is reminiscent of a Victorian dollhouse, with elegant table settings and rich wood floors and furnishings. Every morning, there's a delicious European-style breakfast buffet; at night, cocktail parties are held. There's also a really nice patio, on which, from time to time, there's live entertainment.

511 Caroline St., Key West, FL 33040. www.currymansion.com. ☏ **800/253-3466** or 305/294-5349. Fax 305/294-4093. 28 units. Winter $240–$300 double, $315–$365 suite; off season $195–$235 double, $260–$285 suite. Rates include breakfast buffet. AE, DC, MC, V. No children 11 and under. **Amenities:** Dining room; bike rental; concierge; pool. *In room:* A/C, TV, minibar.

Hyatt Key West Resort & Spa ★ After an $11-million renovation, the Hyatt is now up to speed with other luxe resorts in the area. Sitting on the bay and nicknamed "The Sanctuary off of Duval," the Hyatt features a waterfront pool, small beach area, and guest rooms with white porcelain tile floors, flatscreen TVs, and fabulous bathrooms. New spa cabanas allow for outdoor treatments, and a restaurant overlooking the water is great for lunch or dinner but spotty on breakfast service. Located right near Duval Street and next door to several lively bars, the Hyatt offers the best of both worlds when it comes to Key West relaxation—and partying. The property's new signature restaurant, the **SHOR American Seafood Grill,** serves great, well, seafood. You also shouldn't miss a trip to the **Jala Spa** while you are there. Voted one of the best spas in the United States, Jala offers a variety of natural treatments and uses a new skin-care line, Amala, which is green-certified.

601 Front St., Key West, FL 33040. www.keywest.hyatt.com. © **800/55-HYATT** (554-9288) or 305/809-1234. Fax 305/809-4050. 118 rooms. Winter $485–$550 double; off season $335–$450 double. AE, DC, DISC, MC, V. **Amenities:** Restaurant; bar; fitness center; pool; spa; watersports equipment/rentals. *In room:* A/C, TV, hair dryer, minibar, Wi-Fi.

Island City House Hotel ★★ The oldest running B&B in Key West, the Island City House consists of three separate buildings that share a common junglelike patio and pool. The first building is a historic three-story wooden structure with wraparound verandas on every floor. The warmly outfitted interiors here include wood floors and antiques. The tile bathrooms could use more counter space, but eccentricities are part of this hotel's charm. The unpainted wooden Cigar House has large bedrooms, similar in ambience to those in the Island City House. The Arch House has newly renovated floors and features six airy Caribbean-style suites. Built of Dade County pine, this house's cozy bedrooms are furnished in wicker and rattan, and come with small kitchens and bathrooms. A shaded brick courtyard and pretty pool are surrounded by lush gardens where, every morning, a delicious continental breakfast is served. *Note:* Those who have an allergy to or dislike of cats should know that there are several friendly "resident" felines who call Island City House home.

411 William St., Key West, FL 33040. www.islandcityhouse.com. © **800/634-8230** or 305/294-5702. Fax 305/294-1289. 24 units. Winter $230–$420 double; off season $150–$300 double. Rates include breakfast. AE, DC, MC, V. **Amenities:** Bike rental; concierge; access to nearby health club; outdoor heated pool. *In room:* A/C, TV, hair dryer, kitchen.

La Mer Hotel & Dewey House ★★★ 📖 If we were to build a beach house, this is exactly what it would look like. And although it's technically one bed-and-breakfast, La Mer Hotel is Victorian-style while the adjoining Dewey House is more quaint and cottagey. Between the two, there are 19 rooms, each with a turn-of-the-19th-century feel but with modern amenities including granite wet bars, Wi-Fi, and luxurious linens that may have you lingering in the comfy beds for longer than you'd like, especially when you look out from your balcony or private patio and check out the views of the ocean. Stunning. Every morning there's a deluxe continental breakfast of fresh breads, made-to-order waffles, fresh-squeezed juices, and more on the Dewey Terrace overlooking the beach that's shared with La Mer & Dewey House's sister hotel, the more party-hearty Southernmost on the Beach. To keep with the old-school theme, there's a daily **afternoon tea** service, also included in the rates, from 3:30 to 5:30pm.

506 South St., Key West, FL 33040. www.southernmostresorts.com. © **800/354-4455** or 305/296-6577. Fax 305/294-8272. 19 units. Winter $249–$449 double; off season $159–$299 double. Rates include continental breakfast, daily afternoon tea, and parking. AE, DISC, MC, V. **Amenities:** Restaurant; bar; concierge; pool shared w/Southernmost on the Beach. *In room:* A/C, TV, minifridge, hair dryer, free Wi-Fi.

Marquesa Hotel ★★★ 📖 The exquisite Marquesa offers the charm of a small historic hotel coupled with the amenities of a large resort. It encompasses four buildings, two pools, and a three-stage waterfall that cascades into a lily pond. Two of the hotel's buildings are luxuriously restored Victorian homes outfitted with plush antiques and contemporary furniture. The rooms in the two newly constructed buildings are even cushier; many have four-poster wrought-iron beds with bright floral spreads. If you can, try to get a room with its own private porch overlooking the pool. These are sublime. The bathrooms in the new buildings are lush and spacious; those in the older buildings are also nice, but not nearly as huge and luxe. The decor is simple, elegant, and spotless. The hotel also boasts one of Key West's most elegant restaurants, **Café Marquesa** (p. 253).

600 Fleming St. (at Simonton St.), Key West, FL 33040. www.marquesa.com. ✆ **800/869-4631** or 305/292-1919. Fax 305/294-2121. 27 units. Winter $330–$395 double, $495–$520 suite; off season $190–$290 double, $270–$330 suite. AE, DC, MC, V. No children 14 and under. **Amenities:** Restaurant; bike rental; concierge; access to nearby health club; 2 outdoor pools (1 heated); limited room service. *In room:* A/C, flatscreen TV, fridge, hair dryer, Internet access, minibar.

Parrot Key Resort ★★★ Parrot Key's waterfront Conch-style cottages, suites, and rooms are the epitome of beachy luxury and are the largest available in Key West. Accommodations options include deluxe king or double queen rooms, deluxe one- and two-bedroom suites, and luxury two- and three-bedroom guest cottages. Guest cottages feature gourmet kitchens and all rooms offer private patio, porch, or balcony; flatscreen TVs; premium cable service; and DVD/stereo systems. All rooms are smoke free. Situated on 5 acres of award-winning tropical landscaping, the resort boasts four private pools (each in its own sculpture-garden setting), private white-sand sunbathing terraces, and the poolside **Café Blue** and Tiki bar. Minutes from the action on Duval Street, Parrot Key is an idyllic retreat.

2801 N. Roosevelt Blvd., Key West, FL 33040. www.parrotkeyresort.com. ✆ **305/809-2200.** Fax 305/292-3322. 104 units. Winter $349–$1,199 double; off season $169–$799 double. AE, DC, DISC, MC, V. **Amenities:** Poolside cafe and Tiki bar; bike rental; concierge; fitness center; high-speed Internet access property-wide; outdoor pools; spa services; watersports equipment/rentals; complimentary Wi-Fi. *In room:* A/C, TV, hair dryer.

Pier House Resort and Caribbean Spa ★ If you're looking for something a bit more intimate than the Reach Resort (see below), Pier House is an ideal choice. Its location—at the foot of Duval Street and just steps from Mallory Docks—is the envy of every hotel on the island. Set back from the busy street, on a short strip of private beach, this place is a welcome oasis of calm. The accommodations vary tremendously—no two rooms are alike—from simple business-style rooms to romantic quarters with whirlpool tubs. Although every unit has a balcony or a patio, not all overlook the water. Our favorites, in the two-story spa building, don't have any view at all. But what they lack in scenery, they make up for in opulence: Each well-appointed spa room has a sitting area and a huge Jacuzzi bathroom.

1 Duval St. (near Mallory Docks), Key West, FL 33040. www.pierhouse.com. ✆ **800/327-8340** or 305/296-4600. Fax 305/296-9085. 142 units. Winter $309–$529 double, $479–$3,000 suite; off season $229–$369 double, $389–$2,000 suite. AE, DC, MC, V. **Amenities:** 3 restaurants; 3 bars; babysitting; bike rental; concierge; fitness center; 2 Jacuzzis; heated pool; limited room service; sauna; full-service spa; watersports equipment/rentals. *In room:* A/C, TV, hair dryer, Internet access, minibar.

The Reach, A Waldorf Astoria Resort ★★★ Fresh from a $41-million renovation, the boutique-style Reach Resort features gingerbread balconies, tin roof accents, and shaded Spanish walkways characteristic of historic Key West. Newly refurbished guest rooms are large, with modernized decor and custom furnishings that are vibrant and crisp. Every room features comfortable sectional sofas and sliding glass doors that open onto balconies, some with ocean views. Sixty-eight boutique and 10 executive suites are also available. A new pool deck and 450-foot natural-sand beach are the perfect settings to enjoy a massive array of watersports, available right on the premises. The resort is also home to the Manhattan-based **Strip House** restaurant, which is as delicious as it is gorgeous. Unlike most area resorts, which are smallish, this one seems infinitely larger and, in many ways, worlds away from the rest of Key West.

1435 Simonton St., Key West, FL 33040. www.reachresort.com. ✆ **866/397-6427** or 305/296-5000 for reservations. Fax 305/296-3008. 150 units. Winter $249–$499 double, $299–$549 suite; off season $149–$399 double, $199–$449 suite. AE, DC, DISC, MC, V. **Amenities:** 2 restaurants; bar; bike rental; concierge; outdoor heated pool; room service; spa; watersports equipment/rentals. *In room:* A/C, TV, minifridge, hair dryer, high-speed Internet, minibar.

Simonton Court ★★★ 🎁 This is one of our favorite stays in Key West—too bad it's always booked. Once a cigar factory, Simonton Court features meticulously appointed restored historic cottages and suites amid sparkling pools and luxuriant private gardens. There are several options to choose from: bed-and-breakfast, cottages, guesthouse, mansion, and inn. Some cottages even have their own pools. There's no restaurant, but the well-informed concierge will help you with reservations anywhere no matter what you crave. People love the place so much, they book years in advance. Once you stay here, if you're lucky, you'll understand why.

320 Simonton St., Key West, FL 33040. www.simontoncourt.com. ✆ **800/944-2687** or 305/294-6386. Fax 305/293-8446. 30 units. Winter $260–$400 double in mansion, $480–$515 cottage, $260–$400 inn, $330–$430 manor house, $260–$520 town house; off season $160–$270 double in mansion, $360–$395 cottage, $160–$270 inn, $220–$320 manor house, $160–$400 town house. Rates include continental breakfast. AE, DISC, MC, V. **Amenities:** Concierge; 4 outdoor pools; Wi-Fi throughout the 2 acres. *In room:* A/C, TV/VCR/DVD, fridge, hair dryer.

Southernmost on the Beach ★★★ Revamped in 2008, this beachfront hotel—one of the few in Key West—offers 127 rooms, all with views of the Atlantic, a huge oceanfront pool, and a lively pool bar. Eighty luxury suites feature flatscreen TVs, MP3 docking stations, sleek mahogany furniture, and blue-and-white decor made to resemble a yacht. The best part about this resort is its location directly on an actually sandy private beach. Grounds have been beautifully landscaped with lush gardens and palm trees. The open-air Southernmost **Beach Café** is a nice place for lunch or sunset dinner, but the poolside Tiki bar is where most of the action is. Because of its impressive, beautiful beach, Southernmost is the site of many weddings. In addition to its more subdued, romantic sister bed-and-breakfast La Mer Hotel & Dewey House, Southernmost on the Beach has another property across the street, also with a great pool scene, albeit not on the water—the **Southernmost Hotel in the USA,** 1319 Duval St. (✆ **800/354-4455**), where rates range from $159 to $299 in winter and $99 to $199 in summer.

508 South St., Key West, FL 33040. www.southernmosthotels.com. ✆ **800/354-4455** or 305/295-6550. Fax 305/294-8272. 127 units. Winter $279–$475 double; off season $159–$299 double. Rates include parking. AE, DC, DISC, MC, V. **Amenities:** Restaurant; bar; bike rental; concierge; health club; pool; spa; watersports equipment rental. *In room:* A/C, TV, hair dryer, minifridge, free Wi-Fi.

Weatherstation Inn ★ 🎁 Originally built in 1912 as a weather station, this beautifully restored, meticulously maintained, Renaissance-style inn is just 2 blocks from Duval Street but seems worlds away. It's on the tropical grounds of the former Old Navy Yard, now a private gated community. Presidents Truman, Eisenhower, and JFK all visited the station. Spacious and uncluttered, each guest room is uniquely furnished to complement the interior architecture: hardwood floors, tall sash windows, and high ceilings. The large, modern bathrooms are especially appealing. The staff is both friendly and accommodating.

57 Front St., Key West, FL 33040. www.weatherstationinn.com. © **800/815-2707** or 305/294-7277. Fax 305/294-0544. 8 units. Winter $235–$335 double; off season $180–$245 double. Rates include continental breakfast. AE, DISC, MC, V. **Amenities:** Concierge; outdoor pool. *In room:* A/C, TV/VCR, hair dryer.

MODERATE

Ambrosia Key West ★★ 🎁 Despite countless visits each year to the tiny island of Key West, we discover yet another hidden treasure every time. Ambrosia is one of them, a private compound set on 2 lush acres just a block from Duval Street. Three lagoon-style pools, suites, town houses, and a cottage are spread around the grounds. Town houses have living rooms, kitchens, and spiral staircases leading to master suites with vaulted ceilings and private decks. The cottage, overlooking a dip pool, is a perfect family retreat, with two bedrooms, two bathrooms, a living room, and a kitchen. All rooms, several of which recently received major renovations, have private entrances, most with French doors opening onto a variety of intimate outdoor spaces, including private verandas, patios, and gardens with sculptures, fountains, and pools. The breakfast buffet rocks, with eggs, biscuits, gravy, bacon, sausage, and pretty much anything you'd want. Fantastic service, bolstered by the philosophy that it's better to have high occupancy than high rates, explains why Ambrosia has a 90% year-round occupancy—a record in seasonal Key West.

622 Fleming St., Key West, FL 33040. www.ambrosiakeywest.com. © **800/535-9838** or 305/296-9838. Fax 305/296-2425. 20 units. Winter $279–$609 suite; off season $179–$389 suite. Rates include breakfast buffet. AE, DISC, MC, V. Off- and on-street parking. Pets accepted. **Amenities:** 3 outdoor heated pools. *In room:* A/C, TV, CD player, fridge, hair dryer, kitchen (in some), Wi-Fi.

Eden House ★ 🎁 Owned and operated by Mike Eden for over 34 years, Eden House is a fabulous spot for everyone from budget travelers to those seeking a more private retreat. With a variety of rooms ranging from semiprivate with shared bathrooms to suites with private Jacuzzi, full kitchen, washer, dryer, porch, and private entrance, Eden House does have something for everyone. A free happy hour from 4 to 5pm daily is a great way to meet people, grab a drink, and relax amid the beautifully landscaped grounds complete with waterfalls and porch swings. For those not in the social mood, steal away to a hammock—there are several throughout the property. Other amenities include a pool, Jacuzzi, sun deck, and grill area. Owner Eden is hilarious and if you have a chance, chat with him. As he says, "Key West is a bowl of granola. What's not fruits and nuts, is flakes."

1015 Fleming St., Key West, FL 33040. www.edenhouse.com. © **800/533-5397** or 305/296-6868. Fax 305/294-1221. 40 units. Winter $155–$195 semiprivate, $190–$230 private, $230–$330 deluxe, $335–$475 apt or conch house; off season $155–$180 semiprivate, $125–$150 private, $175–$240 deluxe, $255–$300 apt or conch house. MC, V. **Amenities:** Restaurant; garden pool; Wi-Fi. *In room:* A/C, TV/VCR, fridge, hair dryer.

La Pensione ★★ This classic B&B, set in a stunning 1891 home, is a total charmer. The comfortable rooms all have air-conditioning, ceiling fans, and king-size beds. Many also have French doors opening onto spacious verandas. Although the rooms have no TVs, the distractions of Duval Street, only steps away, should keep you adequately occupied. Breakfast, which includes Belgian waffles, fresh fruit, and a variety of breads or muffins, can be taken on the wraparound porch or at the communal dining table. Recent guests, however, have informed us that service here is not as friendly as it used to be and that the inn's location on U.S. 1 isn't so hot when it comes to the noise and traffic levels.

809 Truman Ave. (btw. Windsor and Margaret sts.), Key West, FL 33040. www.lapensione.com. ℃ **800/893-1193** or 305/292-9923. Fax 305/296-6509. 9 units. Winter $168–$328 double; off season $118–$168 double. Rates include breakfast. Discount of 10% for readers who mention this book. AE, DC, DISC, MC, V. No children. **Amenities:** Bike rental; outdoor pool; Wi-Fi. *In room:* A/C.

Orchid Key Inn ★ What happens to an old-school motor lodge located smack in the middle of Duval Street? It becomes a new-school, trendy motor lodge complete with wine bar and 24 modern, albeit tiny, rooms. And although it's in the middle of the action, the Orchid Key Inn is surprisingly a quiet and peaceful place. We stayed in the very first room right on Duval and heard hardly any noise. Paths lead you through lush tropical landscapes which surround the rooms and suites. Tranquil waterfalls and water features surround the sun deck, heated pool, and spa, all of which are hidden from the main drag. Free daily breakfast and sunset happy hours make it a great place for socializing or just getting your day or party started.

1004 Duval St., Key West, FL 33040. www.orchidkey.com. ℃ **800/845-8384** or 305/296-9915. Fax 305/2924886. 24 units. Winter $189–$289 King Deluxe; $209–$309 1-bedroom suite; off season $119–$169 King Deluxe, $149–$209 1-bedroom suite. Rates include continental breakfast and happy hour. AE, DISC, MC, V. Pets allowed with advance arrangements. **Amenities:** Bar; concierge; Jacuzzi; heated pool. *In room:* A/C, HDTV, hair dryer, MP3 docking station, Wi-Fi.

Seascape, An Inn ★ This romantic retreat located on a quiet street behind the Hemingway House and within walking distance of the water and the action was built from native pine in the Bahamas in the 1840s and transported by ship to Key West, where it was rebuilt in 1889. Fast-forward to 2010 and you have a splendidly renovated, tropical-style inn with turn-of-the-19th-century charm. Rooms are decorated in colorful, tropical decor and have private bathrooms. Most have French doors that open out to a heated pool and Jacuzzi, upstairs sun deck, or lush gardens and courtyard where guests indulge in a delicious champagne continental breakfast. The two-story Havana Suite has a private entrance as well as a kitchenette.

420 Olivia St., Key West, FL 33040. www.seascapetropicalinn.com. ℃ **888/765-6438** or 305/296-7776. Fax 305/296-6283. 6 units. Winter $194–$214 double, $204–$224 suite; off season $129–$149 double, $169 suite. Rates include champagne breakfast. AE, DISC, MC, V. **Amenities:** Jacuzzi; pool. *In room:* A/C, TV, hair dryer, Internet access.

Silver Palms Inn ★ Emerging from the wreckage of the mom-and-pop El Rancho Motel is this brand-new, affordable 50-room boutique hotel on the edge of Duval Street featuring modern, immaculately clean rooms and suites surrounding a courtyard, deck, and sparkling pool. Amenities are aplenty here, from 40-inch LCD TVs and hypoallergenic pillows and duvets to free Wi-Fi, free parking, and free breakfast. Eco-conscious travelers will appreciate the green initiatives, including water and energy conservation and use of eco-friendly insulation and products.

830 Truman Ave., Key West, FL 33040. www.silverpalmsinn.com. ℃ **888/294-8783** or 305/294-8700. 50 units. Winter $189–$309 double, $239–$369 suite; off season $149–$199 double, $219–$269 suite. AE, DISC, MC, V. Free parking. Rates include free breakfast, parking, Wi-Fi. **Amenities:** Fitness room; pool; free Wi-Fi. *In room:* A/C, TV, hair dryer, minifridge, Wi-Fi.

Southernmost Point Guest House ★★ ☺ 🎁 One of the few inns here that welcomes children and pets, this romantic guesthouse is a real find. The antiseptically clean rooms are not as fancy as the house's ornate 1885 exterior, but each is unique and includes rattan furniture with Mombasa-style netting on the beds. Room no. 5 is best, with a private porch, an ocean view, and windows that let in lots of light. Every unit comes with fresh flowers, wine, and a full decanter of sherry. There's also a barbecue grill under a grapevine for those in the mood to pretend it's their home and just grill out. Mona Santiago, the kind, laid-back owner, provides chairs and towels for the beach, which is just a block away. Guests can help themselves to free wine as they soak in the 14-seat hot tub. Kids will enjoy the backyard swings and the pet rabbits.

1327 Duval St., Key West, FL 33040. www.southernmostpoint.com. 🕻 **305/294-0715.** Fax 305/296-0641. 6 units. Winter $125–$200 double, $260–$285 suite; off season $75–$120 double, $165–$175 suite. Rates include breakfast. AE, MC, V. Pets accepted ($5 in summer, $10 in winter). **Amenities:** Pool; Wi-Fi. *In room:* A/C, TV/VCR, fridge, hair dryer.

Westwinds Inn ★ A close second to staying in your own private 19th-century, tin-roofed clapboard house is this tranquil inn, just 4 blocks from Duval Street in the historic seaport district. And although it looks 19th century, it's got a foot in the 21st with wireless Internet and HDTV. Lush landscaping keeps the place private and secluded; at times, you'll feel as if you're alone. Two pools, one heated in winter, are offset by alcoves, fountains, and the well-maintained whitewashed inn, which is actually composed of five separate buildings. Rooms are Key West comfortable, with private bathrooms, wicker furnishings, and fans. All rooms are smoke free.

914 Eaton St., Key West, FL 33040. www.westwindskeywest.com. 🕻 **800/788-4150** or 305/296-4440. Fax 305/293-0931. 22 units. Winter $185–$220 double; $225–$275 suite; off season $90–$180 double, $140–$195 suite. Rates include continental breakfast. DISC, MC, V. No children 11 and under. **Amenities:** Bike rental; 2 pools (1 heated); Wi-Fi. *In room:* A/C, TV (in some), kitchenette (in some).

INEXPENSIVE

Angelina Guest House ★★ This former bordello and gambling-hall-turned-youth-hostel-type guesthouse is one of the cheapest in town—and it's conveniently near a hot hippie restaurant called **Blue Heaven** (p. 256). Though the neighborhood is urban, it's generally safe and full of character. Accommodations are furnished uniquely in a modest style. Four rooms have private bathrooms; the rest have shared bathrooms. A gorgeous lagoon-style heated pool, with waterfall and tropical landscaping, is an excellent addition. Even better is the poolside hammock—get out there early, as it goes quickly! Even though the Angelina is sparse (perfect for bohemian types who don't mind a little grit), it's a great place to crash if you're traveling on the cheap.

302 Angela St. (at Thomas St.), Key West, FL 33040. www.angelinaguesthouse.com. 🕻 **888/303-4480** or 305/294-4480. Fax 305/272-0681. 13 units. Winter $109–$199 double; off season $79–$139 double. Rates include continental breakfast. DISC, MC, V. **Amenities:** Concierge; outdoor heated pool. *In room:* A/C, no phone.

The Grand Guesthouse ★★ 🗲 Don't expect cabbies or locals to know about this well-kept secret, in a residential section of Old Town, about 5 blocks from Duval Street. It's got almost everything you could want, including a moderate price tag. Proprietors Jim Brown, Jeffrey Daubman, and Derek Karevicius provide any and all services for their appreciative guests. All units have private bathrooms, air-conditioning, and private entrances. The best deal is room no. 2; it's small and lacks a closet, but it has a porch and the most privacy. Suites are a real steal: The large two-room units come with kitchenettes. This place is the best bargain in town.

1116 Grinnell St. (btw. Virginia and Catherine sts.), Key West, FL 33040. www.grandkeywest.com. ☎ **888/947-2630** or 305/294-0590. Fax 305/294-0477. 10 units. Winter $148–$208 double, $198–$268 suite; off season $98–$148 double, $128–$188 suite. Rates include expanded continental breakfast. DISC, MC, V. Free parking. **Amenities:** Bike rental; concierge. *In room:* A/C, TV, fridge, Wi-Fi.

Key West Hostel & Seashell Motel This well-run hostel is a 3-minute walk to the beach and Old Town. Very popular with European backpackers, it's a great place to meet people. The dorm rooms are dark, grimy, and sparse, but livable if you're desperate for a cheap stay. There are all-male, all-female, and co-ed dorm rooms for couples. The higher-priced private motel rooms are a good deal, especially those equipped with kitchens. Amenities include a pool table under a Tiki roof; bike rentals; cheap food at breakfast, lunch, and dinner; and discounted prices for snorkeling, diving, and sunset cruises. There's also free Wi-Fi access throughout the property.

718 South St., Key West, FL 33040. www.keywesthostel.com. ☎ **800/51-HOSTEL** (514-6783) or 305/296-5719. Fax 305/296-0672. 92 dorm beds, 10 motel rooms. Year-round $44 dorm room. Winter $75–$105 motel room; off season $55–$85 motel room. MC, V. Free parking. **Amenities:** Bike rental. *In room:* Motel rooms have A/C, TV, fridge, hair dryer; dorm rooms have A/C only.

Where to Dine

With its share of the usual drive-through fast-food franchises—mostly up on Roosevelt Boulevard—and Duval Street succumbing to the lure of a Hard Rock Cafe and Starbucks, you might be surprised to learn that, over the years, an upscale and high-quality dining scene has begun to thrive in Key West. Just wander Old Town or the newly spruced-up Bahama Village and browse menus after you've exhausted our list of picks below.

If you're staying in a condominium or an efficiency, you may want to stock your fridge with groceries, beer, wine, and snacks from the area's oldest grocer, **Fausto's Food Palace.** Open since 1926, Fausto's has two locations: 1105 White St. and 522 Fleming St. The Fleming Street location will deliver with a $25-minimum order (☎ **305/294-5221** or 305/296-5663).

VERY EXPENSIVE

Café Marquesa ★★★ CONTEMPORARY AMERICAN If you're looking for fabulous, upscale dining (and service), this is the place. The intimate, 50-seat restaurant is something to look at, but it's really the food that you'll want to admire. Specialties include macadamia-crusted yellowtail snapper, prosciutto-wrapped black Angus filet, and roast duck breast with red curry coconut sauce. If you're looking to splurge, this is the place.

In the Marquesa Hotel, 600 Fleming St. ☎ **305/292-1919.** Reservations highly recommended. Main courses $21–$39. AE, DC, MC, V. Summer daily 7–11pm; winter daily 6–11pm.

Hot Tin Roof ★★★ FUSION SEAFOOD Ever hear of conch fusion cuisine? Neither did we, until we experienced it firsthand at Hot Tin Roof, Ocean Key Resort's chichi restaurant which transforms South American, Asian, French, and Keys cuisine into an experience unlike any other in this part of the world. The 3,000-square-foot space features both indoor and outdoor deck seating overlooking the harbor. Live jazz/fusion adds to the stunning environment—it's the epitome of casual elegance. Signature dishes include an irresistible lobster with garlic, chilies, and Cuban mojo sauce; broiled yellowtail snapper with papaya pink shrimp salsa and poppy seed vinaigrette; and chocolate-lava cake that makes this tin roof very hot, to say the least, especially for Key West. If you like truffles, try the polenta fries with truffle dip. It's divine. Last time we ate here, Meryl Streep was sitting next to us with her family, looking as impressed as she was impressive.

In the Ocean Key Resort, Zero Duval St. ℂ **305/296-7701.** Reservations highly recommended. Main courses $21–$39. AE, DC, MC, V. Daily 7:30–11am and 5–10pm.

Louie's Backyard ★★ CARIBBEAN Nestled amid blooming bougainvillea on a lush slice of the Gulf, Louie's remains one of the most romantic restaurants on earth. It's off the beaten path, which makes it even more romantic. Famed chef Norman Van Aken, of Norman's in Miami, brought his talents farther south and started one of the finest dining spots in the Keys. It's also one of the hardest places to score a reservation: Either call way in advance or hope that your hotel concierge has some pull. Try the sensational oyster, sweet corn, and shiitake-mushroom potpie for starters, and for a main course, the grilled Berkshire pork chop with beer-braised cabbage and sweet potatoes is to die for. After dinner, sit at the dockside bar and watch the waves crash, almost touching your feet, while enjoying a cocktail at sunset. You can't go wrong with the fresh catch of the day, or any seafood dish, for that matter. The weekend brunches are also great. And a ritual for many in Key West is sunset cocktails at the oceanfront Tiki bar. If you can't stay for dinner, go for lunch; this is one dining experience you won't want to miss. If you're not in the mood for a full-blown meal, consider the restaurant's stellar **Upper Deck Lounge,** serving tapas, including focaccia, bruschetta, *carpaccio,* roasted clams, flaming Ouzo shrimp, grilled Mongolian barbecued lamb ribs, a daily assortment of cheeses, and pizzas Tuesday through Saturday from 5 to 10pm.

700 Waddell Ave. ℂ **305/294-1061.** www.louiesbackyard.com. Reservations highly recommended. Main courses $30–$40; lunch $10–$20; tapas $5–$15. AE, DC, MC, V. Daily 11:30am–3pm and 6–10:30pm.

EXPENSIVE

Antonia's ★★ REGIONAL ITALIAN The food is great, but the atmosphere is a bit fussy for Key West. If you don't have a reservation in season, don't even bother. Still, if you don't mind paying high prices for dishes that go for much less elsewhere, try this old favorite. From the perfectly seasoned homemade focaccia to an exemplary crème brûlée, this elegant little standout is amazingly consistent. The menu includes a small selection of classics, linguine with shrimp, delicious pillowy gnocchi, and *zuppa di pesce* (fish soup). And don't miss the outstanding warm goat-cheese soufflé served with pan-seared asparagus, baby green beans, carrots, and Belgian endive over a roasted tomato vinaigrette. You can't go wrong with any of the handmade pastas. And the owners, Antonia Berto and Phillip Smith, travel to Italy every year to research recipes, so you can be sure you're getting an authentic taste of Italy in small-town Key West.

615 Duval St. ℂ **305/294-6565.** Fax 305/294-3888. www.antoniaskeywest.com. Reservations suggested. Main courses $19–$35. AE, DC, MC, V. Daily 6–11pm.

La Trattoria ★ ITALIAN Have a true Italian feast in a relaxed atmosphere. Each dish here is prepared and presented according to old Italian tradition. Try the delicious bread-crumb-stuffed mushroom caps; they're firm yet tender. The stuffed eggplant with ricotta and roasted peppers is light and flavorful. Or have the seafood salad of shrimp, calamari, and mussels, which is fish-market fresh and tasty. The pasta dishes are also great—go for the penne Venezia, with mushrooms, sun-dried tomatoes, and crabmeat. For dessert, don't skip the homemade tiramisu; it's light yet full-flavored. The dining room is spacious but still intimate, and the waiters are friendly. Before you leave, visit **Virgilio's,** the restaurant's resplendent indoor/outdoor cocktail lounge with live jazz until 2am.

524 Duval St. ✆ **305/296-1075.** www.latrattoria.us. Main courses $14–$37. AE, DC, DISC, MC, V. Daily 5:30–11pm.

Michael's ★★★ 🎁 STEAKHOUSE Tucked away in a residential neighborhood, Michael's is a meaty oasis in a sea of fish. With steaks flown in daily from Chicago, this is *the* steakhouse for when you're craving meat, from New York strip to porterhouse. Unlike most steakhouses, Michael's exudes a relaxed, tropical ambience with a fabulous indoor/outdoor setting that's romantic but not stuffy. A fantastic fondue menu makes for a tasty snack or even a meal, complemented by an excellent, reasonably priced wine list.

532 Margaret St. ✆ **305/295-1300.** www.michaelskeywest.com. Reservations recommended. Main courses $15–$40. AE, DC, DISC, MC, V. Daily 5–11pm.

Nine One Five ★★★ ECLECTIC Housed in a restored Victorian mansion, Nine One Five is a cozy, romantic restaurant with such good food that it was selected to host a six-course dinner at the James Beard House in NYC. Twice. The cuisine is simple yet flavorful with everything from Devils on Horseback, bacon-wrapped dates stuffed with garlic and served with a soy ginger dipping sauce, to duck liver pâté. A tapas platter can be enjoyed as an appetizer or as a main course up in the restaurant's loft lounge area. For main courses, we suggest the Thai whole fish with sizzling chili garlic sauce and steamed basmati rice, or the Soul Mama Seafood soup, a mix of Key West shrimp, mussels, clams, and black grouper in a Thai green-curry coconut broth with lemongrass, cilantro, and Basmati rice. Service is seamless and attentive, although if you sit up on the quaint second-floor porch, you may be there for a while. But this is the kind of place where you want to linger.

915 Duval St. ✆ **305/296-0669.** www.915duval.com. Reservations recommended. Main courses $25–$34. AE, DISC, MC, V. Mon–Sat noon–3pm; daily 6–11pm. Upstairs lounge daily until 2am.

Seven Fish ★★★ 🎁 SEAFOOD "Simple, good food" is Seven Fish's motto, but this little secret is much more than simple. One of the most popular restaurants with locals, Seven Fish is a chic seafood spot serving some of the best fish on the island. Sea scallops with pea purée and spinach, and gnocchi with blue cheese and sautéed fish are among the dishes to choose from. For dessert, do not miss the Key lime cake over tart lime curd with fresh berries.

632 Olivia St. ✆ **305/296-2777.** www.7fish.com. Reservations recommended. Main courses $17–$29. AE, MC, V. Wed–Mon 6–10pm.

MODERATE

Alonzo's Oyster Bar ★ SEAFOOD Alonzo's serves good seafood in a casual setting. It's on the ground floor of the A&B Lobster House, at the end of Front Street in the marina; if you want to dress up, go upstairs for the "fine dining." To start your meal, try the steamed beer shrimp—tantalizingly fresh jumbo shrimp in a sauce of garlic, Old Bay seasoning, beer, and cayenne pepper. A house specialty is white-clam chili, a delicious mix of tender clams, white beans, and potatoes served with a dollop of sour cream. The staff is cheerful and informative, and the service is very good.

700 Front St. ☎ **305/294-5880.** www.alonzosoysterbar.com. Main courses $19–$28. MC, V. Daily 11am–11pm.

Ambrosia ★ SUSHI Trendy sushi spot Ambrosia, in the Santa Maria condo turned hotel, features some of the freshest fish in town. Chef-owner Masa offers you expertly prepared sushi—if you're a fan of tuna, try his *toro* (tuna belly). Specialty rolls include the Key West, a mix of stone crab, avocado, and smelt roe, and the Florida, tempura lobsters wrapped in pink soybean protein. Ambrosia is also a vegetarian hot spot, with excellent tofu dishes.

1401 Simonton St. ☎ **305/293-0304.** http://keywestambrosia.com. Sushi $4–$15. AE, DISC, MC, V. Daily 11am–11pm.

Banana Café ★★★ 🎁 FRENCH Banana Café benefits from a French-country-cafe look and feel. The upscale local eatery discovered by savvy visitors on the less-congested end of Duval Street has retained its loyal clientele with affordable prices and delightful, light preparations. The crepes are legendary, for breakfast or lunch; the fresh ingredients and French-themed menu bring daytime diners back for the casual, classy, tropical-influenced dinner menu. There's live jazz every Thursday night.

1211 Duval St. ☎ **305/294-7227.** www.banana-cafe-key-west.com. Main courses $19–$35; breakfast and lunch $3–$17. AE, DC, MC, V. Breakfast/lunch daily 8am–3pm; Dinner Tues–Sat 6–10pm.

Blue Heaven ★★★ 🎁 SEAFOOD/AMERICAN/NATURAL This hippie-run restaurant has become the place to be in Key West—and with good reason. Be prepared to wait in line. The food is some of the best in town—especially at breakfast, which features homemade granola, tropical-fruit pancakes (owner Richard often makes his pancakes with beer), and seafood Benedict. Dinners are just as good and run the gamut from fresh-caught fish and Jamaican jerk chicken to curried soups and vegetarian stews. Some people are put off by the dirt floors and roaming cats and birds, but frankly, it adds to the charm. The building used to be a bordello, where Hemingway was said to hang out watching cockfights. It's still lively here, but not *that* lively!

305 Petronia St. ☎ **305/296-8666.** www.blueheavenkw.com. Main courses $10–$36; lunch $6–$15; breakfast $5–$15. DISC, MC, V. Daily 8–11:30am, noon–3pm, and 6–10:30pm; Sun brunch 8am–1pm. Closed mid-Sept to early Oct.

Pepe's ★ 🎁 AMERICAN This old dive has been serving good, basic food for nearly a century. Steaks and Apalachicola Bay oysters are the big draws for regulars, who appreciate the rustic barroom setting and historical photos on the walls. Look for original scenes of Key West in 1909, when Pepe's first opened. If the weather is nice, choose a seat on the patio under a stunning mahogany tree. Burgers, fish sandwiches, and standard chili satisfy hearty eaters. Buttery sautéed mushrooms and rich mashed potatoes are the best comfort foods in Key West. There's always a wait, so stop by early for breakfast, when you can get old-fashioned chipped beef on toast and all the usual egg dishes. In the evening, reasonably priced cocktails are served on the deck.

806 Caroline St. (btw. Margaret and Williams sts.). ☎ **305/294-7192.** www.pepescafe.net. Main courses $11–$30; breakfast $3–$17; lunch $3–$18. DISC, MC, V. Daily 6:30am–10:30pm.

Sarabeth's ★★ 🏙 AMERICAN An offshoot of the New York City breakfast hot spot, Sarabeth's brings a much-needed shot of cosmopolitan comfort food to Key West in the form of delicious breakfasts with Sarabeth's signature homemade jams and jellies. Choose from buttermilk to lemon ricotta pancakes or almond-crusted cinnamon French toast. For lunch, the traditional Caesar salad, burger, or Key West pink shrimp roll with avocado are all excellent choices. Dinner is simple, but savory, with top-notch dishes from chicken potpie and meatloaf to a divine green-chili-pepper macaroni with three cheeses or meaty shrimp-and-crabmeat cakes. The dining room is cozy and intimate, and it feels like you're eating in someone's house; a few tables are on a small outdoor patio.

530 Simonton St. ✆ **305/293-8181.** www.sarabethskeywest.com. Main courses $15–$26; breakfast $7–$11; lunch $12–$15. MC, V. Mon 8am–3pm; Wed–Sun 8am–3pm and 6–10pm.

Turtle Kraals Wildlife Grill ★ ☺ 🏙 BARBECUE/SEAFOOD You'll join lots of locals in this out-of-the-way converted warehouse with indoor and dockside seating, which serves innovative seafood at great prices. Try the twin lobster tails stuffed with mango and crabmeat, stone crabs when in season (Oct–May), or any of the big quesadillas or fajitas. If you're not in the mood for seafood, there's also a barbecue menu created by an award-winning pit master from Chicago who presides over an on-premise smoker on which ribs, pork butts, beef brisket, and chicken are slow-smoked for up to 14 hours. Kids will like the wildlife exhibits, the turtle cannery, and the very cheesy menu. Blues bands play most nights, and for drinks the restaurant's roof deck, **The Tower Bar,** has fabulous views of the marina.

213 Margaret St. (at Caroline St.). ✆ **305/294-2640.** www.turtlekraals.com. Main courses $10–$25. DISC, MC, V. Mon–Thurs 11am–10:30pm; Fri–Sat 11am–11pm; Sun noon–10:30pm. Bar closes at midnight.

White Street Bistro ★★★ 🏙 FRENCH On the edge of Old Town Key West, White Street Bistro is one of Key West's best-kept secrets. Featuring an exceptionally creative menu and stellar ambience with an intimate dining room and stunning and secluded garden, White Street Bistro is a place you'll want to linger in, especially in the garden or at the indoor zinc-topped bar. The menu changes often and features moderate prices. Among the specialties, chicken liver pâté, shrimp seviche, roast lemon chicken with potatoes and vegetables, and a South of France–style pizza with caramelized onions, garlic, and mozzarella that's out of this world. Desserts are also great, including *tarte tartin* and chocolate mousse, but we especially love the option of ordering a cheese plate with dates and almonds and just hanging out in the garden. Local artists display their works here, and musicians perform on certain nights.

1019 White St. ✆ **305/294-1943.** Main courses $8–$9; small plates, salads, and sandwiches $6–$9. AE, DC, MC, V. Mon–Fri 11:30am–2pm; Mon–Thurs 5–9pm; Fri–Sat 5–10pm.

INEXPENSIVE

Hogfish Bar & Grill ★ 🏙 SEAFOOD A ramshackle, rough-and-tumble seafood bar and grill on Safe Harbor in "downtown" Stock Island (there's no town, just fisheries, boats, and artists and craftsmen working out of shacks), Hogfish is a popular spot for its namesake sandwich. Similar to grouper, hogfish is a delicious, rare fish with a scalloplike flavor, and the sandwich they make out of it, served on Cuban bread, is so popular it's usually sold out by noon. Other fish sandwiches are available, but it's the "world famous killer hogfish sandwich" that you want to come here for. Key West pink shrimp are aplenty here, so peel and eat is another popular pastime while you're waiting for your hogfish. Live music and a lively, salty bar scene created by locals and tourists alike make Hogfish a quintessential Key West experience. Kids especially like feeding the fish in the harbor.

6810 Front St., Stock Island. ✆ **305293-4041.** www.hogfishbar.com. Main courses $10–$19. AE, DISC, MC, V. Daily 11am–10pm. Take U.S. 1 N. out of Key West and across the Cow Key Channel Bridge. At the 3rd stoplight, bear to the right and onto MacDonald Ave. Follow this for approx. 1 mile and make a right on 4th Ave. (across from Boyd's Campground). Take your next left on Front St. and drive almost to the end—you'll see the Hogfish Bar and Grill on the right.

Island Dogs Bar ★ AMERICAN This islandy, Tommy Bahama–esque bar purchased in 2010 by former Pirate Soul owner Pat Croce (who still owns the popular Rum Barrel bar and restaurant across the street) is a cool spot to throw back a few while catching a game or a live band. But more important is the fare—not typical bar fare, but upscale pub fare including Captain Crunch–breaded chicken fingers, the Jamaican dog with plantains and jerk seasoning, or the Hawaiian dog with coconut and pineapple—and, well, you get the picture. Sit at the bar or at one of the few outdoor tables ideally placed for watching the crowds stumble—literally—off Duval Street.

505 Front St. ✆ **305/295-0501;** www.islanddogsbar.com. Main courses $5–$10. AE, DISC, MC, V. Daily 11am–2am.

Key West After Dark

Duval Street is the Bourbon Street of Florida. Amid the T-shirt shops and clothing boutiques, you'll find bar after bar serving neon-colored frozen drinks to revelers who bounce from bar to bar from noon to dawn. Bands and crowds vary from night to night and season to season. Your best bet is to start at Truman Avenue and head up Duval to check them out for yourself. Cover charges are rare, except in gay clubs (see "The Gay Scene," below), so stop into a dozen and see which you like. Key West is a late-night town, and most bars and clubs don't close until around 3 or 4am.

Captain Tony's Saloon Just around the corner from Duval's beaten path, this smoky old bar is about as authentic as you'll find. It comes complete with old-time regulars who remember the island before cruise ships docked here; they say Hemingway drank, caroused, and even wrote here. The late owner, Capt. Tony Tarracino, was a former controversial Key West mayor—immortalized in Jimmy Buffett's "Last Mango in Paris." 428 Greene St. ✆ **305/294-1838.** www.capttonyssaloon.com.

Cowboy Bill's Honky Tonk Saloon "The Southernmost Country Bar in the USA" features two boot-scootin' locations of indoor and outdoor bars, pool, darts, video games, 26 TVs, line dancing, live music, and the only mechanical bull in the Keys that gets kicking every Tuesday through Saturday from 10pm to 2am, with a special "sexy" bull-riding competition every Wednesday at 11:30pm. Participate or watch, but note that there are webcams catching all the action. And after several dollar Pabst Blue Ribbons, trust us, there's a lot of action going on here from 10pm to 4am daily. 618 Duval St. and 430 Greene St. ✆ **305/295-8219.** www.cowboybillskw.com.

The Green Parrot Bar A Key West landmark since 1890, the Green Parrot is a locals' favorite featuring stiff drinks, salty drinkers, and excellent live music from bluegrass and country to Afro-punk. 601 Whitehead St. ✆ **305/294-6133.** www.greenparrot.com.

You might have a magical night on Duval Street.

Sloppy Joe's You'll have to stop in here just to say you did. Scholars and drunks debate whether this is the same Sloppy Joe's that Hemingway wrote about, but there's no argument that this classic bar's early-20th-century wooden ceiling and cracked-tile floors are Key West originals. There's live music nightly, as well as a cigar room and martini bar. 201 Duval St. © **305/294-5717,** ext. 10. www.sloppyjoes.com.

The Gay & Lesbian Scene

Key West's live-and-let-live atmosphere extends to its thriving and quirky gay community. Before and after Tennessee Williams, Key West has provided the perfect backdrop to a gay scene unlike that of many large urban areas. Seamlessly blended with the prevailing culture, there is no "gay ghetto" in Key West, where the whole place is fabulous.

In Key West, the best music and dancing can be found at the predominantly gay clubs. While many of the area's other hot spots are geared toward tourists who like to imbibe, the gay clubs are for those who want to rave, gay or not. Covers vary, but are rarely more than $10.

Two popular adjacent late-night spots are the **801 Bourbon Bar/One Saloon** (801 Duval St. and 514 Petronia St.; © **305/294-9349** for both; www.801Bourbon.com), featuring great drag and lots more disco. A mostly male clientele frequents this hot spot from 9pm to 4am. Another Duval Street favorite is **Aqua,** 711 Duval St. (© **305/292-8500;** www.aquakeywest.com), where you might catch drag queens belting out torch songs or judges voting on the best package in the wet-jockey-shorts contest.

Sunday nights are fun at La-Te-Da, proper name: **La Terraza de Martí,** 1125 Duval St. (© **305/296-6706;** www.lateda.com), the former Key West home of Cuban exile José Martí. This is a great spot to gather poolside for the best martini in town—don't bother with the food. Upstairs is the **Crystal Room** (© **305/296-6706**), with a high-caliber cabaret performance featuring the popular Randy Roberts in winter. For more entertainment, check out the **Keys, A Key West Piano Bar,** 114 Duval St. (© **305/294-8859;** www.akeywestpianobar.com), featuring live music from show tunes and standards to rock 'n' roll.

Key West celebrates the New Year with "Lowering of the Wench."

An outdoor garden bar, the Off-Key Bar, is the place to be if you happen to be there during a time when a tone-deaf customer takes advantage of the open-mic policy.

THE DRY TORTUGAS ★★

70 miles W of Key West

Few people realize that the Florida Keys don't end at Key West, as about 70 miles west is a chain of seven small islands known as the Dry Tortugas. Because you've come this far, you might wish to visit them, especially if you're into bird-watching, their primary draw.

Ponce de León, who discovered this far-flung cluster of coral keys in 1513, named them Las Tortugas because of the many sea turtles, which still flock to the area during nesting season in the warm summer months. Oceanic charts later carried the preface "dry" to warn mariners that fresh water was unavailable here. Modern intervention has made drinking water available, but little else.

These undeveloped islands make a great day trip for travelers interested in seeing the natural anomalies of the Florida Keys—especially the birds. The Dry Tortugas are nesting grounds and roosting sites for thousands of tropical and subtropical oceanic birds. Visitors will also find a historic fort, good fishing, and terrific snorkeling around shallow reefs.

Getting There

BY BOAT *Yankee Freedom II* (© **800/634-0939** or 305/294-7009; www. yankeefreedom.com), a high-speed boat complete with A/C, cushioned seats, three restrooms, freshwater rinse shower, and full galley selling snacks, soft drinks, beer, wine, mixed drinks (on return trip only), film, and souvenirs, zips you to and from the Dry Tortugas in 2 hours and 15 minutes. The round-trip fare ($165 for adults, $155 for seniors, $120 for children 4 to 16) includes continental breakfast, water, lunch, and a 40-minute guided tour of the fort led by an expert naturalist. The boat leaves Key West for Fort Jefferson at 8am and returns by 5:15pm.

BY PLANE Key West Seaplane Adventures at the Key West International Airport (© 305/293-9300; www.keywestseaplanecharters.com) offers morning, afternoon, and full-day trips to the Dry Tortugas National Park via 10 passenger DHC-3T Turbine Otter seaplanes. Prices are $249 and $435 for adults, $199 and $349 for children, not including the $5-per-person park entry fee. Flights include free soft drinks and snorkeling equipment.

Exploring the Dry Tortugas

Of the seven islands that make up the Dry Tortugas, Garden Key is the most visited because it is where Fort Jefferson and the visitor center are located. Loggerhead Key, Middle Key, and East Key are open only during the day and are for hiking. Bush Key is for the birds—literally! It's a nesting area for birds only, though it is open from October to January for special excursions. Hospital and Long keys are closed to the public.

Fort Jefferson, a six-sided, 19th-century fortress, is set almost at the water's edge of Garden Key, so it appears to float in the middle of the sea. The monumental structure is surrounded by 8-foot-thick walls that rise from the sand to a height of nearly 50 feet. Impressive archways, stonework, and parapets make this 150-year-old monument a grand sight. With the invention of the rifled cannon, the fort's masonry construction became obsolete and the building was never completed. For 10 years, however, from 1863 to 1873, Fort Jefferson served as a prison, a kind of "Alcatraz East." Among its prisoners were four of the "Lincoln Conspirators," including Samuel A. Mudd, the doctor who set the broken leg of fugitive assassin John Wilkes Booth. In 1935, Fort Jefferson became a national monument administered by the National Park Service. Today, Fort Jefferson is struggling to resist erosion from the salt and sea, as iron used in the gun openings and the shutters in the fort's walls has accelerated the deterioration, and the structure's openings need to be rebricked. The National Park Service has designated the fort as the recipient of a $15-million

You can snorkel off Fort Jefferson in the Dry Tortugas.

face-lift, a project that may take up to a decade to complete.

For more information on Fort Jefferson and the Dry Tortugas, call the **Everglades National Park Service** (© 305/242-7700) or visit www.fort jefferson.com. Fort Jefferson is open during daylight hours. A self-guided tour describes the history of the human presence in the Dry Tortugas while leading visitors through the fort.

Outdoor Activities

BIRD-WATCHING Bring your binoculars and your bird books: Bird-watching is *the* reason to visit this cluster of tropical islands. The Dry Tortugas, in the middle of the migration flyway between North and South America, serve as an important rest stop for the more than 200 winged varieties that pass through annually. The season peaks from mid-March to mid-May, when thousands of birds show up, but many species from the West Indies can be found here year-round.

FISHING In July 2001, a federal law closed off all fishing in a 90-square-mile tract of ocean called the Tortugas North and a 61-square-mile tract of ocean called the Tortugas South. It basically prohibits all fishing in order to preserve the dwindling population of fish (a result of commercial fishing and environmental factors). However, rules have been alleviated and some sport fishing is now allowed in Dry Tortugas. We recommend a charter such as **Dry Tortugas Fishing Adventures** (© 305/797-6396; www.tortugas fishing.com), which will take you on a 42-foot sport-fishing catamaran into deep water where you'll catch dolphin (fish, not mammals), tuna, wahoo, king mackerel, sailfish, and an occasional marlin. Trips are overnight and rates are steep: from $3,400 to $3,600 and $1,000 per extra day. If you don't have the money or the time, **Captain Andy Griffiths** (© 305/296-2639; www.fishandy.com) will take you on 3-hour custom fishing trips to the Tortugas at $99 per passenger with a minimum of four anglers.

SCUBA DIVING & SNORKELING The warm, clear, shallow waters of the Dry Tortugas produce optimum conditions for snorkeling and scuba diving. Four endangered species of sea turtles—green, leatherback, Atlantic Ridley, and hawksbill—can be found here, along with myriad marine species. The region just outside the seawall of Fort Jefferson is excellent for underwater touring; an abundant variety of fish and coral live in 3 to 4 feet of water.

Camping on Garden Key

The rustic beauty of **Garden Key** (the only island of the Dry Tortugas where you can pitch tents) is a camper's dream. There are no RVs or motor homes: They can't get here. The abundance of birds doesn't make it quiet, but the camping—a stone's throw from the water—is as beautiful as it gets. Picnic tables, cooking grills, and toilets are provided, but there are no showers. All supplies must be packed in and out. Sites are $3 per person per night and available on a first-come, first-served basis. The 10 sites book up fast. For more information, call the **National Park Service** (© 305/242-7700).

THE EVERGLADES & BISCAYNE NATIONAL PARK

The vast ecosystem of Everglades National Park—and most of South Florida, really—is a shallow, 40-mile-wide, slow-moving river. Its current 1.5 million acres (less than 20% of its mass when preserved in 1947) remain one of few places to see endangered American crocodiles, leatherback turtles, and West Indian manatees. Take your time: The rustling of a bush might be a tiny, red-throated anole lizard; that splash of purple might be a mule-ear orchid.

Active Pursuits Popular day hikes like the **Coastal Prairie** and **Gumbo Limbo** trails wend their way through canopies of cypress and gumbo-limbo trees and past waterways with alligators and pink-hued roseate spoonbills. Shark Valley is South Florida's most scenic bicycling trail, a flat, paved route frequented by sunbathing alligators and turtles. Canoeing through the Everglades allows serene, close-up views of this junglelike ecosystem.

Flora & Fauna A river of saw grass marks Everglades National Park, punctuated with islands of gumbo-limbo hammocks, royal palms, and pale, delicate orchids. The **Anhinga Trail** teems with native wildlife: the swallowtail butterfly, American crocodile, leatherback turtle, West Indian manatee, and, rarely, the Florida panther.

Tours Shallow-draft, fan-powered airboats careen through bayous, rising ever so slightly above swaying saw grass and alongside flocks of snowy egrets. The high-speed runabouts operate just outside park boundaries, including **Gator Park** and **Coopertown Airboat Tours.** At the Shark Valley entrance **Shark Valley Tram Tours** transport visitors on 2-hour, naturalist-led explorations through the heart of the Everglades. A highlight is the climb up a 65-foot observation for a bird's-eye view of the "river of grass."

EVERGLADES NATIONAL PARK ★★

Before visiting it, my conception of the Everglades was that it was one big swamp swarming with ominous creatures, like something generated by the programming geeks at the Syfy Channel. For someone who'd rather endure an endless series of root canals than audition for a role on *Survivor* (the closest I'd ever been to nature was sleep-away camp), the Everglades might as well have been the *Never*glades—that is, until I finally decided to venture there. And I found that the Everglades isn't really a swamp at all, but one of the country's most fascinating natural resources.

For first-timers or those with dubious athletic skills, the best way to see the 'Glades is probably via airboats, which aren't actually allowed in the park proper, but cut through the saw grass on the park's outskirts, taking you past the amazing flora and fauna. A walk on one of the park's many trails will provide you with a different vantage point: up-close interaction with an assortment of tame wildlife. But the absolute best way to see the 'Glades is via canoe, which allows you to get incredibly close to nature. Whichever method you choose, I guarantee that

PREVIOUS PAGE: **Everglades National Park provides habitat for beautiful avians like the great blue heron.**

Alligators rest on the banks of a sunny spot in the Everglades.

you will marvel at the sheer beauty of the Everglades. Despite the multitude of mosquito bites (the bugs seem to be immune to repellent—wear long pants and cover your arms), an Everglades experience will definitely contribute to a new-found appreciation for Florida's natural (and beautiful) wonderland.

This vast, unusual ecosystem is actually a 40-mile-wide, slow-moving river. Rarely more than knee-deep, the water is the lifeblood of this wilderness, and the subtle shifts in water level dictate the life cycles of the native plants and animals. In 1947, 1.5 million acres—less than 20% of the Everglades' wilderness—were established as Everglades National Park. At that time, few lawmakers understood how neighboring ecosystems relate to each other. Consequently, the park is heavily affected by surrounding territories and is at the butt end of every environmental insult that occurs upstream in Miami.

While there has been a marked decrease in the indigenous wildlife, Everglades National Park remains one of the few places where you can see dozens of endangered species in their natural habitat, including the swallowtail butterfly, American crocodile, leatherback turtle, Southern bald eagle, West Indian manatee, and Florida panther.

Take your time on the trails, and a hypnotic beauty begins to unfold. Follow the rustling of a bush, and you might see a small green tree frog or tiny brown anole lizard, with its bright-red spotted throat. Crane your neck to see around a bend, and discover a delicate, brightly painted mule-ear orchid.

The slow and subtle splendor of this exotic land may not be immediately appealing to kids raised on video games, but they'll certainly remember the experience and thank you later. There's enough dramatic fun around the park, such as airboat rides, hiking, and biking, to keep them satisfied for at least a day.

Lazy River
It takes a month for 1 gallon of water to move through Everglades National Park.

Essentials

GETTING THERE & ACCESS POINTS Although the Everglades may seem overwhelmingly large, it's easy to get to the park's two main areas: the northern section, accessible via Shark Valley and Everglades City, and the southern section, accessible through the Ernest F. Coe Visitor Center, near Homestead and Florida City.

NORTHERN ENTRANCES A popular day trip for Miamians, **Shark Valley,** a 15-mile paved loop road (with an observation tower in the middle of the loop) overlooking the pulsating heart of the Everglades, is the easiest and most scenic way to explore the park. Just 25 miles west of the Florida Turnpike, Shark Valley is best reached via the Tamiami Trail, South Florida's preturnpike, two-lane road, which cuts across the southern part of the state along the park's northern border. Roadside attractions (boat rides and alligator farms, for example) along the Tamiami Trail are operated by the Miccosukee Indian Village and are worth a quick, fun stop. An excellent tram tour (leaving from the Shark Valley Visitor Center) goes deep into the park along a trail that's also terrific for biking. Shark Valley is about an hour's drive from Miami.

A little less than 10 miles west along the Tamiami Trail from Shark Valley, you'll discover **Big Cypress National Preserve,** in which stretches of vibrant green cypress and pine trees make for a fabulous Kodak moment. If you pick up S.R. 29 and head south from the Tamiami Trail, you'll hit a modified version of civilization in the form of Everglades City (where the Everglades meet the Gulf of Mexico), where there's another entrance to the park and the **Gulf Coast Visitor Center.** From Miami to Shark Valley: Go west on I-395 to S.R. 821 South (Florida Tpk.). Take the U.S. 41/Southwest 8th Street (Tamiami Trail) exit. The Shark Valley entrance is just 25 miles

The ancient denizens of Big Cypress National Preserve.

west. To get to Everglades City, continue west on the Tamiami Trail and head south on S.R. 29. Everglades City is approximately a 2½-hour drive from Miami, but because it is scenic, it may take longer if you stop or slow down to view your surroundings.

SOUTHERN ENTRANCE (VIA HOMESTEAD & FLORIDA CITY) If you're in a rush to hit the 'Glades and don't care about the scenic route, this is your best bet. Just southeast of Homestead and Florida City, off S.R. 9336, the southern access to the park will bring you to the Ernest F. Coe Visitor Center. Inside the park, 4 miles beyond the Ernest F. Coe Visitor Center, is the Royal Palm Visitor Center, the starting point for the two most popular walking trails, Gumbo Limbo and Anhinga, where you'll witness a plethora of birds and wildlife roaming freely. Thirteen miles west of the Ernest F. Coe Visitor Center, you'll hit Pa-hay-okee Overlook Trail, which is worth a trek across the boardwalk to reach the observation tower, over which vultures and hawks hover protectively amid a resplendent, picturesque, bird's-eye view of the Everglades. From Miami to the southern entrance: Go west on I-395 to S.R. 821 South (Florida Tpk.), which will end in Florida City. Take the first right through the center of town (you can't miss it) and follow signs to the park entrance on S.R. 9336. The Ernest F. Coe Visitor Center is about 1½ hours from Miami.

VISITOR CENTERS & INFORMATION General inquiries and specific questions should be directed to **Everglades National Park Headquarters,** 40001 S.R. 9336, Homestead, FL 33034 (✆ **305/242-7700**). Ask for a copy of *Parks and Preserves,* a free newspaper that's filled with up-to-date information about goings-on in the Everglades. Headquarters is staffed by helpful phone operators daily from 8:30am to 4:30pm. You can also try **www.nps. gov/ever**.

Note that all hours listed are for the high season, generally November through May. During the slow summer months, many offices and outfitters keep abbreviated hours. Always call ahead to confirm hours of operation.

The **Ernest F. Coe Visitor Center,** at the Park Headquarters entrance, west of Homestead and Florida City, is the best place to gather information. In addition to details on tours and boat rentals, and free brochures outlining trails, wildlife, and activities, you will find state-of-the-art educational displays, films, and interactive exhibits. A gift shop sells postcards, film, an impressive selection of books about the Everglades, unusual gift items, and a supply of your most important gear: insect repellent. The shop is open daily from 8am to 5pm.

The **Royal Palm Visitor Center,** a small nature museum located 3 miles past the park's main entrance, is a smaller information center. The museum is not great (its displays are equipped with recordings about the park's ecosystem), but the center is the departure point for the popular Anhinga and Gumbo Limbo trails. The center is open daily from 8am to 4pm.

Knowledgeable rangers, who provide brochures and personal insight into the park's activities, also staff the **Flamingo Visitor Center,** 38 miles from the main entrance, at the park's southern access, with natural-history exhibits and information on visitor services, and the **Shark Valley Visitor Center,** at the park's northern entrance. Both are open daily from 8:30am to 5pm.

ENTRANCE FEES, PERMITS & REGULATIONS Permits and passes can be purchased only at the main park or Shark Valley entrance station. Even if you are just visiting for an afternoon, you'll need to buy a 7-day permit, which costs $10 per vehicle. Pedestrians and cyclists are charged $5 each. An **Everglades Park Pass,** valid for a year's worth of unlimited admissions, is available for $25. You may also purchase a 12-month America the Beautiful National Parks and Federal Recreation Lands Pass–Annual Pass for $50, which is valid for entrance into any U.S. national park. U.S. citizens ages 62 and older pay only $10 for the America the Beautiful National Parks and Federal Recreation Lands Pass–Senior Pass that's valid for life. An America the Beautiful National Parks and Federal Recreation Lands Pass–Access Pass is available free to U.S. citizens with disabilities.

Permits are required for campers to stay overnight either in the backcountry or at the primitive campsites. See "Camping in the Everglades," on p. 276.

Those who want to fish without a charter captain must obtain a State of Florida saltwater fishing license. These are available in the park, at any tackle shop or sporting-goods store nearby. Nonresidents pay $30 for a 7-day license or $17 for a 3-day license. Florida residents pay $17 for an annual fishing license. A snook license must be purchased separately at a cost of $10; a lobster permit is $5. For more information on fishing licenses, go to **http://myfwc.com/License/LicPermit_SWFishing.htm**.

Charter captains carry vessel licenses that cover all paying passengers, but ask to be sure. Freshwater fishing licenses are available at various bait-and-tackle stores outside the park at the same rates as those offered inside the park. A good one nearby is **Don's Bait & Tackle,** 30710 S. Federal Hwy., right on U.S. 1 in Homestead (© **305/247-6616;** www.donsbaitand tackle.com). *Note:* Most of the area's freshwater fishing, limited to murky canals and artificial lakes near housing developments, is hardly worth the trouble when so much good saltwater fishing is available.

SEASONS There are two distinct seasons in the Everglades: high season and mosquito season. High season is also dry season and lasts from late November to May. Most winters here are warm, sunny, and breezy—a good combination for keeping the bugs away. This is the best time to visit because low water levels attract the largest variety of wading birds and their predators. As the dry season wanes, wildlife follows the receding water; by the end of May, the only living things you are sure to spot will make you itch. The worst, called no-see-ums, are not even swattable. If you choose to visit during the buggy season, be vigilant in applying bug spray. Also, realize that many establishments and operators either close or curtail offerings in summer, so always call ahead to check schedules.

RANGER PROGRAMS More than 50 ranger programs, free with entry, are offered each month during high season and give visitors an opportunity to gain an expert's perspective. Ranger-led walks and talks are offered year-round from Royal Palm Visitor Center, and at the Flamingo and Gulf Coast visitor centers, as well as Shark Valley Visitor Center during winter months. Park rangers tend to be helpful, well informed, and good humored. Some programs occur regularly, such as Royal Palm Visitor Center's Glade Glimpses, a walking tour on which rangers point out flora and fauna, and discuss issues affecting the Everglades' survival. Tours are scheduled at 1:30pm daily.

Ranger walks can clue you in to the natural wonders of the Everglades.

The Anhinga Amble, a similar program that takes place on the Anhinga Trail, starts at 10:30am daily and lasts about 50 minutes. Because times, programs, and locations vary from month to month, check the schedule, available at any of the visitor centers.

SAFETY There are many dangers inherent in this vast wilderness area. *Always* let someone know your itinerary before you set out on an extended hike. It's mandatory that you file an itinerary when camping overnight in the back-country (which you can do when you apply for your overnight permit at either the Flamingo Visitor Center or the Gulf Coast Visitor Center). When you're on the water, watch for weather changes; thunderstorms and high winds often develop rapidly. Swimming is not recommended because of the presence of alligators, sharks, and barracudas. Watch out for the region's four indigenous poisonous snakes: diamondback and pygmy rattlesnakes, coral snakes (identifiable by their colorful rings), and water moccasins (which swim on the surface of the water). Bring insect repellent to ward off mosquitoes and biting flies. First aid is available from park rangers. The nearest hospital is in Homestead, 10 miles from the park's main entrance.

Seeing the Highlights

Shark Valley, a 15-mile paved road (ideal for biking) through the Everglades, provides a fine introduction to the wonders of the park, but don't plan on spending more than a few hours here. Bicycling and taking a guided tram tour (p. 275) are fantastic ways to cover the highlights.

If you want to see a greater array of plant and animal life, make sure that you venture into the park through the main entrance, pick up a trail map, and dedicate at least a day to exploring from there.

Stop first along the Anhinga and Gumbo Limbo trails, which start right next to each other, 3 miles from the park's main entrance. These trails provide a thorough introduction to the Everglades' flora and fauna and are highly recommended to first-time visitors. Each is a half-mile round-trip. **Gumbo Limbo Trail** (my pick for best walking trail in the Everglades) meanders through a gorgeous, shaded, junglelike hammock of gumbo-limbo trees, royal palms, ferns, orchids, air plants, and a general blanket of vegetation, though it doesn't put you in close contact with much wildlife. **Anhinga Trail** is one of the most popular trails in the park because of its abundance of wildlife: There's more water and wildlife in this area than in most parts of the Everglades, especially during dry season. Alligators, lizards, turtles, river otters, herons, egrets, and other animals abound, making this one of the best trails for seeing wildlife. Arrive early to spot the widest selection of exotic birds, such as the anhinga bird, the trail's namesake, a large black fishing bird so accustomed to humans that many of them build their nests in plain view. Take your time—at least an hour is recommended for each trail. Both are wheelchair accessible. If you treat the trails and modern boardwalk as pathways to get through quickly, rather than destinations to experience and savor, you'll miss out on the still beauty and hidden treasures that await you.

To get closer to nature, a few hours in a canoe along any of the trails allows paddlers the chance to sense the park's fluid motion and to become a part of the ecosphere. Visitors who choose this option end up feeling more like explorers than observers. (See "Sports & Outdoor Activities," below.)

No matter which option you choose, I strongly recommend staying for the 7pm program, available during high season at the Long Pine Key Amphitheater. This ranger-led talk and slide show will give you a detailed overview of the park's history, natural resources, wildlife, and threats to its survival.

And while the nature tours and talks are fascinating, so are the tours of **Nike Hercules Missile Base HM-69 ★**, a product of collective thinking by President John F. Kennedy and his advisors that arose out of very real Cold War fears. The base was turned back over to the park in 1979 but wasn't open to the public until 2009. From January 1 to March 28, free ranger-led tours take visitors on a 90-minute driving and walking tour of the missile assembly building, three barns where 12 missiles were stored, the guardhouse, and the underground control room. Tours depart from the Ernest Coe Visitor Center at 2pm Saturday and Sunday and at 10am and 2pm Tuesday. The tour is free but the $10 park admission still applies. Definitely call for reservations (© **305/242-7700**).

Sports & Outdoor Activities

BIKING The relatively flat, 38-mile paved **Main Park Road** is great for biking because of the multitude of hardwood hammocks (treelike islands or dense stands of hardwood trees that grow only a few inches above land) and a dwarf cypress forest (stunted and thinly distributed cypress trees, which grow in poor soil on drier land).

Shark Valley, however, is the best biking trail by far. If the park isn't flooded from excess rain (which it often is, especially in spring), this is South Florida's most scenic bicycle trail. Many locals haul their bikes out to the 'Glades for a relaxing day of wilderness-trail riding. You'll share the flat, paved road only with other bikers, trams, and a menagerie of wildlife. (Don't be surprised to see a gator lounging in the sun or a deer munching on some grass. Otters, turtles, alligators, and snakes are common companions in the area.) There are no shortcuts, so if you become tired or are unable to complete the 15-mile trip, turn around and return on the same road. Allow 2 to 3 hours to bike the entire loop.

Those who love to mountain-bike and who prefer solitude might check out the **Southern Glades Trail,** a 14-mile unpaved trail lined with native

The Everglades is a birder's paradise.

trees and teeming with wildlife, such as deer, alligators, and the occasional snake. The trail runs along the C-111 canal, off S.R. 9336 and Southwest 217th Street.

Bicycles are available from **Shark Valley Tram Tours,** at the park's Shark Valley entrance (✆ **305/221-8455;** www.sharkvalleytramtours. com), for $7.25 per hour; rentals can be picked up anytime between 8:30am and 3pm and must be returned by 4pm.

BIRD-WATCHING More than 350 species of birds make their home in the Everglades. Tropical birds from the Caribbean and temperate species from North America can be found, along with exotics that have flown in from more distant regions. Eco and Mrazek ponds, located near Flamingo, are two of the best places for birding, especially in early morning or late afternoon in the dry winter months. Pick up a free birding checklist from one of the visitor centers (p. 267) and inquire about what's been spotted in recent days. In late 2009, a survey revealed that there were more than 77,000 nests in the Everglades. The endangered woo stork increased its nesting activity 1,776% from the previous year. For a guided birding tour, consider the **Everglades Area Tours** (✆ **239/695-9107;** www.evergladesareatours.com) **National Park and Grand Heritage Birding Tour,** a comprehensive, 6- to 7-hour naturalist-led tour with multiple forms of transportation—powerboats, kayaks, and even a beach walk, so you don't miss any of the spectacular feathered (among others) species who call the park home. The tour is a steep $250 per person and limited to six per tour.

CANOEING Canoeing through the Everglades may be one of the most serene, diverse adventures you'll ever have. From a canoe (where you're incredibly close to the water level), your vantage point is priceless. Canoers in the 'Glades can coexist with the gators and birds in a way no one else can; the creatures behave as if you're part of the ecosystem—something that won't happen on an airboat. A ranger-guided boat tour is your best bet, and oftentimes they are either free or very inexpensive at around $7 to $12 per person. As always, a ranger will help you understand the surroundings and what you're seeing. They don't take reservations, but for more information on the various boat tours, call ✆ **239/695-3311.**

Everglades National Park's longest "trails" are designed for boat and canoe travel, and many are marked as clearly as walking trails. The **Noble Hammock Canoe Trail,** a 2-mile loop, takes 1 to 2 hours and is recommended for beginners. The **Hell's Bay Canoe Trail,** a 3- to 6-mile course for hardier paddlers, takes 2 to 6 hours, depending on how far you choose to go. Fans of this trail like to say, "It's hell to get in and hell to get out." Park rangers can recommend other trails that suit your abilities, time limitations, and interests.

You can rent a canoe at the **Ivey House B&B** (✆ 877/577-0679; www.evergladesadventures.com) for $62 for 24 hours, $35 per full day (any 8-hr. period), or for $25 per half-day (1–5pm only). Kayaks and tandem kayaks are also available. The rental agent will shuttle your party to the trail head of your choice and pick you up afterward. Rental facilities are open daily from 8am to 5pm.

During ideal weather conditions (stay away during bug season!), you can paddle right out to the Gulf and camp on the beach. However, Gulf waters at beach sites can be extremely rough, and people in small watercraft such as a canoe should exercise caution.

You can also take a canoe tour from the Parks Docks on Chokoloskee Causeway on S.R. 29, ½ mile south of the traffic circle at the ranger station in Everglades City. Call **Everglades National Park Boat Tours** (✆ 800/445-7724) for information. And for an eco-tour of the 'Glades, **Everglades Area Tours** (✆ 239/695-9107; www.evergladesareatours.com) offers not only guided kayak fishing, but also guided half-day kayak eco-tours, customized bird-watching expeditions, and full-moon paddling, as well as bicycle and aerial tours of the Everglades. Capt. Charles Wright can put six kayaks and six passengers into the Yak Attack shuttle motorboat for the trip out to the Wilderness Waterway, deep within Everglades National Park's Ten Thousand Islands, where you will paddle in the absolute wilderness, spotting birds, dolphins, manatees, sea turtles, and perhaps even the elusive American crocodile. The shuttle then brings you back to Everglades City. The trip costs $195 per angler and includes transportation, guide services, outfitted kayaks, and all safety equipment.

FISHING About a third of Everglades National Park is open water. Freshwater fishing is popular in brackish **Nine-Mile Pond** (25 miles from the main entrance) and other spots along the Main Park Road, but because of the high mercury levels found in the Everglades, freshwater fishers are warned not to eat their catch. Before casting, check in at a visitor center, as many of the park's lakes are preserved for observation only. Fishing licenses are required; see p. 268 for more information.

Saltwater anglers will find snapper and sea trout plentiful. For an expertly guided fishing trip through the backcountry, **Adventures in Backwater Fishing** (✆ 239/643-1261) will send you out with Capt. Dave Harding and Capt. George LeClair, who promise unique fishing—flyfishing and spin casting, among other things—without breaking the bank. Six-hour trips will set you back around $385. A great list of charters and guides can be found at the Flamingo Marina or at **www.fishing-florida.com/adventures**.

MOTORBOATING Motorboating around the Everglades seems like a great way to see plants and animals in remote habitats, and, indeed, it's an interesting and fulfilling experience as you throttle into nature. However, environmentalists are taking stock of the damage inflicted by motorboats (especially airboats) on the delicate ecosystem. If you choose to motor, remember that most of the areas near land are "no wake" zones and that, for the protection of nesting birds, landing is prohibited on most of the little mangrove islands. Motorboating is allowed in certain areas, such as Florida Bay, the backcountry toward Everglades City, and the Ten Thousand Islands area. In all the freshwater lakes, however, motorboats are prohibited if they're above 5 horsepower. There's a long list of restrictions and restricted areas, so get a copy of the park's boating rules from Park Headquarters before setting out.

The Everglades' only marina—accommodating about 50 boats with electric and water hookups—is **Flamingo Marina,** 1 Flamingo Lodge Hwy., Everglades City (𝄐 **239/695-3101**). The marina is the only remnant of the now-demolished Flamingo Lodge, which suffered terrible damage from Hurricanes Katrina and Wilma in 2005. Word is that if enough funds can be rounded up, it'll be replaced with a hurricane-resistant lodging complex featuring a small hotel, cottages, and eco-tents. The well-marked channel to the Flamingo is accessible to boats with a maximum 4-foot draft and is open year-round. Reservations can be made through the marina store (𝄐 **239/695-3101**). Seventeen-foot skiffs with 15-horsepower motors are available for rent. These low-power boats cost $80 for 2 hours, $150 for 4 hours, $195 for 8 hours, and $390 for 24 hours. A $100 deposit is required.

Organized Tours

AIRBOAT TOURS Shallow-draft, fan-powered airboats were invented in the Everglades by frog hunters who were tired of poling through the brushes. Airboats cut through the saw grass and are sort of like hydraulic boats; at high enough speeds, a boat actually rises above the saw grass and into the air. Even though airboats are the most efficient (not to mention fast and fun!) way to get around, they are not permitted in the park—these shallow-bottom runabouts tend to inflict severe damage on animals and plants. Just outside the boundaries of the Everglades, however, you'll find a number of outfitters offering rides. *Tip:* Consider bringing earplugs, as these high-speed boats are *loud.* Sometimes operators provide plugs, but bring a pair just in case.

One of the best outfitters is **Gator Park,** 12 miles west of the Florida Turnpike at 24050 SW Eighth St. (𝄐 **305/559-2255;** www.gatorpark.com; open daily 9am–5pm), which happens to be one of the most informative and entertaining airboat-tour operators around, not to mention the only one to give out free earplugs. Some of the guides deserve a medal for getting into the water and poking around a massive alligator, even though they're not really supposed to. After the boat ride, there's a free interactive wildlife show that features alligator wrestling and several other frightening acts involving scorpions. Take note of the peacocks that live in the trees here. Admission for the boat ride and show is $22 for adults, $11 for children 6 to 11; check for Web discounts. They also offer $45 airboat tours (departing every 20 min.), which include transportation to and from hotels on Miami Beach, Bal Harbour, Surfside, and Sunny Isles.

Airboat tours are a traditional way to see The Everglades.

Another outfitter I recommend is **Coopertown Airboat Tours** (© 305/226-6048; www.coopertownairboats.com), about 11 miles west of the Florida Turnpike on the Tamiami Trail (U.S. 41), in a town that boasts a total population of eight humans! The superfriendly staff has helped the company garner the title of "Florida's Best" by the *Miami Herald* for 40 years in a row. You never know what you're going to see, but with great guides, you're sure to see *something* of interest on the 40-minute, 8-mile round-trip tours. There are also a restaurant and a small gator farm on the premises. Airboat rides cost $22 for adults, $11 for children 7 to 11. Private airboat tours are $50 per hour, per person. The company is open daily from 8am to 6pm; tours leave frequently.

The **Miccosukee Indian Village,** just west of the Shark Valley entrance on U.S. 41/Tamiami Trail and MM 70 (© 305/223-8380; www.miccosukeetours.com), offers 30-minute airboat tours for $10 per person, with cheaper rates online. However, *be advised:* I am not recommending this outfit over others—it's merely the one closest to the Shark Valley entrance. As always, the quality of your tour is only as good as the quality of your guide, and, unfortunately, I've gotten some complaints about the Miccosukee tours.

The **Everglades Alligator Farm,** 4 miles south of Palm Drive on Southwest 192nd Avenue (© 305/247-2628; www.everglades.com), offers half-hour guided airboat tours daily from 9am to 6pm. The price, which includes admission to the park, is $23 for adults and $16 for children 4 to 11.

Another reputable company is **Captain Doug's,** 35 miles south of Naples and 1 mile past the bridge in Everglades City (© 800/282-9194).

CANOE TOURS Slink through the mangroves, slide across saw grass prairies, and walk the sands of the unfettered Ten Thousand Islands—a canoe tour is a great way to explore the Everglades backcountry. Contact **Everglades Adventures** (© 877/567-0679; www.evergladesadventures.com) at the Ivey House B&B (p. 276) for an expert guide.

ECO-TOURS Although it's fascinating to explore on your own, it would be a shame for you to tour the Everglades without a clue about what you're seeing. **Everglades Adventures** (see "Canoe Tours," above) can guide and entertain you, as well as explain such key issues as the differences between alligators and crocodiles, or between swamps and the Everglades.

MOTORBOAT TOURS Both Florida Bay and backcountry tours are offered Thursday to Monday at the **Flamingo Marina** (see "Motorboating," above). Florida Bay tours cruise nearby estuaries and sandbars, while six-passenger backcountry boats visit smaller sloughs. Passengers can expect to see birds and a variety of other animals (I once saw a raccoon and some wild pigs). Both cost $27 for adults, $13 for children 5 to 12. Tours depart throughout the day; reservations are recommended. Charter-fishing and sightseeing boats can also be booked through the resort's main reservation number (✆ **239/695-3101**). If you're on the Gulf Coast side of things, the naturalist-guided Gulf Coast boat tour of the Ten Thousand Islands departs from the **Gulf Coast Marina** (located in the **Gulf Coast Visitor Center,** 5 miles south of Hwy. 41/Tamiami Trail on S.R. 29, in the Everglades City area; ✆ **239/695-2591**) and lasts an hour and a half. There's also a mangrove wilderness tour through the swampier part of the park. Tour prices are the same as the tours at the Flamingo Marina.

TRAM TOURS At the park's Shark Valley entrance, open-air tram buses take visitors on 2-hour naturalist-led tours that delve 7½ miles into the wilderness and are the best quick introduction you can get to the Everglades. At the trail's midsection, passengers can disembark and climb a 65-foot observation tower with good views of the 'Glades (though the tower on the Pa-hay-okee Trail is better). Visitors will see plenty of wildlife and endless acres of saw grass. Tours run December through April, daily on the hour between 9am and 4pm, and May through November at 9:30am, 11am, 1pm, and 3pm. The tours are sometimes stalled by flooding or particularly heavy mosquito infestation. Reservations are recommended from December to March. The cost is $17 for adults, $11 for children 12 and under. For further information, contact **Shark Valley Tram Tours** (✆ **305/221-8455;** www.sharkvalleytramtours.com).

Where to Stay

With the destruction of the Flamingo Lodge, there is no lodging within Everglades National Park proper unless you count your tent as lodging. However, there are a few accommodations just outside the park that are clean and reasonably priced. A $45-million casino hotel, **Miccosukee Resort** (www.miccosukee.com; ✆ **877/242-6464**), is adjacent to the Miccosukee bingo and gaming

The Shark Valley Tram Tour is a great introduction to The Everglades.

hall on the northern edge of the park. Although bugs can be a major nuisance, especially in the warm months, camping (the best way to fully experience South Florida's wilderness) is really the way to go in this very primitive environment.

CAMPING IN THE EVERGLADES

Campgrounds are open year-round in Flamingo and Long Pine Key. Both have drinking water, picnic tables, charcoal grills, restrooms, and tent and trailer pads, and welcome RVs (Flamingo allows up to 40-ft. vehicles, while Long Pine Key accepts up to 60-footers), though there are no electrical hookups. Flamingo has cold-water showers; Long Pine Key does not have showers or hookups for showers. Private ground fires are not permitted, but supervised campfire programs are conducted during winter months. Long Pine Key and Flamingo are popular and require reservations in advance, which can be made through the National Park Reservations Service (www.nps.gov; ✆ **800/365-CAMP** [2267]). Campsites are $16 per night; during winter season (Nov–Apr), there's a 14-day consecutive-stay limit, and a maximum of 30 days a year.

Camping is also available year-round in the **backcountry** (those remote areas accessible only by boat, foot, or canoe—basically, most of the park), on a first-come, first-served basis. Campers must register with park rangers and get a permit in person or by phone no less than 24 hours before the start of their trip. The permit costs $10 plus $2 per camper per night. For more information, contact the **Gulf Coast Visitor Center** (✆ **239/695-3311**) or the **Flamingo Visitor Center** (✆ **239/695-2945**), which are the only two places that sell the permits. Once you have one, camping sites cost $16 (with a maximum of 8 people per site), or $30 for a group site (maximum of 15 people). Campers can use only designated campsites, which are plentiful and well marked on visitor maps.

Many backcountry sites are **chickee huts**—covered wooden platforms (with toilets) on stilts. They're accessible only by canoe and can accommodate free-standing tents (without stakes). Ground sites are located along interior bays and rivers, and beach camping is also popular. In summer especially, mosquito repellent is necessary gear.

LODGING IN EVERGLADES CITY

As Everglades City is 35 miles southeast of Naples and 83 miles west of Miami, many visitors choose to explore this western entrance to Everglades National Park, located off the Tamiami Trail, on S.R. 29. An annual seafood festival held the first weekend in February is a major event that draws hordes of people. Everglades City (the gateway to the Ten Thousand Islands), where the 'Glades meet the Gulf of Mexico, is the closest thing you'll get to civilization in South Florida's swampy frontier, with a few tourist traps—er, shops—a restaurant, and one bed-and-breakfast.

Ivey House B&B ★★ 🎒 The first certified Green Lodging in Collier County, the Ivey House offers a variety of accommodations: the Ivey House Inn, featuring spacious rooms with private bathrooms, TVs, phones, and a view of the courtyard pool and waterfall; the Ivey House Lodge, housed in what used to be a recreational center for the men who built the Tamiami Trail, featuring 10 small rooms with communal bathrooms (one each for women and men), no TVs or phones; and the Ivey House Cottage, with two bedrooms, a full kitchen, a private bathroom, and a screened-in porch. Owners Sandee and David Harraden are extremely knowledgeable about the Everglades and assist guests, providing a variety of daily excursions. Rates include a continental breakfast. A full hot breakfast is provided during peak season. Box lunches are available year-round for $11. *Note:* There is no smoking in any of the buildings.

107 Camellia St., Everglades City, FL 34139. www.iveyhouse.com. © **877/567-0679** or 239/695-3299. Fax 239/695-4155. 28 units. Winter $100–$200 in Inn, $60–$105 in Lodge, $175–$235 in Cottage; off season $75–$85 in Inn, $60–$65 in Lodge, $135 in Cottage. 2-night minimum in all facilities during Everglades Seafood Festival in Feb. Rates include continental breakfast. MC, V. **Amenities:** Restaurant; pool; Wi-Fi. *In room:* A/C, TV, fridge (in inn and cottages), kitchen (in cottages).

Rod & Gun Lodge ★ Set on the banks of the sleepy Baron River, this rustic, old white-clapboard house has plenty of history and all kinds of activities for sports enthusiasts, including a pool, bike rentals, a tennis center, and nearby boat rentals and private fishing guides. Hoover vacationed here after his 1928 election victory, and Truman flew in to sign Everglades National Park into existence in 1947 and stayed over as well. Other guests have included Richard Nixon, Burt Reynolds, and Mick Jagger. The public rooms are beautifully paneled and hung with tarpon, wild boar, deer antlers, and other trophies. Guest rooms in this single-story building are unfussy but comfortable. All have porches looking out on the river. Out by the pool, a screened veranda with ceiling fans is a pleasant place for a libation. The excellent seafood **restaurant** serves breakfast, lunch, and dinner. The entire property is smoke free.

Riverside Dr. and Broadway (P.O. Box 190), Everglades City, FL 34139. www.everglades rodandgun.com. © **239/695-2101.** 17 units. Winter $110–$140 double; off season $95 double. No credit cards. Closed after July 4th for the summer. **Amenities:** Restaurant; bike rental; pool; tennis courts. *In room:* A/C, TV.

LODGING IN HOMESTEAD & FLORIDA CITY

Homestead and Florida City, two adjacent towns that were almost blown off the map by Hurricane Andrew in 1992, have come back better than before. About 10 miles from the park's main entrance, along U.S. 1, 35 miles south of Miami, these somewhat rural towns offer several budget options, including chain hotels. There is a **Days Inn** (© **305/245-1260**) in Homestead and a **Ramada Inn** (© **800/272-6232** or 305/247-8833) right off the turnpike in Florida City. The best options are both in Florida City: **The Best Western Gateway to the Keys,** 411 Krome Ave. (U.S.1; www.bestwestern.com; © **800/528-1234** or 305/246-5100), and the **Everglades International Hostel,** 20 SW 2nd Ave. (www.evergladeshostel.com; © **800/372-3874** or 305/248-1122).

Where to Eat in & Around the Park

Here for nearly a quarter of a century, **El Toro Taco Family Restaurant,** 1 S. Krome Ave., near Mowry and Campbell drives, Homestead (© **305/245-8182**), opens daily at 9:30am and stays crowded until at least 9pm most days. The fresh grilled meats, tacos, burritos, salsas, guacamole, and stews are all mild and delicious. No matter how big your appetite, it's hard to spend more than $15 per person at this Mexican outpost. Bring your own beer or wine.

Housed in a one-story, windowless building that looks something like a medieval fort, the **Capri Restaurant,** 935 N. Krome Ave., Florida City (© **305/247-1542;** www.dinecapri.com), has been serving hearty Italian-American fare since 1958. Great pastas and salads complement a menu of meat and fish dishes; portions are big. Lunch and dinner are served Monday through Friday until

9:30pm and Saturday until 10:30pm. The **White Lion Café,** 146 NW 7th St., Homestead (✆ **305/248-1076;** www.whitelioncafe.com), is a quaint home-and-gardens-cum-cafe with live blues, jazz, and swing music at night, and a menu with Blue Plate specials and cheekily named appetizers and entrees such as Dirty Little Shrimp and Garlic Romanian, which is actually delicious skirt steak sliced thin and served with fresh mushrooms, spinach, and garlic over real mashed potatoes and gravy. Entree prices range from $10 to $22. Dinner is served Tuesday through Saturday from 5pm until "the fat lady sings."

The **Miccosukee Restaurant,** just west of the Shark Valley entrance on the Tamiami Trail/U.S. 41 (✆ **305/223-8380**), serves authentic pumpkin bread, fry bread, and fish, and not-so-authentic Native American interpretations of tacos and fried chicken. It's worth a stop for brunch, lunch, or dinner.

Near the Miccosukee reservation is the **Pit Bar-B-Q,** 16400 SW 8th St. (✆ **305/226-2272;** www.thepitbarbq.com), a total pit of a place known for some of the best smoked ribs, barbecued chicken, and corn bread this side of the Deep South. It's open daily from 11am to 8pm.

In Everglades City, the **Oyster House,** on Chokoloskee Causeway, S.R. (the locals call it Hwy.) 29 S. (✆ **239/695-2073;** www.oysterhouserestaurant. com), is a large, homey seafood restaurant with modest prices, excellent service, and a fantastic view of the Ten Thousand Islands. Try the hush puppies. For more authentic local flavor, try the **Camellia Street Grill,** 208 Camellia St. (✆ **239/695-2003**), an off-the-beaten-path, rusty waterfront fish joint fusing Southern hospitality with outstanding seafood served with a gourmet twist. An on-site herb and veggie garden provides the freshest ingredients and stellar salads. Everything is homemade, including the Key lime pie, and there's live music on Fridays and Saturdays.

BISCAYNE NATIONAL PARK ★

With only about 500,000 visitors each year (mostly boaters and divers), the unusual Biscayne National Park is one of the least-crowded parks in the country. Perhaps that's because the park is a little more difficult than most to access—more than 95% of its 181,500 acres is underwater.

The park's significance was first formally acknowledged in 1968 when, in an unprecedented move (and despite intense pressure from developers), President Lyndon B. Johnson signed a bill to conserve the barrier islands off South Florida's east coast as a national monument—a protected status just a rung below national park. After being twice enlarged, once in 1974 and again in 1980, the waters and land surrounding the northernmost coral reef in North America became a full-fledged national park—the largest of its kind in the country.

To be fully appreciated, Biscayne National Park should be thought of as more preserve than destination. Use your time here to explore underwater life, but also to relax. The park's small mainland mangrove shoreline and keys are best explored by boat. Its extensive reef system is renowned by divers and snorkelers worldwide.

The park consists of 44 islands, but only a few are open to visitors. The most popular is **Elliott Key,** which has campsites and a visitor center, plus freshwater showers (cold water only), restrooms, trails, and a buoyed swim area. It's about 9 miles from **Convoy Point,** the park's official headquarters on land. During Columbus Day weekend, there is a very popular regatta for which a lively crowd of party people gathers—sometimes in the nude—to celebrate the long weekend. If you'd prefer to rough it a little more, the 29-acre island known as **Boca Chita**

Visit the old lighthouse at the tip of Boca Chita Key.

Key, once an exclusive haven for yachters, has now become a popular spot for all manner of boaters. Visitors can camp and tour the island's restored historic buildings, including the county's second-largest lighthouse and a tiny chapel.

Essentials

GETTING THERE & ACCESS POINTS Convoy Point, the park's mainland entrance, is 9 miles east of Homestead. To reach the park from Miami, take the Florida Turnpike to the Tallahassee Road (SW 137th Ave.) exit. Turn left, then left again at North Canal Drive (SW 328th St.), and follow signs to the park. Another option is to rent a speedboat in Miami and cruise south for about 1½ hours. From U.S. 1, whether you're heading north or south, turn east at North Canal Drive (SW 328th St.). The entrance is approximately 9 miles away. The rest of the park is accessible only by boat.

Because most of Biscayne National Park is accessible only to boaters, mooring buoys abound, as it is illegal to anchor on coral. When no buoys are available, boaters must anchor on sand or on the docks surrounding the small harbor off Boca Chita. Boats can also dock here overnight for $20. Even the most experienced boaters should carry updated nautical charts of the area, which are available at Convoy Point's Dante Fascell Visitor Center. The waters are often murky, making the abundant reefs and sandbars difficult to detect—and there are more interesting ways to spend a day than waiting for the tide to rise. There's a boat launch at adjacent Homestead Bayfront Park and 66 slips on Elliott Key, available free on a first-come, first-served basis.

Round-trip transportation to and from the visitor center to Elliott Key costs $50 (plus tax) round-trip per person and takes about an hour. This is a convenient option, *available only if you have six people to fill a boat,* ensuring that you don't get lost on some deserted island by boating there yourself. If you don't have six people, you can charter the boat to and from the key for $300. Round-trip transportation to and from Boca Chita Key, however, is $50 per person regardless of how many people are going out. Call ✆ **305/230-1100** for the seasonal schedule.

A ranger-led tour is a great way to see Biscayne National Park.

VISITOR CENTERS & INFORMATION Open daily from 9am to 5pm, the **Dante Fascell Visitor Center** (often referred to by its older name, Convoy Point Visitor Center), 9700 SW 328th St., Homestead, FL 33033-5634, at the park's main entrance (✆ **305/230-7275;** fax 305/230-1190; www.nps.gov/bisc), is the natural starting point for any venture into the park without a boat. It provides comprehensive information about the park; on request, rangers will show you a short video on the park.

For information on transportation, glass-bottom boat tours, and snorkeling and scuba-diving expeditions, contact the park concessionaire, **Biscayne National Underwater Park, Inc.,** P.O. Box 1270, Homestead, FL 33030 (✆ **305/230-1100;** fax 305/230-1120; www.biscayneunderwater.com). It's open daily from 8:30am to 5pm.

ENTRANCE FEES & PERMITS Park entrance is free, but there is a $20 overnight docking fee at both Boca Chita Key Harbor and Elliott Key Harbor, which includes a campsite. Campsites are $15 for those staying without a boat. Group camping costs $30 a day and covers up to six tents and 25 people. See p. 268 for information on fishing permits. Backcountry camping permits are free and can be picked up from the Dante Fascell Visitor Center. For more information on fees and permits, call the park ranger at ✆ **305/230-1144.**

Seeing the Highlights

Because the park is primarily underwater, the only way to truly experience it is with snorkel or scuba gear. Beneath the surface of Biscayne National Park, the aquatic universe pulses with multicolored life: abounding bright parrotfish and angelfish, gently rocking sea fans, and coral labyrinths. (See the "Snorkeling & Scuba Diving" section, below, for more information.) Afterward, take a picnic out to Elliott Key and taste the crisp salt air blowing off the Atlantic. Or head to Boca Chita, an intriguing island that was once the private playground of wealthy yachters.

Sports & Outdoor Activities

CANOEING & KAYAKING Biscayne National Park affords excellent canoeing, both along the coast and across the open water to nearby mangroves and artificial islands dotting the longest uninterrupted shoreline in the state. Because tides can be strong, only experienced canoeists should attempt to paddle far from shore. If you do plan to go far, first obtain a tide table from the visitor center and paddle with the current. Free ranger-led canoe tours are scheduled from 9am to noon on the second and fourth Saturdays of the month between January 10 and April 24; phone for information. You can rent a canoe at the park's concession stand for $16 to $25 for the 90 minutes, and 50% of the initial cost per additional hour. Paddleboats are also available for $30 to $40 for the 90 minutes, and 50% of the initial cost per additional hour. Call ✆ **305/230-1100** for reservations, information, ranger tours, and boat rentals. You can also visit the website of the park's concession at www.biscayneunderwater.com.

FISHING Ocean fishing is excellent year-round at Biscayne National Park; many people cast their lines from the breakwater jetty at Convoy Point. A fishing license is required. (See p. 268 for more information.) Bait is not available in Biscayne National Park, but it is sold in adjacent Homestead Bayfront Park. Stone crabs and Florida lobsters can be found here, but you're allowed to catch these only on the ocean side when they're in season. There are strict limits on size, season, number, and method of take (including spearfishing) for both freshwater and saltwater fishing. The latest regulations are available at most marinas, bait-and-tackle shops, and the park's visitor centers; or you can contact the **Florida Fish and Wildlife Conservation Commission,** Bryant Building, 620 S. Meridian St., Tallahassee, FL 32399-1600 (✆ **850/488-0331**). For those looking to learn a little about fishing, Biscayne National Park offers a free Fisheries Awareness Class on the third Wednesday of every month (during even-numbered

At Convoy Point, you can walk along the boardwalk out to a jetty.

months, classes are in Spanish) from 6 to 9:30pm at Suniland Park, 12855 S. Dixie Hwy. (© **305/230-1144,** ext. 3089), in Miami.

HIKING & EXPLORING As the majority of this park is underwater, hiking is not the main attraction here, but there are some interesting sights and trails nonetheless. At Convoy Point, you can walk along the 370-foot boardwalk and along the half-mile jetty that serves as a breakwater for the park's harbor. From here, you can usually see brown pelicans, little blue herons, snowy egrets, and a few exotic fish.

Elliott Key is accessible only by boat, but once you're there, you have two good trail options. True to its name, the Loop Trail makes a 1.5-mile circle from the bayside visitor center, through a hardwood hammock and mangroves, to an elevated oceanside boardwalk. You'll likely see land crabs scurrying around the mangrove roots.

Reopened in 1998, Boca Chita Key was once a playground for wealthy tycoons, and it still has the peaceful beauty that attracted elite anglers from cold climates. Many of the historic buildings are still intact, including an ornamental lighthouse that was never put to use. Take advantage of the 3-hour tours, including a boat trip, that usually are led by a park ranger and available every Sunday in winter at 1:30pm. The price is $35 for adults, $25 for seniors, and $20 for children 11 and under. However, call in advance to see if the sea is calm enough for the trip—the boats won't run in rough waters. See "Glass-Bottom Boat Tours," below, for information about the daily 10am excursions.

SNORKELING & SCUBA DIVING The clear, warm waters of Biscayne National Park are packed with colorful tropical fish that swim in the offshore reefs. If you didn't bring your own gear, you can rent or buy snorkeling and scuba gear at the full-service dive shop at Convoy Point. Rates are in line with those at mainland dive shops.

The best way to see the park from underwater is to take a snorkeling or diving tour operated by **Biscayne National Underwater Park, Inc.** (© **305/230-1100;** www.biscayneunderwater.com). The Snorkel Mangrove Eco Adventure takes you inside the barrier islands of Elliott Key at 10am daily; it's $80 for adults, $40 for seniors and children. The other tour, the Snorkel Reef Adventure, takes you inside the Biscayne Bay and around the shoreline of the barrier islands and the finger channels at 10am and 1:30pm daily for $45 per person. There are also private two-tank dives for certified divers; the price is $99, including two tanks and weights. Make your reservations in advance. The shop is open daily from 9am to 5pm.

Before entering the water, be sure to apply waterproof sunblock—once you begin to explore, it's easy to lose track of time, and the Florida sun is brutal, even during winter.

SWIMMING You can swim off the protected beaches of Elliott Key, Boca Chita Key, and adjacent Homestead Bayfront Park, but none of these matches the width or softness of other South Florida beaches. Check the water conditions before heading into the sea: The strong currents that make this a popular destination for windsurfers and sailors can be dangerous, even for strong swimmers. Homestead Bayfront Park is really just a marina next to Biscayne National Park, but it does have a beach and picnic facilities, as well as fishing areas and a playground. It's located at Convoy Point, 9698 SW 328th St., Homestead (© **305/230-3034**).

Get a gander at the sights below the surface in a glass-bottom boat.

Glass-Bottom Boat Tours

If you prefer not to dive, the best way to see the sights is on a glass-bottom boat. **Biscayne National Underwater Park, Inc.** (*©* **305/230-1100;** www.biscayneunderwater.com), has daily trips to view some of the country's most beautiful reefs and tropical fish. Boats depart year-round from Convoy Point at 10am and last about 3 hours. At $45 for adults, $35 for seniors, and $30 for children 12 and under, the scenic, informative tours are pricey, but if you don't enjoy the trip, they promise a full refund. Boats carry fewer than 50 passengers; reservations are almost always necessary.

Where to Stay

Besides campsites, there are no facilities available for overnight guests to this watery park. Most noncamping visitors come for an afternoon, on their way to the Keys, and stay overnight in nearby Homestead (see p. 277 for listings). The good news is that Biscayne National Park boasts some of the state's most pristine **campsites.** Because they are inaccessible by motor vehicle, you'll be sure to avoid the mass of RVs so prevalent in many of the state's other campgrounds. The sites on Elliott Key and Boca Chita can be reached only by boat. If you don't have your own boat, call *©* **305/230-1100** to arrange a drop-off. Transportation to Elliott Key from the visitor center costs $50 (plus tax). They do not provide transportation to Boca Chita, so you'll have to rent a boat. Boca Chita has only saltwater toilets (no showers or sinks); Elliott Key has freshwater, cold-water showers and toilets, but is otherwise no less primitive. If you didn't pay for the overnight docking fee, campsites are $15.

With a backcountry permit, available free from the visitor center, you can pitch your tent somewhere even more private. Ask for a map and be sure to bring plenty of bug spray. Sites cost $15 a night for up to six persons staying in one or two tents. Backcountry camping is allowed only on Elliott Key, which is a very popular spot (accessible only by boat) for boaters and campers. It is approximately 9 miles from the Dante Fascell Visitor Center and offers hiking trails, fresh water, boat slips, showers, and restrooms. While there, don't miss the Old Road, a 7-mile tropical hammock trail that runs the length of Elliott Key. This trail is one of the few places left in the world to see the highly endangered Schaus swallowtail butterfly, recognizable by its black wings with diagonal yellow bands. These butterflies are usually out from late April to July.

THE GOLD COAST:

8

COAST:

HALLANDALE TO
THE PALM BEACHES

Named not for the sun-kissed skin of the area's residents, but for the gold salvaged from shipwrecks off its coastline, the Gold Coast embraces more than 60 miles of beautiful Atlantic shoreline—from the pristine sands of Palm Beach to the legendary strip of beaches in Fort Lauderdale.

If you haven't visited the cities along Florida's southeastern coast in the past few years, you'll be amazed at how much has changed. Miles of grassland and empty lots have been replaced with luxurious resorts and high-rise condominiums. Taking advantage of their proximity to Miami, the cities that make up the Gold Coast have attracted millions looking to escape crowded sidewalks, traffic, and the everyday routines of life.

Fortunately, amid all the building, much of the natural treasure of the Gold Coast remains. There are 300 miles of Intracoastal Waterway, Fort Lauderdale's Venetian-inspired canals, and the splendor of the Everglades just a few miles inland.

The most popular areas in the Gold Coast are Fort Lauderdale, Boca Raton, and Palm Beach. While Fort Lauderdale is a favored beachfront destination, Boca Raton and Palm Beach are better known for their country-club lifestyles and shopping. Farther north is the quietly popular Jupiter, best known for spring training at the Roger Dean Stadium. In between these better-traveled destinations are a few things worth stopping for. Driving north along the coastline is one of the best ways to fully appreciate what the Gold Coast is all about—it's a perspective you certainly won't find in a shopping mall.

Tourists come here by the droves, but they aren't the only people coming; thousands of transplants, fleeing the increasing population influx in Miami and the frigid winters up north, have made this area their home. As a result, there was a brief construction boom in the existing cities and even westward, into the swampy areas of the Everglades. The boom is at a standstill now, obviously, though you'll still see construction on some homes contracted before the recession, in Broward County, for instance. There has also been a great revitalization of several downtown areas, including Hollywood, Fort Lauderdale, and West Palm Beach. These once-desolate urban centers have been spruced up and now attract more young travelers and families than ever.

Unfortunately, like its neighbors to the south, the Gold Coast can be prohibitively hot and buggy in summer. The good news is that bargains are plentiful May through October, when many locals take advantage of package deals and uncrowded resorts.

For the purposes of this chapter, the Gold Coast will consist of the towns of Hallandale, Hollywood, Pompano Beach, Fort Lauderdale, Dania, Deerfield, Boca Raton, Delray Beach, Boynton Beach, and Palm Beach.

FACING PAGE: **On the Gold Coast, you'll find many marvelous mansions.**

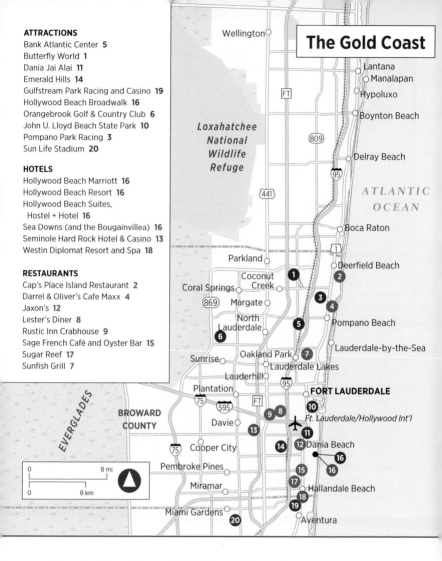

ATTRACTIONS
Bank Atlantic Center **5**
Butterfly World **1**
Dania Jai Alai **11**
Emerald Hills **14**
Gulfstream Park Racing and Casino **19**
Hollywood Beach Broadwalk **16**
Orangebrook Golf & Country Club **6**
John U. Lloyd Beach State Park **10**
Pompano Park Racing **3**
Sun Life Stadium **20**

HOTELS
Hollywood Beach Marriott **16**
Hollywood Beach Resort **16**
Hollywood Beach Suites,
  Hostel + Hotel **16**
Sea Downs (and the Bougainvillea) **16**
Seminole Hard Rock Hotel & Casino **13**
Westin Diplomat Resort and Spa **18**

RESTAURANTS
Cap's Place Island Restaurant **2**
Darrel & Oliver's Cafe Maxx **4**
Jaxon's **12**
Lester's Diner **8**
Rustic Inn Crabhouse **9**
Sage French Café and Oyster Bar **15**
Sugar Reef **17**
Sunfish Grill **7**

The Gold Coast

Exploring the Gold Coast by Car

Like most of South Florida, the Gold Coast consists of a mainland and adjacent barrier islands. You'll have to check maps to keep track of the many bridges that allow access to the islands where most tourist activity is centered. Interstate 95, which runs north-south, is the area's main highway. Farther west is the Florida Turnpike, a toll road that can be worth the expense, as the speed limit is higher and it's often less congested than I-95. Also on the mainland is U.S. 1, which generally runs parallel to I-95 (to the east) and is a narrower thoroughfare that is mostly crowded with strip malls and seedy hotels.

We recommend taking Fla. A1A, a slow oceanside road that connects the long, thin islands of Florida's east coast. Although the road is narrow, it is the most scenic and ushers you properly into the relaxed atmosphere of these resort towns.

FORT LAUDERDALE

Once famous (or infamous) for the annual mayhem it hosted during Spring Break, **Fort Lauderdale** now attracts a more affluent, better-behaved crowd. Its 300 miles of navigable waterways and innumerable canals permit thousands of residents to anchor boats in their backyards. On land, institutions like the Museum of Art Fort Lauderdale and Museum of Discovery & Science give the city cultural resonance.

Things to Do Spend at least an afternoon or evening cruising Fort Lauderdale's waterways by **water taxi.** Stroll the **Hollywood Beach Boardwalk** for a people-watching extravaganza. Head to **Fort Lauderdale Beach** to sun and swim or hike the nature trails at **Lloyd Beach.** Get in 18 holes at **Emerald Hills** or take a dive off **Pompano Beach.**

Shopping Bargain hunters scavenge the off-brand merchandise in the "fashion" stores along **Hallandale Beach Boulevard. Hollywood Boulevard** offers everything from Indonesian artifacts to used and rare books to handmade hats. Called the antiques capital of the South, **Dania** boasts more than 100 dealers. For upscale boutiques, browse the only beachfront mall, **The Gallery at Beach Place.**

Restaurants & Dining Fort Lauderdale can finally boast the presence of several fine restaurants, and ethnic options now join the legions of surf-and-turf joints in **Pompano Beach** and **downtown. Las Olas Boulevard** is packed with good eateries, from fusion and southwestern to Caribbean and seafood.

Nightlife & Entertainment Over the years, Fort Lauderdale has vastly improved the quality of its nightlife by welcoming earthy and sophisticated bars and clubs, especially downtown on **Las Olas Boulevard.** For a quieter night out, consider **Hollywood.**

Visiting Broward County

But even with the shine of Fort Lauderdale, the city's home county of Broward is less exposed and a lot calmer than highly hyped Miami-Dade County; according to some, it's much friendlier than the Magic City, too. In fact, a friendly rivalry exists between residents of both counties. Miamians consider themselves more sophisticated and cosmopolitan than their northern neighbors, who, in turn, dismiss the alleged sophistication as snobbery and actually prefer their own county's gentler pace.

With more than 300 miles of navigable waterways, Broward County attracts lots of marine traffic.

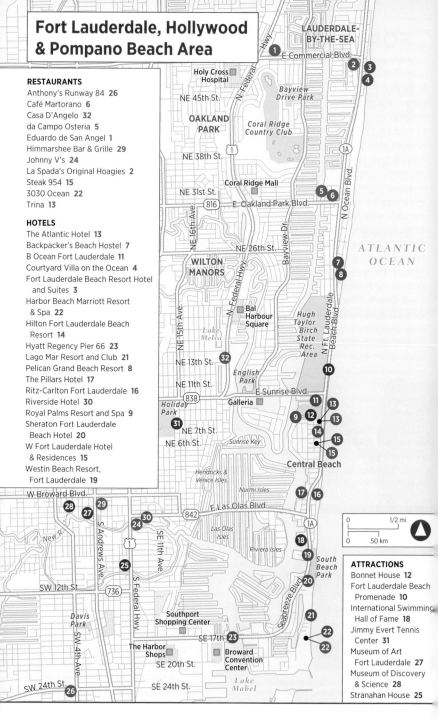

Fort Lauderdale, Hollywood & Pompano Beach Area

RESTAURANTS
Anthony's Runway 84 **26**
Café Martorano **6**
Casa D'Angelo **32**
da Campo Osteria **5**
Eduardo de San Angel **1**
Himmarshee Bar & Grille **29**
Johnny V's **24**
La Spada's Original Hoagies **2**
Steak 954 **15**
3030 Ocean **22**
Trina **13**

HOTELS
The Atlantic Hotel **13**
Backpacker's Beach Hostel **7**
B Ocean Fort Lauderdale **11**
Courtyard Villa on the Ocean **4**
Fort Lauderdale Beach Resort Hotel and Suites **3**
Harbor Beach Marriott Resort & Spa **22**
Hilton Fort Lauderdale Beach Resort **14**
Hyatt Regency Pier 66 **23**
Lago Mar Resort and Club **21**
Pelican Grand Beach Resort **8**
The Pillars Hotel **17**
Ritz-Carlton Fort Lauderdale **16**
Riverside Hotel **30**
Royal Palms Resort and Spa **9**
Sheraton Fort Lauderdale Beach Hotel **20**
W Fort Lauderdale Hotel & Residences **15**
Westin Beach Resort, Fort Lauderdale **19**

ATTRACTIONS
Bonnet House **12**
Fort Lauderdale Beach Promenade **10**
International Swimming Hall of Fame **18**
Jimmy Evert Tennis Center **31**
Museum of Art Fort Lauderdale **27**
Museum of Discovery & Science **28**
Stranahan House **25**

With more than 23 miles of beachfront and 300 miles of navigable waterways, Broward County is also a great outdoor destination. Scattered amid the shopping malls, condominiums, and tourist traps is a beautiful landscape lined with hundreds of parks, golf courses, tennis courts, and, of course, beaches.

The City of Hallandale Beach is a small, peaceful oceanfront town just north of Dade County's Aventura. Condos are the predominant landmarks in Hallandale, which is still pretty much a retirement community, although the revamped multimillion-dollar **Westin Diplomat Resort** (p. 300) is slowly trying to revitalize and liven up the area.

Just north of Hallandale is the more energetic, burgeoning city of Hollywood. Once a sleepy community wedged between Fort Lauderdale and Miami, Hollywood is now a bustling area of 1.5 million people with an array of ethnic and racial identities, from white and African American to Jamaican, Chinese, and Dominican. (*Money* magazine trumpeted the self-described "City of the Future" as having an ethnic makeup that mirrors what the U.S. will look like by the year 2022.) In 2004, the $300-million **Seminole Hard Rock Hotel & Casino** (p. 304) debuted, with a 500-room hotel, spa, and 130,000-square-foot casino.

This was exactly what the city needed to kick its renaissance up a notch. A spate of redevelopment has made the pedestrian-friendly center along Hollywood Boulevard and Harrison Street, east of Dixie Highway, a popular destination for travelers and locals alike. Some predict Hollywood will be South Florida's next big destination. While the prediction is dubious, Hollywood is awakening from its long slumber. Prices are a fraction of those at other tourist areas, and a quasi-bohemian vibe is apparent in the galleries, clubs, and restaurants that dot the new "strip." Its gritty undercurrent, however, prevents it from becoming too trendy.

Fort Lauderdale, with its well-known strip of beaches, restaurants, bars, and souvenir shops, has undergone a major transformation. Consider the recent hotel openings: Starwood's **W Fort Lauderdale** (p. 301), a 346-room boutique hotel, opened at the end of 2008, as did the swanky **Ritz-Carlton** (p. 300). And in 2009, Sir Richard Branson debuted his fleet of Virgin America jetliners in Florida with service from Fort Lauderdale, not Miami, to L.A. and San Francisco, with more destinations, but not Miami, to come. Walk into the W or the Ritz or check out the new B Ocean Fort Lauderdale Hotel, opened in early 2011, or the Sheraton Fort Lauderdale Beach Hotel, revamped to the tune of $30 million, and ask yourself, "What recession?"

Huge cruise ships also take advantage of Florida's deepest harbor, Port Everglades. The seaport is on the southeastern coast of the Florida peninsula, near the Fort Lauderdale Hollywood International Airport on the outskirts of Hollywood and Dania Beach. And with a $75-million cruise terminal expansion, Port Everglades is on its way to being the busiest cruise port in the world.

Essentials

GETTING THERE If you're driving from Miami, it's a straight shot north to Hollywood or Fort Lauderdale. Visitors on their way to or from Orlando should take the Florida Turnpike to exit 53, 54, 58, or 62, depending on the location of your accommodations. The **Fort Lauderdale–Hollywood International Airport** is easy to negotiate, and just 15 minutes from both of the downtown areas it services. However, its user-friendliness may not last much longer: Due to its popularity, the airport is *still* undergoing a $700-million runway expansion and renovation that often renders it just as maddening as any other major metropolitan airport. Completion is expected in 2015. In 2009, Sir Richard Branson introduced his **Virgin America** (✆ **877/FLY-VIRGIN** [359-8474]; www.virginamerica.com) service from the West Coast to FLL, offering two daily nonstop round-trips from San Francisco International Airport and two daily nonstop round-trips from Los Angeles International Airport. Some two dozen other airlines, large and small, serve the airport, with plenty of connections to and from the U.S., Canada and the Caribbean.

The airport has wireless Internet access and a fantastic car-rental center where 10 rental companies are under one roof—very convenient. Levels 1 through 4 are home to Alamo, Avis, Budget, Dollar, Enterprise, E-Z, Hertz, National, Royal, and Thrifty. Levels 5 to 9 provide 5,500 spaces for public parking.

Amtrak (✆ **800/USA-RAIL** [872-7245]; www.amtrak.com) stations are at 200 SW 21st Terrace (Broward Blvd. and I-95), Fort Lauderdale (✆ **954/587-6692**), and 3001 Hollywood Blvd. (northwest corner of Hollywood Blvd. and I-95), Hollywood (✆ **954/921-4517**).

VISITOR INFORMATION The **Greater Fort Lauderdale Convention & Visitors Bureau,** 1850 Eller Dr., Ste. 303 (off I-95 and I-595 E), Fort Lauderdale, FL 33316 (✆ **800/22-SUNNY** [227-8669] or 954/765-4466; fax 954/765-4467; www.sunny.org), is an excellent resource for area information in English, Spanish, and French. Call in advance to request a free comprehensive guide covering events, accommodations, and sightseeing in Broward County. New for iPhone users: **iVisitLauderdale,** a free app featuring all sorts of convenient travel tips, is available at **www.sunny.org/iPhone**.

The **Greater Hollywood Chamber of Commerce,** 330 N. Federal Hwy. (at U.S. 1 and Taylor St.), Hollywood, FL 33020 (✆ **800/231-5562** or 954/923-4000; fax 954/923-8737; www.hollywoodchamber.org), is open Monday through Friday from 9am to 5pm. Here you'll find the lowdown on all of Hollywood's events, attractions, restaurants, hotels, and tours.

Hitting the Beach

The southern part of the Gold Coast, Broward County, has the region's most popular and amenities-laden beaches, which stretch for more than 23 miles. Most do not charge for access and all are well maintained. Here's a selection of some of the county's best, from south to north:

Hollywood Beach, stretching from Sheridan Street to Georgia Street, is a major attraction in the city of Hollywood, a virtual carnival of young hipsters, big families, and sunburned French Canadians who dodge bicyclers and skaters along the rows of tacky souvenir shops, T-shirt shops, game rooms, snack bars, beer stands, hotels, and miniature-golf courses. **Hollywood Beach Broadwalk,** modeled after Atlantic City's legendary boardwalk, is the town's popular beach-front pedestrian thoroughfare, a cement promenade that's 30 feet wide and stretches along the shoreline for 3 miles. A recent makeover added, among other things, a concrete bike path, a crushed-shell jogging path, new trash receptacles, and the relocation of beach showers to each street end (all of are them are accessible for people with disabilities). Popular with runners, skaters, and cruisers, the Broadwalk is also renowned as a hangout for thousands of retirement-age snowbirds who get together for frequent dances and shows at a faded outdoor

Visitors can stroll and bike the Fort Lauderdale Beach Promenade.

amphitheater. Despite efforts to clear out a seedy element, the area remains a haven for drunks and scammers, so keep alert.

If you tire of the hectic diversity that defines Hollywood's Broadwalk, enjoy the natural beauty of the beach itself, which is wide and clean. There are lifeguards, showers, restroom facilities, and public areas for picnics and parties.

The **Fort Lauderdale Beach Promenade,** along the beach, underwent a $26-million renovation and looks fantastic. It's especially peaceful in the mornings, when there's just a smattering of joggers and walkers; but even at its most crowded on weekends, the expansive promenade provides room for everyone. Note, however, that the beach is hardly pristine; it is across the street from an uninterrupted stretch of hotels, bars, and retail outlets. Also nearby is a retail-and-dining megacomplex, the **Gallery at Beach Place** (p. 287), in the throes of its own renovation that will add newer, hipper stores, bars, and restaurants, on Fla. A1A, midway between Las Olas and Sunrise boulevards.

On the sand just across the road, most days you'll find hard-core volleyball players who always welcome anyone with a good spike, and you'll find an inviting ocean for swimmers of any level. The unusually clear waters are under the careful watch of some of Florida's best-looking lifeguards. Freshen up afterward in the clean showers and restrooms conveniently located along the strip. Pets have been banned from most of the beach in order to maintain the impressive cleanliness; a designated area for pets exists away from the main sunbathing areas.

Especially on weekends, parking at the oceanside meters is nearly impossible. Try biking, skating, or hitching a ride on the water taxi instead. The strip is located on Fla. A1A, between SE 17th Street and Sunrise Boulevard.

Dania Beach's **John U. Lloyd Beach State Park,** 6503 N. Ocean Dr., Dania (℃ **954/923-2833;** www.floridastateparks.org/lloydbeach), consists of

251 acres of barrier island, situated between the Atlantic Ocean and the Intracoastal Waterway, from Port Everglades on the north to Dania on the south. Its natural setting contrasts sharply with the urban development of Fort Lauderdale. Lloyd Beach, one of Broward County's most important nesting beaches for sea turtles, produces some 10,000 hatchlings a year. The park's broad, flat beach is popular for both swimming and sunning. Self-guided nature trails are great for those too restless to sunbathe. Admission to the park is $6 per vehicle with two to eight people, $4 for a single occupant, and $2 for pedestrians and bicyclists.

Outdoor Activities & Spectator Sports

BOATING Often called the "yachting capital of the world," Fort Lauderdale provides ample opportunity for visitors to get out on the water, either along the Intracoastal Waterway or on the open ocean. If your hotel doesn't rent boats, try **Aloha Watersports,** Marriott's Harbor Beach Resort, 3030 Holiday Dr., Fort Lauderdale (☏ **954/462-7245;** www.alohawatersports.com). It can outfit you with a variety of craft, including jet skis, WaveRunners, and catamarans. Rates start at $65 per half-hour for WaveRunners ($15 each additional rider; doubles and triples available), $70 to $125 for catamarans, $25 an hour for paddleboards or $100 for a 1-hour lesson, and $75 per person for a 15-minute parasailing ride. Aloha also offers a thrilling speedboat ride for $50 for a half-hour or $100 for a 90-minute excursion, a Surfing School ($50—though the waves are hardly rippin' here!), and a Coast Guard class (9am daily), through which adults can obtain their Florida Boaters License for $3. Treasure hunters can rent a metal detector here for $20 per hour.

FISHING The **IGFA** (International Game Fish Association) **World Fishing Center,** 300 Gulf Stream Way, Dania Beach (☏ **954/922-4212;** www.igfa.org), is an angler's paradise. One of the highlights of this museum, library, and park is the virtual reality fishing simulator that allows visitors to actually reel in their own computer-generated catch. Also included in the 3-acre park are displays of antique fishing gear, record catches, famous anglers, various vessels, and a wetlands lab. To get a list of local captains and guides, call **IGFA headquarters** (☏ **954/927-2628**) and ask for the librarian. Admission is $8 for adults, $5 for seniors and children 3 to 16. The museum and library are open daily from 10am to 6pm. On the grounds is also **Bass Pro Shops Outdoor World,** a huge retail complex set on a 3-acre lake.

GOLF More than 50 golf courses in all price ranges compete for players. Among the best is **Emerald Hills,** 4100 N. Hills Dr., Hollywood (☏ **954/**

961-4000; www.theclubatemeraldhills.com), just west of I-95 between Sterling Road and Sheridan Street. This beauty consistently lands on the "best of" lists of golf writers nationwide. The 18th hole, on a two-tier green, is the course's signature; it's surrounded by water and is more than a bit rough. Greens fees range from $54 during summer to $149 during winter. Rates depend on day and time and are cheaper during the brutally hot summers.

Another great course is the Howard Watson–designed 18-hole Pembroke Lakes course at the **Pembroke Lakes Golf Club,** 10500 Taft St., Pembroke Pines (✆ **954/431-4144;** www.pcmgolf.com), run by the same management company that runs the Miami Beach Golf Club; it was also the recipient of a $7-million renovation that saw the addition of Paspalum Supreme Grass. Best of all, greens fees are almost rock-bottom, ranging from $30 to $60 depending on the time and season.

The **Diplomat Golf Resort and Spa,** 501 Diplomat Pkwy., Hallandale Beach (✆ **954/602-6000;** www.diplomatgolfresortandspa. com), is across the Intracoastal from the Westin Diplomat Resort. It has fabulous golf facilities, with 8 acres of lakes and 7,000 yards of rolling fairways, plus a fantastic delivery service that brings lunch and drinks to your cart. You pay for the services, however, with greens fees of $139 to $179 during high season and $89 to $99 off season. Twilight fees at 2pm cost from $39 to $89.

For one of Broward's best municipal challenges, try the 18-holer at the **Orangebrook Golf & Country Club,** 400 Entrada Dr., Hollywood (✆ **954/967-GOLF** [4653]; www.orangebrook.com). Built in 1937, this is one of the state's oldest courses and one of the area's best bargains. Morning and noon rates are around $17 to $23. After 3pm, you can play for about $13, including a cart. Men must wear collared shirts to play here, and no spikes are allowed.

SCUBA DIVING In Broward County, the best dive wreck is the *Mercedes I,* a 197-foot freighter that washed up in the backyard of a Palm Beach socialite in 1984 and was sunk for divers the following year off Pompano Beach. The artificial reef, filled with colorful sponges, spiny lobsters, and barracudas, is 97 feet below the surface, a mile offshore between Oakland Park and Sunrise boulevards. Dozens of reputable dive shops line the beach. Ask at your hotel for a nearby recommendation, or contact **Neil Watson's Undersea Adventures,** 1525 S. Andrews Ave., Fort Lauderdale (✆ **954/462-3400;** www.nealwatson.com).

SPECTATOR SPORTS During the season, the Florida Marlins play (for now, until the zillion-dollar new baseball stadium built on the ruins of the Orange Bowl in Miami opens sometime in 2012) just south of Hallandale at **Sun Life Stadium,** near the Dade–Broward County line. Tickets go on sale in January for $4 to $100; call **Ticketmaster** (✆ **305/358-5885;** www. ticketmaster.com) to purchase them.

Pompano Park Racing, 1800 SW 3rd St., Pompano Beach (✆ **954/ 972-2000**), has parimutuel harness racing from October to early August. Admission is free to both grandstand and clubhouse.

Wrapped around an artificial lake, **Gulfstream Park Racing and Casino,** at U.S. 1 and Hallandale Beach Boulevard, Hallandale (✆ **954/454-7000;** www.gulfstreampark.com), is pretty and popular, especially after its multimillion-dollar renovation, with a spanking-new casino and restaurants. Large purses and important horse races are commonplace at this recently refurbished suburban course, and the track is often crowded. The most recent renovation has transformed it into a world-class, state-of-the-art facility with shops, bars, higher-end restaurants, 20 luxury suites, private accommodations for top players, and more. It hosts the Florida Derby each March. Call for schedules. Admission and parking are free. From January 3 to April 25, post times are 1:15pm Wednesday through Sunday, and the doors open at 11:30am.

Broward's only fronton, **Dania Jai Alai,** 301 E. Dania Beach Blvd., at Fla. A1A and U.S. 1 (©**954/920-1511**), is a great place to spend an afternoon or evening.

In the sport of ice hockey, the NHL's **Florida Panthers** (©**954/835-7000;** http://panthers.nhl.com) play in Sunrise at the **BankAtlantic Center,** 2555 NW 137th Way (©**954/835-8000**). Tickets range from $15 to $100. Call for directions and ticket information.

TENNIS There are hundreds of courts in Broward County, and plenty are accessible to the public. Many are at resorts and hotels. If yours has none, try the **Jimmy Evert Tennis Center,** 701 NE 12th Ave. (off Sunrise Blvd.), Fort Lauderdale (©**954/828-5378**), famous as the spot where Chris Evert trained. There are 18 lighted clay courts and 3 hard courts here. Nonresidents of Fort Lauderdale pay $9 per hour before 5pm and $11 after. Or, play all day for $18.

Seeing the Sights

Billie Swamp Safari ★ Billie Swamp Safari is an up-close-and-personal view of the Seminole Indians' 2,200-acre Big Cypress Reservation. There are daily tours into reservation wetlands, hardwood hammocks, and areas where wildlife (seemingly strategically placed deer, water buffalo, bison, wild hogs, ornery ostriches, rare birds, and alligators) reside. Tours are provided aboard "swamp buggies," customized motorized vehicles designed to provide visitors with an elevated view of the frontier while they comfortably ride through the wetlands and cypress heads. The more adventurous may want to take a fast-moving airboat ride or trek a nature trail. Airboat rides run about 20 minutes, while swamp-buggy tours last about an hour. A stop at an alligator farm reeks of Disney, but the kids won't care. You can stay overnight in a native Tiki hut for $35 per night if you're really looking to immerse yourself in the culture.

Big Cypress Seminole Reservation, 1½-hr. drive west of Fort Lauderdale. ©**800/949-6101.** www.semtribe.com/safari. Free admission. Swamp-buggy tours $25 adults, $23 seniors 62 and over, $15 children 4–12. Airboat tours $15 for all ages. Daily 8:30am–6pm. Airboats depart every 30 min. 9:30am–4:30pm. Swamp-buggy tours leave on the hour 10am–5pm. Reptile and Critter Shows daily. Day and overnight packages available.

Butterfly World ★ 🐛 After moving to Florida from Illinois in 1968, electrical engineer Ronald Boender decided to actively pursue his passion, raising local butterflies at his home and recording data on each. After realizing there was a need for farmed butterflies, Boender set up a company in 1984 and went one step further, building this butterfly house along with the founder of the world-renowned London Butterfly House across the pond. Enter Butterfly World, renowned globally for its butterfly farm and research facility as well as its 10 acres of aviaries and botanical gardens. Kids especially love the "bug museum," which features some of the insect world's biggest celebrities—all of which kids are able

ONE IF BY LAND, taxi IF BY SEA

Plan to spend at least an afternoon or evening cruising Fort Lauderdale's 300 miles of waterways the only way you can: by boat. The **Water Bus of Fort Lauderdale** (📞 **954/467-6677;** www.watertaxi.com) is one of the greatest innovations for water lovers since those cool Velcro sandals. A trusty fleet of older port boats serves the dual purpose of transporting and entertaining visitors as they cruise through the "Venice of America." Because of its popularity, the water taxi fleet has welcomed several sleek, 70-passenger "water buses" (featuring indoor and outdoor seating with an atrium-like roof).

Taxis operate on demand and also along a fairly regular route, carrying up to 48 passengers to 20 stops. If you're staying at a hotel on the route, you can be picked up there, usually within 15 minutes of calling, and then be shuttled to any of the dozens of restaurants, bars, and attractions on or near the waterfront. If you aren't sure where you want to go, ask one of the personable captains, who can point out historic and fun spots along the way.

Starting daily at 8am, boats run until midnight 7 days a week, depending on the weather. Check the website for exact times of pickup. The cost is $15 for an all-day pass with unlimited stops on and off, $11 for seniors and children 4 to 11, and $7 if you board after 7pm. If you want to go to South Beach (Fri–Tues, Dec–Apr), it's $33 adults, $30 seniors, and $16 for children 4 to 11. Tickets are available onboard; no credit cards are accepted.

to touch, if they dare, with the help of an expert. There's lots to see here in terms of flitting, fluttery things, so set aside at least 2 hours to, uh, flit around yourself.
Tradewinds Park, 3600 W. Sample Rd., Coconut Creek. 📞 **954/977-4400.** www.butterflyworld. com. Admission $25 adults and seniors, $20 children 3–11. Mon–Sat 9am–5pm; Sun 11am–5pm.

Bonnet House ★★★ This historic 35-acre plantation home and estate, accessible by guided tour only, will provide you with a fantastic glimpse of Old Florida. Built in 1921, the sprawling two-story waterfront home (surrounded by formal tropical gardens) is really the backdrop of a love story, which the very chatty volunteer guides will share with you if you ask. Some have actually lunched with the former resident of the house, the late Evelyn Bartlett, wife of world-acclaimed artist Frederic Clay Bartlett. The worthwhile 1¼-hour tour introduces you to quirky people, whimsical artwork, lush grounds, and interesting design.
900 N. Birch Rd. (1 block west of the ocean, south of Sunrise Blvd.), Fort Lauderdale. 📞 **954/563-5393.** www.bonnethouse.org. Admission $20 adults, $18 seniors, $16 children 6 to 12, free for children 5 and under. Call for hours and tour times.

Hillsboro Inlet Lighthouse ★ Completed in 1907, the Hillsboro Inlet Lighthouse, which rises 136 feet above water and marks the northern end of the Florida Reef, isn't just any lighthouse. It contains a 5,500,000-candlepower light and is the most powerful light on the East Coast of the United States. And there's more history. This lighthouse was also made famous thanks to one of the "barefoot mailmen," carriers of the first U.S. mail route between Palm Beach and Miami. Because there was no paved road on that route, the mailmen had to get through by boat and by walking the sand along the beach. James Hamilton was the most famous of these after disappearing delivering mail on the route just after October 10, 1887, presumably the victim of drowning or an encounter with a hungry alligator while trying to swim across the Hillsboro inlet to retrieve his boat from the far side. His body was never recovered. A big trial ensued and his death still remains a mystery today. An original stone statue called *The Barefoot Mailman* by Frank Varga is permanently displayed on the shores of the Hillsboro inlet next to the Hillsboro lighthouse with an inscription dedicated to Hamilton. A fascinating story, it can be told in much more detail with a tour by the Hillsboro Lighthouse Preservation Society, which is given once every other month, usually on Saturdays. If the tour isn't available, go see it for yourself.

Hillsboro Inlet, off A1A, Pompano Beach. © **954/942-2102.** www.hillsborolighthouse.org. Tours $15. Call for hours and tour times. Take I-95 to Atlantic Blvd. Go east across the Intracoastal and left at A1A for 2 miles to Pompano Beach City Park. Stop at the SE corner of the Hillsboro Inlet bridge where there is an excellent view of the Hillsboro Lighthouse. Tours meet on the dock across from Riverside Dr. To get there, go east, cross the Intracoastal and make an immediate left on North Riverside Dr. Go 1 block to the parking lot. Park and head west to the dock across Riverside Dr.

International Swimming Hall of Fame (ISHOF) ★★★ Any aspiring Michael Phelps (who may or may not donate one of his million gold medals to the museum) or those who appreciate the sport will love this splashy homage to the best backstrokers, front crawlers, and divers in the world. The museum houses the world's largest collection of aquatic memorabilia and is the single largest source of aquatic books, manuscripts, and literature. Among the highlights are Johnny Weissmuller's Olympic medals, Mark Spitz's starting block used to win six of his seven 1972 Olympic gold medals, and more than 60 Olympic, national, and club uniforms, warm-ups, and swimsuits. For those who don't mind getting their feet wet, the ISHOF Aquatic Complex is the only one of its kind in the world with two 50m pools, a diving well, and a swimming flume.

1 Hall of Fame Dr., Fort Lauderdale. © **954/462-6536.** www.ishof.org. Admission $8 adults, $6 seniors, $4 children 12 and over. Call for hours and tour times.

Museum of Art Fort Lauderdale ★ 🎨 A fantastic modern-art facility, the Museum of Art Fort Lauderdale has permanent collections, including those from William Glackens; the CoBrA Movement in Copenhagen, Brussels, and Amsterdam, with more than 200 paintings; 50 sculptures; 1,200 works on paper from 1948 to 1951, including the largest repository of Asger Jorn graphics outside the Silkeborg Kunstmuseum in Denmark; stunning Picasso ceramics; and contemporary works from more than 90 Cuban artists in exile around the world. Traveling exhibits and continuing art classes make the museum a great place to spend a rainy day, or night—on Thursdays, the cafe and wine bar have happy hour from 5 to 7pm. On the third Thursday of every month, the museum offers free admission from 5 to 8pm.

1 E. Las Olas Blvd., Fort Lauderdale. © **954/525-5500.** www.moafl.org. Admission $10 adults, $7 seniors and children 6-17, free for children 5 and under. Oct–May Fri–Wed 11am–5pm, Thurs 11am–8pm; June–Sept Mon and Wed–Sun 11am–5pm.

Museum of Discovery & Science ★★ 🎁 This museum's high-tech, interactive approach to education proves that science can equal fun. Adults won't feel as if they're in a kiddie museum, either. Kids ages 7 and under enjoy navigating their way through the excellent explorations in the Discovery Center. Florida Ecoscapes is particularly interesting, with a living coral reef, bees, bats, frogs, turtles, and alligators. Most weekend nights, you'll find a diverse crowd ranging from hip high-school kids to 30-somethings enjoying a rock film in the IMAX theater, which also shows short science-related films daily. Out front in the atrium, see the 52-foot-tall *Great Gravity Clock,* the largest kinetic-energy sculpture in the state.

401 SW 2nd St., Fort Lauderdale. ℂ **954/467-6637.** www.mods.org. Admission (includes IMAX film) $16 adults, $15 seniors, $12 children 2–12; without IMAX film $11 adults, $10 seniors, $9 children 2–12. Mon–Sat 10am–5pm; Sun noon–6pm. Movie theater closes later. From I-95, exit on Broward Blvd. E. Continue to SW 5th Ave., turn right; garage is on the right.

Stranahan House ★★★ In a town where nothing appears to date back earlier than 1940, visitors may want to take a minute to see Fort Lauderdale's very oldest standing structure and a prime example of classic "Florida Frontier" architecture. Built in 1901 by the "father of Fort Lauderdale," Frank Stranahan, this house once served as a trading post for Seminole trappers who came here to sell pelts. It's been a post office, town hall, and general store, and now serves as a worthwhile little museum of South Florida pioneer life, containing turn-of-the-20th-century furnishings and historical photos of the area. It is also the site of occasional concerts and social functions; call for details. *Note:* Self-guided tours are not allowed, so make sure to arrive on time for the 1, 2, or 3pm tours or else you're shut out.

335 SE 6th Ave. (Las Olas Blvd. at the New River Tunnel), Fort Lauderdale. ℂ **954/524-4736.** www.stranahanhouse.org. Admission $12 adults, $11 seniors, $7 students and children. Daily

Tour and explore the fascinating grounds and furnishings of Bonnet House.

The Great Gravity Clock dominates the atrium of the Museum of Discovery & Science.

1–3pm. Tours are on the hour; last tour at 3pm. Accessible by water taxi.

Shopping

It's all about malls in Broward County and, while most of the best shopping is within Fort Lauderdale proper, other areas are also worth browsing.

Malls here include the upscale **Galleria,** at Sunrise Boulevard near the Fort Lauderdale Beach, and **Broward Mall,** west of I-95 on Broward Boulevard, in Plantation.

If you're looking for unusual boutiques, especially art galleries, head to quaint **Las Olas Boulevard ★**, located west of A1A and a block east of Federal Highway/U.S. 1, off SE 8th Street, where there are hundreds of shops with alluring window decorations (like kitchen utensils posing as modern-art sculptures) and intriguing merchandise, such as mural-size oil paintings. For bargains, there's no better place than **Sawgrass Mills,** 12801 W. Sunrise Blvd. (✆ **954/846-0179**), featuring more

Explore the galleries along Las Olas Boulevard for the perfect *objet.*

than 350 name-brand outlets such as Off Fifth and Nordstrom Rack. Nearby is Florida's first-ever **Ikea,** 151 NW 136th Ave. (✆ **954/838-9292;** www.ikea.com), purveyor of all things sleek and Swedish—from furniture to meatballs.

Where to Stay

The Fort Lauderdale beach has a hotel or motel on nearly every block, ranging from run-down to luxurious. **Fort Lauderdale Beach Resort Hotel and Suites,** 4221 N. Ocean Blvd. (www.ftlbeachresort.com; ✆ **800/329-7466** or 954/563-2521), has clean, oceanside rooms starting at about $65.

The landmark Sheraton Yankee Clipper received a $30-million makeover and debuted in 2010 as the **Sheraton Fort Lauderdale Beach Hotel** (see later); the renovation is highlighted by revamped guest rooms, new fitness center, kids' club, restaurants, and a bar. And first in 2011: **B Ocean Fort Lauderdale,** 999 N. Ft. Lauderdale Beach Blvd. (www.bhotelsandresorts.com; ✆ **888/66-BHOTEL** [662-4683]), the flagship property of the W-like B Hotels & Resorts rising from the ashes of an old Holiday Inn and featuring 240 high-tech, chic rooms with white, leather-faced cabinetry, and all with ocean views. A spa, an infinity pool, a lounge, a bistro, and a sushi restaurant round out the amenities. Rates range from $189 to $499 in winter and start at $129 in summer.

In Hollywood, where prices are generally cheaper, the **Hollywood Beach Resort,** 101 N. Ocean Dr. (www.hollywoodbeach-resort.com; ✆ **954/921-0990**), operates a full-service hotel right on the ocean. With prices starting at around $149 in season and discounts for AAA members, it's a great deal. **Hollywood Beach Marriott,** 2501 N. Ocean Dr. (I-95 to Sheridan St. E. to A1A S.; www.marriott.com; ✆ **866/306-5453** or 954/924-2202), is a recently renovated beach resort with a fantastic location right on the Hollywood Beach Broadwalk. Breaking ground in late 2011 with an anticipated late 2012 debut: **Margaritaville Resort Hotel,** Jimmy Buffett's 17-story, $130-million hotel and entertainment complex.

For rentals for a few weeks or months, check the annual list of small lodgings compiled by the **Greater Fort Lauderdale Convention & Visitors Bureau** (✆ **954/765-4466**); they're especially helpful if you're looking for privately owned, charming, affordable lodgings.

VERY EXPENSIVE

The Atlantic Hotel ★★★ Overlooking 23 miles of white sand, the Atlantic is a 16-story study in minimal modernity—soothing colors and comfortable, stylish decor. Besides the usual high-tech amenities found in all rooms of this category—flatscreen TVs, Wi-Fi—each room has a fully equipped granite kitchen or kitchenette. The Atlantic also has a fantastic award-winning restaurant, **Trina** (p. 309), and a spectacular 10,000-square-foot spa. On the hotel's fifth-floor ocean terrace you'll find a heated pool, casual bar, and restaurant. It's an ideal spot for a frozen drink paired with a sensational view. For those looking to stay here in rock-star style, the Penthouse Collection includes two- and three-bedroom suites, ranging from 3,500- to 4,000-plus square feet, some with private elevators. Service is usually stellar, though we've had some complaints of a bit of attitude.

601 N. Fort Lauderdale Beach Blvd., Fort Lauderdale, FL 33304. www.atlantichotelfl.com. ✆ **866/318-1101** or 954/567-8020. Fax 954/567-8040. 124 units. Winter $299–$619 double, $399–$999 suite; off season $199–$329 double, $499 suite. AE, DC, DISC, MC, V. Valet parking $28. **Amenities:** 2 restaurants; bar; bike rentals; concierge; outdoor heated pool; room service; spa; watersports equipment/rentals; free Wi-Fi in lobby. *In room:* A/C, TV, hair dryer, minibar, Wi-Fi.

Harbor Beach Marriott Resort & Spa ★★ 👶 Harbor Beach is loaded with the same amenities as Pier 66 (below), but has a more secluded setting on 16 oceanfront acres just south of Fort Lauderdale's "strip." Everything in this place is huge—from the quarter-mile of private beach to the 8,000-square-foot pool and the $8-million, 22,000-square-foot European spa. Accommodations feature pillow-top bedding, marble, crown molding, and bathrooms with granite vanities, marble flooring, designer lighting, and wraparound mirrors. Most units open onto private balconies overlooking the pool, the city, the ocean, or the Intracoastal Waterway. The hotel's **3030 Ocean** is an excellent seafood restaurant and raw bar helmed by Executive Chef Dean James Max; the Riva, a Mediterranean-style oceanfront eatery, is also top-notch. Return guests include many convention groups and families who enjoy the space and great location. The hotel's Surf Club ($45 half-day; $80 full day) includes lunch, and provides arts and crafts, watersports, and games to keep the young 'uns happily occupied. Speaking of watersports, this hotel has the most comprehensive list, from surfing to parasailing.

3030 Holiday Dr., Fort Lauderdale, FL 33316. www.marriottharborbeach.com. ✆ **800/222-6543** or 954/525-4000. Fax 954/766-6152. 650 units. Winter $345–$659 double; off season $298–$401 double; year-round from $630 suite. AE, DC, DISC, MC, V. Valet parking $27; self-parking $22. From I-95, exit on I-595 E. to U.S. 1 N.; proceed to SE 17th St.; make a right and go over the Intracoastal Bridge past 3 traffic lights to Holiday Dr.; turn right. **Amenities:** 4 restaurants; 3 bars; babysitting can be arranged; bike rentals; children's programs; concierge; health club; outdoor heated pool; room service; European-style spa; 4 clay tennis courts; extensive watersports equipment/rentals. *In room:* A/C, TV, hair dryer, high-speed Internet, minibar.

Hyatt Regency Pier 66 ★★ Set on 22 tropical acres on the Intracoastal Waterway, this landmark hotel is best known for its world-class marina and a rooftop ballroom and brunch spot that spins a complete 360 degrees every 66 minutes. If you experience vertigo after sitting in the revolving ballroom, an invigorating treatment at the hotel's exquisite **Spa 66** will help relocate your sense of balance. Equally invigorating are the recreational amenities, which include a three-pool complex with a 40-person hydrotherapy pool, tennis courts, and an aquatic center with watersports. **Grille 66 & Bar,** a classy, upscale steakhouse, is a welcome addition. A $40-million refurbishment has transformed the lobby, lawn, and remaining guest rooms with a retro modern decor. New lanai guest rooms have cherrywood furnishings and bathrooms with marble floors and granite vanities. All units have flatscreen televisions, wireless Internet access, and balconies with views of the Intracoastal Waterway and the hotel's lushly landscaped gardens.

2301 SE 17th St. Causeway, Fort Lauderdale, FL 33316. www.pier66.com. ✆ **800/233-1234** or 954/525-6666. Fax 954/728-3541. 384 units. Winter $249–$309 double; off season $119–$200 double; year-round from $899 suite. Rates are cheaper on the hotel's website. AE, DC, DISC, MC, V. Valet parking $23; self-parking $19. **Amenities:** 5 restaurants; 3 bars; bike rentals; concierge; 3 pools; room service; spa; 2 lighted clay Har-Tru tennis courts; watersports equipment/rentals. *In room:* A/C, TV, hair dryer, Internet access.

The Ritz-Carlton Fort Lauderdale ★★★ The first and only AAA Five Diamond hotel in Fort Lauderdale, this $160-million property formerly run by St. Regis has elevated the strip to an entirely new level of luxury. The 192 rooms, including 26 "residential suites," all feature views of the Atlantic or the Intracoastal Waterway, and have Wi-Fi Internet access, a state-of-the-art DVD theater/entertainment system with a 32-inch LCD panel TV, a 13-inch LCD panel TV in each bathroom, Italian linens, designer bath amenities, and a refrigerated minicellar of refreshments. We particularly like Chef Christian Claire's stellar Italian grill, **Via Luna,** and the 5,000-bottle wine vault with nightly wine tastings upon request. The oceanfront pool is nice, yet understated, with a VIP cabana level; the luxury spa, with its 99% organic treatment menu, is sublime. Some people have complained that service is snooty, while others deem it refined and top-notch. What's universal is that this is a welcome departure from the norm for the area. *Reservation tip:* All rooms ending in "10" offer floor-to-ceiling windows and spectacular views!

1 N. Fort Lauderdale Beach Blvd., Fort Lauderdale, FL 33316. www.ritzcarlton.com. ✆ **800/241-3333** or 954/465-2300. Fax 954/465-2340. 192 units. Winter from $399 double; off season from $209 double; year-round from $600 suite. AE, DC, DISC, MC, V. Valet parking $30; no self-parking. From I-95, exit on I-595 E. to U.S. 1 N.; proceed to SE 17th St.; make a right and go over the Intracoastal Bridge past 6 traffic lights to Castillo St.; turn left. **Amenities:** 2 restaurants; 2 bars; concierge; fitness center; outdoor heated pool; room service; European-style spa. *In room:* A/C, TV/DVD, hair dryer, minibar, Wi-Fi.

Westin Diplomat Resort & Spa ★★ The Diplomat is a 1,058-room, full-service beach resort—the only one of its kind in the somewhat desolate, residential area—loaded with amenities. The main building is a 39-story oceanfront tower. A gorgeous bridged, glass-bottom pool with waterfalls, private cabanas, and a slew of watersports adds a tropical touch. Rooms are a cross between those in a subtle boutique hotel and in an Art Deco throwback, with dark woods, hand-cut marble, and the 10-layer Heavenly Bed, a Westin trademark, with custom-designed pillow-top mattresses and very cushy down blankets. Dining options are aplenty, from the fine-dining steakhouse to several more-casual places. **Diplomat Landing**, the hotel's shopping-and-entertainment complex across the street, features shops and a waterfront sports bar. The resort's golf resort and spa is located across the Intracoastal, featuring 60 luxurious guest rooms, yacht slips, a 155-acre golf course, and a world-class spa and tennis club.

3555 S. Ocean Dr. (A1A), Hollywood, FL 33019. www.diplomatresort.com. ℂ **888/627-9057** or 954/602-6000. Fax 954/602-7000. 998 units. Winter $305–$515 double, $675–$875 suite; off season $220–$340 double, $475–$675 suite. AE, DC, DISC, MC, V. Valet parking $22. **Amenities:** 9 restaurants; 3 lounges; golf course; health club; 2 pools; room service; spa; 10 clay tennis courts; watersports equipment/rentals. *In room:* A/C, TV, fax, hair dryer, high-speed Internet access, minibar.

W Fort Lauderdale ★★★ Wow. Until this W (and the one on South Beach, frankly) opened, we thought that if you'd seen one W hotel you'd seen 'em all. Not anymore. Designed to resemble a sailboat, this W comprises two 24-story towers of hotel rooms and condos. Inspired by the sand and sea, the hotel's *pièce de résistance* is the stunning oceanfront pool deck with a glass-enclosed stairway that provides splashy, up-close-and-personal views of the pool from the lobby. Rooms exude a beach-house vibe with neutral colors and gorgeous bathrooms that open into the main living area. There's also a Bliss Spa, and hipster-heavy Whiskey Blue bar/lounge. Unique to this W is a restaurant by Stephen Starr, whose empire includes Buddakan and Morimoto in Philadelphia and New York City, in the form of his latest concept, **Steak 954,** a sexy, see-and-be-sceney steakhouse. *Note:* If the W is too sceney for you, consider its more laid-back sister hotel up the block, the **Westin Beach Resort, Fort Lauderdale,** 321 N. Fort Lauderdale Beach Blvd. (ℂ **954/467-1111;** www.starwoodhotels. com), the recipient of a multimillion-dollar face-lift, featuring 433 rooms and an 8,100-square-foot Heavenly Spa.

401 N. Fort Lauderdale Beach Blvd., Fort Lauderdale, FL 33304. www.wfortlauderdalehotel.com. ℂ **866/837-4203** or 954/414-8200. Fax 954/414-8250. 517 units. Winter $305–$515 double, $675–$875 suite; off season $220–$340 double, $475–$675 suite. AE, DC, DISC, MC, V. Valet parking $30. **Amenities:** 2 restaurants; 2 lounges; fitness center; 2 pools; room service; spa. *In room:* A/C, TV, hair dryer, minibar, Wi-Fi.

EXPENSIVE

Lago Mar Resort and Club ★★ 🎁 A charming lobby with a rock fireplace and saltwater aquarium sets the tone of this utterly inviting resort, a casually elegant piece of Old Florida that occupies its own, 10-acre lush little island between Lake Mayan and the Atlantic. Guests have access to the broadest and best strip of 500 feet of private beach in the entire city, not to mention two wonderful pools—one large enough for lap swimming and the other a 9,000-square-foot swimming pool lagoon edged with tropical plants and bougainvillea. Lago Mar is very family oriented, with many facilities and supervised activities for children. Service is spectacular. The plush rooms and suites have Mediterranean or Key West influences. A full-service spa offers a wide array of treatments, while the 1,000-square-foot exercise facility may come in handy after you indulge in the hotel's modern American bistro restaurant, **Acquario,** which is worth a visit even if you don't stay here. The six-story wing of one- and two-bedroom oceanfront suites with individual balconies and larger luxurious bathrooms includes a deck of native tropical landscaping and a 5,000-square-foot saltwater lagoon.

1700 S. Ocean Lane, Fort Lauderdale, FL 33316. www.lagomar.com. © **800/524-6627** or 954/523-6511. Fax 954/524-6627. 204 units. Winter from $315; off season from $155. AE, DC, MC, V. Free valet parking. From Federal Hwy. (U.S. 1), turn east onto SE 17th St. Causeway; turn right onto Mayan Dr.; turn right again onto S. Ocean Dr.; turn left onto Grace Dr.; then turn left again onto S. Ocean Lane to the hotel. **Amenities:** 4 restaurants; bar; wine room; children's programs during holiday periods; concierge; exercise room; mini-golf course; outdoor pool and lagoon; room service; 4 tennis courts; watersports equipment/rentals. *In room:* A/C, TV, fridge, hair dryer, complimentary high-speed Internet.

The Pillars Hotel ★ 🏨 One of Fort Lauderdale's best-kept secrets, the Pillars transports you from the neon-hued flash and splash of Fort Lauderdale's strip and takes you to a two-story British colonial, Caribbean-style retreat tucked away on the bustling Intracoastal Waterway. Because it has just 22 rooms, you'll feel as if you have the grand house all to yourself—albeit a house with white-tablecloth room service, an Edenistic courtyard with a free-form pool, lush landscaping, access to a water taxi, and a private chef. Rooms are luxurious and loaded with amenities such as flatscreen TVs, DVD players, private-label bath products, ultraplush bedding, and, if you're so inclined, a private masseuse to iron out your personal kinks. The hotel's restaurant, the **Secret Garden,** open only to hotel guests and members of its Secret Garden Society, provides gourmet dinner served under the stars and overlooking the Intracoastal. A library area (with more than 500 books) is at your disposal, as is pretty much anything else you request here.

111 N. Birch Rd., Fort Lauderdale, FL 33304. www.pillarshotel.com. © **954/467-9639.** Fax 954/763-2845. 22 units. Winter $285–$355 double, $399–$575 suite; off season $195–$235 double, $275–$469 suite. AE, DC, DISC, MC, V. Free off-street parking. **Amenities:** Restaurant; concierge; pool; room service; free Wi-Fi. *In room:* A/C, TV/DVD, hair dryer, high-speed Internet, minibar.

Riverside Hotel ★★ A touch of New Orleans hits Fort Lauderdale's popular Las Olas Boulevard in the form of this charming, six-story 1936 hotel. There's no beach here, but the hotel is set on the sleepy and scenic New River, capturing the essence of that ever-elusive Old Florida. Guest rooms, outfitted in Mexican tile and wicker furnishings, are spacious and well maintained. Such details as intricately tiled bathrooms and old-style furniture enhance the charm of the otherwise stark building. The best units face the river, but it's hard to see the water past the parking lot and trees. Twelve rooms offer king-size beds with mirrored canopies and flowing drapes. There are also seven elegantly decorated suites with wet bars and French doors that lead to private balconies. The hotel has two restaurants worth trying: **Indigo,** a fantastic seafood spot, and the **Grill Room,** for old-world elegance.

620 E. Las Olas Blvd., Fort Lauderdale, FL 33301. www.riversidehotel.com. © **800/325-3280** or 954/467-0671. Fax 954/462-2148. 217 units. Winter $229–$279 suite; off season $139–$185 suite. Online discounts available. Special packages available. AE, DC, MC, V. Valet

---

The Luxe Life

Catering to the growing crowds of gay tourists to the Fort Lauderdale area is the Royal Palms Resort and Spa, 717 Breakers Ave. (www.royalpalms.com; © **800/237-7256**), a circa-1991 gay guesthouse that was reopened in January 2011 after an $8-million renovation and expansion. Owner Richard Gray added 50 rooms to the existing 12-room guesthouse and noted, "We definitely want to take the gay guesthouse theme to a new level, giving it a more European feel." Rates start at $159.

parking $8–$10. From I-95, exit onto Broward Blvd.; turn right onto Federal Hwy. (U.S. 1); turn left onto Las Olas Blvd. **Amenities:** 2 restaurants; concierge; outdoor pool; limited room service. *In room:* A/C, TV, fridge, hair dryer, high-speed Internet access, minibar.

MODERATE

Courtyard Villa on the Ocean ★ Nestled between a bunch of larger hotels, this small historic hotel is a romantic getaway right on the beach. Courtyard Villa offers spacious oceanfront efficiencies with private balconies; larger suites overlook the pool. Accommodations are plush, with chenille bedspreads and carved four-poster beds; fully equipped kitchenettes are an added convenience. The tiled bathrooms have strong, hot showers to wash off the beach sand. Room nos. 7 and 8 are especially nice, with French doors that open to a private balcony overlooking the ocean. Relax in the hotel's unique heated pool/spa or on the second-floor sun deck. You can also swim from the beach to a living reef just 50 feet offshore. Located on the same street is Courtyard Villa's sister property, **Buena Vista Hotel and Beach Club,** 4225 El Mar Dr. (© **800/291-3560**), where in-season rates range from $179 to $279 and off-season rates are $99 to $169.

4312 El Mar Dr., Lauderdale-by-the-Sea, FL 33308. www.buenavistacorp.com. © **800/291-3560** or 954/776-1164. Fax 954/491-0768. 10 units. Winter $159–$359 unit; off season $109–$225. Rates include full breakfast. AE, MC, V. Pets less than 35 lb. accepted with $200 deposit; must be caged while outside; no pit bulls, Dobermans, or Rottweilers. **Amenities:** Free use of bikes; Internet access; Jacuzzi; outdoor heated pool. *In room:* A/C, TV/VCR, hair dryer, kitchenette.

Hilton Fort Lauderdale Beach Resort ★★ This 25-story landmark property is located on the shoreline of Fort Lauderdale's famous A1A between the palm-shaded boulevards of Sunrise and Las Olas. Guests enter the resort through a gracious porte-cochere into a dramatic two-story lobby. The sixth-floor Sunrise Terrace offers unobstructed views of the Atlantic Ocean and features an infinity pool and private poolside cabanas and is reminiscent of the deck of a luxury yacht. The resort's commitment to personal service can be experienced through a dedicated beach concierge, kids' poolside program, accommodating staff, and deluxe turndown service. Each of the 374 studios and suites is outfitted with a separate shower and soaking tub, high-definition flatscreen TV, kitchen or kitchenette, and private oceanview balcony with expansive views of the Atlantic. The resort features the Spa Q and two distinct dining options, including **ilios**—an upscale signature restaurant of contemporary Mediterranean cuisine—and **Le Marche Gourmet Market & Bakery,** featuring Starbucks drinks, pizzas, panini, gelato, and more.

505 N. Fort Lauderdale Beach Blvd., Fort Lauderdale, FL 33404. www.fortlauderdalebeachresort. hilton.com. © **800/HILTONS** (445-8667) or 954/414-2222. Fax 954/414-2612. 374 units. Seasonal from $159 double. AE, DISC, MC, V. **Amenities:** 2 restaurants; concierge; high-speed Internet access; pool; room service; spa. *In room:* A/C, TV, fridge.

Pelican Grand Beach Resort ★ 🎐 The Pelican Beach Resort sits on a 500-foot private beach, with 159 oversize accommodations, oceanfront suites with balconies, and a sublimely relaxing, wraparound oceanfront veranda and sun deck with rocking chairs. What also rocks about this place are the zero-entry pool and the Lazy River tubing ride. But if you prefer to feel sand between your toes, the private beach is the best thing about this resort, an amenity not too common in this area, where hotels are generally located across the street from the beach instead of being directly on it. This is a great, low-key luxury resort, especially for families looking for a relaxing vacation, as it has all the amenities of a more harried chain resort overwrought with a slew of people. A popular spot here is the **Emporium,** an old-fashioned ice-cream parlor that's command central for your sweet tooth. The resort is also completely smoke free.

2000 N. Ocean Blvd., Fort Lauderdale, FL 33305. www.pelicanbeach.com. © **800/525-OCEAN** (6232) or 954/568-9431. Fax 954/565-2662. 159 units. Winter $299–$349 double, $520 suite; off season $220–$270 double, $420 suite. AE, DC, MC, V. Parking $24. **Amenities:** Restaurant; ice-cream parlor; bar; fitness center; pool. *In room:* A/C, TV, fridge, hair dryer, high-speed Internet.

Seminole Hard Rock Hotel & Casino ★★★ The Seminole Tribe of Florida has created a miniature Vegas within Hollywood, Florida, and it's doing a booming business, especially after the massive, 130,000-square-foot **casino** added blackjack in addition to thousands of Vegas-style slot machines, baccarat, and all kinds of poker tables that are always packed. The main draw here is the casino, but the guest rooms are surprisingly cushy and swank, with flatscreen TVs, Egyptian-cotton linens, and big bathrooms with massive shower heads; the suites are hyper-luxurious. Equally impressive is the 4½-acre lagoon-style pool area with waterfalls, hot tubs, wireless Internet access, and, of course, a bar. Actually, there are lots of bars here, especially at the attached entertainment complex, with two clubs open 24/7, as well as restaurants and stores. There's also a food court, or you can choose from several on-site, full-service restaurants, including **Council Oak,** a swanky steakhouse, Gloria and Emilio Estefan's **Bongo's Cuban Café,** and a branch of Fort Lauderdale's disco-licious Italian hot spot, **Café Martorano** (p. 306). If all this action has you feeling wiped out, there's always the **Body Rock Spa,** which, in Seminole Hard Rock fashion, is also pretty sizable.

1 Seminole Way, Hollywood, FL 33314. www.seminolehardrockhollywood.com. © **800/937-0010** or 954/327-7625. Fax 954/327-7655. 500 units. $189–$259 double; $279 luxury room; $650–$2,000 suite. AE, DC, DISC, MC, V. **Amenities:** 17 restaurants; 13 nightclubs and lounges; Jacuzzi; pool; room service; spa. *In room:* A/C, TV, CD player, hair dryer, high-speed Internet access.

Sheraton Fort Lauderdale Beach Hotel ★★ A dramatic change has taken place at the former Sheraton Yankee Clipper to the tune of $30 million and it's all for the better. The iconic beachfront property now features a refreshed, playful design throughout its 486 inviting guest rooms and suites, most with views of the Atlantic Ocean or the Intracoastal. The better-than-ever Sheraton features great dining and entertainment enticements, including the poolside **Baja Beach Bar and Grill,** the **Link@Sheraton** Internet cafe, and the famed **Wreck Bar** where guests of all ages come to catch a glimpse of mermaids swimming from porthole to porthole. There's also a branch of haute NYC Mexican restaurant **Dos Caminos,** a chic lobby area (aka Living Room), an expanded pool deck and infinity pool as well as a new fitness center, a kids' club, restaurants, and bars.

1140 Seabreeze Blvd., Fort Lauderdale, FL 33305. www.sheraton.com/fortlauderdalebeach. © **954/524-5551.** Fax 954/523-5376. 486 units. Winter $159–$189 studio, $229–$449 suite; off season $159–$189 studio, $269–$319 suite. AE, DC, MC, V. Free valet parking. **Amenities:** Restaurant; bar; kids' programs; fitness center; Jacuzzi; 2 pools; room service; watersports. *In room:* A/C, TV, hair dryer, free Wi-Fi.

INEXPENSIVE

Backpacker's Beach Hostel For the young, or for backpackers on a budget, this hostel is a great option, with both dorm beds and private rooms at bargain-basement prices. Clean and conveniently located, the hostel is just 654 feet from the ocean. It features free parking, free phones, free food for self-cooking, free breakfast buffet, and, if you're lucky, free use of the surfboards or in-line skates lying around.

2115 N. Ocean Blvd., Fort Lauderdale, FL 33305. www.fortlauderdalehostel.com. ℰ **954/567-7275.** 12 units. Dorm beds $20 per night, $145 per week; private rooms $55 double. Rates include breakfast buffet. MC, V. **Amenities:** Free Internet access. *In room:* A/C, TV.

Hollywood Beach Suites, Hostel + Hotel ★ 🎁 🛎 From the owners of Miami's hotelier to the hipster on a budget (South Beach Group) comes this beachy, kitschy hotel and hostel that pays homage to nomadic surfer culture. Rooms—shared female, male, mixed sex, and private rooms and suites—are Key West style, decorated in blues and yellows and featuring bunk beds, queen beds, security lockers, and minikitchenettes with microwave, refrigerator, and sink. The main house is where the action is, with a full kitchen, living room, outdoor lounge area, deck, Mexican outdoor restaurant, and bar. It's steps from Hollywood Beach and Broadwalk. Amenities here are exceptional, from free Wi-Fi to free use of surfboards, bikes, and pool tables. Beach access and parking are also free. New to the property in late 2010 is the **Taco Beach Shack,** a 5,000-square-foot hip outdoor taco joint.

334 Arizona Ave., Hollywood Beach, FL 33109. www.southbeachgroup.com. ℰ **877/762-3477** or 954/391-9448. 24 units. Dorm beds from $22 per night; private rooms from $79 double. MC, V. **Amenities:** Free use of bikes; free Wi-Fi. *In room:* A/C, TV.

Sea Downs (and the Bougainvillea) ★★ This bargain lodging is often booked months in advance by return guests (mostly Europeans) who want to be directly on the beach without paying a fortune. The hosts of this superclean 1950s motel, Claudia and Karl Herzog, live on the premises and keep things running smoothly. All rooms have fully equipped kitchens with fridges, stoves, utensils, and glassware and have been redecorated here and at the Herzogs' other, even less expensive property next door, the 11-unit Bougainvillea. Guests at both hotels share the Sea Downs' pool. All rooms are now smoke free.

2900 N. Surf Rd., Hollywood, FL 33019. www.seadowns.com or www.bougainvilleahollywood.com. ℰ **954/923-4968.** Fax 954/923-8747. 12 units. Winter $111–$168 studio, $127–$198 1-bedroom apt; off season $88–$144 studio, $106–$144 1-bedroom apt. Weekly discounted rates available. No credit cards. From I-95, exit Sheridan St. E. to A1A and go south; drive ½ mile to Coolidge St.; turn left. **Amenities:** Concierge; freshwater outdoor pool. *In room:* A/C, TV, Internet access, fully equipped kitchen.

Where to Eat

Fort Lauderdale—and, to some extent, Hollywood—finally has several fine restaurants. **Las Olas Boulevard** has so many eateries that the city has put a moratorium on the opening of new restaurants on the 2-mile street. And despite the so-called recession, a slew of high-end restaurants staked their culinary claims to Fort Lauderdale, including star chef Todd English's first and second South Florida restaurants, **da Campo Osteria** and **Wild Olives** (in nearby Boca Raton), and Morimoto restaurateur Stephen Starr's **Steak 954**, kicking off a trend of big-name, high-end restaurants bypassing Miami for Fort Lauderdale for a change.

VERY EXPENSIVE

Café Martorano ★★★ ITALIAN This small storefront eatery doesn't win any awards for decor or location, but when it comes to food that's good enough for an entire Italian family, Café Martorano, which also opened to rave reviews in Las Vegas, is one of the best. People wait for a table for upwards of 2 hours because the restaurant accepts no reservations and can get away with it. An almost-offensive sound system (playing disco tunes and Sinatra) has a tendency to turn off many a diner, but you don't come here for an intimate dinner. Dining here is like being at a big, fat, Italian wedding, where eating, drinking, and dancing are paramount. The menu changes daily, but regulars can request special off-the-menu items. If you don't ask, you don't get, so open your mouth. Also keep your eyes open for such celebrities as Liza Minnelli, James Gandolfini, and Little Steven Van Zandt, among others, who make it a point to stop here for a meal while in town. An outpost of the restaurant opened at the Seminole Hard Rock Hotel & Casino in 2010.

3343 E. Oakland Park Blvd., Fort Lauderdale. ℭ **954/561-2554.** www.cafemartorano.com. Reservations not accepted. Main courses $13–$34. MC, V. Daily 5–11pm.

Casa D'Angelo ★★★ ITALIAN Although Fort Lauderdale may be transforming into a thoroughly modern 21st-century beach city, Casa D'Angelo remains steeped in old-school, old-world style and service with an impeccable reputation for some of the best Tuscan-style Italian food in South Florida. Don't be intimidated by the 40-plus-page wine list of regional Italian varietals. The waiters here are friendly and knowledgeable and will help guide you through it if need be. As for chef/owner Angelo Elio's cuisine, insert superlatives here, but you won't truly understand until you taste some of the handmade pastas—handmade ravioli filled with spinach and ricotta, homemade fettuccine with roasted veal ragout, pappardelle with porcini mushrooms. After a while, saying the word *homemade* becomes redundant because, well, it's the standard here. In addition to pastas, there are expertly grilled chops and fresh and simply prepared seafood such as the superb snapper *oreganatta* with sun-dried tomatoes or jumbo prawns sautéed in white wine, garlic, fresh tomato, and imported Ligurian olives, which make the word *flavorful* seem like an understatement. A newer sibling opened in Boca Raton at 171 E. Palmetto Park Rd. (ℭ **561/996-1234**), which some say is quieter than the original, but the food is just as exceptional.

1201 N. Federal Hwy., Fort Lauderdale. ℭ **954/564-1234.** www.casa-d-angelo.com. Reservations recommended. Main courses $14–$34. AE, DC, DISC, MC, V. Sun–Thurs 5:30–10pm; Fri–Sat 5:30–11pm.

da Campo Osteria ★★★ ITALIAN Why star chef Todd English chose to open in a condo hotel off the beaten track is beyond us, but fans of English's gourmet Northern Italian fare, however, would go through an *Amazing Race*–type challenge to find it. You'll stop wondering about the bizarre location as soon as a server arrives to prepare mozzarella tableside. Skip the simple spaghetti and meatballs—as good as it is, there's better in the form of the ricotta ravioli, prepared old-school Bolognese-style or the pork Milanese on the bone with olive caper relish. Some people wonder whether to choose da Campo over the neighborhood's reigning Italian royalty, Café Martorano. We say you can't choose between the two—da Campo is a refined, gourmet dining experience, while Martorano is like eating your Italian grandma's cooking—in a disco. Depends on your mood, we guess. English has since expanded in South Florida, opening **Wild Olives by Todd English** in Boca Raton, 5050 Town Center Circle (📞 **561/544-8000;** www.wildolives.com).

In Il Lugano Suite Hotel, 3333 NE 32nd Ave. (btw. Oakland Park Blvd. and NE 34th Ave.). 📞 **954/226-5002.** www.dacampofl.com. Reservations recommended. Main courses $14–$42. AE, DC, DISC, MC, V. Mon–Sat 7am–11pm; Sun 8am–9pm. From I-95, exit at Oakland Park Blvd. Cross the bridge and make a left on NE 32nd Ave. The hotel is straight ahead on the water.

Darrel & Oliver's Cafe Maxx ★★ FLORIBBEAN/NEW WORLD Despite its bleak location in an unassuming storefront, Darrel & Oliver's Cafe Maxx is one of the best restaurants in Broward County. When it opened in 1984, it was the first restaurant to have an open kitchen, and what a stir that caused! Now, instead of the kitchen, the marvel is what comes out of it. Consider brown sugar–rubbed veal chop with rutabaga and sun-dried pear gratin, charred asparagus, and demi-glace; or hoisin-glazed local cobia with udon noodles and Asian vegetable stir-fry. Yum. But save room for dessert—the vanilla bean crème brûlée in an almond lace cup with pineapple rum caramel sauce and cookies or the Hawaiian vintage chocolate soufflé are just two of many diet- and mind-blowing options.

2601 E. Atlantic Blvd., Pompano Beach. 📞 **954/782-0606.** Fax 954/782-0648. www.cafemaxx. com. Reservations recommended. Main courses $10–$49. AE, DC, DISC, MC, V. Mon–Thurs 5:30–10:30pm; Fri–Sat 5:30–11pm; Sun 5:30–10pm. From I-95, exit at Atlantic Blvd. E. The restaurant is 3 lights east of Federal Hwy.

Steak 954 ★ STEAKHOUSE Housed in the W Fort Lauderdale, this playful creation of restaurant mogul Stephen Starr, of Morimoto fame, puts the emphasis on the simple flavors of dry-aged meats, but the taste and the scene are anything but simple. While the menu may be steakhouse simple, with steaks, chops, seafood, sandwiches, raw bar, and sides, this is Fort Lauderdale's newest "it" girl, a virtual meat market of seeing and being seen in between stabs at beautiful hunks of steak. For a great alternative to meat, try the miso-glazed black cod. The restaurant is tops for ambience too—dark woods and bold floral silk wall panels, with the restaurant's centerpiece being a 15-foot-long reef aquarium home to hypnotic jellyfish. Also be sure to check out the restaurant's popular Saturday and Sunday brunch.

W Fort Lauderdale, 401 N. Fort Lauderdale Beach Blvd., Fort Lauderdale. 📞 **954/414-8333.** www.steak954.com. Reservations recommended. Main courses $26–$65. AE, DC, DISC, MC, V. Sun–Thurs 7am–10pm; Fri–Sat 7am–11pm.

EXPENSIVE

Anthony's Runway 84 ★★★ ITALIAN Meet Anthony, the gregarious owner of this Fort Lauderdale restaurant with an interior all about jet-setting—albeit in the mid- to late '70s—and a bar crafted out of a plane fuselage. Once you meet him, he will introduce your server, whose name is likely to be Tony. Same goes for the bartender. The quintessential, convivial Italian vibe in here (think Travolta in *Saturday Night Fever*) is conducive to one of the most enjoyable meals you'll ever have. The best way to go is—what else?—family-style, in which you'll be able to share lots of dishes such as mussels marinara, fried clams, roasted red peppers in garlic, shrimp parmigiana, an out-of-this-world rigatoni with cauliflower (although it sounds boring, order it no matter what!), and stellar meat and poultry dishes that frequent fliers to Anthony's rave about each time, as if it were their last meal. For the best pizza, try nearby **Anthony's Coal Fired Pizza,** 2203 S. Federal Hwy.

(☎ **954/462-5555;** http://anthonyscoalfiredpizza.com), which is quickly on its way to becoming a bona fide chain with locations all over South Florida and more up north (New York, New Jersey, Pennsylvania). This one is the original though.

330 S.R. 84, Fort Lauderdale. ☎ **954/467-8484.** Reservations strongly recommended. Main courses $15–$50. AE, DC, DISC, MC, V. Tues–Thurs and Sun noon–10pm; Fri–Sat 5–11pm.

Eduardo de San Angel ★★★ MEXICAN Gourmet Mexican is *not* an oxymoron, and for those who don't believe that, take one meal at the sublime Eduardo de San Angel and you'll see how true it is. Chef Eduardo Pria has a masterful way with food, as seen in dishes such as sautéed Florida blue crab and yellow corncakes with smoked chipotle chili sauce and Puebla-style mole, or the ancho chili–flavored crepe filled with *cuitlacoche,* serrano chiles, and onions with melted Asadero cheese laced with a squash blossom sauce. Fresh flowers and candlelight, not to mention the fact that the restaurant resembles an intimate hacienda, also drive home the fact that this isn't your mom's Old El Paso taco dinner. Beer and wine only.

2822 E. Commercial Blvd., Fort Lauderdale. ☎ **954/772-4731.** www.eduardodesanangel.com. Reservations essential. Main courses $24–$36. AE, DC, DISC, MC, V. Mon–Thurs 11:30am–10:30pm; Fri–Sat 5:30–10:30pm.

Himmarshee Bar & Grille ★ AMERICAN Located on a popular street of bars frequented by Fort Lauderdale's young professionals, Himmarshee Bar & Grille is known for its scene and cuisine. A mezzanine bar upstairs is ideal for people-watching; outdoor tables are tight, but strategically situated in front of all the street's action. On weekend nights, in particular, it's difficult to get a table. However, if you can deal with cramming into the bar, it's worth the wait of a cocktail or two. Gorgonzola-stuffed dates are a good starter, and the molasses-brined pork chop or even the stout burger with Guinness-stewed onions and stout mustard are really good mains. The wine list is impressive. Check out **Side Bar**, the restaurant's very ski-lodgey bar next door featuring live music and a bustling crowd of young hipsters.

210 SW 2nd St. (south of Broward Blvd., west of U.S. 1), Fort Lauderdale. ☎ **954/524-1818.** www.himmarshee.com. Reservations recommended. Main courses $13–$32. AE, MC, V. Mon–Thurs 11:30am–2:30pm and 6–10:30pm; Fri 11:30am–2:30pm and 6–11:30pm; Sat 6–11:30pm; Sun 6–10:30pm.

Johnny V's ★★★ SOUTHWESTERN South Florida's favorite so-called Caribbean Cowboy, Chef Johnny Vinczencz, has moved around quite a bit—from South Beach's Hotel Astor (twice!) to Delray Beach's Sundy House. But this Las Olas hot spot looks to be his final stop, and that's good news to all Johnny V's faithful foodies who will travel to the end of the earth to sample some of his barbecue and Caribbean-inspired contemporary cuisine. The menu pops with dishes like sage-grilled Florida dolphin with rock shrimp–plantain stuffing, lobster pan gravy, cranberry-mango chutney, baby green beans, and carrots, plus a slew of other dishes you've likely never seen before.

625 E. Las Olas Blvd. ☎ **954/761-7920.** www.johnnyvlasolas.com. Reservations suggested. Main courses $25–$42. AE, DC, MC, V. Mon–Thurs 11:30am–2:30pm and 5:30–11pm; Fri 11:30am–2:30pm and 5:30pm–midnight; Sat 5:30pm–midnight; Sun 5:30–11pm.

Sage French Café and Oyster Bar ★★ FRENCH A cozy, modern, cacophonous Francophile's dream come true, Sage's Hollywood locale is less bawdy than its Fort Lauderdale counterpart, which comes complete with a Moulin Rouge meets Fort Lauderdale Strip burlesque show, but we prefer this less flashy location, because it lets us concentrate more on the food, which is the true star of the show. A far cry from a brassy brasserie, this Sage features a backlit bar, an open grill, a shellfish bar, a see-through wine cellar, and a Chihuly-esque chandelier straight out of an animated Disney flick. As for the fare, Chef Laurent Tasic has his shellfish flown in daily from Canada, California, or the Chesapeake Bay. The menu isn't all seafood, however, with an unabridged list of crepes, and French classic starters such as grilled artichoke, chicken liver pâté, escargot, and a hearty French-onion soup. Entrees include a fabulous cassoulet, a superb plate of steak frites, coq au vin, short ribs Parisienne, and Chef Laurent's meatloaf—ground veal and filet mignon with fresh herbs in a savory mushroom garlic merlot sauce. For those who want a side of bawdy with their bourguignon, Sage's Fort Lauderdale location is at 2378 N. Federal Hwy. (© **954/565-2299**).

2000 Harrison St., Hollywood. © **954/391-9466.** www.sagecafe.net. Reservations recommended. Main courses $18–$30. AE, MC, V. Sun–Thurs 11am–10pm; Fri–Sat 11am–11pm.

Sunfish Grill ★★★ SEAFOOD Unlike its fellow contemporary seafood restaurants, the Sunfish Grill chooses to focus on fish, not fusion. Chef Anthony Sindaco is content to leave the spotlight on his fantastic fish dishes, which are possibly the freshest in town, because he buys it at local markets and often from well-known fishermen who appear at his back door with their catches of the day. Chef Tony's tuna tartare is legendary. Chilean sea bass, expertly cooked with roast beef–potato hash, glazed turnips, and crispy parsnip fries in a natural sauce, is wonderful. The best dish, in our opinion, is the truffle-crusted black grouper. But the menu changes often so you never know what you may get here, but whatever it is, it's going to be good. In fact, almost everything at the Sunfish Grill is better than at most seafood restaurants.

2775 E. Oakland Park Blvd., Pompano Beach. © **954/788-2434.** www.sunfishgrill.com. Reservations recommended. Main courses $20–$35. AE, MC, V. Mon–Thurs 6–9:30pm; Fri–Sat 6–10:30pm.

Trina Restaurant ★★★ MEDITERRANEAN Yes, it's expensive, but the Mediterranean-infused seafood dishes are worth every penny. Try the skewers of diver scallops and braised short ribs with summer truffle reduction and truffled cauliflower, or the fire-roasted Chilean sea bass with basil crumbs, white beans, and garlic spinach in a tomato basil broth. Out of this world. The menu changes often so you may find other dishes equally excellent, such as the crab-crusted black grouper. Reservations here are hard to come by, especially in season, but the Trina Lounge is also a great option, offering lighter—and cheaper—fare with high-style ambience. Although we love the buzz of the indoor dining room, request a table outside overlooking the ocean.

601 N. Fort Lauderdale Beach Blvd., Fort Lauderdale. © **954/567-8070.** www.trinarestaurant andlounge.com. Reservations recommended. Main courses $20–$42. AE, DC, DISC, MC, V. Sun–Thurs 5:30–10pm; Fri–Sat 5:30–10:30pm. Lounge stays open later.

MODERATE

Cap's Place Island Restaurant ★ 📖 SEAFOOD Opened in 1928 by a bootlegger who ran in the same circles as gangster Meyer Lansky, this barge-turned-restaurant is one of the area's best-kept secrets. Although it's no longer a rum-running restaurant and casino, its illustrious past (FDR and Winston Churchill dined here together) landed it a spot on the National Register of

Historic Places. To get here, you have to take a ferryboat, provided by the restaurant. The short ride across the Intracoastal definitely adds to the Cap's Place experience. The food is good, not great. Traditional seafood dishes such as Florida or Maine lobster, clams casino, and oysters Rockefeller will take you back to the days when a soprano was just an opera singer.

2765 NE 28th Court, Lighthouse Point. ☎ **954/941-0418.** www.capsplace.com. Reservations recommended. Main courses $14–$33. MC, V. Daily 5:30pm–midnight. Motor-launch from I-95, exit at Copan's Rd., and go east to U.S. 1 (Federal Hwy.). At NE 24th St., turn right and follow the double lines and signs to the Lighthouse Point Yacht Basin and Marina (8 miles north of Fort Lauderdale). From here, follow the CAP'S PLACE sign pointing you to the shuttle.

Rustic Inn Crabhouse ★ SEAFOOD A Fort Lauderdale rough-and-tumble landmark for more than 50 years, Rustic Inn isn't the place for a romantic, intimate, quiet dinner. The minute you walk into this inn that's more reminiscent of a trailer, you're assaulted by fluorescent interrogation-style lighting and cacophonous banging—a symphony from a packed house of happy diners cracking their crabs with wooden mallets. Although you don't *have* to crack your own crabs—diva Barbra Streisand didn't when she dined here (she requested them already cracked—god forbid she should break a nail!)—it's all part of the experience. Although the restaurant is known for its "world-famous garlic crabs" (and we think they are totally deserving of that lofty tag line), we especially loved the Dungeness garlic crabs, but you can also order lobster, pasta, and all sorts of fried fish—even fried alligator (it's chewier than chicken!). The fried clams are especially good, but if you want to gorge yourself, try the Reef Raft, a basket of fried oysters, fried scallops, and fried fish. Dress very casually and prepare to wait awhile for a table; but trust us, it's worth it.

4331 Ravenswood Rd., Fort Lauderdale. ☎ **954/584-1637.** www.rusticinn.com Reservations not accepted. Main courses $10–$36; crabs are market price. AE, DC, DISC, MC, V. Mon–Sat 11:30am–10:45pm; Sun 2–9:45pm.

Sugar Reef ★★ FRENCH CARIBBEAN We could go on about this restaurant's priceless ocean view, but the menu of Mediterranean, Caribbean, and French dishes is just as outstanding. A funky fish-shack vibe is bolstered by fresh air wafting in from the Atlantic. Seafood bouillabaisse in green curry and coconut broth and Sugar Reef *pho*—a Vietnamese noodle dish with chicken, shrimp, ginger, and spices—are among the restaurant's most popular dishes. The kitchen puts a savory spin on duck, roasted and topped with mango salsa. This is not a place you'd expect to find on a beach boardwalk, which makes it all the more delightful.

600 N. Surf Rd. (on the Broadwalk, just north of Hollywood Blvd.), Hollywood. ☎ **954/922-1119.** www.sugarreefgrill.com. Reservations accepted for parties of 6 or more. Main courses $16–$33. AE, DISC, MC, V. Mon 4–10:30pm; Tues–Thurs 11am–10:30pm; Fri–Sun 11am–11pm (sometimes later in winter).

INEXPENSIVE

Jaxon's ★ 🍴 ICE CREAM South Florida's best and only authentic old-fashioned ice-cream parlor and country store attracts those with sweet tooths from all over the area. Their cravings are satisfied with an unabridged assortment of homemade ice cream served any which way. Kids love the candy store in the front of the restaurant, and adults love the pre–Ben & Jerry's authenticity. For the calorie-conscious, the sugar-free and fat-free versions are pretty good. Jaxon's most famous everything-but-the-kitchen-sink sundae has countless scoops and endless toppings.

128 S. Federal Hwy., Dania Beach. ✆ **954/923-4445.** Sundaes $2.75–$11. AE, DISC, MC, V. Mon– Thurs 11:30am–11pm; Fri–Sat 11:30am–midnight; Sun noon–11pm.

La Spada's Original Hoagies ★★ SANDWICHES An institution since 1973, La Spada's is a hero to every sandwich fan whether you call it a sub or a hoagie. That said, we think the so-called sandwich artists at Subway could stand to take a lesson or two on the art that has been so perfected here. The artful arranging of layers of fresh meats piled into a chewy roll with lettuce, tomato, onion, pickles, and their own blend of marinated sweet peppers make us rethink the whole sandwich-artist moniker. Here, they're sandwich scientists.

4346 Seagrape Dr., Lauderdale-by-the-Sea. ✆ **954/776-7893.** www.laspadashoagies.com. Sand- wiches $6–$11. AE, MC, V. Mon–Sat 10am–8pm; Sun 11am–8pm (open at 10am on game days).

Lester's Diner ★ AMERICAN Since 1968, Lester's Diner has been serving swarms of South Floridians large portions of great greasy-spoon fare until the wee hours. Try the eggs Benedict and the 14-ounce "cup" of classic coffee, or sample one of Lester's many homemade desserts. The place serves breakfast 24 hours a day and is a Fort Lauderdale institution that attracts locals, club crowds, city offi- cials, and a generally motley, friendly crew of hungry people craving no-nonsense food served by seasoned waitresses with beehive hairdos that contribute to the campy atmosphere. A second Lester's opened in Sunrise, right near Sawgrass Mills and Ikea, at 1399 NW 136th Ave. (✆ **954/838-7473**).

250 S.R. 84, Fort Lauderdale. ✆ **954/525-5641.** Main courses $5–$15. AE, MC, V. Daily 24 hr.

Le Tub ★★ 🏠 AMERICAN Hands down, this is one of the coolest, most un- pretentious, quintessential pre–swanky So Flo restaurants, if not one of the cool- est restaurants, period. Established in 1959 as a Sunoco gas station, Le Tub was purchased in 1974 by a man who personally transformed the place into this wa- terfront restaurant, made out of flotsam, jetsam, and ocean-bone treasures gath- ered over 4 years of jogging on Hollywood Beach. But the waterfront location and unique building aren't the only things to marvel at. As you walk in, take note of the hand-painted bathtubs and toilet bowls (it's not at all gross; they're used as plant- ers) lining the walkway. Inside is a divey bar complete with pool table and jukebox; but outside seating on the deck is the real gem. Le Tub is famous for its burgers (which *Esquire* magazine and Oprah have declared the country's best, thereby increasing the masses who flock here a millionfold), chili, and seafood, but more appealing than the food is the peaceful, easy feeling exuded by the place.

1100 N. Ocean Dr., Hollywood. ✆ **954/931-9425.** Main courses $6–$17. No credit cards. Daily 10:30am–4am.

BOCA RATON & DELRAY BEACH

26 miles S of Palm Beach; 40 miles N of Miami; 21 miles N of Fort Lauderdale

Boca Raton ★★ is one of South Florida's most expensive, well-maintained cit- ies—home to ladies who lunch and SUV-driving yuppies. The city's name liter- ally translates as "rat's mouth," but you'd be hard-pressed to find rodents in this area's fancy digs.

If you're looking for funky, wacky, and eclectic, look elsewhere. Boca is a luxurious resort community and, for some, the only place worth staying in South

Florida. With minimal nightlife, entertainment in Boca is restricted to leisure sports, excellent dining, and upscale shopping. The city's residents and vacationers happily comply.

Delray Beach ★, named after a suburb of Detroit, is a sleepy-yet-starting-to-awaken beachfront community that grew up completely separate from its southern neighbor. Because of their proximity, Boca and Delray can easily be explored together. Budget-conscious travelers would do well to eat and sleep in Delray and dip into Boca for sightseeing and beaching only. The 2-mile stretch of beach here is well maintained and crowded, though not mobbed. Delray's "downtown" area is confined to Atlantic Avenue, which is known for restaurants from casual to chic, quaint shops, and art galleries. During the day, Delray is slumbering, but thanks to the recent addition of trendy restaurants and bars, nighttime is a much more animated hotbed of hipster activity. Still, compared to Boca, Delray is much more laid-back; it's trendy, but hardly as chichi, and definitely more cute little beach town than sprawling, swanky, suburban Boca.

Essentials

GETTING THERE Like the rest of the cities on the Gold Coast, Boca Raton and Delray are easily reached from I-95 or the Florida Turnpike. Both the Fort Lauderdale Hollywood International Airport and the Palm Beach International Airport are about 20 minutes away. **Amtrak** (✆ **800/USA-RAIL** [872-7245]; www.amtrak.com) trains make stops in Delray Beach at an unattended station at 345 S. Congress Ave.

VISITOR INFORMATION Contact or stop by the **Palm Beach County Convention and Visitors Bureau,** 1555 Palm Beach Lakes Blvd., Ste. 800, West Palm Beach, FL 33401 (✆ **800/554-PALM** [7256] or 561/233-3000; fax 561/471-3990; www.palmbeachfl.com). It's open Monday through Friday from 8:30am to 5:30pm and has excellent coupons and discounts. Monday through Friday from 8:30am to at least 4pm, stop by the **Greater Boca Raton Chamber of Commerce,** 1800 N. Dixie Hwy., 4 blocks north of Glades Road, Boca Raton, FL 33432 (✆ **561/395-4433;** fax 561/392-3780; www.bocaratonchamber.com), for information on attractions, accommodations, and events in the area. You can also try the **Greater Delray Beach Chamber of Commerce,** 64 SE 5th Ave., half a block south of Atlantic Avenue on U.S. 1, Delray Beach, FL 33483 (✆ **561/278-0424;** fax 561/278-0555; www.delraybeach.com), but we recommend the Palm Beach County Convention and Visitors Bureau as it has information on the entire county.

Beaches & Outdoor Activities

BEACHES Thankfully, Florida had the foresight to set aside some of its most beautiful coastal areas for the public's enjoyment. Many of the area's best beaches are located in state parks and are free to pedestrians and bikers, though most do charge for parking. Among the beaches we recommend are Delray Beach's **Atlantic Dunes Beach,** 1600 S. Ocean Blvd., which charges no admission to access a 7-acre developed beach with lifeguards, restrooms, changing rooms, and a family park area; and Boca Raton's **South Beach Park,** 400 N. Ocean Blvd., with 1,670 feet of beach, 25 acres, lifeguards, picnic areas, restrooms, showers, and 955 feet of developed beach south of the Boca Inlet, accessible for an admission charge of $16 Monday

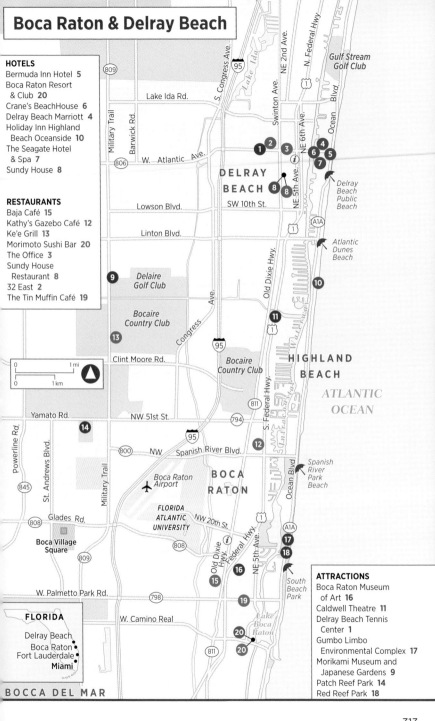

Boca Raton & Delray Beach

HOTELS
Bermuda Inn Hotel **5**
Boca Raton Resort
 & Club **20**
Crane's BeachHouse **6**
Delray Beach Marriott **4**
Holiday Inn Highland
 Beach Oceanside **10**
The Seagate Hotel
 & Spa **7**
Sundy House **8**

RESTAURANTS
Baja Café **15**
Kathy's Gazebo Café **12**
Ke'e Grill **13**
Morimoto Sushi Bar **20**
The Office **3**
Sundy House
 Restaurant **8**
32 East **2**
The Tin Muffin Café **19**

ATTRACTIONS
Boca Raton Museum
 of Art **16**
Caldwell Theatre **11**
Delray Beach Tennis
 Center **1**
Gumbo Limbo
 Environmental Complex **17**
Morikami Museum and
 Japanese Gardens **9**
Patch Reef Park **14**
Red Reef Park **18**

DELRAY BEACH

HIGHLAND BEACH

ATLANTIC OCEAN

BOCA RATON

Delray Beach Public Beach

Atlantic Dunes Beach

Spanish River Park Beach

South Beach Park

Gulf Stream Golf Club

Delaire Golf Club

Bocaire Country Club

Bocaire Country Club

Boca Raton Airport

FLORIDA ATLANTIC UNIVERSITY

Boca Village Square

Lake Ida

Lake Boca Raton

Intracoastal Waterway

FLORIDA
Delray Beach
Boca Raton
Fort Lauderdale
Miami

BOCCA DEL MAR

Lake Ida Rd.
W. Atlantic Ave.
Lowson Blvd.
SW 10th St.
Linton Blvd.
Clint Moore Rd.
Yamato Rd.
NW 51st St.
NW Spanish River Blvd.
NW 20th St.
Glades Rd.
W. Palmetto Park Rd.
W. Camino Real
Swinton Ave.
NE 2nd Ave.
N. Federal Hwy.
Ocean Blvd.
NE 6th Ave.
NE 5th Ave.
S. Congress Ave.
Military Trail
Barwick Rd.
Congress Ave.
Old Dixie Hwy.
S. Federal Hwy.
Powerline Rd.
St. Andrews Blvd.
Old Dixie Hwy.
Federal Hwy.
NE 5th Ave.

313

Boca Raton's South Beach Park is one of the area's most popular.

through Friday, and $18 Saturday and Sunday. The two beaches below are also very popular.

Delray Beach, on Ocean Boulevard at the east end of Atlantic Avenue, is one of the area's most popular hangouts. Weekends especially attract a young and good-looking crowd of active locals and tourists. Refreshments, snack shops, bars, and restaurants are just across the street. Families enjoy the protection of lifeguards on the clean, wide strip. Gentle waters make it a good swimming beach, too. Restrooms and showers are available, and there's limited parking at meters along Ocean Boulevard.

Spanish River Park Beach, on North Ocean Boulevard (A1A), 2 miles north of Palmetto Park Road in Boca Raton, is a huge 95-acre ocean-front park with a half-mile-long beach with lifeguards as well as a large grassy area, making it one of the best choices for picnicking. Facilities include picnic tables, grills, restrooms, showers, and a 40-foot observation tower. You can walk through tunnels under the highway to access nature trails that wind through fertile grasslands. Volleyball nets always have at least one game going on. The park is open from 8am to 8pm. Admission is $16 for vehicles Monday through Friday; $18 on Saturday, Sunday, and major holidays.

Also see the description of **Red Reef Park** under "Scuba Diving & Snorkeling," below.

GOLF This area has plenty of good courses. The best ones that are not in a gated community are **Boca Raton Resort & Club** (p. 318) and the **Inn at Ocean Breeze Golf and Country Club,** formerly known as the Inn at Boca Teeca. Another great place to swing clubs is at the **Deer Creek Golf Club,** 2801 Country Club Blvd., Deerfield Beach (© **954/421-5550;** www.deercreekflorida.com), which also features a 300-plus-yard driving range and practice facility. Rates at the Deer Creek Golf Club are seasonal and range from $35 to $110. However, from May to October or November, about a dozen private courses open their greens to visitors staying in Palm Beach County hotels. This "Golf-A-Round" program is free or severely discounted (carts are additional), and reservations can be made through most major hotels. Ask at your hotel or contact the **Palm Beach County Convention and Visitors Bureau** (© **561/471-3995**) for information on which clubs are available for play.

The **Boca Raton Municipal Golf Course,** 8111 Golf Course Rd. (✆ 561/483-6100), is the area's best public golf course. Renovated in 2010, there's an 18-hole, par-72 course covering approximately 6,200 yards, as well as a 9-hole, par-30 course. Facilities include a snack bar and a pro shop where clubs can be rented. In addition to greens, tees, bunkers, and landscaping, all the bathrooms and locker rooms have been freshly renovated. Greens fees range from $15 to $60. Ask about special summer discounts.

SCUBA DIVING & SNORKELING Moray Bend, a 58-foot dive spot about ¾ mile off Boca Inlet, is the area's most popular. It's home to three moray eels that are used to being fed by scuba divers. The reef is accessible by boat from **Force E Dive Center,** 877 E. Palmetto Park Rd., Boca Raton (✆ 561/368-0555; www.force-e.com). Phone for dive times. Dives cost $55 to $70 per person.

Red Reef Park, 1400 N. Ocean Park Blvd. (✆ 561/393-7974), a 67-acre oceanfront park in Boca Raton, has good swimming and yearround lifeguard protection. There's snorkeling around the shallow rocks and reefs that lie just off the beach. The park has restrooms and a picnic area with grills. Located a half-mile north of Palmetto Park Road, it's open daily from 8am to 10pm. The cost is $16 per car Monday through Friday, $18 on Saturday and Sunday; walkers and bikers get in free.

TENNIS The snazzy **Delray Beach Tennis Center,** 201 W. Atlantic Ave. (✆ 561/243-7360; www.delraytennis.com), has 14 lighted clay courts and 5 hard courts available by the hour. Phone for rates and reservations.

The 17 public lighted hard courts at **Patch Reef Park,** 2000 NW 51st St. (✆ 561/367-7090), are available by reservation. The fee for non-residents is $5.75 per person per 1½ hours. Courts are available Monday through Saturday from 7:30am to 10pm, and Sunday from 7:30am to dusk; call ahead to see if a court is available. To reach the park from I-95, exit at Yamato Road West and continue past Military Trail to the park.

Seeing the Sights

Boca Raton Museum of Art ★★ In addition to a relatively small but well-chosen permanent collection that's strongest in 19th-century European oils (Degas, Klee, Matisse, Picasso, Seurat), the museum stages a wide variety of excellent temporary exhibitions by local and international artists. Lectures and films are offered on a fairly regular basis, so call ahead, or check the website, for details.

Mizner Park, 501 Plaza Real, Boca Raton. ✆ 561/392-2500. www.bocamuseum.org. Admission $8 adults, $6 seniors, $4 students, free for children 12 and under. Additional fees may apply for special exhibits and performances. Free on Wed except during special exhibitions. Tues, Thurs, and Sat 10am–5pm; Wed and Fri 10am–9pm; Sun noon–5pm.

Daggerwing Nature Center ★ Seen enough snowbirds? Head over to this 39-acre swampy splendor where birds of another feather reside, including herons, egrets, woodpeckers, and warblers. The trails come complete with a soundtrack provided by songbirds hovering above (watch your head). The park's night hikes will take you on a nocturnal wake-up call for owls at 6pm. Bring a flashlight. A $2-million expansion in 2007 added a 3,000-square-foot exhibit hall, a laboratory classroom, and exciting wet forest and conservation exhibits. Best part about the addition is the elevated boardwalk over a swamp featuring two trails and an observation tower from which a keen eye can view the abundant plant and animal life, including osprey, woodpeckers, butterflies (including the park's namesake S. Ruddy Daggerwing), endangered wood storks, alligators, and a wide variety of bromeliads.

South County Regional Park, 11200 Park Access Rd., Boca Raton. ℰ **561/488-9953.** Free admission. Tues–Sun 10am–4:30pm. Call for tour and activity schedule.

Gumbo Limbo Environmental Complex ★★★ If manicured lawns and golf courses aren't your idea of communing with nature, then head to Gumbo Limbo. Named for an indigenous hardwood tree, the 20-acre complex protects one of the few surviving coastal hammocks, or forest islands, in South Florida. Walk through the hammock on a half-mile-long boardwalk

A tri-color heron on the grounds of the Daggerwing Nature Center.

that ends at a 40-foot observation tower, from which you can see the Atlantic Ocean, the Intracoastal Waterway, and much of Boca Raton. From mid-April to September, sea turtles come ashore here to lay eggs.

1801 N. Ocean Blvd. (on A1A btw. Spanish River Blvd. and Palmetto Park Rd.), Boca Raton. ℰ **561/338-1473.** www.gumbolimbo.org. Free admission ($5 donation suggested). Mon–Sat 9am–4pm; Sun noon–4pm.

Morikami Museum and Japanese Gardens ★★★ Slip off your shoes and enter a serene Japanese garden that dates from 1905, when an entrepreneurial farmer, Jo Sakai, came to Boca Raton to build a tropical agricultural community.

Enjoy the serenity of the Morkami Museum and Japanese Gardens.

The Yamato Colony, as it was known, was short-lived; by the 1920s, only one tenacious colonist remained: George Sukeji Morikami. But Morikami was quite successful, eventually running one of the largest pineapple plantations in the area. The 200-acre Morikami Museum and Japanese Gardens, which opened to the public in 1977, was Morikami's gift to Palm Beach County and the state of Florida. A stroll through the garden is almost a mile long. An artificial waterfall that cascades into a koi- and carp-filled moat; a small rock garden for meditation; and a large bonsai collection with miniature maple, buttonwood, juniper, and Australian pine trees are all worth contemplation. There's also a cafe with an Asian-inspired menu if you want to stay for lunch.

4000 Morikami Park Rd., Delray Beach. © **561/495-0233.** www.morikami.org. Museum $12 adults, $11 seniors, $7 children 6–17. Museum and Gardens Tues–Sun 10am–5pm. Closed major holidays.

Shopping

Even if you don't plan to buy anything, a trip to Boca Raton's **Mizner Park** is essential for capturing the essence of the city. Mizner is the place to see and be seen, where Rolls-Royces and Ferraris are parked curbside, freshly coiffed women sit amid shopping bags at outdoor cafes, and young movers and shakers chat on their constantly buzzing cellphones. Beyond the human scenery, however, Mizner Park is scenic in its own right, with beautiful landscaping. It's really an outdoor mall, with 45 specialty shops, seven good restaurants, and a multiplex. Each shop front faces a grassy island with gazebos, potted plants, and garden benches. Mizner Park is on Federal Highway, between Palmetto Park and Glades roads (© **561/362-0606**).

Boca's **Town Center Mall,** on the south side of Glades Road, just west of I-95, has seven huge department stores, including Nordstrom, Bloomingdale's, Burdines, Lord & Taylor, and Saks Fifth Avenue. Add hundreds of specialty

The palm-tree lined streets around Mizner Park are a haven for shopping, browsing, and people-watching.

shops, an extensive food court, and a range of other restaurants, and you have the area's most comprehensive shopping center.

On Delray Beach's Atlantic Avenue, especially east of Swinton Avenue, you'll find a few antiques shops, clothing stores, and galleries shaded by palm trees and colorful awnings. Pick up the *Downtown Delray Beach* map and guide at almost any of the stores on this strip, or call ✆ **561/278-0424** for more information.

Where to Stay

A number of national chain hotels worth considering include the moderately priced **Holiday Inn Highland Beach Oceanside,** 2809 S. Ocean Blvd., on A1A, southeast of Linton Boulevard (www.highlandbeachholidayinn.com; ✆ **800/234-6835** or 561/278-6241). Although you won't find rows of cheap hotels as in Fort Lauderdale and Hollywood, a handful of mom-and-pop motels have survived along A1A between the towering condominiums of Delray Beach. Look along the beach just south of Atlantic Boulevard. Especially noteworthy is the pleasant little two-story, shingle-roofed **Bermuda Inn Hotel,** 64 S. Ocean Blvd. (www.thebermudainn.com; ✆ **561/276-5288**). The **Delray Beach Marriott,** 10 N. Ocean Blvd. (www.marriottdelraybeach.com; ✆ **561/274-3200**), is a popular but expensive stay, directly across from the beach with pool and spa. Rates range from $329 during high season to a lot lower in the summer.

Even more economical options can be found in Deerfield Beach, Boca's neighbor, south of the county line. A number of beachfront efficiencies offer great deals, even in the winter months. Try the **Panther Motel and Apartments,** 715 S. A1A (✆ **954/427-0700**), a clean and convenient motel with rates starting as low as $49 (in season, you may have to book for a week at a time; rates then start at $450 to $525).

VERY EXPENSIVE

Boca Raton Resort & Club ★★ 👜 This landmark resort is a sprawling 350-acre collection of oddly matched buildings: the original Cloister (which is undergoing a long, drawn-out renovation with some of the old rooms still available at lesser prices, which are a decent option only if you don't mind being the only one on an entire floor or you've ever wondered what mustiness smelled like back in 1927); the drab pink 27-story Tower; the renovated Beach Club and Pool Oasis, accessible by water shuttle or bus and featuring three redesigned pools, oceanfront bar, beach access, cabana, modern rooms, and sunning terraces; and Yacht Club, a Venetian-style wing of 112 luxury rooms and suites. Fans of the old-school resort should feel right at home as Old World blends beautifully with New World, modern twists. Everything at this resort, which straddles the Intracoastal, is at your fingertips, but may sometimes require some effort to reach. Thankfully, the resort provides transportation shuttles every 10 minutes. Amenities include the grand Spa Palazzo, two 18-hole championship golf courses, a $10-million tennis and fitness center, a 32-slip marina, and a private beach with watersports equipment. The resort's also foodie heaven, with a choice of 12 places to dine, including **Morimoto Sushi Bar** (p. 320), **Cielo, 501 East,** and a bustling branch of NYC's venerable **Serendipity** ice-cream parlor.

501 E. Camino Real (P.O. Box 5025), Boca Raton, FL 33432. www.bocaresort.com. ✆ **888/495-BOCA** (2622) or 561/447-3000. Fax 561/447-3183. 1,047 units. Winter $259–$760 double; off season $169–$329 double. Seasonal packages available. AE, DC, DISC, MC, V. From I-95 N., exit onto Palmetto Park Rd. E. Turn right onto Federal Hwy. (U.S. 1), then left onto Camino Real. **Amenities:**

12 restaurants; 5 bars; extensive children's programs; concierge; 3 fitness centers; 2 18-hole championship golf courses; 7 pools; room service; spa; 30 hydrogrid tennis courts; watersports equipment/rentals. *In room:* A/C, TV, hair dryer, minibar.

The Seagate Hotel & Spa ★★★ Located just 1 block from the beach on Delray's bustling East Atlantic Avenue, the Seagate Hotel & Spa offers you the best of the beach and the city. The best part about the hotel besides its location is the nearby Seagate Beach Club, located less than a mile from the hotel and offering casual and fine dining with gorgeous coastal views, access to watersports equipment rentals, an outdoor swimming pool, and free transportation to and from the hotel. Decor is beachy-chic, featuring a 5,000-gallon aquarium in the main lobby and rooms boasting upscale designer furnishings with Egyptian-cotton linens and all the stylish, tranquil, neutral tones you'd find in, say, Martha Stewart's beach house. The pool on the actual hotel property is pretty large and tropically landscaped. An on-site restaurant, the **Atlantic Grille,** offers indoor and terrace seating and seafood, pasta, and steak dishes. The world-class 8,000-square-foot spa has seven treatment rooms and signature treatments, including the Hot Shell Massage.

1000 E. Atlantic Ave., Delray Beach, FL 33483. www.theseagatehotel.com. ✆ **877/57-SEAGATE** (577-3242) or 561/665-4800. Fax 561/665-4801. 162 units. Winter $349–$669 double; off season $169–$559 double. AE, DC, MC, V. **Amenities:** Restaurant; bar; pool; room service; watersports; free Wi-Fi in public areas. *In room:* A/C, TV/DVD, hair dryer, high-speed Internet, MP3 docking station.

Sundy House ★★★ The oldest residence in Delray Beach, Sundy House is a bona fide 1902 Revival-style home that has been restored to its Victorian glory—on the outside, at least. Inside, the four one- and two-bedroom apartments are in a style best described as Caribbean funky or tropical chic, adorned in brilliant colors and outfitted with state-of-the-art electronics, full modern kitchens, and laundry facilities. Six guest rooms known as the Stables are equestrian chic, with rustic appointments in dark woods. While the rooms here are outstanding, it's the surrounding property that garners the most oohs and aahs. Set on an acre of lush gardens, the Sundy House is surrounded by more than 500 species of exotic plants, streams, and parrots, making an escape here seem more Hawaii than Florida. You can even swim with fish in the hotel's swimming pond! The on-site restaurant features exquisite New Florida cuisine, often using fresh fruits and herbs straight from Sundy House's botanical Taru Gardens.

106 S. Swinton Ave., Delray Beach, FL 33444. www.sundyhouse.com. ✆ **877/439-9601** or 561/272-5678. Fax 561/272-1115. 11 units. Winter $219–$549 1- or 2-bedroom or cottage; off season $169–$499 1- or 2-bedroom or cottage. AE, DC, DISC, MC, V. **Amenities:** Restaurant; bar; swimming pond; limited room service. *In room:* A/C, TV/DVD, CD player, hair dryer, kitchen.

EXPENSIVE

Crane's BeachHouse ★★ If you can't afford your own South Florida beach house—and why bother with all the maintenance, anyway?—Crane's BeachHouse, meticulously run and maintained by husband and wife Michael and Cheryl Crane, is a haven away from home, located just 1 block from the beach and right in the middle of historic Delray Beach. The main draws here are the whimsical, tropical suites, in which every piece of furniture and bric-a-brac is completely original and often crafted by local artists. Although each unit has its own theme—Hawaii, Amazon, Anacapri, and Capetown, for instance—the beds are all the same, in that they are downright heavenly. Lush gardens, a Tiki bar, and a pool leave you with little reason to flee the premises, but when you do, you'll want to return as quickly as possible.

82 Gleason St., Delray Beach, FL 33483. www.cranesbeachhouse.com. ☎ **866/372-7263** or 561/278-1700. Fax 561/278-7826. 27 units. Winter $189–$239 double, $289–$499 suite; off season $139–$169 double, $199–$299 suite. AE, DC, DISC, MC, V. Free parking. **Amenities:** 2 small outdoor pools. *In room:* A/C, TV/VCR, hair dryer, Internet access, full kitchen, minibar.

Where to Eat

Nightlife in Boca means going out to a restaurant. But who cares? This is some of the best dining in South Florida. Delray Beach, on the other hand, has an excellent cuisine and nightlife scene. Best of both worlds.

VERY EXPENSIVE

Kathy's Gazebo Cafe ★★★ CONTINENTAL An elegant, old-school Continental restaurant with chandeliers and white linen tablecloths, Kathy's white-glove restaurant is an ideal spot for special occasions or culinary nostalgia. The food is superb—the Dover sole is flown in from Holland and prepared with nothing fancier than an almandine or meunière sauce; chateaubriand is also spectacular and, in a city smitten by plain ol' steak and sushi, it's a perfect throwback to simpler, delicious days. Fresh homemade pastries and peach Melba are among the desserts. While jackets aren't commonly required at restaurants in South Florida, you'll want to wear one here just to fit in with the dapper moneyed types who frequent the place.

4199 N. Federal Hwy., Boca Raton. ☎ **561/395-6033.** www.kathysgazebo.com. Reservations required. Main courses $20–$43. AE, MC, V. Daily 5:30–10pm.

Morimoto Sushi Bar ★★★ SUSHI A tiny outpost of Iron Chef Masaharu Morimoto's original Philly sushi spot, Morimoto is one of the hottest tickets in Boca, and South Florida in general. If you can snag a reservation at this tiny, ultramodern eatery, take it, even if it's at the unfashionably early hour of, say, 5pm. Don't come expecting a huge selection of dishes, either. It's all about the sushi and sashimi, and if you're a true fan of both, you won't hesitate to order the Omakase Tasting Menu in which the skilled sushi chef trained by the Iron Chef himself will choose for you. Fans of tuna will be thrilled to indulge in a variety of grades of tuna, many rare in South Florida, including *otoro, maguro,* and *chutoro.* In addition to the sushi, there's also excellent rock shrimp tempura, which many say is better than Nobu's, and a sensational seared Kobe beef with abalone mushrooms.

501 E. Camino Real (in the Boca Raton Resort), Boca Raton. ☎ **561/447-3640.** www.boca resort.com. Sushi/sashimi $3–$9 per piece; *maki* $6–$14; Omakase Tasting Menu $50 and $75 per person. AE, MC, V. Daily noon–3pm and 5–10pm.

EXPENSIVE

Ke'e Grill ★★★ SEAFOOD Owners Jim and Debbie Taube respect the seafood they serve, some of the freshest in all of South Florida, by leaving off the bells, whistles, and soppy sauces found on so many fish dishes these days. Boasting a beautiful, bustling dining room overlooking a tropical garden, Ke'e Grill used to not take reservations until the lines out the door got out of control. Appetizers include a sensational blue crab cake or perfectly crispy, fried calamari with dipping sauce that's delicious but not even necessary. For entrees, choose from a papaya, roasted garlic, and sweet chili–glazed Chilean sea bass, which may sound like a lot going on, but it's really a flawless union. Sautéed yellowtail snapper, sautéed yellowfin tuna, or crab cakes all come with two sides: a choice of pasta, rice, veggies, or potato. The house specialty, the Ke'e Grill Cioppino, is a study in fresh seafood—specifically shrimp, scallops, grouper, clams, mussels, lobster—with pearl pasta in a spicy seafood broth, kind of an all-in-one explanation of why this is one of South Florida's finest seafood spots.

17940 N. Military Trail, Boca Raton. ℰ **561/995-5044.** Reservations strongly suggested. Main courses $20–$28. AE, DC, DISC, MC, V. Daily 4:30–9:30pm.

Sundy House Restaurant ★★ FLORIBBEAN This restaurant is a stunning place that combines elegant indoor dining and lush tropical outdoor settings with a gastronomic wizardry of fresh fruits, vegetables, and spices grown on the Sundy House's 5-acre farm. Each dish is prepared with palpable precision. Consider the following: pan-roasted Chilean sea bass with garlic broccolini, balsamic marinated plum tomatoes, and truffled sweet pea and lobster risotto, or the mojo-seared salmon with Manchego cheese corn *arepa*, sweet bell peppers, hearts of palm, watercress salad, and papaya chili vinaigrette. Save room for dessert, including a decadent vanilla-bean crème brûlée and mandarin-orange chocolate torte. A decadent Sunday-brunch buffet makes the day before you return to work infinitely more bearable. On the negative side, the service here can be surly and spotty.

In the Sundy House, 106 S. Swinton Ave., Delray Beach. ℰ **561/272-5678.** www.sundyhouse. com. Reservations essential. Main courses $24–$36. AE, DC, DISC, MC, V. Daily 11:30am–2:30pm; Tues–Thurs 6–9pm; Fri–Sat 6–10pm; Sun brunch 10:30am–2:30pm. Closed Monday. Lunch Nov–May only.

32 East ★★ NEW AMERICAN The menu changes daily at this popular people-watching outpost of tasty, contemporary American food with a focus on local, seasonal ingredients. Standouts include the sauté of Gulf Coast grouper with Yukon gold potatoes on creamed butternut squash and bacon; brine-cured pork chop with pancetta-braised escarole and cinnamon-spiced mashed yams with autumn fruits brown butter; and local mahimahi on potato purée with sweet corn and green beans in a Sherry-mushroom sauce. The buzzing scene makes 32 East a popular hangout for the cocktail set, and while the menu may be sophisticated, the vibe is pure neighborhood bistro, casual and comfortable with two levels of seating—the upper dining room provides better views, while the lower one is obviously in the middle of the action. But we prefer the outdoor seating, a prime vantage point for catching the action on Atlantic Avenue. New from the restaurant's owners: **Tryst,** a gastropub with gourmet versions of fish and chips and mac and cheese, plus shared plates, at 4 E. Atlantic Ave. (ℰ **561/921-0201;** www.trystdelray.com).

32 E. Atlantic Ave., Delray Beach. ℰ **561/276-7868.** www.32east.com. Reservations recommended. Main courses $21–$38. AE, DC, MC, V. Sun–Thurs 5:30–10pm; Fri–Sat 5:30–11pm. Bar until 2am.

MODERATE

The Office ★ AMERICAN A gastropub whose cuisine is described as "modern American casual fare with style," the Office is one of those places in which you don't mind doing overtime. Cuisine features an emphasis on local growers, products, and seafood. Think grass-fed pork honey-braised ribs with fennel pollen and celery-root apple slaw; burgers like the Florida Blue Crab Burger, salads, sandwiches; and bar snacks like heirloom black kernel popcorn with black truffle and Black Sea salt. Decor is reminiscent of an industrial chic, yet cozy, library. Oh, and there's a selection of 35 to 40 beers.

210 E. Atlantic Ave., Delray Beach. ℂ **561/276-3600.** www.theofficedelray.com. Reservations recommended. Entrees $9–$28. AE, DC, MC, V. Daily 11am–11pm.

INEXPENSIVE

Baja Cafe ★ MEXICAN A jeans–and–T-shirt kind of place with wooden tables, Baja Cafe serves fantastic Mexican food at even better prices. Although the salsa borders on somewhat sweet, they do have the hottest sauces; if you like spicy, they will be happy to slap plenty on your meal if you request it. Dishes have kitschy names like Hellfire and Damnation Enchiladas and Chimichanga Cha Cha Cha, but when it comes to flavor, they aren't kidding. This place is located right by the Florida East Coast Railway tracks, so don't be surprised if you feel a little rattling. Live music and entertainment make this place a hot spot for an unpretentious crowd. A second location is at 1310 S. Federal Hwy. in Deerfield Beach (ℂ **954/596-1305**).

201 NW 1st Ave., Boca Raton. ℂ **561/394-5449.** Reservations not accepted. Main courses $6–$15. No credit cards. Mon–Thurs 11:30am–10pm; Fri–Sat 11:30am–11pm; Sun 5–10pm.

The Tin Muffin Cafe ★ BAKERY/SANDWICH SHOP Popular with the downtown lunch crowd, this excellent storefront bakery keeps folks lining up for big sandwiches on fresh bread, plus muffins, quiches, and good homemade soups such as split pea or lentil. The curried-chicken sandwich is stuffed with chunks of white meat doused in a creamy curry dressing and fruit. There are a few cafe tables inside and even one outside on a tiny patio. Be warned, however, that service is (forgivably) slow and parking is a nightmare. Try looking for a spot a few blocks away at a meter.

364 E. Palmetto Park Rd. (btw. Federal Hwy. and the Intracoastal Bridge), Boca Raton. ℂ **561/392-9446.** Sandwiches and salads $7–$14. No credit cards. Mon–Fri 11am–5pm; Sat 11am–4pm.

Boca Raton & Delray Beach After Dark

THE BAR, CLUB & MUSIC SCENE

Atlantic Avenue in Delray Beach has finally gotten quite hip to nightlife and is now lined with sleek and chic restaurants, lounges, and bars that attract the Palm Beach County "in crowd," along with a few random patrons such as New Age musician Yanni, who has a house nearby. Although it's hardly South Beach or Fort Lauderdale's Las Olas and Riverfront, Atlantic Avenue holds its own as far as a vibrant nightlife is concerned. In Boca Raton, **Mizner Park** is the nucleus of nightlife, with restaurants masking themselves as nightclubs or, at the very least, sceney bars.

Boston's on the Beach This is a family restaurant with a somewhat lively bar scene. It's a good choice for post-sunbathing, supercasual happy hours Monday through Friday from 4 to 8pm, with live reggae on Monday. With two decks overlooking the ocean, Boston's is an ideal place to mellow out and take in the scenery. Open daily from 7am to 2am. 40 S. Ocean Blvd., Delray Beach. ℂ **561/278-3364.** www.bostonsonthebeach.com.

Dada Dada is a nocturnal outpost of food, drink, music, art, culture, and history. In other words, here you can expect to find neobohemian, arty types lingering in

Crowds gather in Boca Raton to see shows at the Mizner Park Amphitheater.

their dark glasses and berets on one of the living room's cozy couches, listening to music, poetry, or dissertations on life. Live music, great food, a bar, an outdoor patio area, and a very eclectic crowd make Dada the coolest hangout in Delray. Open daily from 5:30pm to 2am. 52 N. Swinton Ave., Delray Beach. ℂ 561/330-DADA (3232). www.sub-culture.org/dada/home-dada.com.

Delux Believe it or not, this red-hued dance club on Atlantic Avenue is cooler than some of South Beach's big-shot clubs, thanks to a soundtrack of sexy house music, bedlike seating, and a beautiful crowd in which someone as striking as past patron Gwen Stefani can actually blend in without being noticed. Open Wednesday through Sunday from 7pm to 2am. 16 E. Atlantic Ave., Delray Beach. ℂ 561/279-4792. www.deluxdelraybeach.com.

Dubliner A bustling, authentic Irish pub that's popular with the young professional set, Mizner Park's Dubliner features traditional pub fare; pints and pints of Guinness; an impressive selection of beers on tap; assorted spirits; flatscreen TVs for soccer, rugby, and American sporting events; and live music and DJs. Open 4pm to 2am daily. 435 Plaza Real, Boca Raton. ℂ 561/6202540. www.dublinerboca.com.

Falcon House A cozy wine and tapas bar also known as 888 Lounge on a side street off the Atlantic Avenue bustle, Falcon House is reminiscent of a bar you'd find in Napa Valley, with an impressive selection of wine and a hip, well-heeled crowd. It's a haven for those who are over the whole hip-hop scene on Atlantic Avenue. Open Monday through Saturday from 5pm to 2am. 116 NE 6th Ave., Delray Beach. ℂ 561/243-9499. www.thefalconhouse.com.

THE PERFORMING ARTS

For details on upcoming events, check the *Boca News* or the *Sun-Sentinel,* or call the **Palm Beach County Cultural Council** information line at ℂ 800/882-ARTS (2787). During business hours, a staffer can give details on current performances. After hours, a recorded message describes the week's events.

For live concerts, featuring everyone from Dolly Parton and Kelly Clarkson to Weird Al Yankovic, the **Count de Hoernle Amphitheater at the Schmidt Family Centre for the Arts** in Mizner Park (✆ 866/571-ARTS [2787]) is the place to see them in an open-air format, under the stars and, at times, rain. If you're not that big a fan, you'll still hear the concerts from Mizner Park!

Boca's best theater company is the **Caldwell Theatre,** and it's worth checking out. Located in a strip shopping center at 7873 N. Federal Hwy., this Equity showcase does well-known dramas, comedies, classics, off-Broadway hits, and new works throughout the year. Ticket prices are reasonable—usually $38 to $45. Full-time students with ID will be especially interested in the little-advertised student rush: When available, tickets are sold for $5 if you arrive at least an hour early. Call ✆ 561/241-7432 or go to www.caldwelltheatre.com for details.

PALM BEACH ★★ & WEST PALM BEACH ★

65 miles N of Miami; 193 miles E of Tampa; 45 miles N of Fort Lauderdale

For generations, Palm Beach has been the traditional winter home of American aristocracy—the Kennedys, Rockefellers, and Trumps, among others, have all fled northern climes for this slice of paradise. Beyond the upscale resorts that cater to such a crowd, Palm Beach holds some surprises, including the world-class Norton Museum of Art, top-notch birding, and the sparkling Intracoastal Waterway.

Beaches Public beaches are a rare commodity in Palm Beach. **Midtown Beach** is a notable exception, a golden island of undeveloped strand in a sea of glitz and glamour. Groomed beach sand, picnic facilities, and outdoor recreation dominate at **Phipps Ocean Park,** another public beach especially popular with families.

Things to Do Wherever there is an abundance of sun, sand, and sightseers, there is **golf,** and Palm Beach is no exception. Downtown, the **Norton Museum of Art** displays works by the world's most recognizable names: O'Keeffe, Pollock, Monet, Renoir, and Picasso.

Eating & Drinking Leave the Bermuda shorts behind in favor of crisply ironed linen for swanky, oceanfront dining in Palm Beach. Overlook the surf dining on platters of freshly caught **seafood,** from Florida lobster to snapper, at beachside dining rooms. **Southern barbecue** reminds visitors that Florida *is* part of the South.

Nightlife & Entertainment Artists' lofts, sidewalk cafes, bars, restaurants, and galleries dot **Clematis Street,** the pumping heart of Palm Beach nightlife. On weekends, yuppies mingle with stylish Europeans and disheveled artists **sipping tropical cocktails** at sidewalk tables or **dancing** to electronic mixes at youthful bars. The moneyed set in Palm Beach is most likely found sipping high-end ports and brandies at **oceanfront hotel bars.**

Essentials

GETTING THERE If you're driving up or down the Florida coast, you'll probably reach the Palm Beach area by way of I-95. Exit at Belvedere Road or Okeechobee Boulevard, and head east to reach the most central part of Palm Beach.

Gaze upon the art at the Norton Museum in Palm Beach.

Visitors on their way to or from Orlando or Miami should take the Florida Turnpike, a toll road with a speed limit of 65 mph. Tolls are pricey, though; you may pay upwards of $9 from Orlando and $4 from Miami. If you're coming from Florida's west coast, you can take either S.R. 70, which runs north of Lake Okeechobee to Fort Pierce, or S.R. 80, which runs south of the lake to Palm Beach.

All major airlines fly to the **Palm Beach International Airport,** at Congress Avenue and Belvedere Road (© 561/471-7400). **Amtrak** (© 800/USA-RAIL [872-7245]; www.amtrak.com) has a terminal in West Palm Beach, at 201 S. Tamarind Ave. (© 561/832-6169).

GETTING AROUND Although a car is almost a necessity in this area, a recently revamped public transportation system is extremely convenient for getting to some attractions in both West Palm and Palm Beach. **Palm Tran** (www.palmtran.org) covers 32 routes with more than 140 buses. The fare is $1.50 for adults, 75¢ for children 3 to 18, seniors, and riders with disabilities. Free route maps are available by calling © 561/233-4BUS (4287). Information operators are available Monday through Saturday from 6am to 7pm.

In downtown West Palm, free shuttles from City Place to Clematis Street operate Sunday through Wednesday from 11am until 9pm, and Thursday through Saturday 11am until 11pm. Allegedly, the shuttles come every 5 minutes, but count on them taking longer. Look for the bubble gum–pink minibuses throughout downtown. Call © 561/833-8873 for details.

VISITOR INFORMATION The **Palm Beach County Convention and Visitors Bureau,** 1555 Palm Beach Lakes Blvd., Ste. 204, West Palm Beach, FL 33401 (© 800/554-PALM [7256] or 561/471-3995; www.palmbeachfl.com), distributes an informative brochure and answers questions about visiting the Palm Beaches. Ask for a map as well as a copy of the *Arts and Attractions Calendar,* a day-to-day guide to art, music, stage, and other events in the county.

Palm Beach & West Palm Beach

HOTELS
Fairfield Inn and Suites Palm Beach 35
Best Western 4
Comfort Inn 3
Brazilian Court Hotel & Beach Club 19
The Breakers Palm Beach 17
Four Seasons Resort Palm Beach 30
The Omphoy Ocean Resort 33
Palm Beach Marriott Singer Island
  Beach Resort & Spa 1
The Ritz-Carlton, Palm Beach 34
Chesterfield Hotel 20
The Colony 23
Palm Beach Historic Inn 21
Hibiscus House 6
Hotel Biba 13
Parkview Motor Lodge 28

RESTAURANTS
Café Boulud 19
Cafe l'Europe 18
Echo 14
Michelle Bernstein's at The Omphoy 33
Bice Restaurant 22
City Cellar Wine Bar & Grill 9
Rhythm Café 27
Green's Pharmacy 15
Tom's Place for Ribs 5

ATTRACTIONS
City Place 11
Currie Park 7
Flagler Museum 16
Lion Country Safari 24
Mar-A-Lago 29
Norton Museum of Art 12
Palm Beach Public Golf Course 32
Palm Beach Zoo at Dreher Park 26
Phipps Ocean Park 31
Rapids Water Park 2
Raymond F. Kravis Center for the
  Performing Arts 10
Richard and Pat Johnson Palm Beach
  County Museum 8
South Florida Science Museum 25

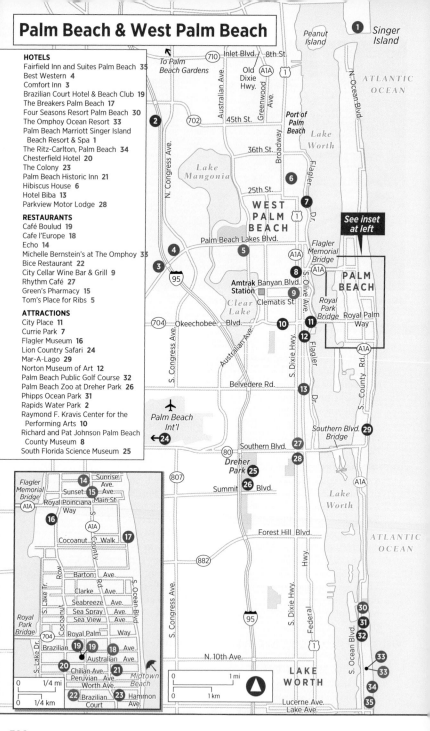

Beaches & Outdoor Activities

BEACHES Public beaches are a rare commodity here in Palm Beach. Most of the island's best beaches are fronted by private estates and inaccessible to the general public. However, there are a few notable exceptions, including **Midtown Beach,** east of Worth Avenue, on Ocean Boulevard between Royal Palm Way and Gulfstream Road, which boasts more than 100 feet of undeveloped sand. This newly widened coast is now a centerpiece and a natural oasis in a town dominated by commercial glitz. There are no restrooms or concessions here, though a lifeguard is on duty until sundown. A popular hangout for locals lies about 1½ miles north of here, near Dunbar Street; they prefer it to Midtown Beach because of the relaxed atmosphere. Parking is available at meters along A1A. At the south end of Palm Beach, there's a less-popular but better-equipped beach at **Phipps Ocean Park.** On Ocean Boulevard, between the Southern Boulevard and Lake Avenue causeways, there's a lively public beach encompassing more than 1,300 feet of groomed oceanfront. With picnic and recreation areas and plenty of parking, the area is especially good for families.

BIKING Rent anything from an English single-speed to a full-tilt mountain bike at the **Palm Beach Bicycle Trail Shop,** 223 Sunrise Ave. (✆ 561/659-4583; www.palmbeachbicycle.com). Rates are $15 per hour, $29 per half-day (9am–5pm), and $39 for 24 hours, and include a basket and lock (not that a lock is necessary in this fortress of a town). The most scenic route is called the Lake Trail, running the length of the island along the Intracoastal Waterway. On it, you'll see some of the most magnificent mansions and grounds, and enjoy the views of downtown West Palm Beach as well as some great wildlife.

GOLF There's good golfing in the Palm Beaches, but many private-club courses are maintained exclusively for members' use. Ask at your hotel or contact the **Palm Beach County Convention and Visitors Bureau** (✆ 561/471-3995) for information on which clubs are available for play. In the off season, some private courses open to visitors staying in Palm Beach County hotels. This Golf-A-Round program boasts no greens fees; reservations can be made through most major hotels.

The best hotel for golf in the area is the **PGA National Resort & Spa** (p. 335; ✆ 800/633-9150), which features a whopping 90 holes of golf.

The **Palm Beach Public Golf Course,** 2345 S. Ocean Blvd. (✆ 561/547-0598; www.golfontheocean.com), a popular public 18-hole course, is a par-3 that was redesigned in 2009 by Raymond Floyd and includes a new layout, more holes by the ocean, and, down the road, a state-of-the-art clubhouse. The course opens at 8am on a first-come, first-served basis. Club rentals are available. Greens fees are $14 to $45 per person depending on the time, season, and number of holes played. Cart fees are an extra $7 to $10.

SCUBA DIVING Year-round warm waters, barrier reefs, and plenty of wrecks make South Florida one of the world's most popular places for diving. One of the best-known artificial reefs in this area is a vintage Rolls-Royce Silver Shadow, which was sunk offshore in 1985. Nature has taken its toll, however, and divers can no longer sit in the car, which has been ravaged by time

THE sport OF KINGS

The posh **Palm Beach Polo and Country Club** and the **International Polo Club** are two of the world's premier polo grounds and host some of the sport's top-rated players. Even if you're not a sports fan, you must attend a match at one of these fields, which are on the mainland in a rural area called Wellington. Rest assured, however, that the spectators, and many of the players, are pure Palm Beach. After all, a day at the pony grounds is one of the only good reasons to leave Palm Beach proper. You need not be a Vanderbilt or a Kennedy to attend—matches are open to the public and are surprisingly affordable.

Even if you haven't a clue how the game is played, you can spend your time people-watching. In recent years, stargazers have spotted Prince Charles, Sylvester Stallone, Tommy Lee Jones, Bo Derek, and Ivana Trump, among others. Dozens of lesser-known royalty keep box seats right on the grounds.

Dress is casual; a navy or tweed blazer over jeans or khakis is the standard for men, while neat-looking jeans or a pantsuit is the norm for women. On warmer days, shorts and, of course, polo shirts are fine, too.

General admission is $15 to $45; box seats cost $75 to $100 but are usually for members only. Call for more information. Special polo brunches are often available, too, at $85 per person. Matches are held throughout the week. Schedules vary, but the big names usually compete on Sunday at 3:30pm from January to April.

The fields are located at 11809 Polo Club Rd. and 3667 120th Ave.,

South Wellington, 10 miles west of the Forest Hill Boulevard exit off I-95. Call ✆ **561/793-1440** or 204-5687, or visit www.internationalpoloclub.com for tickets and a detailed schedule of events.

and saltwater. For gear and excursions, call the **Scuba Club,** 4708 N. Flagler Dr., West Palm Beach (✆ **561/844-2466;** www.thescubaclub.com).

TENNIS There are hundreds of tennis courts in Palm Beach County. Wherever you are staying, you're bound to be within walking distance of one. In addition to the many hotel tennis courts (see "Where to Stay," below), you can play at **Currie Park,** 2400 N. Flagler Dr., West Palm Beach (✆ **561/835-7025**), a public park with three lighted hard courts. They're free and available on a first-come, first-served basis.

WATERSPORTS Call the **Blue Water Boat Rental,** 200 E. 13th St., Riviera Beach (✆ **561/840-7470;** www.bluewaterboatrental.com), to arrange sailboat, jet-ski, bicycle, kayak, water ski, and parasail rentals.

Oil tycoon Henry Flagler's mansion is now a fine museum.

Seeing the Sights

Flagler Museum ★★★ The Gilded Age is preserved in this luxurious mansion commissioned by Standard Oil tycoon Henry Flagler as a wedding present to his third wife. Whitehall, also known as the Taj Mahal of North America, is a classic Edwardian-style mansion containing 55 rooms, including a Louis XIV music room and art gallery, a Louis XV ballroom, and 14 guest suites outfitted with original antique European furnishings. Out back, you can climb aboard the *Rambler*, Mr. Flagler's private restored railroad car. Allow at least 1½ hours to tour the stunning grounds and interior. Group tours are available, but for the most part, this is a self-guided museum.

1 Whitehall Way (at Cocoanut Row and Whitehall Way), Palm Beach. ✆ **561/655-2833.** www.flaglermuseum.us. Admission $18 adults, $10 youth 13–18, $3 children 6–12. Tues–Sat 10am–5pm; Sun noon–5pm.

Norton Museum of Art ★★★ The Norton is world famous for its prestigious permanent collection and top temporary exhibitions. The museum's major collections are divided geographically. The American galleries contain major works by Hopper, O'Keeffe, and Pollock. The French collection contains Impressionist and post-Impressionist paintings by Cézanne, Degas, Gauguin, Matisse, Monet, Picasso, Pissarro, and Renoir. The Chinese collection contains more than 200 bronzes, jades, and ceramics, as well as monumental Buddhist sculptures. Allow about 2 hours to see this museum, depending on your level of interest. On the second Thursday of every month from 5 to 9pm, it's Art After Dark, featuring music, film, special tours with curators and docents, hands-on art activities, a cash bar, and menu options from Café 1451 at the Norton. General admission applies, but it's worth it for an arty night out.

1451 S. Olive Ave., West Palm Beach. ✆ **561/832-5196.** Fax 561/659-4689. www.norton.org. Admission $12 adults, $5 ages 13–21. Mon–Sat 10am–5pm; Thurs until 9pm; Sun 1–5pm. Closed Mon May–Oct and all major holidays. Take I-95 to exit 52 (Okeechobee Blvd. E.). Travel east on Okeechobee to Dixie Hwy., then south ½ mile to the Norton. Access parking through entrances on Dixie Hwy. and S. Olive Ave.

No trip to Palm Beach is complete without at least a glimpse of **Mar-A-Lago** (pictured at right), the stately residence of Donald Trump, the 21st century's answer to Jay Gatsby. In 1985, Trump purchased the estate of cereal heiress Marjorie Merriweather Post for a meager $8 million (for a fully furnished beachfront property of this stature, it was a relative bargain), to the great consternation of locals, who feared that he would turn the place into a casino. Instead, Trump, who sometimes resides in a portion of the palace, opened the house to the public—for a price, of course—as a tony country club (membership fee: $100,000). A long-running, unconfirmed rumor has it that Trump is selling the place. In the meantime, he continues to make his presence loudly known in Palm Beach.

While there are currently no tours open to the public, you can glimpse the gorgeous manse as you cross the bridge from West Palm Beach into Palm Beach. It's located at 1100 S. Ocean Blvd., Palm Beach.

Playmobil FunPark ★★ 🎁 For a child, it doesn't get any better than this. The 17,000-square-foot Playmobil FunPark is housed in a replica castle and loaded with themed areas for imaginative play: a medieval village, a Western town, a fantasy dollhouse, and more. Kids can play with the Playmobil boats on two water-filled tables. Tech-minded youths may get bored, but tots up to age 5 or so will love this place. You *could* spend hours here and not spend a penny, but parents, beware: Everything is available for purchase. There's another Playmobil park in Orlando.

8031 N. Military Trail, Palm Beach Gardens. © **800/351-8697** or 561/691-9880. Fax 561/691-9517. www.playmobil.com. Admission $1. Mon–Sat 10am–6pm; Sun noon–5pm. From I-95, go north to Palm Beach Lakes Blvd., then west to Military Trail. Turn left; the park is about a mile down on the right.

Nature Preserves & Attractions

Lion Country Safari ★★ 🎁 More than 1,300 animals on this 500-acre preserve (the nation's first cageless drive-through safari) are divided into their indigenous regions, from the East African preserve of the Serengeti to the American West. Elephants, lions, wildebeest, ostriches, American bison, buffalo, watusi, pink flamingos, and many other unusual species roam the preserve. When we visited, most of the lions were asleep; when awake, they travel freely throughout the cageless grassy landscape. In fact, you're the one who's confined in your own car without an escort (no convertibles allowed). You're given a detailed pamphlet with photos and descriptions, and are instructed to obey the 15 mph speed limit—unless you see the rhinos charge (a rare occasion), in which case you're encouraged to floor it. Driving the loop takes slightly more than an hour, though you could make a day of just watching the chimpanzees play on their secluded

islands. Included in the admission is Safari World, an amusement park with paddleboats, a carousel, miniature golf, and a baby animal nursery. Picnics are encouraged, and camping is available. The best time to go is late afternoon, right before the park closes; it's much cooler then, so the lions are more active.

Southern Blvd. W. at S.R. 80, West Palm Beach. © **561/793-1084,** or 561/793-9797 for camping reservations. www.lioncountrysafari.com. Admission $27 adults, $24 seniors, $20 children 3–9. Van rental $10 to $18 per hour. Daily 9:30am–5:30pm (last vehicle admitted at 4:30pm). From I-95, exit on Southern Blvd. Go west for about 18 miles.

Palm Beach Zoo at Dreher Park ★

A happy visitor feeds an (also presumably happy) giraffe at Lion Country Safari.

If you want animals, go to Lion Country Safari (above). Unlike big-city zoos, this intimate 23-acre attraction is more like a stroll in the park than an all-day excursion. It features more than 1,400 animals representing more than 100 different species. The zoo also features a colorful wildlife carousel, an interactive water-play fountain, a full-service restaurant, and daily performances of the "Wings Over Water" bird show and the "Wild Things" stage show. The zoo also offers guests the opportunity to view more than 50 animal encounters, keeper talks, or training sessions per week. The Cornell Tropics of the Americas exhibit showcases both the animals and the native culture found in the Central and South American regions. Jaguars, bush dogs, Baird's tapirs, and giant anteaters are just a few of the animals that make their home in this 3-acre re-creation of a Central and South American rain forest. Other animal highlights include Malayan tiger, Florida panther, Queensland koala, Komodo dragon, black bear, river otter, and the Florida Reptile House. Allow at least 2 hours to see all of the sights here.

1301 Summit Blvd. (east of I-95 btw. Southern and Forest Hill boulevards). © **561/547-WILD** (9453). www.palmbeachzoo.org. Admission $17 adults, $13 seniors, $12 children 3–12. Daily 9am–5pm. Closed Thanksgiving and Christmas.

Rapids Water Park ★ 🎁

It may not be on the same grand scale as the theme parks in Orlando, but Rapids is a great way to cool off on a hot day. There are 12 acres of water rides (including an aquatic obstacle course), a children's area, and a miniature-golf course. Check out the Superbowl, a tubeless water ride that spins and swirls before dumping you into the pool below, and the Big Thunder, a giant funnel that plunges you down 50 feet in a four-person tube. Claustrophobia, anyone?

6566 N. Military Trail, West Palm Beach (1 mile west of I-95 on Military, btw. 45th St./exit 54 and Blue Heron Blvd./exit 55 in West Palm Beach). © **561/842-8756.** www.rapidswaterpark.com. Admission $33 Mon–Fri, $36 Sat–Sun; free for children 2 and under. Parking $10. Mid-Mar to Sept Mon–Fri 10am–5pm; Sat–Sun 10am–6pm.

Richard and Pat Johnson Palm Beach County History Museum ★ There's more to Palm Beach history than Donald Trump and well-preserved octogenarians. Opened to the public in 2008 within the historic 1916 Courthouse in downtown West Palm Beach, the museum has two permanent exhibits—the People Gallery, a tribute to approximately 100 individuals and families who have contributed to the growth of Palm Beach County, and the Place Gallery, featuring models and photographs exploring Palm Beach county's natural environment and the animals and ecology that make it unique—that are worth a spin through.

300 N. Dixie Hwy., West Palm Beach. Entrance is on 2nd floor of courthouse. ✆ **561/832-4164.** www.historicalsocietypbc.org. Free admission. Tues–Sat 10am–5pm.

South Florida Science Museum ★ 🎁 It's hands-on at this veteran West Palm science museum, which boasts a planetarium, an aquarium, interactive galleries, and traveling exhibitions. But the museum got a big boost in 2009 when its Marvin Dekelboum Planetarium became one of only a handful of planetariums in the country to showcase state-of-the-art, full-dome digital projection capability that allows visitors to take a virtual space walk or to explore the realms of the sea. Upgrades also include a new, programmable laser system to continue the popular laser concerts, LED lighting, and Blu-ray high-definition video technology. For those so inclined there's also a mini-golf course, Galaxy Golf, where, for $2 you can putt around the planets.

4801 Dreher Trail N., West Palm Beach (at the north end of Dreher Park). ✆ **561/832-1988.** www.sfsm.org. Admission $12 adults, $10 seniors, $8.95 children. Planetarium shows $4 adults, $2 children in addition to museum admission. Laser shows $5 per person. Mon–Fri 10am–5pm; Sat 10am–6pm; Sun noon–6pm.

Shopping

No matter what your budget, be sure to take a stroll down Worth Avenue, the "Rodeo Drive of the South" and a window-shopper's dream. Between South Ocean Boulevard and Cocoanut Row, there are more than 200 boutiques, shops, art galleries, and restaurants. If you want to fit in, dress as if you are going to an elegant luncheon, not the mall down the street.

You'd never know there was ever a recession based on the swarms of shoppers armed with bags from **Gucci, Chanel, Armani, Hermès,** and **Louis Vuitton,** among others. And besides the boldface collection of couturiers, there are also a good number of unique, independent boutiques. For privileged feet, **Stubbs & Wooton,** 4 Via Parigi (✆ **561/655-4105**), sells velvet slippers that are a favorite of the loofahed locals. For rare and estate jewelry, **Richter's of Palm Beach,** 224 Worth Ave. (✆ **561/655-0774**), has been specializing in priceless gems since 1893. Just off Worth Avenue is the **Church Mouse,** 378 S. County Rd. (✆ **561/659-2154**), a great consignment/thrift shop with antique furnishings and tableware, as well as lots of good castoff clothing and shoes from socialites who've moved on to the next designers or, worse than that, to the big gala in the sky. This shop usually closes for 2 months during the summer; call to be sure. Oh, and if you plan to put something up for consignment, make sure to use the special "donor's door" (a nice way of saying service entrance) on the south side of the building.

City Place, Okeechobee Road (at I-95), West Palm Beach (✆ **561/820-9716**), is a $550-million, Mediterranean-style shopping, dining, and entertainment complex that's responsible for revitalizing what was once a lifeless downtown

West Palm Beach. Among the 78 mostly chain stores are **Macy's, Barnes & Noble, Banana Republic, Armani Exchange, Pottery Barn, Sephora, Lucky Brand,** and **SEE** eyewear. Restaurants include McCormick & Schmick's; Cheesecake Factory; Miami Beach, Fort Lauderdale, and Hollywood's Taverna Opa; City Cellar Wine Bar and Grill; Brewzzi; BB King's Blues Club; Blue Martini; and Improv Comedy Club and Dinner Theater. Best of all is the Muvico IMAX, a 20-screen movie theater where you can wine and dine while watching a feature.

Check your net worth before you hit Worth Avenue.

Where to Stay

The island of Palm Beach is the epitome of *Lifestyles of the Rich and Famous* or, for our younger readers, VH1's *The Fabulous Life Of,* oozing with glitz, glamour, and the occasional scandal. Royalty and celebrities come to winter here, and there are plenty of lavishly priced options to accommodate them. Happily, there are also a few special inns that offer reasonably priced rooms in elegant settings. But most of the more modest places to lay your straw hat surround the island.

A few of the larger hotel chains operating in Palm Beach include the **Fairfield Inn and Suites Palm Beach,** 2870 S. Ocean Blvd. (© **800/228-2800** or 561/582-2581), across the street from the beach. In West Palm Beach, chain hotels are mostly on the main arteries close to the highways and a short drive from downtown. They include **Best Western,** 1800 Palm Beach Lakes Blvd. (© **800/331-9569** or 561/683-8810), and, just down the road, **Comfort Inn,** 1901 Palm Beach Lakes Blvd. (© **800/221-2222** or 561/689-6100). Farther south is **Parkview Motor Lodge,** 4710 S. Dixie Hwy., just south of Southern Boulevard (© **561/833-4644**). This 28-room motel is the best of many along Dixie Highway (U.S. 1). With rates starting at about $75 for a room with TV, air-conditioning, and phone (don't laugh, some don't have any), you can't ask for more.

For other options, contact **Palm Beach Accommodations** (© **800/543-SWIM** [7946]).

VERY EXPENSIVE

Brazilian Court Hotel & Beach Club ★★★ This elegant, old-world, Mediterranean-style hotel dates from the 1920s and almost looks like a Beverly Hills bungalow. Much like Palm Beach residents, the hotel debuted a new youthful glow after a remake in 2008. The 80 custom-designed rooms and suites all feature mahogany case goods and crown molding, Provence-style wood shutters, and king-size beds topped with imported linens. Pampered pets under 20 pounds (you know the type: held hostage in Mummy's Gucci bag) receive gift bags full of treats for a (required) one-time $100 pet fee. A large hotel by Palm Beach standards (the Breakers notwithstanding), Brazilian Court sprawls over half a block and features fountains and private courtyards. The only downside? A tiny, yet intimate, pool where you feel you have to whisper. To counter the size is stellar poolside service—order drinks or food and *voilà!* A small Jacuzzi hidden from the pool is where shy types and celebs like to hide. Celebrity stylist Frederic Fekkai offers the hotel's premier salon and spa. With the addition of renowned Chef Daniel Boulud's hauter-than-thou **Café Boulud** (p. 339), which provides a great bar scene with live music, Brazilian Court is Palm Beach's number-one place to see and be seen.

301 Australian Ave., Palm Beach, FL 33480. www.thebraziliancourt.com. ✆ **800/552-0335** or 561/655-7740. Fax 561/655-0801. 80 units. From $550 studio; from $950 1-bedroom suite; from $1,145 2-bedroom suite. Special packages available. AE, DC, DISC, MC, V. Pampered pet fee $100. **Amenities:** Restaurant; concierge; exercise room; heated outdoor pool; room service; spa treatments. *In room:* A/C, TV, hair dryer, minibar, Wi-Fi.

The Breakers Palm Beach ★★★ 🎁 This 140-acre beachfront hotel is quintessential Palm Beach, where old money mixes with new money, and the Old World gives way to a bit of modernity. The seven-story building is a marvel, with a frescoed lobby and long, palatial hallways. Plush rooms feature marble bathrooms and views of the ocean or the magnificently manicured grounds. The Mediterranean-style Beach Club features outstanding vistas of the ocean and is reminiscent of a panoramic island escape. After a $15-million beachfront redevelopment project, the Beach Club now features five pools, four whirlpool spas, expansive pool decks, lush tropical landscaping, and lawn space; a 6,000-square-foot rooftop terrace, 20 private, luxury beach bungalows, and 10 pool cabanas for daytime rental, with a dedicated staff of concierges; a beach gazebo; and two casual oceanside restaurants. The hotel's available spa treatments can be performed indoors or out. A revamp of Florida's oldest existing golf course transformed the Ocean Course into a 6,100-yard, championship-level par-70, and the Breakers Rees Jones Course underwent a $6-million redesign and reconstruction in 2004. Both courses feature state-of-the-art golf learning centers. Kids aren't neglected either at the impressive Family Entertainment Center, a 6,160-square-foot space that includes an arcade, a toddler's playroom, an arts-and-crafts area, a children's movie theater, and a video game room all filled with the latest in high-tech toys and games.

1 S. County Rd., Palm Beach, FL 33480. www.thebreakers.com. ✆ **1-888-BREAKERS** (273-2537) or 561/655-6611. Fax 561/659-8403. 540 units. Winter $499–$1,340 double, $1,310–$6,100 suite; in summer rooms start as low as $259. AE, DC, DISC, MC, V. Valet parking $20. From I-95, exit Okeechobee Blvd. E., head east to S. County Rd., and turn left. **Amenities:** 9 restaurants; 5 bars; babysitting; bike rentals; children's programs; concierge; 2 championship golf courses; 2 fitness centers; 5 outdoor pools; room service; indoor/outdoor spa; 10 Har-Tru tennis courts; watersports equipment/rentals. *In room:* A/C, TV/DVD, CD player, hair dryer, minibar, MP3 docking station, Wi-Fi.

Four Seasons Resort Palm Beach ★★ 🎁 Situated on the pristine Palm Beach oceanfront, Four Seasons is a quiet retreat from Worth Avenue—a pricey cab ride from the hotel. Guest rooms, renovated in the summer of 2010 to reflect a more chic beach-house vibe (as opposed to a stuffy, swanky hotel vibe) arc spacious, with private balconies and lavish new bathrooms. The full-service spa is excellent and also new; at 10,000 square feet, it features 11 treatment rooms including a "Man Room," wet room, spa suite, and full-service salon. The main dining room, known simply as the **Restaurant,** has been updated as a casual seafood-oriented eatery with lovely lounge seating on the outdoor terrace where you can just have a cocktail (try their "organic" drinks) and a small plate from the restaurant's raw bar. Two other restaurants, the **Ocean Bistro**—which is subpar for this kind of hotel—and the **Atlantic Bar & Grill,** round out the dining options. The resort offers a complimentary kids' program, and teens will enjoy the game room with Xbox, a pool table, and a large-screen TV. Meanwhile, parents can entertain themselves in the Living Room, a swank lounge, or at the Restaurant's outdoor lounge.

2800 S. Ocean Blvd., Palm Beach, FL 33480. www.fourseasons.com/palmbeach. © **800/432-2335** or 561/582-2800. Fax 561/547-1557. 210 units. Winter $649–$969 double, from $2,200 1-bedroom suite, from $3,970 2-bedroom suite; off season $195–$665 double, $1,100 1-bedroom suite, $2,600 2-bedroom suite. AE, DC, DISC, MC, V. Valet parking $25. From I-95, take the 6th Ave. exit east and turn left onto Dixie Hwy. Turn east onto Lake Ave. and north onto A1A (S. Ocean Blvd.); the resort is just ahead on your right. Pets less than 20 lb. accepted. **Amenities:** 3 restaurants; lounge/outdoor patio; babysitting; children's programs; concierge; fitness center; outdoor heated pool; spa; 2 tennis courts; watersports equipment/rentals. *In room:* A/C, TV/DVD/VCR, CD player, fridge, hair dryer, high-speed Internet access, minibar, MP3 docking station.

The Omphoy Ocean Resort When it opened in 2009, this 134-room waterfront boutique hotel was the first new resort to open in Palm Beach in nearly 20 years. Owned by the same company that owns the fabulous Brazilian Court, the stylish Omphoy features an open lobby and a minimalist South Beach modern vibe, and it may be the island's hippest hotel, catering to a younger clientele than many of the area hotels. Rooms feature sleek, high-end furnishings and plush linens and offer panoramic ocean or Intracoastal views. The resort also features surfside cuisine, by Miami's star chef **Michelle Bernstein** (p. 340), and New York–based **exhale spa,** with 5,000 square feet of dedicated spa space with indoor and outdoor treatments combining fitness and movement with spa and healing.

2842 S. Ocean Blvd., Palm Beach, FL 33480. www.omphoy.com. © **561/540-6440.** 130 units. Winter $450–$700 suite; off season $279–$450 suite. AE, DC, DISC, MC, V. **Amenities:** 2 restaurants; bar; pool; spa; watersports equipment/rentals; free Wi-Fi. *In room:* A/C, TV/DVD.

Palm Beach Marriott Singer Island Beach Resort & Spa ★ 🏨 Part of Riviera Beach and located on the water in eastern Palm Beach County is Singer Island, sort of like Marco Island, with condos dotting the shore. Rebranded by Marriott in 2010, this all-suite Singer Island resort offers a condolike experience with luxurious one- and two-bedroom all-suite accommodations ranging from 800 to 2,100 square feet and featuring high-tech kitchens and spectacular views of either the ocean or the Intracoastal. Ideal for big families or extended stays, the rooms also feature washers and dryers so you don't have to schlep your dirty laundry back home. Resort amenities include a spa—the only full-service spa on Singer Island—two pools, beach and pool cabanas, a fantastic kids' club, and a restaurant. If you want to stay in Palm Beach and feel like you live there, this is the place to do it. The hotel is completely smoke free.

3800 N. Ocean Dr., Singer Island, FL 33404. www.marriottpalmbeach.com. © **561/340-1700.** Fax 561/340-1705. 222 units. Winter $224–$489 suite; off season $199–$489 suite. AE, DC, DISC, MC, V. **Amenities:** 3 restaurants and lounges; babysitting; concierge; fitness center; 2 pools; room service; spa; watersports equipment/rentals; Wi-Fi. *In room:* A/C, TV, hair dryer, minibar, Wi-Fi.

PGA National Resort & Spa ★★★ This expansive Northern Palm Beach resort is a premier golf-vacation spot, but its top-rated 40,000-square-foot European spa could be a destination in itself. With five 18-hole championship courses on more than 2,300 acres, the PGA National Golf Academy complete with Leadbetter and Pelz golf schools, and tour-level club fitting, golfers and other sports-minded travelers will find plenty to keep them occupied; in addition to golf there's croquet, tennis, swimming, a complete health and fitness center, and a sublime spa. The par-72 Champion Course, redesigned in 1990 by Jack Nicklaus and upgraded again in 2007 and 2008, is the resort's most valuable asset and home to the PGA Tour's Honda Classic. Guest rooms are spacious and comfortable, bordering on residential, with immense bathrooms and private terrace or patio. Club cottages are especially convenient, offering great privacy and serenity. In 2008, the resort completed a $65-million renovation, including extensive renovations to the resort's public spaces, a new lobby and restaurant, a lush new zero-entry resort pool, and a complete renovation of the Palmer course. This is not a beach resort, but multiple resort pools, including a lap pool, main pool, soothing whirlpools, and a collection of outdoor therapy pools, create a true oasis.

400 Ave. of the Champions, Palm Beach Gardens, FL 33418. www.pgaresort.com. © **800/533-9391** or 561/627-2000. Fax 561/225-2595. 339 guest rooms and suites, 40 cottages. Winter $299–$339 double, $369–$829 suite; off season $144–$169 double, $174–$659 suite. Children 16 and under stay free in parent's room. Special packages available. AE, DC, DISC, MC, V. From I-95, take exit 57B (PGA Blvd.) going west and continue for approx. 2 miles to the resort entrance on the left. **Amenities:** 9 restaurants and lounges; babysitting; concierge; 5 18-hole tournament-ready golf courses; 8 pools; room service; European spa; 19 Har-Tru clay tennis courts; Wi-Fi. *In room:* A/C, TV, hair dryer, Internet access, minibar.

The Ritz-Carlton, Palm Beach ★★★ 🎁 If the Breakers is too mammoth for your taste, consider the Ritz. A lot warmer than the Four Seasons, the Ritz, located on a beautiful beach in a tiny town about 8 miles from Worth Avenue, lacks pretension and feels more like a boutique hotel. A $130-million renovation in 2007 added flatscreen HDTVs, bedside electronic control "pamper panels," and Italian custom mahogany furniture. Oceanfront suites have oceanview stone soaking tubs, a sofa sleeper, two-line phones, and two HDTVs. Two pools are perfect for families and/or ideal for relaxation. The 42,000-square-foot Eau Spa by Cornelia debuted in 2009, complete with a custom Scrub and Polish Bar, Bath Lounge, Spa Villas with outdoor verdant gardens, and the Self-Centered Garden featuring swings, dipping pools, and water-massage benches. A casual oceanfront all-day restaurant called **Temple Orange** features Italian/Mediterranean fare with fresh seafood; you can also dine at **Angle,** a local and seasonal fish and beef restaurant. **Breeze,** the "gourmet" burger patio and bar, sits on the ocean's edge; while **Stir Bar** serves cocktails and light bites.

100 S. Ocean Blvd., Manalapan, FL 33462. www.ritzcarlton.com. © **800/241-3333** or 561/533-6000. Fax 561/588-4202. 309 units. Winter $479–$849 double, $849–$1,599 suite, $6,000 presidential suite; off season $279–$619 double, $639–$969 suite, $2,999 presidential suite. AE, DISC, MC, V. Valet parking $28. From I-95, take exit for Lantana Rd., heading east. After 1 mile, turn right onto Federal Hwy. (U.S. 1/Dixie). Continue south to the next light and turn left onto Ocean Ave. Cross the Intracoastal Waterway and turn right onto A1A. **Amenities:** 2 restaurants; bar; bike rental; children's programs; concierge; fitness center; Jacuzzi; 2 outdoor pools; room service; spa; watersports equipment/rentals. *In room:* A/C, HDTV/DVD, hair dryer, minibar, Wi-Fi.

EXPENSIVE

Chesterfield Hotel ★★★ Reminiscent of an English country manor, the Chesterfield in all its flowery, Laura Ashley–inspired glory is a magnificent, charming hotel with exceptional service. Warm and inviting, the Chesterfield is one of the only places in South Florida where the idea of a fireplace (there's one in the hotel's library) doesn't seem ridiculous. Traditional English tea is served every afternoon, including fresh-baked scones, petits fours, and sandwiches. Rooms are decorated with antiques and with bright fabrics and wallpaper. In 2010, the Chesterfield refurbished 16 rooms and suites to feature new carpeting, draperies, upholstery, and headboards. The roomy marble bathrooms are stocked with an array of luxurious toiletries. A small heated pool and courtyard are nice, and the beach is only 3 blocks away, but the real action is inside: The hotel's retro-elegant **Leopard Lounge,** also refurbished in 2010, serves decent Continental cuisine, but is better as a late-night hangout for live music, schmoozing, and eyeing the local cognoscenti.

363 Cocoanut Row, Palm Beach, FL 33480. www.chesterfieldpb.com. © **800/243-7871** or 561/659-5800. Fax 561/659-6707. 52 units. Winter $395–$465 queen, $495–$570 king, $675–$1,585 suite; off season $175–$249 queen, $259–$319 king, $339–$719 suite. Rollaway bed $15. Packages available. AE, DC, DISC, MC, V. Free valet parking. From I-95, exit onto Okeechobee Blvd. E., cross the Intracoastal Waterway, and turn right onto Cocoanut Row. **Amenities:** Restaurant; lounge; concierge; access to nearby health club; hot tub and heated pool; room service; Wi-Fi. **In room:** A/C, TV, DVD/CD player (in kings/suites only), fridge (in kings/suites only), hair dryer, high-speed Internet access.

MODERATE

The Colony ★ For years, the Colony has been a favorite hangout—hide-out, perhaps—for old-timers, socialites, and mysterious luminaries. The very old-school Polo Lounge features an eclectic mix of local lounge and A-list cabaret singers and entertainers, but the people-watching there is priceless as octogenarian sugar daddies proudly and boldly sashay by with bedecked, bejeweled arm candy at least half their age. The hotel's **Royal Room Cabaret** is also a nocturnal fave, saturated with cocktails, song, and an occasional cameo appearance by the likes of Connie Francis, Jack Jones, and Steve Tyrell. Rooms at the Georgian-style hotel have been totally renovated with a dark wood British West Indies theme featuring comfy feather duvets, lots of pillows, pale yellow and gold walls, and fabrics in distinctive palm-tree motif. All rooms feature large flatscreen TVs, cable, comfortable desks for those who need to perform business tasks, and comfy chairs and reading lamps. There are also seven two-bedroom villas and three recently renovated penthouses, including the Presidential Penthouse (Presidents Bush, Clinton, Carter, and Ford have all stayed there) and the Duke of Windsor Penthouse, where the Duke and Duchess of Windsor spent part of their time in exile.

155 Hammon Ave., Palm Beach, FL 33480. www.thecolonypalmbeach.com. © **800/521-5525** or 561/655-5430. Fax 561/659-8104. 90 units. Winter $400 double, $500 1-bedroom suite; off season $175 double, $250 1-bedroom suite. AE, DC, MC, V. From I-95, exit onto Okeechobee Blvd. E. and cross the Intracoastal Waterway. Turn right on S. County Rd. and then left onto Hammon Ave. **Amenities:** Restaurant; bar; concierge; heated pool; limited seasonal room service; spa. *In room:* A/C, TV, hair dryer, Internet access.

Palm Beach Historic Inn ★★ Built in 1923, the Palm Beach Historic Inn is an area landmark within a block's walking distance of the beach (chairs and towels are provided for guests of the hotel), Worth Avenue, and several good restaurants. The small lobby is filled with antiques, books, magazines, and an old-fashioned umbrella stand, all of which add to the homey feel of this intimate B&B. In-room wine, fruit, snacks, tea, and cookies ensure that you won't go hungry—never mind the excellent continental breakfast that is brought to you daily. All bedrooms are uniquely decorated and have hardwood floors, down comforters, Egyptian-cotton linens, fluffy bathrobes, and plenty of good-smelling toiletries. Here you'll find a casual elegance that's comfortable for everyone. In addition, a baby grand piano and guitars for the musically inclined, as well as movies to keep the kids entertained, have been added to the hotel's amenities. *Note:* Smoking is not permitted.

365 S. County Rd., Palm Beach, FL 33480. www.palmbeachhistoricinn.com. ☏ **561/832-4009.** Fax 561/832-6255. 13 units. Winter $185–$345 double, $345–$395 suite; off season $145–$175 double, $225 suite. Rates include continental breakfast. Children stay free in parent's room. AE, MC, V. Small pets accepted. *In room:* A/C, TV/VCR, fridge, hair dryer.

INEXPENSIVE

Hibiscus House ★★ 🏠 Inexpensive bed-and-breakfasts are a rarity in Southeast Florida, making the Hibiscus House, one of the area's first, a true find. Located a few miles from the coast in a quiet residential neighborhood, this 1920s-era B&B is filled with handsome antiques and tapestries. Every room has a private terrace or balcony. The Red Room has a fabulous bathroom with Jacuzzi. The peaceful backyard retreat has been transformed into a tropical garden, with a heated pool and lounge chairs. There are pretty indoor areas for guests to enjoy; one little sitting room is wrapped in glass and is stocked with playing cards and board games. Huge gourmet breakfast portions are as filling as they are beautiful. Make any special requests in advance; owners Raleigh Hill and Colin Rayer will be happy to oblige.

501 30th St., West Palm Beach, FL 33407. www.hibiscushouse.com. ☏ **800/203-4927** or ☏/fax 561/863-5633. 8 units. Winter $125–$210 double; off season $100–$150 double. Rates include breakfast. AE, DC, DISC, MC, V. From I-95, exit onto Palm Beach Lakes Blvd. E. and continue 4 miles. Turn left onto Flagler Dr. and continue for about ½ mile; then turn left onto 30th St. Pets accepted. **Amenities:** Concierge; heated pool. *In room:* A/C, TV, hair dryer.

Hotel Biba ★ 🏠 Located in the historic El Cid neighborhood, just 1 mile from City Place and Clematis Street, the very cool Biba answers the call for an inexpensive, chic hotel that young hipsters can call their own. Housed in a renovated Colonial-style 1940s motor lodge, Biba has been remarkably updated by de rigueur designer Barbara Hulanicki and features a sleek lobby to complement a hip hotel bar, and a gorgeously landscaped outdoor pool area with Asian-inspired gardens. Guest rooms are shabby chic, with private patios, mosaic-tile floors, custom mahogany furniture, Egyptian-cotton linens, down pillows, and flatscreen TVs. The bold color schemes mix nicely with the high-fashion crowd that convenes here. *A word of advice:* This place is not exactly soundproof. Rooms may be cloistered by fence and gardens, but they're still extremely close to a major thoroughfare. Ask for a room that's on the quieter Belvedere Road, as opposed to those facing South Olive Avenue.

320 Belvedere Rd., West Palm Beach, FL 33405. www.hotelbiba.com. ☏ **561/832-0094.** Fax 561/833-7848. 41 units. $110–$215 double; $200–$300 suite. Rates include breakfast. Online discounts available. AE, MC, V. **Amenities:** Lounge; concierge; outdoor pool. *In room:* A/C, TV, CD player, hair dryer, free Wi-Fi.

Where to Eat

Palm Beach has some of the area's swankiest restaurants. Thanks to the development of downtown West Palm Beach, however, there is also a great selection of trendier, less expensive spots. Dress here is slightly more formal than in most other areas of Florida: Men wear blazers, and women generally put on modest dresses or chic suits when they dine out, even on the oppressively hot days of summer.

VERY EXPENSIVE

Café Boulud ★★★ FRENCH Snowbird socialites and foodies rejoiced over the opening of star chef Daniel Boulud's eponymous restaurant in the Brazilian Court hotel. Nonsocialites said, "Figures, another restaurant where we can't afford even a bread crumb." But if you're out to splurge, Boulud is ideal, with an exquisite menu divided into four sections—*La Tradition* (French and American classics), *La Saison* (seasonal dishes), *Le Potager* (dishes inspired by the vegetable market), and *Le Voyage* (world cuisine). The roasted barramundi with squash, pomegranate, and brown butter is superb. There's also a light and somewhat reasonably priced menu offering salads, sandwiches—including possibly the best we've ever had, the BLT with smoked beef brisket, lettuce slaw, Creole mustard, fried green tomatoes, and homemade pickles—and even a cheeseburger if you prefer; try the chickpea fries with *piquillo*-pepper ketchup. If star chefs, stuffy socialites, and froufrou cuisine aren't your thing, don't even bother.

In the Brazilian Court, 301 Australian Ave., Palm Beach. ℂ **561/655-6060.** www.danielnyc.com. Reservations essential. Main courses $32–$40. AE, DC, MC, V. Daily 9am–10pm.

Cafe l'Europe ★★★ CONTINENTAL One of Palm Beach's finest and most popular spots, this 3-decades-plus-old, award-winning, romantic, and formal restaurant gives you a good reason to get dressed up. The enticing appetizers served by a superb staff might include crispy veal sweetbreads, wild mushroom and asparagus, or lobster bisque. Main courses run the gamut from Wiener schnitzel with herbed spaetzle to sautéed potato-crusted Florida snapper to Dover sole in an anchovy tomato sauce. Seafood dishes and steaks in sumptuous but light sauces are always exceptional. For those looking to indulge, the menu offers a caviar collection that may set you back a few hundred bucks. Caviar, we get, but the cheapest pasta dish here is around $41 for a seafood linguine. And as much as this is a haven for Palm Beach see-and-be-scenesters, Café l'Europe, run by husband-and-wife team chef Norbert and Lidia Goldner, is still a mom-and-pop shop, albeit one with French doors, mirrored surfaces, piano bar, and $40-plus pasta.

331 S. County Rd. (at Brazilian Ave.), Palm Beach. ℂ **561/655-4020.** www.cafeleurope.com. Reservations recommended. Main courses $34–$47. AE, DC, DISC, MC, V. Tues–Sat noon–3pm and 6–10pm; Sun 6–10pm.

Echo ★★ ASIAN This hyperstylish, sleek eatery is the Breakers hotel's homage to young and hip. The hotel runs the restaurant, even though it's off premises, and it's worth leaving the comfy, upper-crust confines of the Breakers for this resounding Echo. The menu is broken down into categories: earth, wind, fire, water, and flavor, which doesn't do the food any real justice. Sushi bar specialties, such as the *hamachi kama*, grilled *hamachi*, Asian greens, and citrus soy, and the outstanding echo roll with shrimp tempura, cucumber, avocado, and tobiko in a sesame soy sheet with superspicy *sriracha* sauce, are two of our favorites. But it's not all sushi. There are Chinese dim sum specialties too. The dim sum sampler, at $27, feeds two and is an ideal starter or full-blown meal. Then there's the Thai roast duck, and the open-flame wok specialties. There's too much to choose from, but it's all good. Be sure to check out the restaurant's **Dragonfly Lounge** after dinner. It's a hopping scene, especially by Palm Beach standards.

230 Sunrise Ave., Palm Beach. ℂ **561/802-4222.** www.echopalmbeach.com. Reservations essential. Sushi $4–$23; main courses $18–$60. AE, DC, MC, V. Tues–Sun 5:30–9:30pm.

Michelle Bernstein's at The Omphoy ★★ MEDITERRANEAN Miami's culinary "it" girl takes on finicky Palm Beach diners with her latest, located in a trendy, swanky hotel featuring spectacular water views. Fans of Bernstein's will say this sounds familiar, as Bernstein rose up in the culinary ranks via Azul at Miami's Mandarin Oriental. Bernstein brings her culinary sense of whimsy up to Palm Beach, with dishes such as shrimp *tiradito,* her own spin on popcorn shrimp, prepared with a blend of lime, cilantro, and spices. Bernstein's channeling of her Judeo-Latino heritage in the kitchen is where she really shines, taking an old-fashioned Cuban *croquetta* and sending it off to the Med where it receives an infusion of feta and spinach instead of the usual ham. Other dishes include the finger-lickin'-good Michy's Famous Fried Chicken, a Miami import marinated in a mix of buttermilk and tarragon; a bouillabaisse with Latin accents in the form of *sofrito*-flavored broth; and another of Michy's signature dishes, beautifully braised short ribs. Prices are steep, but worth it—especially if you consider the gas money saved from not having to drive down to Miami for a Bernstein fix.

The Omphoy Ocean Resort, 2842 S. Ocean Blvd., Palm Beach. ☎ **561/540-6444.** www.omphoy.com. Reservations recommended. Main courses $24–$36. AE, DC, DISC, MC, V. Daily noon–2:30pm and 6–10pm.

EXPENSIVE

Bice Restaurant ★★ NORTHERN ITALIAN Bice's Milanese cuisine is excellent, but as far as atmosphere, the air in here is a bit haughty and stuffy, bordering on rude. Servers and diners alike have attitudes, but you should forget all that with one bite of the juicy veal cutlet with tomato salad or the *pasta e fagioli* (pasta with beans). Another standout is the grilled swordfish with sautéed escarole and polenta. Ladies who lunch love the chopped salad. As outdated as the interior may seem, wait until you see some of the octogenarians sporting painted-on jeans and makeup. This is the upper crust's bingo hall, for sure, where servers and managers seem to know everyone's names from their first marriage all the way to their last. And for great people-watching and actually nice service, consider the bar, where you can linger over a glass of wine and, if the bartender likes you, free pizza, for hours.

313½ Worth Ave., Palm Beach. ☎ **561/835-1600.** Reservations essential. Main courses $20–$40. AE, DC, MC, V. Daily noon–10pm.

MODERATE

City Cellar Wine Bar & Grill ★★ AMERICAN If the Palm Beach–proper dining scene is too stuffy, head over to City Place to find this yuppie brick-and-pressed-tin enclave where people-watching is at a premium. Despite its all-American appearance, City Cellar offers a varied menu, from pizzas and pastas to steak and sea bass. We love the onion-and-mushroom soup with pinot grigio, and the twin 7-ounce pork chops with potato purée, sweet-and-sour shallots, and sherry mustard butter. The place is mobbed on weekends, so plan for a long wait that's best spent at the action-packed bar.

700 S. Rosemary Ave., West Palm Beach. ☎ **561/659-1853.** Reservations suggested. Main courses $21–$36; pizzas $12–$14; sandwiches and salads $12–$19. AE, MC, V. Sun–Wed 11:30am–10:30pm; Thurs–Sat 11:30am–11pm. Bar Sun–Wed 11:30am–1am; Thurs–Sat 11:30am–2am.

Rhythm Café ★ 🍴 ECLECTIC AMERICAN This funky hole in the wall is where those in the know come to eat some of West Palm Beach's most laid-back gourmet food. On the handwritten, photocopied menu (which changes daily), you'll always find a fish specialty accompanied by a hefty dose of greens and garnishes. Reliably outstanding is the pork tenderloin with mango chutney. Salads and soups are a great bargain, as portions are relatively large, but there's an extensive menu of appetizers and tapas which can be ordered in small or entree form. The kitschy decor of this tiny cafe comes complete with vinyl tablecloths and a changing display of paintings by local amateurs. Young, handsome waiters are attentive, but not solicitous. The old drugstore where the restaurant now resides features an original 1950s lunch counter and stools.

3800 S. Dixie Hwy., West Palm Beach. ℂ 561/833-3406. www.rhythmcafe.cc. Reservations recommended Sat–Sun. Main courses $18–$26; tapas $4–$13. AE, DISC, MC, V. Tues–Sat 6–10pm; Sun (Dec–Mar) 5:30–9pm. Closed in early Sept. From I-95, exit east on Southern Blvd. Go 1 block north of Southern Blvd.; restaurant is on the right.

INEXPENSIVE

Green's Pharmacy ★ 🍴 AMERICAN This neighborhood pharmacy offers one of the best meal deals in Palm Beach. Both breakfast and lunch are served coffee-shop-style, either at a Formica bar or at tables on a black-and-white checkerboard floor. Breakfast specials include eggs and omelets served with home fries and bacon, sausage, or corned-beef hash. The grill serves burgers and sandwiches, as well as ice-cream sodas and milkshakes, to a loyal crowd of pastel-clad Palm Beachers.

151 N. County Rd., Palm Beach. ℂ 561/832-0304. Fax 561/832-6502. Breakfast $2–$7; burgers and sandwiches $3–$9; soups and salads $2–$9. AE, DISC, MC, V. Mon–Sat 7am–2pm; Sun 7am–3pm.

Tom's Place for Ribs ★★ 🍴 BARBECUE There are two important factors in a successful barbecue: the cooking and the sauce. Tom and Helen Wright's no-nonsense shack wins on both counts, offering flawlessly grilled meats paired with well-spiced sauces. Beef, chicken, pork, and fish are served soul-food-style, with corn bread and your choice of sides such as rice with gravy, collard greens, black-eyed peas, coleslaw, or mashed potatoes. There's another very popular branch of Tom's in Boca Raton, at 7251 N. Federal Hwy. (ℂ 561/997-0920).

1225 Palm Beach Lakes Blvd., West Palm Beach. ℂ 561/832-8774. www.tomsplaceforribs.com. Reservations not accepted. Main courses $11–$23; sandwiches $9–$10. AE, MC, V. Tues–Thurs 11:30am–10:30pm; Fri 11:30am–10pm; Sat noon–10pm.

Palm Beach After Dark

THE PERFORMING ARTS

With a number of dedicated patrons and enthusiastic supporters of the arts, this area happily boasts many good venues for those craving culture. Check the *Palm Beach Post* or the *Palm Beach Daily News* for up-to-date listings and reviews.

The **Raymond F. Kravis Center for the Performing Arts,** 701 Okeechobee Blvd., West Palm Beach (ℂ 561/832-7469; www.kravis.org), is the area's largest and most active performance space. With a huge curved-glass facade and more than 2,500 seats in two lushly decorated indoor spaces, plus a new outdoor amphitheater, the Kravis stages more than 300 performances each year. Phone or check the website for a current schedule of Palm Beach's best music, dance, and theater.

9

THE TREASURE COAST:
STUART TO SEBASTIAN

Through area north of Palm Beach is known as the Treasure Coast for the same reason that the area from Fort Lauderdale to Palm Beach is known as the Gold Coast—it was the site of many shipwrecks that date back more than 300 years, which led to the discovery of priceless treasures in the water (some historians believe that treasures still lie buried deep beneath the ocean floor).

The difference, however, is that while the Gold Coast is a bit, well, tarnished as far as development is concerned, the Treasure Coast remains, for the most part, an unspoiled, quiet, natural jewel. Miles of uninterrupted beaches and aquamarine waters attract swimmers, boaters, divers, anglers, and sun worshipers. If you love the great outdoors and prefer a more understated environment than hyperdeveloped Miami and Fort Lauderdale, the Treasure Coast is a real find.

For hundreds of years, Florida's east coast was a popular stopover for European explorers, many of whom arrived from Spain with full coffers of gold and silver. Rough weather and poor navigation often took a toll on their ships, but in 1715, a violent hurricane stunned the northeast coast and sank an entire fleet of Spanish ships laden with gold. Although Spanish salvagers worked for years to collect the lost treasure, much of it remained buried beneath the shifting sand. Workers hired to excavate the area in the 1950s and 1960s discovered centuries-old coins under their tractors.

Today you can still see shipwrecks and incredible barrier reefs in St. Lucie County, which can be reached from the beaches of Fort Pierce and Hutchinson Island. On these same beaches, you'll also find an occasional treasure hunter trolling the sand with a metal detector, alongside swimmers and sunbathers who come to enjoy the stretches of beach that extend into the horizon. The sea, especially around Sebastian Inlet, is a mecca for surfers, who find some of the largest swells in the state.

Along with the pleasures of the talcum-powder sands, the Treasure Coast has good shopping and sports, and numerous other opportunities to take a reprieve from the hubbub of the rat race. Visitors to this part of South Florida should not miss the extensive array of wildlife, which includes the endangered West Indian manatee, loggerhead and leatherback turtles, tropical fish, alligators, deer, and exotic birds. Sports enthusiasts will find boundless opportunities here—from golf and tennis to polo, motorcar racing, the New York Mets during spring training, and the best freshwater fishing around.

FACING PAGE: **Vero Beach is home to the Citrus Museum;** ABOVE: **Who knows if there's still booty waiting to be found on the Treasure Coast?**

The downtown areas of the Treasure Coast have been experiencing a very slow rebirth in the past few years, along with an unprecedented influx of new residents. Fortunately, growth has occurred at a reasonable pace, allowing the neighborhoods to retain their small-town feel. The result is a batch of freshly spruced-up accommodations, shops, and restaurants from Stuart to Sebastian.

For the purposes of this chapter, the Treasure Coast runs roughly from Hobe Sound in the south to Sebastian Inlet in the north, encompassing some of Martin, St. Lucie, and Indian River counties, and all of Hutchinson Island.

Treasure Coast Essentials

GETTING THERE

Because virtually every town described in this chapter runs along a straight route by the Atlantic Ocean, we've given all directions below.

BY PLANE The **Palm Beach International Airport** (✆ **561/471-7420**), about 35 miles south of Stuart, is the closest gateway to this region if you're flying. See the "Getting There" section on Palm Beach, on p. 324, for complete information. If you're traveling to the northern part of the Treasure Coast, **Melbourne International Airport,** off U.S. 1 in Melbourne (✆ **321/723-6227**), is less than 25 miles north of Sebastian and about 35 miles north of Vero Beach.

BY CAR If you're driving up or down the Florida coast, you'll probably reach the Treasure Coast via I-95. If you're heading to Stuart or Jensen Beach, take exit 61 (Rte. 76/Tanner Hwy.) or 62 (Rte. 714); to Port St. Lucie or Fort Pierce, take exit 63 or 64 (Okeechobee Rd.); to Vero Beach, take exit 68 (S.R. 60); to Sebastian, take exit 69 (County Rd.). You can also take the Florida Turnpike; this toll road is the fastest (but not the most scenic) route, especially if you're coming from Orlando. If you're heading to Stuart or Jensen Beach, take exit 133; to Fort Pierce, take exit 152 (Okeechobee Rd.); to Port St. Lucie, take exit 142 or 152; to Vero Beach, take exit 193 (S.R. 60); to Sebastian, take exit 193 to S.R. 60 east and connect to I-95 North.

If you're staying in Hutchinson Island, which runs almost the entire length of the Treasure Coast, you should check with your hotel or see the listings below to find the best route to take.

Finally, if you're coming directly from the west coast, you'll probably take S.R. 70, which runs north of Lake Okeechobee to Fort Pierce, up the road from Stuart.

BY RAIL Amtrak (✆ **800/USA-RAIL** [872-7245]; www.amtrak.com) stops in West Palm Beach, at 201 S. Tamarind Ave.; and in Okeechobee, at 801 N. Parrot Ave., off U.S. 441 North.

BY BUS Greyhound (✆ **800/231-2222;** www.greyhound.com) serves the area with bus terminals in Stuart, at 1308 S. Federal Hwy.; in Fort Pierce, at 7005 Okeechobee Rd. (✆ **772/461-3299**); and in Vero Beach, at U.S. 1 and S.R. 60 (✆ **772/562-6588**).

GETTING AROUND

A car is a necessity in this large and rural region. Although heavy traffic is not usually a problem here, on the smaller coastal roads, such as Fla. A1A, expect to travel at a slow pace, usually between 25 and 40 mph.

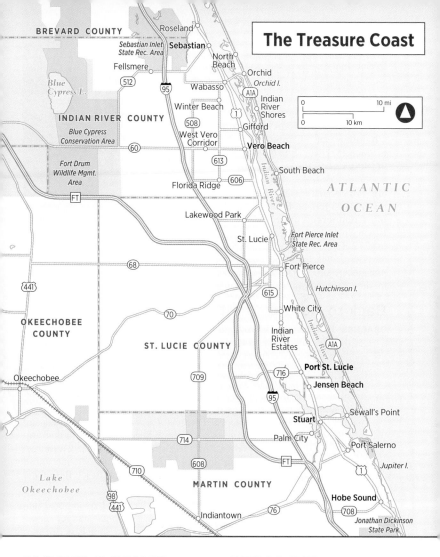

HOBE SOUND ★★★, STUART (NORTH HUTCHINSON ISLAND) ★★ & JENSEN BEACH

Hobe Sound: 45 min. N of Palm Beach; 12 miles S of Stuart

Once just a stretch of pineapple plantations, the towns of Martin County, which include Hobe Sound, Stuart, and Jensen Beach, retain much of their rural character. Between the citrus groves and mangroves are modest homes and an occasional high-rise condominium. Although the area is definitely quiet, the atmosphere is pure small town. Even in historic downtown Stuart, the result of a successful, ongoing restoration, expect the storefronts to be dark and the streets abandoned after 10pm.

Essentials

The **Stuart/Martin County Chamber of Commerce,** 1650 S. Kanner Hwy., Stuart, FL 34994 (*☎***800/524-9704** or 772/287-1088; fax 772/220-3437; www.goodnature. org), is the region's main source for information. The **Jensen Beach Chamber of Commerce,** 1901 NE Jensen Beach Blvd., Jensen Beach, FL 34957 (*☎***772/334-3444;** fax 772/334-0817; www.jensenbeachchamber.biz), also provides visitors with information about its simple beachfront town.

Stroll along the quiet shores of Bathtub Beach on North Hutchinson Island.

Back to Nature: The Beaches & Beyond

BEACHES Hutchinson Island, one of the most popular beach destinations of the Treasure Coast, is the area just north of Palm Beach on the Atlantic Ocean. Some 70 miles of excellent beaches and laid-back, Old Florida ambience make for an idyllic, frozen-cocktail-on-the-beach resort vacation. The best is **Bathtub Beach,** on North Hutchinson Island. The calm waters here are protected by coral reefs, and visitors can explore the region on dune and river trails. Pick a secluded spot on the wide stretch of sand, or enjoy marked nature trails across the street. Facilities include showers and toilets open during the day. To reach Bathtub Beach from the northern tip of Hutchinson Island, head east on Ocean Boulevard (Stuart Causeway) and turn right onto MacArthur Boulevard. The beach is about a mile ahead on your left, just north of the Hutchinson Island Marriott Beach Resort and Marina. Parking is plentiful.

CANOEING Jonathan Dickinson State Park (see "Wildlife Exploration: From Gators to Manatees to Turtles," below) is the most popular area for canoeing. In 2006, the park debuted the Jonathan Dickinson State Park Environmental Education and Research Center, which hosts educational programs and activities. The route winds through a variety of botanical habitats. You'll see lots of birds and the occasional manatee. Canoes rent for $17 for 2 hours, $5 per additional hour, available through the concessions stand (*☎***561/746-1466**) in the back of the park; it's open Monday through Friday from 9am to 5pm, Saturday and Sunday from 8am to 5pm.

FISHING Several charter captains operate on Hutchinson Island and Jensen Beach. One of the largest operators is the **Sailfish Marina,** 3565 SE St. Lucie Blvd., Stuart (*☎***772/283-1122;** www.sailfishmarinastuart.com), which maintains a half-dozen charter boats for fishing excursions year-round. A bait-and-tackle shop is on-site, as is a knowledgeable, helpful staff. Other reputable charter operators in Stuart include **Hungry Bear Adventures, Inc.,** docked at Indian River Plantation Marriott Resort,

WILDLIFE EXPLORATION: FROM GATORS TO MANATEES TO turtles

One of the most scenic areas on this stretch of the coast is **Jonathan Dickinson State Park** ★, 12 miles south of Stuart at 16450 S. Federal Hwy. (U.S. 1), Hobe Sound (☎ **772/546-2771;** www.floridastateparks.org/jonathan dickinson). The park intentionally receives less maintenance than other, more meticulously maintained parks in order to resemble the rough-around-the-edges, wilderness-like environment of hundreds of years ago, before Europeans started chopping, dredging, and "improving" the area. Dozens of species of Florida's unique wildlife, including alligators and manatees, live on the park's more than 11,300 acres. Bird-watchers will be delighted by glimpses of rare and endangered species such as the bald eagle, the Florida scrub-jay, and the Florida sandhill crane, which still call this park home. You can rent canoes from the concessions stand to explore the Loxahatchee River on your own. Admission is $6 per car of up to eight adults, $4 per single-occupant vehicle, and $2 for hikers, bikers, and walkers. The park is open from 8am to sundown. See p. 350 for details on camping.

Close to Jonathan Dickinson State Park is **Hobe Sound National Wildlife Refuge and Nature Center,** on North Beach Road off S.R. 708, at the north end of Jupiter Island (☎ **772/546-6141**). This is one of the best places to spot sea turtles that nest on the shore in the summer months, especially in June and July. Because it's home to a large variety of other plant and animal species, the park is worth visiting the rest of the year as well. Admission is free but it costs $5 per car to park, and the preserve is open daily from sunrise to sunset. Exact times are posted at each entrance and change seasonally.

For turtle walks on Hutchinson Island, call ☎ **877/375-4386.** These walks take place from May 22 to July 22 at 9pm on Friday and Saturday. Reservations are necessary and should be made well in advance (they're accepted as of May 1); each walk is limited to only 50 people.

4730-1 SE Teri Place (ⓒ **772/285-7552;** www.hungrybear.net); and **Bone Shaker Sportfishing,** 3585 SE St. Lucie Blvd. (ⓒ **772/286-5504;** www. boneshakercharters.com).

GOLF Try the **Champions Club at Summerfield,** on U.S. 1, south of Cove Road in Stuart (ⓒ **772/283-1500;** www.thechampionsgolfclub.com), a somewhat challenging championship course designed by Tom Fazio and renovated in 2010 to include TifEagle grass. This rural course, the best in the area, offers great glimpses of wildlife amid the wetlands. Greens fees are around $15 to $49 depending on time and season; cart rentals are mandatory. Reservations are also a must and are taken 4 days in advance.

SCUBA DIVING & SNORKELING Three popular artificial reefs off Hutchinson Island provide excellent scenery for both novice and experienced divers. The **USS *Rankin*** lies 7 miles east-northeast of the St. Lucie Inlet. The *Rankin* is a 459-foot ship that lies on its port side in 80 feet of water. This ship was used in World War II for troop transportation and was sunk to create the reef in 1988. Deck hatches on the wreck are open and allow exploration. Inside, there are thousands of Atlantic spiny oysters, and a cannon is attached to the bow. The ***Georges Valentine,*** designated as one of Florida's shipwreck preserves in 2006, sits in shallow waters a few hundred feet behind Gilbert's House of Refuge. The **Donaldson Reef** consists of a cluster of steel tanks and barrels sunk in 58 feet of water to create an artificial reef. It's due east of the Gilbert's House of Refuge Museum (see below). The **Ernst Reef,** made from old tires, is a 60-foot dive located 4½ miles east-southeast of the St. Lucie Inlet. Local dive shops have tips on the best spots, along with rules and regulations for safe diving.

Seeing the Sights

Elliott Museum ★★ The Elliott Museum is a tribute to inventors, sports heroes, and collectors. The museum was created by the son of turn-of-the-20th-century inventor Sterling Elliott to display the genius of the American spirit. Among the things you'll see here are displays of an apothecary, an ice-cream parlor, a barbershop, and other old-fashioned commercial enterprises, as well as an authentic hand-carved miniature circus. Sports fans will appreciate the baseball memorabilia, including an autographed item from every player in the Baseball Hall of Fame. A gallery of patents and models of machines, invented by the museum's founder and his son, provides an intriguing glimpse into the business of tinkering. The collection of restored antique cars is also impressive. The museum's in transition; its current home will be torn down, with a new facility to be constructed on same site, scheduled for re-opening in 2013. Much of Elliott's contents can be found at the **House of Refuge Museum** (see below).

House of Refuge Museum (at Gilbert's Bar), 301 SE MacArthur, Blvd. ⓒ **772/225-1961.** www. elliottmuseumfl.org. Admission $8 adults, $4 children 5–12, free for children 4 and under. Mon-Sat 10am–4pm; Sun 1–4pm.

Florida Oceanographic Coastal Center ★★ This is a nature lover's Disney World. Opened by the South Florida Oceanographic Society in 1994, the 44-acre site (surrounded by coastal hammock and mangroves) is its own little ecosystem and serves as an outdoor classroom, teaching visitors about the region's flora and fauna. The modest main building houses saltwater tanks, and wet and dry "discovery tables" with small indigenous animals. The incredibly eager staff

of volunteers encourages visitors to wander the lush, well-marked nature trails. In 2007, the museum began an expansion program to include a fishing center, game fish lagoon, shark pavilion, ray pavilion, children's activity center, and more.

890 NE Ocean Blvd. (across the street from the Elliott Museum), Hutchinson Island, Stuart. © **772/225-0505.** www.floridaoceanographic.org. Admission $8 adults, $4 children 3-12. Mon–Sat 10am–5pm; Sun noon–4pm.

Gilbert's House of Refuge Museum ★

Gilbert's, the oldest structure in Martin County, dates from 1875, when it functioned as one of 10 rescue centers for shipwrecked sailors. After a thorough rehab to its original condition along the rocky shores, the house now displays marine artifacts and turn-of-the-20th-century lifesaving equipment and photographs. It's worth a visit to get a feel for the area's early days.

FROM TOP: **You'll find a host of Americana at the Elliott Museum; you might see a scaly 'gator when you take a ride on the** *Loxahatchee Queen.*

301 SE MacArthur Blvd. (south of Indian River Plantation Resort), Hutchinson Island, Stuart. © **772/225-1875.** www.elliottmuseumfl.org. Admission $6 adults, $3 children 5-12. Daily 10am–4pm.

A BOAT TOUR

The *Loxahatchee Queen* ★★★ (© **561/746-1466;** www.floridapark tours.com/boattours.html), a 35-foot, 44-passenger pontoon boat in Jonathan Dickinson State Park in Hobe Sound, makes daily tours of the area's otherwise inaccessible backwater, where curious alligators, manatees, eagles, and tortoises often peek out to see who's in their yard. Catch the 2-hour tour, given Wednesday through Sunday as the tide permits, when it includes a stop at Trapper Nelson's home. Known as the "Wildman of Loxahatchee," Nelson lived in primitive conditions in a log cabin he built himself, now preserved for visitors. Tours leave four times daily—at 9am, 11am, 1pm, and 3pm and cost $20 for adults, $12 for children 6 to 12. **Staff tip:** Try to avoid tours on Tuesdays or Wednesdays, when Trapper Nelson's is closed. See "Wildlife Exploration: From Gators to Manatees to Turtles" (p. 347) for more information on the state park.

Where to Stay

Although the area boasts some beautiful beaches—and a few excellent beach-front hotels and inns—the bulk of the hotel scene is downtown, where the nicer (and more reasonably priced) accommodations can be found among the shops and restaurants. **Note:** A 4% tax is added to accommodations rates in the Stuart–Hutchinson Island area.

The two-story **Best Western Downtown Stuart,** 1209 S. Federal Hwy. (www.bestwesternstuart.com; ✆ **772/287-6200**), is a nice choice on a busy main road. Rates range from $65 to $109.

VERY EXPENSIVE

Hutchinson Island Marriott Beach Resort and Marina ★★ ☺ This sprawling 200-acre, multibuilding compound offers many diversions for active (and not-so-active) vacationers, and families in particular. This is Hutchinson Island's best resort, occupying the lush grounds of a former pineapple plantation. Activities include tennis, golf, boating, sport fishing, scuba diving, and other watersports. Rooms in the main building overlook the Intracoastal and the resort's marina, the ocean, or the golf course; in the Sandpiper Tower, all rooms have kitchenettes and most have golf course views. All rooms are generously sized. Be sure to sign up for a summer "turtle watch" so you can observe turtles crawling onto the sand to lay their eggs. Another great activity, offered at an extra cost, is a sightseeing cruise along the St. Lucie and Indian rivers. The **Baha Grill** seafood restaurant is a great choice on property.

555 NE Ocean Blvd., Hutchinson Island, Stuart, FL 34996. www.marriott.com. ✆ **800/775-5936** or 772/225-3700. Fax 772/225-0003. 274 units. Winter $229–$259 double, $279–$339 suite; off season $159–$199 double, $209–$269 suite. AE, MC, V. From downtown Stuart, take E. Ocean Blvd. over 2 bridges to NE Ocean Blvd.; turn right. **Amenities:** Restaurant; lounge; babysitting; bike rental; children's programs; 18-hole golf course; fitness center; 3 large pools; limited room service; 13 tennis courts; extensive watersports activities; *In room:* A/C, TV, fridge, hair dryer, high-speed Internet access, kitchenette (in Sandpiper Tower rooms only).

CAMPING

There are comfortable campsites (rustic cabins and sites for your tent or camper) in **Jonathan Dickinson State Park,** in Hobe Sound (see "Wildlife Exploration: From Gators to Manatees to Turtles," on p. 347). The River Camp area of the park offers the benefit of the nearby Loxahatchee River, while the Pine Grove site, renovated in 2010, offers beautiful shade trees. There are concession areas for daytime snacks and campsites with showers, clean restrooms, water, optional electricity, and open-fire pits for cooking. Overnight rates are $26 with electricity.

For a cushier camping experience, reserve a cabin with furnished kitchen, bathroom with shower, heat and air-conditioning, and outdoor grill. Cabins rent for $95 (one bed and a pullout couch), $105 (two beds and a pullout couch), and up per night. They sleep four comfortably, or up to six if your group is really into togetherness. Call ✆ **772/546-2771** Monday through Friday between 9am and 5pm, well in advance, to reserve a spot. A $50 cash deposit is required at check-in. Bring your own linens.

The Treasure Coast RV Resort and Campground of Fort Pierce, 2550 Crossroads Pkwy., Fort Pierce (www.treasurecoastrv.com; ✆ **866/468-2099**), has a small lake, oak trees, clubhouse with kitchen, swimming pool, hot tub (!), and shower facilities. There also are full-service hookups, free Wi-Fi, and free cable TV. Rates are $39 to $46.

Where to Eat

EXPENSIVE

The Courtyard Grill ★★ CONTINENTAL Although this restaurant faces railroad tracks and a station that was never fully built, the Courtyard Grill is the essence of charm, with a warm and inviting vibe. Old-school fare such as clams casino and escargot are juxtaposed with nouveau cuisine such as duck-stuffed ravioli, but old standards such as Dover sole are best. An impressive wine list, a gorgeous garden room, and homemade desserts assure you that you're on the right track for fine food in Hobe Sound.

11970 SE Dixie Hwy., Hobe Sound. ✆ **772/546-2900.** Reservations recommended. Main courses $15–$30. MC, V. Tues–Sat 5:30–9:30pm.

11 Maple Street ★★★ NEW AMERICAN A restaurant that's so good it gets diners from Miami driving up just for dinner, 11 Maple Street occupies a converted old house and features the exceptional cuisine of chef/owner Mike Perrin, whose use of farm-raised meats and organic produce from the restaurant's garden is quite masterful. Dining is both indoors and out, in any one of a series of cozy dining rooms or on a covered patio surrounded by gardens. The menu changes daily and features interesting dishes (small and large plates) not typically found in these parts of Florida, such as wood-grilled North American elk with faro squash, fontina gratin, and a chestnut honey essence; and oak-grilled duck breast with wild huckleberry essence, acorn squash, pine nuts, and warm red-cabbage salad.

11 Maple St., Jensen Beach. ✆ **772/334-7714.** www.11maplestreet.net. Reservations recommended. Small plates $6–$20; large plates $32–$45. AE, DISC, MC, V. Wed—Sun 6–10pm.

Flagler Grill ★★ AMERICAN/FLORIDA REGIONAL In the heart of historic downtown, this seemingly out-of-place Manhattan-style bistro serves sensational, seasonal cuisine such as Atlantic salmon filet, almond-crusted and sautéed with snow peas, pickled red radish in an orange-blossom honey, and black fig balsamic in winter; and Parmesan-crusted salmon with Savannah red rice and jicama slaw in summer. It's hard to go wrong with any of the many salads, pastas, fish dishes, or delectable beef choices on the changing menu. The desserts, too, are worth the calories. Or ask the bartender to make you a chocolate martini—dessert with a kick!

47 SW Flagler Ave. (just before the Roosevelt Bridge), downtown Stuart. ✆ **772/221-9517.** www.flaglergrill.com. Reservations strongly suggested in season. Main courses $16–$35. AE, DC, DISC, MC, V. Winter daily 5–10pm; off season Tues–Sat 5:30–9:30pm. Lounge and bar until 11:30pm. Special sunset menu offered 5–6pm.

MODERATE

Black Marlin ★ FLORIDA REGIONAL Although it looks and feels like a dank English pub with exposed brick walls and cozy wooden booths, the Black Marlin offers full Floridian flavor. The salmon BLT is typical of the dishes here—grilled salmon on a toasted bun topped with bacon, lettuce, tomato, and coleslaw. Pizzas are adorned with shrimp, roasted red peppers, and the like. Main dishes range from lobster tail with honey-mustard sauce to yellowfin tuna with fennel and black pepper. I'd stick with the sandwiches and pizzas, though. That said, ask whether they're serving the panko-crusted hogfish or fried lobster tail special—they're out of this world!

53 W. Osceola St., downtown Stuart. ✆ **772/286-3126.** Reservations not accepted. Salads, pizzas, and sandwiches $8–$15; main courses $15–$35. AE, MC, V. Mon–Thurs 5–10pm; Fri–Sat 5–11pm. Bar open later.

Conchy Joe's Seafood ★★ 🎁 SEAFOOD Known for fresh seafood and Old Florida hospitality, Conchy Joe's enjoys an excellent reputation that's far bigger than the restaurant itself. Shorts and flip-flops are the attire of choice here, and dining is either indoors or out on a covered patio overlooking the St. Lucie River. The menu features a variety of freshly shucked shellfish and daily-catch selections that are baked, broiled, or fried; the conch chowder is sublime and the fish in a bag—tilapia baked in a brown paper bag with sweet peppers, yellow squash, white wine, and butter—is delicious. Beer is the drink of choice here, though other beverages are available. Conchy Joe's has been the most active place in Jensen Beach since it opened in 1983. The large bar is popular at night and during weekday happy hours.

3945 NE Indian River Dr. (½ mile from the Jensen Beach Causeway), Jensen Beach. ✆ **772/334-1130.** www.conchyjoes.com. Reservations not accepted. Main courses $15–$30. AE, DISC, MC, V. Daily 11:30am–2:30pm and 5–10pm.

INEXPENSIVE

Harry and the Natives ★ 🎁 AMERICAN When you dine at this wild and wacky, kitschy Old Florida institution (to which both Harleys and Bentleys flock), you'll get decent bar fare (try the venison burger) with a fabulous dish of humor on the side. They call it Hobe Sounds' only waterfront restaurant—when it rains. It is not at all on the water, but more of a roadside stop instead. The menu is hysterical, especially "Acceptables: Cash, dishwashing, silver rolling, honey dipping, oceanfront homes, table dancing, our gift certificates, Visa, MasterCard & American Express." The food ranges from omelets and pancakes to the "President Obamalette—$789,000,000,000 and still waiting for change." I won't spoil it all, so be sure to read the entire menu. There's live music Wednesday through Saturday; request the Harry and the Natives theme song.

11910 S. Federal Hwy., Hobe Sound. ✆ **772/546-3061.** www.harryandthenatives.com. Main courses $5–$26. MC, V. Daily 6:30am–2:30am.

Stuart & Jensen Beach After Dark

Nightlife on the Treasure Coast may as well be called night*dead* because there really isn't any! That said, Stuart and Jensen Beach offer the closest thing to nightlife in the region; local restaurants serve as the centers of after-dark happenings. "Night" ends pretty early here, even on weekends.

Fiji, at **Arthur's Dockside Waterfront,** is a happening, splashy spot, especially around happy hour, which seems to start earlier than most. The bar at the **Black Marlin** (p. 352) is popular with locals and out-of-towners alike. No list of Jensen nightlife would be complete without mention of **Conchy Joe's Seafood** (p. 352), one of the region's most active spots. Inside, locals chug beer and watch a large-screen TV, while outside on the waterfront patio, live bands perform a few nights a week for a raucous crowd of dancers. Happy hours, Monday through Friday from 3 to 6pm, draw large crowds.

The centerpiece of Stuart's slowly expanding cultural offerings is the restored **Lyric Theatre,** 59 SW Flagler Ave. (𝄏 **772/286-7827;** www.lyric theatre.com). This beautiful 1920s-era theater hosts a variety of shows, readings, concerts, and films throughout the year.

VERO BEACH ★ & SEBASTIAN ★★

Vero Beach: 87 miles S of Orlando; 95 miles N of Fort Lauderdale

Old Florida is thriving in these remote and tranquil villages. Vero Beach, known for its exclusive and affluent winter population, and Sebastian, known as one of the last remaining fishing villages, are set at the northern tip of the Treasure Coast region in Indian River County. These two beach towns are populated with folks who appreciate the area's small-town feel, and that's exactly the appeal for visitors: a laid-back atmosphere, friendly people, and friendlier prices.

Catch a wave at Sebastian Inlet State park.

A crowd of well-tanned surfers from all over the state descend on the region, especially the Sebastian Inlet, to catch some of the state's biggest waves. Other watersports enthusiasts enjoy the area's fine diving and windsurfing. Anglers are also in heaven here. In spring, baseball buffs may still be able to catch some minor-league action as Dodgertown—left vacant by the L.A. team that moved to Arizona—continues its quest for a major-league tenant.

Essentials

The **Indian River County Tourist Council,** 1216 21st St., Vero Beach, FL 32961 (𝄏 **772/567-3491;** fax 772/778-3181; www.indianriver chamber.com), will send visitors a detailed information packet on the county (which includes Vero Beach and Sebastian), with a full-color map, a list of upcoming events, a hotel guide, and more.

Beaches & Outdoor Activities

BEACHES You'll find plenty of free and open beachfront along the coast—most areas are uncrowded and are open from 7am to 10pm.

South Beach Park, on South Ocean Drive, at the end of Marigold Lane, is a busy, developed, lifeguarded beach with picnic tables, restrooms, and showers. It's known as one of the best swimming beaches in Vero Beach and attracts a young crowd that plays volleyball in a tranquil setting. A nature walk takes you onto beautiful secluded trails.

At the very northern tip of the island, **Sebastian Inlet State Park ★**, 9700 S. Fla. A1A, Melbourne (© **321/984-4852**), has flat, sandy beaches with lots of facilities, including kayak, paddleboat, and canoe rentals; a well-stocked surf shop; picnic tables; and a snack shop. The winds seem to stir up the surf with no jetty to stop the swells, to the delight of surfers and boarders who come here to catch the big waves. Campers enjoy fully equipped sites in a woody area. Distant plans for the park include cozy, 1,150- to 1,600-square-foot cabins with both high-tech and woodsy amenities. Stay tuned. Entry fees to the park are $8 per car with two to eight people, $4 for a single-occupant vehicle, and $2 for those who walk or bike in.

FISHING Capt. Terry Lamielle has been fishing the area for more than 40 years and will teach you all about fly-fishing for red fish, snook, and tarpon. His **Easy Days Fishing** (© **321/537-5346;** www.easydaysfishing.com) takes anglers on his *Sterling Flats* fishing boat for private river excursions. Half-day jaunts on the Indian River cost $275 for up to two people, tackle, rigs, and everything included; it's $50 extra for a third person.

Many other charters, guides, party boats, and tackle shops operate in this area. Consult your hotel for suggestions, or call the **Vero Beach Chamber of Commerce** (© **772/567-3491**). You can also contact **Captain Hiram's** (© **772/589-4345;** www.hirams.com), a restaurant/bar/hotel/marina that houses many charter boats.

GOLF Hard-core golfers insist that of the dozens of courses in the area, only a handful are worth their plots of grass. Set on rolling hills with uncluttered views of sand dunes and sky, the **Sandridge Golf Club,** 5300 73rd St., Vero Beach (© **772/770-5000;** www.sandridgegc.com), is one of them, offering two par-72 18-holers. The Dunes is a long course with rolling fairways, while the newer Lakes course has lots of water. Both charge $29 to $50, including cart. Reservations are recommended and are taken 2 days in advance.

Although less challenging, the **Sebastian Municipal Golf Course,** 1010 E. Airport Dr. (© **772/589-6801;** www.sebastiangolfcourse.org), is a good 18-hole par-72 course. It's scenic and well maintained, and greens fees are just $25 to $44 per player, with cart.

TENNIS Many of the tennis courts around Vero Beach and Sebastian are at hotels and resorts, and are thus closed to nonguests. Try **Riverside Racquet Complex,** 350 Dahlia Lane, at Royal Palm Boulevard, at the east end of Barber Bridge, Vero Beach (© **772/231-4787**). This popular park has 10 hard courts (6 lighted) that can be rented for $5 per person per hour if you're a county resident, and $6 to $7.50 if not. Reservations are accepted up to 24 hours in advance.

Seeing the Sights

Environmental Learning Center ★★ ☺ The Indian River is not really a river at all, but a large, brackish lagoon that's home to a greater variety of species than any other estuary in North America—it has thousands of species of plants, animals, fish, and birds, including 36 species on the endangered list. The privately funded Environmental Learning Center was created to educate visitors about the Indian River area's environment. Situated on 51 island acres, the center features a 600-foot boardwalk through the mangroves and dozens of hands-on exhibits that are geared to both children and adults. There are touch tanks, exhibits, and microscopes for viewing the smallest sea life up close. The best thing to do is join one of the center's field excursion programs, from guided nature walks and stargazing to river cruise adventures. Prices range from free to $50 depending on the program.

255 Live Oak Dr. (just off the 510 Causeway), Wabasso Island (a 51-acre island in the Indian River Lagoon). ℂ **772/589-5050.** www.elcweb.org. Admission $5, free for children 12 and under. Tues–Fri 10am–4pm; Sat 9am–noon; Sun 1–4pm.

Indian River Citrus Museum The tiny Indian River Citrus Museum exhibits artifacts relating to the history of the citrus industry, from its initial boom in the late 1800s to the present; a small grove displays several varieties. The gift shop sells citrus-themed items along with, of course, ready-to-ship fruit.

2140 14th Ave., Vero Beach. ℂ **772/770-2263.** Admission $1 donation. Tues–Fri 10am–4pm.

McKee Botanical Garden ★★ This impressive 18-acre attraction was originally opened in 1932 and featured a virtual jungle of orchids, exotic and native trees, monkeys, and birds. After years of neglect, it was placed on the National Register of Historic Places in 1998 and renovated; you can now again experience the full charms of this little Eden.

350 U.S. 1, Vero Beach. ℂ **772/794-0601.** www.mckeegarden.org. Admission $9 adults, $8 seniors, $5 children 3–12. Tues–Sat 10am–5pm; Sun noon–5pm.

McLarty Treasure Museum ★ If you're unsure of why this area is called the Treasure Coast, then this is a must-see. Built on the site of a salvage camp from a 1715 shipwreck, this little museum, part of Sebastian Inlet State Park, is full of interesting history. It may not have the treasures of Key West's Mel Fisher museum (p. 235), but it shows an engaging 45-minute video describing the many aspects of treasure hunting. You'll also see household items salvaged from the Spanish fleet and dioramas of life in the 18th century.

13180 N. Fla. A1A, Sebastian Inlet State Recreation Area, Vero Beach. ℂ **772/589-2147.** Admission $2, free for children 5 and under. Daily 10am–4:30pm.

Learn about one of Florida's most popular exports at the Citrus Museum.

Shopping

Ocean Boulevard and Cardinal Drive are Vero's two main shopping streets. Both are near the beach and lined with boutiques, including antiques and home-decor shops.

If you want to send fruit back home, the local source is **Hale Indian River Groves,** 615 Beachland Blvd. (℃ 800/562-4502; www.halegroves.com), a shipper of local citrus and jams since 1947, with four locations in Vero Beach. The grove is closed 2 to 3 months a year, usually from summer to early fall, depending on the crops; the season generally runs from November to Easter.

The **Horizon Outlet Center,** at S.R. 60 and I-95, Vero Beach (℃ 877/ GO-OUTLET [466-8853] or 772/770-6171), contains more than 80 discount stores selling name-brand shoes, kitchenware, clothing, and more. The center is open Monday through Saturday from 9am to 8pm, and Sunday from 11am to 6pm.

Indian River Mall, 6200 20th St. (S.R. 60), about 5 miles east of I-95 (℃ 772/770-6255), is a monster mall, with all the big chains and several department stores. It's open Monday through Saturday from 10am to 9pm, and Sunday from noon to 6pm.

Where to Stay

You can choose to stay on the mainland or on the beach. As you might expect, the beachfront accommodations are a bit more expensive—but, we think, worth it. Thanks to the arrival of a couple new luxury beachfront hotels, what was once known as Zero Beach is now worthy of its proper name. A great spot to know, especially if you're planning to fish, is the **Key West Inn at Captain Hiram's,** 1580 U.S. Hwy. 1, Sebastian (www.hirams.com; ℃ 772/388-8588), where 70 rooms are available adjacent to the restaurant and overlooking the water. (Also see "Fishing," above, and "Vero Beach & Sebastian After Dark," below.)

For those traveling with tots, though we recommend just heading straight to Orlando, there's the newly renovated, all-inclusive **Club Med Sandpiper Bay,** 4500 SE Pine Valley (www.clubmed.us; ℃ 800/CLUB-MED [258-2633] or 772/398-5100), featuring an array of family activities, three pools, tennis academy, fitness academy, and spa; and for true Disney fans who can't wait the 1½-hour drive to Mousetown, there's also **Disney's Vero Beach Resort,** 9250 Island Grove Terrace (http://dvc.disney.go.com; ℃ 407/939-7828), a Disney Vacation Club stay featuring vacation homes and beach cottages.

Comfortable and inexpensive chain options near the Horizon Outlet Center, off S.R. 60, include **Holiday Inn Express** (www.hiexpress.com; ℃ 800/465-4329 or 772/567-2500) and **Hampton Inn** (www.hamptoninn. com; ℃ 800/426-7866 or 772/770-4299). Rates for both run between $85 and $120, and include breakfast and local calls.

EXPENSIVE

Costa d'Este Beach Resort ★★★ Pop star Gloria Estefan and her producer husband Emilio own this fabulous luxury hotel, but thankfully they left the flash and glitz of the Sound Machine back in Miami. Chic is an understatement here, which the Estefans prefer to call a "personal luxury resort," rather than a boutique hotel. Each guest room features modern teak furnishings, flat-panel televisions, and complimentary Wi-Fi. Bathrooms feature tumbled limestone-tile showers with dual shower heads, and beds have buttery-soft Egyptian cotton linens. Choose from an oceanfront suite or a studio. Although there's beach access, we love the infinity-edge pool. A fantastic spa and sleek Oriente restaurant—Cuban cuisine with Spanish and Creole accents—are also on the premises, giving you no reason to really want to leave. Ever.

3244 Ocean Dr., Vero Beach, FL 32963. www.costadeste.com. © **877/562-9919** or 772/562-9919. Fax 772/562-9225. 94 units. Winter from $249 double and suite; off season from $169 double and suite. AE, MC, V. **Amenities:** Oceanfront restaurant; pool bar and grill; concierge; golf privileges at local clubs; fitness center; heated oceanfront pool; room service; spa. *In room:* A/C, TV, MP3 docking station, Wi-Fi.

Vero Beach Hotel & Spa, A Kimpton Hotel ★★★ Located on Vero Beach's famed Ocean Drive along one of the country's most exclusive and pristine beaches, this West Indies–inspired boutique hotel offers 113 designer guest rooms, including one-, two-, and three-bedroom suites that feature dark mahogany woods, Jerusalem-stone flooring, granite countertops, flatscreen televisions, sumptuous bedding, and spacious balconies overlooking the spectacular Atlantic Ocean and unspoiled Treasure Coast beaches. The AAA four-diamond award-winning hotel offers such amenities as the oceanfront Cobalt restaurant and lounge and Heaton's Reef Bar & Grill. Guests can enjoy Kimpton's signature in-room spa services, including massage and body and facial treatments.

3500 Ocean Dr., Vero Beach, FL 32963. www.verobeachhotelandspa.com. © **866/602-VERO** [8376] or 772/231-5666. Fax 772/234-4866. 113 units. From $169 double; from $289 suite. AE, MC, V. Valet parking $10 per day. **Amenities:** Oceanfront restaurant; poolside bar and grill; concierge; golf privileges at private clubs; fitness center; heated oceanfront pool; room service; spa. *In room:* A/C, TV/DVD, fridge, minibar, MP3 docking station, Wi-Fi.

MODERATE

The Caribbean Court Boutique Hotel ★★ 🛏️ This intimate island-style hotel offers a heated pool, private beach access, an excellent on-site French restaurant, **Maison Martinique** (p. 358), and **Havana Nights Piano Bar**, featuring spirits, tropical-lite cuisine, and entertainment. Rooms are nicely furnished with four-poster beds, antique furniture, original Caribbean artwork, French country–style bathrooms with ceramic wash basins, and kitchenettes. Most rooms have balconies or patios. More for couples looking for romance than the area's other beachy-keen hotels, the Caribbean Court has a beautiful honeymoon suite too. It's popular with business travelers during the week. Private beach access is a plus, too.

1601 Ocean Dr., Vero Beach, FL 32963. www.thecaribbeancourt.com. © **772/231-7211.** 18 units. Winter $129–$250 double; off season $99–$199 double. AE, MC, V. Pets accepted. **Amenities:** Restaurant; piano bar; heated pool. *In room:* A/C, TV/DVD, fridge, hair dryer, high-speed Internet, kitchenette.

Driftwood Resort ★★ 🛏️ Originally planned in the 1930s as a private estate by eccentric entrepreneur Waldo Sexton, the Driftwood was opened to the public in the late '30s. All of the guest rooms were renovated in 2000, and each is unique. Some have terra-cotta floors and lighter furniture, while others have a more rustic feel with hardwoods and antiques. Some of the rooms contain Jacuzzis; all are equipped with full kitchens and sleep at least four. Two of the best units: the Captain's Quarters, which overlooks the ocean with a private staircase to the pool; and the town house in the breezeway building, featuring a spiral staircase as well as living room and bedroom views of the ocean. The resort is listed on the National Register of Historic Places and, to say the least, has lots of quirky charm.

3150 Ocean Dr., Vero Beach, FL 32963. www.thedriftwood.com. ☎ **772/231-0550.** Fax 772/234-1981. 100 units. Winter $130–$190 double, $200–$310 apt; off season $100–$130 double, $140–$270 apt. AE, DISC, MC, V. **Amenities:** Restaurant; 2 outdoor heated pools. *In room:* A/C, TV, full or partial kitchen.

Islander Inn ★ This is one of the most comfortable and welcoming inns in the area. Well located in downtown Vero Beach, the small, quaint Key West–meets–Old Florida–style motel is just a short walk to the beach, restaurants, and shops. Every breezy Caribbean-style guest room has a small refrigerator, either a king-size bed or two double beds, paddle fans, wicker furniture, and vaulted ceilings. Rooms open onto a pretty courtyard and sparkling pool. Efficiencies have full kitchens.

3101 Ocean Dr., Vero Beach, FL 32963. http://islanderinnvero.com. ☎ **800/952-5886** or 772/231-4431. 16 units. Winter $135–$165 double; off season $89–$129 double. AE, MC, V. **Amenities:** Cafe; pool. *In room:* A/C, TV, fridge.

CAMPING

The Vero Beach and Sebastian areas of the Treasure Coast are popular with campers, who choose from nearly a dozen camping locations. If you aren't camping at the scenic and popular **Sebastian Inlet State Park** (p. 354), then try the **Vero Beach Kamp RV Park,** 8850 U.S. 1, Wabasso (www.verobeachkamp.com; ☎ **772/589-5665**). This 120-site campground is 2 miles from the ocean and the Intracoastal Waterway, and a quarter-mile from the Indian River, a big draw for fishing fanatics. There's access to running water and electricity, as well as showers, a shop, and hookups for RVs. Rates are $48 per site including water, electric, and cable; $40 per site including just water and electric; and $30 for sites with no hookups. A $4-per-person charge for each additional person over 5 years old is also applied. Cabins are also available at $48 a night for two guests, and cottages are available for $60 a night for four guests. Bring your own linens. To get here, take I-95 to exit 69 East; at U.S. 1, turn left.

Where to Eat

EXPENSIVE

Maison Martinique ★★★ FRENCH/CONTINENTAL Exquisite country-French cooking, a comprehensive wine list, and white-glove service complement the fine linens and imported china at this romantic standout owned and operated by Yannick Martin. Formerly known as Café du Soir, Maison Martinique is in the charming waterfront Caribbean Court Hotel. Excellent starters include Louisiana sausage with sautéed apples, foie gras with caramelized raisins, and exceptional escargot. Main courses include sautéed Dover sole and filet mignon stuffed with Roquefort cheese. Desserts might include raspberry and strawberry napoleons and country apple tarts.

1601 Ocean Dr., Vero Beach. ☎ **772/231-7299.** www.thecaribbeancourt.com. Reservations recommended. Main courses $22–$40. AE, MC, V. Mon–Sat from 6pm; closing time varies based on last reservation.

MODERATE

Ocean Grill ★★ 🍴 STEAKS/SEAFOOD The Ocean Grill attracts faithful devotees with its simple but rich cooking and its stunning locale, right on the ocean's edge; ask for a table along the wall of windows that open onto the sea. Built more than 60 years ago by Vero Beach eccentric Waldo Sexton, the restaurant was once an officers' club for residents of the nearby naval airbase during World War II. All fish can be prepared Cajun-style, wood grilled, or deep-fried. Indian River crab cakes make for a memorable meal, deep-fried with fresh backfin and claw meat rolled in cracker meal. Try stone crab claws when they're in season, or the house shrimp scampi baked in butter and herbs and served with a tangy mustard sauce, or any of the big servings of meats. We especially recommend the Cajun rib-eye, featuring a béarnaise sauce that's delightfully jolting to the taste buds. Dinners are uniformly good here; the only tacky element of this place is the gift shop.

1050 Sexton Plaza (by the ocean at the end of S.R. 60), Vero Beach. © **772/231-5409.** www. ocean-grill.com. Reservations accepted only for parties of 5 or more. Main courses $14–$32. AE, DC, DISC, MC, V. Mon–Fri 11:30am–2:30pm and 5:30–10pm; Sat–Sun 5:30–10pm. Closed Thanksgiving, Super Bowl Sun, and July 4.

INEXPENSIVE

Nino's Cafe ★ ITALIAN This little beachside cafe looks like a stereotypical pizza joint, complete with fake brick walls, murals of the Italian countryside, and red-and-white-checked tablecloths. The atmosphere is pure cheese and so is much of the food—pizza and parmigiana dishes are smothered in the stuff. Still, the thin crust and fresh toppings make pizzas here a cut above the rest— just ask the New York transplants who live for the place. Entrees and pastas are also tasty.

1006 Easter Lily Lane (off Ocean Dr., next to Humiston Park), Vero Beach. © **772/231-9311.** Main courses $9–$15; pizza $11–$22. No credit cards. Mon–Thurs 11am–9pm; Fri–Sat 11am–10pm; Sun 4–9pm.

Vero Beach & Sebastian After Dark

More than half of the residents in this area are retirees, so it shouldn't be a surprise that, even on weekends, this town retires early. Hotel lounges often have live music and a good bar scene, however, especially in high season, and sometimes stay open as late as 1am, if you're lucky. For beachside drinks, go to the **Driftwood Resort** (p. 357).

Vero Beach is also known as an artsy enclave, hosting galleries such as the **Admiralty Gallery,** 3315 Ocean Dr., Vero Beach (© **772/231-3178;** www. admiraltygallery.com). The **Civic Arts Center,** at Riverside Park, is a hub of culture; it includes the **Riverside Theatre** (© **772/231-6990;** www.riverside theatre.com), the **Agnes Wahlstrom Youth Playhouse** (© **772/234-8052**), and the **Center for the Arts** (© **772/231-0707**), known for films and an excellent lecture series.

In Sebastian, you'll find live music every weekend (and daily in season) at **Captain Hiram's,** 1606 N. Indian River Dr. (© **772/589-4345;** www.hirams. com), a salty outdoor restaurant and bar on the Intracoastal Waterway that locals and tourists love at all hours of the day and night (well, until it closes at 11pm, that is). The feel is tacky Key West, complete with a sand floor and thatched-roof bar.

North of the inlet, head for the tried-and-true **Sebastian Beach Inn** (SBI to locals), 7035 S. Fla. A1A (© **321/728-4311;** www.sbiseaside.com), for live music on weekends. Jazz, blues, or sometimes rock 'n' roll starts at 9pm on Friday and Saturday. On Sunday, it's old-style reggae after 2pm. The inn is open daily for drinks from 11am to anytime between midnight and 2am.

A SIDE TRIP: LAKE OKEECHOBEE ★★★

60 miles NW of West Palm Beach

Many visitors to the Treasure Coast come to fish, and they certainly get their fill off the miles of Atlantic shore and on the inland rivers. But if you want to fish freshwater and nothing else, head for "The Lake"—**Lake Okeechobee,** that is. The state's largest, it's chock-full of good eating fish. Only about a 1½-hour drive from the coast, it is located in what is known as the Freshwater Frontier and makes a great day or weekend excursion.

Essentials

GETTING THERE From Palm Beach, take I-95 South to Southern Boulevard (U.S. 98 W.) in West Palm Beach, which merges with S.R. 80 and S.R. 441. Follow signs for S.R. 80 West through Belle Glade to South Bay. In South Bay, turn right onto U.S. 27 North, which leads directly to Clewiston.

VISITOR INFORMATION Contact the **Clewiston Chamber of Commerce,** 544 W. Sugarland Hwy., Clewiston, FL 33440 (© **863/983-7979;** www. clewiston.org), for maps, business directories, and the names of numerous fishing guides throughout the area. In addition, you might contact the **Pahokee Chamber of Commerce,** 115 E. Main St., Pahokee, FL 33476 (© **772/924-5579;** fax 772/924-8116; www.pahokee. com), which will send a complete package of magazines, guides, and accommodations listings.

An angler enjoys the fishing on Lake Okeechobee.

Outdoor Activities

BOATING Head out on the Lake with **Big O Airboat Tours,** 920 E. Del Monte, at Roland Martin Marina (© **863/983-2037;** www.bigofishing.com), and catch a fast glimpse of osprey, roseate spoonbills, bald eagles, and dozens of alligators.

FISHING See "Going After the Big One," below.

SKY DIVING Besides fishing, the biggest sport in Clewiston is jumping out of planes, due to the area's limited air traffic and vast areas of flat, undeveloped land. **Air Adventures** (© **800/533-6151** or 863/

GOING AFTER THE big one

Fishing on Lake Okeechobee is a year-round affair, though the fish tend to bite a little better in the winter, perhaps for the benefit of the many snowbirds who flock here (especially Feb–Mar). RV camps are mobbed almost year-round with fish-frenzied anglers who come down for weeks at a time for a decent catch.

You'll need a fishing license to go out with a rod and reel. It's a simple matter to apply: The chamber of commerce and most fishing shops can sign you up on the spot. The cost for non-Florida residents is $17 for 3 days, $30 for 7 days, or $47 for the year.

You can rent, charter, or bring your own boat to Clewiston; just be sure to schedule your trip in advance. You don't want to show up during one of the frequent fishing tournaments only to find you can't get a room, campsite, or fishing boat. All tournaments are held at Roland Martin's marina (see below). For more information on tournaments, check out www.rolandmartinmarina.com.

There are several marinas where you can rent or charter boats. If it's your first time on the lake, we suggest charter-ing a boat with a guide who can show you the most fertile spots and help you handle your tackle. **Roland Martin,** 920 E. Del Monte (✆ **863/983-3151;** www.rolandmartinmarina.com), is the one-stop spot to find a guide, tackle, rods, bait, coolers, picnic supplies, and a choice of boats. Rates for a guided fishing tour are $250 for a half-day and $350 for a full day, for one or two people. You need a fishing license, which is available here for $17. There are also boat rentals: A 14-footer is $79 for a full day only; an 18-footer is $150 for a full day; and a 21-foot pontoon is $165 for a full day. If you want a guide, rates start at $250 (for two people) for a half-day, though in the summer (June–Oct), when it's slow, you can get a cheaper deal.

983-6151; www.skydivefl.com) operates a year-round program from the Air-glades Airport. If you've never jumped before, you can go on a tandem dive, where you'll be attached to a "jumpmaster." For the first 60 seconds, the two of you free-fall from about 12,500 feet. Then a quick pull of the chute turns your rapid descent into a gentle, balletlike cruise to the ground, with time to see the whole majestic lake from a privileged perspective. Dive packages range from $99 to $195, depending on how many people are jumping and what level of skydiver they are. (*Note:* You must be 18 or older and less than 240 lb.)

Where to Stay

If you aren't camping, book a room at the **Clewiston Inn ★★**, 108 Royal Palm Ave., Clewiston (www.clewistoninn.com; ✆ **800/749-4466** or 863/983-8151). Built in 1938, this allegedly haunted, Southern plantation–inspired hotel is the oldest in the Lake Okeechobee region. Rumor has it that a very friendly, pretty female ghost roams the halls at night. Its 52 rooms are simply decorated and nondescript. The lounge area sports a 1945 mural depicting the animals of the region. Double rooms start at $99 a night; suites begin at $129. All have air-conditioning and TVs.

Another choice, especially if you're here to fish, is **Roland Martin,** 920 E. Del Monte (www.rolandmartinmarina.com; 📞 **800/473-6766** or 863/983-3151), the "Disney of fishing." This RV park (no tent sites) has modest motel rooms, efficiencies, condominiums, apartments, RV hookups, and trailers, with two heated pools, gift and marina shops, and a restaurant. The modern complex, dotted with prefab buildings, is clean and well manicured. Rooms rent from $68 to $95; efficiencies cost from $88 to $105. Condominiums are about $150 to $185 a night, with a 3-night minimum. One- or two-bedroom trailers with full kitchen and living room are $65 to $105. Full-hookup RV sites are $35 a night and include power, water, sewage, and cable TV.

CAMPING

During the winter, campers own the Clewiston area. Campsites are jammed with regulars who come year after year for the simple pleasures of the lake and, of course, the warm weather. Every manner of RV, from simple pop-top Volkswagens to Winnebagos to fully decked-out mobile homes, finds its way to a lakeside campsite.

Okeechobee Landings, U.S. 27 East (www.okeechobeelandingsrv.com; 📞 **863/983-4144**), is one of the best; it has every conceivable amenity included in the price of a site. More than 250 sites are situated around a lake, clubhouse, *pétanque* courts, pool, Jacuzzi, horseshoe pit, shuffleboard court, and tennis court. Full hookup includes a sewage connection, which is not the case throughout the county. Rates start at $39 a day or $193 a week, plus tax, including hookup. Also see Roland Martin, described above.

Where to Eat

If you aren't frying up your own catch for dinner, you may want to reconsider it, as dining options here are few and far between. Thank goodness for the **Clewiston Inn** (see "Where to Stay," above), where you can get catfish, beef stroganoff, ham hocks, fried chicken, and liver and onions in a setting as Southern as the food. The dining room is open daily from 6am to 2pm and 5 to 9pm; entrees cost $10 to $18. Sunday brunch is served from 11:30am to 3pm, and a lunch buffet served Monday through Friday features traditional Southern foods, a salad bar, a dessert assortment, and a beverage for $8.95. **Lightsey's,** 1040 Rte. 78 (📞 **863/763-4276**), housed in a lodge, started as a fish company and has expanded to a full-service restaurant. Any catch of the day can be broiled, fried, grilled, or steamed. Try the frogs' legs, gator, and catfish. Entrees are less than $10. Open daily from 11am to 9pm. **Flora & Ella's Restaurant and Country Store,** 550 State Hwy. 80 (📞 **863/675-2891**), is renowned for its pies (about $3 a slice) and old-fashioned Southern cookin' ($5–$15).

10

SOUTHWEST FLORIDA

Although there are no adobe houses, cactuses, or deserts, and, as far as we know, no extrasensory mystics hawking crystals here, Southwest Florida is definitely the Southwest in terms of serenity, golf, retirees, and expensive homes. While the area itself may be staid, and the ride here, through the Everglades, may be the only adventure you'll have in this neck of the woods, it's definitely an area worth exploring.

As primitive as it gets, **Alligator Alley** (I-75) is the closest thing to a dirt road in South Florida. Once a desolate two-lane road connecting Southeast Florida with the Gulf Coast, Alligator Alley is still pretty quiet, but hardly lifeless, thanks to the presence of the egrets, wood storks, owls, herons, osprey, red-shouldered hawks, belted kingfishers, and, of course, alligators that call the area (behind the fenced-in, protected shoulders) home. As you go through Alligator Alley, en route to or from Southwest Florida, your cellphone will not work and your only option for refueling will be at the Miccosukee Indian Reservation. When you reach the end, you will enter another world, where million-dollar mansions, posh resorts, golf courses, and all the signs of the good life are juxtaposed with nature.

Bordered on the east and south by the Everglades and on the west by an intriguing island-studded coast, Southwest Florida traces its nature-loving roots to inventor and amateur botanist Thomas A. Edison, who was so enamored of it that he spent his last 46 winters in Fort Myers. His friend Henry Ford liked it, too, and built his own winter home next door. The world's best tarpon fishing lured President Theodore Roosevelt and his buddies to the 10,000 or so islands

PREVIOUS PAGE: The wind is right off lovely Captiva Island; ABOVE: You may discover some of Florida's wildlife when you traverse Alligator Alley.

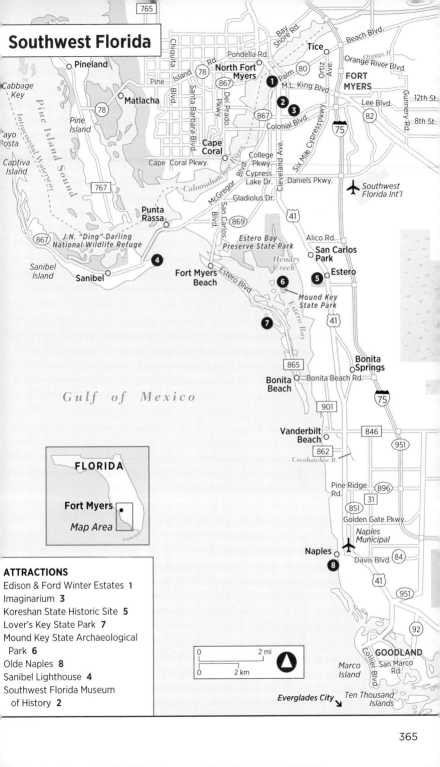

Southwest Florida

ATTRACTIONS

Edison & Ford Winter Estates **1**

Imaginarium **3**

Koreshan State Historic Site **5**

Lover's Key State Park **7**

Mound Key State Archaeological
  Park **6**

Olde Naples **8**

Sanibel Lighthouse **4**

Southwest Florida Museum
  of History **2**

dotting this coast. Some of the planet's best shelling helped entice the du Ponts of Delaware to Gasparilla Island, where they founded the village of Boca Grande. The unspoiled beauty of Sanibel and Captiva islands so entranced Pulitzer Prize–winning political cartoonist J. N. "Ding" Darling that he campaigned to preserve much of those islands in their natural state. Finally, the millionaires who built Naples made their town one of the most alluring—and expensive—in Florida.

Southwest Florida International Airport, on the eastern outskirts of Fort Myers, is this region's major airport (see "Essentials," below). From here it's only 20 miles to Sanibel Island, 35 miles to Naples, and 46 miles to Marco Island. If you have a car, you can see the area's sights and participate in most of its activities easily from one base of operations.

FORT MYERS BEACH ★★

13 miles S of Fort Myers; 28 miles N of Naples; 12 miles E of Sanibel Island

Often overshadowed by trendy Sanibel and Captiva islands to the northwest and by ritzy Naples to the south, down-to-earth Fort Myers Beach, which occupies all of skinny Estero Island, has just as much sun and sand as its affluent neighbors, both a half-hour drive away, but more moderate prices. For Jimmy Buffett–style slacking, Fort Myers Beach is where it's at.

Droves of families and young singles flock to the busy intersection of San Carlos Boulevard and Estero Boulevard, an area so packed with bars, beach-apparel shops, restaurants, and motels that the locals call it "Times Square." That Coney Island image doesn't apply to the rest of Estero Island, where old-fashioned beach cottages, condominiums, and quiet motels beckon couples and families in search of more sedate vacations. Promoters of the southern end of the island don't even say they're in Fort Myers Beach; rather, they're on Estero Island. It's their way of distinguishing their part of town from "Times Square."

Narrow Matanzas Pass leads into broad Estero Bay, which separates the island from the mainland. While the pass is the area's largest commercial fishing port, the bay is an official state aquatic preserve inhabited by a host of birds as well as manatees, dolphins, and other sea life. Nature cruises go forth onto this lovely protected bay, which is dotted with islands.

A few miles south of Fort Myers Beach, a chain of pristine barrier islands includes unspoiled Lovers Key, a state park where a tractor-pulled tram runs through a mangrove forest to one of Florida's best beaches.

Essentials

GETTING THERE This region is served by **Southwest Florida International Airport,** off Daniels Parkway, east of I-75. You can get here on Air Canada, AirTran, American, America West, Continental, Delta, JetBlue, LTU International, Midwest Airlines, Northwest/KLM, Royal, Spirit, Sun Country, United, and US Airways. The two baggage-claim areas have information booths (with maps) and free phones to hotels.

Alamo, Avis, Budget, Dollar, Enterprise, Hertz, National, and Thrifty have rental cars here.

Naples Transportation, Tours & Event Planning (© **239/262-3006;** www.nttep.com) offers an airport-to-hotel shuttle service for $30 per person from Southwest Florida International Airport to greater-Naples-area hotels.

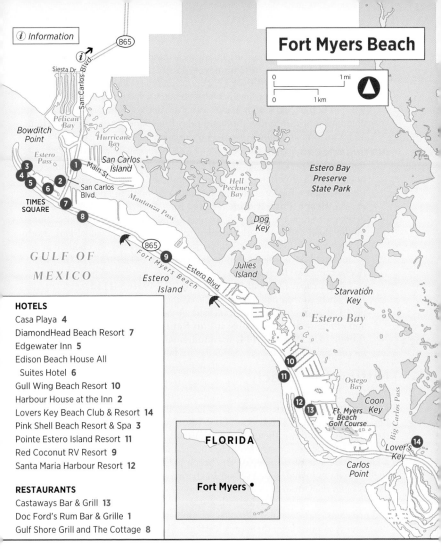

865

Fort Myers Beach

Siesta Dr.

San Carlos Blvd.

Pelican Bay

Bowditch Point

Estero Pass

Hurricane Bay

San Carlos Island

Main St.

San Carlos Blvd.

TIMES SQUARE

Mantanza Pass

Hell Peckney Bay

Estero Bay Preserve State Park

Dog Key

GULF OF MEXICO

865

Fort Myers Beach

Estero Island

Julies Island

Starvation Key

Estero Bay

Ostego Bay

Coon Key

Ft. Myers Beach Golf Course

Big Carlos Pass

Lover's Key

Carlos Point

HOTELS

Casa Playa **4**
DiamondHead Beach Resort **7**
Edgewater Inn **5**
Edison Beach House All
  Suites Hotel **6**
Gull Wing Beach Resort **10**
Harbour House at the Inn **2**
Lovers Key Beach Club & Resort **14**
Pink Shell Beach Resort & Spa **3**
Pointe Estero Island Resort **11**
Red Coconut RV Resort **9**
Santa Maria Harbour Resort **12**

RESTAURANTS

Castaways Bar & Grill **13**
Doc Ford's Rum Bar & Grille **1**
Gulf Shore Grill and The Cottage **8**

FLORIDA

Fort Myers •

Vans and taxis are available at a booth across the street from baggage claim. The maximum fares for one to three passengers are about $35 to downtown Fort Myers, $45 to Fort Myers Beach, $56 to $64 to Sanibel Island, $75 to Captiva Island, $50 to $70 to Naples, and $90 to Marco Island. It's a dollar more for each additional passenger.

Amtrak (℗ **800/USA-RAIL** [872-7245]; www.amtrak.com) provides bus connections between Fort Myers and its nearest station, in Tampa. The Amtrak buses arrive at and depart from **Greyhound/Trailways** (℗ **800/231-2222;** www.greyhound.com) bus station, at 2275 Cleveland Ave.

VISITOR INFORMATION You can get advance information from the **Fort Myers Beach Chamber of Commerce,** 17200 San Carlos Blvd., Fort Myers Beach, FL 33931 (© **800/782-9283** or 239/454-7500; fax 239/454-7910; www.fortmyersbeach.org), which also operates a visitor center on the mainland portion of San Carlos Boulevard, just south of Summerlin Road. The chamber is open Monday through Friday from 9am to 5pm, Saturday from 10am to 5pm, and Sunday from 11am to 5pm.

GETTING AROUND Estero Island is inundated with traffic during the peak winter months, but you can get around on the **Beach Trolley,** which runs every hour, daily from 6:10am to 8:10pm, along the length of Estero Boulevard from Bowditch Regional Park at the north end south to Lovers Key. In winter, the **Beach Park & Ride Trolley** runs daily from 6:10am to 8:10pm between Summerlin Square Shopping Center, on the mainland at Summerlin Road and San Carlos Boulevard, to Bowditch Regional Park. Both trolleys cost $1.25 for adults, 60¢ for seniors, and are free for children under 42 inches. Ask your hotel staff or call **LeeTran** (© **239/275-8726;** www.rideleetran.com) for more info.

For a cab, call **Local Motion Taxi** (© **239/463-4111**).

There are no bike paths, per se, although many folks ride along the paved shoulders of Estero Boulevard. A variety of rental bikes, scooters, and in-line skates are available at **Fun Rentals,** 1901 Estero Blvd., at Ohio Avenue (© **239/463-8844;** www.funrentals.org). Rates start at $90 a day for one-passenger scooters, $25 a day for bikes.

Hitting the Beach

A prime attraction for beachgoers and nature lovers alike is the gorgeous **Lovers Key State Park ★★★**, 8700 Estero Blvd. (© **239/463-4588;** www.floridastateparks.org/loverskey), on Lovers Key, south of Estero Island. Although the highway runs down the center of the island, access to this unspoiled beach from the parking lot is restricted to footpaths and a tractor-pulled tram through a bird-filled forest of mangroves. The beach itself is known for its multitude of shells. Facilities include a snack shop and bathhouses with outdoor showers. The park is open daily from 8am to sunset. Admission is $8 per vehicle with two to eight occupants, $4 for vehicles with a single occupant, and $2 for pedestrians and bicyclists. No alcohol is allowed, nor are pets permitted on the beach or in the water (you must keep them on a leash elsewhere in the park).

On Estero Island, **Lynn Hall Memorial Park** has a fishing pier and beach in the middle of Times Square. It has changing rooms, restrooms, and one of the few public parking lots in the area; the meter costs $2 per hour, so keep it fed. At the island's north end, **Bowditch Regional Park** has picnic tables, showers, and changing rooms. Parking is only for drivers with disabilities permits, but the park is also the turnaround point for the Beach Connection Trolley.

Several beach locations are hotbeds of parasailing, jet skiing, sailboating, and other beach activities. **Times Square,** at San Carlos and Estero boulevards, and the **Best Western Beach Resort,** about a quarter-mile north, are popular spots on Estero's busy north end. Other hot spots are **DiamondHead Beach Resort** (p. 372), just south of Times Square, and the **Junkanoo Beach Bar** (p. 376), in the midbeach area.

SOUTHWEST FLORIDA | Fort Myers Beach

Outdoor Activities

BOATING & BOAT RENTALS Powerboats are available from the **Snook Bight Marina** (📞 239/765-4371; www.snookbightmarina.com), the **Gulf Star Marina** (📞 239/463-9552; www.gulfstar-marina.com), the **Fish Tale Marina** (📞 239/463-3600; www.thefishtailmarina.com), and **Salty Sam's Marina** (📞 239/463-7333; www.saltysamsmarina.com). **Holiday Watersports** (📞 239/765-4386; www.holidaywatersportsfmb.com) rents brand-new boats at the Pink Shell Beach Resort, on Estero Island's northern end. Boat rental costs about $150 to $225 for a half-day, $250 to $325 for a full day depending on the boat.

For canoers and kayakers, the big news is that the beaches of Fort Myers and Sanibel have rolled out the **Great Calusa Blueway** (www.greatcalusablueway.com), a 40-mile paddling trail that covers the waters of Lovers Key State Recreation Area; Mound Key State Archaeological Site; Koreshan State Historic Site; the Caloosahatchee River; Fort Myers Beach; and Sanibel, Captiva, and Pine islands, ending at Cayo Costa. Even cooler, the Blueway utilizes GPS technology, marking key points along the trail to aid navigation. **Kayak Excursions** (📞 239/297-7011; www.kayak-excursions.com) offers rentals; guided tours including wildlife, manatee, and full-moon tours; and kayak classes for kids. Tours cost $50 per person, kayak rentals range from $45 to $100 per day, and classes are $100 per session.

The **Key West Express** (📞 239/463-5733; www.seakeywest.com) offers daily boat service from Fort Myers Beach to Key West for $145 per person, adult round-trip; $135 per senior, round-trip; and $75 per person, children 12 and under, round-trip. The boat leaves from 1200 Main St.

FISHING You can surf-cast, throw your line off the pier at Times Square, or venture offshore on a number of charter-fishing boats here. The staff at **Getaway Marina**, 18400 San Carlos Blvd., about a half-mile north of the Sky Bridge (📞 239/466-3600; www.getawaymarina.com), is adept at matching clients with skilled charter-boat skippers. Expect to spend about $68 per adult and $40 per child 5 to 14 (including rod, reel, bait, tackle, and license) for a full day's fishing. No reservations are required on party boats that take groups out for a half-day of fishing. Operating year-round, the ***Great Getaway*** and ***Great Getaway II*** (📞 239/466-3600) sail from the Getaway Marina, about a half-mile north of the bridge. Boats depart between 9am and 3pm; cost $58 per adult, $40 for kids 5 to 14 (including rod, reel, bait, tackle, and license), and $40 for those who don't fish; and have air-conditioned lounges with bars. Call for details and reservations.

Playing in the Sand

At the **American Sandsculpting Festival,** held each November on Fort Myers Beach, sand sculptors from around the world compete for prize money in two competitions, one for amateurs and one for pros.

SCUBA DIVING & SNORKELING Scuba diving is available at **Seahorse Scuba,** 15600 San Carlos Blvd. (☎ **239/872-6295;** www.seahorsescubaftmyers. com). Two-tank dives start at $75. In business since 1989, the company also teaches diver-certification courses.

The liveaboard dive boat *Ultimate Getaway,* based at Rick's Marina, 18450 San Carlos Blvd. (☎ **239/466-0466;** www.ultimategetaway.net), makes 4- and 5-day voyages to the Dry Tortugas (70 miles west of Key West). This 100-foot vessel carries a maximum of 20 divers and is equipped with a dive platform, chase boat, and TV/DVD. Price varies and includes tanks, weights, belt, food, and soft drinks. Reservations are essential.

Exploring the Area

TOURING THE ESTATES

Edison and Ford Winter Estates ★★ Thomas Edison brought his family to this Victorian retreat—they called it Seminole Lodge—in 1886 and wintered here until his death, in 1931. Mrs. Edison gave the 14-acre estate to the city of Fort Myers in 1947, and today it's Southwest Florida's top historic attraction. It looks exactly as it did during Edison's lifetime. Costumed actors portraying the Edisons, the Fords, and their friends, such as Harvey S. Firestone, give living-history accounts of how the wealthy lived in those days.

Edison experimented with the exotic foliage he planted in the lush tropical gardens surrounding the mansion (he turned goldenrod into rubber and used bamboo for light bulb filaments). Some of his light bulbs dating from the 1920s still burn in the laboratory where he and his staff worked on some of his 1,093 inventions. The monstrous banyan tree that shades the laboratory was 4 feet tall when Firestone presented it to Edison in 1925; today, it's the largest specimen in Florida. A museum displays some of Edison's inventions as well as his unique Model-T Ford, a gift from friend Henry Ford.

In 1916, Ford and his wife, Clara, built Mangoes, the bungalow-style house next door, so they could winter with the Edisons. Like Seminole Lodge, Mangoes is furnished as it appeared in the 1920s.

2350 McGregor Blvd. ☎ **239/334-7419.** www.efwefla.org. Tour of the homes and gardens $20 adults, $11 children 6–12; tour of only botanical gardens $24 adults, $10 children; for only laboratory and museum $12 adults, $5 children. Daily 9am–5:30pm (1½-hr. guided and audio tours depart continuously; last tour departs at 4pm daily). Boat rides Mon–Fri 9am–3pm (weather permitting). Closed Thanksgiving and Christmas Day.

OTHER DOWNTOWN ATTRACTIONS

A good way to explore downtown Fort Myers during the winter season is on a leisurely, 2-hour guided walking tour hosted by the **Southwest Florida Museum of History,** 2300 Peck St., at Jackson Street (☎ **239/321-7430;** www.swflmuseum ofhistory.com). The tours are held on Wednesday (Jan–Apr) from 10am to noon and cost $10 for adults and $5 for children 3 to 12. Reservations are required.

The museum itself is housed in the restored Spanish-style depot served by the Atlantic Coast Line from 1924 to 1971. Inside you'll see exhibits depicting the city's history from the ancient Calusa peoples and the Spanish conquistadors to the first settlers. The remains of a P-39 Aircobra help explain the town's role in training fighter pilots in World War II. Outside stands a replica of an 1800s "cracker" home and the *Esperanza,* the longest and one of the last of the plush

Pullman private cars. Admission is $9.50 for adults, $8.50 for seniors, and $5 for children 3 to 12. Open Tuesday through Saturday from 10am to 5pm.

To avoid the kids going batty on a rainy day, head for the **Imaginarium,** 2000 Cranford Ave., at Dr. Martin Luther King Boulevard (*C* **239/337-3332;** www.imaginariumfortmyers.com), a hands-on museum in the old city water plant. A host of toylike exhibits explain basic scientific principles such as gravity and the weather. Admission is $12 for adults, $10 for seniors, and $8 for children 3 to 12. Open Monday through Saturday from 10am to 5pm, Sunday noon to 5pm. Closed Thanksgiving, Christmas, and Easter.

A NEARBY HISTORIC ATTRACTION

Koreshan State Historic Site Worth a 15-mile drive south of Fort Myers if you're into canoeing or quirky gurus, these 300 acres on the narrow Estero River were home to the Koreshan Unity Movement (pronounced Ko-*resh*-en), a sect led by Chicagoan Cyrus Reed Teed. The Koreshans—who should not be confused with the late, disturbing Branch Davidian leader David Koresh—believed that humans lived *inside* the earth and—ahead of their time—that women should have equal rights. They established a self-sufficient settlement here in 1894. You can visit their garden and several of their buildings, plus view photos from the archives.

Canoeists will find trails winding down the slow-flowing river to **Mound Key,** an islet made of the shells discarded by the Calusa Indians. There's also a picnic and camping area with 60 sites for tents and RVs. For information, contact the park superintendent at 3800 Corkscrew Rd., Estero, FL 33928.

U.S. 41 at Corkscrew Rd., Estero (15 miles south of downtown Fort Myers). *C* **239/992-0311.** www.floridastateparks.org/koreshan. Admission $5 per vehicle for up to 8 people, $4 for a single-occupant vehicle, $2 per pedestrian or biker; tours $2 adults, $1 children 6–12. Canoes $5 per hour, $25 per day. Camping $26. Park daily 8am–sunset; settlement buildings daily 8am–5pm; 1-hr. tours Sat–Sun 1pm. From I-75, take Corkscrew Rd. (exit 19), go 2 miles west, and cross U.S. 41 into the site.

Where to Stay

The **Hyatt Regency Coconut Point Resort & Spa,** 5001 Coconut Rd., Bonita Springs (www.coconutpoint.hyatt.com; *C* **239/444-1234**), a certified Florida Green Lodge, on 26 acres overlooking the Estero Bay Aquatic Preserve, features 454 guest rooms, gardens, water views, and multiple pools. Rates are $299 to $399 in high season and $150 to $279 in the off season.

The hostelries recommended below are removed from the crowds of Times Square, but some chain motels provide comfortable accommodations close to the center of the action: The best one, the midrise **Best Western Beach Resort** (*C* **800/336-4045** or 239/463-6000), is a quarter-mile north, just far enough to escape the noise but still have a lively beach.

Popular with large families and Europeans looking for a longer, more homey stay, condo hotels are aplenty (especially after the real estate bust) on Fort Myers Beach, including **Casa Playa,** 510 Estero Blvd. (www.casaplayaresort.com; *C* **800/569-4876** or 239/765-0510), and the **Lovers Key Beach Club & Resort,** 8771 Estero Blvd. (www.loverskey.com; *C* **877/798-4879** or 239/765-1040). The latter is on the north end of Lovers Key. The less expensive **Santa Maria Harbour Resort,** 7317 Estero Blvd. (*C* **239/765-6700**), is on the bay side of the island.

Sunstream Resorts, 6640 Estero Blvd., Fort Myers Beach (www. sunstream.com; ℂ 800/625-4111), manages "condominium hotels" that include the older, 16-story Pointe Estero Island Resort, 6640 Estero Blvd. (www. pointeestero.com; ℂ 239/765-1155), offering whirlpool tubs and screened balconies with Gulf or bay views; the GullWing Beach Resort, 6620 Estero Blvd. (www.gullwingfl.com; ℂ 239/765-4300), featuring large one-, two-, and three-bedroom condos with screened balconies and views of the Gulf or bay; and the DiamondHead Beach Resort (see below). Not so far from FMB in Cape Coral is Sunstream's newest high-rise condo hotel, The Resort at Marina Village, 5951 Silver King Blvd. (www.marinavillageresort.com; ℂ 239/541-5000), also featuring one-, two-, and three-bedroom residences up to a whopping 2,225 square feet as well as waterfront dining, shopping, and a spa.

New on Fort Myers Beach in 2010: Harbour House at the Inn, 450 Old San Carlos Blvd. (www.harbourhouseattheinn.com; ℂ 239/463-0700), a 34-unit condo-hotel featuring colorful, beachy studio, one-, and two-bedroom condo units with views of Matanzas Pass and the beach. Rates start at $175 in the winter and $85 during summer.

For campers, the somewhat-cramped Red Coconut RV Resort, 3001 Estero Blvd. (www.redcoconut.com; ℂ 239/463-7200; fax 239/463-2609), has sites for RVs and tents both on the Gulf side of the road and right on the beach. Rates range from $48 to $85.

EXPENSIVE

DiamondHead Beach Resort ★ This 12-story beachside resort, Florida Green Lodging certified, sports large, comfortable one-bedroom apartments. Sliding-glass doors lead from both the living quarters and the bedrooms to screened balconies. The beachfront apartments are the most appealing, but every unit has a view (spectacular from the upper floors). Each room has a private 700-square-foot balcony, a sleeper sofa, two TVs, and a kitchen area. Enjoy casual beach-side dining at Cabañas Beach Bar & Grill or live entertainment at Chloë's Restaurant & Lounge. In 2009, the full-service Esterra Spa & Salon opened. During the winter season, evidence of nightlife can be found at the hotel's lounge, which has live music. If it's summer, however, you're on your own.

2000 Estero Blvd. (at Palm Ave.), Fort Myers Beach, FL 33931. www.diamondheadfl.com. ℂ 888/765-5002 or 239/765-7654. Fax 239/765-1694. 124 units. Winter $259–$499 suite; off season $149–$329 suite. AE, DISC, MC, V. Amenities: 2 restaurants; 2 bars; children's programs; exercise room; Jacuzzi; heated outdoor pool; limited room service; watersports equipment/rental. In room: A/C, TV, hair dryer, Internet access, kitchen.

Edison Beach House All Suites Hotel ★★ No standardized list of amenities does justice to this obsessive-compulsively clean, intimate, five-story, nonsmoking beachside inn; when owner Larry Yax built it in 1999, he equipped every unit as if he were going to live in it. Each of the light and airy rooms has a balcony, ceiling fan, fully equipped kitchen (look for your complimentary bag of popcorn in the microwave), writing desk stocked with office supplies, and linen closet packed with extra towels. Also, 47-inch HDTVs and high-speed Internet access have been added to every room. All suites also have stackable washer/dryers. The freshly laundered bedspreads provided to each new guest are but one example of the premium Larry puts on cleanliness. The beachfront units have the best views, but much more romantic are the "A" suites, whose queen-size beds are almost surrounded by windows formed by a turret on one corner of the building—you'll wake up to a panoramic view.

830 Estero Blvd., Fort Myers Beach, FL 33931. www.edisonbeachhouse.com. © **800/399-2511** or 239/463-1530. Fax 239/765-9430. 24 units. Winter $170–$300 double; off season $135–$295 double. AE, DISC, MC, V. **Amenities:** Heated outdoor pool; Wi-Fi. *In room:* A/C, TV, hair dryer, high-speed Internet access, kitchen.

Pink Shell Beach Resort & Spa ★★ ☺ At the tip of Estero Island between tony Naples and laid-back Sanibel and Captiva islands, the 12-acre Pink Shell features deluxe studio and villa-style accommodations all overlooking the beach. Located along a quarter-mile stretch of sugar-white sands along the Gulf of Mexico, the resort offers an array of activities, including various watersports. In addition, guests will experience a broad range of facilities and amenities, including sailing with Colgate Offshore Sailing School or a dolphin-sightseeing tour on a WaveRunner. Sip cocktails poolside at **Bongo's** or enjoy waterfront dining at JoJo's. The 6,000-square-foot **Aquagene Spa** offers a slew of relaxing treatments. The kids will love Octopool, an undersea fantasy pool, or spending a day of adventure with the Kidds Kampp crew. There's also a state-of-the-art gym for workout fiends.

275 Estero Blvd., Fort Myers Beach, FL 33931. www.pinkshell.com. © **800/237-5786** or 239/463-6181. Fax 239/463-1229. 215 units. Winter $359–$619 villas or studios; off season $169–$519 villas or studios. Packages available. AE, DC, DISC, MC, V. **Amenities:** 3 restaurants (1 closed in off season); 2 bars; bike rentals; children's programs; 3 heated outdoor pools and kids' wading pool; watersports equipment/rentals. *In room:* A/C, TV, hair dryer, high-speed Internet, kitchen.

MODERATE

Sanibel Harbour Marriott Resort & Spa ★★★ ☺ This bayside resort is on a tranquil 85-acre peninsula overlooking San Carlos Bay and Sanibel and Captiva islands. The resort's 347 units are in the Sanibel and Captiva towers, all modern and luxurious. All have balconies with water and island views. Three outdoor pools and a bayside beach offer relaxing sunning areas. The spa features more than 60 treatments, including the incredible BETAR bed, one of only 16 such systems in the world, in which the body is bathed in sound waves to create a state of total relaxation. There's also a world-class fitness center, five clay tennis courts, and an assortment of classes and clinics daily. The resort is a fabulous vacation destination for families. When the resort became a Marriott in 2009, it added an upgraded bedding package and installation of flatscreen high-definition televisions throughout the resort. Other upgrades are in store throughout the hotel and are expected to be complete by the end of 2011.

17260 Harbour Pointe Rd., Fort Myers, FL 33908. www.sanibel-resort.com. © **800/767-7777** or 239/466-4000. Fax 239/466-2150. 347 units. Winter from $229 double, from $279 suite; off-season from $129 double, from $179 suite. Daily resort fee $15 per unit, per day, plus tax. Packages available. AE, DC, DISC, MC, V. Valet parking $20; self-parking $12. Take the last exit off Summerlin Rd. before the Sanibel Causeway toll plaza. **Amenities:** 6 restaurants and lounges; children's programs; concierge; health club; 4 pools (1 indoor); room service; 5 clay tennis courts; spa; watersports equipment/rentals. *In room:* A/C, TV, hair dryer, high-speed Internet access, minibar.

INEXPENSIVE

Edgewater Inn ★ 🥄 On the quiet, north end of Estero Island right on the bay, the three-story Edgewater Inn has two one-bedroom and four two-bedroom apartments, all with screened lanais. They're available on a weekly basis in winter and for 3-day-minimum stays off season and are closed from July to September. Free beach chairs, bicycles, and barbecue grills are available for guests' use. Just 300 feet from the beach, Edgewater is an ideal spot for peace, quiet, location, and value.

781 Estero Blvd., Fort Myers Beach, FL 33931. www.edgewaterinnfmb.com. ℭ **800/951-9975** or 239/765-5959. Fax 239/765-0090. 6 units. Winter $900–$1,700 apt per week; off season $450–$950 apt per week. MC, V. **Amenities:** Access to nearby health club; heated outdoor pool. *In room:* A/C, TV, hair dryer, full kitchen.

Where to Dine

The busy area around Times Square has fast-food joints to augment several local restaurants catering to the beach crowd. The best of these is the **Beach Pierside Grill,** on the beach at the foot of Lynn Hall Memorial Pier (ℭ **239/765-7800;** www.piersidegrill.com), a pub with blond-wood trim and vivid colors whose greatest asset isn't the food, but the views. It opens onto a large beachside patio with dining at umbrella tables, outstanding sunsets, and live bands playing at night. The reasonably priced fare is a catchall of conch fritters, shrimp and fish baskets, burgers, and seafood main courses. Reservations are accepted; food is served daily from 11am to 11pm.

MODERATE

Gulf Shore Grill and The Cottage SEAFOOD/AMERICAN On the southern fringes of Times Square, this old clapboard building has splendid views of the Gulf and the beach. It began life in the 1920s as the Crescent Beach Casino and has seen various incarnations as a bathhouse, gambling casino, dance hall, and rooming house. The menu is all over the place, from traditional Florida-style main courses including baked grouper imperial, grilled mahimahi, and shrimp wrapped in bacon and coated with honey, to Mexican classics including tacos, burritos, and quesadillas. This is one of the best breakfast spots on the beach, with items ranging from biscuits and gravy to eggs on a muffin with Alaskan crabmeat and a charon (tomato-hollandaise) sauce. The kitchen also provides the pub fare for the **Cottage Bar,** an open-air drinking establishment next door.

1270 Estero Blvd. (on the beach at Ave. A). ℭ **239/765-5440.** www.gulfshoregrill.com. Reservations recommended for dinner. Main courses $10–$40; breakfast $5–$15; sandwiches and burgers $9–$13. AE, DISC, MC, V. Daily 8am–3pm and 5–10pm.

INEXPENSIVE

Castaways Bar & Grill AMERICAN Formerly known as Loggerheads, this is the best bet on the island's south end. Charter-boat captains and other locals congregate around a big square bar on one side of the knotty pine–accented dining room. The new menu offers ribs, lasagna, spaghetti and meatballs, and meatloaf. There's also some seriously excellent pizza. The new owners, New Jersey expats, added pool tables, dart board, jukebox, and video games. They even host free Texas Hold 'em Sundays at 7pm and there's live entertainment 5 nights a week.

In Santini Marina Plaza, 7205 Estero Blvd. (at Lennel Rd.). ℭ **239/463-4644.** Reservations recommended on weekends. Main courses $10–$15. AE, DISC, MC, V. Daily 11am–2am.

Doc Ford's Rum Bar & Grille ★★ AMERICAN Epitomizing the realtor mantra of "location, location, location," Doc Ford's may also have a swankier

Sanibel Island outpost, but the Fort Myers Beach location is the place to be for water views, tropical drinks, happy hours, and a menu that features everything from simple bar fare and raw bar to finer foods, including a fantastic cedar-plank salmon topped with a mango glaze. We especially love Doc Ford's original lime panko-crusted fish sandwich, one of the best we've had on both coasts of Florida. Doc Ford's on Sanibel is at 975 Rabbit Rd. (ⓒ **239/472-8311;** www.docfords sanibel.com).

708 Fisherman's Wharf. ⓒ **239/765-9660.** www.docfordsfortmyersbeach.com. Main courses $14–$25; sandwiches $8–$14. AE, MC, V. Daily 11am until close (around 1am).

Farmer's Market Restaurant ★★ 🏢 SOUTHERN It's off the beach, but it's worth drying off for. Cabbage, okra, green beans, and tomatoes at the retail farmers' market next door provide fodder for some of Florida's best country-style cooking at this plain and simple restaurant, frequented by everyone from business executives to truck drivers. Specialties are beef and pork barbecue from the tin smokehouse out by Edison Avenue, plus other Southern favorites such as country-fried steak, fried chicken livers and gizzards, fried Lake Okeechobee catfish, and smoked ham hocks with a bowl of lima beans. Yankees can order fried chicken, roast beef, or pork chops, and hash browns instead of grits with the big breakfast. But forget about Southern Comfort: No alcohol is served.

2736 Edison Ave. (at Cranford Ave.). ⓒ **239/334-1687.** www.farmersmarketrestaurant.com. Breakfast $4–$8; main courses $6–$12. No credit cards. Mon–Sat 6am–8pm; Sun 6am–7pm.

Survey Cafe ★ SOUTHERN Off the main drag in "downtown" Bonita Springs, this tiny cottage-cum-restaurant is an ideal spot for fantastic breakfasts, coffee, wine, and tapas. With limited seating, if weather permits, sit outside on the porch and take advantage of the peaceful surroundings—and free Wi-Fi. Everything here is homemade by a hardworking staff. Be patient, as it's not as well staffed as some of the area's larger restaurants. It's totally worth it. For breakfast, try French toast with cinnamon, brown sugar, and vanilla, or a frittata. At lunchtime the brave may want to check out Grandpa's Gator Cakes. We didn't, but drop us a note and tell us if it doesn't taste like chicken. At night it's all about small plates (Fri and Sat only) from 5 to 9pm, when you can choose from an amazing artesian cheese plate, bacon-wrapped quail breast, or *osso buco*—all for $6 to $10. We couldn't resist stopping by here for one of their homemade Monkey Bars—a cross between a brownie, a cookie, and heaven.

10530 Wilson St., Bonita Springs. ⓒ **239/992-0133.** www.thesurveycafe.com. Breakfast $4–$8; lunch $7–$10; small plates $6–$10. AE, MC, V. Daily 7:30am–3pm; Fri–Sat 5–9pm.

Fort Myers Beach After Dark

To find out what's going on, pick up a copy of the daily *News-Press* (www.news press.com). The two local tabloids, *Beach Bulletin* and *Fort Myers Beach Observer,* are available at the chamber of commerce (p. 368).

The area around Times Square is always active, every day in winter and on weekends in the off season. At the foot of Lynn Hall Memorial Pier, the **Beach Pierside Grill,** 1000 Estero Blvd. (ⓒ **239/765-7800;** www.piersidegrill.com), has live entertainment on its beachside patio. It's not directly on the beach, but locals in the know head for the rooftop bar at **Beached Whale,** 1249 Estero Blvd. (ⓒ **239/463-5505;** www.thebeachedwhale.com), which supplies free chicken wings during its nightly happy hour. Rock and reggae music are played downstairs for dancing. **Castaways Bar & Grill** (ⓒ **239/463-4644**) features live entertainment 5 nights a week, as well as free Texas Hold 'em every Sunday night at 7pm; and **Doc Ford's Rum Bar & Grille,** 708 Fisherman's Wharf (📞 **239/765-9660;** www.docfordsfortmyersbeach.com), is usually open until 1am and features a lively bar scene and live music.

Away from the crowds in the "middle beach" area, the **Junkanoo Beach Bar,** under Anthony's on the Gulf, 3040 Estero Blvd. (📞 **239/463-2600**), attracts a more affluent crowd for its bohemian-style parties that run from 11:30am to 1:30am daily. Live bands here specialize in reggae and other island music. On the menu are inexpensive subs, sandwiches, burgers, and pizzas, and a concessionaire rents beach cabanas and watersports toys, making it a good place for a lively day at the beach.

A great place for an afternoon or evening drink or three, **Nervous Nellie's,** 1131 First St. (📞 **239/463-8077;** www.nervousnellies.com), located next to the Sky Bridge on the docks along Matanzas Pass, is a hugely popular happy hour spot thanks to its "Ugly Waterside Bar," where the only things unsightly may be the customers after several drinks.

SANIBEL & CAPTIVA ISLANDS ★★★

14 miles W of Fort Myers; 40 miles N of Naples

Sanibel and Captiva are Florida's unfussy cousins. Here you'll find none of the neon signs, amusement parks, or high-rise condominiums that clutter most beach resorts in the state. Sanibel's main drag, Periwinkle Way, runs under a canopy of whispery pines and gnarled oaks so thick they almost obscure the small signs for chic shops and restaurants. The residents have saved their trees and tropical foliage, permitted no building higher than the tallest palm, and allowed no WaveRunner or other noisy beach toy within 300 yards of their gorgeous, shell-strewn beaches. Legend says that Ponce de León named the larger of these two barrier islands San Ybel, after Queen Isabella of Spain. Another legend claims that Captiva's name comes from the captured women kept here by the pirate Jose Gaspar.

Beaches Of the area beaches, some of the most popular are at **Sanibel Lighthouse,** which has a fishing pier, and **Turner Beach,** popular at sunset because it faces due west.

Things to Do Sanibel and Captiva are famous for their seashells, and residents and visitors alike can be seen in the "Sanibel stoop" or the "Captiva crouch" while searching for some 200 species.

Eating & Drinking There's lots of fine dining in these affluent communities, ranging from **Ellington's Jazz Bar & Restaurant,** where music accompanies your entree, to the kitschy **Bubble Room,** to fresh seafood at the occasionally star-studded yet casual hangout **Cabbage Key Restaurant.**

Nature More than half of Sanibel Island is preserved in its natural state as a wildlife refuge. You can ride, walk, bike, canoe, or kayak through the **J. N. "Ding" Darling National Wildlife Refuge,** one of Florida's best.

Essentials

GETTING THERE See the section on Fort Myers Beach, beginning on p. 366, for information on air, train, bus, and rental-car services. The Amoco station at 1015 Periwinkle Way, at Causeway Road, is the Sanibel agent for **Hertz** (📞 **239/472-2125**).

Sanibel & Captiva Islands

HOTELS

Beachview Cottages **16**
Captiva Island Inn Bed & Breakfast **7**
Casa Ybel Resort **22**
Castaways Beach and Bay Cottages **9**
Gulf Breeze Cottages **30**
Island Inn **15**
Jensen's on the Gulf **2**
Jensen's Twin Palm Resort & Marina **3**
Periwinkle Trailer Park **29**
Sanibel Inn **32**
Sanibel Sunset Beach Resort **14**
Song of the Sea **33**
South Seas Island Resort **1**
Sundial Beach and Golf Resort **26**
Tarpon Tale Inn **35**
' Tween Waters Inn Island Resort **8**

RESTAURANTS

The Bubble Room **5**
Ellington's Jazz Bar and Restaurant **27**
Gramma Dot's Seaside Saloon **34**
The Green Flash **6**
Hungry Heron **19**
The Island Cow **20**
Jacaranda **28**
Jerry's Family Restaurant **24**
The Lazy Flamingo II **31**
Lighthouse Café **36**
Mad Hatter **10**
McT's Shrimp House & Tavern **25**
Mucky Duck **4**
R. C. Otter's Island Eats **5**
Sanibel Café **23**
The Timbers Restaurant & Fish Market **18**

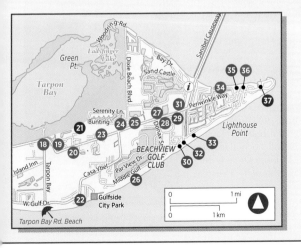

ATTRACTIONS

Bailey-Matthews Shell Museum **17**
J.N. ("Ding") Darling National Wildlife Refuge **12**
Sanibel/Captiva Conservation Foundation **13**
Sanibel Historical Village & Museum **21**
Sanibel Lighthouse **37**
Clinic for the Rehabilitation of Wildlife **11**

VISITOR INFORMATION The **Sanibel & Captiva Islands Chamber of Commerce,** 1159 Causeway Rd., Sanibel Island, FL 33957 (✆ **239/472-1080;** fax 239/472-1070; www.sanibel-captiva.org), maintains a visitor center on Causeway Road, as you drive onto Sanibel from Fort Myers. The chamber gives away an island guide and sells a detailed street map for $5. Also for sale are books, such as a shelling guide and a collection of menus from the islands' restaurants. Phones are available for making hotel and condominium reservations; check the brochure racks for discounts in summer and the month of December. It's open Monday through Sunday from 9am to 5pm. Another great resource for area information is **www.fortmyers sanibel.com**.

GETTING AROUND Neither Sanibel nor Captiva has public transportation. No parking is permitted on any street or road on Sanibel. Free beach parking is available on the Sanibel Causeway. Other municipal lots are reserved for local residents or have a $2 hourly fee. Accordingly, many residents and visitors get around by bicycle (see "More Ways to Enjoy the Outdoors," below). If you need a cab, call **Sanibel Taxi** (✆ **239/472-4160**).

Parks & Nature Preserves

Named for the *Des Moines Register* cartoonist who was a frequent visitor and who started the federal Duck Stamp program, the **J. N. "Ding" Darling National Wildlife Refuge** ★★★ (www.fws.gov/dingdarling), on Sanibel-Captiva Road, is home to alligators, raccoons, otters, and hundreds of species of birds. Occupying more than half of Sanibel Island, this 6,000-plus-acre area of mangrove swamps, winding waterways, and uplands has a 2-mile boardwalk nature trail and a 5-mile, one-way **Wildlife Drive.** The visitor center shows brief videos on the refuge's inhabitants every half-hour and sells a map keyed to numbered stops along the Wildlife Drive. The best times for viewing wildlife are early morning, late afternoon, and at low tide (tables are posted at the visitor center and available at the chamber of commerce). Mosquitoes and no-see-ums (tiny, biting sand flies) are especially prevalent at dawn and dusk, so bring repellent.

Admission to the visitor center is free. The Wildlife Drive costs $5 per vehicle, $1 for hikers and bicyclists (free to holders of federal Duck Stamps and National Park Service access passports). The visitor center is open January through April, daily from 9am to 5pm; off season, daily from 9am to 4pm. It's open on federal holidays January through April, but closed on holidays the rest of the year. The Wildlife Drive is open year-round Saturday through Thursday, from 1 hour after sunrise to 1 hour before sunset. For more information, contact the refuge at 1 Wildlife Dr., Sanibel Island, FL 33957 (✆ **239/472-1100**).

You might see a wood stork at the J.N. "Ding" Darling Wildlife Refuge.

Newly opened to the public in 2010: **Clinic for the Rehabilitation of Wildlife's Healing Winds Visitor Education Center,** 3883 Sanibel Captiva Rd. (℃ **239/472-3644;** www.crowclinic.org), offering an up-close look at how one of the nation's leading rehab hospitals cares for and rescues injured animals. Admission is a donation of $5.

You'll get a lot more from your visit by taking a naturalist-narrated tram tour operated by **Tarpon Bay Explorers,** at the north end of Tarpon Bay Road (℃ **239/472-8900;** www.tarponbayexplorers.com). The tours last 1½ hours and cost $13 for adults, $8 for children 12 and under. Schedules are seasonal, so call ahead.

Tarpon Bay Explorers also offers a variety of guided **canoe and kayak tours,** $30 adults, $20 kids, with an emphasis on the historical, cultural, and environmental aspects of the refuge (call for schedule and reservations, which are required). It also rents canoes, kayaks, and small boats with electric trolling motors (see "More Ways to Enjoy the Outdoors," below).

A short drive from the visitor center, the nonprofit **Sanibel/Captiva Conservation Foundation,** 3333 Sanibel-Captiva Rd. (℃ **239/472-2329;** www.sccf.org), maintains a nature center, a native-plant nursery, and 4.5 miles of nature trails on 1,100 acres of wetlands along the Sanibel River. You can learn more about the islands' ecosystems through environmental workshops, guided 1½-hour trail walks, beach walks, and a 2-hour natural-history boat cruise (call for seasonal schedules and reservations). Various items are for sale, including native plants and publications on the islands' birds and other wildlife. Admission is $3 for adults, free for children 16 and under. The nature center is open year-round, Monday through Friday from 8:30am to 4pm, Saturday from 10am to 3pm.

Also nearby, the **Clinic for the Rehabilitation of Wildlife (C.R.O.W.),** 3883 Sanibel-Captiva Rd. (℃ **239/472-3644;** www.crowclinic.org), is dedicated to the care of sick, injured, and orphaned wildlife. C.R.O.W.'s Visitor Education Center is open Tuesday through Sunday from 10am to 4pm. Admission is $5 for adults and children 4 and older.

Hitting the Beach

BEACHES Sanibel has four public beach-access areas with metered parking: the eastern point around **Sanibel Lighthouse,** which has a fishing pier; **Gulf-side City Park,** at the end of Algiers Lane, off Casa Ybel Road; **Tarpon Bay Road Beach,** at the south end of Tarpon Bay Road; and **Bowman's Beach,** off Sanibel-Captiva Road. **Turner Beach,** at Blind Pass between Sanibel and Captiva, is popular at sunset because it faces due west; there's a small free parking lot on the Captiva side, but parking on the Sanibel side is limited to holders of local permits. All except Tarpon Bay Road Beach have restrooms. *Note:* Although nude bathing is illegal, the north end of Bowman's Beach often sees more than its share of bare straight and gay bodies.

Another popular beach on Captiva is at the end of Andy Rosse Lane in front of the Mucky Duck Restaurant. It's the one place here where you can rent motorized watersports equipment (see "More Ways to Enjoy the Outdoors," below), but you'll have to use the Mucky Duck's restrooms if you need to go. There's limited free parking just north of here, at the end of Captiva Drive (go past the entrance to South Seas Resort to the end of the road).

SHELLING Sanibel and Captiva are famous for their seashells, and residents and visitors alike can be seen in the "Sanibel stoop" or the "Captiva crouch" while searching for some 200 species. Only if you're a hard-core shell fanatic should you check out the **Bailey-Matthews Shell Museum** ★★, 3075 Sanibel-Captiva Rd. (✆ **888/679-6450** or 239/395-2233; www.shellmuseum.org), the only museum in the United States devoted solely to saltwater, freshwater, and land shells (yes, snails are included). The museum is a far cry from the tourist-trap shell factories you'll see throughout the state. Shells from as far away as South Africa surround a 6-foot globe in the middle of the main exhibit hall, showing their geographic origins. A spinning wheel–shaped case identifies shells likely to wash up on Sanibel. Other exhibits are devoted to shells in tribal art, fossil shells found in Florida, medicinal qualities of various mollusks, the endangered Florida tree snail, and "sailor's valentines"—shell crafts made by natives of Barbados for sailors to bring home to their loved ones. The library attracts serious malacologists—those who study mollusks—and a shop has clever shell-themed gifts. The museum is open daily from 10am to 5pm; admission is $7 for adults and $4 for children 5 to 16.

For a great shelling excursion, **Sanibel Island Cruise Line** (✆ **239/472-5799;** www.sanibelislandcruiseline.com) takes you on a 3-hour shelling and dolphin cruise to Cayo Costa for $50 per adult and $40 per child 12 and under.

The months from February to April, or after any storm, are prime times of the year to look for whelks, olives, scallops, sand dollars, conch, and many other varieties of shells. Low tide is the best time of day. The shells can be sharp, so wear Aqua Socks or old running shoes whenever you go walking on the beach.

> ### Don't Take Live Shells
>
> Florida law prohibits taking live shells (those with living creatures inside them) from the beaches, and federal regulations prevent them from being removed from the J. N. "Ding" Darling National Wildlife Refuge.

10

You can see visitors doing the "Sanibel stoop" on the shores of the island.

More Ways to Enjoy the Outdoors

BIKING, WALKING, JOGGING & IN-LINE SKATING On Sanibel, paved bike paths run alongside most roads, including the length of Periwinkle Way and along Sanibel-Captiva Road to Blind Pass, making the island a paradise for cyclists, walkers, joggers, and in-line skaters. You can also walk or bike the 5-mile, one-way nature trail through the J. N. "Ding" Darling National Wildlife Refuge. There are no bike paths on Captiva, where trees next to the narrow roads can make for dangerous riding.

The chamber of commerce's visitor center has bike maps, as do Sanibel's rental outlets: **Finnimore's Cycle Shop,** 2353 Periwinkle Way (✆ 239/472-5577; www.finnimores.com); **Billy's Rentals,** 1470 Periwinkle Way (✆ 239/472-5248; www.sanibelsegway.com); and **Tarpon Bay Explorers,** at the north end of Tarpon Bay Road (✆ 239/472-8900; www.tarponbayexplorers). On Captiva, **Jim's Bike & Scooter Rentals,** on Andy Rosse Lane (✆ 239/472-1296; www.yolowatersports.com), rents bikes and beach equipment. Bike rates range from about $8 to $14 for 4 hours to $16 to $22 a day for basic models. Finnimore's and Jim's also rent in-line skates. Billy's rents Segways and conducts Wildlife-Eco tours on Segways. Call ✆ 239/472-3620 for pricing.

BOATING & FISHING On Sanibel, rental boats and charter-fishing excursions are available at the **Boat House,** at the Sanibel Marina, North Yachtsman Drive (✆ **239/472-2531**), off Periwinkle Way east of Causeway Road. **Tarpon Bay Explorers,** at the north end of Tarpon Bay Road (✆ **239/472-8900;** www.tarponbayexplorers.com), rents boats with electric trolling motors and tackle for fishing.

On Captiva, check with **Beach Bums Rentals,** at the 'Tween Waters Inn Marina (✆ **239/472-6336**); **Jensen's Twin Palms Marina** (✆ **239/472-5800;** www.jensen-captiva.com); and **McCarthy's Marina** (✆ **239/472-5200;** www.mccarthysmarina.com), all on Captiva Road. Rental boats cost about $200 for a half-day, $350 for a full day.

Many charter-fishing captains have boats docked at these marinas. Half-day rates are about $250 to $350 for up to four people. The skippers leave free brochures at the chamber of commerce's visitor center (p. 378), and they're also listed in the free tourist publications found there.

CANOEING & KAYAKING As noted under "Parks & Nature Preserves," above, **Tarpon Bay Explorers** (✆ **239/472-8900;** www.tarponbayexplorers.com) has guided canoe and kayak trips in the J. N. "Ding" Darling National Wildlife Refuge. Do-it-yourselfers can rent canoes and kayaks. They cost $20 for the first 2 hours, $10 for each additional hour. **Captiva Kayak Co./WildSide Adventures,** at McCarthy's Marina (✆ **877/395-2925** or 239/395-2925; www.captivakayaks.com), rents canoes and kayaks on Captiva for $15 per hour, $35 for 4 hours, and $55 for 8 hours, as does **'Tween Waters Inn Marina** (✆ **239/472-5161;** www.tween-waters.com), for $20 to $30 per 2 hours and $5 to $10 per additional hour.

Tarpon Bay Explorers also offers naturalist-led kayaking trips through the mangrove forest along the Commodore Creek water trail. Learn about the rich back-bay ecosystem and the wildlife that lives there. You'll be surrounded by red mangroves, wading birds, and more for $30 per adult and $20 per child (✆ **239/472-8900**). **Captiva Kayak Co./WildSide Adventures,**

10

SOUTHWEST FLORIDA

Sanibel & Captiva Islands

based at McCarthy's Marina, on Captiva (© **877/395-2925** or 239/395-2925; www.captiva kayaks.com), has day and night back-bay ecology trips for $45 for adults and $35 for children (add $10 for sunset/twilight tours). The company will customize tours, including camping on Cayo Costa (see "Nearby Island Hopping," beginning on p. 393) for advanced kayakers. **Adventure in Paradise** (© **239/472-9443;** www.adventureinparadiseinc. com) offers eco-nature canoe and kayak tours through the wildlife-studded Engine Trail and Ibis Isle. Cost is $30 adults, $15 children. Reservations are essential for all operators.

Cast a line off the shores of Captiva.

For information on the 40-mile **Great Calusa Blueway** paddling trail, see p. 369.

GOLF & TENNIS Golfers may view a gallery of wild animals while playing the 5,600-yard, par-70, 18-hole course at the **Dunes Golf & Tennis Club,** 949 Sandcastle Rd., Sanibel (© **239/472-2535;** www.dunesgolfsanibel. com), whose back 9 runs across a wildlife preserve. Call a day in advance for seasonal greens fees and a tee time. The Dunes also has seven tennis courts.

You can also play 18 water-bordered holes at **Beachview Golf Club,** 1100 Par View Dr., Sanibel (© **239/472-2626;** www.beachviewgolfclub. com).

The **South Seas Island Resort,** on Captiva (p. 386), has tennis courts and a 9-hole golf course, but they're for guests only.

SAILING If you want to learn how to sail or polish your skills, noted yachters Steve and Doris Colgate have a branch of their **Offshore Sailing School** at the South Seas Island Resort on Captiva (© **800/221-4326** or 239/454-1700; www.offshore-sailing.com). Clinics range from a half-day to a full week. Also ask about the popular women-only, father-son, and mother-daughter programs.

Also based on Captiva are two sailboats that take guests out on the waters of Pine Island Sound: the 30-foot *Adventure* (© **239/472-5300;** www.captivacruises.com), a sailing sloop offering private tours for up to six guests, at $125 per hour with a 2-hour minimum, or group tours at $45 for adults and $35 for children; and the *New Moon* (© **239/395-1782;** www. newmoonsailing.com), a 40-foot sloop carrying up to 40 passengers from the 'Tween Waters Marina, on 3-hour half-day and 7-hour full-day and sunset charters. Half-day and sunset trips for up to six people cost $300; full-day trips are $600. Reservations are required well in advance, but Captain Mick Gurley tells us "don't be afraid to try last minute."

Do-it-yourselfers can rent small sailboats from **Captiva Kayak Co./ WildSide Adventures,** based at McCarthy's Ma-rina (© **877/395-2925** or 239/395-2925; www.captivakayaks.com). Prices start at $35 an hour to $100 for a half-day, depending on the size of the craft and number of sailors.

WATERSPORTS Sanibel prohibits motorized watersports equipment on its beaches, but Captiva doesn't. **Yolo Watersports** (© 239/472-9656; www.yolo-jims.com) offers parasailing and WaveRunner rentals on the beach in front of the Mucky Duck Restaurant, at the Gulf end of Andy Rosse Lane.

More to See & Do

Worth a stop after you've done everything else here, the **Sanibel Historical Village & Museum,** 950 Dunlop Rd. (© 239/472-4648), includes the 1913-vintage Rutland home and the 1926 versions of Bailey's General Store (complete with Red Crown gasoline pumps), the post office, and Miss Charlotta's Tea Room. Displays highlight the islands' prehistoric Calusa peoples, as well as old photos from pioneer days, turn-of-the-20th-century clothing, and a variety of memorabilia. It's open from November to May, Wednesday through Saturday from 10am to 4pm; from June to mid-August, Wednesday through Saturday from 10am to 1pm. Admission is by $3 donation.

In addition to its other trips, **Captiva Cruises** (© 239/472-5300; www.captivacruises.com) goes on daily sunset cruises from South Seas Island Resort, on Captiva. The cruise costs $25 adults, $15 children 6 to 12. Call for times and reservations.

Where to Stay

Sanibel & Captiva Central Reservations, Inc. (© 800/325-1352 or 239/405-7848; fax 239/405-7847; www.rescen.com) and **Reservation Central** (© 800/290-6920) are reservations services that can book you into most condominiums and cottages here.

In general, Sanibel and Captiva room and condominium rates are highest during the shelling season, February through April. January is usually somewhat less expensive. But note that most rates fall drastically during the off season; don't hesitate to ask for a discount or special deal then. Because most properties on the islands are geared to 1-week vacations, you can save by purchasing a package for stays of 7 nights or longer.

The islands' sole campground, the **Periwinkle Trailer Park,** 1119 Periwinkle Way, Sanibel Island (www.sanibelcamping.com; © 239/472-1433), is so popular it doesn't even advertise. No other camping is permitted on either Sanibel or Captiva.

SANIBEL ISLAND
Very Expensive
Casa Ybel Resort ★★★ One of the best resorts on Sanibel, this all-condo property sits on 23 acres beside the beach on the site of the island's first beachfront hotel, the Thistle Lodge. The present-day Casa Ybel's turn-of-the-20th-century main building houses a restaurant named **Thistle Lodge** as a nostalgic reminder of that first hotel, where both guests and other island visitors can enjoy wonderful cuisine—butter-poached lobster tail, pan-steamed Maine lobster, crackling coconut prawns with Thai orange-chili sauce—and Gulf views. The pool in front of the restaurant is one of Florida's most picturesque. There are

also 14 miles of seashell-studded white sand. This is bliss. The one- and two-bedroom condominiums, housed in beach-washed four-story buildings on the island's most beautifully landscaped grounds, all have screened porches (complete with outdoor gas grills facing the Gulf). With upstairs bedrooms, the town house–style units provide more privacy than most condominiums on Sanibel.

2255 W. Gulf Dr., Sanibel Island, FL 33957. www.casaybelresort.com. © **800/276-4753** or 239/472-3145. Fax 239/472-2109. 114 suites. Winter $339–$649 condo; off season $289–$349 condo. Packages and weekly rates available. AE, DISC, MC, V. **Amenities:** Restaurant; pool bar; babysitting; bike rental; children's programs; concierge; Jacuzzi; heated outdoor pool; tennis courts; watersports equipment/rentals. *In room:* A/C, TV/DVD, hair dryer, high-speed Internet, kitchen.

Sundial Beach and Golf Resort ★★ ☺ The largest resort on Sanibel on a mile-long stretch of shell-strewn beach, this condominium complex has lots to keep families occupied (even jogging strollers are provided), from a palm-studded, beachside pool area to Sunny's Kids Club—a hands-on ecology center with daily programs. The one-, two-, and three-bedroom condominium suites are housed in two- and three-story buildings (as high as they get on Sanibel) and have screened balconies overlooking the beach or landscaped gardens. Rooms have a great tropical modern vibe. **Beaches** is the signature restaurant overlooking the pool and the Gulf of Mexico serving breakfast and an ever-changing surf and turf dinner menu. And what's better than made-to-order pizza in paradise? Now, pizza is delivered directly to suites. **Croc's,** located poolside, is the place to be for full bar and frozen cocktails until dusk. They also serve light lunch and snack food. Guests receive access to nearby Dunes Golf & Tennis Club, the island's only PGA-rated course.

1451 Middle Gulf Dr., Sanibel Island, FL 33957. www.sundialresort.com. © **800/237-4184** or 239/481-3636. Fax 239/481-4947. 265 units. Rates from $149–$399 per night for studios; $169–$479 for 1- to 3-bedroom residences available with full kitchens. AE, DC, DISC, MC, V. **Amenities:** 2 restaurants; 2 bars; bike rental; children's programs; concierge; exercise room; Jacuzzi; 5 heated pools; limited room service; 12 tennis courts; nonmotorized watersports equipment/rentals. *In room:* A/C, TV/VCR/DVD, hair dryer, kitchen.

Moderate

Island Inn ★★ It's difficult to get accommodations here during the winter season, but it's worth trying because this classic beach resort featuring old Florida-style cottages and cozy guest rooms on 10 acres of Gulf beach has been in business for more than a century. Its original central building houses a genteel dining room slash restaurant, **Traditions** (closed Apr 26–Dec 17), a spacious lounge, and a library furnished with old-style bentwood and wicker sofas and chairs. This is the kind of place where guests dress for dinner—jackets aren't required but collared shirts are (and ties are recommended) for men at dinner—and seating is assigned (some guests have had the same table for years). Don't oversleep and miss the sticky buns served at breakfast. Motel rooms (with or without kitchens) are fine, and most have screened porches or balconies, but we say go for a cottage. They aren't luxurious, but are private and give off that beach-house vibe.

3111 W. Gulf Dr., Sanibel Island, FL 33957. www.islandinnsanibel.com. © **800/851-5088** or 239/472-1561. Fax 239/472-0051. 57 units, including 9 cottages. Winter $180–$325 double, $415–$510 cottage; off season $125–$159 double, $280–$315 cottage. Rates include breakfast. AE, DISC, MC, V. **Amenities:** Restaurant (seasonal); bar (seasonal); small heated outdoor pool; tennis court; free Wi-Fi. *In room:* A/C, TV, fridge, hair dryer, kitchen (in some).

Sanibel Inn ★ ☺ A back-to-nature theme prevails at this beachside inn, in both the room decor and the grounds planted with native Florida foliage specifically designed to attract butterflies and hummingbirds. In fact, back-to-nature children's programs make this a great choice for eco-friendly families. Kids can experience shell safaris, nature walks, and nature-oriented crafts. The hotel rooms and one-bedroom suites have been renovated to feel like a modern, yet warm, beach house with bamboo floors, wicker furnishing, and just-right lighting. Fully equipped two-bedroom, two-bathroom condominium apartments (some of Sanibel's most luxurious) are also available. Every unit has a screened porch to enjoy the warm gulf breezes and keep pesky mosquitoes at bay. A pool bar serves drinks and light fare. Guests receive access to nearby Dunes Golf & Tennis Club.

937 E. Gulf Dr., Sanibel Island, FL 33957. www.sanibelcollection.com. ℭ **800/237-1491** or 239/472-3181. Fax 239/472-5234. 94 units. Winter $179–$399 double, $199–$599 suite; off season $149–$249 double, $169–$399 suite. Packages available. AE, DC, DISC, MC, V. **Amenities:** 2 bars; complimentary bikes; children's programs; access to nearby health club; heated outdoor pool; tennis courts. *In room:* A/C, TV, small fridge, hair dryer, free Internet access.

Sanibel Sunset Beach Resort ★ Set on more than 4 tropical acres of swaying palms, the Sanibel Sunset Beach Resort is situated along a stretch of pristine white beach lined with a stunning canopy of seashells. The resort features lush landscaping and modernized guest rooms with screened terraces and all new furnishings and full kitchens with brand-new warm brown granite countertops. All have amazing Gulf views. Poolside cabanas are an ideal spot for relaxation. For the more active types, there are tennis and volleyball courts with free use of equipment. Bikes are free to use, too. Guests receive access to nearby Dunes Golf & Tennis Club.

3287 W. Gulf Dr., Sanibel Island, FL 33957. www.sanibelcollection.com. ℭ **800/831-7384** or 239/472-1700. Fax 239/472-5032. 46 units. Winter $179–$399 double, $349–$599 suite; off season $149–$229 double, $279–$429 suite. Rates include continental breakfast. Packages available. AE, DC, DISC, MC, V. **Amenities:** Complimentary bikes; heated pool; tennis courts. *In room:* A/C, TV, hair dryer, kitchenettes or kitchens (in some).

Song of the Sea ★★ Perfect for couples and popular with Europeans, this beachside inn welcomes guests to reconnect with a complimentary bottle of wine upon check-in. The inn has efficiencies and one-bedroom suites with plantation-style shutters behind sliding-glass doors opening to screened porches. Furnished in French-country style (the hotel calls it West Indies style, so consider it a cross between the two), the rooms are designed for intimacy with oak tables and chairs, and pine Bahamian shutters on patio doors and windows. A pathway leads to the next-door Sanibel Inn (see above), where guests can enjoy the facilities. An extensive continental breakfast is served in the charming lobby and enjoyed outdoors on a brick patio under umbrella tables. Guests receive access to nearby Dunes Golf & Tennis Club, the island's only PGA-rated course.

863 E. Gulf Dr., Sanibel Island, FL 33957. www.sanibelcollection.com. ℭ **800/231-1045** or 239/472-2220. Fax 239/472-8569. 30 units. Winter $199–$429 double, $249–$549 suite; off season $149–$229 double, $229–$399 suite. Rates include continental breakfast. Packages available. AE, DC, DISC, MC, V. **Amenities:** Complimentary bikes; access to nearby health club; Jacuzzi; heated outdoor pool. *In room:* A/C, TV, fax, hair dryer, kitchenette, Wi-Fi.

Tarpon Tale Inn ★ 🛏 Owners Dawn and Joe Ramsey preside over this low-slung gray building in Sanibel's Old Town, the island's first settlement, where the ferries from Fort Myers used to dock near the lighthouse. White walls and tile floors make the comfortable units bright; French doors lead to gardens dense with sea grape, palm, and ficus trees, which provide privacy for a large outdoor hot tub. Three of the five units (which are attached yet completely private bungalows hidden amid palms, bougainvillea, hibiscus, ferns, sea grape, gumbo-limbo, and Key lime) have separate bedrooms, while two other "deluxe studios" are actually two-bedroom suites. All units have shower-only bathrooms. The makings for a continental breakfast are delivered the night before. Smoking is not permitted inside the inn's rooms. There is no daily maid service, though towels and linens are exchanged every 3 days or as needed.

367 Periwinkle Way, Sanibel Island, FL 33957. www.tarpontale.com. ✆ **888/345-0939** or 239/472-0939. Fax 239/472-6202. 5 units. Winter $189–$220 double; off season $109–$149 double. Rates include continental breakfast. AE, DC, DISC, MC, V. Some pets accepted for a fee; call first. **Amenities:** Free use of bikes; Jacuzzi. *In room:* A/C, TV/VCR, CD player, hair dryer (upon request), kitchen, no phone.

CAPTIVA ISLAND
Expensive
South Seas Island Resort ★★ ☺ A former Key lime plantation, this family-friendly "resort village" is on the eco-balanced island of Captiva and uniquely manages the natural habitat with resort amenities and programs. Occupying 335 acres—all of Captiva's northern third—the resort sits on 2½ miles of gorgeous beach, world renowned for shelling, sunsets, and the resident dolphins and manatees. It's so spread out that a free trolley shuttles back and forth through the mangrove forests. Its Gulfside golf course is one of the most picturesque 9-holers anywhere, and its two marinas host multiple fishing charter boats and guides. Rooms—from standard hotel rooms to one-, two-, and three-bedroom beach condos (more like someone's grandma's apartment, which for some is a good thing, for others not so much) and private homes—shine in a soothingly swank West Indies decor. If you want new and modern, request to stay by the marina, where rooms are redone in a Caribbean-chic decor. There's also a fantastic pool complex that overlooks Pine Island Sound with three pools, one with kids' water slides and another with private cabanas. Activities include tennis, golf, Sanibel Sea School—a nonprofit marine education center which, for $55 per person, per session, will teach you everything you ever wanted to know about manatees, snorkeling, and even surfing—and day cruises to Cabbage Key and Useppa. Several restaurants and a Starbucks will keep you well-fed and energized on the property.

5400 Plantation Rd., Captiva Island, FL 33924. www.southseas.com. ✆ **866/565-5089** or 239/432-6760. Fax 239/472-5111. 470 units. Winter $249–$949 double, $379–$3,500 condo or house; off season $169–$399 double, $179–$2,500 condo or house. Packages available. AE, DC, DISC, MC, V. **Amenities:** 4 restaurants; 2 bars; babysitting; bike rental; children's programs; concierge; 9-hole golf course; fitness center; Jacuzzis; 18 heated outdoor pools; limited room service; 19 tennis courts; watersports equipment/rentals. *In room:* A/C, TV, hair dryer, kitchen (in larger units), Wi-Fi.

Moderate
Captiva Island Inn Bed & Breakfast ★ This B&B complex sits surrounded by restaurants, art galleries, and boutiques along Captiva's block-long commercial street. Two suites in the Key West–style main building open to porches overlooking the lane, while four Dutch clapboard cottages sit out back on the fringes

of a gravel parking lot (you get just enough yard here for hammocks and a gas grill). The ceiling in one cottage that once housed aviator Charles Lindbergh has clouds painted against a blue sky. All units have ceiling fans, kitchens, large bathrooms, queen-size sofa beds in the living rooms, cool tile floors, and designer bed linens (including down comforters for the occasional chilly night). Some rooms have shower-only bathrooms. Guests get free use of towels and chairs for the beach (a block away), as well as a complimentary full breakfast at RC Otters or the **Keylime Bistro,** which has good American-style food and superb Key lime cheesecake; it's open daily from 8am to 10pm.

11509 Andy Rosse Lane (P.O. Box 848), Captiva Island, FL 33924. www.captivaislandinn.com. ℂ **800/454-9898** or 239/395-0882. Fax 239/395-0862. 18 units, including 1 5-bedroom house. Winter $255–$300 double; off season $99–$180 double. Rates include full breakfast. AE, MC, V. **Amenities:** Pool. *In room:* A/C, TV, fridge.

'Tween Waters Inn Island Resort ★★ Wedged between the Gulf beach and the bay on the narrowest part of Captiva, this venerable establishment was the haunt of cartoonist J. N. "Ding" Darling. Anne Morrow Lindbergh also dined here while writing *A Gift from the Sea.* In a sandy palm grove, these pink cottages have been upgraded, but still capture that Old Florida spirit. Some face the Gulf, others the bay. Themed to honor famous guests, they range in size from the honeymoon cottage, with barely enough room for its king-size bed and a tiny kitchen, to the three-bedroom, two-bathroom house. The spacious hotel rooms and apartments are in three modern buildings on stilts; all have screened balconies facing the Gulf or the bay. The Old Captiva House restaurant appears much as it did in Ding Darling's days (his cartoons adorn the dining room walls). A **spa** offers prime pampering. Charter captains dock at the full-service marina here.

15951 Captiva Rd., Captiva Island, FL 33924. www.tween-waters.com. ℂ **800/223-5865** or 239/472-5161. Fax 239/472-0249. 138 units. Winter $160–$270 double, $260–$640 suite, $230–$710 cottage; off season $150–$215 double, $230–$475 suite, $205–$495 cottage. Rates include continental breakfast and wireless Internet. Packages available. AE, DC, MC, V. Pets accepted in some units ($15 per day). **Amenities:** 2 restaurants; 2 bars; bike rental; exercise room; Jacuzzi; outdoor pool; spa; 3 tennis courts; watersports equipment/rentals *In room:* A/C, TV, fridge, hair dryer, kitchen (in suites and cottages), Wi-Fi.

COTTAGES

The islands have several Old Florida–style cottages that are charming, often affordable alternatives to hotels and condos. Some of the best are members of the **Sanibel-Captiva Small Inns & Cottages Association.** Contact the association (via its website only) at **www.sanibelsmallinns.com** for a listing.

Sitting between two condominium complexes off Middle Gulf Drive, **Gulf Breeze Cottages ★★**, 1081 Shell Basket Lane, Sanibel (www.gbreeze.com; ℂ **800/388-2842** or 239/472-1626), is a collection of clapboard cottages separated from the beach by a lawn with a covered picnic area and outdoor shower. One two-story building is divided into four efficiencies (the pick is no. 7, with a view of the Gulf from its big picture windows). Rates are $240 to $395 per day in winter, $140 to $295 off season.

Barely updated since the 1960s are the 32 pink-clapboard structures at **Beachview Cottages,** 3325 W. Gulf Dr., Sanibel (www.beachviewsanibel.com; ℂ **800/860-0532** or 239/472-1202; fax 239/472-4720), the sister property to 'Tween Waters Inn. None of the cottages has a phone, and some have shower-only bathrooms. The outdoor pool is heated. Rates are $199 to $329 in winter, $169 to $239 during the off season. 'Tween Waters also owns the **Castaways Beach and Bay Cottages,** 6460 Sanibel-Captiva Rd. (www.castawayssanibel. com; ☎ **800/375-0152**), featuring waterview cottages and efficiencies on the Gulf and Sunset Bay.

On Captiva, **Jensen's on the Gulf,** 15300 Captiva Dr. (www.jensen-captiva.com; ☎ **239/472-4684**), rents homes and cottages year-round from $325 to $700 and Gulf- and gardenview suites from $165 to $465. **Jensen's Twin Palm Resort & Marina** (www.jensen-captiva.com; ☎ **239/472-5800**), on the bay near Andy Rosse Lane, has cottages ranging from $180 to $285 in winter and from $145 to $190 off season.

Where to Dine

SANIBEL ISLAND

Much of the "help" on this affluent island dines at **Jerry's Family Restaurant,** 1700 Periwinkle Way, at Casa Ybel Road (☎ **239/472-9300**; www.jerrysfoods. com), which serves wholesome, inexpensive diner fare. Both the restaurant and adjacent supermarket are open daily from 6am to 11pm. Breakfast is served from 6am to 4pm, and you can usually get a table quickly (which can't be said of Sanibel's other popular breakfast spots).

You'll find reasonably priced pub fare at Sanibel's sports bars, such as the **Lazy Flamingo II** (below) and **Sanibel Grill,** 703 Tarpon Bay Rd., near Palm Ridge Road (☎ **239/472-3128**), which serves as the bar for **Timbers** (p. 389), the fine seafood restaurant next door.

For picnics at Sanibel's beaches or on a canoe, the deli and bakery in **Bailey's General Store,** at Periwinkle Way and Tarpon Bay Road (☎ **239/472-1516;** www.baileys-sanibel.com), carries a gourmet selection of breads, cheeses, and meats. **Huxter's Deli and Market,** 1203 Periwinkle Way, east of Donax Street (☎ **239/472-6988;** www.huxtersmarket.com), has sandwich fixings and "beach box" lunches to go.

Very Expensive

Ellington's Jazz Bar and Restaurant ★ SEAFOOD With live jazz 7 nights a week, this Sanibel hepcat serves equally jazzy cuisine, from the Gillespie's Pork Shank with braised purple cabbage and buttermilk mashed potatoes to Lady Day's Lobster Ravioli. Be sure to try the Croquettes a la Ellington, which are made with mission fig chutney.

1244 Periwinkle Way. ☎ **239/472-5555.** www.ellingtonsjazz.com. Reservations highly recommended. Main courses $22–$45. AE, MC, V. Daily 5–11pm.

Mad Hatter ★★ ECLECTIC One of Sanibel's best choices for a romantic waterfront dinner, this New American Gulf-front restaurant has only 12 tables, but each has a view that's perfect at sunset. The ever-changing menu features flavors from around the world, such as black truffle sea scallops finished with a caramelized shallot beurre blanc served atop whipped Yukon potatoes and julienned zucchini and squash; and a marinated grilled maple-syrup-and-herb-glazed black grouper served with mascarpone risotto and mixed vegetables.

6467 Sanibel-Captiva Rd., at Blind Pass. ☎ **239/472-0033.** www.madhatterrestaurant.com. Reservations highly recommended. Main courses $26–$37. AE, MC, V. Tues–Sun 6–9:30pm.

Moderate

Jacaranda SEAFOOD/PASTA/STEAKS This friendly and casual restaurant (named for the purple-flowered jacaranda tree) attracts an affluent over-40 crowd for its nightly live music at the Patio Lounge. (After midnight, a 20-something crowd which lovingly refers to the place as the Jacko sweeps in.) Although the Jacaranda is best known as a local gathering spot, it has also received several dining awards. Fish is well prepared here, or you can choose steaks or prime rib. The linguine with a dozen littleneck clams tossed in a piquant red or white clam sauce is excellent. For dessert, the turtle pie—ice cream, caramel, fudge sauce, chopped nuts, and whipped cream—will send you away stuffed.

1223 Periwinkle Way (east of Donax St.). *℃* **239/472-1771.** www.jacarandaonsanibel.com. Reservations recommended. Main courses $18–$35. AE, MC, V. Daily 5–10pm. Lounge daily 4pm–2:30am.

McT's Shrimp House & Tavern SEAFOOD Shrimp reigns at this casual Old Florida–style establishment, where at 4pm you'll see a line of people waiting outside for the early-bird specials served to the first 100 in the door. Shrimp here is prepared in at least a dozen ways, from steamed to fried in a coconut-and-almond batter. There is also grouper and swordfish, plus steaks and chicken for the land-minded, but we recommend sticking to the shrimp here. (The Timbers Restaurant & Fish Market, below, does a much better job of cooking fish.) McT's Tavern has an extensive choice of appetizers and light dinners. All-you-can-eat peel-and-eat shrimp and stone crabs are available nightly, though if it's not stone crab season (Oct–May), the crab will likely be frozen.

1523 Periwinkle Way (at Fitzhugh St.). *℃* **239/472-3161.** www.eatmoreshrimp.com. Main courses $16–$22. AE, DC, DISC, MC, V. Shrimp House daily 4–9pm. McT's Tavern daily 4pm–close. Closed Christmas.

The Timbers Restaurant & Fish Market ★★ SEAFOOD/STEAK This casual upstairs restaurant, with bamboo railings, oversize canvas umbrellas, and paintings of tropical scenes through faux windows, is Sanibel's best place for fresh fish and aged beef hot off the charcoal grill. It's true what they say—"We serve it fresh or we don't serve it at all." In the fish market out front, you can view the catch and have the chef chargrill or blacken it to order. The steaks, cut on the premises, are the island's best. You can order a drink from the adjoining Sanibel Grill sports bar and wait for a table out on the shopping center's porch.

703 Tarpon Bay Rd. (btw. Periwinkle Way and Palm Ridge Rd.). *℃* **239/472-3128.** www.prawnbroker.com. Main courses $15–$27. AE, MC, V. Winter daily 4:30–9:30pm; off season daily 5–9:30pm.

Inexpensive

Gramma Dot's Seaside Saloon SEAFOOD One of Sanibel's most popular lunch spots, this open-air but screened cafe on the docks of Sanibel Marina has excellent salads (try the seafood Caesar) and fine sandwiches (fried grouper is tops), great fish and chips, plus, for dinner, a few main courses led by broiled grouper, in a sauce of lemon, dill, butter, and white wine. And while steaks are good, what we really love is the coconut shrimp.

At Sanibel Marina, 634 N. Yachtsman Dr. *℃* **239/472-8138.** Main courses $15–$30; salads and sandwiches $9–$15. MC, V. Daily 11:30am–8pm.

Hungry Heron ★★ ☺ AMERICAN This tropically decorated eatery is Sanibel's most popular family restaurant. There's something for everyone on the huge, tabloid-size menu—from hot and cold appetizers and overstuffed "sea-wiches" to pasta and steamed shellfish. If the 280 regular items aren't enough, there's a list of nightly specials. Seafood, steaks, and stir-fries from a sizzling skillet are popular with local residents, who bring the kids here for fun and the children's menu.

In Palm Ridge Place, 2330 Palm Ridge Rd. (at Periwinkle Way). ☏ **239/395-2300.** www.hungryheron.com. Call for preferred seating. Main courses $9–$24; sandwiches, burgers, and snacks $6–$12. AE, DISC, MC, V. Daily 11am–9pm.

The Island Cow ★ ☺ AMERICAN A fun, albeit bovine-themed, restaurant, Island Cow has a great raw bar, not to mention an unabridged menu of burgers, sandwiches, wraps, quesadillas, and, of course, seafood. Fried is the theme here, but kids love the cow motif. They also serve old-fashioned egg creams. I also highly recommend the breakfast and the free homemade muffins that come with it.

2163 Periwinkle Way. ☏ **239/472-0606.** www.sanibelislandcow.com. Main courses $11–$22; sandwiches, burgers, and snacks $7–$12. AE, DISC, MC, V. Daily 8am–8pm (breakfast served daily until 11am and noon Sun).

The Lazy Flamingo II 🖋 SEAFOOD/PUB FARE The Lazy Flamingo is a down-homey type of place where the food is consistently good. Locals and visitors alike become repeat customers, flocking here for the reasonably priced food, a wide choice of beers iced down in a huge box behind the bar, and the sports TVs. Some of that beer is used to steam shrimp and a collection of oysters, clams, and spices known as "The Pot." Best pick, however, is grouper from the charcoals, as either a main course or a sandwich. The flamingo-pink menu has sandwiches, burgers, fish platters, and atomically spicy Dead Parrot Wings (they're so hot they can raise the dead). Fillet your own catch, and the chef will cook it to order for you. Happy-hour prices prevail whenever football games are on.

A sister institution, the **Lazy Flamingo I,** 6520-C Pine Ave., at Sanibel-Captiva Road, a quarter-mile south of Blind Pass (☏ **239/472-5353**), has the same menu and hours.

1036 Periwinkle Way, west of Causeway Blvd. ☏ **239/472-6939.** www.lazyflamingo.com. Main courses $9–$15; sandwiches and snacks $6–$13. Cook your catch $9. AE, DISC, MC, V. Daily 11:30am–midnight.

Lighthouse Cafe ★ 🖋 AMERICAN This storefront establishment dishes up breakfast omelets that are meals in themselves, especially the ocean frittata containing delicately seasoned scallops, crabmeat, shrimp, broccoli, and mushrooms, and crowned with an artichoke-heart-and-creamy-Alfredo sauce. Seafood Benedict is one of the more decadent offerings. For the light(er) eater, a slew of creative sandwiches is served after 11am. Reasonably priced, cafe-style dinners are served during winter only. For the best pancakes ever, the Lighthouse Cafe has cornered the market, using a special recipe that draws up to 700 people a day in season. For just $5, go nuts on malted-blueberry or banana pancakes, or pretend to be healthy with granola-nut whole-wheat hot cakes with sliced bananas.

In Seahorse Shops, 362 Periwinkle Way (at Buttonwood Lane, east of Causeway Rd.). ☏ **239/472-0303.** www.lighthousecafe.com. Call ahead for preferred seating. Main courses $7–$15; breakfast $6–$12; sandwiches and salads $8–$13. MC, V. Daily 7am–3pm.

Sanibel Cafe ★ *⚑* AMERICAN Seashells are the not-so-original theme at this locals' favorite, whose tables are glass cases containing delicate fossilized specimens from the Miocene and Pliocene epochs. Lunch is really dinner, and it's served all day. Fresh-squeezed orange and grapefruit juice, Havarti omelets, and homemade muffins and biscuits highlight the breakfast menu. Lunch features everything from country-fried steak, meatloaf, and surf and turf to specialty sandwiches and shrimp, Greek, and chicken-and-grape salads made with a light, fat-free dressing. Fatten up on homemade red-raspberry jam, apple or cherry crisp, or terrific Key lime pie.

In the Tahitian Gardens, 2007 Periwinkle Way. ℂ **239/472-5323.** www.sanibelcafe.com. Call ahead for preferred seating. Main courses $9–$15; breakfast $6–$11; salads, sandwiches, and burgers $6–$13. MC, V. Daily 7am–3pm.

CAPTIVA ISLAND

Sandwiches and picnic fare are available at the **Captiva Island Store,** Captiva Road at Andy Rosse Lane (ℂ **239/472-2374;** www.captivaislandstore.com). The beach is a block from here.

Moderate

The Bubble Room ★ ☺ STEAK/SEAFOOD The kitschiest restaurant you'll probably ever find, the Bubble Room has tongue-in-cheek American cuisine complemented by a decor filled with Christmas and Hollywood memorabilia from the '30s, '40s, and '50s. Distracting, to say the least—but in a good way—the Bubble Room makes it hard to decide which is more amusing, the name of the dishes on the menu—Porky Pig a la Bobby Phillips and the Eddie Fisherman—or the thousands of movie stills, puppets, antique jukeboxes, and toy trains. **Note:** We've gotten complaints about the "awful" food here, but we still think the Bubble Room is fun, with decent (though not fabulous) food and a great atmosphere.

15001 Captiva Rd. (at Andy Rosse Lane). ℂ **239/472-5558.** www.bubbleroomrestaurant.com. Call ahead for preferred seating. Main courses $20–$35. AE, DC, DISC, MC, V. Daily 11:30am–3pm; Fri–Sat 4:30–9:30pm; Sun–Thurs 4:30–9pm. Closed Christmas.

The Green Flash ★ SEAFOOD You can't miss this restaurant, which sits at the infamous "curve" where Captiva Road takes a sharp turn to the north. You won't see the real "green flash" as the sun sets here because this modern building looks eastward across Pine Island Sound, but it does make for a nice view at lunch. Seeing the full moon turn the Sound into glistening silver is worth having an evening drink here. The quality of the cuisine is good, and the prices are reasonable for Captiva. Start with oysters Rockefeller or shrimp bisque. Both are house specialties, as is the garlicky grouper "cafe de Paris" and the salmon with a dill-accented béarnaise sauce.

15183 Captiva Rd. ℂ **239/472-3337.** www.greenflashcaptiva.com. Reservations recommended. Main courses $17–$45; lunch sandwiches and salads $7–$13. AE, DC, DISC, MC, V. Daily 11:30am–3:30pm and 5:30–9:30pm. Bar daily 11:30am–9:30pm.

Inexpensive

The Cabbage Key Restaurant ★★★ AMERICAN You can get here only by boat, but there are constant shuttles from Captiva, so get onboard and experience the true meaning of cheeseburgers in paradise. Jimmy Buffett allegedly wrote his famous song here, and when you arrive, you'll understand why. The cheeseburgers rock, the setting is sublime, and there are no microwaves in sight.

It's a place rich in history, and in money: Thousands of dollar bills are signed and stuck to the walls and ceiling with masking tape.

Intracoastal Water Marker 60, N. Fort Myers. ✆ **239/283-2278.** www.cabbagekey.com. Main courses $18–$28; burgers and sandwiches $5–$10. MC, V. Daily 7:30am–9pm.

Mucky Duck ★ SEAFOOD/PUB FARE A Captiva institution since 1976, this British-style pub, named after a pub of the same name in Shakespeare's Stratford-upon-Avon, is the only place on either island where you can dine right by the beach. If you don't get a seat with this great view, the humorous staff will gladly roll over a fake window to appease you. The menu offers a selection of fresh seafood items, plus English fish and chips, steak-and-sausage pie, and a ploughman's lunch. There's also a vegetarian platter. You can't make a reservation, but you can order drinks, listen to live music (Mon–Sat), and bide your time at beachside picnic tables out front (come early for sunset).

Andy Rosse Lane (on the Gulf). ✆ **239/472-3434.** www.muckyduck.com. Main courses $3–$18 lunch, $18–$38 dinner. AE, DC, DISC, MC, V. Mon–Sat 11am–3pm and 5–9:30pm.

R. C. Otter's Island Eats ★ ✦ AMERICAN Occupying an old clapboard-sided cottage, this Key West–style cafe brings informality and good, inexpensive food to Captiva. In contrast to the island's more formal restaurants, you can dine here in your bare feet and not spend a fortune for a great breakfast, snack, lunch, or full meal. The choice seats are under ceiling fans on the front porch or umbrellas on the brick patio. In hot weather, opt for the air-conditioned dining room. The wide-ranging menu includes salads, hot dogs, burgers, sandwiches, meatloaf, country-fried steak, fish, and delicious nightly specials. The island's best breakfasts are equally varied, from bacon and eggs to a seafood quesadilla. Musicians perform out in the yard every day—you might find yourself dancing on the front porch.

11506 Andy Rosse Lane. ✆ **239/395-1142.** Call ahead for preferred seating. Main courses $10–$20; breakfast $6–$12; salads, sandwiches, and burgers $6–$12. AE, DISC, MC, V. Daily 8–10pm (breakfast to 11am).

Sanibel & Captiva Islands After Dark

You won't find glitzy nightclubs, but night owls do have places to roost at the resorts and restaurants listed above. Here's a brief recap:

SANIBEL ISLAND The **Patio Lounge,** in the Jacaranda, 1223 Periwinkle Way (✆ 239/472-1771), attracts an affluent crowd of everyone from 20-somethings to seniors to its live music every evening. **McT's Tavern,** 1523 Periwinkle Way (✆ 239/472-3161), has a large-screen TV for sports fans. Other popular sports bars are the **Sanibel Grill,** 703 Tarpon Bay Rd. (✆ 239/472-4453), and the two **Lazy Flamingo** branches, at 1036 Periwinkle Way (✆ 239/472-6939) and 6520-C Pine Ave. (✆ 239/472-5353).

A group of professional actors performs Broadway dramas and comedies from October to August in Sanibel's state-of-the-art, 150-seat **Schoolhouse Theater,** 2200 Periwinkle Way (✆ 239/472-6862; www.bigarts.org/theatre.php).

CAPTIVA ISLAND Local songwriters perform their works nightly at **R. C. Otter's Island Eats,** 11500 Andy Rosse Lane (✆ 239/395-1142). The **Crow's Nest Lounge,** in the 'Tween Waters Inn on Captiva Road (✆ 239/472-

5161), is Captiva's top nightspot for dancing. Our favorite is the **Keylime Bistro** (☏ **239/395-4000**), where the musicians performing on the restaurant's resplendent outdoor patio aren't just your local garage band—last time we were there, one of Aaron Neville's band members showed up and played an extra-long set. Best of all, there's no cover and entertainment is almost on a nightly basis. Call ahead for schedules.

Nearby Island Hopping

Sanibel and Captiva are jumping-off points for island-hopping boat trips to barrier islands and Keys teeming with ancient legends and *Robinson Crusoe*–style beaches. You don't have to get completely lost out here, however, because several islets have comfortable inns and restaurants. The trip itself across shallow Pine Island Sound is a sightseeing adventure, with playful dolphins surfing on the boat's wake and a variety of cormorants, egrets, frigate birds, and (in winter) rare white pelicans flying above.

Captiva Cruises (☏ **239/472-5300;** www.captivacruises.com) makes daily trips from the South Seas Island Resort on Captiva Island. One vessel goes to Cabbage Key, departing at 10am and returning at 3pm. It stops at Useppa Island, going and coming, daily. Another vessel goes to Boca Grande by way of Cayo Costa State Park, departing daily at 10am and returning at 4pm. These day trips cost $45 for adults, $35 for children 6 to 12 to Boca Grande; $35 for adults, $20 for children 6 to 12 to Cabbage Key or Useppa. Reservations are required.

From Pine Island off Fort Myers, **Tropic Star Cruises** (☏ **239/283-0015;** www.tropicstarcruises.com) operates daily ferry service to Cayo Costa. Tickets are $35 for adults and $25 for children 7 and under.

CABBAGE KEY ★★

You never know who's going to get off a boat at 100-acre Cabbage Key and walk into the funky **Cabbage Key Inn ★★,** a rustic house built in 1938. Ernest Hemingway liked to hang out here, and novelist John D. MacDonald was a frequent guest years later. Today, you could find yourself rubbing elbows at the bar with the likes of Ted Koppel, Sean Connery, or Julia Roberts. Singer and avid yachtie Jimmy Buffett likes Cabbage Key so much that it inspired his hit song "Cheeseburger in Paradise."

A path leads from the tiny marina across a lawn dotted with coconut palms to this white-clapboard house that sits atop an ancient Calusa shell mound. Guests dine in the comfort of two screened porches and seek libations in the library-turned-bar, its pine-paneled walls now plastered with dollar bills left by visitors. The straight-back chairs and painted wooden tables show their age, but that's part of Cabbage Key's laid-back, don't-give-a-you-know-what charm.

Where Chocolate Grows on Trees

From December to February, the area's Black Sapote trees bear a most interesting fruit. Known as the "chocolate pudding fruit," it is round with thin olive-green skin and contains a mass of glossy, chocolate-colored pulp that's soft, sweet, and mild, very much like pudding. It makes a tasty and healthy dessert, a delicious pie filling, or an exotic tropical beverage when mixed with pineapple juice. The **Sunburst Tropical Fruit Company,** on Pine Island (☏ **239/283-1200**), has the fruit for sale, so you needn't pick from the trees.

Watching the sunset off Cabbage Key.

In addition to the famous thick, juicy cheeseburgers so loved by Jimmy Buffett, the house specialties are fresh broiled fish and shrimp steamed in beer. Lunches range from $6 to $13; main courses at dinner are $18 to $29.

Most visitors come out here for the day, but if you want to stay overnight, the Cabbage Key Inn has six rooms and six cottages. The more expensive cottages, four of which have kitchens, are preferable to the rooms. Although the units have private bathrooms and air-conditioners, they are very basic by today's standards, and some of their original 1920s furnishings have seen better days. Service for overnight guests can leave a lot to be desired, and there's no place on the islet to buy snacks or sundries. If you do decide to rough it, rates are $99 to $139 single or double for rooms, $150 to $389 for cottages. For information and reservations, contact Cabbage Key Inn, P.O. Box 200, Pineland, FL 33945 (www.cabbagekey.com; ℂ 239/283-2278; fax 239/283-1384).

CAYO COSTA ★★★

Short of *Lost,* you can't get any more deserted than at **Cayo Costa State Park ★★★** (pronounced *Cay*-oh *Cos*-tah), which occupies a 2,132-acre, unspoiled barrier island with miles of white-sand beaches, pine forests, mangrove swamps, oak-palm hammocks, and grasslands. Other than natural wildlife, the only permanent residents here are park rangers.

Day-trippers can bring their own supplies and use a picnic area with pavilions. A free tram carries visitors from the dock on the sound side to the Gulf beach. The state maintains 12 basic cabins and a primitive campground on the northern end of the island near Johnson Shoals, where the shelling is spectacular. Cabins cost $40 a day, and campsites are $22 a day year-round. For camping or cabin reservations, call ℂ **800/326-3521** or go to www.reserveamerica.com. There's running water on the island, but no electricity.

The park is open daily from 8am to sundown. There's a $2-per-person honor-system admission fee for day visitors. You can rent single-seat kayaks for $40 a day, two-seaters for $50 a day; for reservations, call **Tropic Star Cruises,** on Pine Island (ℂ **239/283-0015;** www.tropicstarcruises.com).

For more information, contact **Cayo Costa State Park,** P.O. Box 1150, Boca Grande, FL 33921 (✆ **941/964-0375;** www.floridastateparks.org/cayo costa). Office hours are Monday through Friday from 8am to 5pm.

UPPER (NORTH) CAPTIVA

Cut off by a pass from Captiva, its northern barrier-island sibling is occupied by the upscale resort of **North Captiva Island Club,** P.O. Box 1000, Pineland, FL 33945 (✆ **800/576-7343** or 239/395-1001; fax 239/472-5836; www.north captiva.com). Despite the development, about 750 of the island's 1,000 acres are included in a state preserve. The club rents accommodations ranging from efficiencies to luxury homes. There's scheduled water-taxi service with **Island Girl Charters** (✆ **239/633-8142;** www.islandgirlcharters.org). Call for rates, as they change often.

USEPPA ISLAND

Useppa was a refuge of President Theodore Roosevelt and his tarpon-loving industrialist friends at the turn of the 20th century. New York advertising magnate Barron G. Collier bought the island in 1906 and built a lovely wooden home overlooking Pine Island Sound. His mansion is now the **Collier Inn,** where day-trippers and overnight guests can partake of lunches and seafood dinners in a place with country club ambience. You can also visit the **Useppa Museum** (✆ **239/283-1061;** www.useppa.com/society.html), which explains the island's history and displays 4,000-year-old Calusa artifacts. Admission is by $5 donation.

The Collier Inn is the centerpiece of the **Useppa Island Club** (✆ **239/283-1061;** www.useppa.com), an exclusive development with more than 100 luxury homes, all in the clapboard-sided, tin-roofed style of Old Florida. For information, rates, and reservations, contact **Collier Inn & Cottages,** P.O. Box 640, Bokeelia, FL 33922 (www.useppa.com; ✆ **888/735-6335** or 239/283-1061; fax 239/283-0290).

PINE ISLAND ★

Just about 40 miles north of Sanibel Island and 30 miles north of Fort Myers is **Pine Island** (www.pineislandfl.com), a tiny 17 × 2-mile island connected to the mainland by a causeway that's time-warped back to Old Florida circa the 1950s and 1960s. Known for palm tree nurseries, fishing villages, mango orchards, and a burgeoning artist's colony, Pine Island features a year-round population of 10,000. As small as it is, it's composed of five small villages—St. James City, Pine Island Center, Pineland, Bokeelia, and Matlacha. At the island's southern end is the Calusa Land Trust's **St. Jude Nature Trail,** featuring spectacular ocean views, bald eagles, herons, roseate spoonbills, egrets, and osprey.

In Pineland, farming is alive and well with a slew of nurseries growing organic veggies, palm trees, hibiscus, and mangoes. Also in Pineland is the **Tarpon Lodge & Restaurant,** 13771 Waterfront Dr. (✆ **239/283-3999;** www.tarpon lodge.com), an old-school Florida resort-lodge dating back to 1926 and known for its blue crab and roasted corn chowder. Rooms and cottages have views of Pine Island Sound, and rates range from $110 to $320. Over in Bokeelia, you'll see some nice beach homes, a few condos, and art galleries. The **Bokeelia Tarpon Inn** (see below), 8241 Main St. (www.tarponinn.com; ✆ **239/283-8961**), is a bed-and-breakfast overlooking Charlotte Harbor with rates ranging from $159 to $299. If you'd rather rough it, try the **Jug Creek Cottages** (www.tropicstar cruises.com; ✆ **239/283-0015**), on 5 acres of state parkland in Bokeelia,

Some of Pine Island's winged residents chill out on a pier.

featuring rustic accommodations with kitchenettes, bathrooms, and air-conditioning, at $90 a night. In Matlacha, you'll discover a groovy group of cottages, art galleries, and restaurants priding themselves on catching the freshest fish from their very own "World's Fishingest Bridge." Among the best restaurants here are **Moretti's Waterfront Seafood Restaurant,** 4200 Pine Island Rd. (☎ **239/283-5825;** www.morettisseafoodrestaurant.com), and **Bert's Bar & Grill,** 4271 Pine Island Rd. (☎ **239/282-3232;** www.bertsbar.us), a lively watering hole featuring great food and live music. If you can't stay overnight, Pine Island is definitely worth a day trip, with an emphasis on the word *trip*. This is as trippy as this area gets!

To get there, we suggest stopping at the Sanibel Chamber of Commerce, where they will guide you through a somewhat tricky set of directions. If not, try following these guidelines, which came straight from a Pine Island resident: Take McGregor Boulevard S.R. 867 and get to College Parkway, where you will take a left, heading to Cape Coral Bridge. Exiting the toll plaza at the bridge, you will be on Cape Coral Parkway for several miles until you come to Chiquita Boulevard. Then turn right (north) and go all the way to the Pine Island Road S.R. 78 intersection. Left here (westerly) will land you in Matlacha and Pine Island.

NAPLES ★★★

42 miles S of Fort Myers; 106 miles W of Miami; 185 miles S of Tampa

Ah, sleepy, swanky Naples. This is a place that may have defined the meaning of R & R, since there's not much to do here besides linger on the beach, play golf, and dream. Naples is also easily Southwest Florida's most sophisticated city. But while Naples has its requisite waterfront mansions, country-club fairways, and a thoroughfare of pricey boutiques and restaurants, it's not nearly as upper-crust as, say, Palm Beach. Although the people are indeed Ralph Lauren types, heavy on the starch, the snobbery factor and upper-tax-bracket lockjaw are conspicuously absent here—unlike the east coast of Florida, which is just as moneyed, but nowhere near as friendly or laid-back.

The long-bearded man dressed in ratty shorts and a Hawaiian T-shirt might just walk past you and hop into a Bentley or zillion-dollar yacht. Therein lies the beauty of Naples. People are wealthy here, but have no need to flaunt it—what they do flaunt are St. Tropez tans and a general *joie de vivre*. Leave the kids at home—even though there's a zoo here, it's not a place where the little ones will have fun. Naples is a romantic spot for couples; it's not a swinging singles scene whatsoever. The median age in Naples can't be much lower than 45, but Naples itself isn't a spring chicken, either.

Naples was born in 1886, when a group of 12 Kentuckians and Ohioans bought 8,700 acres fronted by a gorgeous beach, laid out a town, and started selling lots. They built a pier and the 16-room Naples Hotel, whose first guest was President Grover Cleveland's sister, Rose. She and other notables soon built a line of beach homes known as "Millionaires' Row." Today the area is known as Olde Naples and is protected by its modern residents. Despite a building boom that expanded the city, the original settlement still retains the air of that time more than a century ago.

Although high-rise buildings now line the beaches north of the old town, the newer sections of Naples still have their charm, thanks to Ohio manufacturer Henry B. Watkins, Sr. In 1946, Watkins and his partners bought the old hotel and all the town's undeveloped land, and laid out the Naples Plan, which created the wealthy but environmentally conscious city you see today.

About 4 miles north of Olde Naples, Vanderbilt Beach has a more traditional beach-resort character than the historic district. Lined with high-rise hotels and condominiums, the main beach here sits like an island of development between two preserved areas: Delnor-Wiggins Pass State Park to the north, and a county reserve fronting the expensive Pelican Bay golf course community to the south.

Essentials

GETTING THERE Most visitors arrive at the **Southwest Florida International Airport,** 35 miles north of Naples in Fort Myers (p. 366). **Naples Municipal Airport,** on North Road off Airport-Pulling Road (☏ **239/643-6875;** www.flynaples.com), is served by the commuter arms of **American**

---

bokeeli-HUH?

In Spanish, it means "little mouth," but in terms of traveling through Southwest Florida, Bokeelia means "heaven." West of Fort Myers on the northern tip of Charlotte Harbor, Bokeelia joins Pine Island and St. James City as peaceful places where they've yet to pave paradise. The **Bokeelia Tarpon Inn,** 8241 Main St. (☏ **866/TARPON-2** [827-7662] or 239/283-8961; www.tarponinn.com), is set in the historic Poe Johnson House. Johnson's lineage dates back to 1914. Revamped as an inn, without ruining its historical charm, the six-room house has pine floors and walls, a fireplace, Indonesian wicker furniture, and spacious rooms with louvered shutters and queen-size beds. Because the waters around here are swimming with tarpon, the inn has a fly-tying room where a local fisherman demonstrates the finer points of fly-fishing. The inn can also arrange boat charters. Complimentary breakfast, wine, and hors d'oeuvres, as well as stunning views of Boca Grande and Charlotte Harbor, mean there's absolutely no reason to leave this unfettered little piece of Starbucks-free paradise.

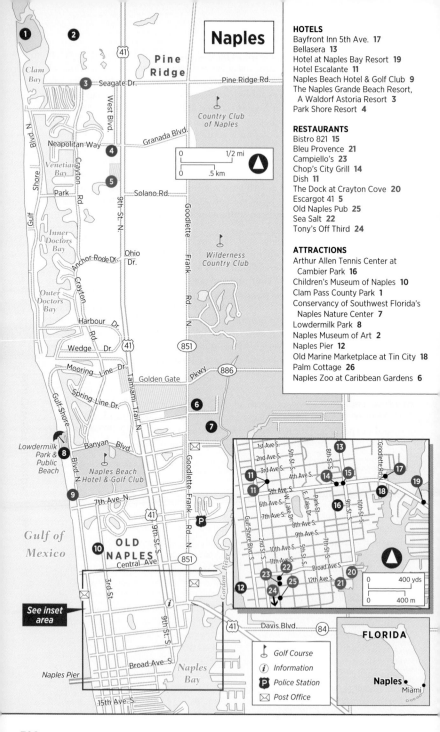

Naples

HOTELS
Bayfront Inn 5th Ave. **17**
Bellasera **13**
Hotel at Naples Bay Resort **19**
Hotel Escalante **11**
Naples Beach Hotel & Golf Club **9**
The Naples Grande Beach Resort,
A Waldorf Astoria Resort **3**
Park Shore Resort **4**

RESTAURANTS
Bistro 821 **15**
Bleu Provence **21**
Campiello's **23**
Chop's City Grill **14**
Dish **11**
The Dock at Crayton Cove **20**
Escargot 41 **5**
Old Naples Pub **25**
Sea Salt **22**
Tony's Off Third **24**

ATTRACTIONS
Arthur Allen Tennis Center at
Cambier Park **16**
Children's Museum of Naples **10**
Clam Pass County Park **1**
Conservancy of Southwest Florida's
Naples Nature Center **7**
Lowdermilk Park **8**
Naples Museum of Art **2**
Naples Pier **12**
Old Marine Marketplace at Tin City **18**
Palm Cottage **26**
Naples Zoo at Caribbean Gardens **6**

Golf Course
Information
Police Station
Post Office

FLORIDA
Naples
Miami

(© 800/433-7300) and **United/US Airways** (© 800/428-4322), which means you'll have to connect in Miami, Tampa, or Orlando.

Taxis await all flights outside the small terminal building. **Avis** (© 800/331-1212), **Budget** (© 800/527-0700), **Hertz** (© 800/654-3131), and **National** (© 800/CAR-RENT [227-7368]) have booths at the airport. **Enterprise** (© 800/325-8007) is located in town.

VISITOR INFORMATION The most comprehensive source of information is the **Naples Area Chamber of Commerce,** which maintains a visitor center at 895 5th Ave. S. (at U.S. 41), Naples, FL 34102 (© 239/262-6141; fax 239/435-9910; www.napleschamber.org). The center has a lot of free information and phones for making hotel reservations. By mail, it will send you a free list of accommodations and other basic information. The center is open Monday through Saturday from 9am to 5pm.

GETTING AROUND The **Naples Trolley** (© 239/262-7300; www.naples trolleytours.com) clangs around 25 stops between the Naples Trolley General Store and Welcome Center, 1010 6th Ave. S., at 10th Street South (2 blocks west of Tin City in Olde Naples), and Vanderbilt Beach. It runs daily from 9:30am to 5:30pm. Daily fares are $25 for adults and $13 for children 4 to 12, with free reboarding. Schedules are available in brochure racks in the lobbies of most hotels and motels. The drivers provide narration, so the entire loop makes a good 2-hour sightseeing tour.

For a taxi, call **Yellow Cab** (© 239/262-1312), **Checker Cab** (© 239/455-5555), **Maxi Taxi** (© 239/262-8977), or **Naples Taxi** (© 239/775-0505).

Hitting the Beach

Unlike many Florida cities, where you have to drive over to a barrier island to reach the beach, this city's beach is right in Olde Naples. Rather than being fronted by tall condo buildings, the beach here has as its backdrop the mansions along Millionaires' Row. Access to the gorgeous white sand is at the Gulf end of each avenue, although parking in the neighborhood can be brutal. Try the metered lots on 12th Avenue South near the **Naples Pier,** the town's most popular beach spot (see "Exploring the Town," below), where there are also restrooms and food concessions. Families gather on the beach north of the pier, while bored local teens congregate on the south side.

Also popular, the Norman Rockwellian **Lowdermilk Park,** on Millionaires' Row, at Gulf Shore and North Banyan boulevards, has a pavilion, restrooms, showers, a refreshment counter, professional-quality volleyball courts, a duck pond, and picnic tables. There's also metered parking, so bring quarters. A few blocks farther north is another metered parking lot with beach access, beside the Naples Beach Hotel & Golf Resort, 851 Gulf Shore Blvd. N., at Golf Drive.

Nature lovers head to the Pelican Bay development north of the historic district and 35-acre **Clam Pass County Park ★★** (© 239/353-0404). A free tram takes you along a 3,000-foot boardwalk winding through mangrove swamps and across a back bay to a beach of fine white sand. It's strange to see high-rise condominiums beyond the mangrove-bordered backwaters, but this is actually a miniature wilderness. Some 6 miles of canoe and kayak trails—with multitudes of birds and an occasional alligator—run from Clam Pass into the winding streams. The beach pavilion here has a bar (drinking is a sport in Naples), restrooms with foot showers only, picnic tables, and beach equipment rentals,

Clam Pass County Park is within sight of the high-rise condos of Naples.

including one- and two-person kayaks and 12-foot canoes. Entry is from a metered parking lot beside the Naples Grande Beach Resort, at the end of Seagate Drive. There's an $8-per-vehicle parking fee. You can push, but not ride, bicycles on the boardwalk.

At Vanderbilt Beach, about 4 miles north of Olde Naples, the **Delnor-Wiggins Pass State Park ★★★**, at the west end of Bluebill Avenue–111th Avenue North (𝄐 239/597-6196; www.floridastateparks.org/delnorwiggins/default.cfm), has been listed among America's top 10 stretches of sand. It has bathhouses, a boat ramp, and the area's best picnic facilities. A concessionaire sells hot dogs, sandwiches, and ice cream, and rents beach chairs, umbrellas, kayaks, canoes, and snorkeling gear. Fish viewing is great over a small reef under 12 feet of water about 150 feet offshore. Fishing from the beach is excellent, too. Rangers provide nature tours throughout the year, with the most interesting during the loggerhead-turtle nesting season from June to October (call or check the park's website for the schedule). The sand is an ideal spot for shellers. The park is open daily from 8am to sunset. Admission is $4 per vehicle with one occupant, $6 per vehicle with two to eight occupants, and $2 per pedestrian or biker. To get here from Olde Naples, go north on U.S. 41 about 4 miles and take a left onto 111th Avenue, which turns into Bluebill Avenue before it reaches the beach. Note that 111th Avenue is known as Immokalee Road east of U.S. 41.

Outdoor Activities

BOATING Powerboats are available from **Extreme Rentals,** at the Bayfront Inn Hotel, 1221 5th Ave. South (𝄐 239/774-0061; www.extremerentals.us); and from **Naples Boat and Jet Ski Rentals** at the **Port-O-Call Marina,** 550 Port O Call Way (𝄐 239/774-0479; www.naples-boatrentals.com).

CRUISES Day Star Charters features the double-decked *Double Sunshine* (𝄐 239/263-4949; www.tincityboats.com), which sallies forth onto the river and bay daily from Tin City, where it has a ticket office. The 1½-hour cruises leave at 10am, noon, 2pm, and an hour before sunset. They cost $25 for adults and $13 for children 11 and under.

The *Sweet Liberty* (𝄐 239/793-3525; www.sweetliberty.com), a 53-foot sailing catamaran, makes 3-hour morning shelling cruises to Keewaydin Island. The vessel then spends the afternoon on 2-hour sightseeing cruises (you'll usually see dolphins playing in the river on this one) and 2-hour sunset cruises on Naples Bay before docking at Naples City Dock, 880 12th Ave. S.

Shelling cruises cost $40 for adults, $15 for children 12 and under; sightseeing and sunset cruises cost $30 for adults, $15 for children 12 and under.

For a good deal more luxury, the 83-foot *Naples Princess* (© 800/728-2970 or 239/649-2275; www.naplesprincesscruises.com) has narrated breakfast, lunch, and sunset dinner cruises from Port-O-Call Marina, on the eastern shore of the Gordon River. With their extensive buffets, the sightseeing, sunset, and shelling cruises are good values, ranging from $15 to $54 per person. Prices for children 12 and under vary on all cruises. Call for schedules and reservations.

For a more scientific type of cruise, **Sea Excursions** (© 239/642-6899; www.dolphin-explorer.com) offers an educational experience aboard the scientific research vessel, *Dolphin Explorer,* on which you will actually work along naturalists to gather data for the 10,000 Islands Dolphin Project (**http://dolphinstudy.com**). Cost is $54 per person.

FISHING The locals like to fish from the **Naples Pier** (see "Exploring the Town," below). The pier has tables on which to clean your catch, but watch out for the ever-present pelicans, which are master thieves. You can buy tackle and bait from the local marinas (see "Boating," above). The pier is open round-the-clock, and admission is free. No fishing license is required.

The least expensive way for singles, couples, and small families to fish without paying for an entire boat is on the 45-foot *Lady Brett* (© 239/263-4949; www.tincityboats.com), which makes two daily half-day trips from Tin City for $69 for adults, $35 for kids 11 and under. Rod, reel, bait, and fishing license are included, but bring your own drinks and lunch. For the same prices, its sister boat, the *Captain Paul,* goes on half-day backcountry fishing trips, departing daily at 9am.

A number of charter boats are based at the marinas mentioned under "Boating," above; call or visit them for booking information and prices.

GOLF Naples has an extraordinary number of fine golf courses. Most are out in the suburbs, though not the flat but challenging 18 holes at the **Naples Beach Hotel & Golf Club ★★** (p. 407), right in the middle of town. Nonguests can play here, but should call ahead for a tee time.

Two of the best-known are the **Lely Flamingo Island Club ★★** and the **Lely Mustang Golf Club,** both on U.S. 41 between Naples and Marco Island (© **800/388-GOLF** [4653] or 239/793-2223; www.lely-resort.net). Robert Trent Jones, Sr., designed the Lely Flamingo course; its hourglass fairways and fingerlike bunkers present many challenges. The Lee Trevino–designed Lely Mustang course is more forgiving, but still fun. Former PGA Tour player Paul Trittler has his golf school at these courses. You'll pay a price here in winter, when 18-hole fees are about $145 at Lely Flamingo and $165 at Lely Mustang, including cart and range balls, but they drop progressively after Easter to about $50 in the muggy summer months.

Eagle Lakes Golf Club, on U.S. 41 between Fla. 931 and Fla. 92 (© **239/732-5108;** www.eaglelakesgolfclub.net), is another winner, with lots of wildlife inhabiting its many lakes (a 16-ft. alligator reportedly resides near the 17th hole). On-site is a driving range, a practice facility, and a restaurant; instruction is available. Wintertime fees are about $39 to $59, but in the off season they drop to $29 or less. Tee times are taken up to 4 days in advance.

Another local favorite is the player-friendly **Hibiscus Golf Club,** a half-mile east of U.S. 41 off Rattlesnake Hammock Road, East Naples

(📞 **239/774-0088**; www.hibiscusgolf.com). A pro shop and teaching pro are available. Fees are about $40 to $85 in winter, cart included, and drop to about $35 in summer.

At the intersection of Vanderbilt Beach and Airport-Pulling roads, the Greg Norman–designed 27 championship holes at the **Tiburón Golf Club ★★**, 2620 Tiburón Dr. (📞 **877/WCI-PLAY** [924-7529] or 239/594-2040; www.tiburongolf.com), play like a British Open course—but without the thick-thatch rough. Greens fees have been reduced in recent years, starting as low as $35 for 18 holes, with cart, on a weekend day. The course is home to the **Rick Smith Golf Academy** (📞 **877/464-6531** or 239/593-1111) and the **Ritz-Carlton Golf Resort** (p. 409).

The area also has several other courses worth playing, most described in the Naples–Fort Myers edition of the *Golfer's Guide,* available at the chamber of commerce's visitor center (or check the magazine's website at www.golfersguide.com). Online, **www.naplesgolf.com** is also a good source of information about area courses.

SCUBA DIVING Kevin Sweeney's **SCUBAdventures,** 971 Creech Rd., at Tamiami Trail (📞 **239/434-7477;** www.scubadventureslc.com), which also has a base on Marco Island (see later section in this chapter), teaches diver-certification courses and rents watersports equipment.

TENNIS In Olde Naples, the city's **Arthur Allen Tennis Center at Cambier Park ★★**, 755 8th Ave. S., at 9th Street South (📞 **239/213-3060;** www.allentenniscenter.com), is one of the country's finest municipal facilities. In fact, it matches those found at many luxury resorts. To play on its 12 lighted Har-Tru clay courts, it costs $12 per adult and $5 for children 18 and under for 1½ hours' play time. Book at the pro shop, which has restrooms but no showers. The shop is open Monday through Friday from 8am to 9pm, Saturday and Sunday from 8am to 5pm.

WATERSPORTS **Naples Watersports,** 550 Port A Call Way (📞 **239/774-0479;** www.naples-boatrentals.com), will hook you up with WaveRunners, jet skis, and other water toys. Hobie Cats and windsurfers can also be rented on the beach at the **Naples Beach Hotel & Golf Club,** 851 Gulf Shore Blvd. N. (📞 **239/261-2222**); and at **Clam Pass County Park,** at the end of Seagate Drive (📞 **239/353-0404**). See p. 399 for more about Clam Pass.

Exploring the Town

OLDE NAPLES ★★★

Its history may go back only to 1886, but the beach skirting **Olde Naples** still has the charm of that Victorian era. The heart of the district lies south of 5th Avenue South (where U.S. 41 takes a 45-degree turn). The town docks are on the bay side, the stunning **Naples Beach** along the Gulf. Laid out on a grid, the tree-lined streets run between many houses, some dating from the town's beginning, and along Millionaires' Row between Gulf Shore Boulevard and the beach. With these gorgeous homes virtually hidden in the palms and casuarinas, Naples Beach seems a century removed from the high-rise condominiums farther north.

The **Naples Pier,** at the Gulf end of 12th Avenue South, is a focal point of the neighborhood. Built in 1888 to let steamers land real estate customers, the original 600-foot-long, T-shape structure was destroyed by hurricanes and

Palm Cottage is one of the historic houses of Olde Naples.

damaged by fire. Local residents have rebuilt it because they like strolling its length to catch fantastic Gulf sunsets—and to get a glimpse of Millionaires' Row from the Gulf side. The pier is now a state historic site. It's open 24 hours a day, but parking in the nearby lots is restricted between 11pm and 7am.

Nearby **Palm Cottage,** 137 12th Ave. S., between 1st Street and Gordon Drive (*©* **239/261-8164;** www.napleshistoricalsociety.org), was built in 1885 by one of Naples's founders, *Louisville Courier-Journal* publisher Walter Haldeman, as a winter retreat for his chief editorial writer. After World War II, its socialite owners hosted many galas attended by Hollywood stars such as Hedy Lamarr, Gary Cooper, and Robert Montgomery. One of the few remaining Southwest Florida houses built of tabby mortar (made by burning shells), Palm Cottage today is the home of the Naples Historical Society, which maintains it as a museum filled with authentic furniture, paintings, photographs, and other memorabilia. Tours are given in winter Monday through Friday from 1 to 3:30pm. Admission is $8 for adults, $5 for children 12 and under.

Near the Gordon River Bridge on 5th Avenue South, the old corrugated waterfront warehouses are now a shopping-and-dining complex known as the **Old Marine Marketplace at Tin City,** to which tourists throng and which local residents assiduously avoid. It does, however, look cool from the outside.

For a historic look at Naples, hop on the **Historic Naples Trolley Tour** (*©* **239/825-8251;** www.dolphinnaples.com/naples-tour.html), on a turn-of-the-19th-century trolley (albeit, with A/C), led by witty conductor Gene Ratcliff, who proves that Naples's history is a lot richer than some of its residents. Tours go Mondays, Wednesdays, Saturdays, and Sundays.

MUSEUMS & ZOOS

Children's Museum of Naples (CMON) ★★ When it opens in the fall of 2012, this museum will feature 10 intricately designed, child-scaled exhibits, from a working art studio and grocery store, to re-creations of space, the Everglades, and the beach. At the heart of the exhibits is the Banyan Tree and Tree House, a soaring, two-story banyan tree with cubbies nestled in vertical prop roots, a lookout platform, and crawling branches that lead to the fascinating treehouse at the top, inspiring children's imaginations as well as body coordination.

North Naples Regional Park, 15000 Livingston Rd. *©* **239/597-1900.** www.cmon.org. Admission and hours of operation not currently available.

Naples Botanical Garden ★ This may be the prettiest strip mall in all of Florida. Strip mall? That's right. In 1993, a group of eight Naples residents fused together their aspirations of creating a world-class botanical garden. In 2000, an endowment enabled the purchase of a 170-acre site with seven different habitats just south of Old Naples. An existing strip mall and parking lot were transformed

There's a brand-new Children's Museum in Naples.

into a garden experience to introduce the community to what was to come. In June 2008, the garden closed for a remarkable makeover. Reopened in 2009 as a world-class tropical garden featuring the plants and cultures found along 26 degrees latitude north and south, Naples Botanical Garden includes cultivated gardens of Brazil, the Caribbean, and a hands-on interactive Children's Garden along with 90 acres of restored natural Florida habitat. Newly cultivated Asian and Florida gardens debuted in mid-2010.

4820 Bayshore Dr. ℰ **239/643-7275.** www.naplesgarden.org. Admission $9.95 adults, $4.95 children 4-14. Daily 9am–5pm.

Naples Museum of Art ★★ The first full-scale art museum in Southwest Florida, the Naples Museum of Art has an impressive 15 galleries highlighting paintings, sculptures, and drawings, with major permanent collections concentrating on both the American Modern and Ancient Chinese genres. Touring shows and exhibitions bring a welcome element of eclecticism to the museum, whose very structure, including a 90 × 45-foot glass dome and 14-foot-high entrance gates, is a work of art on its own. October through May, free guided tours are given at 11am and 2pm Tuesday through Saturday.

5833 Pelican Bay Blvd. (at West Blvd.). ℰ **239/597-1900.** www.thephil.org. Admission $8 adults, $4 students. October 1-June 30 Tues–Sat 10am–4pm; Sun noon–4pm. Closed New Year's Eve, New Year's Day, Memorial Day, July 4, Thanksgiving, Christmas Eve, Christmas Day, and Aug 1 to Labor Day.

Naples Zoo at Caribbean Gardens ★ ☺ This is the only zoo in the Southeast where you can see the fosas of Madagascar (an agile carnivore that can even catch lemurs). You'll also find the rarest tigers in America and the largest black bear exhibit at an accredited zoo east of the Mississippi. A historic botanical garden dating to 1919 is the setting for animals from alligators to zebras, including a new herd of giraffe. Glass walls get you thrillingly close to leopards, pumas, hyenas, ocelots, and more. In addition to exhibits and the 43-acre tropical garden, the zoo offers a guided boat ride through islands of monkeys, lemurs, and apes. In the natural rock-work Safari Canyon theater shows, live animals from free-flying hawks to porcupines do natural behaviors highlighted by video clips and live cam close-ups. During the day, you'll also **Meet the Keeper,** watch professional handlers with venomous snakes, and see a hand-feeding of giant reptiles in Alligator Bay. There are three play areas for the kids including one by the pavilion where lunch and treats are offered by Wynn's, a Naples tradition in fine foods. There are also picnic facilities. Along with offering a day of family fun, this nonprofit organization participates in Species Survival Plans for the long-term survival of endangered species and supports regional and international conservation projects.

1590 Goodlette-Frank Rd. (at Fleischmann Blvd.). ℂ **239/262-5409.** www.napleszoo.com. Admission $20 adults, $19 seniors, $12 children 4–15. Daily 9am–5pm. Closed Thanksgiving and Christmas.

A NATURE PRESERVE

Experience Southwest Florida's abundant natural life without leaving town at the **Conservancy of Southwest Florida's Naples Nature Center ★**, 14th Avenue North, east of Goodlette-Frank Road (ℂ **239/262-0304;** www. conservancy.org), one of two preserves operated by the Conservancy. Here, you'll find nature trails and an aviary (with bald eagles and other birds). You can take guided boat rides on the hour, between 10am and 3pm, weather permitting. The Conservancy was working with Collier County to secure the proper legal permitting and is cooperating with the County to clear the area as safely and quickly as possible, so call ahead to see if boat tours are available. The wildlife is interesting—including an occasional monkey escapee from the Naples Zoo next door (see "Museums & Zoos," above). You can also rent a kayak and see the area by yourself. An excellent nature store carries gift items. There's also a multimedia exhibit dedicated to the imperiled Florida panther, showcasing it in its natural environment, and a "touch tank" with plants, animals, and marine life on display. Construction on a $17-million sustainable, eco-friendly new Nature Center began in 2010 with completion expected in 2012 to include new trails, gardens, and walkways. New additions in 2010 included more programming, such as animal encounters and electric boat cruises. Admission fees of $9 for adults and $4 for children 3 to 12 include the boat rides. Single kayaks cost $20 for 2 hours, and tandems are $35. The center is open year-round Monday through Saturday from 10:30am to 4:30pm; February through April, it's also open Sunday from 1 to 5pm. Closed July 4, Labor Day, Thanksgiving, Christmas Eve, and Christmas Day.

Shopping

A 2-block stretch of **3rd Street South ★★**, at Broad Avenue, aspires to be the Rodeo Drive of Naples, but with the conspicuous absence of Gucci, Prada, and Tiffany, it remains an ordinary (albeit lovely), pricey place for browsing. The window-shopping here is unmatched. Pick up a free brochure from the chamber of commerce's visitor center (p. 399); it lists the merchants and has a map of the area.

The **5th Avenue South ★** shopping area, between 3rd and 9th streets south, is Naples's hottest wining-and-dining spot, complete with requisite Starbucks. The avenue is longer and a bit less chic than 3rd Street South, with its stock brokerages and real-estate offices along with boutiques and antiques dealers.

You can find all kinds of tacky, fun things at Tin City.

Also in Olde Naples, the rustic, tacky **Old Marine Marketplace at Tin City,** 1200 5th Ave. S., at the Gordon River (✆ **239/262-4200**), has 50 boutiques selling everything from souvenirs to avant-garde resort wear and imported statuary. There are more boutiques in the **Dockside Boardwalk,** a half-block west on 6th Avenue South.

Where to Stay

Branches of most chain hotels sit along U.S. 41, but these tend to be of higher quality and better value than their counterparts elsewhere in Southwest Florida.

One of the most reasonably priced condominium complexes, **Park Shore Resort,** 600 Neapolitan Way, Naples (www.parkshorefl.com; ✆ **800/548-2077** or 239/263-2222; fax 239/263-0946), has 156 attractive one- and two-bedroom condominiums surrounding an artificial lagoon with waterfalls cascading on its own island. Guests can walk across a bridge to the artificial island, where they can swim in the heated pool, barbecue on gas grills, or order a meal from the restaurant or a drink from the bar. There's also once-a-day (11am) complimentary transport to the beach. (To return from the beach, make a reservation at the front desk to catch a ride back at 2pm.) The condominiums range from $259 to $199 in winter, and $139 to $179 during the off season.

One of the biggest condominium-rental agents here is **Bluebill Properties,** 26201 Hickory Blvd., Bonita Springs (✆ **800/237-2010** or 239/992-6620).

And newer to the Naples hotel scene is the **Hotel at Naples Bay Resort,** 1500 5th Ave. S. (www.naplesbayresort.com; ✆ **230/530-1199**), an 85-room condo-hotel with condos and cottages on sceney 5th Avenue South, with rates ranging from $159 to $459.

The accommodations below are organized geographically in Olde Naples and north of the historic district, including Vanderbilt Beach.

IN OLDE NAPLES
Very Expensive

Bellasera ★★★ Inspired by the villas of Tuscany, the hotel's rooms are all suites that feature crown molding, gorgeous bathrooms with marble tubs, Kiehl's products, granite counters, and beds you may never want to leave. An outdoor heated pool has private cabanas, as well as an Italian-style courtyard with fountain. **ZiZi Restaurant and Lounge** serves excellent Tuscan fare. Although the hotel is not on the beach, judging by the service here, they'd probably bring the beach to you if you asked. A new spa, **Esterra,** offers organic products and massage services, including Swedish Massage, Bamboosage, Hot Stones, Ashiatsu Oriental Bar Therapy, and Thai Yoga Massage. The top-notch service makes this one of Naples's best hotels, so it's worth having to take a short walk to the beach (or the complimentary beach shuttle).

221 9th St. S., Naples, FL 34102. www.bellaseranaples.com. ✆ **888/612-1115** or 239/649-7333. Fax 239/649-6233. 100 units. Winter $207–$695 double; off season $124–$225 double. AE, DC, DISC, MC, V. **Amenities:** Restaurant; fitness center; Jacuzzi; heated outdoor pool; limited room service; spa. *In room:* A/C, TV, fridge, hair dryer, Internet access, minibar.

Hotel Escalante ★★ On the quiet end of the 5th Avenue shopping district and 1½ blocks from the beach, this romantic 10-suite boutique hotel is perfect for couples who want convenience, no crowds, and a bit of pampering. The Mediterranean villa–style hotel is ensconced in 4 acres of private gardens with more than 300 species of plants, walkways of old brick from Chicago, and fountains from France. All units are luxuriously appointed, and the bathrooms come with two hand basins, ample vanity space, and big shower heads (the majority of bathrooms have walk-in showers as opposed to tubs). Special services include a day spa, lunch served on the beach, an evening wine reception, and an honor bar and complimentary cookies in the library. There is also a restaurant, **Dish** (p.411), which serves fresh seafood and homemade pastas and grows their own herbs and spices on-site in a homemade garden.

290 5th Ave. S., Naples, FL 34102. www.hotelescalante.com. ℰ **239/659-3466.** Fax 239/262-8748. 10 units. Winter $225–$295 double, $305–$895 suite; off season $155–$165 double, $175–$345 suite. Extra person $25. Rates include continental breakfast. AE, MC, V. **Amenities:** Bar; exercise room; Jacuzzi; heated outdoor pool. *In room:* A/C, TV, hair dryer, Internet access, minibar.

LaPlaya Beach & Golf Resort ★★★ There's no dearth of beach resorts in Naples, but what *has* been missing until now is a more intimate resort on the beach, where you don't feel underdressed or socially inappropriate when walking through the lobby in a bathing suit coverup. Located on pristine Vanderbilt Beach, this resort filled the void with plush, beautifully decorated rooms overlooking the Gulf and bay (each with private balcony), a 4,500-square-foot spa, the gourmet seafood restaurant **Baleen,** and a sprawling, scenic, and challenging Bob Cupp–designed golf club and the David Leadbetter Golf Academy. In the rooms, the French-country decor and goose-down pillows are hardly what you'd expect at a beach resort, but it works! Rooms were refurbished in 2010 with new bed linens, decor, and fresh paint. Big bathrooms are luxurious, decked out in marble. Everything has a distinct personality, especially the impressive staff that will go to any lengths to accommodate you, without being overly doting.

9891 Gulf Shore Dr., Naples, FL 34108. www.laplayaresort.com. ℰ **800/237-6883** or 239/597-3123. Fax 239/597-6278. 189 units. Winter $519–$789 double, $1,300–$1,500 suite; off season $229–$399 double, $419–$900 suite. AE, DC, DISC, MC, V. Valet parking $18. **Amenities:** Restaurant; bar; pool bar; concierge; golf course; 4 outdoor pools; room service; spa; watersports equipment/rentals. *In room:* A/C, TV, CD player, hair dryer, Internet access, minibar.

Naples Beach Hotel & Golf Club ★★★ ☺ This beachy-keen retro-resort definitely belongs in Olde Naples. It's also Southwest Florida's only resort with its own 18-hole golf course, tennis center, and full-service spa on the premises. Accommodation options include the Florida Wing, a two-story relic from 1948 that was beautifully renovated in 2010, featuring updated units opening to a long porch with views of the pool and Gulf. Tower units are over the main dining room and across the boulevard from the golf course. Suites in the Cabana Wing boast redesigned, large bathrooms. The Watkins Wing houses the most spacious suites. Rooms in the Penthouse Wing, removed from the action at the north end of the property, face the beach and are the best choice for couples, especially during holidays and summer, when many families stay here—the excellent Beach Klub 4 Kids is *free*. All guest rooms and suites at the resort were remodeled as part of a $22-million renovation. Guest rooms and suites now feature newly remodeled bathrooms, new bedding and fabrics, flat-panel televisions, and accents in calming tropical shades. In addition, the resort completed a multimillion-dollar remodeling of the bathrooms in all guest rooms and suites, and added a new $5-million beachfront pool complex, featuring two new pools—a free-form pool for families, and a quiet oval-shaped pool for adults, as well as new whirlpools, restrooms, and a pool shop. The championship golf course was also renovated, with new grass on 12 of the greens and on all 18 tee boxes, and new bridges over some of the water features.

851 Gulf Shore Blvd. N., Naples, FL 34102. www.naplesbeachhotel.com. © **800/237-7600** or 239/261-2222. Fax 239/261-7380. 317 units. Winter $325–$605 double, $495–$825 suite; off season $190–$305 double, $300–$475 suite. Packages available. AE, DC, DISC, MC, V. Free valet parking. **Amenities:** 4 restaurants; 4 bars; babysitting; bike rental; children's programs; concierge; 18-hole golf course; fitness center; 2 heated outdoor pools; room service; full-service spa; 6 tennis courts; watersports equipment/rentals. *In room:* A/C, TV, fridge, hair dryer, Wi-Fi.

An Open-Air Bar

Because the **Naples Beach Hotel** predates the city's strict historic-district zoning laws, it also has Olde Naples's only restaurants and bar directly on the beach. Of these, the **Sunset Beach Bar** (pictured below) is one of the region's most famous beachside open-air bars; it's always crammed as the sun sets over the Gulf, with nightly live bands and a very popular Sunday-evening pool party.

Expensive

Bayfront Inn 5th Ave. ★★ A great downtown waterfront boutique hotel, Bayfront Inn is a Caribbean chic lodging within walking distance to shopping, dining, and, best of all, the waterfront. A heated waterfall pool and spa and waterfront restaurant with live entertainment keep guests happily ensconced here, with no real reason to leave. Guest rooms are plush and posh, with luxe linens, pillow-top mattresses, and the most sublime Trillium gel pillows you've ever laid your head on. Rooms overlook the water and, in season, you can even charter or rent a boat to ride along the bayfront. The hotel also offers Segway tours and bikes for rent.

1221 5th Ave. S., Naples, FL 34102. www.bayfrontinnnaples.com. © **239/649-5800.** Fax 239/649-0523. 98 units. Winter $210–$310 double, $285–$595 suite; off season $95–$155 double, $145–$395 suite. AE, DC, DISC, MC, V. **Amenities:** Restaurant; concierge; heated outdoor pool; seasonal room service; watersports equipment/rentals. *In room:* A/C, TV/DVD, fridge (in some), hair dryer, high-speed Internet.

NORTH OF OLDE NAPLES

Very Expensive

The Ritz-Carlton, Naples ★★★ ☺ This opulent Mediterranean-style resort, one of Florida's finest, is a favorite among affluent guests who like standard Ritz amenities—marble floors, Waterford-crystal chandeliers, British-style afternoon tea, and a staff that starts fawning over you from the moment you arrive. Still, it lacks the wonderful Old Florida charm of the Naples Beach Hotel & Golf Club (see above). Nor is it as close to the beach: You have to walk through a narrow mangrove forest to reach the sands. The beach here is part of a public park, but hotel staff is out there to answer phones, deliver drinks and snacks, and rent cabanas, boats, and other toys (only towels, chairs, and ice water are complimentary). The plush guest rooms and suites overlook the Gulf, and only six don't have balconies. A $50-million full-service **spa** is bliss, and after your pampering you can now enjoy fresh, healthy, and creative cuisine at a new restaurant on the third floor of the spa. A $6-million upgrade added a high-tech virtual reality interactive entertainment lounge, a new sushi bar, a new Tiki bar, and a new tapas **restaurant** featuring an innovative menu of global cuisine in the recently renovated Lobby Lounge. Guests here can play the golf course and use the other amenities at the Ritz-Carlton Golf Resort, Naples (see below).

280 Vanderbilt Beach Rd., Naples, FL 34108. www.ritzcarlton.com. © **888/856-4372** or 239/598-3300. Fax 239/598-6690. 450 units. Winter $599–$699 double, $1,599–$4,999 suite; off season $299–$359 double, $599–$2,199 suite. AE, DC, DISC, MC, V. Valet parking $25. From Olde Naples, go north 3½ miles on U.S. 41. Turn left on Vanderbilt Beach Rd. (C.R. 862) to the hotel on the left. **Amenities:** 9 restaurants; 3 bars; babysitting; children's programs; concierge; concierge-level rooms; access to golf course; Jacuzzi; 2 heated outdoor pools and children's play pool; room service; sauna; full-service spa; 4 tennis courts; watersports equipment/rentals. *In room:* A/C, TV/DVD/CD player, hair dryer, Internet access, minibar.

The Ritz-Carlton Golf Resort, Naples ★★ This Mediterranean-style resort opened in 2002 at the 36-hole (two 18-hole courses), Greg Norman–designed Tiburón Golf Club, in an exclusive residential enclave at the intersection of Vanderbilt Beach and Airport-Pulling roads. This is a golf lover's version of its sister resort, the Ritz-Carlton, Naples (see above), and guests can use the spa, beach, and other facilities at its older sibling, a 5-minute drive away. Each of the luxuriously appointed guest units has a private balcony overlooking the course. Head to **Global,** the new tapas restaurant in the Bella Vista, to enjoy bar food from around the world after a day at the course. Complimentary shuttle service is provided daily from 6:30am to 11:30pm between the resorts. Guests are encouraged to enjoy the services and amenities at both of the Ritz-Carlton Resorts of Naples.

2600 Tiburón Dr., Naples, FL 34109. www.ritzcarlton.com. © **888/856-4372** or 239/593-2000. Fax 239/254-3300. 333 units. Winter $499–$549 double, $799–$2,300 suite; off season $239–$279 double, $399–$1,649 suite. Packages available. AE, DC, DISC, MC, V. From Olde Naples, go north 3½ miles on U.S. 41. Turn right on Vanderbilt Beach Rd. (C.R. 862) to Airport-Pulling Rd. Hotel is on the left. **Amenities:** 4 restaurants; 2 bars; babysitting; children's programs; concierge; concierge-level rooms; 2 golf courses; health club; Jacuzzi; heated outdoor pool; room service; sauna; 4 tennis courts. *In room:* A/C, TV/DVD/CD player, hair dryer, Internet access, minibar.

Expensive/Moderate

The Inn at Pelican Bay ★ Just 1 mile away from the sands and waters of the Gulf of Mexico, this charming inn features 100 newly renovated guest rooms in the upscale North Naples neighborhood of Pelican Bay. It's quiet and not unlike staying in someone's apartment, but you don't have to make the bed. Decor is "Mediterranean meets Old World," with dark-wood furniture, but amenities are New World, with LCD TVs and complimentary wireless Internet access, and, in some rooms (request these), bathrooms have a jetted tub, separate shower, and huge vanity area. A complimentary deluxe continental breakfast is offered, as is afternoon tea. The lobby bar overlooks a fountain-filled lake. It's peaceful and quiet here.

800 Vanderbilt Beach Rd., Naples, FL 34108. www.innatpelicanbay.com. © **800/597-8770** or 239/597-8777. Fax 239/597-8012. 147 units. Winter $159–$209 double; off season $109–$149 double. Weekly rates available. AE, DC, DISC, MC, V. **Amenities:** Restaurant; bar; heated outdoor pool; free Wi-Fi. *In room:* A/C, TV, hair dryer, Wi-Fi.

The Naples Grande Beach Resort, A Waldorf Astoria Resort ★★ ☺ This luxury boutique high-rise is not directly on the beach: Guests may ride the free Clam Pass County Park tram (p. 399) to the Gulf or enjoy a walk through a mangrove forest and pristine estuary via a .6-mile scenic boardwalk to the 3-mile stretch of beach. To compensate, the resort has a big outdoor complex with three pools, a water slide, and cabanas. There's also a 15–Har-Tru–court tennis center and superb **Golden Door Spa** complete with plunge pools and multisensory massages. The Naples Grande radiates a more relaxed ambience than the traditional Ritz-Carlton, but none of the Old Florida charm of its other chief rival, the Naples Beach Hotel & Golf Club (see above). But thanks to a complete revamp, the lobby and rooms are now on par with trendy boutique hotels that use 300-thread-count linens, backlit headboards, and sleek furniture. Bungalow suites, 50 of them, are incredible, with plush mattresses and bathrooms with rain-shower heads—only 25 have tubs. Kids' programs are impressive, and the little ones (and their parents) will love the pool's 100-foot water slide. Also here: a branch of the **Strip House,** the chain steakhouse known for its racy decor (and excellent steaks).

475 Seagate Dr., Naples, FL 34103. www.naplesgranderesort.com. ✆ **888/422-6177** or 239/597-3232. Fax 239/597-3147. 474 units. Winter $199–$399 double, $329–$649 suite, $899–$1,299 Grande suite; off season $109–$209 double, $279–$429 suite, $499–$799 Grande suite. Resort fee $27 per day. Packages available. AE, DC, DISC, MC, V. From Olde Naples, go about 1½ miles north on U.S. 41 and turn left on Seagate Dr. Hotel is on the right. **Amenities:** 4 restaurants; 2 bars; babysitting; bike rental; children's programs; concierge; access to golf course; fitness center; 3 heated outdoor pools; room service; Golden Door Spa; 15 tennis courts; watersports equipment/rentals. *In room:* A/C, TV, hair dryer, Wi-Fi.

Inexpensive

Lighthouse Inn Motel A relic from decades gone by, this no-frills but spotlessly clean motel sits across the street from other, more expensive Gulf-side properties on Vanderbilt Beach and within walking distance of the Ritz-Carlton, Naples. The efficiencies and apartments are simple, with cinder block walls and small kitchens. The one kitchenless room has a small fridge and coffeemaker, but note that no units have phones, and four have shower-only bathrooms. Most guests take advantage of weekly and monthly rates in winter, when the motel is heavily booked. The hotel also operates **Buzz's Lighthouse Cafe** next door, a pleasant place for an inexpensive dockside breakfast, lunch, or dinner.

9140 Gulf-Shore Dr. N., Naples, FL 34108. ✆ **239/597-3345.** Fax 239/597-5541. 15 units. Winter $135 double, $145 efficiency; off season $65 double, $75 efficiency. MC, V. From Olde Naples, go 3½ miles north on U.S. 41; take a left on Vanderbilt Beach Rd. (C.R. 862). Turn right on Gulf Shore Dr. to hotel on the right. **Amenities:** Restaurant; bar; heated outdoor pool. *In room:* A/C, TV, fridge, kitchen, no phone.

Where to Dine

Naples's beaches are ideal for picnics. In Olde Naples, you can get freshly baked breads and pastries, gourmet sandwiches, and fruit plates at **Tony's Off Third,** 1300 3rd St. S. (✆ **239/262-7999;** www.tonysoffthird.com).

IN OLDE NAPLES

Expensive

Campiello's ★★ ITALIAN It's not about the homemade pasta at this see-and-be-seen spot in Naples, where the open-air bar is command central for local Naples luminaries and suntanned socialites. The martini menu is impressive, featuring more than 20 creative concoctions. The balsamic glazed short ribs with Sicilian onions and smoked tomatoes or the pan-roasted grouper with baby artichokes and potato purée are two of many great choices. Daily specials are the most interesting: There's a slew of fabulous wood-oven pizzas and handmade pastas to confound your menu selection.

1177 3rd St. (at Broad Ave.). © **239/435-1166.** www.campiello.damico.com. Reservations recommended. Main courses $19–$36. AE, DC, DISC, MC, V. Sun–Thurs 11:30am–2:30pm and 5–10:30pm; Fri–Sat 11:30am–2:30pm and 5–11pm.

Chop's City Grill ★ STEAK/SEAFOOD The smells of steak and money waft through this urbane bistro that's more Miami hip than Naples nautical. Aged, top-quality steaks and lamb chops are the house specialties, either chargrilled and served with onion rings and mashed potatoes, or peppered and served with a blackberry-and-cabernet-wine sauce. Whichever cut you choose, you get a free side dish, which is a nice touch considering most steakhouses charge for all sides. Fresh fish from the grill is another good choice. Asian influences appear here, too, such as spiced yellowfin tuna with mango-chili glaze and served with a "sexy" sweet pepper–coriander sauce, wasabi whipped potatoes, and sesame "chop sticks." And because no restaurant these days is complete without it, there's also a good sushi menu, but it's a steakhouse first and foremost.

837 5th Ave. S. (btw. 8th and 9th sts. S.). © **239/262-4677.** Reservations recommended. www.chopscitygrill.com. Main courses $23–$45. AE, DC, DISC, MC, V. Mon–Sun 5pm–closing.

Dish ★★ SEAFOOD Tucked away in the Hotel Escalante, Dish is the brainchild of Bryan "Bubba" Sutton, who closed his restaurant Tropical Reef in favor of this smaller, swankier eatery. Sutton focuses on fresh seafood and homemade pasta and changes the menu based on the catch of the day. He also grows his own herbs and spices in a garden on the hotel's premises. The house specialty? Hotn-Crunchy Grouper breaded in cornflakes and sautéed with almonds, sesame seeds, and chili flakes and served with a spicy mango chutney. Other excellent dishes include a chianti-braised rabbit pappardelle; grilled dry packed sea scallops with a cilantro beurre blanc; and Bubba's Chicken Rhumbera, marinated chicken grilled with rice and mango curry butter.

Hotel Escalante, 290 5th Ave. S. © **239/325-DISH** (3474). Reservations recommended. Main courses $24–$38. AE, DC, DISC, MC, V. Tues–Sat 5:30–9:30pm.

Escargot 41 ★★★ FRENCH Fancy French food in a strip mall may have been oxymoronic at one point, but then came Escargot 41. Chef Patrick Fevrier's cuisine is so stellar you'll feel like you're on the Champs-Elysées and not on the Tamiami Trail. True to its namesake, the house specialty is escargot, which comes in seven varieties, including the Escargot Dr. Ivan, a mix of snails, sweetbreads, and trumpet mushrooms in a creamy Marsala sauce. For more grounded dishes, the beef tenderloin finished with anchovy butter is exceptional. Even the sautéed chicken breast tastes special with mushrooms, smoked sausage, garlic, and Italian thyme in a lightly creamed brown sauce. Desserts are no less impressive—homemade profiteroles with a warm chocolate sauce, or *moelleux au chocolat,* a duo of bittersweet dark chocolate filled with a homemade truffle and served with raspberry sauce, which is baked to order and entirely worth the wait.

4339 U.S. 41 N. © **239/793-5000.** Reservations recommended. www.escargot41.com. Main courses $19–$35. AE, DC, DISC, MC, V. Tues–Sat 5:30–10pm.

Sea Salt ★★★ ITALIAN The most foodie-oriented, exciting opening to hit Naples in the past decade, Sea Salt is a hot ticket thanks to Venice-born Fabrizio Aielli and his wife, Ingrid, best known for their Washington, D.C., restaurant Teatro Goldoni. Chef Aielli's constantly evolving menu emphasizes seafood with an Italian accent and, as is the trend lately, features wild-caught local fish and organic produce. A modern restaurant with sidewalk seating, Sea Salt serves an exceptional lunch as well, putting a gourmet twist on sandwiches and salads. We love the place for a glass of wine and a selection of cheeses, *carpaccio,* and oysters. But it's dinner everyone's raving about, and you'll see why, with dishes such as roasted Irish organic salmon marinated in limoncello and served with fava beans, oven-dried grape tomato, and black truffle; or simply grilled hogfish snapper with asparagus, tomato, and Parmesan polenta. In fact, the only complaints heard here are those from D.C. residents who mourn the loss of their favorite Italian chef who stole away to balmy Naples. Smart guy.

1186 3rd St. S. ✆ **239/434-7258.** www.seasaltnaples.com. Reservations recommended. Main courses $21–$48. AE, DC, DISC, MC, V. Sun–Thurs noon–10pm; Fri–Sat noon–10:30pm.

Moderate

Bistro 821 ★ MEDITERRANEAN FUSION This South Beachy bistro is an excellent choice for Mediterranean-influenced fusion cuisine. Although the quarters are too close for private conversations, small ceiling spotlights romantically illuminate each table. The house specialty is rotisserie chicken, and a daily risotto leads a menu featuring penne in vodka sauce and a seasonal vegetable plate with herb couscous. But in our opinion, the best dishes on the menu are the miso sake–roasted sea bass with roast shallot mashed potatoes, and the coconut, ginger, and lemon grass encrusted snapper with Gulf shrimp and stir-fry veggies in spicy Thai chili peanut sauce. Dishes are huge, but you can order many of them in either full or half portions. There's sidewalk dining here, too.

821 5th Ave. S. (btw. 8th and 9th sts. S.). ✆ **239/261-5821.** www.bistro821.com. Reservations recommended. Main courses $17–$34; small plates $10–$15. AE, DC, MC, V. Daily 5–10pm.

Bleu Provence ★★ FRENCH It's hard to believe Chef Lysielle Cariot had no formal training in the kitchen when you taste the recipes she learned as she grew up in Nigeria and France. Traditional French fare is fine—seared foie gras with raspberry sauce or sautéed sweetbreads—but it's Cariot's daring culinary moves that shine, from Kobe beef short ribs cooked in red wine to crispy walnut-crusted jumbo shrimp with guacamole on a bed of arugula, mangoes, and papaya. For a culinary tour around Cariot's world, consider the Menu Decouverte, offered daily from 5:30 to 6:30pm, featuring one appetizer or salad or soup, and one entree item, plus your choice of cabernet sauvignon, merlot, chardonnay, or pinot grigio for $24.

1234 8th St. S. ✆ **239/261-8239.** www.bleuprovencenaples.com. Reservations recommended. Main courses $24–$38. AE, DC, MC, V. Daily 4:30–11pm.

The Dock at Crayton Cove ★★ 🎁 SEAFOOD Right on the City Dock, this locals' hangout is the best place in town for a supercasual open-air meal or a cool drink while watching the boats. Servers are friendly and conversational. The chow ranges from chowders by the mug to seafood with a Floribbean fare, with Jamaican-style jerk shrimp thrown in for spice; main courses are moderately priced. Grilled seafood, Caesar salad, and a good selection of sandwiches, hot dogs, and other pub-style fare also appear on the menu. On Tuesday, don't miss the happy hour and a half-price raw bar (don't miss the steamed mussels with French bread for dipping into the garlic sauce) from 5 to 6:30pm. The Great Dock Canoe Race draws thousands on the second Saturday in May.

12th Ave. S. (at the City Dock in Olde Naples). ✆ **239/263-9940.** www.dockcraytoncove.com. Main courses $15–$28; sandwiches $11–$15. AE, DISC, MC, V. Daily 11am–midnight.

Naples Tomato ★★★ ITALIAN For OMG organic Italian, Naples Tomato is the place to be and, for many people, ahem, worth even a little road trip across Alligator Alley. People rave about the lasagna, but don't dismiss the other entrees, such as the one called "Date Night," which is an 8-ounce filet, Montepulciano *porcini* demi glace, *truffle melange raviolinni,* and broccoli rabe. There's even a section on the menu called Qualche Cosa Di Inatteso, which translates to "something unexpected" and features creative dishes such as Nadine's Favorite, butternut squash *raviolinni,* duck leg confit, sage butter, and amoretti cookie dust. For truffle fans, there's the Bomb (and it truly is), black-truffle ravioli in a white-truffle sauce. A mozzarella bar features a variety of homemade cheeses with all sorts of condiments and sauces. A self-serve Enomatic wine-by-the-glass system is also pretty cool, if not dangerous. The place is always packed, especially during daily happy hours from 4:30 to 6:30pm, the same time the restaurant also features early dining for those who want to beat the later dinner and mozzarella bar rush.

147000 U.S. 41 N. *©* **239/598-9800.** www.naplestomato.com. Reservations recommended. Main courses $14–$35. AE, DISC, MC, V. Daily 11:30am–11pm.

Inexpensive

Old Naples Pub ★★ 🍴 AMERICAN/PUB FARE You would never guess that the person sitting next to you at the bar here is a mogul of some sort, so relaxed is this small, somewhat-cramped pub near the fabulous 3rd Street South shops. Diners find more room at tables on the shopping center's patio. The menu features very good pub fare (and at inexpensive prices for Olde Naples), including homemade soups, nachos, burgers, and sandwiches ranging from chargrilled bratwurst to fried grouper. Platters include fish and chips, New York strip steak, grilled tuna, the catch of the day, fried grouper or clam strips, and baby back ribs. Best bets are the chicken salad with grapes and walnuts, along with the burgers, steaks, and fish from the charcoal grill. You can catch live entertainment here nightly during winter, Wednesday through Saturday during off season.

255 13th Ave. S. (btw. 3rd and 4th sts. S.). *©* **239/649-8200.** www.oldnaplespub.com. Main courses $12–$20; salads, sandwiches, and burgers $7–$10. AE, DISC, MC, V. Mon–Sat 11am–10pm; Sun noon–9pm.

Naples After Dark

To see what's on, check the *Naples Daily News* (**www.naplesnews.com**), especially the "Neapolitan" section in Friday's edition.

THE PERFORMING ARTS Known locally as "The Phil," the impressive **Philharmonic Center for the Arts** ★★, 5833 Pelican Bay Blvd., at West Boulevard (*©* **800/597-1900** or 239/597-1900; www.thephil.org), is the home of the Naples Philharmonic, but its year-round schedule is also filled with cultural events, concerts by celebrated artists and internationally known orchestras, and Broadway plays and shows aimed at families. Call or check the website for the seasonal calendar.

A fine local theater group, the **Naples Players,** holds its winter-season performances in the new Sugden Community Theatre, 701 5th Ave. S. (*©* **239/263-7990**). Tickets can be hard to get, so call well in advance.

THE CLUB & BAR SCENE Naples is not South Beach, nor does it pretend to be. It does, however, realize that some people like to party past early-bird hours, and, as a result, there are a few good spots here to get your groove on.

The restaurants and bistros along 5th Avenue South are popular watering holes, especially for young professional singles who make the area a meat market on Friday nights. **McCabe's Irish Pub,** 699 5th Ave. S. (✆ **239/403-7170**), features traditional Irish music nightly. For a lot of camp with your cabaret, the **Ridgway Bar and Grill,** 3rd Street South and 13th Avenue (✆ **239/262-5500**), is a hot spot, thanks to pianist Jim Badger, whose bawdy shows bring in crowds of all ages (not recommended for those 17 and under). New to the scene, **The Jolly Cricket,** 720 5th Ave. S. (✆ **239/304-9460;** www.thejollycricket.com), is a gastropub with live entertainment, food, and, of course, an unabridged menu of beer, stouts, ales, and ciders.

MARCO ISLAND

15 miles SE of Naples; 53 miles S of Fort Myers; 100 miles W of Miami

Marco Island is reminiscent of a sleepy, albeit swanky, beachfront retirement community. When the sun goes down, you can hear a pin drop. Which is how the locals prefer it. There's some nightlife—a new comedy club for the night owls and some local watering holes—but if you're looking for a club scene, Marco isn't for you.

That said, Capt. William Collier would hardly recognize Marco Island if he were to come back from the grave today. No relation to Collier County founder Barron Collier, the captain settled his family on the north end of this island, the largest of Florida's Ten Thousand Islands, back in 1871. He traded pelts with the Native Americans, caught and smoked fish to sell to Key West and Cuba, and charged fishermen and other guests $2 a day for a room in his home. A few turn-of-the-20th-century buildings still stand here, but Collier would be shocked to come across the high-rise bridge and see it now sliced by man-made canals and covered by resorts, condominiums, shops, restaurants, and winter homes.

Marco's only real attractions are its crescent-shaped beach and access to the nearby waterways running through a maze of small islands, its excellent boating and fishing, and the island's proximity to acres of wildlife preserves.

Essentials

GETTING THERE See p. 366 and 397, respectively, for information on the **Southwest Florida International Airport** and the **Naples Municipal Airport.** Also see p. 367 for details on Amtrak train service and Greyhound/Trailways bus service to Fort Myers.

VISITOR INFORMATION The **Marco Island Area Chamber of Commerce,** 1102 N. Collier Blvd., Marco Island, FL 34145 (✆ **800/788-6272** or 239/394-7549; fax 239/394-3061; www.marcoislandchamber.org), provides free information. A message board and a phone are outside the office for making hotel reservations even outside of operating hours. In winter, the chamber is open Monday through Friday from 9am to 5pm, and Saturday from 10am to 3pm. You can also get a free visitor's guide by contacting the **Naples, Marco Island, Everglades Convention and Visitor's Bureau** at ✆ **800/688-3600,** or via their website at www.paradisecoast.com.

GETTING AROUND Enterprise **Rent-a-Car** (✆ 800/325-8007 or 239/642-4488) has an office here. For a cab call **Action Taxi** (✆ 239/394-4400), **Classic Taxi** (✆ 239/394-1888), or **A-Okay Taxi** (✆ 239/394-1113).

Depending on the type, rental bicycles cost from $10 an hour to $40 a week at **Scootertown,** 845 Bald Eagle Dr. (𝄢 **239/394-8400;** www. islandbikeshops.com), north of North Collier Boulevard, near Olde Marco. Scooters go for about $70 for 24 hours.

Hitting the Beach

The sugar-white **Crescent Beach** curves for 3½ miles down the western shore of Marco Island. Its southern 2 miles are fronted by an unending row of high-rise condominiums and hotels, but the northern 1½ miles are preserved in **Tigertail Beach** (𝄢 **239/252-4000**), at the end of Hernando Drive. Restrooms, cold-water outdoor showers, a children's playground, watersports rentals, and a snack bar are available here. The park is open daily from dawn to dusk. There's no charge for the beach, but parking in the lot costs $8 per vehicle. The beaches in front of the Marriott, Hilton, and Radisson resorts have parasailing, windsurfing, and other watersports activities, all for a fee.

Outdoor Activities

Marco River Marina, 951 Bald Eagle Dr. (𝄢 **239/394-2502;** www.marco river.com), is the center for boat rentals, fishing, and cruises. Operating from a booth on the marina's dock, **Sunshine Tours** (𝄢 **239/642-5415;** www. sunshinetoursmarcoisland.com) will book offshore fishing charters and arrange back-bay fishing ($60 for adults, $50 for children 9 and under), shelling excursions to the small islands ($50 adults, $40 children 9 and under), and sunset and dinner cruises on the *Marco Island Princess* ($37–$57 per person). The back-bay fishing trips go at high tide, the shelling trips at low tide; call for the schedule and reservations.

Sea Excursions (𝄢 **239/642-6400;** www.seaexcursions.com) also has a booth at the marina and books fishing, boating, and shelling cruises on the *Dolphin Explorer* (www.dolphin-explorer.com).

SCUBAdventures, based at 845 Bald Eagle Dr., Olde Marco (𝄢 **239/389-7889;** www.scubamarco.com), charges $75 to $95 for two-tank dives, depending on the distance offshore.

Find out more about the plants and animals at Rookery Bay with a guided tour.

The closest public golf course is **Marriott's The Rookery at Marco** (𝄢 **239/353-7061;** www.therookery atmarco.com), in the marshlands off Fla. 951 north of the island. A sign at the course warns: PLEASE DON'T DISTURB THE ALLIGATORS. Fees range $45 to $129 in winter, less in summer.

A Nature Preserve

You'll find the **Rookery Bay National Estuarine Research Reserve** is at 300 Tower Rd. (𝄢 **239/417-6310;** www.rookerybay.org). Join a Rookery Bay Naturalist for a 2-hour guided kayak tour of the bays and mangrove forests of Rookery Bay. Discover the unique plants and animals that make this coastal ecosystem so valuable. Tours are offered weekly and times vary due to tides. Registration is required as trips are limited to 10 participants ages 12 and up and cost $40. Back on land, the **Rookery Bay Environmental Learning Center** is a 16,500-square-foot facility with research laboratories, classrooms, a 140-seat auditorium, a nature store, an art gallery, a two-story visitor center with a 2,300-gallon aquarium, a variety of interactive exhibits, and a new bridge and nature trail. Included with admission are 45-minute guided tours or programs by naturalists on everything from sea shells to orchids, offered daily at 11am and 2pm. Admission is $5 adults and $3 children 6 to 12. Open 9am to 4pm Monday through Friday, and also on Saturdays November through April.

Where to Stay

There are no chain hotels on Marco Island other than the large Marriott and Hilton properties (listed below), along Crescent Beach on the island's southwestern corner. **Century 21 First Southern Trust** (*℮* **800/523-0069** or 239/394-7653; fax 239/394-8048; www.c21marco.com) is one of the largest agents representing rental-property owners.

As elsewhere in South Florida, the high season here is from mid-December to mid-April. Rates drop precipitously in the off season.

EXPENSIVE

Marco Beach Ocean Resort ★★ Making up for the lack of a Ritz-y resort on Marco Island is this posh, all-suite, Florida Green Lodgings–certified place with a full-service **spa.** The suites are comfy, complete with full kitchens and patios overlooking the Gulf. Bathrooms are large and have delicious Molton Brown bath products. Although the marble lobby is mausoleum-like, with little or no activity, it is a sight to see. After a recent $1-million renovation to landscaping and suites (fresh paint and new carpet, draperies, and lamps, along with new suite and patio furniture, iPod docking station, flatscreen LCD televisions, and wireless Internet technology), the owners decided to add a new lobby seating area, so you can actually sit and enjoy the scenery. While the pool has private cabanas and great butlers, the beach and the service there is what really matters. There's also a rooftop pool, where you can enjoy massages, butler service, and luxe rental cabanas. New state-of-the-art exercise equipment has been installed in the Resort's Fitness Center, including TRUE® elliptical machines, recumbent bicycles, and treadmills each with a mounted 15-inch television. The restaurant, **Sale e Pepe,** features an award-winning Italian-born chef whipping up exquisite northern Italian cuisine with French influences.

480 S. Collier Blvd., Marco Island, FL 34145. www.marcoresort.com. *℮* **800/260-5089** or 239/393-1400. Fax 239/393-1401. 98 units. Winter $339–$419 double, $650–$800 suite; off season $189–$209 double, $220–$279 suite. AE, DC, DISC, MC, V. Valet parking $15. **Amenities:** 4 restaurants; 2 bars; concierge; golf at nearby facility; fitness center; Jacuzzi; heated outdoor pool; room service; sauna; spa; tennis at nearby facility; watersports equipment/rentals. *In room:* A/C, TV, hair dryer, Internet access, kitchen.

MODERATE

Hilton Marco Island Beach Resort and Spa ★★ About half the size of the Marco Island Marriott Beach Resort, Golf Club & Spa (see below), but nevertheless a group-oriented resort, this 11-story beachside tower overlooks the Gulf and a courtyard with a multi-angled pool wrapped around four coconut palms.

The spacious units were all recently renovated and have curved balconies angled to give water views. This resort has recently completed a major upgrade and renovation of its lobby and restaurant areas. New features include floor-to-ceiling windows in the main entrance lobby and a revamped menu at the **Sandcastles Restaurant** and **Paradise Café.** Guest-room and penthouse renovations round out the $15-million project. There's also a 10,000-square-foot **spa** with 10 treatment rooms and state-of-the-art fitness center. **Sandcastles Lounge** has a piano bar with nightly entertainment. *Note:* The hotel is 100% nonsmoking.

560 S. Collier Blvd., Marco Island, FL 34145. www.hiltonmarcoisland.com. ✆ **800/HILTONS** (445-8667) or 239/394-5000. Fax 239/394-8410. 297 units. Year-round $149–$449 double. Packages available. AE, DC, DISC, MC, V. Valet parking $14; self-parking $10. **Amenities:** 2 restaurants; 2 bars; babysitting; children's programs; concierge; fitness center; heated outdoor pool; room service; sauna; full-service spa; 2 tennis courts; watersports equipment/rental; Wi-Fi. *In room:* A/C, TV, fridge, hair dryer.

Marco Island Marriott Beach Resort, Golf Club & Spa ★★★ ☺ Marco Island is far from Disney World, so if you plan to bring the kids while you experience the utmost in R & R, the sprawling Marco Island Marriott will make sure they're entertained with activities, from watersports and Everglades excursions to Guitar Hero on the beach, Dance Dance Revolution, and dive-in movies, where families can enjoy a movie while floating or lounging poolside. Parents can play, too, or simply sign up children for the resort's daily kids' camp, **Tiki Tribe.** A $225-million renovation has refreshed all the guest rooms and suites, redesigned the Quinn's Pool and kid-friendly Tiki Pool with water slide, added two restaurants (**Pazzi's** oven-fired pizzas and **Korals** cocktails and sushi bar), renovated the golf clubhouse and 18-hole resort-private golf club 7 miles away, and built a 24,000-square-foot Balinese **spa** with private pool. Luxuriously furnished and decorated, the accommodations range from hotel rooms to two-bedroom suites. All have balconies or patios with indirect views of the Gulf. If you don't want to be bored during your Marco Island sojourn (a common affliction after too much of the pool or beach), definitely stay here, where there actually are things to do off—and on—the beach.

400 S. Collier Blvd., Marco Island, FL 34145. www.marcoislandmarriott.com. ✆ **800/438-4373** or 239/394-2511. Fax 239/642-2672. 732 units. Winter $339–$679 double, from $1,059 suite; off season $219–$619 double, from $659 suite. Packages available. AE, DC, DISC, MC, V. Valet parking $20; self-parking $12. **Amenities:** 6 restaurants; 4 bars; babysitting; children's programs; concierge; exercise room; golf course; Jacuzzi; 3 heated outdoor pools; limited room service; tennis court; watersports equipment/rentals. *In room:* A/C, TV, fridge, hair dryer, Wireless Internet access, minibar.

Olde Marco Island Inn & Suites ★★ Considered by many to be one of Florida's most romantic resorts, the Victorian-style Olde Marco Island Inn & Suites dates from 1883, when Capt. Bill Collier built it on the Calusa Indian Grounds. While maintaining its historical charm, the place has been remodeled and updated, and now has 51 one- and two-bedroom, two-bathroom suites decorated with a tropical flair. In addition to stellar service, the inn has one of the area's nicest restaurants, **Bistro Soleil,** featuring the fine French fare of Chef Denis Meurgue. Couples looking for a first, second, or third honeymoon should stay here, without question.

100 Palm St., Marco Island, FL 34145. www.oldemarcoinn.com. ✆ **877/475-3466.** Fax 239/394-4485. 50 units. Winter $129–$289 1- and 2-bedroom suites; off season $119–$159 1-bedroom,

$149–$189 2-bedroom. AE, DC, DISC, MC, V. **Amenities:** Restaurant; bar; concierge; fitness center; outdoor pool; spa. *In room:* A/C, TV/VCR, hair dryer, full kitchen.

Where to Dine

MODERATE

Cafe de Marco ★★ SEAFOOD Purveyor of some of the island's finest cuisine, this homelike establishment was originally constructed as housing for maids at Capt. William Collier's Olde Marco Inn. The chef specializes in excellent treatments of fresh seafood, from your choice of shrimp or baked fish with mushrooms, seasoned shallots, and garlic butter, to his own creation of seafood and vegetables combined in a lobster sauce served over linguine. If your waistline can stand it, finish with homemade Key lime pie. You can dine inside or on a screened patio.

244 Palm St., Olde Marco. 239/394-6262. www.cafedemarco.com. Reservations recommended. Main courses $20–$30. AE, MC, V. Winter daily 5–10pm; off season Mon–Sat 5–10pm. Early-bird specials 5–6pm.

Kretch's ★★ SEAFOOD/CONTINENTAL Noted pastry chef Bruce Kretschmer rules this shopping center roost, Marco's best all-around restaurant. Bruce has created a sinfully rich seafood strudel by combining shrimp, crab, scallops, cheeses, cream, and broccoli in a flaky Bavarian pastry and serving it all under a lobster sauce. It's available as either an appetizer or an entree. Cholesterol-counters can choose from broiled or chargrilled fish, while the rest of us can indulge in shrimp, Florida lobster tail, steaks, or lamb chops. Bruce's Mexican Friday lunches feature delicious tacos and other inexpensive south-of-the-border selections. In winter, Sunday is home-cooking night, with chicken and dumplings, Yankee pot roast, and braised lamb shanks. An expanded and renovated bar area features TVs. Happy hour is from 4 to 6pm and 9pm to closing, with $1 draft beer, $2 bottled beer, $3.50 well drinks, and $3 glasses of house wine. The regular menu is served until 9pm and a light bar menu is served until closing.

527 Bald Eagle Dr. (south of N. Collier Blvd.). 239/394-3433. www.kretchs.com. Reservations recommended in winter. Main courses $16–$27. DISC, MC, V. Mon–Fri 11am–3pm and 5–9pm; Sat–Sun 5–9pm. Closed Sun off season and Easter, July 4, Thanksgiving, Christmas Eve, and Christmas Day.

Snook Inn SEAFOOD The choice dinner seats at this Old Florida establishment are in an enclosed dock right on the scenic Marco River, but for lunch or libation (such as a fabulous bloody mary with pickled okra), head to the dockside Chickee Bar, a fun place anytime, but especially at sunset. The new garden courtyard isn't a bad place to be, either, as long as it's not mosquito season, in which case you should avoid all outdoor areas unless you've covered in repellent. There's live entertainment day and night during the winter season, and nightly the rest of the year. Although seafood is the specialty, tasty steaks, chicken, burgers, and sandwiches are among the choices. Even the sandwiches come with a trip to the salad bar at dinner, making them a fine bargain. Bring a filet of that fish you caught, and the chef will cook it up for you. Call **A-Okay Taxi** (p. 414) for a free ride from anywhere on Marco Island to Snook Inn.

1215 Bald Eagle Dr. (at Palm St.), Olde Marco. 239/394-3313. www.snookinn.com. Main courses $14–$28; sandwiches $9–$15; cook-your-catch $13. AE, DC, DISC, MC, V. Daily 11am–4pm and 4:30–10pm. Closed Thanksgiving and Christmas.

11

THE TAMPA BAY AREA

W hen some people hear the word Tampa, they think of Busch Gardens and never even mention Tampa's bay area. They're missing out: Tampa is a stunning city, with a sparkling array of colors reflecting off its waters. If you haven't had a chance to explore Florida's bay area, here's your chance. There's so much more to the area than beer and amusement parks.

As Florida's own city by the bay, Tampa has a vibrant culture, with roots planted in Cuban and American history. On August 27, 2012, the city will add to its rich history when it hosts the 2012 Republican National Convention.

The city of Tampa is the commercial center of Florida's west coast—a growing seaport and center of banking and high-tech manufacturing. You can come downtown during the day to observe the sea life at the Florida Aquarium and stroll through the Henry B. Plant Museum, housed in an ornate, Moorish-style hotel built more than a century ago to lure tourists to the city. A short trolley ride will take you from downtown Tampa to Ybor City, the historic Cuban enclave, now a bustling, often rowdy nightlife and dining hot spot.

Two bridges and a causeway will whisk you west across Old Tampa Bay to St. Petersburg, Pinellas Park, Clearwater, Dunedin, Tarpon Springs, and other cities on the Pinellas Peninsula, one of Florida's most densely packed urban areas. Over here on the bay, photo-ready downtown St. Petersburg is famous for wintering seniors, a shopping and dining complex built on a pier, and, surprisingly, the world's largest collection of Salvador Dalí's surrealist paintings.

Keep driving west and you'll come to a line of barrier islands, where St. Pete Beach, Clearwater Beach, and other Gulf-side communities boast 28 miles of sunshine, surf, and white sand.

Heading south, I-275 will take you across the mouth of Tampa Bay to Sarasota and another chain of barrier islands that stretches 42 miles along the coast. One of Florida's cultural centers, affluent Sarasota is the gateway to St. Armands and Longboat keys, two playgrounds of the rich and famous, and to Lido and Siesta keys, both attractive to families of more modest means.

TAMPA

200 miles SW of Jacksonville; 85 miles SW of Orlando; 254 miles NW of Miami

Even if you stay on the beaches 20 miles to the west, you should consider driving into Tampa for a taste of metropolis. If you have children, they may *demand* that you go there so they can enjoy the rides and see the animals at Busch Gardens Tampa Bay. Once there, you can also educate them (and yourself) at the Florida Aquarium and the city's other museums. And historic Ybor City has the bay area's liveliest and hottest nightlife.

PREVIOUS PAGE: **The exterior of the Dalí Museum reflects the artist's surreal style.**

Tampa was a sleepy little port when Cuban immigrants founded Ybor City's cigar industry in the 1880s. A few years later, Henry B. Plant put Tampa on the tourist map by building a railroad that ran into town and by constructing bulbous minarets atop his garish Tampa Bay Hotel, now a museum. During the Spanish-American War, Teddy Roosevelt trained his Rough Riders here and walked the Ybor City streets with Cuban revolutionary José Martí. A land boom in the 1920s gave the city its charming, Victorian-style Hyde Park suburb, now a gentrified redoubt for the baby boomers just across the Hillsborough River from downtown.

Today's downtown skyline is the product of the 1980s and 1990s booms, when banks built skyscrapers and the city put up an expansive convention center, a performing arts center, and the St. Pete Times Forum (formerly the Ice Palace), a 20,000-seat bayfront arena that is home to professional hockey's Tampa Bay Lightning. The renaissance hasn't been as rapid as planned, given the recent economic recession, but it is continuing into the 21st century with redevelopment of the seaport area east of downtown. There, the existing Florida Aquarium and the Garrison Seaport Center (a major home port for cruise ships bound for Mexico and the Caribbean) are joined by office buildings, apartment complexes, and a major shopping-and-dining center known as Channelside (in the Channel District) at Garrison Seaport.

You won't necessarily want to spend your entire vacation in Tampa, but it offers a lot as a somewhat fast-paced, modern city on the go.

Essentials

GETTING THERE **Tampa International Airport** (✆ 813/870-8770; www. tampaairport.com), 5 miles northwest of downtown Tampa, is the major air gateway to this area (**St. Petersburg–Clearwater International Airport** has limited service; see "St. Petersburg," later in this chapter). Most major and many no-frills airlines serve Tampa International, including **Air Canada, AirTran, American, America West, British Airways, Continental, Delta, JetBlue, Lufthansa, MetroJet, Midway, Midwest Airlines, Northwest, Southwest, Spirit, United,** and **US Airways.**

Alamo, Avis, Budget, Dollar, Enterprise, Hertz, National, and Thrifty all have rental-car operations here.

The **Limo/SuperShuttle** (✆ 800/282-6817 or 727/527-1111; www.supershuttle.com) operates van services between the airport and hotels throughout the Tampa Bay area. Fares for one person will range from $20 for a one-way trip to $40 to $60 round-trip, depending on your destination. Taxis are plentiful at the airport; the ride to downtown Tampa takes about 15 minutes and costs $15 to $25.

Amtrak trains arrive downtown at the **Tampa Amtrak Station,** 601 Nebraska Ave. N. (✆ 800/872-7245; www.amtrak.com).

VISITOR INFORMATION Contact the **Tampa Bay Convention & Visitors Bureau,** 400 N. Tampa St., Tampa, FL 33602-4706 (✆ 800/448-2672, 800/368-2672, or 813/223-2752; www.visittampabay.com), for advance information. If you're downtown, you can head to the bureau's **visitor information center** at 400 N. Tampa St. (Channelside), Ste. 2800 (✆ 813/223-1111). It's open Monday through Saturday from 9:30am to 5:30pm.

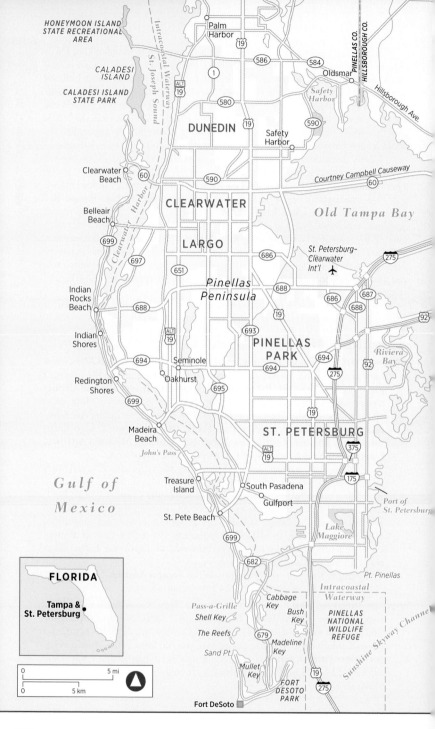

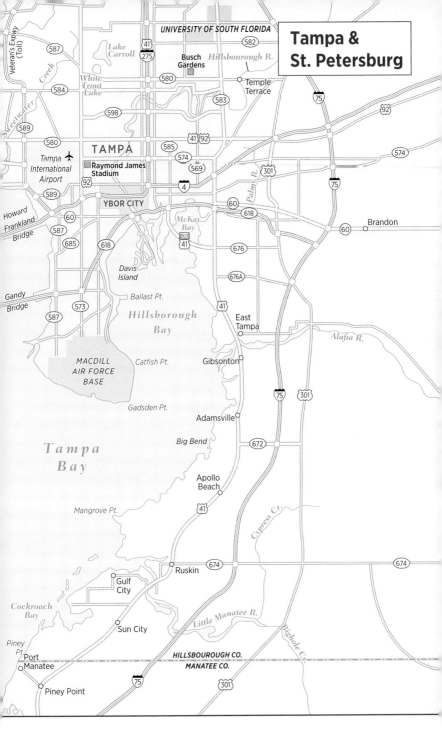

Tampa & St. Petersburg

Operated by the Ybor City Chamber of Commerce, the **Centro Ybor Museum and Visitor Information Center,** in Centro Ybor, 1514½ E. 8th Ave. (btw. 15th and 16th sts. E.), Tampa, FL 33605 (✆ **813/248-3712;** www.ybor.org), distributes information and has exhibits on the area's history. A 7-minute video will orient you to this area—an 8-block stretch of 7th Avenue. The center is open Monday through Saturday from 10am to 6pm, Sunday from noon to 6pm.

GETTING AROUND Like most other Florida destinations, it's all but impossible to see Tampa's sights and enjoy its best restaurants without a car. You can get around downtown via the **In Town Trolley,** which runs north-south between Harbor Island and the city's North Terminal bus station on Marion Street at I-275. The trolleys run every 10 minutes from 6am to 6pm Monday through Friday. Southbound, they follow Tampa Street between Tyler and Whiting streets, and Franklin Street between Whiting Street and Harbor Island. Northbound trolleys follow Florida Avenue from the St. Pete Times Forum to Cass Street. The trolleys cost 25¢ and are operated by the **Hillsborough Area Regional Transit/HARTline** (✆ **813/254-4278;** www.hartline.org), the area's transportation authority, which also provides scheduled **bus service** ($1.75–$2.75) between downtown Tampa and the suburbs. Pick up a route map at the visitor center (see above).

The transportation situation has gotten somewhat better, not to mention nostalgic, with the **TECO Line Street Car System** (✆ **813/254-HART** [4278]; www.tecolinestreetcar.org), a new but old-fashioned 2⅓-mile streetcar system, complete with overhead power lines, that hauls passengers between downtown and Ybor City via the St. Pete Times Forum, Channelside, Garrison Seaport, and the Florida Aquarium. The cars run every 30 minutes; one-way fares are $2.50, $1.25 seniors and children 17 and under. Check with the visitor center or call HARTline for schedules.

Taxis in Tampa don't normally cruise the streets for fares, but they do line up at public places, such as hotels, the performing arts center, and bus and train depots. If you need a taxi, call **Tampa Bay Cab** (✆ **813/251-5555**), **Yellow Cab** (✆ **813/253-0121**), or **United Cab** (✆ **813/253-2424**). Fares are $2 at flag fall, plus $2.25 for each mile.

Exploring Animal & Theme Parks

Adventure Island ☺ If the summer heat gets to you before one of Tampa's famous thunderstorms bring late-afternoon relief, you can take a break at this 30-acre outdoor water theme park near Busch Gardens Tampa Bay (see below). You can also frolic here during the cooler days of spring and fall, when the water is heated. The Key West Rapids, Riptide, Gulf Scream, and other exciting water rides will drench the teens, while other, calmer rides are geared toward younger kids. Wahoo Run plunges up to five riders more than 15 feet per second as the half-enclosed tunnel corkscrews more than 600 feet to a waiting splash pool. There are also places to picnic and sunbathe, an arcade, a volleyball complex, and two outdoor cafes.

10001 Malcolm McKinley Dr. (btw. Busch Blvd. and Bougainvillea Ave.). ✆ **813/987-5600.** www. adventureisland.com. Admission at least $42 adults, $38 children 3–9, plus tax; free for children 2 and under. Pick Two tickets with Busch Gardens Tampa Bay (1-day admission per park) $80–$90, free for children 2 and under. Website sometimes offers discounts. Parking $12. Mid-Mar to Labor Day daily 10am–5pm; early Sept to mid-Oct Fri–Sun 10am–5pm (extended hours on holidays).

Big Cat Rescue is a sanctuary for some of nature's largest felines.

Closed mid-Oct to mid-Mar Check website for exact opening dates. Take exit 50 off I-275 and go east on Busch Blvd. for 2 miles. Turn left onto McKinley Dr. (N. 40th St.); entry is on the right.

Big Cat Rescue ☺ Not your typical animal theme park, this one bills itself as an educational sanctuary in which visitors can get up-close and "purrsonal" with more than 150 big wildcats. The world's largest accredited sanctuary for exotic cats, this one is a unique experience for animal lovers because not only can you view and visit with bobcats and tigers, but you also can feed them, take photo safaris, and even spend a night in one of the sanctuary's cabins.

12802 Easy St. ☏ **813/920-4130.** www.bigcatrescue.org. Day tours for ages 10 and over $25 per person Mon–Fri 9am–3pm; special kids' tour for all ages $15 per person Sat 9am; night tour for ages 18 and over $50 per person, last Fri of the month at dusk; feeding tours for ages 18 and over $50 per person, reservations required; Keeper for a Day tour for ages 18 and over $100 per person, reservations required. Take Busch Blvd. exit west off I-275 for 9 miles (it becomes Gunn Hwy.). Watch for the dirt road near the McDonald's.

Busch Gardens Tampa Bay ★★ ☺ Although its heart-pounding thrill rides get much of the ink, this venerable theme park (it predates Disney World) ranks among the largest zoos in the country. It's a don't-miss attraction for children and adults who can see, in person, all those wild beasts they've watched on *Animal Planet*—and they'll get better views of them here than at Disney's Animal Kingdom in Orlando (p. 538). Busch Gardens Tampa Bay has more than 2,000 exotic animals

An orangutan gets face-to-face with a young visitor at Busch Gardens.

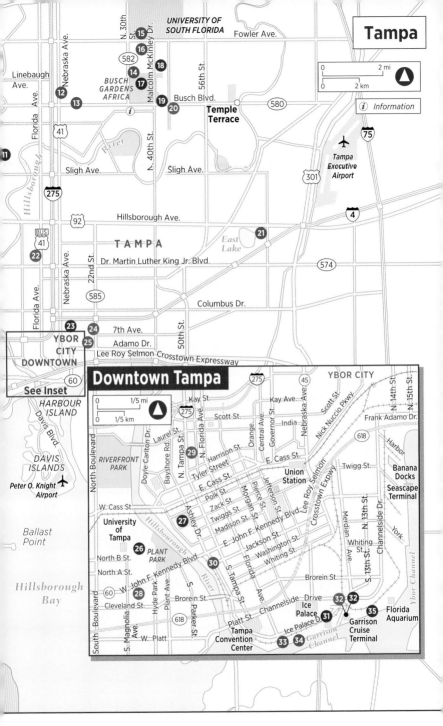

Tampa

0   2 mi
0   2 km

i Information

UNIVERSITY OF SOUTH FLORIDA

Fowler Ave.

N. 30th St.

15

16

582

18

14

17

56th St.

Linebaugh Ave.

Nebraska Ave.

12

BUSCH GARDENS AFRICA

Malcolm McKinley Dr.

Busch Blvd.

580

13

i

19

20

Temple Terrace

Florida Ave.

41

River

11

275

Sligh Ave.

N. 40th St.

Sligh Ave.

301

Tampa Executive Airport

75

92

Hillsborough Ave.

4

BUS 41

T A M P A

East Lake

21

22

Nebraska Ave.

22nd St.

Dr. Martin Luther King Jr. Blvd.

574

585

Columbus Dr.

23

24

7th Ave.

50th St.

25

Adamo Dr.

Florida Ave.

Nebraska Ave.

Lee Roy Selmon Crosstown Expressway

YBOR CITY

DOWNTOWN

See Inset

60

HARBOUR ISLAND

Davis Blvd.

DAVIS ISLANDS

Peter O. Knight Airport

Ballast Point

Hillsborough Bay

Downtown Tampa

0   1/5 mi
0   1/5 km

275

45

YBOR CITY

N. 14th St.

N. 15th St.

Kay St.

Kay Ave.

Scott St.

Frank Adamo Dr.

275

Scott St.

Central Ave.

Governor St.

India

Nick Nuccio Pkwy.

618

Harbor

North Boulevard

Doyle Carlton Dr.

Laurel St.

Bayshore Rd.

N. Tampa St.

N. Florida Ave.

Orange

RIVERFRONT PARK

29

Harrison St.

E. Cass St.

Twigg St.

Banana Docks

Tyler Street

E. Cass St.

Union Station

Seascape Terminal

Polk St.

Pierce St.

Jefferson St.

Scott St.

Lee Roy Selmon Crosstown Expwy.

S. 13th St.

Merdian Ave.

Channelside Dr.

York

W. Cass St.

Zack St.

27

Ashley Dr.

Twiggs St.

Morgan St.

E. John F. Kennedy Blvd.

Whiting Ave.

University of Tampa

Madison St.

Jackson St.

Hillsborough River

26

PLANT PARK

Washington St.

Florida

Whiting St.

North B St.

North A St.

W. John F. Kennedy Blvd.

Hyde Park Ave.

Plant Ave.

S. Tampa St.

Brorein St.

60

28

Cleveland St.

30

S. Parker St.

Brorein St.

618

S. Magnolia Ave.

W. Platt

W. Platt

Platt St.

Channelside Drive

Ice Palace

32

32

35

Florida Aquarium

South Boulevard

Ice Palace Dr.

31

Garrison Cruise Terminal

Tampa Convention Center

33

34

Garrison Channel

Ybor Channel

427

living in natural-style environments. Most authentic is the 65-acre plain, reminiscent of the real Serengeti of Tanzania and Kenya, upon which zebras, rhinos, giraffes, and other animals graze. Unlike the animals on the real Serengeti, however, these grazing creatures have nothing to fear from lions, hyenas, crocodiles, and other predators, which are confined to enclosures—as are the hippos and elephants. The park's seventh roller coaster, **SheiKra** (see below), was the nation's first dive coaster, carrying riders up 200 feet at 45 degrees and then hurtling them 70 mph back at a 90-degree angle.

New in 2011 is **Cheetah Run,** a Linear Synchronous Motor (LSM) Launch Coaster, which uses the force of repelling magnets to launch riders from 0 to 60 in a matter of seconds. Located in the area that formerly housed the Budweiser Clydesdales, this new habitat will give visitors the opportunity to get closer to cheetahs than ever with elevated, glass-paneled viewing areas.

The park has eight areas, each with its own theme, animals, live entertainment, thrill rides, kiddie attractions, dining, and shopping. A Skyride cable car soars over the park, offering a bird's-eye view of it all. Turn right after the main gate and head to **Morocco,** a walled city with exotic architecture, crafts demonstrations, and an exhibit featuring alligators and turtles. Over in **Egypt,** you can visit King Tut's tomb, with its replicas, and youngsters can dig for their own ancient treasures in a sand area. Adults and kids 54 inches or taller can ride **Montu,** the tallest and longest inverted roller coaster in the world, with seven upside-down loops.

From Egypt, walk to the **Edge of Africa,** home to most of the large animals. Go to the Adventure Tours tent and see if you can get on a Serengeti Safari, one of the park's most popular zoologist-led wildlife tours.

Next stop is **Nairobi,** where you can see gorillas and chimpanzees in their lush rainforest habitat in the Myombe Reserve. In the middle of all the excitement, you will find **Timbuktu,** where two of the smaller roller coasters are located: **Scorpion,** a high-speed number with a 60-foot drop and 360-degree loop (42-in. height minimum); and **Cheetah Chase,** a five-story "wild mouse"-style coaster (46-in height minimum). For visual amusement, there's *Sesame Street Presents "Lights, Camera, Imagination!"*

Now head to the **Congo,** where the highlights are the rare white Bengal tigers that live in **Jungala,** the park's 4-acre attraction within the Congo featuring a colorful village hidden deep in the jungle, up-close animal interactions, multistory family play areas, rides, and live entertainment. The Congo is also home to **Kumba,** which plunges riders from 110 feet into a diving loop, where you get a full 3 seconds of feeling weightless while spiraling 360 degrees, before tearing through one of the world's largest vertical loops (54-in. minimum height for riders). You will also get drenched—and refreshed on a hot day—by riding the Congo River Rapids, where you're turned loose in round boats that float down the swiftly flowing "river" (42-in. height minimum).

From the Congo, walk south into **Stanleyville,** a prototype African village, with a shopping bazaar, and the Stanleyville Theater, featuring shows for all ages. Two more water rides here are the **Tanganyika Tidal Wave** (48-in. minimum height for riders), where you'll come to a very damp end, and the **Stanley Falls Flume** (an aquatic version of a roller coaster), or if you're really crazy, check out the floorless **SheiKra,** where for 200 feet up and 90 degrees straight down, you can view the world—from a floorless perspective and a water-feature finale, all packed into a half-mile of steel track. Also, the Zambia Smokehouse serves ribs and chicken—some of the best chow in the park.

Up next is **Sesame Street Safari of Fun** for the young ones and those, ahem, too frightened to partake in some of the other rides. You'll see Sesame Street characters in a family-friendly African adventure filled with kid-size rides, cool water fun, and other adventures. Dip and dive through the desert on the Air Grover junior coaster. Climb and play in Elmo's Tree House. Splash and refresh in Bert and Ernie's fun-filled water play area. The Sesame Street characters take part in shows, and you can have a meal with them.

The next stop is **Bird Gardens,** the park's original core, offering rich foliage, lagoons, and Florida flamingos. New this year is **Walkabout Way,** an immersive animal attraction that gives an up-close look at animals indigenous to the Land Down Under. Hand-feed kangaroos and wallabies in Kangaloom during scheduled feedings throughout the day. Laugh with a kookaburra and other Australian birds in the free-flight aviary, Kookaburra's Nest.

If your stomach can take another hair-raising ride, try **Gwazi** (48-in. minimum height for riders), an adrenaline-pumping attraction in which a pair of old-fashioned wooden roller coasters (named the Lion and the Tiger) start simultaneously and whiz within a few feet of each other six times as they roar along at 50 mph and rise to 90 feet.

Added up-close tours are available, including a 6-hour zookeeper-for-a-day program and a nighttime safari by lantern light. Tour components and prices are subject to change without notice and park admission is required, but not included. For reservations, call © **813/984-4043** or 984-4073.

You can exchange foreign currency in the park, and interpreters are available. *Note:* Daily round-trip transportation is available from Orlando to Busch Gardens Tampa Bay (a 1-hour ride). Buses pick up at Orlando-area hotels between 8:30am and 9:40am, with a return trip at park close or 7pm during peak seasons. Round-trip fares are $10 per person and free with Busch Gardens combination tickets. Call © **800/221-1339** for schedules, pickup locations, and reservations.

3000 E. Busch Blvd. (at McKinley Dr./N. 40th St.). © **888/800-5447.** www.buschgardens.com. Note: Admission prices and hours vary, so call ahead, check website, or get brochure at visitor centers. Admission $75 plus tax adults, $65 plus tax children 3–9, free for children 2 and under. Prices subject to change without notice. Combination tickets and Passport Memberships available. Discounts available for guests with disabilities, senior citizens, military personnel, and AAA members. Normal park hours 10am–6pm; hours extended during select weekends, summer, and holidays. Parking $12 for cars, $14 for trucks and campers. Take I-275 north of downtown to Busch Blvd. (exit 50) and go east 2 miles. From I-75, take Fowler Ave. (exit 54) and follow the signs west.

Florida Aquarium ★★ ☺ There are more than 20,000 aquatic animals and plants at this entertaining attraction. The exhibits follow a drop of water from the springs of the Florida Wetlands Gallery, through a mangrove forest in the Bays and Beaches Gallery, and out onto the Coral Reefs, where an impressive 43-foot-wide, 14-foot-tall panoramic window lets you look out at schools of fish and lots of sharks and stingrays. Also worth visiting are the educational Explore a Shore playground, a deepwater exhibit, and a tank housing moray eels. You can look for birds and sea life on 90-minute Eco Tour cruises in the *Bay Spirit,* a 64-foot catamaran. The aquarium also offers a **Dive with the Sharks** program (© **813/367-4005**) that gives certified divers the chance to swim with blacktip, sand tiger, and nurse sharks for 30 minutes. Don't be surprised if you come face to face with the 250-pound Goliath Grouper during the dive. The $150 price tag includes a souvenir photo and T-shirt. The Penguin Promenade allows you to get up close and personal with the cute creatures. Also popular and interactive is Ocean Commotion, a high-tech gallery utilizing state-of-the-art technology like "smart Wi-Fi," floor-to-ceiling interactive displays, virtual dolphins and whales, animation, and multimedia presentations. Guests can even upload their own videos to become part of the exhibit. Also fun for the adventurous: **Swim With the Fishes,** in which you can scuba through the ½-million-gallon Coral Reef Exhibit. Kids must be 6 or over and those under 9 must have an adult with them. Cost is $85 per person, which includes aquarium admission. Accompanying parents must pay, too. Expect to spend 3 to 4 hours here.

A mysterious sea dragon is one of the residents of Florida Aquarium.

701 Channelside Dr. ℂ **813/273-4000.** www.flaquarium.org. Admission $20 adults, $17 seniors, $15 children 3–11, free for children 2 and under. Eco Tour $22 adults, $20 seniors, $18 children 3–11, free for children 2 and under. Combination aquarium admission and Eco Tour $36 adults, $32 seniors, $28 children 3–11, free for children 2 and under. Website sometimes offers discounts. Daily 9:30am–5pm. Dolphin Quest Mon–Fri 2pm; Sat–Sun 1 and 3pm. Eco Tour Sun–Fri 2 and 4pm; Sat noon, 2, and 4pm. Parking $6. Closed Thanksgiving and Christmas.

Tampa's Lowry Park Zoo ★ ☺ Recognized as the #1 Zoo in the U.S. by *Parents* magazine (2009) and *Child* magazine (2004), Tampa's Lowry Park Zoo features 2,000 animals from Africa, Asia, Australia, South America, and Florida, on nearly 60 acres of natural outdoor habitats year-round. Guests will find many interactive exhibits and opportunities to get closer to wildlife—feed a giraffe, ride a dromedary camel, hold a lorikeet, touch a stingray, and more. The Zoo's **Manatee and Aquatic Center** and **David A. Straz, Jr., Manatee Hospital** expand the traditional boundaries of a zoo, focusing efforts on critical care for injured, sick, and orphaned wild manatees. The Zoo also offers splash ground/water play areas, wild rides, educational shows, and a variety of eateries. Guests can enhance their Zoo experience by going on the **River Odyssey EcoTour,** a relaxing 1-hour journey up the Hillsborough River aboard the Zoo's own vessel, the *Sirenia,* to view animals and plant life that abound along the river's path. EcoTour tickets are $14 for adults, $13 for seniors, and $10 for children 3 to 11. Combo tickets (Zoo/EcoTour) and group tickets are available.

1101 W. Sligh Ave. ℂ **813/935-8552.** www.LowryParkZoo.com. Zoo admission $21 adults, $19 seniors (60 and over), $16 children 3–11, free for children 2 and under. Zoo daily 9:30am–5pm. Free parking. Closed Thanksgiving and Christmas. Take I-275 to Sligh Ave. (exit 48) and follow the signs.

Visiting the Museums

Henry B. Plant Museum Built in 1891 by railroad tycoon Henry B. Plant as the superchichi 511-room Tampa Bay Hotel, this ornate building is worth a trip

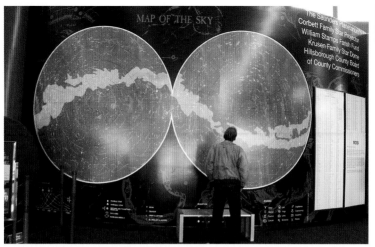

The Museum of Science and Industry is the largest science center in the region.

across the river from downtown to the University of Tampa campus. Its 13 silver minarets and Moorish architecture, modeled after the Alhambra in Spain, make this National Historic Landmark a focal point of the Tampa skyline. Although the building is the highlight of a visit, don't skip its contents: art and furnishings from Europe and Asia, plus exhibits that explain the history of the railroad resort, Florida's early tourist industry, and the hotel's role as a staging point for Theodore Roosevelt's Rough Riders during the Spanish-American War. If you're here in December, do not miss the **Victorian Christmas Stroll,** in which the museum is transformed into a holiday wonderland with each room dolled up in 19th-century Yuletide garb with carolers and Dickens-style stories and decor.

401 W. Kennedy Blvd. (btw. Hyde Park and Magnolia aves.). ✆ **813/254-1891.** www.plant museum.com. Admission Jan–Nov $10 adults, $7 seniors and students, $5 children 4–12. Special pricing in Dec for Victorian Christmas Stroll. Tues–Sat 10am–4pm; Sun noon–4pm. Closed Thanksgiving, Christmas Eve, and Christmas Day. Take Kennedy Blvd. (Fla. 60) across the Hillsborough River.

MOSI (Museum of Science and Industry) ★★ ☺ MOSI is the largest science center in the Southeast, with more than 450 interactive exhibits. Step into the Gulf Hurricane to experience 74-mph winds, explore the human body in The Amazing You, and, if your heart is up to it, ride a bicycle across a 98-foot-long cable suspended 30 feet above the lobby. (Don't worry: You'll be harnessed to the bike.) You can also watch stunning movies in Florida's first IMAX dome theater. Outside, trails wind through a nature preserve with a butterfly garden. The museum is one of very few in the world to feature the articulated remains of a sauropod dinosaur.

4801 E. Fowler Ave. (at N. 50th St.). ✆ **813/987-6100.** www.mosi.org. Admission $21 adults, $19 seniors, $17 children 2–12, free for children 1 and under. Admission includes IMAX movies. Daily 9am–5pm or later. From downtown, take I-275 N. to Fowler Ave. E., exit 51. Take this 2 miles east to museum on right.

Tampa Bay History Center ★ ☺ Opened in early 2009, this 60,000-square-foot museum covers everything from Native Americans to tycoons and sports legends who have inhabited Tampa. The museum features interactive exhibits, theaters, a map gallery, a research center, an event hall, a museum store, and Columbia Cafe, a branch of the internationally acclaimed Columbia Restaurant. The permanent exhibits explore approximately 500 years of recorded history and 12,000 years of human habitation in the region.

801 Old Water St. © **813/228-0097.** www.tampabayhistorycenter.org. Admission $12 adults, $10 seniors and children 10–17, $7 children 4–12. Mon–Fri 9am–5pm.

Tampa Museum of Art ★ The museum recently moved into a brand-new 66,000-square-foot space in downtown's $43.6-million waterfront Curtis Hixon Waterfront Park with state-of-the-art gallery spaces featuring translucent ceilings and polished stone floors. The new space is an impressive site, art notwithstanding. You'll find five interior galleries, one exterior sculpture gallery, and a high-tech classroom. The museum features world-class traveling exhibitions and a growing collection of contemporary and classical art.

120 W. Gasparilla Plaza, downtown. © **813/274-8130.** www.tampamuseum.com. Admission $10 adults, $7.50 seniors, $5 children 6–18 and students with ID, free for children 5 and under; "pay what you will" 2nd Sat of the month 9am–11am and Thurs 5–9pm. Mon–Wed and Fri 11am–7pm; Thurs 11am–9pm; Sat–Sun 11am–5pm. Take I-275 to exit 44 (Ashley Dr.).

Ybor City

Northeast of downtown, the city's historic Latin district takes its name from Don Vicente Martinez Ybor (*Eeee*-bore), a Spanish cigar maker who arrived here in 1886 via Cuba and Key West. Soon, his factory and others in Tampa were producing more than 300,000 hand-rolled stogies a day.

It may not be the cigar capital of the world anymore, but Ybor is still a smokin' part of Tampa, and it's one of the best places in Florida to buy hand-rolled cigars. It's not on par with New Orleans's Bourbon Street, Washington's Georgetown, or Miami's South Beach, but good food and great music dominate the scene, especially on weekends when the streets bustle until 4am. Live-music offerings run the gamut from jazz and blues to rock.

At the heart of it all is **Centro Ybor,** a dining-shopping-entertainment complex between 7th and 8th avenues and 16th and 17th streets (© **813/242-4660;** www.centroybor.com). Here you'll find a multiscreen cinema, a comedy club, several restaurants, and a large open-air bar. The Ybor City Chamber of Commerce has its visitor center here (see "Essentials," earlier in this chapter), and the Ybor City State Museum's gift shop is here as well (see below).

Check with the visitor center about walking tours of the historic district.

The Ybor City State museum commemorates the craft of cigar makers.

Ghost Tours of Tampa Bay (© 727/398-5200; www.ghosttour.com) offers candlelight walking tours of Tampa Bay's most haunted locations with nightly tours in Tampa, St. Petersburg, and John's Pass Village. Gather your courage and scare up some fun on these uniquely entertaining haunted history tours. Reservations required. Cost is $15 per adult and $8 ages 4 to 12. For those who enjoy an even darker side, **Secret Ybor: Scandals, Crimes, and Shady Ladies** (© 813/831-5214; http://historicguides.com/secretybor.htm) explores the more scandalous side of the city. Tours depart at various times from locations throughout Ybor City. The tours are only for groups of 20 or more and are prearranged. Minimum fee is $200 for 20 people.

Even if you're not a cigar smoker, you'll enjoy a stroll through the **Ybor City State Museum ★**, 1818 9th Ave., between 18th and 19th streets (© 813/247-6323; www.ybormuseum.org), housed in the former Ferlita Bakery (1896–1973). You can take a self-guided tour to see the collection of cigar labels, cigar memorabilia, and works by local artisans. Admission is $4, free for children 6 and under. Walking tours of Ybor City are every Saturday morning at 10:30am, cost $8 (which includes admission to the museum), and start at the Ybor City Museum State Park. Depending on the availability of volunteer docents, admission includes a 15-minute guided tour of **La Casita,** a renovated cigar worker's cottage adjacent to the museum; it's furnished as it was at the turn of the 20th century. The museum is open daily from 9am to 5pm, but you have the best chance for the guided tour if you visit between 11am and 3pm. Better yet, plan to catch a cigar-rolling demonstration (ongoing; no specific schedule), held Friday through Sunday from 10am to 3pm.

Like any area with trendy bars and restaurants, things are always changing, opening, and going out of business, so you may want to check **www.ybortimes. com** for the latest in Ybor City.

Organized Tours

When in the Tampa area, be sure to check out the **Tampa Bay Visitor Information Center,** 3601 E. Busch Blvd. (© 813/985-3601), opposite Busch Gardens, which operates guided bus tours of Tampa, Ybor City, and environs. Tampa native Jim Boggs will guide you through the city on 4-hour tours, which are given from 10am to 3pm daily, with a stop for lunch at the Columbia Restaurant in Ybor City. The tour costs $45 for adults and $40 for children 12 and under. The full-day tours (10am–5pm) of Tampa, Clearwater, and St. Petersburg give a good overview of the cities and the beaches; this tour costs $75 for adults and $65 for children. Reservations are required at least 24 hours in advance; passengers are picked up at major Tampa hotels.

Outdoor Activities & Spectator Sports

BIKING, IN-LINE SKATING & JOGGING Bayshore Boulevard, a 7-mile-long promenade, is famous for its sidewalk on the shores of Hillsborough Bay and is a favorite with runners, walkers, and in-line skaters. The route goes from the western edge of downtown in a southward direction, passing stately old homes in Hyde Park, a few high-rise condos, retirement communities, and houses of worship, ending at Ballast Point Park. The view from the promenade across the bay to the downtown skyline is matchless. (Bayshore Blvd. is also great for a drive.)

Bayshore Boulevard is a favorite route for Tampa runners.

BOATING Check out the Hillsborough River by canoe with **Canoe Escape of Tampa** (② 813/986-2067; www.canoeescape.com), which offers all sorts of paddling programs, from a 3-hour religious journey and moonlight trips to a 3-hour nighttime tour down the river. Or rent your own canoe or kayak and take a self-guided tour through Wilderness Park, a 16,000-acre wildlife preserve. Guided-tour prices range from $130 per person to $60 per person for groups of six or more, and self-guided rentals range from $25 to $56 per person.

FISHING For charters, try **Captain Jim's Inshore Sportfishing Charters,** 512 Palm Ave., Palm Harbor (② 727/439-9017; www.captainhud.com), which offers private sport-fishing trips for tarpon, redfish, trout, and snook. Rates are $350 to $625 for two anglers. Call for schedule and reservations. Rave reviews have come in for **Capt. Gus's Crabby Adventures** (② 813/645-6578; www.crabbyadventures.com), whose 4-hour boating, eating, and eco-experience includes interaction with blue crabs, stone crabs, and all the creatures of the bay, including manatees, dolphins, laughing gulls, pelicans, herons, egrets, and osprey. Gus instructs guests on how crab traps are pulled and baited. Guests also learn to grade, clean, steam, and eat blue crabs and stone crabs at the Bay Chop Villa, an open-air, waterfront shack and gazebo overlooking a Zen rock garden. Parties of two cost $300; additional passengers are $50 each. The boat leaves at 8am and 2pm.

GOLF Tampa has three municipal golf courses where you can play for about $30 to $35, a relative pittance compared to fees at private courses. The **Babe Zaharias Municipal Golf Course,** 11412 Forest Hills Dr., north of Lowry Park (② 813/631-4374; www.babezahariasgc.com), is an 18-hole, par-70 course with a pro shop, putting greens, and a driving range. It is the shortest of the municipal courses, but its small greens and narrow fairways present ample challenges. Water provides obstacles on 12 of the 18 holes at **Rocky Point Golf Course,** 4151 Dana Shores Dr. (② 813/673-4316; www.rockypointgc.com), between the airport and the bay. It's a par-71 course with a pro shop, a practice range, and putting greens. On the Hillsborough River in north Tampa, the **Rogers Park Golf Course,** 7910 N. 30th St. (② 813/673-4396; www.rogersparkgc.com), is an 18-hole, par-72 championship course with a lighted driving and practice range. The courses are open daily from 7am to dusk, and lessons and club rentals are available.

You can book starting times and get information about area courses by calling **Tee Times USA** (✆ 800/374-8633; www.teetimesusa.com).

If you want to do some serious work on your game, the **Arnold Palmer Golf Academy World Headquarters** is at Saddlebrook Resort, 5700 Saddlebrook Way, Wesley Chapel, 12 miles north of Tampa (✆ 800/729-8383 or 813/973-1111; www.saddlebrookresort.com). Half-day and hourly instruction is available, as well as 2-, 3-, and 5-day programs for adults and juniors. You have to stay at the resort or enroll in the golf program to play at Saddlebrook. See p. 438 for more information.

For course information online, go to www.floridagolfing.com or www.golf.com or; or call the **Florida Sports Foundation** (✆ 850/488-8347) or **Florida Golfing** (✆ 866/833-2663).

SPECTATOR SPORTS Major-league baseball fans were thrilled when the **Tampa Bay Rays** made it to the World Series against Philly in 2008. Although they lost, the games remain a hugely popular draw for sports fans flocking to Tropicana Field, 1 Tropicana Dr., St. Petersburg (✆ 727/825-3250). Tickets range from as low as $10 to as high as in the hundreds, depending on how good their season is. In 2009, the Rays moved to a new spring-training facility in Port Charlotte.

New York Yankees fans can watch the Bronx Bombers during baseball's spring training, from mid-February to the end of March, at **George Steinbrenner Field** (✆ 813/879-2244 or 813/875-7753; www.steinbrennerfield.com), opposite Raymond James Stadium. This scaled-down replica of Yankee Stadium is the largest spring-training facility in Florida, with a 10,000-seat capacity. Tickets are $10 to $20. Season tickets range from $240 to $460. The club's minor-league team, the **Tampa Yankees** (same contact info), plays at Legends Field April through August.

National Football League fans can catch the **Tampa Bay Buccaneers** at the modern, 66,000-seat Raymond James Stadium, 4201 N. Dale Mabry Hwy., at Dr. Martin Luther King, Jr., Boulevard (✆ 813/879-2827; www.buccaneers.com), August through December. Single-game tickets are very hard to come by, as they are usually sold out to the plethora of season-ticket holders. This is a huge football city!

The National Hockey League's **Tampa Bay Lightning,** winners of the 2004 Stanley Cup, play in the St. Pete Times Forum starting in October (✆ 813/301-6500; www.tampabaylightning.com). You can usually get single-game tickets ($30–$349) on game day.

The only thoroughbred racetrack on Florida's west coast is **Tampa Bay Downs,** 11225 Racetrack Rd., Oldsmar (✆ 800/200-4434 in Florida, or 813/855-4401; www.tampadowns.com), home of the Tampa Bay Derby. Races are held from December to May ($2 general admission, $3 clubhouse), and the track presents simulcasts year-round. Call for post times.

TENNIS Sharpen your game at the **Saddlebrook Tennis Academy,** at the Saddlebrook Resort (p. 438). You must be a member or a guest to play here.

Shopping

Hyde Park and Ybor City are two areas of Tampa worth some window-shopping, perhaps sandwiched around lunch at one of the fine restaurants (see "Where to Dine," below).

On the mall front, there's the upscale **International Plaza** (✆813/342-3790;** www.shopinternationalplaza.com), near Tampa International Airport, where the headliners include Neiman Marcus and Nordstrom.

CIGARS Ybor City is no longer a major producer of hand-rolled cigars, but you can still watch artisans making stogies at the **Columbia Cigar Store.** Rollers are on duty Monday through Saturday from 10am to 6pm. You can stock up on domestic and imported cigars at **El Sol,** 1728 E. 7th Ave. (✆813/247-5554), the city's oldest cigar store; **King Corona Cigar Factory,** 1523 E. 7th Ave. (✆813/241-9109); and **Metropolitan Cigars & Wine,** 2014 E. 7th Ave. (✆813/248-3304).

SHOPPING CENTERS **Old Hyde Park Village,** 1507 W. Swann Ave., at South Dakota Avenue (✆813/251-3500; www.oldhydeparkvillage.com), is a terrific alternative to cookie-cutter malls despite the fact that it's almost always inexplicably devoid of people. It's perfect for a peaceful, quiet shopping experience. Walk around the little boutiques in the sunshine and check out Hyde Park, one of the city's most historic and picturesque neighborhoods. The cluster of 50 upscale shops is set in a village layout. The selection includes Williams-Sonoma, Pottery Barn, Restoration Hardware, Brooks Brothers, Crabtree & Evelyn, and Godiva, to name a few. There are also several restaurants, including the Wine Exchange, Timpano Italian Chophouse, the Cobb CineBistro movie theater and restaurant, and our favorite, Restaurant BT (see later). There's a free parking garage on South Oregon Avenue. Most shops are open Monday through Saturday from 10am to 7pm and Sunday from noon to 5pm. Throughout the year, the village hosts various events from concerts to art festivals.

The centerpiece of the downtown seaport renovation is the massive tourist trap, **Channelside at Garrison Seaport,** on Channelside Drive between the Garrison Seaport and the Florida Aquarium (✆813/223-4250). It has stores, restaurants, bars, a **Splitsville Lanes** bowling alley (✆813/514-2695; www.splitsvillelanes.com), and a multiscreen cinema with an IMAX screen.

In Ybor City, **Centro Ybor,** on 7th Avenue East at 16th Street (✆813/242-4660; www.centroybor.com), is primarily a dining-and-entertainment complex, but you'll find a few chains, such as American Eagle and Urban Outfitters.

Where to Stay

The listings below are organized into three geographic areas: **near Busch Gardens Tampa Bay, downtown,** and **Ybor City.** If you're going to Busch Gardens, Adventure Island, Lowry Park Zoo, or the Museum of Science and Industry (MOSI), the motels near Busch Gardens are much more convenient than those downtown, about 7 miles to the south. The downtown hotels are geared to business travelers, but staying there will put you near the Florida Aquarium, the Tampa Museum of Art, the Henry B. Plant Museum, the Tampa Bay Performing Arts Center, scenic Bayshore Boulevard, and the dining and shopping opportunities in the Channelside and Hyde Park districts. Staying in Ybor City will put you within walking distance of numerous restaurants and the city's liveliest nightspots.

The Westshore area, near the bay, west of downtown, and south of Tampa International Airport, is another commercial center, with a wide range of chain hotels catering to business travelers and conventioneers. It's not far from Raymond

James Stadium and the New York Yankees' spring-training complex. Check with your favorite chain for a Westshore-Airport location.

Room rates at most hotels in Tampa vary little from season to season. This is especially true downtown, where the hotels do a brisk convention business year-round. Hillsborough County adds 12% tax to your hotel bill.

NEAR BUSCH GARDENS TAMPA BAY

The chain motels nearest to the park are the **Econo Lodge,** 1701 E. Busch Blvd. (www.econolodge.com; ✆ 813/933-7681), and the **Comfort Inn,** 820 E. Busch Blvd. (www.comfortinn.com; ✆ 813/933-4011), offering very cheap rooms. Stay at either if it's your last, no pun intended, resort, or if you are on a supertight budget. They are 1½ blocks east of the main entrance. The 500-room **Embassy Suites Hotel and Conference Center,** 3705 Spectrum Blvd., facing Fowler Avenue (✆ 800/362-2779 or 813/977-7066), is the plushest, most expensive establishment near the park. **The Tampa All Suites Inn,** 3001 University Center Dr. (✆ 813/971-8930), features a heated pool and fun Tiki bar. Nearby stands **LaQuinta Inn & Suites,** 3701 E. Fowler Ave. (✆ 800/687-6667 or 813/910-7500). Just south of Fowler Avenue are side-by-side branches of **Hyatt Place,** 11408 N. 30th St. (✆ 813/979-1922), and **Holiday Inn Suites Tampa Bay,** 11310 N. 30th St. (✆ 813/971-7690).

DOWNTOWN TAMPA

Seminole Hard Rock Hotel & Casino ★ Despite its location in a somewhat run-down part of town, Tampa's Seminole Hard Rock Hotel & Casino is full of nonstop action. The 12-story building has 250 rooms, each with modern amenities and large bathrooms. The casino has 178,000 square feet of Vegas-style slots, as well as blackjack, baccarat, Pai Gow poker, Asia poker, Let It Ride poker, Texas Hold 'em, and minibaccarat. They also have Florida's largest (and smoke-free) poker room, with 92 live-action tables with 52 dedicated to no-limit, high-stakes Texas Hold 'em, Omaha Hi-Lo, and Seven-Card Stud. The pool area is fine, but not as nice as those at the Hard Rock in Vegas or in Hollywood, Florida. The **fitness center** is top-notch and even does outdoor treatments in its Zen garden. A recent major expansion added new restaurants including the swanky **Council Oak Steaks & Seafood** and **Fresh Harvest,** a restaurant with a live-action show kitchen.

5223 Orient Rd., Tampa, FL 33605. www.seminolehardrocktampa.com. ✆ 866/502-PLAY (7529) or 813/627-7625. Fax 813/623-6862. 250 units. Winter $169–$329 double; off season $219–$309 double. AE, DC, DISC, MC, V. **Amenities:** 5 restaurants; 5 bars; Jacuzzi; heated outdoor pool; full-service spa. *In room:* A/C, TV, CD player, fridge, hair dryer, high-speed Internet access.

Sheraton Tampa Riverwalk Hotel ★ Set on the east bank of the Hillsborough River, this six-story Green Lodging hotel remains one of Tampa's better bets. Half the rooms face west and have views from their balconies of the Arabesque minarets atop the Henry B. Plant Museum and the University of Tampa across the river—lovely at sunset. These rooms cost more but are preferable to units on the east side of the building, which face downtown's skyscrapers and lack balconies. Rooms feature Sweet Sleeper beds. Set beside the river, the **Ashley**

Street Grille serves indoor-outdoor breakfasts and lunches, then offers fine dining in the evenings. There's also wireless Internet in all public spaces of the hotel. Unless you're here on business or need to stay downtown, there's not much here to entice a mainstream traveler. The hotel is also completely smoke free.

200 N. Ashley Dr. (at Jackson St.), Tampa, FL 33602. www.sheratontampariverwalk.com. ℰ **800/333-3333** or 813/223-2222. Fax 813/221-5929. 277 units. Winter $249–$299 double, $425–$450 suite; off season $229–$279 double, from $240 suite. AE, DC, DISC, MC, V. Valet parking $16. Pets up to 80 lb. accepted. **Amenities:** 2 restaurants; bar; concierge; concierge-level rooms; exercise room; access to nearby health club; heated outdoor pool; limited room service; sauna; Wi-Fi. *In room:* A/C, TV, hair dryer, Internet access.

Tampa Marriott Waterside Hotel and Marina ★★ This luxurious 22-story hotel occupies downtown's most strategic location in the emerging Channel District—beside the river and between the Tampa Convention Center and the St. Pete Times Forum. Opening onto a riverfront promenade, the three-story lobby is large enough to accommodate the many conventioneers drawn to the two neighboring venues and to the hotel's 50,000 square feet of meeting space. The third floor has a fully equipped **spa,** a modern exercise facility, and an outdoor heated pool. About half of the guest quarters have balconies overlooking the bay or city (choice views are high up on the south side). Although spacious, the regular rooms are dwarfed by the 720-square-foot suites. There's also a 32-slip marina. In 2009, the hotel wrapped up a $12-million renovation to its 719 guest rooms, which now feature flatscreen TVs and new bathrooms.

700 S. Florida Ave. (at St. Pete Times Forum Dr.), Tampa, FL 33602. www.tampamarriott waterside.com. ℰ **800/228-9290** or 813/221-4900. Fax 813/221-0923. 719 units. Winter $259–$285 double, $399–$575 suite; off season $179–$259 double, $350–$500 suite. Weekend rates available. AE, DC, DISC, MC, V. Valet parking $21;, self-parking in garage across the street $10–$25. **Amenities:** 3 restaurants; 3 bars; babysitting; concierge; concierge-level rooms; health club; Jacuzzi; heated outdoor pool; limited room service; spa. *In room:* A/C, TV, fax, fridge, hair dryer, high-speed Internet access.

The Westin Tampa Harbour Island ★★★ Close enough to downtown but still worlds away on its own 177-acre island, this hotel insists that you're here on vacation and not stuck in some downtown convention hotel. Rooms overlook the harbor and are hypercomfortable, with pillow-top mattresses and large bathrooms featuring dual shower heads. There's also an elegant waterfront restaurant, **725 South,** that's popular for business dinners and power lunches. A new Westin Workout **gym** is a highlight for those into working out. Stroll the boardwalk to fully appreciate your surroundings.

725 S. Harbour Island Blvd., Tampa, FL 33602. www.starwoodhotels.com. ℰ **877/999-3223** or 813/229-5000. Fax 813/229-5322. 299 units. $249–$399 double; $495–$895 suite. Weekend rates available. AE, DC, DISC, MC, V. Valet parking $16; self-parking $14. **Amenities:** Restaurant; 3 bars; babysitting; concierge; access to nearby health club; Jacuzzi; heated outdoor pool; limited room service; access to spa. *In room:* A/C, TV, fax, hair dryer, high-speed Internet access.

A NEARBY SPA & SPORTS RESORT

Saddlebrook Resort–Tampa ★★ ☺ Set on 480 rolling acres of countryside, Saddlebrook is a landlocked condominium development off the beaten path (30 min. north of Tampa International Airport). But if you're interested in spas, tennis, or golf, we recommend this resort, which offers complete **spa** treatments, the **Saddlebrook Tennis Academy** (Jennifer Capriati pitches a tent here), and the **Arnold Palmer Golf Academy** (see "Outdoor Activities & Spectator Sports," earlier in this chapter). Guests are housed in hotel rooms with Tommy Bahama–esque decor, or one-, two-, or three-bedroom suites. Much more appealing than the rooms, the suites come with a kitchen and either a patio or a balcony overlooking lagoons, cypress and palm trees, and the resort's two 18-hole championship golf courses. There are shops, restaurants, a half-million-gallon "super pool," and a kids' club with supervised activities.

5700 Saddlebrook Way, Wesley Chapel, FL 33543. www.saddlebrookresort.com. ℭ **800/729-8383** or 813/973-1111. Fax 813/973-4504. 800 units. Winter $259–$399 suite; off season $159–$249 suite. Packages available. AE, DC, DISC, MC, V. Valet parking $10. **Amenities:** 4 restaurants; 3 bars; bike rental; children's program; concierge; 2 golf courses; health club; Jacuzzi; heated outdoor pool; limited room service; sauna; spa; 45 grass, clay, and hard tennis courts. *In room:* A/C, TV, hair dryer, Internet access, kitchen, minibar.

Where to Dine

The restaurants below are organized by geographic area: near Busch Gardens, in or near Hyde Park (across the Hillsborough River from downtown), and in Ybor City. Although Ybor City is better known, Tampa's trendiest dining scene is along South Howard Avenue—"SoHo" to the locals—between West Kennedy Boulevard and the bay in Hyde Park.

NEAR BUSCH GARDENS

You'll find the national fast-food and family restaurants east of I-275 on Busch Boulevard and Fowler Avenue.

Inexpensive

Mel's Hot Dogs ☺ AMERICAN Catering to everyone from businesspeople to hungry families craving all-beef hot dogs, Mel Lohn's red-and-white cottage offers everything from traditional Chicago-style and "bagel-dogs" to bacon/cheddar Reuben-style hot dogs. All choices are served on poppy seed buns and can be ordered with fries and a choice of coleslaw or baked beans. Even the decor is dedicated to wieners: The walls and windows are lined with hot dog memorabilia, and a wiener-mobile is usually parked out front. Mel's chili is outstanding, too. And just in case hot dog mania hasn't won you over, there are a few alternatives (chicken, beef, and veggie burgers, and terrific onion rings).

4136 E. Busch Blvd., at 42nd St. ℭ **813/985-8000.** www.melshotdogs.com. Most items $2.75–$11. No credit cards (but there's an ATM on the premises). Sun–Thurs 11am–8pm; Fri–Sat 11am–9pm.

HYDE PARK
Expensive

Bern's Steak House ★★ STEAKHOUSE The exterior of this famous steakhouse is so unassuming you'd never know you were about to enter meat—and wine—heaven. The interior is an opulent foodie fantasyland containing eight ornate dining rooms with themes such as Rhône, Burgundy, and Irish Rebellion. This is a carnivore's paradise. At Bern's, you order and pay for grilled steaks of perfectly aged beef according to the thickness and weight (the 60-oz. strip sirloin can feed six adults). A surprisingly good deal for a fancy steakhouse, all entrees come with French onion soup, salad, baked potato, onion rings, and a selection of organic vegetables. Bern's also offers a "Kitchen Within a Kitchen" menu page that changes every 3 weeks. The phone book–size wine list—one of the restaurant's most famous attributes—has more than 6,500 labels, many available by the glass. Upstairs, the restaurant's other most famous attribute—the **Harry Waugh Dessert Room**—has 50 romantic, semiprivate casks paneled in aged California redwood; each can privately seat from 2 to 12 guests. All of these little chambers are equipped with phones for placing your requests with the piano player. The dessert menu has 35 to 40 tough choices—and with ice-cream flavors, choices become 100 times harder—plus some 1,400 after-dinner drinks, wines, and spirits. You can go here just for desserts, but the dessert room is first come, first served unless you have dinner, which will get you a coveted cask upstairs. For those who love cheese, Bern's has two indoor caves storing artisanal cheeses from around the world.

The big secret here is that steak sandwiches are available at the bar but are not mentioned on the menu.

SideBern's, 2208 W. Morrison Ave., at South Howard Avenue (✆ **813/258-2233**), is the restaurant's New American offshoot. It's also quite good, but if you have only 1 night, choose the original: Missing original Bern's would be like watching the remake of *Psycho* without seeing the original. If you have two nights or more, then do *not* miss the stellar seasonal menus created by executive chef Chad Johnson, who cooks only with locally grown ingredients. There's also an exceptional cheese-and-wine-pairing menu.

1208 S. Howard Ave. (at Marjory Ave.). ✆ **813/251-2421.** www.bernssteakhouse.com. Reservations recommended. Main courses $21–$70. AE, DC, DISC, MC, V. Sun–Thurs 5–10pm; Fri–Sat 5–11pm. Closed Christmas and Labor Day. SideBern's: Mon–Thurs 6–10pm; Fri–Sat 6–11pm. Valet parking $5.

Restaurant BT ★★★ VIETNAMESE I live in Miami and when I heard about this restaurant, I drove the 5 hours to Tampa to see what all the hype was about. It was worth every service plaza, toll fare, and then some! One reviewer called it one of the hippest, most innovative Vietnamese restaurants in the United States. Chef Trina Nguyen-Batley creates a chic, sophisticated, stylish oasis of French Vietnamese fare that's as gorgeous as it is delicious. An appetizer of filet mignon tartare with ginger, garlic, chili, opal basil, cilantro, peanuts, shallots, and lime juice prepares the palate for an outstanding onslaught of flavors and textures to come. A Vietnamese bouillabaisse of Gulf prawns, Manila clams, calamari, salmon, pineapple, okra, bean sprout, lily stem, and tomato in a tangy aromatic seafood broth is equally spectacular. Come to think of it, you can't go wrong with anything here.

1633 W. Snow Ave. ✆ **813/258-1916.** www.restaurantbt.com. Reservations recommended. Main courses $20–$38. AE, DC, DISC, MC, V. Mon–Thurs 11:30am–2:30pm and 5:30–9:30pm; Fri–Sat 11:30am–2:30pm and 5:30–10:30pm.

Moderate
Fly Bar & Restaurant ★★ TAPAS A trendy hot spot in downtown Tampa, Fly Bar & Restaurant is in a restored building and features a buzzing rooftop bar and lounge that's hot with the après-work crowds. The San Francisco import is all about small plates, to be shared in the dining room, on the sidewalk tables, at the bar, or on the rooftop. Among the plates: fish tacos with roasted tomatillo salsa; Kobe beef sliders with Gruyère, sautéed mushrooms, and onions; shrimp and grits with chorizo and spring onions; and truffled mac and cheese. There's usually live music, too.

1202 N. Franklin St. (at E. Royal St.). ℰ **813/275-5000.** www.flybarandrestaurant.com. Reservations recommended. Tapas $6–$13. AE, DC, DISC, MC, V. Mon–Sat 5:30–11pm.

Mise en Place ★★ NEW AMERICAN Look around at all those happy, stylish people soaking up the trendy ambience, and you'll know why Chef Marty Blitz and his wife, Maryann, have been among the culinary darlings of Tampa since 1986. They present the freshest of ingredients in a creative, award-winning menu broken down into first, second, and main plates that changes weekly. Main courses often include such choices as mole-crusted duck breast with kabocha squash pork-belly posole, blackberry ancho gastrique, and haricot vert chayote chili salad; or *sous vide* halibut, fennel salsify asparagus, bay scallops, trumpet mushroom ragout, golden lentil marcona almond quinoa, verjus vinaigrette, Maldon sea salt, and roast grapes. Ingredients may read like an unabridged culinary dictionary, but trust us, the mouthfuls are worth every word. The tasting menus, with wine, are listed on the menu under "Get Blitzed" (four-courses) and "Get a Little Blitzed" (three courses).

In Grand Central Place, 442 W. Kennedy Blvd. (at S. Magnolia Ave., opposite the University of Tampa). ℰ **813/254-5373.** www.miseonline.com. Reservations recommended. Main courses $19–$35; 4-course tasting menu $69 with wine, $49 without; 3-course tasting menu $44 with wine, $29 without. AE, DC, DISC, MC, V. Tues–Thurs 11:30am–2:30pm and 5:30–10pm; Fri 11:30am–2:30pm and 5:30–11pm; Sat 5–11pm.

The Refinery ★ GASTROPUB Hands down the most popular restaurant to hit the Tampa area since, well, we're not sure, The Refinery's culinary MO is "sustainably and ethically right." Ingredients come from farmers, not cans. And those ingredients are assembled into menus that change every Thursday night, but on any given night you may be offered a starter of pork belly with tamarind, roasted radish, pumpkin mole, pepitas, and polenta cake; a main course of roasted chicken with black-eyed peas, collards, pedron cornbread, and honey-Crystal lacquer; and a dessert of cardamom pound cake. Housed in a restored Craftsman-style home, The Refinery's cuisine may be refined, but its vibe is pure laid-back casual.

5137 N. Florida Ave. ℰ **813/281-0770.** www.thetamparefinery.com. Reservations recommended. Main courses $10–$20. AE, DC, DISC, MC, V. Tues–Thurs 5–10pm; Fri–Sat 5–11pm; Sun brunch 11am–3pm.

Whiskey Joe's Bar & Grill ★ BARBECUE Gorgeous ocean views trump the bar menu at Whiskey Joe's (formerly known as Castaway), where pan-seared grouper, whole snapper, po' boy sandwiches, fried chicken, and barbecue ribs reel in a steady crowd of locals and visitors alike. Insist on sitting on the deck and time your meal around sundown; the vantage point for sunsets here makes developers drool. Live reggae on Sunday and daily happy hours make Whiskey Joe's a popular gathering spot for locals.

7720 Courtney Campbell Causeway. ℰ **813/281-0770.** www.whiskeyjoestampa.com. Reservations recommended. Main courses $10–$20. AE, DC, DISC, MC, V. Daily 11am–11pm.

Wine Exchange ★★ MEDITERRANEAN This Tampa hot spot is an oenophile's dream come true, as each dish is paired with a particular wine available by the bottle or the glass. The menu is rather simple, featuring pizzas, pastas, salads, and sandwiches, but daily specials are more elaborate, including macadamia nut–crusted mahi, stuffed pork chop, or chili-rubbed flank steak. The outdoor patio is a great place to sit. There's almost always a wait—and free Wi-Fi—at this buzz-worthy eatery.

1611 W. Swan Ave. ✆ **813/254-9463.** www.wineexchangetampa.com. Main courses $17–$24; pizza and pasta $9–$18. AE, DC, DISC, MC, V. Mon–Fri 11:30am–10pm; Sat 11am–11pm; Sun 11am–9pm; brunch Sat–Sun 11am–3pm.

Inexpensive

Bella's Italian Cafe ★ ITALIAN While trendy restaurants come and go, Bella's has been open for more than 20 years and for good reason. A casual, rustic ambience with a wood-fired oven and indoor and outdoor seating attract a sophisticated crowd of foodies of all ages. The restaurant's authentic Italian fare is delicious, from the paper-thin carpaccio with garlic, olives, capers, and basil, to the old-fashioned spaghetti and meatballs. You can also create your own combination of pasta and sauce, choosing from a large list of options, or just order a pizza cooked in the oak-burning oven. Executive chef and co-owner Joanie Corneil studied cooking in Italy, and you can tell. For those who like a strong drink with their dinner, the Bellarita is a popular potion of Conmemorativo tequila and Grand Marnier. On second thought, save that for after dinner so you can at least appreciate your meal as it's going down!

1413 S. Howard Ave. ✆ **813/254-3355.** www.bellasitaliancafe.com. Reservations recommended. Main courses $13–$26; pizza $9–$12. AE, DC, DISC, MC, V. Mon–Wed 11:30am–11:30pm; Thurs 11:30am–12:30am; Fri 11:30am–1:30am; Sat 4pm–1:30am; Sun 4–11:30pm.

YBOR CITY
Moderate

Columbia Restaurant ★★★ SPANISH Columbia celebrated 100 years in 2005. Its tile building occupies an entire city block in the heart of Ybor City. Tourists flock here to soak up the ambience, and so do the locals because it's so much fun to clap along during the fire-belching Spanish flamenco floor shows Monday through Saturday evenings ($6 per person additional charge besides dinner charge). You can't help coming back time after time for the Spanish bean soup and original "1905" salad. The *paella a la Valencia* is outstanding, with more than a dozen ingredients ranging from shrimp to calamari, mussels, clams, chicken, and pork. Another favorite is *boliche* (eye of round stuffed with chorizo), accompanied by plantains and black beans and rice. Entrees come with a crispy hunk of Cuban bread with butter. Lighter appetites can choose from a 16-item tapas menu. The decor throughout is graced with hand-painted tiles, wrought-iron chandeliers, dark woods, rich red fabrics, and stained-glass windows.

2117 E. 7th Ave. (btw. 21st and 22nd sts.). ✆ **813/248-4961.** www.columbiarestaurant.com. Reservations recommended, especially for flamenco shows. Main courses $15–$30. AE, DC, DISC, MC, V. Mon–Thurs 11am–10pm; Fri–Sat 11am–11pm; Sun noon–9pm.

Inexpensive

Carmine's Seventh Avenue ★ CUBAN/ITALIAN/AMERICAN Bright blue poles hold up an ancient pressed-tin ceiling above this noisy corner cafe. It's not the cleanest joint in town, but a great variety of loyal local patrons gather here for genuine Cuban sandwiches—smoked ham, roast pork, Genoa salami, Swiss cheese, pickles, salad dressing, mustard, lettuce, and tomato on crispy Cuban bread. There's a vegetarian version, too. The combination of a half-sandwich and choice of black beans and rice or a bowl of Spanish soup made with sausages, potatoes, and garbanzo beans is a filling meal just by itself. Main courses are led by Cuban-style roast pork, thin-cut pork chops with mushroom sauce, spaghetti with a blue crab tomato sauce, and a few seafood and chicken platters.

1802 E. 7th Ave. (at 18th St.). © **813/248-3834.** Main courses $10–$20; sandwiches $5–$10. AE, MC, V. Mon–Tues 11am–11pm; Wed–Thurs 11am–1am; Fri–Sat 11am–3am; Sun 11am–6pm.

Tampa After Dark

The Tampa/Hillsborough Arts Council maintains an **Artsline** (© **813/229-2787**), a 24-hour information service providing the latest on current and upcoming cultural events. Racks in many restaurants and bars have copies of *Creative Loafing Tampa* (**www.tampa.creativeloafing.com**) and *Accent on Tampa Bay* (**www.ampubs.com**), two free publications detailing what's going on in the entire bay area. You can also check the "BayLife" and "Friday Extra" sections of the *Tampa Tribune* (**www.tampatrib.com**), as well as the Thursday "Weekend" section of the *St. Petersburg Times* (**www.sptimes.com**). The visitor center usually has copies of the week's newspaper sections (see "Essentials," earlier in this chapter).

THE CLUB, BAR & MUSIC SCENE Ybor City is Tampa's favorite nighttime venue. Stroll along 7th Avenue East between 15th and 20th streets, and you'll hear music blaring from the clubs. On Friday and Saturday, from 9pm to 3am, the avenue is packed with people, the majority high-school kids and early-20-somethings; but you'll also find something going on Tuesday through Thursday, and even on Sunday. The clubs change names frequently, so you don't need names, addresses, or phone numbers; your ears will guide you along 7th Avenue East. With all of the sidewalk seating, it's easy to judge what the clientele is like and make your choice from there. Another hipster haven is the Hyde Park area of town, where restaurant bars buzz with late-night activity. Most recently the downtown scene has been on the verge of a hipster takeover thanks to places like **Fly Bar & Restaurant** (see above) and a slew of new watering holes frequented by the young and fabulous. Among them: **Tapas Wine & Beer Merchants,** 777 N. Ashley Dr. (© **813/463-1968**); **Club Underground,** a popular hip-hop club at 802 E. Whiting St. (© **813/857-5872;** www.clubundergroundtampa.com); and **Kelly's Pub,** 206 N. Morgan St. (© **813/228-0870**).

And while downtown is still emerging, the center of all things nightlife still remains **Centro Ybor,** on 7th Avenue East at 16th Street (© **813/242-4660;** www.centroybor.com), the district's large dining-and-entertainment complex. The restaurants and pubs in this family-oriented center tend to be tamer than many of those along 7th Avenue, at least on nonweekend nights. You don't have to pay to listen to live music in the center's patio on weekend afternoons.

THE PERFORMING ARTS With a prime downtown location on 9 acres along the east bank of the Hillsborough River, the huge **David Straz Jr., Center for the Performing Arts ★**, 1010 N. MacInnes Place, next to the Tampa Museum of Art (© **800/955-1045** or 813/229-7827; www.strazcenter. org), is the largest performing arts venue south of the Kennedy Center. This four-theater complex is the focal point of Tampa's performing arts scene, presenting a wide range of theater, classical and pop concerts, operas, improvisation, and special events.

The restored **Tampa Theatre,** 711 Franklin St., between Zack and Polk streets (🕿 **813/274-8286;** www.tampatheatre.org), dates from 1926 and is on the National Register of Historic Places. It presents a varied program of classic, foreign, and alternative films, as well as concerts and special events (and it's said to be haunted!).

The 66,321-seat **Raymond James Stadium,** 4201 N. Dale Mabry Hwy. (🕿 **813/673-4300;** www.raymondjames.com/stadium), is sometimes the site of headliner concerts. The **USF Sun Dome,** 4202 E. Fowler Ave. (🕿 **813/974-3111;** www.sundome.org), on the University of South Florida campus, hosts major concerts by pop stars, rock bands, jazz groups, and other artists.

One of the busiest spots in town for live music, rustic-style, is **Skipper's Smokehouse,** 910 Skipper Rd. (🕿 **813/971-0666;** www. skipperssmokehouse.com), a Key West–style former smokehouse turned blues, jazz, zydeco, ska, and reggae hot spot.

Ticketmaster (🕿 **813/287-8844;** www.ticketmaster.com) sells tickets to most events and shows.

ST. PETERSBURG ★

20 miles SW of Tampa; 289 miles NW of Miami; 84 miles SW of Orlando

On the western shore of the bay, St. Petersburg stands in contrast to Tampa, much as San Francisco compares to Oakland. Whereas Tampa is the area's business, industrial, and shipping center, St. Petersburg was conceived and built a century ago primarily for tourists and snowbirds. Here you'll find one of the most picturesque and pleasant downtowns of any city in Florida, with a waterfront promenade and the famous inverted-pyramid-shaped Pier offering great views across the bay, quality museums, interesting shops, and a few good restaurants. Thanks to an urban redevelopment program, St. Pete has awoken from its slumber and actually resembles a city that could be considered hip, with renewed, restored streetscapes full of punk'd-out skateboarders, clubs, bars, and a vibrancy that goes beyond the excitement surrounding bingo night at the "adult" communities in town.

Essentials

GETTING THERE **Tampa International Airport,** approximately 16 miles northeast of St. Petersburg, is the prime gateway to the area (see "Essentials," earlier in this chapter). The primary carrier at **St. Petersburg–Clearwater International Airport,** on Roosevelt Boulevard (Fla. 686), about 10 miles north of downtown St. Petersburg (🕿 **727/453-7800;** www.fly2pie. com), is **Allegiant;** another carrier during the winter months is Canadian **Air Transat** (🕿 **877/872-6728;** www.airtransat.com). **Amtrak** (🕿 **800/ USA-RAIL** [872-7245]; www.amtrak.com) has bus connections from its Tampa station to downtown St. Petersburg. (See "Getting There," earlier in this chapter.)

VISITOR INFORMATION For information on St. Petersburg and the beaches before you leave, contact the **St. Petersburg/Clearwater Area Convention & Visitors Bureau,** 14450 46th St. N., Clearwater, FL 34622 (🕿 **800/345-6710,** or 727/464-7200 for hotel reservations; fax 727/464-7222; www.floridasbeach.com for information about the beaches).

After you arrive, you can head to the **St. Petersburg Area Chamber of Commerce,** 100 2nd Ave. N. (at 1st St.), St. Petersburg (© **727/821-4069;** fax 727/895-6326; www.stpete.com). Across the street from the BayWalk shopping-and-dining complex, this downtown main office and visitor center is open Monday through Friday from 8am to 5pm, Saturday from 10am to 4pm, and Sunday from noon to 4pm. Ask for a copy of the chamber's visitor guide, which lists hotels, motels, condominiums, and other accommodations.

Also downtown, you'll find walk-in **information centers** on the first level of the Pier and in the lobby of the Florida International Museum. The chamber also operates the **Suncoast Welcome Center,** 100 2nd Ave. N. (© **727/573-1449**). The center is open daily from 9am to 5pm except New Year's Day, Easter, Thanksgiving, and Christmas.

GETTING AROUND The **Pinellas Suncoast Transit Authority/PSTA** (© **727/530-9911;** www.psta.net) operates regular bus service through-out St. Petersburg and the rest of the Pinellas Peninsula. Rides cost $2 for adults, $1 for seniors, and $1.25 for students.

If you need a cab, call **Yellow Cab** (© **727/821-7777**), $2.25 at flag fall, $1 gas surcharge, and $2 each additional mile; or **Independent Cab** (© **727/327-3444**), $2 at flag fall, $2.20 each additional mile.

Seeing the Top Attractions

The Dalí Museum ★★★ This, well, surreal museum houses the world's most comprehensive (and most valuable, at $125 million) collection of works by the renowned Spanish surrealist. Housing six of the artist's masterworks, the muse-um was given three stars by the Michelin Guide. It includes oil paintings, water-colors, drawings, and more than 1,000 graphics, plus posters, photos, sculptures,

The St. Petersburg Pier provides a lovely view across the bay.

objets d'art, and a 5,000-volume library on Dalí and surrealism. Take one of the free docent-led tours to get the most out of the museum. In early 2011, the museum moved into a new, 66,450-square-foot facility north of its original location and more than twice the size. The building is a work of art, too, nicknamed "The Glass Enigma" and featuring 900 triangular-shaped glass panels—a 21st-century expression of Buckminster Fuller's geodesic dome, as utilized in Dalí's Teatro Museo in Figueres, Spain.

1 Dali Blvd. ✆ **727/823-3767.** www.thedali. org. Admission $17 adults, $15 seniors, $12 students, $4 children 5–9, free for children 4 and under, $5 for all Thurs 5–8pm. Mon–Wed and Fri–Sat 9:30am–5:30pm; Thurs 9:30am–8pm; Sun noon–5:30pm. Closed Thanksgiving and Christmas.

Visitors head up the spiral staircase at the Dalí Museum.

Florida Holocaust Museum ★ This thought-provoking museum has exhibits about the Holocaust (Jewish life before the Holocaust, the rise of the Nazi party, and so on), including a boxcar used to transport human cargo to Auschwitz and a gallery of art relating to the Holocaust. Its main focus, however, is to promote tolerance and understanding in the present. It was founded by Walter P. Loebenberg, a local businessman who escaped Nazi Germany in 1939 and fought with the U.S. Army in World War II.

55 5th St. S. (btw. Central Ave. and 1st Ave. S.). ✆ **800/960-7448** or 727/820-0100. www.fl holocaustmuseum.org. Admission $14 adults, $12 seniors, $10 college students, $8 students 17 and under, free for children 5 and under. Mon–Fri 10am–5pm; Sat–Sun noon–5pm (last admission at 4pm). Closed Easter, Rosh Hashanah, Yom Kippur, Thanksgiving, and Christmas.

Museum of Fine Arts ★★ Resembling a Mediterranean villa on the waterfront, this museum houses an excellent collection of European, American, pre-Columbian, and Far Eastern art, with works by such artists as Fragonard, Monet, Renoir, Cézanne, and Gauguin. Other highlights include period rooms with antique furnishings, plus a gallery of Steuben crystal, a new decorative-arts gallery, and world-class rotating exhibits. The best way to see it all is on a guided tour, which takes about 1 hour. Ask about classical-music performances from October to April.

255 Beach Dr. NE (at 3rd Ave. N.). ✆ **727/896-2667.** www.fine-arts.org. Admission $16 adults, $14 seniors 65 and over, $10 students with ID, free for children 6 and under (special exhibits cost

Open-Air Mail

St. Petersburg residents don't have to go inside to get mail out of their boxes at St. Petersburg's open-air **post office,** at the corner of **1st Avenue North** and **4th Street North.** Built in 1917, this granite, arcaded Spanish Colonial structure is a local landmark and is often photographed by those enchanted by its charm.

Downtown St. Petersburg

(i) Information
☒ Post Office

8th Ave. N.
7th Ave. N.
6th Ave. N.
5th Ave. N.
4th Ave. N.
3rd Ave. N.
2nd Ave. N.
1st Ave. N.
Central Ave.
1st Ave. S.
2nd Ave. S.
3rd Ave. S.
4th Ave. S.
5th Ave. S.
6th Ave. S.
14th Ave. S.

Round Lake Park
Coliseum Ballroom
Mirror Lake
Williams Park
Post Office
Vinoy Park
North Straub Park
South Straub Park
The Pier
Tampa Bay
Demens Landing Park
Progress Energy Park
Al Lang Field
Bayfront Center
Albert Whitted Park
ALBERT WHITTED AIRPORT (PRIVATE)
Poynter Park
Univ. of South Florida at St. Petersburg
Port of St. Petersburg

Beach Dr. NE
Bayshore Dr.
Beach Dr.
Bay St. SE

FLORIDA
St. Petersburg

0 — 1/4 mi
0 — .25 km

HOTELS
The Dickens House **3**
Hilton St. Petersburg Bayfront **11**
Mansion House Bed & Breakfast **5**
Vinoy Renaissance Resort and Golf Club **4**

RESTAURANTS
Chateau France **6**
Ceviche Tapas Bar & Restaurant **9**
Fourth Street Shrimp Store **1**
The Moon Under Water **7**
Red Mesa Cantina **14**

ATTRACTIONS
The Dalí Museum **12**
Florida Holocaust Museum **13**
Museum of Fine Arts **8**
The Pier **10**
Sunken Gardens **2**

extra). Admission includes guided tour. Tues–Sat 10am–5pm; Sun 1–5pm. Guided tours Tues–Sat 11am and 1, 2, and 3pm; Sun 1 and 2pm. Closed New Year's Day; Martin Luther King, Jr., Day; Thanksgiving; and Christmas.

Sunken Gardens Dating from 1935, this former tourist attraction is now operated as a 7-acre botanical garden by the city of St. Petersburg. It contains an array of 5,000 plants, flowers, and trees; a butterfly aviary; a display of snakes, spiders, and scorpions; and a rainforest information center. There's also a wildlife show. Call for a schedule.

1825 4th St. N. (btw. 18th and 19th aves. NE). © **727/551-3102.** www.stpete.org/sunken/index.asp. Admission $8 adults, $6 seniors, $4 children 2–11. Mon–Sat 10am–4:30pm; Sun noon–4:30pm.

Outdoor Activities & Spectator Sports

 Pier Around by Trolley

You can spend a small fortune in a parking garage or by feeding the meters in St. Petersburg, or you can cut costs substantially by parking at the **Pier** ($3 all day) and taking the **Looper,** the city's trolley service, which operates between the Pier and all major downtown attractions.

BIKING, IN-LINE SKATING & HIKING With miles of flat terrain, the St. Petersburg area is ideal for bikers, in-line skaters, and hikers. The **Pinellas Trail** is especially good, as it follows an abandoned railroad bed 47 miles from St. Petersburg north to Tarpon Springs (✆ 727/464-8201; www. pinellascounty.org/trailgd). The **St. Pete trail head** is on 34th Street South (U.S. 19), between 8th and Fairfield avenues south. It's packed on weekends. Free maps of the trail are available at the St. Petersburg Area Chamber of Commerce (see "Visitor Information," above). The 2½-mile-long **Friendship TrailBridge,** linking Tampa and St. Petersburg, is another popular venue for hikers, bikers, bicyclists, anglers, and in-line skaters, but be careful going up and down the steep center span, especially if you're on skates.

GOLF One of the nation's top 50 municipal courses, the **Mangrove Bay Golf Course ★★**, 875 62nd Ave. NE (✆ 727/893-7800), hugs Old Tampa Bay and offers 18-hole, par-72 play. Facilities include a driving range. Lessons and golf-club rental are also available. Fees are about $31 with cart, $23 without in winter, slightly lower during off season.

In Largo, the **Bardmoor Golf & Tennis Club,** 8001 Cumberland Rd. (✆ 727/392-1234; www.bardmoorgolf.com), is often the venue for major tournaments. Lakes punctuate 17 of the 18 holes on this par-72 championship course. Lessons and rental clubs are available, as is a Tom Fazio–designed practice range. Call for info on greens fees, which usually range from $25 to $75 depending on the season/time. The course is open daily from 7am to dusk.

Call **Tee Times USA** (✆ 800/374-8633; www.teetimesusa.com) to reserve times at these and other area courses.

For course information online, go to www.golf.com or www.florida golfing.com; or call the **Florida Sports Foundation** (✆ 850/488-8347) or **Florida Golfing** (✆ 866/833-2663).

SAILING Steve and Doris Colgate's **Offshore Sailing School** (✆ 888/454-8002 or 239/454-1700; www.offshore-sailing.com) and the **Annapolis Sailing School** (✆ 800/638-9192 or 727/867-8102; www.annapolis sailing.com) have operations here. Various courses, lasting from 2 days to a week, are offered. Contact the schools for prices and schedules.

SPECTATOR SPORTS St. Petersburg has always been a baseball town, and **Tropicana Field,** a 45,000-seat domed stadium alongside I-175 between 9th and 16th streets (✆ 727/825-3100), is the home of the American League's **Tampa Bay Rays** (✆ 888/326-7297 or 727/825-3137; http://tampabay. rays.mlb.com). Baseball season runs from April to October. Single-game tickets are $3 to $75 and are usually available on game days. Call or check the website for the schedule. The Rays moved outdoors to a new facility in Port Charlotte in 2009 for spring-training workouts and games from mid-February to March. See the team's website for more information.

The **Philadelphia Phillies** play their spring-training season in new digs in Clearwater, at Bright House Networks Field, 601 Old Coachman Rd. (© **727/442-8496**). Their minor-league affiliate, the **Clearwater Threshers** (© **727/441-8638;** www.threshersbaseball.com; $4–$9), plays in the stadium April through August. The **Toronto Blue Jays** do their spring thing at Knology Park, 311 Douglas Ave., in Dunedin (© **800/707-8269** or 813/733-9302; www.bluejays.mlb.com; $13–$70), which is also home to their minor-league affiliate, the **Dunedin Blue Jays** (© **727/733-9302;** www.dunedinbluejays.com), April through August.

A Town Runs Through It

The scenic **Pinellas Trail** happens to run right through downtown Dunedin, a charming Gulf Coast town known for fishing, beaching, and the Toronto Blue Jays' (see below) spring training. The 6-block downtown area is dotted with shops, restaurants, old-fashioned street lamps, and brick sidewalks, and it's a world apart from neighboring big-city Tampa and St. Pete. Just off the coast are Honeymoon and Caladesi islands (see later in this chapter). For more information contact the **Dunedin Chamber of Commerce** (© **727/733-3197;** www.dunedin-fl.com).

TENNIS You can learn to play or hone your game at the **Phil Green Tennis Academy,** at Safety Harbor Resort and Spa (p. 452).

Where to Stay

The **St. Petersburg/Clearwater Area Convention & Visitors Bureau** (see "Essentials," earlier in this section) operates a free **reservations service** (© **800/345-6710**), through which you can book rooms at most hotels and motels in St. Petersburg and at the beaches. The bureau also publishes a brochure that lists members of its Superior Small Lodgings program; these establishments have fewer than 50 rooms and have been inspected and certified for cleanliness and value.

Other than the Vinoy Renaissance Resort and Golf Club (see below), the only chain hotel downtown is the **Hilton St. Petersburg Bayfront,** 333 1st St. S., between 3rd and 4th avenues south (© **800/445-8667** or 727/894-5000; fax 727/823-4797), a 15-story convention hotel near the Salvador Dalí Museum, Florida Power Park at Al Lang Field, and the Bayfront Center's theaters.

Note: Sales and hotel taxes will add 13% to your bill.

EXPENSIVE

Vinoy Renaissance Resort and Golf Club ★★★ Built in 1925, this elegant Spanish-style establishment has hosted everyone from Jimmy Stewart to Bill Clinton, and is on the National Register of Historic Places after a total and meticulous $93-million restoration that made it, once again, the city's finest hotel. Dominating the northern part of downtown, it overlooks Tampa Bay and is within walking distance of the Pier, Central Avenue, and other attractions. All guest rooms, many with views of the bay, offer the utmost in comfort and include three phones, flatscreen TVs, and high-speed Internet access. Some rooms in the original building have standing-room-only balconies; if you need enough room to sit outside, request a balconied unit in the new Tower Wing. Overlooking the bay, **Marchand's Bar and Grill** serves award-winning American cuisine with a Floribbean flair. The Vinoy also has a steakhouse—**Fred's Chophouse**—12 tennis courts, an 18-hole golf course, a day spa, and a private marina. The hotel is nonsmoking.

501 5th Ave. NE (at Beach Dr.), St. Petersburg, FL 33701. www.marriott.com. ℂ **888/303-4430** or 727/894-1000. Fax 727/822-2785. 360 units. Winter $259–$525 double; off season $149–$329

ANCIENT BURIAL MOUNDS & manatees

Drive north of St. Petersburg for an hour on congested U.S. 19, and you'll come to one of Florida's original tourist attractions, the famous **Weeki Wachee Springs** (ℂ **877/469-3354** or 352/596-2062; www.weekiwachee.com). "Mermaids" (pictured at right) have been putting on acrobatic swimming shows here every day since 1947. It's a sight to see them doing their dances in waters that come from one of America's most prolific freshwater springs, pouring some 170 million gallons of 72°F (22°C) water each day into the river. There's more than mermaids here; you can also take a Wilderness River Cruise across the Weeki Wachee River and send the kids on the flume ride at Buccaneer Bay, the water park part of the attraction. Admission to Weeki Wachee only is $13 for adults, $5 for children 6 to 12. To Buccaneer Bay *and* Weeki Wachee, it's $26 for adults, $12 for children 6 to 12. Weeki Wachee Springs is open Monday through Thursday from 10am to 3pm, Friday through Sunday from 10am to 4pm. Buccaneer Bay water park is open only on Friday from 10am to 4pm, Saturday and Sunday from 10am to 5pm. Parking is free.

You can rent kayaks on the Weeki Wachee River for $30 for a one-person kayak, $35 for a two-person kayak, and $35 for a canoe per day (ℂ **352/597-0360**; www.floridacanoe.com).

From Weeki Wachee, travel 21 miles north to the **Homosassa Springs Wildlife State Park,** 4150 S. Suncoast Blvd. (U.S. 19), in Homosassa Springs (ℂ **352/628-5343;** www.florida stateparks.org/homosassasprings). The highlight here is a floating observatory where visitors can "walk" underwater and watch manatees in a rehabilitation facility, as well as see thousands of fresh- and saltwater fish. You'll also spot deer, bear, bobcats, otters, egrets, and flamingos along unspoiled nature trails. The park is open daily from 9am to 5:30pm (last tickets sold at 4pm). There are also very educational, entertaining wildlife programs, including the alligator and hippo program and the manatee program. Admission is $13 for adults and $5 for children 3 to 12; it includes a 20-minute narrated boat ride.

About 7 miles north of Homosassa Springs, more than 300 manatees spend the winter in Crystal River. You can **swim or snorkel with the manatees** ★★ in the warm-water natural spring of Kings Bay. **American Pro Diving Center,** 821 SE Hwy. 19, Crystal River (ℂ **800/291-3483** or 352/563-0041; www.americanprodive.com), offers daily swimming and snorkel tours. Early morning is the best time to see the manatees, so try to take the 6:30am departure. The trips range from $30 to $50 per person. Call for schedule and reservations. American Pro Diving also rents cottages on the Homosassa River.

Tour the Crystal River with Captain Russ Holliday's **Native Sun Tours** (ℂ **352/212-6142**) via a three-tiered airboat that glides over the shallow water.

double. Packages available. AE, DC, DISC, MC, V. Valet parking $18; self-parking $12. **Amenities:** 4 restaurants; 2 bars; concierge; golf course; health club; Jacuzzi; 2 heated outdoor pools; room service; spa; 12 tennis courts. *In room:* A/C, TV, hair dryer, Internet access, minibar.

MODERATE

The Dickens House ★★★ No relation to Charles Dickens, this Dickens House once belonged to Henry and Sadie Dickens, early St. Pete settlers.

For a sublime stay, the **Blue Moon Bed & Breakfast** (ⓒ 352/621-1960; www. thebluemoonbb.com), located amid the thick forest along the Homosassa River, offers themed rooms and a lodgelike lobby with fireplace from $155. Don't miss an afternoon in Heritage Village in downtown Crystal River, with delicious cafes including **Café on the Avenue** (ⓒ 352/795-3656; www.dineonthe avenue.com), known for the best three-layer banana-pineapple-pecan cake in the South, and **Back Porch Garden & Tea Bar** (ⓒ 352/564-1555; www.back porchgarden.com), where you can sip an iced tea under an oak tree.

Also check out the **Weedon Island Preserve,** 4801 37th St. S. (ⓒ 727/893-2627; www.weedon islandcenter.org), in the upper Tampa Bay waters of Pinellas County, on the western shore of the entrance to Old Tampa Bay directly west of Port Tampa.

The island was named for Dr. Leslie Weedon, a renowned authority on yellow fever, who acquired the 1,250-acre island in 1898 in what is now north St. Petersburg. Weedon had a fascination with Indian culture and developed a weekend retreat on the island, from which he began excavations that first revealed the importance of the site as an Indian burial mound. A Smithsonian expedition to the island in 1923 and 1924 further documented the importance, which is now managed as a county preserve. Today it's home to an assortment of fish, snakes, raccoons, and dolphins. Rent a canoe to explore, and find yourself "becoming one" with nature.

Baseball fans won't want to miss the **Ted Williams Museum & Hitters Hall of Fame,** Tropicana Field, One Tropicana Dr., St. Pete (ⓒ 352/527-6566; www.tedwilliamsmuseum.com). The museum holds the great hitter's personal memorabilia, including his two Triple Crown batting titles. The museum opens 2 hours before home games, and stays open through the last inning. Admission is exclusive to fans attending games at the stadium.

For more information about the area, contact the **Citrus County Chamber of Commerce,** 28 NW Hwy. 19, Crystal River, FL 34428 (ⓒ 352/795-3149; fax 352/795-4260; www.citruscountychamber.com). The chamber's visitor center is open Monday through Friday from 8:30am to 4:30pm, Saturday from 9am to 1pm.

Purchased in 1995 by mural artist Ed Caldwell, a graduate of the Rhode Island School of Design, the Dickens House was restored to its original Craftsman-style architecture. Caldwell goes above and beyond design to make this inn more than just a place to sleep. The charming inn has five guest rooms. The Cracker Suite has a custom-made bent-willow queen bed and a twin bed. The Orange Blossom Room, while the smallest in the house, nevertheless has a queen bed and a tiny bathroom with a whirlpool. Our personal fave is the second-floor Cottage Suite, which resembles a Victorian-age beach cottage with white wicker, sea-grass carpet, roll-up awnings, and nightstands displaying shells. It also sleeps three. All rooms but the cottage suite have whirlpool tubs. Don't miss complimentary snacks and wine every afternoon in the house's living room.

335 8th Ave. NE, St. Petersburg, FL 33701. www.dickenshouse.com. *©* **727/822-8622.** 5 units. Winter $129–$235 double; off season $109–$199 double. Rates include full breakfast. AE, DISC, MC, V. **Amenities:** Free use of guest computer with high-speed Internet. *In room:* A/C, TV/VCR/DVD, fridge, hair dryer, Wi-Fi.

Mansion House Bed & Breakfast ★★ Mirror images of each other, the two houses of Mansion House are separated by a landscaped courtyard and were built between 1901 and 1912. The comfortable living room in the main house, which has 6 of the 12 units, opens to a sunroom, off which a small screened porch provides mosquito-free lounging. Both houses have upstairs front parlors with TVs, DVDs, and libraries. Tall, old-fashioned windows let lots of light into the attractive guest rooms. The pick of the litter is the Pembroke Room, upstairs over the carriage house. It has a four-poster bed with mosquito netting, along with its own whirlpool tub in an outdoor screened hut. The brick courtyard garden between the two houses (there's a heated pool and Jacuzzi out there) is a popular spot for weddings and receptions. The rates include "wine time," with snacks and home-made cookies. There's also an on-site massage therapist and spa.

105 5th Ave. NE (at 1st St. NE), St. Petersburg, FL 33701. www.mansionbandb.com. *©* **800/274-7520** or 727/821-9391. Fax 727/821-6909. 12 units. $129–$250 double. Rates include full breakfast. AE, DC, DISC, MC, V. **Amenities:** Bike rentals; Jacuzzi; heated outdoor pool. *In room:* A/C, TV, hair dryer, Wi-Fi.

A NEARBY SPA

Safety Harbor Resort and Spa ★★ *✦* Hernando de Soto thought he found Ponce de León's fabled Fountain of Youth when, in 1539, he happened upon five mineral springs in what is now Safety Harbor on the western shore of Old Tampa Bay (see the "Tampa & St. Petersburg" map on p. 422). You may not recover your youth at this venerable, 50,000-square-foot spa, the recipient of a multimillion-dollar renovation, but you will be rejuvenated. The healing mineral springs are the site of acclaimed water-fitness programs. There's also a tennis academy. The complex of beige-stucco buildings with Spanish-tile roofs offers upgraded rooms with new furniture and understated, yet crisp, soothing shades of tropical earth tones. It sits on 22 waterfront acres in the sleepy town of Safety Harbor, north of St. Petersburg, with a number of shops and restaurants just steps away.

105 N. Bayshore Dr., Safety Harbor, FL 34695. www.safetyharbor-resort.com. *©* **888/237-8772** or 727/726-1161. Fax 727/724-7749. 175 units. Winter $169–$359 double; off season $149–$259 double; year-round from $345 suite. Packages available. AE, DC, DISC, MC, V. Valet parking $12; self-parking free. **Amenities:** 2 restaurants; lobby cocktail lounge; free use of bikes; fitness center (w/classes); 3 indoor/outdoor pools; room service; spa; 9 tennis courts. *In room:* A/C, TV, hair dryer, high-speed Internet access.

Where to Dine

Don't overlook the food court at the **Pier,** where the inexpensive chow is accompanied by a rich, but free, view of the bay. Among the Pier's restaurants is a branch of Tampa's famous **Columbia Restaurant** (✆ **727/822-8000**; p. 442).

EXPENSIVE

Chateau France ★★ CLASSICAL FRENCH Chef Antoine Louro provides St. Petersburg's most romantic setting in this cozy Victorian house built in 1910. He specializes in French classics such as homemade pâté, Dover sole meunière, filet mignon au poivre, coq au vin, and rich seafood bouillabaisse. The wine list is excellent, as are the bananas flambé and crêpes suzette.

136 4th Ave. N. (btw. Bayshore Dr. and 1st St. N.). ✆ **727/894-7163.** www.chateaufranceonline. com. Reservations recommended. Main courses $23–$43. AE, DC, DISC, MC, V. Daily 5–11pm.

MODERATE

Ceviche Tapas Bar & Restaurant ★★ TAPAS A bustling see-and-be-seen spot in downtown St. Pete, Ceviche is a hot spot thanks to pitchers of the area's best sangria and a selection of 45 tapas for all taste buds, reflecting traditional dishes from the small tapas bars in old Spain. All contain the purest sherry, almonds, tomatoes, garlic, olive oil, olives, Spanish ham, cheeses, great mussels, sea bass, pork, and quail. There's also live flamenco and late-night dining, making it a haven for area hipsters. A Tampa outpost is at 2109 Bayshore Blvd. (✆ **813/250-0134**) and there are also locations in Orlando, Sarasota, and Clearwater.

95 Central Ave. ✆ **727/209-2302.** www.cevichetapas.com. Reservations recommended. Tapas $5–$15; paellas $19–$30. AE, DC, DISC, MC, V. Tues–Sat 5pm–2am (tapas served until 12:30am); Sun 5–10pm.

Chouinard's Cuisine ★★★ ECLECTIC Chef Joseph Chouinard cooked for Madonna. But what earns him the acclaim is his cooking, not his clientele. An eclectic, constantly changing menu with a global theme is what makes this place one of the best to hit St. Petersburg in a long time. Dishes are artfully presented, but don't fret over ruining the visuals—Chouinard's food is meant to be eaten. On the heavier, yet savory side is a roast rack of lamb crusted in macadamia nuts and served with a side of pineapple-mint chutney. For lighter, yet no less delicious fare, try the grouper Francaise, lightly battered and fried and topped with a lemon-caper butter or the hearty lobster roll full of fresh chunks of meat. The place is located in a strip mall, but if you're looking for fantastic food, you'll forget the location.

9617 Bay Pines Blvd. (across from Bay Pines VA Medical Center). ✆ **727329-8717.** www. chouinardscuisine.com. Reservations recommended. Main courses $15–$26. AE, DC, DISC, MC, V. Tues–Sat 5–9pm.

INEXPENSIVE

Fourth Street Shrimp Store ★★ 🐟 SEAFOOD If you're anywhere in the area, drive by to see the colorful, cartoonlike mural on the outside of this eclectic and casual establishment just north of downtown. On first impression, it looks like graffiti, but it's a gigantic drawing of people eating. Inside it gets even better, with paraphernalia and murals on two walls that make the main dining room seem like a warehouse with windows that look onto an early-19th-century seaport (one painted sailor permanently peers in to see what you're eating). You'll pass a seafood market counter when you enter, from which comes the fresh shrimp, the star here. You can also pick from grouper, clam strips, catfish, or oysters fried, broiled, or steamed, all served in heaping portions. This is the best and certainly the most interesting bargain in town. There's limited outdoor seating.

1006 4th St. N. (at 10th Ave. N.). ✆ **727/822-0325.** www.theshrimpstore.com. Main courses $8–$19; sandwiches $5–$12. MC, V. Daily 11am–9pm.

The Moon Under Water ★ ASIAN/BRITISH/MIDDLE EASTERN/AMERI-CAN Tables on the veranda or sidewalk in front of this waterfront pub are a great place to take a break downtown. The British Raj rules supreme inside the dark-paneled dining room with its slowly twirling ceiling fans and colonial arti-facts, including obligatory pith helmets. The bill of fare covers a number of for-mer British outposts, including America (burgers and Philly cheesesteaks), but the emphasis is on mild, medium, or blazing-hot Indian curries—with a recom-mended Irish, British, or Australian beer to slake the resulting thirst. For lighter fare, consider Middle Eastern tabbouleh. There's live music on weekends.

332 Beach Dr. NE (btw. 3rd and 4th aves.). ✆ **727/896-6160.** www.themoonunderwater.com. Main courses $11–$20; sandwiches and salads $7.50–$12. AE, DC, DISC, MC, V. Sun–Thurs 11:30am–11pm; Fri–Sat 11:30am–midnight. Closed New Year's Day, Thanksgiving, and Christmas.

Red Mesa Cantina ★★ MEXICAN Although the vibe at this hip, downtown Mexican restaurant is unpretentious, the food's good enough to have a bit of at-titude. Salsa and guacamole are made fresh and are addictive, as is the stuffed shrimp with chipotle sauce. The Grouper Al Mojo De Ajo sautéed with garlic, tomato, parsley, and chile arbol is a refreshing, spicy twist on our favorite Florida grouper and should not be missed if you are a fan of the fish. The menu is cre-ative and not your typical Mexican combo-plate fare; we highly doubt you'll see duck enchiladas and filet mignon *chimichurri* at your corner chips and salseria! We threw in an extra star for the restaurant's amazing outdoor, brick-walled and fountained courtyard and bustling bar scene. There's another, less sceney Red Mesa at 4912 4th St. N. (✆ **727/527-8728**), but for that one we'd take a star off.

128 3rd St. S. (✆ **727/510-0034.** www.redmesarestaurant.com. Reservations not taken Fri–Sat. Main courses $13–$25. AE, DC, DISC, MC, V. Mon–Thurs 11am–9:30pm; Fri–Sat 11am–10:30pm; Sun 9am–9pm.

Skyway Jack's ★ BREAKFAST This is a real down-home country kitchen with kitsch *and* outstanding breakfast fare. *Food Network Magazine* declared Skyway Jack's the best breakfast place in Florida for its famous, somewhat in-scrutable "scrapple" dish—a concoction of pretty much every part of a pig you'd normally never eat. We tried it and weren't impressed, but see for yourselves. You can always start the day off with eggs Florentine, stuffed French toast, even sweetbreads and eggs; or go old school with eggs, grits, hash browns, and biscuits 'n' gravy. For early risers or late-night partiers, Skyway Jack's greases its griddle starting at 5am. There's a **Skyway Jack's Pancake House,** 11140 4th St. N., St. Petersburg (✆ **727/576-2900**), which serves 95% of the menu at the origi-nal, but some die-hard devotees say it's nothing like the original.

2795 34th St. S. ✆ **727/867-1907.** Main courses $3–$10. No credit cards (but there's an ATM on the premises). Daily 5am–3pm.

St. Petersburg After Dark

Good sources of nightlife information are the Thursday "Weekend" section of the *St. Petersburg Times* (**www.sptimes.com**), the "BayLife" and "Friday Extra" sections of the *Tampa Tribune* (**www.tampatrib.com**), and *Creative Loafing Tampa* (**www.tampa.creativeloafing.com**), a tabloid available at visitor centers and in many hotel and restaurant lobbies.

The bars on Central Ave. and 3rd and 4th Streets are the heart of downtown's nighttime scene. Avoid the bleak **BayWalk,** an aspiring shopping-dining-entertainment complex bordered by 1st and 2nd streets and 2nd and 3rd avenues north with more SPACE AVAILABLE signs than shops, dining, or entertainment.

THE BAR, CLUB & MUSIC SCENE Ever since St. Pete started upping its hipster quotient, cool bars began appearing. Among them are **A Taste for Wine,** 241 Central Ave. (© 727/895-1623; www.tasteforwine.net), an upscale spot with polished woods and a granite bar offering terrific by-the-glass vintages, appetizers, and a gorgeous outdoor balcony; the **Haymarket Pub,** 8308 4th St. N. (© 727/577-9621), the gay-friendly "Cheers" of St. Pete, where audible conversation and reasonably priced drinks aren't implausible demands; **Jannus Landing Courtyard,** 16 2nd St. N. (© 727/896-2276; www.jannuslandingconcerts.com), a fantastic outdoor concert venue and bar; **Ringside Cafe,** 2742 4th St. N. (© 727/894-8465), a laid-back jazz and blues bar; and **Push Ultra Lounge,** 128 3rd St. S. (© 727/871-7874), a bi-level, 10,000-square-foot upscale dance club with a fabulous rooftop deck overlooking the city.

A historic attraction, the Moorish-style **Coliseum Ballroom,** 535 4th Ave. N. (© 727/892-5202; www.stpete.org/coliseum), has been hosting dancing, big bands, boxing, and other events since 1924 (it even made an appearance in the 1985 movie *Cocoon*). Come out and watch the town's many seniors jitterbug as if it were 1945 again! Call for schedule and prices.

THE PERFORMING ARTS The **Bayfront Center,** 400 1st St. S. (© 727/892-5767,** or 892-5700 for information), houses the 8,100-seat Bayfront Arena and the 2,000-seat Mahaffey Theater (www.mahaffeytheater.com). The schedule includes a variety of concerts, Broadway shows, big bands, ice shows, and circus performances. **Ticketmaster** (© 813/287-8844) sells tickets to most events and shows.

Tropicana Field, 1 Stadium Dr. (© 727/825-3100), has a capacity of 50,000, but also hosts smaller events when the Rays aren't playing baseball.

ST. PETE & CLEARWATER BEACHES ★★

St. Pete Beach: 20 miles SW of Tampa; 289 miles NW of Miami; 84 miles SW of Orlando. Clearwater Beach: 90 miles W of Orlando; 20 miles W of Tampa; 20 miles N of St. Petersburg.

If you're looking for sun and sand, you'll find plenty on the 28 miles of slim barrier islands that skirt the Gulf shore of the Pinellas Peninsula. With some one million visitors every year, don't be surprised if you have lots of company. But you'll also discover quieter neighborhoods and some of the nation's finest beaches, including some protected from development by parks and nature preserves.

At the southern end of the strip, St. Pete Beach is the granddaddy of the area's resorts: Visitors started coming here a century ago, and they haven't quit. Today St. Pete Beach is heavily developed and often overcrowded during the winter season. If you like high-rises and mile-a-minute action (albeit before 9pm, when things start to slow down a bit), St. Pete Beach is for you. But even here, Pass-a-Grille, on the island's southern end, is a quiet residential enclave with eclectic shops and a fine, though crowded, public beach.

A more gentle lifestyle begins to the north on the 3½-mile-long Treasure Island. From here, you cross John's Pass to Sand Key, a 12-mile-long island occupied primarily by residential Madeira Beach, Redington Shores, Indian Shores, Indian Rocks Beach, and Belleair Beach. The road crosses a soaring bridge to Clearwater Beach, whose sands attract active families and couples.

If you like your great outdoors unfettered by development, the jewels here are **Fort DeSoto Park,** south of St. Pete Beach at the mouth of Tampa Bay, and **Caladesi Island State Park,** north of Clearwater Beach. They are consistently rated among America's top beaches. **Sand Key Park,** on the southern shores of Little Pass (which separates Clearwater Beach from Belleair Beach), is one of Florida's finest local beach parks.

Essentials

GETTING THERE See "Getting There" (p. 444) for information on getting to the beaches.

VISITOR INFORMATION See "Visitor Information" (p. 444) for the St. Petersburg/Clearwater Area Convention & Visitors Bureau and the St. Petersburg Area Chamber of Commerce. The visitor bureau's website, at www.floridasbeach.com, has information specific to the beaches.

Once you're here, you can get beach info at the **Gulf Beaches of Tampa Bay Chamber of Commerce,** 6990 Gulf Blvd. (at 70th Ave.), St. Pete Beach (© **800/944-1847** or 727/360-6957; fax 727/360-2233; www.tampabaybeaches.com). It's open Monday through Friday from 9am to 5pm.

For information on Clearwater Beach, contact the **Clearwater Regional Chamber of Commerce,** 1130 Cleveland St., Clearwater, FL 33755 (© **727/461-0011;** fax 727/449-2889; www.clearwaterflorida.org). You can also walk into the **Clearwater Visitor Information Center,** on Causeway Boulevard in the lobby of the Clearwater Beach Marina Building (© **727/462-6531**). It's open Monday through Saturday from 9am to 5pm, Sunday from 1 to 5pm.

GETTING AROUND The **Pinellas Suncoast Transit Authority/PSTA** (© **727/ 530-9911;** www.psta.net) operates motorized trolley service along Gulf Boulevard (Fla. 699) between the Hurricane restaurant (p. 466) in St. Pete Beach and the Sheraton Sand Key Resort (the one-way trip takes about an hour), where it connects with the **Suncoast Beach Trolley** (© **727/445-1200**), which continues on Gulf Boulevard through Clearwater Beach. The PSTA trolley runs daily, every 20 minutes from 5am to 10pm, until midnight on Friday and Saturday. Rides cost $1.75, or you can buy a daily pass for $4. Call for schedules, or pick up printed copies at the Gulf Beaches of Tampa Bay Chamber of Commerce.

Along the beach, the major cab company is **BATS Taxi** (✆ 727/367-3702). Fares are $2.50 at flag fall, plus $2.40 each additional mile.

Hitting the Beach

This entire stretch of coast is one long beach, but because hotels, condominiums, and private homes occupy much of it, you may want to sun and swim at one of the public parks. The best are described below, but there's also the fine **Pass-a-Grille Public Beach,** on the southern end of St. Pete Beach, where you can watch the boats going in and out of Pass-a-Grille Channel and quench your thirst at the Hurricane restaurant (p. 466). This and all other Pinellas County public beaches have metered parking lots, so bring a supply of quarters. There are public restrooms along the beach.

Sand Key Park ★, on the northern tip of Sand Key facing Clearwater Beach, sports a wide beach and gentle surf, and is relatively off the beaten path in this commercial area. It's a great place to go for a morning walk or jog. The park is open from 8am to dark and has restrooms. Admission is free, but the parking lot has meters. For more information, call ✆ **727/464-3347.**

Clearwater Public Beach (also known as Pier 60; www.pier60fishing. com) has beach volleyball, watersports rentals, lifeguards, restrooms, showers, and concessions. The swimming is excellent, and there's a fishing pier with a bait-and-tackle shop, plus a children's playground and a legendary nightly sunset celebration that features local merchants, musicians, and artists. There's a 50¢ walk-on admission fee. Daily fishing fees are $8 for adults, $6.75 for seniors, and $5.25 for children 5 to 15. Rod rental is $8. There's metered parking in lots across the street from the Clearwater Beach Marina, a prime base for boating, cruises, and other water activities (see "Outdoor Activities," below). A less crowded spot in Clearwater Beach is at the Gulf end of Bay Esplanade.

CALADESI ISLAND STATE PARK ★★★

Occupying a 3½-mile-long island north of Clearwater Beach, **Caladesi Island State Park** boasts one of Florida's top beaches—a lovely, relatively secluded stretch with fine, soft sand edged in sea grass and palmettos. Dolphins often cavort in the waters offshore. In the park is a nature trail, where you might see rattlesnakes, raccoons, armadillos, or rabbits. A concession stand, a ranger station, and bathhouses (with restrooms and showers) are available. Caladesi Island is accessible only by ferry from **Honeymoon Island State Recreation Area,** which is connected by Causeway Boulevard (Fla. 586) to Dunedin, north of Clearwater. As for the name, well, the pioneers called it Hog Island, but in 1939 when a New York developer built 50 palm-thatched bungalows for honeymooners, its name was forever changed for the better.

You'll first have to pay the admission to Honeymoon Island: $8 per vehicle with two to eight occupants, $4 per single-occupant vehicle, $2 for a pedestrian or bicyclist. Beginning daily at 10am, the ferry (✆ **727/734-5263**) departs Honeymoon Island every hour. Round-trip rides cost $10 for adults, $6 for kids ages 4 to 12.

Neither Caladesi nor Honeymoon allows camping, but pets are permitted in the inland and on South Beach (bring a leash and use it at all times). The two parks are open daily from 8am to sunset and are administered by Gulf Islands Geopark, 1 Causeway Blvd., Dunedin, FL 34698 (✆ **727/469-5918;** www.floridastateparks.org/caladesiisland and www.floridastateparks.org/honeymoonisland).

St. Pete & Clearwater Beaches

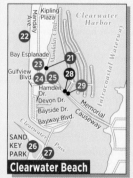

Clearwater Beach

Caladesi Island's beaches are for the birds.

FORT DESOTO PARK ★★★

South of St. Pete Beach at the very mouth of Tampa Bay, **Fort DeSoto Park** encompasses all of Mullet Key, set aside by Pinellas County as a 900-acre bird, animal, and plant sanctuary. Besides the stunning white-sugar sand, it is best known for a Spanish-American War–era fort, which has a museum that's open daily from 9am to 4pm. Other diversions include fishing from piers (7am–11pm), large playgrounds for kids, and 4 miles of trails winding through the park for in-line skaters, bicyclists, and joggers. Park rangers conduct nature and history tours, and you can rent canoes and kayaks to explore the winding mangrove channels along the island's bay side. The park has changing rooms and restrooms as well.

Sitting by itself on a heavily forested island, the park's **campground ★★** is one of Florida's most picturesque (many sites are beside the bay). It's such great camping that the 233 tent and RV sites usually are sold out, especially on weekends, so it's best to reserve well in advance. But there are a few catches: You must appear in person no more than 30 days in advance at the campground office, at 631 Chestnut St. in Clearwater, or at 150 5th St. N. in downtown St. Petersburg. You must pay when you make your reservation, in cash or by traveler's check (no credit cards or personal checks). And you must reserve for at least 2 nights, but you can stay no more than 14 nights in any 30-day period. Sites cost $30 to $41. All sites have water and electricity hookups.

Entry to the park is free. It's open daily from 8am to dusk, although campers and persons fishing from the piers can stay later. To get here, take the Pinellas Bayway (50¢ toll) east from St. Pete Beach and follow Florida 679 (35¢ toll) and the signs south to the park. For more information, contact the park at 3500 Pinellas Bayway, Tierra Verde, FL 33715 (© **727/582-2267;** www.pinellas county.org/park/05_Ft_DeSoto.htm).

Outdoor Activities

BOATING, FISHING & OTHER WATERSPORTS You can indulge in parasailing, boating, deep-sea fishing, wave running, sightseeing, dolphin-watching, water-skiing, and just about any other waterborne diversion your heart could desire in the St. Pete and Clearwater beaches area. All you have to do is head to one of two beach locations: **Hubbard's Marina,** at John's Pass Village and Boardwalk (© **800/755-0677** or 727/393-1947; www.

hubbardsmarina.com), in Madeira Beach on the southern tip of Sand Key; or **Clearwater Beach Marina,** at Coronado Drive and Causeway Boulevard (✆ **800/772-4479** or 727/461-3133), which is at the beach end of the causeway leading to downtown Clearwater. Agents in booths there will give you the schedules and prices (expect to pay $35–$65 for a half-day of fishing on a large party boat, $65–$100 for a full day), answer any questions you have, and make reservations, if necessary.

SCUBA DIVING You can dive on reefs and wrecks with **Dive Clearwater** (✆ **800/875-3483** or 727/443-6731; www.divingclearwater.com), which also operates manatee, scalloping, and fishing tours. Call for schedules and prices.

Attractions on Land

Clearwater Marine Aquarium ★★ ☺ This little jewel of an aquarium on Clearwater Harbor is low-key and friendly; it's dedicated to the rescue and rehabilitation of marine mammals and sea turtles. Exhibits include otters, sea turtles, sharks, stingrays, mangroves, and sea grass. There's a slew of education programs too, from dolphin encounters to trainer-for-a-day programs. A popular attraction is the **Sea Life Safari,** a 2-hour boat trip that scouts dolphins, sea birds, and other marine life en route to a shell island. Tickets are $23 adults, $20 seniors, and $15 for children 3 to 12. Combo packages are available. One of the star residents is Winter, a dolphin rescued off the east coast of Florida who wasn't expected to survive after losing her tail. Not only did she survive, and learn to swim with a prosthesis, but she inspired *Dolphin Tale,* a full-length 3D film due out in September 2011, starring Winter, along with Morgan Freeman, Ashley Judd, Kris Kristofferson, and Harry Connick, Jr. Expect a surge of interest (and visitors) when the film comes out.

249 Windward Passage, Clearwater Beach. ✆ **888/239-9414** or 727/441-1790. www.seewinter. com. Admission $15 adults, $11 seniors, $10 children 3–12, free for children 2 and under. Sea Life Safari/admission combo tickets $38 adults, $35 seniors, $29 children 3–12. Mon–Thurs 9am–5pm; Fri–Sat 9am–8pm; Sun 10am–5pm. The aquarium is off the causeway btw. Clearwater and Clearwater Beach; follow the signs.

Rescue and rehabilitation is the focus of the Clearwater Marine Aquarium.

John's Pass Village and Boardwalk Casual and charming, albeit too touristy, this Old Florida, turn-of-the-20th-century fishing village on John's Pass consists of a string of wooden structures topped by tin roofs and connected by a 1,000-foot boardwalk. Most have been converted into shops, art galleries, restaurants, and saloons. The focal points are the boardwalk and marina, where many water-sports are available for visitors (see "Outdoor Activities," above). If you don't go out on the water, enjoy an alfresco lunch—**Sculley's** (℃ **727/393-7749;** www.sculleysrestaurant.com) is the best restaurant here—and watch the boats go in and out of the pass.

12901 Gulf Blvd. (at John's Pass), Madeira Beach. ℃ **800/944-1847** or 727/394-0756. www.johnspass.com. Free admission. Shops and activities daily 9am–6pm or later.

Suncoast Seabird Sanctuary ★ At any one time, there are usually more than 500 sea and land birds living at this sanctuary, from cormorants, white herons, and birds of prey to the ubiquitous brown pelican. The nation's largest wild-bird hospital, dedicated to the rescue, medical care, recuperation, and release of sick and injured wild birds, is also here.

18328 Gulf Blvd., Indian Shores. ℃ **727/391-6211.** www.seabirdsanctuary.com. Free admission; donations welcome. Daily 9am–sunset. Free tours Wed and Sun 2pm.

Where to Stay

St. Pete Beach and Clearwater Beach have national chain hotels and motels of every name and description. You can use the St. Petersburg/Clearwater Convention & Visitors Bureau's free **reservations service** (℃ **800/345-6710**) to book rooms at most of them. The **St. Petersburg Area Chamber of Commerce** (p. 449) lists a wide range of hotels, motels, condominiums, and other accommodations in its annual visitor guide, and also publishes a brochure listing members of its Superior Small Lodgings program.

As is the case throughout Florida, there are more short- and long-term rental condominiums than hotel rooms here. Many of them are in high-rise buildings right on the beach. Among local rental agents, **JC Resort Management,** 17200 Gulf Blvd., North Redington Beach, FL 33708 (℃ **800/535-7776** or 727/397-0441; fax 727/397-8894; www.jcresort.com), has many from which to choose.

ST. PETE BEACH

Very Expensive

Don CeSar Beach Resort, A Loews Hotel ★★★ ☺ This Moorish-style "Pink Palace" on the National Register of Historic Places has a rich history and appeals to groups, families, and couples. Sitting majestically on 7½ acres of beachfront, this landmark sports a lobby of classic high windows and archways, crystal chandeliers, marble floors, and original artwork. Some of the 275 rooms under the minarets of the original building may seem small, but they offer views of the Gulf or Boca Ciega Bay. Some have balconies. If you want more space but less charm, go for one of the resort's 70 luxury condominiums in the **Don CeSar Beach House,** a midrise building ¾ mile to the north (there's 24-hr. complimentary transportation between the two). Two beachfront pools and a spa make relaxing very easy. An excellent kids' program features supervised activities, including cake decorating classes with the hotel's pastry chef who, incidentally, makes nearly 300 wedding cakes a year at the hotel.

3400 Gulf Blvd. (at 34th Ave./Pinellas Byway), St. Pete Beach, FL 33706. www.doncesar.com. ☏ **866/728-2206** or 727/360-1881. Fax 727/367-6952. 277 units. Winter $279–$541 double, $393–$3,000 suite; off season $189–$429 double, $299–$2,000 suite. Packages available. AE, DC, DISC, MC, V. Valet parking $20 overnight, $13–$18 day; self-parking free. Pet-friendly. **Amenities:** 4 restaurants; 4 bars; babysitting; children's programs; concierge; exercise room; Jacuzzi; 2 heated outdoor pools; room service; spa; watersports equipment/rentals. *In room:* A/C, TV, hair dryer, minibar, Wi-Fi.

Expensive

Sirata Beach Resort & Conference Center ★ A ton of money was spent a few years ago to completely renovate this older property and bring it up to second-tier status, on par with the TradeWinds Island Grand Resort, but below that of Don CeSar Beach Resort & Spa. A yellow-and-green Old Florida–style facade now disguises the eight-story main building, which houses (all nonsmoking) hotel rooms and one-bedroom suites upstairs (upper-level units have nice views), and a convention center. Some guest rooms in this two-story building face the courtyard, but the choice quarters are the Gulf-side rooms, the only units with patios or balconies opening directly onto the beach. The most spacious units are efficiencies and one-bedroom suites in two-story buildings; they all have kitchenettes, but they look out primarily on parking lots. For activities, there are three pools, beachfront cabanas, hammocks, a beach bar, a restaurant, and beach volleyball. Sirata was recently awarded a Green Lodging certification, too.

5300 Gulf Blvd. (at 53rd Ave.), St. Pete Beach, FL 33706. www.sirata.com. ☏ **727/363-5100.** Fax 727/363-5195. 380 units, including 170 suites. Summer, fall, winter $134–$224 double, $164–$444 suite; spring $199–$269 double, $229–$489 suite. AE, DC, DISC, MC, V. **Amenities:** 2 restaurants; 4 bars; concierge; exercise room; 3 heated outdoor pools; room service; watersports equipment/rentals. *In room:* A/C, TV/DVD, CD player, hair dryer, kitchen, Wi-Fi.

TradeWinds Island Grand Resort ★ ☺ Don't be dismayed by the outward appearance of this six- and seven-story concrete-and-steel monstrosity, for underneath and beside it runs a maze of brick walkways, patios, and lily ponds connected by a quarter-mile of waterways. Many of the guest units, which look out on the Gulf or the 20 acres of grounds, have full kitchenettes, and most have private balconies. Choice units face the Gulf, but this hotel has a variety of accommodations, so consult the reservations advisor when booking. Although the resort draws large meetings and conventions, it's a big hit with families too. It's not a fancy place, but when it comes to beach hotels, this one's location can't be beat. One of the four heated pools is reserved for adults, and there's lots more to keep grown-ups busy, including a fun **bar** with live music, and free use of paddleboats. A massive renovation in 2010–11 spruced up the rooms and brought them up to 21st-century speed with flatscreen TVs and new everything. For a quieter, more intimate experience, check out the resort's sister property, **TradeWinds Sandpiper Suites,** 6000 Gulf Blvd. (☏ **800/237-0707**), where winter rates go from $269 to $323 double, $373 to $409 suite, and off season $195 to $246 double and $296 to $308 suite.

5500 Gulf Blvd. (at 55th Ave.), St. Pete Beach, FL 33706. www.justletgo.com. ☏ **800/237-0707** or 727/363-2212. Fax 727/363-2222. 584 units. Winter $269–$409 double, $366–$528 suite; off season $195–$329 double, $287–$421 suite. Packages, special rates, and offers available year-round. AE, DC, DISC, MC, V. Valet parking $8; self-parking free. **Amenities:** 7 restaurants; 3 lounges; children's programs; concierge; mini-golf; fitness center; Jacuzzi; 4 heated outdoor pools; room service; sauna; spa services; 2 tennis courts; watersports equipment/rentals. *In room:* A/C, TV, fridge, hair dryer, Wi-Fi.

Moderate

Island's End Resort ★★★ 🏖 A wonderful respite from the crowds, and a great bargain to boot, this little all-cottage hideaway sits right on the southern tip of St. Pete Beach, smack-dab on Pass-a-Grille, where the Gulf of Mexico meets Tampa Bay. Because the island curves sharply here, nothing will block your view of the emerald bay. Strong currents run through the pass, but you can safely swim in the Gulf or watch a brilliant sunset at the Pass-a-Grille's public beach, just one door removed. Linked to one another by boardwalks, the comfortable one- and three-bedroom cottages have dining areas, living rooms, VCRs and DVD players, and fully equipped kitchens. You will love the one monstrous unit with two living rooms (one can be converted to sleeping quarters), two bathrooms (one with a whirlpool tub and separate shower), and private bayside swimming pool. Maid service is available on request.

1 Pass-a-Grille Way (at 1st Ave.), St. Pete Beach, FL 33706. www.islandsend.com. 📞 **727/360-5023.** Fax 727/367-7890. 6 units. Winter $192–$354 cottage; off season $148–$354 cottage. Weekly rates available. Complimentary breakfast Tues, Thurs, and Sat. MC, V. **Amenities:** Free Wi-Fi. *In room:* A/C, TV/DVD/VCR, hair dryer, kitchen, Wi-Fi.

Postcard Inn on the Beach ★★★ 🏖 Created as a "Vintage American Getaway," Postcard Inn on the Beach was trendy before it opened in the fall of 2009 thanks to the fact that its owner founded a slew of NYC restaurant hot spots and the trendy James Hotel chain in Scottsdale. But there's nothing dry about this place, located on a prime stretch of St. Pete beachfront. Rooms are done up in surfer-chic decor with quirky refurbished surfer gear, vintage lighting, and plush bedding. Though each room comes with the usual trappings of modernity—flatscreen TVs and the like—no two rooms are alike. Rooms overlook the Gulf, garden, or pool. If you choose a room with a private poolside patio, expect to hear noise coming from the pool, which was created with the words *pool party* in mind. Because Postcard Inn was designed with youth culture in mind, as low-key as it is, it's also party central thanks to its fun and funky **PCI Beach Bar and Snack Shack,** featuring fabulous Gulf views and live music, and its restaurant, **Wildwood BBQ & Burger,** featuring slow-smoked fare from skilled Pit Master Big Lou Elrose. Whether you want to relax in a hammock, sit by the fire pit, watch a movie on the sun deck, play beach volleyball, or do nothing, we highly recommend you do it here.

6300 Gulf Blvd., St. Pete Beach, FL 33706. www.postcardinn.com. 📞 **727/367-2711.** Fax 727/367-7068. 196 units. Winter from $189; off season from $99. Rates include complimentary hot and cold continental breakfast. AE, DC, DISC MC, V. **Amenities:** 2 restaurants; 2 bars; bike rental; gym; heated pool. *In room:* A/C, TV/DVD, hair dryer, MP3 docking station, Wi-Fi.

Inexpensive

Beach Haven ★ 🏖 Nestled on the beach between two high-rise condos, these low-slung, pink-with-white-trim structures look like the early-1950s motel they once were. The former owners (who still own Island's End) replaced the innards and installed bright tile floors, vertical blinds, pastel tropical furniture, and many modern amenities, including DVDs and refrigerators. Five of the original quarters remain motel rooms (with shower-only bathrooms), but the others are linked to make 12 one-bedroom units and one two-bedroom unit, all with kitchens. The top choice is the one-bedroom suite with sliding-glass doors opening onto a tiled patio beside an outdoor heated pool. There's also a sunning deck with lounge furniture by the beach. The 1950s rooms are smallish, but every unit is bright, airy, and comfortable. Beach Haven's sister motel, the **Miramar Resort,** 4200 Gulf Blvd. (📞 **727/367-2311;** www.miramarbeachresort.com), is nearby, also on the Gulf, with rates from $85 to $250.

4980 Gulf Blvd. (at 50th Ave.), St. Pete Beach, FL 33706. www.beachhavenvillas.com. 📞 **727/367-8642.** Fax 727/360-8202. 18 units. Winter $85–$180 double; off season $75–$125 double. AE, DISC, MC, V. **Amenities:** Concierge-level rooms; heated outdoor pool. *In room:* A/C, TV, hair dryer, kitchen, free Wi-Fi.

Plaza Beach Hotels Beachfront Resort 😊 A no-frills, family-friendly beach resort, Plaza Beach Resort sits right on St. Pete Beach and features 39 rooms—nothing fancy, but immaculately clean and all with flatscreen TVs and full kitchens. In addition to the beachfront pool, there's shuffleboard, mini-golf, human-sized chess board, BBQ area, beach cabanas, and wireless Internet. Some rooms have balconies overlooking the Gulf of Mexico. The down-to-earth staff contributes to its reputation as the coolest mom-and-pop hotel in the area!

4506 Gulf Blvd. (at 50th Ave.), St. Pete Beach, FL 33706. www.plazaresorts.com. 📞 **727/257-8998.** Fax 727/367-3620. 39 units. Winter $99–$239 double; off season $59–$139 double. AE, DISC, MC, V. **Amenities:** Heated outdoor pool. *In room:* A/C, TV, hair dryer, kitchen, free Wi-Fi.

CLEARWATER BEACH

Very Expensive

Sandpearl Resort ★★★ For nearly a century, the original Clearwater Beach Hotel—built as a summer bungalow by a Florida lumberman in 1917—reigned as the crown jewel of the area, eventually passing its rich legacy onto its newest incarnation as the Sandpearl. Opened in 2007, the resort sits on 700 feet of beachfront. Rooms are open and airy, with balconies and high ceilings. The **Sandpearl Spa** is swank (and Florida Green Lodging certified), with treatments focusing on ocean therapy. A lagoon-style beachfront pool is the way to go, unless, of course, you want to dip into Sandpearl's life-enriching programs that take you on guided kayaking tours, naturalist tours of Caladesi Island, behind-the-scenes tours of Clearwater Marine Aquarium, and more. A Sunset Celebration invites a chosen guest to ring the dinner bell salvaged from the old Clearwater Beach Resort. Tradition is still here, albeit with a more 21st-century twist. Fine dining options are aplenty. Camp Ridley is for children, and it offers campfire storytelling, singalongs, and more.

500 Mandalay Ave., Clearwater Beach, FL 33767. www.sandpearl.com. 📞 **877/726-3111** or 727/441-2425. Fax 727/449-9024. 253 units, including 52 suites. Guest rooms, including Gulf Front Junior Suites, off season $169–$299 double, peak season $289–$509 double; 1- and 2-bedroom suites off season $289–$659, peak season $479–$1,189. AE, DC, DISC, MC, V. **Amenities:** 2 restaurants; 2 bars; coffee bar; children's programs; concierge; fitness center; lagoon-style pool; room service; full-service spa; watersports equipment/rentals. *In room:* A/C, TV, fridge, hair dryer, free Internet access, minibar.

Moderate

Clearwater Beach Marriott Suites on Sand Key ★ 😊 You'll see the beauty of Sand Key Island from the suites in this boomerang-shaped, 10-story, all-suite hotel across the boulevard from the Sheraton Sand Key Resort (see below). Although the resort sits on the bay and not the Gulf, it has a large swimming pool complex next to the water, and the beach and Sand Key Park are just a short walk or trolley ride away. The resort has a good children's program and

The Laughing Lizard: A B&B on the Rocks

The **Laughing Lizard B&B,** on Indian Rocks Beach, was built in 2005 and is billed as a contemporary throwback to island-style architecture. Inside the three-story Key West–style home, you'll find the antithesis of quaint B&Bs with an elevator; 56 windows, many with a view of the Gulf or of Gulf Boulevard; and guest rooms with private bathrooms and kitschy names such as Nautical Newt, Crimson Chameleon, and Gallivanting Gecko. The newest addition, Island Iguana, is an efficiency apartment with partial kitchen and separate entrance. Innkeeper Bill Ockunzzi, a former mayor of Indian Rocks Beach, holds an evening wine tasting in Lizard Hall just as the sun sinks into the water. Other amusements can be found in the collection of clay, glass, wood, and plastic lizards lounging around in some of the most unexpected places. Rates are $145 to $200. Head to 2211 Gulf Blvd., Indian Rocks Beach (© 727/595-7006; www.laughinglizardbandb.com).

an excellent steakhouse, **Watercolour Steakhouse and Grille,** and the family will enjoy exploring the adjacent boardwalk's 25 shops and restaurants, including a branch of Ybor City's excellent Columbia Restaurant (p. 442). Each suite has a bedroom with a balcony offering water views, as well as a living room with sofa bed, wet bar, and entertainment unit. The gorgeous heated pool with cascading waterfalls is reminiscent of an exotic resort in Mexico, Hawaii, or even Las Vegas.

1201 Gulf Blvd., Clearwater Beach, FL 33767. www.clearwaterbeachmarriottsuites.com. © **800/228-9290** or 727/596-1100. Fax 727/595-4292. 220 units. Winter $199–$289 suite; off season $199–$259 suite. Packages available. AE, DC, DISC, MC, V. Valet parking $12. **Amenities:** 2 restaurants; 2 bars; babysitting; children's programs; golf course; exercise room; Jacuzzi; heated outdoor pool; limited room service; sauna. *In room:* A/C, TV, hair dryer, Internet access, minibar.

Sheraton Sand Key Resort ★ Set on 10 acres next to Sand Key Park, away from the honky-tonk of Clearwater, this nine-story Spanish-style hotel is a favorite with groups and watersports enthusiasts. It's only a 450-foot walk across the broad beach in front of the hotel to the water's edge. The moderately spacious guest rooms here all have new bedding, flatscreen TVs, and balconies or patios with views of the Gulf or the bay. The exercise room is on the top floor, affording great workout views. For those who love a little scandal, room no. 538 was the one where infamous former Praise the Lord Ministry leader Jim Bakker was busted with his then-assistant Jessica Hahn. In 2009, the resort became a member of Florida Green Lodging.

1160 Gulf Blvd., Clearwater Beach, FL 33767. www.sheratonsandkey.com. © **800/325-3535** or 727/595-1611. Fax 727/596-1117. 390 units. Winter $199–$412 double; off season $179–$345 double. AE, DC, DISC, MC, V. **Amenities:** 2 restaurants; 2 bars; babysitting; children's programs (summer only); concierge; concierge-level rooms; exercise room; Jacuzzi; heated outdoor pool; limited room service; sauna; 3 tennis courts; watersports equipment/rentals; Wi-Fi. *In room:* A/C, TV, hair dryer, high-speed Internet access.

Inexpensive

Barefoot Bay Resort and Marina ★ ◀ A family-owned-and-operated motel on the bay, Barefoot Bay offers clean, comfortable apartment-like accommodations at great prices. There are four types of rooms, including a two-bedroom apartment with full kitchen. But the best part about the place, besides its location, is its backyard pool deck, complete with tropical landscaping and heated pool. It's more like hanging out at a friend's house than a motel. Even better, the beach is across the street.

401 E. Shore Dr., Clearwater Beach, FL 33767. www.barefootbayresort.com. ✆ **866/447-3316** or 727/447-3316. Fax 727/447-1016. 10 units. Winter $75–$200 double; off season $65–$170 double. AE, DC, MC, V. **Amenities:** Heated pool. *In room:* A/C, TV, fridge.

TWO NEARBY GOLF RESORTS

Innisbrook, a Salamander Golf & Spa Resort ★★ *Golf Digest, Golf,* and others pick this as one of the country's best places to play golf. Between Palm Harbor and Tarpon Springs, this 900-acre, all-condominium resort has 72 holes on championship courses more like the rolling links of the Carolinas than the usually flat courses found in Florida. Some pros think the **Copperhead Course** ★★ is number one in Florida. If you want to learn, Innisbrook has one of the largest resort-owned-and-operated golf schools in North America. In addition, it boasts a tennis center with instruction. It's similar to the sports-oriented Saddlebrook Resort near Tampa (p. 438), except that the courses are more challenging and you're closer to the beach. A free shuttle runs around the property, and another goes to the beach three times a day. Ranging in size from suites to two-bedroom models, the quarters are privately owned condos all over the premises.

36750 U.S. 19 N., Palm Harbor, FL 34684. www.innisbrookgolfresort.com. ✆ **877/752-1480** or 727/942-2000. Fax 727/942-5576. 700 units. Winter $189–$485 suite; off season $129–$289 suite. Golf packages available. AE, DC, DISC, MC, V. **Amenities:** 5 restaurants; 4 bars; babysitting; children's programs; concierge; 4 golf courses; health club; Jacuzzis; heated outdoor pools; limited room service; sauna; 15 tennis courts. *In room:* A/C, TV, hair dryer, Internet access, kitchen, minibar.

Where to Dine

The restaurants here are grouped by geographic location: St. Pete Beach, including Pass-a-Grille; Indian Rocks Beach, including Madeira Beach, Redington Beach, North Redington Beach, Redington Shores, and Indian Shores; and Clearwater Beach.

ST. PETE BEACH

Crabby Bill's ☺ SEAFOOD This member of a local chain sits right on the beach. It has an open-air rooftop bar, as well as a large dining room enclosed by big windows. There are fine water views from picnic tables, which are equipped with paper towels and buckets of saltine crackers, the better with which to eat the blue, Alaskan, snow, and stone crabs. The crustaceans fall into the moderate price category or higher, but most other main courses, such as fried fish or shrimp, are inexpensive—and they aren't overcooked or overbreaded. This is a good place to feed the family.

5300 Gulf Blvd. (at 53rd Ave.), St. Pete Beach. ✆ **727/360-8858.** www.crabbybills.com. Main courses $11–$33; market price for lobster and stone-crab claws; sandwiches $6–$10. AE, MC, V. Mon–Thurs 11:30am–10pm; Fri–Sat 11:30am–11pm; Sun noon–10pm.

Hurricane SEAFOOD A longtime institution, across the street from Pass-a-Grille Public Beach, this three-level gray Victorian building with white gingerbread trim is a great place to toast the sunset, especially from the rooftop bar. It's more beach pub than restaurant, but the grouper sandwiches are excellent, and there's always fresh fish. Downstairs, you can dine inside the knotty-pine-paneled dining room or on the sidewalk terrace, where bathers from across Gulf Way are welcome (there's a walk-up bar for beach libation). You must be at least 21 to go up to the Hurricane Watch rooftop bar or to join the revelry when the second level turns into Stormy's Nightclub, at 10pm Wednesday through Saturday.

807 Gulf Way (at 9th Ave.), Pass-a-Grille. © **727/360-9558.** www.thehurricane.com. Main courses $9–$21; sandwiches $5–$12. AE, MC, V. Daily 8am–1am.

Maritana Grille ★★ SEAFOOD/FLORIBBEAN If you're not staying at Don CeSar Resort, consider eating there, at this bastion of fabulous Floribbean cuisine. It's known for elegant dinners of steaks and seafood, and, after a major revamp in 2010, modern and chic decor. That said, the dining room is still adorned with 1,500 gallons of saltwater aquariums and Florida fish. A specialty that's one of the most innovative dishes we've had is the orange habanero barbecued grouper with warm pineapple, vanilla-bean stew, glazed banana, and rum pepper sauce. The chef's table is a degustation that takes place in the kitchen, at a private table from which guests are able to interact with the chef and observe him in action.

At Don CeSar Resort, 3400 Gulf Blvd. (at 9th Ave.), St. Pete Beach. © **727/360-1882.** Reservations recommended. Main courses $20–$44. AE, MC, V. Tues–Sat 6–10pm.

Ted Peters' Famous Smoked Fish ★ ⌗ SEAFOOD This open-air eatery is an institution in these parts: Ted's has been around since the '50s. Some folks bring their catches for the staff to smoke, while others figure fishing is a waste of time and come right to Ted's for mullet, mackerel, salmon, and other fish slowly cooked over red oak. Enjoy the aroma and sip a cold one while you wait for your order.

1530 Pasadena Ave. (just across St. Pete Beach Causeway), Pasadena. © **727/381-7931.** Main courses $8–$20. No credit cards. Wed–Mon 11:30am–7:30pm.

Wildwood BBQ & Burger ★ BARBECUE Hailing from NYC, this modern regional American barbecue spot isn't your ordinary grill even if its wooden, rustic, and industrial look may have you believing otherwise. Fired up by Pit Master Big Lou Elrose, the slow cooker here yields some Food Network–worthy pulled pork, brisket, chicken, ribs, and burgers. At the Postcard Inn on the Beach, it's almost like attending someone's poolside barbecue, but this time with a bona fide pit master.

The Postcard Inn on the Beach, 6300 Gulf Blvd., St. Pete Beach. © **727/367-2711.** Main courses $11–$20. AE, DISC, MC, V. Daily 11am–11pm.

INDIAN ROCKS BEACH AREA

Guppy's on the Beach Grill & Bar ★★ SEAFOOD Locals love this bar and grill across from Indian Rocks Public Beach because they know they'll always get terrific chow. You won't forget the salmon coated with potatoes and lightly fried, then baked with a creamy leek-and-garlic sauce; it's fattening, yes, but delicious. Another good choice is the lightly cooked tuna with a brandy peppercorn sauce. All entrees come with Cesar salad, fresh steamed veggies, and a choice of side dish. The atmosphere is casual beach-friendly, with a fun bar. Try the upside-down apple-walnut pie topped with ice cream. You can dine outside on a patio beside the main road.

1701 Gulf Blvd. (at 17th Ave.), Indian Rocks Beach. © **727/593-2032.** www.3bestchefs.com/guppys. Main courses $13–$40; sandwiches $9–$13. AE, DC, DISC, MC, V. Sun–Thurs 11:30am–10:30pm; Fri–Sat 11:30am–11pm.

Lobster Pot ★★★ SEAFOOD/STEAK Step into this weathered-looking restaurant near the beach and experience some of the finest seafood in the area. The prices are high, but the variety of Maine lobster dishes is amazing. The pan-seared lobster with sweet corn sauté and gazpacho sauce is baked to succulent perfection. In addition to lobster, there's a wide selection of grouper, snapper, salmon, shrimp, scallops, crab, and steaks, most prepared with elaborate sauces. The children's menu here is definitely out of the ordinary: It features half a Maine lobster and a petite filet mignon. A four-course prix-fixe dinner is offered nightly from 4:30 to 6pm at $17, or if you want to taste some new menu items, check out the restaurant's Martini Bar on Thursdays from 5 to 9pm when they pass around items for review and offer live jazz on Fridays and Saturdays.

17814 Gulf Blvd. (at 178th Ave.), Redington Shores. ℂ **727/391-8592.** www.lobsterpotrestaurant. com. Reservations recommended. Main courses $20–$45. AE, DC, MC, V. Daily 4:30–10pm.

The Salt Rock Grill ★★★ SEAFOOD/STEAK Affluent professionals and so-called beautiful people pack this waterfront restaurant, making it *the* place to see and be seen. The big dining room is built on three levels, thus affording every table a view over the creeklike waterway out back. In fair weather, you can dine out by the dock or slake your thirst at the lively Tiki bar (bands play Sat–Sun during the summer). Thick, aged steaks are the house specialties, but it's the seafood everyone comes for. Pan-seared peppered tuna and salmon cooked on a cedar board lead the seafood. A fresh market cioppino gives you an all-in-one seafood experience with day-boat fish, king crab, shrimp, lobster, clams, mussels, and sourdough toast. Avoid spending a fortune by showing up for the early-bird specials (daily 4–5:30pm), or by ordering the Mile High meatloaf with mashed potatoes and onion straws ($13) or the half-pound sirloin steak ($16).

19325 Gulf Blvd. (north of 193rd Ave.), Indian Shores. ℂ **727/593-7625.** www.saltrockgrill.com. Reservations strongly advised. Main courses $18–$40; early-bird specials $20. AE, DC, DISC, MC, V. Sun–Thurs 4–10pm; Fri–Sat 4–11pm. Tiki bar Sat 2pm–midnight (or later); Sun 2–10pm.

CLEARWATER BEACH

Bobby's Bistro & Wine Bar ★★ AMERICAN Son of Bob Heilman's Beachcomber (see below), this chic bistro draws a more urbane crowd. A wine-cellar theme is justified by the real thing: a walk-in closet with several thousand bottles kept at a constant 55°F (13°C). Walk through and pick your vintage, then listen to jazz while you dine inside at tall, bar-height tables or outside on a covered patio. The chef specializes in gourmet pizzas with homemade focaccia crusts, plus chargrilled lamb chops, filet mignon, fresh fish, and monstrous pork chops with caramelized Granny Smith apples and a Mount Vernon mustard sauce. Everything's served a la carte here, so watch your wallet. There's a less expensive sandwich menu featuring bronzed grouper and chicken with a spicy Jack cheese.

447 Mandalay Ave. (at Papaya St., behind Bob Heilman's Beachcomber). ℂ **727/446-9463.** www.bobbysbistro.com. Reservations recommended. Main courses $13–$28; sandwiches and pizzas $8–$13. AE, DC, DISC, MC, V. Sun–Thurs 5–11pm; Fri–Sat 5pm–midnight. Bar stays open later.

Bob Heilman's Beachcomber ★ AMERICAN In a row of restaurants, bars, and T-shirt shops, this establishment has been popular with the locals since 1948. Each dining room here is unique: Large models of sailing crafts create a nautical theme in one, a pianist makes music in a second, works of art create a gallery in the third, and booths and a fireplace make for a cozy fourth. The menu presents a variety of well-prepared fresh seafood and beef, veal, and lamb selections. If you tire of fruits-of-the-sea, the "back to the farm" fried chicken—from an original 1910 Heilman family recipe—is incredible. The Beachcomber shares valet parking and an extensive wine collection with Bobby's Bistro & Wine Bar (see above).

447 Mandalay Ave. (at Papaya St.). 📞 727/442-4144. www.heilmansbeachcomber.com. Reservations recommended. Main courses $18–$35. AE, DC, DISC, MC, V. Mon–Sat 11:30am–11pm; Sun noon–10pm.

Frenchy's Original Cafe SEAFOOD Popular with locals and visitors in the know since 1981, this casual pub makes the best grouper sandwiches in the area and has all the awards to prove it. The sandwiches are fresh, thick, juicy, and delicious. We love the grouper sandwich served Buffalo-style. The atmosphere is pure Florida casual. There can be a wait during winter and on weekends year-round. For a similarly relaxed setting, directly on the beach, **Frenchy's Rockaway Grill,** at 7 Rockaway St. (📞 727/446-4844), has a wonderful outdoor setting and keeps a charcoal grill going to cook fresh fish. Same goes for two more Frenchy's-owned eateries: **Frenchy's Salt Water Café,** 419 Poinsettia Ave. (📞 727/461-6295), and Frenchy's South Beach Café, 351 S. Gulfview Blvd. (📞 727/441-9991).

41 Baymont St. 📞 727/446-3607. www.frenchysonline.com. Sandwiches and burgers $7–$13. AE, MC, V. Mon–Thurs 11:30am–11pm; Fri–Sat 11:30am–midnight; Sun noon–11pm.

Island Way Grill ★★ SEAFOOD/SUSHI Not your ordinary waterfront seafood shanty, the glass-encased, wood-enhanced sleek Island Way prepares the daily catch Pan-Asian style in its open kitchen. Everything is delicious, from the (cooked) fish to the sushi. Even the meatloaf is gourmet, with wasabi mashed potatoes and tumbleweed onions—a bargain at $11. There's also a full sushi bar. The wine list is also superb. Sit on the patio, then gravitate toward the outdoor bar, where the fabulous people—like members and owners of the Tampa Bay Buccaneers—hang out, talk shop, and scope the scene.

20 Island Way. 📞 727/461-6617. www.islandwaygrill.com. Main courses $11–$37. AE, MC, V. Sun–Thurs 4–10pm; Fri–Sat 4–11pm.

The Beaches After Dark

The restored fishing community of **John's Pass Village and Boardwalk,** on Gulf Boulevard at John's Pass in Madeira Beach, has plenty of restaurants, bars, and shops to keep you occupied after the sun sets. Elsewhere, the nightlife scene at the beach revolves around rocking bars that pump out music until 2am. All of the places listed in this section are bars that feature live music.

Pass-a-Grille has the always-lively lounge at **Hurricane,** on Gulf Way at Ninth Avenue, opposite the public beach (p. 466). Up on the northern tip of Treasure Island, **Gators on the Pass** (📞 727/367-8951) claims to have the world's longest waterfront bar, with a huge deck overlooking the waters of John's Pass. The complex also has a nonsmoking sports bar and a three-story tower with a top-level observation deck for panoramic views of the Gulf of Mexico. Live music, from acoustic to blues to rock, is featured most nights.

In Clearwater Beach, the **Palm Pavilion Beachside Grill & Bar,** on the beach at 18 Bay Esplanade (📞 727/446-6777; www.palmpavilion.com), has live music Tuesday through Sunday nights in winter and on weekends in the off season. Nearby, **Frenchy's Rockaway Grill,** at 7 Rockaway St. (📞 727/446-

4844; www.frenchysonline.com/rock_index.html), is another popular hangout.

If you're into laughs, **Coconuts Comedy Club,** at the TradeWinds Sandpiper, 6000 Gulf Blvd., at 61st Avenue in St. Pete Beach (☎ **727/360-5653;** www.coconutscomedyclubs.com), has an ever-changing program of live stand-up, funny men and women. Call for the schedules and prices.

For a more highbrow evening, go to the Clearwater mainland and the 2,200-seat **Ruth Eckerd Hall,** 1111 McMullen-Booth Rd. (☎ **727/791-7400;** www.rutheckerdhall.com), which hosts a varied program of Broadway shows, ballet, drama, symphonic works, popular music, jazz, and country music.

SARASOTA ★★★

52 miles S of Tampa; 150 miles SW of Orlando; 225 miles NW of Miami

Far enough away from Tampa Bay to have an identity of its own, Sarasota is one of Florida's cultural centers. In fact, many retirees spend their winters here because there's so much to keep them entertained and stimulated, including the Van Wezel Performing Arts Hall and the FSU Center for the Performing Arts, home of the annual Asolo Theatre Festival. Sarasota also has an extensive array of first-class resorts, restaurants, and boutiques.

Offshore, more than 40 miles of white beaches fringe a chain of long, narrow barrier islands stretching from Tampa Bay to Sarasota. To the south, **Siesta Key** is a residential enclave popular with artisans and writers, and is home to Siesta Village, this area's funky, laid-back, and often noisy beach hangout. Shielded from the Gulf by **Lido Key,** which has a string of affordable hotels attractive to families, **St. Armands Key** sports a quaint and lively shopping and dining district, while adjacent **Longboat Key** is one of the country's swankiest islands.

Essentials

GETTING THERE You'll probably find less-expensive airfare by flying into **Tampa International Airport** (p. 421), an hour's drive north of Sarasota, and you can save even more because Tampa's rental-car agencies usually offer some of the best deals in Florida. If you don't rent a car, **Sarasota-Tampa Express** (☎ **800/326-2800** or 941/727-1344; www.stexps.com) provides bus connections for $40 for adults, $20 for children 4 to 12. Call in advance for a schedule and pickup locations.

If you fly directly here, **Sarasota-Bradenton International Airport** (☎ 941/359-2770; www.srq-airport.com), north of downtown, off University Parkway between U.S. 41 and U.S. 301, is served by **Continental, Delta, Northwest,** and **US Airways.**

Diplomat Taxi (☎ **941/355-5155;** www.srqtaxi.com) has a monopoly on service from the airport to hotels in Sarasota and Bradenton. Look for the cabs outside baggage claim. Fares are all metered at $2.25 at flag fall and $2.15 per additional mile.

Amtrak has bus connections to Sarasota from its Tampa station (☎ **800/872-7245;** www.amtrak.com).

VISITOR INFORMATION Contact the **Sarasota Convention and Visitors Bureau,** 655 N. Tamiami Trail (U.S. 41), Sarasota, FL 34236 (☎ **800/522-9799** or 941/957-1877; fax 941/951-2956; www.sarasotafl.org). The bureau and its visitor center are in a blue pagoda-shaped building on Tamiami Trail (U.S. 41) at 6th Street. They offer a great, **self-guided architecture tour**

spotlighting structures associated with the Sarasota School of Architecture, as well as other symbols of architectural ingenuity. It is intended as a self-guided driving tour that can be completed in 2 hours. It is available for $6 at the bureau or at www.toursarasota.com. Hours are Monday through Saturday from 9am to 5pm, Sunday from 11am to 3pm; closed holidays.

A new eco-website listing Sarasota's bays, beaches, parks, preserves, rivers, and the best spots for communing with nature is **Discover Natural Sarasota County**'s www.discovernaturalsarasota.org.

You can get a packet of advance information on Bradenton and Manatee County from the **Greater Bradenton Area Convention and Visitors Bureau,** P.O. Box 1000, Bradenton, FL 34206 (©**800/462-6283** or 941/729-9177; fax 941/729-1820; www.floridaislandbeaches.org).

If you're driving from the north via I-75, you can get off at U.S. 301 (exit 224) and head west if you want to go to the **Manatee County Tourist Information Center** (©**941/729-7040**), where volunteers will answer questions and sell excellent road maps for less than you'll pay elsewhere. It's open daily from 8:30am to 5pm except Easter Sunday, Thanksgiving, the day after Thanksgiving, and Christmas Day. The office also has an information kiosk at **Prime Outlets,** across I-75, which is open Monday through Saturday from 10am to 6pm, and Sunday from 11am to 6pm.

GETTING AROUND Sarasota County Area Transit (SCAT; ©**941/861-5000;** www.scgov.net/SCAT/default.asp) operates a fairly reliable bus service around town. Fares are 75¢ for adults, with two children 5 and under free and 35¢ per additional child. Sarasota taxi companies include **Diplomat Taxi** (©**941/355-5155**), **Green Cab Taxi** (©**941/922-6666**), and **Yellow Cab of Sarasota** (©**941/955-3341**).

Hitting the Beach

Many of the area's 40-plus miles of beaches are occupied by hotels and condominium complexes, but there are excellent public beaches as well. The area's most popular is **Siesta Key Public Beach,** rated number 2 on Dr. Beach's 2010 Top Beaches list, with a picnic area, a 700-car parking lot, crowds of families, and quartz sand reminiscent of the white beaches in Northwest Florida. There's also beach access at **Siesta Village,** which has a plethora of casual restaurants and pubs with outdoor seating (see "Where to Dine," later). The more secluded, quiet **Turtle Beach** is at Siesta Key's south end. It has shelters, boat ramps, picnic tables, and volleyball nets. Both beaches have restroom facilities. New to the area is **Passage Key,** a nude beach accessible only by boat, on a protected bird sanctuary. It's in the bay between the Rod 'n' Reel Pier on Anna Maria and Egmont Key.

Unless you're staying on Longboat Key, you won't be able to hit the beach there, as private houses and condos block access to the Gulf. However, do drive the length of Longboat Key and admire the luxury homes. Then take a right off St. Armands Circle onto Lido Key and **North Lido Beach.** The south end of the island is occupied by **South Lido Beach Park,** with plenty of shade—a good spot for picnics and walks.

Outdoor Activities & Spectator Sports

BIKING & IN-LINE SKATING The flat terrain in this area makes for good in-line skating and for fine, though not challenging, bike riding. You can bike and skate from downtown Sarasota to Lido and Longboat keys, because paved walkways/bike paths run alongside the John Ringling Causeway and then up Longboat Key. **Siesta Sports Rentals,** 6551 Midnight Pass Rd., in the Southbridge Mall, just south of Stickney Point Bridge on Siesta Key (✆ 941/346-1797; www.siestasportsrentals.com), rents bikes of various sizes (including trail attachments for kids), plus motor scooters, kayaks, and beach chairs and umbrellas. They can even arrange kayak tours, if you wish. Bike rentals range from about $15 a day to $45 a week; scooters go for $45 for a half-day or $65 for a full day. They also rent three-wheeled scooter cars. The shop is open daily from 9am to 5pm.

BOAT RENTALS **Siesta Key Water Sports,** 1536 Stickney Point Rd. (✆ 941/921-3030; www.siestakeywatersports.com), rents jet skis and kayaks and offers parasailing. At the island end of the bridge, **C. B.'s Saltwater Outfitters,** 1249 Stickney Point Rd. (✆ 941/349-4400; www.cbs outfitters.com), and **Siesta Key Marina,** 1265 Old Stickney Point Rd. (✆ 941/349-8880; www.siestakeymarina.com), both rent runabouts, pontoon boats, and other craft. Bait and tackle are available at the marinas.

CRUISES The area's best nature cruises depart from Mote Aquarium (see "Exploring the Area," later).

FISHING Charter fishing boats dock at most marinas here; check out **www.4sarasota.com/Sarasota/Recreation/fish_charters.html** for a list. In downtown Sarasota, the **Flying Fish Fleet,** at Marina Jack's Marina, U.S. 41 at Island Park Circle (✆ 941/366-3373; www.flyingfishfleet. com), offers party-boat charter-fishing excursions, with bait and tackle furnished. Prices for half-day trips are $55 for adults, $50 for seniors, and $45 for kids 4 to 12. All-day voyages cost $86, $80, and $76, respectively. Call for the schedule. Other charter boats also line up along the dock here.

GOLF The **Bobby Jones Golf Complex ★**, 1000 Circus Blvd. (✆ 941/365-4653; www.bobbyjonesgolfclub.com), is Sarasota's only municipal facility. It has two 18-hole championship layouts—the American (par 71) and British (par 72) courses—and the 9-hole Gillespie executive course (par 30). Tee times are assigned 3 days in advance. Greens fees range from $18 to $50 including cart rental.

The semiprivate **Rolling Green Golf Club,** 4501 Tuttle Ave. (✆ 941/355-6620; www.rollinggreengc.com), is an 18-hole, par-72 course. Facilities include a driving range, rental clubs, and lessons. Tee times are assigned 2 days in advance. Prices, including cart, are about $20 to $55. Also semiprivate, the **Sarasota Golf Club,** 7820 N. Leewynn Dr. (✆ 941/371-2431; www.sarasotagc.com), is an 18-hole, par-72 course. Facilities include a driving range, lessons, club rentals, a restaurant, a lounge, and a golf shop. Fees, including cart, are $16 to $35.

If you have reciprocal privileges, **University Park Country Club,** west of I-75 on University Parkway (✆ 941/359-9999; www.university park-fl.com), is Sarasota's only nationally ranked course. Fees, including cart, are about $40 to $70.

Bradenton is home to the **David Leadbetter Golf Academy,** 1414 69th Ave., at U.S. 41 (✆ 800/872-6425 or 941/755-1000; www. leadbetter.com), a part of the Nick Bollettieri Tennis Academy (see "Tennis," below). Presided over by one of golf's leading instructors, this facility offers practice tee instruction, video analysis, scoring strategy, and more.

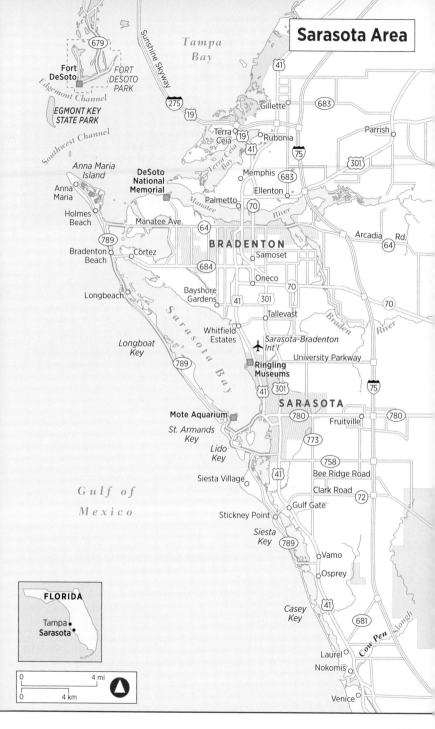

Sarasota Area

Tampa Bay

Egmont Channel

Fort DeSoto

FORT DESOTO PARK

EGMONT KEY STATE PARK

Southwest Channel

Anna Maria Island

Anna Maria

Holmes Beach

Manatee Ave.

Bradenton Beach

Cortez

Longbeach

Longboat Key

DeSoto National Memorial

Manatee River

Palmetto

Memphis

Ellenton

BRADENTON

Samoset

Oneco

Bayshore Gardens

Tallevast

Whitfield Estates

Sarasota-Bradenton Int'l

Ringling Museums

Sarasota Bay

Mote Aquarium

St. Armands Key

Lido Key

Siesta Village

Gulf of Mexico

Stickney Point

Siesta Key

Gulf Gate

SARASOTA

Fruitville

Bee Ridge Road

Clark Road

Braden River

University Parkway

Cow Pen Slough

Vamo

Osprey

Casey Key

Laurel

Nokomis

Venice

Gillette

Rubonia

Terra Ceia

Terra Ceia Bay

Parrish

Sunshine Skyway

Arcadia Rd.

FLORIDA

Tampa

Sarasota

0   4 mi

0   4 km

473

Take a ride along the beach, on horseback, at Palma Sola Bay.

For course information, go to www.golf.com or www.floridagolfing.com; or call the **Florida Sports Foundation** (© 850/488-8347) or **Florida Golfing** (© 866/833-2663).

HORSEBACK RIDING For a unique equestrian experience, **Great World Nature Tours** (© 941/907-7272; www.beachhorses.com) offers horseback riding in the sand and the water at Bradenton's **Palma Sola Bay,** 8400 Manatee Ave. W. Rides are scheduled at low tide and take about an hour. Private rides for up to 4 riders are available at a steep price—around $358 for a half-day and $700 for a full day. Group tours are much more affordable at $60 to $100, depending on the time and date you book. Children as young as 3 are able to ride and no experience is necessary.

KAYAKING Based at Mote Aquarium (see "Exploring the Area," below), **Sarasota Bay Explorers** ★★ (© 941/388-4200; www.sarasotabayexplorers. com) uses a 38-foot pontoon boat to ferry novice and experienced kayakers and their craft to a marine sanctuary, where everyone paddles through tunnels formed by mangroves. The paddling is easy and the waters are shallow. Experienced naturalists serve as guides. Wear a swimsuit and tennis shoes or rubber-soled booties, and bring a towel and lunch. The 3-hour trip is $55 for adults, $45 for children 5 to 17, and free for kids 4 and under (seats are provided for the youngsters). Reservations are required.

SAILING Take a cruise on the waters of Sarasota Bay and the Gulf of Mexico aboard the 41-foot, 12-passenger *Enterprise,* docked at Marina Jack's Marina, U.S. 41 at Island Park Circle (© 888/232-7768 or 941/951-1833; www.sarasotasailing.com). Cruises range from 2 hours for $40 per person to 4 hours for $70 a head, while 2-hour sunset excursions cost $45 per person. Departure times vary, and reservations are required. **Siesta Key Sailing,** 1219 Southport Dr. (© 941/346-7245; www.siestakeysailing.com), charges about the same for cruises in a 42-foot Morgan Outlander sloop. Call for rates and reservations. **Key Sailing,** 2 Marina Plaza (© 941/346-SAIL [7245]; www.siestakeysailing.com), offers various sailing experiences on the historic 41-foot Morgan Classic II sailing yacht, the *Key Breeze,* including "Fresh Air, Fine Chocolates and a Few Hours of Peace on Earth." Rates range from $48 to $80 per person.

You can also get to Egmont Key, 3 miles off the northern end of Anna Maria Island at the mouth of Tampa Bay, on a 30-foot sloop-rigged sailboat with **Spice Sailing Charters** (©941/778-3240; http://charters2.tripod.com), based at the Galati Yacht Basin on Bay Boulevard on northern Anna Maria Island. Rates start at $35 per person for a 2½-hour sail to $50 per person for a 4-hour sail. The company has sunset cruises as well. Call for the schedule and reservations.

Bring your racquet and work on your game at the Nick Bollettieri Tennis Academy.

SPECTATOR SPORTS The **Baltimore Orioles** came to Sarasota in the Spring of 2010 when, after 14 years in Fort Lauderdale, the major-league team began spring training at **Ed Smith Stadium,** 2700 12th St. (©941/954-4101; www.orioles.com). Tickets range from $10 and up. The **Pittsburgh Pirates** (©941/748-4610; www.pirateball.com) do their February through March spring training at 6,562-seat McKechnie Field, 9th Street West and 17th Avenue West, south of downtown Bradenton. Tickets are $10 to $20. After purchasing the Sarasota Reds when Cincinnati moved to Arizona for spring trailing, the Pirates got their own minor-league team, the **Bradenton Marauders** (www.bradentonmarauders.com), who also play at McKechnie Field April through September. Tickets are $5 to $10.

The **Sarasota Polo Club,** 8201 Polo Club Lane (©941/907-0000; www.sarasotapolo.com), at Lakewood Ranch, a planned community midway between Sarasota and Bradenton, is the site of Sunday-afternoon polo matches from mid-December to early April. General admission is $10 for adults, free for children 12 and under. Call for the schedule.

TENNIS The **Nick Bollettieri Tennis Academy,** 5500 34th St. W., Bradenton (©800/872-6425 or 941/755-1000; www.imgacademies.com), is one of the world's largest tennis training facilities, with over 70 grass, clay, and hard courts, and a pro shop. It's open year-round; reservations are required for all activities.

WATERSPORTS You'll find watersports activities in front of the major hotels on the Keys (see "Where to Stay," beginning on p. 479). **Siesta Sports Rentals,** 6551 Midnight Pass Rd., on Siesta Key (©813/346-1797; www.siestasportsrentals.com), rents kayaks and sailboats, plus beach chairs and umbrellas.

Exploring the Area

IN SARASOTA

Art Center Sarasota In addition to the John and Mable Ringling Museum of Art (see below), Sarasota is home to more than 40 galleries and exhibition spaces, all open to the public. A convenient starting point is this downtown community art center, next to the Sarasota Convention and Visitors Bureau. It contains three galleries and a small sculpture garden, presenting the area's largest display of works by national and local artists, ranging from paintings and pottery to sculpture, cartoons, jewelry, and enamelware. There are also art demonstrations and special events.

707 N. Tamiami Trail (at 6th St.). ☎ **941/365-2032.** www.artsarasota.org. Free admission ($2 suggested donation). Tues–Sat 10am–4pm; Sun noon–4pm.

FSU Ringling Center for the Cultural Arts ★★★ The (big) top attraction here, this 66-acre site is where showman and circus legend John Ringling and his wife, Mable, collected art and built a house on a grand scale. Now under the aegis of Florida State University, the **John and Mable Ringling Museum of Art** is the state's official art museum. Over 500 years of the history of European and American art are represented in the collections of the Museum of Art, which also presents a vibrant schedule of special exhibitions. The collections of 17th-century baroque paintings are world-renowned, and include five vast, famous tapestry cartoons by Peter Paul Rubens. Built between 1924 and October 1925 at a cost of $1.5 million and modeled after several Venetian palaces on the Grand Canal, the Ringling's 56-room palatial bayfront, five-story winter residence, **Ca'd'Zan** (House of John in Venetian dialect) has recently been restored. A 13,000-square-foot marble terrace leads down to the lower dock where John and Mable Ringling moored several luxury yachts and a gondola. Don't miss the tour of the house to see the period furniture and stunning architecture and artwork; in fact, make it the first stop on your Ringling itinerary. The **Ringling Circus Museum** is devoted to circus memorabilia, including parade wagons, calliopes, costumes, and colorful posters. The grounds include a classical courtyard, a rose garden, a museum shop, and the historic **Asolo Theater,** an 18th-century Italian court theater, which the Ringling's first director, Chick Everett Austin, moved here in the 1950s. It's now one of the centerpieces of the Florida State University Center for the Performing Arts. If you're hungry, check out the museum's on-site restaurant, **Treviso,** an elegant spot serving fine Italian fare for lunch and dinner depending on the time of year. You can dine inside or, better yet, outside overlooking the Ringling's pristine grounds. A museum admission ticket isn't required to dine in the restaurant. You'll need most of a day to see everything here.

5401 Bay Shore Rd., at N. Tamiami Trail (U.S. 41). ☎ **941/359-5700** or 941/351-1660 for recorded information. www.ringling.org. Admission $25 adults, $20 seniors, $10 students and children 6–17, free for children 5 and under. Prices subject to change. Daily 10am–5pm. Closed New Year's Day, Thanksgiving, and Christmas. From downtown, take U.S. 41 N. to University Pkwy. and follow signs to the museum.

Some of the art is circus-related at the Ringling Center.

G. Wiz (Gulfcoast Wonder & Imagination Zone) This hands-on, state-of-the-art science center has two floors of fun exhibits that cover the physical, earth, and health sciences. The ExploraZone features rotating interactive exhibits from San Francisco's renowned Exploratorium. The 35 exhibits have themes ranging from sound and music to mathematics and motion, color and optics, sight and illusion, and more.

1001 Blvd. of the Arts (in the Blivas Science and Technology Center, 1 block west of U.S. 41). ℂ **941/906-1851.** www.gwiz.org. Admission $10 adults, $9 seniors, $7 children 3 to 16. Tues–Sat 10am–5pm; Sun noon–5pm.

Marie Selby Botanical Gardens ★★ A must-see for serious plant lovers and a should-see for those looking for good photo ops, this peaceful retreat on the bay, just south of downtown, is said to be the only botanical garden in the world specializing in the preservation, study, and research of epiphytes—that is, "air plants" such as orchids. It's home to more than 20,000 exotic plants, including more than 6,000 orchids, as well as a bamboo pavilion, a butterfly and humming-bird garden, a medicinal-plant garden, a waterfall garden, a cactus and succulent garden, a fernery, a hibiscus garden, a palm grove, two tropical-food gardens, and a native shore-plant community. Selby's home and the Payne Mansion (both on the National Registry) are also located here.

811 S. Palm Ave. (south of U.S. 41). ℂ **941/366-5731.** www.selby.org. Admission $17 adults, $6 children 6–11, free for children 5 and under with an adult. Daily 10am–5pm. Closed Christmas.

Sarasota Classic Car Museum In operation since 1953, this is now a non-profit museum dedicated to preserving antique automobiles. But there's more to the place than its 90-plus classic and "muscle" autos, from Rolls-Royces and Pierce Arrows to the four cars used personally by circus czar John Ringling. Also here are more than 1,200 antique music boxes and several of Thomas Edison's early phonographs, including a 1909 diamond-tipped-needle model. Check out the Penny Arcade's antique games (with original prices), and grab a cone at the ice-cream and sandwich shop.

5500 N. Tamiami Trail (at University Pkwy.). ℂ **941/355-6228.** www.sarasotacarmuseum.org. Admission $8.50 adults, $7.50 seniors, $6.50 children 6–12, free for children 5 and under. Daily 9am–6pm. Take U.S. 41 north of downtown; museum is 2 blocks west of the airport.

ON ST. ARMANDS KEY

Mote Aquarium ★★ ☺ Kids get to touch such cool stuff as stingrays (minus the stinger) and watch sharks in the shark tank at this excellent aquarium. Part of the noted Mote Marine Laboratory complex, it is more broad-based than Tampa's Florida Aquarium, which concentrates primarily on local sea life. See manatees in the Marine Mammal Center, a block's walk from the aquarium, as well as many research-in-progress exhibits. Start by watching the aquarium's 12-minute film on the feeding habits of sharks; allow at least 90 minutes to take in every-thing on land. Add another 2 hours for a narrated sea-life encounter cruise with the **Sarasota Bay Explorers** (ℂ **727/388-4200;** www.sarasotabayexplorers. com). These fun, informative cruises visit a deserted island, and the guides throw out nets and bring up sea life for inspection. Try to make reservations a day in advance. This company has unusual kayaking adventures too (p. 474).

1600 Ken Thompson Pkwy. (on City Island). ℂ **800/691-6683** or 941/388-2541. www.mote.org. Admission $17 adults, $16 seniors, $12 children 4–12, free for children 3 and under. Combination aquarium-cruise tickets $36 adults, $29 children. Daily 10am–5pm. Nature cruises daily 11am and 1:30 and 4pm. From St. Armands Circle, head north toward Longboat Key; turn right just before the Lido-Longboat bridge.

IN & NEAR BRADENTON

DeSoto National Memorial Nestled on the Manatee River, west of downtown, this park attracts history buffs by re-creating the look and atmosphere of the period when Spanish explorer Hernando de Soto landed in 1539. It includes a restoration of de Soto's campsite and a scenic .5-mile nature trail that circles a mangrove jungle and leads to the ruins of one of the first settlements in the area. Start by watching the 21-minute film about de Soto in America. From December to March, park employees dress in 16th-century costumes and portray the early settlers' way of life, including cooking and the firing of an arquebus, one of the world's earliest firearms.

DeSoto Memorial Hwy. (north end of 75th St. W.). ✆ **941/792-0458.** www.nps.gov/deso. Free admission. Daily 9am–5pm. Take Manatee Ave. (Fla. 64) west to 75th St. W. and turn right; follow the road to its end and the entrance to the park.

Gamble Plantation ★ Northeast of downtown Bradenton, this is the oldest structure on the southwestern coast of Florida, and a fine example of an antebellum plantation home—something that's rare in Florida. It was constructed during a 6-year period in the late 1840s by Maj. Robert Gamble, made primarily of "tabby mortar" (a mixture of oyster shells, sand, molasses, and water), with 10 rooms, verandas on three sides, 18 exterior columns, and eight fireplaces. Now maintained as a state historic site, it includes a fine collection of 19th-century furnishings. Entrance to the house is by tour only, although you can explore the grounds on your own.

3708 Patten Ave. (U.S. 301), Ellenton. ✆ **941/723-4536.** www.floridastateparks.org/gamble plantation. Free admission. Tour $6 adults, $4 children 6–12, free for children 5 and under. Thurs–Mon 9am–4:30pm; 30-min. guided house tour at 9:30 and 10:30am and at 1, 2, 3, and 4pm. Take U.S. 301 north of downtown to Ellenton; the site is on the left, just east of Ellenton-Gillette Rd. (Fla. 683).

Robinson Preserve ★★★ A 487-acre conservation land is an eco-tourism haven featuring restored coastal habitat and 2.5 miles of kayaking and canoe trails. In addition, there are 100 acres of open water tidal systems, 56 acres of marshland, and 30 acres of uplands. If you prefer to stay on land, there are two piers, a 500-foot boardwalk, six bridges, and 10 miles of coastal, shell, and paved trails, along with two 400-foot-long pathways through mangrove forests. Naturalist-led wagon tours through the preserve are the way to go! Trips run an hour and are usually given twice a day and cost $3 for adults and $2 for children.

1704 99th St. W., Bradenton. ✆ **941/748-4501.** www.mymanatee.org/home/government/departments/natural-resources/resource-management/robinson-preserve.html. Free admission. Daily 8am–sunset. From U.S. 41, head north toward 33rd Ave. W. Turn right and then left on 26th St. W. Turn left at Manatee Ave. W. and then right at 75th St. W. Turn left at 9th Ave. NW and then right at 99th St.

Solomon's Castle ★★ This attraction gets the award in the Weirdest and Wackiest (and, boy, are there many) of Florida category. In 1974, Howard Solomon began building what has become a 60-foot-tall, 12,000-square-foot castle in a Manatee County swamp. Solomon, a metal and wood sculptor by trade, built the huge structure (where he now lives) out of 22 × 34-inch offset aluminum printing plates discarded by a local newspaper. He and the other tour guides (try to get the tour led by Solomon, or at least talk with him about his work) lead guests on a pun-filled tour of the castle, which is decked out with some of his smaller artistic creations, mostly made of other people's "trash," including a chair made out of 86 beer cans, an elephant pieced together with seven oil drums, a unicorn fashioned out of coat hangers, and about 80 stained-glass windows. Howard is continually building new things—you never know what you'll find. If you're hungry, check out the **Boat in the Moat** restaurant, which is literally just that. You *have* to experience this to believe it.

4533 Solomon Rd., Ona. ✆ **863/494-6007.** www.solomonscastle.com. Admission $10 adults, $4 children 11 and under. Tours Oct–June Tues–Sun 11am–4pm. Closed July–Sept. Take Hwy. 64 east of I-75 29 miles to Hwy. 665, go south 9 miles, and turn left at the sign to the castle.

South Florida Museum, Bishop Planetarium & Parker Manatee Aquarium ☺

The star at this downtown complex is Snooty, the oldest manatee born in captivity (1948) and Manatee County's official mascot. The South Florida Museum tells the story of Florida's history, from prehistoric times to the present; it includes a Native American collection with life-size dioramas, and a Spanish courtyard containing replicas of 16th-century buildings. The Bishop Planetarium is a state-of-the-art domed theater with one of the most advanced projection systems in the world.

201 10th St. W. (on the riverfront, at Barcarrota Blvd.). ✆ **941/746-4131.** www.southflorida museum.org. Admission $16 adults, $14 seniors, $12 children 5–12, free for children 4 and under. Jan–Apr and July Mon–Sat 10am–5pm, Sun noon–5pm; rest of year Tues–Sat 10am–5pm, Sun noon–5pm. Closed New Year's Day, Thanksgiving, and Christmas. From U.S. 41, take Manatee Ave. west to 10th St. W. and turn right.

Where to Stay

The beaches here are lined with condominiums, many of which are actually all-condo projects operated as hotels. Among the rental agencies requiring stays of less than a month are **Argus Property Management,** 2477 Stickney Point Rd., Sarasota, FL 34231 (✆ **941/927-6464;** fax 941/927-6767; www. argusmgmt.com); and **Florida Vacation Connection,** 3720 Gulf of Mexico Dr., Longboat Key, FL 34228 (✆ **877/702-9981** or 941/387-9709; www.flvacation connection.com). The hotels below are organized by geographic region: in downtown Sarasota, on Lido Key, on Longboat Key, and on Siesta Key. The high season is from January to April. The bed tax in Sarasota County of 5% plus 7% sales tax adds a 12% total tax to your bill.

DOWNTOWN SARASOTA

Most visitors stay out at the beaches, but cost-conscious travelers will find some good deals on the mainland, such as the **Best Western Midtown,** 1425 S. Tamiami Trail (U.S. 41) at Prospect Street (www.bwmidtown.com; ✆ **800/722-8227** or 941/955-9841; fax 941/954-8948). This older but well-maintained motel features newly renovated rooms and is 2 miles in either direction from the main causeways leading to the Keys. Rates range from $89 to $99, sometimes lower if booked online.

Downtown's top hotel before the opening of the Ritz-Carlton (see below), the **Hyatt Sarasota,** 1000 Blvd. of the Arts (www.sarasota.hyatt.com; ✆ **800/233-1234** or 941/953-1234; fax 941/952-1987), is adjacent to the Civic Center and the Van Wezel Performing Arts Hall, and within walking distance of downtown shops and restaurants.

Oh, the huge manatee (at the Parker Manatee Aquarium).

Hyatt Place, 950 University Pkwy., Sarasota (www.sarasotabradenton. place.hyatt.com/hyatt/hotels/place/index.jsp; *©* **941/554-5803**), opened in the summer of 2009, is 3 miles from downtown Sarasota and features free continental breakfast, free Wi-Fi, and plasma TVs.

Most other chain motels are near the airport, including **Quality Inn** (*©* **800/228-5151** or 941/355-7091), **Days Inn** (*©* **800/329-7466** or 941/355-9721), and **Comfort Inn** (*©* **800/521-2121** or 941/351-7734). All stand side by side on Tamiami Trail (U.S. 41) near the FSU Ringling Center for the Cultural Arts and the Asolo Center for the Performing Arts.

The Cypress ★★★ A throwback to the 1940s, the Cypress is a two-story, tin-roofed inn tucked amid giant mango trees and hovering palms. Best of all, it overlooks the bay. You can't get accommodations much better than this, with its antiques, a grand piano, and guest rooms with private bathrooms, queen-size beds, hardwood floors, ceiling fans, and Oriental rugs. The best unit is the Essie Leigh Key West Room, which has its own side entrance, a front-porch view of the bay, a brass-and-pewter bed, an antique oak chest, and Spanish-pine side tables. Others disagree and say the best is the Martha Rose Suite and its romantic French-Victorian decor and balcony with views of the Sarasota Bay. It's up to you. Other rooms are distinctly "Victorian meets Ralph Lauren," some with French doors and others with neoclassical twists.

621 Gulfstream Ave. S., Sarasota, FL 34236. www.cypressbb.com. *©* **941/955-4683.** 5 units. Winter $259–$289 double; off season $150–$199 double. AE, DISC, MC, V. *In room:* A/C, TV, Wi-Fi.

The Ritz-Carlton Sarasota ★★★ Downtown's swankiest digs, just north of the Ringling Causeway, the Ritz occupies the bottom eight floors of an 18-story Mediterranean-style building (the top floors are private residences). It sits perpendicular to the bay, so most of the spacious guest units have views looking across the water to the Keys and the Gulf. The rooms are luxuriously appointed in typical Ritz-Carlton fashion, including marble bathrooms. The hotel's four restaurants are led by **Vernona,** while the **Bay View Bar & Grill** offers casual dining both indoors and out. The elegantly appointed lobby opens to a bayside courtyard with a heated pool. There is no beach on-site, but a shuttle will take you to the hotel's fabulous, private beach club on Lido Key. Also offsite but another plus is the Ritz-Carlton Member's Golf Club, 13 miles from the hotel, featuring a Tom Fazio–designed 18-hole championship course.

1111 Ritz-Carlton Dr. (at Tamiami Trail/U.S. 41), Sarasota, FL 34236. www.ritzcarlton.com. **©** 800/241-3333 or 941/309-2000. Fax 941/309-2100. 266 units. Winter $329–$695 double; off season $299–$519 double. AE, DC, DISC, MC, V. **Amenities:** 3 restaurants (2 additional at off-site beach and golf club); 3 bars (2 additional at off-site beach and golf club); babysitting; children's programs; concierge; concierge-level rooms; golf course; health club; Jacuzzi; 2 outdoor pools (heated, including a children's pool); room service; sauna; spa; 3 tennis courts. *In room:* A/C, TV, hair dryer, high-speed Internet access, minibar.

A BRADENTON B&B

The **Londoner Bed & Breakfast,** 304 15th St. W. (www.thelondonerinn.com; **©** 941/748-5658), is Bradenton's only B&B and a famous one at that. Serving as the backdrop for psychic thriller *The Message,* the Londoner, a restored 1926 house, is a quaint, not creepy, seven-bedroom, seven-bath B&B with wood floors and modern amenities including Wi-Fi and flatscreen TVs, daily afternoon tea, and a traditional English breakfast. Rates range from $120 to $180.

ON LONGBOAT KEY

Longboat Key Club & Resort ★★ A 410-acre beachfront resort and private club on the southern end of Longboat Key, this award-winning, green-certified destination resort pampers the country club set with upscale restaurants and a variety of world-class recreational facilities and social activities all in a lush, private tropical setting. The spacious, newly renovated 218 luxurious rooms and suites have flatscreen TVs and private balconies overlooking the Gulf, a lagoon, or golf-course fairways. All have custom-designed furnishings and neoclassical decor, full-size kitchens or kitchenettes, and washer/dryer. Among several dining options here, the **Sands Pointe Restaurant** has the feel of an informal but elegant supper club, serving inspired organic cuisine in a romantic setting by the Gulf, while the adjacent lounge offers casual dining and live entertainment.

301 Gulf of Mexico Dr. (P.O. Box 15000), Longboat Key, FL 34228. www.longboatkeyclub.com. **©** 800/237-8821 or 941/383-8821. Fax 941/383-0359. 218 units. Winter $360–$650 double, $650–$1,560 suite; off season $179–$275 double, $225–$720 suite. Packages available. AE, DISC, MC, V. From St. Armands Key, take Gulf of Mexico Dr. north; take 1st left after bridge. **Amenities:** 6 restaurants; 6 bars; babysitting; complimentary bikes; children's programs; concierge; 2 golf courses (45 holes); fitness center and Mind & Motion Studio; Jacuzzi; heated outdoor pool; room service; sauna; signature spa; 25 Har-Tru tennis courts; watersports equipment/rentals. *In room:* A/C, TV, DVD, hair dryer, high-speed Internet, fully equipped kitchen/kitchenette.

ON SIESTA KEY

Captiva Beach Resort ★ 🍃 About half a block from the beach in a tropical oasis with other small resorts, Captiva Beach Resort, Sarasota's first Green Lodging, eco-friendly resort, is popular with longer-term guests during winter, Europeans during the summer. Every one of the comfortable, sparkling-clean units here has some form of cooking facility and five-star queen-size pillow-top beds, and some have separate living rooms with sleeper sofas. These are older buildings, so you'll find window air-conditioners mounted through the walls; however, the property has been upgraded for all the modern conveniences, such as high-speed Internet connection and bottle-quality water at every faucet. Rooms also have personal barbecues, beach chairs, and umbrellas. You'll get fresh linens and towels daily except Sunday. Daily maid service is available for a small fee. Guests get complimentary use of sand toys.

6772 Sara Sea Circle, Siesta Key, FL 34242. www.captivabeachresort.com. ℭ **800/349-4131** or 941/349-4131. Fax 941/349-8141. 20 units. Winter $255–$285 double, $215–$370 bungalow and suite; off season $115–$165 double, $115–$250 bungalow and suite. Weekly and monthly rates available. See website for packages. AE, DISC, MC, V. **Amenities:** Heated outdoor pool; watersports equipment/rentals. *In room:* A/C, TV/VCR, hair dryer, high-speed Internet access, kitchen.

Tropical Breeze Resort & Spa ★ On the Gulf side of Siesta Key Village, Tropical Breeze exudes romance and relaxation, with lush gardens and private units across the street from the beach. All the units are walking distance to the beach, shops, restaurants, and nightlife. Rooms are spacious—sizes ranging from a standard to a five-bedroom suite—and decorated in comfortable furniture, nothing fancy, but completely beachy and most with kitchens. Complimentary amenities include but are not limited to continental breakfast, Wi-Fi, gas grills, beach chairs and umbrellas, beach towels, and three heated pools. Pets are also welcome.

153 Av. Messina, Siesta Key, Sarasota, FL 34242. www.tropicalbreezeinn.com. ℭ **941/349-1125.** Fax 941/349-0057. 67 units. Year-round $99–$129 double, $119–$199 1-bedroom suite, $229–$349 2-bedroom. Weekly and monthly rates available. AE, DISC, MC, V. Pets accepted for an extra charge. **Amenities:** Cafe; pool; spa. *In room:* A/C, TV/VCR, hair dryer, kitchen, Wi-Fi.

Turtle Beach Resort Hotel & Marina ★★★ On Siesta Key's south end, this intimate bayside charmer is one of Florida's most romantic retreats. Some units are close to a small bayside swimming pool, heavy tropical foliage provides a reasonable degree of privacy, and high wooden fences surround each unit's private outdoor hot tub. Sitting right on the bay, all units also have one-way privacy mirror windows. The cottages are done in various styles, such as Caribbean and Nantucket, and have at least one bedroom each. There's no restaurant on the grounds, but there are two waterfront restaurants and a pub right next door, and all units have kitchens. Guests can use bikes, fishing poles, kayaks, and canoes for free. Boaters especially love the property's 10 boat docks. Turtle Beach is only a 5-minute walk. Ten new studios and one-bedroom luxury units, called the **Inn at Turtle Beach,** have been added across the street on the Gulf side. All units have hot tubs with aromatherapy jets. Facilities include kitchenettes and bathrooms, two boat docks, fountains, and a heated pool.

9049 Midnight Pass Rd., Sarasota, FL 34242. www.turtlebeachresort.com. ℭ **941/349-4554.** Fax 941/312-9034. 10 units. Winter $350–$430 cottage, $340–$430 Inn studios; off season $235–$365 cottage, $175–$365 Inn studios. Weekly rates available. AE, DISC, MC, V. Pets accepted for an extra charge. **Amenities:** Free use of bikes; outdoor pool; free use of watersports equipment. *In room:* A/C, TV/DVD/VCR, hair dryer, kitchen, free Wi-Fi.

Where to Dine

The restaurants below are organized geographically: in downtown Sarasota, in Southside Village (the city's hottest new dining scene), on St. Armands Key (next to Lido Key), on Longboat Key, and on Siesta Key.

IN DOWNTOWN SARASOTA

Downtown's best breakfast spot is the local branch of **First Watch,** 1395 Main St., at Central and Pineapple avenues (ℭ **941/954-1395**). Like its siblings in Naples and elsewhere, First Watch offers a wide variety of breakfast and lunch fare. It's open daily from 7:30am to 2:30pm. If the wait's too long, walk south along Central Avenue; this block has several coffeehouses and cafes with sidewalk seating.

Bijou Cafe ★★ INTERNATIONAL South African chef Jean-Pierre Knaggs prepares award-winning cuisine from around the world in his cafe, a former gas station, in the heart of the theater district. Although the more casual Michael's on East (see below) bistro draws a hefty after-theater crowd, this is the best place to dine within walking distance of the downtown venues. Jean-Pierre artfully presents the likes of crisp, roasted duck with bread pudding stuffing, sour cherry merlot sauce, seasonal vegetables, and simmered lamb shanks with rosemary and garlic. An African staple of shrimp *piri-piri* is spicy, hot, and sautéed with garlic, lemon, and cayenne pepper. His outstanding wine list has won accolades from *Wine Spectator* magazine.

1287 1st St. (at Pineapple Ave.). ✆ **941/366-8111.** www.bijoucafe.net. Reservations recommended. Main courses $18–$39. AE, DC, MC, V. Mon–Sat 11:30am–2pm and 5–9:30pm; Sun 5–9:30pm. Closed Sun June–Dec. Free valet parking nightly in winter, on weekends off season.

Derek's Culinary Casual ★★★ PROGRESSIVE AMERICAN Despite its name as "culinary casual," Derek's is casual in vibe, but completely off the wall and original in terms of cuisine. Pushing the gastronomic envelope, chef/owner Derek Barnes does the whole small- and large-plate thing but in a way that no one else, with the exception of Libby's (see below), does in this town. Fish and chips with corvine beignets, artichoke aioli, crispy potato, and malt vinegar is just an example of Barnes's culinary savvy. A double-cut "boutique farmed" pork chop served with root vegetable purée, pecan praline, crispy onion, house-made bacon, and smoked shallot sauce is exceptional, as is a yellowfin tuna with oyster mushroom, caramelized parsnips, garlicky broccoli, bacon preserves, and roasted pear jus. A Thursday-night "Supper Club" features some of the chef's latest experiments. Everything here is seasonal and sensational.

1 N. Lemon Ave. ✆ **941/330-0440.** www.dereks-sarasota.com. Reservations recommended. Small plates $4–$12; main courses $21–$30. AE, DC, MC, V. Tues–Fri 11am–2:30pm; Tues–Sat 5–10pm.

Main Street Oyster Bar ★ SEAFOOD The sleek and stylish space formerly known as Zoria is now an oyster bar with a mostly seafood menu with simple dishes of snapper, yellowfin, grouper, salmon, flounder, and, well, you get the picture. There are also sandwiches and pastas, and while you'd think the focus would be on the restaurant's namesake, a small selection of oysters is somewhat of a letdown. Fans of Zoria were baffled by the transformation, but thanks to a prime location on Main Street, perhaps the Main Street Oyster Bar has slowly but surely rediscovered its identity.

1991 Main St. ✆ **941/955-4457.** www.zoria.net. Reservations recommended. Main courses $14–$29; sandwiches $12–$21; small plates $10–$14. AE, DC, MC, V. Mon–Sat 5–10pm; Sun 5–9pm.

Marina Jack's SEAFOOD/CONTINENTAL Overlooking the waterfront with a 270-degree view of Sarasota Bay and both Siesta and Lido keys, this establishment has spectacular vistas and a carefree "on vacation" attitude, especially on the open-air raw-bar deck, which is often packed all afternoon on weekends and at sunset every day. The food is good but not the best in town, so come here for a fun time. You may have to wait for a table or bar stool down on the portside patio bar, but be sure to make reservations if you want to have a meal in the upstairs dining room. Fresh local seafood is the star both upstairs and down— grilled grouper is your best bet. The downstairs piano lounge and raw bar also serves sandwiches and burgers.

In Island Park, Bayfront at Central Ave. ☎ **941/365-4232.** www.marinajacks.com. Reservations recommended in dining room. Dining room main courses $25–$45; lounge menu $9–$43; patio bar $10–$14; sandwiches and salads $8–$14. AE, DISC, MC, V. Daily 11:30am–2am. Closed Christmas.

Mattison's City Grille ★★ ITALIAN Downtown Sarasota's premier alfresco hot spot, Mattison's features Italian fare, including pretty good pizza as well as tapas, burgers, and salads, but the main draw here isn't the food, per se, it's the live jazz and blues bands that play nightly. Mattison's is also a hot spot for Saturday and Sunday brunch.

1 N. Lemon Ave. ☎ **941/330-0440.** www.mattisons.com. Reservations recommended. Tapas $9–$16; pizza $15–$25; burgers and salads $9–$16; main courses $17–$29. AE, DC, MC, V. Mon–Thurs 11am–11pm; Fri 11am–midnight; Sat 9am–midnight; Sun 11am–10pm.

Michael's on East ★★ NEW AMERICAN At the rear of the Midtown Plaza shopping center on U.S. 41 south of downtown, Michael Klauber's chic bistro is one of the top places for fine dining—it's the locals' favorite after-theater haunt. Huge cut-glass walls create three intimate dining areas, one a piano bar for pre- or after-dinner drinks. Prepared with fresh ingredients and a creative flair, the offerings here will tempt your taste buds. House specialties are pan-roasted blue fin crab cakes; pan-roasted Chilean sea bass with artisanal Sardinian fregola, green onions, fire-roasted corn, royal trumpet and shiitake mushrooms, oven-roasted herbed tomatoes, and micro licorice; and the roasted, bone-in Kurubuta pork chop with Snake River Farms heirloom pork, caramelized sweet potatoes, cumin-spiced chestnuts, quince-cranberry chutney, and ancho-glazed carambola with poblano-tomatillo reduction. A great bargain is the three-course $25 Epicurean Adventures menu. For just $10 more you can add wine pairings.

1212 East Ave. S. (btw. Bahia and Prospect sts.). ☎ **941/366-0007.** www.michaelsoneast.com. Reservations recommended. Main courses $16–$38. AE, DC, DISC, MC, V. Mon–Fri 11:30am–2pm and 5:30–10pm; Sat–Sun 5:30–10pm. Free valet parking.

Morel ★★ NEW AMERICAN A warm, sophisticated, bistrolike ambience (that could use a remodel to go with the "new" in New American) and an innovative menu created by chef/owner Fredy Mayer have made Morel one of Sarasota's hottest and "hautest" restaurants. Of all the excellent fare, we recommend the potato-and-leek latkes with house-smoked salmon, the sautéed pork loins, and the Chilean sea bass in a hoisin-teriyaki reduction. A $17 prix-fixe menu is also available from 4:30 to 5:30pm.

3809 S. Tuttle Ave. ☎ **941/927-8716.** www.morelrestaurant.com. Reservations recommended. Main courses $16–$26. AE, MC, V. Tues–Sat 4:30–9:30pm.

Yoder's ★ 🍴 AMISH/AMERICAN Just 3 miles east of downtown is an award-winning, value eatery operated by an Amish family (Sarasota and Bradenton have sizable Amish communities and several Amish restaurants). Evoking the Pennsylvania Dutch country, the dining room displays handicrafts, photos, and paintings celebrating the Amish way. The menu emphasizes plain, made-from-scratch cooking such as home-style meatloaf, Southern fried chicken, country-smoked ham, and fried filet of flounder. Burgers, salads, soups, and sandwiches are also available. Leave room for Mrs. Yoder's shoofly and other homemade pies, one of the restaurant's biggest draws. *Note:* Alcohol is neither served nor allowed here.

3434 Bahia Vista St. (west of Beneva Rd.). ℭ **941/955-7771.** www.yodersrestaurant.com. Main courses $7–$17; breakfast $3–$8; sandwiches, burgers, and salads $4–$10. No credit cards (ATM on premises). Mon–Sat 6am–8pm.

IN SOUTHSIDE VILLAGE

Sarasota's hottest dining area is **Southside Village,** centered on South Osprey Avenue between Hyde Park and Hillview streets, about 15 blocks south of downtown. Here you'll find several hip restaurants, including Fred's and Pacific Rim (see below). The village landmark is **Morton's Gourmet Market ★**, 1924 S. Osprey Ave. (ℭ **941/955-9856;** www.mortonsmarket.com), which offers a multitude of deli items, sandwiches, salads, fresh pastries and desserts, and cooked meals dispensed from a cafeteria-style steam table. You can dine picnic-fashion at sidewalk tables. Most ready-to-go items cost less than $10. The market is open Monday through Saturday from 8am to 8pm, Sunday from 10am to 5pm.

Hillview Grill ★ ECLECTIC A locals' favorite, Hillview Grill offers an unabridged menu of burgers, salads, small plates ranging from fish tacos to escargot, and large plates including ancho chili seared scallops, and grilled meatloaf with applewood bacon and mushroom gravy. A late-night bar scene Wednesday through Saturday nights brings in the hip cocktail set and features a late-night menu.

In Hillview Centre, 1920 Hillview St. (btw. Osprey Ave. and Laurent Place). ℭ **941/952-0045.** www.hillviewgrill.com. Main courses $10–$24; small plates $6.75. AE, DISC, MC, V. Mon–Fri 11am–1pm and 5–9pm; Sat–Sun 4pm–midnight.

Libby's Café & Bar ★★★ NEW AMERICAN A popular newcomer on the Southside dining scene, Libby's features Chef Fran Casciato's fabulous Florida-inspired cuisine that emphasizes locally grown produce and ingredients. Everything on the menu seems refreshingly special and original, from the deviled eggs with Mote Marine American sturgeon caviar and the cheesesteak egg roll to the "Libbsticker," a truffled Kobe meatloaf club stacked with prosciutto di parma, melted white cheddar, crispy shoestring onions, roasted mushrooms, romaine lettuce, beefsteak tomatoes, and truffle aioli. And those are just starters and sandwiches or, rather, "Hands On." Main courses include the 7-Day Famous Mahi Tacos served in soft tortillas, with Aztec-style slaw, *pico de gallo,* and chipotle sour cream; and the citrus chipotle skirt steak with cheddar jalapeño cornbread and tortilla salad. Choosing from this menu isn't an easy task. Take advantage of early dining specials and happy hours if you can.

1917 S. Osprey (at Hillview). ℭ **941/487-7300.** www.libbyscafebar.com. Main courses $10–$36; small plates $5–$17. AE, DISC, MC, V. Mon–Sat 11:30am–3pm; daily 5pm–close.

Pacific Rim ★ ✦ JAPANESE/THAI Sarasotans love this chic and casual restaurant for exceptional cuisine at economical prices. Japanese influence is felt at the sushi bar along one side of the dining room, while Thai spices make a strong impact on the regular menu. The chargrilled shrimp with Thai curry and coconut-milk sauce is especially tasty, as is the combination of chicken and vegetables stir-fried in a wok. Here you can select your meat and vegetables separately from the sauce, and the chefs will combine them on the grill, in the wok, or in the bowl (as in rice dishes).

In Hillview Centre, 1859 Hillview St. (btw. Osprey Ave. and Laurent Place). ℭ **941/330-8071.** www.pacificrimsarasota.com. Main courses $10–$25; sushi $3–$12. AE, DISC, MC, V. Mon–Thurs 11:30am–2pm and 5–9pm; Fri 11:30am–2pm and 5–10pm; Sat 5–10pm.

ON ST. ARMANDS KEY

While locals are hanging out in Southside Village, part-year residents and visitors flock to St. Armands Circle. Plan to spend at least 1 evening here: The nighttime scene is like a fair, with everyone strolling around the circle, poking heads into the few stores that stay open after dark, and window-shopping the others. It's fun and safe, so come early and plan to stay late.

The circle has a branch of Tampa's famous **Columbia Restaurant** (p. 442), between John Ringling Boulevard and John Ringling Parkway (℡ **941/388-3987**). The Spanish food is excellent, there's outdoor seating, and the Patio Lounge is one of the liveliest spots for evening entertainment Thursday through Sunday. Like its sibling in Naples, the local edition of **Tommy Bahama's Tropical Cafe,** 300 John Ringling Blvd. (℡ **941/388-2446**), draws a lively crowd of young professionals for its moderately priced seafood. It's upstairs over the Tommy Bahama's clothing store.

At dinner, you may wish to forgo an expensive dessert and wander over to the local branch of **Kilwin's,** 312 John Ringling Blvd. (℡ **941/388-3200**), for some gourmet chocolate, Mackinac Island fudge, or ice cream or yogurt in a home-made waffle cone. Enjoy your sweets on one of the sidewalk park benches—everyone else does.

Café L'Europe ★★★ CONTINENTAL Café L'Europe has been the recipient of countless awards and praise for its Continental fare that fuses French, Caribbean, and Spanish influences into what the chef prefers to call New European cuisine. An elegant ambience makes Café L'Europe the place to celebrate special occasions, whether over the classic Dover sole (served for two people) or an updated version of sweetbreads—with brandied demi-glace and mushrooms. Grouper—pan roasted and served with a risotto of shrimp, scallops, lobster, and mussels—is a sublime choice as well, especially when matched with one of the restaurant's many vintages. Service, as to be expected in an establishment of this caliber, is outstanding.

431 St. Armands Circle (at John Ringling Blvd.). ℡ **941/388-4415.** www.cafeleurope.net. Reservations recommended. Main courses $29–$42. AE, DC, MC, V. Daily 11am–10:30pm.

ON LONGBOAT KEY

Euphemia Haye/The Haye Loft ★★★ INTERNATIONAL This area's most extraordinary restaurant, the romantically lit Euphemia Haye is known for Chef Raymond Arpke's crispy roast duckling filled with bread stuffing and accompanied by a tangy fruit sauce. His prime strip steak rolled in cracked peppercorns and served with an orange, brandy, and butter sauce is another winner, as is his Indian-style shrimp in curry sauce, spiced with jalapeño peppers and enhanced with tomato, lemon, coconut, onion, and ginger. Appetizers also take a trip around the globe with dishes hailing from the Middle East (hummus) to Russia (smoked salmon on buckwheat crepes). If all this sounds sweet, wait until you go upstairs to the **Haye Loft,** his casual dessert bar and lounge with live entertainment. Up here, you can take your pick from fabulous pies topped with thick whipped cream. You can also sample the kitchen's offerings because the loft has its own light-fare menu, including soups, appetizers, small pizzas, and sandwiches. If you're lucky, the night's special sandwich will be steak topped with Raymond's peppercorn sauce, available for sale by the bottle if you like it.

5540 Gulf of Mexico Dr. (at Gulfbay Rd.). ℡ **941/383-3633.** www.euphemiahaye.com. Reservations recommended downstairs, not accepted in the Haye Loft. Main courses $27–$50;

sandwiches, pizzas, and salads $10–$20. DC, DISC, MC, V. Restaurant Sun–Thurs 5–10pm; Fri–Sat 5–10:30pm. Haye Loft daily 6pm–midnight.

Moore's Stone Crab ★★ SEAFOOD In Longbeach, the old fishing village on the north end of Longboat Key, this bayfront restaurant began in 1967 as an offshoot of a family seafood business established 40 years earlier. From the outside, it still looks a little like a packing house, but the view of the bay dotted with mangrove islands makes a fine complement to stone crabs fresh from the family's own traps from October 15 to May 15. Otherwise, the menu offers an incredibly large variety of seafood, most of it fried or broiled. Sandwiches and salads are served all day.

800 Broadway (at Bayside Dr.). ✆ **941/383-1748.** Main courses $15–$27; stone crab market price (as much as $40–$45 in season, mid-Oct to mid-May); sandwiches and salads $9–$13. AE, DISC, MC, V. Winter daily 11:30am–9:30pm; off season Mon–Fri 4:30–9:30pm, Sat–Sun 11:30am–9:30pm.

Pattigeorge's ★★ SEAFOOD A bayside eatery with views of mangrove-covered islands, PG's, as it's known by regulars, offers fantastic coastal cuisine, including a miso-glazed sea bass in a lobster consommé and crispy Bahamian lobster tails served with Asian slaw, red bliss potatoes, and honey-mustard sauce. The Thai-green curried grouper is one of the house specialties. Try the panko-crusted fried banana for dessert, or if you'd rather stay healthy—okay, *healthier*—check out the hashed Brussels sprouts, thinly shredded and sautéed with butter and poppy seeds. If you don't dig the Asian influences, there's also a selection of sandwiches, pastas, and pizzas.

4120 Gulf of Mexico Dr. ✆ **941/383-0102.** www.pattigeorges.com. Main courses $13–$40. AE, DISC, MC, V. Daily 6–11pm (bar from 5:30pm).

ON SIESTA KEY

Ocean Boulevard, which runs through **Siesta Village,** the area's funky, laid-back beach hangout, is lined with restaurants and pubs. Most have bars and outdoor seating, which attracts the beach crowd during the day. At night, rock-'n'-roll bands draw teens and college students to this lively scene.

Blasé Café ★★ 🖍 INTERNATIONAL Tongue-in-cheeky, to say the least, this restaurant doesn't take itself seriously, hence the oxymoronic name. This super-casual establishment has tables indoors and a few under the cover of the Village Corner shopping center's walkway, but most are alfresco, on a wooden deck built around a palm tree in the center's asphalt parking lot. Never mind the cars pulling in and out next to your chair: The food is so good it draws droves of locals who don't mind waiting for a table. Dinner includes the likes of soft-shell crab served Provençal-style with tomato, capers, and olives, or a kicky New Orleans–style jambalaya. There are also pasta, sandwiches, and burgers for the pickier eaters. You can while away the rest of the evening in the martini bar, where the owners have installed the original bar from Don CeSar Beach Resort & Spa in St. Pete Beach. Live music is featured on weekends.

In Village Corner, 5263 Ocean Blvd. (at Calle Miramar), Siesta Village. ✆ **941/349-9822.** www.theblasecafe.com. Reservations recommended. Main courses $5–$16. MC, V. Mon–Thurs 6–9:30pm; Fri–Sat 6–10pm. Closed Mon June–Nov.

SKOB ★★ SEAFOOD Siesta Key Oyster Bar, or SKOB to the locals, features live music, daily drink specials, and, of course, oysters of all varieties, raw on the half shell, fried, or steamed. There are also a slew of sandwiches, salads, and a kids' menu, but what the place is known for is one of the best happy hours in town, daily from 3 to 6pm, when there are two-for-one appetizers, live bands, and drink specials.

5238 Ocean Blvd. ☎ **941/346-5443.** www.skob.com. Raw bar $6–$12; sandwiches and salads $7–$14; main courses $12–$22. AE, DISC, MC, V. Mon–Sat 11am–close; Sun 11:30am–close.

Sun Garden Cafe ★★ BREAKFAST/LUNCH Hands down the best breakfast place on Siesta Key, this indoor-outdoor cafe features a breezy ambience and superb service, along with a seasonal menu of fantastic and freshly made egg dishes, breakfast sandwiches (the Ham-n-Egger—ham steak, cheddar, and a fried egg on sourdough with jalapeño mustard kick-started my day), waffles, pancakes (try the banana ones), French toast, omelets, biscuits, and other breakfast items undoubtedly contributing to ordering anxiety. Whatever you choose, you won't be disappointed. If you take long enough to figure out what you want, you may as well order lunch, whose menu is equally delicious—and distracting with a bounty of burgers, salads, and sandwiches not found at your corner Subway. Our recommendation? Grilled bologna smothered in cheese and spicy pickles.

210 Avenida Madera. ☎ **941/346-7170.** www.sol-food.net. Main courses $3–$15. AE, DISC, MC, V. Daily 7am–2:30pm.

Turtles AMERICAN With tropical overtones and breathtaking water vistas across from Turtle Beach, this informal restaurant on Little Sarasota Bay has tables indoors and on an outdoor deck. Unique seafood offerings include snapper New Orleans and potato-encrusted mahimahi. You can't go wrong ordering grouper grilled, broiled, blackened, or fried. A selection of pastas is also available. Early-bird specials are available daily 4 to 6pm. The daily happy hour from 3 to 6pm features great two-for-one drink specials.

8875 Midnight Pass Rd. (at Turtle Beach Rd.). ☎ **941/346-2207.** www.turtlesrestaurant.com. Main courses $11–$25; salads and sandwiches $6–$10. AE, DISC, MC, V. Mon–Sat 11:30am–9:30pm; Sun 10am–9pm.

Sarasota After Dark

The cultural capital of Florida's west coast, Sarasota is home to a host of performing arts, especially during the winter season. To get the latest on what's happening any time of year, call the city's 24-hour **Artsline** (☎ **941/365-2787**). Also check the "Ticket" section in Friday's *Herald-Tribune* (**www.newscoast.com**), the local daily newspaper; copies are usually available at the Sarasota Convention and Visitors Bureau (p. 470).

THE PERFORMING ARTS At the **FSU Ringling Center for the Cultural Arts** (p. 476), the **Florida State University Center for the Performing Arts,** 5555 N. Tamiami Trail (U.S. 41; ☎ **800/361-8388** or 941/351-8000; www. asolo.org), presents the **Asolo Repertory Theatre** ★★★. The Asolo Rep has a reputation as one of the finest regional theaters in the country, and hosts a conservatory for training professional actors. In addition to the Asolo Theatre, a 19th-century Italian court playhouse moved here from Asolo, Italy, in the 1950s by the Ringlings, the center uses the 487-seat Harold E. and Ethel M. Mertz Theatre, originally constructed in Scotland in 1900 and transferred piece by piece to Sarasota in 1987. The 161-seat **Asolo Conservatory Theatre** was later added as a smaller venue for experimental and alternative offerings. The complex is under the direction of Florida State University (FSU).

The city's other prime venue is the lavender, seashell-shaped **Van Wezel Performing Arts Hall ★★★**, 777 N. Tamiami Trail (U.S. 41), at 9th Street (© **800/826-9303** or 941/953-3368; www.vanwezel.org). Recently renovated, it offers excellent visual and acoustic conditions, and a wide range of year-round programming, including touring Broadway shows and visiting orchestras and dance troupes. It and the FSU Center host performances by the **Florida West Coast Symphony** (© **941/953-4252;** www.fwcs.org), the **Jazz Club of Sarasota** (© **941/366-1552** or 941/316-9207; www.jazzclubsarasota.

Classic and modern plays are presented at the Asolo Repertory Theatre.

com), the **Sarasota Pops** (© **941/795-7677**), and the **Sarasota Ballet** (© **800/361-8388** or 941/351-8000; www.sarasotaballet.org).

Downtown Sarasota's theater district is home to the **Florida Studio Theatre,** 1241 N. Palm Ave., at Cocoanut Avenue (© **941/366-9000;** www.floridastudiotheatre.org), which has contemporary performances from December to August, including a New Play Festival in May. Built in 1926 as the Edwards Theater, the **Opera House,** 61 N. Pineapple Ave., between Main and 1st streets (© **941/366-8450;** www.sarasotaopera.org), presents classical operas (in their original languages) as well as highbrow concerts. Next door to the Opera House, the **Golden Apple Dinner Theatre,** 25 N. Pineapple Ave. (© **941/366-5454;** www.thegoldenapple.com), presents cocktails, dinner, and a professional Broadway-style show year-round. The non-Equity **Theatre Works,** 1247 1st St., at Cocoanut Avenue (© **941/952-9170**), presents musical revues and other works year-round.

THE CLUB & MUSIC SCENE One of downtown's most popular places for a night out is **Mattison's City Grille,** 1 N. Lemon Ave. (© **941/330-0440;** www.mattisons.com). In Siesta Key Village, the **Old Salty Dog,** 5023 Ocean Blvd. (© **941/349-0158;** www.theoldsaltydog.com), offers a selection of British ales and an outdoor patio. Strolling St. Armands Circle provides for an entertaining night out, especially if you stop into some of the bustling bars and restaurants. Also on St. Armands Circle, the **Patio Lounge** in the Columbia Restaurant (© **941/388-3987;** p. 442) is one of the liveliest spots along the beach strip, featuring live, high-energy dance music Tuesday through Sunday evenings. And on Siesta Key, the pubs and restaurants along Ocean Boulevard in Siesta Village have noisy rock-'n'-roll bands entertaining a mostly young crowd—**SKOB**, 5238 Ocean Blvd. (© **941/346-5443;** www.skob.com), is a major hot spot, featuring fabulous happy hours and live music nightly; or you can retire to the pleasant confines of the martini bar at **Blasé Café** (© **941/349-9822;** p. 487) for live jazz. On Longboat Key, it's the **Haye Loft** at **Euphemia Haye,** 5540 Gulf of Mexico Dr., at Gulfbay Road (© **941/383-3633;** www.euphemiahaye.com), command central for the cocktail set. Be sure to check out all the beach bars on Anna Maria Island and Bradenton Beach for some salty, sandy nights.

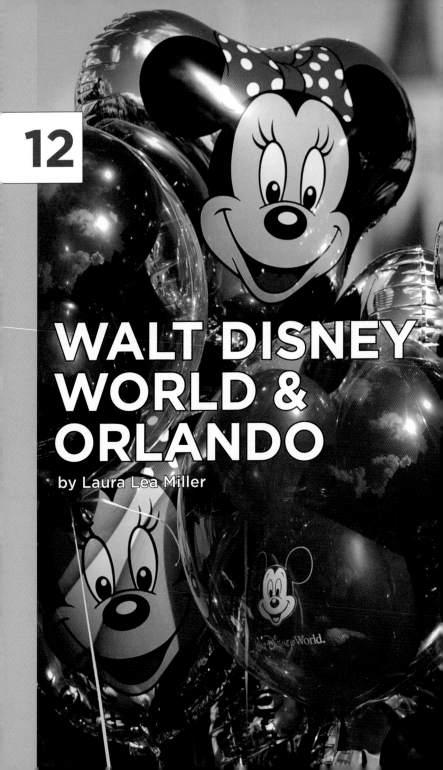

12

WALT DISNEY WORLD & ORLANDO

by Laura Lea Miller

W hen Walt Disney World opened its gates just over 40 years ago, I doubt even Walt himself, could have imagined the transformation that would follow. Orlando, once known for its citrus groves and cattle ranches, has evolved into an international vacation destination. An extraordinary and diverse array of activities, shopping and dining experiences, and world-class accommodations await those who visit the "Happiest Place on Earth," amid the natural beauty of Central Florida.

Walt Disney World (WDW), practically a city unto itself at 47 square miles, is home to four major theme parks; two water parks; an incredible shopping, dining, and entertainment complex; thousands of hotel rooms; scores of restaurants; and a cruise line!

When **Universal Orlando** (consisting of two major theme parks; an entertainment, dining, and shopping complex; and three luxury resorts), **SeaWorld** (including Discovery Cove and Aquatica, SeaWorld's water park), and the handful of smaller players toss their wonders into Orlando's mix, it can get quite overwhelming.

To help you plan your Orlando stay, we've included the lowdown on the area's best hotels, restaurants, and attractions. You'll also find tips to help you plan and budget, making it not only easier to arrange, but, we hope, more affordable too.

Note: For a more in-depth look at WDW as well as Orlando's other offerings, check out Frommer's *Walt Disney World® & Orlando,* as well as *Frommer's Walt Disney World® with Kids* (Wiley).

ESSENTIALS
Getting There

BY PLANE More than 33 scheduled airlines and several more charter companies serve just under 34 million Orlando-bound passengers who arrive at the **Orlando International Airport** (☎ 407/825-2001; www.orlandoairports. net) each year. The best travel fares to Orlando are often available during the months of November, December, and January, excluding holidays (when fares go way up).

Southwest Airlines brings 24% of the flights in and out of the airport. Other major airlines serving Orlando include **AirTran Airways, JetBlue, Delta, Continental, United Airlines, Air Canada, American, British Airways, Spirit,** and **US Airways,** among many others.

Located 25 miles from Walt Disney World, Orlando International is a relatively easy drive from the most popular tourist destinations. If you're

FACING PAGE: Walt Disney World leaves many visitors feeling buoyant.

not renting a car, **Mears Transportation** (☎ **407/423-5566;** www.mearstransportation.com) provides town-car and shuttle service to and from the airport; vans run 24 hours a day and depart every 15 to 25 minutes. Round-trip fares are $30 to $46 for adults and $24 to $37 for children ages 4 to 11 (actual price depends on your destination); children 3 and under ride free. **Quicksilver Tours and Transportation** (☎ **888/468-6939** or 407/299-1434; www.quicksilver-tours.com) provides town-car, shuttle, and limo service, along with such extras as meet and greet, luggage assistance, safety seats for the kids, and a 30-minute grocery stop included. One-way shuttle fares run $75 to $80, round-trip $125 to $135, for up to 10 passengers.

Harry Potter's Hogsmeade can be found at Universal Orlando.

BY CAR From Atlanta, take I-75 South to the Florida Turnpike to I-4 West. From the northeast, take I-95 South to I-4 West. From Chicago, take I-65 South to Nashville, then I-24 South to I-75, then south to the Florida Turnpike to I-4 West. From Dallas, take I-20 East to I-49 South, then head south to I-10, east to I-75, and south to the Florida Turnpike to I-4 West.

BY TRAIN **Amtrak** trains (☎ **800/872-7245;** www.amtrak.com) pull into stations in both Downtown Orlando (23 miles from WDW) and Kissimmee (15 miles from WDW). Winter Park (10 miles north of downtown) and Sanford (23 miles northeast of Downtown Orlando) have stations as well; Sanford is the terminus for Amtrak's Auto Train.

Package Tours

If you plan to spend most of your time at Walt Disney World, contact **Walt Disney World Central Reservation Operations (CRO)** at ☎ **407/934-7675** for a wide assortment of packages. **AAA,** the American Automobile Association (☎ **800/222-6953;** www.aaa.com), is another good source for WDW packages. Another good place to look for packages is **www.mousesavers.com**—it's an "unofficial" site, but it provides plenty of useful information and deals. **Universal Orlando** packages can be booked at ☎ **877/801-9720;** information is available online at **www.universalorlando.com**. For **SeaWorld** package information, call ☎ **800/557-4268** or go to **www.seaworldorlando.com**.

Many of the major airlines also have Orlando packages.

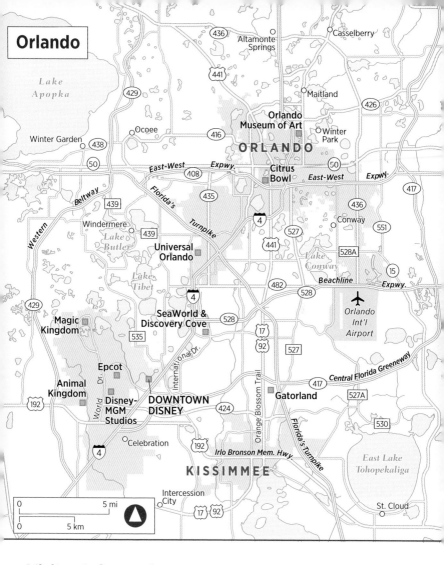

Visitor Information

Visit Orlando, 8723 International Dr., Ste. 101, Orlando, FL 32819 (© **800/972-3304** or 407/363-5872; www.orlandoinfo.com), can answer questions and will send you an array of maps and brochures, including the *Official Vacation Guide* and a calendar of events. The packet takes a few weeks to arrive—be sure to request it far enough in advance—and includes the "Orlando Magicard," good for discounts on rooms, car rentals, attractions, and more. You can also order the guide by calling © **800/643-9492.**

For information about **Walt Disney World**—including vacation brochures, DVDs, and such—contact Walt Disney World, Box 10000, Lake Buena Vista, FL 32830-1000 (© **407/934-7639** or 407/939-6244; www.disneyworld.com).

Disney's official website is an especially good bet; it's easy to navigate and provides detailed information, photos, and videos of the Disney parks, restaurants, and resorts. A very comprehensive unofficial website worth checking out is **www. allearsnet.com**. For information about **Universal Orlando,** call ✆ **800/837-2273,** 407/363-8000, or 407/224-4233; surf the Internet to **www.universal orlando.com**; or write to Universal Orlando, 1000 Universal Studios Plaza, Orlando, FL 32819.

You can obtain **SeaWorld** information online at **www.seaworld.com** or by calling ✆ **888/800-5447** or 407/351-3600.

City Layout

Interstate 4 (I-4) will take you everywhere you want to go in and around Orlando, with several exits along the way to get you to Walt Disney World, SeaWorld, and Universal Orlando, not to mention the areas of International Drive (or I-Dr.), Lake Buena Vista, Celebration, and Kissimmee. *Note:* I-4 can often be jam-packed with traffic—though recent improvements near the Walt Disney World entrances have helped to alleviate a good portion of the tourist traffic tie-ups that plague the area. Consult a detailed local map before heading out to find one of the many alternative routes best suited to your touring plans. If you must use the highway, it's least congested from late morning to midafternoon.

The **Florida Turnpike** crosses I-4 and links with I-75 to the north. U.S. 192, a major east-west highway, runs along Kissimmee's major motel area to U.S. 27, where it crosses I-4 near the Disney World entrance. The **Beachline Expressway** runs east from I-4 past Orlando International Airport to Cape Canaveral and Cocoa Beach.

The Neighborhoods in Brief

WALT DISNEY WORLD WDW is southwest of the city of Orlando. Encompassing more than 47 square miles, it includes within its boundaries four major theme parks, two smaller water parks, several themed resorts, and a plethora of restaurants and shops. It's also home of Downtown Disney, Disney Quest, and the ESPN Wide World of Sports Complex.

LAKE BUENA VISTA Lake Buena Vista encompasses all of WDW, and includes much of the area bordering the resort. Here you can find the "official" (but not Disney-owned) hotels along Hotel Plaza Boulevard. The area along Highway 535, or Apopka-Vineland as it is also known, is home to many a resort and restaurant. Most, though not all, resorts, restaurants, and shops are far off enough from the main thoroughfare to maintain a quieter atmosphere.

CELEBRATION This 4,900-acre community of gingerbread-trimmed houses, some with white picket fences and shade trees in the front yard, evokes Disney-esque perfection. It should come as no surprise that Disney had a hand in its creation—experts as they are at creating the perfect vision of almost anything. The Market Street area, filled with upscale shops, restaurants, and a boutique hotel, is a throwback to a bygone era.

DOWNTOWN DISNEY Downtown Disney encompasses Disney's entertainment district (what remains of it following the demise of the Pleasure Island clubs) known as Disney's West Side, the shopping and dining district known as the Marketplace, and Pleasure Island (soon to be renamed Hyperion Wharf), where upscale restaurants, specialty shops, and attractions have begun to line the more tourist-friendly streetscape. At Downtown Disney you can shop 'til you drop, tempt your taste buds, and take in a show.

KISSIMMEE Brought back to life by a "Rebeautivacation" project, U.S. 192, Kissimmee's main tourist area, sports extrawide sidewalks, colorful streetlamps, landscaping, and location markers. Once home to mostly budget hotels, it now has a handful of moderate hotels, and even a few high-end luxury resorts, a myriad of eateries, and a handful of minor attractions. That said, U.S. 192 still remains frustratingly busy.

INTERNATIONAL DRIVE AREA (HWY. 536) This busy thoroughfare, better known as **I-Drive,** is home to more than 100 resorts and hotels, countless restaurants, attractions big and small, and great shopping. It's even got its own transportation system—the I Ride Trolley. The endless array provides something for every taste and budget.

DOWNTOWN ORLANDO Located some 25 miles or so northeast of Walt Disney World on I-4, downtown Orlando has been revitalized by the addition of ultrachic eateries, nightclubs, shops, and cultural venues (including theaters, museums, parks, and the Orlando Science Center), and in recent years has reemerged as a center of new urbanism.

GETTING AROUND

In a city that thrives on tourism, getting from point A to point B is certainly easy enough, especially by car; it's the time it takes to get there that can wreak havoc on your schedule. If you're traveling by highway, it's best to avoid the 7-day-a-week rush hour (7–9am and 4–6pm) whenever possible. Note that alternate routes can remain congested later into the evening thanks to the dinner rush.

Tip: Generally speaking, unless you will be confining your touring solely to Disney World or Universal Orlando (and staying at those parks' hotels), you're better off renting a car in Orlando. All the major rental chains have desks at or adjacent to the airport, and some have desks at select area hotels.

INTERNATIONAL DRIVE Traffic on I-Drive can be infuriating, compounded exponentially if you are visiting at Easter or Christmas or during select conventions in the early spring. Two of the best ways to conquer the traffic are to travel by foot (points of interest can be reasonably close together, but heavy traffic can be hazardous to pedestrians) and to travel by the **I-Ride Trolley** (© **407/248-9590;** www.iridetrolley.com), which stops about every 2 blocks as it moves from one end of I-Drive to the other. The trolley runs from 8am to 10:30pm ($1.25 adults, 25¢ seniors, free for children 12 and under; *exact change is required*). Unlimited trolley passes covering between 1 and 14 days are available as well. It's a fun and easy way to get around that's often a timesaver when I-Drive is at a standstill.

BY THE DISNEY TRANSPORTATION SYSTEM If you plan to stay at WDW and spend most of your time there, an extensive, free transportation network runs throughout the property. Disney resorts and official hotels offer unlimited free transportation via bus, monorail, ferry, or water taxi to all WDW properties throughout the day and, at times, well into the evening.

The free system saves you money on a rental car, insurance, and gas, as well as parking fees (though Disney resort guests get free parking). The drawback is that you're at the mercy of the Disney departure schedules and routes, which can often be slow and sometimes *very* indirect (especially from Disney's cheaper resorts). Check Disney's website (**www.disneyworld.com**), or ask your concierge to determine the best route.

BY SHUTTLE Operating town cars, vans, and buses, **Mears Transportation** (✆ 407/423-5566; www.mearstransportation.com) goes to all of the theme parks, as well as the Kennedy Space Center and Busch Gardens Tampa Bay, among others. **Quicksilver Tours and Transportation** (✆ 888/468-6939 or 407/299-1434; www.quicksilver-tours.com) offers similar services. Rates for both companies vary according to destination; call or check their websites for current prices.

BY TAXI Taxis gather at the major resorts, and smaller properties will be happy to call a cab for you. **Yellow Cab** (✆ 407/699-9999) and **Ace Metro** (✆ 407/855-0564) are both good choices, but keep in mind that taxis are expensive and charges may run as high as $3.25 for the first mile and $1.75 or more per mile thereafter.

[FastFACTS] WALT DISNEY WORLD & ORLANDO

Babysitters Many Orlando hotels, including all of Disney's resorts, offer in-room babysitting services, usually from an outside service such as **Kids Night Out** (✆ 800/696/8105 or 407/828-0920; www.kidsniteout.com) or **All About Kids** (✆ 800/728-6506 or 407/812-9300; www.all-about-kids.com). Rates for in-room sitters usually run $14 to $16 per hour for the first child and another $2 to $3 per hour for each additional child. A premium fee of $2 per hour (not per child) is often added for services provided during very early or late hours. A transportation fee of $10 to $12 is usually charged as well. Several resorts offer child-care facilities with counselor-supervised activity programs on the premises, including select Disney resorts (for kids ages 4–12; ✆ 407/939-3463). This type of child-care usually costs between $10 and $15 per hour, per child. Reservations are highly recommended, and are often required for either type of service.

Doctors & Dentists There are basic first-aid centers in all of the theme parks. To find a dentist, call **Dental Referral Service** at ✆ 800/235-4111 or go online to **www.dentalreferral.com**. **Doctors on Call Service** (✆ 407/399-3627) makes house and room calls in most of the Orlando area (including the Disney resorts). **Centra-Care** lists several walk-in clinics in the Yellow Pages, including a location in Lake Buena Vista, near Disney (✆ 407/934-2273). The **East Coast Medical Network** (✆ 407/648-5252; www.themedical concierge.com) offers similar services.

Emergencies Dial ✆ 911 for the police, the fire department, or an ambulance.

Hospitals Dr. Phillips Hospital, 9400 Turkey Lake Rd. (✆ 407/351-8500), is about 2 miles south of Sand Lake Road. **Florida Hospital Celebration Health** (✆ 407/303-4000), in the near-Disney town of Celebration, is at 400 Celebration Place.

Kennels The theme parks board pets during the day for about $15 (Disney charges $15 to $69 per pet per day depending on length of stay and type of accommodations—even for day care). WDW also offers overnight boarding at the Best Friends Pet Care kennel ($12–$76 for the general public or $10–$69 for Disney resort guests, again depending on the size and type of pet, as well as the level of accommodations). (Pets are not allowed to stay at the Disney resorts—the sole exception: select campsites at Disney's Fort Wilderness Resort & Campground.) Universal Orlando's kennel is in the parking garage ($15 per day, no overnight boarding). All of Universal Orlando's resorts welcome pets to stay with you right in your room (additional charges apply). SeaWorld boards pets as well ($15 per day, no overnight boarding); the kennel is located near the park entrance.

Lost Children Every theme park has a designated spot where parents can reunite with lost children. Ask a park employee or check at guest services for details.

Pharmacies Walgreens (www.walgreens.com) has a 24-hour drive-through pharmacy at 5935 W. Irlo Bronson Memorial Hwy. (U.S. 192; ✆ **407/396-2002**). It has another location at 12650 International Dr., in the Regency Shopping Center (✆ **407/238-5344**).

Post Office The post office most convenient to both Disney and Universal is at 10450 Turkey Lake Rd. (✆ **800/275-8777**). It's open Monday through Friday from 8am to 7pm and Saturday from 9am to 5pm.

Taxes In Florida, a 6% to 7.5% sales tax (depending on which local county you happen to be in) is charged on all goods, with the exception of most edible grocery-store items and medicines. Hotels add up to an additional 7% in resort taxes to your bill, so the total tax on accommodations can run up to 14.5%.

Telephone If you make a local call in Orlando, even to someone just across the street, *you must dial the 407 area code followed by the number you wish to call,* for a total of 10 digits.

Weather Call ✆ **321/255-0212** for the local weather forecast, or check out the Weather Channel at **www.weather.com** for the most up-to-date information.

WHERE TO STAY

There are just shy of 116,000 rooms in the Orlando area, with hundreds, sometimes thousands, added annually. Don't let that number fool you, as occupancy can be high much of the time. Even with the economy in a state of disarray, it's a wise idea to book your room as far ahead as possible—especially if you're coming during peak season, around the holidays and in the summer. The lowest rates are usually available September through the first 2 weeks of December (excluding the week of Thanksgiving) and January through April (excluding the weeks of Spring Break).

Walt Disney World Central Reservations Office

To reserve a room or book packages at Disney's resorts, villas, campgrounds, and official hotels, contact **Central Reservation Operations (CRO),** P.O. Box 10000, Lake Buena Vista, FL 32830-1000 (✆ **407/934-7639** or 407/939-6244; www.disneyworld.com), or the **Walt Disney Travel Company** by calling ✆ **407/939-7675** for packages or 407/939-7429 for room-only reservations.

They can recommend accommodations suited to your price range and specific needs, such as proximity to your favorite park or to those with supervised child-care centers. Though the people who answer the telephones can be very helpful and knowledgeable, they won't volunteer information about a better deal or a special, so be sure to ask.

We've included a good selection of some of our favorite Disney Resorts below, but for a complete listing of all the Disney Resorts, as well as even more area lodgings, check out Frommer's *Walt Disney World® & Orlando,* as well as *Frommer's Walt Disney World® with Kids* (Wiley).

Disney Resorts

VERY EXPENSIVE

Disney's BoardWalk Inn & Villas ★★★ This 1940s-style "seaside" resort lures romantics and families. Here you will find an array of restaurants, shops, clubs, and carnival-style entertainment along a quarter-mile boardwalk directly behind the resort, overlooking the water. The resort recaptures the spirit of Coney Island and Atlantic City back in their heydays. The BoardWalk's Cape Cod–style rooms comfortably sleep four, and some feature balconies. The priciest rooms overlook the boardwalk (most provide a good view of Epcot's nightly fireworks) and the pool; the less expensive rooms face the parking lot, but are sheltered from the activity and noise of the boardwalk. Hang onto your swimsuit if you hit the pool's famous—or infamous—200-foot "keister coaster" water slide. The BoardWalk's accommodations range from studios to grand villas that can sleep up to 12 people. All rooms are nonsmoking. Epcot and Hollywood Studios are only minutes away by walkway or water taxi.

2101 N. Epcot Resorts Blvd. (off Buena Vista Dr.; P.O. Box 10000), Lake Buena Vista, FL 32830-1000. www.disneyworld.com. ✆ **407/934-7639** or 407/939-5100. Fax 407/934-5150. 654 units, including 282 villas. $345–$620 double; $655–$2,865 suite; $480–$2,135 club; $345–$2,330 villa. Extra person $25. Children 17 and under stay free in parent's room. AE, DC, DISC, MC, V. Valet parking $12; self-parking free. Take I-4 to the Hwy. 536/Epcot Center Dr. exit and follow the signs. **Amenities:** 4 restaurants; grill; 2 lounges; 3 clubs; babysitting; bike rentals; concierge; concierge-level rooms; health club; Jacuzzi; 2 outdoor heated pools and kids' pool; room service; 2 lighted tennis courts; limited Wi-Fi access (fee); WDW Transportation System; transportation to non-Disney parks for a fee. *In room:* A/C, TV, fridge, hair dryer, high-speed Internet (fee), kitchen (in villas).

Disney's Contemporary Resort ★★ and Bay Lake Tower ★★★ If location is one of your priorities, it's hard to beat these Disney resorts, right beside the Magic Kingdom, and on the monorail system. Both the Contemporary and the all-new Bay Lake Tower offer great views of the Magic Kingdom as well as the Seven Seas Lagoon. The main resort, a 15-story concrete A-frame, dates to WDW's infancy, though top-to-bottom renovations bring it into the modern era. Rooms reflect an upscale Asian/retro look that should appeal to adults (along with flatscreen TVs, there are in-room computers with free Internet and online concierge), and those with kids in tow will appreciate the rounded corners, kid-proof locks on the sliding doors, and breakables placed high above a little one's reach. Notable changes to public areas in recent years include the addition of **The Wave**—a new full-service restaurant—and **Contempo,** an all-new high-tech, quick-service eatery sporting touch-screens rather than menus. The pool at the Contemporary, while less spectacular than most, is large and has a wading pool for toddlers with a small beach area nearby. The rooms can fit up to five people instead of the usual four (though space will be tight). The best views are from the upper floors of the tower (ninth floor and up), where the rooms are a tad quieter than those on the lower floors, which are exposed to public areas and the monorail (which runs right through the hotel). Come here for dinner at **Chef Mickey's** or the **California Grill** (p. 519), but if you have very young kids, you may be better off elsewhere.

The Bay Lake Tower, the newest member of the Disney Vacation Club resorts, opened its doors in 2009. Connected by a sky bridge to the existing resort (its restaurants, shops, and the monorail), the Tower sports a rooftop lounge, a fireworks viewing deck, and a lakeside zero-entry pool and interactive water-play area. Spacious public areas, accents of modern artwork, suite-style rooms, and an innovative contemporary design add up to Disney chic from top to bottom. *Note:* While guests staying at the Bay Lake Tower have access to the numerous amenities at the Contemporary, the privileges are not reciprocal—only Bay Lake Tower guests have access to the resort and its recreational areas.

4600 N. World Dr. (P.O. Box 10000), Lake Buena Vista, FL 32830-1000. www.disneyworld.com. ✆ **407/939-6244** or 407/824-1000. Fax 407/824-3539. 950 units, including 295 villas. $300–$675 double; $555–$3,040 club; $645–$3,040 suite; $395–$2,550 villa. Extra person $25. Children 17 and under stay free in parent's room. AE, DC, DISC, MC, V. Valet parking $12; self-parking free. **Amenities:** 3 restaurants; cafe; 2 lounges; babysitting; concierge; concierge-level rooms; fitness center; Jacuzzi; 3 outdoor heated pools and kids' pool; room service; watersports equipment; limited Wi-Fi access (fee); WDW Transportation System; transportation to non-Disney parks for a fee. *In room:* A/C, TV, fridge, hair dryer, high-speed Internet access (fee), kitchen (in villas).

Disney's Grand Floridian Resort & Spa ★★★ As an orchestra plays in the background, the elegance of this turn-of-the-20th-century-style Victorian resort transports guests to a bygone era. The crystal chandeliers that hang above the five-story domed lobby are just one of the opulent touches you'll find throughout. High tea is served in the afternoon. If you prefer, you can spend the day at the **spa**, the best in WDW. The Grand Floridian is one of the most romantic resorts for couples, though families will appreciate the children's programs, recreational facilities, and character dining experiences. The Victorian-style rooms sleep at least four; almost all overlook a garden, a pool, a courtyard, or the Seven Seas Lagoon. Located on the monorail system, the resort makes for a quick trip to the Magic Kingdom or Epcot. Note that all rooms are nonsmoking.

4401 Floridian Way (P.O. Box 10000), Lake Buena Vista, FL 32830-1000. www.disneyworld.com. ✆ **407/934-7639** or 407/824-3000. Fax 407/824-3186. 867 units. $440–$800 double; $545–$3,145 club; $1,140–$3,145 suite. Extra person $25. Children 17 and under stay free in parent's room. AE, DC, DISC, MC, V. Valet parking $12; self-parking free. Take I-4 to the Hwy. 536/Epcot Center Dr. exit and follow the signs. **Amenities:** 5 restaurants; grill; 3 lounges; character meals; babysitting; children's club; concierge; concierge-level rooms; health club; heated outdoor pool and kids' pool; room service; spa; 2 lighted tennis courts; watersports equipment; limited Wi-Fi access (fee); WDW Transportation System; transportation to non-Disney parks for a fee. *In room:* A/C, TV, fridge, hair dryer, high-speed Internet access (fee), minibar.

Disney's Polynesian Resort ★★ ☺ Located right on the Disney monorail line, the 25-acre Polynesian features extensive recreational areas, including a stretch of beach along a lagoon dotted with hammocks and palm trees, a volcano-themed pool, and watercraft rentals. An on-site child-care facility makes it a good choice for those traveling with kids, as do the casual on-site dining options. Its landscaped and torch-lit walkways, along with its longhouse-style thatched-roof

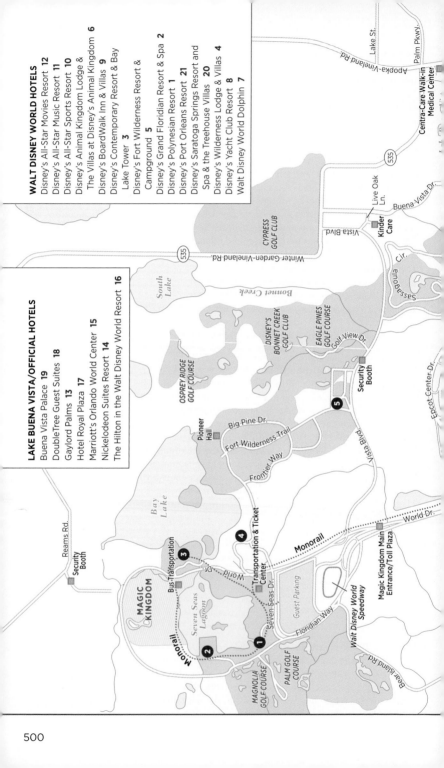

WALT DISNEY WORLD HOTELS
Disney's All-Star Movies Resort **12**
Disney's All-Star Music Resort **11**
Disney's All-Star Sports Resort **10**
Disney's Animal Kingdom Lodge &
The Villas at Disney's Animal Kingdom **6**
Disney's BoardWalk Inn & Villas **9**
Disney's Contemporary Resort & Bay
Lake Tower **3**
Disney's Fort Wilderness Resort &
Campground **5**
Disney's Grand Floridian Resort & Spa **2**
Disney's Polynesian Resort **1**
Disney's Port Orleans Resort **21**
Disney's Saratoga Springs Resort and
Spa & the Treehouse Villas **20**
Disney's Wilderness Lodge & Villas **4**
Disney's Yacht Club Resort **8**
Walt Disney World Dolphin **7**

LAKE BUENA VISTA/OFFICIAL HOTELS
Buena Vista Palace **19**
DoubleTree Guest Suites **18**
Gaylord Palms **13**
Hotel Royal Plaza **17**
Marriott's Orlando World Center **15**
Nickelodeon Suites Resort **14**
The Hilton in the Walt Disney World Resort **16**

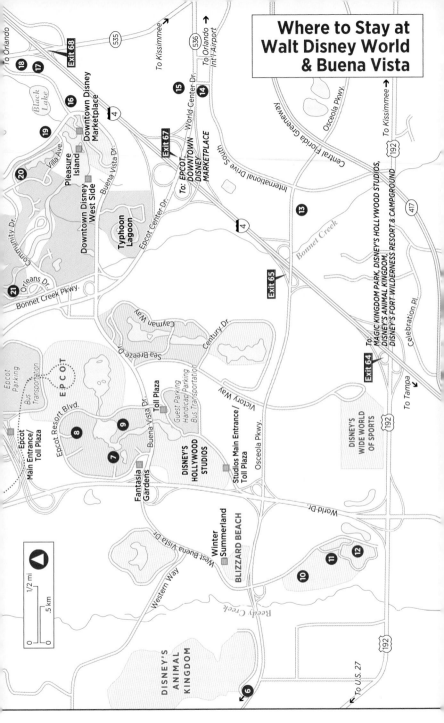

Where to Stay at Walt Disney World & Buena Vista

To Orlando

535

18

17

Exit 68

Black Lake

16

Downtown Disney Marketplace

19

4

Villa Ave.

Pleasure Island

Downtown Disney West Side

Buena Vista Dr.

20

Epcot Center Dr.

Typhoon Lagoon

Community Dr.

Orleans Dr.

21

Bonnet Creek Pkwy.

To Kissimmee

536

To Orlando Int'l Airport

15

14

World Center Dr.

Exit 67

To: EPCOT, DOWNTOWN DISNEY MARKETPLACE

International Drive South

Central Florida Greenway

Osceola Pkwy.

To Kissimmee

192

13

Bonnet Creek

4

417

Exit 65

Celebration Pl.

To: MAGIC KINGDOM PARK, DISNEY'S HOLLYWOOD STUDIOS, DISNEY'S ANIMAL KINGDOM, DISNEY'S FORT WILDERNESS RESORT & CAMPGROUND

Exit 64

To Tampa

Epcot Parking

Bus Transportation

EPCOT

Sea Breeze Dr.

Cayman Way

Century Dr.

Main Entrance/ Epcot Toll Plaza

Epcot Resort Blvd.

8

9

7

Buena Vista Dr.

Toll Plaza

Guest Parking Handicap Parking Bus Transportation

Victory Way

DISNEY'S WIDE WORLD OF SPORTS

192

Fantasia Gardens

DISNEY'S HOLLYWOOD STUDIOS

Studios Main Entrance/ Toll Plaza

Osceola Pkwy.

World Dr.

Winter Summerland

BLIZZARD BEACH

West Buena Vista Dr.

11

12

10

1/2 mi

.5 km

0

0

Western Way

Reedy Creek

192

DISNEY'S ANIMAL KINGDOM

6

To U.S. 27

buildings, give the resort a South Pacific ambience. The entire resort underwent extensive renovations a few years back, and rooms sport space-conscious furnishings, a muted earth-tone color scheme, and such upscale amenities as flatscreen TVs and refrigerators. Rooms can accommodate up to five people and are all nonsmoking.

1600 Seven Seas Dr. (P.O. Box 10000), Lake Buena Vista, FL 32830-1000. www.disneyworld.com. ℂ **407/934-7639** or 407/824-2000. Fax 407/824-3174. 847 units. $385–$815 double; $520–$3,100 club; $650–$3,100 suite. Extra person $25. Children 17 and under stay free in parent's room. AE, DC, DISC, MC, V. Valet parking $12; self-parking free. Take I-4 to the Hwy. 536/Epcot Center Dr. exit and follow the signs. **Amenities:** Restaurant; cafe; 2 lounges; dinner show; character meals; babysitting; children's club; concierge; concierge-level rooms; 2 heated outdoor pools and kids' pool; room service; watersports equipment; WDW Transportation System; transportation to non-Disney parks for a fee. *In room:* A/C, TV, fridge, hair dryer, high-speed Internet (fee).

Disney's Yacht Club Resort ★★★ The nautically themed Yacht Club shares its extensive recreational facilities with its sister resort, the Beach Club, next door. White sandy beaches and an immense, beautifully landscaped swimming area (with sand-bottom pools, water slides, and a life-size shipwreck to explore) line the lagoon side of the resort. The atmosphere is geared more toward adults and families with older children, although young kids are certainly catered to (this *is* Disney). The turn-of-the-20th-century New England theme can be felt throughout, as the public areas are filled with brass accents, nautical instruments, and a lighthouse to help you find your way home. Rooms have space for up to five people, and most have balconies. All rooms are nonsmoking. Epcot is just a short walk away.

1700 Epcot Resorts Blvd. (off Buena Vista Dr.; P.O. Box 10000), Lake Buena Vista, FL 32830-1000. www.disneyworld.com. ℂ **407/934-7639** or 934-7000. Fax 407/924-3450. 621 units. $335–$555 double; $475–$2,875 club; $1,375–$2,875 suite. Extra person $25. Children 17 and under stay free in parent's room. AE, DC, DISC, MC, V. Valet parking $12; self-parking free. Take I-4 to the Hwy. 536/Epcot Center Dr. exit and follow the signs. **Amenities:** 3 restaurants; grill; lounge; babysitting; children's club; concierge; concierge-level rooms; Jacuzzi; 2 heated outdoor pools and kids' pool; room service; 2 lighted tennis courts; watersports equipment; limited Wi-Fi access (fee); WDW Transportation System; transportation to non-Disney parks for a fee. *In room:* A/C, TV, fridge, high-speed Internet (fee), minibar.

Walt Disney World Dolphin ★★ If Antonio Gaudí and Dr. Seuss had teamed up on an architectural design, they might have created something like this Starwood resort (and its adjacent sister, the Swan). The Dolphin centers on a 27-story pyramid with two 11-story wings crowned by 56-foot twin dolphin sculptures. Not nearly as theme-intensive as the other Disney resorts, it's popular with business travelers. Rooms (all nonsmoking) feature a contemporary decor and the public areas are a bit more avant-garde, with upscale furnishings. Rooms comfortably sleep four (the Swan's are a tad smaller). The resort's grotto pool is lined by waterfalls, a water slide, and whirlpools; a small children's play area is close by. The Swan and Dolphin share a stretch of beach, a Body by Jake health club, a **Mandara Spa,** and a plethora of restaurants, including **Todd English's bluezoo** and **Il Mulino New York Trattoria,** as well as other trimmings. The Beach & Yacht Club Resorts as well as the BoardWalk Inn are also a short walk away (and are all on the water-taxi route). Epcot and Hollywood Studios are a water-taxi ride away (adventurous guests could walk—though I wouldn't suggest it with kids in tow). *Tip:* The beach next to the pool has a great view of Epcot's IllumiNations fireworks.

1500 Epcot Resorts Blvd. (off Buena Vista Dr.; P.O. Box 22653), Lake Buena Vista, FL 32830-2653. www.swandolphin.com. © **800/227-1500** or 407/934-4000. Fax 407/934-4884. 1,509 units. $219–$574 double; $600–$4,300 suite. Resort fee $10 per day. Extra person $25. Children 17 and under stay free in parent's room. AE, DC, DISC, MC, V. Valet parking $16; self-parking $12. Take I-4 to the Hwy. 536/Epcot Center Dr. exit and follow the signs. **Amenities:** 4 restaurants; grill; 2 lounges; character meals; babysitting; children's club; concierge; concierge-level rooms; health club; 4 heated outdoor pools; room service; spa; 4 lighted tennis courts; watersports equipment; limited Wi-Fi access (fee); WDW Transportation System; transportation to non-Disney parks for a fee. *In room:* A/C, TV, fridge, hair dryer, high-speed Internet (fee).

EXPENSIVE

Disney's Animal Kingdom Lodge & The Villas at Disney's Animal Kingdom—Jambo House and Kidani Village ★★★ 🏊 Enter this resort's grand lobby, with its thatched roof and ornate shield chandeliers, and you'll feel like you've stepped into a lodge in an African game preserve. The resort's *kraal* design (a semicircular layout), with many rooms overlooking a 33-acre savanna, allows guests an occasional view of the animals that roam the savanna below. Families will appreciate the array of activities, including storytelling by the fire, singalongs, and more. Those in the mood for romance will appreciate the more remote and relaxed setting. Standard rooms are slightly smaller than at Disney's other "deluxe" resorts, but the distinctive theme and surroundings are unparalleled. Vacation Club villas are available on the top floors of the Lodge for those needing additional room and homey amenities. In 2009, the Kidani Village opened it doors. Adjacent to the existing lodge, the all-new Vacation Club village features its own check-in, full-service restaurant (**Sanaa,** featuring African-inspired cuisine with an Indian touch and inspired decor), themed pool, and water-play area. **Boma** (p. 519), one of Orlando's best restaurants, is a must. The lodge and villas are adjacent to Animal Kingdom, but most everything else on WDW property is quite a distance away. Note that all rooms are nonsmoking.

2901 Osceola Pkwy., Bay Lake, FL 32830. www.disneyworld.com. © **407/939-6244** or 407/938-3000. Fax 407/939-4799. 1,421 units. $250–$615 double; $365–$2,990 club; $740–$2,299 suite; $280–$2,330 villa. Extra person $25. Children 17 and under stay free in parent's room. AE, DC, DISC, MC, V. Valet parking $12; self-parking free. Take I-4 to the Hwy. 536/Epcot Center Dr. exit and follow the signs. **Amenities:** 4 restaurants; lounge; babysitting; children's center; concierge; concierge-level rooms; health club; heated outdoor pool and kids' pool; limited room service; WDW Transportation System; transportation to non-Disney parks for a fee. *In room:* A/C, TV, fridge, hair dryer.

Disney's Saratoga Springs Resort and Spa and the Treehouse Villas at Disney's Saratoga Springs Resort and Spa ★★ The first phase of this Disney Vacation Club resort opened in May 2004, its final phase—or so we thought—in 2007. While lying idle and unoccupied for several years, Disney's Treehouse Villas were resurrected (and completely redesigned) in 2009—adding 60 new Vacation Club villas to the lineup. The main resort transports guests back to the heyday of upstate New York's 19th-century resorts. The resort town of Saratoga Springs is evoked through lavish gardens, Victorian architecture, and bubbling springs. The resort's main pool brings to mind its namesake's natural springs, with "healing" waters spilling over the rocky landscaping. The renowned

spa provides an array of services and treatments. Accommodations resemble those of the other Disney timeshare properties and range from studios that sleep 4 to villas that can sleep up to 12. The Treehouse Villas are elevated some 10 feet off the ground by pedestals and beams, nestled amid the trees. Each three-bedroom "cabin casual" villa sleeps up to nine and features such modern touches as cathedral ceilings, granite countertops, and flatscreen TVs. Downtown Disney is a short ferry ride across the lake, but getting to the parks will require a bit more effort.

1960 Broadway St., Lake Buena Vista, FL 32830. www.disneyworld.com. ✆ **407/827-1100** or 407/934-3400. Fax 407/827-1151. 924 units (including 60 treehouse villas). $305–$455 studio; $415–$1,780 villa; $555–$935 treehouse villa. Children 17 and under stay free in parent's room. AE, DC, DISC, MC, V. Free parking. Take I-4 to exit 67; take Community Dr. to Broadway and follow the signs. **Amenities:** Restaurant; lounge; babysitting; biking; golf; health club; themed heated pool and kids' interactive pool area; limited room service; spa; tennis; free WDW transportation. *In room:* A/C, TV, VCR (in villas), fridge, hair dryer, high-speed Internet (fee), full kitchen (in villas), kitchenette (in studios).

Disney's Wilderness Lodge & Villas ★★★

The Wilderness Lodge is surrounded by a forest of pines, cypress, and oaks far away from the rest of Mickey's world. Beyond the "spring fed" pool, set amid the rocky landscape, a geyser erupts periodically. The grand log-framed lobby is adorned by a mammoth stone hearth, gigantic twin totem poles, and four massive tepee chandeliers, giving the resort an old-time national-park feel. Standard rooms at the lodge sleep four, while the villas next door can accommodate up to 12. The decor is among Disney's best, and the restaurants have some of the most spectacular views in WDW. Though it's not that far from the Magic Kingdom, the bus ride can be a long haul.

901 W. Timberline Dr. (on the southwest shore of Bay Lake just east of the Magic Kingdom; P.O. Box 10000), Lake Buena Vista, FL 32830-1000. www.disneyworld.com. ✆ **407/934-7639** or 407/938-4300. Fax 407/824-3232. 909 units. $250–$540 lodge; $425–$1,500 club; $455–$1,500 suite; $340–$1,245 villa. Extra person $25. Children 17 and under stay free in parent's room. AE, DC, DISC, MC, V. Valet parking $12; self-parking free. Take I-4 to the Hwy. 536/Epcot Center Dr. exit and follow the signs. **Amenities:** 2 restaurants; 2 lounges; babysitting; children's club; concierge-level rooms; 2 Jacuzzis; heated outdoor pool and kids' pool; limited room service; watersports equipment; WDW Transportation System; transportation to non-Disney parks for a fee. *In room:* A/C, TV, fridge, hair dryer, high-speed Internet (fee), full kitchen (in villas), kitchenette (in villa studios).

MODERATE

Disney's Port Orleans Resort ★ 🎈

Two separate resorts, each with a distinctive Southern theme, Port Orleans boasts the best landscaping and coziest atmosphere of Disney's moderate resorts. The **French Quarter** reflects the charm of New Orleans at the turn of the 20th century, with accents of Mardi Gras; **Riverside,** filled with grand mansions and back bayous, is reflective of the Old South. The dragon-themed Doubloon Lagoon pool, the Ol' Man Island swimming hole, and a nearby playground are a huge hit with kids. Guest rooms are large enough for four, but it'll be a tight fit. (Bayou Rooms have a trundle bed, offering room for an extra child.) It's just east of Epcot and Disney's Hollywood Studios; there's boat service to Downtown Disney.

2201 Orleans Dr. (off Bonnet Creek Pkwy.; P.O. Box 10000), Lake Buena Vista, FL 32830-1000. www.disneyworld.com. ✆ **407/934-7639** or 934-5000. Fax 407/934-5353. 3,056 units. $154–$269 double. Extra person $15. Children 17 and under stay free in parent's room. AE, DC, DISC, MC, V. Free parking. Take I-4 to the Hwy. 536/Epcot Center Dr. exit and follow the signs. **Amenities:**

2 restaurants; grill/food court; 2 lounges; babysitting; Jacuzzi; 6 heated outdoor pools and 2 kids' pools; limited room service; watersports equipment/rentals; WDW Transportation System; transportation to non-Disney parks for a fee. *In room:* A/C, TV, fridge, hair dryer, high-speed Internet access (fee).

INEXPENSIVE

Disney's All-Star Music Resort Oversize instruments are scattered about the grounds—a musical motif that runs throughout this resort. As at all of the Disney value resorts, standard rooms are on the small side and lacking in frills. But thanks to a recent redesign, two-bedroom suites are available too. It's these family suites that set this resort apart. The suites, which sleep up to six, feature upgraded amenities, including two full bathrooms, a separate master bedroom, flatscreen TVs, and a kitchenette with a small fridge and a microwave.

Note: Disney has two other All-Star resorts—the **All-Star Movies Resort** and the **All-Star Sports Resort**—both identical to the All-Star Music Resort where it counts (like standard room size and layout—but no suites). The only real difference is the theme: One sports an athletic theme, the other features movies (of the Disney variety). Any of the All-Star resorts is a good choice for the budget-conscious family who wants to stay on Disney property—but they're out in the Disney boonies, so a car is almost a must. The closest park is Animal Kingdom.

1701 W. Buena Vista Dr. (at World Dr. and Osceola Pkwy.; P.O. Box 10000), Lake Buena Vista, FL 32830-1000. www.disneyworld.com. **407/939-6000.** Fax 407/939-7333. 1,704 units, including 215 family suites. $82–$179 double; $194–$365 suite. Extra person $10. Children 17 and under stay free in parent's room. AE, DC, DISC, MC, V. Free parking. Take I-4 to the Hwy. 536/Epcot Center Dr. exit and follow the signs. **Amenities:** Food court; lounge; babysitting; 2 heated outdoor pools and kids' pool; limited room service; WDW Transportation System; transportation to non-Disney parks for a fee. *In room:* A/C, TV, fridge (upon request for a fee in standard rooms; included in family suites).

ROUGHING IT, DISNEY-STYLE

Disney's Fort Wilderness Resort & Campground ★ Pine trees, cypress trees, and fish-filled lakes and streams surround this woodsy 780-acre camping resort. The closest park is the Magic Kingdom, which you can reach by boat. If you're an outdoors type, you'll enjoy the breath of fresh air away from the hustle and bustle of the parks. There are 110- to 220-volt outlets, grills, and comfort stations with private showers and restrooms. Tents and RVs are welcome. The 409 cabins sleep up to six and have full kitchens and daily housekeeping service. The wide variety of outdoor recreational activities just adds to the appeal of this resort. Standouts include a Segway tour, an Archery Experience, nightly campfires, and movies under the stars. It is also home to the *Hoop De Doo Musical Revue* dinner show (p. 555) and Mickey's Backyard Barbeque (offered seasonally).

Some sites are open to pets— at a cost of $5 per site—which is much cheaper than using the WDW overnight kennel, where you pay $10 to $69 per pet.

 In the Lineup at Priceline

Beginning in November 2011, Disney will list its hotel rooms on **Priceline.** Be aware, the Mouse is only taking baby steps—listing rooms on the site's conventional booking engine rather than its "Name Your Own Price" service. Disney also lists rooms on **Travelocity** and **Orbitz.** *Note:* Disney involvement with Priceline does not extend to its European booking site (Booking.com).

3520 N. Fort Wilderness Trail (P.O. Box 10000), Lake Buena Vista, FL 32830-1000. www.disney world.com. ☏ **407/934-7639** or 407/824-2900. Fax 407/824-3508. 799 campsites, 409 wilderness cabins. Campsite $46–$125 double; wilderness cabin $275–$450 double. Extra person $2 for campsite, $5 for cabin. Children 17 and under stay free in parent's room. AE, DC, DISC, MC, V. Free parking. Take I-4 to the Hwy. 536/Epcot Center Dr. exit and follow the signs. Pets $5 at select campsites. **Amenities:** 2 restaurants; grill; lounge; babysitting; 2 heated outdoor pools and kids' pool; 2 lighted tennis courts; watersports equipment/rentals; limited Wi-Fi access (fee); WDW Transportation System; transportation to non-Disney parks for a fee. *In room:* A/C, TV/VCR, fridge, hair dryer (in cabins), kitchen.

Lake Buena Vista/Official Hotels

"Official" Disney hotels, though not owned and operated by Disney, line Hotel Plaza Boulevard, on the northeast side of Disney property and adjacent to Downtown Disney. Guests can enjoy some of the perks of staying in a WDW resort (like free transportation to the Disney parks) while staying in a location more central to the rest of Orlando's offerings. You can reserve a room through **Central Reservations Operations** (☏ **407/934-7639**), but it's best to call (or check online) the individual hotel or parent chain to check for deals and packages.

EXPENSIVE

Buena Vista Palace ★ The most upscale of the "official" properties, popular with business and leisure travelers alike, now sports a chic, trendy look. Recently renovated guest rooms sleep at least four—corner rooms feature a bit of extra space. Many have balconies or patios; ask for one above the fifth floor with a "recreation view" facing the pools and Downtown Disney. Recreation Island is home to the resort's three pools (one partially indoors), game center, playground, tennis courts, beach volleyball, and the Island Suites. The resort is known for its full-service, European-style **spa.** Downtown Disney's numerous shopping, dining, and entertainment venues are just across the road.

1900 Buena Vista Dr. (just north of Hotel Plaza Blvd.; P.O. Box 22206), Lake Buena Vista, FL 32830. www.buenavistapalace.com or www.downtowndisneyhotels.com. ☏ **866/397-6516** or 407/827-2727. Fax 407/827-6034. 1,013 units. $89–$239 double; $142–$1,520 suite. Daily resort fee $17. Extra person $20. Children 17 and under stay free in parent's room. AE, DC, DISC, MC, V. Valet parking $22; self-parking free. From I-4, take the Hwy. 535/Apopka-Vineland Rd. exit north to Hotel Plaza Blvd. and go left. At 1st stoplight, turn right onto Buena Vista Dr. It's the 1st hotel on the right. **Amenities:** 3 restaurants; 3 lounges; character brunch; babysitting; concierge;

 WDW Check-In Made Easy

In an effort to make check-in a bit easier, Disney is now offering resort guests the option of checking in ahead of time. Go online within 10 days of your arrival date, enter the requested check-in information, and advise the resort of your arrival time. You can also make room requests at this time should you have any (keeping in mind that requests are not guaranteed). You'll need to register the names of all the people in your party and provide a credit card to cover any WDW resort charges. Upon arrival at the resort, simply head to the special welcome area, where you'll find your room keys and other registration material waiting for you.

Jacuzzi; 3 heated outdoor pools and kids' pool; room service; sauna; spa; tennis court; complimentary bus service to WDW parks; transportation to non-Disney parks for a fee. *In room:* A/C, TV, fridge, hair dryer, high-speed Internet access, minibar, limited Wi-Fi (fee).

MODERATE

Note: Accommodations in this category are usually a step above the "moderate" resorts inside WDW.

DoubleTree Guest Suites in the Walt Disney World Resort ★ ☺ Children get their own check-in desk and a gift upon arrival at this hotel, which is the best of the official hotels for families with little ones. All of the accommodations in this seven-story hotel are two-room suites, large by most standards (with space for up to six). Be sure to sample the cookies given to guests at check-in, a tasty tradition at the DoubleTree properties. It's the farthest "official" hotel from Downtown Disney, but a bus is available for those not quite up to the lengthy though pleasant walk.

2305 Hotel Plaza Blvd. (just west of Hwy. 535/Apopka-Vineland Rd.), Lake Buena Vista, FL 32830. www.downtowndisneyhotels.com or www.doubletreeguestsuites.com. © **800/222-8733** or 407/934-1000. Fax 407/934-1011. 229 units. $99–$289 double. Extra person $20. Children 17 and under stay free in parent's room. AE, DC, DISC, MC, V. Free parking. From I-4, take the Hwy. 535/Apopka-Vineland Rd. exit north to Hotel Plaza Blvd. and go left. It's the 1st hotel on the left. **Amenities:** Restaurant; 2 lounges; concierge; fitness center; heated outdoor pool and kids' pool; limited room service; 2 lighted tennis courts; complimentary bus service to WDW parks; transportation to non-Disney parks for a fee. *In room:* A/C, 2 TVs, fridge, hair dryer.

The Hilton in the Walt Disney World Resort ★★ This resort is the only official resort on Hotel Plaza Boulevard to offer guests Disney's Extra Magic Hour option. The hotel's array of guest services, dining options, upscale yet friendly atmosphere, and prime location across from Downtown Disney make it one of the best bets on the boulevard. The rooms sport an upscale and contemporary Shaker-style decor; junior suites, featuring sleeper sofas, are more spacious and a better option for families. Rooms on the upper three floors (on the boulevard side, or front side of the resort) offer a glimpse of Disney's nightly fireworks displays.

1751 Hotel Plaza Blvd., Lake Buena Vista, FL 32830. www.hilton.com or www.downtowndisney hotels.com. © **407/827-4000.** Fax 407/827-6369. 814 units. $89–$259 double. Extra person $20. Children 17 and under stay free in parent's room. AE, DC, DISC, MC, V. Valet parking $17; self-parking $10. From I-4 take exit 68, turn right onto S.R. 535, then left onto Hotel Plaza Blvd. Follow the boulevard, and the resort is near the end on the left. **Amenities:** 4 restaurants; 3 lounges; character breakfast; babysitting; concierge; concierge-level rooms; 2 outdoor heated pools; room service; complimentary bus service to WDW parks; transportation to non-Disney parks for a fee. *In room:* A/C, TV, fridge (fee), hair dryer, minibar, Wi-Fi access (fee).

Hotel Royal Plaza ★ The Royal Plaza is one of the boulevard's original hotels, but renovations throughout its 25-year history have ensured it remains one of the best. A favorite with the budget-minded, its hallmark is a friendly staff, many of whom have been here since the hotel opened. The nicely decorated rooms, now sporting new furnishings and an updated decor (pullout sofas and plasma TVs are standard in every room), are of good size, with enough space for five. Poolside rooms have balconies and patios. Tower rooms have separate sitting areas, and some have whirlpool tubs in the bathrooms. If you want a view from up high, ask for a room facing west toward WDW.

1905 Hotel Plaza Blvd. (btw. Buena Vista Dr. and Hwy. 535/Apopka-Vineland Rd.), Lake Buena Vista, FL 32830. www.royalplaza.com or www.downtowndisneyhotels.com. © **800/248-7890** or 407/828-2828. Fax 407/827-6338. 394 units. $69–$139 double; $189–$269 suite. Resort fee $8. Children 17 and under stay free in parent's room. AE, DC, DISC, MC, V. Valet parking $16; self-parking $10. From I-4, take the Hwy. 535/Apopka-Vineland Rd. exit north to Hotel Plaza Blvd. and go left. It's the 2nd hotel on the left. **Amenities:** Restaurant; lounge; babysitting; children's activity program; fitness center; whirlpool; heated outdoor pool; limited room service; 2 lighted tennis courts; complimentary bus service to WDW parks; transportation to non-Disney parks for a fee. *In room:* A/C, TV, hair dryer, minibar, Wi-Fi (fee).

Other Lake Buena Vista Hotels

The hotels in this section are within a few minutes' drive of the WDW parks, offering the location but not privileges of a stay at an "official" hotel.

VERY EXPENSIVE

Gaylord Palms ★★★ 🖌 It's the most extensively themed resort outside of Disney's not-so-little world. Practically a destination unto itself, this place offers its own entertainment, themed dining, shops, recreational facilities, and a Relache Spa Club for working out the kinks from the day's activities. The 4½-acre octagonal Grand Atrium, topped by an impressive glass dome, surrounds a replica of the Castillo de San Marcos, a Spanish fort in St. Augustine. Waterfalls, lush foliage, live alligators, cobblestone walkways, and a rocky landscape complete the setting. The Emerald Bay, a 362-room hotel within the hotel, has the most elegant air about it, while other themed areas include Key West, St. Augustine, and the Everglades. The rooms are spacious and well-appointed, each with a balcony overlooking the interior Floridian landscapes. The service is impeccable, friendly, and welcoming.

6000 Osceola Pkwy., Kissimmee, FL 34747. www.gaylordpalms.com. © **877/677-9352** or 407/586-0000. Fax 407/239-4822. 1,406 units. $139–$299 double; $635–$2,700 suite. Daily resort fee $15. Extra adult $20. Kids 17 and under stay free in parent's room. AE, DC, DISC, MC, V. Valet parking $20; self-parking $13. Take the I-4 Osceola Pkwy. exit east to the hotel. **Amenities:** 3 restaurants; 4 lounges; babysitting; children's center; concierge; concierge-level rooms; fitness center; 2 outdoor heated pools; room service; spa; free transportation to Disney parks; transportation to non-Disney parks for a fee. *In room:* A/C, TV, hair dryer, high-speed Internet access.

Marriott's Orlando World Center ★★★ Golf, tennis, and spa lovers will find plenty to do at this 230-acre upscale resort, thanks to the array of recreational activities (it welcomes a lot of business trade, too). The largest of its five pools has water slides and waterfalls surrounded by space to relax among the palm trees and tropical landscaping. The location, set back from the main thoroughfare and 2 miles from the Disney parks, is a plus. The large, comfortable rooms sleep four, and the higher poolside floors have views of Disney. Discounts and special packages are often offered, making this a more affordable option than at first glance.

8701 World Center Dr. (on Hwy. 536 btw. I-4 and Hwy. 535), Orlando, FL 32821. www.marriott worldcenter.com or www.marriott.com. © **800/621-0638** or 407/239-4200. Fax 407/238-8777. 2,004 units. $224–$399 for up to 5; $750–$1,600 suite. Children 17 and under stay free in parent's room. AE, DC, DISC, MC, V. Valet parking $24; self-parking $14. Take I-4 to the Hwy. 535/Apopka-Vineland Rd. exit, go south 1½ miles, proceed right/west on Hwy. 536, and continue ⅓ mile. **Amenities:** 4 restaurants; 2 lounges; babysitting; concierge; 18-hole golf course; health club; whirlpool; 3 heated outdoor pools, heated indoor pool, and kids' pool; room service; sauna; spa; 8 lighted tennis courts; Wi-Fi (fee); transportation to all theme parks for a fee. *In room:* A/C, TV, hair dryer, high-speed Internet access (fee), minibar.

MODERATE

Nickelodeon Suites Resort ★★ ☺ 🍴 This all-suite property is the first Nickelodeon-branded resort, and one of the best resorts in the area for families (as long as you can deal with the overstimulating atmosphere that comes along with staying here). Its brightly colored Kid Suites feature a separate bedroom for the kids (with bunks or twin beds, TV, video game system, and more), minikitchens, and pullout sofas in the living areas. Three-bedroom suites (sporting a trendier decor) include a second bathroom and a full kitchen. The lobby and mall area are filled with casual kid-friendly restaurants, an arcade, shops, and nightly entertainment venues. Kids get a kick out of the Nickelodeon characters and color schemes (neon-Nick green and orange) that run throughout the resort. The resort's two pool areas are veritable water parks, with multilevel water slides, flumes, climbing nets, and water jets. "Nick After Dark," an evening supervised activity program for kids ages 5 to 12, allows parents a night off on their own. Budget-minded parents will appreciate that up to four kids can eat free per paying adult at the hotel's extensive breakfast buffet (not including the character breakfast).

14500 Continental Gateway (off Hwy. 536), Lake Buena Vista, FL 32821. www.nickhotel.com. ✆ **877/387-5437,** 407/387-5437, or 866/GO2-NICK (462-6425). Fax 407/387-1489. 789 units. $130–$1,050 suite. Daily resort fee $25. AE, DC, DISC, MC, V. Free parking. From I-4, take the Hwy. 536/International Dr. exit east 1 mile to the resort. **Amenities:** Restaurant; lounge; food court; character breakfast; mini-golf course; fitness center; 2 Jacuzzis; 2 water-park pools; kids' spa; free shuttle to Disney, Universal Orlando, and SeaWorld parks. *In room:* A/C, TV/VCR, fridge, hair dryer, high-speed Internet access (free), kitchen (in some suites).

On U.S. 192/Kissimmee

This somewhat appealing, yet busy, stretch of highway within proximity of the Disney parks is lined with shops, restaurants, and smaller attractions. The hotels and restaurants generally cater to the budget-conscious traveler. However, a few luxury resorts are beginning to sprout a few miles to the south of the highway.

MODERATE

Comfort Suites Maingate East ★ 🍴 Set back from the main drag, this welcoming hotel still remains one of the nicest in its class in the area. The lobby and accommodations—consisting of studio and one-bedroom suites—are bright and inviting. The main pool and the children's pool, with an umbrella fountain to keep everyone cool, are open around the clock. Entertainment is a stone's throw away: Old Town (a small-scale shopping, dining, and entertainment complex) is just next door, and a great miniature-golf course is located in front of the property.

2775 Florida Plaza Blvd., Kissimmee, FL 34746. www.comfortsuitesfl.com. ✆ **888/782-9772** or 407/397-7848. Fax 407/396-7045. 198 units. $79–$159 double. Extra person $10. Rates include continental breakfast. Children 17 and under stay free in parent's room. AE, DC, DISC, MC, V. Free parking. From I-4 take the U.S. 192 E. exit; continue 1¾ miles, then turn right on Florida Plaza Blvd. **Amenities:** Concierge; fitness center; outdoor heated pool and kids' pool; free shuttle to Disney, Universal, and SeaWorld. *In room:* A/C, TV, fridge, hair dryer, free high-speed Internet access.

International Drive Area

The hotels and resorts here are 7 to 10 miles northeast of the Walt Disney World parks and 1 to 3 miles from Universal Orlando and SeaWorld, which makes this area the most centrally located for those who want to sample all that Orlando offers. The disadvantages: The northern end of International Drive is horribly congested. The shops, motels, eateries, and attractions along this stretch can vary greatly in quality; as a general rule, the closer you get to the convention center, the better the class of hotels and dining.

VERY EXPENSIVE

Peabody Orlando ★★★ ✦ The five Peabody mallards continue to march into the main lobby fountain each and every morning at 11am and then back out at 5pm, accompanied by John Philip Sousa's *King Cotton March,* and are only a small part of the appeal of this upscale hotel. Primarily a business and convention destination, the Peabody also appeals to adults looking for an ultraclassy hotel that provides top-of-the-line service, amenities, and atmosphere (families with older children will find the array of recreational offerings and spacious accommodations to their liking as well). Combining with the main hotel's elegant ambience and so-phisticated decor is the new Peabody Tower (a $450-million addition that added 870 guest rooms and suites in late 2010); the transition between the two buildings is seamless (a particularly impressive feat given the Tower's chic retro-inspired de-cor and Sinatra-esque ambience) and is stunning from top to bottom. The tower brings with it a full-service **spa** and athletic club, a salon, a gourmet deli, a coffee bar, a full-service restaurant (**Napa**—a wine-themed restaurant and bar with pa-tios overlooking the landscaped grotto-style pool below), and a piano lounge (**The Rocks**) adding to the already impressive lineup of offerings. Rooms sleep up to five (suites are available), and are tastefully decorated and well-appointed. Be sure to remember your room and floor number—the chip-based key cards are coded for safety reasons. Those on the west side of the main hotel (6th floor and higher) and the west end of the Tower offer distant views of Disney and its fireworks dis-plays, and the remaining tower rooms (the 10th floor and higher) offer impressive after-dark views of International Drive. *As a note:* Dux (once the hotel's signature restaurant) is now used only for private dining, and the **B-Line Diner** now sports a more contemporary yet diner-inspired decor. Self-parking is once again available (in the new parking garage).

9801 International Dr. (btw. Beachline Expwy. and Sand Lake Rd.), Orlando, FL 32819. www. peabodyorlando.com. **℃ 800/732-2639** or 407/352-4000. Fax 407/354-1424. 891 units. $150–$495 standard (up to 3 persons); $575–$2,500 suite. Daily resort fee $15. Extra person $25. Chil-dren 17 and under stay free in parent's room. AE, DC, DISC, MC, V. Valet parking $20; self-parking $12. From I-4, take the Sand Lake Rd./Hwy. 482 exit east to International Dr., then go south. Hotel is on the left across from the Convention Center. **Amenities:** 3 restaurants; 4 lounges; grill; 2 ca-fes; concierge; concierge-level rooms; fitness center; Jacuzzi; outdoor heated pool and kids' pool; room service; spa; 2 lighted tennis courts; shuttle to WDW and other parks for a fee. *In room:* A/C, TV, hair dryer, high-speed Internet access (fee), minibar.

Renaissance Orlando Resort at SeaWorld ★★ A simple hotel exterior gives way to a beautiful, inviting interior, which is peppered with luxurious touch-es. A glass-covered atrium soars high above a stunning and chic indoor courtyard area filled with cascading waterfalls, a trendy lounge, and a sushi bar. The taste-fully decorated rooms are oversize, providing plenty of space to spread out and relax. SeaWorld and Aquatica fans will appreciate the location—it's across the street from both parks.

6677 Sea Harbour Dr., Orlando, FL 32821. www.renaissanceseaworld.com. © **800/327-6677** or 407/351-5555. Fax 407/351-1991. 778 units. $161–$249 double. Children 17 and under stay free in parent's room. AE, DC, DISC, MC, V. Valet parking $20; self-parking $15. From I-4, take the Hwy. 528/Beachline Expwy. exit east to International Dr., then go south to Sea Harbor Dr. and turn right. **Amenities:** 3 restaurants; grill; 3 lounges; babysitting; concierge; golf privileges at nearby courses (fee); health club; 2 Jacuzzis; outdoor heated pool and kids' pool; room service; sauna; spa; 4 lighted tennis courts; Wi-Fi (fee); transportation to all the parks for a fee. *In room:* A/C, TV, fridge (in some), hair dryer, high-speed Internet access (fee), minibar.

MODERATE

Hyatt Place ★ This modern and stylish property sports an inviting lobby—the perfect spot for catching up on the news, surfing the Net on your laptop, or grabbing a snack at the semi-self-service cafe. The chic, upscale decor carries through to the oversized rooms, where you'll find comfy bedding, a sleeper sofa, a mini-fridge, a work desk, and 42-inch flat-panel TVs. Self-service check-in and check-out kiosks offer an efficient alternative to standing in line, and complimentary Wi-Fi (available throughout the hotel) keeps you connected without costing you a bundle. A free continental breakfast is part of the package, but for those with a heartier appetite, hot breakfast entrees are available (they'll cost you extra).

8741 International Dr., Orlando, FL 32819. www.orlandoconventioncenter.place.hyatt.com. © **800/833-1516** or 407/370-4720. Fax 407/331-4721. 149 units. $79–$259 for up to 4. Rates include free full breakfast. Children 17 and under stay free in parent's room. AE, DC, DISC, MC, V. Free parking. **Amenities:** Exercise room; outdoor heated pool. *In room:* A/C, TV, hair dryer, Wi-Fi.

Universal Orlando Resorts

Universal Orlando has three unique, upscale themed properties, all run by the Loews hotel group. Like the Disney resorts, Universal gives its resort guests additional privileges, including preferred access to the Universal parks' rides and attractions.

VERY EXPENSIVE

Portofino Bay Hotel ★★★ Universal's first hotel has the stature and magnificence of Disney's Grand Floridian. This romantic, upscale resort is designed to resemble the village of Portofino, Italy, complete with a harbor and canals that lead you via water taxi to the theme parks. The stylish rooms sleep up to five. Ask for a view overlooking the piazza and "bay" area. For those with young children, there are a select number of Seuss-themed kids' suites. The Portofino doesn't just have swimming pools: Its beach pool has a stone fort with a water slide, while the villa pool is lined with cabanas with laptop hookups, fridge, and TV for the perfect mix of business and pleasure. The resort's **Mandara Spa** includes a state-of-the-art fitness center and full-service spa. The drawbacks: There are stairs everywhere you turn, and the size of the resort can make it difficult to find your way around.

5601 Universal Blvd., Orlando, FL 32819. www.loewshotels.com/hotels/Orlando or www.universalorlando.com. © **888/322-5541** or 407/503-1000. Fax 407/224-7118. 750 units. $284–$564 double; $574–$2,500 suite and villa. Extra person $25. Children 17 and under stay free in parent's room. AE, DC, DISC, MC, V. Valet parking $22; self-parking $15. From I-4, take the Kirkman Rd./Hwy. 435 exit and follow the signs to Universal. Pets $25. **Amenities:** 4 restaurants; deli; 3 lounges; babysitting; kids' club; concierge; concierge-level rooms; fitness center; 3 outdoor heated pools (1 for concierge-level and suite guests only) and kids' pool; room service; spa; watersports equipment; free water taxi and bus transportation to Universal Studios, Islands of Adventure, and CityWalk; free shuttle to SeaWorld; transportation to WDW parks for a fee. *In room:* A/C, TV/DVD, CD player, fridge (fee), hair dryer, high-speed Internet access (fee), minibar.

EXPENSIVE

Hard Rock Hotel ★★★ ☺ You can't get any closer than this to Universal Studios Florida. This California mission–style resort sports a rock-'n'-roll theme with rates a shade less expensive than the Portofino's. The atmosphere is more casual than those of its fellow Universal resorts, though with an air of chic sophistication. Public areas are filled with rock memorabilia, but it's the pool area that takes center stage—the large free-form pool's underwater sound system ensures that you won't miss a beat. Thanks to a recent renovation, the stylish and modern rooms now have flat-panel TVs, MP3 docking stations, and upgraded bedding. Unfortunately, though the units are fairly soundproof, a few notes seep through the walls, so ask for one away from the lobby area. If you're bringing school-age kids or teens, it's the best bet of the three Universal resorts. *Tip:* The Hard Rock is a cut above some of Disney's comparable properties.

5000 Universal Blvd., Orlando, FL 32819. www.loewshotels.com/hotels/Orlando or www.universalorlando.com. © **800/232-7827** or 407/503-2000. Fax 407/224-7118. 650 units. $244–$524 double; $474–$2,020 suite. Extra person $25. Children 17 and under stay free in parent's room. AE, DC, DISC, MC, V. Valet parking $22; self-parking $15. From I-4, take the Kirkman Rd./Hwy. 435 exit and follow the signs to Universal. Pets $25. **Amenities:** 3 restaurants; grill; 2 lounges; babysitting; kids' club; concierge; concierge-level rooms; fitness center; outdoor heated pool and kids' pool; room service; free water taxi or bus transportation to Universal Studios, Islands of Adventure, and CityWalk; free shuttle to SeaWorld; transportation to WDW parks for a fee. *In room:* A/C, TV, CD player, fridge (fee), hair dryer, high-speed Internet access (fee), minibar.

Royal Pacific Resort ★★★ ☺ The Royal Pacific features a spectacular beachfront lagoon-style pool. It's lined with palm trees, winding walkways, waterfalls, and an orchid garden, all giving it a remote island feel (apart from the screams emanating from the nearby Islands of Adventure). The rooms, smaller than those at other Universal resorts, are decorated with wooden carvings and accents. Recent renovations include the addition of Jurassic Park kids' suites— they feature a separate bedroom for the kids with a flatscreen TV, twin beds, and a dino-themed decor. The public areas are impressive and worth exploring. The addition of the **Wantilan Luau Pavilion** ensures that the weekly luau is held rain or shine. If you're traveling with young children, the Royal Pacific is the best choice at Universal.

6300 Hollywood Way, Orlando, FL 32819. www.loewshotels.com/hotels/Orlando or www.universalorlando.com. © **800/232-7827** or 407/503-3000. Fax 407/503-3202. 1,000 units. $229–$479 double; $339–$1,950 suite. Extra person $25. Children 17 and under stay free in parent's room. AE, DC, DISC, MC, V. Valet parking $22; self-parking $15. From I-4, take exit 75B, Kirkman Rd./Hwy. 435 and follow the signs to Universal. Pets $25. **Amenities:** 2 restaurants; 3 lounges; babysitting; kids'

Universal Resort Guests Get to Harry Early!

Universal resort guests get **early access to the Wizarding World of Harry Potter** a full hour prior to the official park opening.

club; concierge; concierge-level rooms; Jacuzzi; outdoor heated pool and kids' pool; sauna; free water-taxi and bus transportation to Universal Studios, Islands of Adventure, and CityWalk; free shuttle to SeaWorld; transportation for a fee to WDW parks. *In room:* A/C, TV, fridge (fee), hair dryer, high-speed Internet access (fee).

WHERE TO DINE

From family-style restaurants to fast food to five-star dining, Orlando has restaurants to please every palate and every budget. As most Orlando visitors spend the majority of their time at Disney, most of the dining options below can be found there, too. I do list plenty of other restaurants, including the better places at Universal and along International Drive.

Advanced Reservations at Disney Restaurants

"Advanced Reservations" *aren't* really reservations. They are simply a way of claiming the first table that becomes available close to the time of your choosing. You'll be given priority over walk-ups. There may still be a wait (usually 10–20 min.), but it will be significantly shorter than without reservations. If you don't make Advanced Reservations, you may miss out altogether, as they're usually booked well in advance, leaving little or no room at all for drop-ins. To make Advanced Reservations at any WDW restaurant (in the parks or at the resorts), call ✆ **407/939-3463** or go online to **http://disneyworld.disney.go.com/dining**. You can book as far as 180 days in advance of your arrival for most restaurants. An added perk for guests staying at a Disney-owned resort (which excludes the Swan, Dolphin, and Hotel Plaza Boulevard resorts, or Shades of Green) is the ability to make Advanced Dining Reservations for their entire vacation (up to 10 days' worth) on the 180th day out.

Disney's **dinner shows** (the most popular dining experiences at WDW), Mickey's BBQ, and Fairytale Dining at Cinderella's Royal Table can also be booked 180 days in advance, but you must pay in full at the time of booking. Restaurants requiring a credit card guarantee include Victoria & Albert's, Citricos' Chef's Domain, the Fantasmic Dining Experience, and the Princess Storybook Breakfast (at Epcot's Norway pavilion).

If you're staying on Disney property and haven't made arrangements prior to coming, you can make Advanced Reservations at your resort. At Epcot, you can do it at Guest Relations near Innoventions East; at the Magic Kingdom, head to City Hall or the guest relations counter near the park entrance; and at Disney's Hollywood Studios head to Hollywood Junction for help. You can also go directly to the restaurant of your choice and make arrangements in person.

Inside the Walt Disney World Theme Parks

The food offered throughout the parks is fairly decent, though you won't find Disney's park restaurants winning gourmet awards. While portions are generally on the large side, so are prices. Children's entrees now include healthy options such as milk, veggies, and fruit (soda and fries are still available). And all of WDW (theme parks and resorts) is transitioning to trans-fat-free menu items. The following list includes Magic Kingdom, Epcot, Disney's Hollywood Studios, and Animal Kingdom. You can get information on Disney restaurants by calling ✆ **407/939-3463** or visiting **www.disneyworld.com**.

TIPS FOR dining AT WALT DISNEY WORLD

- All park restaurants (as well as all restaurants in Florida) are nonsmoking.

- Magic Kingdom restaurants don't serve alcohol, but those at Animal Kingdom, Epcot, and Disney's Hollywood Studios do.

- Sit-down restaurants in WDW take American Express, Diners Club, Discover, MasterCard, Visa, and the Disney Card.

- Unless otherwise noted, *restaurants in the parks require park admission.*

- Unless you're using WDW transportation, there is a $14 parking fee.

- Nearly all WDW restaurants with sit-down or counter service offer children's menus with items ranging from $5 to $9.

EPCOT

World Showcase

The World Showcase has some of the best dining options inside the WDW theme parks, thanks to the cultural cuisine of its 11 nation pavilions. Although many consider a meal here an essential part of the park experience, the food (as in all the parks) is priced higher than comparable fare in the free world, though of course you're paying for the atmosphere and architectural surroundings.

The restaurants below are arranged geographically, beginning at the Canada pavilion and proceeding counterclockwise around the World Showcase Lagoon. Note that the United States pavilion is not listed below; it's a burger-and-fries-style counter service eatery. *Prices below are for entrees only.*

CANADA Le Cellier Steakhouse's vaulted archways, stone walls, and lanterns create a cozy atmosphere, much like that of a centuries-old wine cellar. While sandwiches and salads are offered at lunch, steaks are the main menu item at dinner, with a variety of cuts to choose from, including filet, porterhouse, and prime rib. Lunch runs $13 to $31; dinner is $20 to $37.

UNITED KINGDOM The Tudor-beamed **Rose & Crown** is an English pub where folk music and saucy servers entertain as you dine. The short menu has British favorites, including fish and chips, bangers and mash, cottage pie, and warm bread pudding. Head over later in the evening for a pint of Bass ale or Guinness stout, as the patio is one of the best places to see the IllumiNations fireworks display. Lunch is $11 to $19; dinner is $15 to $27.

FRANCE One of Disney's priciest park restaurants, **Les Chefs de France** has a glass exterior that's among the prettiest around. Three French chefs can take credit for the menu, which includes such entrees as roasted perch with lobster mousse; potato scales on sautéed fennel with a lobster reduction; and grilled tenderloin of beef with a black pepper sauce, original potato gratin of Savoy, and green beans. Lunch is $16 to $20; dinner is $19 to $35, with prix-fixe sampling options ($20 and $37, respectively) available as well.

MOROCCO Of all the Epcot restaurants, **Marrakesh ★** best exemplifies the spirit of the park. The setting is grand; the interior is filled with tile mosaics, carpets, and brass chandeliers. Belly dancers and Moroccan music often entertain guests as they feast on options such as roast lamb, marinated beef or chicken shish kebabs, and a host of seafood and salad choices. The combination appetizer (for two) is a great way to start. Couscous accompanies most entrees. Lunch costs $15 to $28; dinner is $25 to $29.

JAPAN At **Teppan Edo,** guests are seated around large grill tables while white-hatted chefs rapidly dice, slice, stir-fry, and launch the occasional shrimp onto your plate with amazing skill. The culinary acrobatics are a sight to see; the cuisine is average. Lunch and dinner range from $15 to $26. **Tokyo Dining** features a menu of traditional Japanese cuisine with an emphasis on sushi. Lunch and dinner range from $16 to $30. **Yakitori House,** a small bamboo-roofed teahouse, features such fare as teriyaki chicken, beef simmered in a spicy curry sauce and served with vegetables and rice, sushi rolls, and tempura vegetables with shrimp. Meals here are generally between $8 and $10.

ITALY **Tutto Italia** is one of Epcot's most popular restaurants even after recently changing hands. This elegant establishment features a menu filled with traditional pastas, fish, chicken, and pork. If you want a quieter setting, ask for a seat on the veranda overlooking the center courtyard. Lunch costs $15 to $30; dinner runs $23 to $36. **Via Napoli,** an authentic Neapolitan pizzeria featuring a menu of handcrafted pizzas, pastas, sandwiches, and Italian wines with extensive seating both indoors and out, opened in 2010. The open kitchen along the perimeter gives way to tables that run the length of the room (with smaller more intimate tables set along the edges). The menu at lunch and dinner is the same and costs $17 to $26; pizzas run $16 for an individual pie and are upwards of $39 for a 12-slice pie.

GERMANY The **Biergarten ★** feels like a Bavarian village at Oktoberfest. The mood is due in part to the Bavarian musicians who perform during the dinner hour, and possibly due to the beer—it's served in tremendous steins. Diners are encouraged to join the fun by singing and dancing with the performers. The all-you-can-eat buffet is heaped with Bavarian fare (assorted sausages, pork schnitzel, sauerbraten, seafood, roast chicken, spaetzle with gravy, sauerkraut, salads, and plenty of other trimmings). The lunch buffet is $26 for adults, $14 for kids 3 to 11; dinner is $35 for adults, $17 for kids.

CHINA The **Nine Dragons ★**, after months of renovations, now reflects a more modern motif with sleek and stylish furnishings, trendy dishware, and an updated decor complimented by colorful lanterns and silk hangings. The menu features a selection of familiar favorites—but don't overlook the light and tasty Dioa Yu Tai Cucumber Salad or the shrimp summer rolls wrapped in rice paper and served with a rich-and-creamy peanut sauce. Lunch runs $13 to $18; dinners, $13 to $26.

NORWAY **Akershus** is a re-created 14th-century castle with iron chandeliers hanging high above the banquet hall. An impressive smorgasbord of *smavarmt* (hot) and *koldtbord* (cold) dishes are on the menu. While the Storybook breakfast features American fare, a sampling of more traditional Norwegian fare is added to the menu of seared salmon, citrus-marinated mahimahi, sautéed chicken, and herb-dusted beef tips (among other tasty choices) during the Storybook lunch and dinner. Several Disney princesses make their way around the hall. Storybook Breakfast costs $40 for adults,

$24 for kids 4 to 9; Storybook Lunch costs $42 for adults, $25 for kids; and Storybook Dinner costs $47 for adults, $26 for kids.

MEXICO It's always night at the **San Angel Inn ★**, where amid the marketplace, candlelit tables set a romantic mood under a faux star-lit sky. Reasonably authentic food, including the *mole poblano* (chicken simmered in spices, ground tortillas, and a hint of cocoa), is on the menu. Lunch runs $15 to $22, and dinners around $24 to $28. **La Cava del Tequila,** a tequila bar serving up 70 types of tequila alongside a selection of tapas-style treats, is inside the pavilion. Outside, **La Cantina de San Angel,** a quick-service eatery, offers a menu of tacos, empanadas, nachos, and guacamole dip for $7 to $12, and features a large outdoor semicovered patio overlooking the lagoon. Recent renovations added a new indoor table-service establishment. Adjacent to the Cantina is **La Hacienda de San Angel.** Entrees here include flank steak, roast pork tenderloin, grilled tilapia, and marinated chicken—all with a Mexican twist and running about $25, with a dinner for two running $50. Kids will appreciate the tacos, nachos, and chicken tenders.

Future World

Inside the Living Seas pavilion, the **Coral Reef** features tables scattered around a 5.6-million-gallon aquarium filled with tropical fish. Diners can observe Disney's denizens of the deep swim by; tiered seating ensures that everyone gets a decent view. The menu features mainly fresh seafood and shellfish with favorites such as mahimahi, tilapia, salmon, and ahi tuna (for landlubbers, prime rib and grilled chicken). Lunch is $12 to $29; dinner is $19 to $32.

The **Sunshine Season Food Faire,** an upscale food court just inside the Land pavilion, consists of six eateries, each offering a small menu of items, including Asian dishes, salads, chicken, fish, and beef entrees, sandwiches, and desserts. The contemporary earthy decor continues the look and feel of the intricate mosaic leading to the entrance while variations in the carpet and carefully placed partitions separate the large open seating area into smaller sections. Open to the second story, and with no real walls, it retains an airy feel. Most items cost between $8 and $10.

IN THE MAGIC KINGDOM

In addition to the restaurants listed below, there are plenty of fast-food outlets throughout the park, of which Pecos Bill Cafe, Cosmic Ray's Starlight Cafe, and the Columbia Harbour House are your best choices. You may find that a quiet, sit-down meal is an essential, if brief, break from the activities of the day.

FANTASYLAND Atop the winding stone staircase inside Cinderella Castle is the medieval-themed **Cinderella's Royal Table ★**. Stained-glass windows line the stone walls, and servers treat you like a lord or lady while fetching you such entrees as pan-seared salmon, roast prime rib, and spice-rubbed roasted chicken as Disney princesses and members of the royal family visit your table. Breakfast costs $30 for children ages 3 to 9 and $45 for adults; lunch costs $32 for children ages 3 to 9 and $49 for adults; dinner costs $34 for children ages 3 to 9 and $59 for adults. Advanced Reservations are a must.

The **Crystal Palace,** named for its glass exterior, is a favorite with families because of its all-you-can-eat character buffets. Breakfast costs $23 for adults and $13 for children ages 3 to 9. Lunch costs $25 for adults and $14 for children 3 to 9. Dinner runs $37 for adults and $18 for children 3 to 9. Advanced Reservations are strongly suggested.

AT DISNEY'S HOLLYWOOD STUDIOS

There are more than a dozen places at which to refuel in this Hollywood-style theme park. Most feature more fun than fabulous food; the ones listed below are the best of the bunch. Again, Advanced Reservations are a must.

Modeled after the old Los Angeles celebrity haunt, the **Hollywood Brown Derby** re-creates the feel and atmosphere of a 1930s supper club. Caricatures of Hollywood's most famous celebrities line the walls. Highlights include the Cobb salad and spiced pan-roasted pork; the Derby's signature dessert, grapefruit cake with cream-cheese icing, is a perfect meal capper. Entrees go for $15 to $32 at lunch, $22 to $36 at dinner.

The **50's Prime Time Café** is like going home to Mom's for dinner—back in the 1950s. The atmosphere delivers, with black-and-white TV sets showing *My Little Margie* and servers threatening to withhold dessert if you don't eat all your veggies. The mainstays are the meatloaf and pot roast. Kids will get a kick out of the neon ice cubes glowing in their drinks. Lunch costs $12 to $19; dinner costs $13 to $21. Advanced Reservations are a must to eat here.

The best bets at the casual **Mama Melrose's Ristorante Italiano** are the wood-fired and brick-baked specialties, including the flatbreads (grilled pepperoni, portobello mushroom, and four cheeses). The warm and welcoming atmosphere makes you feel like you're at your local mom-and-pop-run restaurant. Lunch costs $12 to $20; dinner costs $12 to $22.

At the **Sci-Fi Dine-In Theater Restaurant,** diners sit in chrome-plated convertibles with the Hollywood Hills as a backdrop and are treated to newsreels, cartoons, and "B" horror flicks. Sandwiches, burgers, and salads make up the lunch menu; dinner features heartier fare such as steak, pasta, ribs, and chicken. Lunches run $12 to $22; dinners are $14 to $23. Eating here is a bit pricey for what you get (and adding a cosmic concoction or two can really blow your budget), but the unique atmosphere is worth it (at least once). Advanced Reservations are a must.

IN THE ANIMAL KINGDOM

You'll find only a few meal options in the Animal Kingdom, and most of those are of the grab-and-go variety (of these, the Flame Tree BBQ is the best). There are three spots where you can sit yourself down for a spell.

Expect California fare with an island spin at the **Rainforest Cafe.** Menu offerings tend to be tasty and creative, but the prices run on the high side for what you get—most people come for the junglelike tropical atmosphere. Lunch and dinner run anywhere from $13 to $32. **Note:** The restaurant is accessible from outside the park, so you don't have to pay park admission to eat here.

The thatched-roof **Tusker House,** in Harambe village, features a buffet with a bit of flair. The slightly shaded patio out back, with a view over the trees, allows you to relax and enjoy your meal away from the crowds. Out front, the pavilion provides shade and, if timed right, a view of the live entertainment. Options include a variety of salads, vegetarian dishes, and meats ranging from Blatjang Chutneys with South African preserves, *sambals*, tabbouleh, hummus, and baba ghanouj to vegetable couscous, root vegetables, and cabbage to salmon filets. Kids will likely find the PB&J, mac and cheese, or corn dog nuggets more to their liking. Lunch runs $12 for kids, $21 for adults; dinner, $14 for kids, $29 for adults. A character meal is available at breakfast ($14 for kids, $25 for adults).

Yak & Yeti is a Pan-Asian eatery that offers both sit-down and counter-service dining in a meticulously detailed setting that blends into the Himalayan village surrounding it. The menu inside features specialties including crispy wok-fried green beans; lettuce cups filled with minced chicken, chopped veggies, and a yummy maple tamarind sauce; seared miso salmon; crispy mahimahi; and maple tamarind chicken. Be sure to leave room for dessert—the mango pie and fried wontons (filled with cream cheese and served with skewers of fresh pineapple, vanilla ice cream, and a sweet honey-vanilla drizzle) are delish. Kids will appreciate the miniburgers, veggie lo mein, egg rolls, and chicken bites. Entrees run between $18 and $25 (the same for lunch and dinner), while kids' meals cost just under $8.

In the Walt Disney World Resorts

Most of these restaurants set their prices higher than outside, but the food generally is a few notches higher than what you find in the theme parks. Advanced Reservations are a must for dinner, but they can be far less crowded at lunch and during off hours.

VERY EXPENSIVE

Citricos ★ FRENCH ECLECTIC Here you'll be treated to a fabulous view of the Seven Seas Lagoon; a warm, Mediterranean atmosphere filled with orange and yellow hues; and a fine meal created by the fusion of French and Mediterranean cuisine with a Florida twist. The oft-changing menu might offer a citron rotisserie pork chop with creamy polenta, garlic-wilted red kale, and cilantro lime drizzle; or sautéed wild king salmon with oven-roasted leeks and an herb butter sauce.

4401 Floridian Way, in Disney's Grand Floridian Resort & Spa. © **407/939-3463**. www.disney world.com. Advanced Reservations recommended. Main courses $29–$46. AE, DC, DISC, MC, V. Wed–Sun 5:30–10pm. Valet parking $12.

Victoria & Albert's ★★★ INTERNATIONAL It's not often that dinner can be described as "an event," but Disney's most elegant restaurant earns that distinction. If the portions seem small, it's simply so you can better enjoy all seven courses. The setting is romantic; a violinist or harpist often plays softly in the background. The fare changes nightly, but you might find main events such as lamb seared with foie gras over brioche with imported Fuji apples; tamarind-glazed blue-fin tuna over bok choy stir-fry; or Colorado lamb with corn risotto. The dining room is crowned by a domed, chapel-style ceiling; 20 tables are lit softly by Victorian lamps; and your waitstaff (always named Victoria and Albert) provide superb service. In addition to the **Chef's Table** (an intimate dining experience set in an alcove in the kitchen) is **Queen Victoria's Room**—Disney's most exclusive dining experience. Behind closed doors with just four tables, discerning diners will experience a 10-course meal with French gueridon service and personalized attention. The price tag is $200 per person (with wine pairing, add an additional $95 per person). To reserve a table (a single seating is offered nightly) call the restaurant's private line at © **407/939-3862.** Advanced Reservations can now be made 180 days in advance for the main dining room, the

Chef's Table, and Queen Victoria's Room. Plan on a leisurely dining experience (allowing at least 3–4 hr.). Reservations can now be made online (with the exception of Queen Victoria's Room).

4401 Floridian Way, in Disney's Grand Floridian Resort & Spa. © **407/939-3463**. www.disney world.com. Reservations required. Jackets required for men. Not recommended for children. Prix fixe $125 per person, $185 with wine pairing; $175 Chef's Table, $245 with wine; $200 Queen Victoria's Room, $295 with wine. AE, DC, DISC, MC, V. 2 main dining room seatings daily Sept–June 5:45-6:30pm and 9–9:45pm; 1 seating July–Aug 6:45-8pm. Chef's Table 6pm only. 1 seating daily for Queen Victoria's Room. Valet parking $12.

Yachtsman Steakhouse ★ SEAFOOD/STEAK Even by outside-the-park standards, this is a solid steakhouse with a cordial staff. In keeping with the resort, the atmosphere is nautical New England, with a brighter decor than at most steakhouses. The exhibition kitchen provides a peek at steaks, chops, and seafood being seared over oak and hickory. Options range from an 8-ounce filet to a 12-ounce strip to a belly-busting 24-ounce T-bone. The menu also has rack of lamb, salmon, and chicken.

1700 Epcot Resorts Blvd., in Disney's Yacht Club Resort. © **407/939-3463.** Advanced Reservations recommended. Main courses $24–$43. AE, DC, DISC, MC, V. Daily 5:30-10pm. Free self- and valet parking.

EXPENSIVE

Artist Point ★★ 🍴 SEAFOOD/STEAK Enjoy a grand view of Disney's Wilderness Lodge in this rustically elegant establishment. Hand-painted murals of Southwestern scenery adorn the raised center ceiling, and ornate lanterns hang from timber columns. Select from a seasonally changing menu that might include grilled buffalo sirloin with a sweet potato–and–hazelnut gratin, or cedar-plank-roasted king salmon. Note: Artist Point has a more relaxed atmosphere than some WDW resort restaurants, but kids will have more fun at the lively Whispering Canyon Café next door.

901 W. Timberline Dr., in Disney's Wilderness Lodge. © **407/939-3463** or 407/824-1081. www. disneyworld.com. Advanced Reservations recommended. Main courses $25–$41; 3-course wine pairing $30. AE, DC, DISC, MC, V. Daily 5:30-10pm. Free valet and self-parking.

Boma ★★ INTERNATIONAL One of the Animal Kingdom Lodge's signature restaurants, Boma offers a diversion from the usual Disney fare, and a warm atmosphere in a setting that evokes an African marketplace. In front of the open exhibition kitchens lies an incredible buffet of international cuisine featuring authentic African dishes from more than 50 countries alongside a few more familiar favorites—including dishes especially for kids. Chefs are close by to answer questions and make suggestions throughout the various stations. A specialty of the house is the very delicious watermelon rind. Everything is fresh and tasty. *Note:* An American buffet breakfast is served here daily.

2901 Osceola Pkwy., at Disney's Animal Kingdom Lodge. © **407/938-3000.** www.disneyworld. com. Advanced Reservations recommended. All-you-can-eat buffet $25–$40 adults, $14–$20 children 3-9. AE, DC, DISC, MC, V. Daily 7:30-11am and 5:30-10pm.

California Grill ★★ CALIFORNIA Make your way to the 15th floor of the Contemporary Resort and enjoy views of the Magic Kingdom—and its fireworks— while your meal is prepared in an exhibition kitchen. Headliners change often, but usually include brick-oven flatbreads, Atlantic salmon, and grilled pork tenderloin with goat-cheese polenta, cremini mushrooms, and a zinfandel glaze. A vegetarian selection is available as well. The Grill also features a sushi and sashimi menu. This is one of the few spots in WDW that isn't particularly well suited to kids. The upbeat and charged atmosphere is enhanced by the contemporary yet colorfully artistic decor. Reservations are required to ride the elevator to the restaurant, so make arrangements well ahead of time—this is a tough spot to get a table.

4600 N. World Dr., at Disney's Contemporary Resort. ✆ **407/939-3463** or 407/824-1576. www. disneyworld.com. Reservations required. Main courses $28–$44; sushi and sashimi $21–$28. AE, DC, DISC, MC, V. Daily 5:30–10pm.

Todd English's bluezoo ★★ SEAFOOD Here's the hippest, hottest place in town, with a contemporary and sophisticated marine-themed decor, an impressive exhibition kitchen, and an intimate lounge where live music is occasionally featured. Celebrity chef Todd English has created an ever-changing menu of fresh seafood and coastal dishes. Start off with "Olive's" *classico* flatbread and the teppan seared scallops, both tasty signature treats, before moving on to the main event (where the daily "Dancing Fish" has been added to the lineup of signature entrees). Worth noting, however, is the fact that several menu items (even the drink menu) are overly complicated, and while a true foodie might find this to his or her liking, many may find it a bit off-putting. Thankfully, a selection of fresh grilled fish (aptly named "simply fish") complimented by several unique sauces helps to offset the overly complicated dishes. Portions are large, but side dishes will run you an extra $7 to $11. Dress is casual, but the upscale atmosphere is chic and adult (and even though there's a children's menu, I wouldn't suggest bringing them along).

1500 Epcot Resort Blvd., at the WDW Dolphin. ✆ **407/934-1111.** www.disneyworld.com. Advanced Reservations recommended. Main courses $27–$60. AE, DISC, MC, V. Daily 5–11pm. Validated valet and self-parking free.

MODERATE

ESPN Club ★ AMERICAN Upon entering, you will be surrounded by monitors showing every possible sporting event. The all-American fare includes such choices as "Boo-Yeah" chili, hot wings, and burgers. Sandwiches and salads are available as well. The star here is for service, which is impeccable—never have I had a waiter so quick on his feet. While the food is quite good, it's really the atmosphere that draws the crowds here.

2101 N. Epcot Resorts Blvd., at Disney's BoardWalk. ✆ **407/939-1177.** www.disneyworld.com. Advanced Reservations not available. Lunch and dinner $10–$16. AE, DC, MC, V. Mon–Thurs 11:30am–1am; Fri–Sat 11:30am–2am.

Kouzzinas ★ MEDITERRANEAN Run by celebrity Iron Chef Cat Cora, this newish restaurant offers a chef's table, an upscale prix-fixe dining experience, and a video screen in the lobby with images that showcase the chef and her views on food and family. The menu also includes an olive oil tasting experience! The decor is warm golden hues, wrought-iron accents, wood beams, old-world-inspired murals, and show kitchen (recently updated and accented with soft drapes, new artwork, and marble finishes since the previous tenant), and the menu is now filled with authentic family recipes with a Mediterranean flavor. Simple yet creative dishes might include cinnamon stewed chicken, chargrilled lamb burgers, or fisherman's stew with sides ranging from smashed garlic fried potatoes to chilled salt-roasted beets. The pizza window, a popular late-night stop, is open for business till midnight—you can pick up a slice ($3.50–$4) or order an entire pie to go (starting at $18, add $1.50 for each additional topping).

2101 N. Epcot Resorts Blvd., at Disney's BoardWalk. ℂ **407/939-3463.** www.disneyworld. com. Advanced Reservations recommended. Main courses $10–$13 breakfast, $20–$32 dinner; pizza $3.50–$18. AE, DC, DISC, MC, V. Daily 7:30am–11am and 5:30–10pm. Pizza window 5pm–midnight.

'Ohana ★ ☺ PACIFIC RIM The decibel level here may turn off those without children in tow. As your luau is prepared exhibition-style over an 18-foot-wide fire pit, the staff keeps you busy with coconut races, hula lessons, and other shenanigans. Servers come around the tables with 3-foot skewers of pork, turkey, steak, and vegetables, while starters and sides are served family-style. More kid-friendly fare can be requested. *Note:* A daily character breakfast with Lilo, Stitch, Mickey, and Pluto is available.

1600 Seven Seas Dr., at Disney's Polynesian Resort. ℂ **407/939-3463** or 407/824-2000. www. disneyworld.com. Advanced Reservations strongly encouraged. $21–$33 adults; $12–$16 children 3-11. AE, DC, DISC, MC, V. Daily 7:30–11am and 5–10pm.

The Wave . . . of American Flavors ★ AMERICAN The Contemporary Resort eatery lures diners with a modern but welcoming atmosphere and seasonal menus of fresh and healthy American fare accented with flavors from around the world. Dishes are prepared with local and regional products whenever possible, and entrees might include whole-wheat linguine with clams, rock shrimp, and fresh thyme in a chunky tomato broth; or a scrumptious braised lamb shank smothered in a bulgur lentil stew and red-wine sauce. Look for a selection of organic beers, trendy cocktails, and an innovative wine list from around the globe to top off your meal.

4600 N. World Dr., in Disney's Contemporary Resort. ℂ **407/939-3463.** www.disneyworld. com. Advanced Reservations recommended. Main courses $9–$18 breakfast, $12–$21 lunch, $18–$30 dinner. AE, DC, DISC, MC, V. Daily 7:30–11am, noon–2pm, and 5:30–11pm.

Downtown Disney

VERY EXPENSIVE

Fulton's Crab House ★★ SEAFOOD Oysters and stone crab claws are the specialties of this upscale eatery, in a replica of a 19th-century Mississippi riverboat. Outdoor decks offer the best views of the lake and Downtown Disney. As it's one of the area's best seafood houses, you might want to bring along some extra cash. The menu changes often, at times even daily, but with more than 50 fresh seafood selections, you won't be disappointed (and a "crab map" ensures that diners are well-versed on exactly what it is they're dining on). Though you may not see many of them, kids are welcome.

1670 Buena Vista Dr., aboard the riverboat docked at Downtown Disney. ℂ **407/934-2628.** www.levyrestaurants.com. Advanced Reservations recommended. Main courses $11–$18 lunch, $20–$52 dinner. AE, DC, DISC, MC, V. Daily 11:30am–4pm and 5–11pm. Valet parking $7.

MODERATE

Rainforest Cafe ☺ CALIFORNIA Don't arrive starving (or expecting a peaceful meal—the jungle atmosphere entertains most kids but can be noisy). Waits here average 2 hours if you fail to call ahead to make an Advanced Reservation. The menu can be tasty and creative, though somewhat overpriced. The choices seem endless, but a few of the more fun dishes include Mogambo Shrimp (sautéed in olive oil and served with penne pasta), Rumble in the Jungle Turkey Wrap (with romaine, tomatoes, and bacon), and Maya's Mixed Grill (ribs, chicken breast, and shrimp).

Downtown Disney Marketplace, near the smoking volcano. ℂ **407/827-8500.** www.rainforest cafe.com. Advanced Reservations strongly recommended. Main courses $12–$32 (most less than $25). AE, DISC, MC, V. Sun–Thurs 10:30am–11pm; Fri–Sat 10:30am–midnight.

T-Rex ☺ CALIFORNIA A sibling of the Rainforest Cafe and Downtown Disney's latest addition, T-Rex adds another unique element to its lineup of family-friendly dining options. Bubbling geysers, a fossil dig site, life-size animatronic dinosaurs, and themes of fire and ice run throughout this prehistoric eatery. Each themed room will entertain even the squirmiest kids, but be aware—it can be overload for those easily bothered by loud noises and flashing lights. Waits here average 2 hours without Advanced Reservations. The menu can be tasty and creative, though, like most Disney restaurants, somewhat overpriced. The choices seem endless but a few of the more fun dishes include Footprints Flatbread (cheddar, mozzarella, Parmesan, and goat cheese with rotisserie chicken, caramelized onions, and a balsamic glaze) and Fire-Roasted Rotisserie Chicken (with a choice of yummy sides). Don't forget to save room for dessert—the Chocolate Extinction is fabulous (chocolate-fudge cake with vanilla ice cream, whipped cream, chocolate, and caramel drizzle, as well as Butterfinger crumbles—this one's big enough for two or more).

Downtown Disney Marketplace. ℂ **407/828-8739.** www.trexcafe.com. Advanced Reservations strongly recommended. Main courses $11–$30 (most less than $25). AE, DISC, MC, V. Sun–Thurs 11am–11pm; Fri–Sat 11am–midnight.

Wolfgang Puck Café ★★ CALIFORNIA The wait can be distressing, but the energized, upscale, and contemporary atmosphere, along with the eclectic mix of menu choices, makes it worth the effort. An exhibition kitchen in the more casual downstairs section allows you to watch as your food is prepared. A favorite stop is the sushi bar, a copper-and-terrazzo masterpiece that delivers some of the best sushi in Orlando. The upstairs dining room has a more refined atmosphere, with its own menu and service to match (the floor-to-ceiling windows allow for a view of the lake and a glimpse of the fireworks if you time it right). Puck's is noisy, making conversation difficult no matter which level you choose. *Note:* In a hurry? Try the Wolfgang Puck Express at the West Side or Marketplace.

1482 Buena Vista Dr., at Disney's West Side. ℂ **407/938-9653.** www.wolfgangpuck.com or www.levyrestaurants.com. Reservations not accepted on lower level; Advanced Reservations recommended for upstairs dining room. Main courses upstairs $27–$41; main courses cafe $18–$26, pizza and sushi $13–$18; Express $10–$16. AE, DC, DISC, MC, V. Daily 11am–1am.

Universal Orlando

Universal Orlando's CityWalk and its resorts are home to a number of diverse dining spots—some of the best in Orlando.

VERY EXPENSIVE

Emeril's ★★ NEW ORLEANS It's next to impossible to get short-term reservations for dinner unless you're willing to take your chances with no-shows or visiting during the off-peak season. But once in, you'll find the dynamic, Creole-inspired cuisine worth it. The back half of the building is a glass-walled, 12,000-bottle aboveground cellar. If you want a show, we recommend one of eight counter seats, where you can watch chefs work their magic; but reservations are required *excruciatingly* early (2–3 months, at least). **Note:** Lunch costs about half what you'll spend on dinner, and the menu and portions are almost the same. No matter when you come, leave the kids at home.

6000 Universal Studios Blvd., in CityWalk. ☏ **407/224-2424.** www.emerils.com/restaurants. Reservations recommended. Main courses $18–$28 lunch, $31–$50 dinner. AE, DISC, MC, V. Sun–Thurs 11:30am–2pm and 5:30–10pm; Fri–Sat 11:30am–2pm and 5:30–11pm. Self-parking $14 ($3 after 6pm). From I-4, take the Kirkman Rd./Hwy. 435 exit and follow the signs to Universal.

EXPENSIVE

Tchoup Chop ★★★ PACIFIC RIM Culinary perfection is pronounced "chop chop." Emeril Lagasse's second restaurant in Orlando is named for the location of his original restaurant, Tchoupitoulas Street in New Orleans. Think bluezoo (see above) with an Asian Pacific twist—very chic, contemporary, and impressive. The service is impeccable, and the relaxing atmosphere, decor, and food ensure that the experience is memorable and worth the price. Some of the Polynesian- and Asian-influenced dishes include macadamia nut–crusted Atlantic salmon, ki-awe grilled New York strip steak, and Hawaiian-style rotisserie chicken. Recently Tchoup Chop began serving up Sunday brunch featuring a three-course prix-fixe menu along with $4 "eye opener" drinks—bloody marys, mimosas, and mai tais.

6300 Hollywood Way, in Universal's Royal Pacific Hotel. ☏ **407/503-2467.** www.emerils.com/restaurants. Reservations strongly recommended. Main courses $19–$35. AE, DISC, MC, V. Sun–Thurs 11:30am–2pm and 5:30–10pm; Fri–Sat 11:30am–2pm and 5:30–11pm. Valet parking $5. From I-4, take the Kirkman Rd./Hwy. 435 exit, and follow the signs to Universal.

MODERATE

Pastamore Ristorante SOUTHERN ITALIAN The *antipasto amore* here is a meal unto itself, and includes bruschetta, melon with prosciutto, grilled portobello mushrooms, sliced Italian meats, marinated olives, tomato *caprese,* and mozzarella. This casual family eatery has a menu of Italian classics, seafood, pastas, and grilled specialties. Options include veal Marsala, chicken piccata, shrimp scampi, fettuccine Alfredo, and pizza, among several others. An open kitchen allows diners a view of the chefs at work. You can also eat in a cafe, where lighter fare—breakfast and sandwiches—is served from 8am to 2am.

1000 Universal Studios Plaza, in CityWalk. ☏ **407/363-8000.** www.universalorlando.com. Reservations accepted. Main courses $11–$23. AE, DISC, MC, V. Daily 5pm–midnight. Self-parking $14 ($3 after 6pm). From I-4, take the Kirkman Rd./Hwy. 435 exit and follow the signs to Universal.

The International Drive Area

International Drive has one of the area's larger collections of fast-food joints, but its midsection and southern reaches have some of this region's better restaurants. It's about 10 minutes by car from the Disney parks.

MODERATE

Ming Court ★★ CHINESE Its diverse menu and tasty dishes make this one of Orlando's most popular Chinese restaurants. The lightly battered, deep-fried chicken breast gets zip from a delicate lemon-tangerine sauce. If you're in the mood for beef, try the grilled filet mignon seasoned Szechuan-style. Portions are sufficient and the service is excellent. The 250-foot, ornately carved dragons that greet you at the entrance are a hint at what awaits inside. Kids get their own menu, featuring beef, shrimp, chicken, and pork served with an Asian flair.

12

Bring On the Barbecue

Bubbalou's Bodacious BBQ ★, 5818 Conroy Rd., Orlando (℡ **407/423-1212;** www.bubbalous.com), offers what some say is the best barbecue in Florida. Go for the full pork platter that comes with a heaping helping and all the fixin's. The uninitiated should stay away from the "Killer" sauce if you value your taste buds; you might even taste-test the mild sauce before moving up to the hot. Sandwiches run $5 to $9; main courses run $10 to $16. Hours are Monday through Saturday from 10am to 9pm. To get here, take exit 75B off of I-4, follow Kirkman, and then make a left onto Conroy and follow your nose; Bubbalou's is on the left.

9188 International Dr. (btw. Sand Lake Rd. and Beachline Expwy.). ℡ **407/351-9988.** www. ming-court.com. Reservations recommended. Main courses $6–$28 lunch, $11–$43 dinner, $50–$60 dinner for 2; dim sum mostly $3–$8. AE, DC, DISC, MC, V. Daily 11am–2:30pm and 4:30–11:30pm. From I-4, take the Sand Lake Rd./Hwy. 528 exit east to International Dr., then south. Ming Court is on the right, opposite Pointe Orlando.

Only in Orlando: Dining with Disney Characters

Dining with Disney characters is a treat for any Disney fan, but it's a special one for those 9 and under. The characters will greet you, sign autographs, pose for photos, and interact with the family. These dining experiences are *very* popular, so make Advanced Reservations (℡ **407/939-3463**) as early as possible (up to 180 days in advance), and call for schedules. Prices vary, but generally expect breakfast (most serve it) to be $20 to $36 for adults, $11 to $24 for kids 3 to 9. Restaurants that serve dinner charge $28 to $56 for adults and $14 to $28 for kids.

Character meals are offered at **Cape May Café** (in Disney's Beach Club Resort), **Chef Mickey's** (at Disney's Contemporary Resort), **Cinderella's Royal Table** (in Cinderella Castle, Magic Kingdom), **Crystal Palace Buffet** (at the Crystal Palace, Magic Kingdom), **Donald's Safari Breakfast at the Tusker House** (in Africa, Animal Kingdom), **Garden Grill** (in the Land Pavilion, Epcot), **'Ohana** (at Disney's Polynesian Resort), **Akershus Royal Banquet Hall** (in Epcot's Norway Pavilion), **Hollywood & Vine** (at Disney's Hollywood Studios), **1900 Park Fare** (at Disney's Grand Floridian Resort & Spa), and the **Garden Grove Café** and **Gulliver's Grill** (at the WDW Swan).

TIPS FOR VISITING WALT DISNEY WORLD ATTRACTIONS

Walt Disney World, home to the four major theme parks including the Magic Kingdom, Epcot, Disney's Hollywood Studios, and Animal Kingdom, welcomes around 50 million guests in a typical year.

Besides its larger theme parks, Disney boasts an assortment of other venues, including Downtown Disney (Cirque du Soleil, DisneyQuest, Pleasure Island (aka Hyperion Wharf upon completion of the area's reinvention), West Side, and the Marketplace), Blizzard Beach, and Typhoon Lagoon, just to name a few.

PARKING Cars, light trucks, and vans pay $14. Visitors with disabilities can park in special areas near the entrances; ask the parking lot attendants or call ✆ **407/824-4321.** *Don't forget* to write down where you parked (area and row number); after a long day at the parks, Minnie, Mickey, Goofy, and Donald all start to look and sound alike.

WHEN YOU ARRIVE Grab a printed park guide. It tells you not only where the fun is (including current ride-restriction and FASTPASS information), but when and where to eat and shop. Pick up a copy of the *Times Guide* too—it includes a schedule for the parks' daily shows and parades. Arrive early (about 20–30 min., depending on the season) to get a good seat.

BEST TIMES TO VISIT There isn't really an off season in Orlando, but crowds are usually thinner from early January to mid-March and from mid-September until the week before Thanksgiving. The busiest days are generally Saturday and Sunday, when the locals visit. Major holidays attract scores of visitors: Christmas to New Year's is by far the busiest time; with the week preceding and following Easter a close second. **Note:** Summer, though one of the least expensive times to visit, can also be the worst. The crowds are heavy with locals, and the heat and humidity can be intolerable.

OPERATING HOURS Park hours vary and are influenced by special events as well as the economy. Call ahead or go to **www.disneyworld.com** to check operating times; otherwise, you could find yourself expecting to stay all night when the park closes at 6pm. Hours will vary not only from park to park, but also from week to week, and even day to day. Don't just assume that a park is open; check the schedule ahead of time and once you arrive.

Tip: If you are a WDW Resort guest (or are staying at the WDW Hilton, the WDW Swan, or the WDW Dolphin), you can take advantage of Disney's **Extra Magic Hour** program. This allows WDW Resort guests early entry (or extended evening hours) at select theme parks (including the water parks) on select days. The Extra Magic Hour schedule can change frequently, so it's best to check with your resort upon arrival for the most up-to-date information.

TICKETS Disney's ticketing structure (**Magic Your Way**) gives visitors who stay here for a few days far better deals than those who come for a day. The system allows guests to customize tickets by purchasing a base ticket for a set fee, and then purchasing add-ons, including a Park-Hopper option, a no-expiration option, and the option to include admission to some of Disney's smaller venues.

Ticket durations can vary from a single day to 10 days (after 7 days, however, an annual pass becomes a wise purchase), and the more you stay, the less you pay per day. Do note, however, that unlike in years past, unless you purchase a no-expiration add-on to your ticket, it will now expire within 14 days of the first day of use. (However, you don't have to use your tickets on consecutive days.)

The following prices don't include 6.5% sales tax unless noted. **Note:** Price hikes are frequent, so call ✆ **407/824-4321** or visit WDW's website (www.disneyworld.com) for the most up-to-the-minute pricing.

One-day/one-park tickets, for admission to the Magic Kingdom, Epcot, Animal Kingdom, or Disney's Hollywood Studios, are $82 for adults,

$74 for children 3 to 9. **Multiday tickets** allow you to visit *one park per day.* A 7-day ticket costs $247 for adults (about $35 a day), $224 for kids (about $32 a day).

A **Park-Hopper** add-on ($54 *per ticket,* per person) allows visitors unlimited admission to the Magic Kingdom, Epcot, Animal Kingdom, and Disney's Hollywood Studios for the length of their ticket. A 1-day adult Park-Hopper ticket costs $136, while the 7-day version costs $301—making the latter a far better deal. Because the $54 fee applies per ticket and not per day, the longer you stay, the better the deal.

Water Park Fun & More tickets also allow visitors their choice of 2 to 10 admissions (the number depends on the length of your pass) to Typhoon Lagoon, Blizzard Beach, DisneyQuest, or Disney's Oak Trail Golf Course, and the ESPN Wide World of Sports. Prices range from an obscene $136 for a 1-day adult pass to $301 for a 7-day pass (a very good deal).

A **1-day ticket** to **Typhoon Lagoon** or **Blizzard Beach** is $45 for adults, $39 for children, while a 1-day ticket to **DisneyQuest** costs $41 for adults and children alike.

If you're planning an extended stay or are going to visit Walt Disney World more than once during the year, **annual passes** ($499–$629 adults, $450–$567 children) are another great option.

THE MAGIC KINGDOM

The Magic Kingdom is the most enchanting of all the Disney parks. Taking center stage is Cinderella Castle, the best-known, most recognized symbol of Disney. The park's seven "lands" surround the castle.

Main Street, U.S.A.

The gateway to the Kingdom, Main Street resembles a turn-of-the-20th-century American street (okay, so it leads to a 13th-c. European castle, but nobody complains). It has shops, restaurants, and outdoor entertainment. Main Street, however, is best left for the end of the day when you're heading back to your hotel.

As soon as you arrive at Main Street, you can board the **Walt Disney World Railroad,** an authentic 1928 steam-powered train, for a 20-minute trip around the perimeter of the park. It's a good way to travel if you're headed to Frontierland or back to the park entrance (the station at Mickey's Toontown Fair is no longer operational during the expansion of Fantasyland).

Adventureland

Cross a bridge and stroll through an exotic jungle of foliage, thatched roofs, and totems. Amid dense vines and stands of bamboo, drums are beating and swash-buckling adventures are beginning.

On the 10-minute **Jungle Cruise,** you sail through an African veldt in the Congo, an Amazon rainforest, and the Nile River in Egypt. Dozens of animatronic creatures inhabit the vines, waterfalls, and tropical foliage.

The **Magic Carpets of Aladdin ★** delights wee ones and a few older kids too. Its 16 four-passenger carpets circle a giant genie's bottle while the camels spit water at the passengers and passersby. The flying carpets spin gently around, move up, down, forward, and back.

In the **Pirates of the Caribbean ★★**, pillaging pirates wreak havoc upon a small Caribbean town as your boat passes by. Audio-animatronic figures include a seedy cast of yo-ho-ho-ing characters; spurred by the popularity of the movie *Pirates of the Caribbean: Curse of the Black Pearl* and its sequels (the most recent in the summer of 2011), Jack Sparrow, Barbossa, and Davy Jones have signed on as part of the crew. A tweak in the story line to mirror the movies and a mix of updated special effects have been added. Still, the ride may be scary for kids 4 and under due to the unexpected drops and moments of darkness. **Captain Jack's Pirate Tutorial** takes place nearby and allows pint-size pirates (pulled from the audience) to train alongside Captain Jack himself—learning the art of swordplay and swashbuckling silliness before being sworn in as honorary members of the crew.

The **Enchanted Tiki Room Under New Management** is a very upbeat and enchanting show featuring a slew of tropical birds singing and telling jokes. It is a bit loud on the decibel front, but is otherwise cute and entertaining.

Frontierland

Step into the wild and woolly past of the American frontier. The landscape is straight out of the Wild West, complete with log cabins and rustic saloons.

The **Big Thunder Mountain Railroad ★★** roller coaster, situated on a 200-foot-high red-stone mountain, has tight turns and dark descents rather than sudden, steep drops. Your train careens through caves and canyons, under waterfalls, past geysers and mud pots, and over a bottomless volcanic pool. It's tailor-made for kids and grown-ups who want a thrill but aren't quite up to tackling the big coasters. **Note:** You must be 40 inches or taller to ride.

The **Country Bear Jamboree ★** is a hoot. It's a 15-minute show featuring audio-animatronic bears belting out rollicking country tunes and crooning plaintive love songs. It's a great place to cool off too.

Take the curves at high speed on Big Thunder Mountain.

Cinderella's Castle is where the princesses and their princes might be found.

FASTPASS: GETTING ahead OF THE CROWD

Don't like standing in long lines? Take advantage of Disney's FASTPASS system. Here's the drill:

Hang onto your ticket stub when you enter, and head to the hottest ride of your choosing. If it's a FASTPASS attraction (they're noted in the park guide) and there's a line, feed your ticket stub into the FASTPASS ticket taker. Retrieve both your ticket stub and the FASTPASS stub that comes with it. Two times will be stamped on the FASTPASS—come back during that 1-hour window, bypass the regular line, and head straight for the FASTPASS entrance, where you'll have little or almost no wait.

Note: Early in the day, your window may begin as close as only 40 minutes after you feed the FASTPASS machine, but later in the day it could be hours. Initially, Disney allowed you to do this on only one ride at a time; however, now you can get a pass for a second attraction 2 hours after you get your first FASTPASS stamp (a time frame that's subject to change). Note, however, that the passes go quickly at times and the system can max out, sometimes by noon, so be sure to head to the rides most important to you earliest in the day.

Based on Disney's 1946 film *Song of the South,* **Splash Mountain ★★★** takes you flume-style past 26 colorful scenes that include swamps, bayous, caves, and waterfalls. Riders are caught up in the schemes of Brer Fox and Brer Bear as they chase the ever-wily Brer Rabbit. Your hollow-log vehicle twists, turns, and splashes, sometimes plummeting in darkness, as the ride leads to a 52-foot-long, 40-mph splashdown in a briar-filled pond. **Note:** You must be at least 40 inches tall to ride.

Liberty Square

Step back into 18th-century America. Thirteen lanterns, symbolizing the colonies, hang from the Liberty Tree, an immense live oak in the center of the courtyard. You may even encounter a fife-and-drum corps on the cobblestone streets.

Every American president is represented by a lifelike audio-animatronic figure in the **Hall of Presidents ★**, reopened after a lengthy refurbishment,. Look closely, and you'll see them fidget and whisper. The show begins with a film, and then the curtain rises on America's leaders. Each president's costume reflects his period's fashion, fabrics, and tailoring techniques.

Once you're inside the **Haunted Mansion ★★**, darkness, spooky music, howling, and screams enhance the ambience. After a brief and somewhat ominous welcome, the slow-motion ride takes you past a host of bizarre scenes. It's a classic that's more amusing than terrifying for anyone older than 5. A recent refurbishment has further enhanced its unearthly special effects and spectral silliness.

Fantasyland

The attractions in this happy land are themed after classics such as *Snow White, Peter Pan,* and *Dumbo.* If your kids are 8 and under, you may want to make this your primary stop in the Magic Kingdom.

There's not a lot to do at **Cinderella Castle** ★ (an expansion will change this dramatically), but its status as the Magic Kingdom's icon makes it a must. Mickey, along with a slew of Disney characters, appears daily on the castle forecourt stage in "Dream along with Mickey," while Cinderella's Royal Table restaurant and the Bibiddi Bobiddi Boutique are located inside. Beginning in 2011, the castle is transformed (after dark) into a royal projection screen, where hundreds of images of parkgoers (taken throughout the day) are projected for all to see.

The elaborate and beautiful **Prince Charming Regal Carrousel** ★★ was constructed by Italian carvers in 1917 and refurbished by Disney artists, who added 18 hand-painted scenes from the Cinderella story on a wooden canopy above the horses (originally Cinderella's Golden Carrousel before being renamed in 2010). Kids of all ages (and parents) will enjoy this ride.

Dumbo the Flying Elephant ★ is a very tame kids' ride, in which the Dumbos go around in a circle, gently rising and dipping. If you can stand the lines (and they are usually quite long), it's exciting for wee ones.

Built for the 1964 New York World's Fair, **It's a Small World** ★ takes you to countries inhabited by appropriately costumed audio-animatronic dolls singing "It's a Small World After All," in tiny doll voices. Every adult who has ever ridden this will remember the tune, as it can be difficult to get out of your head.

Mad Tea Party is a traditional amusement park ride with an *Alice in Wonderland* theme that's always a hit with the younger set. Riders sit in big pastel-hued teacups on saucers that careen around a circular platform at the same time that they too are spinning. Adults may want to ground themselves when they get off, as the kids tend to spin as fast as physically possible.

Mickey's PhilharMagic ★★★ is the most amazing 3-D film I've seen. Covering one of the largest screens made for a 3-D movie, the special and sensory effects are incredible. Many of Disney's most beloved characters make an appearance to help (or in some cases hinder) the attempts of Donald Duck to retrieve Mickey's sorcerer's hat. This is a must-see for everyone.

Climb aboard the little elephant with the big ears: Dumbo.

On **Peter Pan's Flight ★** you'll ride in airborne versions of Captain Hook's ship, and take a calm flight over nighttime London to Never-Never Land. You will fly above the mermaids, the ticking crocodile, the Lost Boys, Princess Tiger Lilly, Tinker Bell, Hook, and Smee. This is a fun ride for younger kids and Peter Pan fans of all ages. Just be prepared for one of the longest waits in the park.

A bit too scary for kids 4 and under, **Snow White's Scary Adventure** is as scary as the name implies. The story line, while bright in spots, still plays up the movie's darker scenes. The title heroine, however, does appear in a few pleasant scenes as she rides off to live happily ever after. *Note:* Disney's expansion plan includes replacing this ride with a princess meet-and-greet area (aptly named Princess Fairytale Hall)—how long the ride will remain operational is unknown.

Note: Look for major changes in the near future as a major expansion is underway in Fantasyland. Disney recently began construction on the largest expansion in Magic Kingdom history. Over a 3-year period (set to finish in 2013), this enormous undertaking promises to bring with it a slew of new rides, interactive attractions, and eateries. The majority of additions are said to revolve around Disney's ever-popular princesses, though Disney is taking the approach that boys as well as girls should be taken into account. Once completed, the expansion will practically double the size of Fantasyland. Details regarding the changes had yet to be released at press time. Noticeable changes that may affect your touring plans include the closure of **Mickey's Toontown Fair, Ariel's Grotto,** and **Pooh's Playful Spot** (the latter incorporated into the queue at **The Many Adventures of Winnie the Pooh**).

Tomorrowland

Stitch's Great Escape recruits riders to help capture and contain "experiment 626" (aka Stitch), who is wreaking havoc on the galaxy. Disney animatronics bring the mischievous character to life, and sensory effects and overhead restraints help provide atmosphere. *Tip:* Younger kids who reach the 38-inch maximum height restriction may not care for the long periods of darkness and silence.

On **Buzz Lightyear's Space Ranger Spin ★★★**, join Buzz and try to save the universe while flying your cruiser through a world you'll recognize from the *Toy Story* movies. Kids can use the laser cannons as they spin through the sky (filled with gigantic toys instead of stars). If they're good shots, they can set off sight and sound gags. You may be riding this more than once if you have kids.

The cosmic coaster **Space Mountain ★** usually has *long* lines (if you don't use FASTPASS), especially after the completion of recent refurbishments (bringing this iconic ride, once well past its prime, into the 21st century). The updates, however, are subtle—the special effects have been enhanced but the ride itself remains much the same (albeit somewhat smoother). Once aboard the "rocket," you'll climb and dive through the inky, starlit blackness of outer space. The hairpin turns and plunges make it seem as if you're going at breakneck speed, but your car doesn't go any faster than 28 mph. *Note:* Riders must be at least 44 inches tall.

The immersive **Monsters, Inc., Laugh Floor** takes its cue from the hit Disney/Pixar flick *Monsters, Inc.,* as Mike, along with an entire cast of monster comedians, pokes fun at audience members in hopes of getting enough laughs to fill the gigantic laugh canister. This new immersive experience is live and unscripted, using real-time animation, digital projection, sophisticated voice-activated animation, and a tremendous cast of talented improv comedians.

Younger kids love **Tomorrowland Indy Speedway,** especially if their adult companion lets them drive (without a big person, there's a 52-in. height minimum for driving a lap). Teens and other fast starters find it just too slow—the cars go only 7 mph and are loosely locked into lanes.

Parades, Fireworks & More

For up-to-the-moment information, see the entertainment schedule in the park-guide map as well as the *Times Guide & New Information* card that you can (and should) pick up when entering the park.

Wishes ★★★, the Magic Kingdom's fireworks display, debuted in October 2003 to great acclaim. Its precise mix of choreographed bursts, music, and story is just amazing and has to be experienced to be appreciated. This is absolutely the best way to end your day in the Magic Kingdom. The fireworks go off nightly during peak periods, but only on selected nights the rest of the year.

A 20-minute after-dark display, **SpectroMagic ★★,** combines fiber optics, holographic images, old-fashioned twinkling lights, and a soundtrack featuring classic Disney tunes. The parade runs on a *very limited basis.*

Disney's famed **Electrical Parade ★★** along Main Street U.S.A. made a return in the summer 2010 (it was originally planned as a seasonal offering; however, its popularity ensured that it remains a regular nightly event).

Seasonal celebrations, including *Holidays Around the World* and *Summer Nightastic!* (making its debut in the summer of 2010), bring specially ticketed after-hours parties, specially themed parades, and enhanced fireworks displays to the already lengthy lineup of entertaining enticements and offerings at the parks. Check the latest *Times Guide* for details.

EPCOT

Epcot is an acronym for Experimental Prototype Community of Tomorrow, and it was Walt Disney's dream for a planned residential community. However, long after his death, it opened in 1982 as Central Florida's second Disney theme park.

The 260-acre park has two distinct sections: **Future World** and **World Showcase.** It's so large that hiking World Showcase from tip to tip (1⅓ miles) can be exhausting. That's why some folks say Epcot really stands for "Every Person Comes Out Tired." Depending on how long you intend to linger at each of the 11 countries in World Showcase, this park can be seen in 1 day, but it's better to do it in 2 days to take it all in properly.

Future World

Future World is centered on Epcot's icon, a giant geosphere known as **Spaceship Earth.** Major corporations sponsor most themed areas, with a focus on discovery, scientific achievements, and tomorrow's technologies in areas running from energy to undersea exploration. Here are the headliners:

The fountains at the **Imagination ★★** pavilion are magical—they fire "water snakes" that arch in the air and dare kids to avoid their "bite." The 3-D **Captain EO ★★** has guests flashing back some 24 or so years as Michael Jackson sings and dances his way across the galaxy, conquering the forces of evil. **Journey into Your Imagination ★** features a park favorite, Figment the dragon.

Innoventions ★ is divided into two sections (both constantly updated, so it's always worth stopping in). House of Innoventions in **Innoventions East**

heralds Storm Struck, where guests can experience the effects of hurricane-force winds; Don't Waste It, where educating guests on the importance of recycling is the main message; and The Sum of All Thrills, where guests can design and ride their own simulated thrill ride. The exhibits in **Innoventions West** are led by the Video Game Playground (good luck getting the kids out); Where's the Fire, where fire safety lessons are aimed at the kid set; and The Great Piggy Bank Adventure, where financial responsibility is made fun for everyone.

FROM TOP: The futuristic geosphere called Spaceship Earth presides over EPCOT. Kids can hang out with Nemo (and his dad) and other undersea friends.

The **Land** ★ looks at human relationships with food and nature. **Living with the Land** ★ is a 13-minute boat ride through a rainforest, an African desert, and the windswept American plains. *Circle of Life* ★ blends spectacular live-action footage with animation in a 15-minute movie based on *The Lion King,* and it delivers a cautionary environmental message. **Soarin'** ★★★ allows guests a bird's-eye view of the California landscape. With feet dangling 40 feet above the ground, you'll soar above scenery projected onto the domed screen. Sensory elements and gentle winds add realism to the experience. There's a 40-inch height minimum to ride.

The **Seas with Nemo & Friends** ★ pavilion has been completely renovated, save the 5.7-million-gallon aquarium that holds a reef and more than 4,000 sea creatures, including, among other aquatic creatures, sharks, barracudas, parrotfish, rays, and dolphins. Also inside is a family-friendly "clamobile" ride that slowly moves you along several stunning undersea scenes in search of Nemo; using new animation technology, the characters seemingly swim right along with the live inhabitants in the aquarium. Kids will get a kick out of **Turtle Talk with Crush** ★★, as Crush, the turtle from *Finding Nemo,* engages them in a real-time conversation right from his movie-screen tank.

Get set to blast off to Mars on **Mission: SPACE ★★★**, Epcot's most intense attraction. Sophisticated simulator technology, developed in partnership with NASA and Hewlett-Packard, launches you on an amazing ride through space that feels like the real deal. The original, or orange, version is definitely not for the faint of heart—the green, however, is far less intense, allowing astronauts-in-training (those not ready for G-forces and spinning simulators) a chance to experience space travel. *Note:* Riders must be at least 44 inches tall for both.

Spaceship Earth, Epcot's icon, is a large, silvery geosphere with an audio-visual adventure through time awaiting guests inside. Slow-moving cars take you on a 15-minute journey through the history of communications which, thanks to recent updates and enhancements, has improved (though not significantly). The addition of interactive touch-screens enables guests to create their own idea of what the future will look like—and to see themselves in it. An all-new interactive exhibit area, where guests can test their skills in the areas of medicine, transportation, and energy management through interactive games and displays, has been added as well.

Test Track ★★ is a marvel that combines GM engineering and Disney Imagineering. Once you're in your six-passenger convertible, the 5-minute ride follows what looks like a real highway and includes a brake test, a climb, and tight S-curves. There's also a 12-second burst of speed that reaches 65 mph on the straightaway. *Note:* Riders must be at least 40 inches tall.

Sponsored by Exxon, the **Universe of Energy ★★** pavilion is home to a 32-minute ride, **Ellen's Energy Adventure,** which features comedian Ellen DeGeneres being tutored by Bill Nye the Science Guy to be a *Jeopardy!* contestant. In the process, you learn about energy resources from fossil fuels and take a ride through the age of the dinosaurs.

World Showcase

Surrounding the nearly 40-acre lagoon at the north end of the park is this community of 11 miniaturized nations, each re-created with meticulous detail and featuring indigenous architecture, landscaping, restaurants, and shops. The nations' cultural facets are explored in art exhibits, dance and live performances, or films. The cast members working at each pavilion are natives of that country. The World Showcase opens at 11am and remains open generally up to 2 hours after Future World closes, so plan on heading there after Future World.

The architecture in **Canada ★★** ranges from a mansard-roofed replica of Ottawa's 19th-century, French-style Château Laurier (here called Hôtel du Canada) to a British-influenced stone building. But the highlight is *O Canada! ★*, a 22-minute, 360-degree CircleVision film that shows Canada's scenic splendor, from a dog sled race to the thundering flight of thousands of snow geese.

Bounded by a serpentine wall that wanders its perimeter, the **China ★★** pavilion is entered via a triple-arched ceremonial gate inspired by the Temple of Heaven in Beijing, a summer retreat for Chinese emperors. Passing through the gate, you'll see a half-size replica of this ornately embellished, red-and-gold circular temple, built in 1420 during the Ming dynasty. Inside, the CircleVision film, *Reflections of China,* shows off China's greatest cities. Gardens simulate those in Suzhou, with miniature waterfalls, fragrant lotus ponds, bamboo groves, corkscrew willows, and weeping mulberry trees. Outside, the amazing **Dragon Legend Acrobats** provide live thrills.

The **France** pavilion focuses on La Belle Epoque, a period from 1870 to 1910 during which French art, literature, and architecture flourished. It's entered via a replica of the Pont des Arts footbridge over the Seine and leads to a ¹⁄₁₀-scale model of the Eiffel Tower, constructed from Gustave Eiffel's original blueprints. The big attraction is *Impressions du France* ★★, a 20-minute film featuring the country's top sights and scenery set to the music of French composers.

Enclosed by castle walls and towers, the **Germany** pavilion is centered on a cobblestone square with pots of colorful flowers girding a fountain statue of St. George and the Dragon. The adjacent clock tower's glockenspiel figures herald each hour with quaint melodies. The 16th-century facades replicate a merchant's hall in the Black Forest and the town hall in Römerberg Square. Model-train enthusiasts and kids shouldn't miss the detailed **miniature German village ★**.

One of the prettiest World Showcase pavilions, **Italy ★**, lures visitors over an arched footbridge to a replica of Venice's pink-and-white Doge's Palace. Other highlights include an 83-foot-tall bell tower, Venetian bridges, and a central piazza enclosing a version of Bernini's Neptune Fountain.

At **Japan ★★**, a flaming-red *torii* (gate of honor) leads the way to the Goju No To pagoda, inspired by a shrine built at Nara in A.D. 700. In a traditional Japanese garden, cedars, yews, bamboos, willows, and flowering shrubs frame pebbled footpaths, rustic bridges, waterfalls, rock landscaping, and a pond of koi. The Yakitori House is based on the 16th-century Katsura Imperial Villa in Kyoto, considered the crowning achievement of Japanese architecture. Another highlight is the **White Heron Castle,** a replica of the Shirasagi-Jo, a 17th-century fortress overlooking the city of Himeji. The drums of **Matsuriza ★★**—one of the best performances in the World Showcase—entertain guests daily.

You'll hear marimbas and mariachi bands (including **Mariachi Cobre**) as you approach the **Mexico ★** showcase, fronted by a Mayan pyramid modeled on the Aztec temple of Quetzalcoatl (God of Life) and surrounded by Yucatán jungle landscaping. Upon entering the pavilion, you'll find yourself in a museum of pre-Columbian art and artifacts. Down a ramp, after you have passed through the marketplace and its shops, the newly refurbished **Gran Fiesta Tour Starring the Three Caballeros** offers an 8-minute cruise through Mexico, with a new story line and an overlay of animation starring Donald Duck, Jose, and Carioca.

When you enter **Morocco ★★**, note the imperfections in the mosaic tile in the Koutoubia Minaret, the prayer tower of a 12th-century mosque in Marrakech. They were put there intentionally in accordance with the belief that only Allah is perfect. The **Medina (Old City),** entered via a replica of an arched gateway in Fez, leads to Fez House (a traditional Moroccan home) and the narrow, winding streets of the souk, a bustling marketplace where all manner of handcrafted

A Grand Nightcap

IllumiNations ★★ is a blend of fireworks, lasers, and fountains in a display that's signature Disney. The show is worth the crowds that flock to the parking lot when it's over—don't miss it! *Tip:* Stake your claim to the best viewing areas a half-hour before showtime (listed in your *Times Guide*). The ones near Showcase Plaza have a head start for the exits. The Rose & Crown Pub in the U.K. pavilion (see earlier in this chapter), La Hacienda de San Angel, and La Cantina de San Angel all offer a great view of the proceedings.

Mickey's sorcerer hat can be found in Disney's Hollywood Studios.

merchandise is on display. **Treasures of Morocco** is a daily, 35-minute guided tour that highlights this country's culture, architecture, and history.

Inside **Norway** ★, a *stavekirke* (stave church), styled after the 13th-century Gol Church of Hallingdal, features changing exhibits. A replica of Oslo's 14th-century **Akershus Castle,** next to a cascading woodland waterfall, is the setting for the pavilion's restaurant (p. 515). **Maelstrom** ★, a ride in a dragon-headed Viking vessel, traverses fiords before you crash through a gorge into the North Sea, where you're hit by a storm (albeit a relatively calm one). Passengers disembark at a 10th-century Viking village to view the 70-millimeter film *Norway,* which documents Norwegian history.

The **United Kingdom** ★ beckons you with **Britannia Square,** a London-style park, complete with copper-roofed gazebo bandstand, red phone booth, and a statue of the Bard. Four centuries of architecture are represented along cobblestone streets. *Tip:* Don't miss the **British Invasion** ★, a group that impersonates the Beatles daily except Sunday, and live entertainment at the pub most evenings.

Housed in a Georgian-style structure, the 29-minute **U.S.A.—The American Adventure** ★ is a dramatization of U.S. history using video, rousing music, and a cast of audio-animatronic figures, including narrators Mark Twain and Ben Franklin. You'll see Jefferson writing the Declaration of Independence, the attack on Pearl Harbor, and the *Eagle* heading for the moon, among other historic scenes. Entertainment includes the **Spirit of America Fife & Drum Corps** and **Voices of Liberty,** an a cappella group that sings patriotic songs.

DISNEY'S HOLLYWOOD STUDIOS

Disney bills this park as "the Hollywood that never was and always will be." Hollywood's golden era, around 1940 or so, and done up a la Disney, surrounds you with Art Deco–style buildings accented with pastel colors and neon lights. You'd be hard-pressed to miss Mickey's giant sorcerer's hat on Hollywood Boulevard, or the Tower of Terror and the Earful Tower rising above the landscape. This park is home to two of Disney's most pulse-quickening rides, a variety of movie- and TV-themed shows, and themed restaurants.

Major Attractions & Shows

The 35-minute **Hollywood Studios Backlot Tour ★** takes you behind the scenes via tram for a look at the vehicles, props, costumes, sets, and special effects used in movies and TV shows. But the real fun begins once you reach **Catastrophe Canyon,** where an earthquake causes canyon walls to rumble. A raging oil fire, explosions, torrents of rain, and flash floods threaten you and other riders before you're taken behind the scenes to see how filmmakers use special effects to make such disasters. Over at soundstage 4, on Mickey Avenue, the magical world of Narnia comes alive.

Producers adapted the 30-minute show **Beauty and the Beast Live on Stage ★** from the movie of the same name. The sets and costumes are lavish, and the production numbers are pretty spectacular. Arrive early to get a good seat.

On the **Great Movie Ride,** film footage, audio-animatronic movie stars, and miniature movie sets re-create some of the most famous scenes in film, including clips from *Casablanca, Mary Poppins,* and *Alien.* The ride is longer than most at 22 minutes, but movie buffs will find this ride down memory lane sheer bliss.

Peek into the world of movie stunts at the 30-minute **Indiana Jones Epic Stunt Spectacular ★★★**, which re-creates the most memorable scenes from the Indiana Jones films. Arrive early and sit near the stage for your shot at being an audience participant. Alas, this is a job for adults only.

Kermit and Miss Piggy are the stars of **Jim Henson's Muppet*Vision 3D ★★**, a film that marries Jim Henson's puppets with Disney audio-animatronics, special effects, and 3-D technology. The coming-at-you action includes flying Muppets, cream pies, and cannonballs, high winds, fiber-optic fireworks, bubble showers, even an actual spray of water. This comical 25-minute show runs continuously.

Younger kids will appreciate the **Honey, I Shrunk the Kids Movie Set Adventure,** as they can crawl and climb their way through the larger-than-life set filled with 30-foot blades of grass and gigantic spider webs.

The **Magic of Disney Animation** begins with a theater presentation co-hosted by Mushu the dragon (from Disney's *Mulan*), who reveals the secrets behind the creation of Disney's animated characters. The Q&A session that follows allows guests a chance to ask questions before attempting to draw their own Disney characters under the supervision of a working animator (the best part of the experience). You'll also get the chance to meet and greet Disney characters.

Younger audiences (ages 2–5) love the 20-minute **Disney Junior—Live on Stage!** (replacing Playhouse Disney), where they meet characters from *Jake and the Never Land Pirates, Mickey Mouse Clubhouse, Little Einsteins, Handy Manny,* and others. It encourages preschoolers to dance, sing, and play along with the cast. It shows several times a day. Check your schedule.

Want the best thrill ride WDW has to offer? Then tackle the fast-and-furious **Rock 'n' Roller Coaster ★★★**. Sitting in a 24-passenger "stretch limo" with 120 speakers blaring Aerosmith tunes at 32,000 watts, you'll blast from 0 to 60 mph in 2.8 seconds, then fly into the first inversion at 5Gs. The wild ride continues on through a make-believe California freeway system in the semidarkness (to the tune of Aerosmith's hit "Sweet Emotion"). **Note:** Riders must be at least 48 inches tall.

Cutting edge when it opened, **Star Tours,** based on the original *Star Wars* trilogy, was a few rungs below today's technological standards—but thankfully, in 2011, the ride underwent a complete overhaul—the result being an updated

Wow! Looks like "I Shrunk the Kids!"

3-D version based on Episodes III and IV, boasting enhanced special effects, a new Starspeeder (with C-3PO piloting). So hop aboard the 40-seat "spacecraft," and you'll be off on a journey that takes you through some of the more famous *Star Wars* scenes, full of sudden drops, crashes, and oncoming laser blasts. **Note:** Riders must be at least 40 inches tall. Just next door, pint-size padawan can train alongside Jedi masters at the all-new interactive **Jedi Training Academy.**

The **Twilight Zone Tower of Terror ★★★** is one of the most exciting rides at WDW. As legend has it, during a violent storm on Halloween night 1939, lightning struck the Hollywood Tower Hotel, causing an entire wing and an elevator full of people to disappear—and you're about to meet them as you star in a special episode of *The Twilight Zone.* The ride features random drop sequences, allowing for a real sense of the unknown. New visual, audio, and olfactory effects have also been added to make the experience more frightening. Because it offers a different experience every time you dare to ride, it's the best attraction of its kind. **Note:** You must be at least 40 inches tall to ride.

Hazy lighting and special effects create an underwater effect in a reef-walled theater, helping set the mood for the 17-minute musical **Voyage of the Little Mermaid ★★**, which combines live performers with puppets, film clips, and more. Many of the movie's songs, including "Under the Sea," are featured.

Lights, Motors, Action! Extreme Stunt Show features high-flying high-speed movie stunts full of pyrotechnic effects and more. It's similar to the Indiana Jones Stunt Spectacular, but far faster paced and action packed.

Toy Story Mania made its debut in the summer of 2008. Donning 3-D glasses, guests shrink to the size of a toy, hop into fanciful vehicles, and then travel and twist along a midway-themed route. Think Buzz Lightyear's Space Ranger Spin (at the Magic Kingdom) but with a classic midway twist. Hidden targets lead to different levels of play, ensuring that each experience is unique—just be prepared to wait in a lengthy line as it's quickly become one of the most popular rides in the park.

It's *American Idol* a la Disney at the **American Idol Experience.** Debuting in early 2009, this all-new high-energy show follows in the footsteps of the hit TV show. Staged on a set that replicates the TV original, guests audition and compete—and are judged live and on stage. It's definitely the hottest ticket in the park.

Pixar Pals Countdown to Fun, filled with Pixar characters that seemingly jump off the big screen and onto vibrantly colored floats, takes to the streets each and every afternoon. Fan favorites from such flicks as *Toy Story, Monsters Inc., The Incredibles, Up, Ratatouille,* and *A Bug's Life* are all part of the lively celebration that made its debut in the spring of 2011 (replacing Disney's Block Party Bash).

A Nighttime Spectacle

The fireworks, laser lights, and choreography of **Fantasmic!** ★★★ make it a spectacular, 25-minute, end-of-day experience. The extravaganza features shooting stars, fireballs, animated fountains, a cast of 50, a dragon, a king cobra, and 1 million gallons of water. Everything is orchestrated by a familiar sorcerer mouse. Throughout, musical scores and characters from Disney classics will entrance you.

ANIMAL KINGDOM

Disney's fourth major park combines the elaborate, impressive landscapes of Asia and Africa, including the exotic (and real!) creatures that inhabit them, with the prehistoric lands of the dinosaur. A conservation venue as much as an attraction ensures that you won't find the animals blatantly displayed throughout the 500-acre park; instead, naturalistic habitats blend seamlessly into the surroundings. This means that, at times, you'll have to search a bit to find the inhabitants. Your experience will be far different from that at Disney's other parks because the focus is on the surroundings, meticulously re-created architecture, and detailing, not so much on the attractions themselves. *A bonus:* Although it's the largest of Disney's four theme parks, the Animal Kingdom is easily enjoyed in a single day, making it a good choice when you need to slow it down to a less frenetic pace.

Discovery Island

Like Cinderella Castle in the Magic Kingdom, the 14-story **Tree of Life** ★★ is the Discovery Island's central landmark. The tree has 8,000 limbs, 103,000 leaves, and 325 mammals, reptiles, amphibians, bugs, birds, Mickeys, and dinosaurs carved into its trunk, limbs, and roots. It's worth a walk around its roots on the way to see **It's Tough to Be a Bug!** ★★, a fun 3-D movie with impressive special effects. Grab your glasses and settle into a creepy-crawly seat. It's not a great choice for younger kids or bug haters, but for others, it's a fun, sometimes poignant look at life from a smaller perspective.

Dinoland U.S.A.

Enter beneath "Olden Gate Bridge," a 40-foot Brachiosaurus reassembled from fossils. You'll also find a replica of "Sue," a 67-million-year-old Tyrannosaurus Rex skeleton that was worked on by paleontologists here before being shipped to her home at Chicago's Field Museum.

Kids love the chance to slip, slither, slide, and slink through the **Boneyard** ★★, a giant playground where they can discover and uncover the realistic-looking remains of Triceratops, T-Rex, and other vanished giants. It's also a great place for parents to take a break while the kids frolic.

DINOSAUR ★ hurls you through the darkness in a CTX Rover "time machine" to the time when dinosaurs ruled the earth. The expedition takes you past an array of snarling and particularly ferocious-looking dinosaurs, one of which thinks that you would make a great lunchtime treat. Young children may find the dinos and darkness a bit frightening and the ride a bit jarring. **Note:** You must be 40 inches or taller to climb aboard.

Primeval Whirl is a spinning, freestyle twin roller coaster, where you control the action through its wacky maze of curves, peaks, and dippity-do-dahs. This is a modern version of those old carnival roller coasters of the '50s and '60s. **Note:** It carries a 48-inch height minimum.

A young visitor joins in the Festival of the Lion King.

TriceraTop Spin is a minithrill for youngsters. Friendly-looking dinosaur "cars" circle a hub while moving up and down and all around, much like Dumbo and the Magic Carpets of Aladdin (p. 526) at the Magic Kingdom.

Finding Nemo—The Musical ★★★, Disney's new enchanting stage production, sees Nemo, Marlin, Dory, Crush, and Bruce (among others) come to life, as live actors in creatively designed, puppetlike costumes work together to re-create the undersea adventure made popular by the hit film. Stunning special effects and a moving musical score (created especially for the show) complete and complement the experience. Even the squirmiest toddler will sit mesmerized through this 30-minute show—it's a must for the entire family.

Camp Minnie-Mickey

A character meet-and-greet zone and one of the best theme park shows in town are the main attractions in this small area of Animal Kingdom.

If your kids are hooked on filling their autograph books, the **Character Greeting Trails** should be your first stop (though lines can get excruciatingly long). Various Disney characters have separate trails where you can meet and mingle, snap photos, and get those autographs.

Everyone in the audience comes alive when the music starts at the rousing, 28-minute ***Festival of the Lion King*** ★★★ in the Lion King Theater. The festival celebrates nature's diversity with a talented troupe of singers, dancers, and life-size critters. It's a sight-and-sound spectacular that shouldn't be missed. Make sure to arrive at least 20 minutes early.

Africa

Enter through **Harambe,** a re-creation of an African coastal village at the edge of the 21st century. A central marketplace is surrounded by structures built of coral stone, thatched with reed by African craftsmen.

Kilimanjaro Safaris might get you a close-up look at some amazing wild animals.

Animal Kingdom has expanded its collection of rides, but the **Kilimanjaro Safaris** ★★★ is still one of the most popular. As you bump along through a simulated African savanna in a large truck, you may spot black rhinos, hippos, crocodiles, antelopes, wildebeests, zebras, giraffes, and lions. The downside: If the animals aren't feeling cooperative, you may not see much. They're scarce at midday most of the year (in cooler months you may get lucky), so *ride this one as close to the park's opening or closing as you can.* Adventurous guests (with fat wallets) can book a trek through the Harambe Wildlife Reserve, navigate along the bushwalk, cross the rope bridges hanging precariously above the Safi River (all the while tethered to a safety line—the bridge, of course, actually well secured), hang over the cliffs above pools filled with hippos and crocodiles, and experience, firsthand, remote areas of the reserve (via open-air vehicles). The adventure ends at a private safari camp elevated above the savanna for optimal wildlife viewing— a sampling of African fare and beverages ready and waiting. Limited to 12 adventurous guests, the **Wild Africa Trek** currently costs $129 per person (though expect this to increase).

Hippos, tapirs, ever-active mole rats, and other critters are often on the **Pangani Forest Exploration Trail** ★★ for your viewing, but the real prize is getting a look at the gorillas. Don't expect full cooperation, however, because in hot weather, they spend most of the day in shady areas and out of view. Those who come early, stay late, are patient, or make return visits should be rewarded with a close-up look.

Asia

Disney's Imagineers did an amazing job of creating the mythical kingdom of **Anandapur.** The intricately painted artwork is just another example of the lengths to which Disney has gone to transport you from the everyday real world to the places of your imagination.

Kali River Rapids ★ is a good raft ride. Its churning waters and optical illusions will have you wondering if you're about to drop over the falls. Expedition Everest makes a brief but impressive appearance along the way. You *will* most likely get wet. **Note:** There's a 38-inch height minimum.

Take the fast way down Mt. Everest.

Impressively detailed surroundings and up-close views of the animals make **Maharajah Jungle Trek ★★** an often-overlooked jewel. If you don't show up in the midday heat, you may see Bengal tigers through the thick glass, while nothing but air divides you from dozens of giant fruit bats (with wingspans up to 6 ft.) and other smaller inhabitants. Be sure to pick up one of the guides that list the many unusual and often rare inhabitants to look for along the way.

Expedition Everest ★★★, the newest attraction in the park, transports guests to the small Himalayan village of Serka Zong. Guests board the Anandapur Rail Service bound for Mount Everest; after passing through bamboo forests and waterfalls, diving through fields of glaciers, and climbing to the snowcapped peaks, the train suddenly veers "out of control," sending riders careening down Mount Everest's rough, rugged terrain. You'll be thrust forward and backward, in and out of the darkness. And that's not the end . . . a close encounter with a legendary Yeti will have your hair standing on end before it's over.

OTHER WDW ATTRACTIONS
Typhoon Lagoon ★★★

A storm-stranded fishing boat—*Miss Tilly*—teeters atop 95-foot-high Mount Mayday overlooking this Disney water park. Guests can be tossed about on a number of twisting and turning wild rides and slides here. There are more relaxing activities as well.

Castaway Creek's rafts and inner tubes glide along a 2,100-foot-long river that circles most of the park, passing through a rainforest, caves, and grottoes. At **Water Works,** jets of water spew from shipwrecked boats.

Ketchakiddie Creek is for the 2- to 5-year-old set. It has bubbling fountains in which to frolic, mini water slides, a pint-size "white-water" tubing run, spouting whales and squirting seals, rubbery crocodiles to climb on, grottoes to explore, and waterfalls to loll under.

At **Shark Reef,** guests get free equipment and a few instructions—and then you're off for a 15-minute swim through a snorkeling area that's home to a simulated reef and shipwreck, populated by parrotfish, rays, and small sharks.

541

The **Surf Pool ★★**, the park's 2.75-million-gallon wave pool, is one of the world's largest. Every 90 seconds, a foghorn sounds, warning you of the impending and crashing waves, just in case you want to head for cover. Young children will appreciate wading in the lagoon's more peaceful tidal pools of **Blustery Bay** and **Whitecap Cove;** the bigger, more powerful waves of the Surf Pool would most likely sweep them away.

Humunga Kowabunga consists of three 214-foot Mount Mayday slides that send you plummeting down the mountain on a serpentine route through waterfalls and bat caves and past nautical wreckage before depositing you into a catch pool. *Note:* You must be 48 inches or taller to ride this. **White-Water Rides** at Mount Mayday is the setting for three white-water rafting adventures—**Keelhaul Falls, Mayday Falls,** and **Gangplank Falls**—all offering steep and drenching drops coursing through caves and passing lush scenery.

The newest thrill to splash onto the scene is the **Crush 'n' Gusher,** a first-of-its-kind water coaster with three separate experiences to choose from: the **Banana Blaster, Coconut Crusher,** and **Pineapple Plunger,** each offering steep drops, twists, and turns of varying degrees.

Typhoon Lagoon is open from 10am to 5pm, with extended hours during holiday periods and summer (*©* **407/560-4141;** www.disneyworld.com). A 1-day ticket is $46 for adults, $40 for children 3 to 9.

Blizzard Beach ★★★

Snowcapped mountaintops in the middle of sunny Orlando—who else but Disney could have created this 66-acre "ski resort," set in the midst of a tropical lagoon and centered on the 90-foot Mount Gushmore? *Note:* The majority of this park's attractions are geared to thrill-seekers, making it a better choice for families with kids at least 8 years of age.

The 2,900-foot-long **Cross Country Creek** is a lazy river ride that runs the perimeter of the park, but watch out for the brisk melting "ice" as you pass through the Polar Caves. The waves of Melt-A-Way Bay offer yet another relaxing and less heart-pounding option. **Runoff Rapids,** however, will send you and your tube careening down one of three twisting runs through semidarkness.

Ski-Patrol Training Camp, designed for 'tweens and teens, features a rope swing, a T-bar hanging over the water, the wet and slippery **Mogul Mania** slide, and an ice-floe walk along slippery floating icebergs.

Snow Stormers has three flumes descending from the top of Mount Gushmore, following a switchback course through slalom-type gates.

Summit Plummet ★★ is one of the most breath-defying adventures in any water park. Read every speed, motion, vertical-dip, wedgie, and hold-onto-your-breastplate warning before hopping on. This starts slow, with a lift ride to the 120-foot summit. But it finishes as the world's fastest body slide—a test of your courage and swimsuit—that goes nearly straight down and has you moving sans vehicle at 60 mph into the catch pool. *Note:* It has a 48-inch height minimum.

Teamboat Springs is the world's longest white-water raft ride, twisting down a 1,200-foot series of rushing waterfalls.

Tike's Peak is a kid-friendly version of Mount Gushmore. It has short water slides, animals to climb aboard, a snow castle, a squirting ice pond, and a fountain play area for young guests.

Blizzard Beach is open from 10am to 5pm, with extended hours during some holiday periods and summer (*©* **407/560-3400;** www.disneyworld.com). A 1-day ticket is $46 for adults, $40 for children 3 to 9.

Miniature Golf ★

Hippos, ostriches, and alligators decorate the **Fantasia Gardens** course, a good bet for beginners and kids. Seasoned mini-golfers will likely prefer the second 18-hole course, **Fantasia Fairways,** filled with sand traps, water hazards, and trickier putting greens. This one is definitely not for novices.

Santa Claus and his elves provide the theme for **Winter Summerland,** which has two additional 18-hole courses, appropriate for all ages and abilities. The summer course is pure Florida, from sand castles to surfboards; the other course offers a touch of the North Pole and a visit with Santa on the "Winternet."

Tickets are about $13 for adults and $11 for kids 3 to 9. The courses are open from 10am to 10 or 11pm daily. For information about Fantasia Gardens, call ✆ **407/560-4582.** For information on Winter Summerland, call ✆ **407/560-3000.** Find both on the Internet at **www.disneyworld.com**.

BEYOND DISNEY: UNIVERSAL ORLANDO & SEAWORLD

There are so many attractions in Orlando (more than 95) that it's impossible to see even half of them unless you're here for a month. The following should help you finish your must-see list.

Universal Studios in Florida

Lights, camera, and *action, action, action.* Universal is touted as the park where you can "Ride the Movies," and it's filled with fast-paced, high-intensity attractions. There's a lot here for kids too. As a plus, it's a working motion picture and TV studio, so occasional filming takes place at the sound stages. There are also plenty of characters on hand to meet and greet visitors throughout the park.

TICKET PRICES Universal recently revised its entire ticketing schedule; it's now a system similar to (but not exactly like) Disney's, with single-park tickets and multipark tickets good for between 1 and 7 days. Currently a **1-day, one-park ticket** costs $82 for adults, $74 for children 3 to 9. A **2-day, one-park-per-day admission ticket,** good for admission to either of Universal's major theme parks (Universal Studios or Islands of Adventure) on each day your ticket is valid, runs $115 for adults, $102 for children. As the number of days increases, so does the ticket price (up to a 4-day, one-park-per-day ticket costing $140 for adults, $123 for children).

A **1-day park-to-park access ticket** (which allows you to park-hop btw. Universal Studios and Islands of Adventure) costs $112 for adults, $104 for children ages 3 to 9. A **2-day park-to-park ticket** costs $135 for adults, $122 for children—and again, as the number of days increases, so does the ticket price (up to a 7-day park-to-park access ticket at a cost of $175 for adults, $155 for children). Park-to-park access tickets purchased at the gate will run you $10 more per ticket. A **two-park premier annual pass** runs $350 (any age). The latter includes unlimited admission to the parks (no blackout dates), free self-parking, free valet parking on most days, Universal Express Plus privileges after 4pm, all-club access at CityWalk, and a slew of discounts good at Universal parks and resorts. The **two-park preferred annual pass** is less expensive at $230 (any age) and includes unlimited admission to the parks (no blackout dates), free self-parking, and numerous discounts good at Universal parks and resorts.

Like Disney, Universal offers savings on ticket purchases if you purchase them before you leave home. Buy your park-to-park access tickets online and you'll save $10 a ticket (adding up to a substantial savings for families). You can pick up your tickets at the front gate of either park or have them sent (for a delivery charge) to your home.

THE FLEXTICKET The least expensive way to see Universal, SeaWorld, Aquatica, *and* Wet 'n Wild is with a **FlexTicket.** This pass lets you pay one price for unlimited admission to participating parks during a 14-day period. The Orlando FlexTicket, which includes admission to Universal Studios Florida, Islands of Adventure, Wet 'n Wild, SeaWorld, and Aquatica, is $275 for adults and $255 for children 3 to 9. The Orlando FlexTicket Plus, which adds Busch Gardens in Tampa Bay (p. 425), is $315 for adults and $295 for kids. FlexTickets can be ordered through Universal (✆ **800/711-0080** or 407/363-8000; www.universalorlando.com) as well the other participating parks. Free shuttle service between all of the parks, even Busch Gardens, is included in the ticket price.

PARKING Parking is $15 for cars, light trucks, and vans—after 6pm it's $3. Valet parking is $25.

MAJOR ATTRACTIONS

Set in a parklike theater-in-the-round, the 25-minute musical *A Day in the Park with Barney* stars that big purple dinosaur, Baby Bop, and BJ. It uses song, dance, interactive play, and special effects to entertain younger guests. It's a must for preschoolers, though parents will need strength to endure it.

Not long after you climb on a San Francisco BART train at **Disaster ★★**, there's an earthquake that's 8.3 on the Richter scale! As you sit helplessly trapped, concrete slabs collapse around you, a propane truck bursts into flames, a runaway train hurtles your way, and the station begins to flood with no way out.

Revenge of the Mummy ★★★ is a high-speed, twisting, turning, pulsating adventure through Egyptian tombs, with creepy skeletal warriors in hot pursuit. This one is packed full of amazing pyrotechnic effects, a state-of-the-art propulsion system, and hair-raising robotic creatures.

Soar with E.T. on a mission to save his ailing planet at **E.T. Adventure ★**; you'll pass through the dense forest and gently glide into space aboard a bicycle.

The $45-million **Jaws ★★** begins calmly enough, with a leisurely boat ride through New England coastal waters, when suddenly a 3-ton, 32-foot-long great white shark is spotted. You can pretty much figure out what happens next. There are plenty of special effects, including a wall of flame that surrounds your boat as you chargrill the fish before landing safely back at the dock.

Buckle up for **Jimmy Neutron's Nicktoon Blast ★★**, as Jimmy's Rocket Pod hurtles you through hyperspace thanks to sophisticated computer graphics, state-of-the-art ride technology, animation, and programmable motion-based seats.

In **Men in Black Alien Attack ★★★**, board a six-passenger cruiser, buzz the streets of New York, and use your "zapper" to splatter up to 120 bug-eyed targets. You have to contend with return fire as well as light, noise, and clouds of liquid nitrogen (also known as fog) that can spin you out of control. Your laser tag–style gun fires infrared bullets. ***Note:*** Guests must be at least 42 inches tall for this ride.

Hollywood Rip Ride Rockit is Universal Studios' newest (and Central Florida's tallest) coaster to date. Located between Jimmy Neutron's Nicktoon Blast and the AQUOS Theater (home to the Blue Man Group), on a track spilling out beyond the boundaries of the park, twisting high above CityWalk, riders are sent careening through corkscrews, tight turns, and dramatic drops—oh, and did I mention the record-breaking loop? Check it out for yourself—head to **www. hollywoodripriderockit.com**.

Shrek 4-D ★ is a 20-minute show that can be seen, heard, felt, and smelled, thanks to motion-simulator technology, OgreVision glasses, and special sensory effects. I expected more from Universal in the seating-effects department, but the preshow and the movie are definitely worthwhile.

The **Simpsons Ride ★★★** replaced "Back to the Future: The Ride" a few years back. Though the simulated coaster ride remains much the same (albeit a bit smoother), guests are now rocketed along with the entire Simpson family on an amusing adventure through a side of Springfield that has yet to be explored.

James Cameron, who directed *Terminator 2,* supervised the $60-million **Terminator 2: 3-D Battle Across Time ★★**, which features Arnie and other original cast members (on film). It combines three huge screens with technical effects and live action on stage, including a custom-built Harley and six 8-foot-tall cyberbots. The crisp 3-D effects are among the best in any Orlando park. *Note:* Universal has given this show a PG-13 rating.

Two million cubic feet of air per minute create a funnel cloud five stories tall at **Twister . . . Ride It Out ★★**. The roar of a freight train, at rock-concert decibel level, fills the theater as cars, trucks, and a cow fly by, while the audience watches just 20 feet away. *Note:* This show has a PG-13 rating—and although not listed as such, it has, in the past, been open only seasonally.

Woody Woodpecker's Nuthouse Coaster ★★ is a kiddie coaster that will thrill some moms and dads too. Although only 30 feet at its peak, it offers quick, banked turns. The ride lasts only about 60 seconds and the wait can be 30 minutes or more. *Note:* The coaster has a 36-inch height minimum.

For a good dose of reality, reality TV that is, be sure to catch **Fear Factor Live.** Audience members can sign up to be the stars of the show, but be prepared—the stunts, while toned down, are similarly challenging (and just as disgusting), so be sure you're up for the task before volunteering. *Note:* At press time, the show was being offered only seasonally.

The Blue Man Group, a visually exciting and wildly unique stage show, can be seen daily at the all-new redesigned AQUOS Theater (previously Nickelodeon Studios in Production Central). Show-only tickets start at $64 for adults, $25 for children ages 3 to 9 (park ticket packages are also available for an additional cost). Theme park admission is not required.

Islands of Adventure

Universal's second theme park is even more impressive architecturally than its big brother, Universal Studios Florida. Roller coasters roar above pedestrian walkways, and water rides make some rather big splashes throughout the park. It is, bar none, *the* Orlando theme park for thrill-ride junkies, and also offers some of the best, and most unique, dining around—theme park or otherwise.

A few words of caution: *Nine of the park's 14 major rides (not including those yet to become operational) have height restrictions.* Many rides may not be suitable for those who are tall enough but who are pregnant or have health

Oh the places you'll go on the High in the Sky Trolley!

problems—physical restrictions; heart, neck, or back problems; or a tendency for motion sickness.

PARKING Parking is $15 for cars, light trucks, and vans—$3 after 6pm. Valet parking is $25.

MAJOR ATTRACTIONS
Port of Entry
A towering lighthouse marks the entrance to this seemingly centuries-old marketplace, which serves as a gateway to the Islands of Adventure's five (soon to be six) themed "islands." Guest Services can be found near the gates; the remaining area is filled with shops and restaurants.

Seuss Landing
You'll feel as if you have jumped into the pages of a Dr. Seuss classic as you enter colorful Seuss Landing. Main attractions are aimed at youngsters, but anyone who loved the good doctor as a child will enjoy the fun.

It's hard to miss the cat's candy-striped hat marking the entrance to the **Cat in the Hat** ★★, where guests follow the famous story from beginning to end. You'll pass through scenes right out of the famous tale of a day gone very much awry. This chaotic ride has a few swirls and whirls along the way, making it a bit spunkier than most, though that's part of the fun.

The **High in the Sky Seuss Trolley Train Ride** is a kid-friendly ride that runs along two separate tracks suspended high above Seuss Landing. Traveling in individual "cars," you'll pass by classic Seussian scenes and colorful characters—with the occasional view of Seuss Landing below. Lines for this one can be quite long, but high-power fans will keep you cool while you wait.

One Fish, Two Fish, Red Fish, Blue Fish ★ is a family favorite similar to the Magic Carpets of Aladdin and Dumbo rides at WDW (including the long, long lines). Here, controls let you move your funky fish up or down as you circle a central hub. Watch out for "squirt posts" that spray unsuspecting riders.

Hop on **Caro-Seuss-El** ★★★ for a chance to ride whimsical characters from Dr. Seuss, including cowfish, elephant birds, and Mulligatawnies.

The outdoor interactive play area **If I Ran the Zoo** ★ features flying water snakes and a chance to tickle the toes of a Seussian animal. Kids can also spin wheels, explore caves, fire water cannons, climb, slide, and otherwise burn off excited energy.

Marvel Super Hero Island

Adrenaline junkies and thrill-seekers thrive on the twisting, turning, stomach-churning rides on this island of larger-than-life comic superheroes and villains.

The original web master is the star of the exceptional, special effects–laden ride the **Amazing Adventures of Spider-Man ★★★**. Passengers wearing 3-D glasses squeal as their 12-passenger cars twist and spin, plunge, and soar through a comic book universe. A simulated 400-foot drop feels a lot like the real thing.

Look! Up in the sky! It's a bird, it's a plane . . . uh, it's you falling 150 feet, if you're courageous enough to climb aboard **Doctor Doom's Fearfall ★**. The screams that can be heard far from the ride's entrance add to the anticipation. You're fired to the top, with feet dangling, and dropped in intervals, leaving your stomach at several levels. The fall isn't quite up to Disney's Tower of Terror's (p. 537), but it's still frightening. ***Note:*** Minimum height is 52 inches.

On the **Incredible Hulk Coaster ★★★**, you're launched from a dark tunnel and hurtled into the lower ozone while accelerating from 0 to 40 mph in 2 seconds. You will spin upside down 128 feet from the ground, feel weightless, and career through the center of the park. Coaster lovers will be pleased to know that this ride, which lasts 2 minutes and 15 seconds, includes seven inversions and two deep drops. ***Note:*** Riders must be at least 54 inches tall.

Toon Lagoon

More than 150 life-size cartoon images let you know you've entered an island dedicated to your favorites from the Sunday funnies.

Dudley Do-Right's Ripsaw Falls ★★ has a lot more speed and drop than onlookers think. Six-passenger logs launch you into a 75-foot dip at 50 mph. You *will* get wet on this ride. ***Note:*** Riders must be 44 inches or taller.

The three-story boat *Me Ship, The Olive ★* is family-friendly from bow to stern. Kids can toot whistles, clang bells, or play the organ. Sweet Pea's Playpen is fun for young guests. Adults and kids 6 and over love Cargo Crane, which lets you drench riders on Popeye & Bluto's Bilge-Rat Barges.

Popeye & Bluto's Bilge-Rat Barges ★★ are similar to the rafts at WDW's Kali River Rapids (p. 540), but they're faster and bouncier. Adding to the fun, you'll be squirted by water cannons fired from *Me Ship, The Olive* (see above). The rafts bump and dip 14 feet at one point, as you travel a *c-c-cold* white-water course. You will get *soaked!* Riders must be at least 42 inches tall.

Jurassic Park

All of the basics and some of the high-tech wizardry from Steven Spielberg's films are incorporated in this lushly landscaped tropical locale that includes a replica of the visitor center from the *Jurassic Park* movie.

The **Camp Jurassic ★★★** play area has everything from lava pits with dino bones to a rainforest. Watch out for the spitters that lurk in dark caves. The multilevel play area has plenty of places to crawl through, explore, and expend energy. But keep an eye on young ones: It's easy to get confused in the caverns.

Jurassic Park Discovery Center, a virtual replica of the lab from the movie set, is an amusing, somewhat educational pit stop that offers life-size dinosaur replicas and interactive games.

On the **Jurassic Park River Adventure ★★**, after a leisurely raft tour along a faux river, things go awry (don't they always?). An immense T-Rex thinks you look like a rather tasty morsel, with spitters launching "venom" your way just to add insult to injury. The only way out: an 85-foot, almost vertical plunge in your log-style life raft. It's steep and quick enough to lift your fanny out of the seat. Expect to get wet. *Note:* Guests must be at least 42 inches tall.

The Lost Continent

Although it's mixed its millennia—ancient Greece with a medieval forest sprinkled in with the magical world of witches and wizards—Universal has done a good job of creating a foreboding mood in this section of the park, whose entrance is marked by menacing stone griffins.

Those who notice it have fun at the **Mystic Fountain** ★, a "smart" fountain that delights kids. It can "see," "hear," and "talk," leading to a lot of kibitzing with those who stand before it and take the time to kibitz back. But be careful: It can squirt you.

One of the park's shows, ***Poseidon's Fury*** ★ revolves around a battle between Poseidon, god of the sea, and Darkenon, an evil sorcerer. The most impressive effect occurs as you pass through a small vortex, where 17,500 gallons of water swirl around before you enter a room to experience the battle's pyrotechnic glories.

The Wizarding World of Harry Potter

In June 2010, the **Wizarding World of Harry Potter,** after 3 years of preparation, finally cast its magical spell. Based on the wildly popular series of books by J. K. Rowling (as well as the blockbuster movies), the Wizarding World brings to life the adventures of the young wizard through immersive rides and next-generation interactive attractions—including re-creations of Hogwarts Castle and the village of Hogsmeade—plus an array of shops and restaurants (think Diagon Alley, albeit on a much smaller scale) created from areas within the Lost Continent and beyond.

In **The Village of Hogsmeade** you'll find **Zonko**'s joke shop filled with a collection of tricks and jokes, Extendable Ears, Boxing Telescopes, and Sneakoscopes; **Honeydukes** candy shop, filled with candy treats from Chocolate Frogs to Bertie Bott's Every-Flavour Beans; **The Owlery,** where roosting owls await their next delivery, the **Owl Post,** where you can mail letters to the muggle world with a Hogsmeade postmark and Wizarding World stamps; **Ollivanders** wand shop, featuring an unprecedented interactive experience where the wand chooses the wizard; **Dervish and Banges,** the place to pick up the latest Quidditch equipment, Triwizard apparel, Spectrespecs, and Remembralls, among other magical gadgets; and **Filch's Emporium of Confiscated Goods,** where merchandise from the Ministry of Magic, magical creatures, Omnioculars, and remote control Golden Snitches line the shelves.

Dining options include **Three Broomsticks** and the **Hog's Head,** where menus of traditional British fare are offered along with Butterbeer (a nonalcoholic beverage) and pumpkin juice.

Welcome to Hogsmeade, where you might run into a wizard or two.

Thrill-seekers will find the **Dragon Challenge** (Dueling Dragons in a previous life) to their liking, while families with younger children may find the **Flight of the Hippogriff** a tamer, less intense option. **Harry Potter and the Forbidden Journey,** located in the iconic Hogwarts castle, will take you soaring over Hogwarts grounds!

SeaWorld

This 200-acre marine-life park explores the mysteries of the deep by combining conservation awareness with entertainment (also known as *edutainment*). Through the years it has expanded, adding a handful of thrill rides (including Manta in the summer of 2009), a large shopping and dining area, additional entertainment venues, and more wildlife. While not as large as its neighbors (Universal and Disney), it won't leave you as thoroughly exhausted, or exasperated by crowds. The unique combination of its animal life, calmer atmosphere, beautifully landscaped grounds, shows, and sprinkling of rides makes it a must-see for anyone visiting the Orlando area.

TICKET PRICES A **1-day ticket** costs $80 for ages 10 and over, $72 for children 3 to 9, plus 6.5% sales tax. If you purchase tickets in advance online, you can save $5 off the price of an adult ticket; in addition, each ticket holder (child or adult) will get a second day free (valid for one additional visit up to 7 days from when you first used your ticket).

MULTIPARK PASSES For information on the **FlexTicket,** see p. 544. The **Fun Card** is a 1-year pass good for unlimited visits to SeaWorld. Prices run $80 for ages 10 and over, $72 for children ages 3 to 9. Fun Cards are available only to Florida residents.

Multiday and multipark tickets are also available. These are good for admission to two or three SeaWorld parks (SeaWorld, Aquatica, and Busch Gardens Tampa) over a consecutive 14-day period. Prices start at $115 for adults and $107 for kids ages 3 to 9 for a two-park ticket. A three-park ticket runs $130 for adults and $122 for kids. Throw in a visit to Discovery Cove and tickets run $199 (including admission to three additional SeaWorld parks) for adults and kids alike. For $279 you can visit all five parks.

Annual passes are good for either 1 or 2 years and cover one, two, three, or four parks. The passes start at $110 and reach as high as $380. For more information, call ✆**407/351-3600** or check **www.seaworld.com**.

PARKING Parking is $14 for cars, light trucks, and vans. For $20, you can park close to the entrance in a specially designated section.

Watch the stingrays soar through the water at SeaWorld.

MAJOR ATTRACTIONS

A lovable sea lion and otter, with a supporting cast of walruses and harbor seals, as well as some quick-witted SeaWorld actors/trainers, appear in **Clyde & Seamore Take Pirate Island ★★**, a fish-breath comedy with a swashbuckling theme. It's corny, but a lot of fun. Watch out if you enter too close to showtime; the mime entertaining the crowds ahead of time may target you for the audience's amusement.

SeaWorld created a story to go with its $30-million water coaster, **Journey to Atlantis ★★**. But what really matters is the drop—a wild plunge from 60 feet with lugelike curves. **Note:** Riders must be at least 42 inches tall, and pregnant women as well as those with heart, neck, or back problems should not ride.

Kraken ★★★, named for a mythological beast, is a floorless, open-sided coaster where 32-passenger trains place you on a pedestal, high above the track, your feet dangling. You'll climb 151 feet, only to fall 144 feet at speeds of up to 65 mph seconds later, passing underground a total of three times (spraying bystanders with water) and making seven loops before you finally touch ground again. It's higher and faster than any coaster at Universal, probably making it the longest 3 minutes and 39 seconds of your life. **Note:** Kraken has a 54-inch height minimum.

Manta is SeaWorld's newest thrill-a-minute megacoaster. It takes riders soaring high into the sky and diving deep into the ocean depths at speeds of up to 60 mph past some of the largest underwater habitats in the park—all the while riding face-down, in a prone horizontal position. Riders will at times find themselves within inches of the sea—at others skimming the sky thanks to the track's four inversions.

In **Manatee Rescue ★**, underwater viewing stations, cinema techniques, and interactive displays combine for a tribute to these marine mammals. While this isn't as good as seeing them in the wild, it's as close as most folks get.

You are transported by moving sidewalk through arctic and antarctic displays at **Penguin Encounter.** You'll get a glimpse of penguins as they preen, socialize, and swim at bullet speed in their 22°F (–6°C) habitat. You'll also see puffins and murres in a similar, separate area. While it gives you a nice view of the penguins, the viewing area's surroundings are in need of a face-lift.

The 4-acre **Shamu's Happy Harbor ★★** play area has a four-story net tower with a 35-foot-high crow's nest, as well as water cannons, remote-controlled vehicles, nine slides, a submarine, as well as water maze, and six kid-friendly rides, including a cool little coaster. Most kids relish the freedom of running, jumping, and climbing (and, of course, getting wet) after hearing, "Don't wander too far away from us," all day long. It is easy to escape a parent's watchful eye here, so little ones are best accompanied by an adult.

Everyone comes to SeaWorld to see Shamu and his friends—the stars of the all-new eco-themed show, **One Ocean** (replacing *Believe* in the spring of 2011). An impressive set and spectacular special effects combine with a top-notch performance to produce a great show (the trainers no longer in the water alongside the killer whales, instead working from the stage). The focus is on introducing parkgoers to the animals themselves, emphasizing the individual personalities of each whale, and highlighting how they interact with each other. A vividly apparent message runs throughout the show regarding the importance of conservation efforts aimed at protecting the ocean and its inhabitants. Be sure to heed the warnings, however, as those sitting in the first 14 rows are sure to get soaked with icy water—and not just once, either. **Blue Horizons** ★★, the park's dolphin show, features aerial acrobatics, exotic birds, and dolphins, of course. **A'Lure—The Call of the Ocean,** replacing *Odyessa* in 2010, is a high-energy show that's visually exciting as acrobatics and spectacular undersea scenery simply entrance the audience.

SeaWorld has added 220 species to its **Shark Encounter** attraction. The pools out front contain small sharks and rays (feeding isn't allowed). The interior aquariums have big eels, lionfish, barracudas, puffer fish, and even larger and more menacing sharks. The eerie music playing in the background adds to the ominous ambience.

Enveloping guests in the beauty, exhilaration, and danger of a polar expedition, **Wild Arctic** ★ combines a high-definition adventure film with flight-simulator technology to display arctic panoramas. After a hazardous flight over the frozen north, visitors emerge into an exhibit where they can see a polar bear, beluga whales, and walruses. Kids and those prone to motion sickness may find the ride bumpy. There's a separate line if you want to skip the flight.

The **Waterfront,** SeaWorld's answer to a shopping and dining district, is a themed 5-acre Mediterranean seaport village filled with unique shops, a wide variety of restaurants (each offering a very different atmosphere and menu), and, for entertainment, formal shows and street performances.

DINING AT SEAWORLD

The park offers an array of casual and entertaining dining experiences in addition to its newly expanded collection of Waterfront eateries. **Dine with Shamu** ($42 adults, $33 kids ages 3–9) gives visitors the experience of seeing Shamu up-close while enjoying a buffet-style meal. *Note:* Dine with Shamu had been temporarily suspended following the tragic death of a SeaWorld trainer in 2010—in the spring of 2011 the up-close dining experience resumed (though details regarding guest access and which meals would be served had yet to be released at press time).

Breakfast with Jack Hanna is the park's popular ask-the-expert dining experience, and includes reserved seating at Jungle Jack's first show of the day ($18 adults, $16 children 3–9). The **Makahiki Luau** serves up island-style entertainment as well as a luau-type meal. The cost is $46 adults, $29 kids ages 3 to 9 (park admission is *not* required). **Sharks Underwater Grill** is an upscale restaurant geared mostly to adults and allows up-close viewing of sharks through a wall of glass. Entrees are a bit pricey, averaging around $18 (and reaching upwards of $36), but the gourmet Floribbean fare is a few cuts above the usual park cuisine. *Note:* The park now offers an "all-day dining deal"—guests pay a flat price ($30 for ages 10 and over, $15 for kids ages 3–9) and can dine all day long at select restaurants. Each time through the line (you can pass through as many times as you wish), you can choose a nonalcoholic beverage, an entree, and either a desert or a side dish, and, if you like, go back for more.

Shuttle Service

SeaWorld and Busch Gardens (p. 425), both owned by Anheuser-Busch, offer round-trip shuttle service ($10 per person) to get you from Orlando to Tampa and back. The 1½- to 2-hour one-way shuttle runs daily and has five pickup locations in Orlando, including at Universal and on International Drive (☎ 800/221-1339). The schedule allows for about 7 hours at Busch Gardens. The service is free if you hold a FlexTicket.

12

WALT DISNEY WORLD & ORLANDO

Beyond Disney

Discovery Cove: A Dolphin Encounter

Anheuser-Busch spent $100 million building SeaWorld's sister park, which debuted in 2000. In 2011, millions more were poured into the park's first expansion as **The Grand Reef** is set to make its debut (in the summer of 2011). Prices vary seasonally but range from $199 to $299 per person (plus 6.5% sales tax) for ages 6 and up—the Grand Reef's Sea Venture experience costs an additional $59 per person. Double-check prices when you make your reservations (required to enter the park).

The **dolphin encounter** ★★★ allows guests the opportunity to swim, touch, play, and interact with these amazingly intelligent creatures. They can even take a brief, albeit thrilling ride with one. The entire experience lasts 90 minutes, 35 to 40 minutes of which are spent in the lagoon with a dolphin. The rest is a classroom experience on these remarkable mammals.

The Grand Reef (set to open in the summer of 2011) brings with it an inviting palm-lined stretch of white-sand beach, and underwater grottoes teaming with vibrantly colored tropical fish, moray eels, and reef sharks (among other denizens of the deep). Guests can venture below the surface in shallow waters surrounded by a variety of sea life; snorkel in deeper waters among velvety rays, angelfish, tangs, and an array of tropical fish; or dive even deeper into the park's newest interactive underwater adventure, *Sea Venture.* This underwater walking tour takes guests (wearing diving helmets) along underwater pathways allowing for an up-close-and-interactive experience. Swimming alongside are thousands of schooling sardines and eagle rays, while some of the reef's more formidable inhabitants (including zebra, nurse, blacktip, and whitetip sharks as well as venomous lionfish) swim behind panoramic windows. Pathways and bridges above the water allow guests to view the waters below (and lead to various islands

OTHER AREA attractions

One of the most notable smaller Orlando-area attractions (that requires less than a full day to experience and doesn't cost a fortune to experience) is **Gatorland** (✆ **800/393-5297** or 407/855-5496; www.gatorland.com). Founded in 1949 and one of Orlando's original attractions, Gatorland now houses thousands of alligators and crocodiles on its 70-acre spread. Headliners include *Gator Wrestlin',* where trainers stick their heads in the mouths of gators—you can even be part of the show and get your photo sitting atop a gator (his mouth wrapped); and *Gator Jumparoo,* a fan favorite that features the park's largest reptilian inhabitants lunging 4 to 5 feet out

of the water to snatch a hunk of meat from a trainer's hand. **The Screamin' Gator Zipline** (debuting in the summer of 2011) is a 60-minute adventure that takes adventurous guests zooming 65 feet above several of the park exhibits at speeds of up to 30 mph—including the park's collection of Cuban jumping crocodiles! The experience is priced separately from park admission ($60 per person). A stop here makes for an entertaining afternoon away from the hustle and bustle of the major parks. The park is generally open from 9am to 5pm (closing time varies seasonally). Admission runs $23 to $30 for adults, $15 to $24 children 3 to 12 (plus tax).

and hidden grottoes). This hour-long experience (limited to six people per group) runs an additional $59 fee per person.

Here's what you get for your money, with or without the dolphin encounter.

○ A limit of *no more than 1,000 guests a day*. (The average daily attendance at Disney's Magic Kingdom is 45,000.) This ensures that your experience will be more relaxing and private.

○ A continental breakfast, lunch, all-day snacks and drinks, a towel, a locker, sunscreen, snorkeling gear including a flotation vest, a souvenir photo, and free self-parking are also part of the deal.

○ Other 9am-to-5:30pm activities include a chance to swim near (but on the other side of the Plexiglas) **barracudas** and **blacktip sharks.** There are no barriers, however, between you and the gentle rays and brightly colored tropical fish swimming amid the 1.3-million-gallon coral reef. The 3,300-foot-long Tropical River is a great place to swim or float in a mild current—it goes through a cave, two waterfalls, and a 100-foot-long, 30-foot-high aviary where you can take a stroll, becoming a human perch. There are also beaches for tanning and relaxing.

○ Seven consecutive days of **unlimited admission** to SeaWorld, Busch Gardens, *or* Aquatica. For an additional $80 per person, you can upgrade this option to 14 days of unlimited admission to all three parks (SeaWorld, Busch Gardens, and Aquatica).

Private cabanas overlooking dolphin lagoon, including a table, chairs, chaise longues, and towels, among other amenities, are available for an additional fee. Additional cabanas are located along the Grand Reef.

Get more information on Discovery Cove by calling ℂ **877/434-7268,** or go to **www.discoverycove.com**. If you want to try it, make a reservation as far in advance as possible. Despite the price, it reaches its capacity almost every day.

Aquatica: SeaWorld's Water Park

SeaWorld's latest adventure park is a 59-acre eco-themed water park that blends its signature up-close animal encounters with thrill rides (including racing tunnels and raft rides, slides, and more) with a plethora of pools, lagoons, winding rivers, and stretches of white sandy beaches.

For information, call ℂ **888/800-5447** or go to www.aquaticabyseaworld.com. Admission runs $48 for adults, $42 for kids ages 3 to 9. As with all other SeaWorld parks, multiday and multipark passes are available.

MAJOR ATTRACTIONS

Dolphin Plunge (near the entrance) is the park's signature ride; it takes riders down through 250 feet of clear tubes, under the water, and right through the dolphin habitat (those not willing to take the plunge can sneak a peak at Dolphin Lookout). Riders must be at least 48 inches tall. Other options include the **Taumata Racer,** an eight-lane 300-foot slide that has riders flying in and out of tunnels and around a 360-degree turn before crossing the finish line; **HooRoo Run** is one of the wildest flume rides anywhere around with three—count 'em three—drops straight down (riders must be at least 42 inches); and **Tassie's Twister,** a 129-foot flume that takes riders on single or double tubes spinning and splashing their way down through a gigantic bowl before dropping them into **Loggerhead Lane** below (a lazy river that, in addition to offering a relaxing

ride through the park, has a great underwater view of the Commerson's
dolphins as well as thousands of exotic
fish). Riders must be able to hold on
unassisted. Making its debut as this
book goes to print is **Omaka Rocka.**
Inspired by skateboarding and snow-
boarding, riders will find themselves
sliding and riding forward, backward,
and up the walls through high-speed
tubes and half-pipe funnels before
reaching the splashdown zone below.

Cool down and get wet at Walkabout Waters.

You can also ride **Whanau Way,**
a five-story 340-foot multilane slide filled with drops, unexpected curves, water
curtains, and other thrills before a drop into the pool below (riders must be able to
hold on unassisted); and **Walhalla Wave,** a family raft ride that takes up to four
riders down six stories of tunnels filled with twists and turns (42-in. minimum
height). You can catch a wave (or two or three . . .) at **Big Surf Shores** (best for
older kids and adults thanks to its crashing waves) and **Cutback Cove** (offering a
gentler rolling surf that's more appropriate for kids), the world's only side-by-side
wave pools. A stretch of beach with what seems like a sea of beach chairs and
chaise longues is nearby—the downside, however, is that there's precious little
shade to protect you from the searing hot sun. If you've got the cash to spare, I recommend renting one of the nearby cabanas, but only if you're here for the day.

If you're so inclined, you can zip through waterfalls, passing geysers and
along over 1,500 feet of rapids on **Roa's Rapids.** The latter is similar to a lazy-
river raft ride, but there's nothing lazy about it. The park also has a family play area
(Walkabout Waters) that sports a large interactive water play area (including a
60-ft. rain fortress, family slides, water cannons, and plenty of fountains), as well
as a children's area **(Kata's Kookaburra Cove)** for tinier tots with miniraft rides
(Mom and Dad can ride along). Life vests are plentiful (with several racks scattered throughout the park) and free (a bonus, because they're required swimwear
for those under 48 in. tall). If you enjoy the water, plan on spending a full day—
and bring plenty of sunscreen.

DINING AT AQUATICA

Dining options include the **Banana Beach Cookout,** an all-you-can-eat buffet
restaurant (it runs $20 for adult all-day pass, $12 for children 3–9 all-day pass);

 Cirque du Soleil: Not Your Ordinary Circus

Cirque du Soleil seems to put all 64
performers onstage at once in the
trampoline routine. The eye-popping *La
Nouba* ★★★, set in a state-of-the-art
theater, is a Fellini-style amalgam of live
music, dance, theater, and acrobatics.

But in a world of pricey attractions,
this is one of the priciest. There are

three ticket categories: Prices range
from $71 to $124 for adults and $57 to
$99 for kids 3 to 9 (including tax). The
90-minute shows are at 6 and 9pm;
days rotate. Call ✆ **407/939-7600** or
check out **www.cirquedusoleil.com** for
details.

the **Mango Market,** a grab-and-go market where you can pick up pizzas, salads, snacks, and other on-the-go items—they'll even pack it up in a picnic basket; and the **WaterStone Grill,** selling a variety of freshly carved sandwiches, salads, and platters. Anheuser-Busch products (for those 21 and over) are available throughout the park.

WALT DISNEY WORLD & ORLANDO AFTER DARK

Central Florida has plenty for night owls to do. Parties last into the wee hours at **CityWalk,** and other hot spots too.

Disney Dinner Shows

Disney's Spirit of Aloha Dinner Show 📷 POLYNESIAN The Polynesian Resort's 2-hour luau is worth attending. It features Tahitian, Samoan, and Hawaiian singers, drummers, and dancers who entertain while you feast on tropical appetizers, Lanai roasted chicken, Polynesian wild rice, South Seas vegetables, dessert, wine, beer, and other beverages. The action takes place in an open-air theater (dress for nighttime weather). 1600 Seven Seas Dr. (at Disney's Polynesian Resort). ℂ **407/939-3463.** www.disneyworld.com. Reservations required. $53–$62 adults, $27–$32 children 3–9 (depends on seating), including tax and gratuity. Holiday surcharge applies on select days. Tues–Sat 5:15 and 8pm. Free parking.

Hoop De Doo Musical Revue ★★★ ☺ AMERICAN Featuring singing and dancing sprinkled with comedy, this show is the most popular of the Disney dinner shows—with good reason. Dinner consists of country-fried chicken served in a bucket, along with corn on the cob, biscuits, and dessert. And though the food is pretty good, you could almost forget to eat, thanks to all the action going on around you. 4510 N. Fort Wilderness Trail, at Disney's Fort Wilderness Resort and Campground. ℂ **407/WDW-DINE** (939-3463). Reservations required. $53–$62 adults, $27–$32 children 3–11 (depends on seating, including tax and gratuity). Holiday surcharge applies on select days. Nightly 5, 7:15, and 9pm. Free parking.

Entertainment Meccas

DOWNTOWN DISNEY WEST SIDE

CityWalk

Between Islands of Adventure and Universal Studios Florida, this 30-acre club-and-restaurant district (ℂ **407/363-8000;** www.citywalk.com) is filled with some of the hottest clubs and lounges in the tourist district. Most CityWalk clubs open around 4pm and don't close until 2am. With few exceptions, only those 21 and over can enter after 9pm, and usually a cover of around $7 applies after 9pm.

You can walk the entire area for free, but select clubs charge a cover to enter their doors. CityWalk also offers two types of **party passes.** A pass that includes access to all the clubs costs $12 plus tax. For $15 plus tax, you get a club pass and a movie at Universal Cineplex (ℂ **407/354-5998**). **Note:** Daytime parking in the Universal Orlando garages costs $15, $3 after 6pm.

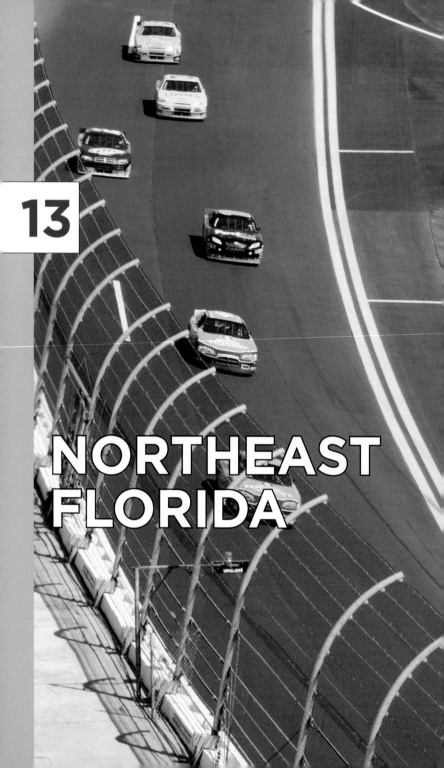

13

NORTHEAST FLORIDA

When driving through the elongated state of Florida, many people make the grave mistake of speeding through the Northeast without as much as a single stop beyond the Cracker Barrels, Denny's, and gas stations lining the highways. Thankfully, Juan Ponce de León made the fortunate mistake of discovering just how magnificent the northeast part of the state is. You would do well to follow in his footsteps.

Northeast Florida traces its roots back to 1513, when the wandering de León, who later undertook a misguided quest for the Fountain of Youth, landed somewhere between present-day Jacksonville and Cape Canaveral. (He was a bit off course—he meant to land in what is now Bimini—but who can blame a guy who didn't have GPS?) Observing the land's lush foliage, he named it *La Florida,* or "the flowery land."

In 1565, the Spanish established a colony at St. Augustine, the country's oldest continuously inhabited European settlement. Not much, if anything at all, has changed in St. Augustine (in a wonderful way). The streets of the restored Old City look much as they did in Spanish times.

Not everything in Northeast Florida is antiquated, however. To the south, there's the "Space Coast," where rockets blast off from the Kennedy Space Center at Cape Canaveral. In Cocoa Beach, you can watch surfers riding the rather sizable waves. In Daytona, brace yourself for the deafening roar of the stock cars and motorbikes that make this beach town the "World Center of Racing." And don't blink, because you wouldn't want to miss Daytona's other pop-cultural phenomenon, known as Spring Break. In recent years, it has dwindled from a whopping 400,000 party-hearty kids down to a crowd so tame, the Daytona Beach Area Convention & Visitors Bureau no longer maintains student visitor estimates!

Going north along the coast, you'll come to a place that's a far cry from being populated with Spring Breakers on a budget: the moneyed haven of Ponte Vedra Beach, where golf takes precedence over manual labor. In Jacksonville, Florida's largest metropolis and a thriving port city and naval base, you can get a taste of city life before retreating to the beach.

Up near the state line, cross a bridge to Amelia Island, where you'll discover exclusive resorts that take advantage of 13 miles of beautiful beaches. Amelia's Victorian-era town, Fernandina Beach, is another throwback to the past, helping to further render the northeast region a fascinating juxtaposition of the old, the new, and somewhere in between.

THE SPACE COAST

46 miles SE of Orlando; 186 miles N of Miami; 65 miles S of Daytona

The "Space Coast," the area around Cape Canaveral, was once a sleepy place where city dwellers escaped the urban centers of Miami and Jacksonville. But

FACING PAGE: **The Daytona 500 is one of the highlights of the NASCAR circuit.**

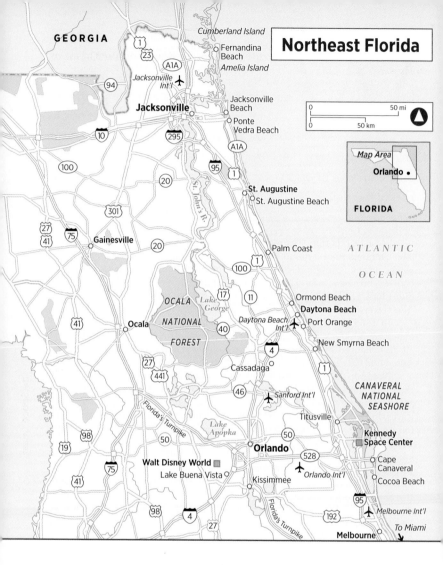

Northeast Florida

GEORGIA

Cumberland Island
Fernandina Beach
Amelia Island

Jacksonville Int'l

Jacksonville

Jacksonville Beach
Ponte Vedra Beach

St. Johns R.

St. Augustine
St. Augustine Beach

Gainesville

Palm Coast

ATLANTIC

OCEAN

OCALA
NATIONAL
FOREST

Lake George

Ocala

Ormond Beach
Daytona Beach
Daytona Beach Int'l
Port Orange
New Smyrna Beach

Cassadaga

Sanford Int'l

CANAVERAL
NATIONAL
SEASHORE

Florida's Turnpike

Lake Apopka

Titusville

Kennedy Space Center

Orlando

Walt Disney World
Lake Buena Vista
Kissimmee
Orlando Int'l

Cape Canaveral
Cocoa Beach

Florida's Turnpike

Melbourne Int'l
To Miami
Melbourne

0 ——— 50 mi
0 ——— 50 km

Map Area
Orlando •
FLORIDA

then came NASA. Today the region produces and accommodates its own crowds, including the hordes who come to visit the Kennedy Space Center and enjoy the area's 72 miles of beaches (this is the closest beach to Orlando's mega-attractions), as well as excellent fishing, surfing, and golfing. And although the shuttle program is winding down, the area isn't completely kaput.

Thanks to NASA, this is also a prime destination for nature lovers. The space agency originally took over much more land than it needed to launch rockets. Rather than sell off the unused portions, it turned them over to the **Canaveral National Seashore** and the **Merritt Island National Wildlife Refuge** (www.nbbd.com/godo/minwr), which have preserved these areas in their pristine natural states.

A handful of Caribbean-bound cruise ships also depart from Port Canaveral. The south side of the port is lined with seafood restaurants and marinas, which serve as home base for gambling ships and the area's deep-sea charter and group fishing boats.

Essentials

GETTING THERE The nearest airport is **Melbourne International Airport** (✆ **321/723-6227;** www.mlbair.com), 22 miles south of Cocoa Beach, served by **Continental** and **Delta. Orlando International Airport** (p. 491), about 35 miles to the west, is a much larger hub with many more flight options and generally less expensive fares. It's an easy 45-minute drive from the Orlando Airport to the beaches via the Bee Line Expressway (Fla. 528, a toll road)—it can take almost that long from the Melbourne Airport, where **Avis, Budget, Hertz,** and **National** all have car-rental desks. The **Melbourne Airport Shuttle** (✆ **321/724-1600**) will take you from the Melbourne Airport to most local destinations for about $10 to $30 per person.

VISITOR INFORMATION For information on the area, contact the **Florida Space Coast Office of Tourism/Brevard County Tourist Development Council,** 8810 Astronaut Blvd., Ste. 102, Cape Canaveral, FL 32920 (✆ **800/872-1969** or 321/868-1126; www.space-coast.com). The office is in the Sheldon Cove building, on Fla. A1A a block north of Central Boulevard, and is open Monday through Friday from 8am to 5pm. It also operates an information booth at the Kennedy Space Center Visitor Complex (p. 560).

GETTING AROUND A car is essential in this area. If you're not coming by car, you can rent one at the airport. **Space Coast Area Transit** (✆ **321/633-1878;** www.ridescat.com) operates buses ($1.25 adults, 60¢ seniors and students), but routes tend to be circuitous and extremely time-consuming.

Attractions

In addition to the attractions below, Brevard College's **Astronaut Memorial Planetarium and Observatory,** 1519 Clearlake Rd., Cocoa Beach (✆ **321/634-3732;** www.brevardcc.edu/planet), south of Florida 528, has its own International Hall of Space Explorers, but its big draw are sound-and-light shows in the planetarium. Call or check the website for schedules and prices.

Brevard Zoo ★★ ☺ This delightful small-town zoo houses more than 550 animals, including giraffes, white rhinos, red kangaroos, cheetahs, alligators, siamang gibbons, giant anteaters, jaguars, wallabies, crocodiles, howler monkeys, bald eagles, red wolves, and river otters. Enjoy a 10-minute train tour of the grounds ($3); hand-feed gentle giraffes and lorikeets in a free-flight aviary; get friendly with the wildlife at the Paws On play area, featuring a 22,000-gallon aquarium, water play, and petting zone; and kayak around an animal exhibit or through a 22-acre restored wetlands for just $6. For an up-close-and-personal view of the animals, try a rhino encounter, offered daily from noon to 1pm for $15 per person. The zoo also offers eco-tours on the Indian River Lagoon (www.lagoonadventures.org). For $50, you get kayak rental, kayak instruction, snacks and drinks, a trained environmental educator guide, lunch on an island, and close viewing of manatees, dolphins, and wading birds. Plan to spend 1 to 4 hours here.

Try out the Shuttle Launch Experience at the Kennedy Space Center.

8225 N. Wickham Rd., Melbourne (just east of I-95 exit 73/Wickham Rd.). © **321/254-9453.** www.brevardzoo.org. Admission $14 adults, $13 seniors, $10 children 3–12, free for children 2 and under. Daily 9:30am–5pm (last admission 4:15pm).

John F. Kennedy Space Center ★★★ Whether or not you're a space buff, you'll appreciate the sheer grandeur of the facilities and technological achievements displayed at NASA's primary space launch facility. Astronauts departed Earth from here in 1969 en route to the most famous "small step" in history—the first moon walk—and space shuttles recently lifted off from here on missions to the International Space Station. Today, military and commercial rockets regularly launch from Cape Canaveral Air Force Station.

Because all roads other than State Road 405 and State Road 3 are closed to the public in the Space Center, you must begin your visit at **Kennedy Space Center Visitor Complex.** A bit like an amusement theme park, this privately operated complex continuously receives renovations, so check beforehand to see if tours and exhibits have changed since we wrote this. Call ahead to see what's happening the day you intend to be here and arrive early. You'll need at least 2 hours to see the Space Center's highlights on the bus tour, up to 5 hours if you linger at stops along the way, and a full day to see and do everything. Buy a copy of the *Official Tour Book,* and you can take it home as a colorful souvenir (though the bus tours are narrated and the exhibits have good descriptions).

The Visitor Complex has real NASA rockets and the actual Mercury Mission Control Room from the 1960s. Exhibits portray space exploration in its early days and where it's going in the new millennium. There are hands-on activities for kids, a daily "encounter" with a real astronaut, dining venues, and a shop selling space memorabilia. IMAX movies shown on five-and-a-half-story-high screens are both informative and entertaining.

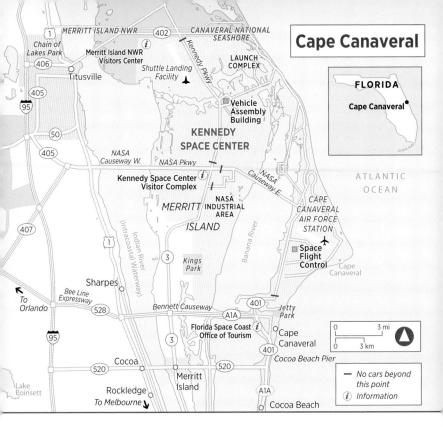

While you could spend an entire day at the Visitor Complex, you must take a **KSC Tour** to get a behind-the-scenes glimpse of Kennedy Space Center. Buses depart every 15 minutes or so, and you can reboard as you wish. They stop at the LC-39 Observation Gantry, with a dramatic 360-degree view over launchpads where shuttles once blasted off into space, and the Apollo/Saturn V Center, a tribute to the Apollo moon program, which includes artifacts, shows, photos, interactive exhibits, and the 363-foot-tall *Saturn V,* the most powerful rocket ever launched by the United States.

Don't miss the **Astronaut Memorial.** Dedicated in 1991, the memorial honors the U.S. astronauts who gave their lives for space exploration. The 43 × 50-foot "Space Mirror" brilliantly illuminates the names cut through the monument's black granite surface.

Today, the U.S. Air Force operates Cape Canaveral Air Force Station on Cape Canaveral, the barrier island east of the Banana River, where military and commercial rockets are launched. Launch days are great days to visit the Visitor Complex. Rocket launches taking place during operating hours can be viewed from the main Visitor Complex with the regular admission price of $41 plus tax per adult and $31 plus tax per child (ages 3–11).

For an out-of-this-world experience, do **Lunch With an Astronaut,** a once-in-a-lifetime opportunity available every day ($23 plus tax for adults, $16 plus tax for kids ages 3–11, in addition to Visitor Complex admission). Astronauts who have participated in the past include some of the greatest, such as Jim Lovell, Al Worden, Story Musgrave, and Jon McBride. Seating is limited; call ✆ **877/313-2610** to make a reservation.

Kennedy Space Center Visitor Complex also offers the **Astronaut Training Experience,** a combination of hands-on training and preparation for the rigors of spaceflight. You'll hear first-hand from veteran astronauts as you progress through an authentic half-day of mission simulation and exploration and even get to check out true-to-training simulator exercises. Due to the program's highly interactive nature, ATX crews are small and advance reservations are required. Cost is $145 per person; call ✆ **877/313-2610** to make a reservation.

Note: Make sure to stop by the **U.S. Astronaut Hall of Fame,** on State Road 405, on your way to Kennedy Space Center Visitor Complex or on your way home. The Hall of Fame, approximately 6 miles west of the main Visitor Complex, is included with regular admission to the Visitor Complex. The Hall of Fame features exhibits and tributes to the heroes of the Mercury, Gemini, Apollo, and Space Shuttle programs. There's also the world's largest collection of personal astronaut memorabilia and a Mercury *Sigma* 7 capsule on display. Separate admission to the Hall of Fame only is $20 plus tax adults, and $16 plus tax children 3 to 11.

NASA Pkwy. (Fla. 405), 6 miles east of Titusville, ½ mile west of Fla. 3. ✆ **877/313-2610** for general information and reservations. For more information to plan your trip, visit www. kennedyspacecenter.com. Admission $41 plus tax adults, $31 plus tax children 3–11, free for children 2 and under. Annual passes $53 plus tax adults, $43 plus tax children 3–11. Audio guides $6 plus tax per person. Daily 9am to closing times that vary according to season. Bus tours depart daily beginning at 10am. Closed Dec 25.

Beaches & Wildlife Refuges

To the north of the Kennedy Space Center, **Canaveral National Seashore ★★★** is a protected 13-mile stretch of barrier-island beach backed by cabbage palms, sea grapes, palmettos, marshes, and Mosquito Lagoon. This is a great area for watching herons, egrets, ibises, willets, sanderlings, turnstones, terns, and other birds. You might also glimpse dolphins and manatees in Mosquito Lagoon. Canoeists can paddle along a marked trail through the marshes of Shipyard Island, and backcountry camping is possible November through April (permits required; see below).

The main **visitor center** is at 7611 S. Atlantic Ave., New Smyrna Beach, FL 32169 (✆ **321/867-4077,** or 321/867-0677 for recorded information; www.nps.gov/cana), on Apollo Beach, at the north end of the island. The southern access gate to the island is 8 miles east of Titusville on Florida 402, just east of Florida 3. A paved road leads from the gate to undeveloped **Playalinda Beach ★★★**, one of Florida's most beautiful. Though illegal, nude sunbathing has long been a tradition here (at least, for those willing to walk a few miles to the more deserted areas). The beach has toilets, but no running water or other amenities, so bring everything you'll need. There's also a **pontoon boat tour** of the Indian River Lagoon for $20 per person and a turtle-watch program for $14 per person. For those looking for a little more history, The **Eldora Statehouse** is a step back in time, a well-preserved example of earlier life along Mosquito Lagoon. It is in Canaveral National Seashore's Apollo district, and is open year-round. The seashore is open daily from 6am to 8pm during daylight saving time, daily from 6am to 6pm during standard time. Entry fees are $3 per person. National Park

Birds, bathers and surfers all share the sand by Cocoa Beach Pier.

Service passports are accepted. Backcountry camping permits cost $10 for up to six people per day and $20 for more than six people per day, and must be obtained from the New Smyrna Beach visitor center (✆ **386/428-3384**, ext. 10). For single-day access to backcountry beaches between Playalinda and Apollo beaches, it's $2 per day. For advance information, contact the seashore headquarters at 308 Julia St., Titusville, FL 32796 (✆ **321/867-4077** or 321/267-1110; www.nps. gov/cana).

Canaveral National Seashore's neighbor to the south and west is the 140,000-acre **Merritt Island National Wildlife Refuge** ★★, home to hundreds of species of shorebirds, waterfowl, reptiles, alligators, and mammals, many of them endangered. Pick up a map and other information at the visitor center, on Florida 402 about 4 miles east of Titusville (it's on the way to Playalinda Beach). The center has a quarter-mile boardwalk along the edge of the marsh. Displays show the animals you may spot from 6-mile Black Point Wildlife Drive or from one of the nature trails through the hammocks and marshes. The visitor center is open Monday through Friday from 8am to 4:30pm, Saturday and Sunday from 9am to 5pm (closed Sun Apr–Oct). Entry is free. For more information and a schedule of programs, contact the refuge at P.O. Box 6504, Titusville, FL 32782 (✆ **321/861-0667**; www.nbbd.com/godo/minwr).

Note: Parts of the national seashore near the Kennedy Space Center and all of the refuge close 4 days before a shuttle launch and usually reopen the day after.

Another good beach area is **Lori Wilson Park,** on Atlantic Avenue at Antigua Drive in Cocoa Beach (✆ **321/868-1123**), which preserves a stretch of sand backed by a forest of live oaks. It's home to a small but interesting nature center, and restrooms are available. The park is open daily from sunrise to sunset; the nature center, Monday through Friday from 1 to 4pm.

The beach at **Cocoa Beach Pier,** on Meade Avenue east of A1A (✆ **321/783-7549**), is a popular spot with surfers, who consider it the East Coast's surfing capital. The rustic pier was built in 1962 and has 842 feet of fishing, shopping, and dining overlooking a wide, sandy beach (see "Where to Dine," below). Because this is not a public park, there are no restrooms other than the ones in restaurants on the pier.

Jetty Park, 400 E. Jetty Rd., at the south entry to Port Canaveral (✆ 321/783-7111; www.jettypark.org), has lifeguards, a fishing pier with bait shop, a playground, a volleyball court, a horseshoe pit, picnic tables, a snack bar, a grocery store, restrooms, changing facilities, and the area's only campground. From here, you can watch the big cruise ships as they enter and leave the port's narrow passage. The park is open daily from 7:30am to dusk; the pier is open 24 hours for fishing. Admission is $10 per car for nonresidents of Brevard County ($5 for residents), $15 per RV. The 150 tent and RV campsites (some of them shady, most with hookups) cost $25 to $47 a night, depending on the location and time of year. Properly immunized pets are allowed in some areas of the park.

Outdoor Activities & Spectator Sports

BASEBALL The **Washington Nationals** play spring-training games at **Space Coast Stadium,** 5800 Stadium Pkwy., Viera (✆ 321/633-4487), located south of Cape Canaveral and north of Melbourne. Tickets are $10 to $30. The stadium also hosts minor-league action from the Brevard County Manatees, an affiliate of the Nationals.

ECO-TOURS **Funday Discovery Tours** (✆ 321/725-0796; www.fundaytours. com) offers a variety of day trips, including dinner and sunset cruises, airboat and swamp-buggy rides, dolphin-watching cruises, bird-watching expeditions, and personalized tours of the Kennedy Space Center and Merritt Island National Wildlife Refuge. Reservations are required.

FISHING Head to Port Canaveral for catches such as snapper and grouper. **Jetty Park** (✆ 321/783-7111), at the south entry to the port, has a fishing pier equipped with a bait shop (see "Beaches & Wildlife Refuges," above). The south bank of the port is lined with charter boats. Try deep-sea fishing on *Miss Cape Canaveral* (✆ 321/783-5274, or 407/648-2211 in Orlando; www.misscape.com), one of the party boats based here. All-day voyages departing daily at 8am cost $80 adults, $75 seniors, $70 kids 11 to 17; all trips come with parking, a hot meal, unlimited soda, coffee, two cans of cold beer, bait, and tackle.

GOLF You can read about Northeast Florida's best courses in the free *Golfer's Guide,* available at the tourist information offices and in many hotel lobbies. See p. 45 for information on ordering copies.

The municipal **Cocoa Beach Country Club,** 500 Tom Warringer Blvd. (✆ 321/868-3351), has 27 holes of golf and 10 lighted tennis courts set on acres of natural woodlands, rivers, and lakes. Greens fees (including cart) are $22 to $40 depending on the time and season.

On Merritt Island south of the Kennedy Space Center, the **Savannahs at Sykes Creek,** 3915 Savannahs Trail (✆ 321/455-1377; www.golfthe savannahs.com), has 18 holes over 6,636 yards bordered by hardwood forests, lakes, and savannas inhabited by a host of wildlife. You'll have to hit over a lake to reach the 7th hole. Fees with a cart are about $25 to $34, and $19 to $24 without.

The best nearby course is the Gary Player–designed **Baytree National Golf Club,** 8010 N. Wickham Rd., a half-mile east of I-95 in Melbourne (✆ 321/259-9060; www.baytreenational.com), where challenging marshy holes are flanked by towering palms. This par-72 course has 7,043 yards with a red-shale waste area. Fees are $24 to $40 depending on the time and season, including cart.

For course information, go to www.golf.com or www.floridagolfing.com, or call the **Florida Sports Foundation** (𝄫 **850/488-8347**) or **Florida Golfing** (𝄫 **866/833-2663**).

KAYAKING For those who want to see Merritt Island National Wildlife Refuge at night, **A Day Away Kayak Tours** (𝄫 **321/268-2655;** www.adayaway kayaktours.com) offers guided bioluminescent trips—meaning besides the moon, the only light you'll see on this fabulous tour is that of tiny, illuminated creatures swirling beneath the surface of the water and providing a lanternlike pathway across the water—through the Refuge, Thursday through Monday nights, June through September. Tours start at 7:30pm and last for about 2 hours. Cost is $32 for adults and $24 for children. Book early and don't forget the mosquito repellent!

SURFING Rip through some occasionally awesome waves (by Florida's standards, not California's or Hawaii's) at the **Cocoa Beach Pier** area or down south at **Sebastian Inlet.** Get outfitted at **Ron Jon Surf Shop,** 4151 N. Atlantic Ave. (𝄫 **321/799-8888;** www.ronjons.com), and then learn how to hang five or ten with **Ron Jon Surf School ★**, 150 E. Columbia Lane (𝄫 **321/868-1980;** www.cocoabeachsurfingschool.com). The school offers equipment and lessons for beginners and pros at area beaches. Be sure to bring along a towel, flip-flops, sunscreen, and a lot of nerve. Rates range from $50 to $135 depending on how many people are in the group and how many hours of lessons are wanted.

Where to Stay

Most of the hotels listed below are in Cocoa Beach, the closest resort area to the Kennedy Space Center, about a 30-minute drive to the north. (For pop-culture junkies, Cocoa Beach was where the TV show *I Dream of Jeannie* took place.) Closest to the space center and Port Canaveral is the **Radisson Resort at the Port,** 8701 Astronaut Blvd. (A1A), in Cape Canaveral (www.radisson.com; 𝄫 **800/333-3333** or 321/784-0000). It isn't on the beach, but you can relax in its landscaped courtyard, where a waterfall cascades over fake rocks into a heated pool. Rooms aren't fancy but are clean and comfortable. The hotel caters to business travelers and passengers waiting to board cruise ships (with free transportation to the port and free parking while you cruise); it offers a substantial hot and cold complimentary breakfast.

The newer chain motels in this area are the **Hampton Inn Cocoa Beach,** 3425 Atlantic Blvd. (www.hamptoninncocoabeach.com; 𝄫 **877/492-3224** or 321/799-4099), and **Courtyard by Marriott,** 3435 Atlantic Blvd. (www. courtyardcocoabeach.com; 𝄫 **800/321-2211** or 321/784-4800). They stand side by side and access the beach via a pathway through a condominium complex.

The **Florida Space Coast Office of Tourism,** 8810 Astronaut Blvd., no. 102, Cape Canaveral, FL 32920 (𝄫 **800/93-OCEAN** [936-2326] or 321/868-1126; www.space-coast.com), publishes a booklet of the area's *Superior Small Lodgings.*

The area has a plethora of rental condominiums and cottages. **King Rentals, Inc.,** 102 W. Central Blvd., Cape Canaveral, FL 32920 (www.kingrentals.com; 𝄫 **888/295-0934** or 321/784-5046), has a wide selection in its inventory.

Given the proximity to Orlando, the generally warm weather year-round, and the business travelers visiting the space complex, there is little, if any, seasonal fluctuation in room rates here. They are highest on weekends, holidays, and during special events, such as space shuttle launches.

Tent and RV camping are available at **Jetty Park,** in Port Canaveral (see "Beaches & Wildlife Refuges," above).

You'll pay a 5% hotel tax on top of the Florida 6.5% sales tax here.

Hilton Cocoa Beach Oceanfront ★★ Recently renovated to reflect the newer, more modern Hilton decor, the Hilton Cocoa Beach Oceanfront is a popular pre- and post-cruise and business hotel. The rooms at this seven-story Hilton lack balconies or patios; instead, they have small, sealed windows, and only 16 of the rooms face the beach. These and other architectural features make this seem more like a downtown hotel transplanted to a beachside location. Nevertheless, it's one of the few upscale beachfront properties here. No doubt you'll run into a crew of conventioneers, as it's especially popular with groups. Despite their lack of fresh air, the rooms are spacious and comfortable.

1550 N. Atlantic Ave., Cocoa Beach, FL 32931. www.hiltoncocoabeach.com. ✆ **800/445-8667** or 321/799-0003. Fax 321/799-0344. 296 units. Year-round $139–$189 double, $209–$249 suite. AE, DC, DISC, MC, V. **Amenities:** Restaurant; 2 bars; concierge-level rooms; exercise room; heated outdoor pool; limited room service; watersports equipment/rentals. *In room:* A/C, TV, hair dryer, Internet access.

The Inn at Cocoa Beach ★★★ Despite having 50 units, this seaside inn has an intimate B&B ambience and is far and away the most romantic place in the area. Owner Karen Simpler, a skilled interior decorator, has furnished each unit with an elegant mix of pine, tropical, and French-country pieces. Rooms in the three- and four-story buildings are much more spacious and have better sea views from their balconies than the "standard" units in the original two-story motel wing (all but six units here have balconies or patios). The older units open onto a courtyard with a pool tucked behind the dunes. Highest on the romance scale are the two rooms with Jacuzzi tubs and easy chairs. Guests are treated to continental breakfast and evening wine and cheese. There's also an honor bar and a library.

4300 Ocean Blvd., Cocoa Beach, FL 32932. www.theinnatcocoabeach.com. ✆ **800/343-5307** or 321/799-3460. Fax 321/784-8632. 50 units. $125–$325 double. Rates include continental breakfast and afternoon tea. AE, DISC, MC, V. No children 11 and under accepted. **Amenities:** Bar (guests only); outdoor pool; sauna. *In room:* A/C, TV, Internet access.

Where to Dine

On the **Cocoa Beach Pier** (www.cocoabeachpier.com), at the beach end of Meade Avenue, you'll get a fine view down the coast to accompany the seafood offerings at **Atlantic Ocean Grill** (✆ **321/783-7549**) and the mediocre pub fare at **Marlins Good Times Bar & Grill** (same phone). The restaurants may not justify spending an entire evening on the pier, but the outdoor, tin-roofed **Mai Tiki Bar ★**, where live music plays most nights, is a prime spot to have a cold one while watching the surfers or a sunset.

Rusty's Seafood & Oyster Bar ✦ SEAFOOD This lively sports bar beside Port Canaveral's man-made harbor serves inexpensive chow ranging from spicy seafood gumbo to a pot of seafood that will give two people their fill of steamed oysters, clams, shrimp, crab legs, potatoes, and corn on the cob. Raw or steamed fresh oysters and clams from the raw bar are first-rate and a good value, as is a weekday lunch buffet. Seating is indoors or out, but the inside tables have the best view of the fishing boats and cruise liners going in and out of the port. Daily happy hour from 3 to 6pm offers two-for-one well drinks, beers drafted at $1.60 a mug, and tons of raw or steamed oysters and spicy Buffalo wings go for 65¢ each. The joint is busy and sometimes noisy, especially on weekend afternoons, but the clientele tends to be older—especially during the $10 Early Bird Special hours of 3pm to 6pm—and better behaved than those at other pubs along the banks of Port Canaveral.

628 Glen Cheek Dr. (south side of the harbor), Port Canaveral. ☏ **321/783-2033.** www.rustys seafood.com. Main courses $11–$24; sandwiches and salads $7–$12. AE, DC, DISC, MC, V. Mon-Thurs 11am–10pm; Fri-Sun 11am–11pm.

The Surf Bar & Grill ★ SEAFOOD/STEAK What started as Bernard's Surf in 1948, serving standard steak-and-seafood fare in a nautical setting, is now a regular ol' bar and grill (still with the old-school astronaut memorabilia) featuring a fine dining room, The Surf, with a menu of seafood specials such as stone crab claws, chargrilled red snapper, and a belly-busting platter of shrimp, scallops, grouper, crab cakes, lobster, and oysters. The fresh seafood also finds its way into the less expensive Surf Bar & Grill, a *Cheers*-like lounge popular with locals featuring a discounted early-bird menu daily from 4pm to 6pm. The menu features fried combo platters and mussels with a wine sauce over pasta, as well as burgers and other pub fare. Also located within the complex, **Shuckleberry Finn's Oyster Bar,** which has a 35¢ happy hour of oysters and spicy wings every day from, we kid you not, 11am to 7pm.

2 S. Atlantic Ave. (at Minuteman Causeway Rd.), Cocoa Beach. ☏ **321/783-2401.** www.the surfbarandgrill.com. Main courses $18–$40. Bar & Grill main courses $6–$20; sandwiches and salads $9–$11. AE, DC, DISC, MC, V. Mon-Fri 4-10pm; Sat 4-11pm. Shuckleberry Finn's Oyster Bar Mon-Fri 10am-10pm; Sat 11am-11pm.

The Space Coast After Dark

For a rundown of current performances and exhibits, call the **Brevard Cultural Alliance's Arts Line** (☏ 321/690-6819). For live music, walk out on the **Cocoa Beach Pier,** on Meade Avenue at the beach, where **Oh Shucks Seafood Bar & Grill** (☏ 321/783-7549), **Marlins Good Times Bar & Grill** (☏ 321/783-7549), and the alfresco **Mai Tiki Bar** ★ (same phone as Marlins) feature bands on weekends, more often during the summer season.

DAYTONA BEACH ★★

54 miles NE of Orlando; 251 miles N of Miami; 78 miles S of Jacksonville

Daytona Beach is a town with many personalities. It is at once the self-proclaimed "World's Most Famous Beach" and "World Center of Racing," a mecca for tattooed motorcyclists and pierced Spring Breakers (though it lost its Spring Break crown to Panama City Beach), *and* the home of a surprisingly good art museum. Though the city and developers spent millions to turn the beachfront area (complete with the requisite T-shirt and souvenir shops) around the famous Main Street Pier into Ocean Walk Village, a redevelopment area of shops, entertainment, and resort facilities, there's still something bleak about Daytona's famous strip. Many of its '70s-style beachfront condos and hotels are badly in need of a face-lift. Thank goodness for Ponce Inlet, a scenic fishing village that has seemingly remained impervious to development.

Racing fans, however, don't care what the place looks like. Daytona Beach has been a destination for them since the early 1900s, when "horseless carriages" raced on the hard-packed sand beach. One thing is for sure: Daytonans still love their cars. Recent debate over the environmental impact of unrestricted driving on the beach caused an uproar from citizens who couldn't imagine it any other way. As it worked out, they can still drive on the sand, but not everywhere, and especially not in areas where sea turtles are nesting.

Today, hundreds of thousands of race enthusiasts come to the home of the National Association for Stock Car Auto Racing (NASCAR) for the **Daytona 500,** the **Pepsi 400,** and other races throughout the year.

Be sure to check the "Calendar of Events" (p. 36) in chapter 2 to know when the town belongs to college students on Spring Break, thousands of leather-clad motorcycle buffs during Bike Week (Mar) and Biketoberfest (Oct), or racing enthusiasts for big competitions. You won't be able to find a hotel room, drive the highways, or enjoy a peaceful vacation when they're in town.

Essentials

GETTING THERE **Continental** and **Delta** fly into the small, pleasant, and calm **Daytona Beach International Airport** (© 386/248-8030; www.fly daytonafirst.com), 4 miles inland from the beach on International Speedway Boulevard (U.S. 92), but you can usually find less-expensive fares to **Orlando International Airport** (p. 491), about an hour's drive away. **Daytona-Orlando Transit Service** (**DOTS;** © 800/231-1965 or 386/257-5411; www.dots-daytonabeach.com) provides van transportation to and from Orlando International Airport. One-way fares are about $35 for adults, $18 for children ages 11 and under. The service takes passengers to the company's terminal at 1034 N. Nova Rd., between 3rd and 4th streets, or to beach hotels for an additional fee.

If you fly into the Daytona, rates for the **Daytona Shuttle** (© 386/255-2294; www.dots-daytonabeach.com), which has a station near, not at, the airport, also cost $35 per adult, $18 per child. The ride from the airport to most beach hotels via **Yellow Cab Co.** (© 386/255-5555) is between $10 and $20.

Alamo (© 800/327-9622), **Avis** (© 800/831-2847), **Budget** (© 800/527-0700), **Dollar** (© 800/800-4000), **Enterprise** (© 800/325-8007), **Hertz** (© 800/654-3131), and **National** (© 800/227-7368) have booths at the airport. Or why not rent a Harley? This is Daytona, home of Biketoberfest, after all. Contact **Destination Daytona,** 1637 N. U.S. Hwy. 1 (© 386/673-2677; www.destinationdaytona.com). Rates are $140 daily, $372 for 3-day rental, $798 for 7-day rental.

Amtrak (© 800/872-7245; www.amtrak.com) trains stop at Deland, 15 miles southwest of Daytona Beach, with bus service from Deland to the beach.

VISITOR INFORMATION The **Daytona Beach Area Convention & Visitors Bureau,** 126 E. Orange Ave. (P.O. Box 910), Daytona Beach, FL 32115 (© 800/544-0415 or 386/255-0415; www.daytonabeach.com), can help you with information on attractions, accommodations, dining, and events.

Daytona Beach

HOTELS

Bahama House **15**
Hilton Garden Inn Daytona
  Beach Airport **11**
Shoreline All Suites Inn &
  Cabana Colony
  Cottages **13**
The Plaza Resort & Spa **4**
The Shores Resort & Spa **14**
The Villa Bed & Breakfast **3**
Wyndham Ocean Walk
  Resort **5**

RESTAURANTS

Azure **14**
The Cellar **7**
Down the Hatch **18**
Frappes North **1**
Inlet Harbor Restaurant
  and Marina **17**
Ocean Deck Restaurant &
  Beach Club **6**
Stonewood Tavern & Grill **2**

ATTRACTIONS

Daytona Flea and Farmers'
  Market **12**
Daytona International
  Speedway **10**
Halifax Historical Museum **8**
Marine Science Center **19**
Museum of Arts and
  Sciences **9**
Ponce de León Inlet
  Lighthouse & Museum **16**

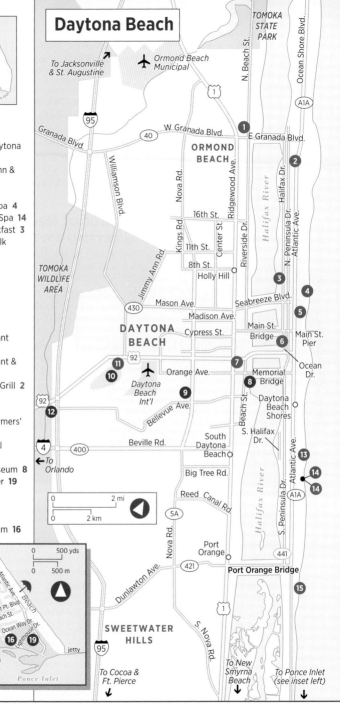

The office is on the mainland just west of the Memorial Bridge. The information area of the lobby is open daily from 9am to 5pm. The bureau also maintains a kiosk at the airport.

GETTING AROUND Although Daytona is primarily a driver's town, Volusia County's public transit system, **VOTRAN** (✆ **386/761-7700;** www.votran.org), runs a pay **trolley** along Atlantic Avenue on the beach, Monday through Saturday from noon to 7pm (a select few trolleys do run until midnight) January through Labor Day. Fares are $1.25 for adults, 60¢ for seniors and children ages 6 to 17, and free for kids ages 5 and under who are riding with an adult. VOTRAN also runs **buses** through downtown and the beaches.

For a taxi, call **Yellow Cab** (✆ **386/255-5555**) or **Southern Komfort Cab** (✆ **386/252-2222**).

A Visit to the World Center of Racing

Daytona International Speedway/DAYTONA 500 Experience ★★ You don't have to be a racing fan to enjoy a visit to the **Daytona International Speedway,** 4 miles west of the beach. Opened in 1959 with the first Daytona 500, this 480-acre complex is one of the key reasons for the city's fame. The track presents about nine weekends of major racing events annually, featuring stock cars, sports cars, motorcycles, and go-karts, and is used for automobile and motorbike testing and other events the rest of the year. Its grandstands can accommodate more than 146,000 fans.

The DAYTONA 500 Experience is a 60,000-square-foot, state-of-the-art interactive motor-sports attraction. Here you can learn about the history, color, and excitement of stock car, go-kart, and motorcycle racing in Daytona. In Daytona Dream Laps, you get the feel of what it's like to zoom around the track from a 32-seat motion simulator. If that doesn't get your stomach churning, hop inside your own 80%-scale NASCAR vehicle in Acceleration Alley, buckle up, and roar up to 200 mph in a spectacular simulator for the ultimate virtual reality–like racing experience ($5 per ride). On the milder side, you can participate in a pit stop on a NASCAR Sprint Cup stock car, see an actual winning Daytona 500 car still covered in track dust, talk via video with favorite competitors, and play radio or television announcer by calling the finish of a race. On the newer side: Champions at Daytona, an exhibit paying tribute to speed demons with photos, racing memorabilia, and, of course, cars.

An action-packed IMAX film will put you in the winner's seat of a Daytona 500 race. To experience what it's like, you can make three laps around the track in a stock car from April to October with the **Richard Petty Driving Experience Ride-Along Program** (✆ **800/237-3889;** www.drivepetty.com). Professional drivers (sorry, none is named Petty) are at the wheel as you see and feel what it's like to travel an average of 160 mph. For less intensive tours, the speedway offers an **All Access Tour** that takes you into the garages, press box, drivers' meeting room, and victory lap; and a **Speedway Tour** that takes you through the infield and into the garages. Allow at least 4 hours to see everything, and bring your video camera.

1801 W. International Speedway Blvd. (U.S. 92, at Bill France Blvd.). ✆ **800/PITSHOP** (748-7467) for race tickets, or 386/947-6800 for DAYTONA 500 Experience. www.daytona internationalspeedway.com and www.daytona500experience.com. All Access Tour $22 adults, $17 children 6–12; Speedway Tour $15 adults, $10 children 6-12. DAYTONA 500 Experience $25 adults, $20 seniors, $20 children 6–12, free for children 5 and under. Speedway daily 10am–6pm;

Suit up for a ride around Daytona's famous speedway.

trams depart every 30 min. except during races and special events. DAYTONA 500 Experience daily 9am–7pm (later during race events). Closed Christmas.

Hitting the World's Most Famous Beach

The beautiful and hard-packed beach here runs for 24 miles along a skinny peninsula separated from the mainland by the Halifax River. The bustling hub of activity is at the end of Main Street, where you'll find the **Main Street Pier** (also known as the Daytona Beach Pier or Ocean Pier), the longest wooden pier on the East Coast. Out here you'll find a restaurant, bar, bait shop, beach-toy concessions, chairlift running its length, and views from the 180-foot-tall Space Needle. Admission as far out as the restaurant and bar is free (at about a third of the way, this is far enough for a good view down the beach), but you'll have to pay $1 to walk beyond that point, and more than that if you fish (see "Outdoor Activities," below). Beginning at the pier, the city's famous oceanside **Boardwalk** is lined with restaurants, bars, and T-shirt shops, as are the 4 blocks of Main Street nearest the beach. The city's $400-million **Ocean Walk Village** redevelopment project begins here and runs several blocks north, featuring a movie theater, boutiques, restaurants, and even a 175-room hotel/condo, the **Ocean Walk Resort** (© 877/845-WALK [9255]).

There's another busy beach area at the end of **Seabreeze Boulevard,** which has a multitude of restaurants, bars, and shops.

Folks seeking privacy usually prefer the northern or southern extremities of the beach. **Ponce Inlet,** at the very southern tip of the peninsula, is especially peaceful, as there is little commerce or traffic to disturb the silence. **Lighthouse Point Park** is the best beach, consisting of 52 acres of pristine beaches on the northern end of Ponce Inlet. It features fishing, nature trails, an observation deck and tower, swimming, and picnicking. Admission is $5 per vehicle.

Outdoor Activities

ECO-TOURS Aqua Safari, 601 Earl St. (© 386/405-3445), provides a 4-hour water tour of the area's ecosystem with free admission to Ponce de León Inlet Lighthouse and the Marine Science Center. Refreshments are also provided. All-inclusive admission is $50 adults and $30 children 12 and under.

Driving on the Beach at Daytona

You can drive and park on sections of the sand along 18 miles of the beach from 1 hour after sunrise to 1 hour before sunset. During turtle nesting season, May 1 to October 31, driving hours are from 8am to 7pm. Traffic lanes and speed limits are clearly marked at low tide, but watch for signs warning of nesting sea turtles. There's a $5-per-vehicle access fee and 10-mph speed limit. *Watch out for the tides.* If you park at low tide and lose track of time, your vehicle may become an inadvertent rust bucket or artificial reef at high tide!

FISHING The easiest and least expensive way to fish offshore for cobia, sea bass, sharks, king mackerel, grouper, red snapper, and more is with the **Critter Fleet,** 4950 S. Peninsula Dr., just past the lighthouse in Ponce Inlet (*℃* **800/338-0850** or 386/767-7676; www.critterfleet.com), which operates two party boats. One goes on all-day trips (about $80 for adults, $50 for kids 16 and under), while the other makes morning and afternoon voyages (about $50 for adults, $40 for kids 7 and over, 6 and under free). The fares include a rod, reel, and bait. Call for schedules, prices, and reservations.

Save the cost of a boat by fishing with the locals on the **Sunglow Pier** at **Crabby Joe's Deck and Grill,** 3701 S. Atlantic Ave. (*℃* **386/788-3364;** www.sunglowpier.com). Admission for anglers is $6 for adults, $3 for kids 11 and under. Rod rentals are $5.25 for all day, bait ranges from $2.50 to $3.50, and no license is required.

GOLF There are more than 25 courses within 30 minutes of the beach, and most hotels can arrange starting times for you. **Golf Daytona Beach,** 126 E. Orange Ave., Daytona Beach (*℃* **800/881-7065** or 386/239-7065; fax 386/239-0064), publishes an annual brochure describing the major courses. It's available at the tourist information offices (see "Essentials," above).

For course information, go to www.golf.com or www.floridagolfing.com; or you can call the **Florida Sports Foundation** (*℃* **850/488-8347**) or **Florida Golfing** (*℃* **866/833-2663**).

Two of the nation's top-rated links for women golfers are at the **LPGA International ★★**, 1000 Championship Dr. (*℃* **386/274-5742;** www.lpgainternational.com): the Champions course, designed by Rees Jones, and the Legends course, designed by Arthur Hills. Each boasts 18 outstanding holes. LPGA International is a center offering workshops and teaching programs for professional and amateur women golfers, and the pro shop carries a great selection of ladies' equipment and clothing. Greens fees with a cart are usually about $35 to $100, lower in summer. *Pssst*—they let guys play here, too!

A Lloyd Clifton–designed course, the centrally located 18-hole, par-72 **Indigo Lakes Golf Course,** 2620 W. International Speedway Blvd. (*℃* **386/254-3607;** www.indigolakesgolf.com), has flat fairways and large bunkered Bermuda greens. Fees here are about $20 to $35 (including a cart).

The semiprivate South Course at **Pelican Bay Country Club,** 550 Sea Duck Dr. (*℃* **386/756-0034;** www.pelicanbaygolfclub.com), is one of the area's favorites, with fast greens to test your putting skills. Fees are about $25 to $50 with cart (no walking allowed). The North Course is for members only.

The city's prime municipal course is the **Daytona Beach Golf Club,** 600 Wilder Blvd. (*C* **386/258-3119;** www.daytonabeachgc.com), which has 36 holes. Winter fees are about $15 to $25 to walk, $25 to $35 to share a cart. Rates drop in summer.

HORSEBACK RIDING **Shenandoah Stables,** 1759 Tomoka Farms Rd., off U.S. 92 (*C* **386/257-1444**), offers daily trail rides and lessons. Call for prices and schedules.

SPECTATOR SPORTS The **Daytona Cubs** (*C* 386/872-2827; www.daytona cubs.com), a Class A minor-league affiliate of the Chicago Cubs, play April through August at **Jackie Robinson Ballpark ★**, on City Island downtown. A game here is a treat, as the park has been restored to its classic 1914 style by the designers of Baltimore's Camden Yards and Cleveland's Jacobs Field. Tickets are $6 to $12.

WATERSPORTS Watersports equipment, bicycles, beach buggies, and mopeds can be rented along the Boardwalk, at the ocean end of Main Street (see "Hitting the World's Most Famous Beach," above), and in front of major beachfront hotels.

Museums & Attractions

Halifax Historical Museum ★ On Beach Street, Daytona's original riverfront commercial district on the mainland side of the Halifax River (see "Shopping," below), this local museum is worth a look for the 1912 neoclassical architecture of its home, a former bank. A mural of Old Florida wildlife graces one wall, the stained-glass ceiling reflects sunlight, and across the room is an original teller's window. The eclectic collection includes tools and household items from the Spanish and British periods, thousands of historic photographs, possessions of past residents (even a ball gown worn at Lincoln's inauguration), and, of course, model cars. A race exhibit opens annually in mid-January as a stage setter for Race Week.

252 S. Beach St. (just north of Orange Ave.). *C* **386/255-6976.** www.halifaxhistorical.org. Admission $5 adults, $1 children 11 and under; free Sat for children. Tues–Sat 10am–4pm.

Marine Science Center ★ ☺ This marine museum has interior displays (with exhibits on mangroves, mosquitoes, shells, artificial reefs, dune habitats, and pollution solutions), a 5,000-gallon aquarium, and educational programs and activities. Though the exhibit area is small, there's more than enough information for a child to digest at one time. Perhaps the most interesting part is the area reserved for the rehabilitation of endangered and threatened sea turtles and seabirds. You can watch them in any of seven turtle tanks—look for the ones that need life jackets to stay afloat!

100 Lighthouse Dr., Ponce Inlet. *C* **386/304-5545.** www.marinesciencecenter.com. Admission $5 adults, $4 seniors, $2 children 3–12, free for children 2 and under. Tues–Sat 10am–4pm; Sun noon–4pm. See directions for Ponce de León Inlet Lighthouse & Museum (below).

Museum of Arts and Sciences ★★ An exceptional institution for a town of Daytona's size and reputation (sometimes thought of as culturally devoid beyond NASCAR), this hard-to-find museum is best known for its "Cuba: A History of Art" exhibit, with paintings acquired in 1956, when Cuban dictator Fulgencio Batista donated his collection to the city. The Dow Gallery displays American decorative arts, while the Bouchelle Study Center for the Decorative Arts contains American and European jewelry, furniture, mirrors, and more. Other rooms include the Schulte Gallery of Chinese Art; Africa: Life and Ritual, with the largest collection of Ashante gold ornaments in the U.S. (these are stunning); and the Center for Florida History, with the skeleton of a 13-foot-tall, 130,000-year-old giant ground sloth. Check out the unique collection of the late Chapman S. Root, a Daytona philanthropist and a founder of the Coca-Cola empire; among the memorabilia are the mold for the original Coke bottle and the Root family's two private railroad cars. The **planetarium** presents 30-minute shows of what the night sky will look like on the date of your visit. Don't miss **The Charles and**

CROSSING OVER INTO Cassadaga

If you're in the Daytona Beach/Orlando area, you might have an intuition to make a pit stop in Cassadaga, the tiny 115-year-old community composed of psychics and mediums who will be happy to tell you your fortune or put you in touch with the deceased—for a price, of course.

Should you find the whole concept of psychics and talking to the dead a bit far-fetched, consider the history of Cassadaga, which is fascinating in its own right.

The story goes that, as a young man from New York, George Colby was told during a séance that he would someday establish a spiritualist community in the South. In 1875, the prophecy came true when Colby was led through the wilderness of Central Florida by his spiritual guide to a 35-acre area that became the Cassadaga Spiritualist Camp.

Consisting of about 57 acres and 55 no-nonsense clapboard houses, Cassadaga caters to those who have chosen to share in a community of like-minded people who happen to believe in the otherworldly. Yes, the people are eccentric, to say the least, but they're all friendly. About 25 of the camp's residents are mediums who channel their skills from their homes. Designated a Historic District on the National Register of Historic Places, Cassadaga is one of the few remaining "spiritualist" communities, like Lily Dale in upstate New York.

When you get to town, head straight for the information center (see below for directions), where you can find out which psychics and mediums are work-

ing that day, and make an appointment for a session, which ranges from $25 and up for a palm reading to $50 and up for a session with a medium. A general store, a restaurant, a hotel, and a few shops selling crystals and potions of sorts will keep you occupied while you wait for your appointment. Whether you're a believer or not, an hour or two in Cassadaga will make for interesting cocktail conversation.

From Daytona, take I-4 exit 114. Turn right onto Highway 472 at the end of the exit ramp toward Orange City/Deland. At the traffic light, turn right onto Dr. Martin Luther King, Jr., Parkway. Turn right at the first light, which is Cassadaga Road. Continue 1½ miles to the intersection with Stevens Street. The information center is on the right. For more information call ✆ **386/228-3171** or go to **www.cassadaga.org**.

Linda Williams Children's Museum, a world-class science center featuring over 9,000 square feet of hands-on science activities. For nature lovers, MOAS just happens to be on a 90-acre nature preserve that features over ½ mile of boardwalk nature trails and learning stations. The museum displays new temporary exhibits bimonthly.

352 S. Nova Rd. (btw. International Speedway Blvd. and Bellevue Ave.). © **386/255-0285.** www. moas.org. Museum $13 adults, $11 seniors, $6.95 children and students with ID, free for children 5 and under. Planetarium shows included with paid admission. Mon–Sat 9am–5pm; Sun 11am–5pm. Closed Thanksgiving, Christmas Eve, and Christmas Day. Take International Speedway Blvd. west, make a left on Nova Rd. (Fla. 5A), and look for a sign on your right.

Ponce de León Inlet Lighthouse & Museum ★★ This National Historic Landmark is worth a stop even if you're not a lighthouse enthusiast. The 175-foot brick-and-granite structure is the second-tallest lighthouse in the United States. Built in the 1880s, the lighthouse and the graceful Victorian brick buildings surrounding it have been restored. There are no guided tours, but you can walk through the 12 areas, which feature different exhibits (lighthouse lenses, historical artifacts, and a film of early car racing on the nearby beach), and stroll around the tugboat *F. D. Russell,* now sitting high and dry in the sand. There are 203 steps to the top of the lighthouse; it's a grinding ascent, but the view from up there is spectacular.

4931 S. Peninsula Dr., Ponce Inlet. © **386/761-1821.** www.ponceinlet.org. Admission $5 adults, $1.50 children 11 and under. Memorial Day to Labor Day daily 10am–9pm; rest of year daily 10am–5pm. Follow Atlantic Ave. south, make a right on Beach St., and follow the signs.

Shopping

On the mainland, Daytona Beach's main riverside drag, **Beach Street,** is one of the few areas in town where people actually stroll. The street is wide and inviting, with palms down its median, and decorative wrought-iron archways and fancy brickwork overlooking a branch of the Halifax River. Today the stretch of Beach Street between Bay Street and Orange Avenue offers antiques and collectibles shops, galleries, clothiers, a magic shop, a historical museum (see "Museums & Attractions," above), and several good cafes. At 154 S. Beach St., you'll find the home of the **Angell & Phelps Chocolate Factory** (© **386/252-6531;** www. angellandphelps.com), which has been making candy for more than 75 years. Watch the goodies being made (and get a free sample)!

"Hog" riders will find several shops along Beach Street, north of International Speedway Boulevard, including **Bruce Rossmeyer's Daytona Harley-Davidson** (© **866/642-3464;** www.brucerossmeyer.com), a 20,000-square-foot retail outlet and diner serving breakfast and lunch. It's one of the nation's largest Harley dealerships. In addition to hundreds of gleaming new and used Hogs, you'll find as much fringed leather as you've ever seen in one place. For Harley fanatics, check out Rossmeyer's **Destination Daytona,** 1635 N. U.S. Hwy. 1 (www.destinationdaytona.com), a virtual Harley theme park with motel, Hog-themed bars, and restaurants. Rossmeyer, incidentally, was killed in a motorcycle accident en route to the Sturgis Rally in South Dakota in July 2009.

The **Daytona Flea and Farmers' Market,** 2987 Bellvue Ave. (© **386/253-3330;** www.daytonafleamarket.com), is huge, with 1,000 covered outdoor booths plus 100 antiques and collectibles vendors in an air-conditioned building. Most of the booths feature new (though not necessarily first-rate) wares along the lines of socks, sunglasses, luggage, handbags, jewelry, tools, and the like. It's open year-round Friday through Sunday from 9am to 5pm. Admission and parking are free.

Where to Stay

Room rates here are among the most affordable in Florida. Some lodgings have several rate periods during the year, but generally they are somewhat higher from the beginning of the races in February to Labor Day. Rates skyrocket during major events at the speedway, during bikers' gatherings, and during Spring Break (see the "Calendar of Events," beginning on p. 36). Even if you find a room, there's often a minimum-stay requirement.

A slew of hotels and motels line Atlantic Avenue along the beach, many of them family owned and operated. The **Daytona Beach Area Convention & Visitors Bureau** (see "Essentials," earlier in this chapter) distributes a brochure that lists "Superior Small Lodgings" for Daytona Beach, Deland, and New Smyrna Beach. All of the small motels listed below are members.

If you're going to the races and don't care about staying on the beach, some upper-floor rooms at the **Hilton Garden Inn Daytona Beach Airport,** 189 Midway Ave. (✆ **877/944-4001** or 386/944-4000), overlook the international speedway track.

Thousands of rental condominiums line the beach. Among the most luxurious is the 175-unit condominium hotel **Wyndham Ocean Walk Resort,** 300 N. Atlantic Ave., Daytona Beach, FL 32118 (www.oceanwalk.com; ✆ **800/649-3566** or 386/323-4800), which is part of the Ocean Walk Village redevelopment. Near the Main Street Pier, it's in the center of the action and has one-, two-, and three-bedroom apartments with full kitchens, washers and dryers, and all of the usual hotel amenities, plus a wondrous computer-golf simulator, a "lazy river" in one of the three outdoor pools (there are also two pools indoors), an island putting green, and much more. Rates are $170 to $399. One of the largest rental agents is **Peck Realty,** 2340 S. Atlantic Ave., Daytona Beach Shores, FL 32118 (✆ **800/447-3255** or 386/257-5000; www.peckrealty.com).

In addition to the 6.5% state sales tax, Volusia County levies a 6% tax on hotel bills.

Bahama House ★★ A Caribbean-style beach hotel, Bahama House is a family-owned, 10-story oceanfront stay on a quiet stretch of the Atlantic coastline. All rooms, each named after an area of the Caribbean, offer private balconies with ocean and Intracoastal Waterway views and tropical decor. In addition to complimentary deluxe continental breakfast served daily, there's also a nightly cocktail reception from 5:30 to 6:30pm that features free snacks, house wines, beer, and highballs. During the day, there are freshly baked cookies available in the lobby, giving this place more of a B&B feel. A heated pool; beach activities, including family surfing lessons; and a great selection of nearby beach rentals make Bahama House an ideal place for families. All resort guests also have access to nearby tennis at the USTA Florida tennis complex and LPGA golf courses.

2001 S. Atlantic Ave., Daytona Beach Shores, FL 32118. www.daytonabahamahouse.com. ✆ **800/571-2001** or 386/248-2001. Fax 386/248-0991. 87 units, including 74 efficiencies. $99–$189 double. Rates include continental breakfast and evening cocktail reception. Specials, packages, and discounts offered year-round. AE, DC, DISC, MC, V. Free parking. **Amenities:** Jacuzzi; 2-tiered heated pool. *In room:* A/C, TV, minifridge, hair dryer, kitchenette (in efficiencies), Wi-Fi.

The Plaza Resort & Spa ★★ After $70 million in renovations, these elegant adjoining 7- and 13-story buildings hold some of Daytona Beach's best rooms (in a much more tasteful atmosphere than many of the neighboring hotels)—provided you don't need a large bathroom. The best units are the corner suites, each with a sitting area and two balconies overlooking the Atlantic; some even have a Jacuzzi. All units have balconies, plasma TVs, and microwaves. The full-service **Ocean Waters Spa** ★★ (✆ **386/267-1660;** www.oceanwatersspa.com) has 16 treatment rooms and a soothing menu of facials, massages, and wraps.

600 N. Atlantic Ave. (at Seabreeze Ave.), Daytona Beach, FL 32118. www.plazaresortandspa.com. ✆ **800/874-7420** or 386/255-4471. Fax 386/238-7984. 323 units. $119–$199 double; $189–$449 suite. AE, DC, DISC, MC, V. **Amenities:** Restaurant; bar; babysitting; concierge-level rooms; exercise room; Jacuzzi; heated outdoor pool; limited room service; spa; watersports equipment/ rentals. *In room:* A/C, TV, fridge, hair dryer, Internet access.

Shoreline All Suites Inn & Cabana Colony Cottages ★ 🐾 The Shoreline All Suites Inn has one- and two-bedroom suites that occupy two buildings separated by a walkway leading to the beach. Most have small bathrooms with scant vanity space and—shall we say—intimate shower stalls. Every unit has a full kitchen, and there are barbecue grills on the premises. For a change of scenery, consider the Shoreline's sister property, the **Cabana Colony Cottages** ★★. All 12 of the cottages were built in 1927 but have since been upgraded. They aren't much bigger than a motel room with a kitchen, but they're light, airy, and attractively furnished. The cottages share a heated pool with the Shoreline.

2435 S. Atlantic Ave. (A1A, at Dundee Rd.), Daytona Beach Shores, FL 32118. www.daytona shoreline.com. ✆ **800/293-0653** or 386/252-1692. Fax 386/239-7068. 30 units, including 12 cottages. $69–$299 suite and cottage. Rates include continental breakfast. Golf packages available. AE, DISC, MC, V. **Amenities:** Heated outdoor pool. *In room:* A/C, TV/VCR, kitchen.

The Shores Resort & Spa ★★★ Far enough south to escape the madding crowds of Main Street, and in a residential area directly on the beach, this hotel is the most luxurious hotel here hands down, despite its location on a somewhat shoddy stretch of Atlantic Ave. That said, the beach in back is lovely. The large guest rooms are grouped in pairs and can be joined to form suites; only one of each pair has a balcony. All have plush bedding with high-thread-count linens and flatscreen TVs. Oceanfront rooms are preferable; all have a sea and/or river view. The restaurant, **Azure,** is one of Daytona's nicest, offering stellar seafood with a gourmet and regional twist; patio dining overlooking the ocean is a fine option. Private cabanas and fire pits surround the pool deck area, and, for a fee, you can make your own s'mores every night. The **spa** offers an Indonesian-inspired menu of treatments, and a kids' club ensures that children 2 to 12 are fully entertained and occupied with trained child-care counselor-led daytime activities indoors and outdoors, day and night.

2637 S. Atlantic Ave. (A1A, btw. Florida Shores Blvd. and Richard's Lane), Daytona Beach Shores, FL 32118. www.shoresresort.com. ✆ **866/934-SHORES** (7467) or 386/767-7350. Fax 386/760-3651. 212 units. Winter $249–$489 double, $549–$1,129 suite; off season $169–$359 double, $509–$829 suite. AE, DC, DISC, MC, V. Amenities: Restaurant; bar; babysitting; kids' club; exercise room; heated outdoor pool; room service; spa. *In room:* A/C, TV, hair dryer, kitchen, Wi-Fi.

The Villa Bed & Breakfast ★★★ You'll think you're in Iberia upon entering this more-than-70-year-old Spanish mansion's great room with its fireplace, baby grand piano, and terra-cotta floors. If you want out-of-place opulence (bordering on cheesy), this is the place. A sunroom equipped with a TV and DVD, a formal dining room, and a breakfast nook are also located downstairs. The lush backyard surrounds a pool and a covered Jacuzzi. Upstairs, the nautically themed Christopher Columbus room has a vaulted ceiling and a small balcony overlooking the pool. The largest unit here is the King Carlos suite, once the original master bedroom, with a four-poster bed, an entertainment system, a fridge, a rooftop deck with hot tub, and a bathroom equipped with a seven-head shower. The Queen Isabella room has a royal crown hanging above a queen-size bed, while the Marco Polo room features Chinese black-lacquer furniture and Oriental rugs. No children 13 and under allowed. Rates include free use of beach bikes, towels, and beach chairs.

801 N. Peninsula Dr. (at Riverview Blvd.), Daytona Beach, FL 32118. www.thevillabb.com. ©/fax **386/248-2020.** 4 units. $100–$200 double. Rates include continental breakfast. AE, MC, V. No children 13 and under accepted. **Amenities:** Jacuzzi; heated outdoor pool. *In room:* A/C, TV/DVD, CD player, hair dryer, Wi-Fi.

Where to Dine

Daytona Beach has a few interesting dining venues. A profusion of fast-food joints line the major thoroughfares, especially along Atlantic Avenue on the beach and International Speedway Boulevard (U.S. 92) near the racetrack. Restaurants come and go in the Beach Street district, and along Main Street and Seabreeze Boulevard on the beach. A casual restaurant out on the Main Street Pier serves burgers, chicken wings, and lots of suds.

One chain restaurant is worth a mention: **Stonewood Tavern & Grill,** 100 S. Atlantic Ave., in Ormond Beach (© **386/671-1200;** www.stonewoodgrill. com), is a casual upscale restaurant with a nice but dark mahogany interior, good American food, and excellent service. It's open only for dinner and usually packed; you won't be disappointed with its menu of steaks, seafood, and the like.

AT THE BEACHES

Azure ★★ SEAFOOD The chicest restaurant in Daytona, Azure is all about swanky, gourmet seafood with priceless water views. Start with caramelized diver scallops with a warm three-bean salad in a blood orange sauce, or grilled shrimp with a roasted corn, bacon, and spring-onion johnnycake with New Orleans barbecue butter. Entrees include an excellent crispy-skin striped bass with corn and jalapeño griddle cake, *chimichurri* sauce, and marinated cherry tomatoes, and a fantastic plate of shrimp and grits, gourmet-style, of course, with black-eyed peas and Smithfield ham in a spiced Southern Comfort butter sauce.

In the Shores Resort & Spa. © **386/767-7356.** www.shoresresort.com. Reservations strongly recommended. Main courses $19–$29. AE, DC, DISC, MC, V. Daily 7am–11pm.

Down the Hatch ★ 🍴 SEAFOOD Occupying a 1940s fish camp on the Halifax River, Down the Hatch serves big portions of fresh fish and seafood (note its shrimp boat docked outside). Inexpensive burgers and sandwiches are available, too. The scenic views include boats and shorebirds visible through the picture windows. At night, arrive early to catch the sunset over the river, and also to beat the crowd to this very popular place. In summer, light fare is served on a covered deck.

4894 Front St., Ponce Inlet. © **386/761-4831.** www.down-the-hatch-seafood.com. Call ahead for priority seating. Main courses $15–$41; burgers and sandwiches $9–$14. AE, MC, V. Daily

11:30am–9pm. Closed 1st week in Dec. Take Atlantic Ave. south, make a right on Beach St., and follow the signs.

Inlet Harbor Restaurant and Marina ★ SEAFOOD For great water-front views, outdoor and indoor dining, live music, and a view of the Ponce Inlet Lighthouse, Inlet Harbor is one of those places that reminds you why you're here. In addition to the good sea fare—peel-and-eat shrimp, pan-fried grouper, deep-water lobster tails—there's also Florida fresh gator tail, fried and served with a honey mustard sauce. Try it—it tastes like chicken! The restaurant also has charter captains on-site to take you out boating; and, if you get lucky out there, the restaurant will even cook your catch for you. The *Sea Spirit*, a 65-passenger party boat, also departs daily from the restaurant's dock, in case you haven't partied enough already.

133 Inlet Harbor Rd., Ponce Inlet. ✆ **386/757-5590.** www.inletharbor.com. Main courses $9–$23; sandwiches and burgers $6–$9. AE, MC, V. Daily 11am–midnight. Take A1A S.; make a right on Inlet Harbor Rd.

Ocean Deck Restaurant & Beach Club 🍴 SEAFOOD/PUB FARE Known by Spring Breakers, bikers, and other beachgoers as Daytona's best "beach pub" since 1940, the three-story Ocean Deck is also the best restaurant in the area around the Main Street Pier. The downstairs reggae bar is as sweaty and packed as ever (a band plays nightly 9pm–2:30am). The upstairs dining room can be noisy, but come here for good food, reasonable prices, and great ocean views. You can choose from a wide range of seafood, chicken, sandwiches, and the best burgers on the beach, but don't pass up the mahimahi (look for "trophy" on the menu), a bargain at $14. There's valet parking after dark, or you can park free at the lot behind the Ocean Deck's Reggae Republic surf shop, a block away.

127 S. Ocean Ave. (at Kemp St.). ✆ **386/253-5224.** www.oceandeck.com. Main courses $14–$22; salads and sandwiches $6–$10. AE, DISC, MC, V. Daily 11am–2am. Bar to 3am.

ON THE MAINLAND

The Cellar ★★ ITALIAN This fine-dining classical Italian eatery occupies the basement of a 1907 Victorian built as President Warren G. Harding's winter home, and it is listed on the National Register of Historic Places. Brick walls make for a cozy, un-Florida-like ambience. While the restaurant's history is authentically American, an all-Italian menu features some tempting options. Chef/owner Sam Moggio is a graduate of the Culinary Institute, and boy does it show! All pastas are homemade, and there are outstanding entrees. Among them: a snapper filet sautéed with artichokes, diced tomatoes, basil, saffron, and white wine; and braised lamb shanks with vegetable risotto. For dessert: a sinful, semi-sweet flourless chocolate torte.

220 Magnolia Ave. (btw. Palmetto and Ridgewood aves.). ✆ **386/258-0011.** www.thecellar restaurant.com. Main courses $17–$36. AE, DISC, MC, V. Tues–Sun 5–10pm.

Frappes North ★★ NEW AMERICAN It's worth the 6-mile drive north to Bobby and Meryl Frappier's sophisticated, hip establishment, which provides this area's most entertaining cuisine. Some like to call the food served here "organically groovy." We just call it great. Several chic dining rooms set the stage for an ever-changing "Menu of the Moment," fusing a multitude of styles. Ingredients are always fresh, and herbs come from the restaurant's garden. Bobby and Meryl offer at least one vegetarian main course. Main courses include cheekily titled dishes such as the Organically Groovy Chicken Breast with lemon basil sun-dried tomato beurre blanc, goat-cheese and leek soufflé, and sautéed spinach. Lunch is a steal here, and Sunday brunch features a stellar spinach, tomato, and cheddar cheese frittata. The restaurant is in a storefront on the mainland stretch of Granada Boulevard, Ormond Beach's main drag.

123 W. Granada Blvd. (Fla. 40, btw. Ridgewood Ave. and Washington St.), Ormond Beach. ✆ 386/615-4888. www.frappesnorth.com. Reservations recommended. Main courses $16–$27 dinner, $6–$12 lunch. AE, MC, V. Mon–Fri 11:30am–2:30pm and 5–10pm; Sat 5–10pm; Sun 10am–1:30pm and 5–8pm. From the beaches, drive 4 miles north on A1A and turn left on Granada Blvd. (Fla. 40); cross Halifax River to restaurant on right.

Daytona Beach After Dark

Check the Friday edition of the Daytona Beach *News-Journal* (**www.n-jcenter. com**) for its weekly "Go-Do," and the Sunday edition for the "Master Calendar" section, which lists upcoming events. Other good sources listing nighttime

---

SIDE TRIP TO Ocala, FLORIDA'S HORSE COUNTRY

Just 78 miles west of Daytona Beach is **Ocala,** a different world that is more Kentucky than Central Florida. Known for its rolling hills, cow pastures, and Derby-caliber horse farms (www.horsecapitaldigest.com), Ocala is a nature lover's paradise and home to the stunning **Ocala National Forest ★** (✆ 877/HIKE-FLA [445-3352]; www.floridatrail.org), with 600 lakes, 23 spring-fed streams, and two rivers and lakes, including **Lake George,** the second-largest lake in Florida, whose west side is encompassed within the forest and features springs and an impressive variety of wildlife and fish, including Atlantic stingray, mullet, striped bass, and blue crab.

In fact, there's so much blue crab in Lake George that it supports a local fishery, making it one of the few fresh-water blue crab fisheries in the world. Designated a National Scenic Trail in 1983, the forest's Florida Trail features the remains of homesteads made famous by Marjorie Kinnan Rawlings's classic *The Yearling.*

Just outside of Ocala is **Silver Springs,** 5656 E. Silver Springs Blvd. (✆ 352/236-2121; www.silversprings. com), a 350-acre natural theme park whose main attraction is the country's largest collection of artisan springs. The park is listed on the National Register of Historic Landmarks and features wild animal displays, glass-bottom boat rides, a jungle cruise, and a jeep safari. Ocala, in Marion County, which has been called the "Horse Capital of the World," also has a quaint, historic downtown district, with renovated Victorian homes and buildings, boutiques, antiques shops, restaurants, and cafes. While Ocala isn't necessarily somewhere to spend a week, it is worth exploring the **Heart of Florida Scenic Trail** (www. floridaseden.org), which comprises the college town of Gainesville, the horse country of Ocala, Old Florida towns including the very Victorian McIntosh and Micanopy, and the scenic Rainbow River (www.therainbowriver.com). For more information on the area, contact the **Marion County Visitors and Convention Bureau,** 2102 SW 20th Place (✆ 888/356-2252; www.ocala marion.com).

---

entertainment are *Happenings Magazine* and *Backstage Pass Magazine,* two tabloids available at the visitor center (see "Essentials," earlier in this chapter) and in many hotel lobbies.

Ghost tours are led by certified ghost hunters who merge legend with science. You're guaranteed to have a spooky time (at least more interesting than most touristy ghost tours). A portion of all proceeds goes to cemetery preservation and restoration. Tickets are $10 per person, free for children 5 and under. The tour leaves from the gas station parking lot on the northwest corner of the Main Street and Peninsula intersection at 7:30pm nightly. Contact **Haunts of Daytona** (✆ 386/253-6034; www.hauntsofdaytona.com).

THE PERFORMING ARTS The city-operated **Peabody Auditorium,** 600 Auditorium Blvd., between Noble Street and Wild Olive Avenue (box office ✆ 386/671-3460; www.peabodyauditorium.org), is Daytona's major venue for serious art, including concerts by the Symphony Society (✆ 386/253-2901). Professional actors perform popular musicals during winter and summer at the **Seaside Music Theater,** 176 N. Beach St., downtown (✆ 800/854-5592 or 386/252-6200). The **Oceanfront Bandshell** (✆ 386/671-8250; www.daytonabandshell.com), on the Boardwalk, hosts a series of free big-name concerts every Sunday night from June to Labor Day. Daytona also has a great relationship with the **London Symphony Orchestra,** which considers the city its official summer home, having performed more times in Daytona than any city outside London. For more cultural affairs, check out **www.daytonabeach.com/whattosee.cfm/mode/culturallydb**.

THE CLUB & BAR SCENE Main Street and **Seabreeze Boulevard** on the beach are happening areas where dozens of bars (and a few topless shows) cater to leather-clad bikers. The **Boot Hill Saloon,** 310 Main St. (✆ 386/258-9506; www.boothillsaloon.com), is a bluesy, brewsy honky-tonk, especially popular during race and bike weeks. A popular beachfront bar for more than

---

Paynes **PRAIRIE PRESERVE**

Just 40 minutes north from Ocala is **Micanopy** (www.welcometomicanopy.com), Florida's oldest inland settlement that's full of great antiques shops and home to the **Paynes Prairie Preserve State Park,** 100 Savannah Blvd. (✆ 352/466-3397; www.floridastateparks.org/paynesprairie), a bird-watcher's dream, featuring more than 270 species, as well as alligators and bison. Exhibits and an audiovisual program at the visitor center explain the area's natural and cultural history. A 50-foot-high observation tower near the visitor center provides a panoramic view of the preserve. Eight trails provide opportunities for hiking, horseback riding, and bicycling. Ranger-led activities are offered on weekends, November through April. Admission is $6 per vehicle with up to eight people, $4 single-occupant vehicle, and $2 pedestrians. From I-75 South, take exit 374, the Micanopy exit, and turn right at the end of the exit ramp. You will then be traveling east on C.R. 234. Stay on this road 1¼ miles until it intersects with U.S. 441. Turn left onto 441 and go about ⅔ mile to Paynes Prairie Preserve State Park.

40 years, the **Ocean Deck Restaurant & Beach Club,** 127 S. Ocean Ave. (*©* **386/253-5224;** see "Where to Dine," above), is packed with a mix of locals and tourists, young and old, who come for live music and cheap drinks. Reggae or ska bands play daily and nightly. There's valet parking after dark, or leave your vehicle at Ocean Deck's Reggae Republic surf shop on Atlantic Avenue. New in 2010 was **Vince Carter's,** 2150 LPGA Blvd. (*©* **386/274-0015;** www.vincecarter15.com), a 10,700-square-foot restaurant and sports entertainment complex owned by the Daytona native and Orlando Magic player of the same name.

ST. AUGUSTINE: AMERICA'S FIRST CITY ★★

105 miles NE of Orlando; 302 miles N of Miami; 39 miles S of Jacksonville

America's oldest permanent European settlement, St. Augustine draws history buffs and romantics to its Colonial Spanish Quarter and 18th-century buildings. With its coquina buildings and sprawling, moss-draped live oaks, visitors can do more than just museum hop. St. Augustine encourages guests to sit down for a while, and to drink in scenes from the past along with a chilled glass of sweet tea.

Things to Do Historic sites top the list in this 16th-century town. The top attractions include the **Oldest House,** the **Oldest Wooden Schoolhouse** from the earliest days of Florida, and the amazing **Lightner Museum,** a Victorian-era mansion packed with all kinds of curios and memorabilia.

Shopping Spanish-influenced home decor and furniture fill the antique shops and galleries in the historic district. Glossy oak tables, Mediterranean-style tiles, and silver bric-a-brac fill display windows along **Aviles Street** and **St. George Street.**

Nightlife & Entertainment Old Town St. Augustine amps it up on weekends. Check out the **Mill Top Tavern,** a warm and rustic bar housed in a 19th-century mill building (the water wheel is still outside).

Restaurants & Dining Spicy food lovers, St. Augustine has something special for you: the Datil, one of the hottest peppers you'll ever find. Restaurants across town add whole and ground Datils to their menus. **Hot Stuff Mon** sells an assortment of

Tour the magnolia-lined streets of old St. Augustine.

Datil delicacies you can take home with you. The gaudy neon stripes covering its exterior are just the beginning at **Gypsy Cab Co.,** where the inventive menu constantly changes.

Tourism is St. Augustine's main industry these days. However, despite the number of visitors, it's an exceptionally charming town, with good restaurants, a small-town nightlife, and shopping bargains. Give yourself 2 days here to see the highlights, longer to savor this historic gem.

Essentials

GETTING THERE The **Daytona Beach International Airport** (p. 568) is about an hour's drive south of St. Augustine, but service is more frequent—and fares usually lower—at **Jacksonville International Airport** (p. 604), about the same distance north.

VISITOR INFORMATION Before you go, contact the **St. Augustine, Ponte Vedra & The Beaches Visitors and Convention Bureau,** 88 Riberia St., Ste. 400, St. Augustine, FL 32084 (✆ **800/653-2489** or 904/829-1711; www.visitoldcity.com). Request the *Visitor's Guide,* which details attractions, events, restaurants, accommodations, shopping, and more.

The **St. Augustine Visitor Information Center** is at 10 S. Castillo Dr., at San Marco Avenue, 10 W. Castillo Dr. just off U.S. 1 and opposite the Castillo de San Marcos National Monument (✆ **904/825-1000;** www.st augustinegovernment.com). There are numerous ways to see the city, depending on your interests and schedule; this makes a good first stop. For $1, you can watch *Struggle to Survive,* a 42-minute video about the town's difficult first 14 years. (History buffs will enjoy it; otherwise, it's a good way to kill an hour on a rainy day.) The free 22-minute orientation video is more helpful in planning a visit. Once you've looked through the extensive information and made plans, you can buy tickets for the sightseeing trains and trolleys, which include discounted admissions to the attractions (see "Getting Around," below). The center is open daily from 8:30am to 5:30pm.

GETTING AROUND Once you've parked at the visitor center, you can walk or take one of the sightseeing trolleys, trains, or horse-drawn carriages around the historic district. The trolleys and trains follow 7-mile routes, stopping at the visitor center and at or near most attractions between 8:30am and 5pm daily. You can get off at any stop, visit the attraction, and step aboard the next vehicle that comes along about every 20 minutes. If you don't get off at any attractions, it takes about 1 hour and 10 minutes

 In the Beginning . . .

In 1562, a group of French Huguenots settled near the mouth of the St. Johns River, in present-day Jacksonville. Three years later, a Spanish force under Pedro Menéndez de Avilés arrived, wiped out the Huguenot men (de Avilés spared their women and children), and established a settlement he named St. Augustín. The colony survived a succession of attacks by pirates, Indians, and the British over the next 2 centuries. The Treaty of Paris, ending the French and Indian War, ceded the town to Britain in 1763, but the British gave it back to Spain 20 years later. The United States took control when it acquired Florida from Spain in 1821.

to complete the tour. The vehicles don't all go to the same sights, so speak with their agents at the visitor center in order to pick the right one for you. You can buy tickets, as well as discounted tickets to some attractions, at the visitor center or from the drivers.

Old Town Trolley Tours (©800/213-2474; www.historictours. com) takes you on an hour tour with more than 20 stops at the historic district and its most famous sites. Best of all, you can hop on and off at your leisure all day. Tickets include admission to the Florida Heritage Museum and the St. Augustine Beach Bus, which picks up and drops off passengers at various resorts and attractions around town. The tour costs $23 for adults, $10 for kids 6 to 12. Rates are cheaper online.

St. Augustine Sightseeing Trains (©800/226-6545 or 904/824-1606; www.redtrains.com) cover all the main sights except the Authentic Old Jail and the Florida Heritage Museum at the Authentic Old Jail, but its red open-air trains, operated by "Ripley's Believe It or Not," are small enough to go down more of the narrow historic-district streets. Tickets are $19 for adults, $8 for kids 6 to 12, and are good for 3 consecutive days. The company also sells package tickets for your convenience, and rates are cheaper online.

You may want to see the sights by horse-drawn carriage. **St. Augustine Transfer Company** (©904/829-2391; www.staugustinetransfer.com) has been showing people around town since 1877. Its carriages line up on Avenida Menendez, south of Castillo de San Marcos National Monument. Slow-paced, entertaining, driver-narrated 45-minute to 1-hour rides past major landmarks and attractions are offered from 8am to midnight. Private tours and hotel and restaurant pickups are available for $85 per person. There is also a cool, spooky ghost ride from 6pm to closing every night. Carriage tours cost $20 for adults, $10 for kids 5 to 11. Private carriage rides are $85.

For a tasty tour of St. Augustine, **City Walks Guided Tours** (©904/540-3476; www.staugustinecitywalks.com) has a delicious tour, **The Savory Faire,** a 2½-hour walking tour exploring historical and cultural influences on St. Aug cuisine from tapas to desserts. For those who prefer shopping over eating, they also offer a 3-hour shopping tour of the most unique shops in the city (and there's a cart that will carry all your bags). Cost is $45 per person.

For more personalized group excursions, call **Tour Saint Augustine** (©800/797-3778 or 904/825-0087; www.staugustinetours.com), which offers guided walking tours around the historic area. Rates vary based on the number of people in the group.

You can search for old spirits with the nightly **Ghost Tours of St. Augustine ★★** (©888/461-1009 or 904/461-1009; www.ghosttoursof staugustine.com), in which guides in period dress lead you through the historic district or to the St. Augustine Lighthouse. Tickets are $10 to $26 per person, depending on the tour. Also offered are 1-hour ghost cruises on the river in a 72-foot-tall mast schooner. These cost $35 per person, including soft drinks and snacks. Call for schedules and reservations. Or, if your feet hurt from touring all day, **Shivers and Awe,** 98 St. George St. (©904/377-1447; www.sagpstours.com), offers a GPS-guided pedicab ghost tour of St. Augustine. Cost is $35 per ride, for two people.

The **Sunshine Bus Company** (☎ 904/823-4816; www.sunshine bus.net) operates public bus routes Monday through Saturday from 6am to 7pm. The line runs between the St. Augustine Airport on U.S. 1 and the historic district via San Marco Avenue and the Greyhound bus terminal on Malaga Street. Rides cost $1 per person. All-day tickets are $3 for adults and $1.50 for seniors. Call for the schedule.

For water views, **Country Carriages** (☎ 904/826-1982; www. countrycarriages.net) offers 1-hour guided tours on horseback on St. Augustine's beaches. Tours are $75 per person and require advance reservations.

For a taxi, call **Yellow Cab** (☎ 904/824-6888).

Solano Cycle, 61 San Marco Ave., at Locust Avenue, 2 blocks north of the visitor center (☎ 904/825-6766; www.solanocycle.com), rents bicycles and scooters. Bikes cost $18 a day, while scooters are $75 for a single passenger and $80 for two. Open daily from 10am to 6pm.

Seeing the Top Historic Attractions

St. George Street, from King Street north to the Old City Gate (at Orange St.), is the heart of the historic district. Lined with restaurants and boutiques selling everything from T-shirts to antiques, these 4 blocks get the lion's share of the town's tourists. You'll have much less company if you poke around the narrow streets of the primarily residential neighborhood south of King Street. Most of the town's attractions do not have guided tours, but many do have docents on hand to answer questions.

Be sure to drive through the parking lot of the Howard Johnson Express Inn, at 137 San Marco Ave., to see a gorgeous and stately **live oak tree ★★** that is at least 600 years old; then continue east to **Magnolia Avenue ★★**, a spectacularly beautiful street with a lovely canopy of old magnolia trees.

Castillo de San Marcos National Monument ★ As far as fortresses are concerned, this one's pretty cool. America's oldest and best-preserved masonry fortification took 23 years (1672–95) to build. It is stellar in design, with a double drawbridge entrance (the only way in or out) over a 40-foot dry moat. Diamond-shaped bastions in each corner, which enabled cannons to set up a deadly crossfire, contained sentry towers. The Castillo was never captured in battle, and its coquina (limestone made from broken seashells and corals) walls did not crumble when pounded by enemy artillery or violent storms over more than 300 years. Today the old bombproof storerooms surrounding the central

Costumed re-enactors inhabit the Colonial Spanish Quarter.

plaza have exhibits about the history of the fort, a national monument since 1924. You can tour the vaulted powder magazine, a dank prison cell (supposedly haunted), the chapel, and guard rooms. Climb the stairs to get a great view of Matanzas Bay. A self-guided tour map and brochure are provided at the ticket booth. If available, the 20- to 30-minute ranger talks are well worth attending. Popular torchlight tours of the fort are offered in winter.

If you like forts, you should also check out **Fort Matanzas,** built on an island in the 1740s to warn St. Augustine of enemy attacks from the south (which were out of reach of Castillo de San Marcos). For information, call ✆ **904/471-0116** or visit www.nps.gov/foma. Fort Matanzas is open daily from 8:30am to 5:30pm, and admission and the ferry ride to the island are free, though donations are accepted.

1 E. Castillo Dr. (at San Marco Ave.). ✆ **904/829-6506.** www.nps.gov/casa. Admission $6 adults for 7-day pass, free for children 15 and under. Fort daily 8:45am–4:45pm; grounds daily 5:30am–midnight.

Colonial Spanish Quarter and Spanish Quarter Museum ★★ If H. G. Wells were alive, he'd get a load of this re-created colonial Spanish village—complete with costumed folks doing things they used to do back in the 1700s—and think he was witnessing living proof of a time-travel machine. Watch as the blacksmiths, carpenters, leather workers, and homemakers demonstrate their skills and show you what life was like before the Internet. All of the architecture and landscape have been re-created within this 2-square-block park, which, in my opinion, is infinitely more fun than the museum itself. Take a 20-minute guided tour of the **DeMesa-Sanchez House** (ca. 1740–60), the only authentic colonial-era structure in the compound (the others are reproductions). If you're into this re-created history, then don't miss the **Old St. Augustine Village Museum,** which covers even more history.

33 St. George St. (btw. Cuna and Orange sts.). ✆ **904/825-6830.** www.historicstaugustine.com. Admission $7 adults, $6 seniors, $4.25 students 6–18, free for children 5 and under, $17 per family (2 adults and children 6–17 living in the same household). Daily 9am–5:30pm (last entry at 4:30pm).

Dow Museum of Historic Houses ★★ More time travel in St. Augustine is available at this museum re-creating life back in the old days. Operated by Daytona Beach's Museum of Arts and Sciences (p. 573), this museum brings to life each period of the city's history, from Spanish colonial times to the early 20th century. The eight restored homes here—built between 1790 and 1910—are on their original building sites. Some homes are decorated with period furniture and decor, while others serve as galleries. The reconstructed Star General Store sells preserves and other Victorian-era goods. You'll need 2 hours to see it all, including the 30-minute guided tour. Admission is good all day, so if you miss the start of a tour, you can leave and come back.

149 Cordova St. (entry on Bridge St. btw. St. George and Cordova sts.). ✆ **904/823-9722.** www.dowmuseum.com. Admission $9 adults, $8 seniors, $7 children 11 and under. Tues–Sat 10am–4:30pm; Sun 11am–4:30pm. Guided tours on the hour 10am–3pm, except 1pm.

Lightner Museum ★★★ Now *this* is a museum. Henry Flagler's opulent Spanish Renaissance–style Alcazar Hotel, built in 1889, closed during the Depression and stayed vacant until Chicago publishing magnate Otto C. Lightner bought the building in 1948 to house his vast collection of Victoriana. The lobby of the museum is exactly as the hotel lobby was back in the 1800s. The

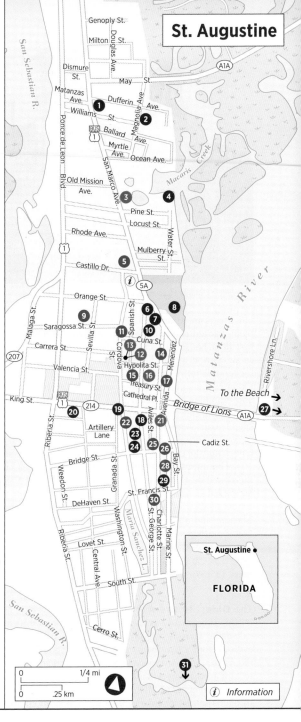

St. Augustine

HOTELS
Alexander Homestead **9**
Bayfront Westcott House Bed & Breakfast Inn **28**
Best Western Spanish Quarter Inn **5**
Carriage Way Bed & Breakfast **11**
Casa de Solana Bed & Breakfast **30**
Casa Monica Hotel **22**
Casablanca Inn on the Bay **17**
Kenwood Inn **26**
Monterey Inn **14**
Pirate Haus Inn & Hostel **15**
Victorian House **25**

RESTAURANTS
A1A Ale Works **21**
The Bunnery Bakery & Café **16**
Collage **13**
Columbia **12**
Raintree **3**

ATTRACTIONS
Authentic Old Jail/Florida Heritage Museum **1**
Castillo de San Marcos National Monument **8**
Colonial Spanish Quarter and Spanish Quarter Museum **10**
Dolphin Conservation Center at Marineland **31**
Dow Museum of Historic Houses **23**
Old St. Augustine Villiage Museum **24**
Fountain of Youth Archaeological Park **2**
Lightner Museum/Flagler College **19**
Mission of Nombre de Dios **4**
The Oldest House **29**
The Oldest Wooden Schoolhouse in the U.S.A. **6**
Spanish Military Hospital **18**
St. Augustine Lighthouse & Museum **27**
St. Augustine Pirate & Treasure Museum **7**
Villa Zorayda **20**

i Information

The opulent Lightner Museum was once the Alcazar Hotel.

building is an attraction in itself and makes a gorgeous museum, centering on a palm-planted courtyard with an arched stone bridge spanning a fishpond. The first floor houses a Victorian village, with shop fronts representing emporiums selling period wares. The Victorian Science and Industry Room displays shells, rocks, and Native American artifacts in beautiful turn-of-the-20th-century cases. Other exhibits include stuffed birds, an Egyptian mummy, steam-engine models, and examples of Victorian glass blowing. (Yes, it's a strange amalgamation for a museum, but there's sure to be *something* you're interested in here.) Plan to spend about 90 minutes exploring, and be sure to be here at 11am or 2pm, when a room of automated musical instruments erupts into concerts of period music. Check out the cafe too, housed in what used to be a stunning indoor pool.

The imposing building across King Street was Henry Flagler's rival resort, the Ponce de León Hotel. It now houses **Flagler College,** which runs not-to-be-missed 45-minute tours daily (at 10am and 2pm) of its magnificent Tiffany stained-glass windows, ornate Spanish Renaissance architecture, and gold-leafed Maynard murals ($6 adults, $5 kids 11 and under). Call ✆ **904/823-3378,** or visit www.flagler.edu for more information. Across Cordova Street stands another competitor of the day, the 1888-vintage **Casa Monica Hotel** (p. 596).

75 King St. (at Granada St.). ✆ **904/824-2874.** www.lightnermuseum.org. Admission $10 adults, $5 students with ID and youth 12–18, free for children 11 and under. Daily 9am–5pm (last tour 4pm).

The Oldest House ★★ Archaeological surveys indicate that a dwelling stood on this site as early as the beginning of the 17th century. What you see today, called the Gonzáles-Alvarez House (named for two of its prominent owners), evolved from a two-room coquina dwelling built between 1702 and 1727. The rooms are furnished to evoke various historical eras. Admission also entitles you to explore the adjacent **Manucy Museum of St. Augustine History,** where artifacts, maps, and photographs document the town's history from its origins through the Flagler era a century ago. Allow about 30 minutes here.

14 St. Francis St. (at Charlotte St.). ℂ **904/824-2872.** www.staugustinehistoricalsociety.org. Admission $8 adults, $7 seniors 55 and over, $4 students, free for children 6 and under, $18 per family. Daily 9am–5pm; tours depart every half-hour (last tour 4:30pm).

The Oldest Wooden Schoolhouse in the U.S.A. ★ ☺ Photo ops abound at this old-fashioned schoolhouse. One of three structures in town dating from the Spanish colonial period, this cedar-and-cypress structure is held together by wooden pegs and handmade nails, its hand-wrought beams still intact. The last class was held in 1864. Today the old-time classroom is re-created using animated pupils and a teacher, complete with a dunce and below-stairs "dungeon" for unruly children, which will make your kids count their lucky stars that they weren't in school back then.

14 St. George St. (btw. Orange and Cuna sts.). ℂ **904/824-0192.** www.oldestwoodenschool house.com. Admission $4 adults, $3 children 6–12, free for children 5 and under. Daily 9am–5pm (later in summer).

Spanish Military Hospital Hypochondriacs, doctors, and fans of medicine in general will love this place—but if you're squeamish in hospitals, this one isn't an exception. The clapboard building is a reconstruction of part of a hospital that stood here during the second Spanish colonial period, from 1784 to 1821. A 20-minute guided tour will show you what the apothecary, administrative offices, patients' ward, and herbarium probably looked like in 1791. The ward and a collection of actual surgical instruments of the period will enhance your appreciation of modern medicine. They say it's haunted and, as a result, there's a great ghost tour here every night at 8pm, with a 9:30pm tour on Saturdays, for $12 a person at the door and $10 prepaid over the phone.

3 Aviles St. (south of King St.). ℂ **904/827-0807.** www.spanishmilitaryhospital.com. Admission $5.30 adults, $4.50 seniors, $3 children 6–12. Mon–Sat 10am–5pm; Sun noon–5pm.

More Historic Attractions

Authentic Old Jail It's no Alcatraz, but in a sinister way, this old jail is kind of quaint. The compact prison, a mile north of the visitor center, may be authentic, but it's not particularly historic. It was built in 1890 and served as the county jail until 1953. The sheriff and his wife raised their children upstairs and used the same kitchen facilities to prepare the inmates' meals and their own. Among the "regular" cells, you can also see a maximum-security cell where murderers and horse thieves were confined, a cell housing prisoners condemned to hang (they could see the gallows being constructed from their window), and a grim solitary-confinement cell—with no windows or mattress. A restaurant here serves inexpensive lunch fare.

167 San Marco Ave. (at Williams St.). ℂ **904/829-3800.** Admission $9 adults, $5 children 6–12, free for children 5 and under. Rates are cheaper at www.trustedtours.com. Daily 8:30am–5pm.

Florida Heritage Museum at the Authentic Old Jail Compared to the other museums in town, this one isn't so special. After you've seen the Authentic Old Jail, you can spend another 30 minutes wandering through this museum documenting 400 years of Florida's past, focusing on the life of Henry Flagler, the Civil War, and the Seminole Wars. Highlights are a collection of toys and dolls, mostly from the 1870s to the 1920s, and a replica of a Spanish galleon filled with weapons, pottery, and treasures, along with display cases filled with gold, silver, and jewelry recovered by treasure hunters. A typical wattle-and-daub hut of a Timucuan Indian in a forest setting illustrates the lifestyle of St. Augustine's first residents.

167 San Marco Ave. (at Williams St.). ☏ **904/829-3800.** Admission $6 adults, $5 children 6–12, free for children 5 and under. Free admission with purchase of Old Town Trolley Tour and cheaper at www.trustedtours.com. Daily 8:30am–5pm.

Fountain of Youth Archaeological Park ✋ Never mind that Juan Ponce de León never found the Fountain of Youth; this 25-acre archaeological park bills itself as North America's first historic site. Smithsonian Institution archaeological digs have established that a Timucuan Indian village existed here some 1,000 years ago, but there's no evidence that Ponce de León visited the spot during his 1513 voyage. You can wander the not-so-interesting grounds yourself, but you'll learn more on a 45-minute guided tour or at a planetarium show about 16th-century celestial navigation. *Be warned:* This place could define the phrase *"tourist trap"* (not to mention that the fountain's water smells and tastes *awful*). Nevertheless, the grounds are lovely and the nonfountain exhibits are okay, which is good because many people still feel the need to visit.

11 Magnolia Ave. (at Williams St.). ☏ **800/356-8222** or 904/829-3168. www.fountainofyouth florida.com. Admission $9 adults, $8 seniors, $5 children 6–12, free for children 5 and under. Daily 9am–5pm.

Mission of Nombre de Dios This serene setting overlooking the Intracoastal Waterway is believed to be the site of the first permanent mission in the United States, founded in 1565. The mission is a popular destination of religious pilgrimages. Whatever your beliefs, it's a beautiful tree-shaded spot, ideal for quiet meditation.

27 Ocean Ave. (east of San Marco Ave.). ☏ **904/824-2809.** Free admission; donations appreciated. Daily 8am–5:30pm.

Old Florida Museum ★★ ☺ For those who can't resist touching things in museums, it's okay to do so here, and even encouraged! This mostly outdoors museum gives you the chance to experience historic Florida, with many hands-on activities (shelling and grinding corn, pumping water, writing with a quill pen) that kids may enjoy. Showcasing daily activities, everyday objects (games, weapons, tools, and more), and recreational pastimes, the museum demonstrates how three different eras of people in the area—the native Timucuan Indians, colonial Spaniards, and American pioneers—lived, worked, and played from the 16th to the early 20th century. Admission includes excellent, informative, and entertaining guided tours all day, so be sure to take one.

259 San Marco Ave. ☏ **800/813-3208** or 904/824-8874. www.oldfloridamuseum.com. Admission $11 adults, $7 children 6–18. Daily 10am–5pm.

St. Augustine Lighthouse & Museum ★ This 165-foot-tall structure, Florida's first official lighthouse, was built in 1875 to replace the old Spanish lighthouse that had stood at the inlet since 1565. The lightkeeper's cottage was destroyed by fire in 1970, but was meticulously restored to its Victorian splendor. The Victorian-style visitor center houses a museum explaining the history of the lighthouse and the area. You should be in good condition (children must be at least 7 years old *and* 4 ft. tall) to climb the 219 steps to the top of the lighthouse. In 2007, the SyFy Network's popular show *Ghost Hunters* filmed an episode here and found that, after a thorough investigation, the lighthouse is, indeed, haunted!

81 Lighthouse Ave. (off A1A east of the Bridge of Lions). ℂ **904/829-0745.** www.staugustine lighthouse.com. Admission to museum and tower $9 adults, $7.50 seniors, $7 children 7–11, free for children 6 and under and all active-duty and retired military personnel. Daily 9am–6pm. Follow A1A S. across the Bridge of Lions; take the last left before the turnoff to Anastasia State Park.

Villa Zorayda After being closed for over a decade, the renovated and restored Gilded Age, castlelike winter home of architect Franklin Smith has reopened to the public and features a big collection of antiques. Audio tours in English and Spanish are available with an admission ticket.

83 King St. ℂ **904/829-9887.** www.villazorayda.com. Admission $10 adults, $9 seniors, $8 students, $4 children 8–13. Mon–Sat 10am–5pm (last tour 4:30pm).

Other Entertainment Attractions

Dolphin Conservation Center at Marineland ★★ What once was a schlocky 7-acre tourist trap is now a world-class Dolphin Conservation Center. This, the descendant of the former Marineland of Florida (home of Flippy, the first-ever trained dolphin) and Marine Studios (1938), is 15 minutes south of St. Augustine and is on the National Register of Historic Places. Today, you can swim with dolphins in shallow and deep-water programs, create one-of-a-kind paintings with dolphin artists, enjoy summer camp for children focusing on science and exploration, and experience what it's like to be a dolphin trainer from 1 to 3 full days. The very young and those not inclined to participate may observe dolphins as they swim, play, and interact with guests, while more adventurous souls may take part in kayak tours exploring the estuaries of the Guana Tolomato Matanzas National Estuarine Research Reserve provided by Ripple Effect Ecotours. We also recommend the Touch and Feed Program, perfect for anyone who has ever wanted to touch a dolphin, but was discouraged by the cost of swimming with them. Cost is only $26 per person. (*Note:* Swimming with dolphins has both its critics and its supporters. You may want to visit the Whale and Dolphin Conservation Society's website at **www.wdcs.org**.)

9600 Ocean Shore Blvd. ℂ **904/460-1275.** www.marineland.net. Admission $8.50 adults, $7.25 seniors, $4 children 12 and under. Dolphin encounters $26–$330; kayak tours $50 (includes admission to Marineland). Daily 8:30am–4:30pm. South of St. Augustine on A1A.

St. Augustine Alligator Farm Zoological Park ★★ ☺ At the St. Augustine Alligator Farm Zoological Park, gators and crocs are a dime a dozen. In fact, there are more than 2,700 of them—including some rare white ones—at this more-than-a-century-old attraction. It houses the world's only complete collection of all 23 species of crocodilians, a category that includes alligators, crocodiles, caimans, and gavials. There are ponds and marshes filled with ducks, swans, herons, egrets, ibises, and other native wading birds. Entertaining (and educational) 20-minute alligator and reptile shows take place hourly throughout the day, and you can often see narrated feedings spring through fall. Don't miss Maximo, an Australian croc that weighs 1,250 pounds and is 15 feet, 3 inches long, or the 12-foot King cobra, the 21-foot reticulated python, and the Komodo dragon.

999 Anastasia Blvd. (A1A), east of Bridge of Lions at Old Quarry Rd. ℂ **904/824-3337.** www. alligatorfarm.com. Admission $22 adults, $11 children 3–10, free for children 2 and under. Discounts available online. Daily 9am–5pm; summer 9am–6pm.

St. Augustine Pirate & Treasure Museum ★ Adding a little swashbuckling to St. Augustine's rich, pristine history is this brand-new museum (opened in

Avast ye! It's the new St. Augustine Pirate & Treasure Museum.

November 2010) dedicated to all things pirate. This offshoot of the now-closed Key West original known as Pirate Soul and owned by the colorful Pat Croce, entrepreneur turned author turned Philadelphia 76ers former president, features rare relics from the days when pirates weren't just characters in Disney movies and rides.

12 Castillo Dr., St. Augustine. ℭ **877/GO-PLUNDER** (467-5863). www.piratesoul.com. Admission $12 adults, $6 children 6–12. Tickets cheaper on website. Winter Mon–Fri 9am–7pm, Sat–Sun 10am–7pm; summer Mon–Fri 9am–5pm, Sat–Sun 10am–5pm.

Hitting the Beach

There are several places to find sand and sea: **Vilano Beach,** on the north side of St. Augustine Inlet; and **St. Augustine Beach,** on the south side (the inlet dumps the Matanzas and North rivers into the Atlantic). Be aware, however, that erosion has almost swallowed the beach from the inlet as far south as Old Beach Road in St. Augustine Beach. The U.S. Army Corps of Engineers is reclaiming the sand (not without controversy as they are taking sand from the St. Augustine Inlet, which some say is harming the area's north beaches), but in the meantime, hotels and homes here have rock seawalls instead of sand bordering the sea.

Erosion has made a less noticeable impact on **Anastasia State Park ★★**, on Anastasia Boulevard (A1A) across the Bridge of Lions and just past the Alligator Farm, where the 4 miles of beach (on which you can drive and park) are still backed by picturesque dunes. On its river side, the area faces a lagoon. Amenities include shaded picnic areas with grills, restrooms, windsurfing, sailing and canoeing (on a saltwater lagoon), a nature trail, and saltwater fishing (for bluefish, pompano, redfish, and flounder; a license is required for nonresidents). In summer, you can rent chairs, beach umbrellas, and surfboards. There's good bird-watching here, especially in spring and fall; pick up a brochure at the entrance. The 139 wooded campsites are in high demand year-round; they come with picnic tables, grills, and electricity. Admission to the park is $8 per vehicle,

$4 single-occupant vehicle, $2 per bicyclist or pedestrian. Campsites cost $28. For camping reservations, call ✆ **800/326-3521** or go to www.reserveamerica. com. The day-use area is open daily from 8am to sunset. You can bring your pets. For information, contact Anastasia State Park, 1340A Fla. A1A S., St. Augustine, FL 32084 (✆ **904/461-2033;** www.floridastateparks.org/anastasia).

From Memorial Day to Labor Day, all St. Augustine beaches charge a fee of $3 per car at official access points; the rest of the year, you can park free, but there are no lifeguards on duty or restroom facilities on the beach.

Outdoor Activities

For additional outdoor options, contact the St. Augustine, Ponte Vedra & The Beaches Visitors and Convention Bureau (p. 583) and request a copy of its *Outdoor Recreation Guide.*

CRUISES The Usina family has been running **St. Augustine Scenic Cruises** (✆ **904/824-1806;** www.scenic-cruise.com) on Matanzas Bay since the turn of the 20th century. They offer 75-minute narrated tours aboard the double-decker *Victory III,* departing from the Municipal Marina just south of the Bridge of Lions. You can sometimes spot dolphins, brown pelicans, cormorants, and kingfishers. Snacks, soft drinks, beer, and wine are sold on-board. Departures are usually at 11am and 1, 2:45, and 4:30pm daily except Christmas, with an additional tour at 6:15pm from April 1 to May 21 and from Labor Day to October 15. From May 22 to Labor Day, there are two additional tours, at 6:45 and 8:30pm. Call ahead—schedules can change during inclement weather. Fares are $17 for adults, $14 for seniors, $9.75 for youths ages 13 to 18, and $7.75 for children ages 4 to 12. If you're driv-ing, allow time to find parking on the street.

You can also take the free ferry to Fort Matanzas on Rattlesnake Island. There are often dolphins in the water as you make the trip, and the fort is interesting. Ferries take off from 8635 Hwy. A1A (follow A1A S. out of St. Augustine for about 15 miles). Call ✆ **904/471-0116** or visit www.nps. gov/foma for more information.

ECO-TOURS St. Augustine Eco Tours (✆ **904/377-7245;** www.staugustine ecotours.com), offers several kayak and boat tours through St. Augustine's waterways, including Guana River and Lake, Moultrie Creek, Moses Creek, Washington Oaks, Faver-Dykes, and Six Mile Landing. Prices range from $40 to $50 adults, $30 to $40 kids. They also have a 27-foot catamaran sailing into the remote backwaters, creeks, and estuaries for glimpses of manatees, sea turtles, dolphins, and birds. Cost is $50 for adults, $35 for kids 12 and under.

Ripple Effect Eco Tours (✆ **904/347-1565;** www.rippleeffecteco tours.com) offers Hobie Mirage pedal-drive kayaks, eliminating the splash-es of paddles that startle subjects into flight, ensuring an ideal platform for nature photography. Rates start at $50 per person.

For the more adventurous types, **Adrenaline Alligator Adventures** (✆ **904/607-6399;** www.adrenalinealligators.com) is led by a licensed al-ligator trapper and takes you from swamps to golf course fairways on a mis-sion to subdue and remove nuisance gators. Cost is $45 per person or, if you're really insane, $145 will get you right into the middle of the action as you assist in the snaring, subduing, and taping of the gator's monster jaws. Good luck and, please, send us a picture.

WHERE golf IS KING

Passionate golf fans can easily spend a day at the **World Golf Hall of Fame** ★ (📞 **904/940-4123;** www.wgv.com), a state-of-the-art museum honoring professional golf, its great players, and the sport's famous supporters (including comedian Bob Hope and singer Dinah Shore). It's the centerpiece of **World Golf Village,** a complex of hotels, shops, offices, and 18-hole golf courses (see "Outdoor Activities," below). There's an IMAX screen next door.

Museum admission is $21 for adults, $19 for seniors and students, and $10 for children 4 to 12, and includes an IMAX film and a round of golf on the putting green. IMAX tickets range from $8.50 to $13 for adults, $7.50 to $12 for seniors and students, and $6 to $9 for children. The museum is open daily from 10am to 6pm; IMAX movies run until 8pm Friday and Saturday.

The village is built around a lake with a "challenge hole" sitting out in the middle, 132 feet from the shoreline. You can hit balls at it or play a round on the nearby putting course. Admission to the Hall of Fame includes a round on the putting course. The **Walkway of Champions** (whose signatures appear in pavement stones) circles the lake and passes a shopping complex where the main tenant is the two-story **Tour Stop** (📞 **904/940-0422**), offering pricey apparel and equipment.

If you'd like to stay overnight, contact the **World Golf Village Renaissance Resort,** 500 S. Legacy Trail, St. Augustine, FL 32092 (📞 **888/740-7020** or 904/940-8000; www.worldgolf renaissance.com), whose newly remodeled rooms and suites include flatscreens, new bathrooms, and new furniture.

The village is at exit 95A off I-95. For more information, contact World Golf Village, 21 World Golf Place, St. Augustine, FL 32092 (📞 **904/940-4000;** www.wgv.com).

FISHING You can fish to your heart's content at **Anastasia State Park** (see "Hitting the Beach," above). Or you can cast your line off **St. Johns County Fishing Pier,** at the north end of St. Augustine Beach (📞 **904/461-0119**). The pier is open 24 hours daily and has a bait shop with rental equipment that's open from 6am to 10pm. Admission is $3 ($1.50 children 11 and under) for fishing, $1 for sightseeing.

For full-day, half-day, and overnight **deep-sea fishing** excursions (for snapper, grouper, porgy, amberjack, sea bass, and other species), contact the **Sea Love Marina,** 250 Vilano Rd. (A1A N.), at the eastern end of the Vilano Beach Bridge (📞 **904/824-3328;** www.sealovefishing.com). Full-day trips on the party boat *Sea Love II* cost about $80 for adults, $75 for seniors, and $70 for kids 14 and under; half-day trips $60 for adults, $55 for seniors, and $50 for kids 14 and under. No license is required, and rod, reel, bait, and tackle are supplied. Bring your own food and drink.

GOLF The area's best golf resorts are in Ponte Vedra Beach—a half-hour's drive north on A1A, closer to Jacksonville than St. Augustine (see p. 610 for details).

The **Tournament Players Club Sawgrass** (📞 **888/421-8555;** www.pgatourexperience.com) offers the **Tour Player Experience,** where duffers will be treated like pros and have access to the exclusive wing of the 77,000-square-foot clubhouse where only actual pros, such as Vijay Singh

You can play the famous Tournament Players Club course at Sawgrass.

and Jim Furyk, are allowed. You also get a personal caddy wearing a bib with your name on it. The experience also includes a stay at the Sawgrass Marriott Resort and Spa, dinner, spa services, instruction at the Tour Academy, and a golf gift bag that includes balls, marker, and shirt. Packages are available from $423 to $901 per person.

At World Golf Village, 12 miles north of St. Augustine, at exit 95A off I-95 (see the box "Where Golf Is King," above), the **Slammer & The Squire** and the **King & The Bear** (✆ 904/940-6088; www.wgv.com) together offer 36 holes amid a wildlife preserve. Locals say they're not as challenging as their greens fees, which start at around $119 and go up, way up, from there. Specials, however, are available off season and off times. For those not schooled in golf history, the "Slammer" is in honor of Sam Sneed, the "Squire" is for Gene Sarazen, the "King" is Arnold Palmer, and the "Bear" is Jack Nicklaus. Palmer and Nicklaus collaborated in designing their course.

Nicklaus also had a hand in the stunning course at the **Ocean Hammock Golf Club** ★★ at the Hammock Beach Resort (✆ 386/477-4600; www.hammockbeach.com), on A1A, in Palm Coast, about halfway between St. Augustine and Daytona Beach. With 6 of its holes skirting the beach, it is the first truly oceanside course built in Florida since the 1920s.

There are only a few courses in St. Augustine, including the **St. Augustine Shores Golf Club,** 707 Shores Blvd., off U.S. 1 (✆ 904/794-4653), a par-70, 18-hole course with lots of water, a lighted driving range and putting green, and a restaurant and lounge. Greens fees usually are less than $30, including cart.

For more course information, go to www.golf.com or www.florida golfing.com, or call the **Florida Sports Foundation** (✆ 850/488-8347) or **Florida Golfing** (✆ 866/833-2663).

WATERSPORTS Jet skis and equipment for surfing and windsurfing can be rented at **Surf Station,** 1020 Anastasia Blvd. (A1A), a block south of the Alligator Farm (✆ 904/471-9463; www.surf-station.com); and at **Raging Water Sports,** at the Conch House Marina Resort, 57 Comares Ave. (✆ 904/829-5001; www.ragingwatersports.com), off Anastasia Avenue (A1A) halfway between the Bridge of Lions and the Alligator Farm.

Shopping

The winding streets of the historic district are home to dozens of **antiques stores** and **galleries** stocked full of original paintings, sculptures, bric-a-brac, fine furnishings, china, and other treasures. Brick-lined **Aviles Street,** a block from the river, has an especially good mix of shops for browsing, as does **St. George Street** south of the visitor center, and the Uptown area on **San Marco Avenue** a few blocks north of the center. The **Alcazar Courtyard Shops,** at the Lightner Museum (*C* 904/824-2874; p. 586), have a decent selection of antiques. Check at the visitor center for lists of art galleries and antiques shops, or contact the **Antique Dealers Association of St. Augustine,** 60 Cuna St., St. Augustine, FL 32084 (no phone).

Experience chocolate heaven at **Whetstone Chocolates,** 2 Coke Rd. (Fla. 312), between U.S. 1 and the Mickler O'Connell Bridge (*C* 904/825-1700; www.whetstonechocolates.com). Free self-guided tours of the store and factory usually take place Monday through Saturday from 10am to 5pm, but call ahead to confirm the schedule. Whetstone has a retail outlet at 42 St. George St., in the historic district.

Where to Stay

There are plenty of moderate and inexpensive motels and hotels in St. Augustine. Most convenient to the historic district is the 40-room **Best Western Spanish Quarter Inn,** 6 Castillo Dr. (www.staugustinebestwestern.com; *C* 800/528-1234 or 904/824-4457), directly across from the visitor center. It's completely surrounded by an asphalt parking lot, but it does have a pool and hot tub.

Another nice spot on the beach is **La Fiesta Ocean Inn & Suites,** 810 A1A Beach Blvd. (www.lafiestainn.com; *C* 800/852-6390 or 904/471-2220). Each room or suite features a microwave and refrigerator. There's a heated pool and gardens. Best of all, guests enjoy a daily complimentary breakfast, delivered to your room, with fresh-baked scones and muffins, bagels and cream cheese, yogurt, and fruit cup. Rates start at $99 in the winter and $150 in the summer.

Once a ramshackle fishing camp, the **Devil's Elbow Fishing Resort,** 7507 A1A S., St. Augustine (www.devilselbowfishingresort.com; *C* 904/471-0398), offers 10 newly remodeled resort-style waterfront rental cottages built in the classic Old Florida style with covered porches, tin roofs, roof-top cupolas, and hardwood floors. Rates range from $175 to $450 daily.

If you're coming on a weekend, expect the higher end of the listed rates—almost all accommodations increase their prices on weekends, when the town is most crowded with visitors. St. Johns County charges a 10% tax on hotel bills (4% bed tax plus 6% state tax).

HOTELS & MOTELS

Casa Monica Hotel ★★★ This Moorish Revival hotel is the best in town, with top-notch rooms and services. In 2010, the hotel joined Marriott's Autograph Collection, a new brand of upscale and independent hotels with distinctive personalities in major cities. Personality it has, but more important, it still has autonomy from Marriott (though you can now book a room here through the megachain's reservations system and collect points through their rewards systems). Most of the guest rooms have spacious, all-new luxury interiors with Moorish-style rouge carpet, elegantly appointed furnishings with gold accents, and plush red-velvet-tufted headboards. All units have big bathrooms equipped with high-end toiletries and either a large walk-in shower or a tub/shower combination. More interesting are the seven "signature suites" in the building's two tile-topped towers and fortresslike central turret. Each of these one- to four-bedroom units is unique. The **95 Cordova** restaurant has an excellent wine list, great service, and beautiful decor.

95 Cordova St. (at King St.), St. Augustine, FL 32084. www.casamonica.com. © **800/648-1888** or 904/827-1888. Fax 904/819-6065. 138 units. $159–$1,059 double. Packages available. AE, DC, DISC, MC, V. Valet parking $20. **Amenities:** Restaurant; cafe; bar; babysitting; concierge; access to nearby health club; exercise room; Jacuzzi; heated outdoor pool; room service; Wi-Fi. *In room:* A/C, TV, fridge (in some rooms), hair dryer, high-speed Internet access.

Monterey Inn ♨ For the price, you can't find a better choice than this modest, wrought-iron-trimmed motel overlooking the Matanzas Bay and close to the attractions of the Old City. Three generations of the Six family have run this two-story motel, and they keep the 1960s building and grounds clean and functional. Rooms are not especially spacious, but they're good enough to sleep in after a day at the beach.

16 Av. Menendez (btw. Cuna and Hypolita sts.), St. Augustine, FL 32084. www.themontereyinn. com. © **904/824-4482.** Fax 904/829-8854. 59 units. $109–$199 double. AE, DC, DISC, MC, V. **Amenities:** Restaurant; heated outdoor pool. *In room:* A/C, TV, hair dryer, Wi-Fi.

BED & BREAKFASTS

St. Augustine has more than two dozen bed-and-breakfasts in restored historic homes—and one boat! They all provide free parking, breakfast, 24-hour refreshments, and plenty of atmosphere, but most accept neither young children nor smokers (check before booking). Those listed below are in the historic district. For more choices, contact **St. Augustine Historic Inns,** P.O. Box 5268, St. Augustine, FL 33085-5268 (no phone; www.staugustineinns.com), for descriptions of its member properties.

Alexander Homestead ★★ This restored 1888 Victorian beauty is spectacular, not to mention romantic, and makes a popular place for weddings and honeymoons. One room has a Jacuzzi, two have fireplaces, and all have private porches, bathrooms, and antiques. Gourmet breakfasts include baked French toast with almond syrup; at night, you can enjoy a complimentary brandy along with your complimentary chocolate. Even better, coffee is delivered directly to your door in the morning, so there's no need to stir too much before your caffeine fix.

14 Sevilla St., St. Augustine, FL 32084. www.alexanderhomestead.com. © **888/292-4147** or 904/826-4147. 4 units. $169–$229 double. Rates include full breakfast. AE, DISC, MC, V. *In room:* A/C, TV, free Wi-Fi.

Bayfront Westcott House Bed & Breakfast Inn ★ Overlooking Matanzas Bay, this romantic, Key West–style wood-frame house offers rare opportunities for uncluttered views from the porch, the second-story veranda, and a shady courtyard. The rooms—some with private balconies, two-person whirlpool tubs, and fireplaces—are immaculate and exquisitely furnished. Yours might have authentic Victorian furnishings and a brass bed made up with a white quilt and lace dust ruffle. A nightly social hour features wine, beer, sodas, and hors d'oeuvres.

146 Av. Menendez (btw. Bridge and Francis sts.), St. Augustine, FL 32084. www.westcotthouse. com. © **800/513-9814** or 904/825-4602. Fax 904/824-4301. 15 units. $139–$349 double. Rates include full breakfast and social hour. AE, DISC, MC, V. **Amenities:** Access to nearby health club; Jacuzzi; free Wi-Fi. *In room:* A/C, TV, hair dryer.

Carriage Way Bed & Breakfast ★ Primarily occupying an 1883 Victorian wood-frame house fronted by Mexican petunias and topiaries, this family-owned B&B isn't fancy or formal, but it is comfortable *and* a good value. TV, books, and games are provided in a homey parlor. Guest rooms in the main house are furnished with simple reproductions, including king and queen beds with pillow-top mattresses and plush, luxe sheets. One room retains its original fireplace. Two rooms can accommodate more than two people. For more privacy, two more rooms are down the street in the Cottage, a clapboard house built in 1885. The Cottage has a living room and kitchen, and both of its bedrooms have claw-foot tubs. The Miranda room also sports a two-person Jacuzzi, while the Ashton has a small back porch. Full breakfasts include freshly baked breads, and to work it all off, the B&B offers free use of bikes to tool around town. Special packages provide nice little touches such as a gourmet picnic lunch, a horse-drawn carriage ride, and breakfast in bed.

70 Cuna St. (btw. Cordova and Spanish sts.), St. Augustine, FL 32084. www.carriageway.com. **800/908-9832** or 904/829-2467. Fax 904/826-1461. 11 units. $99–$199 double; $159–$269 Cottage rooms. Rates include full breakfast. AE, DISC, MC, V. Free onsite parking. **Amenities:** Free beverages, free use of bikes. *In room:* A/C, free Wi-Fi.

Casablanca Inn on the Bay ★ This 1914 Mediterranean-style white-stucco house, listed on the National Register of Historic Places, faces the bay, although only a few of the rooms have views. The most stunning are the second-floor suites with hammocks and private porches. The furnishings—a mix of turn-of-the-20th-century American oak, European, and Victorian pieces—are of a higher quality than those at many other inns. Modern conveniences in rooms include flatscreen TVs, DVD players, and sound machines. This may be appreciated, especially if you're in a ground-floor room that unfortunately suffers from the noise of the street and the next-door bar and grill. Pillow-top mattresses, however, make up for some of that distraction. A gourmet, sit-down breakfast is served alfresco on the porch or in a glass-enclosed conservatory. A porch with rocking chairs is an ideal spot to chill out, read a book, or sip a cocktail.

24 Av. Menendez (btw. Hypolita and Treasury sts.), St. Augustine, FL 32084. www.casablanca inn.com. **800/826-2626** or 904/829-0928. Fax 904/826-1892. 20 units. In season $99–$349

A SWASHBUCKLING hostel

International travelers on the cheap congregate at the **Pirate Haus Inn & Hostel,** 32 Treasury St., at Charlotte Street (www.piratehaus.com; **904/808-1999**), in the middle of the historic district. Done up in a pirate theme, this Spanish-style building has a communal kitchen, living room, and rooftop terrace. The inn has five private rooms (three with their own bathrooms), each equipped with a queen-size or double bed, plus one or two bunk beds. Two other rooms have dormitory-style bunks. Rooms cost $50 to $85 a night (higher on some weekends), while dorm beds go for $20. There's a $3 charge for children 12 and under. MasterCard and Visa are accepted. Reservations are advised, especially on weekends. Rates include the hostel's famous all-you-can-eat pancake breakfast.

double; off season $99–$279 double. Rates include full breakfast. AE, DISC, MC, V. **Amenities:** Free use of bikes; access to nearby health club. *In room:* A/C, TV (in 18 units), no phone (in 6 units).

Casa de Solana Bed & Breakfast ★★★ Owned by an interior designer, this St. Augustine landmark has been beautifully restored with British colonial furnishings and accessories. Just 1 block from the bayfront, the B&B offers a delicious Southern breakfast, evening wine in the inn's stunning garden courtyard, bikes, desserts, coffee, and free parking. Eight out of the 10 rooms have fireplaces and whirlpool tubs.

24 Aviles St., St. Augustine, FL 32084. www.casadesolana.com. © **877/824-3555** or 904/824-3355. Fax 904/824-3316. 10 units. In season $135–$265 double; off season $119–$249 double. Rates include full breakfast and complimentary social hour and dessert. AE, DISC, MC, V. **Amenities:** Free use of bikes; free Wi-Fi. *In room:* A/C, TV/DVD, CD player.

Kenwood Inn ★ Built in 1865, the Kenwood Inn is the only remaining hotel structure of its size from St. Augustine's Gilded Age. In St. Augustine's most historic district, the Victorian-style inn boasts two living rooms, two dining rooms, and guest rooms and suites that are larger and more private than most other B&B accommodations in converted single-family homes. Some feature DVD players, Jacuzzi tubs, and balconies with hammocks. Also unique to St. Augustine, it boasts a large outdoor pool and spacious sunning patio with chaise longues. A gourmet buffet breakfast features coffee, juices, pastries, muffins, an assortment of cereals, granolas, yogurts, fresh fruit, and parfaits plus hot entrees such as eggs Benedict, quiches, egg casseroles, waffles, and more. Bloody marys and champagne mimosas are offered on weekends. The nightly social includes wines, snacks, and an opportunity to meet the other guests.

38 Marine St. (at Bridge St.), St. Augustine, FL 32084. www.thekenwoodinn.com. © **800/824-8151** or 904/824-2116. 13 units, including some 2-bedroom suites. $129–$259 double. Rates include breakfast. AE, DISC, MC, V. **Amenities:** Bikes; pool; Wi-Fi. *In room:* A/C, TV, hair dryer.

Victorian House ★★ ☺ This 1897-vintage Victorian B&B has a wraparound porch and an adjoining old store, now dubbed the Carriage House. The latter is divided into four units, one of which has a kitchenette. What's unusual is that children can stay in the Carriage House units, all of which have TVs and private entrances, but the main house is adults only. Victorian antiques adorn all units. All rooms feature private bathrooms, some with double Jacuzzi tubs, fireplaces, and private porches. Victorian House's location between the two oldest streets is an added perk for history buffs, but for those who relish privacy and quiet, its location away from the noise—with the exception of the clopping of a horse or two—is priceless.

11 Cadiz St. (btw. Aviles and Charlotte sts.), St. Augustine, FL 32084. www.victorianhousebnb. com. © **877/703-0432** or 904/824-5214. Fax 904/824-7990. 10 units. $99–$199 double. Rates include full breakfast. AE, DISC, MC, V. **Amenities:** Free Wi-Fi. *In room:* A/C, TV (in 4 units), kitchen (in 1 unit), no phone.

Where to Dine

In a town with as much tourist traffic as St. Augustine, there are, of course, a number of "tourist trap" restaurants. But on the whole, the food here, even at the popular eateries, is fairly priced and of good quality. But before you eat, check out a local winery, the **San Sebastian Winery,** 157 King St. (© **904/826-1594;**

www.sansebastianwinery.com), in one of Henry Flagler's old East Coast Railway buildings a few blocks from downtown St. Augustine. The winery offers free guided tours and free (!) tastings of wines produced by their vineyards in Central Florida. Apparently, Florida's muscadine grapes are high in fiber and antioxidants, so drink up! The third floor of the winery, the **Cellar Upstairs,** is a wine and jazz bar that serves appetizers, wines, and beer.

Fans of chilies and hot peppers will be thrilled to know that St. Augustine is the home of the Datil pepper, one of the hottest around. Lots of local restaurants have their own Datil pepper sauces and even "Datil Dust," which is used to heat up any dish. **Hot Stuff Mon,** in the historic shopping district at 34 Treasury St. (✆ **904/824-4944;** www.hotstuffmon.com), features an assortment of hard-to-find sauces and sauces made exclusively with Datils in St. Augustine. Also check out **www.datildoit.com**.

The historic district has a branch of Tampa's famous **Columbia,** 98 St. George St., at Hypolita Street (✆ **904/824-3341**). Like the original in Ybor City (p. 442), this one sports Spanish architecture, including intricate tile work and courtyards with fountains.

A1A Ale Works ★ SEAFOOD Anyone who has ever chugged from a beer bong, entered a beer-drinking contest, or just simply loves beer must visit this brewpub. You can't miss the two-story Victorian-style building, on the waterfront opposite the Bridge of Lions. One of the city's most popular watering holes (owned by chain gastropub Gordon Biersch Brewery), the downstairs bar offers nightly entertainment, which sometimes filters upstairs into the restaurant. Despite the noise potential, the kitchen turns out a surprisingly good blend of New World Floribbean, Cuban, Caribbean, and Latino styles, in a nice setting with big windows and outdoor seating. Most of the seafood is very fresh, and the sauces are made to order. For an appetizer, try the Boniachos—a Floridian twist on nachos with *boniato* chips piled with black beans, black olives, jalapeño peppers, and cheese. Don't overlook nightly specials, either, especially the fresh fish. The house brew ranges from a very light lager to a nonalcoholic root beer.

1 King St. (at Av. Menendez). ✆ **904/829-2977.** www.a1aaleworks.com. Call for preferred seating. Main courses $13–$38; sandwiches $8–$11. AE, DC, DISC, MC, V. Sun–Thurs 11am–10:30pm; Fri–Sat 11am–11pm. Late-night menu served downstairs.

The Bunnery Bakery & Café ★ 🍴 BAKERY/DELI If you suffer from a raging sweet tooth, get thee to the Bunnery. Alluring aromas waft from this bakery and cafe in the heart of the historic district. It's a lovely spot for breakfast (stick to the pastries) or for a pastry and cappuccino anytime you need a break from sightseeing. At lunch, plop yourself into one of the colorful booths and indulge in the soups, salads, burgers, or panini—or perhaps a croissant stuffed with walnut-and-pineapple chicken salad. Order at the counter; the staff will call your number when it's ready.

121 St. George St. (btw. Treasury and Hypolita sts.). ✆ **904/829-6166.** Breakfast $3–$10; sandwiches and salads $4–$10. No credit cards. Daily 8am–6pm. Closed New Year's Day, Easter, Thanksgiving, Christmas Eve, and Christmas Day.

Collage ★★ INTERNATIONAL Collage (formerly La Parisienne) is a welcome respite from all the nearby Americana. The creative, frequently changing menu includes tasty dishes including the baked brie appetizer—a wheel of brie baked in phyllo and served with a caramelized onion and apple chutney; and a fantastic Florida bouillabaisse. The restaurant also serves homemade ice cream and a sinful Bougainvillea Dessert of strawberries sautéed in butter and black pepper, homemade vanilla-bean ice cream, and a cabernet vanilla sauce served in a leaf-shaped phyllo cup.

60 Hypolita St. (btw. Spanish and Cordova sts.). ✆ **904/829-0055.** www.collagestaug.com. Reservations recommended. Main courses $22–$41. AE, DISC, MC, V. Daily 5:30–9pm.

Gypsy Cab Co. ★★ 🍴 NEW AMERICAN Billing itself as a temple of "urban cuisine," Ned Pollack's high-energy establishment, with gaudy neon stripes outside and art-filled dining rooms inside, is the town's most interesting culinary experience. Ned's creative menu changes daily, though black-bean soup is a constant winner. If it's available, try the veal with bacon-horseradish cream or the grouper in a tomato-basil sauce. As a capper, I recommend peanut butter mousse or Key lime pie. Also of note is the house salad dressing, which is so good they sell it by the bottle. Lunch is served (Mon–Fri 11am–4pm) in the **Corner Sports Bar & Grill** (✆ 904/808-1305) next door, which features live music and entertainment.

828 Anastasia Blvd. (A1A, at Ingram St., east of the Bridge of Lions). ✆ **904/824-8244.** www. gypsycab.com. Main courses $15–$22. AE, DC, DISC, MC, V. Mon–Thurs 4:30–10pm; Fri 4:30–11pm; Sat 11am–11pm; Sun 10:30am–10pm.

The Purple Olive ★ INTERNATIONAL A local favorite, the Purple Olive is a cozy bistro with a menu that's sort of like one of those old Choose Your Own Adventure books in which you get to build your own plate, with more than a dozen choices of entrees, sauces, condiments, and side items. For those who'd rather, leave it in the expert hands of chef/owner Peter Kenney, who may recommend starting with mussels in a fragrant coconut curry broth or a Southern-accented fresh baby-spinach salad with candied pecans, apples, crispy bacon, and warmed brie. The South is well represented in entrees too, with shrimp and grits served in a sausage ragout over grit cakes with grilled vegetables. Or you can go back to the Asian and choose a tofu, chicken, or seafood Thai curry for your main course. Speaking of tofu, even if you aren't a vegetarian, it's worth trying the blue-crusted corn tofu with mole sauce, avocado *crema,* grit cakes, and grilled vegetables. As if your choices weren't confusing enough, the Purple Olive also features a selection of nightly specials, as well as fresh-baked artisan breads, and homemade soups, sauces, salad dressings, and desserts made from scratch.

4255 A1A S. ✆ **904/461-1250.** www.purple-olive.com. Reservations recommended. Main courses $14–$33. AE, DC, MC, V. Tues–Sat 5–9pm.

Raintree ★ INTERNATIONAL Even if you don't have a full meal at this romantic 1879 Victorian house (about a half-mile north of the historic district), the tempting variety of crepes and an exemplary crème brûlée are worth a visit. Sweetness works its way onto the main menu, as in crisp roasted half duckling in a raspberry demi glace. More traditional choices include beef Wellington and rack of New Zealand lamb. The food is all very good, though not as modern as at Gypsy Cab Co. or as expertly prepared as at Collage (see above). The list of more than 300 vintages has won *Wine Spectator* awards. The Dessert Bar is heavenly, with choices such as a lace cookie basket, Granny Smith apple pie, or triple-chocolate torte with chocolate ganache in a graham cracker crust. Keep in mind that Raintree is a destination restaurant, which means hordes of people are constantly traipsing through and marveling at the lovely old-world ambience.

102 San Marco Ave. (at Bernard St.). ☎ **904/824-7211.** www.raintreerestaurant.com. Reservations recommended. Main courses $10–$30; dessert bar from $6. AE, DC, MC, V. Sun–Thurs 6–9:30pm; Fri–Sat 6–10pm. Courtesy car provides transportation from/to downtown hotels.

St. Augustine After Dark

Especially on weekends, the Old Town is full of strollers and partiers making the rounds of dozens of bars, clubs, and restaurants. For up-to-date details on what's happening in town, check the local daily, the *St. Augustine Record* (**www. staugustine.com**), or the irreverent *Folio Weekly* (**www.folioweekly.com**). Another nighttime activity is taking one of the many ghost tours.

The best-looking and rowdiest crowd in town can be found at the **A1A Ale Works** (p. 600). Twenty-something hipsters and middle-aged partiers mingle at this New Orleans–style microbrewery and restaurant. You'll find live music Thursday through Saturday at the bar—usually light rock and R&B tunes.

Ann O'Malley's, 23 Orange St., near the Old City Gate (☎ **904/825-4040;** www.annomalleys.com), is an Irish pub that's open until 1am. Besides the selection of ales, stouts, and drafts, this is one of the only spots where you can grab a late-night bite. And, on rainy days, the bar pours $1 Yuengling drafts.

Also popular with locals, **Mill Top Tavern,** 19½ St. George St., at the Fort (☎ **904/829-2329;** www.milltop.com), is a warm and rustic tavern in a 19th-century mill building (the water wheel is still outside). Weather permitting, it's an open-air space. There's music here every day from 1pm to 1am.

Scarlett O'Hara's, 70 Hypolita St., at Cordova Street (☎ **904/824-6535;** www.scarlettoharas.net), a catacomb of cozy rooms with working fireplaces in a rambling, 19th-century wood-frame house, is the setting for everything from DJs and karaoke to live music. Sporting events are aired on a large-screen TV; and, if you're hungry, check out the Southern fried chicken.

Across the river, the **Gypsy Bar & Grill,** part of the Gypsy Cab Co. restaurant (p. 601), 828 Anastasia Blvd. (☎ **904/824-8244**), often has live music, as well as a comedy club next door.

JACKSONVILLE

36 miles S of the Georgia border; 134 miles NE of Orlando; 340 miles N of Miami

Once infamous for its smelly paper mills, the sprawling metropolis of Jacksonville—residents call it "Jax," from its airport abbreviation—is now one of the South's insurance and banking capitals. Development was rampant throughout Duval County during the 1990s, with hotels, restaurants, attractions, and clubs springing up, especially in suburban areas near the interstate highways. Aside from that, there are 20 miles of Atlantic Ocean beaches upon which to sun and swim, championship golf courses, and an abundance of beautiful and historic national and state parks to roam.

Spanning the broad, curving St. Johns River, downtown Jacksonville is a vibrant center of activity weekdays and on weekend afternoons and evenings, when many locals head to the restaurants and bars of Jacksonville Landing and Southbank Riverwalk. These two dining-and-entertainment complexes face each other across the river and have helped to revitalize the downtown area.

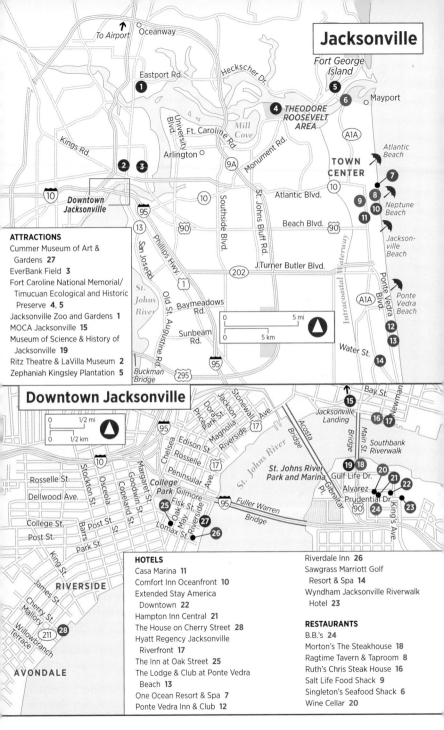

Jacksonville

To Airport
Oceanway
Eastport Rd. **1**
Heckscher Dr.
Fort George Island
5
6 Mayport
4 THEODORE ROOSEVELT AREA
University Blvd.
Ft. Caroline Rd.
Mill Cove
A1A
Atlantic Beach
Kings Rd.
Arlington
2 **3**
9A
Monument Rd.
TOWN CENTER
7
Atlantic Blvd.
10
8
9 **10** Neptune Beach
Downtown Jacksonville
10
95
13
Southside Blvd.
St. Johns Bluff Rd.
Beach Blvd.
90
11
Jacksonville Beach
Phillips Hwy.
90
San Jose Rd.
J. Turner Butler Blvd.
202
Ponte Vedra Blvd.
Ponte Vedra Beach
A1A
12
St. Johns River
Old St. Augustine Rd.
Baymeadows Rd.
1
Sunbeam Rd.
13
0   5 mi
0   5 km
Water St.
14
Buckman Bridge
295
95

ATTRACTIONS

Cummer Museum of Art & Gardens **27**
EverBank Field **3**
Fort Caroline National Memorial/ Timucuan Ecological and Historic Preserve **4, 5**
Jacksonville Zoo and Gardens **1**
MOCA Jacksonville **15**
Museum of Science & History of Jacksonville **19**
Ritz Theatre & LaVilla Museum **2**
Zephaniah Kingsley Plantation **5**

Downtown Jacksonville

0   1/2 mi
0   1/2 km
10
95
Stockton St.
Rosselle St.
Dellwood Ave.
Oscoola
Margaret St.
Goodwin St.
Copeland St.
College St.
Post St.
Barrs St.
Park St.
King St.
James St.
Cherry St.
Mallory
Willowbranch Terrace
28
211
RIVERSIDE
AVONDALE
Dora St.
Price St.
Jackson St.
Magnolia
Stonewall St.
Riverside Ave.
Chelsea
Edison St.
Rosselle
17
17
Peninsular
Gilmore
Fisk St.
Oak St.
May St.
Lomax St.
College Park
25
95
27
26
Fuller Warren Bridge
Bay St.
Jacksonville Landing
St. Johns River
Acosta Bridge
Gibralter Pl.
St. Johns River Park and Marina
15
16 **17**
Main St.
Newman
Southbank Riverwalk
Gulf Life Dr.
19 **18**
20
21 **22**
Alvarez
Prudential Dr.
24 **23**
90
King's Ave.

HOTELS

Casa Marina **11**
Comfort Inn Oceanfront **10**
Extended Stay America Downtown **22**
Hampton Inn Central **21**
The House on Cherry Street **28**
Hyatt Regency Jacksonville Riverfront **17**
The Inn at Oak Street **25**
The Lodge & Club at Ponte Vedra Beach **13**
One Ocean Resort & Spa **7**
Ponte Vedra Inn & Club **12**
Riverdale Inn **26**
Sawgrass Marriott Golf Resort & Spa **14**
Wyndham Jacksonville Riverwalk Hotel **23**

RESTAURANTS

B.B.'s **24**
Morton's The Steakhouse **18**
Ragtime Tavern & Taproom **8**
Ruth's Chris Steak House **16**
Salt Life Food Shack **9**
Singleton's Seafood Shack **6**
Wine Cellar **20**

Essentials

GETTING THERE **Jacksonville International Airport,** on the city's north side, about 12 miles from downtown (℡ 904/741-2000; www.jia.aero), is served by **Air Canada, AirTran, American, Continental, Delta, JetBlue, Metrojet, Northwest, Southwest, United,** and **US Airways.**

    Alamo (℡ 800/327-9633), **Avis** (℡ 800/331-1212), **Budget** (℡ 800/527-0700), **Dollar** (℡ 800/800-4000), **Enterprise** (℡ 800/325-8007), **Hertz** (℡ 800/654-3131), and **National** (℡ 800/227-7368) have rental-car booths at the airport.

    Airport shuttles and all sorts of taxicabs are available, and even though **Gator City Taxi** is the official JAX taxi company (℡ 904/355-8294), we recommend **Yellow Cab** (℡ 904/260-1111). Fares are around $1.50 when the flag drops and about $1.85 per additional mile thereafter.

    There's an **Amtrak** station in Jacksonville at 3570 Clifford Lane, off U.S. 1, just north of 45th Street (℡ 800/USA-RAIL [872-7245]; www.amtrak.com).

VISITOR INFORMATION Contact the **Jacksonville and the Beaches Convention & Visitors Bureau,** 201 E. Adams St., Jacksonville, FL 32202 (℡ 800/733-2668 or 904/798-9111; fax 904/789-9103; www.jaxcvb.com), for maps, brochures, calendars, and advice. The bureau is open Monday through Friday from 8am to 5pm. It has a walk-in information office in **Jacksonville Beach,** at 403 Beach Blvd., between 3rd and 4th streets (℡ 904/242-0024), open Monday through Saturday from 10am to 6pm.

GETTING AROUND In general, you're better off having a car if you want to explore this vast area. To get around downtown Jacksonville, you can take the **Skyway,** an elevated and completely automated train that runs down Hogan Street from Florida Community College's Jacksonville campus through downtown and across the river via the Acosta/Florida 13 bridge to the Southbank Riverwalk. The Skyway operates Monday through Friday from 6am to 11pm, Saturday from 10am to 11pm, and Sunday only for special events. The fare is 50¢.

    The **Trolley** connects with the Skyway and runs east-west through downtown, primarily along Bay Street. It's free and operates Monday through Friday from 6:30am to 7pm and Saturday from 8am to 6pm. In 2010, the **Riverside Trolley** expanded its weekday service from 5am to 7:30pm with stops at The Shoppes of Avondale. The **Beaches Trolley** goes from South Beach Parkway Shopping Center to the Atlantic Village Shopping Center, stopping at all points along the beach from 7pm to 2am Fridays, noon to 2am Saturdays, and noon to 6pm Sundays. Fare is free for the downtown route and $1 for the Riverside and Beaches routes. Get maps and schedules from the visitor's bureau or information booths (see above). Both the Skyway and the Trolley are operated by the **Jacksonville Transportation Authority** (℡ 904/630-3181; www.jtafla.com), which also provides local bus service.

    You can hail a cab downtown if you spot one, though it's usually best to call **Yellow Cab** (℡ 904/260-1111) for a pickup. Fares are around $1.50 when the flag drops and about $1.85 per additional mile thereafter.

    Out at the beaches, the **St. Johns River Ferry** (℡ 904/241-9969; www.stjohnsriverferry.com) shuttles vehicles across the river between

Mayport, an Old Florida fishing village on the south side, and Fort George, on the north shore. The boats run daily; times vary, so call for the current schedule. One-way fare is $5 per two-axle private vehicle, $1 per pedestrian or bicyclist. Even if you have to wait 30 minutes for the next ferry, the 5-minute ride greatly shortens the trip between the Jacksonville beaches and Amelia Island.

Bikers and hikers traveling along the 3,000-mile East Coast Greenway connecting major cities from Calais, Maine, to Key West can now take the "Blueway Bypass" thanks to the **Cumberland Sound Ferry Service** (✆ **877/264-9972;** www.ameliarivercruises.com), which runs a minimum of three round-trips per day from Amelia Island, Florida, to St. Marys, Georgia, on Thursday, Friday, and Saturday. The trip takes approximately 1 hour and features live narration of the region's history, natural features, and wildlife. You'll also get to explore each of the cities. Trip costs $20 round-trip per person.

Exploring the Area

Camp Milton ★ ☺ A key Confederate installation during the Civil War, Camp Milton served as a base for skirmishes between Union and Confederate soldiers. After years of neglect, the 124-acre park was preserved and is now home to pines, magnolias, blackberries, foxes, bobcats, armadillos, and hawks. A boardwalk leads into the woods where the remains of earthworks built by Confederate soldiers still stand. For true history buffs, reenactors dressed in period costumes talk about life in Jacksonville circa 1884, and for Civil War buffs, there are reenactors dressed in Union and Confederate regalia who tell the story of the not-so-bloody spats on the site back in the day. Every year the park holds a reenactment of events leading up to the Battle of Olustee, usually around the last week in January. In addition to the historical markers throughout the park, there are bike paths, nature trails, and an interpretive center.

1175 Halsema Rd. ✆ **904/824-1606.** www.campmilton.com. Free admission. Daily 9am–5pm. Take I-10 west, exit 351; turn left onto Chaffee Rd. N; turn left onto Beaver St., U.S. 90; turn right onto Halsema Rd.

Cummer Museum of Art & Gardens ★★ Built on the grounds of a private Tudor mansion, this impressive museum is worth a visit for anyone who appreciates the visual arts. The permanent collection encompasses works from 2000 B.C. to the present. It's especially rich in American Impressionist paintings, 18th-century porcelain, and 18th-century Japanese woodblock prints. I find the art here a bit boring and too focused on landscapes, but that's my taste. Frankly—and art snobs may gasp at this statement—the landscaping of the museum is more spectacular. Don't miss the stunning Italian and English gardens set on the scenic St. Johns River. The museum hosts temporary and traveling exhibits, and sponsors a multitude of activities, so call ahead to see what's happening.

829 Riverside Ave. (btw. Post and Fisk sts.). ✆ **904/356-6857.** www.cummer.org. Admission $10 adults, $6 seniors 66 and over and military, $6 students and children 5 and under, free Tues after 4pm. Tues 10am–9pm; Wed–Sat 10am–4pm; Sun noon–5pm.

Jacksonville Zoo and Gardens ★ ☺ Located between downtown and the airport, this environmentally sensitive zoo has become one of the Southeast's best. While the zoo's Wild Florida area presents local wildlife—including black bears, red wolves, Florida panthers, reptiles, birds, and alligators—the main exhibits feature an extensive and growing collection of lions, rhinos, elephants, antelopes, cheetahs, western lowland gorillas, and other African wildlife. You'll enter the 120-acre park through an authentic thatched roof built in 1995 by 24 Zulu craftsmen. Whether you go on foot or by train, allow at least 3 hours to tour this vast zoo. When you arrive, ask about current animal shows and special events. Strollers and wheelchairs are available for rent. The **Range of the Jaguar** exhibit focuses on a neotropical rainforest setting that can be found in Central or South America. Although this attraction spotlights the jaguar, you will also see other animals, such as golden lion tamarins, tapirs, capybaras, giant river otters, anteaters, and a variety of bird, amphibian, fish, and reptile species, including the anaconda. New to the zoo is the **Asian Bamboo,** host to 111 plant species and varieties and 29 species and varieties of bamboo. The tallest bamboo in the garden includes the Parker's Hawaiian Giant, which can grow to 70-plus feet. Kids will especially love the 2½-acre, $6.7-million **Kids' Zone** with mazes, a splash ground, a treehouse, and a rock-climbing area. For a great overview of the zoo, take the train, which costs $4 for adults and $2 for children 3 to 12. Combo tickets are also available. In September 2010, a rare Amur leopard cub was born—in the wild, there are only 44 of these animals.

370 Zoo Pkwy. ✆ **904/757-4462** or -4463. www.jacksonvillezoo.org. Admission $14 adults, $12 seniors, $8.95 children 3–12, free for children 2 and under. Combo tickets $18 adults, $16 seniors, $11 children 3–12. Daily 9am–5pm. Closed Thanksgiving and Christmas. Take I-95 N. to Heckscher Dr. (exit 358A) and follow the signs.

MOCA Jacksonville ★★ This museum of contemporary art is one of the Southeast's largest, housed in the renovated Western Union Telegraph Building and featuring five changing exhibition galleries, an ArtExplorium Loft, a children's interactive center, education studios, an auditorium, a cafe, and a shop. Permanent works are impressive and include works by Ed Paschke, Hans Hoffmann, Joan Mitchell, and James Rosenquist.

333 N. Laura St. ✆ **904/366-6911.** www.mocajacksonville.org. Admission $8 adults; $5 seniors 60 and over, military, students,; free Wed after 5pm; free for families on Sun. Tues–Wed and Fri–Sat 10am–4pm; Thurs 10am–8pm; Sun noon–4pm.

Ritz Theatre & LaVilla Museum From 1921 to 1971, the Ritz Theatre was the center of cultural life in LaVilla, an African-American neighborhood so vibrant that it was known as the Harlem of the South. Many entertainers played the Ritz before moving on to the Apollo Theater in the real Harlem. Most of LaVilla's small clapboard "shotgun" houses (so called because you could fire a shotgun through the central hallway to the back room and not hit anything) have been torn down in anticipation of urban renewal, but the Ritz has been rebuilt and is once again a center of the city's cultural life. Only the northwest corner of the building, including the Ritz sign, is original, but the new 426-seat theater captures the spirit of vaudevillian times. Off the lobby, the LaVilla Museum recounts local African-American history and exhibits artwork. Regularly scheduled events include free spoken-word nights, free art walks, and Amateur Night at the Ritz, modeled after the famous talent show at Harlem's Apollo Theater, at 7:30pm on the first Friday of every month. Tickets are $5.50.

829 N. Davis St. (btw. State and Union sts.). ✆ **904/632-5555.** www.ritzlavilla.org. Admission $6 adults, $3 seniors and children 17 and under. Tues–Fri 10am–6pm; Sat 10am–2pm; Sun 2–5pm. From downtown, take Main St. north, turn left (west) on State St. to theater and museum on Davis St.

Southbank Riverwalk ☺ Bordering the St. Johns River, opposite Jacksonville Landing this 1¼-mile wooden zigzag boardwalk is usually filled with joggers, tourists, folks sitting on benches, and lovers walking hand-in-hand, all of them watching the riverboats, the shorebirds, and downtown's skyline reflected in the water. At 200 feet in diameter, the **Friendship Fountain,** near the west end, is the nation's largest self-contained fountain; it's especially beautiful at night when illuminated by 265 colored lights. Nearby, you'll pass military memorials, a small museum dedicated to the city's history, and the **Museum of Science & History of Jacksonville (MOSH),** at Museum Circle and San Marco Boulevard (📞 904/396-6674; www.themosh.org). MOSH is an interactive children's museum focusing on the science and history of Northeast Florida. One of its stars is an Allosaurus dinosaur skeleton. It also has a small planetarium, with shows included in museum admission: $10 for adults, $8.50 for seniors, and $8 for children ages 3 to 12. The museum is open Monday through Friday from 10am to 5pm, Saturday from 10am to 6pm, and Sunday from 1 to 6pm. The Riverwalk is the scene of special MOSH programs, seafood fests, parties, parades, and arts-and-crafts festivals.

On the south bank of St. Johns River, flanking Main St. Bridge, btw. San Marco Blvd. and Ferry St. 📞 **904/396-4900.** Take I-95 N. to Prudential Dr. exit, make a right, and follow the signs.

An Unusual Breed of National Park

Named after the American Indians who inhabited Central and North Florida some 1,000 years before European settlers arrived, the **Timucuan Ecological and Historic Preserve** provides visitors an opportunity to explore untouched wilderness, historic buildings, and informative exhibits on the area's natural history. Unusual for a national park, this 46,000-acre preserve hasn't been hacked off from the rest of the community and drawn within arbitrary boundaries. The result is a vast, intriguing system of sites joined by rural roads alongside tumbledown fish camps, trailer parks, strip malls, condominiums, and stately old homes.

Entry to all park facilities is free (though donations are accepted). The **visitor centers** at Fort Caroline National Memorial and Zephaniah Kingsley Plantation (see below) are open daily from 9am to 5pm, except New Year's Day, Thanksgiving, and Christmas. The Theodore Roosevelt Area is open daily from 7am to 8pm during daylight saving time and daily from 7am to 5pm during standard time; closed for Christmas.

SOUTH OF THE RIVER

The preserve's prime attractions are 14 miles northeast of downtown on the south bank of the St. Johns River. Your starting point is the **Fort Caroline National Memorial ★,** 12713 Ft. Caroline Rd. (📞 904/641-7155; www.nps.gov/timu), which serves as the preserve's visitor center. This was the site of the 16th-century French Huguenot settlement that was wiped out by the Spanish who landed at St. Augustine. This two-thirds-size replica shows you what the original was like. You can see archaeological artifacts and two well-produced half-hour videos highlighting the area as well.

The fort sits at the northwestern edge of the 600-acre **Theodore Roosevelt Area,** a beautiful woodland and marshland rich in history, which has been undisturbed since the Civil War. On a 2-mile hike along a centuries-old park trail, you'll see a wide variety of birds, wildflowers, and maritime hammock forest. Bring binoculars, because such birds as endangered wood storks, great and snowy egrets, ospreys, hawks, and painted buntings make their homes here in spring and summer.

On the ground, you might catch sight of a gray fox or raccoon. You may also want to bring a picnic basket and blanket to spread beneath the ancient oak trees that shade the banks of the wide and winding St. Johns River. After the trail crosses Hammock Creek, you're in ancient Timucuan country, where their ancestors lived as far back as 500 B.C. Farther along is the site of a wilderness cabin that belonged to the reclusive brothers Willie and Saxon Browne, who lived without the modern conveniences of indoor plumbing or electricity until the last brother's death in 1960.

> ### Escaping Intolerance
>
> Zephaniah Kingsley, the white man who, from 1817 to 1829, owned the plantation that is now part of the Timucuan Ecological and Historic Preserve, held some seemingly contradictory views on race. Although he owned more than 200 slaves, he believed that "the coloured race were superior to us, physically and morally." He married a Senegalese woman—one of his former slaves—and in 1837 moved his mixed-race family to what is now the Dominican Republic to escape what he called the "spirit of intolerant injustice" in Florida.

If you're here on a weekend, take the fascinating 1½-hour guided tour of the fort and Theodore Roosevelt Area, offered every Saturday and Sunday (when weather and staffing permit). Call the fort for details and schedules.

The **Ribault Monument,** on St. Johns Bluff about a half-mile east of the fort, was erected in 1924 to commemorate the arrival in 1562 of French Huguenot Jean Ribault, who died defending Fort Caroline from the Spanish. It's worth a stop for the dramatic view of the area.

To get here from downtown Jacksonville, take Atlantic Boulevard (Fla. 10) east, make a left on Monument Road, and turn right on Fort Caroline Road; the Theodore Roosevelt Area is entered from Mt. Pleasant Road, about 1 mile southeast of the fort (look for the trail-head parking sign and follow the narrow dirt road to the parking lot).

NORTH OF THE RIVER

On the north side of the river, history buffs will appreciate the **Zephaniah Kingsley Plantation** ★, at 11676 Palmetto Ave., on Fort George Island (© **904/251-3537**). A winding 2½-mile dirt road runs under a canopy of dense foliage to the remains of this 19th-century plantation. The National Park Service maintains the well-preserved two-story clapboard residence, kitchen house, barn/carriage house, and remnants of 23 slave cabins built of "tabby mortar"— oyster shell and sand. Exhibits in the main house and kitchen focus on slavery as it existed in the rice-growing areas of Northern Florida, Georgia, and South Carolina. You can see it all on your own, but 40-minute ranger-guided tours are much more informative. They're usually given at 1pm Monday through Friday, 1 and 3pm Saturday and Sunday; call to confirm. Allot time to explore the grounds. The well-stocked book-and-gift shop will keep you even longer. The plantation is open daily from 9am to 5pm, except Christmas Day.

To get here from I-95, take Heckscher Drive East (Fla. 105) and follow the signs. From Fort Caroline, take Florida 9A North over St. Johns River to Heckscher Drive East. The plantation is 12 miles east of Florida 9A, on the left. From the beaches, take A1A to the St. Johns River Ferry and ride it from Mayport to Fort George; the road to the plantation is a half-mile east of the ferry landing.

The Zephaniah Kingsley Plantation has exhibits on plantation life in the Old South.

Hitting the Beach

You can fish, swim, snorkel, sail, sunbathe, or stroll on the sand dunes—at least from March to November, as winter can get downright chilly here. All of these activities are just a 20- to 30-minute drive east of downtown at Jacksonville's four beach communities.

Atlantic Boulevard (Fla. 10) will take you to **Atlantic Beach** and **Neptune Beach.** The boulevard divides the two towns, and where it meets the ocean, you'll come to **Town Center,** a quaint community with shops, restaurants, pubs, and a few inns.

Beach Boulevard (U.S. 90) dead-ends at **Jacksonville Beach,** where you'll find beach concessions, rental shops, and a fishing pier. This is also the most popular local surfing beach.

To the south, J. Turner Butler Boulevard (Fla. 202) leads from I-95 to the boundary between Jacksonville Beach and Ponte Vedra Beach. A right turn there will take you to **Ponte Vedra Beach** (pronounced here as *Pon*-ti *Vee*-dra). This ritzy, golf-oriented enclave is actually in St. Johns County (St. Augustine), but it's so much closer to Jacksonville that it's included in this section.

Outdoor Activities & Spectator Sports

CRUISES Jacksonville River Cruises (© 904/396-2333; www.jaxrivercruises. com) operates sightseeing, dinner, and dancing cruises on the stern-wheel paddleboats, the *Lady St. Johns* and the *Annabelle Lee.* They usually dock at 1501 Riverplace Blvd. Cost is $40 to $45 and includes a meal; schedules vary greatly by season, so call ahead or check the website.

FISHING The least expensive way to fish for red snapper, grouper, sea bass, small sharks, amberjack, and more, 15 to 30 miles offshore in the Atlantic Ocean, is aboard the *Majesty,* a modern, 65-foot, air-conditioned deep-sea party boat that has a galley offering hot meals. The full-day trips depart at 7:30am daily from Monty's Marina, 4378 Ocean St. (A1A), a half-mile south of the Mayport Ferry landing (☏ 904/246-7575; www.kingneptunefishing.com); they return at 4:30pm. The price is $75 per adult, $65 per child 6 to 14, including bait and tackle. Those who just want to sunbathe and watch the anglers pay $30. You don't need a license, but reservations are required.

GOLF The Jacksonville area has a great variety of golf courses, some of which are ranked among the top in the country. In Ponte Vedra Beach, the Sawgrass Marriott Resort sits on the most famous course, the Players Stadium

You might see a Jaguar (or a real big fan of the NFL team) in Jacksonville.

Course at **TPC at Sawgrass ★★★**, home of the Players Championship in March. Ranked among the nation's top courses, its island hole is one of the most photographed in the world. Nearby are the Ocean and Lagoon courses at the Ponte Vedra Inn & Club. See "Where to Stay," below, for information on the resorts.

Top courses open to the public include the **Golf Club of Jacksonville,** 10440 Tournament Lane (☏ 904/779-0800; www.golfbentcreek.com), which is managed by the PGA Tour. It's a great bargain, with greens fees between $27 and $49. The semiprivate **Cimarrone,** 2690 Cimarrone Blvd. (☏ 904/287-2000; www.cimarronegolf.com), is a fast and watery course with greens fees ranging from $33 to $65. But the best public course in the city, hands down, is the 18-hole Mill Cove course at the **Mill Cove Golf Club,** 1700 Monument Rd. (☏ 904/642-6140; www.millcovegolfcourse.com), which features a newly renovated par-71, 6,671-yard course with a slope rating of 129, designed by Arnold Palmer. Rates are exceptionally affordable at $25 to $45.

Be on the lookout for the free *Golfer's Guide* in visitor centers and hotel lobbies (see p. 45 for information on how to order a copy).

For course information, go to www.golf.com or www.floridagolfing.com; or call the **Florida Sports Foundation** (☏ 850/488-8347) or **Florida Golfing** (☏ 866/833-2663).

HORSEBACK RIDING For lessons or a scenic ride along the dunes or through Jennings State Forest, try **Diamond D Ranch,** located 3 miles West of Cecil Commerce Center and the Jacksonville Equestrian Center, off Normandy Boulevard (☏ 904/289-9331; www.diamonddranchinc.com). Call for rates and reservations.

SPECTATOR SPORTS The 73,000-seat **EverBank Field,** 1 Stadium Place, at East Duval and Haines streets (☏ 904/633-6100 for tickets), hosts the annual Florida–Georgia football game every October, and other college football games September through December. It's also the home field of the National Football League's **Jacksonville Jaguars** (☏ 877/452-4784, or 904/633-2000 for ticket information; www.jaguars.com). One of the stadium's biggest draws is the **Konica Minolta Gator Bowl,** usually held on New Year's Day.

The 16,000-seat **Jacksonville Veterans Memorial Arena,** 300 A. Phillip Randolph Blvd. (℃ **904/630-3900** for information, or 904/353-3309 for tickets), hosts National Hockey League exhibition games, college basketball games, ice-skating exhibitions, wrestling matches, and family shows.

Shopping

Jacksonville has plenty of shopping opportunities, including the upscale **The Avenues,** south of town at 10300 Southside Blvd.; **St. John's Town Center,** 4663 River City Dr.; and a number of flea markets. At **Beach Boulevard Flea and Farmers' Market,** on Beach Boulevard/Florida 90 (℃ **904/645-5961**), more than 600 vendors show up Saturday and Sunday from 9am to 5pm to sell their wares in the partially covered facility. Some booths are open other days of the week as well.

San Marco Square, at San Marco and Atlantic boulevards, south of the river, is a quaint shopping district in the middle of a stunning residential area. Shops housed in meticulously refashioned Mediterranean Revival buildings sell antiques and home furnishings, in addition to clothing, books, and records.

Another worthwhile neighborhood to explore is the **Avondale/Riverside** historic district, southwest of downtown on St. Johns Avenue between Talbot Avenue and Boone Park, on the north bank of the river. More than 60 boutiques, antiques stores, art galleries, and cafes line the wide, tree-lined avenue. **The Riverside Arts Market** (℃ **904/554-6865;** www.riversideartsmarket.com), located under the Fuller Warren Bridge near downtown, is the largest free weekly arts and entertainment venue in the state and is open every Saturday from 10am to 4pm from March to December.

Nearby, the younger set hangs out at **Five Points** (www.5pointsjax.com), on Park Street at Avondale Avenue, where used-record stores, vintage clothiers, coffee shops, and funky galleries stay open late.

Like St. Augustine, Jacksonville is a mecca for chocoholics. If you've never tried chocolate-covered popcorn or pretzels, **Peterbrooke Chocolatier Production Center,** 1470 San Marco Blvd., on San Marco Square (℃ **904/398-2489;** www.peterbrooke.com), is the place, if you're up for the experience. It's open Monday through Friday from 10am to 5pm. Peterbrooke also has a retail shop on St. Johns Avenue in Avondale.

Where to Stay

Because Jacksonville hasn't yet made it onto the hip list, there are no boutique hotels—yet. Instead, you have a choice of either a too-cool-for-its-location **Loft Jacksonville Airport** (see below); a large chain hotel, a la Hilton or Omni; or a much cozier, more charming bed-and-breakfast.

The accommodations listed below are arranged geographically, in and around downtown first, followed by the beach scene. The suburbs have dozens more options, especially along I-95. Many are clustered south of downtown in the **Southpoint** (exit 101, Turner Butler Blvd./Fla. 202) and **Baymeadows** (exit 101, Baymeadows Rd./Fla. 152) areas. These locales have a multitude of chain restaurants, and you can hop on the highways and zoom to the beach or downtown.

Rates in the downtown hotels are higher midweek, when rooms are in demand by business travelers. Beach accommodations are somewhat less expensive in the colder months from December to March.

Note: Hotel taxes in the area tack on an additional 13%!

IN JACKSONVILLE

Prudential Drive in the Southbank Riverwalk area is home to the **Wyndham Jacksonville Riverwalk Hotel** (*C* **800/996-3426** or 904/396-5100), the **Hampton Inn Central** (*C* **800/426-7866** or 904/396-7770), and the all-suites **Extended Stay America Downtown** (www.extendedstay.com; *C* **800/398-7829** or 904/396-1777).

Loft Jacksonville Airport, 751 Skymarks Dr., Jacksonville (www.starwood hotels.com; *C* **904/714-3800**), the first of the W Hotel offshoots in Florida (the second is in Tallahassee), opened in August 2009 and features ultramodern decor, a hip lounge, and free Wi-Fi. The hotel is so very hip we think it belongs somewhere else—say in downtown Jax. But we'll take what we can get.

The House on Cherry Street ★★ This colonial-style wood-frame house, on the St. Johns River in the Historic District, is ideal for a romantic getaway. French doors open onto a screened-in porch furnished with rocking chairs; it overlooks a tree-shaded lawn (where guests play croquet) leading through the organic garden to the river (where guests can watch ospreys and sunrises). You might go for the Riverside Room or the Duck Room, each with a canopied four-poster bed and river view. Florida artists are rather a theme here, with original art in each room. All units have adjacent sitting rooms, private bathrooms, ceiling fans, and fresh flowers. No smoking is permitted inside. This place gets booked up fast, so reserve early.

1844 Cherry St. (on St. Johns River), Jacksonville, FL 32205. www.houseoncherry.com. *C* **904/384-1999.** Fax 904/384-5013. 4 units. $89–$115 double. 2-night minimum on weekends. Rates include full breakfast. AE, MC, V. No young children accepted. *In room:* A/C, TV, hair dryer, no phone.

Hyatt Regency Jacksonville Riverfront ★★ After $15 million in renovations, this Green Lodging–designated Hyatt is now one of the city's most elegant lodgings. In the heart of downtown, it's popular with the suit-and-tie crowd, but also with those who want to be within walking distance of Jacksonville Landing. Renovations to the hotel included extensive changes to guest rooms, restaurants, bars, and the rooftop pool area. All units sport the Hyatt Grand Bed, 250-thread-count triple sheeting, down comforters, and very plush pillows. Bathrooms also received a much-needed makeover, with new tiles, paint, and marble countertops. The hotel features a rooftop pool and hot tub, dry sauna, and state-of-the-art 24-hour Hyatt Stay Fit.

225 E. Coast Line Dr., Jacksonville, FL 32202. www.jacksonvillehyatt.com. *C* **904/588-1234.** Fax 904/634-4554. 963 units. $89–$269 double. AE, DC, MC, V. Valet parking $20, self-parking $15. **Amenities:** 4 restaurants; bar; concierge; concierge-level rooms; fitness center; pool; room service; Wi-Fi in lobby and public areas. *In room:* A/C, TV, hair dryer, high-speed Internet access, MP3 docking station.

The Inn at Oak Street ★★★ A luxury B&B in the historic Riverside area, the Inn at Oak Street is just 2 miles from downtown Jax, but worlds away. The Inn's 6,000-square-foot main house has an eclectic, upscale ambience—no tchotchkes or clutter are found here. Instead, it just has peace, quiet, and a bit of chic too, with chandeliers; silk, linen, and bamboo window treatments; and touches of exposed brick. Guest rooms are spacious, with a funky mix of antiques and reproductions fused with modern comforts such as fine linens, a wine fridge, and flatscreen TVs with DVD players. Three units have balconies, and one (the Boudoir) has a gas fireplace. Wi-Fi is available throughout the house—even on the 70-foot wraparound front porch on which we recommend you enjoy your full gourmet breakfast with a menu that changes daily. Private bathrooms have whirl-pool spa tubs, Italian fixtures, and fantastic bath products. Every night in the parlor, guests can enjoy wine hour, or just chill out in the tranquil spa room.

3114 Oak St., Jacksonville, FL 32205. www.innatoakstreet.com. © **904/379-5525.** 6 units. $135–$180 suite. Rates include full breakfast. AE, MC, V. No young children accepted. **Amenities:** Coffee bar; spa. *In room:* A/C, TV/DVD, wine fridge, hair dryer, Wi-Fi.

Riverdale Inn ★★ In turn-of-the-20th-century Jacksonville, more than 50 mansions lined Riverside Avenue in an area known as "the Row." Today, sadly, only two of these Victorian-style homes remain. Riverdale Inn is one of them, and thank goodness for preservation. Ten period guest rooms are available with antique rugs and furniture, some featuring canopy and four-poster beds and fire-places, and all with free Wi-Fi connection for those who insist on the true retro-modern experience. Plush robes are found in all the bathrooms. For a nightcap, there's the **Gum Bunch Pub,** a cozy bar serving all sorts of spirits.

1521 Riverside Ave., Jacksonville, FL 32204. www.riverdaleinn.com. © **866/808-3400** or 904/354-5080. Fax 904/354-6859. 10 units. $109–$189 double; $278–$527 combination suites. Rates include full breakfast. AE, DISC, MC, V. **Amenities:** Restaurant; bar. *In room:* A/C, TV, hair dryer, Wi-Fi.

AT THE BEACHES

A dozen modest hotels line Jacksonville Beach's First Street, along the Atlantic. The **Comfort Inn Oceanfront,** 1515 N. First St., 2 blocks east of A1A (www.comfortinnjaxbeach.com; © **800/654-8776** or 904/241-2311; fax 904/249-3830), is one of the better values. Its rooms have balconies or screened patios, and guests can enjoy a large pool with four rock waterfalls and a palm-fringed deck, a secluded grotto whirlpool, an exercise room, a gift/sundries shop, and a multicourt sand volleyball park.

If you'd like to rent an old-fashioned cottage or a luxurious condominium in the affluent enclave of Ponte Vedra, contact **Ponte Vedra Club Realty,** 280 Ponte Vedra Blvd., Ponte Vedra Beach, FL 32082 (www.pvclubrealty.com; © **800/278-8171** or 904/285-6927; fax 904/285-5218). The company has more than 100 properties in its rental inventory, about 75% of them on the ocean. Its renters get a discount on use of facilities at the Lodge & Club at Ponte Vedra Beach, and at the Ponte Vedra Inn & Club (see below).

Casa Marina ★★ A member of the Historic Hotels of America, this beachfront resort may be old, but when it comes to service and style, it's completely new in a boutiquey sort of way. With just 25 rooms and suites, Casa Marina isn't the kind of place to go to if you feel like partying, making noise, or entertaining the kids. Rather, it's a romantic getaway, a popular place for weddings, and, most of all, period-style peace and quiet.

691 N. 1st St., Jacksonville Beach, FL 32250. www.casamarinahotel.com. © **904/270-0025.** Fax 904/270-1159. 25 units. $199–$349 double. AE, DC, DISC, MC, V. **Amenities:** Restaurant; 2 bars; outdoor pool; room service; spa; watersports equipment/rentals. *In room:* A/C, TV/DVD, fax, fridge, hair dryer, Internet access, minibar.

The Lodge & Club at Ponte Vedra Beach ★★★ This gorgeous two-story Mediterranean-style, Green Lodging–approved building is right on the beach. A stunning lobby is decked out in stone floors and hand-carved Tommy Bahama furniture. All 66 rooms are the epitome of high-end luxury, with gorgeous artwork, two-person settees recessed in front of windows looking onto the beach, and huge bathrooms with two-person tubs and separate showers. The "preferred" rooms and all of the suites also have gas fireplaces; ceiling fans hang from vaulted ceilings in the upstairs units. Some suites have marble-faced fireplaces and French doors. The beach has a couples-only pool and hot tub. Guests here have access to all the facilities at Ponte Vedra Inn & Club (see below). The Innlet Dining Room has gorgeous views, plus afternoon tea daily in the lounge, where a pianist performs by the fireplace on weekend nights. *Note:* There is resort fee of $18 per room for the bellman, doorman, and chambermaid, so *don't double tip.*

607 Ponte Vedra Blvd. (at Corona Rd.), Ponte Vedra Beach, FL 32082. www.pvresorts.com. ℂ **800/243-4304** or 904/273-9500. Fax 904/273-0210. 66 units. Winter $250–$300 double, $350–$400 suite; summer $290–$350 double, $390–$440 suite. Packages available. AE, DC, DISC, MC, V. **Amenities:** 2 restaurants; 2 bars; babysitting; bike rental; concierge; health club (w/ lap pool); Jacuzzi; 2 heated outdoor pools; room service; sauna; access to nearby spa; watersports equipment/rentals. *In room:* A/C, TV, fax, hair dryer, Internet access, kitchen (in suites).

One Ocean Resort & Spa ★★★ This hyperluxe eight-story beachfront hotel, formerly known as the Sea Turtle Inn, has received a major multimillion-dollar makeover and is incomparable in terms of service, style, and amenities. Need help unpacking or just aren't in the mood to do so at all? Let them do it for you. All rooms and suites feature ocean views and are decorated in shades of azure, sand, and pear, outfitted with custom-designed, plush One Ocean mattresses, plasma-screen TVs, and fantastic mood lighting. A world-class spa and gourmet restaurant, **Azurea,** which uses locally produced food and ingredients, not to mention a pristine stretch of sand and a great kids' club, make for a luxurious beach vacation.

1 Ocean Blvd. (at beach end of Atlantic Blvd.), Atlantic Beach, FL 32233. www.oneoceanresort.com. ℂ **800/874-6000** or 904/247-0305. Fax 904/247-0308. 193 units. $199–$349 double. AE, DC, DISC, MC, V. **Amenities:** Restaurant; 2 bars; babysitting; outdoor pool; room service; spa; watersports equipment/rentals. *In room:* A/C, TV/DVD, fax, fridge, hair dryer, Internet access, minibar.

Ponte Vedra Inn & Club ★★ This luxurious 300-acre Green Lodging oceanfront resort features 250 spacious and upscale guest rooms and suites housed in 10 low-rise buildings. All have patios or balconies overlooking either the Atlantic Ocean or the golf course; some have four-poster or sleigh beds. In addition to the Inn's two 18-hole golf courses, its excellent tennis center, and its fully equipped gym with four-lane Olympic pool, guests can use the resort facilities at the nearby Lodge & Club at Ponte Vedra Beach (see above). Between rounds of golf or games of tennis, guests can enjoy the on-site 28,000-square-foot spa, which provides fabulous treatments. Dining options include the resort's oceanfront Seahorse Grille, which features seafood fare in a casual environment. Shopping enthusiasts will appreciate the resort's several boutiques. *Note:* There is a nightly resort fee of $15 per room for the bellman, doorman, chambermaid, and valet-parking staff, so *don't double tip.*

200 Ponte Vedra Blvd. (off A1A), Ponte Vedra Beach, FL 32082. www.pontevedra.com. ℂ **800/234-7842** or 904/285-1111. Fax 904/285-2111. 250 units. Winter $200–$290 double, $320–$450 suite;

summer $220–$310 double, $340–$470 suite. Packages available. AE, DC, DISC, MC, V. **Amenities:** 3 restaurants; 3 bars; babysitting; bike rental; children's programs (summer only); concierge; 2 golf courses; health club; indoor pool; room service; spa; 15 tennis courts; watersports equipment/rentals. *In room:* A/C, TV, hair dryer, Internet access, kitchen (in some), minibar.

Sawgrass Marriott Golf Resort & Spa ★★★ One of the nation's largest golf resorts, this luxury destination in prestigious Ponte Vedra Beach is virtually surrounded by golf, including the Pete Dye–designed THE PLAYERS Stadium Course at TPC Sawgrass, home of the annual THE PLAYERS Championship in May. The resort was ranked the best golf resort in Florida and ninth best in the country by *Travel + Leisure Golf* magazine in 2008. Overlooking the 13th hole, the seven-story hotel sits beside one of the lakes that make the course so challenging. The view augments the gourmet fusion cuisine served in the resort's restaurants, including **Augustine Grille, 619 Ocean View,** and **V. Kelly's.** The guest rooms in the hotel are exceptional and have recently been refurbished with new furniture and decor. Fully equipped one- and two-bedroom "villa suites" (condominium apartments) on or near the golf course have large patios. A complimentary shuttle takes guests to the oceanside Cabana Beach Club for a day at the beach.

1000 PGA Tour Blvd. (off A1A, btw. U.S. 210 and J. Turner Butler Blvd.), Ponte Vedra Beach, FL 32082. www.sawgrassmarriott.com. © **800/228-9290** or 904/285-7777. Fax 904/285-0906. 508 units. $109–$179 double; $179–$769 suite. Golf packages available. AE, DC, DISC, MC, V. Valet parking $20; self-parking $10. **Amenities:** 7 restaurants; 4 bars; babysitting; bike rental; children's programs; concierge; concierge-level rooms; 8 golf courses; 2 health clubs; Jacuzzi; 4 outdoor pools (2 heated); limited room service; watersports equipment/rentals. *In room:* A/C, TV, hair dryer, Internet access, kitchen (in condos), minibar.

Where to Dine

The **Jacksonville and the Beaches Convention & Visitors Bureau** (p. 604) puts out an annual guide that contains a complete list of restaurants. For more choices, check listings in the "Shorelines" and "Go" sections of Friday's *Florida Times-Union* (**www.jacksonville.com**) and in *FolioWeekly* (**www.folio weekly.com**), the free local alternative paper available at restaurants, hotels, and nightspots all over town. I've concentrated here on restaurants in downtown Jacksonville and at the beaches.

IN DOWNTOWN JACKSONVILLE

Southbank Riverwalk is the city's up-and-coming mecca for eating out. In addition to B.B.'s, the area has riverfront branches of **Ruth's Chris Steak House,** in the Crowne Plaza Jacksonville Riverfront, 1201 Riverplace Blvd. (© **904/396-6200**); **Morton's The Steakhouse,** 1510 Riverplace Blvd. (© **904/399-3933**); and the **Wine Cellar,** 1314 Prudential Dr. (© **904/398-8989;** www.winecellarjax.com), which offers very good Continental fare and has a wine list to justify its name.

You'll also find a plethora of good cafes and restaurants in the San Marco Square and Avondale neighborhoods.

Don't forget that on the north side of the river, **Jacksonville Landing** has several full-service restaurants and a food court with outdoor seating.

B.B.'s ★★ NEW AMERICAN South of the Southbank Riverwalk, this bistro son of Biscotti's (see below) is one of the city's hottest restaurants. You'll find local yuppies congregating at the big marble-top bar on one side of the sometimes-noisy Art Deco dining room, especially during weekday "wine-downs," featuring beer and wine specials and discounted appetizers (the mozzarella bruschetta is a big hit), from 4 to 7pm. A small but inventive selection of sandwiches, salads, and pizzas is available all day. The nightly specials feature local seafood and run the gamut from blue corn tortilla crusted wahoo with saffron cream, and bacalao picholine-stuffed purple peppers, to the chargrilled filet with bacon shallot potato gratin, asparagus, boursin cheese, red-onion marmalade, toasted hazelnuts, and sauce bordelaise. Save room for the famous desserts. Saturday brunch sees the likes of yummy Benedict-style crab cakes and flaming Bananas Foster.

1019 Hendricks Ave. (btw. Prudential Dr. and Home St.). ✆ **904/306-0100.** www.bbs restaurant.com. Call for priority seating. Main courses $21–$29; sandwiches and salads $7–$12; pizzas $10–$12. AE, DC, DISC, MC, V. Mon–Thurs 11am–10:30pm; Fri 11am–midnight; Sat 10am–midnight (Sat brunch 10am–2pm).

Biscotti's ★★ 🍴 NEW AMERICAN/MEDITERRANEAN This brick-walled gem in the Avondale neighborhood might easily have come out of New York's East Village. Start your day here (except on Mon) with a pastry and cup of joe. At lunch and dinner, daily specials, such as pan-seared tuna or pork loin, are always fresh and beautifully presented. The Parmesan-crusted rainbow trout with short rib ragout, shiitake mushroom risotto, and wilted spinach is divine. But if that's too heavy for you, the huge and inventive salads are especially good: Try the Asian version, with chicken breast, orange slices, roasted peppers, and creamy sesame dressing. Pizzas, too, are served with wonderfully exotic and delicious toppings—ever try balsamic duck confit on your slice? And by all means, don't leave without sampling the wonderful desserts. On warm days, choose a tiny sidewalk table for great people-watching. *Note:* If the wait's too long here, other choices line these 2 blocks of St. Johns Avenue, ranging from a neighborhood diner to expensive haute cuisine.

3556 St. Johns Ave. (btw. Talbot and Ingleside aves.), Avondale. ✆ **904/387-2060.** www. biscottis.net. Main courses $10–$25; sandwiches and salads $6–$10; pizzas $7–$10. AE, DC, DISC, MC, V. Mon 11am–10pm; Tues–Thurs 7am–10pm; Fri 7am–midnight; Sat 8am–midnight; Sun 8am–3pm.

AT THE BEACHES

In addition to the Ragtime Tavern & Taproom (see below), you'll find several dining (and drinking) choices in the brick storefronts of **Town Center,** the old-time beach village at the end of Atlantic Boulevard.

Ragtime Tavern & Taproom ★★ SEAFOOD/CAJUN In the heart of Town Center, this lively sister of St. Augustine's A1A Ale Works (p. 600) and product of Gordon Biersch Brewery offers six hand-crafted brews, including a refreshing Pilsener known as Dolphin's Breath. You can imbibe at one of two bars on either end of the building. In between, a rabbit warren of dining rooms provides fine enough fare to keep it filled with local professionals, right through the cool winter months. Try the barbecued oysters or the Louisiana crawfish as an appetizer. For a main course, choose from blackened Cajun snapper or several other treatments of fish, shrimp, chicken, and pasta. Save room for New Orleans–style beignets for dessert. Also from the Big Easy, po' boy sandwiches are served at all hours. Good local bands play here Thursday through Sunday evenings.

207 Atlantic Blvd. (at 1st Ave.), Atlantic Beach. ✆ **904/241-7877.** www.ragtimetavern.com. Call ahead for priority seating. Main courses $13–$25; sandwiches and salads $6–$11. AE, DC, DISC, MC, V. Sun–Thurs 11am–10:30pm; Fri–Sat 11am–11pm. Bar stays open later.

Salt Life Food Shack ★ SEAFOOD Based on the Salt Life, a cult lifestyle of avid divers, surfers, fishermen, and beach bums in general, this hip, laid-back Jax Beach restaurant 3 blocks off the sand offers a menu of fresh fare, including hearty sandwiches (or, as they call them, "Hand Helds"), fresh rolled sushi, tacos, local fried shrimp, and our fave, Backyard Beer Can Chicken made with the poor-man-turned-hipster's beer of choice: Pabst Blue Ribbon. There's also beer, oysters, booze, and did we mention beer and booze? As their motto says, "Eat. Drink. And Be Salty."

1018 3rd St. N., Jacksonville Beach. © **904/372-4456.** Main courses $8–$15; sandwiches $6–$10. AE, DISC, MC, V. Sun–Tues 11am–10pm; Wed–Thurs 11am–11pm; Fri–Sat 11am–midnight.

Singleton's Seafood Shack ★★ 🍴 SEAFOOD This rustic fish camp has been serving every imaginable kind of fresh-off-the-boat seafood since 1969. And rustic it is, constructed primarily of unpainted, well-weathered plywood nailed to two-by-fours. Unlike most other fish camps that tend to overwork the deep-fryer, here the fried standbys, such as conch fritters, shrimp, clam strips, oysters, and squid, retain their seafood taste! Singleton's also offers other preparations such as blackened mahimahi and Cajun shrimp. Best bets at lunch are the fried shrimp or oyster po' boy sandwiches covered in crispy onion rings. At dinner, your Styrofoam plate will come stacked with a choice of sides such as black beans and rice, marvelous horseradishy coleslaw, fries, and hush puppies. There's a selection of chicken dishes, too, but stick to the seafood.

4728 Ocean St. (A1A, at St. Johns River Ferry landing), Mayport. © **904/246-4442.** Main courses $10–$20; sandwiches $5–$10. AE, DISC, MC, V. Sun–Thurs 10am–9pm; Fri–Sat 10am–10pm.

Jacksonville After Dark

In addition to the spots recommended below, check the listings in the "Shorelines" and "Go" sections of Friday's *Florida Times-Union* (**www.jacksonville.com**) and *FolioWeekly* (**www.folioweekly.com**), the free local alternative paper available all over town. Another source is **www.jaxevents.com**.

THE PERFORMING ARTS Jacksonville has plenty of seats for concerts, touring Broadway shows, dance companies, and big-name performers at the 73,000-seat **Jacksonville Municipal Stadium,** at East Duval and Haines streets (© **904/630-3900**); the 16,000-seat **Jacksonville Veterans Memorial Arena,** 300 A. Phillip Randolph Blvd. (© **904/630-3900** for information, or 904/353-3309 for tickets); the 4,400-seat **Times-Union Center for the Performing Arts,** 300 Water St., between Hogan and Pearl streets (© **904/630-3900**); and the revitalized **Ritz Theatre** (© **904/632-5555;** p. 606). A good website of event listings is **www.jaxevents.com**. Call or check the sources above for what's playing.

THE BAR SCENE You will find several libation options downtown at **Jacksonville Landing** including, if you must, a waterfront **Hooters** (© **904/356-5400**), plus free outdoor rock, blues, country, and jazz concerts every Friday and Saturday night, except during winter.

Out at Town Center, at the ocean end of Atlantic Boulevard, one of several popular spots is **Ragtime Tavern & Taproom** (above), where local groups play live jazz and blues Wednesday through Sunday nights. On weekends, especially, the place is really jumping and the crowd is young, but it's lively rather than rowdy. Across the street is the **Sun Dog,** 207

You'll probably hear "Freebird" or another Skynyrd favorite at Freebird Live.

Atlantic Blvd. (© **904/241-8221;** www.sundogjax.com), with nightly acoustic music and decent diner food. New to the Town Center in 2010 is **Whisky River,** 4850 Big Island Dr. (© **904/645-5571;** www.the whiskyriver.com), a brand-new restaurant and live music venue owned and operated by NASCAR star Dale Earnhardt, Jr. If these don't fit your mood, walk around Town Center until you find something you like.

Freebird Live, 200 N. 1st St. (© **904/246-2473;** www.freebirdlive. com), is a two-story homage to native Jacksonville band Lynyrd Skynyrd, run by late lead singer Ronnie Van Zant's widow and his daughter, and featuring live music 6 nights a week.

AMELIA ISLAND ★★

32 miles NE of Jacksonville; 192 miles NE of Orlando; 372 miles N of Miami

Paradise is found on the northernmost barrier island of Florida. With 13 beautiful miles of beach and a quaint Victorian town, Amelia Island is a charming getaway about a 45-minute drive northeast of downtown Jacksonville. This skinny barrier island, 18 miles long by 3 miles wide, has more in common with the Low Country of Georgia (across Cumberland Sound from here) and South Carolina. In fact, it's more like St. Simons Island in Georgia or Hilton Head Island in South Carolina than other beach resorts in Florida.

Amelia has five distinct personalities. First is its southern end, an exclusive real estate development built in a forest of twisted, moss-laden live oaks. Here you'll find world-class tennis and golfing at two of Florida's most luxurious resorts. Second is modest **American Beach,** founded in the 1930s so that African Americans would have access to the ocean in this then-segregated part of the country. Today it's a modest, predominantly black community tucked away among all that south-end wealth. Third is the island's middle, a traditional beach community with a mix of affordable motels, cottages, condominiums, and a seaside inn. Fourth is the historic bayside town of **Fernandina Beach ★★★**, which boasts a 50-square-block area of gorgeous Victorian, Queen Anne, and Italianate homes listed on the National Register of Historic Places. And fifth is lovely **Fort Clinch State Park,** which keeps developers from turning the island's northern end into more ritzy resorts.

The town of Fernandina Beach dates from the post–Civil War period, when Union soldiers who had occupied Fort Clinch began returning to the island. In the late 19th century, Amelia's timber, phosphate, and naval-stores industries boomed. Back then, the town was an active seaport, with 14 foreign consuls in residence. You'll see (and occasionally smell) the paper mills that still stand near the small seaport here. The island experienced another economic explosion in the 1970s and 1980s, when real estate developers built condominiums, cottages, and two big resorts on the island's southern end. In recent years, Fernandina Beach has seen another big boom, this time in bed-and-breakfast establishments.

Essentials

GETTING THERE The island is served by **Jacksonville International Airport** (p. 604), 12 miles north of Jacksonville's downtown and 43 miles from the island. Skirting the Atlantic in places, the scenic drive here from downtown Jacksonville is via A1A and the St. Johns River Ferry. The fast, four-lane way is via I-95 North and the Buccaneer Trail East (A1A).

VISITOR INFORMATION For information, contact the **Amelia Island–Fernandina Beach–Yulee Chamber of Commerce,** 102 Centre St. (P.O. Box 472), Fernandina Beach, FL 32035 (© **800/226-3542** or 904/277-0717; fax 904/261-6997; www.ameliaisland.org). The chamber's visitor center, in the rustic train station at the bay end of Centre Street, is open Monday through Friday from 9am to 5pm, and Saturday from 10am to 2pm.

GETTING AROUND There's no public transportation on this 13-mile-long island, so you'll need a vehicle. An informative and entertaining way to tour the historic district is a 30-minute ride with **Old Towne Carriage Company** (© **904/277-1555;** www.ameliacarriagetours.com), whose horse-drawn carriages leave from the waterfront on Centre Street between 6:30 and 9pm. Advance reservations are essential. Rides cost $15 for adults and $7.50 for kids 12 and under; private 30-minute tours are the same but with a minimum of $60 per ride, 1-hour tours with a minimum of $120 per ride. The carriage company closes from November to April, when the horses get a much-deserved rest.

Another excellent way to see the town is on a walking tour sponsored by the Amelia Island Museum of History (p. 623).

Hitting the Beach

Thanks to a reclamation project, the widest beaches here are at the exclusive enclave on the island's southern third. Even if you aren't staying at one of the swanky resorts, you can enjoy this section of beach at **Peters Point Beach Front Park,** on A1A, north of the Ritz-Carlton. The park has picnic shelters and restrooms. North of the resort, the beach has public-access points with free parking every quarter-mile or so. The center of activity is **Main Beach,** at the ocean end of Atlantic Avenue (A1A), with good swimming, restrooms, picnic shelters, showers, a food concession, a playground, and lots of free parking. This area is popular with families.

The beach at **Fort Clinch State Park** ★★, which wraps around the island's heavily forested northern end, is backed by rolling dunes and is filled with shells and driftwood. A jetty and pier jutting into Cumberland Sound are popular with anglers. There are showers and changing rooms at the pier. Elsewhere in the park, you might see an alligator—and certainly some of the 170 species of birds that live here—by hiking the Willow Pond nature trail. Rangers lead nature tours on the trail, usually beginning at 10:30am on Saturday. There are also 6 miles of off-road bike trails here. Construction on the remarkably well-preserved **Fort Clinch** began in 1847 on the northern tip of the island and was still underway when Union troops occupied it in 1862. The fort was abandoned shortly after the Civil War, except for a brief reactivation in 1898 during the Spanish-American War. Reenactors gather the first full weekend of each month to re-create how the Union soldiers lived in the fort in 1864 (including wearing their wool underwear, even in summer!). Rangers are on duty at the fort year-round, and they lead candlelight tours ($3 per person) on Friday and Saturday evenings during summer, beginning about an hour after sunset. You can arrange guided tours at other times for an extra fee. The park entrance is on Atlantic Avenue near the beach. Entrance fees are $6 per vehicle with up to eight occupants, $2 per pedestrian or bicyclist. Admission to the fort costs $2, free for children 4 and under. The park is open daily from 8am to sunset; the fort, daily from 9am to 5pm. For a schedule of tours and events, contact the park at 2601 Atlantic Ave., Fernandina Beach, FL 32034 (© **904/277-7274;** www.floridastateparks.org/fortclinch).

The park also has 62 **campsites**—some behind the dunes at the beach (no shade out there), most in a forest along the sound side. They cost $26 per night,

Fort Clinch State Park offers beaches, beautiful scenery, hiking, and nature tours.

Amelia Island

HOTELS
Elizabeth Pointe Lodge **2**
Fairbanks House **13**
Florida House Inn **11**
Hampton Inn & Suites **9**
Omni Amelia Island Plantation **4**
Ritz-Carlton Amelia Island **3**

ATTRACTIONS
Amelia Island Museum of History **14**
Fort Clinch State Park **1**

RESTAURANTS/NIGHTLIFE
Beech Street Grill **12**
Brett's Waterway Café **5**
Frisky Mermaid Bar & Grill **11**
Joe's 2nd Street Bistro **10**
Marina Restaurant **8**
Palace Saloon **6**
Salt 29 South **7**

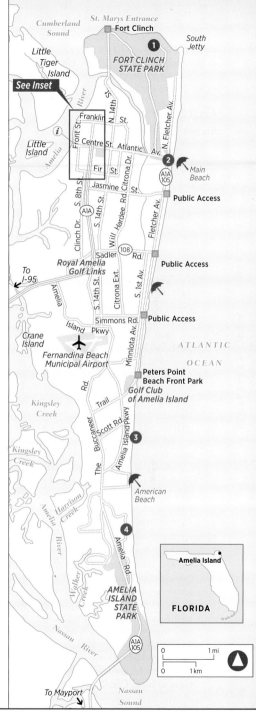

621

including tax. You can reserve a site up to 11 months in advance (a very good idea in summer) by calling © 800/326-3521 or going to www.reserveamerica.com.

Pets on leashes are allowed on all of the island's public beaches and in Fort Clinch State Park.

Outdoor Activities

BIKING Cumberland Sound Ferry (© 877/264-9972; www.ameliariver cruises.com) has been designated an official connection as part of the East Coast Greenway, a route from Maine to Key West for cyclists. The ferry facilitates day trips and overnight visits and eliminates the need for a 35-mile trip by car on narrow two-lane roads without shoulders for cyclists. See below.

BOATING, FISHING, SAILING & KAYAKING The **Amelia Island Charter Boat Association** (© 800/229-1682 or 904/261-2870), at Tiger Point Marina on 14th Street, north of the historic district (though the boats dock at Centre St.), can help arrange deep-sea fishing charters, party-boat excursions, and dolphin-watching and sightseeing cruises. Other charter boats also dock at Fernandina Harbor Marina, downtown at the foot of Centre Street.

Windward Sailing School, based at Fernandina Harbor Marina, 3977 First Ave. (© 904/261-9125; www.windwardsailing.com), will teach you to skipper your boat; it also has charters and boat rentals. Call for details and reservations.

You have to be careful in the currents, but the backwaters here are great for kayaking, whether you're a beginner or a pro. However, you'll have to travel just off the island to do it. Ray and Jody Hetchka's **Kayak Amelia** ★★ (© 888/305-2925 or 904/251-0016; www.kayakamelia.com) is based near Talbot Island State Park (technically in Jacksonville) and offers beginner and advanced-level trips on back bays, creeks, and marshes. Half-day trips go for about $55 to $60 per person. Kayak and canoe rentals go from $32 to $62. Reservations are required.

A fabulous company that takes you along the salt marshes, wilderness beaches, and historic riverbanks of Amelia, Fernandina Beach, and Cumberland Island, Georgia, where wild horses roam the unfettered beaches, **Amelia River Cruises and Cumberland Sound Ferry** (© 877/264-9972; www.ameliarivercruises.com) offers all sorts of tours ranging from $20 to $26 for adults, $18 to $24 for seniors, and $14 to $20 for children 12 and under.

ECO-TOURS EcoMotion Tours (© 904/251-9477; www.ecomotiontours.com) provides Segway excursions through Florida's state park trails on Fort George Island and Little Talbot Island. The guided tours will take you through the sandy paths of these two protected islands and through the lush vegetation, where you'll see butterflies, tortoises, dunes, and waterside bluffs. During winter months they conduct a custom tour of Little Talbot Island, a 2-hour trip through sandy state park trails and a rarely found, totally undeveloped beach on the Atlantic. Tours are $55 to $85 per person and highly recommended.

For a high(er)-tech way to explore Amelia Island's most popular sites and for those who own their own GPS systems, check out **The Amelia Island Geocaching Challenge,** www.geocacheamelia.com, which will guide you around by way of a very cool GPS-based treasure hunt.

GOLF If you're not staying in a resort with a golf course (see "Where to Stay," below, and note these courses can be extremely expensive), try the 36-hole **Amelia Links** (𝄐 904/261-6161; www.omniameliaisland plantation.com), featuring two signature courses designed by Pete Dye and Bobby Weed at the Omni Amelia Island Plantation, where greens fees range from $150 to $180 per person depending on the time and season. The **Long Point ★★** course, a mind-blowingly beautiful Tom Fazio–designed 18-holer, has two par-3s in a row bordering the ocean. Fees are high—from $175 to $200 depending on the time and season. Or play the older and less expensive 27-hole **Fernandina Municipal Golf Course** (𝄐 904/277-7370; www.fernandinabeachgolfclub. com), where prices are $18 to $44.

Take a Segway tour through some of Florida's state park trails.

For course information go to www.golf.com or www.floridagolfing.com; or you can call the **Florida Sports Foundation** (𝄐 850/488-8347) or **Florida Golfing** (𝄐 866/833-2663).

HORSEBACK RIDING You can go riding on the beach with the **Kelly Seahorse Ranch** (𝄐 904/491-5166; www.kellyranchinc.com), on the southernmost tip of Amelia Island within the Amelia Island State Park. The cost is $60 per person for a 1-hour ride; the ranch is open daily from 8am to 6pm. Reservations are required. *Note:* Riders must be 13 or older, at least 4½ feet tall, and weigh less than 230 pounds. No experience is necessary.

TENNIS Ranked among the nation's top 50 by *Tennis* magazine, the Omni Amelia Island Plantation's **Racquet Park** (𝄐 904/261-6161; www.aipfl. com/Tennis/tennis.htm), with 23 Har-Tru tennis courts (naturally shaded by a canopy of gorgeous trees), hosts many professional tournaments, including the annual Bausch & Lomb Championships, and is home to the renowned Gunterman Tennis School.

An Old Jail Turned Historic Museum

Amelia Island Museum of History ★ Housed in the old Nassau County jail, built of brick in 1878, this award-winning local museum explains Amelia Island's history, from Timucuan Indian times through its possession by France, Spain, Great Britain, the United States, and the Confederacy. Only an upstairs photo gallery is open for casual inspection, so plan to take the 1-hour, 15-minute docent-led tour of the newly remodeled ground floor if you want to get the most out of this museum.

The museum also offers excellent **walking tours** of historic Centre Street on Thursday and Friday from September to June. These depart at 3pm from the chamber of commerce (p. 619) and cost $10 for adults, $5 for students. You can't make a reservation; just show up. Longer tours of the 50-square-block historic district can be arranged with 24-hour notice; these cost $10 per person with a minimum of four persons required. We especially recommend the ghost tour or the pub crawl that leaves Thursday evenings at 5:30pm to tour four of the small town's most popular, notorious, or otherwise historic pubs and bars. Cost is $25 per person (21 and over only) and reservations for this one are a must.

233 S. 3rd St. (btw. Beech and Cedar sts.). ℂ **904/261-7378.** www.ameliamuseum.org. Admission $7 adults, $4 students. Tours $10 adults, $5 students. Mon–Sat 10am–4pm. Tours Mon–Sat 11am and 2pm.

Where to Stay

More than two dozen of the town's charming Victorian and Queen Anne houses have been restored and turned into B&Bs. For a complete list, contact the chamber of commerce (p. 619) or the **Amelia Island Bed & Breakfast Association** (ℂ **888/277-0218;** www.ameliaislandinns.com). You can tour all the B&Bs during an island-wide open house the first weekend in December.

Your best camping option here is **Fort Clinch State Park** (p. 620).

Note: Rates are subject to an 11% hotel tax (7% sales tax, 4% bed tax).

Elizabeth Pointe Lodge ★★ This three-story, Nantucket-style shingled beauty sits overlooking the beach on Amelia Island. Built in 1991 by David and Susan Caples, it has big-paned windows that look out from the comfy library (with stone fireplace) and a dining room to an expansive front porch and the surf beyond. Antiques, reproductions, and other touches lend the 20 rooms in the main building a turn-of-the-20th-century cottage ambience. All have oversize tubs. The recently restored Ocean Lodge next door has four large guest rooms in a West Indies motif, and the two-bedroom, two-bathroom Miller Cottage is great for small groups.

98 S. Fletcher Ave. (just south of Atlantic Ave.), Fernandina Beach, FL 32034. www.elizabeth pointelodge.com. ℂ **800/772-3359** or 904/277-4851. Fax 904/277-6500. 25 units, including 1 cottage. $185–$395 double; $450 cottage. Rates include full seaside buffet breakfast, parking, and wine hour. Packages available. AE, DISC, MC, V. **Amenities:** Bike rentals; room service; Wi-Fi. *In room:* A/C, TV, hair dryer.

Fairbanks House ★★ Boasting all the amenities and almost as much privacy as a first-class hotel, this superbly refurbished, romantic 1885 Italianate home is a top B&B choice in the historic district. As gorgeous as it is, it used to be known as "Fairbanks's Folly," because of its standout decor. Many rooms and all of the cottages offer private entrances for guests who prefer not to walk through the main house. Room no. 3 is one of the finest units, with a private entrance, a sitting room, a plush king-size bed, period antiques, and fresh flowers. The two-bedroom Tower Suite, occupying the entire top floor, has plenty of room to spread out, plus 360-degree views and its own whirlpool tub. Five other units here have whirlpool tubs as well. The Fairbanks also has a great pool. No smoking is permitted, indoors or out. Speaking of outdoors, all landscaping has been renovated to eco-friendly standards and includes a new butterfly garden.

227 S. 7th St. (btw. Beech and Cedar sts.), Fernandina Beach, Amelia Island, FL 32034. www. fairbankshouse.com. ℂ **888/891-9882** or 904/277-0500. 12 units, including 3 cottages.

$175–$265 double; $265–$365 cottage; $395 tower suite. Rates include full breakfast and evening social hour (beverages and hors d'oeuvres). Packages available. AE, DISC, MC, V. No children 11 and under. **Amenities:** Free use of bikes; pool. *In room:* A/C, TV, fridge, hair dryer, kitchen (in some rooms and cottage), Wi-Fi.

Florida House Inn ★ 🍴 Built in 1857 by one of Florida's founding fathers, David Yulee, this clapboard Victorian building is Florida's oldest operating hotel. Ulysses S. Grant stayed here, as did Cuban revolutionary José Martí. Rockefellers and Carnegies broke bread at the boardinghouse-style dining room now called the **Frisky Mermaid Bar & Grill** that still provides family-style traditional Southern fare, live bluegrass music, and old-school Carolina shag dancing! You can rock away on the two gingerbread-trimmed front verandas or on a back porch overlooking a brick courtyard shaded by a huge oak tree. The 18 rooms in the original building, all mostly up to modern standards, are loaded with antiques. Most have working fireplaces; some have claw-foot tubs. One of these has log-cabin walls, the others are done in country or Victorian style. Some have fireplaces and Jacuzzi tubs. The 10-room Carriage House has a variety of bedrooms, including a pair of two-bedroom efficiency apartments.

22 S. 3rd St. (btw. Centre and Ash sts.), Fernandina Beach, FL 32034. www.floridahouseinn.com. © **800/258-3301** or 904/261-3300. Fax 904/277-3831. 28 units. $99–$249 double; $299–$349 carriage house. Rates include full breakfast. AE, DISC, MC, V. Pets accepted ($15–$25 nightly fee). **Amenities:** Restaurant; bar. *In room:* A/C, TV, hair dryer, Wi-Fi.

Hampton Inn & Suites ★★ A Hampton Inn that garners two stars, you ask? It's true. One of the most unusual Hampton Inns I've ever seen, although there's only one building, the exterior looks like a row of different structures, all in the styles and sherbet hues of the Victorian storefronts lining Centre Street. Wooden floors taken from an old Jacksonville church, slatted door panels evocative of 19th-century schooners, and many other touches add to the Victorian ambience inside. About half of the guest rooms are near the top of the romance scale, with king-size beds, gas fireplaces, and two-person whirlpool tubs. The standard suites are large enough for families, and the other rooms are adequately equipped for business travelers. About a third of the units have balconies. Those higher up on the west side have fine views over the river and marshes. The only drawback: Trains slowly rumble by the west side a few times a day.

29 S. 2nd St. (btw. Centre and Ash sts.), Fernandina Beach, FL 32034. www.hamptoninnand suites.net. © **800/426-7866** or 904/491-4911. Fax 904/491-4910. 122 units. $119–$209 double. Rates include extensive breakfast buffet. AE, DC, DISC, MC, V. **Amenities:** Babysitting; exercise room; Jacuzzi; pool. *In room:* A/C, TV, fridge, hair dryer, Wi-Fi.

Omni Amelia Island Plantation ★★ An immense state-designated Green Lodging property (nontoxic pest control, clean and green housekeeping, re-sortwide recycling, smart HVAC in the resort that shuts off when sliding-glass doors open and returns to a preset temperature when the guest leaves the room for an extended period), this resort occupies 1,350 lush beachfront acres of manicured golf greens, bike trails, and a breathtaking coastal wilderness of marshes and lagoons. The resort is so spread out that a free tram runs around the grounds every 15 minutes. The Plantation is known for its outstanding sports offerings (see "Golf" and "Tennis," above) and all golf courses are Audubon International Certified sanctuaries. A 20-room, all-natural spa also features a meditation garden, plus nontoxic, paraben-free products and services. The eight-story,

Mediterranean-style resort offers 249 spacious, upscale rooms. Traditionally furnished, the rooms boast oceanview patios or balconies. Other accommodations here are one- to three-bedroom privately owned condominium apartments (or "villas," in Florida-speak). All but a few have balconies or patios. All have fully equipped kitchens. For larger accommodations, **The Villas of Amelia Island Plantation Resort** offer one-, two-, and three-bedroom villas. The **Ocean Grill** restaurant serves exceptional and expensive contemporary regional cuisine, accompanied by stunning ocean views. Other restaurants and nightspots are also on the property. ***Note:*** You can Segway your way around the massive resort. Prices for Segway transportation devices range from $40 for a 30-minute kids' excursion to $80 for a 1½-hour safari tour of the property. All tours include orientation, coaching, and tour guides. In 2010, Omni Hotels & resorts acquired the resort with plans to expand development with approximately 125 additional guest rooms and suites.

6800 First Coast Hwy., Amelia Island, FL 32034-3000. www.omniameliaislandplantation.com. ✆ **800/834-4900** or 904/261-6161. Fax 904/277-5945. 573 units (249 oceanfront guest rooms plus 324 1-, 2-, and 3-bedroom villas). $99–$409 double; $129–$949 villa. Packages available. AE, DC, DISC, MC, V. Valet parking $15; self-parking free. **Amenities:** 9 restaurants; 5 bars; babysitting; bike rental; age-specific youth programs; concierge; 4 golf courses; health club; Jacuzzi; heated indoor pool and 20 outdoor pools (1 heated); limited room service; sauna; spa; 23 tennis courts. *In room:* A/C, TV, hair dryer, kitchen (in condos), minibar (in resort only), Wi-Fi.

Ritz-Carlton Amelia Island ★★★ ☺ Sprawling over 13 acres of stunning beachfront, the Ritz offers slightly glitzier accommodations than its neighbor, the Omni Amelia Island Plantation. While some may like the fact that it's perfectly acceptable to walk through the lobby of this Ritz in shorts (it's downright relaxed in this way), others may find the service and surroundings not as polished as they have experienced in other Ritz-Carltons. The kids' program makes well-heeled families feel just as much at home as the conventioneers who flock here to meet and make use of the extensive recreational facilities, including a beautiful 18-hole championship golf course. The spacious guest rooms—all with oceanfront or oceanview balconies or patios—have many amenities, such as scales, cosmetic mirrors, and phones in their marble bathrooms. The playfully gourmet **Salt** ★★★, the longest-running AAA Five Diamond restaurant in Florida, leads the hotel's restaurants, with an ocean view that accompanies exceptional seafood and seasonal dishes by Chef Richard Gras; the restaurant is named after the 30-plus international salts the kitchen collects. You could easily plan your stay around one of their fantastic, hands-on cooking classes. Check the website for dates. There's also a state-of-the-art **spa.**

4750 Amelia Island Pkwy., Amelia Island, FL 32034. www.ritzcarlton.com. ✆ **800/241-3333** or 904/277-1100. Fax 904/277-1145. 444 units. $199–$439 coastalview double; $409–$629 oceanview suite. Golf, tennis, and other packages available. AE, DC, DISC, MC, V. Valet parking $17. **Amenities:** 5 restaurants; 3 bars; babysitting; bike rental; children's programs; concierge; concierge-level rooms; golf course; fitness center; heated indoor and outdoor pools; room service; spa; 9 tennis courts; watersports equipment/rentals. *In room:* A/C, TV, hair dryer, high-speed Internet access, minibar.

Where to Dine

You'll find several restaurants, pubs, and snack shops along Centre Street, between the bay and 8th Street (A1A), in Fernandina Beach's old town. Two good dining options stand opposite the Hampton Inn & Suites on South 2nd Street, between Centre and Ash streets: the hip **Joe's 2nd Street Bistro** (© 904/321-2558; www.joesbistro.com) and the more formal but still relaxed **Le Clos** (© 904/261-8100; www.leclos.com). Joe's serves fine international fare in an old store, while Le Clos provides provincial French fare in a charming old house. Both are open for dinner only; reservations are recommended. Drop by during the day for a look at the menus posted outside each.

And don't forget **Salt** at the Ritz-Carlton Amelia Island (see above); a world-class four-course "Chef's Adventure" menu is worth the $80 per-person price tag ($120 per person paired with wines).

Lastly, the **Florida House Inn's Frisky Mermaid** (p. 625) serves everything from all-you-can-eat fried chicken and fried pork chops to pizzas and Thai food. The restaurant also features live blues, bluegrass, and local singers every night.

Beech Street Grill ★★ NEW AMERICAN The cosmopolitan-chic Beech Street Grill pleases all palates with a rich menu of fish, chicken, and meat choices, including seasonal game dishes such as roasted venison loin in a black-currant sauce with sweet-potato-and-onion hash. Nightly fish specialties are always exceptional. The crab stuffed shrimp with roasted corn cream, collards, and Falls Mills stone-ground grits cake is one of several stellar Southern-accented entrees. Housed in a century-old landmark home and in a newer wing to one side, the five dining rooms have a lively atmosphere. The upstairs section features a pianist. A well-known fact on the island is that Beech Street Grill catered the secret wedding of the late John F. Kennedy, Jr., and Carolyn Bessette when they married on nearby Cumberland Island, Georgia.

801 Beech St. (at 8th St./A1A), Fernandina Beach. © **904/277-3662.** www.beechstreetgrill.com. Reservations strongly recommended. Main courses $17–$32. AE, DC, DISC, MC, V. Daily 6–10pm.

Brett's Waterway Cafe SEAFOOD/STEAK You'll pay for the view, but this friendly waterfront cafe at the foot of Centre Street is the only place in town to dine while watching the boats coming and going on the river—and to sip a drink (try one of the excellent martinis) while watching the sun setting over the marshes between here and the mainland. In fine weather, grab a table out by the docks. One of the best dishes is Carolina BBQ grilled shrimp with Anson Mills cheese grits, collard greens, and Vidalia onion threads, and the fried-green-tomatoes béarnaise sauce with goat cheese are an addictive starter. The nightly fresh-fish specials are well prepared. Steaks and chops are also served.

1 S. Front St. (at Centre St., on the water), Fernandina Beach. © **904/261-2660.** www.bretts waterwaycafe.com. Main courses $14–$28; sandwiches $10–$12. AE, MC, V. Mon–Sat 11:30am–2:30pm and 5:30–9:30pm; Sun 5:30–9:30pm.

Joe's 2nd Street Bistro ★★★ NEW AMERICAN In the heart of the Fernandina Beach historic district is this restored 1900s home that's filled with flavor. The island-inspired dining room features a brick fireplace, and upstairs is a private dining room, but I suggest grabbing a table out on the covered porch. A meal here is almost like eating in a chef's home, a quaint and delectable experience, to say the least. Try the grilled leg of lamb rubbed with black pepper, garlic, and herbs and served with tomato mint salsa, potatoes, and "cotton fried onions." Yowza! For dessert, the apple bread pudding kicks that part of your body where perhaps the calories will end up. It rocks. Joe's rocks. Don't miss it. Eat at Joe's.

14 S 2nd St. (at Front St.), Fernandina Beach. ℭ **904/321-2558.** www.joesbistro.com. Reservations recommended. Main courses $15–$30. AE, DC, MC, V. Daily 6–9:30pm.

Marina Restaurant ⚓ AMERICAN Occupying a brick store built in the 1880s, this quintessential small-town restaurant has been feeding low-country fare to locals since 1965. A lot of the seafood here is fried and broiled, but you can order grouper topped with scallops and a garlicky wine sauce. Budgeters love the $10-and-under list of Southern favorites, such as country-fried steak and breaded veal cutlet. Meatloaf with tomato-and-basil gravy, stuffed peppers with a Greek-style tomato sauce, and other lunch specials come with three fresh country-style vegetables, which are themselves worth the price of the meal. In fact, stick with the less expensive items as the pricier entrees aren't worth the money. Hearty breakfasts feature eggs, omelets, French toast, and hot cakes.

101 Centre St. (at Front St.), Fernandina Beach. ℭ **904/261-5310.** Main courses $10–$30; sandwiches $5–$10; breakfast $3–$10. DC, MC, V. Daily 7–10am and 11:30am–9pm.

29 South ★★★ NEW AMERICAN Chef Scotty Schwartz presides over this chic neighborhood bistro where nothing is ordinary. Signature items include lobster corn dogs with spicy horseradish ketchup spiked with Ketel One vodka, sweet tea–brined DelKat Family Farm pork chop on macaroni gratin with warm blackberry preserves, and grilled heart of romaine salad with Maytag blue vinaigrette with bacon and toasted walnuts. You get the idea. Best of all, it's not a trendy snobby spot but a casual eatery that manages to turn everything into something extraordinary. Even coffee and doughnuts are served here—as glazed doughnut bread pudding with butterscotch drizzle and mocha ice cream.

29 S. 3rd St., Fernandina Beach. ℭ **904/277-7919.** www.29southrestaurant.com. Reservations strongly suggested. Main courses $18–$32; sandwiches $13–$20. AE, MC, V. Sun 10am–2pm; Tues–Sat 11:30am–2:30pm; Mon–Thurs 5:30–9:30pm; Fri–Sat 5:30–10pm.

After Dark

Palace Saloon ★ AMERICAN The state's oldest continuously operating drinking establishment, the Palace Saloon is a must before or after dinner if but for a drink and to drink in the ambience of inlaid mosaic floors, embossed tin ceiling, and murals depicting scenes from Shakespeare to Dickens. While the Saloon used to serve food, they now only cater to, as they say, "those on a liquid diet." Nightly entertainment from DJs to live bands is good, but not nearly as enthralling as the history of the place. It was originally constructed as a haberdashery in 1878 until 1903, when hats were replaced with booze, even on the very last night before Prohibition, when the Saloon was the last to close, staying open until midnight and grossing $60,000 in a single day. Incidentally, the Saloon was also the first hard liquor bar to begin serving Coca-Cola, around 1905.

117 Centre St. (at Front St.), Fernandina Beach. ℭ **904/491-3332.** www.thepalacesaloon.com. AE, DC, MC, V. Daily noon–2am.

14

NORTHWEST FLORIDA:
THE PANHANDLE

T he Florida Panhandle is to the state as Jan Brady of TV's *The Brady Bunch* is to her family. Cindy, the cute younger sister, could represent Orlando and Tampa, with their amusements. South and Southwest Florida could be Marcia, the gorgeous older sister whom everyone fawns over. Then there's the misunderstood, underestimated, Jan—in this case, Northwest Florida, also known as the Panhandle—always getting the shaft, even though she has great qualities, if only people took the time to discover them. For the Panhandle, this is a particular shame, as it is a dynamic, uncommonly beautiful part of Florida.

If you like beaches, you'll love the Panhandle, the land of the two-way sun, which runs east to west along the Gulf of Mexico and, therefore, has sunrises *and* sunsets. It was once known—and sometimes erroneously still is known—as the Redneck Riviera (thanks to a steady crowd from Georgia, Alabama, and Louisiana), a refreshing change from the glitz and glamour oozing from South Florida. The Panhandle, while still rugged in a sexy, Marlboro Man kind of way, has slowly shed that reputation with the emergence of upscale residential developments and boutique hotels.

Three other reasons to love this zone: water as turquoise as colored contact lenses, smaller crowds than at other Florida beaches, and ghost-white sand so talcumlike that it squeaks when you walk on it. The sand in these parts is brilliantly white because, over thousands of years, quartz particles were washed downstream from the eroding Appalachian Mountains and pummeled into grains as fine and soft as baby powder before finally landing at their resting place: under the towels of the three million sunbathers who flock here every year. Speaking of walking, you can, because some 100 miles of these incomparable sands are protected in state parks and the Gulf Islands National Seashore.

Pensacola, Destin, Fort Walton Beach, and Panama City Beach are summertime meccas for families, couples, and singles from the aforementioned adjoining states—a geographic proximity that lends this area the languid charm of the Deep South. Indeed, Southern specialties such as collard greens and cheese grits appear frequently on menus here.

And so people don't ignore the 227 miles of coastline on Northwest Florida's Gulf Coast, a marketing plan came up with the nifty, collective moniker of THE Beach to represent Escambia, Santa Rosa, Okaloosa, Walton, Bay, Gulf, and Franklin counties, all of which exude that small-beach-town charm that is strictly preserved and staunchly thwarting extinction.

But there's more to the northwestern Panhandle than beaches and Southern charm. Record catches of grouper, amberjack, snapper, mackerel, cobia, sailfish, wahoo, tuna, and blue marlin have made Destin one of the world's fishing capitals. In the interior, near Pensacola, the Blackwater, Shoal, and Yellow rivers teem

PREVIOUS PAGE: **The waves wash gently over the beach at St. George Island State Park, a barrier island just off Apalachicola.**

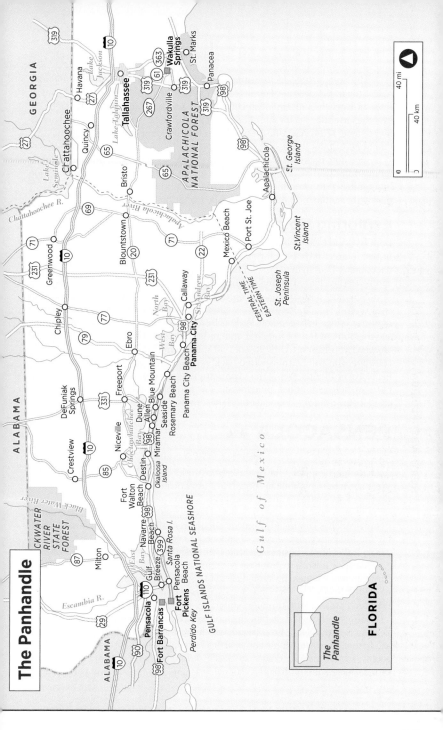

The Panhandle

GEORGIA

ALABAMA

Gulf of Mexico

FLORIDA

The Panhandle

with bass, bream, and catfish and also allow for some of Florida's best canoeing and kayaking adventures.

The area is steeped in history as well. Rivaling St. Augustine as Florida's oldest town, picturesque Pensacola preserves a heritage derived from Spanish, French, English, and American conquests. Famous for its oysters, Apalachicola saw the invention of the air conditioner. Tallahassee, seat of the state government since 1824, has a host of 19th-century buildings, including the majestic Old State Capitol.

One note to those traveling the entire state: While "season" in South Florida tends to fall in the winter months, due to the Panhandle's geographic location and tendency to get chilly or downright cold during the winter, its "season" is during the summer, so hotel rates will be higher during that time.

Exploring Northwest Florida by Car

Both I-10 and U.S. 98 link Tallahassee and Pensacola, some 200 miles apart. The fastest route is I-10, but all you'll see is a huge pine forest divided by two strips of concrete. Plan to take U.S. 98 instead, a scenic excursion in itself. Although it can be traffic clogged during summer, U.S. 98 has some beautiful stretches out in the country, particularly as it skirts the bay east of Apalachicola and the Gulf west of Port St. Joe. It's also lovely along skinny Okaloosa Island and across the high-rise bridge between Fort Walton Beach and Destin. From the bridge, you'll see the brilliant hue of the Gulf and understand why this is called the Emerald Coast. If you turn off U.S. 98 onto 30A, a magnificent 20-mile drive along the coastline, you will be transported back in time to the pre–Golden Arches–lined highways of Florida. Along this scenic stretch, you'll see not only sand and surf but also, believe it or not, pine forests, saw palmettos, the Choctawhatchee Bay, and Hogtown Bayou, a magnet for fiery sunsets.

PENSACOLA ★★

191 miles W of Tallahassee; 354 miles W of Jacksonville

A charming blend of Old Spanish brickwork, colonial French balconies, and Victorian mansions built by British and American lumber barons, Pensacola is worthy of its motto, "City of Five Flags." However, it's much more than pretty buildings and a nice vibe. Thanks to the Pensacola Downtown Improvement Board, work has continued to progress on the revitalization of downtown, promoting the full occupancy of once-abandoned 125-year-old buildings and the emergence of downtown businesses, stores, historic theaters, restaurants, and bars.

West of town, the National Museum of Naval Aviation at the U.S. Naval Air Station celebrates the storied past of U.S. Navy and Marine Corps pilots who trained at Pensacola. The Blue Angels are based here, and they demonstrate the high-tech present with thrilling exhibitions of precision flying.

Also on the naval station, historic Fort Barrancas looks across the bay to Perdido Key and Santa Rosa Island, which reach out like narrow pincers to form the harbor. Powdery white-sand beaches beckon sun-and-surf lovers to the Gulf shores, which include Pensacola Beach, a family-oriented resort, and most of Florida's share of Gulf Islands National Seashore, home of historic Fort Pickens.

HOTELS
New World Inn **10**
Solé Inn and Suites **3**
Springhill Guesthouse **2**

RESTAURANTS
Dharma Blue **8**
Five Sisters Blues Café **1**
McGuire's Irish Pub **5**
Wintzell's Oyster House **6**

ATTRACTIONS
Civil War Soldiers Museum **13**
Historic Pensacola Village **9**
Pensacola Civic Center **4**
Pensacola Historical
  Museum **11**
Pensacola Museum of Art **12**
Vietnam Memorial **7**

Downtown Pensacola

North Hill
Preservation District

Post
Office

Palafox
Historic District

Seville
Historic District

Government
Center

Historic
Pensacola Village

Municipal
Auditorium

Pensacola
Port

Sanders
Beach

FLORIDA

Pensacola

0   1/4 mi
0   .25 km

Essentials

GETTING THERE Pensacola Gulf Coast Regional Airport, 12th Avenue, at
Airport Road (© **850/436-5005;** www.flypensacola.com), underwent an
$80-million renovation in 2009 and is served by **AirTran, Continental,
Delta, United, Northwest,** and **US Airways.** In 2010, the airport intro-
duced direct flights to Chicago, Miami, and Washington, D.C., via United,
American Eagle, and US Airways, respectively.

Alamo, Avis, Budget, Dollar, Enterprise, Hertz, and National have
rental-car operations here.

Taxis wait outside the modern terminal. Fares are $2 at flag drop and
$2.25 for each additional mile.

The **Amtrak** (☎ 800/872-7245; www.amtrak.com) transcontinental *Sunset Limited* stops in Pensacola at 980 E. Heinberg St.

VISITOR INFORMATION The **Pensacola Visitor Information Center,** 1401 E. Gregory St., Pensacola, FL 32501 (☎ 800/874-1234 or 850/434-1234; fax 850/432-8211; www.visitpensacola.com), gives away helpful information about the Greater Pensacola area, including maps of self-guided tours of the historic districts, and sells a detailed street map of the area. The office is at the mainland end of the Pensacola Bay Bridge and is open daily from 8am to 5pm (until 4pm Sat–Sun Oct–Mar).

For information specific to the beach, contact the **Pensacola Beach Chamber of Commerce,** 735 Pensacola Beach Blvd. (P.O. Box 1174), Pensacola Beach, FL 32561 (☎ 800/635-4803 or 850/932-1500; fax 850/932-1551; www.visitpensacolabeach.com). The chamber's offices and visitor center are on the right as you drive onto Santa Rosa Island across the Bob Sikes Bridge. It's open daily from 9am to 5pm.

Northwest Florida's Gulf Coast has been rebranded by the tourism honchos as THE Beach, consisting of 227 miles of white-sand beaches stretching from Pensacola to Carrabelle. Check out **www.thebeachfla.com**, which offers comprehensive information on everything worth seeing and doing in Escambia, Santa Rosa, Okaloosa, Walton, Bay, Gulf, and Franklin counties.

GETTING AROUND For a trolley tour around town, check out **Beach Bum Trolley** (☎ 850/941-2876; www.beachbumtrolley.com), which operates one to eight tours of all the historic sights. Prices range from as low as $18 per person for a 50-minute narrated tour of Pensacola, to $150 per person for a 7-hour trolley tour and a full day of deep-sea fishing. To see the historic sights during the warmer months, take the **Beach Trolley,** which leaves every 30 minutes from Portofino Boardwalk and runs to Fort Pickens Gate on the west side of the island, and to Portofino Island Resort & Spa on the east side. The trolley is free from Memorial Day weekend to Labor Day weekend, Friday 5pm to midnight, Saturday noon to midnight, and Sunday 5 to 10pm. New in 2010: **Pensacola Trolley Tours** (☎ 850/941-4363; www. pensacolatrolleytours.com), 90-minute narrated tours of historic districts on a replica 1880s streetcar. Prices are $16 for adults; $14 for students, seniors, and military; and free for kids 12 and under. For a more swashbuckling look at Pensacola, **The Five Flags Trolley Company** (☎ 850/435-0914; www.piratetrolley.com) offers pirate-themed tours on vintage red trolleys complete with treasure hunts, pirate fare, and tour guides in costume. Cost is $20 for adults, $5 for kids 10 and under.

> ## A Friendly Feud
>
> Native Americans left pottery shards and artifacts in the dunes in Pensacola centuries before Tristan de Luna arrived with a band of Spanish colonists in 1559. Although his settlement lasted only 2 years, modern Pensacolans claim that their town is the oldest in North America. Pensacola actually dates its permanence from a Spanish colony established here in 1698, however, so St. Augustine wins this friendly feud, having been continuously settled since 1565. France, Great Britain, the United States, and the Confederacy subsequently captured (and, in one case, recaptured) this strategically important deepwater port.

You can explore the remains of Fort Pickens near Pensacola Beach.

ECAT (☎ 850/595-3228; www.goecat.com) also runs public buses (some of which have Wi-Fi) around town Monday through Saturday ($1.75 adults, 85¢ seniors)—but not to the beach. Call for schedules.

If you need a cab, call **Airport Express Taxi/City Cab** (☎ 850/478-4477), **Orange Cab** (☎ 850/478-0222), or **Yellow Cab** (☎ 850/433-3333). Fares are $2 at flag fall, plus $2.25 a mile.

TIME Pensacola is in the Central Time zone, 1 hour behind Miami, Orlando, and Tallahassee.

Gulf Islands National Seashore & More

Stretching eastward 47 miles, from the entrance to Pensacola Bay to Fort Walton Beach, skinny Santa Rosa Island is home to the resorts, condominiums, cottages, restaurants, and shops of **Pensacola Beach,** the area's prime vacation spot. This small, low-key resort began life a century ago as the site of a beach pavilion, or "casino," as such facilities were called back then; and the heart of town—at the intersection of Pensacola Beach Boulevard, Via de Luna, and Fort Pickens Road—is still known as Casino Beach. This lively area has restaurants, snack bars, an arcade, a miniature golf course, public restrooms, walk-up beach bars with live bands blaring away, an indoor sports bar, and an outdoor concert pavilion. The shops, restaurants, and bars of Quietwater Boardwalk are across the road on the bay side of the island. If you want an active beach vacation, it's all here.

One reason Pensacola Beach is so small is that most of Santa Rosa Island is included in the **Gulf Islands National Seashore ★★★**. Jumping from island to island from Mississippi to Florida, this magnificent preserve, possibly the best beach in the state, includes 150 miles of undeveloped and federally protected white-sand beach and dunes covered with sea grass and sea oats. Established in 1971, the national seashore is a protected environment for more than 280 species of birds. In the aftermath of the 2010 BP oil-spill disaster, Gulf Islands National Seashore is on a constant oil vigil, an official National Park Service statement saying, "The nature of oil's movement means we cannot predict which, if any, beaches will have oil on them or the quantity of oil to be found at any given time." During the spill, more than 700 sea-turtle nests along the gulf coast were carefully excavated and relocated across the Florida peninsula to be hatched and released in the Atlantic.

The most interesting part of the seashore is **Fort Pickens** (📞 **850/934-2635**; www.nps.gov/guis), on the western end of Santa Rosa Island, about 7 miles west of Pensacola Beach. Built in the 1830s to team with Fort Barrancas in guarding Pensacola's harbor, this brick structure saw combat during the Civil War, but it's best known as the prison home of Apache medicine man Geronimo from 1886 to 1888. The visitor center has a small museum featuring displays about Geronimo, coastal defenses, and the seashore's ecology. Plan to be here at 2pm, when rangers lead 45-minute tours of the fort (the schedule can change, so call the fort to make sure). Seven-day admission permits (that's the minimum you can get) to the Fort Pickens area are $8 per vehicle, $3 per pedestrian or bicyclist, and free for holders of National Park Service passes. The fort and museum are open March through October daily from 9:30am to 5pm, November through February daily from 8:30am to 4pm. Both are closed Christmas Day.

The Fort Pickens area has 200 **campsites** (135 with electricity) in a pine forest on the bay side of Santa Rosa Island. Nature trails lead from the camp through Blackbird Marsh and to the beach. Camping fees range from $10 to $30. Call 📞 **800/365-2267** for reservations (enter code GUL) or 850/934-2623 for recorded information.

The national seashore's headquarters are in the 1,378-acre **Naval Live Oaks Area,** on U.S. 98, a mile east of Gulf Breeze (📞 **850/934-2600**). This former federal tree plantation is a place of primitive beauty, with nature trails leading through the oaks and pines to picnic areas and a beach. Pick up a map at the headquarters building, which has a small museum and a gorgeous view through the pines to Santa Rosa Sound. Picnic areas and trails are open from 8am to sunset year-round, except Christmas. Admission is free. The visitor center is open daily from 8am to 5:30pm.

The national seashore maintains historic **Fort Barrancas,** on the U.S. Naval Air Station west of town. See "Pensacola's Other Fort" (p. 641) for details.

Outdoor Activities

FISHING Red snapper, grouper, mackerel, tuna, and billfish are abundant off the Panhandle. The easiest way to drop a line into the Gulf is off the new **Pensacola Beach Gulf Fishing Pier,** on Fort Pickens Road in Pensacola Beach (📞 **850/934-7200;** www.fishpensacolabeachpier.com). At 1,471 feet, it's the longest fishing pier on the Gulf Coast. The pier is open 24 hours a day, year-round. Fees for fishing are $7.50 per day for adults, $6.50 for seniors, and $4.50 for children 6 to 12. Bait and equipment cost extra. Observers can watch for $1.25 per person.

Fishing-charter services are offered at Pensacola by the **Beach Marina Fishing Fleet** (📞 **877/650-3474** or 850/932-0304), and at Pensacola Beach by **Reel Eazy Charters** (📞 **877/733-5329** or 850/932-8824; www.reeleazy.com). Expect to pay between $300 and $2,200 for 1 to 10 passengers, depending on the length of your trip. You may be able to save by driving to Destin, where party boats charge less per person (p. 652). Sightseeing and evening cruises here go for $50 to $225 per person.

FLORIDA'S canoe CAPITAL

The little town of **Milton,** the official "Canoe Capital of Florida" (by an act of the state legislature, no less), is about 20 miles northeast of Pensacola via U.S. 90. Its title is well earned, as the nearby Blackwater River, Coldwater River, Sweetwater Creek, and Juniper Creek are perfect for canoeing, kayaking, tubing, rafting, and paddleboating.

The Blackwater is considered one of the world's purest sand-bottom rivers. It has remained a primordial backwoods beauty, thanks chiefly to Florida's largest state forest (183,000 acres of oak, pine, and juniper) and **Blackwater River State Park ★★**, 7720 Deaton Bridge Rd., Holt, FL 32564 (*C* **850/983-5363;** www.floridastateparks.org/blackwater river), where you can observe plant life and wildlife along nature trails. The park has facilities for fishing, picnicking, and camping. Admission is $4 per day per vehicle with driver, $2 per extra vehicle passenger, $2 per pedestrian or bicyclist. Campsites cost $20. For camping reservations, call *C* **800/326-3521** or go to www.reserveamerica.com.

Adventures Unlimited, 8974 Tomahawk Landing Rd., Milton (*C* **800/239-6864** or 850/623-6197; fax 850/626-3124; www.adventures unlimited.com), is a year-round resort with canoeing, kayaking, and tubing trips. Canoe trips start at $25 per person with a two-person minimum charge per canoe. Kayaking adventures are from $30. Tubes start at $18. There are 12 fur-

nished cabins, including five riverfront cabins, three creekfront cabins, and several bungalows in the woods. Cabin prices range from $99 to $249 a night. Some cabins have fireplaces and tubs. Two-night minimum stays are required, 3 nights on holidays and from Memorial Day to Labor Day. Rustic cabins range in price from $49 to $59 per night and do not have indoor kitchens or bathrooms. There's also the School House Inn (eight rooms, all with private bathroom), whose rooms range $89 to $129 per night. Campsites are priced from $20 per night and one- and two-room camping cabins are $39 to $59. Call for reservations.

Blackwater Canoe Rental, 10274 Pond Rd. in Milton (*C* **800/967-6789** or 850/623-0235; www.blackwater canoe.com), also rents canoes, kayaks, floats, tubes, and camping equipment. It has two kinds of camping trips by canoe or kayak: a day trip, ranging from $20 to $28 per person, and an overnight excursion, ranging from $30 to $40 per person. Tents, sleeping bags, and coolers are all available for rent.

GOLF The Pensacola area has its share of Northwest Florida's numerous championship golf courses. Look for free copies of *South Coast Golf Guide,* an annual directory describing all of them, at the visitor center and in many hotel lobbies (see p. 46 for information on ordering copies). Reasonably priced golf packages can be arranged through many local hotels and motels.

For course information, go to www.golf.com or www.floridagolfing.com, or call the **Florida Sports Foundation** (℃ 850/488-8347) or **Florida Golfing** (℃ 866/833-2663).

Among this region's best courses is **Marcus Pointe,** on Marcus Pointe Boulevard, off North W Street (℃ 800/362-7287 or 850/484-9770; www.golfmarcuspointe.com), which has hosted the Nike Tour, the American Amateur Classic, and the Pensacola Open. *Golf Digest* described this 18-hole course as a "great value," and that's not far off: Greens fees with cart are about $25 to $50, depending on the season.

Other courses worth considering are the **Lost Key Golf Club,** on Perdido Key (℃ 888/256-7853 or 850/492-1300; www.lostkey.com), one of the area's more difficult courses; **Scenic Hills,** on U.S. 90 northwest of town (℃ 850/476-9611; www.scenichills.com), with rolling fairways unique in this mostly flat area; the 36-hole **Tiger Point,** 1255 Country Club Rd., east of Gulf Breeze by Santa Rosa Sound (℃ 850/932-1330; www.tigerpointclub.com), overlooking the water (the 5th-hole green of the East Course sits on an island); **Hidden Creek,** 3070 PGA Blvd., in Navarre, between Gulf Breeze and Fort Walton Beach (℃ 850/939-4604; www.hiddengolf.com); **Creekside Golf Course,** 2355 W. Michigan Ave. (℃ 850/944-7969; www.creeksidegolf.com); and **Osceola Municipal Golf Course,** 300 Tonawanda, off Mobile Highway (℃ 850/456-2761; www.osceolagolf.com).

The renovated **Perdido Bay Golf Club,** 1 Doug Ford Dr. (℃ 866/319-2471 or 850/492-1223; www.perdidobaygolf.com), on the mainland north of Perdido Key, has accommodations available for visiting golfers. It was the home of the PGA Pensacola Open from 1978 to 1987. Greens fees range from $29 to $79.

WATERSPORTS Visibility in the waters around Pensacola can range from 30 to 50 feet deep inshore, to 100 feet deep 25 miles offshore. Although the bottom is sandy and the area is too far north for coral, the battleship USS *Massachusetts,* submerged in 30 feet of water 3 miles offshore, is one of some 35 artificial reefs where you can spot loggerhead turtles and other creatures. Among the other military-oriented reefs: the Russian freighter *San Pablo,* a Navy barge, an A-7 Corsair that fell off the deck of the carrier USS *Lexington,* Vietnam-era tanks, and the USS *Oriskany,* a retired aircraft carrier. There are also good snorkeling sites just off the beach; get a map from the Gulf Islands National Seashore (see "Gulf Islands National Seashore & More," above).

Scuba Shack, 711 S. Palafox St. (℃ 850/433-4319; www.scubashackpensacola.com), offers sales, rentals, classes, and diving and fishing charters on the *Wet Dream,* moored behind the office. **MBT Divers** (℃ 850/455-7702; www.mbtdivers.com) has rentals, instruction, and trips to several sites, including the habitats of sea turtles, manta rays, and nurse sharks.

Key Sailing Center, 500 Quietwater Beach Rd., on the Quietwater Beach Boardwalk (℃ 877/932-7272 or 850/932-5520; www.keysailing.

com), and **Radical Rides,** 444 Pensacola Beach Blvd., near the Bob Sikes Bridge (*€* **850/934-9743;** www.radicalrides.com), rent Hobie Cats, pontoon boats, WaveRunners, jet skis, and windsurfing boards.

Exploring Historic Pensacola

Adjacent to the Historic Pensacola Village, the city's **Vietnam Memorial,** on Bayfront Parkway at 9th Avenue, is known as the "Wall South," as it is a three-quarter-size replica of the Vietnam Veterans' Memorial in Washington, D.C. Look for the "Huey" helicopter atop the wall.

Civil War Soldiers Museum ★ Founded by Dr. Norman Haines, Jr., a physician who started collecting Civil War relics when he was growing up in Sharpsburg, Maryland, this 4,200-square-foot museum in the heart of the Palafox Street business district emphasizes how ordinary soldiers lived during that bloody conflict. The doctor's collection of military medical equipment and treatment methods is especially informative. A 23-minute video tells of Pensacola's role during the Civil War. The museum's bookstore carries more than 600 titles about the war.

108 S. Palafox St. (south of Romana St.). *€* **850/469-1900.** www.cwmuseum.org. Admission $6 adults, $5 military, $2.50 children 6–12. Tues–Sat 10am–4:30pm. Closed New Year's Day, Thanksgiving, Christmas Eve, and Christmas Day.

Historic Pensacola Village ★★★ History buffs, as well as those who appreciate delightful architecture, will *love* this retro-fabulous old-school village, comparable to Virginia's Colonial Williamsburg. Bounded by Church, Zaragoza, Jefferson, Tarragona, and Adams streets, this original part of Pensacola resembles a shady English colonial town—albeit with Spanish street names—complete with town green and its own Christ Church, built in 1832. Some of Florida's oldest homes, now owned and preserved by the state, are here, and the village is in the heart of the broader historic district, home to charming boutiques and interesting restaurants.

Start your visit by buying tickets at **Tivoli High House,** 205 E. Zaragoza St., just east of Tarragona Street and one street above the Port of Pensacola, where you can get free maps and brochures. Try to take one of the 90-minute guided walking tours, which will lead you through buildings not otherwise open to the public: the French Creole–style **1805** Charles Lavalle House, the Victorian 1871 Dorr House, Old Christ Church, and the 1890 Lear-Rocheblave House. Tours are given daily at 11am, 1pm, and 2:30pm. Among the landmarks you can self-guide through with your ticket are the Museum of Industry, the Museum of Commerce, and the Manuel Barrios Cottage, all interpreting Pensacola from the late 1800s

Some of Florida's oldest homes are in Historic Pensacola Village.

Soar into the history of naval aviation with historic and modern military aircraft.

through the Roaring Twenties. The 1805 Julee Cottage displays an African-American heritage exhibit, telling the story of the African-American experience in Pensacola from Spanish exploration to the reconstruction periods.

Don't miss the **T. T. Wentworth, Jr., Florida State Museum,** 330 S. Jefferson St. (*(C)* 850/595-5985), a 1907 Renaissance Revival building originally built on Plaza Ferdinand as the city hall. It is open to the public for free as a local history museum, displaying exhibits of regional and Pensacola history. The third floor houses the Discovery Gallery, a hands-on children's exhibit, appropriate for children of preschool age through second grade.

205 E. Zaragoza St. (east of Tarragona St.). *(C)* **850/595-5985.** www.historicpensacola.org. Admission $6 adults, $5 seniors, $3 children 4-16. Tues–Sat 10am–4pm; 90-min. guided tours 11am, 1pm, and 2:30pm. Closed New Year's Day, Thanksgiving, Christmas Eve, Christmas Day, and all other state holidays. May be closed for further hours during holiday season; call in advance.

National Museum of Naval Aviation ★★ This museum gives you a look into just how much blood, sweat, and tears go into defending this country. The U.S. Navy and Marine Corps have trained at the U.S. Naval Air Station since they began flying planes early in the 20th century. Celebrating their heroics, this museum has more than 100 aircraft dating from the 1920s to the space age, plus exhibits on subjects such as POWs. There's even a torpedo bomber flown by former U.S. president George H. W. Bush during World War II. Children and adults can sit at the controls of a jet trainer, and the mock-ups of aircraft-carrier conning towers and hangar decks are realistic. You can almost feel the tug of gravity while watching the Blue Angels and other naval aviators soaring about the skies in the *Magic of Flight,* one of two IMAX films shown at the museum. If the movie doesn't get your stomach churning, then a 15-minute ride in the flight-motion simulator will. Using high-tech video and real motion, it simulates a high-speed, low-level mission in the navy's F-18 Hornet jet fighter. A ride on a Top Gun Air Combat Simulator is $25 per person and memorable to say the least! All guides are retired naval and Marine Corps aviators, which adds a personal touch to the hour-long museum tours. Allow at least half a day here, and save 20 minutes for a Flight Line bus tour of more than 40 aircraft parked outside the museum's restoration hangar. New in 2011: Special events and exhibits will commemorate 100 years of naval aviation.

Radford Blvd., U.S. Naval Air Station. ℭ **850/452-3604.** www.naval-air.org. Free admission. IMAX movies $8–$8.50 adults; $7.50–$8 seniors, military, and children 5–13; add $5 for 2nd movie. Flight-motion simulator rides $5–$5.50 per person. Daily 9am–5pm. Guided tours daily at 9:30 and 11am, 1 and 2:30pm. Flight Line bus tours daily every 30 min. 10am–noon and 1–4pm. IMAX movies on the hour daily 10am–4pm. Flight-motion simulator every 15 min. 9am–4:45pm. Closed New Year's Day, Thanksgiving, and Christmas. Enter naval station either at the Main Gate at the south end of Navy Blvd. (Fla. 295) or at the Back Gate on Blue Angel Pkwy. (Fla. 173) and follow the signs. No passes required.

Pensacola Historical Museum To learn more about Pensacola's five-flag history, spend 30 to 60 minutes at this museum in the Arbona Building, a structure built around 1882. An archaeological dig of the Spanish commanding officer's compound across Zaragosa Street has a boardwalk with explanatory signposts. The museum is operated by the Pensacola Historical Society, which has a resource center and library at 117 E. Government St. (ℭ **850/434-5455**). Around Halloween, the museum offers walking ghost tours in which you can rent a ghost meter (EMF sensor) for $5. Tours are $10 for adults, $2 for children 12 and under.

115 E. Zaragosa St. (btw. Tarragona and Jefferson sts.). ℭ **850/433-1559.** www.pensacolahistory. org. Free admission. Mon–Sat 10am–4:30pm.

Pensacola Museum of Art ★ Housed in what was the city jail from 1906 to 1954, this museum showcases an impressive collection of decorative glass, some African tribal art, and sometimes minor works by Salvador Dalí, John Marin, Ansel Adams, Thomas Hart Benton, Milton Avery, Alexander Calder, and Andy Warhol, among others, all displayed in the former cellblocks. It also sponsors cool events such as **Art After Dark,** in which you are invited to use the walls of the museum as your personal canvas for personal, artistic expression. Call before going to see what's on.

PENSACOLA'S other fort

Standing on Taylor Road near the National Museum of Naval Aviation, **Fort Barrancas** ★★ (ℭ **850/455-5167**) is worth a visit while you're at the naval station. This imposing brick structure sits on a bluff overlooking the pass into Pensacola Bay. The Spanish built the water battery in 1797. Linked to it by a tunnel, the intricate brickwork of the fort's upper section was constructed by American troops between 1839 and 1844. Entry is by means of a drawbridge across a dry moat, and an interior scarp gallery goes all the way around the inside. Meticulously restored and operated by the National Park Service as part of Gulf Islands National Seashore,

the fort is open March through October daily from 9:30am to 4:45pm, November through February daily from 8:30am to 3:45pm. Ranger-led, 1-hour guided tours are well worth taking. The schedule changes seasonally, so call for the latest information. Admission and tours are free.

The **Pensacola Lighthouse** (www. pensacolalighthouse.org), opposite the museum entrance on Radford Boulevard, has guided ships to the harbor entrance since 1825. Tours of the lighthouse are given on Saturdays from noon to 4pm May through October. Admission is $5 adults and $3 seniors and children 3 to 12.

407 S. Jefferson St. (at Main St.). ℭ **850/432-6247.** www.pensacolamuseumofart.org. Admission $5 adults, $2 students and active-duty military, free for children 5 and under. Tues–Fri 10am–5pm; Sat–Sun noon–5pm.

HISTORIC DISTRICTS

In addition to Historic Pensacola Village (see above) in the Seville Historic District, the city has two other interesting preservation areas. The Pensacola visitor center (p. 634) provides free walking-tour maps, if you're interested.

PALAFOX HISTORIC DISTRICT ★★ Running up Palafox Street from the water to Wright Street, the Palafox Historic District is also the downtown business district. Beautiful Spanish Renaissance and Mediterranean-style buildings, including the ornate Saenger Theatre, still stand from the early days. In 1821, Gen. Andrew Jackson accepted Florida into the United States during a ceremony in Plaza Ferdinand VII, now a National Historic Landmark. His statue commemorates the event.

For architecture buffs, this district offers the 1902 Theisen Building and its vivid displays of Beaux Arts details, as well as the 1925 Saenger Theatre, with its terra-cotta ornamentation and grillwork on the front facade, showcasing it as an elegant gem of the Spanish baroque style.

The Palafox District is home to the **Pensacola Historical Museum;** the **Pensacola Museum of Art,** in the old city jail; and the **T. T. Wentworth, Jr., Florida State Museum** (see "Exploring Historic Pensacola," above).

For booze hounds, the **Palace Cafe** at **Seville Quarter,** 130 E. Government St. (ℭ **850/434-6211;** www.sevillequarter.com), a Disney World for drinkers, has a bar from the old Palace Hotel circa 1810, where Florida's first liquor license was issued.

NORTH HILL PRESERVATION DISTRICT ★ Another entry in the National Register of Historic Places, the North Hill Preservation District covers the 50 square blocks north of the Palafox Historic District bounded by Wright, Blount, Palafox, and Reus streets. Descendants of Spanish nobility, timber barons, British merchants, French Creoles, buccaneers, and Civil War soldiers still live in some of the more than 500 homes. They are not open to the public, but fascinating for their architecture. In 1863, Union troops erected a fort in Lee Square, at Palafox and Gadsden streets. It later was dedicated to the Confederacy, complete with a 50-foot-high obelisk and sculpture based on John Elder's painting *After Appomattox.* For more information on homes and sites, visit **www.historicnorthhill.com**.

Where to Stay

The Pensacola visitor center (p. 634) publishes a complete list of rental condominiums and cottages. Among the leading rental agents are **JME Management,** 22-A Via de Luna, Pensacola Beach (www.jmevacations.com; ℭ **800/554-3695**), and **Tristan Realty,** 1591 Via de Luna Dr., Pensacola Beach (www.realtymarts.com/tristanrealty; ℭ **800/445-9931** or 850/932-7363; fax 850/932-8361).

The **Fort Pickens Area** of Gulf Islands National Seashore is your best bet for camping (p. 636).

Escambia County adds an 11.5% tax to all hotel and campground bills; however, at certain properties on Pensacola Beach, there is an additional 2.5% fee charged by Santa Rosa Island Authority.

The accommodations listed below are arranged by geographic area: downtown Pensacola and Pensacola Beach. Bear in mind that Pensacola Beach is at least a 15-minute drive from downtown.

DOWNTOWN PENSACOLA

The University Mall complex at I-10 and Davis Highway, about 5 miles north of downtown, has a host of chain motels, and there's an ample supply of inexpensive restaurants on Plantation Road and in the adjacent mall. Another good bet is the **Hampton Inn Airport,** 2187 Airport Blvd. (© **800/426-7866** or 850/478-1123; fax 850/478-8519), in an area that's not as congested as that around University Mall; there's a free shuttle to nearby Cordova Mall and its adjacent restaurants.

Several of the town's Victorian homes have been turned into bed-and-breakfasts. Among the best is **Springhill Guesthouse,** 903 N. Spring St. (www.springhillguesthouse.com; © **800/475-1956** or 850/438-6887), in a turreted 1900 Victorian and featuring paradoxical amenities such as DVD players and high-speed Internet connections. Rates are reasonable at $115 a night.

One of downtown Pensacola's newer stays: **Solé Inn and Suites,** opened on Palafox Street, in the heart of downtown Pensacola, 200 N. Palafox St. (www.soleinnandsuites.com; © **850/470-9298**). Rates at the 1950s-style, retro hotel start at $89 and include free Wi-Fi, breakfast, and cocktails from 5 to 7pm.

New World Inn ★ Near the bay and in the historic district, this urban, boutiquey version of a country inn (it looks more like a concrete fortress) is part of a meeting facility known as New World Landing. Inside, however, is an entirely different—and more pleasing to the eye—story. From the colonial-style lobby, a grand staircase leads to high-ceilinged, spacious rooms. There's a fresh, contemporary twist to the rooms, which offer a sleek decor. **The 600 South,** a wine and martini bar, has happy hour Tuesday through Friday from 4 to 6pm and features a tapas menu with items ranging from $5 to $11.

600 S. Palafox St. (at Pine St.), Pensacola, FL 32501. www.newworldlanding.com. © **850/432-4111.** Fax 850/432-6836. 16 units. $129 double; $149–$169 suite. Rates include continental breakfast. AE, MC, V. **Amenities:** Restaurant; bar; access to nearby health club. *In room:* A/C, TV, high-speed Internet access.

PENSACOLA BEACH

Hampton Inn Pensacola Beach ★ ☺ This pastel, four-story hotel sits on a sliver of land—600 feet, specifically—between Santa Rosa Sound and the Gulf, next to the action on Casino Beach. The bright lobby opens to a sun deck with beachside pools on either side (one is heated). Half of the oversize rooms—recipients of a $6.5-million renovation in 2007—have balconies overlooking the Gulf; these are more expensive than rooms on the bay side, which have nice views but no outside sitting areas. A **Tiki bar** is directly on the beach, making it a fun place to spend some time.

2 Via de Luna, Pensacola Beach, FL 32561. www.hamptonbeachresort.com. © **800/320-8108** or 850/932-6800. Fax 850/932-6833. 181 units. Summer $169–$199 double, $459 suite; off season $109–$149 double, $299 suite. Rates include continental breakfast. AE, DC, DISC, MC, V. **Amenities:** Bar; exercise room; 2 heated outdoor pools. *In room:* A/C, TV, fridge, hair dryer, Wi-Fi.

Margaritaville Beach Hotel ★★ ☺ Music mogul Jimmy Buffett didn't let a little oil spill stop him from opening this 162-room homage to the Buffettbranded Margaritaville lifestyle. In other words, it's beachy keen and laid-back, and brand-new. Rooms are nice, if nondescript—some come with balconies and all have beach or lagoon views. Opened in June 2010, Margaritaville Beach Hotel sits on 800 feet of Gulf-front beach, with Tiki bars, live entertainment, the **Land Shark Restaurant,** and a **Frank and Lola Love Pensacola Café** named after the 1982 Buffett hit about a couple on their second honeymoon in Pensacola. The only oil that seems to matter here is of the suntan kind, and frankly nothing seems to spoil the party at this place—not even a lost shaker of salt.

 When Room Rates Are Lowest

Room rates at Panhandle beaches are highest from mid-May to mid-August, and premiums are charged at Easter, Memorial Day, July 4, and Labor Day. Hotel or motel reservations are essential then. There's another high-priced peak in March, when thousands of college students invade during Spring Break. Economical times to visit are April (except Easter) and September—the weather is warm, most establishments are open, and room rates are significantly lower. The lowest rates are during winter, but many attractions and some restaurants may be closed.

165 Fort Pickens Rd., Pensacola Beach, FL 32561. www.margaritavillebeachhotel.com. ☎ **850/916-9755.** Fax 850/916-9756. 162 units. Summer $299–$309 double, $329 suite; off season $179–$209 double, $279 suite. AE, DC, DISC, MC, V. **Amenities:** 3 bars/restaurants; live entertainment on pool deck; concierge; fitness center; free high-speed Internet; pool. *In room:* A/C, TV, fridge, hair dryer, Wi-Fi.

Portofino Island Resort and Spa ★★★ ☺ The only luxe spot in the area, the Portofino is a stunning, Mediterranean-style, 28-acre condominium resort at the quieter east end of Pensacola Beach, adjacent to the pristine beaches of the Gulf Islands National Seashore. The resort's fifth tower offers more than 300 residences (they call 'em Sky Homes), most of which are vacant and have been converted into hotel rooms. The richly decorated suites are spectacular and feel much like luxury apartments, with panoramic views of the Gulf and Santa Rosa Bay. The resort boasts an indoor Olympic-size pool and seven heated pools; whirlpool spas, saunas, and steam rooms; a **spa** offering many treatments; indoor and outdoor dining restaurant; and a complimentary water shuttle to the Pensacola Boardwalk for shopping and entertainment and tram service to Tiger Point, a 36-hole championship golf course. Guests who book direct enjoy spa towels upon arrival, a beach chair set for two, tennis court time, access to the 40,000-square-foot Lifestyle Center with state-of-the-art fitness center, and unlimited DVD rentals. Guests also enjoy one round of golf per day on any of the four Emerald Coast Golf Trail courses as well as a deep-sea fishing excursion (per party). One word of caution: Because this place is a massive condo/hotel, maid service can be spotty in the condo units. Be sure you request daily service when booking.

10 Portofino Dr., Pensacola Beach, FL 32561. www.portofinoisland.com. ☎ **866/478-3400** or 850/916-5000. Fax 850/916-5010. 315 units. Summer $388–$529 2- or 3-bedroom apt; off season $250–$309 2- or 3-bedroom apt. AE, DC, DISC, MC, V. **Amenities:** 2 restaurants; bar; children's program; fitness center; 8 pools; 5 Rubico tennis courts; watersports equipment/rentals. *In room:* A/C, TV, hair dryer, high-speed Internet access, gourmet kitchen.

Where to Dine

PENSACOLA

Dharma Blue ★★★ CAFE Occupying a Victorian home overlooking Seville Square in Historic Pensacola Village, Dharma Blue is a cozy cafe with an expansive menu featuring everything from sushi to an excellent peach barbecue glazed pork tenderloin with country corn and lima beans served over red-bliss potatoes. For lunch, try the rib-eye sandwich of shaved beef with melted provolone cheese and *chimichurri* sauce on po' boy bread.

300 S. Alcaniz St. *℃* **850/433-1275**. www.dharmablue.com. Reservations recommended. Main courses $13–$27. AE, DISC, MC, V. Mon–Sat 11am–4pm; Mon–Thurs 5–10pm; Fri–Sat 5–11pm; Sun 5–9pm.

Five Sisters Blues Café ★ SOUTHERN A lively downtown eatery in a restored 1913 building, Five Sisters Blues Café, named for by the owner's mother and her sisters from Kentucky, features a Creole-accented Southern menu and live blues music. Menu highlights include gumbo, fried green tomatoes, secret-recipe blue crab cakes, Southern fried chicken, and pulled-pork BBQ. There's also an a la carte Sunday brunch with all sorts of egg dishes, chicken and waffles, grits, pork chops, and more.

421 W. Belmont St. *℃* **850/912-4850.** http://fivesistersbluescafe.com. Reservations recommended. Main courses $7–$13. AE, DISC, MC, V. Tues–Thurs 11am–9pm; Fri–Sat 11am–2am; Sun 9am–3pm. Closed Mon.

Marina Oyster Barn ★ 🍴 SEAFOOD Exuding the ambience of the quickly vanishing Old Florida fish camps, this plain but clean restaurant at the Johnson-Rooks Marina is a local legend. It's been a favorite since 1969, for its view and its down-home seafood. Freshly shucked oysters, served raw, steamed, fried, or Rockefeller-style, are the main feature; but the seafood salad is also first-rate, and the fish, shrimp, and oysters are breaded with cornmeal in true Southern fashion. The daily luncheon specials give you a light meal at a bargain price.

505 Bayou Blvd. (on Bayou Texar). *℃* **850/433-0511.** www.marinaoysterbarn.com. Main courses $9–$17; sandwiches $6–$9; lunch specials $5–$8. AE, DISC, MC, V. Tues–Sat 11am–9pm (lunch specials 11am–2pm). Go east on Cervantes St. (U.S. 90) across the Bayou Texar Bridge, then take 1st left on Stanley Ave., and turn left again to the end of Strong St.

McGuire's Irish Pub ★ STEAKS/SEAFOOD Every day is St. Patrick's Day at this bustling pub with the motto "Feasting, Imbibery, and Debauchery." The menu is delectably Irish, with Irish stew and corned beef and cabbage. Supersize steaks are the best offerings, as are hickory-smoked ribs and chicken. You can also order seafood, including a hearty bouillabaisse with shrimp, red snapper, clams, mussels, and oysters. The big burgers come with a choice of more than 20 toppings, from smoked Gouda cheese to sautéed Vidalia onions. For the high roller, try the $100 Grand Burger—custom-ground and chargrilled grand filet mignon, served with a side order of caviar and chopped red onions, and a grand magnum of Moët & Chandon White Star Champagne. You can watch your ale being brewed in copper kettles and dine in a cellarlike room where 8,000 bottles of wine are on display. Live music is offered most nights. There's another McGuire's on Destin Beach, 33 Hwy. 98 (*℃* **850/650-0000**).

600 E. Gregory St. (btw. 11th and 12th aves.). *℃* **850/433-6789.** www.mcguiresirishpub.com. Main courses $18–$35; snacks, burgers, and sandwiches $8–$12. AE, DC, DISC, MC, V. Daily 11am–midnight, later on weekends.

Wintzell's Oyster House ★★ SEAFOOD The Mobile, Alabama, landmark continues its spread through the southeast with its newest location in Pensacola. The menu features all sorts of seafood, pasta, sandwiches, salads, and appetizers. The restaurant, known for its namesake, the oyster—served either "fried, stewed, or nude," Wintzell's is no longer the mom and pop shop it was, but it's a worthy throwback to a Gulf coast tradition.

400 E. Chase St. (℗ **850/432-7752.** www.wintzellsoysterhouse.com. Main courses $12–$20; sandwiches and salads $8–$12; oysters market price. AE, DISC, MC, V. Sun–Thurs 11am–10pm; Fri–Sat 11am–11pm.

PENSACOLA BEACH

Flounder's Chowder & Ale House ★★ SEAFOOD Floundering around for a place where you can get fresh fish cooked any way, accompanied by live reggae? Then you need to be at Flounder's Chowder & Ale House, on the boardwalk overlooking the Santa Rosa Sound, where you'll find great food for breakfast, brunch, lunch, dinner, or late-night snacks. The best offerings include the Maine lobster and chargrilled tuna, grouper, and mahimahi. If you're lucky, a big smoker grill outside will be producing more fish and exceptional ribs. Burgers, salads, and sandwiches are offered all day. The dining room is cool and not what you'd expect from a fish house; its bookshelves, confessional booth walls straight from a New Orleans church, and stained-glass windows imported from a convent contribute to a cozy, Nantucket-in-the-winter kind of feel. But when the weather's warm, you'll definitely want to be outdoors.

800 Quietwater Beach Rd. (at Via de Luna and Fort Pickens Rd.). (℗ **850/932-2003.** www. flounderschowderhouse.com. Main courses $8–$23; burgers and sandwiches $8–$10. AE, DC, DISC, MC, V. Mon–Thurs noon–10pm; Fri noon–2am; Sat–Sun 11am–midnight.

The Last Great Road House

Sitting on the Florida-Alabama state line on Perdido Key, about 15 miles west of downtown Pensacola, the **Flora-Bama Lounge** (pictured at right), 17401 Perdido Key Dr. (℗ **850/492-0611;** www.flora bama.com), is almost a shrine to country music. Billing itself as the "Last Great American Road House," this Gulf-side pub is famous for its Saturday and Sunday jam sessions from noon to way past midnight. Flora-Bama is the prime sponsor and a key venue for the **Frank Brown International Songwriters' Festival,** the first week of November. But the wackiest shindig here has to be the **Interstate Mullet Toss and Beach Party** (the last weekend in Apr), which defies more in-depth description. The raw oyster bar is popular all the time. Granted, the joint can get a bit rough, but you won't soon

forget the great Gulf views while sipping a cold one at the Deck Bar. The Flora-Bama is open daily from 11am to 2:30am.

Pensacola After Dark

For what's hip and happening when the sun goes down, pick up the daily *Pensacola News-Journal* (**www.pensacolanewsjournal.com**), especially its Friday entertainment section. Another good source for nightly events is the *Pensacola Downtown Crowd* (**www.downtownpensacola.com**), a free publication available at the visitor center (p. 634).

THE PERFORMING ARTS Pensacola has a sophisticated array of entertainment choices for such a small city. Pick up **Sneak Preview,** a calendar of events at the Pensacola Civic Center and the Saenger Theatre. Both publications are available at the visitor center (p. 634). Tickets for all major performances can be purchased from **Ticketmaster** (*✆* **800/488-5252** or 850/433-6311; www.ticketmaster.com).

The highlight venue here is the **Saenger Theatre ★**, 118 S. Palafox St., near Romana Street (*✆* **850/444-7686;** www.pensacolasaenger.com), a restored masterpiece of Spanish baroque architecture. Presentations feature the local opera company and symphony orchestra, Broadway musicals, and touring performers. The 10,000-seat **Pensacola Civic Center,** 201 E. Gregory St., at Alcaniz Street (*✆* **850/432-0800;** www.pensacola civiccenter.com), hosts a variety of concerts, exhibitions, sports events, and conventions.

THE CLUB & BAR SCENE Pensacola's downtown nighttime entertainment center is **Seville Quarter,** 130 E. Government St., at Jefferson Street (*✆* **850/434-6211;** www.rosies.com), in the Seville Historic District. This restored antique-brick complex with New Orleans–style wrought-iron balconies is a collection of pubs and restaurants whose names capture the ambience: Rosie O'Grady's Goodtime Emporium, Palace Cafe (see earlier in this chapter), Lili Marlene's Aviator's Pub, Apple Annie's Courtyard, End o' the Alley Bar, Phineas Phogg's Balloon Works (a dance hall, not a balloon shop), and Fast Eddie's Billiard Parlor (which has electronic games too). The pubs serve up libations, food, and live entertainment from Dixieland jazz to country and western. Get a calendar at the information booth next to Rosie O'Grady's. Seville Quarter is open daily from 11am to 2am.

Every night is party time at **McGuire's Irish Pub,** the city's popular Irish pub, brewery, and eatery (p. 645). Irish bands appear nightly during summer, and on Saturday and Sunday the rest of the year.

Beach nightlife centers on **Quietwater Boardwalk,** Via de Luna at Fort Pickens Road (no phone), a complex on Santa Rosa Sound. With the lively beach-and-reggae bar at **Flounder's Chowder & Ale House** (p. 646) just a few steps away, it's easy to barhop until you find a band to your liking. Across Via de Luna, at Casino Beach, is **The Dock** (*✆* **850/934-3314**), which has live bands nightly in summer, and on weekends off season. Finally, **Sidelines Sports Bar & Restaurant** (*✆* **850/934-3660;** www.sidelinessportsbarandrestaurant.com) has a great game lineup.

DESTIN & FORT WALTON BEACH

40 miles E of Pensacola; 160 miles W of Tallahassee

The major tourist destination in Florida's Panhandle, **Destin and Fort Walton Beach ★★★**, along with Okaloosa Island, draws beach lovers and golfers year-round. White, sandy strips stretch the entire length of what has become known as the Emerald Coast. Destin and Fort Walton Beach are home to the state's largest fishing fleet. Myriad golf courses give visitors reason to head inland as well.

Beaches   The 1½ miles of sandy beachfront at **Henderson Beach State Park** sit like an oceanfront oasis in the middle of Destin. **Fort Walton Beach** bums while away the hours on the white sands of Okaloosa Island, just one bridge away from town.

Things to Do   Head for the greens at Destin-area golf courses. The **Sandestin Golf and Beach Resort** offers 72 holes over three courses landscaped with palms and bougainvillea.

Eating & Drinking   Fresh seafood rules along Florida's Emerald Coast. If you spent your day fishing, bring your catch to **Destin's Fisherman's Wharf Seafood House,** where they'll prepare and grill, broil, or blacken your fish for dinner. Or stop in at **Sexton's Seafood** on the way for a fresh-off-the-boat feast.

Nightlife & Entertainment   A thatched-roof deck shelters visitors and live reggae bands at **AJ's Club Bimini** in Destin, as 20-somethings groove with Caribbean rum drinks within sight of the Gulf of Mexico. The sounds of Jimmy Buffett fill the air at Destin's **Nightown,** where a single price admits you to live music and amateur boxing matches.

Lay of the Land

Sitting on a round harbor off East Pass, which lets broad and beautiful Choctawhatchee Bay flow into the Gulf of Mexico, Destin, along with Fort Walton Beach and Okaloosa Island, is Northwest Florida's fastest-growing and most upscale vacation destination.

Although Fort Walton Beach has its own strip of white sand on Okaloosa Island, the city's economy is supported less by tourism than by the sprawling Eglin Air Force Base. Covering more than 700 square miles, Eglin is the world's largest air base and is home to the U.S. Air Force's Armament Museum and the 33rd Tactical Fighter Wing, the "Top Guns" of Operation Desert Storm in 1991.

To the east of Destin and south of I-10 along the Emerald Coast Parkway are the spectacular sugar-white-sand beaches of **South Walton County.** In fact, it's the only destination in the entire country to have all 26 miles of coastline certified as "Blue Wave" beaches by the Clean Beaches Council. While there is some development in the area (in the form of the new urbanist beach town of **Alys Beach**), this picturesque area has mostly cottages nestled among rolling sand dunes covered with sea oats. As you drive along the scenic highway **30A,** you will discover quirky, cozy, and quaint communities each with distinct personalities. Here you'll find **Grayton Beach State Park,** which sports one of America's finest beaches, and the quaint, albeit Stepford-esque planned village of **Seaside ★★★**, which served as the set for Jim Carrey's movie *The Truman Show.* Seaside was built on a lovely stretch of beach in the 1980s, but with Victorian architecture that makes it look a century older. Seaside also has meandering white-picket-fenced footpaths; waterfront dining; 26-miles of white-sand beaches and architecturally unique beach pavilions; the alfresco Seaside Repertory Theatre; interesting shops and galleries; a stamp-size, Greek Revival–style post office; and a resident population of artists, writers, and other creative folks, who permit only their own cars in their relatively expensive little enclave. Don't worry, there are parking spaces for tourists on the one main road through Seaside. Seaside is the filling of a multilayered gourmet sandwich of several more Kodak-worthy communities. **Water**

Color ★★★ is located in Santa Rosa Beach and boasts 140 vacation homes, a stellar hotel, and nature trails. Also nearby is a sister community called **WaterSound Beach ★**, featuring vacation residences and a mile-long beach with pedestrian bridges, footpaths, and dunes.

The aforementioned **Alys Beach ★★** is a stunning, Antiguan/Bermudan/ Guatemalan/Mediterranean-style, environmentally friendly beach community of three- to five-bedroom homes, all with their own courtyards and most with private pools. It's on 30A, near **Rosemary Beach ★★★**, another fabulous, neo-traditional planned beach town, whose design is a compelling fusion of St. Augustine, the West Indies, New Orleans, and Charleston.

Essentials

GETTING THERE The big news is that it's now much easier to get to the area with the opening of **Northwest Florida Beaches International Airport,** 6300 West Bay Pkwy., Panama City Beach (✆ 850/763-6751; www. pcairport.com), the first international airport built in the U.S. since 9/11, in Panama City Beach. It's located within St. Joe's West Bay Sector, with service by **Southwest Airlines** (✆ 800/435-9792). Southwest is offering daily flights to and from Orlando, Nashville, and Baltimore/Washington, D.C. In addition, Southwest offers direct or connecting service to more than 58 destinations, including Dallas, Hartford, Chicago, and Fort Lauderdale, along with the New York and Boston regions. The airport has the unofficial title of "America's Greenest Airport," planned with the help of several of the state's environmental organizations, developers, and local, state, and federal agencies. The airport also aims to boast the first LEED-certified terminal building in the country.

Flights arriving at and departing from **Okaloosa Regional Airport** (✆ 850/651-7160; www.flyvps.com) actually use the enormous strips at Eglin Air Force Base. The terminal is on Florida 85, north of Fort Walton Beach, and is served by **American Eagle** (✆ 800/433-7300), **Continental** (✆ 800/525-0280), **Delta** (✆ 800/221-1212), **Northwest** (✆ 800/225-2525), and **US Airways** (✆ 800/428-4322).

Avis (✆ 800/331-1212), **Budget** (✆ 800/527-0700), **Hertz** (✆ 800/654-3131), and **National** (✆ 800/CAR-RENT [227-7368]) have rental cars at the airport, while **Enterprise** (✆ 800/325-8007) is located in town.

Bayside Shuttle (✆ 850/581-1505; www.baysideshuttle.com) provides 24-hour van transportation to and from the airport. Fares are based on a three-person minimum: $24 to Fort Walton Beach, $40 to Destin, $18 to Sandestin, and $75 to southern Walton County.

The **Amtrak** (✆ 800/872-7245; www.amtrak.com) *Sunset Limited* transcontinental service stops at Crestview, 26 miles north of Fort Walton Beach.

VISITOR INFORMATION For information on both Fort Walton Beach and Destin, contact the **Emerald Coast Convention and Visitors Bureau,** P.O. Box 609, Fort Walton Beach, FL 32549 (✆ 800/322-3319 or 850/651-7122; fax 850/651-7149; www.destin-fwb.com). The bureau shares quarters with the **Okaloosa County Visitors Welcome Center** in a tin-roofed, beachside building on Miracle Strip Parkway (U.S. 98), on Okaloosa Island at the eastern edge of Fort Walton Beach. Stop here for brochures, maps, and other information. This visitor center is open Monday through Friday from 8am to 5pm, Saturday and Sunday from 10am to 4pm.

The **Destin Area Chamber of Commerce,** 4484 Legendary Dr., Destin, FL 32541 (✆ **850/837-6241;** fax 850/654-5612; www.destin chamber.com), offers free brochures and sells maps of the area. The chamber is in an office complex at the entry to Regatta Bay Golf & Country Club, on U.S. 98, a half-mile east of the Mid-Bay Bridge. It's open Monday through Friday from 9am to 5pm; closed holidays.

For information on Rosemary Beach, WaterSound, Alys Beach, Seaside, WaterColor, Santa Rosa, Sandestin, and about eight more beach towns, contact **Beaches of South Walton,** P.O. Box 1248, Santa Rosa Beach, FL 32459 (✆ **800/822-6877** or 850/267-1216; fax 850/267-3943; www.beachesofsouthwalton.com). Its visitor center is at the intersection of U.S. 98 and U.S. 331, in Santa Rosa Beach (✆ **850/267-3511**); open daily from 8:30am to 5:30pm.

GETTING AROUND The **Okaloosa County Tourist Development Council** (✆ **850/651-7131;** www.destin-fwb.com) operates a free **Island Shuttle** trolley during the summer months along the length of Santa Rosa Boulevard on Okaloosa Island. The two trolleys run every 30 minutes Sunday through Thursday from 7am to 10pm, and Friday and Saturday from 7am to 1am. They also connect the island to the uptown bus station, on Eglin Parkway Northeast, on the Fort Walton Beach mainland.

For a cab in Fort Walton Beach, call **Black and Gold Taxi** (✆ **850/244-7303**) or **Yellow Cab** (✆ **850/244-3600**). In Destin, call **Destin Taxi** (✆ **850/654-5700**). Fares are usually $2.25 at flag fall and $2.25 each additional mile.

HOW TO FIND A street address

Don't worry about getting lost, as most of what you'll want to see and do in Destin and Fort Walton Beach is either on, or a few blocks from, U.S. 98, the area's main east-west drag. Finding a street address is another matter, because even many local residents don't fully comprehend the bizarre naming and numbering system along U.S. 98.

In Fort Walton Beach, U.S. 98 is known as "Miracle Strip Parkway," with "southwest" and "southeast" addresses on the mainland and "east" addresses on Okaloosa Island.

In Destin, U.S. 98 is known as "Highway 98 East" from the Destin Bridge east to Airport Road, and street numbers get higher as you head east from the bridge. East of Airport Road, however, the post office calls U.S. 98 the "Emerald Coast Parkway"—although locals still say a place is on "98 East." The highway is also known as the

Emerald Coast Parkway in Walton County, but the street-numbering system changes completely once you pass the county line.

Adding to the confusion in Destin, "Old Highway 98 East" is a short spur from Airport Road to the western side of Henderson Beach State Park, and "Scenic Highway 98 East" parallels the real U.S. 98 along the beach from the eastern side of Henderson Beach to Sandestin.

In other words, call and ask for directions if you're not sure how to find a place.

TIME The area is in the Central Time zone, 1 hour behind Miami, Orlando, and Jacksonville.

Hitting the Beach

DESTIN Like an oasis in the middle of Destin's development, the 208-acre **Henderson Beach State Park ★★**, east of Destin Harbor on U.S. 98, allows easy access to swimming, sunning, surf fishing, picnicking, and seabird-watching along its 1½ miles of beach. There are restrooms, outdoor showers, and surf chairs for people with disabilities. The area is open daily from 8am to sunset. Admission is $6 per vehicle with up to eight occupants, $4 single-occupant vehicle, $2 per pedestrian or cyclist. Several good restaurants are just outside the park's western boundary. Pets on leashes are allowed in the park, including the beach and campground. Campers will find 60 sites in a wooded setting here; they cost $30, including electricity, and can be reserved up to 11 months in advance. For camping reservations, call ✆ **800/326-3521** or go to www.reserveamerica.com. For more information, contact the park at 1700 Emerald Coast Pkwy., Destin, FL 32541 (✆ **850/837-7550;** www.floridastateparks.org/hendersonbeach).

The **James W. Lee Park,** between Destin and Sandestin, on Scenic Highway 98, has a long white-sand beach and overlooking it are covered picnic tables, a playground, an ice-cream parlor, and a seafood restaurant with great views.

FORT WALTON BEACH Do your loafing on the white sands of **Okaloosa Island,** joined to the mainland by the high-rise Brooks Bridge over Santa Rosa Sound. Most resort hotels and amusement parks are grouped around the Gulfarium marine park on U.S. 98, east of the bridge. Here you'll find the **Boardwalk,** a collection of tin-roofed beachside buildings that have an arcade for the kids, a saloon for adults, covered picnic areas, a summertime snack bar, and a seafood restaurant. Just to the east, you can use the restrooms, cold-water showers, and other free facilities at **Beasley Park,** home of the Okaloosa County Visitor Welcome Center.

Across U.S. 98, the Okaloosa portion of the **Gulf Islands National Seashore** has picnic areas and sailboats for rent on Choctawhatchee Bay, plus access to the Gulf. Admission to this part of the national seashore is free.

SOUTHERN WALTON COUNTY Sporting the finest stretch of white sand on the Gulf, **Grayton Beach State Park ★★★**, on C.R. 30A, also has 356 acres of pine forests surrounding scenic Western Lake. A self-guided nature-trail system allows for a close-up look at the ecological diversity in the area, including sand dunes, a coastal dune lake, pine flat woods, a marsh area, and, of course, miles of beach. Get a leaflet at the main gate for a self-guided tour of the trail. There's a boat ramp and a campground with electric hookups on the lake. Pets are not allowed anywhere in the recreation area. The park is open daily from 8am to sunset. Admission is $5 per vehicle with up to eight occupants, $4 for a single occupant, and $2 per pedestrian or bicyclist. New campsites were built and cost $25, including electricity. Older campsites are a dollar cheaper. There are also cabins that range from $110 to $130 per night. For camping reservations, call ✆ **800/326-3521** or go to www.reserveamerica.com. For general information, contact the park at 357 Main Park Rd., Santa Rosa Beach, FL 32459 (✆ **850/231-4210;** www.floridastateparks.org/graytonbeach).

Seaside has free parking along 30A and is a good spot for a day at the beach, a stroll or bike ride around the village, and a meal at one of its restaurants. The same goes for **Seagrove Beach,** which also has some charming eateries.

Outdoor Activities

For a comprehensive listing of outdoor activities in the area, go to **www. waltonoutdoors.com**.

BOATING Pontoon boats are highly popular for use on the back bays and for Sunday-afternoon floating parties in East Pass. Several companies rent them, including **Gilligan's Watersports** (© 850/650-9000; www. gilligansofdestin.com) and **Brooks Bridge Bait and Tackle** (© 850/243-5721; www.destin-ation.com/adventuremarina). Expect to pay about $150 for a half-day, $250 for a full day.

FISHING Billing itself as the "World's Luckiest Fishing Village," Destin has Florida's largest charter-boat fleet, with more than 140 vessels based at the marinas lining the north shore of Destin Harbor, on U.S. 98, east of the Destin Bridge. Arranging a trip is as easy as walking along the Destin Harbor waterfront, where you'll find the booking booths of several agents, the best being **Harborwalk Charters** (© 800/242-2824 or 850/837-2343; www. harborwalkfishing.com). Rates for private charters range from about $100 per person to $300 per person, depending on the length of the voyage.

For additional information on small- and large-group charters, check out **FishDestin.com** (© 850/837-9401 or 850/585-0049; www.fish destin.com). If you're a die-hard angler, consider coming in October for the **Destin Fishing Rodeo** (© 850/837-6734; www.destinfishingrodeo.org), a month-long fishing extravaganza.

You don't have to go to sea to fish from the catwalk of the 3,000-foot **Destin Bridge,** over East Pass. The marinas and bait shops at Destin Harbor can provide gear, bait, and fishing licenses. In Fort Walton Beach, you can cast a line off **Okaloosa Island Fishing Pier,** 1030 Miracle Strip Pkwy. E./U.S. 98 (© 850/244-1023; www.okaloosaislandpier.com), open 24 hours a day. Adults pay $7.50 to fish, seniors $6.50; children 12 and under pay $4.50. Observers pay $2. Bait and equipment rentals are available for $7 to $8.

For those angling for something different, WaterColor Inn's **Orvis Fly Fishing School** (© 850/534-5008; www.orvis.com/store/product. aspx?pf_id=9C0G) offers a 2-day course year-round on select Tuesdays/Wednesdays and Saturdays/Sundays and is open to participants of all levels at $470 per person, including equipment and lunch.

GOLF For advance information on area courses, contact the **Emerald Coast Golf Association,** P.O. Box 304, Destin, FL 32540. Also look for *South Coast Golf Guide,* the free annual directory published in Pensacola; see p. 46 for details. Be sure to ask whether your choice of accommodations offers golf packages, which can mean significant savings.

For course information, go to www.golf.com or www.floridagolfing.com, or call the **Florida Sports Foundation** (© 850/488-8347) or **Florida Golfing** (© 866/833-2663).

On the mainland, nonresidents are welcome to play at the city-owned **Fort Walton Beach Golf Club,** on Lewis Turner Boulevard (C.R. 189) north of town (☎ 850/833-9530). The club has two 18-hole courses—the **Pines** and the **Oaks** (☎ 850/833-9528)—plus a pro shop. Greens fees at both courses are about $18 to $27 year-round, including cart.

In Destin, **Indian Bayou Golf and Country Club,** off Airport Road (☎ 850/837-6191; www.indianbayougolf.com), has three 9-hole courses with large greens and wide fairways. They look easy, but watch out for water hazards and hidden bunkers! Greens fees, including cart, are about $30 to $65.

Sandestin Golf and Beach Resort (p. 660), on U.S. 98 East, in southern Walton County (☎ 850/267-8211 for tee times; www.sandestin. com), is the largest facility here. Its 72 holes are spread over three outstanding championship courses. The Baytowne and Links courses overlook Choctawhatchee Bay. Fees for 18 holes are $49 to $135, with specials for hotel guests.

Some of the 18 championship holes at **Emerald Bay Golf Club,** 2 miles east of the Mid-Bay Bridge on U.S. 98 (☎ 850/837-5197; www. emeraldbaygolfclub.com), run along Choctawhatchee Bay; the water adds both beauty and challenges to the otherwise wide and forgiving fairways. Greens fees are $35 to $105, depending on time and season.

In southern Walton County, the semiprivate **Santa Rosa Golf & Beach Club,** off 30A in Dune Allen Beach (☎ 850/267-2229; www. santarosaclub.com), offers a challenging 18-hole course through tall pines looking out to vistas of the Gulf. The club has a pro shop, a beachside restaurant, a lounge, and tennis courts. Fees are about $49 to $99.

In Niceville, a 20-minute drive north via the Mid-Bay Bridge, nonguests may play golf (four 9-hole courses; $45–$62) or tennis (21 courts; $6–$10 per hour) at the **Bluewater Bay Resort** (☎ 850/897-3241; www.bwb resort.com), which also has condominiums for rent.

Call ahead for reservations and current fees at all these clubs; also ask about afternoon and early-evening specials.

HIKING Meanderers will find plenty of opportunities to get lost in this area, from the new Deer Lake State Park (see below) and nature trails of WaterColor (see later in this chapter) to **Point Washington State Forest,** 5865 E. U.S. Hwy. 98 (☎ 850/231-5800; www.beachesofsouthwalton.com/point_ washington.aspx), a 15,810-acre forest featuring the Eastern Lake Bike/ Hike Trails established by the Florida Division of Forestry. Trails consist of three double-track loop trails of 3.5, 5, and 10 miles, and weave through a variety of plant communities, cypress ponds, wet prairies, and swamps. Maps are available at the field office.

HORSEBACK RIDING Seaside Stables, 613 Hwy. 393 (☎ 850/622-2202; www.seasidestables.com), offers horseback rides through the forest by appointment only. Prices start at $50 for an hour.

KAYAKING Sunny Days Bikes and Kayaks, 2129 S. County Hwy. 83, Santa Rosa Beach (☎ 850/267-0040; www.sunnydaysbikes.com), rents kayaks for $65 a day.

SAILING The 54-foot schooner *Nathaniel Bowditch* (☎ 850/650-8787; www.bowditchsailing.com) will take you on sunset cruises Monday through Saturday, $40 per person, or $50 per person for a wine-and-cheese cruise.

SCUBA DIVING & SNORKELING Military buffs will find the waters off Destin littered with sunken barges, tugs, Liberty ships, landing craft, airplanes,

14

Destin & Fort Walton Beach

army tanks, and bridge rubble populated with grouper, flounder, and cobia. At least a dozen dive shops are along the beaches. Considered one of the best, **Scuba Tech Diving Charters** has two locations in Destin: at 301 U.S. 98 E. (☎ 850/837-2822; www.scubatechnwfl.com) and at 10004 U.S. 98 E. (☎ 850/837-1933), about a half-mile west of the Sandestin Beach Resort.

WATERSPORTS Hobie Cats, WaveRunners, jet boats, jet skis, and parasailing are available all along the beach. The largest selection of operators is at the marina just east of the Destin Bridge, behind the Hooters. These include **Boogies** (☎ 850/654-4497; www.boogieswatersports.com) and **Gilligan's of Destin** (☎ 850/650-9000; www.gilligansofdestin.com).

If surfing the wild surf is a bit too adventurous for you, check out **YOLO Boarding,** 820 N. County Hwy. 393, in Santa Rosa Beach (☎ 850/622-5760; www.yoloboard.com), a not-so-new kind of "surfing" (aka stand-up paddleboarding) that suits those who love the water but not the wave action. YOLO (an acronym for You Only Live Once) involves standing up and paddling on a big, safe, comfortable longboard, offering a whole new point of view—from paddling with dolphins or sneaking up on blue crabs to dropping in at your favorite surf-break or just enjoying the view toward the beach. YOLO-ing, or stand-up paddling, has evolved from its surfing roots to a far more gentle way to enjoy time on the water from a new perspective.

Exploring the Area

Deer Lake State Park ★ South Walton's newest state park, Deer Lake consists of 172 acres south of 30A, as well as 1,700 acres south of the highway in which hikers can wander through unmarked trails that meander through native vegetation. Future plans call for the installation of organized hiking trails—that's how new this park is. A boardwalk across the dunes offers easy access to the beach, where you can picnic, swim, and fish. It also offers a spectacular view of the dune ecosystem, one of 11 natural communities found in the park. The park shares its name with the coastal dune lake within its boundaries and is home to southern magnolias, golden asters, woody goldenrod, scrub oaks, and various species of migratory birds and butterflies. Rare plants such as Gulf Coast lupine, spoonflower, pitcher plants, and Curtiss' sand grass are also found here.

357 Main Park Rd., Santa Rosa Beach. ☎ 850/267-8300. www.floridastateparks.org/deerlake/default.cfm. Honor box requires correct change of $3 per vehicle, $2 per pedestrian or bicyclist. Daily 8am to sundown. Located on 30A in Santa Rosa Beach.

Eden Gardens State Park ★ Evoking images from *Gone With the Wind,* these 115 acres house the 1895 Greek Revival–style **Wesley Mansion,** which has been restored and richly furnished with period antiques. The second-largest collection of Louis XVI furniture in the country is here, along with a Chippendale nightstand worth about $1 million. The mansion overlooks Choctawhatchee Bay and is surrounded by Spanish moss–draped oak trees. The house is particularly stunning during Christmastime, when it is draped in lights and decoration. The Eden Gardens are resplendent with camellias and azaleas. Your visit won't be complete without a guided tour, so avoid coming here on a Tuesday or Wednesday. Picnicking is allowed on the grounds. In 2010, the park received over $1 million in enhancements, including new picnic pavilions, a kayak/canoe launch, scenic overlook deck, and new visitor and ranger facilities.

181 Eden Gardens Rd. (off C.R. 395), Point Washington. ℂ **850/231-4214.** www.florida stateparks.org/edengardens. Grounds and gardens $4 per vehicle, $2 per pedestrian or bicyclist. Mansion tours $4 adults, $2 children 12 and under. Gardens and grounds daily 8am–sunset. 45-min. mansion tours on the hour Thurs–Mon 10am–3pm. Take C.R. 395 north from Hwy. 98. Proceed for a mile; park entrance is on the left.

Explore native fauna like this palmetto in Tate's Hell State Forest.

Florida's Gulfarium ☺ The country's second-oldest marine park (it opened in 1955) presents ongoing 25-minute shows with dolphins, sea lions, Peruvian penguins, loggerhead turtles, sharks, stingrays, moray eels, and alligators. Exhibits include the **Living Sea,** with windows for viewing undersea life. During one of the shows, a scuba diver explains the sea life while swimming among the various creatures. The **Spotted Dolphin Encounter** is a terrific program in which brave participants receive an up-close-and-personal hand-to-flipper encounter with two of the dolphins, Kiwi and Daphne. A trainer will guide you through the 40-minute interactive session. You could spend about 3 hours here between all the shows and exhibits. (Be aware that swimming with dolphins has both its critics and its supporters. You may want to visit the Whale and Dolphin Conservation Society's website at **www.wdcs.org.**)

1010 Miracle Strip Pkwy. (U.S. 98), on Okaloosa Island. ℂ **850/244-5169.** www.gulfarium.com. Admission $19 adults, $18 seniors, $12 children 4–11; Dolphin Encounter $150. Mid-May to Labor Day daily 9am–8pm (last entry 6pm); Labor Day to mid-May daily 9am–6pm (last entry 4pm).

Indian Temple Mound and Museum This ceremonial mound, one of the largest ever discovered, dates from A.D. 1200. The museum showcases some of its 6,000 ceramic artifacts from southeastern American Indian tribes, the nation's largest such collection. Exhibits depict the lifestyles of the four tribes that lived in the Choctawhatchee Bay region for 12,000 years.

139 Miracle Strip Pkwy. SE, on the mainland. ℂ **850/833-9595.** Park admission free; museum $5 adults, $4.50 seniors, $3 children 4–17. Park daily dawn–dusk. Museum Sept–May Mon–Fri 11am–4pm, Sat 9am–4pm; June–Aug Mon–Sat 9am–4:30pm, Sun 12:30–4:30pm.

Tate's Hell State Forest ★ Offbeat and off the beaten path, this 202,000-acre forest in Franklin County, between the Apalachicola and Ochlockonee rivers near Carrabelle, Florida, is a dream come true for outdoorsy types looking to explore 35 miles of rivers, streams, creeks, nature trails, and wildlife, including the bald eagle, Florida black bear, gopher tortoise, and red-cockaded woodpeckers. In fact, the forest is part of the Great Florida Birding Trail. It's also a great spot for fishing and hunting (permits required). As for how it got its name, well, apparently it involves a farmer who went off into the forest looking for the panther that killed his livestock. The farmer got lost for 7 days and was bitten by a snake, and when he finally emerged in Carrabelle, he said, "My name is Cebe Tate, and I just came from hell!" That said, it's a heavenly place for nature lovers, we swear. For a night in Hell, primitive campsites are available at $8 a night.

290 Airport Rd., Carrabelle. ℂ **850/697-3734.** www.fl-dof.com/state_forests/tates_hell. html. Free admission. Daily 9:30am–4:30pm.

U.S. Air Force Armament Museum ★ Although this museum is not on a par with Pensacola's National Museum of Naval Aviation (p. 640), you'll love it if you're into warplanes. Located on the world's largest air base, it traces military developments from World War II to Operation Desert Storm. Reconnaissance, fighter, and bomber planes, including the SR-71 Blackbird spy plane, are on display.

100 Museum Dr., off Eglin Pkwy. (Fla. 85) at Eglin Air Force Base, 5 miles north of downtown. ℂ **850/882-4062.** www.afarmamentmuseum.com. Free admission. Daily 9:30am–4:30pm. Closed federal holidays.

Shopping

Silver Sands Factory Stores ★★, on U.S. 98 between Destin and Sandestin (ℂ **800/510-6255** or 850/864-9771; www.silversandsoutlet.com), has more than 120 upscale stores, such as Liz Claiborne, DKNY, J. Crew, Brooks Brothers, Coach, Bose, and so on. Shops are open Monday through Saturday from 10am to 9pm (to 7pm Jan–Feb), Sunday from 10am to 6pm (noon–6pm Jan–Feb). There are also electronic games for kids and a sports bar for adults. **Destin Commons,** 4300 Legendary Dr. (ℂ **850/337-8700;** www.destincommons. com), at the corner of Highway 98 and Mid-Bay Bridge Road, offers shops and restaurants including Banana Republic, Crocs, Forever 21, Williams-Sonoma, Lucky Brand Jeans, Chico's, Talbots, Bass Pro Shops, Johnny Rockets, Sushi Siam, Cold Stone Creamery, and a 14-screen movie theater. Destin Commons is open Monday to Thursday from 10am to 9pm, Friday and Saturday from 10am to 10pm, and on Sunday from 11am to 7pm. Along similar lines is Sandestin's **Grand Boulevard,** 215 Grand Blvd. (ℂ **850/654-5929;** www.grandboulevard. com), featuring shops and restaurants.

Over at the Sandestin Beach Resort on U.S. 98, you can window-shop in the **Market at Sandestin,** where boutiques sell expensive clothing, gifts, and Godiva chocolates. Nearby is the half-charming, half Disney-esque **Village of Baytowne Wharf,** 9300 U.S. Hwy. 98 W. (ℂ **850/267-8117;** www.baytowne wharf.com), on the water in the Sandestin resort development, featuring restaurants, shops, and bars.

For a funkier, artier shopping experience, consider the beachside artist colony **Artists at Gulf Place** (ℂ **850/662-0400**), on the corner of Highway 393 and 30A in Santa Rosa Beach, a collection of nine local artists who sell their works from colorful, open-air kiosks. For more art, check out Seaside's **Ruskin Place Artist Colony,** 123 Quincy Circle (ℂ **850/231-1091**), the largest and most impressive collection of art galleries along the Gulf Coast housed in some of Seaside's most architecturally appealing buildings. For handcrafted jewelry, furniture, sculptures, pottery, art, and vintage items, do not miss the **Big Mama Hula Girl Gallery,** 1300 B Hwy. 283 S., in Santa Rosa Beach (ℂ **850/231-6201**), and for fans of folk art, **Woodie's Folk Art,** 1066 Bay Dr. (ℂ **850/231-1783**), in Santa Rosa Beach, features fantastic paintings by a man with a fantastic story.

Find unique handcrafted art at Artists at Gulf Place.

Do not miss the individual shopping villages of Rosemary Beach (℡ **850/278-2100**) and Seaside (℡ **850/231-5424**), where mom-and-pop shops selling fashion, fragrances, art, and kitsch thrive and are proof that not every successful store these days has to be chained down to a mall.

Where to Stay

The area has a wide range of condominiums and cottages for rent. One good-value example is **Venus by the Sea** (see below). The visitor information offices (p. 649) will provide lists of others. The largest rental agent is **Resort Quest,** 3500 Emerald Coast Pkwy., Destin (www.abbott-resorts.com; ℡ **888/909-6807;** fax 850/654-2937), which publishes an annual brochure picturing and describing its many properties.

The **Flamingo Cottage,** on Santa Rosa Beach (www.flamingocottage.com; ℡ **832/309-5866**), is perfect for families or groups (it can sleep up to 16), with fabulous features such as stone tiles, 9-foot bead-board ceilings, crown moldings, an oak staircase, and a master suite with Jacuzzi and private covered balcony. In addition to a large den and kitchen, laundry room, and outdoor gas grill, the cottage has four bedrooms and three bathrooms. Rates are $250 to $340 nightly, or $1,475 to $3,200 per week, depending on the season.

There are several commercial campgrounds here, but the best camping is at **Henderson Beach State Park,** in Destin, and at **Grayton Beach State Park,** in south Walton County (p. 651 for both).

State and local governments add 11% tax to all hotel and campground bills.

DESTIN & DESTIN BEACH

Henderson Park Inn ★★★ Overlooking 6,000 feet of undisturbed coastline, this Nantucket-style bed-and-breakfast is nestled at the end of a quiet road on the eastern edge of the Henderson State Park. Featuring Victorian-inspired furnishings, a large veranda, and private terraces overlooking the Gulf of Mexico, Henderson Park Inn is a stellar option for couples looking to rekindle the romance, with wine and grapes provided in your room upon arrival, a nightly wine reception at sunset, rooms with whirlpools, and even some with fireplaces. Best of all, it's an adults-only inn. Free boxed lunches are ideal to take to a picnic on the beach; for those with a sweet tooth, the community fridge is stocked with candy bars.

2700 Scenic Hwy. 98, Destin, FL 32541. www.forhendersonparkinn.com. ℡ **866/398-4432** or 850/269-8646. Fax 850/654-7116. 35 units. Summer $169–$400 suite; off season $329–$600 suite. Rates include continental breakfast, gourmet boxed lunches, unlimited beer and wine at happy hour, candy bars and sodas, wine/grapes/flowers in room upon arrival. AE, DISC, MC, V. **Amenities:** Free use of bikes; exercise room; Jacuzzi; indoor and outdoor pools; free use of kayaks. *In room:* A/C, TV, fridge, hair dryer, high-speed Internet access.

FORT WALTON BEACH

The managers of Venus by the Sea (see below) also run the **Sea Crest Condominiums,** at 895 Santa Rosa Blvd. (www.seacrestcondos.com; ℡ **800/476-1885** or 850/301-9600; fax 850/301-9205). The 112 units in this seven-story building aren't as spacious as those in Venus, but they're more luxurious, and those on the higher floors have great views toward the west. The complex has indoor and outdoor pools (actually one pool—you can swim under a glass partition between them), and it sits next to a county park with a boardwalk leading over the dunes to the beach.

Among the chain motels is the **Hampton Inn Fort Walton Beach,** 1112 Santa Rosa Blvd. (http://hamptoninn1.hilton.com; *©* **800/426-7866** or 850/301-0906).

Venus by the Sea ★ 🏊 Offering considerably more space than a hotel normally would at these rates, this three-story enclave on western Okaloosa Island was built in the 1970s and has been well-maintained ever since, though the decor is still stuck in that era (think retirement home) and should be updated. Each of the one-, two-, and three-bedroom units has a long living/dining/kitchen area, with a rear door leading to a balcony or a patio that opens onto a grassy courtyard. The beach is a short walk across the dunes, and you can stroll along the undeveloped beach at an Eglin Air Force Base auxiliary facility about 600 feet away. The same management operates the new and much more luxurious **Sea Crest Condominiums** (see above), and Venus guests can use the indoor/outdoor pool there.

885 Santa Rosa Blvd., Fort Walton Beach, FL 32548. www.venuscondos.com. *©* **800/476-1885** or 850/301-9600. Fax 850/301-9205. 45 units. Summer $140–$205 apt; off season $90–$180 apt. Weekly and monthly rates available. Ask about off-season specials. MC, V. **Amenities:** Outdoor pool; tennis court. *In room:* A/C, TV/VCR, kitchen.

 luxurious **COTTAGES, VILLAS & LUSCIOUS SURROUNDINGS**

Rosemary Beach (pictured at right), at the east end of 30A, just 8 miles east of Seaside (www.rosemarybeach.com; *©* **888/855-1551**), a larger, Seaside-style community that's a fusion of West Indies and Southern American architecture, has a collection of about 300 Pan-Caribbean–style cottages and carriage houses (from studios to six bedrooms) for rent, all of which are nonsmoking. This is another pedestrian-friendly community—almost everything on the 107 acres is within a 5-minute walk of the town center—and most of the homes are owned by people who live here part-time and lease to vacationers the rest of the year. The white-sand beach is ridiculously gorgeous, though guests can also choose from among four pools. Nothing on the architecturally stunning, strikingly planted property is higher than four stories, and all the homes telescope in from the beach, so everyone can have a view (or partial view) of the Gulf.

Other amenities include a health club, bike rental, racquet club, 2.3-mile fitness trail, spa, shops, town hall, post office, and a few good restaurants, including the delightful **Onano Neighborhood Café,** 78 Main St. (*©* **850/231-2436;** www.onanocafe.com). Cottages are individually decorated, so check online to see pictures of the properties before deciding. Though all come with a full kitchen, washer/dryer, and TV/DVD, some have added amenities such as a Jacuzzi or private pool. There is also an 11-room inn, the **Pensione** (*©* **888/855-1551**), on the premises, and the town is building a full-service hotel. The inn's daily rates are $175 to $195 spring and fall, from $195 in summer, and $150 in winter. Opening sometime this century, **Hotel Saba** (*©* **800/310-5768**) is a 53-room boutique hotel in Rosemary Beach's Town Center.

Sandwiched on 30A between Rosemary Beach and Seaside is the

SOUTHERN WALTON COUNTY

If you want to stay near the Sandestin Golf and Beach Resort (see below) without paying its prices, there's a **Sleep Inn**, 5000 Emerald Coast Pkwy./U.S. 98 (✆ **800/627-5337** or 850/654-7022), just a mile west. **Emerald Grande** (www.legendaryresorts.com; ✆ **866/755-7824**) is a luxury condo/hotel on 15 acres in Destin Harbor. While most units are owned by individuals, some are available for nightly (minimum 3-night stay) and weekly rental. Amenities include a sun deck resting 63 feet above sea level, with pools, waterfront eatery Harry T's (see "Where to Dine," later), a Florida outpost of New Orleans landmark Commander's Palace, a full-service spa and fitness center, a 24-hour concierge, and more.

Hilton Sandestin Beach Golf Resort & Spa ★★ ☺ This all-inclusive, all-suites beachside resort, in two adjacent towers, is the top full-service hotel here. It's nicely situated on the grounds of Sandestin Golf and Beach Resort (see the next listing) and shares its golf and tennis facilities. Enjoy a casual meal overlooking the Gulf at **Barefoots Beachside Bar & Grill,** or dine at the hotel's AAA Four-Diamond award-winning **Seagar's Prime Steaks and Seafood Restaurant.** Have a treatment at **Serenity by the Sea spa** and fitness center,

brand-new **Alys Beach** (✆ **877/259-5500;** www.alysbeach.com), the greenest member of the gang of new urbanists and a sustainable community, featuring 158 acres of million-dollar-plus beachfront villas (all considered "fortified homes" incorporating the latest in green/earth-friendly technology) inspired by the architecture of Bermuda, Antigua, and Guatemala, with 1,500 feet of beach, parks, open spaces, and

a 20-acre environmental preserve trail system and wetlands. Of the few homes that have been completed and sold, several are available for vacation rental.

There are also community pools, one of which is open to the public on select evenings—the **Caliza Pool** (✆ **866/832-1760**). This Ancient Greece-meets-modern-day South Beach complex of a main pool, family pool, lap pool (in which you can plug in your iPod for a custom, underwater soundtrack!), and spa pool also contains the Caliza Restaurant, housed in a loggia with billowing curtains and including dining areas with tables shaded by a gallery roof and seating niches built within a thickened wall punctuated by wood-screened openings. That said, Alys Beach is still a work in progress, with completion of the 600 villas, restaurants, parks, pools, and shops expected within the next 10 years!

which includes separate men's and women's locker areas with steam room, sauna, and cascading whirlpool. Executive suites in one wing are equipped primarily for business travelers and conventioneers, while the junior suites in the old wing are geared toward families, with a special area for children's bunk beds. Parents can send the kids to a supervised summertime program. Miniature golf, three pools, 15 tennis courts, four championship golf courses, and the stunning private beach make for a very enticing stay. The resort offers a tram service to take guests to nearby shopping, dining, and entertainment complexes. *Note:* The hotel is 100% smoke free. In 2010, a fire damaged the popular beach bar and grill, giving way to a fantastic new ocean view and a brand-new bar.

4000 Sandestin Blvd. S., Destin, FL 32541. www.hiltonsandestinbeach.com. ✆ **800/367-1271** or 850/267-9500. Fax 850/267-3076. 598 units. Summer $289–$459 suite; off season $109–$229 suite. Golf and tennis packages available. AE, DC, DISC, MC, V. Valet parking $20, self-parking $10. **Amenities:** 5 restaurants; 2 bars; babysitting; children's programs; concierge; golf course; health club; Jacuzzi; indoor and outdoor pools; room service; spa; tennis courts; watersports equipment/rental. *In room:* A/C, TV, hair dryer, minibar.

Sandestin Golf and Beach Resort ★★★ ☺ Sprawling over 2,400 acres with a spectacular beach 5 miles west of Destin and a marina, this resort is notable for its 72 holes of championship golf, tennis center, spa, and more. An array of luxury accommodations overlook the Gulf, Choctawhatchee Bay, the fairways, lagoons, or a nature preserve. The hotel rooms and suites are in the Bayside Inn; all have kitchenettes and balconies. Private condominiums are individually decorated and each has a full kitchen and a patio or balcony; many have a washer and dryer. The Village of Baytowne Wharf, a 28-acre pedestrian village overlooking the Choctawhatchee Bay, has a collection of more than two dozen specialty merchants ranging from boutiques and eateries to lively bars and nightclubs. It also features hotel rooms and one-, two-, and three-bedroom luxury accommodations surrounding the bay, with rates ranging from $100 to $479 in the off season to $165 to $719 in the summer.

9300 Emerald Coast Pkwy. W. (U.S. 98), Destin, FL 32541. www.sandestin.com. ✆ **800/277-0800** or 850/267-8000 in the U.S., or 800/933-7846 in Canada. Fax 850/267-8222. 1,600 units, including 1,425 condo apts. Summer $165–$719 double, $165–$719 condo apt; off season $100–$479 double, $100–$479 condo apt. Packages and weekly/monthly rates available. AE, DC, DISC, MC, V. **Amenities:** 22 restaurants; 8 bars; babysitting; free use of bikes; children's programs; concierge; 4 golf courses; health club; Jacuzzis; 19 heated outdoor pools; limited room service (hotel only); spa; 15 tennis courts; watersports equipment/rentals. *In room:* A/C, TV, hair dryer, Internet access, kitchen.

SEASIDE

Mayberry meets *Metropolitan Home* in this pastel-hued community, where life is a dreamlike state of mind. If you decide to rent a home or a **romantic honeymoon cottage ★★** in this village, contact the **Seaside Cottage Rental Agency,** P.O. Box 4730, Seaside, FL 32459 (✆ **866/624-1054** or 850/231-1320; fax 850/351-2009; www.seasidefl.com). The agency, which runs the hotels listed below, has several hundred cottages in its rental inventory, from one to six bedrooms. The beachside cottages are one of Florida's best getaways for anyone else looking for a romantic escape, though if you want a little more privacy and less action, you might choose Rosemary Beach or Alys Beach (see above) instead. Fun fact: Every property in Seaside is identified not by address but by name. And the names are everything from cheeky and kitschy—Changes in Attitude, Cork the Whine, Four the Girls, Happy Ours, Salad Days Lockoff—to celebratory, such as Independence Day, the cottage owned by the songwriter who wrote the hit country song of the same name. Another fun fact: No two houses on the same street can have the same type of picket fence.

Inn by the Sea, Vera Bradley ★★★ With its Tuscan columns reminiscent of a Virginia mansion, this nine-room inn, one of the few traditional hotel stays in Seaside, was designed by lifestyle brand Vera Bradley. Straight out of a country-style home-decor magazine, it has fresh bright colors and styling throughout. Each of the nine bedrooms features flatscreen TVs and, even better, a VB-quilted tote filled with bottled water and other niceties. Every room is a different style. Every guest has full privileges at the private swim, tennis, and fitness club in Seaside. Two rooms are in the carriage house and feature king-size beds, private sitting room, and kitchenette. The dining room offers a Southern breakfast. We especially like the welcome bottle of wine upon check in, too. Nice touch.

38 Seaside Ave., Seaside, FL 32459. www.innbytheseavb.com. *C* **866/624-1054.** Fax 850/351-2009. 9 units. $250–$550 double. Rates include gourmet continental breakfast. AE, DISC, MC, V. **Amenities:** Restaurant; Swim, Tennis & Fitness Club. *In room:* A/C, TV, fridge, hair dryer, kitchen (in some), Wi-Fi.

 WaterColor Inn: Picture Perfect

Designed by renowned architect David Rockwell, the **WaterColor Inn,** 34 Goldenrod Circle (www.watercolorresort.com; *C* **866/426-2656** or 850/534-5000), is a 499-acre beachfront boutique hotel. With just 60 rooms, it feels more like a private beach house than a hotel. A ground-floor library with club chairs and a cocktail lounge opening onto the pool deck drive home that feeling even more. Guest rooms feature a walk-in shower with views to the beach, and Adirondack chairs on the balcony. Six ground-floor bungalows have outdoor showers enclosed by striped tents, lending a French Riviera feel. Rotunda guest rooms in the center tower provide 180-degree views from massive balconies. Access to WaterColor community facilities, such as the Tom Fazio–designed Camp Creek Golf Club, 6 miles east, and Greg Norman–designed Shark's Tooth Golf Club, 13 miles east, is a bonus. Five Har-Tru tennis courts are also available. A Gulf-front beach club (with pool deck, children's pool, and beach services), a lakefront boathouse (with canoes, kayaks, and fishing), and **Camp WaterColor,** with supervised kids' activities, will keep you from wanting to leave. Rates range from $225 to $595 for a king room, $395 to $625 for a suite. In addition to the 60 rooms at the Inn, WaterColor has a selection of rental homes, ranging from one to five bedrooms. These are very popular with families and groups of friends traveling together. Rental guests can use all of the resort's facilities, and kayaks and canoes are complimentary. For those looking for more privacy, WaterColor's sister community **WaterSound Beach** (www.watersoundvacationrentals.com; *C* **800/413-2363**), a 256-acre gated residential community 4 miles west near Camp Creek Golf Club on 30A near Deer Lake State Park, features a private beach club, white-sand beaches, and a seasonal restaurant. Rates for one- to five-bedroom private vacation rentals range from $195 to $695.

Seaside Motorcourt ★ We told you Seaside was a throwback to Old Florida, and to prove it is, this renovated, nostalgically hip nine-room motel has been restored and refreshed with courtyards, new landscaping, and interior design. All rooms feature rustic Americana art hung alongside the benchmark of the 21st-century hotel: a plasma TV. Guests can take advantage of complimentary DVD rentals if they insist on staying in, and while rooms are comfy, they are also ideally situated a block from town, 1 minute to the beach, and within walking distance of Seaside's Swim, Tennis & Fitness Clubs, which include three pools, six tennis courts (two hard, four Rubico), croquet lawn, bike rentals, seasonal children's camp, and state-of-the-art fitness center. As with the Inn by the Sea, guests at the Seaside Motorcourt receive a welcome bottle of wine.

2311 E. Scenic Hwy. 30A, Seaside, FL 32459. www.cottagerentalagency.com. ✆ **866/624-1054.** Fax 850/351-2009. 9 units. $199 double. AE, DISC, MC, V. **Amenities:** Restaurant; Swim, Tennis & Fitness Club. *In room:* A/C, TV/DVD, hair dryer, Wi-Fi.

Where to Dine

Except for the strip on Okaloosa Island, a plethora of fast-food and family chain restaurants line U.S. 98.

DESTIN

If you didn't catch a fish to be grilled at Fisherman's Wharf (see below), you can buy one to brag about at **Sexton's Seafood ★**, 602 Hwy. 98 E., opposite Destin Harbor (✆ **850/837-3040**). It's the best market here.

AJ's Seafood & Oyster Bar ★ SEAFOOD Jimmy Buffett tunes set the tone at this fun, Tiki-topped establishment on the picturesque Destin Harbor docks, where fishing boats unload their daily catches right into the kitchen. The best items here are grilled or fried fish, but raw or steamed Apalachicola oysters also headline the menu. You can sample a bit of everything with a "run of the kitchen" seafood platter. AJ's is most famous for its topside bar, Club Bimini, open nightly and featuring live bands (you should have dinner elsewhere if you're not in a partying mood). At lunch, picnic tables on the covered dock make a fine place to eat with a view across the harbor. Locals love this place and you will, too.

116 Hwy. 98 E., Destin Harbor. ✆ **850/837-1913.** www.ajs-destin.com. Main courses $12–$38; sandwiches and salads $9–$15. AE, DISC, MC, V. Apr–Sept Sun–Thurs 11am–10pm, Fri–Sat 11am–midnight; off season daily 11am–9pm. Bar until 4am.

Back Porch ★ SEAFOOD This cedar-shingled seafood shack has glorious beach and Gulf views from its long porch. It also has beach chairs on the sand. They originated chargrilled amberjack, which you'll now see on menus throughout Florida. Other fish and seafood, as well as chicken and juicy hamburgers, also come from the coals. Come early, order a rum-laden Key lime freeze, and enjoy the sunset. The Back Porch sits with a number of other restaurants near the western boundary of the Henderson Beach State Park and is a popular hangout for Frisbee players and sunbathers. A second location is at Panama City Beach's Pier Park (see later in this chapter).

1740 Old Hwy. 98 E. ✆ **850/837-2022.** www.theback-porch.com. Main courses $15–$28; sandwiches, burgers, and pastas $9–$13. AE, DC, DISC, MC, V. Apr–Sept daily 11am–11pm; off season daily 11am–10pm. From U.S. 98, turn toward the beach at the Hampton Inn.

Copper Grill ★★ STEAK An upscale restaurant lit by gas torches, the Copper Grill is a delicious dichotomy of swank and kitsch—check out the zebra prints inside the dining room. Each table has its own DVD player, TV screen, and coffeemaker, and, to add to the distraction, there's an open-pit grill in the middle of the action. The Angus beef is top-notch, but order the African lobster tails with sweet mustard and lemon butter sauce—heaven!

11225 Hwy. 98, Destin. © **850/654-6900.** www.coppergrill.com. Reservations recommended. Main courses $25–$52. AE, DISC, MC, V. Tues–Sat 5–11pm.

Donut Hole Bakery Cafe ★ SOUTHERN Available around the clock, breakfasts at this popular spot include eggs Benedict, fluffy biscuits with sausage gravy, Belgian waffles, and freshly baked doughnuts. Lunch choices are deli sandwiches, half-pound burgers, and big salads. Daily specials are a bargain. The rough-hewn building has booth and counter seating. Be prepared to wait out on the deck, especially on weekends. There's another Donut Hole in southern Walton County, on U.S. 98 E., 2½ miles east of the Sandestin Beach Resort (© **850/267-3239**); it's open daily from 6am to 10pm.

635 U.S. 98 E., Destin. © **850/837-8824.** Main courses $7–$10; breakfast items, sandwiches, salads, and burgers $5–$9. No credit cards. Daily 24 hr. Closed 2 weeks before Christmas.

Fisherman's Wharf Seafood House ★★ SEAFOOD Go fishing, bring your catch here, and then have the chef chargrill it at this atmospheric restaurant next to a charter-fleet marina. (The restaurant hosts most of Destin's fishing competitions.) If you struck out fishing and didn't stop by Sexton's Seafood (see above) on the way, you can select from the restaurant's fresh-off-the-boat catch for grilling, broiling, frying, or blackening. Chargrilling is the house specialty—the triggerfish filet comes white and flaky but still moist. All main courses include a choice of two side dishes including hush puppies, corn on the cob, french fries, rice pilaf, baked potato, or roasted vegetables. For the gastronomically adventurous, try the gator wings—tender bits of alligator tail served in a mild Buffalo sauce. The building, though modern, reminds me of an Old Florida fish camp, with rough-hewn wood walls and double-hung windows looking onto a large harborside deck, a venue during the warmer months for two bars, an oyster bar, live music, and great sunsets.

210D Hwy. 98 E., Destin Harbor. © **850/654-4766.** www.fishermanswharfdestin.com. Main courses $12–$23; sandwiches and burgers $9–$10. AE, DC, DISC, MC, V. Summer daily 11am–11pm (deck bar until later); off season daily 11am–9pm.

Fudpucker's Beachside Bar & Grill ★ AMERICAN A sprawling 26,000-square-foot complex, Fudpucker's is a beachside burger-and-beer joint with a twist—or, rather, many twists. For one, there's also a sushi bar. The decor is funky, with antique beer cans, mirrors, and what they call "Fud Junk." The Fudburger is the menu's most popular, but an unabridged selection of everything from fried crab to Puckeroni Pizza is available. Eight different dining rooms, a playground, and game rooms are nothing compared to Fudpucker's Gator Beach, the restaurant's very own alligator collection in the pond underneath the building. Live music and a new addition, Club Key West, make this place one of the area's most popular nightspots. **Fudpucker's on the Island,** 108 Santa Rosa Blvd., Fort Walton Beach (© **850/243-3833**), is the original, located on Okaloosa Island.

20001 Emerald Coast Pkwy., Destin. © **850/654-4200.** www.fudpuckers.com. Main courses $16–$25; sandwiches $9–$12. AE, DC, DISC, MC, V. Mon–Wed 11am–10pm; Thurs–Sat 11am–4am.

Harbor Docks SEAFOOD/JAPANESE The harbor views are spectacular from indoors or outdoors at this casual, somewhat rustic establishment. You can order

14

NORTHWEST FLORIDA

Destin & Fort Walton Beach

your fill of fried fish, but such specialties as the daily catch sautéed with artichoke hearts are far more enjoyable. Asian influences include a sushi bar and hibachi table, which are open for dinner, and a few Thai specialties that grace the lunch menu. The bar here is popular with charter-boat skippers, and frequent live entertainment keeps the action going on the outdoor deck at night.

538 U.S. 98 E., Destin Harbor. ✆ **850/837-2506.** www.harbordocks.com. Reservations accepted only for hibachi table. Main courses $18–$28; sushi $4–$12. AE, DC, DISC, MC, V. Feb–Oct daily 5:30–10:30am and 11am–11pm; Nov–Jan daily 11am–11pm. Sushi bar daily 5–10pm.

Harry T's Boat House ★ ☺ AMERICAN To honor the memory of trapeze artist "Flying Harry T" Baben, his family opened this lively spot on the ground floor of Destin Harbor's tallest building. Standing guard is the stuffed Stretch, Harry's beloved giraffe. The decor includes circus memorabilia and relics from the luxury cruise ship *Thracia,* which sank off the Emerald Coast in 1927; Harry T was presented with the ship's salvaged furnishings and fixtures for personally leading the heroic rescue of its 2,000 passengers. In 2007, Harry's moved into the lighthouse building along the harborfront in a 13,000-square-foot space in the new HarborWalk Village at Emerald Grande. Luckily the kitsch—and the giraffe—remain. The menu offers traditional seafood, steak, chicken, and pasta dishes. The house specialty is smokehouse ribs, juicy and full of flavor. Call for information on Kids' Night, which features clowns, face painting, and balloon animals.

46 Harbour Blvd., Destin Harbor. ✆ **850/654-4800.** www.harryts.com. Main courses $15–$30; soups, sandwiches and salads $5–$15. Menu cheaper during winter months. AE, DISC, MC, V. Summer Mon–Sat 11am–2am, Sun 10am–2am; off season Mon–Sat 11am–9pm, Sun 10am–9pm. Bar until later. Sun brunch year-round 10am–3pm.

Marina Cafe ★★★ NEW AMERICAN Destin's finest restaurant provides a classy atmosphere with soft candlelight, subdued music, and walls of glass overlooking the harbor. The changing menu offers nouveau preparations of seafood, such as ginger-scallion-crusted Norwegian salmon. Pizzas are topped with the likes of Creole shrimp, caramelized onions, and roasted pepper, while pastas might feature Gulf shrimp. Try the pan-seared andouille-crusted redfish with cayenne butter and chive rémoulade if it's available. Weather permitting, enjoy the outdoor deck for drinks and appetizers. There's also a sushi bar, and, in Rosemary Beach, Marina Café has a sibling restaurant, **Destin Chops 30A** (see below).

404 Hwy. 98 E., Destin Harbor. ✆ **850/837-7960.** www.marinacafe.com. Reservations recommended. Main courses $26–$39; pizza and pasta $11–$20. AE, DC, DISC, MC, V. Daily 5–11pm. Closed 1st 3 weeks in Jan.

Rutherford's 465 ★ NEW AMERICAN An elegant lunch-and-brunch-only restaurant overlooking Lake Regatta, Rutherford's 465 is an eclectic dining experience, thanks to Chef Todd Misener's New American cuisine. Dishes such as the panko-grilled Gulf shrimp with red chili sauce, and the pan-fried local triggerfish in a sunflower-seed crust with blackened jumbo shrimp and golden-pineapple butter sauce are outstanding.

465 Regatta Bay Blvd. (inside the Regatta Bay community), Destin. ✆ **850/337-8888.** www. rutherfords465.com. Main courses $7–$17. AE, DC, DISC, MC, V. Tues–Sat 11am–2pm; Sun 10am–2:30pm.

FORT WALTON BEACH

Big City American Bistro ★★★ AMERICAN BISTRO For a caffeine fix; an inexpensive breakfast, brunch, or lunch; or afternoon tea, head to Tina and Jim Ivanchukov's bright cafe on the mainland near the Brooks Bridge. The owners make great salads—such as herb-roasted chicken with apples, walnuts, and tarragon dressing (sold by the pound)—and sandwiches served on homemade focaccia. Don't miss the sweet-potato fries either. Dinner entrees are also tempting—the cowboy-style flame-grilled skirt steak is served with a coffee-and-black-pepper crust that's sure to awaken both you and your taste buds!

201 Miracle Strip Pkwy. SE (U.S. 98). ℂ **850/664-0664.** Main courses $11–$25; sandwiches and salads $7–$10. MC, V. Mon–Fri 7am–7pm; Sat 8am–5pm; Sun 10:30am–2:30pm.

Caffè Italia ★★ NORTHERN ITALIAN Nada Eckhardt is from Croatia, but she met her American husband, Jim, while working at a restaurant named Caffè Italia in Italy. The Eckhardts duplicated that establishment in this 1925 Sears Roebuck mail-order house on the waterfront. You can dine on the patio, with a view of the sound through live oak trees (one table is set romantically under a gazebo), or sit inside, where Nada has installed floral tablecloths and photos from the old country. A limited but fine menu includes pizzas; pasta dishes, such as lobster ravioli, risotto with asparagus, or smoked salmon; and meat and seafood dishes to fit the season. The cappuccino is first-rate, as are the genuine Italian desserts.

189 Brooks St., on the mainland in the block west of Brooks Bridge. ℂ **850/664-0035.** www.acaffeitalia.com. Reservations recommended. Main courses $17–$20; pizza and pasta $10–$20. AE, DC, DISC, MC, V. Sun and Tues–Fri 11am–10pm; Sat 5–11pm. Closed Thanksgiving and Christmas.

Pandora's Restaurant & Lounge ★ STEAK/SEAFOOD The front of this unusual restaurant is a beached yacht now housing the main-deck lounge. Below is a dining room with ceiling beams and aglow with lights from copper chandeliers. Try for the private Bob Hope Booth, where you can dine beneath two of the great comedian's golf clubs (he used to come here to raise money for a local Air Force widows' home). Anything from the charcoal grill is excellent, including the wonderful appetizer of bacon-wrapped scallops. Several varieties of freshly caught fish are among the main-course choices, but oak-grilled steaks and prime rib keep the locals coming back for more. The tender beef is cut on the premises and grilled to perfection. The delicious breads and pies are homemade. *Note:* Service has been known to be spotty here.

1120B Santa Rosa Blvd. ℂ **850/244-8669.** www.pandorassteakhouse.com. Reservations recommended. Main courses $20–$49. AE, DISC, MC, V. Sun and Tues–Thurs 5–10pm; Fri–Sat 5–10:30pm.

Staff's Seafood Restaurant SEAFOOD/STEAK Considered the first Emerald Coast restaurant, Staff's started as a hotel in 1913 and moved to this barnlike building in 1931. Among the memorabilia on display are an old-fashioned phonograph lamp and a 1914 cash register. Staff's tangy seafood gumbo has gained fame for this casual, historic restaurant. One of the most popular dishes is the chargrilled amberjack served with gazpacho salsa. Main courses are served with baskets of hot, home-baked wheat bread from a secret 70-year-old recipe, plus salad and dessert. A pianist plays at dinnertime year-round.

24 SW Miracle Strip Pkwy. (U.S. 98), on the mainland. (C) **850/243-3526.** www.staffrestaurant. com. Main courses $16–$30. AE, DISC, MC, V. Summer daily 5–11pm; off season Mon–Thurs 5–9pm, Fri–Sat 5–10pm.

BEACHES OF SOUTH WALTON/SCENIC HIGHWAY 30A

Another Broken Egg Cafe ★ AMERICAN Forgive us, but this is an "eggcellent" breakfast chain with locations in Destin, Sandestin, Grayton Beach, Tallahassee, and our favorite, Grayton Beach. With its country-cozy ambience and menu featuring an assortment of delicious, farm-fresh omelets, skillets, scrambles, Benedicts, pancakes, waffles, French toast, and even Bananas Foster, Another Broken Egg Cafe isn't just another breakfast spot.

51 Grayton Uptown Circle, Grayton Beach. (C) **850/231-7835.** www.anotherbrokenegg.com. Reservations not accepted. Main courses $8–$15. AE, DC, MC, V. Tues–Sun 7am–2pm.

Café Tango ★★ AMERICAN Despite the name, this restaurant has nothing to do with Argentina. Housed in a 50-something-year-old vine-covered red cottage, Café Tango is best known for its seafood, steaks, and pastas. We loved the jalapeño shrimp scampi, but all-around faves include pan-seared duck breasts in a plum and Madeira sauce; the Tango Fish, a pan-sautéed fish filet topped with lump crabmeat, mushrooms, roasted red peppers, and scallions, finished with a lemon beurre blanc; and lobster ravioli with fresh Gulf shrimp and diver scallops. With only eight tables, this place is a tiny, romantic find.

14 Vicki St., Santa Rosa Beach. (C) **850/267-0054.** www.letseat.at/CafeTango. Reservations recommended. Main courses $15–$30. AE, MC, V. Daily 6–10pm.

Café Thirty-A ★★★ SEAFOOD/AMERICAN Only 1½ miles east of Seaside, along Scenic Highway 30A, this comfortable yet classy restaurant prepares exquisite seafood, steaks, and wood-oven pizzas. It's mostly a vacationing white-collar crowd here, but anyone can enjoy the remarkable offerings (including drinks from the creative martini menu and wine from the extensive, award-winning list), served up by a friendly and efficient staff. The menu changes daily, but usually available is the fantastic grilled Georgia quail served with creamy grits and sage fritters. For entrees, you can't miss with any of the seafood dishes, such as the wood-oven-roasted grouper with chili-dusted baby tiger shrimp and vegetable risotto, or the grilled Hawaiian butterfish. If you're feeling more turf than surf, the filet mignon served with roasted-garlic whipped potatoes and a balsamic reduction is excellent. Leave room for such desserts as the luscious molten chocolate torte or the heavenly banana beignets.

3899 E. Scenic Hwy. 30A, Seagrove Beach. (C) **800/231-2166.** www.cafethirtya.com. Reservations highly recommended. Main courses $28–$38; wood-oven pizzas $14–$15. AE, DC, DISC, MC, V. Summer daily 6–10pm; off season Mon–Fri 5:30–9pm; Sat–Sun 5:30–9:30pm.

Cowgirl Cafe ★ SOUTHWESTERN This fun, tiny Rosemary Beach cafe has big, bold Texas/Southwestern flavors as seen with hearty lunches, breakfasts, dinners, and even picnic baskets. Salsa and guacamole are homemade and excellent toppers on everything from breakfast tacos and burritos to the Mexican tuna salad sandwich. There are also pizzas such as the Drunken Cowgirl made with a special red sauce of vodka, light cream, garlic, and tomato. Although the small bar serves only beer and wine, it has a reputation as one of the best neighborhood bars on 30A.

54 Main St., Rosemary Beach. (C) **850/303-0708.** www.cowgirlkitchen.net. Main courses $6–$14. AE, DC, MC, V. Mon 11am–9pm; Tues–Sun 8am–9pm.

Destin Chops 30A ★★ STEAKHOUSE Just outside of Rosemary Beach, Destin Chops is a contemporary steakhouse with a sexy cocktail lounge and sushi bar. Forget the sushi, though, and go for the restaurant's namesake featuring USDA prime meats in all shapes and sizes. For a nice surf and turf combo, do the 30A Filet—8 ounces topped with jumbo lump crabmeat, béarnaise sauce, and grilled asparagus. An American Kobe hanger steak with roasted red pepper relish, broccolini, and Yukon gold mashed potatoes is also delicious. For the bar scene, check out the nightly happy hour from 5 to 7pm, and for early birds, there's an early-evening dining menu offering one free entree with the purchase of another from 5 to 6pm.

10343 E. County Hwy. 30A, Seacrest Beach. ✆ **850/231-4050.** www.destinchops30a.com. Reservations recommended. Main courses $25–$55. AE, DC, MC, V. Daily 5–10pm.

Fire ★★ NEW AMERICAN A little bit out of the way, Fire is a gastronaut's hot spot, featuring a funky, seasonal menu that's a little bit Napa Valley and a little bit New Orleans with a gourmet mix of Cajun, natural, and comfort foods. Menus change twice a year, but among the creative fare: buttermilk-fried pheasant breast with black truffle–scented Gruyère grits, white balsamic braised kale, pickled sweet pepper relish, and poached garlic chicken jus; Florida lobster and country ham carbonara with fresh fettuccine, sweet pea purée, crispy poached egg, preserved lemon, and tomato oil; and a fantastic grilled black grouper with *sofrito*, black bean, and potato croquette in a cherry tomato confit with charred corn cream and chili oil. Lunch and brunch are great, too. Don't miss the Cuban sandwich with roast pork, country ham, cherry mustard, house jalapeño pickles, and Gruyère cheese on pressed French bread.

55 Clayton Lane, Grayton Beach. ✆ **850/231-9020.** www.restaurantfire.com. Main courses $24–$35; sandwiches $11–$12. AE, DC, MC, V. Tues-Fri 11:30am-2pm; Tues-Sat 6-11pm; Sun 11am-3pm.

Fish Out of Water ★★★ SEAFOOD WaterColor Inn's signature restaurant was one of 10 in the country hailed by *Bon Appétit* magazine for its Southern-inspired seafood dishes using local catches and freshly harvested and foraged organic fruits, vegetables, and herbs. Chef Philip Krajeck goes out of his way to support local farmers and fishermen. While the views of the Gulf and the modern decor are distractions, nothing compares to the cuisine, which changes seasonally and includes simple, yet dazzling, dishes such as a sensational Florida Hopper Shrimp with herb risotto, hen of the woods mushrooms, and poultry *jus*; line-caught pompano with eggplant, almonds, and raisins; and black grouper with local vegetable stew and tarragon. Stellar side dishes include Anson Mill's Grits with Hobbs' ham hock and roasted Brussels sprouts with lardons. If you can, try the prix-fixe menus, which provide you with a delectable sample of some of the best on the menu.

34 Goldenrod Circle, Santa Rosa Beach. ✆ **850/534-5050.** www.watercolorresort.com. Main courses $13–$36. AE, DC, MC, V. Summer and Spring Break daily 5:30-10:30pm; off-season Tues–Sat 5:30-10pm.

George's at Alys Beach ★ NEW AMERICAN/SEAFOOD Smack in the middle of stunning, work-in-progress Alys Beach is this casual cafe that boasts the best burger on 30A and a famous grouper sandwich. We can justify calling the grouper sandwich "famous," served either fried or wood grilled, which is how we had it. In addition to excellent, freshly prepared fare, including a killer lobster quesadilla with fruit salsa, superb sweet-and-sour fish over Asian slaw, wood-grilled salmon wraps, and Señora Anna's fish tacos, the menu has a serious sense of humor, broken down into two categories—"Behave" and "Misbehave." A great kids' menu and takeout service make this an excellent place for families and picnickers.

30 Castle Harbour Dr., Alys Beach. ☎ **850/641-0017.** www.georgesatalysbeach.com. Reservations recommended. Main courses $19–$32 dinner; $6–$15 lunch. AE, DC, MC, V. Daily 11am–3pm and 5–9pm.

The Red Bar ★ SEAFOOD Housed in a former general store, this funky Grayton Beach spot is best known for its bric-a-brac and chalkboard menu featuring excellent Low Country–esque entrees, such as sautéed shrimp and crawfish. There's live jazz nightly and a buzzing cocktail scene. Celebrities from Sheryl Crow to Jim Carrey have been spotted sipping drinks with the locals. Check out the breakfast, featuring all sorts of omelets, delicious egg dishes, and potent bloody marys.

70 Hotz Ave., Grayton Beach. ☎ **850/231-1008.** www.theredbar.com. Main courses $13–$21; breakfast $4–$11. No credit cards. Daily 7–10:30am, 11am–3pm, and 5pm "until late."

Stinky's Fish Camp Seafood & Wine Bar ★★★ SEAFOOD Only in the case of this rustic seafood house is the word *stinky* a positive adjective. Serving delicious, fresh local seafood, Stinky's is a locals' favorite with a great, lively bar scene. From po' boys and frogs' legs to something called Stinky's Stew, a savory "Who's Who" of local seafood—fresh shrimp, mussels, Gulf fish, crab legs, oysters, Bay scallops—and tomatoes, potatoes, and corn simmered in wine and garlic broth and served with a pressed crab meat po' boy, Stinky's is truly the antithesis of its namesake. There are also great lunch, brunch, and late-night menus.

5994 Hwy. 30A, Santa Rosa Beach. ☎ **850/267-3053.** www.stinkysfishcamp.com. Main courses $15–$25. AE, DC, MC, V. Daily 5pm–midnight.

SEASIDE

Several cafes and sandwich shops in Seaside's Gulf-side shopping complex sell inexpensive snacks to beachgoers.

Bud & Alley's ★★ SEAFOOD/STEAK/MEDITERRANEAN In this cracked-crab-and-champagne-loving village, Bud & Alley's (named for a dog and a cat) has spectacular sunset views from the rooftop bar and a menu that changes frequently, but always has savory surprises. The menu offers an infusion of Basque, Italian, Louisiana, and Floridian dishes that might include seafood stew or sautéed head-on shrimp with garlic, shallots, and cracked pepper. You can dine indoors or out, on the screened porch or under an open-air gazebo where you'll hear waves splashing against the white sand. Jazz is usually in the spotlight on weekends. The roof-deck bar overlooking the water is always hopping and features an impressive menu of frozen cocktails, martinis, and wines. On New Year's Eve, everyone celebrates at Bud & Alley's. Call ahead to see whether a noted guest chef is cooking or a wine-tasting dinner is scheduled. In the same complex is **Bud & Alley's Taco Bar,** where you can toss back tequila and a few tacos

 Building Fences

Seaside's Urban Code requires that all homes sport white-painted wood picket fences at the streetfront and pathfront property lines, and that no two fences be the same on any one avenue. Explore them all; they range from subdued to downright wacky.

or burritos for $3 to $8, and the **Pizza Bar,** featuring eat-in or takeout antipasti, pasta, wood-burning-oven pizzas, wine, and beer for $5 to $15.

Hwy. 30A, in the beachside shops. ℂ **850/231-5900.** www.budandalleys.com. Reservations recommended. Main courses $24–$36; lunch $10–$15. MC, V. Apr–Sept daily 11:30am–3pm, Sun–Thurs 5:30–9:30pm, Fri–Sat 5:30–10pm; Oct–Mar Sun–Mon and Wed–Thurs 5:30–9pm, Fri–Sat 5:30–9:30pm.

Crush Wine Bar ★ TAPAS This funky tapas and wine bar has a great, bohe-mian vibe and a great selection of sandwiches and small plates, including Papas Bravas potatoes with *sriracha* aioli and sweet paprika and a great braised beef short rib panini with caramelized onions and Gruyère cheese. Bar seating is pre-mium, and indoor tables are sparse, but when the weather is great and there's something going on at the Seaside Amphitheater, the alfresco tables are where the action is. It's also a great place for an after-dinner drink or two.

25 Central Sq., Seaside. ℂ **850/468-0703.** www.crush30a.com. Reservations not taken. Sushi and tapas $6–$16. AE, DC, MC, V. Sun–Wed 5–10pm; Thurs–Fri 5pm–midnight. Bar Mon–Fri 5pm–whenever; Sat noon–whenever.

Great Southern Cafe ★★ SOUTHERN Smack in the middle of "down-town" Seaside is this cozy, cracker-style restaurant serving down-home Southern fare (chef/owner Jim Shirley still cooks in his grandma's cast-iron skillets) with a gourmet twist as seen in their house specialty, Grits-a-ya-ya: smoked Gouda cheese grits smothered with a sauce of fresh cream, sautéed Gulf shrimp, spin-ach, portobello mushrooms, applewood-smoked bacon, garlic, and shallots. I also loved the pan-seared crab cakes and fried green tomatoes dusted with a roasted red pepper rémoulade sauce, and for oyster lovers, inside the restaurant is the Littlest Oyster Bar, which is really just a shucking table serving an enormous se-lection of Apalachicola's finest. Choose from outdoor porch dining or inside the cozy houselike dining room. An outdoor side bar is a great spot for observing the concerts and activities on Seaside's great lawn.

83 Central Sq., Seaside. ℂ **850/231-7327.** www.thegreatsoutherncafe.com. Reservations rec-ommended. Main courses $16–$28; lunch $9–$13. AE, DC, MC, V. Daily breakfast 8am–11am; lunch 11am–5pm; dinner 5–9:30pm.

Destin & Fort Walton Beach After Dark

In summer, there's live entertainment at most resorts, including the Ramada Plaza Beach Resort, in Fort Walton Beach; the Hilton Sandestin Beach & Golf Resort; and Sandestin Golf and Beach Resort, in southern Walton County (see "Where to Stay," earlier in this chapter). Call ahead to find out what's scheduled, especially during the slow season (Oct–Feb).

For other ideas and listings of what's happening, pick up a copy of the week-ly *Walton Sun* newspaper.

DESTIN Several restaurants provide entertainment nightly in summer, and on weekends in the off-season. See "Where to Dine," earlier in this chapter, for details about restaurants. The dockside **AJ's Club Bimini,** 116 U.S. 98 E. (ℂ **850/837-1913**), has live reggae under a thatched-roofed deck. A some-what older, if not more sober, crowd gathers at the big harborside deck at **Fisherman's Wharf,** on U.S. 98 E. (ℂ **850/654-4766;** www.fishermans wharfdestin.com), and the **Deck,** on U.S. 98 E. at the Harbor Docks res-taurant, overlooking the harbor (ℂ **850/837-2506**). For Irish tunes nightly

Crack some (crab) legs at AJ's Club Bimini in Destin.

year-round, head for **McGuire's Irish Pub & Brewery,** in the Harborwalk Shops, U.S. 98 east of the Destin Bridge (©850/650-0567). The **Sky Bar,** above Gratzi Italian Restaurant, 1771 Old Hwy. 98 (©850/837-7475; www.skybar.net), draws the after-dinner crowd from the Back Porch and other adjacent restaurants.

Twenty-somethings are attracted to the dance club, rowdy saloon, Jimmy Buffett–style reggae bar, and sports TV and billiards parlor all under one roof at **Nightown,** 140 Palmetto St. (©850/837-6448; www.nightown.com), near the harbor on the inland side of U.S. 98 E. One admission covers it all. There's live music Friday and Saturday nights, and amateur boxing on Tuesday. Nearby, **Hogs Breath Destin,** 541 Hwy. 98 E. (©850/837-5991; www.hogsbreath.com), is a lively sibling of the famous pub in Key West with bands playing rock, blues, and jazz.

Out toward Sandestin, **Fudpucker's Beachside Bar & Grill** (p. 663), opposite the Henderson Beach State Park, offers double the fun with two summertime stages. There's another Fudpucker's at 108 Santa Rosa Blvd., on Okaloosa Island in Fort Walton Beach (©850/243-3833).

FORT WALTON BEACH Country music and dancing fans should head for the **High Tide Oyster Bar,** at Okaloosa Island off the Brooks Bridge (©850/244-2624). **Papa Joe's Hideaway,** 104 S. Perry Ave. (©850/244-5599), is a great hangout for live music—everything from country and blues to experimental jazz—and, on Thursdays and Saturdays at 6:30pm, final table poker.

BEACHES OF SOUTH WALTON/30A For a mellow night out, Rosemary Beach's **Courtyard Wine & Cheese,** 66 Main St. (©850/231-1219; www.courtyardwineandcheese.com), features a fantastic selection of wines by the glass or bottle, excellent cheeses and fondue, live music, and courtyard seating. Over in Seaside, sunset or late-night drinks are a must at the **Tarpon Club Roof-Deck Bar** upstairs at Bud & Alley's (©850/231-5900; www.budandalleys.com). For a great bar and tapas scene, **Crush Wine Bar** (©850/468-0703; www.crush30A.com) is the place. But it's the **Red Bar** (©850/231-1008) that sees the funkiest crowd, from rowdy locals to bona fide celebrities. As the night goes on, the place gets crazier. Brace yourselves.

PANAMA CITY BEACH

100 miles E of Pensacola; 100 miles SW of Tallahassee

Panama City Beach, a Spring Break mecca, has long been known as the "Redneck Riviera." Millions flock here from the bordering states of Georgia, Alabama, Mississippi, and Louisiana. It still has a seemingly unending strip of bars, amusement parks, and old-fashioned motels, but this lively and crowded destination (in season) also has some decent resorts and condos to go along with its 20-plus miles of sandy beaches, golf courses, fishing, boating, and fresh seafood.

Panama City Beach is the most seasonal resort in Northwest Florida, as many restaurants, attractions, and some hotels close between October and March. Spring Break is a big deal here; MTV sets up shop in Panama City Beach for its annual beach-party broadcasts. In an attempt to appeal to a more upscale clientele, Panama City Beach introduced Pier Park, an alfresco shopping, dining, and entertainment complex on the beach.

Essentials

GETTING THERE The commuter arms of **Delta, Northwest,** and **US Airways** will still fly into **Panama City/Bay County International Airport,** on Lisenby Avenue, north of St. Andrews Boulevard, in Panama City (✆ **850/763-6751;** www.pcairport.com). In May 2010, that airport was replaced by the brand-new **Northwest Florida Beaches International Airport,** 6300 West Bay Pkwy., Panama City Beach (✆ **850/763-6751;** www.pcairport.com), which is now serviced by **Southwest Airlines.**

Alamo (✆ 800/327-9633), **Avis** (✆ 800/331-1212), **Budget** (✆ 800/527-0700), **Enterprise** (✆ 800/325-8007), **Hertz** (✆ 800/654-3131), and **National** (✆ 800/CAR-RENT [227-7368]) have rental-car offices here.

Taxi fares to the beach are about $25 to $30.

The **Amtrak** (✆ **800/USA-RAIL** [872-7245]; www.amtrak.com) transcontinental *Sunset Limited* service stops at Chipley, 45 miles north of Panama City.

VISITOR INFORMATION For advance information, contact the **Panama City Beach Convention & Visitors Bureau,** P.O. Box 9473, Panama City Beach, FL 32417 (✆ **800/722-3224** in the U.S., 800/553-1330 in Canada, or 850/233-6503; fax 850/233-5072; www.800pcbeach.com). It operates a visitor center in the City Hall complex, 17001 Panama City Beach Pkwy. (U.S. 98), at Florida 79. The center is open daily from 8am to 5pm; closed New Year's Day, Thanksgiving, and Christmas.

GETTING AROUND The **Bay Town Trolley** (✆ **850/769-0557;** www.baytowntrolley.org) runs along Thomas Drive and on Front Beach Road as far west as Florida 79; it operates year-round Monday through Friday five times a day. Rides cost $1.50 for adults and 75¢ for seniors. Children 5 and younger ride free. Call for the schedule.

For a taxi, call **Yellow Cab** (✆ **850/763-4691**). Fares at the beach are approximately $2 to climb aboard and $2 per mile.

TIME The Panama City area is in the Central time zone, 1 hour behind Miami, Orlando, and Tallahassee.

Hitting the Beach: St. Andrews State Park

A nearly unbroken strand of white sand fronts all 22 miles of Panama City Beach, but the highlight for many is **St. Andrews State Park ★★★**, at the east end. With more than 1,000 acres of dazzling white sand and dunes, this preserved wilderness demonstrates what the area looked like before motels and condominiums lined the beach. Lacy, golden sea oats sway in the Gulf breezes, and rosemary grows wild. Picnic areas (on the Gulf beach and the Grand Lagoon), restrooms, and open-air showers are available for beachgoers. Anglers will find jetties and a boat ramp. A nature trail reveals wading birds and perhaps an alligator or two. Drive carefully here because the area is home to foxes, coyotes, and a herd of deer. A historic turpentine fir tree still on display was formerly used by lumbermen to make turpentine and rosin, both important for caulking old wooden ships.

The park's 176 RV and tent **campsites** are among the state's most beautiful, especially the 40 in a pine forest right on the shores of Grand Lagoon. They are very popular, so reservations are highly recommended—and essential in summer. Call ℂ **800/326-3521** or go to www.reserveamerica.com. Sites cost $28 year-round.

Park admission is $8 per car of up to eight, $4 single occupant, and $2 per pedestrian or cyclist. The area is open daily from 8am to sunset. Pets are not allowed in the park. For more information, contact the park at 4607 State Park Lane, Panama City, FL 32408 (ℂ **850/233-5140;** www.floridastateparks.org/standrews).

Pristine **Shell Island ★★**, a 7½-mile-long, 1-mile-wide barrier island accessible only by boat, sits a few hundred yards across an inlet from St. Andrews State Park. This uninhabited natural preserve is great for shelling and fun for swimming, sun-tanning, or just relaxing. Visitors can bring chairs, beach gear, coolers, food, and beverages. The best way to get here is on the park's **Shell Island Shuttle** (ℂ **800/227-0132** or 850/234-7245; www.shellislandshuttle. com), which runs every 30 minutes daily from 9am to 5pm. Fares are $15 for adults and $6.95 for children 11 and under, plus the admission fees to the state park (see above). A snorkeling package costs $22 for adults and $17 for kids 12 and under, and includes the shuttle ride and equipment. Kayak rentals are $55 a day for a single-seat boat, $65 for a double-seater.

Several cruise boats go to Shell Island, including the glass-bottomed **Captain Anderson III,** which departs from Captain Anderson's Marina, 5500 N. Lagoon Dr., at Thomas Drive (ℂ **850/234-3435;** www.captandersons marina.com). It charges $18 for adults, $10 for kids ages 2 to 11 (Mar–Oct).

Outdoor Activities

BOATING A variety of rental boats are available at some of the marinas near the Thomas Drive bridge over Grand Lagoon. These include the **Captain Davis Queen Fleet,** based at Captain Anderson's Marina, 5500 N. Lagoon Dr. (ℂ **800/874-2415** or 850/234-3435), and the **Shell Island Boat Rentals** at Treasure Island Marina, 3605 Thomas Dr. (ℂ **850/234-7245;** www.shellislandtours.com), which also rents WaveRunners, jet boats, inflatables, and other equipment.

FISHING The least expensive way to try your luck is with **Captain Anderson's Deep Sea Fishing,** at Captain Anderson's Marina, Thomas Drive at Grand Lagoon (ℂ **800/874-2415** or 850/234-5940; www.captandersonsmarina. com). The captain's party-boat trips last 5 to 6 hours, with prices ranging from $50 to $90 per person, including bait and tackle. Observers can go along for $25 to $40.

The more expensive charter-fishing boats depart daily from March to November from the marinas mentioned in "Boating," above.

You definitely won't get seasick casting your line from two recently revamped boardwalks at the **County Pier,** 12213 Front Beach Rd. (© **850/233-3039**), or the **Russell Fields Pier,** 16101 Front Beach Rd. (© **850/233-5080**).

GOLF At Bay Point Marriott Golf Resort & Spa (p. 675), the **Bay Point Marriott Golf Club,** 3900 Marriott Dr., off Jan Cooley Road (© **850/235-6950;** www.baypointgolf.com), offers 36 holes of championship play, including the Jack Nicklaus–designed course the **Nicklaus Course ★★,** rated one of the country's most difficult—and scenic. Hole No. 17 features a green design reminiscent of a fishbowl, where the green is actually recessed below the surrounding landscape, creating a challenging semiblind shot. The signature hole, No. 5, offers panoramic views of the Grand Lagoon and St. Andrews Bay. Both this course and the Club Meadows course have clubhouses, putting greens, driving ranges, clinics, and private instruction. Greens fees with cart start at about $99 in summer and $49 in winter, depending on the time and day of the week.

The **Edgewater Beach Resort,** 11212 U.S. 98A (© **850/235-4044;** www.resortspcbeach.com), also has a 9-hole resort course, and its guests have access to the **Hombre,** 120 Coyote Pass, 3 miles west of the Hathaway Bridge off Panama City Beach Parkway/U.S. 98 (© **850/234-3573;** www.hombregolfclub.com), a par-72 championship course that's a PGA Tour Qualifying School site. Also, 15 of its 18 holes have water hazards (the 7th hole sits on an island). Greens fees are about $39 to $69 with cart.

The course at the semiprivate **Holiday Golf Club,** 100 Fairway Blvd. (© **850/234-1800;** www.holidaygolfclub.com), sports lake-lined fairways and elevated greens. Greens fees with cart are about $25 to $65. You can play at night on a lighted 9-hole, par-29 executive course.

The cheapest place to play here is the flat and forgiving **Signal Hill,** 9516 N. Thomas Dr. (© **850/234-3218;** www.signalhillgolfcourse.com), where you'll pay about $20 to $30 with cart, rates subject to change seasonally.

For course information, go to www.golf.com or www.floridagolfing.com, or call the **Florida Sports Foundation** (© **850/488-8347**) or **Florida Golfing** (© **866/833-2663**).

SCUBA DIVING & SNORKELING Although the area is too far north for extensive coral formations, more than 50 artificial reefs and shipwrecks in the Gulf waters off Panama City attract a wide variety of sea life. The marine institute has sent ships, navy scrap metal, pontoons, towers, bridge spans, tanks, hovercraft, and even a Quonset hut to the bottom of the Gulf since the 1970s. Perhaps the most famous wreck is the *Empire Mica,* a British tanker that was torpedoed by a German U-boat in 1942. It now rests 20 miles off Cape San Blas. The largest local operator is **Dive Locker,** 106 Thomas Dr. (© **850/230-8006;** www.divelocker.net). Others include **Panama City Dive Center,** 4823 Thomas Dr. (© **850/235-3390;** www.pcdivecenter.com), and **Emerald Coast Divers,** 5121 Thomas Dr. (© **800/945-DIVE** [3483] or 850/233-3355; www.divedestin.com). These companies lead dives, teach courses, and take snorkelers to the grass flats off Shell Island.

Exploring the Area

Gulf World Marine Park ☺ This landscaped tropical garden and marine attraction has shows with dolphins, sea lions, penguins, and more. Not to be upstaged, parrots perform daily, too. Scuba demonstrations, shark feedings, and underwater shows keep the crowds entertained. The park has interactive programs, including a trainer-for-a-day program ($199 per person) and a dolphin encounter ($150). Allow about 3½ hours to see it all, more if you do one of the encounters. **Note:** Swimming with dolphins has both its critics and its supporters. You may want to visit the Whale and Dolphin Conservation Society's website at **www.wdcs.org**.

15412 Front Beach Rd. (at Hill Ave.), Panama City Beach. ✆ **850/234-5271.** www.gulfworld marinepark.com. Admission $27 adults, $17 children 5–11. Summer daily 9am–4pm; off season daily 9am–2pm.

Museum of Man in the Sea Owned by the Institute of Diving, this small museum exhibits relics from the first days of scuba diving, historic displays of the underwater world dating from 1500, and treasures recovered from sunken ships. Hands-on exhibits explain water and air pressure, light refraction, and why diving bells work. Both kids and adults can climb through a submarine and see live sea animals in a pool. Videos and aquariums explain the sea life found in St. Andrews Bay.

17314 Panama City Beach Pkwy. (at Heather Dr., west of Fla. 79), Panama City Beach. ✆ **850/235-4101.** http://maninthesea.org. Admission $5 adults, free for children 5 and under. Tues–Sun 10am–4pm. Closed Mon, New Year's Day, Thanksgiving, and Christmas.

ZooWorld Zoological & Botanical Park ★ ☺ Situated in a pine forest, this zoo is an active participant in the Species Survival Plan, which helps protect endangered species by employing specific breeding and housing programs. Among the 350 guests here are orangutans and other primates; lions, tigers, and leopards; and alligators and other reptiles. The zoo's most precious attraction is the Tilghman Infant Care Facility, a nursery facility that allows you to view the baby animals born at ZooWorld.

9008 Front Beach Rd. (near Moylan Dr.), Panama City Beach. ✆ **850/230-4839.** www.zooworldpcb.net. Admission $15 adults, $12 seniors, $10 children 5–11. Mon–Sat 9:30am–4pm; Sun 11am–4pm. Last admission 3pm.

AMUSEMENT PARKS

For that Panama City–meets–Coney Island vibe, there's one amusement park good for killing some time. A 105-foot-high roller coaster is just one of the 30 rides at the **Shipwreck Island Water Park,** 12000 Front Beach Rd., at Alf Coleman Road (✆ **850/234-5810;** www.shipwreckisland.com; $33 adults, $22 seniors, $28 kids 35–50 in. tall). Little ones will love the traditional carousel. The park is lots of fun, with live entertainment and tons of junk food. There's also a variety of water amusements, including the 1,600-foot-long winding Lazy River for tubing and a daring 35-mph Speed Slide. The Tad Pole Hole is exclusively for young kids. Lounge chairs, umbrellas, and inner tubes are free, and lifeguards are on duty. Open Saturday and Sunday from mid-March to Memorial Day, then daily until mid-August, and back to weekends from then to Labor Day weekend.

Where to Stay

There are scores of motels along the beach here, ranging from small mom-and-pop operations to sizable members of national chains. The annual guide distributed by the Panama City Beach Convention & Visitors Bureau (p. 671) has a complete list.

The **Hampton Inn,** 2909 Thomas Dr. (©**850/236-8988**), is just a mile away from the beach and offers reasonably priced, clean rooms. The **Hilton Garden Inn,** 1101 U.S. Hwy. 231 (©**850/392-1093**), is a nice choice, but in the business district and a bit of a way from the beach.

Panama City Beach abounds with condominium complexes, such as the Edgewater Beach Resort, listed below. Among the many rental agents are **Counts Oakes Resort Properties,** 726 Thomas Dr., Panama City Beach (www.panamabeachrentals.com; © **800/621-2462** or 850/235-9920).

The best camping is at the lovely sites in **St. Andrews State Park** (p. 672), one of this area's major attractions.

Rates at even the most expensive properties here drop precipitously during winter, when the town rolls up the sidewalks. Bay County adds 5% tax to all hotel and campground bills, bringing the total add-on tax (with the county's 6.5% sales tax) to 11.5%.

Bay Point Marriott Golf Resort & Spa ★★ ☺ ♠

Ranked among the nation's top golf and tennis resorts, Bay Point Marriott, a Green Lodging property, is a great value, and the centerpiece of a development sprawling over 1,100 acres on a wildlife sanctuary bordered by St. Andrews Bay and the Grand Lagoon. Tucked away in a quieter, residential enclave of Panama City Beach, the resort is beside the lagoon and surrounded by gardens. From the breezy three-story lobby, window walls look out to scenic water views and two pools (one in its own glass-enclosed building). Guest rooms are spacious and luxurious, some with balconies or patios. The recently renovated **Golf Villas at Bay Point Marriott** is a group of seven buildings and 60 units next to the only Nicklaus Golf Course in Northwest Florida. They do seem somewhat away from the rest of the resort's action. Watersports are available at the resort's Grand Lagoon Beach. There's also a free water shuttle to beautiful Shell Island on the Gulf of Mexico. The 12,000-square-foot **Serenity Spa at Bay Point** offers an impressive menu of pampering and primping. Of the four restaurants, we especially liked the seasonal **Lime's Bayside Bar & Grill,** reachable by boardwalk and featuring fab bay views, cocktails, and casual fare. When temps get chillier, stay indoors and have sushi at the **Kingfish Restaurant & Sushi Bar.** During summer months, the resort offers a great kids' camp with all sorts of eco-inspired and generally fun planned events and activities.

4200 Marriott Dr., Panama City Beach, FL 32408. www.marriottbaypoint.com. © **800/874-7105** or 850/236-6000. Fax 850/236-6158. 376 units. Summer $179–$519 double; off season $99–$309 double. Packages available. AE, DC, DISC, MC, V. From Thomas Dr., take Magnolia Beach Rd. and bear right on Dellwood Rd. to resort complex. **Amenities:** 4 restaurants; 4 bars; seasonal children's program; concierge; 2 golf courses; health club; 2 Jacuzzis; 3 heated outdoor pools and 1 indoor pool; room service; 5 tennis courts; watersports equipment/rentals. *In room:* A/C, TV, fridge, hair dryer, high-speed Internet access.

Beachcomber by the Sea

An older, eight-story resort at Front Beach Road and Florida 79, Beachcomber by the Sea is a Panama City Beach veteran, seeing more than its fair share of Spring Breakers. All units have balconies overlooking a Gulf-side pool and hot tub bordered by a concrete deck accented by palm trees. The well-equipped suites come in two sizes. Each of the larger ones has a living room with sleeper sofa, kitchenette, bathroom, and bedroom with either one king-size bed or two double beds. The suites are similar to those at the Flamingo Motel & Tower, except here they have air conditioners in both the living room and the bedroom. The smaller units are more like motel rooms, but do contain microwaves; two have whirlpool tubs as well. For decent beachfront chow there's the **Barefoot Beach Club,** and complimentary continental breakfast is available in the lobby each morning.

17101 Front Beach Rd., Panama City Beach, FL 32413. www.beachcomberbythesea.com. © **888/886-8916** or 850/233-3600. Fax 850/233-3622. 96 units. Summer $169–$189 double; off season $69–$89 double. Rates include continental breakfast. Packages available. AE, DISC, MC, V. **Amenities:** Restaurant; access to nearby health club; Jacuzzi; heated outdoor pool. *In room:* A/C, TV, hair dryer, high-speed Internet access.

Edgewater Beach Resort ★ ☺ One of the Panhandle's largest condominium resorts, this sports-oriented, gated facility enjoys a beachfront location and 110 landscaped acres. Units in five Gulf-side towers have commanding views of the emerald waters and gorgeous sunsets from their private balconies. A pedestrian overpass leads across Front Beach Road to low-rise apartments and town homes fringing the ponds and fairways of the resort's 9-hole golf course. A daytime shuttle runs around the resort to pools, whirlpools, tennis center, and golf course. (Guests also get privileges at the 18-hole Hombre Golf Club, a quarter-mile north.) The Shoppes at Edgewater restaurants are across the road. Last but not least, the 11,000-square-foot, Polynesian-style pool has waterfalls, islands, and a deck with live entertainment daily from 11am to 4pm. Edgewater is part of the Resort Collection of Panama City Beach (**www.resortspcbeach.com**), which also consists of the Majestic Beach Resort, Emerald Beach Resort, Long Beach Resort, the En Soleil, Grand Panama, and Marina Landing.

11212 Front Beach Rd., Panama City Beach, FL 32407. www.edgewaterbeachresort.com. © **800/874-8686** or 850/235-4044. Fax 850/235-6899. 525 units. Summer $174–$595 condo; off season $93–$190 condo. Weekly rates and maid service available for a fee. AE, DC, DISC, MC, V. **Amenities:** 3 restaurants; 2 bars; children's programs; 9-hole executive golf course; health club; 4 Jacuzzis; 11 outdoor pools; limited room service; spa services; 11 Plexicushion tennis courts; watersports equipment/rentals. *In room:* A/C, TV, full kitchen, Wi-Fi.

Holiday Inn SunSpree Resort ★★ ☺ One building removed from the Edgewater Beach Resort and across the road from the Shoppes at Edgewater, this 15-story establishment is the top full-service Gulf-front hotel here. It's designed in an arch, with all rooms' balconies looking down on the beach, where a heated, lagoon-style pool and sun deck are separated from the sand by a row of palms and Polynesian torches. The hotel has won architectural awards for its dramatic lobby with a waterfall and the Fountain of Wishes (the coins go to charity). Each attractive, spacious guest room has a full-size refrigerator, a microwave, and two vanity areas. Decor is dramatically different from that found in your typical Holiday Inn—it's more reminiscent of a resort in the Caribbean, with its pastel colors and tile floors. The Aqualand water playground, Splash Around Kids' Club for ages 5 to 12, and Dive Inn Movies make this resort a favorite for visiting families.

11127 Front Beach Rd., Panama City Beach, FL 32407. www.holidayinnsunspree.com. © **800/633-0266** or 850/234-1111. Fax 850/235-1907. 340 units. Summer $204–$270 double, $280 suite; off season $90–$105 double, $129–$150 suite. AE, DC, DISC, MC, V. **Amenities:** 2 restaurants; bar; babysitting; concierge; concierge-level rooms; exercise room; Jacuzzi; heated outdoor pool; limited room service; watersports equipment/rentals. *In room:* A/C, TV, fridge, hair dryer, high-speed Internet access.

Sunset Inn This well-maintained establishment, near the east end of the beach, is right on the Gulf but away from the crowds. The spacious beachside rooms accommodate families in one- and two-bedroom apartments, while refurbished efficiencies and a new building with tropically furnished one- and two-bedroom condominiums are across the street. The condominiums are the most expensive units here, but the units with patios or balconies right on the beach will better suit sun-and-sand lovers. The best part about this motel is the quiet beach—it offers a sense of peace not necessarily found elsewhere along the strip.

8109 Surf Dr., Panama City Beach, FL 32408. www.sunsetinnfl.com. © **850/234-7370.** Fax 850/234-7370, ext. 350. 62 units. Spring Break and summer $65–$145 rooms and efficiencies, $150–$175 condos (4-6 people); spring $55–$100 rooms and efficiencies, $110–$125 condos; fall and winter $45–$85 rooms and efficiencies, $80–$100 condos. Weekly and monthly rates available during fall and winter. AE, DISC, MC, V. **Amenities:** Heated outdoor pool. *In room:* A/C, TV, kitchen.

Where to Dine

Except for fast-food joints, there aren't many national-chain family restaurants in Panama City Beach (you'll find those along 15th and 23rd sts. over in Panama City). One local chain worth trying is the **Montego Bay Seafood House** (www.montegobaypcb.com), which offers a wide range of sandwiches, burgers, and seafood main courses. Branches are at the "curve" at 4920 Thomas Dr. (© **850/234-8686**), and in the Shoppes at Edgewater, 473 Beckrich Rd., at Front Beach Drive (© **850/233-6033**).

Pay attention to the restaurant hours here—places are closed in winter. Even if they're open, many close early when business is slow; call ahead to make sure.

Billy's Oyster Bar and Crab House 🦐 SEAFOOD More a lively raw bar than a restaurant, Billy and Eloise Poole's casual spot has been serving the best crabs in town since 1982. These are hard-shell blue crabs prepared Maryland-style: steamed with Old Bay seasoning. Unlike at crab houses in Baltimore, however, Billy and Eloise remove the crab's top shell, clean out the "mustard" (intestines), and cut the crabs in two for you; all you have to do is "pick" out the meat. Don't worry, they'll show you how. Other steamed morsels include shrimp, oysters, crabs, and lobster served with corn on the cob and garlic bread. For fried food lovers, don't miss the fried crab. Order anything from the briny deep, but pass over other items.

3000 Thomas Dr. (btw. Grand Lagoon and Magnolia Beach Rd.). © **850/235-2349.** www.billysoysterbar.com. Main courses $6–$20; sandwiches $5–$10. AE, DISC, MC, V. Daily 11am–9pm.

Boar's Head Restaurant ★ STEAK/SEAFOOD An institution since 1978, this shingle-roofed establishment appears from the road to be a South Seas resort. Inside, its beamed ceiling, stone

> ## "We Shuck 'Em, You Suck 'Em"
>
> That's the motto at **Shuckums Oyster Pub & Seafood Grill**, 15614 Front Beach Rd., at Powell Adams Drive (© **850/235-3214;** www.shuckums.com). The bar is virtually papered over with dollar bills signed by old and young patrons who have flocked here since 1967. The specialty is fresh Apalachicola oysters, served raw, steamed, or baked with a variety of toppings. Otherwise, the menu consists of pub fare and mediocre seafood main courses. In summer, Shuckums is open daily from 11am to 2am. During the off season, it closes at 9pm Monday through Friday, at midnight Saturday and Sunday.

walls, and fireplaces create a warm, tavernlike atmosphere suited to the house specialties: tender, marbled prime rib of beef and perfectly cooked steaks. Beefeaters don't have the Boar's Head to themselves, however, as the coals are also used to give a charred flavor to salmon, grouper, and yellowfin tuna. Venison, quail, and other game dishes also find their way here in winter. The extensive wine list has won awards. Try the fried lobster if you're in the mood to indulge. A cozy tavern to one side features live music, usually Wednesday through Saturday evenings.

17290 Front Beach Rd. (just west of Fla. 79). ✆ **850/234-6628.** www.boarsheadrestaurant.com. Main courses $17–$43. AE, DC, DISC, MC, V. Summer daily 4:30–10pm; off season Sun–Thurs 4:30–9pm, Fri–Sat 4:30–10pm.

Captain Anderson's Restaurant & Waterfront Seafood Market ★

SEAFOOD Since 1953, this famous restaurant has been attracting early diners, who come to watch the fishing fleet unload the catch of the day at the busy marina on Grand Lagoon. It's so popular, in fact, that you may have to wait 2 hours for a table during the peak summer months; the three bars help you pass the time. The Captain's menu is noted for grilled local fish (grouper, amberjack, and yellowfin tuna), crab-stuffed jumbo shrimp, and a seafood platter that's heaped high.

5551 N. Lagoon Dr. (at Thomas Dr.). ✆ **850/234-2225.** www.captanderson.com. Main courses $14–$44. AE, DC, DISC, MC, V. Summer Mon–Sat 4–10pm; off season Mon–Sat 4:30–10pm. Closed Sun and Nov–Jan.

Firefly ★★ INTERNATIONAL

The Firefly is a stylish, New York–style, global cuisine restaurant. You can still dine outdoors under a grand old oak tree! The menu changes monthly, but hope you're there the night they are serving tempura-fried Apalachicola oysters. Other selections could include salmon and cream leek pizza with truffle oil; sushi-quality yellowfin tuna in a sherry-soy sauce; a "trio" of tuna, salmon, and pistachio; honey-Dijon-crusted grouper; and sautéed grouper with lump crabmeat in a sherry-butter sauce. Forget the crab cakes. Landlubbers can partake of award-winning beef, veal, lamb, pork, and game dishes. Espresso and tomato braised free-range Texas boar shank, anyone? White-chocolate crème brûlée is among several wonderful sweet endings. There's also an early dining menu and the cozy **535 Library Lounge,** featuring a big-screen TV, bona fide books, live music, and great cocktails.

535 Beckrich Rd. (in Shoppes at Edgewater), Panama City. ✆ **850/872-8444.** www.fireflypcb. com. Reservations recommended. Main courses $22–$42. AE, DC, DISC, MC, V. Daily 5–10pm.

SPECIAL DINING EXPERIENCES

Dinner-dance cruises on the **Lady Anderson** offer a romantic evening; they're available March through October. This modern, three-deck ship boards at Captain Anderson's Marina, 5550 N. Lagoon Dr. (✆ **800/360-0510** or 850/234-5940; www.ladyanderson.com), Monday through Saturday evenings, with the cruises lasting from 7 to 10pm. Buffet dinners are followed by live music for dancing on Monday, Wednesday, Friday, and Saturday nights; comedy on Tuesday; gospel music on Thursday. Dinner-dance and comedy tickets cost $48 for adults, $42 for seniors, $22 for children 6 to 11, and $14 for children 2 to 5. Gospel-music cruises go for $36 adults, $32 seniors, $22 children 6 to 11, and $15 children 2 to 5. Tips are included. Summertime reservations should be made well in advance.

Panama City & Panama City Beach After Dark

THE BAR & CLUB SCENE

The **Breakers,** 12627 Front Beach Rd. (© **850/234-6060;** www.breakerspcb.com), is the area's premier supper club, with unsurpassed Gulf views and music for dining and dancing. The beachfront **Harpoon Harry's Waterfront Cafe** is part of the same complex.

Romantic lounges with live entertainment can be found at the Firefly's **535 Library Lounge** at 535 Beckrich Rd. (in Shoppes at Edgewater; © **850/872-8444**); and at the **Boar's Head** (p. 677), 17290 Front Beach Rd. (© **850/234-6628**).

The 20-something crowd likes to boogie all night at such beach clubs as **Schooners,** 5121 Gulf Dr. (© **850/235-3555;** www.schooners.com), where every table has a Gulf view, and **Club La Vela,** also on the beach at 8813 Thomas Dr. (© **850/234-3866;** www.clublavela.com), a bikini-contest kind of place and one of Florida's largest nightclubs whose motto, to the horror of crowd-phobes, is "party with thousands." The clubs often stay open until 4am in summer. **Pineapple Willy's Lounge,** beachside at 9900 S. Thomas Dr. (© **850/235-0928;** www.pineapplewillys.com), is open from 11am to 2am, serving ribs basted with Jack Daniel's and spotlighting live entertainment during summer and a host of sports on TVs year-round.

Panama City Beach's newest nightlife hot spot is **Pier Park,** 600 Pier Park Dr. (© **850/236-9979**), a Disney/Caribbean-style dining, shopping, drinking complex located right on the "strip," across from the beach and featuring, among other things, a movie theater, Jimmy Buffett's Margaritaville, Reggae J's Island Grill, a branch of Nashville's legendary Tootsies Orchid Lounge, Hofbrau Beer Garden, and a branch of Destin's Back Porch Seafood & Oyster House.

APALACHICOLA ★★

65 miles E of Panama City; 80 miles W of Tallahassee

Sometimes called Florida's Last Frontier (a claim that overlooks the Everglades) or the Forgotten Coast, though Franklin County is now billing itself as "A Natural Escape" (**http://anaturalescape.com**), Apalachicola makes a fascinating day trip from Panama City Beach or Tallahassee, as well as a destination in its own right. The long, gorgeous beaches on St. George Island, 7 miles from town, are among America's best. Justifiably famous for Apalachicola oysters, the bays and estuaries are great for fishing and boating. If you love nature, the area is rich in wildlife preserves.

The lovely little town of Apalachicola (pop. 2,600) was a major seaport each autumn from 1827 to 1861, when plantations in Alabama and Georgia shipped tons of cotton down the Apalachicola River to the Gulf. The town had a racetrack, an opera house, and a civic center that hosted balls, socials, and gambling. The population shrank during the mosquito-infested summer months, however, when yellow fever and malaria epidemics struck. It was during one of these outbreaks that Dr. John Gorrie of Apalachicola tried to develop a method of cooling his patients' rooms. In doing so, he invented the forerunner of the air-conditioner, a device that made Florida tourism possible and life a whole lot more bearable for locals.

Apalachicola has traditionally made its living primarily from the Gulf and the lagoonlike bay protected by a chain of offshore barrier islands.

Today this area produces the bulk of Florida's oyster crop, and shrimping and fishing are major industries, too. The Gulf oil spill never reached this part of the Panhandle, and the eponymous oysters remained safe and delicious.

The town has also been discovered by a number of urban expatriates, who came for a visit and stayed. They've restored old homes, and opened antiques and gift shops (there aren't many towns this size where you can buy Crabtree & Evelyn products). Apalachicola is a hidden gem of a charming Southern small town that manages to balance both its history and its aspirations.

Essentials

GETTING THERE The nearest airport is 65 miles to the west at Panama City Beach (p. 671). From there, you'll have to rent a car or take an expensive taxi ride. The Tallahassee Regional Airport (p. 685) is about 85 miles to the northeast.

The scenic way to drive here is via the Gulf-hugging U.S. 98 from Panama City Beach, or via U.S. 319 and U.S. 98 from Tallahassee. From I-10, take exit 142 at Marianna, then follow Florida 71 south to Port St. Joe; from there, take U.S. 98 East to Apalachicola.

VISITOR INFORMATION The **Apalachicola Bay Chamber of Commerce,** 99 Market St., Apalachicola, FL 32320 (✆ **850/653-9419;** fax 850/653-8219; www.apalachicolabay.org), supplies information about the area from its office on Market Street (U.S. 98) between Avenue D and Avenue E. The chamber is open Monday through Friday from 9:30am to 5pm. The **Franklin County Tourist Development Council** (http://anaturalescape.com) also offers an easily navigable website with information about attractions, events, activities, and lodging.

TIME The town is in the Eastern Time zone, like Orlando, Miami, and Tallahassee (1 hr. ahead of Panama City Beach and the rest of the Panhandle). *Note:* Many shops are closed on Wednesday afternoon, when Apalachicolans go fishing.

Beaches, Parks & Wildlife Refuges

Some experts consider the 9 miles of beaches in the **Dr. Julian G. Bruce St. George Island State Park ★★★** among America's best. This pristine nature preserve occupies the eastern end of St. George Island, about 15 miles east of Apalachicola. A 4-mile-long paved road leads through the dunes to picnic areas, restrooms, showers, and a boat launch. An unpaved trail leads another 5 miles to the island's eastern end, but be careful: It's easy to get stuck in the soft sand, even in a four-wheel-drive SUV. From a hiking trail leading from the campground out to a narrow peninsula on the bay side, you can see countless terns, snowy plovers, black skimmers, and other birds. Entry costs $6 per vehicle with up to eight occupants, $4 single-occupant vehicle, and $2 per pedestrian or bicyclist. East End access costs $6 per person. Campsites go for $24. The park is open daily from 8am to sunset. Pets are allowed only on campgrounds. For more information, contact the park at 1900 E. Gulf Beach Dr., St. George Island, FL 32328 (✆ **850/927-2111;** www.floridastateparks.org/stgeorgeisland).

If you'd rather stay on St. George Island in one of 270 privately owned rental homes, from luxe six-bedroom beach homes to old-fashioned Florida cottages, call **Collins Vacation Rentals** (✆ **800/423-7418;** www.collinsvacation rentals.com). In addition to the state park, the island offers restaurants, bars, and some of the best fishing in the state.

There are no facilities whatsoever at the **St. Vincent National Wildlife Refuge,** southwest of Apalachicola and accessible only by boat. The U.S. Fish & Wildlife Service has left this 12,358-acre barrier island in its natural state, but visitors are welcome to walk through its pine forests, marshlands, ponds, dunes, and beaches. In addition to native species, such as bald eagles and alligators, the island is home to a small herd of sambar deer from Southeast Asia. Red wolves are bred here for relocation in other wildlife areas. **St. Vincents Island Shuttle Service** (© 850/229-1065; www.stvincentisland.com), at Indian Pass, 21 miles west of Apalachicola via

You'll probably see pelicans on the Gulf Coast around Apalachicola.

U.S. 98 and C.R. 30A and 30B, will take you to the island in a pontoon boat. If you bring your bike, the boat will drop you at one end of the island and pick you up at the other. Call for prices and reservations, which are required. The refuge headquarters, at the north end of Market Street in town, has exhibits of wetland flora and fauna; it's open Monday through Friday from 8am to 4:30pm. Admission is free. For more information, contact the refuge at P.O. Box 447, Apalachicola, FL 32329 (© 850/653-8808).

The **Apalachicola National Forest** begins a few miles northeast of town. It has a host of facilities, including canoeing and mountain bike trails.

Outdoor Activities

CRUISES Jeanni McMillan of **Journeys of St. George Island** ★ (© 850/927-3259; www.sgislandjourneys.com) takes guests on narrated nature cruises to the barrier islands, and on canoe and kayak trips in the creeks and streams of the Apalachicola River basin. She also leads night hikes with blue crab netting, shelling excursions, and fishing and scalloping trips, plus excursions tailored exclusively for children. Prices range from $250 to $450 per person. Reservations are required, so call to find out what she's offering when you'll be in town. Jeanni also rents canoes, kayaks, sailboats, and sailboards. Closed January and February.

You can go afternoon or sunset sailing on the bay on Capt. Jerry Weber's 40-foot sloop *Wind Catcher* (© 850/653-3881). The 2½-hour voyages on Apalachicola Bay cost $35 for adults and $30 for children 15 and under, including snacks and soft drinks. Reservations are essential. Or you can rent the entire boat for your own private sail for $210 for 2½ hours.

FISHING You can't go oystering, but fishing is excellent in these waters, where trout, redfish, flounder, tarpon, shark, and drum abound. The chamber of commerce (p. 680) can help arrange charters on the local boats, many of which dock at the Rainbow Inn on Water Street. For guides, contact **Robinson Brothers Guide Service** (© 850/653-8896; www.flaredfish.com). Rates run about $375 for a half-day and $500 to $550 for a full day for up to four anglers.

The renovated Dixie Theatre showcases live performance in Apalachicola.

Exploring the Town

Start your visit by picking up a map and a self-guided tour brochure from the chamber of commerce (p. 680), and then stroll around Apalachicola's waterfront, business district, and Victorian-era homes.

Along Water Street, several tin warehouses date back to the town's seafaring days of the late 1800s, as does the 1840s-era **Sponge Exchange,** at Commerce Street and Avenue E. A highlight of the residential area, centered on Gorrie Square at Avenue D and Sixth Street, is the Greek Revival–style **Trinity Episcopal Church,** built in New York and shipped here in 1837. **Battery Park,** at the water end of Sixth Street, has a children's playground. A number of excellent art galleries and gift shops are grouped on Market Street, Avenue D, and Commerce Street.

The showpiece at the **John Gorrie Museum State Park ★**, Avenue D, at Sixth Street (© 850/653-9347; www.floridastateparks.org/johngorriemuseum), is a replica of Dr. Gorrie's cooling machine, a prototype of today's air-conditioner: It really works! The park is open Thursday through Monday from 9am to 5pm; closed New Year's Day, Thanksgiving, and Christmas. Admission is $2 (free for children 6 and under).

The renovated **Dixie Theatre,** 21 Ave. E (© 850/653-3200; www.dixie theatre.com), a 1912 movie house, hosts live theater productions. It has maintained its original ticket booth and restored its facades to their original glory.

The **Estuarine Walk,** at the north end of Market Street, on the grounds of the Apalachicola National Estuarine Research Reserve (© 850/653-8063), contains aquariums full of fish and turtles, along with displays of other estuarine life. It's open Monday through Friday from 8am to 5pm. Admission is free.

Where to Stay

Built in 1997, the 42-room **Best Western Apalach Inn,** 249 Hwy. 98 W. (www. bwapalachinn.com; © 800/528-1234 or 850/653-9131; fax 850/653-9136), a mile west of downtown, is the only national chain hotel here.

Apalachicola River Inn ★ The town's only waterfront lodging, this two-story motel has rough-hewn exterior timbers that make it look like one of the neighboring warehouses. Units in the main building all have views across a marina to Apalachicola Bay. Those on the second floor are larger and have balconies, making them preferable to the smaller downstairs units, with doors opening directly onto the marina's boardwalk. All accommodations have been renovated, and they have new carpeting, windows, and French doors. Most of the upstairs rooms have shower-only bathrooms; however, there are whirlpool tubs in two of the units, as well as in a two-bedroom apartment in a building next door. The redone lobby now features the **Frog Level Oyster Bar,** a casual bar serving—what else?—oysters. There's also **Boss Oyster,** the inn's popular riverfront restaurant; **Caroline's;** and the **Roseate Spoonbill Lounge**—*the* local watering hole, with a grand view and music on an outdoor deck on weekends.

123 Water St., Apalachicola, FL 32320. www.apalachicolariverinn.com. ✆ **850/653-8139.** Fax 850/653-2018. 26 units. $129–$159 double; $195 suite; $260–$360 River Cottage. AE, DC, DISC, MC, V. Pets accepted in smoking rooms ($10 nightly fee). **Amenities:** Restaurant; 2 bars and lounges. *In room:* A/C, TV.

Coombs House Inn ★★★ The most luxurious place around, this large B&B occupies three Victorian villas. This historic inn is enchanting, with elegant antiques, Oriental carpets, original gilt-framed oil paintings, 15 original carved fireplaces, hardwood floors, romantic gardens, and spacious verandas under the shade of large oak trees. Each of the 23 beautifully furnished rooms, 7 which are Jacuzzi suites, are wonderfully furnished with carved four-poster beds, Egyptian cotton bedding, and complementary amenities such as in-room Starbucks coffee, delicious breakfasts, afternoon cookies and tea, weekend wine receptions, and considerably more. Complimentary as well are bicycles for touring the historic district or beach chairs for an afternoon on the pristine white beaches of adjacent St. George Island. A major truck route, U.S. 98, runs along the north side of both houses; request a south room to escape the periodic road noise.

80 6th St., Apalachicola, FL 32320. www.coombshouseinn.com. ✆ **850/653-9199.** Fax 850/653-2785. 23 units. $99–$299 double. Rates include breakfast, afternoon tea and cookies, wine reception. DISC, MC, V. **Amenities:** Free use of bikes and beach chairs. *In room:* A/C, TV, hair dryer, high-speed Internet access.

Gibson Inn ★★★ Built in 1907 as a seamen's hotel and gorgeously restored, this cupola-topped inn is such a brilliant example of Victorian architecture that it's listed on the National Register of Historic Inns. No two guest rooms are alike (some still have the original sinks in the sleeping areas), but all are richly furnished with period reproductions. Nonguests are welcome to wander upstairs and peek into unoccupied rooms (whose doors are left open). Reservations are advised during summer and on spring and fall weekends, and as much as 5 years in advance for the seafood festival in November. Grab a drink from the **bar** and relax in one of the high-backed rockers on the old-fashioned veranda. The dining room serves excellent seafood and is open to all comers, so don't expect this to be private like a B&B; instead, you'll find yourself in a reborn, absolutely charming, turn-of-the-20th-century hotel—one, albeit, with Wi-Fi access!

51 Ave. C, Apalachicola, FL 32320. www.gibsoninn.com. ✆ **850/653-2191.** Fax 850/653-3521. 30 units. $115–$155 double; $175–$260 suite. AE, MC, V. **Amenities:** Restaurant; bar; passes to local fitness center; Wi-Fi. *In room:* A/C, TV.

Where to Dine

Townsfolk still plop down on the round stools at the marble-topped counter to order Coca-Colas and milkshakes at the **Old Time Soda Fountain & Luncheonette,** 93 Market St. (✆ **850/653-2606**). This 1950s relic was once the town drugstore. It's open Monday through Saturday from 10am to 5pm.

The Boss Oyster ★★★ SEAFOOD You've heard about the aphrodisiac properties of Apalachicola oysters. Well, you can see if those properties are real at this rustic dockside eatery, whose motto is "Shut Up and Shuck." This is one of the best places in Florida to try the bivalves raw, steamed, or under a dozen toppings, ranging from capers to crabmeat. Steamed shrimp are also on offer, as are delicious po' boy sandwiches. Most main courses come from the fryer, so consider this joint a great local experience. Sit at the picnic tables inside, on a screened porch, or out on the dock.

At the Apalachicola River Inn, 125 Water St. (btw. aves. C and D). ✆ **850/653-9364.** Main courses $17–$25; oysters $4.50–$20; sandwiches and baskets $7–$10. AE, DC, DISC, MC, V. Apr-Sept Sun–Thurs 11:30am–10pm, Fri–Sat 11:30am–11pm; Oct–Mar Sun–Thurs 11:30am–9pm, Fri–Sat 11:30am–10pm.

Chef Eddie's Magnolia Grill ★★★ CONTINENTAL/CAJUN One of the top places to dine in Northwest Florida, Boston-bred chef-owner Eddie Cass's pleasant, homey restaurant offers nightly specials ranging from classic French rack of lamb and beef Wellington to fresh local seafood with New Orleans–style sauces. You will long remember Eddie's mahimahi Pontchartrain with cream and artichoke hearts. Start with a bowl of spicy seafood gumbo, a consistent hit during the Florida Seafood Festival.

99 11th St. (btw. aves. E and F). ✆ **850/653-8000.** Reservations recommended. Main courses $12–$24. MC, V. Mon–Sat 6–9:30pm.

The Owl Cafe ★★ SEAFOOD Ensconced on the first floor of a two-story clapboard building in the heart of downtown, this sophisticated restaurant ranks only behind Chef Eddie's Magnolia Grill as having the best cuisine in town. The menu features an emphasis on locally caught seafood. Go for the nightly seafood specials or opt for the terrific black grouper filet with garlic, capers, and artichokes. There's also an impressive, extensive wine list and a great Sunday brunch.

15 Ave. D (at Commerce St.). ✆ **850/653-9888.** www.owlcafeflorida.com. Reservations recommended. Main courses $12–$25. MC, V. Mon–Sat 11:30am–3pm and 5:30–10pm.

Tamara's Cafe Floridita ★★ FLORIBBEAN/LATIN AMERICAN Tamara Suarez's storefront cafe offers a change of pace and, after a bit of a rough patch experienced after she handed the restaurant over to her daughter and son-in-law, things are sizzlin' again. The black-bean soup still has that zing, and the pork tenderloin with black beans and yellow rice is outstanding. Don't miss the savory and sweet caramelized plantains and, for something truly different, fried flounder with pesto macaroni and cheese. You'll also find Latino spices accentuating Floribbean fare, such as a creamy jalapeño sauce putting a little fire into pecan-encrusted grouper. And while the paella is also tops, the snapper served in a broth with chorizo, clams, roasted potatoes, and wild arugula is sensational.

17 Ave. E (at Commerce St.). ✆ **850/653-4111.** www.tamarascafe.com. Reservations recommended. Main courses $12–$26. MC, V. Daily 11am–10pm.

TALLAHASSEE

163 miles W of Jacksonville; 191 miles E of Pensacola; 250 miles NW of Orlando

As a University of Miami alumna, I was practically taught to hate Tallahassee, just because it's the home of the Miami Hurricanes' biggest rivals—Florida State University's Seminoles (or 'Noles, as locals refer to them). Because I couldn't care less about football, I just chalked up Tallahassee as the state capital and, later in life, as command central for that pesky 2000 election bug known as the chad. But it's not just about football and hanging chads. There's a ton of charm and other history, as well.

Tallahassee was selected as Florida's capital in 1823 because it was halfway between St. Augustine and Pensacola, then the state's major cities. That location puts it almost in Georgia—and, in fact, Tallahassee has more in common with Macon than with Miami. There's as much Old South ambience as anywhere else in Florida. You'll find lovingly restored, 19th-century homes and buildings, including the 1845 Old Capitol. They all sit among so many towering pines and sprawling live oaks that you'll think you're in a forest. The trees form virtual tunnels along Tallahassee's five official Canopy Roads, which are lined with historic plantations, ancient Native American settlement sites and mounds, gardens, quiet parks with picnic areas, and beautiful lakes and streams. The nearby Apalachicola National Forest is a virtual gold mine of outdoor pursuits.

While tradition and history are important here, you'll also encounter the modern era, beginning with the New Capitol Building towering 22 stories over downtown. Usually sleepy Tallahassee takes on a very lively persona when the legislature is in session and when the football teams of Florida State University and Florida A&M University take to the gridiron.

If you're inclined to give your credit cards a workout, the nearby town of Havana is Florida's antiques capital.

Essentials

GETTING THERE American, Continental, Delta, Northwest, and US Airways serve **Tallahassee Regional Airport** (℃ 850/891-7802; www.talgov.com/airport), 10 miles southwest of downtown on Southeast Capital Circle.

Alamo, Avis, Budget, Hertz, and **National** have airport sites; **Dollar, Enterprise,** and **Thrifty** are nearby. You can take a **taxi** downtown for about $30.

The **Amtrak** (℃ 800/872-7245; www.amtrak.com) transcontinental *Sunset Limited* train stops in Tallahassee at 918½ Railroad Ave.

VISITOR INFORMATION For advance information, contact the **Tallahassee Area Convention and Visitors Bureau,** 200 W. College Ave. (P.O. Box 1369), Tallahassee, FL 32302 (℃ 800/628-2866 or 850/413-9200; fax 850/487-4621; www.visittallahassee.com). The bureau's excellent quarterly visitors guide has descriptions (including hours and admission fees) of just about everything going on here.

Go to the **Tallahassee Area Visitor Information Center,** 106 E. Jefferson St., across from the capitol (℃ 850/413-9200; www.visit tallahassee.com), for free street and public-transportation maps, brochures, and pamphlets outlining tours of the historic districts and the Canopy Roads. It's open Monday through Friday from 8am to 5pm, Saturday from 9am to noon.

For statewide information, a **Florida Welcome Center** is in the west foyer of the New Capitol Building (see below).

GETTING AROUND The city's public-transportation agency, **StarMetro** (℃ 850/891-5200), provides city **bus** service from its downtown terminal, at Tennessee and Adams streets ($1.25 adults, 60¢ seniors and kids 12 and under). The ticket booths there and at the Tallahassee Area Visitor Information Center have route maps and schedules. Some routes even have free Wi-Fi!

For taxi service, call **Yellow Cab** (© 850/580-8080) or **City Taxi** (© 850/562-4222). Fares are about $2.50 at flag fall, plus $2.50 per mile.

TIME Tallahassee is in the Eastern Time zone, like Orlando, Miami, and Apalachicola. It's 1 hour ahead of the rest of the Panhandle.

Exploring the City

THE CAPITOL COMPLEX

Florida's capitol complex, on South Monroe Street at Apalachee Parkway, dominates the downtown area and should be your first stop after the Tallahassee Area Visitor Information Center, just across Jefferson Street.

The **New Capitol Building** (© 850/488-6167), a $43-million sky scraper, was built in 1977 to replace the 1845-vintage Old Capitol. State legislators meet here for at least 60 days, usually beginning in March. The house and senate chambers have public viewing galleries. For a spectacular view, take the elevators to the 22nd-floor **observatory,** where, on a clear day, you can see all the way to the Gulf of Mexico. You can also view works by Florida artists while up here. The New Capitol is open Monday through Friday from 8am to 5pm.

In front of the skyscraper is the strikingly white **Old Capitol ★** (© 850/487-1902; www.flhistoriccapitol.gov). With its majestic dome, this "Pearl of Capitol Hill" has been restored to its original beauty. An eight-room exhibit portrays Florida's political history. Turn-of-the-20th-century furnishings, cotton gins, and other artifacts are also of interest. The Old Capitol is open Monday through Friday from 9am to 4:30pm, Saturday from 10am to 4:30pm, and Sunday and holidays from noon to 4:30pm. Admission is free to both the old and new capitols.

The twin granite towers of the **Vietnam Veterans Memorial** are across Monroe Street from the Old Capitol. Next to it, facing Apalachee Parkway, the **Union Bank Museum** (© 850/561-2603) is housed in Florida's oldest surviving bank building. For a while, it was the Freedman's Savings and Trust Company, which served emancipated slaves. Now part of Florida Agricultural and Mechanical University's Black Archives Research Center, it houses a small but interesting collection of artifacts and documents reflecting black history and culture and is definitely worth a brief visit. The museum is open Monday through Friday from 9am to 4pm; admission is free.

The Old Town Trolley will take you north of the capitol to the Georgian-style **Governor's Mansion,** at Adams and Brevard streets (© 850/488-4661). Enhanced by a portico patterned after Andrew Jackson's columned antebellum home in Tennessee, the Hermitage, and surrounded by giant magnolia trees and landscaped lawns, the mansion is furnished with 18th- and 19th-century antiques and collectibles. Tours are given when the legislature is in session, usually beginning in March. Call for schedules and reservations.

Adjacent to the Governor's Mansion, the **Grove** was home to Ellen Call Long, known as "The Tallahassee Girl," the first child born after Tallahassee was settled.

MUSEUMS, GALLERIES & ARCHAEOLOGICAL SITES

Black Archives Research Center and Museum ★ Housed in the columned library built by Andrew Carnegie in 1908, and set on the grounds of the Florida Agricultural and Mechanical University (FAMU), this research center and museum displays one of the nation's most extensive collections of African-American artifacts, as well as such treasures as a 500-piece Ethiopian cross collection. The

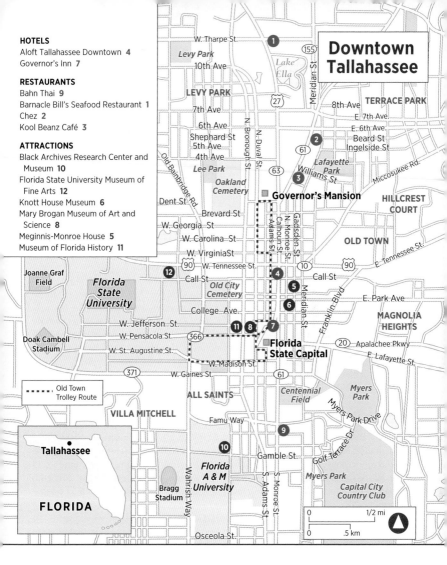

Downtown Tallahassee

archives contain one of the world's largest collections of African-American history. Visitors can listen to tapes of gospel music and of elderly people reminiscing about the past. FAMU was founded in 1887, primarily as a black institution. Today it's acclaimed for its business, engineering, and pharmacy schools.

Martin Luther King, Jr., Blvd. and Gamble St., on the Florida A&M University campus. © **850/599-3020.** www.famu.edu. Free admission. Mon–Fri 9am–4pm. Closed major holidays. Parking lot next to building.

Florida State University Museum of Fine Arts ★ This permanent, 4,000-piece collection includes 16th-century Dutch paintings, 20th-century American paintings, Japanese prints, pre-Columbian artifacts, and much more. Touring exhibits are displayed every few weeks.

250 Fine Arts Building, Copeland and Call sts. (on the FSU campus). ✆ **850/644-6836.** www.mofa.fsu.edu. Free admission. May–Aug Mon–Fri 9am–4pm; Sept–Apr Mon–Fri 9am–4pm, Sat–Sun 1–4pm. Closed holidays and weekends May–Aug.

Knott House Museum ★★ Adorned by a columned portico, this stately mansion was constructed in 1843, probably by a free black builder named George Proctor. Florida's first reading of the Emancipation Proclamation took place here in 1865. In 1928, it was purchased by politician William Knott, whose wife, Louella, wrote eccentric (read: kooky) rhymes about the house and Victorian furnishings (including the nation's largest collection of 19th-c. gilt-framed mirrors). She also wrote about

Florida's Old Capitol stands before the new high-rise Capitol.

social, economic, and political events of the era. Attached by satin ribbons to tables, chairs, and lamps, her poems are the museum's most unusual feature. The house is in the Park Avenue Historic District and is listed on the National Register of Historic Places. It's preserved as it looked in 1928, when the Knott family left it and all of its contents to the city (it's now administered by the Museum of Florida History). The gift shop carries Victorian greeting cards, paper dolls, tin toy replicas, reprints of historic newspapers, and other nostalgic items.

301 E. Park Ave. (at Calhoun St.). ✆ **850/922-2459.** www.museumoffloridahistory.com/about/sites/knott/about.cfm. Free admission. Wed–Fri 1–4pm; Sat 10am–4pm. 1-hr. tours depart on the hour.

Mary Brogan Museum of Art and Science ☺ This museum's mission, "to stimulate interest in and understanding of the visual arts, sciences, mathematics, and technology through experiences that educate and inspire," pretty much says it all. Associated with the Smithsonian Institution, the Mary Brogan Museum has changing exhibitions, educational programs, and lectures, as well as permanent science museum–type exhibits.

350 S. Duval St. (at Pensacola St.). ✆ **850/513-0700.** www.thebrogan.org. Admission $10 adults; $5 seniors 60 and over, college students, military with ID, and children 3–17. Mon–Sat 10am–5pm; Sun 1–5pm.

Meginnis-Monroe House ★★ This restored 1852 antebellum home, listed on the National Register of Historic Places, is a lovely setting for fine art. The **LeMoyne Art Gallery** within it is named in honor of Jacques LeMoyne, a member of a French expedition to Florida in 1564. Commissioned to depict the natives' dwellings and to map the seacoast, LeMoyne was the first European artist known to have visited North America. Exhibits here include permanent displays by local artists, sculpture, pottery, and photography—everything from the traditional to the avant-garde. The gardens, with an old-fashioned gazebo, are spectacular during the Christmas holiday season. Programs of classical music are combined with visual arts during the year.

125 N. Gadsden St. (btw. Park Ave. and Call St.). ✆ **850/222-8800.** www.lemoyne.org. Admission $1 adults, free for children 12 and under. Tues–Sat 10am–5pm. Closed holidays.

Mission San Luís de Apalachee ★ A Spanish Franciscan mission named San Luís was set up in 1656 on this hilltop, already a principal village of the Apalachee Indians. From then until 1704, it served as the capital of a chain of Spanish missions in Northwest Florida. The mission complex included a tribal council house, a Franciscan church, a Spanish fort, and residential areas. Based on archaeological and historical research, the council house and the 10 × 50-foot thatch-roofed church have been reconstructed, and are open to the public. Interpretive markers are found across the 60-acre site, and self-guided tour brochures are available at the visitor center. Call for a schedule of ranger-led guided tours on weekends.

2021 Mission Rd. (btw. W. Tennessee and Tharpe sts.). © **850/487-3711.** www.missionsanluis.org. Admission $5 adults, $3 seniors, $2 children 6-17. Tues–Sun 10am–4pm. Closed Thanksgiving and Christmas. From downtown, take Tennessee St. (U.S. 90 W.) to entrance on right past Ocala St.

Museum of Florida History ★ An 11-foot-tall mastodon greets you at this state history museum, where you can look back 12,000 years to the first Native Americans to live in Florida (mastodons were very much alive back then). Ancient artifacts from Native American tribes are exhibited, along with such relics from Florida's past as a reconstructed steamboat and treasures from 16th- and 17th-century sunken Spanish galleons. Inquire about guided tours and special exhibits.

Lower level of R. A. Gray Building, 500 S. Bronough St. (at Pensacola St.). © **850/245-6400.** http://dhr.dos.state.fl.us/museum. Free admission. Mon–Fri 9am–4:30pm; Sat 10am–4:30pm; Sun and holidays noon–4:30pm. Closed Thanksgiving and Christmas. Parking available in garage around the corner on St. Augustine St., btw. Bronough and Duvall sts.

Where to Stay

There is no high or low season here, but every hotel and motel for miles around is booked during FSU and FAMU football weekends from September to November, at graduation in May, and, to a lesser degree, weekdays during the 60-day legislative session that begins in March. Reserve well in advance—or you may have to stay 60 miles or more from the city. For the game schedules, call or visit the websites of FSU or FAMU.

Most hotels are concentrated in three areas: in downtown Tallahassee; north of downtown, along North Monroe Street, at exit 199 off I-10 (where you'll find most chains); and along Apalachee Parkway, east of downtown.

Tax on all hotel bills is 5% in Leon County. However, certain campgrounds in Leon County are exempt from the 5% Tourist Development Tax.

Aloft Tallahassee Downtown ★★ The latest brand of shabby chic from the folks at W Hotels, Aloft features all the necessities to make the mod squad on a budget very comfy. Located within walking distance of the state capitol, Aloft features modern rooms with nine-foot ceilings, extra-large windows, comfy beds, great walk-in showers, and Bliss Spa products. A high-tech entertainment center has a one-stop connectivity station that recharges your gadgets and links to the 42-inch LCD TV for optimal sound and viewing. The requisite hipster hotel bar and lounge are also here, as is a grab-and-go 24/7 pantry serving sandwiches, snacks, and cappuccino, and an inviting lobby set up like a living room. An outdoor pool even features wireless Internet, which is also available free throughout the hotel.

200 N. Monroe St., Tallahassee, FL 32301. www.alofttallahassee.com. © **850/513-0313.** Fax 850/513-0316. 243 units. Winter $89–$129 double; summer $120–$219 double. AE, DC, DISC, MC, V. **Amenities:** Restaurant; bar; gym; outdoor pool. *In room:* A/C, TV, hair dryer, MP3 docking station, Wi-Fi.

The antebellum Knott House is now a historic home/museum you can visit.

Cabot Lodge North 🗝 It looks like a random motel, really, but look closer: There's charm here. A clapboard plantation-style house with a tin roof and a wraparound porch provides Southern country ease that distinguishes this friendly motel from its nearby competitors. Guests can relax in rockers on the porch or on comfy sofas by the fireplace in the living room. Although the guest rooms in the two-story buildings out back don't hold up their end of the atmosphere factor, they're still quite satisfactory at these rates, and they give quick access to the outdoor pool. Guests can also enjoy a complimentary continental breakfast buffet and evening cocktails.

2735 N. Monroe St., Tallahassee, FL 32303. www.cabotlodgenorthmonroe.com. © **800/223-1964** or 850/386-8880. Fax 850/386-4254. 160 units. $73–$84 double. Rates include continental breakfast and evening reception. AE, DC, DISC, MC, V. **Amenities:** Access to nearby health club; outdoor pool. *In room:* A/C, TV, hair dryer, Wi-Fi.

Governor's Inn ★★ Legislators, lobbyists, groupies, and Southern gentry stay at this elegantly furnished inn, half a block north of the Old Capitol in the Adams Street Commons historic district. The building was once a livery stable, and part of its original architecture has been preserved, including the impressive beams. The guest rooms are distinctive, with four-poster beds, black-oak writing desks, rock maple armoires, and antique accouterments. Of the suites, each one named for a Florida governor, one has a whirlpool tub; another has a loft bedroom with wood-burning fireplace. Complimentary continental breakfast and afternoon cocktails are served in the pine-paneled Florida Room, and a restaurant across the street provides limited room service. Hang out in the bar area and eavesdrop on amusing political banter. The staff here is superfriendly and helpful. Note that all the rooms are nonsmoking.

209 S. Adams St., Tallahassee, FL 32301. www.thegovinn.com. © **800/342-7717** or 850/681-6855. Fax 850/222-3105. 41 units. $169–$189 double; $229–$319 suite. Rates include continental

breakfast and evening cocktails. AE, DC, DISC, MC, V. Free valet parking. **Amenities:** Complimentary access to nearby health club; limited room service. *In room:* A/C, TV, minifridge, Wi-Fi.

Where to Dine

Bahn Thai THAI/CANTONESE Lamoi (Sue) Snyder and progeny have been serving the spicy cuisine of her native Thailand at this storefront since 1979. In deference to local Southerners, who may never have sampled anything spicier than cheese grits, much of her menu is devoted to mild Cantonese-style Chinese dishes. More adventurous diners, however, flock here to order such authentic tongue-burners as *yon voon-sen,* a combination of shrimp, chicken, bean threads, onions, lemon grass, ground peanuts, and the obligatory chili peppers. Sue's specialty is a deliciously sweet, slightly gingered version of Penang curry. You can ask her to turn down the heat in her other Thai dishes. Come at lunch and sample everything from the all-you-can-eat buffet—a real bargain, but make sure you have free time, because service is notoriously slow here.

1319 S. Monroe St. (btw. Oakland Ave. and Harrison St.). ℂ **850/224-4765.** Main courses $10–$20; lunch buffet $7.50. DISC, MC, V. Mon–Thurs 11am–2:30pm and 5–10pm; Fri 11am–2:30pm and 5–10:30pm; Sat 5–10:30pm.

Barnacle Bill's Seafood Restaurant SEAFOOD There's always plenty of action at this noisy, casual spot, a favorite of the downtown crowd, including journalists, bureaucrats, and politicians. Freshly shucked Apalachicola oysters are the stars at the enormous raw bar, but the menu also offers a mélange of seafood. The cooking is simple and usually done by Florida State University students working part-time. Best bets are chargrilled mahimahi, tuna, amberjack, and grouper. For a smoked sensation, try the mahimahi and amberjack cured on the premises. A downstairs bar serves the regular seafood items, plus sushi, deli sandwiches, and salads. A daily happy hour serves $6-a-dozen oysters and $1.50 beers.

1830 N. Monroe St. (north of Tharpe St.). ℂ **850/385-8734.** www.barnaclebills.com. Main courses $10–$20; sandwiches and salads $4–$12. AE, DC, DISC, MC, V. Sun–Thurs 11am–11pm; Fri–Sat 11am–midnight.

Chez ★★ TRADITIONAL FRENCH You become an instant Francophile in Florida at this chic restaurant, situated in a beautifully restored 1920s brick home. French-born chef Eric Favier and his American wife and partner, Karen Cooley, serve traditional French cuisine either inside the house or out on a large deck partly shaded by live oaks draped with Spanish moss. Opening onto the deck, a bistro-style bar provides a light-fare menu between lunch and dinner. The tapaslike starters are fantastic, from the bacon-wrapped medjool dates stuffed with blue cheese and scallions, the beer cheese fondue, and the calamari fries, to classic escargot and duck liver pâté with black truffles. Burgers and sandwiches, including an excellent croque-monsieur, are available at dinnertime for those not in the mood for the heavier, heartier, and sensational beef bourguignon. Live music regularly accompanies dining. Smoking is permitted on the front porch, where you can enjoy stogies and brandy while lounging in wicker chairs. Go for brunch and don't miss the Bananas Foster French toast.

1215 Thomasville Rd. (at 6th Ave.). ℂ **850/222-0936.** www.chezpierre.com. Reservations recommended. Main courses $18–$32; sandwiches $10–$12. AE, DC, DISC, MC, V. Mon–Sat 11am–10pm; Sun 11am–2:30pm and 6–9pm.

SIDE TRIP TO THE scallop CAPITAL

Just 90 minutes outside the state's capital is Florida's so-called "Scallop Capital," **Steinhatchee,** where the summer sport of scalloping—a sport (and for many a livelihood) that involves patience and a keen eye—is all the rage. From July 1 to September 10, hundreds descend on this tiny fishing village, population 1,500, on the hunt for those tiny, tasty mollusks in what can only be described as a combination of snorkeling and stalking. And while it sounds like scallops are tame creatures, they're pretty feisty, making for an interesting hunt. Your best bet is to hire a guide, who will provide you with a saltwater fishing license and some gear. Ask if they provide the necessary snorkel, mask, and fins. Two of the best guides are **Capt. "Casino" Dave Jenkins of Fish 'n Tales Charters** (☎ 352/498-2469) and **Capt. Jim Henley** (☎ 352/498-0792). Trips run for a full day and typically cost $350, six people per boat. For overnight trips, make a reservation at the **Steinhatchee Landing Resort** (☎ 800/584-1709; www.steinhatcheelanding.com), where cottages rent from $185 to $250 a night. These fill up fast, so book early. To get there from Tallahassee: Take I-10 East or U.S. Highway 27 East to U.S. Highway 19. Go south on U.S. 19 to Tennille. (Watch for the blinking yellow caution light and a convenience store/gas station.) Turn right onto Florida Highway 51. Steinhatchee Landing is 8 miles from Tennille on the left.

Kool Beanz Cafe ★★ CARIBBEAN The coolest cafe in town, this noisy emporium of trendy cooking draws lots of patrons in their late 20s and early 30s, who appreciate the exciting blends of flavors. The joint is dimly lit but painted in bright pastels from the Caribbean. You'll find many island-style items on the constantly changing menu, including jerked pork tenderloin, mango-jalapeño salsa, fried plantains, black bean sauce, coconut rice and a mojo spiced chicken, shrimp, chorizo sausage, pepper-jack cheese, black beans, and rice. You may want to get here early: The more inventive items, such as the jerked mahi, mango-jicama "slaw," coconut black bean sauce, *tostones,* and cilantro rice, sell out early, as do the shrimp n' mussel Creole stew, fried green tomato, crawfish toast, red beans, and rice.

921 Thomasville Rd. (at Williams St.). ☎ **850/224-2466.** www.koolbeanz-cafe.com. Main courses $16–$23. AE, DISC, MC, V. Mon–Fri 11am–2:30pm and 5:30–10pm; Sat 5:30–10pm.

Side Trips from Tallahassee

The following excursions are generally on the way to Apalachicola, so if you're headed that way, plan to make a detour or two.

WAKULLA SPRINGS ★★

The world's largest and deepest freshwater spring is 15 miles south of Tallahassee in the 2,860-acre **Edward W. Ball Wakulla Springs State Park** ★★, on Florida 267 just east of its junction with Florida 61. Ball, a financier who administered the du Pont estate, turned the springs and the moss-draped surrounding forest into a preservation area. Divers have mapped an underwater cave system extending more than 6,000 feet back from the spring's mouth. Wakulla has been known to dispense an amazing 14,325 gallons per second of water at certain times. Mastodon bones, including those of Herman, now in Tallahassee's

Museum of Florida History, were found in the caves. The 1930s Tarzan movies, starring Johnny Weissmuller, were also filmed here.

A free 10-minute movie is shown in the park's theater at the waterfront. You can hike or bike along the nature trails, and swimming is allowed in designated areas. *Note:* It's important to observe swimming rules as alligators are present here.

If the spring water is clear enough, 30-minute glass-bottom-boat sightseeing trips depart every 45 minutes daily, from 9:45am to 5pm during daylight saving time, and from 9:15am to 4:30pm the rest of the year. Even if the water is murky, you're likely to see alligators, birds, and other wildlife on 30-minute riverboat cruises, which operate during these same hours. Either boat ride costs $8 for adults, $5 for children 12 and under.

Entrance fees to the park are $6 per vehicle with up to eight passengers, $4 single-occupant vehicle, $2 per pedestrian or bicyclist. The park is open daily from 8am to dusk. For more information, contact the park at 550 Wakulla Springs Dr., Wakulla Springs, FL 32305 (© **850/224-5950;** www.floridastateparks.org/wakullasprings).

Where to Stay & Dine

Wakulla Springs Lodge ★ On the shores of Wakulla Springs, this dated but charming lodge is distinctive for its magnificent Spanish architecture and old-world furnishings, such as rare Spanish tiles, black-granite tables, marble floors, and ceiling beams painted with Florida scenes by a German artist (supposedly Kaiser Wilhelm's court painter). The guest rooms are simple by today's standards (you'll get a marble bathroom and phone, but no TV). By all means, ask for a room in the front so you'll have a lake view. You don't have to be a lodge guest to enjoy the warm, smoky ambience of the lobby, with its huge stone fireplace and arched windows looking onto the springs, or to enjoy reasonably priced meals featuring Southern cuisine in the lovely **Ball Room** (reservations recommended). The fountain (a 60-ft.-long marble drugstore-style counter for old-fashioned ice-cream sodas) provides snacks and sandwiches.

550 Wakulla Park Dr., Wakulla Springs, FL 32305. www.wakullacounty.org/wakulla-24.htm. © **850/224-5950.** Fax 850/561-7251. 27 units. $95–$150 double. AE, DISC, MC, V. **Amenities:** Restaurant. *In room:* A/C.

THE ST. MARKS AREA

Rich history lives in the area around the little village of **St. Marks,** 18 miles south of the capital at the end of both Florida 363 and the Tallahassee–St. Marks Historic Railroad Trail State Park.

After marching overland from Tampa Bay in 1528, the Spanish conquistador Panfilo de Narvaez and 300 men arrived at this strategic point at the confluence of the St. Marks and Wakulla rivers near the Gulf of Mexico. Because their only avenue back to Spain was by sea, they built and launched the first ships made by Europeans in the New World. Some 11 years later, Hernando de Soto and his 600 men arrived here after following Narvaez's route from Tampa. They marked the harbor entrance by hanging banners in the trees, then moved inland. Two wooden forts were built, one in 1679 and one in 1718, and a stone version was begun in 1739. The fort shifted among Spanish, British, and Native American hands until Gen. Andrew Jackson took it away from the Spanish in 1819.

Parts of the old Spanish bastion wall and Confederate earthworks built during the Civil War are in the **San Marcos de Apalachee Historic State Park,** reached by turning right at the end of Florida 363 in St. Marks and following the

See some of Florida's marine mammals, like the manatee, at Wakulla Springs.

paved road. A museum built on the foundation of the old marine hospital contains exhibits and artifacts covering the area's history. The site is open Thursday through Monday from 9am to 5pm (closed New Year's Day, Thanksgiving, and Christmas). Entrance to the site is free; admission to the museum costs $2 (free for children 6 and under). For more information, contact the site at 1022 DeSoto Park Dr., Tallahassee, FL 32301 (© **850/922-6007;** www.florida stateparks.org/sanmarcos).

De Soto's men marked the harbor entrance in what is now the **St. Marks Lighthouse and National Wildlife Refuge** ★, P.O. Box 68, St. Marks, FL 32355 (© **850/925-6121**). Operated by the U.S. Fish and Wildlife Service, this 65,000-acre preserve occupies much of the coast from the Aucilla River east of St. Marks to the Ochlockonee River west of Panacea; it's home to more species of birds than anyplace else in Florida except the Everglades. The visitor center is 3½ miles south of U.S. 98 on Lighthouse Road (Fla. 59); turn south off U.S. 98 at Newport, about 2 miles east of St. Marks. Stop at the center for self-guided tour maps of the roads and hiking trails, some built atop levees running through the marshland.

APALACHICOLA NATIONAL FOREST

The largest of Florida's three national forests, this huge preserve encompasses 600,000 acres stretching from Tallahassee's outskirts southward to the Gulf Coast and westward some 70 miles to the Apalachicola River. Included is a variety of woodlands, rivers, streams, lakes, and caves populated by a host of wildlife. There are picnic areas with sheltered tables and grills, canoe and mountain bike trails, campgrounds with tent and RV sites, and a number of other facilities, some of them especially designed for visitors with disabilities.

The **Leon Sinks Area** is closest to Tallahassee, 5½ miles south of Southeast Capital Circle on U.S. 319 near the Leon-Wakulla county line. Nature trails and boardwalks lead from one sinkhole (a lake formed when water erodes the underlying limestone) to another. The trails are open daily from 8am to 8pm.

A necessary stop before heading into this wilderness is the visitor center at the **Wakulla Area Ranger District,** 57 Taft Dr., Crawfordville, FL 32327 (© **850/926-3561;** fax 850/926-1904), which provides information and sells topographic and canoe trail maps. The station is off U.S. 319, about 20 miles south of Tallahassee and 2 miles north of Crawfordville. It's open Monday through Thursday from 8am to 4:30pm, Friday from 8am to 4pm.

Be careful where you swim at Wakulla Springs, the gators were here first!

15

PLANNING YOUR TRIP

Whether you plan to spend a day, a week, 2 weeks, or longer in the Sunshine State, you'll need to make many "where," "when," and "how" choices before you leave.

As for the where, well, that's a toughie. It depends on what sort of vacation you're looking for. There's relaxing, adventurous, kitschy, beachy, Mickey, Minnie, and, well, you get the picture. . . .

How to get to Florida? We recommend almost every and any way except hitchhiking. And now to the when: That's the biggest question we get. As Florida shifts from a seasonal to a more year-round destination, there's always a good time to visit. Even during Hurricane Season (June 1–Nov 30), when prices are lower, crowds are thinner, and hurricanes are (knock on wood) often elusive. When temperatures freeze elsewhere, that's when Florida starts sinking further into the ocean, as crowds flock to the state for deep thawing and the state feels, well, heavier. For those who love heat, humidity, and sweating, summertime is the ideal time to visit and saves you a trip to the sauna.

GETTING THERE
By Plane

Most major domestic airlines fly to and from many Florida cities. Choose from **American, Continental, Delta, Northwest/KLM, United,** and **US Airways.** Of these, Delta and US Airways have the most extensive network of commuter connections within Florida (see "Getting Around," below).

Several so-called no-frills airlines—with low fares but few amenities—also fly to Florida. The biggest and best is **Southwest Airlines,** which has flights from many U.S. cities to Fort Lauderdale, Jacksonville, Orlando, Tampa, and Panama City.

Others airlines flying to Florida include **AirTran, JetBlue, Virgin America, Midwest Airlines,** and **Spirit.**

The major airports in Florida are Miami International Airport (MIA), Fort Lauderdale Hollywood International Airport (FLL), Southwest Florida International Airport (RSW), Jacksonville International Airport (JAX), Key West International Airport (EYW), Melbourne International Airport (MLB), Orlando International Airport (MCO), Orlando Sanford International Airport (SFB), Sarasota-Bradenton International Airport (SRQ), St. Augustine Airport (SGJ), St. Petersburg Clearwater International Airport (PIE), Tampa International Airport (TPA), the brand-new Northwest Beaches International Airport (ECP) in Panama Beach, and Palm Beach International Airport (PBI).

By Bus

Greyhound (© **800/231-2222;** www.greyhound.com) has more than 50 stops within the state of Florida and more than 2,400 service locations in North America.

PREVIOUS PAGE: **Visitors come from everywhere to the Sunshine State.**

By Car

Florida is reached by **I-95** along the East Coast, **I-75** from the Central States, and **I-10** from the west. The **Florida Turnpike,** a toll road, links Orlando, West Palm Beach, Fort Lauderdale, and Miami (it's a shortcut from Wildwood on I-75 north of Orlando to Miami). **I-4** cuts across the state from Cape Canaveral through Orlando to Tampa.

See "Getting Around," below, for more information about driving in Florida and the car-rental firms that operate here.

International visitors should note that insurance and taxes are almost never included in quoted rental-car rates in the U.S. Be sure to ask your rental agency about additional fees for these. They can add a significant cost to your car rental.

Most car-rental companies in Florida require that you be 25, but if not, there's a hefty surcharge applied to renters 21 to 24 years old.

And because Florida isn't exactly known for stress-free driving, The Florida Department of Transportation has come out with the **Florida 511 Traveler Information** system, a free traffic and travel info system that offers advice on routes, airports, and even traffic to avoid—for free. Just call 511.

For information on car rentals and gasoline (petrol) in Florida, see "By Car" under "Getting Around," below.

By Train

Amtrak (© **800/USA-RAIL** [872-7245]; www.amtrak.com) offers train service to Florida from both the East and West coasts. It takes some 26 hours from New York to Miami, and 68 hours from Los Angeles to Miami.

Amtrak's *Silver Meteor* and *Silver Star* both run twice daily between New York and either Miami or Tampa, with intermediate stops along the East Coast and in Florida. Amtrak's Thruway Bus Connections are available from the Fort Lauderdale Amtrak station and Miami International Airport to Key West; from Tampa to St. Petersburg, Treasure Island, Clearwater, Sarasota, Bradenton, and Fort Myers; and from Deland to Daytona Beach. From the West Coast, the *Sunset Limited* runs three times weekly between Los Angeles and Orlando. It stops in Pensacola, Crestview (north of Fort Walton Beach and Destin), Chipley (north of Panama City Beach), and Tallahassee. Sleeping accommodations are available for an extra charge.

If you intend to stop along the way, you can save money with Amtrak's **Explore America** (or All Aboard America) fares, which are based on three regions of the country.

Amtrak's **Auto Train** runs daily from Lorton, Virginia (12 miles south of Washington, D.C.), to Sanford, Florida (just northeast of Orlando). You ride in a coach while your car is secured in an enclosed vehicle carrier. Make your train reservations as far in advance as possible.

By Boat

While you can't hop on a cruise ship to Florida, you can from Florida with cruise ports located in Miami, Port Everglades, Cape Canaveral, and Tampa.

GETTING AROUND

Having a car is the best and easiest way to see Florida's sights or to get to and from the beach. Public transportation is available only in the cities and larger towns, and even there, it may provide infrequent or inadequate service. Getting from one city to another, cars and planes are the way to go.

By Plane

The commuter arms of **Continental, Delta,** and **US Airways** provide extensive service between Florida's major cities and towns. Fares for these short hops tend to be reasonable.

Cape Air flies between Key West and Fort Myers, which means you can avoid backtracking to Miami from Key West if you're touring the state. (You can also take a 3-hour boat ride btw. Key West and Fort Myers Beach year-round, or Marco Island during the winter months; see p. 230.)

Attention visitors to the U.S. from abroad: Some major airlines offer transatlantic or transpacific passengers special discount tickets under the name **Visit USA,** which allows mostly one-way travel from one U.S. destination to another at very low prices. Unavailable in the U.S., these discount tickets must be purchased abroad in conjunction with your international fare. This system is the easiest, fastest, cheapest way to see the country. Inquire with your air carrier.

By Car

If you're visiting from abroad and plan to rent a car in Florida, keep in mind that foreign driver's licenses are usually recognized in the U.S., but you should get an international one if your home license is not in English.

Jacksonville is about 350 miles north of Miami and 500 miles north of Key West, so don't underestimate how long it will take you to drive all the way down the state. The speed limit is either 65 mph or 70 mph on the rural interstate highways, so you can make good time between cities. Not so on U.S. 1, U.S. 17, U.S. 19, U.S. 41, or U.S. 301; although most have four lanes, these older highways tend to be heavily congested, especially in built-up areas.

Every major car-rental company is represented here, including **Alamo, Avis, Budget, Dollar, Enterprise, Hertz, National,** and **Thrifty.**

State and local **taxes** will add as much as 20% to your final bill. You'll pay an additional $2.05 per day in statewide use tax, and local sales taxes will tack on at least 6% to the total, including the statewide use tax. Some airports add another 35¢ per day and as much as 10% in "recovery" fees. You can avoid the recovery fee by picking up your car in town rather than at the airport. Budget and Enterprise both have numerous locations away from the airports. Competition is so fierce among Florida rental firms that most have now stopped charging **drop-off fees** if you pick up a car at one place and leave it at another. Be sure to ask in advance if there's a drop-off fee.

To rent a car, you must have a valid **credit card** (not a debit or check card) in your name, and most companies require you to be at least 25 years old. Some also set maximum ages and may deny cars to anyone with a bad driving record. Ask about requirements and restrictions when you book, in order to avoid problems once you arrive.

International visitors should note that insurance and taxes are almost never included in quoted rental car rates in the U.S. Be sure to ask your rental agency about additional fees for these. They can add a significant cost to your car rental.

Regular unleaded prices at press time were heading toward the $4 a gallon range for regular unleaded (ouch!). Taxes are already included in the printed price. One U.S. gallon equals 3.8 liters or .85 imperial gallons. For an up-to-the-minute listing of gas prices at stations throughout Florida, go to **www.floridastategasprices.com**.

By Train

International visitors can buy a **USA Rail Pass,** good for 15, 30, or 45 days of unlimited travel on **Amtrak** (✆ **800/USA-RAIL** [872-7245] in the U.S. or Canada; ✆ **001/215-856-7953** outside the U.S.; www.amtrak.com). The pass is available online or through many overseas travel agents. Reservations are generally required and should be made as early as possible.

By Bus

Greyhound (✆ **800/231-2222** in the U.S.; ✆ **001/214/849-8100** outside the U.S. with toll-free access; www.greyhound.com) is the sole nationwide bus line. International visitors can obtain information about the **Greyhound North American Discovery Pass.** The pass, which offers unlimited travel and stopovers in the U.S. and Canada, can be obtained outside the United States from travel agents or through **www.discoverypass.com**. You can travel between Florida's cities fairly easily on Greyhound.

TIPS ON ACCOMMODATIONS

Florida accommodations are as varied in personality as the weather is in mid-July. All sorts of stays line the Sunshine State, ranging from swanky, five-star luxury hotels and beach resorts to cozy one-room cottages, posh penthouses, B&Bs, and beachfront high-rise condominiums to back-to-nature-style Everglades cabins and campsites. For sports or nature lovers there are hotels and motels located

---

 Easy Rider: Camping Out Old School

As time goes by and the remnants of Old Florida become as rare as natural blondes on South Beach, it's nice to jump on the vintage bandwagon—or in this case, the vintage **Volkswagen,** when the opportunity presents itself. Thanks to **Florida Oldschool Campers** (pictured at right), your nostalgic journey through the Sunshine State begins on tricked-out VW mini RVs, complete with two-burner propane stove, icebox, table, cabinet space, and two surprisingly comfy beds with clean linens. Owners Mike and Dixie keep the rides stocked with cookware, linens, and flashlights, and even a water tank. Each of the two buses has full hookups including water

and standard 110-volt outlets. Even the prices are pretty vintage and, uh, far out, at $80 a day, making for a trippy way to explore what's new and old in the state of Florida. Florida Oldschool Campers, Tampa (no street address), **www.florida vwrentals.com**.

on golf courses, marinas, or surrounded by nature preserves and hiking trails. For families and admirers of kitsch, there are themed hotels that transport you from Florida to, say, Colorado, or even the Cartoon Network. For the hipster, there's the requisite boutique hotel with mandatory celebrity sightings. And for those who just want to get away from it all, there are countless hidden hotels, motels, and cottages, even a few on private islands.

[Fast FACTS] FLORIDA

Area Codes 239: For the Southwest coast, including all of Lee County, Collier County, mainland Monroe County, and excluding Florida Keys; includes Cape Coral, Fort Myers, Naples, and the Everglades.

305: All of Miami-Dade County and the Florida Keys of Monroe County: Miami, Homestead, Coral Gables, Key West; **786:** A newer area code covering those Miami-Dade numbers not covered by 305.

321: Orlando, Cocoa Beach, St. Cloud, and central eastern Florida. Is also the exclusive code for the Space Coast: Cape Canaveral, Melbourne, Titusville, Cocoa Beach.

352: Gainesville, Ocala, Inverness, Spring Hill, Dunnellon, and central Florida.

386: Daytona Beach, Lake City, Live Oak, Crescent City, and northern and eastern Florida.

407: Parts of Orlando, Cocoa Beach, Kissimmee, St. Cloud, and central-eastern Florida not covered by 321.

561: Palm Beach County: West Palm Beach, Boca Raton, Boynton Beach, Delray Beach, Belle Glade.

727: Majority of Pinellas County including Clearwater, St. Petersburg, Dunedin.

954: All of Broward County: Fort Lauderdale, Hollywood, Coral Springs.

754: All of Broward County that isn't covered by 954.

772: Vero Beach, Port Saint Lucie, Fort Pierce, Sebastian, Stuart, and central-eastern Florida.

813: All of Hillsborough County, including Tampa and Plant City; inland areas of Pasco County; and parts of Oldsmar in Pinellas County.

850: Pensacola, Tallahassee, Panama City, and the Florida Panhandle.

863: Lakeland, Avon Park, Clewiston, Bartow, Sebring, Winter Haven, and south-central Florida.

904: Jacksonville, St. Augustine, Starke, Green Cove Springs, and northeastern Florida.

941: Gulf Coast immediately south of Tampa Bay: all of Manatee County, Sarasota County, and Charlotte County; includes Bradenton, Port Charlotte, Sarasota, and Punta Gorda.

Business Hours "Normal" business hours are usually 9am to 5pm, but in certain parts of the state—Miami, especially—hours range from "whenever" to "whenever." Always call ahead to ask for hours, as, like the weather, they can change in an instant.

Customs Every visitor 21 years of age or older may bring in, free of duty, the following: (1) 1 U.S. quart of alcohol; (2) 200 cigarettes, 50 cigars (but not from Cuba), or 3 pounds of smoking tobacco; and (3) $100 worth of gifts. These exemptions are offered to travelers who spend at least 72 hours in the United States and who have not claimed them within the preceding 6 months. It is forbidden to bring into the country almost any meat products (including canned, fresh, and dried meat products such as bouillon, soup mixes, and the like). Generally, condiments including vinegars, oils, pickled goods, spices, coffee, tea, and some cheeses and baked goods are permitted. Avoid rice products, as rice can often harbor insects. Bringing fruits and vegetables is prohibited since they may harbor pests or disease. International visitors may carry in or out up to $10,000 in U.S. or foreign currency with no formalities; larger sums must be declared to U.S. Customs on entering or leaving, which includes filing form CM 4790. For details regarding U.S. Customs and Border Protection, consult your nearest U.S. embassy or consulate, or **U.S. Customs** (www.customs.gov).

Disabled Travelers Florida is exceptionally accommodating to those with special needs. In addition to special parking set aside at every establishment, out-of-state vehicles with disability parking permits from other states can park in these spots. Florida state law and the Americans with Disabilities Act (ADA) require that guide dogs be permitted in all establishments and attractions, although some ride restrictions do apply. For those who have hearing impairments, **TDD service** is available by dialing *②* **711** via the Florida Relay Service. There are several resources for people with disabilities who are traveling within Florida, including special wheelchairs with balloon tires provided free of charge at many Florida beaches. For the best information on traveling with disabilities, go to **www.visitflorida.com/Disablities_Travel**.

Drinking Laws The legal age for purchase and consumption of alcoholic beverages is 21, though, strangely and somewhat hypocritically, a person serving or selling alcohol can be 18; proof of age is required and often requested at bars, nightclubs, and restaurants, so it's always a good idea to bring ID when you go out. Do not carry open containers of alcohol in your car or any public area that isn't zoned for alcohol consumption. The police can fine you on the spot. Don't even think about driving while intoxicated. Florida state law prohibits the sale of alcohol between 3am and 7am, unless the county chooses to change the operating hours later. For instance, Miami-Dade County liquor stores may operate 24 hours. Alcohol sales on Sundays vary by county; some, such as Palm Beach and Miami-Dade County, can start serving booze as early as 7am while other counties such as Monroe don't start popping corks until noon. Check with your specific county to see what time spirits start being served. Supermarkets and other licensed business establishments can sell only beer, low-alcohol liquors, and wine. The hard stuff must be sold in dedicated liquor stores, which may be in a separate part of a grocery or a drugstore. Beer must be sold in quantities of 32 ounces or less or greater than 1 gallon. Forty- and 64-ounce alcoholic beverages are illegal.

As for open container laws: Having open alcoholic containers on public property, including streets, sidewalks, or inside a vehicle, is prohibited, though opened bottles of liquor are allowed inside a car trunk. Drivers suspected to be under the influence of alcohol or drugs must agree to breath, blood, or urine testing under "implied consent laws." Penalties for refusing testing can mean suspension of the driver's license for up to 1 year. In Florida, the first conviction carries a mandatory suspension of the driver's license for 6 months; for the second offense, 1 year; for the third offense, 2 years. Underage drivers (20 or younger) have a maximum legal blood-alcohol content percentage of .02%. Above this amount, they are subject to DUI penalties. At .20% above the legal limit of .08%, a driver faces much harsher repercussions. This also applies to drivers refusing chemical testing for intoxication.

Electricity Like Canada, the United States uses 110 to 120 volts AC (60 cycles), compared to 220 to 240 volts AC (50 cycles) in most of Europe, Australia, and New Zealand. Downward converters that change 220–240 volts to 110–120 volts are difficult to find in the United States, so bring one with you.

Embassies & Consulates All embassies are in the nation's capital, Washington, D.C. Some consulates are in major U.S. cities, and most nations have a mission to the United Nations in New York City. If your country isn't listed below, call for directory information in Washington, D.C. (📞 **202/555-1212**) or check **www.embassy.org/embassies**.

The embassy of **Australia** is at 1601 Massachusetts Ave. NW, Washington, DC 20036 (📞 **202/797-3000;** www.usa.embassy.gov.au). Consulates are in New York, Honolulu, Houston, Los Angeles, and San Francisco.

The embassy of **Canada** is at 501 Pennsylvania Ave. NW, Washington, DC 20001 (📞 **202/682-1740;** www.canadainternational.gc.ca/washington). Other Canadian consulates are in Buffalo (New York), Detroit, Los Angeles, New York, and Seattle.

The embassy of **Ireland** is at 2234 Massachusetts Ave. NW, Washington, DC 20008 (📞 **202/462-3939;** www.embassyofireland.org). Irish consulates are in Boston, Chicago, New York, San Francisco, and other cities. See website for complete listing.

The embassy of **New Zealand** is at 37 Observatory Circle NW, Washington, DC 20008 (📞 **202/328-4800;** www.nzembassy.com). New Zealand consulates are in Los Angeles, Salt Lake City, San Francisco, and Seattle.

The embassy of the **United Kingdom** is at 3100 Massachusetts Ave. NW, Washington, DC 20008 (📞 **202/588-6500;** http://ukinusa.fco.gov.uk). Other British consulates are in Atlanta, Boston, Chicago, Cleveland, Houston, Los Angeles, New York, San Francisco, and Seattle.

Emergencies To reach the police, ambulance, or fire department, dial 📞 **911** from any phone. No coins are needed.

Family Travel Florida is a great family destination, with Walt Disney World leading the list of theme parks geared to young and old alike. Consequently, most Florida hotels and restaurants are willing, if not eager, to cater to families traveling with children. Many hotels and motels let children age 17 and younger stay free in a parent's room (be sure to ask when you reserve). To locate accommodations, restaurants, and attractions that are particularly kid-friendly, refer to the "Kids" icon throughout this guide.

At the beaches, it's the exception rather than the rule for a resort not to have a children's activities program (some will even mind the youngsters while the parents enjoy a night off!). Even if they don't have a children's program of their own, most will arrange babysitting services.

Recommended family-travel websites include **Family Travel Forum** (www.familytravelforum.com), a site that offers customized trip planning; **Family Travel Network** (www.familytravelnetwork.com), an online magazine providing travel tips; and **TravelWithYourKids.com** (www.travelwithyourkids.com), a comprehensive site written by parents for parents, offering sound advice for long-distance and international travel with children.

Health Florida doesn't present any unusual health hazards for most people. Folks with certain medical conditions, such as liver disease, diabetes, and stomach ailments, should avoid eating raw **oysters.** Cooking kills the bacteria, so if in doubt, order your oysters steamed, broiled, or fried.

Florida has millions of **mosquitoes** and invisible biting **sand flies** (known as no-see-ums), especially in the coastal and marshy areas. Fortunately, neither insect carries malaria or other diseases. (Although there were a few cases of mosquitoes carrying West Nile virus in the Panhandle, it's really not a problem in Florida.) Keep these pests at bay with a good insect repellent.

It's especially important to protect yourself against **sunburn.** Don't underestimate the strength of the sun's rays down here, even in the middle of winter. Use a sunscreen with a high protection factor and apply it liberally.

Insurance Hurricane season (June 1–Nov 30) is a time when travel insurance may come in handy.

For information on traveler's insurance, trip-cancellation insurance, and medical insurance while traveling, visit **www.frommers.com/planning**.

Internet & Wi-Fi When it comes to Internet and Wi-Fi, we're pretty connected. Most major cities offer free Wi-Fi hot spots. To find cybercafes in your destination, check **www.cybercaptive.com** and **www.cybercafe.com**. Also, most public libraries throughout the state offer free Internet access/Wi-Fi.

Language Although English is obviously the language of choice in the United States, when it comes to some cities in Florida, namely Miami, there are certain parts of the city and people who refuse to speak it. It can be trying on your patience, but it happens. Just a warning.

Legal Aid While driving, if you are pulled over for a minor infraction (such as speeding), never attempt to pay the fine to a police officer; this could be construed as attempted bribery, a much more serious crime. Pay fines by mail, or directly into the hands of the clerk of the court. If accused of a more serious offense, say and do nothing before consulting a lawyer. In the U.S., the burden is on the state to prove a person's guilt beyond a reasonable doubt, and everyone has the right to remain silent. Once arrested, a person can make one telephone call to a party of his or her choice. The international visitor should call his or her embassy or consulate.

LGBT Travelers The editors of *Out and About,* a gay and lesbian newsletter, have described Miami's **South Beach** as the "hippest, hottest, most happening gay travel destination in the world." Today, however, **Fort Lauderdale**—where gays own more than 20 motels, 40 bars, and numerous other businesses—steals its rainbow-colored crown. For many years, that could also be said of **Key West,** which still is one of the country's most popular destinations for gays.

You can contact the **Gay, Lesbian & Bisexual Community Services of Central Florida,** 946 N. Mills Ave., Orlando, FL 32803 (℃ **407/228-8272;** www.glbcc.org), whose welcome packets usually include the latest issue of the *Triangle,* a quarterly newsletter, and a calendar of events pertaining to the gay and lesbian community. Although not a tourist-specific packet, it includes information and ads for the area's gay and lesbian clubs.

Watermark, P.O. Box 533655, Orlando, FL 32853 (℃ **407/481-2243;** fax 407/481-2246; www.watermarkonline.com), is a biweekly tabloid newspaper covering the gay and lesbian scene, including dining and entertainment options, in Orlando, the Tampa Bay area, and Daytona Beach.

The **International Gay and Lesbian Travel Association (IGLTA;** ℃ **800/448-8550** or 954/776-2626; www.iglta.org) is the trade association for the gay and lesbian travel industry, and offers an online directory of gay- and lesbian-friendly travel businesses and tour operators.

Mail At press time, domestic postage rates were 28¢ for a postcard and 44¢ for a letter. For international mail, a first-class letter of up to 1 ounce costs 98¢ (75¢ to Canada and 79¢ to Mexico); a first-class postcard costs the same as a letter. For more information go to **www.usps.com**.

If you aren't sure what your address will be in the United States, mail can be sent to you, in your name, c/o General Delivery at the main post office of the city or region where you expect to be. (Call ℃ **800/275-8777** for information on the nearest post office.) The addressee must pick up mail in person and must produce proof of identity (driver's license, passport, and so forth). Most post offices will hold mail for up to 1 month, and are open Monday to Friday from 8am to 6pm, and Saturday from 9am to 3pm.

Always include zip codes when mailing items in the U.S. If you don't know your zip code, visit **www.usps.com/zip4**.

Medical Requirements Unless you're arriving from an area known to be suffering from an epidemic (particularly cholera or yellow fever), inoculations or vaccinations are not required for entry into the United States.

Mobile Phones Someone without a cellphone in Florida is as rare as an albino crocodile. But it happens. Reception varies from excellent to spotty, depending on where you are. The Everglades used to be an abysmal place to use a mobile phone, but thanks to new cellphone towers, reliable service is almost as guaranteed as a gator sighting. Typically, however, the more remote in the state you are, the less chance your phone will work. But it is getting better.

If you need to stay in touch at a destination where you know your phone won't work, **rent** a phone from **InTouch USA** (✆ **800/872-7626;** www.intouchglobal.com) or a rental-car location, you'll pay $1 a minute or more for airtime. Or you can purchase an inexpensive pay-as-you-go mobile phone—they're all but ubiquitous at convenience stores and other retail outlets.

If you're not from the U.S., you'll be appalled at the poor reach of our **GSM (Global System for Mobile Communications) wireless network,** which is used by much of the rest of the world. Your phone will probably work in most major U.S. cities; it definitely won't work in many rural areas. To see where GSM phones work in the U.S., check out www.t-mobile.com/coverage/national_popup.asp. And you may or may not be able to send SMS (text messaging) home.

Money & Costs Frommer's lists exact prices in the local currency. The currency conversions quoted above were correct at press time. However, rates fluctuate, so before departing consult a currency-exchange website such as **www.oanda.com/currency/converter** to check up-to-the-minute rates.

Beware of hidden credit-card fees while traveling. Check with your credit or debit card issuer to see what fees, if any, will be charged for overseas transactions. Recent reform legislation in the U.S., for example, has curbed some exploitative lending practices. But many banks have responded by increasing fees in other areas, including fees for customers who use credit and debit cards while out of the country—even if those charges were made in U.S. dollars. Fees can amount to 3% or more of the purchase price. Check with your bank before departing to avoid any surprise charges on your statement.

For help with currency conversions, tip calculations, and more, download Frommer's convenient Travel Tools app for your mobile device. Go to **www.frommers.com/go/mobile** and click on the Travel Tools icon.

Newspapers Thanks to technology, you can likely read your own hometown daily newspaper on your mobile. But for those who like to engage in what's going on in their vacation surroundings, the following is a list of some of Florida's more major newspapers: Florida *Times-Union* (Jacksonville), Gainesville *Sun,* Key West *Citizen,* Miami *Herald,* Naples *Daily News Online, El Nuevo Herald* (the Miami *Herald*'s Spanish paper), Orlando *Sentinel,* Palm Beach *Post,* Pensacola *News-Journal,* the St. Augustine *Record,* St. Petersburg *Times,* Sarasota *Herald-Tribune,* South Florida *Sun-Sentinel*

THE VALUE OF THE U.S. DOLLAR VS. OTHER POPULAR CURRENCIES

US$	AUS$	CAN$	EURO (€)	NZ$	UK£
1	A$.93	C$.95	€.68	NZ$1.24	£.63

WHAT THINGS COST IN FLORIDA	$
Taxi from the airport to major destination	$18–$25
Double room, moderate	$179
Double room, inexpensive	$99
Three-course dinner for one without wine, moderate	$25–$50
Bottle of beer	$3–$6
Cup of coffee	$2–$6
1 gallon of gas	$3.75–$4.25
Admission to most museums	Free–$20
Admission to most national parks	$2–$8

(Fort Lauderdale), Tampa *Tribune,* and Tallahassee *Democrat.*

For a comprehensive list of major Florida newspapers, daily and otherwise, go to **http://dlis.dos.state.fl.us/fgils/flnews2.html**.

Packing Florida is typically a warm-weather state, but not always. Be sure to pack a sweater, long sleeves, and pants in case the weather cools or, more likely, you go into a place where the A/C is arctic. Long sleeves and pants also come in handy during pesky mosquito season. For more helpful information on packing for your trip, download our convenient Travel Tools app for your mobile device. Go to **www.frommers.com/go/ mobile** and click on the Travel Tools icon.

Passports Virtually every air traveler entering the U.S. is required to show a passport. All persons, including U.S. citizens, traveling by air between the United States and Canada, Mexico, Central and South America, the Caribbean, and Bermuda are required to present a valid passport. *Note:* U.S. and Canadian citizens entering the U.S. at land and sea ports of entry from within the western hemisphere must now also present a passport or other documents compliant with the Western Hemisphere Travel Initiative (WHTI; see www.getyouhome.gov for details). Children 15 and under may continue entering with only a U.S. birth certificate, or other proof of U.S. citizenship.

Australia Australian Passport Information Service (© 131-232, or visit www. passports.gov.au).

Canada Passport Office, Department of Foreign Affairs and International Trade, Ottawa, ON K1A 0G3 (© 800/567-6868; www.ppt.gc.ca).

Ireland Passport Office, Setanta Centre, Molesworth Street, Dublin 2 (© 01/671-1633; www.foreignaffairs.gov.ie).

New Zealand Passports Office, Department of Internal Affairs, 47 Boulcott St., Wellington, 6011 (© 0800/225-050 in New Zealand or 04/474-8100; www.passports. govt.nz).

United Kingdom Visit your nearest passport office, major post office, or travel agency, or contact the Identity and Passport Service (IPS), 89 Eccleston Sq., London, SW1V 1PN (© 0300/222-0000; www.ips.gov.uk).

United States To find your regional passport office, check the U.S. State Department website (http://travel.state.gov/passport) or call the **National Passport Information Center** (© 877/487-2778) for automated information.

Police To reach the police, dial ✆ **911** from any phone. No coins are needed.

Safety While Florida's a far cry from Juárez, it pays to use common sense when traveling throughout the state. When on beaches, keep close watch on your personal items; when in South Beach, Key West, Fort Lauderdale, and pretty much any other Sunshine State hot spot, watch your drinks and never leave them unattended. And while we completely encourage exploration, avoid areas not heavily trafficked—not the off-the-beaten-path areas, but ones that have sadly remained impervious to gentrification and modernization. Our biggest safety tip, however: sunscreen. Use it generously. You'll still get a tan. Trust us.

Senior Travel With one of the largest retired populations of any state, Florida offers a wide array of activities and benefits for seniors. Don't be shy about asking for discounts, but always carry some kind of identification, such as a driver's license, that shows your date of birth. Mention the fact that you're a senior when you make your travel reservations. In most cities, people 60 and older qualify for reduced admission to theaters, museums, and other attractions, as well as discounted fares on public transportation.

Members of **AARP,** 601 E St. NW, Washington, DC 20049 (✆ **888/687-2277;** www.aarp.org), get discounts on hotels, airfares, and car rentals. Anyone 50 or older can join.

The U.S. National Park Service offers an **America the Beautiful—National Park and Federal Recreational Lands Pass—Senior Pass** (formerly the **Golden Age Passport**), which gives seniors 62 years or older lifetime entrance to all properties administered by the National Park Service—national parks, monuments, historic sites, recreation areas, and national wildlife refuges—for a one-time processing fee of $10. The pass must be purchased in person at any NPS facility that charges an entrance fee. Besides free entry, the American the Beautiful Senior Pass also offers a 50% discount on some federal-use fees charged for camping, swimming, parking, boat launching, and tours. For more information, go to www.nps.gov/fees_passes.htm or call ✆ **888/467-2757.**

Many agencies and organizations target the 50-plus market. **Elderhostel** (✆ **800/454-5768;** www.elderhostel.org) arranges worldwide study programs for those age 55 and older. **ElderTreks** (✆ **800/741-7956** or 416/558-5000 outside North America; www.eldertreks.com) offers small-group tours to off-the-beaten-path or adventure-travel locations, for travelers 50 and older.

Smoking In November 2002, 71% of Florida's citizens voted for a constitutional amendment to prohibit smoking in all enclosed indoor workplaces. The smoke-free law became effective July 1, 2003. All establishments making more profit from food than from beverages are also smoke free, though some renegade bars and restaurants defy the law despite the hefty fees and allow smoking indoors.

Taxes The Florida state sales tax is 6%. Many municipalities add 1% or more to that, and most levy a special tax on hotel and restaurant bills. In general, expect at least 9% to be added to your final hotel bill. The United States has no value-added tax (VAT) or other indirect tax at the national level. Every state, county, and city may levy its own local tax on all purchases, including hotel and restaurant checks and airline tickets. These taxes will not appear on price tags.

Telephones Many convenience groceries and packaging services sell **prepaid calling cards** in denominations up to $50, as well as inexpensive cellphones for which you pay as you go. Many public pay phones at airports now accept American Express, MasterCard, and Visa. **Local calls** made from most pay phones (if you can find one) cost either 25¢ or 35¢. Most long-distance and international calls can be dialed directly from any phone. **To make calls within the United States and to Canada,** dial 1 followed by the area code and the seven-digit number. **For other international calls,** dial 011 followed by the country code, the city code, and the number you are calling.

Calls to area codes **800, 888, 877,** and **866** are toll-free. However, calls to area codes **700** and **900** can be expensive—charges of 95¢ to $3 or more per minute. Some numbers have minimum charges that can run $15 or more.

For **reversed-charge or collect calls,** and for person-to-person calls, dial the number 0 and then the area code and number; an operator will come on the line, and you should specify whether you are calling collect, person-to-person, or both. If your operator-assisted call is international, ask for the overseas operator.

For **directory assistance** ("Information"), dial ⓒ **411** for local numbers and national numbers in the U.S. and Canada. For dedicated long-distance information, dial 1, then the appropriate area code plus 555-1212.

Time The Florida peninsula observes **Eastern Standard Time,** but most of the Panhandle, west of the Apalachicola River, is on **Central Standard Time,** 1 hour behind the rest of the state.

Daylight saving time is in effect from 1am on the second Sunday in March to 1am on the first Sunday in November, except in Arizona, Hawaii, the U.S. Virgin Islands, and Puerto Rico. Daylight saving time moves the clock 1 hour ahead of standard time.

The continental United States is divided into **four time zones:** Eastern Standard Time (EST), Central Standard Time (CST), Mountain Standard Time (MST), and Pacific Standard Time (PST). Alaska and Hawaii have their own zones. For example, when it's 9am in Los Angeles (PST), it's 7am in Honolulu (HST), 10am in Denver (MST), 11am in Chicago (CST), noon in New York City (EST), 5pm in London (GMT), and 2am the next day in Sydney.

For help with time translations and more, download our convenient Travel Tools app for your mobile device. Go to **www.frommers.com/go/mobile** and click on the Travel Tools icon.

Tipping In hotels, tip **bellhops** at least $1 per bag ($2–$3 if you have a lot of luggage), and tip the **chamber staff** $1 to $2 per day (more if you've left a big mess for him or her to clean up). Tip the **doorman** or **concierge** only if he or she has provided you with some specific service (for example, calling a cab for you or obtaining difficult-to-get theater tickets). Tip the **valet-parking attendant** $1 every time you get your car.

In restaurants, bars, and nightclubs, tip **service staff** and **bartenders** 15% to 20% of the check, tip **checkroom attendants** $1 per garment, and tip **valet-parking attendants** $2 per vehicle.

Keep an eye on your bill in tourist hot spots such as South Beach, where as much as an 18% auto gratuity could be already added to the total check.

As for other service personnel, tip **cab drivers** 15% of the fare; tip **skycaps** at airports at least $1 per bag ($2–$3 if you have a lot of luggage); and tip **hairdressers** and **barbers** 15% to 20%.

For help with tip calculations, currency conversions, and more, download our convenient Travel Tools app for your mobile device. Go to **www.frommers.com/go/mobile** and click on the Travel Tools icon.

Toilets You won't find public toilets or "restrooms" on the streets in most U.S. cities, but they can be found in hotel lobbies, bars, restaurants, museums, department stores, railway and bus stations, and service stations. Large hotels and fast-food restaurants are often the best bet for clean facilities. Restaurants and bars in resorts or heavily visited areas may reserve their restrooms for patrons.

Visas The U.S. State Department has a **Visa Waiver Program (VWP)** allowing citizens of the following countries to enter the United States without a visa for stays of up to 90 days: Andorra, Australia, Austria, Belgium, Brunei, Czech Republic, Denmark, Estonia, Finland, France, Germany, Greece, Hungary, Iceland, Ireland, Italy, Japan, Latvia, Liechtenstein, Lithuania, Luxembourg, Malta, Monaco, the Netherlands, New Zealand, Norway, Portugal, San Marino, Singapore, Slovakia, Slovenia, South Korea, Spain, Sweden, Switzerland, and the United Kingdom. (***Note:*** This list was accurate at press time; for the most up-to-date list of countries in the VWP, consult **http://travel.state.gov/visa**.) Even though a visa isn't necessary, in an effort to help U.S. officials check travelers against terror watch lists before they arrive at U.S. borders, visitors from VWP countries must register online through the Electronic System for Travel Authorization (ESTA) before boarding a plane or a boat to the U.S. Travelers must complete an electronic application providing basic personal and travel-eligibility information. The Department of Homeland Security recommends filling out the form at least 3 days before traveling. Authorizations will be valid for up to 2 years or until the traveler's passport expires, whichever comes first. Currently, there is a US$14 fee for the online application. Existing ESTA registrations remain valid through their expiration dates. ***Note:*** Any passport issued on or after October 26, 2006, by a VWP country must be an **e-Passport** for VWP travelers to be eligible to enter the U.S. without a visa. Citizens of these nations also need to present a round-trip air or cruise ticket upon arrival. E-Passports contain computer chips capable of storing biometric information, such as the required digital photograph of the holder. If your passport doesn't have this feature, you can still travel without a visa if the valid passport was issued before October 26, 2005, and includes a machine-readable zone; or if the valid passport was issued between October 26, 2005, and October 25, 2006, and includes a digital photograph. For more information, go to **http://travel.state.gov/visa**. Canadian citizens may enter the United States without visas, but will need to show passports and proof of residence.

Citizens of all other countries must have (1) a valid passport that expires at least 6 months later than the scheduled end of their visit to the U.S., and (2) a tourist visa.

For information about U.S. visas go to **http://travel.state.gov** and click on "Visas." Or go to one of the following websites:

Australian citizens can obtain up-to-date visa information from the **U.S. Embassy Canberra,** Moonah Place, Yarralumla, ACT 2600 (✆ **02/6214-5600**), or by checking the U.S. Diplomatic Mission's website at **http://canberra.usembassy.gov/visas.html**.

British subjects can obtain up-to-date visa information by calling the **U.S. Embassy Visa Information Line** (✆ **09042-450-100** from within the U.K. at £1.20 per minute; or ✆ **866/382-3589** from within the U.S. at a flat rate of $16; payable by credit card only) or by visiting the "Visas to the U.S." section of the American Embassy London's website at **http://london.usembassy.gov/visas.html**.

Irish citizens can obtain up-to-date visa information through the **U.S. Embassy Dublin,** 42 Elgin Rd., Ballsbridge, Dublin 4 (✆ **1580-47-VISA** [8472] from within the Republic of Ireland at €2.40 per minute; **http://dublin.usembassy.gov**).

Citizens of **New Zealand** can obtain up-to-date visa information by contacting the **U.S. Embassy New Zealand,** 29 Fitzherbert Terrace, Thorndon, Wellington (✆ **644/462-6000; http://newzealand.usembassy.gov**).

Visitor Information For the most comprehensive visitor information in the state, check out Visit Florida, **www.visitflorida.com**, a comprehensive site featuring deals, maps, and all sorts of excellent information on the state's beaten- and off-the-beaten-path hot spots. You can also find a list of Frommer's travel apps at **www.frommers.com/go/mobile**.

INDEX

709